KABBALAH
for the
STUDENT

LAITMAN
KABBALAH PUBLISHERS

KABBALAH FOR THE STUDENT

Copyright © 2025 by MICHAEL LAITMAN
All rights reserved
Published by Laitman Kabbalah Publishers
www.kabbalah.info info@kabbalah.info
1057 Steeles Avenue West, Suite 532, Toronto, ON, M2R 3X1, Canada

No part of this book may be used or reproduced in any manner without written permission of the publisher, except in the case of brief quotations embodied in critical articles or reviews.

Library of Congress Cataloging-in-Publication Data

Kabbalah for the student. -- 1st ed.
   p. cm.
ISBN 978-1-77228-203-0

1. Cabala. I. Ashlag, Yehudah. II. Ashlag, Barukh Shalom, ha-Levi, 1907-1991. III. Laitman, Michael.
BM525.K27 2009
296.1'6--dc22

                           2008040178

Copy Editor: Claire Gerus
Associate Editor: Michael R. Kellogg
Proofreading: Natasha Sigmund
Layout: Luba Visotzki
Diagrams: Alex Rain
Cover Design: Rami Yaniv
Printing & Post Production: Uri Laitman
Translator & Executive Editor: Chaim Ratz

Table of Contents

Foreword (Bnei Baruch)..5
The Tree of Life – a Poem (Rav Isaac Luria) 7
Time for Spiritual Attainment..11
    Time to Act (Rav Yehuda Ashlag) 13
    Disclosing a Portion, Covering Two (Rav Yehuda Ashlag)...15
    The Essence of the Wisdom of Kabbalah (Rav Yehuda Ashlag) 21
    The Teaching of the Kabbalah and Its Essence (Rav Yehuda Ashlag).......................31
    The Essence of Religion and Its Purpose (Rav Yehuda Ashlag) 51
    Body and Soul (Rav Yehuda Ashlag)...59
    Exile and Redemption (Rav Yehuda Ashlag)...65
    A Speech for the Completion of The Zohar (Rav Yehuda Ashlag) १९
    Peace in the World (Rav Yehuda Ashlag)..83
    The Wisdom of Kabbalah and Philosophy (Rav Yehuda Ashlag) 99
    Introduction to The Book of Zohar (Rav Yehuda Ashlag) १०९
    A Handmaid that Is Heir to Her Mistress (Rav Yehuda Ashlag)............................. 147
    Messiah's Shofar (Rav Yehuda Ashlag) 153
    Kabbalists Write about the Wisdom of Kabbalah (Assorted Authors) 157
    A Prayer before a Prayer (excerpt from *Noam Elimelech*) 183
Spiritual Attainment...187
    Divinity in Exile (Rav Yehuda Ashlag)...189
    The Reason for the Heaviness in the Work (Rav Yehuda Ashlag) 193
    Lishma Is an Awakening from Above (Rav Yehuda Ashlag)...................................195
    Support in the Torah (Rav Yehuda Ashlag) 199
    Habit Becomes Second Nature (Rav Yehuda Ashlag)..203
    The Difference between a Shade of Kedusha and a Shade of Sitra Achra (Rav Yehuda Ashlag) 205
    The Essence of One's Work (Rav Yehuda Ashlag) 207
    Lishma (Rav Yehuda Ashlag)...208
    The Time of Ascent (Rav Yehuda Ashlag) 211
    You Who Love the Lord Hate Evil (Rav Yehuda Ashlag) 213
    Raising the Slave through the Ministers (Rav Yehuda Ashlag).............................. 214
    PARDESS (Rav Yehuda Ashlag)...217
    Sit and Do Nothing—Better (Rav Yehuda Ashlag)..223
    If I Am Not for Me, Who Is for Me? (Rav Yehuda Ashlag) 224
    Walking the Path of Truth (Rav Yehuda Ashlag)...227
    One Is Where One Thinks (Rav Yehuda Ashlag) 231
    An Allegory about the Rich Man's Son in the Cellar (Rav Yehuda Ashlag)....................232
    The Lord Is Thy Shade (Rav Yehuda Ashlag) 235
    The Labor Is the Most Important (Rav Yehuda Ashlag)...236
    Association of Mercy with Judgment (Rav Yehuda Ashlag)....................................237
Society as a Condition for Attaining Spirituality..239
    Matan Torah (The Giving of the Torah) (Rav Yehuda Ashlag) 241

The Arvut (Mutual Guarantee) (Rav Yehuda Ashlag)	251
The Peace (Rav Yehuda Ashlag)	261
The Message in Matan Torah (Bnei Baruch)	277
Unity of Friends (Rav Yehuda Ashlag)	281
Love of Friends (Rav Yehuda Ashlag)	282
The Influence of the Environment on a Person (Rav Baruch Ashlag)	283
Purpose of Society (Rav Baruch Ashlag)	286
Concerning Love of Friends (Rav Baruch Ashlag)	288
They Helped Every One His Friend (Rav Baruch Ashlag)	290
Purpose of Society (Rav Baruch Ashlag)	291
What Does "Love Thy Friend as Thyself" Give Us? (Rav Baruch Ashlag)	293
Love of Friends (Rav Baruch Ashlag)	294
According to What Is Explained Concerning "Love Thy Friend" (Rav Baruch Ashlag)	295
Which Keeping of Torah and Mitzvot Purifies the Heart (Rav Baruch Ashlag)	299
Which Degree Should One Achieve? (Rav Baruch Ashlag)	301
The First Degree When One Is Born (Rav Baruch Ashlag)	303
Concerning the Importance of Society (Rav Baruch Ashlag)	305
Concerning the Importance of Friends (Rav Baruch Ashlag)	308
The Agenda of the Assembly (Rav Baruch Ashlag)	311

Stages of Attainment 313

Introduction to The Study of the Ten Sefirot (Rav Yehuda Ashlag)	315
The Freedom (Rav Yehuda Ashlag)	375
Concealment and Disclosure of the Face of the Creator (Rav Yehuda Ashlag)	403
Preface to The Book of Zohar (Rav Yehuda Ashlag)	407
Introduction to the Book, Panim Meirot uMasbirot (Rav Yehuda Ashlag)	431
Matter and Form in the Wisdom of Kabbalah (Rav Yehuda Ashlag)	471
This Is for Judah (Rav Yehuda Ashlag)	473
The Acting Mind (Rav Yehuda Ashlag)	477
Introduction to the Book, From the Mouth of a Sage (Rav Yehuda Ashlag)	479
Introduction to the Preface to the Wisdom of Kabbalah (Rav Yehuda Ashlag)	489

The Evolution of the Worlds 497

Foreword to the Preface to the Wisdom of Kabbalah (Rav Michael Laitman)	499
Preface to the Wisdom of Kabbalah (Rav Yehuda Ashlag)	565
HaIlan (The Tree) (Rav Yehuda Ashlag)	645
Explanation of the Article, Preface to the Wisdom of Kabbalah (Rav Baruch Ashlag)	663
Preface to the Sulam Commentary (Rav Yehuda Ashlag)	681
Talmud Eser Sefirot, Part One, Histaklut Pnimit (Rav Yehuda Ashlag)	721
General Preface (Rav Yehuda Ashlag)	745

Appendix A: Kabbalah Glossary (Bnei Baruch)	775
Appendix B: Acronyms and Abbreviations (Bnei Baruch)	811
Appendix C: Diagrams of the Spiritual Worlds (Bnei Baruch)	813
About Bnei Baruch	857

Foreword

Why are we here? What does the future hold? How can we avoid suffering and feel tranquil and safe? These are questions we would all like to answer. The wisdom of Kabbalah provides the answers to these questions and to many more. It allows us to ask any question and experience the intimate, profound fulfillment that comes with answering the deepest questions to the fullest. This is why it is called "the wisdom of the hidden."

Kabbalah teaches that we all want to enjoy. Kabbalists call this desire "the will to receive delight and pleasure," or simply, "the will to receive." This desire propels all of our actions, thoughts, and feelings, and Kabbalah depicts how we can realize our desires and fulfill our wishes.

Although the wisdom of Kabbalah often tends to sound technical or obscure, it is important to remember that this is a very practical science. The people who mastered it and wrote about it were just like you and me. They were seeking solutions to the same questions we all want to answer: "Why are we born?" "What happens after we die?" "Why is there suffering?" and "Can I experience lasting pleasure, and if so, how?" And when they found the answers to these questions and implemented them in their own lives, they wrote the texts within this collection, so we may know them, too.

In this compilation, you will find precise explanations as to how you can achieve that sublime feeling of unbounded pleasure and complete control of your life.

Kabbalah teaches how to enjoy life here and now. It explains such concepts as "the next world," "souls," "reincarnation," and "life and death."

How can we, novices, experience such perceptions? How can we discover the true picture of reality?

Each of us builds his or her own priorities in life. Some matters are more important to us, some are less so, and some we prefer to put off. But regardless of the level of importance, we categorize our priorities according to a single measurement: our purpose in life.

Some people will strive tirelessly for love, some crave money, and others desire honor or knowledge. But most people prefer not to put all their eggs in one basket by focusing on fulfilling one desire. They settle for a little of everything and suppress any strong desire that emerges in them and demands too much of their attention.

The Kabbalists who wrote the texts you will read here are of the first, uncompromising kind. They set a very clear goal before them: to show humankind how to achieve eternal life—filled with pleasure and unbounded, fulfilled emotions. To achieve this, they studied the will to receive delight and pleasure that exists in each of us.

The greatest Kabbalists who lived in our time are also the ones who explained the rules of the wisdom of Kabbalah in the clearest and simplest style. The two prime Kabbalists whose writings appear in this book are Rav Yehuda Ashlag, known as Baal HaSulam (Owner of the Ladder) for his *Sulam* (Ladder) commentary on *The Book of Zohar*, and his son, Rav Baruch Ashlag, who expanded and interpreted his father's explanations. Rav Michael Laitman, Rav Baruch Ashlag's prime student and personal assistant, teaches us how to correctly interpret the texts, and how to use them to achieve the purpose for which we were created.

We, Bnei Baruch, wish you joy and fulfillment in your study, and rapid spiritual growth.

THE TREE OF LIFE – A POEM

Behold that before the emanations were emanated and the creatures were created,
The Upper Simple Light had filled the whole existence.
And there was no vacancy, such as an empty air, a hollow,
But all was filled with that Simple, Boundless Light.
And there was no such part as head, or end,
But everything was One, Simple Light, balanced evenly and equally,
And it was called "the Light of Ein Sof (Infinity)."
And when upon His simple will, came the desire to create the worlds and emanate the emanations,
To bring to light the perfection of His deeds, His names, His appellations,
Which was the cause of the creation of the worlds,
Then the Ein Sof restricted Himself, in His middle point, precisely at the center,
And He restricted that Light, and drew far off to the sides around that middle point.
And there remained an empty space, an empty air, a vacuum
Precisely from the middle point.
And that restriction was equally around that empty, middle point,
So that the space was evenly circled around it.
And after the restriction, when the vacant space remained empty
Precisely in the middle of the Light of Ein Sof,
A place was formed, where the Emanations, Creations, Formations, and Actions might reside.
Then from the Light of Ein Sof, a single line hung down from Above, lowered into that space.
And through that line, He emanated, created, formed, and made all the worlds.

Prior to these four worlds, there was one Light of Ein Sof, whose Name is One, in wondrous, hidden unity,

And even in the angels closest to Him

There is no force and no attainment in The Ein Sof,

As there is no mind of a created that could attain Him,

For He has no place, no boundary, no name.

–The Ari, *The Tree of Life*, Part One, Gate One

The Messiah sits at the gate to Jerusalem and awaits people worthy of redemption. He is fettered, and he needs whole people to untie his chains. He has had more than his fill of pious adherents; now he is fervently seeking men of truth.

–From the sayings of The Rabbi of Kotzk,
There Is None So Whole as a Broken Heart, p 115

Time *for* Spiritual Attainment

Time to Act

For a long time now, my conscience has burdened me with a demand to come out and create a fundamental composition regarding the essence of Judaism, religion, and the wisdom of Kabbalah, and spread it among the nation, so people will come to know and properly understand these exalted matters in their true meaning.

Previously in Israel, prior to the development of the printing industry, there were no fallacious books among us relating to the essence of Judaism, as there were almost no writers who could not stand behind their words, for the simple reason that in most cases, an irresponsible person is not famous.

Therefore, if, by chance, one dared to write such a composition, no scribe would copy it, as he would not be paid for his labor, which, for the most part, was quite considerable. Thus, such a composition was doomed from the start to be lost.

In those days, knowledgeable people, too, had no interest in writing such books, since the populace did not need that knowledge. Quite the contrary, they had an interest in hiding it in secret chambers for the reason that "It is the glory of God to conceal a thing." We were commanded to conceal the essence of the Torah and the work from those who did not need it, or were unworthy of it, and to not degrade it by displaying it in shop windows for the lusting eyes of the boasting, because thus the glory of God demands.

But ever since the printing of books has become popular, and writers are no longer in need of scribes, the price of books has been reduced. This has paved the way for irresponsible writers to publish whatever books they please, for money or for glory. But they do not take their own actions into account and do not examine the consequences of their work.

From that time on, publications of the aforementioned kind have significantly increased, without any learning or reception mouth-to-mouth from a qualified Rav, and even without knowledge of earlier books that dealt with this topic. Such writers fabricate theories of their own empty shells, and relate their words to the most exalted matters, to thus portray the essence of the nation and its fabulous treasure. As fools, they know not how to be scrupulous, nor have a way by which to learn it. They instill faulty views to generations, and in return for their petty lusts they sin and make the nations sin for generations to come.

Recently, their stench has soared upward because they have plunged their nails into the wisdom of the Kabbalah, not minding that this wisdom has been locked and chained behind a thousand doors to this day, that no person may understand the true meaning of even a single word of it, much less the connection between one word and the next.

That is because in all the genuine books that were written to this day, there are but clues that barely suffice for a knowledgeable disciple to understand their true meaning, from the mouth of a wise and qualified Kabbalist sage. And there, too, "the arrowsnake make her nest, and lay, and hatch, and brood under her shadow." These days, such conspirators multiply, who make such delights that disgust those who behold them.

Some of them even go as far as to presume and to assume the place of the leaders of the generation, and they pretend to know the difference between the ancient books and tell which of them is worthy of study and which is not, since it is filled with fallacies, and they arouse contempt and wrath. Until today, the work of scrutiny had been limited to one in ten leaders of a generation; and now the ignorant abuse it.

Therefore, the perception of these matters by the public has been greatly corrupted. In addition, there is an atmosphere of frivolity and people think that a glance at one's leisure is sufficient for the study of such exalted matters. They skim over the ocean of wisdom and the essence of Judaism in a glance, like that angel, and draw conclusions based on their own mood.

These are the reasons that have prompted me to go out of my way and decide that it is time to "do for the Lord" and salvage what can still be salvaged. Thus, I have taken upon myself to reveal some of the true essence, which relates to the above matter, and spread it among the nation.

Disclosing a Portion, Covering Two

There is an idiom among great sages when they come to disclose a profound matter: they begin their words with, "I am disclosing a portion and covering two portions." Our sages took great care not to utter words needlessly, as our sages instructed, "A word is a rock; silence is two."

This means that if you have a priceless word whose worth is one rock, know that not saying it is worth two rocks. This refers to those uttering needless words without pertinent content or use except to decorate the tongue in the eyes of the beholders. This was strictly forbidden in the eyes of our sages, as is known to those who examine their words. Hence, we must be attentive to understand this common idiom of theirs.

THREE KINDS OF CONCEALMENT OF THE WISDOM

There are three parts to the secrets of the Torah. Each part has its own reason for being concealed. They are called by the following names:

1. Unnecessary

2. Impossible

3. The counsel of the Lord is with them that fear Him

There is not a single fraction of this wisdom where scrutinies of these three parts do not apply, and I will clarify them one at a time.

1. UNNECESSARY

This means that no benefit will stem from its disclosing. Of course, this is not such a great loss because there is only the issue of the cleanness of the mind here, to warn of those actions defined as "so what," meaning so what if I did this, there is no harm in it.

But you should know that, in the eyes of the sages, the "so what" is considered the worst corruptor. This is because all the destructors in the world, those that have been and those that will be, are the "so what" kind of people. This means that they occupy themselves and others in needless things. Hence, sages would not accept any student before they were certain that he would be cautious in his ways, so as not to reveal what was not necessary.

2. IMPOSSIBLE

This means that the language does not compel them to say anything of their quality, due to their great sublimity and spirituality. Hence, any attempt to clothe them in words may only mislead the examiners and deflect them to a false path, which is considered the worst of all iniquities. Therefore, to reveal anything in these matters, permission from Above is required. This is the second part of the concealment of the wisdom. Yet, this permission, too, requires explanation.

PERMISSION FROM ABOVE

This is explained in the book, *The Gate to Rashbi's Words*, by the Ari, in *The Zohar, Parashat Mishpatim*, p 100. It reads as follows, "Know that some of the souls of the righteous are of the Surrounding-Light kind, and some are of the Inner-Light kind. Those that are of the Surrounding-Light kind have the power to speak of the secrets of the Torah by way of concealment and intimation, so their words will be understood only by those worthy of understanding them.

"Rabbi Shimon Bar-Yochai's soul was of the Surrounding-Light kind. Hence, he had the power to clothe the words and teach them in a way that even if he taught them to many, only the worthy of understanding would understand. This is why he was given 'permission' to write *The Book of Zohar*.

"The permission was not 'granted' to write a book in this wisdom to his teachers or to the first ones who preceded them, even though they were certainly more proficient in this wisdom than he. But the reason is that they did not have the power to dress the matters as did he. This is the meaning of what is written, 'Yochai's son knew how to guard his ways.' Now you can understand the great concealment in *The Book of Zohar*, written by Rashbi, that not every mind can grasp his words."

His words in essence: Explaining matters in the wisdom of truth is not dependent whatsoever upon the greatness or smallness of the Kabbalist sage. Rather, it is about the illumination of a soul dedicated to this: the illumination of this soul is considered "giving permission" from Above to disclose the Higher

Wisdom. We therefore learn that one who has not been rewarded with this permission must not make clarifications in this wisdom, as he cannot clothe the subtle matters in their suitable words in a way that will not fail the students.

For this reason we did not find a single book in the wisdom of truth that precedes Rashbi's *The Book of Zohar*, since all the books in the wisdom prior to his are not categorized as interpretations of the wisdom. Instead, they are mere intimations, without any order of cause and consequence, as it is known to those who find knowledge, thus far understanding his words.

I should add, as I had received from books and from authors, that since the time of Rashbi and his students, the authors of *The Zohar*, until the time of the Ari there was not a single writer who understood the words of *The Zohar* and the *Tikkunim* (corrections) like the Ari. All the compositions before his time are mere inklings in this wisdom, including the books of the sage, Ramak.

And the same words that were said about the Rashbi should be said about the Ari himself—that his predecessors were not given permission from Above to disclose the interpretations of the wisdom, and that he was given this permission. And also, this does not distinguish any greatness or smallness at all, since it is possible that the virtue of his formers was much greater than the Ari's, but they were not given permission for it at all. For this reason, they refrained from writing commentaries that relate to the actual wisdom, but settled for brief intimations that were not in any way linked to one another.

For this reason, since the books of the Ari appeared in the world, all who study the wisdom of Kabbalah have left their hands from all the books of the Ramak, and all the first and the great ones that preceded the Ari, as it is known among those who engage in this wisdom. They have attached their spiritual lives solely to the writings of the Ari in a way that the essential books, considered proper interpretations of this wisdom, are only *The Book of Zohar*, the *Tikkunim* and following them, the books of the Ari.

3. THE COUNSEL OF THE LORD IS WITH THEM THAT FEAR HIM

This means that the secrets of the Torah are revealed only to those who fear His Name, who keep His Glory with their hearts and souls, and who never commit any blasphemy. This is the third part of the concealment of the wisdom.

This part of the concealment is the strictest, as this kind of disclosure has failed many. From the midst of those stem all the charmers, whisperers, and "practical" Kabbalists, who hunt souls with their cunningness, and the mystics, who use withered wisdom that came from under the hands of unworthy students, to draw bodily benefit for themselves or for others. The world has suffered much from it, and is suffering still.

You should know that the root of the concealment was only this part. From here the sages took excessive strictness in testing the students, as they said (*Hagiga* 13), "heads of chapters are given only to a chief justice, and to one whose heart is worried," and "*Maase Beresheet* is not to be explored in pairs, neither is *Merkava* to be explored alone." There are many others like that, and all this fear is for the above reason.

For this reason, few are the ones who have been rewarded with this wisdom, and even those who passed all their tests and examinations are sworn by the most serious oaths to not reveal anything of those three parts.

Do not misunderstand my words, in that I have divided the concealment of the wisdom into three parts. I do not mean that the wisdom of truth itself is divided into these three parts. Rather, I mean that these three parts stem from every single detail of this wisdom, since they are the only three manners of scrutiny that are always applied to this wisdom.

However, here we should ask, "If it is true that the firmness of the concealment of the wisdom is so strict, from where were all the thousands of compositions in this wisdom taken?" The answer is that there is a difference between the first two parts and the last part. The prime burden lies only in the above third part, for the reason explained above.

But the first two parts are not under constant prohibition. This is because sometimes an issue in the "unnecessary" is reversed, stops being unnecessary for some reason, and becomes necessary. Also, the part, "impossible," sometimes becomes possible. This is so for two reasons: either because of the evolution of the generation or by being given permission from Above, as it happened to the Rashbi and to the Ari, and to smaller extents to their formers. All the genuine books written in the wisdom emerge from these discernments.

This is what they mean by their idiom, "I am disclosing a portion and covering two portions." They mean that it happened that they revealed a new thing that was not discovered by their predecessors. And this is why they imply that they are only revealing one portion, meaning he is revealing the first part of the three parts of concealment, and leaves two parts concealed.

This indicates that something happened, which is the reason for that disclosure: either the "unnecessary" received the form of "necessary," or "permission from Above" was granted, as I have explained above. This is the meaning of the idiom, "I am disclosing a portion."

The readers of these tracts, which I intend to print during the year, should know that they are all innovations, which are not introduced purely as such, in their precise content, in any book preceding mine. I received them mouth to mouth from my teacher, who was authorized for it, meaning he, too, received from his teachers mouth to mouth.

And although I had received them under all the conditions of covering and watchfulness, by the necessity introduced in my essay, "Time to Act," the "unnecessary" part has been inverted for me and became "necessary." Hence, I have revealed this portion with complete permission, as I have explained above. Yet I will keep the other two portions as I am commanded.

THE ESSENCE OF THE WISDOM OF KABBALAH

Before I go about elucidating the history of the wisdom of Kabbalah, conversed about by many, I find it necessary to begin with a thorough clarification of the essence of this wisdom, which I believe so few know. And naturally, it is impossible to speak of the history of something before we know the thing itself.

Although this knowledge is wider and deeper than the ocean, I will make an utmost effort, with all the strength and knowledge I have acquired in this field, to clarify and illuminate it from all angles, enough for any soul to draw the right conclusions, as they truly are, leaving no room for error, as is often the case in such matters.

WHAT DOES THE WISDOM REVOLVE AROUND?

This question comes to the mind of every right-minded person. To properly address it, I will provide a reliable and lasting definition: this wisdom is no more and no less than a sequence of roots, which hang down by way of cause and consequence, by fixed, determined rules, interweaving to a single, exalted goal described as "the revelation of His Godliness to His creatures in this world."

And here there is a conduct of particular and general:

General—the whole of humanity, obligated to eventually come to this immense evolvement, as it is written, "For the earth shall be full of the knowledge of the Lord, as the waters cover the sea" (Isaiah 11, 9). "And they shall teach no more every man his neighbor, and every man his brother, saying, know the Lord: For they shall all know me, from the least of them to the greatest of them" (Jeremiah 31, 33). "Yet thy Teacher shall not hide Himself any more, but thine eyes shall see thy Teacher" (Isaiah 30, 20).

Particular—that even before the perfection of the whole of humanity, this rule is implemented in a chosen few individuals in every generation. These are the ones who are endowed, in each generation, with certain degrees of revelation of His Godliness. And these are the prophets and the men of God.

And as our sages said, "There is no generation without such that are as Abraham and Jacob." Thus you see that the revelation of His Godliness is implemented in each generation, as our sages, whom we find trustworthy, proclaim.

THE MULTIPLICITY OF PARTZUFIM, SEFIROT, AND WORLDS

However, according to the above, a question arises—since this wisdom has but one, special, and clear role, why is there the matter of the multiplicity of *Partzufim*, *Sefirot*, and interchangeable connections, which are so abundant in the books of Kabbalah?

Indeed, if you take the body of a small animal, whose only task is to nourish itself so it may exist in this world for enough time to father and carry on its species, you will find in it a complex structure of millions of fibers and tendons, as physiologists and anatomists have discovered. And there is much there that humans have yet to find. From the above, you can conclude the vast variety of issues and channels that need to connect in order to achieve and to reveal that sublime goal.

TWO CONDUCTS—FROM ABOVE DOWNWARDS AND FROM BELOW UPWARDS

This wisdom is generally divided into two parallel, identical orders, like two drops in a pond. The only difference between them is that the first order extends from Above downwards, to this world, and the second order traverses from below upwards, precisely by the same routes and make-ups imprinted at the root when they appeared from Above downwards.

The first order is called "the order of descent of the worlds, *Partzufim*, and *Sefirot*," in all their occurrences, whether lasting or transient. The second order is called "attainments or degrees of prophecy and Holy Spirit." A person rewarded with it must follow the same trails and inlets, and gradually attain each detail and each degree, precisely by the same rules that were imprinted in them upon their emanation from Above downwards.

A revelation of Godliness does not appear at once, but gradually, over a period of time, depending on the cleansing of the attaining, until one discovers all the degrees from Above downwards. And because they come in an order of attainment, one after the other and one above the other, as do rungs of a ladder, they are called "degrees" (steps).

ABSTRACT NAMES

Many believe that all the words and the names in the wisdom of Kabbalah are a kind of abstract names. This is so because it deals with Godliness and spirituality, which are above time and space, where even our imagination has no hold. For this reason they have decided that surely, these matters speak only of abstract names, or even more sublime and exalted than abstract names, as they are completely and from the outset, devoid of elements that are imagined.

But that is not the case. On the contrary, Kabbalah uses only names and appellations that are concrete and real. It is an unbending rule for all Kabbalists that, "Anything we do not attain, we do not define by a name and a word."

Here you must know that the word "attainment" (Heb: *Hasaga*) implies the ultimate degree of understanding. It derives from the phrase, "that thy hand shall reach" (Heb: *Ki Tasig Yadcha*). That means that before something becomes utterly lucid, as though gripped in one's hand, Kabbalists do not consider it attained, but understood, comprehended, and so on.

THE ACTUALITY OF THE WISDOM OF KABBALAH

Actual things are found even in the corporeal reality set before our eyes, although we have neither perception nor image of their essence. Such are the electricity and the magnet, called "fluidum."

Nevertheless, who can say that these names are not real, when we vividly and satisfactorily know their actions? We could not be more indifferent to the fact that we have no perception of the essence of the subject itself, namely electricity itself.

This name is as tangible and as close to us as though it were entirely perceived by our senses. Even little children are familiar with the word, "electricity," as well as they are familiar with words such as bread, sugar, and so on.

Moreover, if you wish to exercise your tools of scrutiny a bit, I shall tell you that as a whole, as there is no perception of the Creator whatsoever, so is it impossible to attain the essence of any of His creatures, even the tangible objects that we feel with our hands.

Thus, all we know about our friends and relatives in the world of action before us are nothing more than "acquaintance with their actions." These are prompted and born by the association of their encounter with our senses, which render us complete satisfaction although we have no perception whatsoever of the essence of the subject.

Furthermore, you have no perception or attainment whatsoever even of your own essence. Everything you know about your own essence is nothing more than a series of actions extending from your essence.

Now you can easily conclude that all the names and appellations that appear in books of Kabbalah are indeed real and factual, although we have no attainment in the subject matter whatsoever. It is so because those who engage in it have the complete satisfaction with their inclusive perception of its ultimate wholeness, meaning a mere perception of actions, prompted and born of the association of the Upper Light and its perceivers.

However, it is quite sufficient, for this is the rule: "All that is measured and extracted from His Providence so as to be realized into the nature of Creation, is completely satisfactory." Similarly, one cannot wish for a sixth finger on one hand, because the five fingers are quite sufficient.

THE CORPOREAL TERMS AND THE PHYSICAL NAMES IN BOOKS OF KABBALAH

Any reasonable person will understand that when dealing with spiritual matters, much less with Godliness, we have no words or letters with which to contemplate. This is because our whole vocabulary is but combinations of the letters of our senses and imagination. Yet, how can they be of assistance where there are neither imagination nor senses?

Even if we take the subtlest word that can be used in such matters, meaning the word, "Upper Light," or even "Simple Light," it is still imaginary and borrowed from the light of the sun, or a candlelight, or a light of contentment one feels upon resolving some great doubt. Yet, how can we use them in spiritual matters and Godly ways? They offer the examiner nothing more than falsehood and deceit.

It is particularly so where one needs to find some rationale in these words to help one in the negotiations customary in the research of the wisdom. Here the sage must use rigorously accurate definitions for the eyes of the observers.

And should the sage fail with but a single unsuccessful word, he is certain to confuse and mislead the readers. They will not understand at all what he is saying there, before it, after it, and everything connected to that word, as is known to anyone who examines books of wisdom.

Thus, one should wonder how is it possible for Kabbalists to use false words to explain the interconnections in this wisdom? Also, it is known that there is no definition through a false name, for the lie has no legs and no stance.

Indeed, here you need to have prior knowledge of the Law of Root and Branch by which the worlds relate to one another.

THE LAW OF ROOT AND BRANCH BY WHICH THE WORLDS ARE RELATED

Kabbalists have found that the form of the four worlds, named *Atzilut*, *Beria*, *Yetzira*, and *Assiya*, beginning with the first, highest world, called *Atzilut*, and ending in this corporeal, tangible world, called *Assiya*, is exactly the same in every item and event. This means that everything that eventuates and occurs in the first world is found unchanged in the next world, below it, too. It is likewise in all the worlds that follow it, down to this tangible world.

There is no difference between them, but only a different degree, perceived in the substance of the elements of reality in each world. The substance of the elements of reality in the first, Uppermost world, is purer than in all the ones below it. And the substance of the elements of reality in the second world is coarser than in that of the first world, but purer than all that is of a lower degree.

This continues similarly down to this world before us, whose substance of the elements in reality is coarser and darker than in all the worlds preceding it. However, the shapes and the elements of reality and all their occurrences come unchanged and equal in every world, both in quantity and quality.

They compared it to the conduct of a seal and its imprint: all the shapes in the seal are perfectly transferred in every detail and intricacy to the imprinted object. So it is with the worlds, where each lower world is an imprint of the world Above it. Hence, all the forms in the Higher World are meticulously copied, in both quantity and quality, to the lower world.

Thus, there is not an element of reality, or an occurrence of reality in a lower world, that you will not find its likeness in the world Above it, as identical as two drops in a pond. And they are called "Root and Branch." That means that the item in the lower world is deemed a branch of its pattern, found in the Higher World, being the root of the lower element, as this is where that item in the lower world was imprinted and made to be.

That was the intention of our sages when they said, "You haven't a blade of grass below that has not a fortune and a guard above that strike it and tells it,

"Grow"! It follows that the root, called "fortune," compels it to grow and assume its attribute in quantity and quality, as with the seal and the imprint. This is the law of Root and Branch, which applies to every detail and occurrence of reality, in every single world, in relation to the world Above it.

THE LANGUAGE OF THE KABBALISTS IS A LANGUAGE OF BRANCHES

This means that the branches indicate to their roots, being their molds that necessarily exist in the Upper World. This is because there is nothing in the reality of the lower world that does not stem from its Superior World. As with the seal and the imprint, the root in the Upper World compels its branch in the lower one to reveal its entire form and feature, as our sages said, that the fortune in the world Above, related to the grass in the world below, strikes it, forcing it to complete its growth. Because of that, each and every branch in this world well defines its mold, situated in the Higher World.

Thus, Kabbalists have found a set and annotated vocabulary, sufficient to create an excellent spoken language. It enables them to converse with one another of the dealings in the Spiritual Roots in the Upper Worlds by merely mentioning the lower, tangible branch in this world that is well defined to our corporeal senses.

The listeners understand the Upper Root to which this corporeal branch points because it is related to it, being its imprint. Thus, all the beings of the tangible creation and all their instances have become to them like well-defined words and names, indicating the High Spiritual Roots. Although there cannot be a verbal expression in their spiritual place, as it is above any imagination, they have earned the right to be expressed by utterance through their branches, arranged before our senses here in the tangible world.

That is the nature of the spoken language among Kabbalists, by which they convey their spiritual attainments from person to person and from generation to generation, both by word of mouth and in writing. They fully understand one another, with all the required accuracy needed for negotiating in research of the wisdom, with precise definitions one cannot fail in. This is so because each branch has its own natural, unique definition, and this absolute definition indicates to its root in the Higher World.

Bear in mind that this Language of Branches of the wisdom of Kabbalah is better suited to explain the terms of the wisdom than all our ordinary tongues. It is known from the theory of nominalism that the languages have been disrupted in the mouths of the crowd. In other words, due to excessive use of the words, they have been emptied of their accurate contents, resulting in great difficulties to convey precise deductions from one to another by word of mouth or in writing.

This is not case with the Kabbalah's language of branches: it is derived from the names of the creations and their occurrences, set before our eyes, and defined by the unchangeable laws of nature. The readers and the listeners will never be misled into a misunderstanding of the words being offered to them, since the natural definitions are utterly unwavering and cannot be breached.

CONVEYANCE FROM A WISE KABBALIST TO AN UNDERSTANDING RECEIVER

Thus wrote the RAMBAM in his introduction to his commentary on the Torah: "And I bring with true covenant to all who scrutinize this book, that of all the clues that I write in the secrets of the Torah, I resolutely assert that my words will not be grasped by any mind or intelligence, except from the mouth of a wise Kabbalist to the ear of an understanding receiver." Such as that, Rav Chaim Vital wrote in his introduction to *The Tree of Life*, and also, in the words of our sages (*Hagiga*, 11): "One does not study the Kabbalah on one's own, unless he is wise and understands with his own mind."

Their words are thoroughly understood when they say that one must receive from a wise Kabbalist. But why the necessity for the disciple to first be wise and understanding with his own mind? Moreover, if he isn't so, then he must not be taught, be he the most righteous person in the world. Additionally, if one is already wise and understands with his own mind, what need has he to learn from others?

From the aforesaid, their words are understood with utter simplicity: we have seen that all the words and utterances our lips pronounce cannot help us convey even a single word from the spiritual, Godly matters, above the imaginary time and space. Instead, there is a special language for these matters, being the Language of the Branches, indicating their relation to their Upper Roots.

However, this language, though extremely suitable for its task of delving into the studies of this wisdom, more than other languages, is only so if the listener is wise in his own right, meaning that he knows and understands the way the branches relate to their roots. It is because these relations are not at all clear when looking from the lower upwards. In other words, it is impossible to find any deduction or semblance in the Upper Roots by observing the lower branches.

Quite the contrary, the lower is studied from the Higher. Thus, one must first attain the Upper Roots, the way they are in spirituality, above any imagination, but with pure attainment. And once he has thoroughly attained the Upper Roots with his own mind, he may examine the tangible branches in this world and know how each branch relates to its root in the Upper World, in all its orders, in quantity and quality.

When one knows and thoroughly comprehends all that, there is a common language between him and his teacher, namely the Language of the Branches. Using it, the Kabbalist sage may convey the studies in the wisdom, conducted in the Upper, Spiritual Worlds, both the ones he had received from his teachers, as well as his expansions in the wisdom, which he had discovered by himself. This is because now they have a common language and they understand each other.

However, when a disciple is not wise and comprehends the language on his own, meaning how the branches indicate to their roots, naturally, the teacher cannot convey even a single word of this spiritual wisdom, much less negotiate with him in the scrutiny of the wisdom. This is so because they have no common language they can use, and they become like mute. Thus, it is necessary that the wisdom of Kabbalah will not be taught unless he is wise and understands with his own mind.

We must ask further: How then, has the disciple grown so wise as to know the relations of branch and root through tracing the Upper Roots? The answer is that here one's efforts are in vain; it is the Creator's help that we need! He fills those who capture His fondness with wisdom, understanding, and knowledge to acquire sublime attainments. Here it is impossible to be assisted by any flesh and blood!

Indeed, once He has grown fond of a person and has endowed him with the sublime attainment, one is then ready to come and receive the vastness of the wisdom of Kabbalah from a wise Kabbalist, for only now do they have a common language.

APPELLATIONS ALIEN TO THE HUMAN SPIRIT

With all that is said above, you will understand why we sometimes find appellations and terms quite alien to the human spirit in books of Kabbalah. They are abundant in the fundamental books of Kabbalah, which are *The Zohar*, the *Tikkunim*, and the books of the Ari. It is indeed bewildering why these sages used such lowly appellations to express such exalted, holy notions.

Yet, you will fully understand it once you have acquired the above conceptions. This is because it is now clear that no language in the world can be used to explain that wisdom, except one that is intended for just that end, namely the Language of the Branches, relating to their Upper Roots.

Thus, obviously, no branch or occurrence of a branch should be neglected because of its inferior degree, or not be used to express the desired concept in the interconnections in the wisdom, as there is no other branch in our world to take its place.

As no two hairs suck from the same foramen, we do not have two branches that relate to a single root. Hence, by leaving an incident unused, we lose the spiritual concept corresponding to it in the Upper World, as we have not a single word to utter in its place and indicate that root. In addition, such an incident would impair the entire wisdom in all its vastness, since now there is a missing link in the chain of the wisdom connected to that concept.

This mutilates the entire wisdom, for there is no other wisdom in the world where matters are so fused and intertwined by way of cause and effect, primary and consequential, as is the wisdom of Kabbalah, connected head to toe just like a long chain. Therefore, upon the temporary loss of but a small cognizance, the entire wisdom darkens before our eyes, for all its issues are tied to one another very strongly, literally fusing into one.

Now you will not wonder at the occasional use of alien appellations. They have no freedom of choice with appellations, to replace the bad with the good, or the good with the bad. They must always use the branch or the incident, which precisely points to its Upper Root in all its necessary measure. Moreover, the matters must be expanded so as to provide an accurate definition for the eyes of their fellow observers.

The Teaching of the Kabbalah and Its Essence

What is the wisdom of Kabbalah? As a whole, the wisdom of Kabbalah concerns the revelation of Godliness, arranged on its path in all its aspects—those that have emerged in the worlds and those that are destined to be revealed, and in all the manners that can ever appear in the worlds, to the end of time.

THE PURPOSE OF CREATION

Since there is no act without some purpose, it is certain that the Creator had a purpose in the Creation set before us. And the most important thing in this whole diverse reality is the sensation given to the animals—that each of them feels its own existence. And the most important sensation is the noetic sensation, given to man alone, by which one also feels what is in one's other—the pains and comforts. Hence, it is certain that if the Creator has a purpose in this Creation, its subject is man. It is said about him, "All of the Lord's works are for him."

But we must still understand what was the purpose for which the Creator created this lot? Indeed, it is to elevate him to a Higher and more important degree, to feel his God like the human sensation, which is already given to him. And as one knows and feels one's friend's wishes, so will he learn the words of the Creator, as it is written about Moses, "And the Lord spoke unto Moses face to face, as a man speaketh unto his friend."

Any person can be as Moses. Undoubtedly, anyone who examines the evolution of Creation before us will see and understand the great pleasure of the Operator, whose operation evolves until it acquires that wondrous sensation of being able to converse and deal with one's God as one speaks to one's friend.

FROM ABOVE DOWNWARDS

It is known that the end of the act is in the preliminary thought. Before one begins to think about how to build a house, one contemplates the apartment in the house, which is the purpose. Subsequently, one examines the blueprint to make it suitable for this task.

So it is with our matter. Once we have learned about the purpose, it is also clear to us that all the conducts of Creation, in its every corner, inlet, and outlet, are completely prearranged for the purpose of nurturing the human species from its midst, to improve its qualities until it can sense the Creator as one feels one's friend.

These ascensions are like rungs of a ladder, arranged degree-by-degree until it is completed and achieves its purpose. And you should know that the quality and quantity of these rungs is set in two realities: 1) the existence of material substances, and 2) the existence of spiritual concepts.

In the language of Kabbalah, they are called "**from Above downwards**" and "**from below Upwards**." This means that the corporeal substances are a sequence of disclosure of His Light **from Above downwards**—from the first source, when a measure of Light was cut off from His Essence, and was restricted *Tzimtzum* by *Tzimtzum* (restriction by restriction) until the corporeal world was formed off it, with corporeal creatures at its very bottom.

FROM BELOW UPWARDS

Afterwards begins an order of **from below Upwards**. These are all the rungs of the ladder by which the human race develops and climbs up to the purpose of creation. These two realities are explained in their every detail in the wisdom of Kabbalah.

NECESSITY TO STUDY KABBALAH

An opposer might say, "Therefore, this wisdom is for those who have already been rewarded with a measure of Godly revelation, but what necessity can the majority of the people have for knowing this sublime wisdom?"

Indeed, there is a common opinion that the prime goal of religion and the Torah is only the cleansing of actions, that all that is desired concerns observing the physical *Mitzvot* (commandments), without any additions or anything that should result from it. Had that been so, those who say that studying the revealed and practical actions alone is sufficient would be right.

Yet, this is not the case. Our sages have already said, "Why should the Creator mind if one slaughters at the throat or at the back of the neck? After all, the *Mitzvot* were only given to cleanse people." Thus, there is a purpose beyond the observance of the actions, and the actions are merely preparations for this purpose. Hence, clearly, if the actions are not arranged for the desired goal, it is as if nothing exists. And it is also written in *The Zohar*: "A *Mitzva* (commandment) without an aim is like a body without a soul." Hence, the aim, too, should accompany the act.

Also, it is clear that the aim should be a true aim worthy of the act, as our sages said about the verse, "'And I will set you apart from the peoples, that ye should be Mine,' so your separation will be for My Name. Let not one say, 'Pork is impossible.' Rather, let one say 'it is possible, but what can I do, my Father in Heaven has sentenced me.'"

Thus, if one avoids pork because of abomination or because of some bodily harm, this aim does not help at all for it to be considered a *Mitzva*, unless one has the unique and proper intention that the Torah forbade. So it is with every *Mitzva*, and only then is one's body gradually purified by observing the *Mitzvot*, which is the desired purpose.

Hence, the study of **physical conducts** is not enough; we need to study those things that produce **the desirable intention**, to observe everything with faith in the Torah and in the Giver of the Torah, that there is a Judgment and there is a Judge.

Who is so foolish as to not understand that faith in the Torah and in reward and punishment, which have the power to yield this great thing, require much study in the proper books? Thus, even before the act, a study that purifies the body is required, to grow accustomed to faith in the Creator, His Law, and His Providence. Our sages said about that, "I have created the evil inclination; I have created for it the Torah as a spice." They did not say, "I have created for it the *Mitzvot* as a spice," since "your guarantor needs a bondsman himself," as the evil inclination desires licentiousness and will not let him keep the *Mitzvot*.

TORAH AS A SPICE

The Torah is the only spice to annul and subdue the evil inclination, as our sages said, "The Light in it reformed them."

THE MAJORITY OF THE WORDS OF THE TORAH ARE FOR STUDY

This reconciles why the Torah speaks at length on parts that do not concern the practical part but only the study, meaning the introduction to the act of Creation. These are the whole of the book of *Beresheet* (Genesis), *Shemot* (Exodus), most of *Devarim* (Deuteronomy), and, needless to say, legends and commentaries. Yet, since they are what the Light is stored in, his body will be purified, the evil inclination subdued, and he will come to faith in the Torah and in reward and punishment. This is the first degree in the observance of the work.

COMMANDMENT IS A CANDLE, AND TORAH IS LIGHT

It is written, "For the commandment is a candle, and the Torah is light." As one who has candles but no light to light them sits in the dark, one who has *Mitzvot* but no Torah sits in the dark. This is because the Torah is Light, by which the darkness in the body is illuminated and lit up.

NOT ALL PORTIONS OF THE TORAH ARE OF EQUAL LIGHT

According to the above-mentioned power in the Torah, that is, considering the measure of **Light** in it, it is certain that the Torah should be divided into degrees, according to the measure of **Light that one can receive** from studying it. Clearly, when one ponders and contemplates words of Torah that pertain to the revelation of the Creator to our fathers, they bring the examiner more **Light** than when examining practical matters.

Although they are more important with respect to the actions, with respect to the Light, the revelation of the Creator to our fathers is certainly more important. Anyone with an honest heart who has tried to ask to receive the **Light** of the Torah will admit to that.

NECESSITY AND UNFOLDING OF THE EXPANSION OF THE WISDOM

Since the whole of the wisdom of Kabbalah speaks of the revelation of the Creator, naturally, there is none more successful teaching for its task. This is what the Kabbalists aimed for—to arrange it so it is suitable for studying.

And so they studied in it until the time of concealment (it was agreed to conceal it for a certain reason). However, this was only for a certain time, and not forever, as it is written in *The Zohar*, "This wisdom is destined to be revealed at the end of days, and even to children."

It follows that the above-mentioned wisdom is not at all limited to the language of Kabbalah, as its essence is a spiritual Light that emerges from His Essence, as it is written, "Can thou send forth lightnings, that they may go, and say unto thee: 'Here we are,'" referring to the two above ways: **from Above downwards and from below Upwards**.

These matters and degrees expand according to a language suitable for them, and they are truly all the beings in this world and their conducts in this world, which are their branches. This is so because "You have not a blade of grass below that does not have an angel above, which strikes it and tells it, 'Grow!'" Thus, the worlds emerge from one another and are imprinted from one another like a seal and imprint. And all that is in one is in the other, down to the corporeal world, which is their last branch, but contains the world Above it like an imprint of a seal.

Thus, it is easy to know that we can speak of the Higher Worlds only by their corporeal, lower branches, which extend from them, or of their conducts, which is the language of the Bible, or by secular teachings or by people, which is the language of Kabbalists, or according to agreed upon names. This was the conduct in the Kabbalah of the *Geonim* since the concealment of *The Zohar*.

Thus, it has been made clear that the revelation of the Creator is not a one-time disclosure, but an ongoing matter that is revealed over a period of time, sufficient for the disclosure of all the great degrees that appear from Above downwards and from below Upwards. On top of them, and at the end of them, appears the Creator.

It is like a person proficient in all the countries and people in the world, who cannot say that the whole world has been revealed to him before he has completed his examination of the last person and the last country. Until one has achieved that, one has not attained the whole world.

Similarly, the attainment of the Creator unfolds in preordained ways. The seeker must attain all those ways in both the Upper and the lower. Clearly, the Upper Worlds are the important ones here, but they are attained together because there is no difference in their shapes, only in their substance. The substance of a Higher World is purer, but the shapes are imprinted from one another, and what exists in the Higher World necessarily exists in all the worlds below it, since the lower one is imprinted by it. Know that these realities and their conducts, which the seeker of the Creator attains, are called "degrees," since their attainment is arranged one atop the other, like rungs of a ladder.

SPIRITUAL EXPRESSIONS

The spiritual has no image, hence it has no letters to contemplate with. Even if we declare in general that it is Simple Light, which descends and extends to the seeker until one clothes and attains it in the amount sufficient for His revelation, this, too, is a borrowed expression. This is so because everything that is called "Light" in the spiritual world is not like the light of the sun or candlelight.

What we refer to as Light in the spiritual world is borrowed from the human mind, whose nature is such that when a doubt is resolved in a person, one discovers a kind of abundance of light and pleasure throughout the body. This is why we sometimes say "the light of the mind," although this is not so. The light that shines in those parts of the substance of the body that are unsuitable for receiving resolved scrutinies is certainly something inferior to the mind. Hence, those lower, inferior organs can receive it and attain it, too.

Yet, to be able to name the mind by some name, we call it "the light of the mind." Similarly, we call the elements of the reality of the Upper Worlds "Lights," as they bring those who attain them abundance of light and pleasure throughout the body, from head to toe. For this reason, we may call one who attains "clothing," for he has clothed that Light.

We might ask, "Would it not be more correct to call them by names used in scrutiny, such as observation and attainment, or to express oneself with expressions that emphasize the phenomena of the noetic mind?" The thing is that it is nothing like the conducts of the noetic phenomena, since the mind is a particular branch among all the elements of reality. Hence, it has its own ways of manifestation.

This is not so with degrees, as they are a complete whole, which contains all the elements that exist in a world. Each element has its own particular ways. For the most part, the perception of matters in degrees is similar to the perception of animate bodies: when one attains some essence, one attains the whole of it, from head to toe.

If we judge by the laws of the noetic mind, we can say that he has attained everything he could attain in that essence, and even if he contemplated it for another thousand years, he would not add to it even an iota. Yet, in the beginning it is very similar to… meaning he sees everything but understands none of what he sees. Yet, by the passing of time he will have to attain additional matters, similar to *Ibur* (conception), *Yenika* (nursing), *Mochin* (adulthood), and a second *Ibur*. At that time, he will begin to feel and use his attainments in every way he wishes.

However, in truth, he did not add a thing to the attainments he had achieved in the beginning. It is rather like ripening: previously it was unripe, hence he could not understand it, and now its ripening has completed.

Thus, you see the big difference from the conducts of noetic phenomena. For this reason, the definitions we are accustomed to using will not suffice for us with noetic phenomena. We are compelled to use only the conducts that apply to corporeal matters, since their shapes are completely similar, although their substance is utterly remote.

FOUR LANGUAGES ARE USED IN THE WISDOM OF TRUTH

Four languages are used in the wisdom of truth:

1. The language of the Bible, its names, and appellations.
2. The language of laws. This language is very close to the language of the Bible.
3. The language of legends, which is very far from the Bible, since it has no consideration of reality. Strange names and appellations are attributed to this language, and also, it does not relate to concepts by way of root and its branch.
4. The language of *Sefirot* and *Partzufim*. In general, sages had a strong inclination to conceal it from the ignorant, since they believed that wisdom and ethics go hand in hand. Hence, the first sages hid the wisdom in writing, using lines, dots, tops, and bottoms. This is how the alphabet was formed with the twenty-two letters before us.

THE LANGUAGE OF THE BIBLE

The language of the Bible is the primary, rudimentary language, perfectly suited for its task, as for the most part, it contains a root and branch relation. This is the easiest language to understand. This language is also the oldest; it is the Holy Tongue, attributed to *Adam ha Rishon*.

This language has two advantages and one disadvantage. Its first advantage is that it is easy to understand, and even beginners in attainment immediately understand all they need. The second advantage is that it clarifies matters extensively and in depth, more than in all other languages.

Its disadvantage is that it cannot be used for discussing particular issues or connections of cause and consequence. This is so because every matter needs to be clarified in its fullest measure, as it is not self-evident in showing to which element it is referring, unless by presenting the whole matter. Hence, to emphasize the smallest detail, a complete story must be presented. This is why it is unfit for small details or for connections of cause and consequence.

Also, the language of prayers and blessings is taken from the language of the Bible.

THE LANGUAGE OF LAWS

The language of laws is not of reality, but of the existence of reality. This language is taken entirely from the language of the Bible according to the roots of the laws presented there. It has one advantage over the Bible: it greatly elaborates on every matter and hence points to the Upper Roots more accurately.

However, its great disadvantage, compared to the language of the Bible, is that it is very difficult to understand. This is the most difficult of all the languages, and only a complete sage, called "entering and exiting without harm," will attain it. Of course, it also contains the first disadvantage, as it is taken from the Bible.

THE LANGUAGE OF LEGENDS

The language of legends is easy to understand through the allegories that perfectly fit the desired meaning. In superficial examination, it seems even easier to understand than the language of the Bible. Yet, for complete understanding, it is a very difficult language, since it does not confine itself to speaking in sequences of root and branch, but only in allegories and marvelous wit. However, it is very rich in resolving abstruse and odd concepts that concern the essence of the degree in its state, for itself, which cannot be explained in the languages of Bible and law.

THE LANGUAGE OF KABBALISTS

The language of Kabbalists is a language in the full sense of the word: very precise, both concerning root and branch and concerning cause and consequence. It has a unique merit of being able to express subtle details in this language without any limits. Also, through it, it is possible to approach the desired matter directly, without the need to connect it with what precedes it or follows it.

However, despite all the sublime merits that you find in it, there is a great fault to it: it is very difficult to attain, almost impossible, except from a Kabbalist sage and from a wise one who understands with his own mind. This means that even one who understands the rest of the degrees from below Upwards and from Above downwards with his own mind, will still not understand a thing in this language until he receives it from a sage who had already received the language from his teacher face-to-face.

THE LANGUAGE OF KABBALAH IS CONTAINED IN ALL

The names, appellations, and *Gematrias* belong entirely to the wisdom of Kabbalah. The reason they are found in the other languages, too, is that all the languages are included in the wisdom of Kabbalah. This is so because these are all particular cases that the other languages must be assisted with.

But one should not think that these four languages, which serve to explain the wisdom of Godly revelation, evolved one at a time, over time. The truth is that all four appeared before the sages simultaneously.

In truth, each consists of all the others. The language of Kabbalah exists in the Bible, such as the standing on the *Tzur* (rock), the thirteen attributes of mercy in the Torah and in *Micah*, and, to an extent, it is sensed in each and every verse. There are also the chariots in Isaiah and Ezekiel, and atop them all *The Song of Songs*, all of which is purely the language of Kabbalah. It is similar in laws and in legends, and all the more so with the matter of the unerasable names, which bear the same meaning in all the languages.

ORDER OF THE EVOLUTION OF THE LANGUAGES

Within everything is a gradual development, and the easiest language to use is one whose development is completed before the others. Hence, the first products were in the language of the Bible, as it is the most convenient language and was prevalent at the time.

Following it came the language of laws, since it is completely immersed in the language of the Bible, as well as because it was needed in order to show the people how to implement the laws.

The third was the language of legends. Although it is found in many places in the Bible, too, it is only as an auxiliary language because its wit rushes the perception of matters. However, it cannot be used as a basic language, as it lacks the precision of root and its branch. Thus, it was rarely used and hence did not develop.

And even though legends were used extensively during the time of the Tanaaim and the Amoraim, it was only in conjunction with the language of the Bible, to open the words of our sages—Rabbi... started, etc., (and other suffixes). In truth, expansive use of this language by our sages began after the concealment of the language of Kabbalah, during the days of Yohanan Ben Zakai and soon before, meaning seventy years prior to the ruin of the Temple.

The last to evolve was the language of Kabbalah. This was so because of the difficulties in understanding it: in addition to attainment, one needs to understand the meaning of its words. Hence, even those who understood it could not use it, since, for the most part, they were alone in their generation and had no one with whom to study. Our sages called that language, *Maase Merkavah*, since it is a special language by which one can elaborate on the details of the *Herkev* (composition) of the degrees in one another, and not at all with any other.

THE LANGUAGE OF KABBALAH IS LIKE ANY SPOKEN LANGUAGE, AND ITS PREFERENCE IS IN THE MEANING CONTAINED WITHIN A SINGLE WORD!

At first glance, the language of Kabbalah seems like a mixture of the three above-mentioned languages. However, one who understands how to use it will find that it is a unique language in and of itself from beginning to end. This does not pertain to the words, but to their meanings. This is the whole difference between them.

In the first three languages, there is almost no meaning to a single word, allowing the examiner to understand what the word implies. Only by joining a few words, and sometimes issues, can their content and meaning be understood. The advantage in the language of Kabbalah is that each and every word in it discloses its content and meaning to the examiner in utter precision, no less than in any other human tongue: each word carries its own precise definition and cannot be replaced with another.

FORGETTING THE WISDOM

Since the concealment of *The Zohar*, this important language has gradually been forgotten, as it was being used by fewer and fewer people. Also, there was a cessation of one generation, where the receiving sage did not convey it to an understanding receiver. Ever since then, there has been an immeasurable deficit.

You can evidently see that Kabbalist Rabbi Moshe de Leon, who was the last to possess it and by whom it appeared in the world, did not understand a word of it. This is because in those books where he introduces pieces of *The Book of Zohar*, it is clear that he did not understand the words at all, as he interpreted it according to the language of the Bible. He confused the understanding completely, although he himself had a wonderful attainment, as his compositions demonstrate.

So it was for generations: all the Kabbalists dedicated their entire lives to understanding the language of *The Zohar*, but could not find their hands and legs, since they forced the language of the Bible on it. For this reason, this book was sealed before them, as it was to Rabbi Moshe de Leon himself.

KABBALAH OF THE ARI

This was so until the arrival of the unique Kabbalist, the Ari. His attainment was above and beyond any boundary, and he opened the language of *The Zohar* for us and paved our way in it. Had he not passed away so young, it is hard to imagine the amount of Light that would be drawn out of *The Zohar*. The little we have been blessed with has paved a way and inlet, and true hope that over the generations our understanding would grow to fully grasp it.

Yet, you must understand the reason why all the great sages who followed the Ari abandoned all the books that they compiled in this wisdom and in the commentaries on *The Zohar*, and nearly prohibited themselves even from being seen, and dedicated their lives to the words of the Ari. This was not because they did not believe in the sanctity of the sages preceding the Ari; God forbid that we should think so. Anyone with eyes in the wisdom could see that the attainment of those great sages in the wisdom of truth was immeasurable. Only an ignorant fool could doubt them. However, their logic in the wisdom followed the first three languages.

Although each language is true and fitting in its place, it is not completely fitting, and quite misleading to understand the wisdom of Kabbalah contained in *The Zohar* using these orders. This is so because it is a completely different language, since it was forgotten. For this reason, we do not use their explanations, either the explanations of Rabbi Moshe de Leon himself, or his successors', as their words in interpreting *The Zohar* are not true, and to this day we have but one commentator—the Ari.

In light of the above, it follows that the internality of the wisdom of Kabbalah is none other than the internality of the Bible, the Talmud, and the legends. The only difference between them is in their explanations.

This is similar to a wisdom that has been translated into four languages. Naturally, the essence of the wisdom has not changed at all by the change of language. All we need to think of is which translation is the most convenient for conveying the wisdom to the student.

So is the matter before us: the wisdom of truth, meaning the wisdom of the revelation of Godliness in His Ways to the creatures, like secular teachings, must be passed on from generation to generation. Each generation adds a link to its former, and thus the wisdom evolves. Moreover, it becomes more suitable for expansion in the public.

Hence, each sage must pass on to his students and to the following generations everything he has inherited in the wisdom from earlier generations, as well as the additions he himself has been rewarded with. Clearly, the spiritual attainment—as it is attained by the attaining—cannot be passed on to another, and all the more so be written in a book. This is so because spiritual objects cannot come in letters of the imagination whatsoever (and even though it is written, "...and by the ministry of the prophets have I used similitudes," it is not literally so).

ORDER OF PASSING THE WISDOM

Thus, how can one who attains convey one's attainments to the generations and to students? Know that there is only one way for this: the way of root and branch. All the worlds and everything that fills them, in their every detail, emerged from the Creator in One, Unique, and Unified Thought. And the Thought alone cascaded and created all the many worlds and creations and their conducts, as explained in *The Tree of Life* and in the *Tikkuney Zohar*.

Hence, they are all equal to one another, like seal and imprint, where the first seal is imprinted in all. As a result, we call the closer worlds to the Thought about the purpose, "roots," and the farther worlds from the purpose we call "branches." This is so because the end of the act is in the preliminary thought.

Now we can understand the common idiom in the legends of our sages: "and watches it from the end of the world to its end." Should they not have said, "...from the beginning of the world to its end"? But there are two ends: an end according to the **distance from the purpose**, meaning the last branches in this world, and 2) an end called **"the final purpose,"** since the purpose is revealed at the end of the matter.

But as we have explained, "The end of the act is in the preliminary thought." Hence, we find the purpose at the beginning of the worlds. This is what we refer to as **"the first world,"** or **"the first seal."** All other worlds stem from it, and this is why all creations—still, vegetative, animate, and speaking—in all their incidents exist in their fullest form right at the first world. And what does not exist there cannot appear in the world, since one does not give what one does not have.

ROOT AND BRANCH IN THE WORLDS

Now it is easy to understand the matter of roots and branches in the worlds. Each of the manifold still, vegetative, animate, and speaking in this world have their corresponding parts in the world Above it, without any difference in their form, but only in their substance. Thus, an animal or a rock in this world is a corporeal matter, and its corresponding animal or rock in the Higher World is a spiritual matter, occupying no place or time. However, their quality is the same.

And here we should certainly add the matter of relation between matter and form, which is naturally conditioned on the quality of form, too. Similarly, with the majority of the still, vegetative, animate, and speaking in the Upper World, you will find their similitude and likeness in the world Above the Upper. This continues through the first world, where all the elements are completed, as it is written, "And God saw every thing that He had made, and, behold, it was very good."

This is why the Kabbalists wrote that the world is at the center of everything, to indicate the above, that the **end of the act** is the first world, meaning **the goal**. Also, the remoteness from the goal is called "the descent of the worlds from their Emanator" down to this corporeal world, the farthest from the purpose.

However, the end of all the corporeals is to gradually develop and achieve the goal that the Creator had designed for them, meaning the first world. Compared to this world, which we are in, it is the last world, meaning of the end of the matter. This is why it seems that the world of the goal is the last world, and that we, people of this world, are in between them.

ESSENCE OF THE WISDOM OF TRUTH

Now it is clear that as the emergence of the living species in this world and the conduct of their lives are a wondrous wisdom, the appearance of the Divine Abundance in the world, the degrees and the conduct of their actions unite to create a wondrous wisdom, far more than the science of physics. This is so because physics is mere knowledge of the arrangements of a particular kind existing in a particular world. It is unique to its subject, and no other wisdom is included in it.

This is not so with the wisdom of truth, since it is knowledge of the whole of the still, vegetative, animate, and speaking in all the worlds with all their instances and conducts, as they were included in the Creator's Thought, that is, in the purpose. For this reason, all the teachings in the world, from the least of them unto the greatest of them, are wondrously included in it, as it equalizes all the different teachings, the most different and the most remote from one another, as the east from the west. It makes them all equal, meaning the orders of each teaching are compelled to come by its ways.

For example, the science of physics is arranged precisely by the order of the worlds and the *Sefirot*. Similarly, the science of astronomy is arranged by that same order, and so is the science of music, etc. Thus, we find in it that all the teachings are arranged and follow a single connection and a single relation, and they are all like the relation of the child to its progenitor. Hence, they condition one another;

that is, the wisdom of truth is conditioned by all the teachings, and all the teachings are conditioned by it. This is why we do not find a single genuine Kabbalist without comprehensive knowledge in all the teachings of the world, since they acquire them from the wisdom of truth itself, as they are included in it.

UNITY

The greatest wonder about this wisdom is the integration in it: all the elements of the vast reality are incorporated in it, until they come into a single thing—the Almighty, and all of them together.

In the beginning, you find that all the teachings in the world are reflected in it. They are arranged within it precisely by its own orders. Subsequently, we find that all the worlds and the orders in the wisdom of truth itself, which are immeasurable, unite under only ten realities, called "Ten *Sefirot*."

Afterwards, these ten *Sefirot* arrange in four manners, which are the four-letter Name. After that, these four manners are included in the tip of the *Yod*, which implies the *Ein Sof* (Infinity).

In this way, one who begins in the wisdom must begin with the tip of the *Yod*, and from there to the ten *Sefirot* in the first world, called "the world of *Adam Kadmon*." From there one sees how the numerous details in the world of *Adam Kadmon* necessarily extend by way of cause and consequence, by the same laws we find in astronomy and physics, meaning constant, unbreakable laws that necessarily stem from one another, cascading from one another, from the tip of the *Yod* down to all the elements in the world of *Adam Kadmon*. From there they are imprinted by one another from the four worlds by way of seal and imprint, until we arrive at all the elements in this world. Afterwards, they are reintegrated in one another until they all come to the world of *Adam Kadmon*, then to the ten *Sefirot*, then to the four-letter Name, up to the tip of the *Yod*.

We could ask, "If the material is unknown, how can we study and scrutinize it"? Indeed, such as that you will find in all the teachings. For example, when studying anatomy—the various organs and how they affect one another—these organs have no similarity to the general subject, which is the whole, living human being. However, over time, when you thoroughly know the wisdom, you can establish a general relation of all the details upon which the body is conditioned.

So it is here: the general topic is the revelation of Godliness to His creations, by way of the purpose, as it is written, "...for the earth shall be full of the knowledge of the Lord." However, a novice will certainly have no knowledge of the general topic, which is conditioned by all of them. For this reason, one must acquire all the details and how they affect each other, as well as their causes by way of cause and consequence, until one completes the whole wisdom. And when one thoroughly knows everything, if he has a purified soul, it is certain that he will ultimately be rewarded with the general topic.

And even if he is not rewarded, it is still a great reward to acquire any perception of this great wisdom, whose advantage over all other teachings is as the value of their topics, and as the advantage of the Creator over His creations is valued. Similarly, this wisdom, whose subject is Him, is far more valuable than the wisdom whose subject is His creatures.

It is not because it is imperceptible that the world refrains from contemplating it. After all, an astronomer has no perception of the stars and the planets, but only of their moves, which they perform with wondrous wisdom that is predetermined in wondrous Providence. Similarly, the knowledge in the wisdom of truth is not more hidden than that, as even beginners thoroughly understand the moves. Rather, the whole prevention was because Kabbalists very wisely hid it from the world.

GIVING PERMISSION

I am glad that I have been born in such a generation when it is permitted to disclose the wisdom of truth. And should you ask, "How do I know that it is permitted?" I will reply that I have been given permission to disclose. Until now, the ways by which it is possible to publicly engage and to fully explain each word have not been revealed to any sage. And I, too, have sworn by my teacher not to disclose, as did all the students before me. However, this oath and this prohibition apply only to those manners that are given orally from generation to generation, back to the prophets and before. Had these ways been revealed to the public, they would cause much harm, for reasons known only to us.

Yet, the way in which I engage in my books is a permitted way. Moreover, I have been instructed by my teacher to expand it as much as I can. We call it "the manner of clothing the matters." You will see in the writings of Rashbi that he calls this way, "giving permission," and this is what the Creator has given me to the fullest extent. We deem it as dependent not on the greatness of the sage, but on the state of the generation, as our sages said, "Little Samuel was worthy, etc., but his generation was unworthy." This is why I said that my being rewarded with the manner of disclosing the wisdom is because of my generation.

ABSTRACT NAMES

It is a grave mistake to think that the language of Kabbalah uses abstract names. On the contrary, it touches only upon the actual. Indeed, there are things in the world that are real even though we have no perception of them, such as the magnet and electricity. Yet, who would be so foolish as to say that these are abstract names? After all, we thoroughly know their actions, and we could not care less that we do not know their essence. In the end, we refer to them as sure subjects to the actions that relate to them. And this is a real name. Even an infant who is just learning to speak can name them, if he only begins to feel their actions. This is our law: **All that we do not attain, we do not name.**

ESSENCE IS NOT PERCEIVED IN THE CORPOREALS

Moreover, even the things we imagine we attain by their essence, such as rocks and trees, after honest examination we are left with zero attainment in their essence, since we only attain their actions, which occur in conjunction with the encounter of our senses with them.

SOUL

For example, when Kabbalah states that there are three forces, 1) Body, 2) Animate Soul, and 3) Sacred Soul, this does not refer to the essence of the soul. The essence of the soul is fluid; it is what psychologists refer to as "self" and materialists as "electric."[1]

It is a waste of time to speak of its essence, as it is not arranged for impression through the touch of our senses, as with all corporeal objects. However, by observing in the essence of this fluid three kinds of actions in the spiritual worlds, we thoroughly distinguish between them by different names, according to their actual operations in the Upper Worlds. Thus, there are no abstract names here, but rather tangible ones in the full sense of the word.

ADVANTAGE OF MY COMMENTARY OVER PREVIOUS COMMENTARIES

We can be assisted by secular teachings in interpreting matters in the wisdom of Kabbalah, since the wisdom of Kabbalah is the root of everything and they are all included in it. Some were assisted by anatomy, such as in, "then without my flesh shall I see God," and some were assisted by philosophy. Latterly, there is extensive use of the wisdom of psychology. But all these are not considered true commentaries, since they do not interpret anything in the wisdom of Kabbalah

---

1 Rav Laitman explains that by "electric," Baal HaSulam means based on atoms.

itself, only show us how the rest of the teachings are included in it. This is why the observers cannot be assisted by one place, in another place. ...even though the wisdom of serving God is the closest wisdom to Kabbalah from all the external teachings.

And needless to say, it is impossible to be assisted by interpretations according to the science of anatomy, or by philosophy. For this reason, I said that I am the first interpreter by root and branch, and cause and consequence. Hence, if one were to understand some matter through my commentary, one can be certain that everywhere this matter appears in *The Zohar* and in the *Tikkunim*, he can be assisted by it, as with the commentaries on the literal, where you can be assisted by one place for all the other places.

The style of interpreting according to external teachings is a waste of time because it is nothing more than a testimony to the genuineness of one over the other. And an external teaching needs no testimony, as Providence has prepared five senses to testify for it, and in Kabbalah (nevertheless) one should understand the argument prior to bringing testimony to the argument.

STYLE OF INTERPRETING ACCORDING TO EXTERNAL TEACHINGS

This is the source of Rav Shem Tov's mistake: he interpreted *The Guide for the Perplexed* according to the wisdom of Kabbalah, and he did not know, or pretended not to know, that the wisdom of medicine, or any other wisdom, could be interpreted according to the wisdom of Kabbalah no less than the wisdom of philosophy. This is so because all the teachings are included in it and were imprinted by its seal.

Of course, *The Guide for the Perplexed* did not refer at all to what Rav Shem Tov interpreted, and he did not see how... in *The Book of Creation*, he interpreted the Kabbalah according to philosophy. I have already proven that such a style of commentaries is a waste of time, since external teachings need no testimony, and it is pointless to bring testimony to the truthfulness of the wisdom of Kabbalah before its words are interpreted.

It is like a prosecutor who brings witnesses to verify his words before he has explained his arguments (except for books that deal with the work of God, since the wisdom of serving God truly needs witnesses to its truthfulness and success, and we should be assisted by the wisdom of truth).

However, all the compositions of this style are not at all a waste. After we thoroughly understand the wisdom in itself, we will be able to receive much assistance from analogies, how all the teachings are included in it, as well as the manners by which to seek them.

ATTAINING THE WISDOM

There are three orders in the wisdom of truth:

1. The originality in the wisdom. It requires no human assistance, as it is entirely the gift of God, and no stranger shall interfere with it.

2. The understanding of the sources that one has attained from Above. It is like a person who sees that the whole world is set before his eyes, and yet he must exert and study to understand this world. Although he sees everything with his own eyes, there are fools and there are wise. This understanding is called "the wisdom of truth," and *Adam ha Rishon* was the first to receive a sequence of sufficient knowledge by which to understand and to successfully maximize everything he saw and attained with his eyes.

    The order of this knowledge is given only from mouth to mouth. And there is also an order of evolution in them, where each can add to his friend or regress (whereas in the first discernment everyone receives equally without adding or subtracting, like Adam, in understanding the reality of this world. In viewing it, all are equal, but this is not so in understanding it—some evolve from generation to generation and some regress). And the order of its conveyance is sometimes called "conveying the Explicit Name," and it is given under many conditions, but only orally, and not in writing.

3. This is a written order. It is a completely new thing, since besides containing much room for the development of the wisdom, through which each inherits all the expansions of his attainments to the following generations, there is another magnificent power in it: All who engage in it, although they still do not understand what is written in it, are purified by it, and the Upper Lights draw closer to them. And this order contains four languages, as we have explained above, and the language of Kabbalah exceeds them all.

ORDER OF CONVEYING THE WISDOM

The most successful way for one who wishes to learn the wisdom is to search for a genuine Kabbalist and follow all his instructions, until one is rewarded with understanding the wisdom in one's own mind, meaning the first discernment. Afterwards, one will be rewarded with its conveyance mouth to mouth, which is the second discernment, and after that, understand in writing, which is the third discernment. Then, one will have inherited all the wisdom and its instruments from his teacher with ease, and will be left with all one's time to develop and expand.

However, in reality there is a second way: through one's great yearning, the sights of the Heavens will open for him and he will attain all the origins by himself. This is the first discernment. Yet, afterwards one must still labor and exert extensively, until one finds a Kabbalist sage before whom one can bow and obey, and from whom to receive the wisdom by way of conveyance face to face, which is the second discernment, and then the third discernment.

And since one is not attached to a Kabbalist sage from the outset, the attainments come with great efforts and consume much time, leaving one with only little time to develop in it. Also, sometimes the knowledge comes after the fact, as it is written, "and they shall die without wisdom." These are ninety-nine percent and what we call, "entering but not exiting." They are as fools and ignorant in this world, who see the world set before them but do not understand any of it, except the bread in their mouths.

Indeed, in the first way, too, not everyone succeeds. This is because the majority, having attained, become complacent and stop subjugating themselves to their teacher sufficiently, as they are not worthy of the conveyance of the wisdom. In this case, the sage must hide the essence of the wisdom from them, and "they shall die without wisdom," "entering but not exiting."

This is so because there are harsh and strict conditions in conveying the wisdom, which stem from necessary reasons. Hence, very few are regarded highly enough by their teachers for them to find them worthy of this thing, and happy are the rewarded.

The Essence of Religion and Its Purpose

In this article I would like to resolve three issues:

A. What is the essence of religion?

B. Is its essence attained in this world or in the next world?

C. Is its purpose to benefit the Creator or the creatures?

At first glance, the reader might be surprised by my words, and will not understand these three questions that I have set before me as the topic of this essay. For who is it who does not know what religion is, and especially its rewards and punishments, which are destined to come primarily in the afterlife? And we need not mention the third issue, for everyone knows that it is to benefit the creatures and to guide them to delight and happiness, and what else need we add to that?

Indeed, I have nothing more to add. But because they are so familiar with the three concepts from infancy, they do not add or further examine them for the rest of their lives. And that shows their lack of knowledge in these exalted matters, which are necessarily the very foundation upon which the whole structure of religion is based.

Therefore, tell me how it is possible that a child of twelve or thirteen years of age, can already thoroughly grasp these subtle notions, and so sufficiently that he will not need to add any further concepts or knowledge of these matters for the rest of his life?

Indeed, here lies the problem! For this rash conjecture brought with it all the recklessness and wild conclusions that have come into our world in our generation! And it brought us to a state where the second generation has almost completely slipped from under our hands.

THE ABSOLUTE GOOD

To avoid tiring the readers with long discussions, I have relied on all that I wrote in previous essays, especially on the essay, "Matan Torah" (The Giving of the Torah), which are all like a preface to the exalted topic ahead. Here I shall speak briefly and simply, to make it understood for all.

First, we must understand the Creator—He is the Absolute Goodness. This means that it is utterly impossible that He would ever cause any sorrow to any person. And this we take to be the first concept, for our common sense clearly shows that the basis for any evil-doing in the world stems only from the will to receive.

That means that the eagerness to benefit ourselves makes us harm our fellow persons, due to our will to receive self-gratification. Thus, if no being would find contentment in favoring itself, no being would ever harm another. And if we sometimes find some being that harms another, without any will to receive self-gratification, it does that only because of an old habit that originated in the will to receive, which now rids it of the need to find a new reason.

And because we realize that the Creator is, in and of Himself, complete and needs no one to help Him to completion, since He precedes everything, it is therefore clear that He does not have any will to receive. And because He has no will to receive, He is fundamentally devoid of a desire to harm anyone; it is as simple as that.

Furthermore, it is completely agreeable to our mind as the first concept, that He possesses a desire to bestow goodness upon others, meaning to His creatures. And that is evidently shown by the great Creation that He has created and set before our eyes. For in this world there are beings that necessarily experience either a good feeling or a bad one, and that feeling necessarily comes to them from the Creator. And once it is absolutely clear that there is no aim to harm in the nature of the Creator, it necessitates that the creatures receive only goodness from Him, for He has created them only to bestow upon them.

Thus we learn that He has only a desire to bestow goodness, and it is utterly impossible that any harmfulness might be in His domain, which could emit from Him. Hence we have defined Him as "The Absolute Good." And after we have learned that, let us take a look at the actual reality that is guided by Him, and how He bestows only goodness upon them.

HIS GUIDANCE IS PURPOSEFUL GUIDANCE

By observing nature's systems, we understand that any beings of the four types—still, vegetative, animate and speaking—as a whole and in particular, are found to be under purposeful guidance, meaning a slow and gradual growth by way of cause and effect, as a fruit on a tree, which is guided with favourable guidance to finally become a sweet and fine-looking fruit.

Go and ask a botanist how many phases the fruit undergoes from the time it becomes visible until it is completely ripe. Not only do its preceding phases show no evidence of its sweet and fine-looking end, but as if to vex, they show the opposite of the final outcome.

The sweeter the fruit is at its end, the more bitter and unsightly it is in the earlier phases of its development. And so it is with the animate and speaking types: for the beast, whose mind is little at its end, is not so wanting while it grows. Whereas man, whose mind is great at his end, is very wanting while developing. "A day-old calf is called an ox"; that is, it has the strength to stand on its own legs and walk, and the intelligence to avoid hazards on its way.

But a day-old infant lies seemingly senseless. And should one who is not accustomed to the conducts of this world examine these two newborns, he would certainly conclude that the human infant will amount to nothing and the calf will turn out to be a great hero, if he were to judge by the wisdom of the calf compared to the senseless and mindless child.

Thus, it is evident that His guidance over the reality that He has created is in the form of purposeful Guidance, without taking into consideration the order of the phases of development, for they deceive us and prevent us from understanding their purpose, being always opposite to their final shape.

It is about such matters that we say, "There is none so wise as the experienced." Only one who is experienced has the opportunity to examine Creation in all its phases of development, all the way through completion, and can calm things down, so as to not fear those spoilt images that the Creation undergoes in the phases of its development, but believe in its fine and pure end.

Thus, we have thoroughly shown the conducts of His Providence in our world, which is only a purposeful Guidance. The attribute of goodness is not at all apparent before Creation arrives at its completion, its final ripeness. On the contrary, it rather always takes a form of corruption in the eyes of the beholders. Thus you see that the Creator bestows upon His creatures only goodness, but that goodness comes by way of purposeful Guidance.

TWO PATHS: A PATH OF PAIN AND A PATH OF TORAH

We have shown that God is the Absolute Good, and that He watches us in complete benevolence without a hint of evil, and in purposeful guidance. That means that His guidance compels us to undergo a series of phases, by way of cause and effect, preceding and resulting, until we are qualified to receive the desired goodness. And then we shall arrive at our purpose as a ripe and fine-looking fruit. And we understand that this purpose is guaranteed for us all, or else you flaw His Providence, saying it is insufficient for its purpose.

Our sages said, "Divinity in the lower ones—a high need." That means that since His guidance is purposeful and aims to eventually bring us to adhesion with Him, so it would reside within us, this is considered a high need. Meaning, if we do not come to that, we shall find ourselves, regarding His Providence, flawed.

This is similar to a great king who had a son at old age, and he was very fond of him. Hence, since the day he was born, he thought of only good things for him. He collected the finest, wisest, and most precious books in the kingdom and built him a school. He sent after the finest builders and built palaces of pleasure. He gathered all the musicians and singers and built him concert halls, and called the finest bakers and chefs to provide him with all the delicacies in the world.

But alas, the son grew up to be a fool, with no desire for education. And he was blind and could not see or feel the beauty of the buildings. And he was deaf, unable to hear the poems and the music. And he was ill, permitted to eat only coarse flour bread, arising contempt and wrath.

However, such a thing may happen to a flesh and blood king, but that is impossible to say about the Creator, where there cannot be any deceit. Therefore, He has prepared for us two paths of development:

The first is a path of suffering, which is the conduct of development of Creation from within itself. By its own nature it is compelled to follow a way of cause and effect, in varying, consecutive states, which slowly develop us, until we come to a resolution to choose the good and reject the bad, and to be qualified for the purpose as He desires.

And that path is indeed a long and painful one. Therefore, He has prepared for us a pleasant and gentle way, which is the path of torah and *Mitzvot*, which can qualify us for our purpose painlessly and quickly.

It turns out that our final aim is to be qualified for adhesion with Him—for Him to reside within us. That aim is a certainty and there is no way to deviate from it, since His guidance supervises us in both paths, which are the path of suffering and the path of Torah. But looking at the actual reality, we find that His guidance comes simultaneously in both paths, which our sages refer to as "the way of the earth" and "the way of Torah."

THE ESSENCE OF RELIGION IS TO DEVELOP IN US THE SENSE OF RECOGNITION OF EVIL

Our sages say, "Why should the Creator mind whether one slays at the throat or at the back of the neck? After all, the *Mitzvot* were only given to cleanse people." That cleansing has been thoroughly clarified in "Matan Torah" (Item 2), but here I would like to clear up the essence of that development, which is attained through Torah and *Mitzvot*.

Bear in mind that it is the recognition of the evil within us. That engagement in *Mitzvot* can slowly and gradually purify those who delve in them. And the scale by which we measure the degrees of cleansing is the measurement of the recognition of the evil within us.

Man is naturally ready to repel and root out any evil from within him. In that, all people are the same. But the difference between one person and the next is only in the recognition of evil. A more developed person recognizes in himself a greater amount of evil, and hence repels and separates the evil from within to a greater extent. The undeveloped senses in himself only a small amount of evil, and will therefore repel only a small amount of evil. As a result, he leaves all his filth within, for he does not recognize it as filth.

To avoid tiring the reader, we shall clarify the general meaning of good and bad, as it has been explained in "Matan Torah" (Item 12). Evil, in general, is nothing more than self-love, called "egoism," since it is opposite in form from the Creator, who hasn't any will to receive for Himself, but only to bestow.

As we have explained in "Matan Torah" (Items 9,11), pleasure and sublimity are measured by the extent of equivalence of form with the Maker. And pain and intolerance are measured by the extent of disparity of form from the Maker. Thus, egoism is loathsome and pains us, as its form is opposite from the Maker.

But this loathsomeness is not divided equally among all souls, but is given in varying measures. The crude, undeveloped person does not regard egoism as a bad attribute and uses it openly, without shame or restraints. He steals and murders in broad daylight wherever he finds it possible. The somewhat more developed, sense some measure of their egoism to be bad, and are at least ashamed to use it in public, to steal and kill openly. But in secrecy they still commit their crimes.

The even more developed feel egoism to be a loathsome thing indeed, until they cannot tolerate it within and reject it completely, as much as they detect of it, until they cannot, and do not want to enjoy the labor of others. Then begin to emerge in them the sparks of love for others, called "altruism," which is the general attribute of goodness.

And that, too, evolves gradually. First develops love and desire to bestow upon one's family and kin, as in the verse, "thou hide not thyself from thine own flesh." When further developing, one's attribute of bestowal expands to all the people around him, being one's townspeople or one's nation. And so one adds, until he finally develops love for the whole of humanity.

CONSCIOUS DEVELOPMENT AND UNCONSCIOUS DEVELOPMENT

Bear in mind that two forces serve to push us up the rungs of the aforementioned ladder, until we reach its head in the sky, which is the purposeful point of equivalence of form with our Maker. And the difference between these two forces is that the first pushes us from behind, which we defined as "the path of pain" or "the way of the earth."

From that path stems the philosophy of morality called "ethics," which is based on an empirical knowledge, through examination of the practical reason, whose essence is but a summation of the visible damages that result from the nucleons of egoism.

These experiments come to us by chance, not as a result of our conscious choice, but they are certain to lead us to their goal, for the image of evil grows ever clearer to our senses. And to the extent that we recognize its damages, we remove ourselves from it and then climb to a higher rung on the ladder.

The second force pushes us consciously, that is, of our own choice. That force pulls us from before, and that is what we defined as "the path of Torah and *Mitzvot*." For engaging in *Mitzvot*, and the work to bring contentment to our Maker rapidly develops that sense of recognition of evil, as we have shown in "Matan Torah" (Item 13).

And here we benefit twice:

A. We do not have to wait for life's ordeals to push us from behind, whose measure of goading is gauged only by the measure of agony and destructions. On the contrary, through the subtle pleasantness we feel when working sincerely to Him, to please Him, there develops within us a relative recognition of the lowliness of these sparks of self-love—that they are obstacles on our way to receiving that subtle taste of bestowal upon the Creator. Thus, the gradual sense of recognition of evil evolves in us from times of delight and great tranquility, through reception of the good while serving the Creator, out of our sensation of the pleasantness and gentleness that reach us due to the equivalence of form with our Maker.

B. We save time, for He operates to "enlighten" us, thus enabling us to increase our work and hasten time as we please.

RELIGION IS NOT FOR THE GOOD OF THE PEOPLE, BUT FOR THE GOOD OF THE WORKER

Many are mistaken and compare our holy Torah to ethics. But that has come to them because they have never tasted religion in their lives. I call upon them: "Taste and see that the Lord is good." It is true that both ethics and religion aim at one thing—to raise man above the filth of the narrow self-love and bring him to the heights of love-of-others.

But still, they are as remote one from the other as the distance between the Thought of the Creator and the thought of people. For religion extends from the Thoughts of the Creator, and ethics comes from thoughts of flesh and blood and from the experiences of their lives. Hence, there is an evident difference between them, both in practical aspects and in the final aim. For the recognition of good and evil that develops in us through ethics, as we use it, is relative to the success of the society.

With religion, however, the recognition of good and evil that develops in us, as we use it, is relative to the Creator alone, that is, from the disparity of form from the Maker, to equivalence of form with Him, which is called *Dvekut* (adhesion), as clarified in "Matan Torah" (Items 9-11).

And they are also completely removed from one another regarding the goal, for the goal of ethics is the well-being of society from the perspective of practical reason, derived from life's experiences. But in the end, that goal does not promise its follower any elevation above the boundaries of nature. Hence, this goal is still subject to criticism, for who can prove to an individual the extent of his benefit in such a conclusive manner that he will be compelled to even slightly diminish his own self in favor of the well-being of society?

The religious goal, however, promises the well-being of the individual who follows it, as we have already shown that when one comes to love others, he is in direct *Dvekut*, which is equivalence of form with the Maker, and along with it man passes from his narrow world, filled with pain and impediments, to an eternal and broad world of bestowal upon the Lord and upon the people.

You will also find a significant difference regarding the support because following the ethics is supported by the favor of people, which is like a rent that finally pays off. And when man grows accustomed to this work, he will not be able to ascend in degrees of ethics, for he will now be used to such work that is well rewarded by society, which pays for his good deeds.

Yet, by observing Torah and *Mitzvot* in order to please his Maker, without any reward, he climbs the rungs of ethics precisely to the extent that he pursues it, since there is no payment on his path. And each penny is added to a great account. And finally he acquires a second nature, which is bestowal upon others without any self-gratification, except for the bare necessities of his life.

Now he has really been liberated from the incarcerations of Creation. For when one detests any self-reception and his soul loathes the petite physical pleasures and respect, he finds himself roaming free in the Creator's world. And he is guaranteed that no damage or misfortune will ever come upon him, since all the damages come to a man only through the self-reception imprinted in him.

Thus, we have thoroughly shown that the purpose of religion is only for the individual who engages in it, and not at all for the use or benefit of common people, although all his actions revolve around the benefit of people and are measured by these acts. But this is but a passage to the sublime goal, which is equivalence of form with the Maker. And now we can understand that the purpose of religion is collected while living in this world, and examine closely in "Matan Torah," regarding the purpose of the whole and of the individual.

Body and Soul

Before I clarify this exalted matter, it is important for me to note that although all the readers seem to consider it impossible to clarify and bring such a matter closer to the human mind, except by relying on abstract, philosophical concepts, as is usually the case in such scrutinies, since the day I have discovered the wisdom of Kabbalah and dedicated myself to it, I have distanced myself from abstract philosophy and all its branches as the east from the west. Everything that I will write henceforth will be from a purely scientific perspective, in utter precision, and by means of simple recognition of practical, useful things.

Although I will mention their words below, it will be only to indicate the difference between what the human mind can conjure up and what can be understood using the concepts of the Torah and the prophecy, which are based on practical foundations (as I have shown in "The Essence of the Wisdom of Kabbalah").

I would also like to thoroughly clarify the terms "body" and "soul" as they truly are, since truth and sound mind are one and the same. This is because the truth is available for anyone, but only by the spirit of the Holy Torah and by removing all the distorted concepts that have taken root among the people. These are primarily taken from abstract methods from which the spirit of our Holy Torah is utterly removed.

THREE METHODS IN THE CONCEPTS OF BODY AND SOUL

In general, we find that the methods that abound in the world concerning the concepts of body and soul are gathered into three methods:

1) The Method of Faith

The method of faith argues that all that exists is the spirit, or the soul. They believe that there are spiritual objects separated from one another by quality. They are called "souls of people," and that they exist independently, prior to dressing in a human body. Afterwards, when the body dies, the death does not apply to it, since a spiritual object is a simple object. In their view, death is but a separation of the elements comprising the object.

This is possible with physical objects, comprised of several elements which death disintegrates. But the spiritual soul, which is an utterly simple object, lacking any complexity, cannot be separated in any way, as this separation would annul its existence. Hence, the soul is eternal and exists forever.

The body, as they understand it, is like a clothing over this spiritual object. The spiritual soul clothes in it and uses it to manifest its forces: the good qualities and all kinds of concepts. Also, it provides the body with life and motion and guards it from harm. Thus, the body itself is lifeless, motionless, and contains nothing but dead matter, as we see it once the soul departs it—when it dies—and all the signs of life that we see in human bodies are but manifestations of the soul's powers.

2) *The Method of Believers in Duality*

Those who believe in duality think of the body as a complete creation, standing, living, and nourishing, and safekeeping its existence in all that is required. It does not need any assistance from any spiritual object.

Yet, the body is not considered man's essence. Man's primary essence is the perceiving soul, which is a spiritual object, as in the view of the supporters of the first method.

The difference between these two methods is only in the concept of the body. Following the extensive developments in physiology and psychology, they have found that Providence has provided for all of life's needs within the machine of the body itself. This, in their view, restricts the role of the soul's functionality within the body solely to concepts and virtues of the spiritual kind. Thus, while they believe in duality, in both methods together, they say that the soul is the reason for the body, meaning that the body is a result, extending from the soul.

3) *The Method of the Deniers*

The method of deniers of spirituality, who acknowledge only corporeality. Supporters of this method completely deny the existence of any kind of abstract spiritual object within the body. They have evidently proven that man's mind, too, is but a product of the body, and they depict the body as an electronic machine with wires that stretch from the body to the brain, and operate by encounters with external things.

Also, they send their sensations of pain or pleasure to the brain, and the brain instructs the organ what to do. Everything is run by wires and cords built for this task. They move the organ away from sources of pain and towards sources of pleasure. Thus, they clarify all of man's conclusions from life's events.

Also, what we feel as concepts and rationalities within our minds are but images of corporeal occurrences within the body. And man's pre-eminence over all animals is that our minds are developed to such an extent that all the body's events are depicted in our brains as images that we experience as concepts and rationalities.

Thus, the mind and all its deductions are but products that extend from the events of the body. In addition, there are proponents of the second method who completely agree with this method, but add the spiritual, eternal object to it, called "the soul that dresses within the machine of the body." This soul is **man's essence**, and the machine of the body is but its clothing. Thus, I have laid out in general terms all that human science has thus far contrived in the concepts of "body" and "soul."

THE SCIENTIFIC MEANING OF BODY AND SOUL ACCORDING TO OUR HOLY TORAH

Now I shall explain this exalted matter according to our Holy Torah, as our sages have explained it to us. I have already written in several places that there is not a single word of our sages, not even in the prophetic wisdom of Kabbalah, that relies on theoretical bases. This is so because it is a known fact that man is naturally doubtful, and each conclusion that the human mind deems certain, it deems uncertain after some time. Hence, one doubles the efforts of one's study and invents another inference and declares that as certain.

But if one is a genuine student, he will walk around this axis all of one's life, since yesterday's certainty has become today's uncertainty, and today's certainty become tomorrow's uncertainty. Thus, it is impossible to determine any definite conclusions for more than a day.

REVEALED AND CONCEALED

Today's science has sufficiently understood that **there is no absolute certainty in reality**. Yet, our sages arrived at this conclusion several thousand years earlier. Hence, concerning religious matters, they have guided and forbidden us to not only refrain from drawing any conclusions based on theory, but even prohibited us from being assisted by such theories, even by way of negotiations.

Our sages divided the wisdom into two matters: revealed and concealed. The revealed part contains everything we know from our direct consciousness, as well as the concepts built upon practical experience, without any assistance from scrutiny, as our sages said, "a judge has only what his eyes see."

The concealed part contains all those concepts we had heard from trusted people or have acquired by ourselves through general understanding and perception of them. However, we cannot sufficiently approach it so as to criticize it with a healthy mind, with straightforward cognizance. And this is regarded as "concealed," where we were advised to accept matters with "simple faith." And with all that concerns religion, we have been strictly forbidden to even **gaze** at matters that could arouse us to scrutinize and **study them**.

Yet, these names, "revealed" and "concealed," are not permanent names, applying to a certain kind of knowledge, as the uneducated think. Rather, they apply only to the human **consciousness**. Thus, one refers to all those concepts one has already discovered and has come to know through actual experience as "revealed," and regards all the concepts that are yet to be recognized in this manner as "concealed."

Thus, throughout the generations, all people have these two divisions. The revealed part will be permitted for study and research, as it relies on a true basis, and the concealed part is forbidden for even a shred of scrutiny, since one has no real basis there.

PERMITTED AND FORBIDDEN IN USING HUMAN SCIENCE

Hence, we who follow in the footsteps of our sages are not permitted to use the human science, except with knowledge that has been proven by actual experiences, and of whose validity we have no doubt. Therefore, we cannot accept any religious principle from the above three methods, all the more so concerning the concepts of body and soul, which are the fundamental concepts and the subject of religion as a whole. We can only accept concepts of life sciences taken from experiments that no man can doubt.

Clearly, such a proof cannot be found in any spiritual matter, but only in physical matters, set up for perception by the senses. Hence, we are permitted to use the third method, to an extent. It engages only in **matters of the body**, in all those deductions that have been proven by experiments, and which no one doubts. The rest of the concepts, which combine the **reason** of their method and other methods, are forbidden to us. One who uses them breaches, "Turn you not unto the idols."

Yet, this third method is foreign and loathsome to the human spirit. There is hardly any truly educated person who is able to accept it. This is so because according to them, man's humane form has been erased and vanished. Man has been made into a machine that walks and works by other forces. According to them, man has no free choice whatsoever, but is rather pushed by nature's forces, and all his actions are compulsory. Hence, man has no reward or punishment, since no judgment, punishment, or reward apply to one who has no freedom of will.

Such a thing is utterly unthinkable, and not only for the religious, who believe in reward and punishment, since believing in His Providence, that all of nature's forces are guided by Him, assures them that everything has a good and desirable cause. Yet, this method is even stranger in the eyes of the nonreligious, who believe that everyone is given to the hands of a blind, mindless, and aimless nature. These intelligent ones are like toys in its hands, led astray, and who knows where? Hence, this method has become despised and unaccepted in the world.

But you should know that the method of those who conceive duality came only to correct this above-mentioned wrong. For this reason, they have decided that the body, which is but a machine according to the third method, is not at all the real human. Man's real essence is something altogether different—invisible and imperceptible to the senses. It is a spiritual entity, clothed and hidden within the body. This is man's "self," the "I." The body and everything within it are considered possessions of that eternal and spiritual I, as they have written.

Yet, by their own admission, this method is lame, since they cannot explain how a spiritual entity, being the soul or the self, can move the body or decide anything concerning it. This is because following the philosophical precision itself, the spiritual has no contact whatsoever with the physical. It has absolutely no impact on it, as they have written themselves.

THE ACCUSATION AGAINST THE RAMBAM (MAIMONIDES)

Yet, even without this question, their method would have been forbidden among Israel, as we have explained above. It is important to know that the whole accusation of Rambam by Israel's sages and the harsh judgment to burn his books, were not because they had any doubt of the righteousness and piousness of the Rambam himself. Rather, it was only because he used philosophy and metaphysics, which were at their peak at the time, as assistance in his books. The Rambam wished to save them from it, yet the sages did not agree with him.

Needless to say, today our generation has already recognized that metaphysical philosophy contains no real content upon which it is worthwhile to spend one's time. Hence, it is certainly forbidden for anyone to take any spices from their words.

Exile and Redemption

Harmony between religion and the law of development or blind fate

> "And among these nations you shall have no rest."
> —Deuteronomy 28:85

> "And that which comes into your mind shall not be at all; in that you say we will be as the nations, as the families of the countries."
> —Ezekiel 20:32

The Creator will evidently show us that Israel cannot exist in exile, and will find no rest as the rest of the nations that mingled among the nations and found rest, and assimilated in them, until no trace was left of them. Not so is the house of Israel. This nation will find no rest among the nations until it realizes the verse, "And from there you will seek the Lord your God and you will find Him for you will demand Him with all your heart and all your soul" (Deuteronomy 4:29).

This can be examined by studying Providence and the verse which states about us, "The Torah is true and all its words are true," and woe to us as long as we doubt its truthfulness. And we say about all the rebuke that is happening to us that it is chance and blind fate. This has but one cure—to bring the troubles back on us to such an extent that we will see that they are not coincidental but steadfast Providence, intended for us in the Holy Torah.

And we should clarify this matter by the law of development itself: the nature of the steadfast Guidance that we have attained through the Holy Torah, as in the path of Torah in Providence (see "Two Ways"), a far more rapid development than the other nations has come to us. And because the members of the nation developed so, there was always the necessity to go forward and be extremely meticulous with all the *Mitzvot* of the Torah. And because they would not do it, but wished to include their narrow selfishness, meaning the *Lo Lishma*, this developed the ruin of the First Temple, since they wished to extol wealth and power above justice, as other nations.

But because the Torah prohibits it, they denied the Torah and the prophecy and adopted the manners of the neighbors so they could enjoy life as much as selfishness demanded of them. And because they did that, the powers of the nation disintegrated: some followed the kings and the selfish officers, and some followed the prophets. And that separation continued until the ruin.

In the Second Temple, it was even more conspicuous, since the beginning of the separation was publicly displayed by unvirtuous disciples, headed by Tzadok and Bytos. Their mutiny against our sages revolved primarily around the obligation of *Lishma*, as our sages said, "Wise men, be careful with your words." Because they did not want to retire from selfishness, they created communities of this corrupt kind and became a great sect called "Tzdokim," who were the rich and the officers, pursuing selfish desires unlike the path of Torah. And they fought the Prushim and brought the Roman kingdom's rule over Israel. They are the ones who would not make peace with the imperious, as our sages advised by the Torah, until the house was ruined and the glory of Israel was exiled.

THE DIFFERENCE BETWEEN A SECULAR IDEAL AND A RELIGIOUS IDEAL

A secular ideal stems from humanness and hence cannot raise itself above humanness. But a religious idea, which stems from the Creator, can raise itself above humanity. This is because the basis for a secular ideal is in comparing and the price of **glorifying man**, and he acts to boast in the eyes of people. And although one is sometimes disgraced in the eyes of one's contemporaries, one still relies on other generations and it is still a precious thing for him, like a gem that fuels its owner although no one knows of it or cherishes it.

A religious idea, however, is based on **glory in the eyes of God**. Hence, he who follows a religious idea can raise himself above humanness.

And so it is among the nations of our exile. As long as we followed the path of Torah, we remained safe, for it is known to all the nations that we are a highly developed nation and they wanted our cooperation. They exploit us, each according to their own selfish desires. Yet we still had great power among the nations, for after all the exploitation, there still remained a handsome portion left for us, greater than for the civilians of the land.

But because people rebelled against the Torah in their aspiration to execute their selfish ploys, they lost life's purpose, meaning the work of God. And because the sublime goal was swapped for selfish goals of life's pleasures, anyone who attained fortune raised his own goal with glory and beauty. And where the religious man scattered his monetary surplus on charity, good deeds, building seminaries, and other such collective needs, the selfish ones scattered their surplus on the joys of life: food and drink, clothing and jewels, and equalized with the prominent in every nation.

By these words, I only mean to show that the Torah and the natural law of development go hand in hand in wondrous unity even with blind faith. Thus, the bad incidences in the exile, which we have much to tell of from the days of our exile, were all because we embezzled the Torah. And if we kept the commandments of the Torah, no harm would come to us.

CONGRUITY AND UNITY BETWEEN TORAH AND BLIND FATE, AND THE DEVELOPMENT OF HUMAN CALCULATION

Hence, I hereby propose to the House of Israel to say to our troubles, "Enough!" and at the very least, make a human calculation regarding these adventures that they have inflicted us time and time again, and here in our country, as well. We wish to start our own policy, as we have no hope of clutching at the ground as a nation as long as we do not accept our holy Torah without any extenuations, to the last condition of the work *Lishma*, and not for oneself, with any residue of selfishness, as I have proven in the article "Matan Torah."

If we do not establish ourselves accordingly, then there are classes among us, and we will undoubtedly be pushed right and left as all nations are, and much more. This is because the nature of the developed is that they cannot be restrained, for any important notion that comes from an opinionated person will not bow its head before anything and knows no compromise. This is why our sages said, "Israel is the fiercest of the nations," as one whose mind is broader is most obstinate.

This is a psychological law. And if you do not understand me, go and study this lesson among the contemporary members of the nation: While we have only begun to build, time has already disclosed our fierceness and assertiveness of the mind, and that which one builds, the other ruins.

...This is known to all, but there is only one innovation in my words: They believe that in the end, the other side will understand the danger and will bow his head and accept their opinion. But I know that even if we tie them together in one basket, one will not surrender to the other even a little, and no danger will interrupt anyone from carrying out his ambition.

In a word: As long as we do not raise our goal above the corporeal life, we will have no corporeal revival because the spiritual and the corporeal in us cannot dwell in one basket, for we are the children of the idea. And even if we are immersed in forty-nine gates of materialism, we will still not give up the idea. Hence, it is the holy purpose of for His name that we need.

A Speech for the Completion of The Zohar

It is known that the desired purpose of the work in Torah and *Mitzvot* is to cleave unto the Creator, as it is written, "and to cleave unto Him." We should understand what *Dvekut* (adhesion) with the Creator means. After all, the thought has no perception of Him whatsoever. Indeed, our sages have discussed this question before me, asking about the verse, "and to cleave unto Him": "How can one cleave unto Him? After all, He is consuming fire."

And they replied, "Cleave unto His qualities: as He is merciful, you are merciful; as he is compassionate, you are compassionate." This is perplexing; how did our sages drift from the literal text? After all, it is explicitly written, "and to cleave unto Him." Had the meaning been to cleave unto His qualities it would have to write, "cleave unto His ways." So why does it say, "and to cleave unto Him"?

The thing is that in corporeality, which takes up space, we understand *Dvekut* as proximity of place, and we understand separation as remoteness of place. However, in spirituality, which does not occupy any space, *Dvekut* and separation do not mean proximity or remoteness of place. This is because they do not occupy any space at all. Rather, we understand *Dvekut* as equivalence of form between two spirituals, and we understand separation as disparity of form between two spirituals.

As the axe cuts and separates a corporeal object into two, by removing the parts from one another, disparity of form distinguishes the spiritual and divides it in two. If the disparity of form between them is small, we say that they are a little far from one another. And if the disparity of form is great, we say that they are very far from one another. And if they are of opposite forms, we say that they are as far from each other as two extremes.

For example, when two people hate each other, it is said about them that they are as separated from one another as the East from the West. And if they love each other, it is said about them that they are as attached to one another as a single body.

And this does not concern nearness or remoteness of location. Rather, it is about equivalence of form or disparity of form. This is so because when people love each other, it is because there is equivalence of form between them. Because one loves everything that one's friend loves, and hates all that one's friend hates, they are attached to one another and love one another.

However, if there is any disparity of form between them, and one loves something even though one's friend hates that thing, they are hateful of each other and remote from one another to the extent of their disparity of form. And if they are opposite so that everything that one loves, one's friend hates, it is said about them that they are as remote and as separated as the East from the West.

And you find that disparity of form in spirituality acts like the axe that separates in corporeality. Similarly, the measure of remoteness of location and the measure of the separation in them depends on the measure of disparity of form between them. Also, the measure of *Dvekut* between them depends on the measure of equivalence of form between them.

Now we understand how right our sages were when they interpreted the verse, "and to cleave unto Him," as adhesion with His qualities—as He is merciful, you are merciful; as He is compassionate, you are compassionate. They did not deflect the text from the literal meaning. Quite the contrary, they interpreted the text precisely according to its literal meaning, since spiritual *Dvekut* can only be depicted as equivalence of form. Hence, by equalizing our form with the form of His qualities, we become attached to Him.

This is why they said, "as He is merciful." In other words, all His actions are to bestow and benefit others, and not at all for His own benefit, since He has no deficiencies that require complementing. And also, He has no one from whom to receive. Similarly, all your actions will be to bestow and to benefit others. Thus, you will equalize your form with the form of the qualities of the Creator, and this is spiritual *Dvekut*.

There is a discernment of "mind" and a discernment of "heart" in the above-mentioned equivalence of form. The engagement in Torah and *Mitzvot* in order to bestow contentment upon one's Maker is equivalence of form in the mind. This is because the Creator does not think of Himself—whether He exists or whether He watches over His creations, and other such doubts. Similarly, one who wishes to achieve equivalence of form must not think of these things, as well, when it is clear that the Creator does not think of them, since there is no greater disparity of form than that. Hence, anyone who thinks of such matters is certainly separated from Him, and will never achieve equivalence of form.

This is what our sages said, "Let all your actions be for the Creator," that is, *Dvekut* with the Creator. Do not do anything that does not promote this goal of *Dvekut*. This means that all your actions will be to bestow and to benefit your fellow person. At that time, you will achieve equivalence of form with the Creator—as all His actions are to bestow and to benefit others, so you, all your actions will be only to bestow and to benefit others. This is the complete *Dvekut*.

And we could ask about it, "How can one's every action be to benefit others? After all, one must work to sustain oneself and one's family." The answer is that those deeds that one does out of necessity, to receive one's bare necessities for sustenance, that necessity is neither praised nor condemned. This is not considered doing something for oneself whatsoever.

Anyone who delves into the heart of things will certainly be surprised at how one can achieve complete equivalence of form, so all one's actions are to give to others, while man's very essence is only to receive for oneself. By nature, we are unable to do even the smallest thing to benefit others. Instead, when we give to others, we are compelled to expect that in the end, we will receive a worthwhile reward. If one as much as doubts the reward, one will refrain from acting. Thus, how can one's every action be only to bestow upon others and not at all for oneself?

Indeed, I admit that this is a very difficult thing. One cannot change the nature of one's own creation, which is only to receive for oneself, much less invert one's nature from one extreme to the other, meaning to not receive anything for oneself, but rather act only to bestow.

Yet, this is why the Creator gave us Torah and *Mitzvot*, which we were commanded to do only in order to bestow contentment upon the Creator. Had it not been for the engagement in Torah and *Mitzvot Lishma* (for Her Name), to bring contentment to the Creator with them, and not to benefit ourselves, there would have been no tactic in the world that could help us invert our nature.

Now you can understand the rigorousness of engaging in Torah and *Mitzvot Lishma*. If one's intention in the Torah and *Mitzvot* is not to benefit the Creator, but oneself, not only will the nature of the will to receive in him not be inverted, but rather, the will to receive in him will be much more than what he was given by the nature of his creation.

But what are the virtues of one who has been rewarded with *Dvekut* with the Creator? They are not specified anywhere, except in subtle intimations. Yet, to clarify the matters in my essay, I must disclose a little, as much as necessary.

I will explain the matters with an allegory. The body with its organs are one. The whole of the body exchanges thoughts and sensations regarding each of its organs. For example, if the whole body thinks that a specific organ should serve it and please it, this organ will immediately know that thought and provide the contemplated pleasure. Also, if an organ thinks and feels that the place it is in is narrow, the rest of the body will immediately know that thought and sensation and move it to a comfortable place.

However, should an organ be cut off from the body, they will become two separate entities; the rest of the body will no longer know the needs of the separated organ, and the organ will not know the thoughts of the body, to benefit it and serve it. But if a physician came and reconnected the organ to the body as before, the organ would once again know the thoughts and needs of the rest of the body, and the rest of the body would once again know the needs of the organ.

According to this allegory, we can understand the merit of one who has been rewarded with *Dvekut* with the Creator. I have already demonstrated in my "Introduction to The Book of Zohar," Item 9, that the soul is an illumination that extends from His Essence. This illumination has been separated from the Creator by the Creator's clothing it with a will to receive. This is so because the Thought of Creation, to do good to His creations, created in each soul a desire to receive pleasure. Thus, this form of the will to receive separated that illumination from His Essence and turned it into a separate part from Him.

It follows that each soul was included in His Essence prior to its creation. But with creation, meaning along with the will to receive pleasure that has been instilled in it, it acquired disparity of form and was separated from the Creator, whose only wish is to bestow. This is so because, as we have explained above, the disparity of form separates in spirituality as the axe does in corporeality.

Thus, now the soul is completely similar to the allegory about the organ that was cut off and separated from body. Even though, prior to the separation, they—the organ and the whole body—were one, and exchanged thoughts and sensations with one another, after the organ has been cut off from the body they have become two entities. Now one does not know the other's thoughts and needs. It is even more so after the soul is dressed in a body of this world: all the connections it had had prior to the separation from His Essence have stopped, and they are like two separate entities.

Now we can easily understand the merit of one who has been rewarded with cleaving unto Him once more. It means that he has been rewarded with equivalence of form with the Creator by inverting the will to receive, imprinted in him through the power in Torah and *Mitzvot*. This was the very thing that separated him from His Essence, and turned it into a will to bestow. And all of one's actions are only to bestow and benefit others, as he has equalized his form with the Maker. It follows that one is just like the organ that was once cut off from the body and has been reunited with the body: it knows the thoughts of the rest of the body once again, just as it did prior to the separation from the body.

The soul is like that, too: after it has acquired equivalence with Him, it knows His Thoughts once more, as it knew prior to the separation from Him due to the will-to-receive's disparity of form. Then the verse, "know thou the God of thy father," lives in him, as then one is rewarded with complete knowledge, which is Godly knowledge. Also, one is rewarded with all the secrets of the Torah, as His Thoughts are the secrets of the Torah.

This is what Rabbi Meir said: "All who study Torah *Lishma* are granted many things. The secrets of Torah are revealed before them, and they become like an ever-flowing spring." As we have said, through engagement in Torah *Lishma*, meaning by aiming to bring contentment to one's Maker through one's engagement in the Torah, and not at all for one's own benefit, one is guaranteed to cleave to the Creator. This means that one will achieve equivalence of form, and all one's actions will be to benefit others and not oneself at all. This is just like the Creator, whose every action is only to bestow and to benefit others.

By that, one returns to *Dvekut* with the Creator, as was the soul prior to its creation. Hence, one is granted many things, and is rewarded with the secrets and flavors of the Torah, and becomes like an ever-flowing spring. This is so because of the removing of the partitions that parted one from the Creator, so he has become one with Him again, as before one was created.

Indeed, the whole Torah, revealed and concealed, is the Thoughts of the Creator, without any difference. Yet, it is like a person drowning in the river, whose friend throws him a rope to save him. If the drowning catches the rope in its near part, his friend can save him and pull him out of the river.

The Torah is like that, too. Being entirely the Thoughts of the Creator, it is like a rope that the Creator throws to people to save them and pull them out of the *Klipot* (shells). The end of the rope that is near to all the people is the revealed Torah, which requires no intention or thought. Moreover, even when there is a faulty thought in the *Mitzvot*, it is still accepted by the Creator, as it is written, "One must always engage in Torah and *Mitzvot Lo Lishma* (not for Her Name), since from *Lo Lishma* he will come to *Lishma*."

Hence, the Torah and *Mitzvot* are the end of the rope, and there is not a person in the world who cannot grip it. If one tightly grips it, meaning is rewarded with engaging in Torah and *Mitzvot Lishma*, to bring contentment to one's Maker and not to oneself, the Torah and *Mitzvot* lead one to equivalence of form with the Creator. This is the meaning of "and to cleave unto Him."

At that time, one will be rewarded with attaining all the Thoughts of the Creator, called "secrets of the Torah" and "flavors of the Torah," which are the rest of the rope. However, one is granted it only after one has achieved complete *Dvekut*.

The reason we compare the Creator's Thoughts, meaning the secrets of the Torah and the flavors of the Torah, to a rope is that there are many degrees in the equivalence of form with the Creator. Hence, there are many degrees in the rope, in attaining the secrets of the Torah. One's measure of attainment of the secrets of the Torah, of knowing His Thoughts, is as the measure of equivalence of form with the Creator.

Overall, there are five degrees: *Nefesh*, *Ruach*, *Neshama*, *Haya*, *Yechida*, and each is made of all of them. Also, each contains five degrees, and each of those contains at least twenty-five degrees.

They are also called "worlds," as our sages said, "The Creator is destined to grant each righteous 310 worlds." And the reason the degrees of attaining Him are called "worlds" is that there are two meanings to the name *Olam* (World):

1. All those who enter that world have the same sensation; what one sees, hears, and feels, all who are in that world see, hear, and feel, too.

2. All those who are in that "hidden" world cannot know or attain anything in another world. And also, these two degrees are in attainment:

   1. Anyone who has been rewarded with a certain degree knows and attains in it everything that those who came to that degree attained, in all the generations that were and that will be. And he has common attainment with them as though they are in the same world.

   2. All who come to that degree will not be able to know or to attain what exists in another degree. It is like this world: they cannot know anything of what exists in the world of truth. This is why the degrees are called "worlds."

Hence, those with attainment can compose books and put their attainments to writing in intimations and allegories. They will be understood by all who have been rewarded with the degrees that the books describe, and they will have common attainment with them. But those who have not been rewarded with the full measure of the degree as the authors will not be able to understand their intimations. It is even more so with those who have not been rewarded with any attainment; they will not understand a thing about them, as they have no common attainments.

We have already said that the complete *Dvekut* and complete attainment is divided into 125 degrees overall. Accordingly, prior to the days of the Messiah, it is impossible to be granted all 125 degrees. And there are two differences between the generation of the Messiah and all other generations:

1. **Only in the generation of the Messiah is it possible to attain all 125 degrees, and in no other generation.**
2. **Throughout the generations, those who ascended and were rewarded with *Dvekut* were few, as our sages wrote about the verse, "I have found one person in a thousand; a thousand enter the room, and one comes out to teach," meaning to *Dvekut* and attainment. It is as they said, "for the earth shall be full of the knowledge of the Lord." "And they shall teach no more every man his neighbor, and every man his brother, saying: 'Know the Lord'; for they shall all know Me, from the least of them unto the greatest of them."**

An exception is Rashbi and his generation, the authors of *The Zohar*, who were granted all 125 degrees in completeness, even though it was prior to the days of the Messiah. It was said about him and his disciples: "A sage is preferable to a prophet." Hence, we often find in *The Zohar* that there will be none like the generation of Rashbi until the generation of the Messiah King. This is why his composition made such a great impact in the world, since the secrets of the Torah in it occupy the level of all 125 degrees.

Hence, it is said in *The Zohar* that *The Book of Zohar* will be revealed only at the End of Days, the days of the Messiah. This is so because we have already said that if the degrees of the students are not at the full measure of the degree of the author, they will not understand his intimations, since they do not have a common attainment.

And since the degree of the authors of *The Zohar* is at the full level of the 125 degrees, they cannot be attained prior to the days of the Messiah. It follows that there will be no common attainment with the authors of *The Zohar* in the generations preceding the days of the Messiah. Hence, *The Zohar* could not be revealed in the generations before the generation of the Messiah.

And this is a clear proof that our generation has come to the days of the Messiah. We can see that all the interpretations of *The Book of Zohar* before ours did not clarify as much as ten percent of the difficult places in *The Zohar*. And in the little they did clarify, their words are almost as abstruse as the words of *The Zohar* itself.

But in our generation we have been rewarded with the *Sulam* (Ladder) commentary, which is a complete interpretation of all the words of *The Zohar*. Moreover, not only does it not leave an unclear matter in the whole of *The Zohar* without interpreting it, but the clarifications are based on a straightforward analysis, which any intermediate student can understand. And since *The Zohar* appeared in our generation, it is a clear proof that we are already in the days of the Messiah, at the outset of that generation upon which it was said, "for the earth shall be full of the knowledge of the Lord."

We should know that spiritual matters are not like corporeal matters, where giving and receiving come as one. In spirituality, the time of giving and the time of receiving are separate. This is because first it was given from the Creator to the receiver; and in this giving He only gives him a chance to receive. However, he has not received a thing yet, until he is properly sanctified and purified. And then one is rewarded with receiving it. Thus, it may take a long time between the time of giving and the time of receiving.

Accordingly, the saying that this generation has already come to the verse, "for the earth shall be full of the knowledge of the Lord," refers only to the giving. Yet, we have not yet come to a state of reception. When we are purified, sanctified, and study, and exert in the desired amount, the time of reception will arrive, and the verse, "for the earth shall be full of the knowledge of the Lord," will come true in us.

Also, it is known that redemption and the complete attainment are intertwined. The proof is that anyone who is drawn to the secrets of the Torah is also drawn to the land of Israel. This is why we were promised, "for the earth shall be full of the knowledge of the Lord," only at the End of Days, during the time of redemption.

Therefore, as we have not yet been rewarded with a time of reception in the complete attainment, but only with a time of giving, by which we have been given a chance to achieve complete attainment, so it is with redemption. We have been rewarded with it only in the form of giving. The fact of the matter is that the Creator delivered our holy land from the foreigners and has given it back to us, yet we have not received the land into our own authority, since the time of reception has not yet come, as we explained concerning the complete attainment.

Thus, He has given but we have not received. After all, we have no economic independence, and there is no political independence without economic independence. Moreover, there is no redemption of the body without redemption of the soul. And as long as the majority of the people are captive in the foreign cultures of the nations and are incapable of Israel's religion and culture, the bodies, too, will be captive under the alien forces. In this respect, the land is still in the hands of foreigners.

The proof is that no one is excited about the redemption, as it should have been with redemption after two millennia. Not only are those in the Diaspora not inclined to come to us and delight in the redemption, but a large portion of those that have been redeemed, and are already dwelling among us, are anxiously waiting to be rid of this redemption and return to the Diaspora whence they came.

Thus, even though the Creator has delivered the land from the hands of the nations and has given it to us, we have not yet received it. We are not enjoying it. But with this giving, the Creator has given us an opportunity for redemption, to be purified and sanctified and assume the work of God in Torah and *Mitzvot Lishma*. At that time, the Temple will be built and we will receive the land into our own authority. And then we will experience and feel the joy of redemption.

But as long as we have not come to that, nothing will change. There is no difference between the current manners of the land and the way it was while still under the hands of foreigners, in law, in economy, and in the work of God. Thus, all we have is an opportunity for redemption.

It follows that our generation is the generation of the days of the Messiah. This is why we have been granted the redemption of our holy land from the hands of the foreigners. We have also been rewarded with the revelation of *The Book of Zohar*, which is the beginning of the realization of the verse, "for the earth shall be full of the knowledge of the Lord." "And they shall teach no more... for they shall all know Me, from the least of them unto the greatest of them."

Yet, with those two, we have only been rewarded with giving from the Creator, but we have not received anything into our own hands. Instead, we have been given a chance to begin with the work of God, to engage in Torah and

Mitzvot Lishma. Then we will be granted the great success that is promised to the generation of the Messiah, which all the generations before us did not know. And then we will be rewarded with the time of reception of both the complete attainment and the complete redemption.

Thus, we have thoroughly explained our sages' reply to the question, "How is it possible to cleave unto Him, which they said means 'cleave unto His qualities'"? This is true for two reasons:

1. **Spiritual *Dvekut* is not in proximity of place, but in equivalence of form.**
2. **Since the soul was separated from His Essence only because of the will to receive, which the Creator had imprinted in it, once He had separated the will to receive from it, it naturally returned to the previous *Dvekut* with His Essence.**

However, all this is in theory. In fact, they have not answered anything with the explanation of cleaving unto His qualities, which means to separate the will to receive, imprinted in the nature of Creation, and arriving at the will to bestow—the opposite of its nature.

And what we explained, that one who is drowning in the river should firmly grip the rope, and before one engages in Torah and *Mitzvot Lishma* in a way that he will not turn back to folly, it is not considered gripping the rope firmly, the question returns: Where will one find motivation to wholeheartedly exert solely to bring contentment to one's Maker? After all, one cannot make a single movement without any benefit for oneself, as a machine cannot work without fuel. And if there is no self-gratification, but only contentment to one's Maker, one will have no fuel with which to work.

The answer is that anyone who sufficiently attains His greatness, the bestowal that one bestows upon Him is inverted into reception, as it is written in *Masechet Kidushin* (p. 7): with an important person, when the woman gives him money it is considered reception for her, and she is sanctified.

So it is with the Creator: if one achieves His greatness, there is no greater reception than contentment to one's Maker. This is sufficient fuel to toil and wholeheartedly exert to bring contentment to Him. But clearly, as long as one has not sufficiently attained His greatness, one will not regard giving contentment to the Creator as reception enough for one to give one's heart and soul to the Creator.

Hence, each time one truly aims only to bring contentment to one's Maker and not to oneself, one will immediately lose the strength to work, as he will be like a machine without fuel, since one cannot move any organ without drawing some benefit to oneself. It is even more so with such great labor as giving one's heart and soul, as dictated in the Torah. Undoubtedly, one will not be able to do so without drawing some reception of pleasure for oneself.

Indeed, obtaining His greatness in a measure that bestowal becomes reception, as mentioned concerning an important person, is not at all difficult. Everyone knows the greatness of the Creator, who created everything and consumes everything, without beginning and without end, and whose sublimity is endless.

Yet, the difficulty in that is that the measure of the greatness does not depend on the individual, but on the environment. For example, even if one is filled with virtues but the environment does not appreciate one as such, one will always be low-spirited and will not be able to take pride in his virtues, although he has no doubt that they are true. And conversely, a person with no merit at all, whom the environment respects as though he is virtuous, that person will be filled with pride, since the measure of importance and greatness is given entirely to the environment.

And while one sees how one's environment slights His work and does not properly appreciate His greatness, one cannot overcome the environment. Thus, one cannot obtain His greatness, and slights during one's work, as do they.

And since one does not have the basis for obtaining His greatness, he will obviously not be able to work to bestow contentment upon his Maker and not for himself. This is so because one would have no motivation to exert, and "if you did not labor and found, do not believe." And one's only choice is to either work for oneself or to not work at all, since for him, bestowing contentment upon one's Maker will not be tantamount to reception.

Now you can understand the verse, "In the multitude of people is the king's glory," since the measure of the greatness comes from the environment under two conditions:

1. **The extent of the appreciation of the environment.**

2. **The size of the environment. Thus, "In the multitude of people is the king's glory."**

And because of the great difficulty in the matter, our sages advised us: "Make for yourself a rav[2] and buy for yourself a friend." This means that one should choose for oneself an important and renowned person to be one's rav, from whom one will be able to come to engaging in Torah and *Mitzvot* in order to

---

2   Translator's note: a great teacher

bring contentment to one's Maker. This is so because there are two facilitations to one's rav:

1. Since he is an important person, the student can bestow contentment upon him, based on the sublimity of one's rav, since bestowal becomes as reception for him. This is a natural fuel, so one can always increase one's acts of bestowal. And once a person grows accustomed to engage in bestowal upon the rav, one can transfer it to engaging in Torah and *Mitzvot Lishma* towards the Creator, too, since habit becomes a second nature.

2. Equivalence of form with the Creator does not help if it is not forever, that is, "until He who knows all mysteries will testify that he will not turn back to folly." This is not so with equivalence of form with one's rav. Since the rav is in this world, within time, equivalence of form with him helps even if it is only temporary and he later turns sour again.

   Thus, every time one equalizes one's form with one's rav, he is adhered to him for a time. Thus, one obtains the thoughts and knowledge of the rav, according to one's measure of *Dvekut*, as we have explained in the allegory of the organ that has been cut off from the body and was reunited with it.

For this reason, the student can use his rav's attainment of the Creator's greatness, which inverts bestowal into reception and sufficient fuel to give one's heart and soul. At that time, the student, too, will be able to engage in Torah and *Mitzvot Lishma* with one's very heart and soul, which is the remedy that yields eternal *Dvekut* with the Creator.

Now you can understand what our sages said (*Berachot* 7): "Serving in the Torah is greater than studying it, as it is said, 'Elisha the son of Shaphat is here, who poured water on the hands of Elijah.' It did not say studied, but poured." This is perplexing; how can simple acts be greater than studying the wisdom and the knowledge?

But according to the above, we thoroughly understand that serving one's rav with one's body and soul in order to bring contentment to one's rav bring one to *Dvekut* with one's rav, that is, to equivalence of form. Thus, one receives the thoughts and knowledge of the rav by way of "mouth-to-mouth," which is *Dvekut* of spirit with spirit. By that, one is rewarded with obtaining His greatness sufficiently to turn bestowal into reception, to become sufficient fuel for devotion, until one is rewarded with *Dvekut* with the Creator.

This is not so concerning studying Torah with one's rav, as this must be for one's own benefit, and does not yield *Dvekut*. It is considered "from mouth to ear." Thus, serving brings the student the rav's thoughts, and the study—only the rav's words. Also, the merit of serving is greater than the merit of the study as the importance of the rav's thoughts over the rav's words, and as the importance of "mouth-to-mouth" over "from mouth to ear."

However, all this is true if the service is in order to bestow contentment upon Him. Yet, if the service is to benefit oneself, such service cannot bring one to *Dvekut* with one's rav, and certainly the study with the rav is more important than serving him.

Yet, as we have said about obtaining His greatness, an environment that does not properly appreciate Him weakens the individual and prevents one from obtaining His greatness. And this is certainly true for one's rav, as well. An environment that does not properly appreciate the rav prevents the student from being able to properly obtain the greatness of one's rav.

Hence, our sages said, "Make for yourself a rav and buy yourself a friend." This means that one can make a new environment for oneself. This environment will help him obtain the greatness of his rav through love of friends who appreciate the rav. Through the friends' discussing the greatness of the rav, each of them receives the sensation of his greatness. Thus, bestowal upon one's rav will become reception and sufficient motivation to an extent that will bring one to engage in Torah and *Mitzvot Lishma*.

They said about that, "The Torah is acquired by forty-eight virtues, by serving of sages and by meticulousness with friends." This is so because besides serving the rav, one needs the meticulousness of friends, as well, the friends' influence, so they will affect him the obtainment of his rav's greatness. This is so because obtaining the greatness depends entirely on the environment, and a single person cannot do a thing about it whatsoever.

Yet, there are two conditions to obtaining the greatness:

1. **Always listen and assume appreciation of the environment to the extent of their greatness.**
2. **The environment should be great, as it is written, "In the multitude of people is the king's glory."**

To receive the first condition, each student must feel that he is the smallest among all the friends. In that state, one can receive the appreciation of the greatness from everyone, since the great cannot receive from a smaller one, and much less be impressed by his words. Rather, only the small is impressed by the appreciation of the great.

And for the second condition, each student must extol the virtues of each friend and cherish him as though he were the greatest in the generation. Then the environment will affect him as a sufficiently great environment, since quality is more important than quantity.

Peace in the World

> "Mercy and truth are met together; righteousness and peace have kissed each other. Truth springeth out of the earth; and righteousness hath looked down from heaven. Yea, the Lord will give that which is good; and our land shall yield her produce."
> —Psalms 85

EVERYTHING IS EVALUATED NOT BY ITS APPEARANCE AT A GIVEN MOMENT, BUT ACCORDING TO ITS MEASURE OF DEVELOPMENT

Everything in reality, good and bad, and even the most harmful in the world, has a right to exist and should not be eradicated from the world and destroyed. We must only mend and reform it because any observation of the work of Creation is enough to teach us about the greatness and perfection of its Operator and Creator. Therefore, we must understand and be very careful when casting a flaw in any item of Creation, saying it is redundant and superfluous, as that would be slander about its Operator.

It is common knowledge that the Creator did not complete Creation when He created it. And we can see in every corner of reality, in the general and in the particular, that it abides by laws of gradual development, from absence to completion of growth. For this reason, when the fruit tastes bitter at the beginning of its growth, it is not considered a flaw in the fruit, since we all know the reason: the fruit has not yet completed its development.

And so it is in every element of reality: When some element appears bad and harmful to us, it is but a self-testimony of that element; that it is still in the transition phase—in the process of its development. Hence, we cannot decide that it is bad and it is not wise for us to cast a flaw in it.

THE WEAKNESS OF "WORLD REFORMERS"

This is the key to understand the weakness of world-reformers throughout the generations. They regarded man as a machine that is not operating properly and needs mending, meaning to remove the corrupted parts and replace them with good ones.

And that is the tendency of all world reformers—to eradicate any harmful and bad in the human species... and it is true that if the Creator had not stood against them, they would certainly have by now cleansed man entirely, living only the good and useful.

But because the Creator meticulously watches over all the elements in His Creation, not letting anyone destroy a single thing in His Domain but only reform it and make it useful and good, all the reformers of the above-mentioned kind will vanish from the face of the earth, and evil inclinations will not vanish. They live on and count the degrees that they must still traverse until they complete their ripening.

At that time, the bad attributes themselves will turn to good and useful ones, as the Creator had initially perceived them to be, like the fruit on the tree that sits and waits and counts the days and months it must still wait before the completion of its ripeness, at which time its taste and sweetness will become evident to any person.

REWARDED—I WILL HASTEN IT, NOT REWARDED—IN ITS TIME

We must know that the above-mentioned law of development, which is spread over the whole of reality, is guaranteed to return all evil to good and useful acts through the power of the Government of Heaven Above, meaning without asking permission from the people who inhabit the earth. However, the Creator placed knowledge and authority in the hands of man and permitted him to accept the above-mentioned law of development under his own authority and government, and handed him the ability to hasten the process of development as he wishes, freely and completely independent of the boundaries of time.

It turns out that there are two authorities here, acting in the above-mentioned conduct of development: the one is the authority of Heaven, which is sure to turn anything harmful and evil to good and useful, but that will be in due time, in its own way, in a floundering manner and after a long time. And then there is the authority of the earth. And when the "evolving object" is a living being, it suffers horrendous torments while under the "press of development," a press that carves its way ruthlessly.

The "authority of the earth," however, is comprised of people who have taken this above-mentioned law of development under their own government and can free themselves entirely from the chains of time, and who greatly accelerate time, the completion of the ripeness and correction of the object, which is the end of its development.

Such are the words that our sages said (*Sanhedrin* 98) about the complete redemption and complete correction of Israel. And thus they clarified the verse "I the Lord will hasten it in its time" (Isaiah 60:22): Rewarded—I will hasten it, not rewarded—in its time.

Thus, if Israel are rewarded and take the law of development that their bad attributes must go through in order to invert them into good ones, they will bring it under their own government. In other words, they will set their minds and hearts to correct all the bad attributes in them and turn them into good ones by themselves. Then, "I will hasten it," meaning they will be completely freed from the chains of time. And from now on, this end depends on their own will, meaning only by the greatness of the deed and the mindfulness. Thus, they hasten the end.

But if they are not rewarded with developing their bad attributes under their own authority, but leave it under the Authority of Heaven, they, too, are certain to attain the end of their redemption and the end of their correction. This is because there is complete certainty in the Government of Heaven, which operates by the law of gradual development, degree by degree, until it turns any evil and harmful to good and useful, as the fruit on a tree. The end is guaranteed, but in its time, meaning it is completely connected and dependent on time.

According to that law of gradual development, one must go through many degrees, which tend to come heavily and very slowly and lengthily, and stretch over a very long time before one reaches the end. And because the objects we are discussing are evolving, sensing, living beings, they, too, must suffer great agony and pains in those states of development, since the compelling force, which exists in those degrees in order to raise man from a lower degree to a Higher One, is but a pushing force of pain and torment that has accumulated in the lower degree and that can no longer be tolerated. Because of that, we must leave that degree and rise to a Higher One. It is as our sages said, "The Creator places over them a king whose sentences are as harsh as Haman's, and Israel repent and reform."

Therefore, the end is certain to come to Israel by the above-mentioned law of gradual development, and it is called "in its time," meaning tied to the chains of time. And Israel's guaranteed end, by taking the development of their attributes under their own authority is called, "I will hasten it," meaning completely independent of time.

GOOD AND BAD ARE EVALUATED BY THE ACTIONS OF THE INDIVIDUAL TOWARD SOCIETY

Before we examine the correction of evil in the human species, we must first determine the value of those abstract terms, "good" and "bad." When we define an act or an attribute as good or bad, we should clarify whom that attribute or act benefits.

To understand that, we must thoroughly know the proportional value between the individual and the collective, between the individual and the collective that the individual lives in and nourishes from, in both matter and in spirit.

Reality shows us that there is no right to exist for an isolated individual without a sufficient number of people around him to serve him and help him provide for his needs. Hence, a person is born to lead a social life to begin with. And each and every individual in society is like a wheel that is linked to several other wheels, placed in a machine. And this single wheel has no freedom of movement in and of itself, but continues with the motion of the rest of the wheels in a certain direction, to qualify the machine to perform its general role.

And if there is some breakdown in the wheel, the breakdown is not evaluated relating to the wheel itself, but according to its service and role with respect to the whole machine.

And in our subject, the benefit of each and every person within his collective is evaluated not according to his own goodness, but according to his service to the public. And vice-versa, we appreciate the attribute of evil of each and every individual only according to the harm one inflicts upon the public in general, and not by one's own individual value.

These things are crystal clear both from the perspective of the truth in them, and from the perspective of the good in them. This is because what is found in the collective is only what is found in the individual. And the benefit of the collective is the benefit of each and every individual: who harms the collective takes his share in the harm, and who benefits the collective takes his share in the benefit, since individuals are part of the whole, and the whole is not worth in anyway more than the sum of its individuals.

It thus turns out that the collective and the individual are one and the same. And the individual is not harmed because of his enslavement to the collective, since the freedom of the collective and the freedom of the individual are one and the same, too. And as they share the good, they also share the freedom.

Thus, good attributes and bad attributes, good deeds and bad deeds are evaluated only according to the benefit of the public.

Of course, the above words apply if all the individuals perform their role toward the public to the fullest and receive no more than they deserve, and take no more than their friends' share. But if a part of the collective does not behave accordingly, it turns out that not only do they harm the collective but they are also harmed.

We should not discuss further something that is known to all, and the aforesaid is only to show the drawback, the place that needs correction, and that is that each and every individual will understand that his own benefit and the benefit of the collective are one and same thing. In that, the world will come to its full correction.

THE FOUR ATTRIBUTES, MERCY, TRUTH, JUSTICE, AND PEACE, IN THE INDIVIDUAL AND THE COLLECTIVE

Once we know full well the desired attribute of goodness, we should examine the things and the means at our disposal, in order to hasten that delight and happiness.

Four properties are provided for that purpose: mercy, truth, justice, and peace. Those attributes have been used by all world reformers thus far. It is more correct to say that it is with those four attributes that human development has advanced thus far through the government of Heaven, in a gradual path, until it brought humankind to its current state.

It has already been written that it would be better for us to take the law of development under our own hands and government, for then we will rid ourselves of any torment that the developmental history has in store for us from this day forth. Thus, we should scrutinize and examine those four properties in order to thoroughly understand what we have been given thus far and by them we will know what aid we should hope to get from them in the future.

PRACTICAL DIFFICULTIES IN DETERMINING THE TRUTH

When we discuss good attributes, in theory, there is certainly no better attribute than the attribute of truth. This is because all the goodness that we have defined above in the relationship between the individual and the collective is when the individual gives and fully plays his part toward the collective, and also takes his share from the collective justly and honestly. All that is but the truth, but the drawback is that in fact, the collective does not accept this property at all. Thus, the practical difficulty in the above-mentioned truth is proven from itself: there is some drawback and a cause here that makes it unacceptable to the collective. And we must examine what is that drawback.

When you closely examine the above-mentioned truth from the perspective of its practical feasibility, you will necessarily find it vague and complicated, and it is impossible for the human eye to scrutinize it. That is, truth necessitates us to equalize all the individuals in the collective, to receive their share according to their labor, no more and no less. And this is the one true basis, which cannot be doubted, for it is certain that anyone who wishes to enjoy the labor of his friend, his acts are against the above-mentioned reason and clear truth.

But how do we think that we can scrutinize that truth in a way that it is acceptable to the collective? For example, if we evaluate something according to the apparent labor, meaning according to the number of hours, and we compel each and everyone to work an equal number of hours, we will still not discover the attribute of truth at all.

Moreover, there is an evident lie here for two reasons: The first is the physical side and the second is the mental side of the worker.

That is because by nature, the power to work is not equal with each and every person. One person in the society labors in one hour of work, due to his weakness, much more than his friend who works two hours or more.

And there is also a psychological matter here, because he who is very lazy by nature exhausts himself in one hour more than his friend in two hours or more. And according to the perspective of the evident truth, we should not compel one part of society to labor more than the other part for the fulfillment of the needs of their lives. In fact, the naturally strong and nimble in society benefit from the labor of others and exploit them maliciously against the attribute of truth, because they labor very little compared to the weak and the lazy in society.

And if we also consider the natural law, "Taking after the majority," then such a truth that takes the number of hours of apparent work as a basis is completely unfeasible, since the weak and the lazy are always the vast majority in society, and they will not allow the nimble and strong minority to exploit their strength and labor. Thus, you see that the above-mentioned basis, which is the labor of the individual on the condition of the evident truth, and with it the majority in the society, is completely unfeasible, since it cannot be examined and evaluated in any way.

Thus you find that the attribute of truth has no practical ability to organize the path of the individual and the path of the collective in an absolute and satisfactory manner. Also, it is completely insufficient for organizing life at the end of the correction of the world.

Furthermore, there are even greater difficulties here because there is no clearer truth than nature itself. And it is natural that each and every individual feels himself in the world of the Creator, as a sole ruler, that all the others were created only to ease and improve his life, without him feeling any obligation whatsoever to give anything in return.

And in simple words we shall say, that the nature of each and every person is to exploit the lives of all other people in the world for his own benefit. And all that he gives to another is only out of necessity; and even then there is exploitation of others in it, but it is done cunningly, so that his friend will not notice it and concede willingly.

The reason for it is that the nature of every branch is close to its root. And because man's soul extends from the Creator, who is One and Unique, and everything is His, hence, so man, who extends from Him, feels that all the people in the world should be under his own governance and for his own private use. And this is an unbreakable law. The only difference is in people's choices: One chooses to exploit people by attaining lower desires, and one by attaining government, while the third by attaining respect. Furthermore, if one could do it without much effort, he would agree to exploit the world with all three together—wealth, government and respect. However, he is forced to choose according to his possibilities and capabilities.

This law can be called "the law of singularity in man's heart." No person escapes it, and each and every one takes his share in that law: the great according to his size, and the small according to his size.

Thus, the above law of singularity in the nature of every person is neither condemned nor praised, as it is a natural reality and has a right to exist like all parts of reality. And there is no hope to eradicate it from the world or even blur its form a little, just as there is no hope to eradicate the entire human species from the face of the earth. Therefore, we will not be lying at all if we said about this law that it is the absolute truth.

And since it is undoubtedly so, how can we even try to ease one's mind by promising him equality with all the people in the collective? For nothing is further from human nature than that, while one's sole inclination is to soar higher, above the whole collective.

Thus we have thoroughly clarified that there is no real possibility to bring good and joyful conducts to the life of the individual and the lives of the collective by following the attribute of truth in a way that it will ease the mind of each and every individual, so that he may completely agree with it, as it should be at the end of correction.

IN THE ABSENCE OF THE ABILITY TO ESTABLISH THE ATTRIBUTE OF TRUTH, THEY TRIED TO ESTABLISH THE NOBLE ATTRIBUTES

Now let us turn to the remaining three attributes: mercy, justice, and peace. It seems that to begin with, they were created only to be used as support for the weak attribute of truth in our world. And here, developmental history began to climb its slow and straggler degrees in its progress toward organizing the lives of the collective.

In theory, everyone willingly agreed and took it upon themselves to not deviate in any way from the truth. But in fact, they conducted themselves completely opposite from the truth. And since then, it has been the fate of truth to always be in the hands of the most deceitful and never in the hands of the weak and the righteous, so they could even be somewhat assisted by the attribute of truth.

When they could not establish the attribute of truth in the life of the collective, the exploited and the weak increased within society and from here emerged the attributes of mercy and justice and enacted their actions in the conduct of society, because the existence of the whole society compelled the successful among them to support the weak, so as to not harm the society in general. Therefore, they behaved with them indulgently, meaning mercifully and with charity.

But it is only natural that under such conditions the weak and the exploited proliferate, until there are enough of them to protest against the successful and start quarrels and fights. And from here emerged the attribute of "peace" in the world. Thus, all those attributes—mercy, charity, and peace—emerged and were born from the weakness of truth.

This is what caused society to divide into sects. Some adopted the attributes of mercy and charity, giving of their own possessions to others, and some adopted the attribute of truth, meaning "What's mine is mine and what's yours is yours."

In simpler words, we can divide the two sects into "constructors" and "destructors." Constructors are those who want construction, the benefit of the collective, for which they are often willing to give of their own possessions to others. But those who are naturally prone to destruction and profligacy were more comfortable clinging to the attribute of truth, meaning, "What's mine is mine and what's yours is yours," for their own gain, and would never want to give up anything of their own to others without taking into consideration jeopardizing the well-being of the collective, for as by nature they are destructors.

HOPES FOR PEACE

Once those conditions brought society a great deal of strife and risked the well-being of society, the "peacemakers" appeared in society. They have assumed control and power and renewed the social life based on new conditions, which they considered true, to suffice for the peaceful existence of society.

Yet, the majority of those peacemakers, which spring up after every dispute, naturally come from among the destructors, meaning from the seekers of truth, by way of "What's mine is mine and what's yours is yours." This is because they are the powerful and courageous ones in society, called "heroes," for they are always willing to renounce their own lives and the lives of the whole collective, if the collective disagrees with their view.

But the constructors in society, who are the men of mercy and charity, who care for their own lives and for the life of the collective, refuse to risk themselves or the public in order to impose their opinion on the collective. Hence, they are always on the weak side in society, called "the faint-hearted" and "the coward."

It is hence obvious that the hand of the brave profligates will always be on top, and it is natural that the peacemakers will come from among the destructors and not from the constructors.

Thus we see how the hope for peace, which our generation so yearns for, is futile both from the perspective of the subject and the perspective of the predicate.

For the **subjects**, who are the peace-makers of our time and in any generation, meaning those who have the power to make peace in the world, are forever made of the human substance we call "destructors," for they are seekers of truth, meaning to establish the world on the attribute of "What's mine is mine and what's yours is yours."

It is natural that those people defend their opinions firmly, to the point of risking their own lives and the life of the entire collective. And that is what gives them the power to always prevail over the human substance called, "constructors," the seekers of mercy and charity, who are willing to give up of their own for the good of others, in order to save the world, because they are the faint-hearted and the coward.

It turns out that seeking truth and the destruction of the world are one and the same, and the desire for mercy and the construction of the world are one and the same, too. Therefore, we should not hope from the destructors to establish the peace.

And it is hopeless to hope for peace from the predicate, meaning by the conditions of peace itself. This is so because the proper conditions for the well-being of the individual and the well-being of the collective, according to the criterion of truth that these peacemakers so desire, have not yet been established. And it is a must that there will always be a large minority in society who are unsatisfied by the conditions offered to them, as we have shown the weakness of the truth above. This minority will therefore always remain a ready and willing fuel for the new quarrelsome people and the new peacemakers that will always follow.

THE WELL-BEING OF A CERTAIN COLLECTIVE AND THE WELL-BEING OF THE WHOLE WORLD

Do not be surprised if I mix together the well-being of a particular collective with the well-being of the whole world, because indeed, we have already come to such a degree that the whole world is considered one collective and one society. Meaning, because each person in the world draws his life's marrow and his livelihood from all the people in the world, he is coerced to serve and care for the well-being of the whole world.

We have proven above that the total subordination of the individual to the collective is like a small wheel in a machine. He draws his life and his happiness from that collective, and therefore the well-being of the collective and his own well-being are one and the same, and vice-versa. Therefore, to the extent that a person is enslaved to himself, he necessarily becomes enslaved to the collective, as we have spoken at length above.

And what is the extent of that collective? That is determined by the perimeter of the drawing of the individual from them. For example, in historic times, that perimeter was only the perimeter of one family, meaning the individual needed aid only from his own family members. At that time, he had to be subordinated only to his own family.

In later times, families gathered into towns and counties, and the individual became enslaved to his town. Later, when the towns and counties were joined into states, the individual was supported by all his countrymen for the happiness of his life. Thus, he became enslaved to all the people in the country. Therefore, in our generation, when each person is aided for his happiness by all the countries in the world, it is necessary that to that extent, the individual becomes enslaved to the whole world, like a wheel in a machine.

Therefore, the possibility of making good, happy, and peaceful conducts in one state is inconceivable when it is not so in all the countries in the world, and vice versa. In our time, the countries are all linked in the satisfaction of their needs of life, as individuals were in their families in earlier times. Therefore, we can no longer speak or deal with just conducts that guarantee the well-being of one country or one nation, but only with the well-being of the whole world because the benefit or harm of each and every person in the world depends and is measured by the benefit of all the people in the world.

And although this is, in fact, known and felt, still the people in the world have not yet grasped it properly. And why? Because such is the conduct of the development in nature, that the act comes before the understanding, and only actions will prove and push humanity forward.

IN PRACTICAL LIFE, THE FOUR ATTRIBUTES CONTRADICT ONE ANOTHER

If the above practical difficulties, which disturb us helpless people on our way, are not enough, we have in addition a further mix-up and great battle of the psychological predispositions, meaning the attributes themselves within each and everyone of us individually, which are unique and contradictory to one another. For the four above attributes, mercy, truth, justice, and peace, which were divided in the nature of people, whether by development or by rearing, are in and of themselves contradictory to one another. If we take, for example, the attribute of mercy in its abstract form, we find that its government contradicts all other attributes, meaning that by the laws of the rule of mercy, there is no place for the appearance of the other attributes in our world.

What is the attribute of mercy? Our sages defined it, "What's mine is yours and what's yours is yours"—*Hasid*.[3] And if all the people in the world were to behave by this quality, it would cancel all the glory of the attribute of truth and judgment, because if each and every one were naturally willing to give everything he had to others, and take nothing from another, then the whole interest in lying to one another would disappear. Also, it would be irrelevant to discuss the quality of truth, since truth and falsehood are relative to one another. If there were no falsehood in the world, there would be no concept of truth. Needless to say, all the other attributes, which came only to strengthen the attribute of truth because of its weakness, would be cancelled.

---

3   Translator's Note: *Hasid* means one with the quality of *Hesed* (mercy).

Truth is defined in the words: "What's mine is mine, and what's yours is yours." That contradicts the attribute of mercy and cannot altogether tolerate it, since in truth it is unjust to labor and strain for another, because besides failing his friend and accustoming him to exploit others, truth dictates that every person should treasure his own assets for a time of need, so he will not have to be a burden on his fellow man.

Moreover, there is not a person without relatives and heirs that, in fact, should come before others, because so nature dictates that he who gives his property to others lies to his relatives and natural heirs by not leaving them anything.

And peace also contradicts justice because to make peace in the public, there must be conditions that by content promise the nimble and the smart, which invest their energy and wisdom, to become rich, and those who are negligent and naïve, to be poor. Hence, he who is more energetic takes his own share and the share of his negligent friend and enjoys such a good life that there is not enough left for the negligent and naive to merely provide for their necessary livelihood. Hence, they remain completely bare and destitute in many ways.

It is certainly unjust to punish the negligent and the naive so harshly for no evil, for what is their sin and what is the crime of those wretched people, if Providence did not grant them agility and acumen that they should be punished with torments harsher than death?

Therefore, there is no justice whatsoever in the conditions of peace. Peace contradicts justice and justice contradicts peace, because if we order the division of property justly, meaning give to the negligent and naive a substantial portion of the part that the nimble and the energetic have, then these powerful and initiating people will certainly not rest until they overthrow the government that enslaves the great ones, the energetic ones, and exploits them in favor of the weak. Therefore there is no hope for the peace of the collective. Thus, justice contradicts peace.

THE ATTRIBUTE OF SINGULARITY IN THE EGOISM AFFECTS RUIN AND DESTRUCTION

Thus you see how our attributes collide and fight one another; and not only between sects, but within each person, the four attributes dominate him all at once or one at a time and fight within him until it is impossible for common sense to organize them and bring them to complete consent.

The truth is that the root of this whole disorder within us is no more than the above-mentioned attribute of singularity, which exists within each of us, whether more or less.

And although we have clarified that it comes from a sublime reason, that this attribute extends to us directly from the Creator, who is single in the world and the Root of all creations, still, out of the sensation of singularity, when it sits within our narrow egoism, it affects ruin and destruction until it became the source of all the ruins that were and will be in the world.

And indeed, there is not a single person in the world who is free from it, and all the differences are only in the way it is used—for the desires of the heart, for ruling, or for honor—and this is what separates people from one another.

But the equal side in all the people of the world is that each of us stands ready to abuse and exploit all the people for his own private benefit with every means possible, without taking into any consideration that he is going to build himself on the ruin of his friend. And it is inconsequential what allowance each of us gives himself, according to his chosen direction, since the desire is the root of the mind and not the mind the root of desire. In truth, the greater and more outstanding the person, precisely so is his attribute of singularity greater and outstanding.

USING THE NATURE OF SINGULARITY AS A SUBJECT OF EVOLUTION IN THE COLLECTIVE AND IN THE INDIVIDUAL

Now we shall penetrate into the understanding of the direct conditions that will finally be accepted by humanity at the time of the appearance of world peace, and learn how its conditions are good to bring a life of happiness to the individual and to the collective, and the willingness in humanity to want to finally burden themselves with those special conditions.

Let us return to the matter of singularity in the heart of every person, which stands to swallow the whole wide world for his own pleasure. Its root extends directly from the Unique One to the people, which are His branches. Here there is a question that demands an answer: "How can it be that such a corrupted form will appear in us so as to become the father of all harm and ruin in the world, and how from the Source of every construction extends the source of every destruction?" We cannot leave such a question unanswered.

Indeed, there are two sides to the coin of the above-mentioned singularity. If we examine it from its upper side, from the side of its equivalence with the Unique One, it works only in the form of bestowal upon others, for the Creator is all bestowal and has nothing of the form of reception, because He lacks nothing and needs to receive nothing from the creatures He has created. Therefore, the singularity that extends to us from Him must also act only in forms of bestowal to others, and to receive nothing for ourselves.

On the other side of that coin, meaning how it actually works in us, we find that it operates in the complete opposite direction, because it operates only in forms of receptions for oneself, such as the desire to be the only great and rich man in the whole world. Thus, the above two sides are as far apart from one another as the East from the West.

That gives us the solution to our question: "How is it possible that within the same singularity, which stems and comes to us from He Who is Unique in the world, Who is the Source of every construction, serves in us as the source of every destruction?" This has come to us because we use that precious tool in the opposite direction, which is self-reception. And I am not saying that the singularity in us will never act in us in a form of bestowal, because you cannot deny that amongst us are people whose singularity operates in them in the form of bestowal upon others, too, such as those who spend all their money for the common good, and those who dedicate all their efforts to the common good, etc.

But those two sides of the coin that I have described speak only of the two points of the development of Creation, which brings everything to completion, starting in absence, and gradually climbing the degrees of development, from one degree to the next Higher up, and from there to the Higher still, until it comes to the summit, which is its preordained measure of perfection. And there it will remain forever.

The order of development of those two points is, A) the starting point, the lowest degree, which is close to complete absence. It is described as the second side of the coin. B) The summit, where it rests and exists forever. And that is described in the first side of the coin.

But this era that we are in has already developed to a great extent and has already risen many degrees. It has already risen above its lowest phase, which is the above-mentioned second side, and has come significantly closer to the first side.

Therefore, there are already people among us who use their singularity in forms of bestowal upon others. But they are still few, as we are still in the midst of the path of development. When we come to the Highest point of the degrees, we will all be using our singularity only in a form of bestowal upon others, and there will never be any case of any person using it in a form of self-reception.

By those words, we find the opportunity to examine the conditions of life in the last generation—the time of world peace, when the whole of humanity achieves the level of the first side and will use their singularity only in the form of bestowal upon others, and not at all in the form of reception for self. And it is good to copy here the above-mentioned form of life so it will serve to us as a lesson and as a role model to settle our minds under the flood of the waves of our lives. Perhaps it is worthwhile and possible in our generation, too, to experiment in resembling this above form of life.

THE CONDITION OF LIFE IN THE LAST GENERATION

First, everyone must thoroughly understand and explain to his surroundings that the well-being of society, which is the well-being of the state and the well-being of the world, are completely interdependent. As long as the laws of society are not satisfactory to each and every individual in the state, and leave a minority that is unsatisfied with the government of the state, this minority conspires under the government of the state and seeks to overthrow it.

And if its power is not sufficient to fight the government of the state face to face, it will want to overthrow it indirectly, such as to incite countries against each other and bring them to war, because it is natural that at war time there will be a lot more unsatisfied people with which they will have hope of achieving the critical mass to overthrow the government of the state and establish a new leadership that is convenient for them. Thus, peace of the individual is a direct cause for peace of the state.

Furthermore, if we take into consideration that part in the state whose craftsmanship is war, which the state always has, and their every hope of success, such as the scholars of war and those who live by supplying the ammunition, that as far as the social quality is concerned, they are always a very significant minority, and if we add them to the unsatisfied minority from the current rules, at every given moment you have a vast amount of people who crave war and bloodshed.

Thus, peace of the world and peace of the state are interdependent. Hence, we necessarily find that even that part of the state which is currently satisfied with its life, which are the nimble and the clever, still have a lot to be concerned about for the safety of their lives, due to the tensions with those who strive to overthrow them. And if they understood the value of peace, they would be happy to adopt the conduct of living of the last generation, for "all that a man has will he give for his life."

PAIN VS. PLEASURE IN SELF-RECEPTION.

Thus, when we examine and thoroughly grasp the above plan, we will see that the whole difficulty lies in changing our nature from a desire to receive for ourselves, to a desire to bestow upon others, since those two things deny one another. At first glance, the plan seems imaginary, as something that is above human nature. But when we delve deeply into it, we will find that the contradiction from reception for oneself to bestowal upon others is nothing but a psychological matter, because in fact we do bestow upon others without benefiting ourselves. This is so because although self-reception manifests itself in us in various ways, such as property, possessions for pleasure of the heart, the eye, the pallet, etc., all those are defined by one name, "pleasure." Thus, the very essence of reception for oneself that a person desires is nothing but the desire for pleasure.

And now, imagine that if we were to collect all the pleasures one feels during his seventy years of life and put it on one side, and collect all the pain and sorrow one feels on the other side, if we could see the outcome, we would prefer not to have been born at all. And if this is so, then what does one receive during one's life? If we assume that one obtains twenty percent of pleasure during his lifetime and eighty percent of pain, then if we put them one opposite the other, there would still remain sixty percent of suffering unrewarded.

But this is all a private calculation, as when one works for oneself. But in a global calculation, the individual produces more than he takes for his own pleasure and sustenance. Thus, if the direction were to change from self-reception to bestowal, the individual will enjoy the entire produce he produces without much pain.

The Wisdom of Kabbalah and Philosophy

WHAT IS SPIRITUALITY?

Philosophy has gone through a great deal of trouble to prove that corporeality is the offspring of spirituality and that the soul begets the body. Still, their words are unacceptable to the heart in any manner. Their primary mistake is their erroneous perception of spirituality: they determined that spirituality fathered corporeality, which is certainly a fib.

Any parent must somehow resemble its progeny. This relation is the path and the route by which its sequel extends. In addition, every operator must have some regard to its operation by which to contact it. Since you say that spirituality is denied of any corporeal incidents, then such a path does not exist, or a relation by which the spiritual can contact and set it into any kind of motion.

However, understanding the meaning of the word, "spirituality," has nothing to do with philosophy. This is because how can they discuss something that they have never seen or felt? What do their rudiments stand on?

If there is any definition that can tell spiritual from corporeal, it belongs only to those who have attained a spiritual thing and felt it. These are the genuine Kabbalists; thus, it is the wisdom of Kabbalah that we need.

PHILOSOPHY WITH REGARD TO HIS ESSENCE

Philosophy loves to concern itself with His Essence and prove which rules do not apply to Him. However, Kabbalah has no dealings whatsoever with it, for how can the unattainable and imperceptible be defined? Indeed, a negative definition is just as valid as a positive definition. For if you see an object from a distance and recognize its negatives, meaning all that it is not, that, too, is considered seeing and some extent of recognition. If an object is truly out of sight, even its negative characteristics are not apparent.

If, for example, we see a black image from a distance, but can still determine that it is neither human nor bird, it is considered vision. If it had been even farther still, we would have been unable to determine that it is not a person.

This is the origin of their confusion and invalidity. Philosophy loves to pride itself on understanding all the negatives about His essence. However, the sages of Kabbalah put their hand to their mouth at this point, and do not give Him even a simple name, **for we do not define by name or word that which we do not attain.** That is because a word designates some degree of attainment. However, Kabbalists do speak a great deal about His illumination in reality, meaning all those illuminations they have actually attained, as validly as tangible attainment.

THE SPIRITUAL IS A FORCE WITHOUT A BODY

That is what Kabbalists define as "spirituality" and that is what they talk about. It has no image or space or time or any corporeal value (In my opinion, philosophy has generally worn a mantle that is not its own, for it has pilfered definitions from the wisdom of Kabbalah, and made delicacies with human understanding. Had it not been for that, they would never have thought of fabricating such acumen). However, it is only a potential force, meaning not a force that is clothed in an ordinary, worldly body, but a force without a body.

A SPIRITUAL VESSEL IS CALLED "A FORCE"

This is the place to point out that the force that spirituality speaks of does not refer to the spiritual Light itself. That spiritual Light extends directly from His essence and is therefore the same as His Essence. This means that we have no perception or attainment in the spiritual Light that we may define by name. Even the name, "Light," is borrowed and is not real. Thus, we must know that the name, "Force," without a body refers specifically to the "spiritual vessel."

LIGHTS AND VESSELS

Therefore, we must not inquire how the sages of the Kabbalah, which fill the entire wisdom with their insights, differentiate between the various Lights. That is because these observations do not refer to the Lights themselves, but to the impression of the vessel, being the above-mentioned force, which is affected by its encounter with the Light.

VESSELS AND LIGHTS (THE MEANING OF THE WORDS)

Here is where the line between the gift and the love that it creates must be drawn. The Lights, meaning the impression on the vessel, which is attainable, is called "form and matter together." The impression is the form and the above force is the matter.

However, the love that is created is considered a **"form without matter."** This means that if we separate the love from the gift itself, as though it never clothed any gift, but only in the abstract name, "the love of God," then it is regarded as a form. In that event, the practice of it is regarded as **"Formative Kabbalah."** However, it would still be regarded as real, without any similarity to Formative Philosophy, since the spirit of this love remains in the attainment, completely separated from the gift, being the Light itself.

MATTER AND FORM IN KABBALAH

The reason is that although this love is merely a consequence of the gift, it is still far more important than the gift itself. It is like a great king who gives an unimportant object to a person. Although the gift itself is worthless, the love and the attention of the king make it priceless and precious. Thus, it is completely separated from the matter, being the Light and the gift, in a way that the work and the distinction remain carved in the attainment with only the love itself, while the gift is seemingly forgotten from the heart. Therefore, this aspect of the wisdom is called the **"Formative Wisdom of Kabbalah."** Indeed, this part is the most important part of the wisdom.

ABYA

This love consists of four parts that are much like human love: when we first receive the present, we still do not refer to the giver of the gift as one who loves us, all the more so if the giver of the present is important and the receiver is not equal to him.

However, the repetitive giving and the perseverance will make even the most important person seem like a true, equal lover. This is because the law of love does not apply between great and small, as two real lovers must feel equal.

Thus, you can measure four degrees of love here. The incident is called ***Assiya***, the repetition of the giving of gifts is called ***Yetzira***, and the appearance of the love itself is called ***Beria***.

It is here that the study of the **Formative Wisdom of Kabbalah** begins, for it is in this degree that love is separated from the presents. This is the meaning of, "and create darkness," meaning the Light is removed from the *Yetzira* and the love remains without Light, without its gifts.

Then comes **Atzilut**. After it has tasted and entirely separated the form from the matter, as in, "and create darkness," it became worthy of ascending to the degree of *Atzilut*, where the form clothes the substance once more, meaning Light and love together.

THE ORIGIN OF THE SOUL

Everything spiritual is perceived as a separated force from the body because it has no corporeal image. However, because of that, it remains isolated and completely separated from the corporeal. In such a state, how can it set anything corporeal in motion, much less beget anything physical, when it has no relation by which to come in contact with the physical?

THE ACIDIC ELEMENT

However, the truth is that the force itself is also considered a genuine matter, just as any corporeal matter in the concrete world, and the fact that it has no image that the human senses can perceive does not reduce the value of the substance, which is the "force."

Take a molecule of oxygen as an example: It is a constituent of most materials in the world. Yet, if you take a bottle with pure oxygen when it is not mixed with any other substance, you will find that it seems as though the bottle is completely empty. You will not be able to notice anything about it; it will be completely like air, intangible and invisible to the eye.

If we remove the lid and smell it, we will find no scent; if we taste it, we will find no flavor, and if we put it on a scale, it will not weigh more than the empty bottle. The same applies to hydrogen, which is also tasteless, scentless, and weightless.

However, when putting these two elements together, they will immediately become a liquid–drinking water that possesses both taste and weight. If we put the water inside active lime, it will immediately mix with it and become as solid as the lime itself.

Thus, the elements, oxygen and hydrogen, in which there is no tangible perception whatsoever, become a solid body. Therefore, how can we determine about natural forces that they are not a corporeal substance just because they are not arranged in such a way that our senses can perceive them? Moreover, we can evidently see that most of the tangible materials in our world consist preliminarily of the element of oxygen, which human senses cannot perceive and feel!

Moreover, even in the tangible reality, the solid and the liquid that we can vividly perceive in our tangible world might turn to air and fume at a certain temperature. Likewise, the vapors may turn to solids when the temperature drops.

In that event, we should wonder, **how does one give that which one does not possess?** We clearly see that all the tangible images come from elements that are in and of themselves intangible, and do not exist as materials in and of themselves. Likewise, all the fixed pictures that we know and use to define materials are inconsistent and do not exist in their own right. Rather, they only dress and undress forms under the influence of conditions such as heat or cold.

The primary part of the corporeal substance is the "force" in it, though we are not yet able to tell these forces apart, as with chemical elements. Perhaps in the future they will be discovered in their pure form, as we have only recently discovered the chemical elements.

EQUAL FORCE IN SPIRITUAL AND PHYSICAL

In a word: all the names that we ascribe materials are completely fabricated, meaning stem from our concrete perception in our five senses. They do not exist in and of themselves. On the other hand, any definition we ascribe to the force, which separates it from the material, is also fabricated. Even when science reaches its ultimate development, we will still have to regard only the tangible reality. This means that within any material operation we see and feel, we must perceive its operator, who is also a substance, like the operation itself. There is a correlation between them, or they would not have come to it.

We must know that this erring of separating the operator from the operation comes from the **Formative Philosophy**, which insisted on proving that the spiritual act influences the corporeal operation. That resulted in erroneous assumptions such as the above, which Kabbalah has no need for.

BODY AND SOUL IN THE UPPER ONES

The opinion of Kabbalah in this matter is crystal clear, excluding any mixture of philosophy. This is because in the minds of Kabbalists, even the spiritual, separated, conceptual entities, which philosophy denies having any corporeality and displays them as purely conceptual substance, although they are indeed spiritual, more sublime and abstract, they still consist of a **body and soul,** just like the physical human.

Therefore, you need not wonder how two can win the prize and say that they are complex. Furthermore, philosophy believes that anything complex will eventually disintegrate and decompose, meaning die. Thus, how can one declare that they are both complex *and* eternal?

LIGHTS AND VESSELS

Indeed, their thoughts are not our thoughts, for the way of the sages of the Kabbalah is one of finding actual proof of attainment, making its revocation through intellectual pondering impossible. But let me make these matters so that they are clear for every person's understanding.

First, we must know that the difference between Lights and vessels is created immediately in the first emanated being from *Ein Sof* (Infinity). Naturally, the first emanation is also the most complete and purer than everything that follows it. It is certain that it receives this pleasantness and completeness from His Essence, which wishes to grant it every pleasantness and pleasure.

It is known that the measurement of the pleasure is essentially the will to receive it. That is because what we most want to receive feels as the most pleasurable. Because of that, we should discern two observations in this first emanation: the "will to receive" that received Essence, and the received Essence itself.

We should also know that the will to receive is what we perceive as the "body" of the emanated, meaning its primary essence, being the vessel to receive His goodness. The second is the Essence of the good that is received, which is His Light, which is eternally extended to the emanation.

It follows that we necessarily distinguish two discernments that clothe one another even in the most sublime spiritual that the heart can conceive. It is the opposite of the opinion of philosophy, which fabricated that the separated entities are not complex materials. It is necessary that that "will to receive," which necessarily exists in the emanated (for without it there would be no pleasure but coercion, and no feeling of pleasure) is absent in His Essence. This is the reason for the name "emanated," since it is no longer His Essence, for from whom would He receive?

However, the bounty that it receives is necessarily a part of His Essence, for here there need not be any innovation. Thus, we see the great difference between the generated body and the received abundance, which is deemed His essence.

HOW CAN A SPIRITUAL BEGET A CORPOREAL?

It is seemingly difficult to understand how the spiritual can beget and extend anything corporeal. This question is an ancient philosophical query that much ink has been spilt attempting to resolve.

The truth is that this question is a difficult one only if one follows their doctrine. That is because they have determined the form of spirituality without any connection to anything corporeal. That produces a difficult question: how can the spiritual lead to or father anything corporeal?

But it is the view of the sages of Kabbalah that this is not difficult at all, for their terms are the complete opposite to those of philosophers. They maintain that any spiritual quality equalizes with the corporeal quality like two drops in a pond. Thus, the relationships are of the utmost affinity and there is no separation between them, except in the substance: the spiritual consists of a spiritual substance and the corporeal consists of a corporeal substance.

However, all the qualities in spiritual materials abide in corporeal materials, too, as explained in the article, "The Essence of the Wisdom of Kabbalah."

The old philosophy presents three opinions as obstacles before my explanation: The first is their decision that the power of the human intellect is the eternal soul, man's essence. The second is their conjecture that the body is an upshot of the soul. The third is their saying that spiritual entities are simple objects and not complex.

MATERIALISTIC PSYCHOLOGY

Not only is it the wrong place to argue with them about their fabricated conjectures, but also the time of supporters of such views has already passed and their authority revoked. We should also thank the experts of materialistic psychology for that, which built its plinth on the ruin of the former, winning the public's favor. Now everyone admits to the nullity of philosophy, for it is not built on concrete foundations.

This old doctrine became a stumbling rock and a deadly thorn to the sages of Kabbalah because where they should have subdued before the sages of Kabbalah, and assume abstinence and prudence, sanctity, and purity before the sages disclosed before them even the smallest thing in spirituality, they easily received what they had wanted from the formative philosophy. Without payment or price, they watered them from their fountain of wisdom to satiation, and refrained from delving in the wisdom of Kabbalah until the wisdom has almost been forgotten from among Israel. Hence, we are grateful to materialistic psychology for handing it a deadly blow.

I AM SOLOMON

The above is much like a fable that our sages tell: "Asmodeus (the devil) drove King Solomon four hundred parsas (a distant measurement) from Jerusalem and left Him with no money and means of sustenance. Then he sat in King Solomon's throne while the king was begging at the doors. Every place he went, he said: "I am Ecclesiastes!" but none believed him. And so he went from town to town declaring, "I am Solomon!" But when he came to the Sanhedrin (the sages of the Talmud) they said: "A fool does not utter the same folly all the time, saying, 'I was once a king.'"

It seems as though the name is not the essence of a person, but rather the owner of the name is. Therefore, how can a wise man such as Solomon not be recognized if he is indeed the owner of the name? Moreover, it is the person that dignifies the name and he should display his wisdom!

THREE PREVENTIONS

There are three reasons that prevent us from knowing the owner of a name:

1. Because of its truthfulness, the wisdom becomes clear only when all its details appear together. Therefore, before one knows the whole wisdom, it is impossible to see even a fraction of it. Thus, it is the publicity of its truthfulness that we need, so as to have enough prior faith in it to make a great effort.

2. Just as Asmodeus, the demon, wore the clothes of King Solomon and inherited his throne, philosophy sat on the throne of Kabbalah with easier concepts to grasp, for the lie is quickly accepted. Therefore, there is a twofold trouble here: first, the wisdom of truth is profound and laborious, while philosophy is false and easily grasped; and second, it is superfluous, because philosophy is quite satisfying.

3. As the demon claims that King Solomon is mad, philosophy mocks and dismisses Kabbalah.

However, as long as wisdom is sublime, it is elevated above the people and separated from it. Because he was the wisest man, he was also higher than every man. Thus, the finest scholars could not understand him, except those friends, meaning the Sanhedrin, whom he taught his wisdom to every day for days and years. They are the ones who understood him and publicized his name in the entire world.

The reason for it is that minute wisdom is perceived in five minutes, and is thus attainable by anyone and can be easily publicized. However, a weighty concept will not be understood in less than several hours. It may even take days or years, depending on the intelligence. Accordingly, the greatest scholars will be understood only by a selected few in the generation, because profound concepts are founded on much prior knowledge.

It is therefore not surprising that the wisest of all men, who was exiled to a place where he was not known, could not demonstrate his wisdom or even show a hint of his wisdom before they believed that he was the owner of the name.

It is the same with the wisdom of Kabbalah in our time: the troubles and the exile that have come upon us brought us to forget it (and if there are people who do practice it, it is not in its favor, but rather harms it, for they did not receive it from a Kabbalist sage). Hence, in this generation, it is as King Solomon was in exile, declaring, "I am the wisdom, and all the flavors of religion and Torah are in me," yet none believe it.

But this is perplexing, for if it is a genuine wisdom, can it not display itself like all other wisdoms? It cannot. As King Solomon could not display his wisdom to the scholars at the place of his exile and had to come to Jerusalem, the place of the Sanhedrin, who studied and knew King Solomon, and testified to the depth of his wisdom, so it is with the wisdom of Kabbalah: it requires great sages who examine their hearts to study it for twenty or thirty years. Only then will they be able to testify to it.

And as King Solomon could not prevent Asmodeus from sitting on his throne, pretending to be him until he arrived in Jerusalem, sages of Kabbalah observe philosophic theology and complain that they have stolen the upper shell of their wisdom, which Plato and his Greek predecessors had acquired while studying with the disciples of the prophets in Israel. They have stolen basic elements from the wisdom of Israel and wore a cloak that is not their own. To this day, philosophic theology sits on the throne of Kabbalah, being heir under her mistress.

And who would believe the sages of Kabbalah while others sit on their throne? It is as when they did not believe King Solomon in exile, for they knew him to be sitting on his throne, meaning the demon, Asmodeus. As with King Solomon, it is hopeless that the truth will be exposed, for the wisdom is deep and cannot be revealed by testimony or by experimentation except to those believers that dedicate themselves to it with heart and soul.

Just as the Sanhedrin did not recognize King Solomon as long as the falsehood of Asmodeus did not appear, Kabbalah cannot prove its nature and truthfulness, and no revelations will suffice for the world to know it before the futility and falsehood of theological philosophy that has taken its throne becomes apparent.

Therefore, there was no such salvation for Israel as when the materialistic psychology appeared and struck theological philosophy on its head a lethal blow. Now, every person who seeks the Lord must bring Kabbalah back to its throne, and restore its past glory.

Introduction to The Book of Zohar

1) In this introduction, I would like to clarify matters that are seemingly simple. Matters that everyone fumbles with, and for which much ink has been spilled, attempting to clarify. Yet we have not reached a concrete and sufficient knowledge of them. And here are the questions:

1. What is our essence?
2. What is our role in the long chain of reality, of which we are but small links?
3. When we examine ourselves, we find that we are as corrupted and as low as can be. And when we examine the operator who has made us, we are compelled to be at the highest degree, for there is none so praiseworthy as Him. For it is necessary that only perfect operations will stem from a perfect operator.
4. Our mind necessitates that He is utterly benevolent, beyond compare. How, then, did He create so many creatures that suffer and agonize all through their lives? Is it not the way of the good to do good, or at least not to harm so?
5. How is it possible that the infinite, that has neither beginning nor end, will produce finite, mortal, and flawed creatures?

2) In order to clear all that up, we need to make some preliminary inquiries. And not, God forbid, where it is forbidden, in the Creator's essence, of which we have no thought or perception whatsoever, and thus have no thought or utterance of Him, but where the inquiry is a *Mitzva* (commandment/good deed), the inquiry of His deeds. It is as the Torah commands us: "Know thou the God of thy father and serve Him," and as it says in the poem of unification, "By your actions we know you."

Inquiry No. 1: How can we picture a new creation, something new that is not included in Him before He creates it, when it is obvious to any observer that there is nothing that is not included in Him? Common sense dictates it, for how can one give what one does not have?

Inquiry No. 2: If you say that from the aspect of His almightiness, He can certainly create existence from absence, something new that is not in Him, there rises the question—what is that reality, which can be determined as having no place in Him at all, but is completely new?

Inquiry No. 3: This deals with what Kabbalists have said, that one's soul is a part of God Above, in such a way that there is no difference between Him and the soul, but He is the "whole" and the soul is a "part." And they compared it to a rock carved from a mountain. There is no difference between the rock and the mountain, except that He is the "whole" and the rock is a "part." Thus we must ask: it is one thing that a stone carved from the mountain is separated from it by an ax made for that purpose, causing the separation of the "part" from the "whole." But how can you picture that about Him, that He will separate a part of His essence until it departs His essence and becomes separated from Him, meaning a soul, to the point that it can only be understood as part of His essence?

3) Inquiry No. 4: Since the chariot of the *Sitra Achra* (other side) and the *Klipot* (shells) is so far, at the other end of His Holiness, until such remoteness is inconceivable, how can it be extracted and made from Holiness, much less that His Holiness will sustain it?

Inquiry No. 5: The matter of the rising of the dead: Since the body is so contemptible, that immediately at birth it is doomed to perish and to be buried. Moreover, *The Zohar* said that before the body rots entirely, the soul cannot ascend to its place in the Garden of Eden, while there are still remnants of it. Therefore, why must it return and rise at the revival of the dead? Could the Creator not delight the souls without it?

Even more bewildering is what our sages said, that the dead are destined to rise with their flaws, so that they will not be mistaken for another, and after that He will cure their flaws. We must understand why God should mind that they would not be mistaken for another, that for that He would recreate their flaws and then would have to cure it.

Inquiry No. 6: Regarding what our sages said, that man is the center of reality, that the Upper Worlds and this corporeal world and everything in them were created only for him (*The Zohar*, *Tazria*, 40), and obliged man to believe that the world had been created for him (*Sanhedrin* 37). It is seemingly hard to grasp that for this trifling human, whose value is no more than a wisp, with respect to the reality of this world, much less with respect to all the Upper Worlds, whose Height and Sublimity is immeasurable, that the Creator had troubled Himself to create all these for him. And also, why would man need all that?

4) To understand these questions and inquiries, the only tactic is to examine the end of the act, that is, the purpose of Creation. For nothing can be understood in the middle of the process, but only at its end. And it is clear that there is no act without a purpose, for only the insane can act purposelessly.

I know that there are those who cast over their backs the burden of Torah and *Mitzvot* (plural for *Mitzva*), saying the Creator has created the whole of reality, then left it alone, that because of the worthlessness of the creatures it is not fitting for the Exalted Creator to watch over their mean little ways. Indeed, without knowledge they have spoken, for it is impossible to comment on our lowliness and nothingness, before we decide that we have created ourselves with all our corrupted and loathsome natures.

But while we decide that the Creator, who is utterly perfect, is the One who created and designed our bodies, with all their admirable and contemptible attributes, surely, there can never emerge an imperfect act under the hand of the perfect worker, as each act testifies to its performer. And what fault is it of a bad garment, if some no-good tailor has made it?

Such as this we find in *Masechet Taanit*, 20: A tale about Rabbi Elazar who came across a very ugly man. He said to him: "How ugly is that man." The man replied: "Go and tell the craftsman that made me, 'How ugly is this instrument you have made.'" Hence, those who claim that because of our lowliness and nothingness, it is not fitting for Him to watch over us, and therefore He has left us, do nothing but display their ignorance.

Try to imagine, if you were to meet some man who would create creatures, precisely so they would suffer and agonize their whole lives as we do, and not only that, but cast them behind his back, not wanting even to look after them, to help them a little. How contemptible and low you would regard him! Can such a thing be thought of Him?

5) Therefore, common sense dictates that we grasp the opposite of what appears to be on the surface, and decide that we are truly noble and worthy creatures, of immeasurable importance, actually worthy of the Worker who had made us. For any fault you wish to perceive in our bodies, behind all the excuses

that you give to yourself, falls only on the Creator, who created us and the nature within us, for it is clear that He had created us and not we.

He also knows all the ways that stem from the evil nature and attributes He has created in us. It is as we have said, that we must contemplate the end of the act, and then we will be able to understand everything. It is as the saying goes, "Do not show a fool a job half done."

6) Our sages have already said that the Creator created the world for no other reason but to delight His creatures. And here is where we must place our minds and all our thoughts, for it is the ultimate aim of the act of the creation of the world. And we must bear in mind that since the Thought of Creation was to bestow upon His creatures, He had to create in the souls a great measure of desire to receive that which He had thought to give them. For the measure of each pleasure and delight depends on the measure of the will to receive it. The greater the will to receive, the greater the pleasure, and the lesser the will, the lesser the pleasure from reception.

Thus, the Thought of Creation itself necessarily dictates the creation of an excessive will to receive in the souls, to fit the immense pleasure that His Almightiness thought to bestow upon the souls. For the great delight and the great desire to receive go hand in hand.

7) Once we have learned that, we come to a full understanding of the second inquiry, in complete clarity. For we have learned what is the reality that can be clearly determined, which is not a part of His essence, to the extent that we can say that it is a new creation, existence from absence. And now that we know for certain that the Thought of Creation, to delight His creatures, necessarily created a measure of desire to receive from Him all the goodness and pleasantness that He had planned for them, that will to receive was clearly not included in His essence before He had created it in the souls, because from whom could He receive? It follows that He had created something new, which is not in Him.

And yet, we understand that according to the Thought of Creation, there was no need to create anything more than that will to receive. This is because this new creation is sufficient for Him to fulfill the entire Thought of Creation, which He had thought to bestow upon us. But all the filling in the Thought of Creation, all the benefits He had planned to render us, stem directly from His essence, and He has no reason to recreate them, since they are already extracted, existence from existence, to the great will to receive in the souls. Thus we evidently see that all the substance in the generated creation, from beginning to end, is only the "will to receive."

8) Now we have come to understand the words of the Kabbalists in the third inquiry. We wondered how it was possible to say about souls that they were a part of God Above, like a stone that is carved from a mountain, that there is no difference between them except that one is a "part" and the other is a "whole." And we wondered: it is one thing to say that the stone that is carved from the mountain becomes separated by an ax made for that purpose, but how can you say that about His essence? And also, what was it that separated the souls from His essence and excluded them from the Creator, to become creatures?

From the above, we clearly understand that as the ax cuts and divides a physical object in two, the disparity of form divides the spiritual into two. For example, when two people love each other, you say that they are attached to one another as one body. And when they hate each other, you say that they are as far from one another as the east from the west. But there is no question of nearness or remoteness of location here. Rather, this implies the equivalence of form: when they are equal in form, and each loves what the other loves and hates what the other hates, they love each other and are attached to one another.

And if there is some disparity of form between them, and one of them likes something that the other hates, then to the extent that they differ in form, they become distant and hateful of one another. And if, for example, they are opposite in form, and everything that one likes, the other hates, and everything the other hates is liked by the first, they are deemed as remote as the east from the west, meaning from one end to the other.

9) And you find that in spirituality the disparity of form acts like the ax that separates in the corporeal world, and the distance between them is proportional to the oppositeness of form. From this we learn that since the will to receive His delight has been imprinted in the souls, and we have shown that this form is absent in the Creator, because from whom would He receive, that disparity of form that the souls acquired separates them from His essence, as the ax that carves a stone from the mountain. And because of that disparity of form the souls were separated from the Creator and became creatures. However, everything the souls acquire of His Light extends from His essence, existence from existence.

It therefore turns out that with respect to His Light, which they receive in their *Kli* (vessel), which is the will to receive, there is no difference whatsoever between them and His essence. This is because they receive it existence from existence, directly from His essence. And the only difference between the souls and His essence is that the souls are a part of His essence.

This means that the amount of Light that they receive in their *Kli*, being the will to receive, is already separated from the Creator, as it is predicated on the disparity of form of the will to receive. And this disparity of form made it a part by which they were separated from the "whole" and became a "part." Thus, the only difference between them is that one is a "whole" and the other is a "part," as a stone that is carved from a mountain. And scrutinize this meticulously, for it is impossible to expand further on such an exalted place.

10) Now we can begin to understand the fourth inquiry: how is it possible that the chariot of impurity and *Klipot* would emerge from His Holiness, since it is at the other end of His Holiness? And also, how can it be that He supports and sustains it? Indeed, first we must understand the meaning of the existence of impurity and *Klipot*.

Know that this great will to receive, which we determined was the very essence of the souls by creation—for which they are fit to receive the entire filling in the Thought of Creation—does not stay in that form within the souls. If it had, they would have to remain eternally separated from Him because the disparity of form in them would separate them from Him.

And in order to mend that separation, which lays on the *Kli* of the souls, He created all the worlds and separated them into two systems, as in the verse: "God has made them one against the other," which are the four pure worlds ABYA, and opposite them the four impure worlds ABYA. And He imprinted the desire to bestow in the system of the pure ABYA, removed the will to receive for themselves from them, and placed it in the system of the impure worlds ABYA. Because of that, they have become separated from the Creator and from all the worlds of holiness.

For that reason the *Klipot* are called "dead," as in the verse: "sacrifices of the dead" (Psalms 106, 28). And the wicked that follow them, as our sages said, "The wicked, in their lives, are called 'dead,'" since the will to receive imprinted in them in oppositeness of form to His Holiness separates them from the Life of Lives, and they are remote from Him from one end to the other. It is so because He has no interest in reception, only in bestowal, whereas the *Klipot* want nothing of bestowal, but only to receive for themselves, for their own delight, and there is no greater oppositeness than that. And you already know that spiritual remoteness begins with some disparity of form and ends in oppositeness of form, which is the farthest possible distance in the last degree.

11) And the worlds cascaded onto the reality of this corporeal world, to a place where there is a body and a soul and a time of corruption and a time of correction. For the body, which is the will to receive for itself, extends from its root in the Thought of Creation, through the system of the impure worlds, as it is written, "and a wild ass's colt is born a man" (Job 11, 12). And he remains under the authority of that system for the first thirteen years, which is the time of corruption.

And by engaging in Mitzvot from thirteen years of age onwards, in order to bestow contentment upon his Maker, he begins to purify the will to receive for himself, imprinted in him, and slowly turns it to be in order to bestow. By that he extends a holy soul from its root in the Thought of Creation. And it passes through the system of the pure worlds and dresses in the body. This is the time of correction.

And so he accumulates degrees of holiness from the Thought of Creation in Ein Sof (Infinity), until they aid him in turning the will to receive for himself in him, to be entirely in the form of reception in order to bestow contentment upon his Maker, and not at all for himself. By that, one acquires equivalence of form with his Maker, because reception in order to bestow is regarded as pure bestowal.

In Masechet Kidushin it is written that with an important man she gives and he says—by that you are sanctified. Because when his reception is in order to delight her, the giver, it is deemed absolute bestowal and giving. Thus, one buys complete adhesion with Him, for spiritual adhesion is but equivalence of form, as our sages said, "How is it possible to cleave unto Him? Rather, cleave on to His qualities." And by that, one becomes worthy of receiving all the delight and pleasure and the gentleness in the Thought of Creation.

12) Thus we have clearly explained the correction of the will to receive, imprinted in the souls by the Thought of Creation. For the Creator has prepared for them two systems, one opposite the other, through which the souls pass and divide into two discernments, body and soul, which dress in one another.

And through Torah and Mitzvot, they finally turn the form of the will to receive to be as the form of the will to bestow. And then they can receive all the goodness in the Thought of Creation. And along with it, they are rewarded with a solid adhesion with Him, because through the work in Torah and Mitzvot they have been rewarded with equivalence of form with their Maker. This is deemed the end of correction.

And then, since there will no longer be a need for the evil Sitra Achra, it will be eliminated from the earth and death shall cease forever. And all the work in

Torah and *Mitzvot* that was given to the world during the six thousand years of the existence of the world, and to each person for the duration of one's seventy years of life, are to bring them to the end of correction—the above-mentioned equivalence of form.

The issue of the formation and extension of the system of *Klipot* and impurity from His Holiness has also been thoroughly clarified now: it had to be in order to extend by it the creation of the bodies, which would then be corrected through Torah and *Mitzvot*. And if our bodies, with their corrupted will to receive, were not extended through the impure system, we would never be able to correct it, for one cannot correct that which is not in him.

13) Indeed, we still need to understand how the will to receive for oneself, which is so flawed and corrupted, could extend from, and be in the Thought of Creation in *Ein Sof*, whose unity is beyond words and beyond description? The thing is that by the very thought to create the souls, His thought completed everything, for He does not need an act, as do we. Instantaneously, all the souls and worlds that were destined to be created, emerged filled with all the delight and pleasure and the gentleness He had planned for them, in the final perfection that the souls were intended to receive at the end of correction, after the will to receive in the souls has been fully corrected and was turned into pure bestowal, in complete equivalence of form with the Emanator.

This is so because in His Eternalness, past, present, and future are as one. The future is as the present and there is no such thing as time in Him. Hence, there was never an issue of a corrupted will to receive in its separated state in *Ein Sof*.

On the contrary, that equivalence of form, destined to be revealed at the end of correction, appeared instantly in the Infinite. And our sages said about that: "Before the world was created there were He is One and His Name One," for the separated form in the will to receive had not been revealed in the reality of the souls that emerged in the Thought of Creation. Rather, they were cleaved unto Him in equivalence of form by way of, "He is One and His Name One."

14) Thus you necessarily find that on the whole, there are three states to the soul:

The First State is their presence in *Ein Sof*, in the Thought of Creation, where they already have the future form of the End of Correction.

The Second State is their presence in the six thousand years, which were divided by the above two systems into a body and a soul. They were given the work in Torah and *Mitzvot*, in order to invert their will to receive and turn it into a will to bestow contentment upon their Maker, and not at all to themselves.

During the time of that state, no correction will come to the bodies, only to the souls. This means that they must eliminate any form of self-reception, which is considered the body, and remain with but a desire to bestow, which is the form of desire in the souls. Even the souls of the righteous will not be able to rejoice in the Garden of Eden after their demise, but only after their bodies rot in the dust.

The Third State is the end of correction of the souls, after the revival of the dead. At that time the complete correction will come to the bodies, too, for then they will turn reception for themselves, which is the form of the body, to take on the form of pure bestowal. And they will become worthy of receiving for themselves all the delight and pleasure and pleasantness in the Thought of Creation.

And with all that, they will attain strong adhesion by the force of their equivalence of form with their Maker, since they will not receive all that because of their desire to receive, but because of their desire to bestow contentment upon their Maker, since He derives pleasure when they receive from Him. And for purposes of brevity, from now on I will use the names of these three states, namely "first state," "second state," and "third state." And you should remember all that is explained here in every state.

15) When you examine the above three states, you will find that one completely necessitates the other, in a way that, if one were to be cancelled, the others would be cancelled, too.

If, for example, the third state—the conversion of the form of reception to the form of bestowal—had not materialized, it is certain that the first state in *Ein Sof* would never have been able to emerge.

It is because the perfection materialized there only because the future third state was already there, as though it is in the present. And all the perfection that was pictured there in that state is like a reflection from the future into the present. But if the future could be cancelled, there would not be any present. Thus, the third state necessitates the existence of the first.

All the more so when something is cancelled in the second state, where there is all the work that is destined to be completed in the third state, the work in corruptions and corrections and the continuance of the degrees of the souls. Thus, how will the third state come to be? Hence, the second state necessitates the existence of the third.

And so it is with the existence of the first state in *Ein Sof*, where the perfection of the third state resides. It definitely necessitates that it will be adapted, meaning that the second and third states will appear in complete perfection, no less and no more in any way.

Thus, the first state itself necessitates the expansion of two corresponding systems in the second state, to allow the existence of a body in the will to receive, corrupted by the system of impurity, thus enabling us to correct it. And had there not been a system of impure worlds, we would not have that will to receive, and we would not be able to correct it and come to the third state, for "one cannot correct that which is not in him." Thus we need not ask how the impure system came to be from the first state, for it is the first state that necessitates its existence in the form of the second state.

16) Therefore, one must not wonder at how it was that the choice had been taken from us, since we must be completed and come to the third state, since it is already present in the first. The thing is that there are two ways the Creator has set for us in the second state to bring us to the third state:

1. The Path of Keeping Torah and *Mitzvot*.
2. The Path of Suffering, since the pain itself purifies the body and will eventually compel us to invert our will to receive into the form of a will to bestow, and cleave to Him. It is as our sages said (*Sanhedrin*, 97b), "If you repent, good; and if not, I will place over you a king such as Haman, and he will force you to repent." Our sages said about the verse, "will hasten it in its time": "If they are rewarded, I will hasten it; and if not, in its time."

This means that if we are granted through the first path, by keeping Torah and *Mitzvot*, we thus hasten our correction, and we do not need the harsh agony and the long time needed to experience them, so they will compel us to reform. And if not, "in its time," meaning only when the suffering will complete our correction and the time of correction will be forced upon us. On the whole, the path of suffering is also the punishments of the souls in Hell.

But in any case, the end of correction—the third state—is mandatory, because of the first state. Our choice is only between the path of suffering and the path of Torah and *Mitzvot*. Thus we have thoroughly clarified how the three states of the souls are interconnected and necessitate one another.

17) From all the above, we thoroughly understand the third inquiry, that when we examine ourselves, we find ourselves to be as corrupted and contemptible as can be. But when we examine the operator who created us,

we must be exalted, for there is none so praiseworthy as He, as becoming of the Operator who created us, because the nature of the Perfect Operator is to perform perfect operations.

Now we can understand that our body, with all its trifle incidents and possessions, is not at all our real body. Our real, eternal, and complete body already exists in *Ein Sof*, in the first state, where it receives its complete form from the future third state, that is, receiving in the form of bestowal, in equivalence of form with *Ein Sof*.

And if our first state necessitates that we receive the *Klipa* (shell) of our body in the second state, in its corrupted and loathsome form, which is the will to receive for oneself alone, which is the force that separates us from *Ein Sof* so as to correct it and allow us to receive our eternal body in practice, in the third state, we need not protest against it. Our work can only be done in this transitory and wasteful body, for "one does not correct that which is not in him."

Thus, we are already in that measure of perfection, worthy and fitting of the Perfect Operator who had made us, even in our current, second state, for this body does not defect us in any way, since it will expire and die, and is only here for the time necessary for its cancellation and acquisition of our eternal form.

18) This settles our fifth inquiry: How could it be that transitory, wasteful actions would extend from the eternal? And we see that, indeed, we have already been extended as is fitting for His Eternalness—eternal and perfect beings. And our eternalness necessitates that the *Klipa* of the body, which was given to us only for work, will be transitory and wasteful. For if it remained in eternity, we would remain forever separated from the Life of Lives.

We have said before (Item 13), that this form of our body, which is the will to receive for ourselves alone, is not at all present in the eternal Thought of Creation, for there we are in the form of the third state. Yet, it is obligatory in the second state, to allow us to correct it.

And we must not ponder the state of other beings in the world but man, since man is the center of Creation, as will be written below (item 39). And all other creatures do not have any value of their own but to the extent that they help man achieve his perfection. Hence, they rise and fall with him without any consideration of themselves.

19) With that, we also settle our fourth inquiry: Since the nature of the good is to do good, how did He create beings that would be tormented and agonized throughout their lives? As we have said, all this agony is necessitated from our first state, where our complete eternity, which comes from the future third state,

compels us to go either by the path of Torah, or by the path of suffering, and to reach our eternal state in the third state (Item 15).

And all this agony is felt only by the *Klipa* of our body, created only to be perished and buried. This teaches us that the will to receive for himself was created only to be eradicated, abolished from the world, and to turn it into a will to bestow. And the pains we suffer are but discoveries of its nothingness and the harm in it. Indeed, when all human beings agree to abolish and eradicate their will to receive for themselves, and have no other desire but to bestow upon their friends, all worries and jeopardy in the world would cease to exist. And we would all be assured of a whole and wholesome life, since each of us would have a whole world caring for us, ready to fulfill our needs.

Yet, while each of us has only a desire to receive for ourselves, it is the source of all the worries, suffering, wars, and slaughter we cannot escape. They weaken our bodies with all sorts of sores and maladies, and you find that all the agonies in our world are but manifestations offered to our eyes, to prompt us to revoke the evil *Klipa* of the body and assume the complete form of the will to bestow. And it is as we have said, that the path of suffering in itself can bring us to the desired form. Bear in mind that the *Mitzvot* between man and man come before the *Mitzvot* between man and God, because the bestowal upon one's friend brings one to bestow upon his Maker.

20) After all that we have said, we come to the resolution of the first inquiry: What is our essence? Our essence is as the essence of all the details in reality, which is no more and no less than the will to receive (as written in Item 7). But it is not as it is now, in the second state, which is the will to receive for self alone, but as it stands in the first state, in *Ein Sof*, in its eternal form, which is reception in order to bestow contentment upon his Maker (as written in Item 13).

And although we have not yet reached the third state in actual fact, and we still lack time, it does not blemish our essence whatsoever, since our third state is necessitated from the first. Thus "all that is bound to be collected is deemed collected." And the lack of time is regarded a deficiency only where there is doubt whether one will complete what needs to be completed in time.

And since we have no doubt about that, it is as though we have already come to the third state. And our body, too, given to us in its present, corrupted form, does not blemish our essence, since it and all its possessions are to be completely eradicated, along with the whole system of impurity, which is their source, and all that is bound to be burned is deemed burned, considered as though it never existed.

But the soul that is dressed in that body, whose essence is also purely a desire—but a desire to bestow, which extends to us from the system of the four worlds of the Holy *ABYA* (Item 11)—exists forever. This is because this form of a desire to bestow is in equivalence of form with the Life of Lives and is not in any way exchangeable. (This matter will be completed below, from Item 32 on.)

21) And do not be led astray by the philosophers who say that the very essence of the soul is an intellectual substance, and that it only exists through the concepts it learns, that it grows through them, and that they are its very essence. And the question of the continuance of the soul after the departure of the body depends entirely on the extent of concepts it has acquired, until in the absence of such concepts, there remains nothing to continue. This is not the view of Torah. It is also unaccepted by the heart, and anyone who ever tried to acquire knowledge knows and feels that the mind is a possession, not the actual possessor.

But as we have said, the whole substance of creation, both the substance of the spiritual objects and the substance of the corporeal objects, is no more and no less than a will to receive. And although we said that the soul is entirely a desire to bestow, it is only through corrections of Reflected Light that it receives from the Upper Worlds, from which it comes to us.

Yet, the very essence of the soul is a will to receive, as well. And the difference we can tell between one object and another is discerned only by its will, for the will in any essence creates needs, and the needs create thoughts and concepts so as to obtain those needs, which the will to receive demands.

And as human desires differ from one another, so do their needs, thoughts, and ideas. For instance, those whose will to receive is limited to beastly desires, their needs, thoughts, and ideas are dedicated to satisfying that will to receive in its entire beastliness. And although they use the mind and reason as humans do, it is, however, enough for the slave to be as his master. And it is like the beastly mind, since the mind is enslaved and serves the beastly desire.

And those whose will to receive is strong mainly in human desires—such as respect and domination over others—which are absent in the beast, the majority of their needs, thoughts, and ideas revolve solely around satisfying that desire as much as they can. And those whose will to receive is intensified mainly for acquisition of knowledge, the majority of their needs, thoughts, and ideas are to satisfy that desire as much as they can.

22) These three desires are mostly present in every person, but they mingle in different quantities, hence the difference from one person to another. And

from the corporeal attributes we can deduce about the spiritual objects, relating to their spiritual value.

23) Thus, human souls, too, the spiritual ones, have only a desire to bestow contentment upon their Maker, through the dresses of Reflected Light received from the Upper Worlds from which they come. And that desire is their essence and the core of the soul. It turns out that once dressed in a human body, it generates needs and desires and ideas to satisfy its desire to bestow to the fullest, meaning to bestow contentment upon its Maker, according to the size of its desire.

24) The essence of the body is but a desire to receive for itself, and all its manifestations and possessions are fulfillments of that corrupted will to receive, which had initially been created only to be eradicated from the world, in order to achieve the complete third state at the end of correction. For this reason, it is mortal, transitory, and contemptible, along with all its possessions, like a fleeting shadow that leaves nothing in its wake.

And since the essence of the soul is but a desire to bestow, and all its manifestations and possessions are fulfillments of that desire to bestow, which already exists in the eternal first state, as well as in the future third state, it is immortal and irreplaceable. Rather, it and all its possessions are eternal and exist forever. Absence does not affect whatsoever at the departure of the body. On the contrary, the absence of the form of the corrupted body greatly strengthens it, enabling it to rise to the Garden of Eden.

Thus we have clearly shown that the persistence of the soul in no way depends upon the concepts it has acquired, as philosophers claim. Rather, its eternality is in its very essence, in its will to bestow, which is its essence. And the concepts it acquires are its reward, not its essence.

25) From here emerges the full resolution of the fifth inquiry: Since the body is so corrupted that the soul cannot be fully purified before it rots in the ground, why does it return at the revival of the dead? And also the question about the words of our sages: "The dead are destined to be revived with their flaws, so it will not be said, 'It is another'" (*The Zohar*, *Amor*, 17).

And you will clearly understand this matter from the Thought of Creation itself, from the first state. Because we have said that since the Thought was to delight His creatures, He had to create an overwhelmingly exaggerated desire to receive all that bounty, which is in the Thought of Creation, for "the great delight and the great desire to receive go hand in hand" (Items 6-7). We stated there that this exaggerated will to receive is all the substance that He had created, for He needs nothing more than that, to carry out the Thought of Creation. And it is the nature of the Perfect Operator to not perform redundant operations, as written in the Poem of Unification: "Of all Your work, not a thing did You forget, omit, or add."

We also said there that this exaggerated will to receive has been completely removed from the pure system and was given entirely to the system of the impure worlds, from which extend the bodies, their sustenance, and all their possessions in this world. When a man reaches thirteen years of age, he begins to attain a holy soul through engaging in the Torah. At that time, he is nourished by the system of the pure worlds, according to the measure of the purity of soul he has attained.

We also said above, that during the six thousand years that are given to us for work in Torah and *Mitzvot*, no corrections come to the body—to its exaggerated will to receive. All the corrections that come through our work relate only to the soul, which thus climbs the degrees of holiness and purity, which means enhancement of the will to bestow that extends with the soul.

For this reason, the body will ultimately die, be buried, and rot because it did not undergo any correction. Yet, it cannot remain that way, for if the exaggerated will to receive perished from the world, the Thought of Creation would not be realized—meaning the reception of all the great pleasures that He thought to bestow upon His creatures, for "the great will to receive and the great pleasure go hand in hand." And to the extent that the desire to receive it diminishes, so diminish the delight and pleasure from reception.

26) We have already stated that the first state necessitates the third state, to fully materialize as was in the Thought of Creation—in the first state—not omitting a single thing (see Item 15). Therefore, the first state necessitates the revival of the dead. That means that their excessive will to receive, which had already been eradicated and rotted in the second state, must now be revived in all its exaggerated measure, with no restraints whatsoever, meaning with all its past flaws.

Then begins the work anew, to convert that excessive will to receive to be only to bestow. And then we will have doubled our gain:

1. We would have a place to receive all the delight and pleasure and gentleness in the Thought of Creation, since we would already have the body with its greatly excessive will to receive, which goes hand in hand with these pleasures.
2. Since our reception in that manner would only be in order to bestow contentment upon our Maker, that reception would be regarded as complete bestowal (see Item 11). And that would bring us to equivalence

of form, which is *Dvekut* (adhesion), which is our form in the third state. Thus, the first state absolutely necessitates the revival of the dead.

27) Indeed, there cannot be revival for the dead, but only near the end of correction, towards the end of the second state. For once we have been rewarded with denial of our excessive will to receive, and have been granted the will to only bestow, and once we have been endowed with all the wonderful degrees of the soul, called *Nefesh*, *Ruach*, *Neshama*, *Haya*, *Yechida*, through our work at negating this will to receive, we have come to the greatest perfection, until the body could be revived with all its excessive will to receive, and we are no longer harmed by it by being separated from our *Dvekut*.

On the contrary, we overcome it and give it the form of bestowal. And indeed, this is done with every corrupt quality that we wish to remove from it. First, we must completely remove it until there is nothing left of it. Afterwards, we can receive it again and conduct it in the middle way. But as long as we have not fully removed it, it is impossible to conduct it in the desired, medium way.

28) Our sages said, "The dead are destined to be revived with their flaws, and then be healed." This means that in the beginning the same body is revived, which is the excessive will to receive, without any restraints, just as it grew under the nourishment of the impure worlds before the Torah and *Mitzvot* have purified it in any way. This is the meaning of, "in all their flaws."

And then we embark on a new kind of labor—to insert all that exaggerated will to receive in the form of bestowal. Then it is healed, because now it obtained equivalence of form. And they said that the reason is "so it will not be said, 'It is another,'" meaning so it will not be said about it that it is in a different form from the one it had in the Thought of Creation. This is so because that excessive will to receive stands there, aiming to receive all the bounty in the Thought of Creation.

It is only that in the meantime it has been given to the *Klipot* for purification. But in the end, it must not be a different body, for if it were diminished in any way, it would be deemed entirely different, thus unworthy of receiving all the bounty in the Thought of Creation, as it receives there is the first state.

29) Now we can resolve the above second inquiry: what is our role in the long chain of reality, of which we are but tiny links, during the short span of our days? Know that our work during the seventy years of our days is divided in four:

The First Division is to obtain the excessive will to receive without restraints, in its full, corrupted measure from under the hands of the four impure worlds

ABYA. If we do not have that corrupted will to receive, we will not be able to correct it, for "one cannot correct that which is not in him."

Thus, the will to receive imprinted in the body at birth is insufficient. Rather, it must also be a vehicle for the impure *Klipot* for no less than thirteen years. This means that the *Klipot* must dominate it and give it their lights, for their lights increase its will to receive. That is because the fulfillments that the *Klipot* provide the will to receive with only expand and enhance the demands of the will to receive.

For example, at birth, he has a desire for only a hundred, and not more. But when the *Sitra Achra* provides the one hundred, the will to receive immediately grows and wants two hundred. Then, when the *Sitra Achra* provides fulfillment for the two hundred, the desire immediately expands to want four hundred. And if one does not overcome it through Torah and *Mitzvot*, and purifies the will to receive to turn it into bestowal, one's will to receive expands throughout one's life, until eventually he dies without attaining half his desires. This is regarded as being under the *Sitra Achra* and the *Klipot*, whose role is to expand and enhance his will to receive and make it exaggerated and unrestrained in any way, to provide one with all the material he needs to work with and correct.

30) **The Second Division** is from thirteen years and on. At that point, the point in his heart, which is the posterior of holiness, is given strength. Although it is dressed in his will to receive at birth, it only begins to awaken after thirteen years, and then one begins to enter the system of the pure worlds, to the extent that one observes Torah and *Mitzvot*.

The primary aim of that time is to obtain and intensify the spiritual will to receive, because at birth, one has only a will to receive for corporeality. Therefore, although one has obtained the excessive will to receive before he turned thirteen, it is still not the completion of the growth of the will to receive, for the primary intensification of the will to receive is only to spirituality.

This is because if, for example, prior to turning thirteen, one's will to receive wishes to devour all the wealth and respect in this corporeal world. This is apparently not an eternal world, and for all of us it is but a fleeting shadow. But when one obtains the excessive spiritual will to receive, one wishes to devour, for one's own delight, all the wealth and delights in the next, eternal world, which is an eternal possession. Thus, the majority of the excessive will to receive is completed only with the will to receive spirituality.

31) It is written in *New Tikkun* (97b) about the verse (Proverbs 30, 15), "The horseleech hath two daughters: 'Give, give.'": "A leech means Hell. And the evil

caught in that Hell cry as dogs '*Hav, Hav* (Hebrew: Give, Give),'" meaning "give us the wealth of this world, give us the wealth of the next world."

Yet it is a much more important degree than the first, since aside from obtaining the full measure of the will to receive, giving one all the material one needs for one's work, this is the degree that brings one to *Lishma* (for Her Name). It is as our sages said (*Pesachim* 50b): "One should always engage in Torah and *Mitzvot* lo *Lishma* (not for Her Name), as from *Lo Lishma*, one comes to *Lishma*."

Hence, this degree, which comes past the thirteen years, is deemed holiness. This is considered the holy maid that serves her mistress, which is the Holy *Shechina* (Divinity). This is because the maid brings one to *Lishma*, and he is rewarded with the inspiration of Divinity. Yet, one should take every measure suited to bring one to *Lishma*, since if one does not strain for that and does not achieve *Lishma*, he will fall into the pit of the impure maid, which is the opposite of the holy maid, whose role is to confuse a person, that the *Lo Lishma* will not bring him to *Lishma*. It is said about her: "handmaid that is heir to her mistress" (Proverbs 30, 23), for she will not let one near the mistress, which is the Holy Divinity.

And the final degree in this division is that he will fall passionately in love with the Creator, as one falls passionately for a corporeal love, until the object of passion remains before one's eyes all day long and all night long, as the poet says, "When I remember Him, He does not let me sleep." Then it is said of him: "but desire fulfilled is a tree of life" (Proverbs 13, 12). This is because the five degrees of the soul are the Tree of Life, which stretches over five hundred years. Each degree lasts a hundred years, meaning it will bring him to receive all five *Behinot* (discernments) *NRNHY* (*Nefesh, Ruach, Neshama, Haya, Yechida*) clarified in the third division.

32) **The Third Division** is the work in Torah and *Mitzvot Lishma*, in order to bestow and to not receive reward. This work cleanses the will to receive for oneself and replaces it with a will to bestow. To the extent that one purifies the will to receive, he becomes worthy of receiving the five parts of the soul called *NRNHY* (below Item 42). This is because they stand in the will to bestow (see Item 23), and cannot clothe one's body as long as the will to receive—which is opposite, or even different in form from the soul—controls it.

That is because the matter of dressing and equivalence of form go hand in hand (see Item 11). And when one is rewarded with being entirely in the will to bestow and not at all for oneself, he will be rewarded with obtaining equivalence of form with his Upper NRNHY, which extend from one's origin in *Ein Sof* in the first state, through the pure *ABYA*, and will immediately extend and clothe him in a gradual manner.

The Fourth Division is the work conducted after the revival of the dead. This means that the will to receive, which had already been completely absent through death and burial, is now revived in its excessive, worst will to receive, as our sages said: "The dead will be revived in their flaws" (Item 28). And then it is turned into reception in the form of bestowal. However, there are a chosen few who were given this work while still living in this world.

33) Now remains the clarification of the sixth inquiry, which is the words of our sages who said that all the worlds, Upper and lower, were created only for man. It seems very peculiar that for man, whose worth is but a wisp compared to the reality before us in this world, much less compared to the Upper, Spiritual Worlds, the Creator would go to all the trouble of creating all that for him. And even more peculiar is what would man need all these vast Spiritual Worlds for?

And you must know that any contentment of our Maker from bestowing upon His creatures depends on the extent that the creatures feel Him—that He is the giver, and that He is the one who delights them. For then He takes great pleasure in them, as a father playing with his beloved son, to the degree that the son feels and recognizes the greatness and exaltedness of his father, and his father shows him all the treasures he had prepared for him, as it is written (Jeremiah 31): "Ephraim, my darling son, is he joy of his parents? For whenever I speak of him, I earnestly remember him still. Hence, My heart yearneth for him, I will surely have compassion upon him, says the Lord" (Jeremiah 31, 19).

Observe these words carefully and you can come to know the great delights of the Lord with those whole ones that have been granted feeling Him and recognizing His greatness in all those manners He has prepared for them, until they are like a father with his darling son, the joy of his parents. And we need not continue on that, for it is enough for us to know that for this contentment and delight with those whole ones, it was worth His while to create all the worlds, Higher and lower alike.

34) To prepare His creatures to reach the aforementioned exalted degree, the Creator wanted to affect it by an order of four degrees that evolve one out of the other, called, "still," "vegetative," "animate," and "speaking." These are, in fact, the four phases of the will to receive, by which the Upper Worlds is divided. For although the majority of the desire is in the fourth phase of the will to receive, it is impossible for the fourth phase to appear at once, but by its

preceding three phases, in which, and through which, it gradually develops and appears until it is fully completed in the form of Phase Four.

35) In Phase One of the will to receive, called "still," which is the initial manifestation of the will to receive in this corporeal world, there is but a collective force of movement for the whole of the still category. But no motion is apparent in its particular items. This is because the will to receive generates needs, and the needs generate sufficient movements, enough to satisfy the need. And since there is only a small will to receive, it dominates only the whole of the category at once, but its power over the particular items is indistinguishable.

36) The vegetative is added to it, which is Phase Two of the will to receive. Its measure is greater than in the still, and its will to receive dominates each and every item of its items, because each item has its own movement, expanding through its length and breadth, and moving towards the sun. Also, the matter of eating and drinking and secretion of waste is also apparent in each item. However, the sensation of freedom and individuality is still absent in them.

37) Atop that comes the animate category, which is Phase Three of the will to receive. Its measure is already completed to a great extent, for this will to receive already generates in each item a sensation of freedom and individuality, which is the life that is unique to each item separately. Yet, they still lack the sensation of others, meaning they have no preparation to share others' pains or their joys, etc.

38) Above all comes the human species, which is Phase Four of the will to receive. It is the complete and final measure, and its will to receive includes the sensation of others, as well. And if you wish to know the precise difference between Phase Three of the will to receive, which is in the animate, and the fourth phase of the will to receive in man, I shall tell you that it is as the worth of a single creature compared to the whole of reality.

This is because the will to receive in the animate, which lacks the sensation of others, can only generate needs and desires to the extent that they are imprinted in that creature alone. But man, who can feel others, too, becomes needy of everything that others have, too, and is thus filled with envy to acquire everything that others have. When he has a hundred, he wants two hundred, and so his needs forever multiply until he wishes to devour all that there is in the whole world.

39) Now we have shown that the Creator's desired goal for the Creation He had created is to bestow upon His creatures, so they would know His truthfulness and greatness, and receive all the delight and pleasure He had prepared for them,

in the measure described in the verse: "Ephraim my darling son, is he joy of his parents?" (Jeremiah 31, 19). Thus, you clearly find that this purpose does not apply to the still and the great spheres, such as the earth, the moon, or the sun, however luminous they may be, and not to the vegetative or the animate, for they lack the sensation of others, even from among their own species. Therefore, how can the sensation of the Godly and His bestowal apply to them?

Humankind alone, having been prepared with the sensation of others of the same species, who are similar to them, after delving in Torah and *Mitzvot*, when they invert their will to receive to a will to bestow, and come to equivalence of form with his Maker, they receive all the degrees that have been prepared for them in the Upper Worlds, called *NRNHY*. By that they become qualified to receive the purpose of the Thought of Creation. After all, the purpose of the creation of all the worlds was for man alone.

40) And I know that it is completely unaccepted in the eyes of some philosophers. They cannot agree that man, which they think of as low and worthless, is the center of the magnificent Creation. But they are like a worm that is born inside a radish. It lives there and thinks that the world of the Creator is as bitter, as dark, and small as the radish it was born in. But as soon as it breaks the shell of the radish and peeps out, it claims in bewilderment: "I thought the whole world was the size of the radish I was born in, and now I see a grand, beautiful, and wondrous world before me!"

So, too, are those who are immersed in the *Klipa* (singular for *Klipot*) of the will to receive they were born with, and did not try to take the unique spice, which are the practical Torah and *Mitzvot*, which can break this hard *Klipa* and turn it into a desire to bestow contentment upon the Maker. It is certain that they must determine their worthlessness and emptiness, as they truly are, and cannot comprehend that this magnificent reality had been created only for them.

Indeed, had they delved in Torah and *Mitzvot* to bestow contentment upon their Maker, with all the required purity, and would try to break the *Klipa* of the will to receive they were born in and assume the desire to bestow, their eyes would immediately open to see and attain for themselves all the degrees of wisdom, intelligence and clear mind, that have been prepared for them in the Spiritual Worlds. Then they would themselves say what our sages said, "What does a good guest say? 'Everything the host has done, he has done for me alone.'"

41) But there still remains to clarify why would man need all the Upper Worlds the Creator had created for him? What use has he of them? Bear in mind that the reality of all the worlds is generally divided into five worlds, called

a) *Adam Kadmon*, b) *Atzilut*, c) *Beria*, d) *Yetzira*, and e) *Assiya*. In each of them are innumerable details, which are the five *Sefirot KHBTM* (*Keter*, *Hochma*, *Bina*, *Tifferet*, and *Malchut*). The world of *AK* (*Adam Kadmon*) is *Keter*; the world of *Atzilut* is *Hochma*; the world of *Beria* is *Bina*; the world of *Yetzira* is *Tifferet*; and the world *Assiya* is *Malchut*.

And the Lights clothed in those five worlds are called YHNRN. The Light of *Yechida* shines in the world of *Adam Kadmon*; the Light of *Haya* in the world of *Atzilut*; the Light of *Neshama* in the world of *Beria*; the Light of *Ruach* in the world of *Yetzira*; and the Light of *Nefesh* in the world of *Assiya*.

All these worlds and everything in them are included in the Holy Name, *Yod-Hey-Vav-Hey*, and the tip of the *Yod*. We have no perception in the first world, AK. Hence, it is only implied in the tip of the *Yod* of the Name. This is why we do not speak of it and always mention only the four worlds ABYA. *Yod* is the world of *Atzilut*, *Hey*—the world of *Beria*, *Vav*—the world of *Yetzira*, and the bottom *Hey* is the world of *Assiya*.

42) We have now explained the five worlds that include the entire spiritual reality that extends from *Ein Sof* to this world. However, they are included in one the other, and in each of the worlds there are the five worlds, the five *Sefirot KHBTM*, in which the five Lights *NRNHY* are dressed, corresponding to the five worlds.

And besides the five *Sefirot KHBTM* in each world, there are the four spiritual categories—Still, Vegetative, Animate, and Speaking. In it, man's soul is regarded as the speaking, the animate is regarded as the angels in that world, the vegetative category is called "dresses" and the still category is called "halls." And they all robe one another: the speaking category, which is the souls of people, clothes the five *Sefirot*, *KHBTM*, which is the Godliness in that world. The animate category, which are the angels clothes over the souls; the vegetative, which are the dresses, clothe the angels; and the still, which are halls, revolve around them all.

The dressing means that they serve one another and evolve from one another, as we have clarified with the corporeal still, vegetative, animate and speaking in this world (Items 35-38): the three categories—still, vegetative, and animate—did not extend for themselves, but only so the fourth category, which is man, might develop and rise by them. Therefore, their role is only to serve man and be useful to him.

So it is in all the spiritual worlds. The three categories—still, vegetative, and animate—appeared there only to serve and be useful to the speaking category there, which is man's soul. Therefore, it is considered that they all clothe over man's soul, meaning to serve him.

43) When man is born, he immediately has a *Nefesh*[4] of *Kedusha* (Holiness). But not an actual *Nefesh*, but the posterior of it, its last discernment, which, due to its smallness, is called a "point." It dresses in man's heart, in one's will to receive, which is found primarily in one's heart.

Know this rule, that all that applies to the whole of reality, applies to each world, and even in the smallest particles that can be found in that world. Thus, as there are five worlds in whole of reality, which are the five *Sefirot KHBTM*, there are five *Sefirot KHBTM* in each and every world, and there are five *Sefirot* in every little item in that world.

We have said that this world is divided into still, vegetative, animate and speaking (SVAS), corresponding to the four *Sefirot HBTM*. Still corresponds to *Malchut*, vegetative corresponds to *Tifferet*, animate to *Bina*, and speaking to *Hochma*. And the root of them all corresponds to *Keter*. But as we have said, even in the smallest item in each species in the SVAS there are four discernments of SVAS. Hence, even in a single item of the speaking category, meaning even in one person, there are also SVAS, which are the four parts of his will to receive, where the point from the *Nefesh* of *Kedusha* is dressed.

44) Prior to the thirteen years, there cannot be any emergence of the point in one's heart. But after thirteen years, when he begins to delve in Torah and *Mitzvot*, even without any intention, meaning without any love and fear, as is fitting when serving the king, even in *Lo Lishma*, the point in one's heart begins to grow and disclose its action.

This is so because *Mitzvot* do not need an aim. Even acts without an aim can purify one's will to receive, but only in the first degree, called "still." And to the extent that he purifies the still part of the will to receive, one builds the six hundred and thirteen organs of the point in the heart, which is the still of the *Nefesh* of *Kedusha*.

And when one completes all six hundred and thirteen *Mitzvot* in action, it completes the six hundred and thirteen organs in the point in the heart, which is the still category of the *Nefesh* of *Kedusha*, whose two hundred and forty-eight spiritual organs are built by keeping the two hundred and forty-eight positive *Mitzvot*,[5] and its three hundred and sixty-five spiritual tendons are built through observing the three hundred and sixty-five negative *Mitzvot*, until it becomes a

---
4 Translator's note: By *Nefesh* he means the first degree in *NRNHY*.
5 Translator's note: Positive *Mitzvot* are precepts you have to perform in action, and negative *Mitzvot* are precepts you keep by avoiding certain actions.

complete *Partzuf* (spiritual face) of *Nefesh* of *Kedusha*. Then the *Nefesh* rises and clothes the *Sefira* (singular of *Sefirot*) of *Malchut* in the spiritual world of *Assiya*.

And all the spiritual elements of still, vegetative and animate in that world, which correspond to that *Sefira* of *Malchut* of *Assiya*, serve and aid that *Partzuf* of *Nefesh* of one who has risen there, to the extent that the soul perceives them. Those concepts become its spiritual nourishment, giving it strength to grow and multiply, until it can extend the Light of the *Sefira* of *Malchut* of *Assiya* in all the desired perfection, to Light man's body. And that complete Light aids one to add exertion in Torah and *Mitzvot* and receive the remaining degrees.

And we have stated that immediately at the birth of one's body, a point of the Light of *Nefesh* is born and dresses in him. So it is here: when his *Partzuf* of *Nefesh* of *Kedusha* is born, a point from its adjacent Higher degree is born with it—the last degree of the Light of *Ruach* of *Assiya*—and dresses inside the *Partzuf* of *Nefesh*.

And so it is in all the degrees. With each degree that is born, the last discernment in the degree above it instantaneously appears within it. This is because this is the whole connection between Higher and lower through to the top of the degrees. Thus, through this point, which exists in it from the Upper One, it becomes able to rise to the next Higher degree.

45) And that Light of *Nefesh* is called "the Light of the holy still in the world *Assiya*." This is because it corresponds to the purity of the still part of the will to receive in man's body. It shines in spirituality like the still category in corporeality (see Item 35), whose particles have no individual motion, but only collective motion, common to all the items equally. So it is with the Light of *Partzuf Nefesh* of *Assiya*: although there are six hundred and thirteen organs in it, which are six hundred and thirteen forms of receiving the bounty, these changes are not apparent in it, but only a general Light, whose action enfolds them all equally, without distinction of details.

46) Bear in mind that although the *Sefirot* are Godliness, and there is no difference in them from the head of *Keter* in the world of *AK*, through the end of the *Sefira* of *Malchut* in the world of *Assiya*, there is still a great difference with respect to the receivers. This is so because the *Sefirot* are considered Lights and *Kelim* (vessels), and the Light in the *Sefirot* is pure Godliness. But the *Kelim*, called KHBTM in each of the lower worlds—*Beria, Yetzira, Assiya*—are not considered Godliness, but are rather covers that conceal the Light of *Ein Sof* within them and ration a certain amount of Light to the receivers. Each of them will receive only according to the level of its purity.

And in this respect, although the Light itself is one, we name the Lights in the *Sefirot NRNHY* because the Light divides according to the qualities of the *Kelim*. *Malchut* is the coarsest cover, hiding the Light of *Ein Sof*. The Light it passes from Him to the receivers is only a small portion, related to the purification of the still body of man. This is why it is called *Nefesh*.

The *Kli* of *Tifferet* is purer than the *Kli* of *Malchut*. The Light it passes from *Ein Sof* relates to the purification of the vegetative part of man's body, because it acts in it more than the Light of *Nefesh*. This is called "the Light of *Ruach*."

The *Kli* of *Bina* is purer still than *Tifferet*, and the Light it passes from *Ein Sof* relates to the purification of the animate part of man's body, and it is called "the Light of *Neshama*."

The purest of all is the *Kli* of *Hochma*. The Light it passes from *Ein Sof* relates to the purification of the speaking part of man's body. It is called "the Light of *Haya*," and its action is beyond measurement.

47) In *Partzuf Nefesh*, which man one attains through engaging in Torah and *Mitzvot* without the intention, there is already a point from the Light of *Ruach* clothed in there. And when one strengthens and keeps Torah and *Mitzvot* with the desired aim, he purifies the vegetative part of his will to receive, and to that extent builds the point of *Ruach* into a *Partzuf*. And by performing the 248 positive *Mitzvot* with intention, the point expands through its 248 spiritual organs. And by observing the 365 negative *Mitzvot*, the point expands through its 365 tendons.

When it is completed with all 613 organs, it rises and clothes the *Sefira* of *Tifferet* in the spiritual world of *Assiya*, which extends to him a greater Light from *Ein Sof*, called "the Light of *Ruach*," which corresponds to the purification of the vegetative part in man's body. And all the items of the still, vegetative, and animate in the world of *Assiya*, related to the level of *Tifferet*, aid one's *Partzuf* of *Ruach* to receive the Lights from the *Sefira* of *Tifferet* in all its entirety, as was explained above with the Light of *Nefesh*. Because of that, it is called "holy vegetative."

The nature of its Light is like the corporeal vegetative: there are distinct differences in motion in each of its elements, so in the spiritual Light of vegetative there is much strength to shine in unique ways for each and every organ of the 613 organs in *Partzuf Ruach*. Each of them manifests action-power related to that organ. Also, with the extension of *Partzuf Ruach*, the point of the next degree Above it extended from it, a point of the Light of *Neshama*, which dresses in its internality.

48) And by engaging in the secrets of Torah and the flavors of the *Mitzvot*, he purifies the animate part of his will to receive, and to that extent builds the point of the soul, dressed in him in its 248 organs and 365 tendons. When the construction is completed and it becomes a *Partzuf*, it rises and dresses the *Sefira* of *Bina* in the spiritual world of *Assiya*. This *Kli* is much purer than the first *Kelim*, TM (*Tifferet* and *Malchut*). Hence, it extends a great Light from *Ein Sof*, called "Light of *Neshama*."

And all the items of still, vegetative, and animate in the world of *Assiya*, related to the level of *Bina*, aid and serve one's *Partzuf* of *Neshama* in receiving all its Lights from the *Sefira* of *Bina*. And it is also called "holy animate" because it corresponds to the purification of the animate part of man's body. And so is the nature of its Light, as we have seen with the corporeal animate (Item 37), which gives a sensation of individuality to each of the 613 organs of the *Partzuf*, that each of them is alive and free, without any dependence on the rest of the *Partzuf*.

At last, it is discerned that its 613 organs are 613 *Partzufim* (plural for *Partzuf*), unique in their Light, each in its own way. And the advantage of this Light over the Light of *Ruach*, in spirituality, is as the advantage of the animate over the still and the vegetative in corporeality. And there also extends a point from the Light of *Haya* of *Kedusha*, which is the Light of the *Sefira* of *Hochma*, with the emergence of *Partzuf Neshama*, and dresses in its internality.

49) And when he has been rewarded with the great Light called "the Light of *Neshama*," each of the 613 organs in that *Partzuf* Light fully shine in their own unique way, each as an independent *Partzuf*. Then there opens before him the possibility to engage in each *Mitzva* according to its genuine aim, for each organ in the *Partzuf* of *Neshama* lights the path of each *Mitzva* related to that organ.

And through the great power of those Lights, one purifies the speaking part of one's will to receive and inverts it into a desire to bestow. And to that extent, the point of the Light of *Haya*, dressed within him, is built in its spiritual 248 organs and 365 tendons.

When it is completed into a whole *Partzuf* it rises and dresses the *Sefira* of *Hochma* in the spiritual world of *Assiya*, which is an immeasurably pure *Kli*. Therefore, it extends a tremendous Light to it from *Ein Sof*, called "the Light of *Haya*" or *Neshama* to *Neshama*. And all the elements in the world of *Assiya*, which are the still, vegetative, and animate related to the *Sefira* of *Hochma*, aid him in receiving the Light of the *Sefira* of *Hochma* to the fullest.

And it is also called "Holy Speaking," since it corresponds to the purification of the speaking part of man's body. And the value of that Light in Godliness is as the value of the speaking in the corporeal SVAS. This means that one obtains the sensation of others in a way that the measure of that Light over the measure of the spiritual still, vegetative and animate is as the advantage of the corporeal speaking over the corporeal still, vegetative and animate. And the Light of *Ein Sof*, dressed in this *Partzuf*, is called "the Light of *Yechida*."

50) Indeed, you should know that these five Lights, NRNHY, received from the world of *Assiya*, are but NRNHY of the Light of *Nefesh* and have nothing of the Light of *Ruach*. This is because the Light of *Ruach* is only in the world of *Yetzira*, the Light of *Neshama* is only in the world of *Beria*, the Light of *Haya* only in the world of *Atzilut*, and the Light of *Yechida* only in the world of AK.

But everything that exists in the whole appears in all the items, too, down to the smallest possible item. Thus, all five discernments, NRNHY, exist in the world of *Assiya*, as well, although they are only NRNHY of *Nefesh*. Similarly, all five discernments, NRNHY, are found in the world of *Yetzira*, which are the five parts of *Ruach*. And also, there are all five discernments, NRNHY, in the world of *Beria*, which are the five parts of *Neshama*. And so it is in the world of *Atzilut*, which are the five parts of the Light of *Haya*; and so it is in the world of AK, which are the five parts of the Light of *Yechida*. The difference between the worlds is as we have explained in the discernments between each of the NRNHY of *Assiya*.

51) Know that repentance and purification cannot be accepted unless they are totally permanent, that he will not turn back to folly, as it is written, "When is there *Teshuva* (repentance)? When He who knows all mysteries will testify that he will not turn back to folly." Thus, as we have said, if one purifies the still part of his will to receive, he is rewarded with a *Partzuf* of *Nefesh* of *Assiya*, and ascends and clothes the *Sefira* of *Malchut* of *Assiya*.

This means that he will certainly be granted the permanent purification of the still part, in a way that he will not turn back to folly. And then he will be able to rise to the spiritual world of *Assiya*, for he will have definite purity and equivalence of form with that world.

But as for the rest of the degrees, which we have said are *Ruach*, *Neshama*, *Haya*, and *Yechida* of *Assiya*, corresponding to them, one should purify the vegetative, animate, and speaking parts of one's will to receive, so they will clothe and receive those Lights. Yet, the purity does not need to be permanent, "until He who knows all mysteries will testify that he will not turn back to folly."

That is so because the whole of the world of *Assiya*, with all its five *Sefirot* KHBTM, are actually only *Malchut*, which relates only to the purification of the still. And the five *Sefirot* are but the five parts of *Malchut*.

Therefore, since he has already been rewarded with purifying the still part of the will to receive, he already has equivalence of form with the whole of the world of *Assiya*. But since each *Sefira* in the world of *Assiya* receives from its corresponding discernment in the worlds Above it, thus, the *Sefira* of *Tifferet* of *Assiya* receives from the world of *Yetzira*, which is all *Tifferet* and the Light of *Ruach*. And the *Sefira* of *Bina* of *Assiya* receives from the world of *Beria*, which is all *Neshama*. And the *Sefira* of *Hochma* of *Assiya* receives from the world of *Atzilut*, which is all *Hochma* and the Light of *Haya*.

Thus, although he has permanently purified only the still part, if he has purified the remaining three parts of his will to receive, even if not permanently, he can receive the *Ruach*, *Neshama*, and *Haya* from *Tifferet*, *Bina*, and *Hochma* of *Assiya*, though not permanently. This is because when one of the three parts of his will to receive awakens, he immediately loses these Lights.

52) After he permanently purifies the vegetative part of his will to receive, he permanently rises to the world of *Yetzira*, where he attains the permanent degree of *Ruach*. There he can also attain the Lights of *Neshama* and *Haya* from the *Sefirot Bina* and *Hochma* that are there, which are considered *Neshama* and *Haya* of *Ruach*, even before he has been granted with purifying the animate and speaking parts permanently, as we have seen in the world of *Assiya*. Yet, this is not permanent, for after he has permanently purified the vegetative part of his will to receive, he is already in equivalence of form with the whole of the world of *Yetzira*, to its Highest degree, as written about the world of *Assiya*.

53) After he purifies the animate part of his will to receive, and turns it into a will to bestow, "until He who knows all mysteries will testify that he will not turn back to folly," he is already in equivalence of form with the world of *Beria*. And he rises there and receives the permanent Light of *Neshama*. And through the purification of the speaking part of his body, he can rise up to the *Sefira* of *Hochma* and receive the Light of *Haya* that is there, although he has not yet permanently purified it, as with *Yetzira* and *Assiya*. But the Light, too, does not shine for him permanently.

54) And when one is rewarded with permanent purification of the speaking part in his will to receive, he is granted equivalence of form with the world of *Atzilut*, and he rises there and permanently receives the Light of *Haya*. And when he is further rewarded, he receives the Light of *Ein Sof*, and the Light of *Yechida* dresses in the Light of *Haya*, and there is nothing more to add here.

55) Thus, we have clarified what we asked, "Why does man need all the Upper Worlds, which the Creator had created for him? What need has man of them?" Now you will see that one cannot bring contentment to one's Maker, if not with the help of all these worlds. This is because he attains the Lights and degrees of his soul, called NRNHY, according to the measure of the purity of his will to receive. And with each degree he attains, the Lights of that degree assist him in his purification.

Thus, he rises in degrees until he achieves the amusements of the final aim in the Thought of Creation (Item 33). It is written in *The Zohar* (Noah, Item 63), about the verse, "He who comes to be purified is aided." It asks, "Aided with what?" And it replies that he is aided with a holy soul. For it is impossible to achieve the desired purification for the Thought of Creation, except through the assistance of all the NRNHY degrees of the soul.

56) And you should know that the all the NRNHY we have spoken of thus far are the five parts, by which the whole of reality is divided. Indeed, all that is in the whole exists even in the smallest element in reality. For example, even in the still part of the spiritual *Assiya* alone, there are five discernments of NRNHY to attain, which are related to the five general discernments of NRNHY.

Thus, it is impossible to attain even the Light of still of *Assiya* except through the four parts of the work. Therefore, there is not a person from Israel who can excuse himself from engaging in all of them, according to one's stature. And one should engage in Torah and *Mitzvot* with intent, in order to receive the level of *Ruach* of his stature. And he should engage in the secrets of the Torah, according to his stature, to receive the level of *Neshama* according to his stature. And the same applies to the *Taamim* (flavors) of the *Mitzvot*, for it is impossible to complete even the smallest Light in *Kedusha* (holiness) without them.

57) Now you can understand the aridity and the darkness that have befallen us in this generation, such as we have never seen before. It is because even the worshipers of the Creator have abandoned the engagement in the secrets of the Torah.

Maimonides has already given a true allegory about that: If a line of a thousand blind walk along the way, and there is at least one leader amongst them who can see, they are certain to take the right path and not fall in the pits and obstacles, since they are following the sighted one who leads them. But if that person is missing, they are certain to stumble over every hurdle on the way, and will all fall into the pit.

So is the issue before us. If the worshipers of the Creator had, at least, engaged in the internality of the Torah and extended a complete Light from *Ein Sof*, the whole generation would have followed them. And everyone would be certain of their way, that they would not fall. But if even the servants of the Creator have distanced themselves from this wisdom, it is no wonder the whole generation is failing because of them. And because of my great sorrow I cannot elaborate on that!

58) Indeed, I know the reason: it is mainly because faith has generally diminished, specifically faith in the holy men, the wise men of all generations. And the books of Kabbalah and *The Zohar* are filled with corporeal parables. Therefore, people are afraid lest they will lose more than they will gain, since they could easily fail with materializing. And this is what prompted me to compose a sufficient interpretation to the writings of the Ari, and now to the Holy *Zohar*. And I have completely removed that concern, for I have evidently explained and proven the spiritual meaning of everything, that it is abstract and devoid of any corporeal image, above space and above time, as the readers will see, to allow the whole of Israel to study *The Book of Zohar* and be warmed by its sacred Light.

And I have named that commentary *The Sulam* (Ladder) to show that the purpose of my commentary is as the role of any ladder: if you have an attic filled abundantly, then all you need is a ladder to reach it. And then, all the bounty in the world will be in your hands. But the ladder is not a purpose in and of itself, for if you pause on the rungs of the ladder and will not enter the attic, your goal will not be achieved.

And so it is with my commentary on *The Zohar*, because the way to fully clarify these most profound of words has not yet been created. But nonetheless, with my commentary, I have constructed a path and an entrance for any person by which to rise and delve and scrutinize *The Book of Zohar* itself, for only then will my aim with this commentary be completed.

59) And all those who know the ins and outs of the holy *Book of Zohar*, that is, who understand what is written in it, unanimously agree that the holy *Book of Zohar* was written by the Godly Tanna (sage) Rabbi Shimon Bar Yochai. Only some of those who are far from this wisdom doubt this pedigree and tend to say, relying on fabricated tales of opponents of this wisdom, that its author is the Kabbalist Rabbi Moshe de Leon, or others of his contemporaries.

60) And as for me, since the day I have been endowed, by the Light of the Creator, with a glance into this holy book, it has not crossed my mind to question its origin, for the simple reason that the content of the book brings to

my heart the merit of the Tanna Rashbi (Rabbi Shimon Bar Yochai) far more than all other sages. And if I were to clearly see that its author is some other name, such as Rabbi Moshe de Leon, then I would praise the merit of Rabbi Moshe de Leon more than all other sages, including Rashbi.

Indeed, judging by the depth of the wisdom in the book, if I were to clearly find that its writer is one of the forty-eight prophets, I would consider it much more acceptable than to relate it to one of the sages. Moreover, if I were to find that Moses himself received it from the Creator Himself on Mount Sinai, then my mind would really be at peace, for such a composition is worthy of him. Hence, since I have been blessed with compiling a sufficient interpretation that enables every examiner to acquire some understanding of what is written in the book, I think I am completely excused from further toil in that examination, for any person who is knowledgeable in *The Zohar* will now settle for no less than the Tanna Rashbi as its writer.

61) Accordingly, the question arises, "Why was *The Zohar* not revealed to the early generations, whose merit was undoubtedly greater than the latter ones, and were more worthy"? We must also ask, "Why was the commentary on *The Book of Zohar* not revealed before the time of the Ari, and not to the Kabbalists that preceded him"? And the most bewildering question, "Why were the commentaries on the words of the Ari and on the words of *The Zohar* not revealed since the days of the Ari through our generation"?

The answer is that the world, during the six thousand years of its existence, is like one *Partzuf* divided into three thirds: *Rosh* (head), *Toch* (interior), *Sof* (end), meaning *HBD* (*Hochma, Bina, Daat*), *HGT* (*Hesed, Gevura, Tifferet*), *NHY* (*Netzah, Hod, Yesod*). This is what our sages wrote, "Two millennia of *Tohu* (chaos), two millennia of Torah, and two millennia of the days of the Messiah" (*Sanhedrin* 97a).

In the first two millennia, considered *Rosh* and *HBD*, the Lights were very small. They were regarded as *Rosh* without *Guf* (body), having only Lights of *Nefesh*. This is because there is an inverse relation between Lights and vessels: with the *Kelim* (vessels) the rule is that the first *Kelim* grow first in each *Partzuf*; and with the Lights it is the opposite—the smaller Lights dress in the *Partzuf* first.

Thus, as long as only the upper parts are in the *Kelim*, the *Kelim HBD*, only Lights of *Nefesh* dress there, which are the smallest Lights. This is why it is written about the first two millennia that they are considered *Tohu*. And in the second two millennia of the world, which are *Kelim* of *HGT*, the Light of *Ruach* descends and clothes in the world, which is considered the Torah. This is why it is said about the two middle millennia that they are Torah. And the last two millennia are *Kelim* of NHYM (*Netzah*, *Hod*, *Yesod*, *Malchut*). Therefore, at that time, the Light of *Neshama* dresses in the world, which is the greater Light, hence they are the days of the Messiah.

This is also the conduct in each particular *Partzuf*. In its vessels of HBD, HGT, through its *Chazeh* (chest), the Lights are covered and do not begin to shine, which is open *Hassadim*, which means that the appearance of the sublime Light of *Hochma* occurs only from the *Chazeh* down, in its NHYM. This is the reason that before the *Kelim* of NHYM began to show in the *Partzuf* of the world, which are the last two millennia, the wisdom of *The Zohar* in particular and the wisdom of Kabbalah in general were hidden from the world.

But during the time of the Ari, when the time of the completion of the *Kelim* below the *Chazeh* had drawn closer, the Light of the sublime *Hochma* was revealed in the world, through the soul of the Godly Rabbi Isaac Luria (the Ari), who was ready to receive that great Light. Hence, he revealed the essentials in *The Book of Zohar* and the wisdom of Kabbalah, until he overshadowed all his predecessors.

Yet, since these *Kelim* were not yet completed (since he passed away in 1572), the world was not yet worthy of discovering his words, and his holy words were only known only to a chosen few, who were prohibited to tell them to the world.

Now, in our generation, since we are nearing the end of the last two millennia, we are given permission to reveal his words and the words of *The Zohar* throughout the world to a great measure, in such a way that from our generation onwards the words of *The Zohar* will become increasingly revealed in the world, until the full measure is revealed, as the Creator wills it.

63) Now you can understand that there really is no end to the merit of the first generations over the last, as this is the rule in all the *Partzufim* (plural for *Partzuf*) of the worlds and of the souls, that the purer one is the first to be selected into the *Partzuf*. Therefore, the purer *Kelim*, HBD, were selected first in the world and in the souls.

Thus, the souls in the first two millennia were much Higher. Yet, they could not receive the full measure of Light, due to the lack of the lower parts in the world and in themselves, which are HGT NHYM.

And afterwards, in the two middle millennia, when the *Kelim* of HGT were selected into the world and in the souls, the souls were indeed very pure, in and of themselves. This is because the merit of the *Kelim* of HGT is close to that of

HBD. Yet, the Lights were still concealed in the world, due to the absence of the *Kelim* from the *Chazeh* down, in the world and in the souls.

Thus, in our generation, although the essence of the souls is the worst, which is why they could not be selected for *Kedusha* thus far, they are the ones that complete the *Partzuf* of the world and the *Partzuf* of the souls with respect to the *Kelim*, and the work completed only through them.

This is because now, when the *Kelim* of NHY are being completed, and all the *Kelim*, *Rosh*, *Toch*, *Sof* are in the *Partzuf*, full measures of Light, in *Rosh*, *Toch*, *Sof*, are now being extended to all those who are worthy, meaning complete NRN. Hence, only after the completion of these lowly souls can the Highest Lights manifest, and not before.

64) Indeed, even our sages asked this question (*Masechet Berachot*, p 20): "Rav Papa said to Abayei: 'How were the first different, that a miracle had happened to them, and how are we different, that a miracle is not happening to us'? Is it because of the study? During the years of Rav Yehuda, the whole study was in *Nezikin*, whereas we are learning the six volumes (the whole Mishnah). And when Rav Yehuda delved in *Okatzin*, he said, 'I saw Rav and Shmuel here, whereas we are learning thirteen *Yeshivot* in *Okatzin*. And when Rav Yehuda took off one shoe, the rain came, whereas we torment our souls and cry out, and no one notices us.' He replied, 'The first gave their souls to the sanctity of the Lord.'"

Thus, although it is obvious, both to the one who asks and to the one who answers, that the first were more important than they, with respect to the Torah and the wisdom, Rav Papa and Abayei were more important than the first. Thus, although the first generations were more important than the latter generations in the essence of their souls, because the purer is selected to come to the world first, with respect to the wisdom of the Torah, it is increasingly revealed in the latter generations. This is so for the reason we have mentioned, that the overall measure is completed specifically by the latter ones. This is why more complete Lights are extended to them, although their own essence is far worse.

65) Hence, we could ask, "Why, then, is it forbidden to disagree with the first in the revealed Torah?" It is because, as far as the practical part of the *Mitzvot* is concerned, it is to the contrary, the first were more complete in them than the last. This is because the act extends from the holy *Kelim* of the *Sefirot*, and the secrets of the Torah and the *Taamim* (flavors) of the *Mitzva* extend from the Lights in the *Sefirot*.

You already know that there is an inverse relation between Lights and vessels: in the *Kelim*, the Higher ones grow first (see Item 62), which is why the first were more complete in the practical part than the last. But with the Lights, where the lower ones enter first, the last are more complete than the first.

66) Bear in mind that in everything there is internality and externality. In the world in general, Israel, the descendants of Abraham, Isaac and Jacob, are considered the internality of the world, and the seventy nations are considered the externality of the world. Also, there is internality within Israel themselves, which are the wholehearted workers of the Creator, and there is externality—those who do not devote themselves to the work of the Creator. Among the nations of the world, there is internality as well, which are the Righteous of the Nations of the World, and there is externality, which are the rude and the harmful among them.

Additionally, among the servants of the Creator among the Children of Israel, there is internality, being those rewarded with comprehension of the soul of the internality of the Torah and its secrets, and externality, who merely observe the practical part of the Torah.

Also, there is internality in every person from Israel—the Israel within—which is the point in the heart, and externality—which is the inner Nations of the World, the body itself. But even the inner Nations of the World in that person are considered proselytes, since by cleaving to the internality, they become like proselytes from among the Nations of the World, that came and cleaved to the whole of Israel.

67) When a person from Israel enhances and dignifies one's internality, which is the Israel in that person, over the externality, which are the Nations of the World in him, that is, when one dedicates the majority of one's efforts to enhance and exalt one's internality, to benefit one's soul, and gives minor efforts, the mere necessity, to sustain the Nations of the World in him, meaning the bodily needs, as it is written (*Avot*, 1), "Make your Torah permanent and your labor temporary," by so doing, one makes the Children of Israel soar upwards in the internality and externality of the world as well, and the Nations of the World, which are the externality, to recognize and acknowledge the value of the Children of Israel.

And if, God forbid, it is to the contrary, and an individual from Israel enhances and appreciates one's externality, which is the Nations of the World in him, more than the inner Israel in him, as it is written (Deuteronomy 28), "The stranger that is in the midst of thee," meaning the externality in that person rises and soars, and you yourself, the internality, the Israel in you, plunges down? With these actions, one causes the externality of the world in general—the Nations of the World—to soar ever higher and overcome Israel, degrading them to the ground, and the Children of Israel, the internality in the world, to plunge deep down.

68) Do not be surprised that one person's actions bring elevation or decline to the whole world, for it is an unbending law that the general and the particular are as equal as two peas in a pod. And all that applies in the general, applies in the particular, as well. Moreover, the parts make what is found in the whole, for the general can appear only after the appearance of the parts in it, according to the quantity and quality of the parts. Evidently, the value of an act of a part elevates or declines the entire whole.

That will clarify to you what is written in *The Zohar*, that by engagement in *The Book of Zohar* and the wisdom of truth, they will be rewarded with complete redemption from exile (*Tikkunim*, end of *Tikkun* No. 6). We might ask, what has the study of *The Zohar* to do with the redemption of Israel from among the nations?

69) From the above we can thoroughly understand that the Torah, too, contains internality and externality, as does the entire world. Therefore, one who engages in the Torah has these two degrees, as well. When one increases one's toil in the internality of the Torah and its secrets, to that extent, one makes the virtue of the internality of the world—which are Israel—soar high above the externality of the world, which are the Nations of the World. And all the nations will acknowledge and recognize Israel's merit over them, until the realization of the words, "And the people shall take them, and bring them to their place: and the house of Israel shall possess them in the land of the Lord" (Isaiah 14, 2), and also "Thus says the Lord God, Behold, I will lift up my hand to the nations, and set up my standard to the peoples: and they shall bring thy sons in their arms, and thy daughters shall be carried on their shoulders" (Isaiah 49, 22).

But if, God forbid, it is to the contrary, and a person from Israel degrades the virtue of the internality of the Torah and its secrets, which deals with the conduct of our souls and their degrees, and the perception and the tastes of the *Mitzvot* with regard to the advantage of the externality of the Torah, which deals only with the practical part? Also, even if one does occasionally engage in the internality of the Torah, and dedicates a little of one's time to it, when it is neither night nor day, as though it were redundant, by that one dishonors and degrades the internality of the world, which are the Children of Israel, and enhances the externality of the world—meaning the Nations of the World—over them. They will humiliate and disgrace the Children of Israel, and regard Israel as superfluous, as though the world has no need for them, God forbid.

Furthermore, by that, they make even the externality in the Nations of the World overpower their own internality, for the worst among the Nations of the World, the harmful and the destructors of the world, rise above their internality, which are the Righteous of the Nations of the World. And then they make all the ruin and the heinous slaughter our generation had witnessed, may God protect us from here on.

Thus you see that the redemption of Israel and the whole of Israel's merit depend on the study of *The Zohar* and the internality of the Torah. And vise versa, all the destruction and the decline of the Children of Israel are because they have abandoned the internality of the Torah. They have degraded its merit and made it seemingly redundant.

70) This is what is written in the *Tikkunim* (corrections) of *The Zohar* (*Tikkun* 30): "Awaken and rise for the Holy Divinity, for you have an empty heart, without the understanding to know and to attain it, although it is within you." The meaning of it is, as it is written (Isaiah 40), that a voice pounds in the heart of each and every one of Israel, to cry and to pray for raising the Holy Divinity, which is the collection of all the souls of Israel. But Divinity says, "I have no strength to raise myself off the dust, for 'all flesh is grass,' they are all like beasts, eating hay and grass." This means that they keep the *Mitzvot* mindlessly, like beasts, "and all the goodliness thereof is as the flower of the field, all the good deeds that they do, they do for themselves."

That means that with the *Mitzvot* they perform, they have no intention of doing them in order to bring contentment to their Maker. Rather, they keep the *Mitzvot* only for their own benefit, and even the best among them, who dedicate all their time to engagement in the Torah, do it only to benefit their own bodies, without the desirable aim—to bring contentment to their Maker.

It is said about the generation of that time: "A spirit leaves and will not return to the world," meaning the spirit of the Messiah, who must deliver Israel from all their troubles until the complete redemption, to keep the words, 'for the earth shall be full of the knowledge of the Lord.' That spirit had left and does not shine in the world.

"Woe unto them that make the spirit of Messiah leave and depart from the world, and cannot return to the world. They are the ones that make the Torah dry, without any moisture of comprehension and reason. They confine themselves to the practical part of the Torah, and do not wish to try to understand the wisdom of Kabbalah, to know and to understand the secrets of the Torah and the flavors of *Mitzva*. Woe unto them, for with these actions they bring about the existence of poverty, ruin, and robbery, looting, killing, and destructions in the world.

71) The reason for their words is, as we have explained, that when all those who engage in the Torah degrade their own internality and the internality of the Torah, leaving it as though it were redundant in the world, and engage in it only at a time that is neither day nor night, and in this regard, they are like blind searching the wall, by that, they intensify their own externality, the benefit of their own bodies. Also, they consider the externality of the Torah higher than the internality of the Torah. And with these actions they cause all the forms of externality in the world to overpower all the internal parts in the world, each according to its essence.

This is so because the externality in the whole of Israel, meaning the Nations of the World in them, overpowers and revokes the internality in the whole of Israel, which are those who are great in the Torah. Also, the externality in the Nations of the World—the destructors among them—intensify and revoke the internality among them, which are the Righteous of the Nations of the World. Additionally, the externality of the entire world, being the Nations of the World, intensify and revoke the Children of Israel—the internality of the world.

In such a generation, all the destructors among the Nations of the World raise their heads and wish primarily to destroy and to kill the Children of Israel, as it is written (*Yevamot* 63), "No calamity comes to the world but for Israel." This means, as it is written in the above corrections, that they cause poverty, ruin, robbery, killing, and destruction in the whole world.

And through our many faults, we have witnessed to all that is said in the above-mentioned *Tikkunim*, and moreover, the judgment struck the very best of us, as our sages said (*Baba Kama* 60), "And it start with the righteous first." And of all the glory Israel had had in the countries of Poland and Lithuania, etc., there remains but the relics in our holy land. Now it is upon us, relics, to correct that dreadful wrong. Each of us remainders should take upon himself, heart and soul, to henceforth intensify the internality of the Torah, and give it its rightful place, according to its merit over the externality of the Torah.

And then, each and every one of us will be rewarded with intensifying his own internality, meaning the Israel within us, which is the needs of the soul over our own externality, which is the Nations of the World within us, that is, the needs of the body. That force will come to the whole of Israel, until the Nations of the World within us recognize and acknowledge the merit of the great sages of Israel over them, and will listen to them and obey them.

Also, the internality of the Nations of the World, the Righteous of the Nations of the World, will overpower and submit their externality, which are the destructors. And the internality of the world, too, which are Israel, shall rise in all their merit and virtue over the externality of the world, which are the nations. Then, all the nations of the world will recognize and acknowledge Israel's merit over them.

And they shall follow the words (Isaiah 14, 2), "And the people shall take them, and bring them to their place: and the house of Israel shall possess them in the land of the Lord." And also (Isaiah 49, 22), "And they shall bring thy sons in their arms, and thy daughters shall be carried on their shoulders." That is what is written in *The Zohar* (*Nasoh*, p 124b), "through this composition," which is *The Book of Zohar*, "they will be delivered from exile with mercy." Amen, would that be so.

A Handmaid that Is Heir to Her Mistress

This requires a thorough explanation. To make it clear to all, I shall choose to interpret the matter by what appears to us for this reason and extends to us here in the conduct of this world.

THE INTERNALITY OF THE EXTERNALITY

The thing is that the Higher Roots extend their power by cascading until their branches appear in this world, as it is written in the explanation of roots and branch. As a whole, the worlds are considered internality and externality. This is similar to a heavy load, which none can lift or move from place to place. Hence, the advice is to divide the load into small parts and subsequently transfer them one at a time.

It is similar in our matter, since the purpose of Creation is invaluable because a tiny spark such as a person's soul can rise in its attainment Higher than the ministering angels, as our sages said about the verse, "now it will be said to Jacob and to Israel: 'What has God wrought!'" They interpreted that the Higher angels will ask Israel, "What has God wrought?"

THE EVOLUTION OF ISRAEL (INTERNALITY) ONE AT A TIME

This bounty will come to us only by developing one at a time. As in the above allegory, even the heaviest load can be lifted if we split it into pieces and raise them one at a time. Not only the general purpose comes to us in this manner, but even the physical purpose, which is but a preparation for the general purpose, comes to us through gradual and slow development.

Hence, the worlds have been divided into internality and externality, where each world contains illuminations suitable to operate in slow development. And these are called "the internality of the world."

INSTANTANEOUS EVOLUTION OF THE NATIONS OF THE WORLD (EXTERNALITY)

Opposite them are illuminations that can only act instantaneously. Hence, when they appear here in their worldly branches and are given control, not only do they not correct, they ruin.

Our sages call it "unripe," as it is written concerning the Tree of Knowledge and *Adam ha Rishon*, that they ate unripe fruit. This means that it is truly a dainty delight, destined to delight man, but in the future, not at present, as it is still growing and developing. This is why they compared it to an unripe fruit, since the fig, too, which is the sweetest, daintiest fruit, when eaten prematurely, will upset one's stomach and he will die.

Indeed, we should ask, "Who is the one who brings such an act into the world?" After all, it is known that there is no action in our world that comes without the strike of a Higher Root. Know that this is what we call "the dominion of the externality," as in the verse, "God hath made even the one as well as the other." It contains a force that urges and rushes towards the revelation of the dominion of the internality, as our sages have said, "I place upon them a king such as Haman, and he will force them to repent."

THE INTERNALITY ARE THE PEOPLE OF ISRAEL

Once we have clarified the Higher Roots, we will clarify the branches in this world. Know that a branch that extends from the internality is the people of Israel, which has been chosen as an operator of the general purpose and correction. It contains the preparation required for growing and developing until it moves the nations of the worlds, too, to achieve the common goal.

THE EXTERNALITY ARE THE NATIONS OF THE WORLD

The branch that extends from the externality is the nations of the world. They have not been imparted the qualities that make them worthy of receiving the development of the purpose one at a time. Rather, they are fit to receive the correction at once and to the fullest, according to their Higher Root. Hence, when they receive dominion from their Root they destroy the virtues in the children of Israel and cause suffering in the world.

A SLAVE AND A HANDMAID

The Higher Roots, called "Externality," as we have explained above, are generally called "handmaid" and "slave." This aims to show that they do not intend to harm at all, as it may seem in superficial observation. Instead, they serve the internality, like the slave and the handmaid who serve their masters.

THE EXTERNALITY RULE WHEN ISRAEL DOES NOT DEMAND DEPTH IN THEIR WORK

The above-mentioned rule of the externality is called "the exile of Israel among the nations of the world." Through it, they inflict many forms of suffering, degradation, and ruin upon the Israeli nation. However, to be brief, we will explain only what is revealed through a general observation, which is the general purpose. This is the idol worshipping and superstition, as it is written, "But mingled themselves with the nations, and learned their works." This is the most terrible and dangerous poison, which destroys the souls of Israel, as it brings their vanities closer to the human reason. In other words, they do not require great depth to understand and thus plant the foundations of their work in the hearts of the children of Israel. And although an Israeli man is quite unfit to accept their nonsense, in the end they do induce idolatry and filth, down to blatant heresy, until he says, "all faces are equal."

THE REASON FOR THE CONCEALMENT OF THE KABBALAH

Now you can understand the issue of the concealment of the wisdom of the hidden from the eyes of the externals, as well as what the sages said, "A gentile must not be taught Torah." There seems to be a contradiction between this and the Tanah (great sage in the early CE years) Debei Eliyahu, who said, "Even a gentile, even a slave, and even a handmaid who sit and learn Torah, Divinity is with them." Thus, why did the sages prohibited teaching the Torah to gentiles?

TEACHING TORAH TO GENTILES

Indeed, the Tanah Debei Eliyahu relates to a converted gentile, or at least to one who retired from idol worshipping, from superstition. Our sages, conversely, referred to one who did not retire from idol worshipping and wanted to know Israel's law and wisdom in order to strengthen and fortify their idolatry. And you might say, "Why should we care if this gentile has become more pious in his idol worshipping because of our Torah? If it does not help, what harm will it do?"

RASHBI'S WEEPING

Indeed, this is what Rashbi cried for before he explained an important secret in the wisdom of the hidden, as it is written, "Rabbi Shimon wept, 'Woe if I tell, and woe if I do not tell. If I tell, the sinners will know how to serve their idols; and if I do not tell, the friends will lose that word.'"

He was afraid lest this secret would come by the hands of idol worshippers and they would perform their idolatry with the force of this Holy Mind. This is what prolongs our exile and brings upon us all the afflictions and the ruins, as we now see before us, since the sages of the nations of the world studied all the books of the children of Israel and turned them into delicacies to strengthen their faith, meaning their wisdom, called "theology."

TWO HARMS FROM REVEALING ISRAEL'S WISDOM TO THE NATIONS OF THE WORLD

They have done two wrongs:

1. Besides clothing in our robe, saying that all of that wisdom is from the attainment of their own holy spirit, these mimics gained their reputation at our expense. Thus, they strengthen their false teaching and obtain the strength to deny our Holy Torah.

2. But an even greater harm came upon us: one who observes their theology discovers in it concepts and wisdom concerning the work of God that seem truer and more genuine than our wisdom.

This is so for two reasons:

The first is that they are many, and among them are great and proficient philologists who know their work: to make matters acceptable to uneducated people. Philology comes from external teachings, and certainly a society of eight billion people can produce many more and much greater philologists than our society of fifteen million can. Hence, one who observes their books falls into doubting that they might be right, or even worse, of course.

The second, and the most important reason, is that the sages of Israel conceal the wisdom of religion from the masses behind closed doors and in every way. The sages of each generation offer simple explanations to the masses and reject them with all kinds of trickery from the desire to even approach and touch the wisdom of the hidden.

WOE IF I TELL

They do this for fear that the matters will fall into the hands of idol worshippers, as Rashbi wrote, "If I tell, the sinners will know how to serve their idols." After all, we suffer plenty even for the petite things that they have stolen from our vessels, which have seeped to them past all the vigil guarding.

THE REASON FOR THE CONCEALMENT OF KABBALAH

This clarifies what would unfold if our sages revealed the wisdom of the hidden to all. And since we conceal, as long as our commoner is unfit to be given the secrets of the Torah, he has no knowledge at all in the wisdom of religion. Hence, such a person is obviously inspired and elated when he finds the trifling wisdom and explanations in their theology, whose essence is but an assortment of stolen concepts from our hidden, with added literary dainties. Once one sees that, he says and denies our practical law, and ends in complete heresy.

A HANDMAID THAT IS HEIR TO HER MISTRESS

This is called "a handmaid that is heir to her mistress," since the very power of the mistress—the dominion of the internality—is by the force of our wisdom and knowledge, as it is written, "we are distinguished, I and Thy people, from all the people that are upon the face of the earth." And now the handmaid has stepped forth and prides herself in public that she is the heir of this wisdom. And you should know that this power of theirs is the shackle by which the legs of the children of Israel are chained in the exile, under their dominion.

SHACKLES OF EXILE

Thus, the essence of the shackles of exile and its power is from the wisdom of Torah and its secrets, which they have managed to steal and place in their vessels, passed all the watchful guarding we have put up. With it, they mislead the masses, saying they have inherited God's work, and cast doubt and heresy, too, on the souls of Israel.

Messiah's Shofar[6]

REDEMPTION ONLY THROUGH KABBALAH
Know that this is what it means that the children of Israel are redeemed only after the wisdom of the hidden is revealed to a great extent, as it is written in *The Zohar*, "With this composition, the children of Israel are redeemed from exile." This is because at that time there was hope for redemption, as the writing of *The Zohar*, which began in the days of Rashbi, was during the days when Bar-Kokheva appeared. Rabbi Akiva, Rashbi's teacher, said about him: "there shall step forth a star out of Jacob." Thus, after the ruin of Beitar there was great hope.

WRITING THE ZOHAR AND CONCEALING IT
And because of that, Rashbi permitted himself and disclosed the wisdom of the hidden in his books, *The Zohar* and the *Tikkunim*. However, it was with great care, since he only permitted Rabbi Abba, who could disclose with intimation, so only the sages of the children of Israel would understand, and the sages of the nations would not understand, for fear lest the wicked would know how to serve their masters. Therefore, as soon as they saw that the time was too soon for Israel's redemption, they hid it. That was at the time of the sages, the Savoraim, because we find much that our sages, the Savoraim, wrote his matters inside *The Zohar*.

DISCLOSING THE KABBALAH IS GOD'S WILL
Indeed, it was God's will that it would appear. This is why it wandered onto the widow of Rabbi Moshe de Leon. She inherited the manuscript from her husband, and he probably told her nothing of the prohibition to disclose, and she, by chance, put it up for sale.

ISRAEL'S TROUBLES ARE BECAUSE OF THE DISCLOSURE OF KABBALAH
Indeed, to this day, it caused many ruins in the house of Israel for the above reasons.

---
6 Translator's note: A *Shofar* is a ram's horn, used on festive occasions in Jewish holidays.

BENEFIT FROM DISCLOSING THE KABBALAH

However, there is no bad without good. And therefore, this dominion, which the nations have obtained by stealing the secrets of the Torah, propelled a great thrust for the development of holiness. In my assessment, we are in a generation that is standing at the very threshold of redemption, if we only know how to spread the wisdom of the hidden to the masses.

FIRST BENEFIT

Apart for the simple reason of "He hath swallowed down riches, and he shall vomit them up," this will reveal what is between my son and my father-in-law, and the difference between the essence of the nucleus and the upper *Klipa* (shell), from which all the sages of the nations in the world peeled. This is because all the camps of Israel that have denied the Torah are sure to return to the Creator and to His work.

SECOND BENEFIT

There is another reason for it: We have accepted that there is a precondition for the redemption—that all the nations of the world will acknowledge Israel's law, as it is written, "and the land shall be full of the knowledge," as in the example of the exodus from Egypt, where there was a precondition that Pharaoh, too, would acknowledge the true God and His laws, and would allow them to leave.

REDEMPTION THROUGH DIVULGING KABBALAH TO THE NATIONS OF THE WORLD

This is why it is written that each of the nations will hold a Jewish man and lead him to the Holy Land. And it was not enough that they could leave by themselves. You must understand from where the nations of the world would come by such a will and idea. Know that this is through the dissemination of the true wisdom, so they will evidently see the true God and the true law.

DISSEMINATION OF THE WISDOM OF KABBALAH THE WORLD OVER

And the dissemination of the wisdom in the masses is called "a *Shofar*." Like the *Shofar*, whose voice travels a great distance, the echo of the wisdom will spread all over the world, so even the nations will hear and acknowledge that there is Godly wisdom in Israel.

THE REVELATION OF KABBALAH TO ALL THE NATIONS IS THE REVELATION OF ELIYAHU (ELIJAH)

And this task was said about Eliyahu the prophet, since the disclosure of the secrets of the Torah is always referred to as "the disclosure of Eliyahu." It is as they have said, "let it rest until Elijah comes," and also, "the Tishbi will answer the questions and problems." For this reason, they said that three days (a known intimation) prior to the coming of the Messiah, Elijah would walk upon the hilltops and will blow in a great horn, etc.

DISCLOSING KABBALAH TO ALL THE NATIONS IS A PRECONDITION FOR THE COMPLETE REDEMPTION

You must understand these intimations: The issue of the *Shofar* is only the disclosure of the wisdom of the hidden in great masses, which is a necessary precondition that must be met prior to the complete redemption.

And the books that have already been revealed through me in this wisdom will testify to it; that matters of the greatest importance have been spread out like a gown for all to see. This is a true testimony that we are already at the threshold of redemption, and that the voice of the great *Shofar* has already been heard, though not in the distance, for it still sounds very softly.

But indeed, any greatness requires prior smallness, and there is no great voice if it is not preceded by a soft sound, for this is the way of the *Shofar*, that it progressively grows. And who better than I knows that I am not at all worthy of being even a messenger and a scribe for disclosing such secrets, and much less to thoroughly understand them. And why has the Creator done so to me? It is only because the generation is worthy of it, as it is the last generation, which stands at the threshold of complete redemption. And for this reason, it is worthy of beginning to hear the voice of Messiah's *Shofar*, which is the revealing of the secrets, as has been explained.

Kabbalists Write about the Wisdom of Kabbalah

Even if we find people who are great in the Torah, in fear, and in wisdom, yet who are not interested in the secrets of the Torah because of the sublimity of their degree, because they have many possessions with which to occupy their spirit in the treasures of the revealed Torah and wisdom, let it not droop the heart of one who feels an inner sensation, a pressure of the soul's craving for the way of secrets. For even if we decide that this yearning came to him due to his lack of skills in the revealed matters, so what? In the end, this is one's share, and one should be happy with one's lot, for the Lord is near to all them that call upon Him in honest truth.

–The Rav Raiah Kook,
Orot HaTorah (*Lights of the Torah*), Chapter 10, Item 4

Concerning the rule to not roam in the PARDESS, unless one has filled one's stomach with meat and wine, it should be said to one who comes to do only what the Torah commands by law. But one who craves and yearns to learn the inner things, to know His truthfulness, is under the rule, "one should always learn Torah in the place one's heart wishes." And one should be very strong in one's way and know that he will learn and succeed... and make one's soul's craving to adhere to knowing His Name permanently. And if one should see that the majority of the students are not so, he should know that this is right for them, so they will not destroy the sanctity until they walk by gradations. This has nothing to do with ostentation and boasting, only divisions in the soul's nobility.

–The Rav Raiah Kook,
Orot HaTorah (*Lights of the Torah*), Chapter 9, Item 12

Let not the eunuch say, "For I am a dry tree, and who am I to approach the holiness within, in the books of Kabbalah?" This is because all the righteous have already agreed that today this is the counsel of the inclination and a lie. And although he does not understand everything, still, the words of the Holy *Zohar* have power for the soul, and are approachable for every soul of Israel, small or great, each according to one's understanding and the root of one's soul.

–Rabbi Tzvi Hirsh Horovitz of Backshwitz,
Hanhagot Yesharot (*Upright Guidance*), Item 5

Had my people heeded me in this generation, when heresy is increasing, they would have studied *The Book of Zohar* and the *Tikkunim* (corrections), and contemplated them with nine-year-old children.

–Rav Yitzhak Yehudah Yehiel of Komarno,
Notzer Hesed (*Keeping Mercy*), Chapter 4, Teaching 4

There are no limitations on studying *The Zohar* because it is mostly *Midrash* (commentaries). The *Hafetz Chaim* used to evoke everyone to study *The Zohar* of that *Parasha* (weekly portion of the Torah) every Shabbat, even unmarried men.

–Rabbi Yosef Ben Shlomo of Pojin,
Hosafot Binian Yosef (*Yosef's Building Supplements*)

Without knowing the wisdom of Kabbalah, one is like a beast, since one is following the *Mitzva* without flavor, only going through the motions. This is similar to hay-eating beasts, without the taste of human food. And even if one is an important businessperson, occupied with much negotiations, he is not exempted from engaging in this wisdom.

–The Holy Rav of Ziditshov,
Sur MeRa VeAseh Tov (*Depart from Evil, and Do Good*)

The Torah is but a means. Engaging in it should be with a desire and profound desire for *Dvekut* (adhesion) with the Creator. No other intention is permitted in the Hall of God. Clearly, if students of Torah had engaged in it with burning love of God in their hearts, and the desire to cleave unto Him would be filling their whole being, there would be no argument concerning the internality of the Torah. All would flock to the King's Hall to engage in the wisdom of Kabbalah and the Holy *Zohar* for the greater part of their day, and even most of their time.

–*The Path of the PARDESS*, vol. 11,
Parashat VaYishlach, November 1996, Issue 515/3

Kabbalah deals with achieving the knowledge of the Creator, which is His uniqueness... because besides engaging in it and achieving it, one knows The Name and attains the secrets of the Torah and the flavors of the *Mitzvot*, which, in themselves revive the soul. This is so since through them, the soul is fortified and adheres to its Maker. Also extending from it are the proper keeping of the *Mitzvot*, as it excites the heart of those who know it, to do it wholly.

–Avodat HaKodesh (Holy Work),
"The Purpose," Chapter 70

At the time of the Messiah, evil increases and impudence and vice will be led by the heads of the mixed multitude. Then the Hidden Light will appear from the Heaven—*The Book of Zohar*, followed by the writings of the Holy Ari. And this learning will root out the evil in his soul. He will be rewarded with cleaving to the Upper Light, and he will be rewarded all the virtues in the world. It is for this reason that this Light appeared.

And the essence of your study in the internality of the Torah will be to attain illumination and Godly liveliness in your soul during your study and through the rest of the day. The Ari said that at that time the hidden will become revealed, and learning the secrets of the Torah and revealing the secrets to everyone from Israel gives joy to the Creator.

–Heichal HaBrahch (The Hall of Blessing),
Devarim (Deuteronomy) 208

The study of *The Book of Zohar* is above all studies and is a great correction to the soul. Since the whole of the Torah is the Names of the Creator, it is nevertheless clothed in stories, and one who reads the stories thinks of the literal. However, in *The Book of Zohar*, the secrets themselves are revealed, and the reader knows that they are the secrets of the Torah, although it is not understood because of the smallness of the attaining, and the depth of the attained.

–Pointing with the Finger, item 44

Why then did the Kabbalists obligate each person to study the wisdom of Kabbalah? Indeed, there is a great thing in it, worthy of being publicized: There is a wonderful, invaluable remedy to those who engage in the wisdom of Kabbalah. Although they do not understand what they are learning, through the yearning and the great desire to understand what they are learning, they awaken upon themselves the Lights that surround their souls.

This means that every person from Israel is guaranteed to finally attain all the wonderful attainments that the Creator has calculated in the Thought of Creation to delight every creature. One who has not been rewarded in this life will be rewarded in the next life, etc. until one completes the Creator's Thought of him.

-Rav Yehuda Ashlag (Baal HaSulam),
"Introduction to The Study of the Ten Sefirot," Item 155

The merit of contemplating the words of the Living God in *The Book of Zohar* and all that accompany it, and the words of the wisdom of truth, is immeasurable and priceless. It is especially so with the clear words of the Ari.

And even if one has not yet come to understand the heart of the matter through in-depth scrutiny, through constant engagement, the gates of Light and doors of wisdom will appear to all who walk on the path of God in wholeness, whose soul craves nearing the King's Hall. Hence, blessed will be all who volunteer to engage in the wisdom for even an hour or two a day, every day. The Creator adds an act to a good thought, and it will be regarded as standing, always and everyday, in the Lord's Court and His Abode, in the secrets of the Torah.

-The Rav Raiah Kook,
Who Love Israel with Holiness, 232

Those who engage solely in the dresses of the Torah are gravely mistaken, may God have mercy on them. And when the Lord's demand is abandoned and the majority of the multitude of the sages of the Torah do not know its purpose, and they consider the wisdom of the Torah with its purpose as mere addition of some quip to the laws—which, though truly sacred and precious—they will not illuminate our souls.

-The Rav Raiah Kook,
Igrot (Letters), Vol. 2, 8

I write only to evoke the hearts of disciples of sages to engage in the study of the internality of the Torah and to study the Holy *Zohar* as diligently as the Mishnah and the Gemarah. Yet, not all are ready for it by the nature of their souls. Hence, one who is not capable, and whose heart is keen, should certainly prolong the quip in Mishnah and Gemarah. But one who is capable of delving in the wisdom of Kabbalah, should dedicate the greater part of his study to know his Maker.

-The Rav Raiah Kook,
Igrot (Letters), Vol. 1, 41-42

The young, or those who find themselves heavy and of little desire for the Inner Light, must, at the very least, make it a rule to dedicate one or two hours a day to the wisdom of truth. In time, their minds will broaden and abundant success will unfold on their study of the essence of the Torah, as well, and their strength in scrutiny will mount and grow with pure ideas and broadening of the mind.

-The Rav Raiah Kook,
Igrot (*Letters*), Vol. 1, 82

As long as orthodoxy insists on saying, "No! Only Gemarah and Mishnah, no legends, no ethics, no Kabbalah, and no research," it dwindles itself. All the means it uses to protect itself, without taking the true potion of life, the Light of the Torah in its internals, beyond the tangible and obvious—the revealed in the Torah and *Mitzvot*—are utterly incapable of leading to its goal in all the generations, and especially in our generation, unless accompanied by expanding the many spiritual roots.

-The Rav Raiah Kook,
Igrot (*Letters*), Vol. 2, 232-233

We did not heed the voice of the true prophets, the voice of the best of the sages of all the generations, the voice of the righteous and the *Hassidim*, the sages of morals, the sages of study and secrets, who were crying out loudly that the river of the practical study alone will ultimately run dry, unless we constantly draw into it the water of the wisdom of Kabbalah.

-The Rav Raiah Kook,
Orot (*Lights*), 101

Redemption will only come by means of studying the Torah, and redemption is primarily in the study of Kabbalah.

-The Vilna Gaon (GRA),
Even Shlemah (*A Perfect and Just Weight*), Chapter 11, Item 3

When engaging in this composition, one evokes the power of the souls and the power of those righteous with the force of Moses. This is so because while engaging in it, they renew the generated Light, which was created during its composition. And Divinity shines and illuminates from that Light as when it was first created. And all who engage in it reawaken that same benefit and that first Light, which Rashbi and his friends had revealed while composing.

-*Ohr Yakar* (*Precious Light*),
Gate 1, Item 5

Studying the Holy *Zohar* purifies the body and the soul and is capable of bringing redemption soon in our days.

–Rabbi Efraim Ben Avraham Ardot,
Mateh Efraim (*Efraim's Wand*), *The Tip of the Mateh* (wand), Item 23

By the power of this holy study will we be redeemed from exile, and with nothing but that study. The reward of this study is greater than the whole of the Torah and all the *Mitzvot*. If one has engaged in this wisdom after one's soul has departed one's body, he is exempted from all the judgments. One who engages in the wisdom of Kabbalah, to know the secrets of the Torah and the flavors of the *Mitzvot* according to the secret, is called "a son to the Creator."

–*Sefer HaBrit* (*The Book of the Covenant*),
Part 2, Article 12, Chapter 5

One who is not studying this wisdom is as one who lives abroad. It is similar to one who has no other God, whose desire increases and the inclination deflects and brings doubt in the faith. But one who is bold and engages in the wisdom of Kabbalah will have no doubt in the ways of God.

–The Holy Rav of Ziditshov,
Sur MeRa (*Depart from Evil*), 69

And you shall return and distinguish between a righteous... a servant of God, and one who serves Him not: A servant of God is one who engages in the Talmud and *The Zohar*. One who does not serve Him engages only in Talmud, and does not engage in *The Zohar*.

–*Maayan Ganim* (*Fountain of Gardens*), Chapter 1, Item 2

Let fear of studying not come into your heart, for by studying, the 248 organs and 365 tendons will be sanctified and purified. You will be able to sanctify and purify each organ, be a chariot to the *Shechina* (Divinity), and hasten the end of the exile.

–*Heichal HaBracha* (*Hall of Blessing*), *Beresheet*, p 32

It is known that the study of *The Zohar* is capable indeed. Know that the study of *The Zohar* creates desire, and the holy words of *The Zohar* strongly evoke to the work of God.

–Rabbi Nachman of Breslev, *Talks of Rabbi Nachman*, 108

The whole of the wisdom of Kabbalah is only to know the guidance of the Higher Will, why It has created all these creatures, what It wants of them, what will be the end of all the cycles of the world, and how all these cycles in the world, which are so foreign, are interpreted. This is because the Higher Will had already calculated the cycle of this Guidance, which ends in utter completeness. And these measures are what we interpret as *Sefirot* and worlds.

–The Rav Moshe Chaim Luzzato (The Ramchal), *Daat Tvunot*, p 21

Studying Kabbalah, I know that you yourself would not want to study, except from one greater than you. And you will not find it except in studying *The Book of Zohar*. However, prior to each study, resolve within yourself to not make it a habit, but only for the Creator. And not all times are the same: at times you will be able to study for the Creator fervently, if you are rewarded with praying with a pure thought; and sometimes with a small thought, but all with a thought to benefit the Creator.

–The Rav Meshulam Feibush, *Yosehr Divrey Emet (Sincerity, Words of Truth)*, p 25

If he studies in truth, and with fear of sinning, the more he studies, the more he will surrender and see himself far from the truth, and he is certain to come to fear sin. But when he studies to be a quip scholar, savvy in rules to judge and to instruct, the more arguments and opinions he adds, the more he will ache and the greater will the heart become. Indeed, for this reason, the fool walks in the dark, in all sorts of lusts and lies; and he will waste his years with a wanting heart.

–The Rav Meshulam Feibush, *Yosehr Divrey Emet (Sincerity, Words of Truth)*, p 39

All of the sages of the nations do not know in *Yetzira* what the smallest in Israel knows. And the benefit of the rest of the teachings is in being a ladder to the wisdom of knowing the Creator.

–The Rav Moshe Ben Nachman, *The Writings of the Ramban*, Essay *Torat H' Temima* (The Law of the Lord Is Perfect), p 155

When one engages in this wisdom, mentioning the names of the Lights and the vessels related to one's soul, they immediately shine upon him to a certain degree. However, they shine for him without clothing the interior of his soul, for lack of the vessels able to receive them. Yet, the illumination one receives time after time during the engagement draws upon one grace from above, imparting one with abundance of sanctity and purity, which bring one much closer to reaching perfection.

-Rav Yehuda Ashlag (Baal HaSulam),
"Introduction to The Study of the Ten Sefirot," Item 155

It follows, that all the rejections he had experienced had all come from the Creator. They all came to prompt him to develop in spirituality, so he would not settle for his state. These rejections were not punishments for bad deeds, which he did because he could not overcome the obstructions. Rather, only those that the Creator wishes to bring near, the Creator Himself sends them help from above, using these rejections. This help is sent only to one with a true desire to rise above this world. Such a person receives help from above, being constantly shown how he is at fault, that he is not advancing in spirituality, and he is sent thoughts and views against the uniqueness of the Creator's actions.

-Rav Yehuda Ashlag (Baal HaSulam),
Shamati (*I Heard*), Article no. 1, "There Is None Else besides Him"

One must know that he will never come to know the true measure of the importance of the connection between man and the Creator because one cannot assess its true value. Instead, as much as one appreciates it, so he attains its merit and importance. There is a power in that, since thus one can be permanently imparted this illumination.

-Rav Yehuda Ashlag (Baal HaSulam), *Shamati* (*I Heard*), Article no. 4, "The Reason for the Heaviness"

There is no need for asceticism, and there is no need to correct the external. Do not correct your externality, but only your internality, since only your internality is about to be corrected. The primary cause for the corruption of the internality is pride and self-centeredness. If you wish to cleanse your sins, you should engage in annulling self-centeredness instead of asceticism, to feel that you are the lowest and the worst of all the people in the world. Yet, one should take note and lower oneself only before opportune people, before our society, and not before strangers.

-Rav Yehuda Ashlag (Baal HaSulam), *Pri Hacham* (*A Sage's Fruit*), p 75

Study in a book of Kabbalah, and even if you do not understand them, say the words of *The Zohar*, for they can purify the soul.

-*The Rav Yaakov Kapil Prayer Book*, Section "The Intention in the Study"

The internality of the Torah is life to the internality of the body, which is the soul and the externality to the externality of the body. And those who engage in intimations and secrets, the evil inclination cannot provoke them.

-The Vilna Gaon (GRA), *Even Shlemah* (*A Perfect and Just Weight*), Chapter 8, Item 27

One who does ample studying will study mostly in *The Zohar*, even if he does not understand. After all, why should he care that he does not understand, since it is a cure nonetheless?

-*Short Articles of the Old Admor*, p 571

One who has not been granted with understanding will read the words nonetheless, since the words can cleanse the soul and illuminate it with wondrous radiance.

-Rav Chaim HaCohen, *Good Conducts*, Item 45

Hear me my brothers and friends, who are craving and seeking the truth, the truth of the work of the heart—to behold the pleasantness of the Lord and to visit His Hall: My soul shall bend and cling unto *The Book of Zohar*, as the power of engaging in the holy book is known from our ancient sages.

-The Holy Rav of Ziditshov, *Sur MeRa* (*Depart from Evil*), p 4

It is true that we accept that even for one who knows nothing, the words of *The Zohar* can still cleanse the soul.

-Rav Tzvi Elimelech Shapira (MAHARTZA), *The MAHARTZA Additions*, Item 9

A new Light is renewed every moment, until it actually becomes a new creation, through *The Zohar* and our teacher the Ari.

-*Heichal HaBracha* (*Hall of Blessing*), *Devarim* (Deuteronomy), p 11

Each and every letter in *The Book of Zohar* and the writings of our great teacher, by Rav Chaim Vital... are great corrections for the soul, to correct all the incarnations.

-Rav Yitzhak Yehudah Yehiel of Komarno,
Notzer Hesed (*Keeping Mercy*), Chapter 4, Teaching 20

He said, "Prior to the coming of the Messiah, heresy and Epicureanism will increase in the world." The advice for it is to meticulously say *The Zohar* every day, even if one does not understand what one is saying, since saying *The Zohar* can cleanse the heart.

-The Light of the Upright, *Clear Myrrh*

One hour of studying *The Zohar* will correct Above what a whole year of studying the literal will not.

-Rav Shalom Ben Moshe Buzzaglo, *The King's Throne*, Tikkun 43, Item 60

The Creator feels no contentment in His world except when engaging in this wisdom. Moreover, man was created only to study the wisdom of Kabbalah.

-The Rav Chaim Vital, *Preface to the Gate to Introductions*

Should you say, "What benefit is there in these corrections?" Know that there is a great benefit. First, they are no longer lost, but are kept through the end of days. Second, when these great actions unfold within, even though the actions themselves do not come out, an illumination from them does come out, to yield great corrections in the general redemption. But to bring out that small illumination, all these great actions are required, since they are closed within.

-The Rav Moshe Chaim Luzzato (The Ramchal),
Adir BaMarom (The Mighty One on High), p 17

All the *Mitzvot* that are written in the Torah or the accepted ones, which the Patriarchs established, although they are mostly actions or words, they are all to correct the heart, "for the Lord searches all hearts, and understands all the inclinations of the thoughts."

-Rav Avraham Eben Ezra, *Yesod Morah*, p 8b

If one wishes to know, and asks of the Creator to understand the connection, this is called "a prayer." And this is a great and very important thing, since one has connection with the Creator, and wishes something of Him.

-Rav Baruch Ashlag,
Dargot HaSulam (Steps of the Ladder), Vol. 2, Article no. 561, "Prayer"

The prayer is called "the work in the heart," since the heart is *Malchut*, and the heart leads all the organs.

-The Rav Moshe Chaim Luzzato (The Ramchal),
Adir BaMarom (The Mighty One on High), p 234

But prayer is more particular to the heart. It touches it first, and prepares it to properly understand the organs. And the whole correction force is that the heart, in all its aspects, will cling to the Name *HaVaYaH*, meaning ZA, and be included in it.

-The Rav Moshe Chaim Luzzato (The Ramchal),
Adir BaMarom (*The Mighty One on High*), p 242

You can therefore see the utter necessity for anyone from Israel... to engage in the internality of the Torah and its secrets. Without it, the intention of creation will not be completed in man. This is the reason why we reincarnate, generation-by-generation, through our current generation, the remainder of the souls upon which the intention of creation has not been completed, as they have not attained the secrets of the Torah in previous generations.

-Rav Yehuda Ashlag, "Introduction to the Book, From the Mouth of a Sage"

Being favored by the Creator, or the opposite, does not depend on the person himself. Rather, it all depends on the Creator. And one who has not acquired a spiritual mind cannot understand why the Lord has favored him now and hence brought him closer, and subsequently left him, since one understands it only past one's entrance to spirituality.

-Rav Yehuda Ashlag (Baal HaSulam), *Shamati* (*I Heard*),
Article no. 1, "There Is None Else besides Him"

A real place in spirituality is called the place of reality, since anyone who comes to that place sees the same form as the other. However, an imaginary thing is not called a real place, since it is imaginary, and then everyone imagines it differently.

-Rav Yehuda Ashlag (Baal HaSulam), *Shamati* (*I Heard*),
Article no. 98, "Spirituality Is Called That Which Will Never Be Lost"

Angels do not know the secrets of the Torah. Also, they do not attain their Maker as the souls attain—demanding the Torah and, through it, attaining the Creator, the greatness of the Maker, and rise. The whole Torah speaks of nothing but the existence of the Maker and His merit in His *Sefirot* and His operations in them. And the more one studies its secrets, the better, since one utters His merit and does wonders in the *Sefirot*.

-Rav Moshe Cordovero (RAMAK), *Know the God of Thy Father*, 40

We do not know the Creator from the world and through the world, but from within our soul, from His Godly quality.

-The Rav Raiah Kook, *Igrot* (*Letters*), Vol. 1, 45

The Wisdom of the secret is not given to one person, since everyone has a part in the Torah, as the aim is only to know the Creator. Also, it is impossible for one person to attain the whole wisdom if not all the people in the world. Indeed, "Her husband is known in the *She'arim* (gates)." In *Shi'urim* (measures), each has a *Shi'ur* (measure) in the Torah, to know one's Maker.

-Rav Moshe Cordovero (RAMAK), *Know the God of Thy Father*, 93

There are those who only examine the literal Torah and the literal issues. These are in shame for the Next World, since there are no literal matters there, but their secrets, so he can negotiate among the rest of the righteous, the students of the secrets of the Torah that are there. Otherwise, he will be rejected from them, out to the place of students of the literal.

And those who delve in the secret have a part in *Bina*, so they will shine and radiate from there, from the secret of the internality of the Torah, and measuring a level, that is, as the brightness of the firmament. There is no reward as the reward of the disciples of the Torah and knowing its secrets, to the glory of its Creator.

-Rav Moshe Cordovero (RAMAK), *Know the God of Thy Father*, 148

Happy are those who engage in the Torah to know the wisdom of their Lord. They know and observe the Higher Secrets. When a person who has repented leaves this world, and is left with only transgressions for which death atones, through it, meaning death, all the judgments in the world depart from him. Moreover, they open before him thirteen gates from the secrets of the Pure Persimmon, upon which Sublime Wisdom depends.

-*The Book of Zohar* (with the *Sulam* commentary), Song of Songs, p 148

It is not without reason—according to their will—did they determine impure, pure, forbidden, permitted, kosher, and banned. They rather judged from the internality of the Torah, as it is known to those who know the wisdom of the hidden.

-Rav Chaim Vital, *The Writings of the Ari, The Tree of Life*, Part 1, "Introduction of Rav Chaim Vital," 3

One who has not seen the Light of the wisdom of Kabbalah, has never seen Lights. This is because then he understands and learns the secret of His Uniqueness and His Guidance. And all who retire from the wisdom of Kabbalah retire from the eternal, spiritual life.

–Rav Isaiah Horowitz (the Holy Shlah), "First Article," p 30

Who has not seen the Light of *The Book of Zohar* has never seen Light.

–The Rav Tzvi Hirsh of Ziditshov,
Ateret Tzvi (A Crown of Glory) *Parashat BeHaalotcha*

It must be known because we are commanded, "know this day, and lay it to thy heart, that the Lord, He is God." Thus, we must *know*, and not only believe, but matters should make sense.

–The Rav Moshe Chaim Luzzato (The Ramchal), *Moses' War*, "Rules," p 349

There shall be no strange god in thee—God will not be a stranger to you, within you.

–*There Is None More Complete than a Broken Heart* (Sayings of the Rav of Kotzk), p 42

The soul spreads in the parts of the body and is included in a single whole in the heart, by understanding. This is the meaning of "the heart understands" (*Berachot* 61), since the understanding of the heart is actual seeing, since as the eyes see, so is the understanding of the soul, which is only observing.

–The Rav Moshe Chaim Luzzato (The Ramchal),
Adir BaMarom (*The Mighty One on High*), p 274

Each attains individual attainment, according to one's own degree and according to the time.

–The Rav Moshe Chaim Luzzato (The Ramchal),
Adir BaMarom (*The Mighty One on High*), p 279

In truth, one who achieves true knowledge can see three things: the real, hidden Guidance, the superficial appearance of the Guidance, which is not the truth, where this appearance originates, and how it connects to the actual Guidance.

–The Rav Moshe Chaim Luzzato (The Ramchal),
Adir BaMarom (*The Mighty One on High*), p 459

The Baal Shem Tov ordered his people to study the words of *The Zohar* prior to praying.

-Rav Yitzhak Bar Yishaiah Atia,
Doresh Tov (Seeking Good), "Concerning *The Zohar*"

Will not achieve life but only through the study of *The Zohar*... And in this generation it is impossible to draw the Higher *Shechina* (Divinity) but through *The Zohar* and the writings of Rav Chaim Vital.

-*Heichal HaBracha* (Hall of Blessing), *Devarim* (Deuteronomy), 58

On this day, when the holy book—*The Zohar*—was written, which is from the illumination of the hidden, good Light ... it shines for us in the exile until, by its merit, the Messiah will appear. Let this Light be the Light of the Messiah King.

-Rav Tzvi Elimelech Shapira (MAHARTZA), *Bnei Isaschar* (*The Children of Issachar*), "Articles for the Month of *Iyar*," Article no. 3, Item 4

It is known from books and from authors that the study of the wisdom of Kabbalah is an absolute must for any person from Israel. And even if one has learned the whole Torah and has memorized the Mishnah and the Gemarah; if one is also filled with virtues and good deeds more than all his contemporaries, but has not learned the wisdom of Kabbalah, he must reincarnate into this world to study the secrets of Torah and wisdom of truth.

-Rav Yehuda Ashlag, "Introduction to the Book, From the Mouth of a Sage"

I am glad that I have been born in such a generation when it is already permitted to publicize the wisdom of truth. And should you ask, "How do I know that it is permitted?" I will reply that I have been given permission to disclose. This means that until now, the ways by which it is possible to publicly engage, before every nation and denomination, and to fully and correctly explain each word, have not been revealed to any sage.

I, too, have sworn by my teacher to not disclose, as did all the students before me. But this oath and this prohibition apply only to those manners given orally from generation to generation, back to the prophets and before. Had these ways been revealed to the public, they would have caused much harm, for reasons known only to us.

Yet, the way in which I engage in my books is a permitted way. Moreover, I have been instructed by my teacher to expand it as much as I can. We call it "the manner of clothing the matters." This does not depend on the genius of the sage himself, but on the state of the generation, as our sages said, "Little Samuel was worthy, etc., but his generation was unworthy." This is why I said that my being rewarded with the manner of disclosing the wisdom is because of my generation.

–Rav Yehuda Ashlag, *Pri Hacham* (*A Sage's Fruit*), Articles, "The Teaching of Kabbalah and Its Essence," p 165

We must establish seminaries and compose books, to hasten the dissemination of the wisdom throughout the nation. That was not so before, for fear lest unworthy disciples would mingle. And this became the primary reason for the prolonging of the exile, for our many sins, to this day. ...Many will roam, and knowledge will increase among all those worthy of it. By that, we will soon be rewarded with the coming of the Messiah and the redemption of our souls soon in our days, Amen.

–Rav Yehuda Ashlag, *The Book of Introductions*, "Introduction to the Book, The Tree of Life," Item 5, p 205

Due to the comprehensive prevention on the spiritual study of Godly matters, the concept of Godliness is dimming, for lack of purified work in mind and heart. This is the heresy of the days of the Messiah, when Godly wisdom is exhausted in the Assembly of Israel and in the world over.

–The Rav Raiah Kook, *Orot* (*Lights*), p 126

Turning the hearts and occupying the minds with noble thoughts, whose origin is the secrets of the Torah, has become an utter necessity in the last generation.

–The Rav Raiah Kook, *Mist of Purity*, p 65

Indeed, we will never be able to ignore the general, comprehensive cure, whose abandonment caused our fall. This is the thing that I, in my misery and discontent, am used to calling... Precisely at a time of great peril and crisis, we should take the best of cures in all the Torah, with all its spiritual interpretations. ... At such a time, we must protest for the greatest of deficiencies.

–The Rav Raiah Kook, *Igrot* (*Letters*), Vol. 2, pp 123, 125

All the great Kabbalists unanimously cry out like cranes that as long as we deny the Torah of its secrets and do not engage in its secrets, we are destroying the world.

–The Rav Raiah Kook, *Igrot* (*Letters*), Vol. 2, p 231

I have already said on several occasions that precisely this generation, which seems so vain and unruly, is the best suited for the Light of true repentance.

-The Rav Raiah Kook, *Igrot* (*Letters*), Vol. 2, p 34

When knowledge diminishes in Israel, as the exile continues, and the Godly introductions are gone and forgotten, many will fall in the pit of materialization, and make a God that has a place and image. This is because the secrets of the Torah will be hidden from them. And not many will be wise and know the secret, but one out of a city, and many will be in the pit of error.

-Rav Moshe Cordovero (RAMAK), *Know the God of Thy Father*, 139-140

Studying the Holy *Zohar* at this time is much needed to save and protect us from all evil, since the disclosure of this wisdom now is in flawed generations, to now be a shield for us to wholeheartedly cling to our Father in Heaven. Previous generations were men of action and pious, and the good deeds saved them from the accusers. Now we are remote from the Higher Root, like the yeast in the barrel. Who will protect us if not our study of this wisdom?

-The Sage Yaakov Tzemach in his introduction to *The Tree of Life*

And he will know the secrets of the Torah and the flavors of the *Mitzvot*... because the soul is strengthened by them and unites with its Maker... And besides the hidden good, the next world, for one who delves and grows wise in it, one tastes the flavors of the next world in this world, too. ... And by the merit of those who engage, the Messiah will come; for then the earth shall be full of knowledge, because of it, and this will be a reason for His arrival.

-Rav Isaiah Horowitz (the Holy Shlah), "First Article," p 30

All who will be rewarded with Him, will be rewarded with redemption. This is because this lesser work, at this time, is more important than all the rams of Nebaioth that were during the time when the Temple existed.

-Rav Avraham Katz of Kalisk, *Mercy to Abraham*, "First Fountain," 24

I have seen it written that the prohibition from Above to refrain from open study in the wisdom of truth was only for a limited period, until the end of 1490. But from then on the prohibition has been lifted and permission was granted to engage in *The Book of Zohar*. And from the year 1540, it has been a great *Mitzva* (commandment, good deed) for the masses to study, old and young...

And because the Messiah will come because of that, for no other reason, we must not be negligent.

–Avraham Ben Mordechai Azulai,
Ohr HaChama (*Light of the Sun*), Introduction

Through Israel's engagement in the secrets of the Torah, the Messiah will come soon in our days, Amen.

–*The Congregation of Jacob*, Headword Secret

Redemption will come only through the study of Kabbalah.

– The Vilna Gaon (GRA),
Even Shlemah (*A Perfect and Just Weight*), Chapter 11, Item 3

May they begin to teach the holy *Book of Zohar* to children when they are still small, ages nine or ten, as it was written by the great Kabbalist... and redemption would certainly come soon, without any labor pains of the Messiah. And Rabbi Shem Tov had already written in *The Book of Faiths* that Judah and Israel will be redeemed forever only by the wisdom of Kabbalah, since only this is a Godly wisdom, given to the sages of Israel since days and years of old. And by its merit will the glory of God and the glory of His Sacred Law be revealed.

–The Rav Shabtai Ben Yaakov Yitzhak Lifshitz,
Segulot Israel (*The Virtue of Israel*), Set no. 7, Item 5

Listen to my advice and God will be with you: Do not avoid engagement in the wisdom because of fear. After all, what is your life's soul in the world? If, God forbid, there is no wisdom and knowledge in you, your life is not life. The writing says, "See, I have set before thee this day life; therefore choose life." Imagine that a person came upon you to deny you of life; would you wage war against him... or reign him, or would it be to the contrary? "All that a man has will he give for his life," and he will slight all actions and justifications in the world, to cross the sea, to rise up to the Heaven, until he surrenders the one who stands against him and wishes to rob him of life. This is even more so with the Eternal Life, called "life."

–The Holy Rav of Ziditshov, *Sur MeRa* (*Depart from Evil*), 8

Why has God sent for us to reveal in our generation, what He did not reveal except in the generation of Rabbi Akiva and Rabbi Shimon Bar-Yochai and his friends. ... For this is the rudiment of the Torah and the tenet of faith on which the axes of the doors of the Torah and the work revolve. Without it, you will not know what is Torah *Lishma* (for Her Name), since you will not know the root of the images of His Names, blessed is He and blessed is His Name. ... And you are not exempted from the internality of the Torah, for without it, man is like a beast, a hay-eating ox.

–The Holy Rav of Ziditshov, *Sur MeRa* (*Depart from Evil*), 29

I say, I wish the greatest of the generations had not eased the study of the holy wisdom, and I wish they had taught their students a way to engage in this wisdom. Then there would certainly be no pride in external teachings, and all the teachings would be rejected by it, as darkness is rejected by the light. Yet, our sins have caused quite a few of the righteous of the generation to shut the doors of wisdom before the novices and say that they will not teach until they have a degree and the spirit of holiness. For this reason, we have remained bare of the sacred wisdom, and through our many sins, the darkness of the external teachings has increased. The fool walks in the dark and soon in our days the Lord will say, "Let there be light," and we will be enlightened.

–Rav Tzvi Elimelech Shapira (MAHARTZA),
Maayan Ganim (*A Fountain of Gardens*), Chapter 1, Item 5

Due to the intensification of the *Klipot* (shells), the heresy, impudence, and unholy mixture in this generation, permission has been given from Above to disclose the Light of this wisdom, to tie the souls to the life of the Light of Godliness, to truly cleave unto Him... This is because this wisdom has been revealed in this generation only to sanctify, purify, and to remove the vices.

–*Heichal HaBracha* (*Hall of Blessing*), *Devarim* (*Deuteronomy*), p 27

Because Israel are destined to taste from the Tree of Life, which is the holy *Book of Zohar*, through it, they will be redeemed from exile.

–*The Book of Zohar*, Naso, Item 90

When we repent and engage in this wisdom with love, Israel will be redeemed soon in our days, Amen.

–Rav Chaim Vital, "Preface to the Gate to Introductions"

Redemption depends on the study of Kabbalah.

–The Vilna Gaon (GRA),
Even Shlemah (*A Perfect and Just Weight*), Chapter 11, Item 3

I have news about the city of Prague, which is a place of study: Judaism is declining there, retreating day-by-day. Indeed, the thing is that previously, the revealed Torah sufficed. But now, in the days of the Messiah, there is a need for the hidden Torah, as well. Previously, the evil inclination was not so strong, and the revealed Torah was sufficient as a spice against it. But now, prior to the redemption, the evil inclination is intensifying and requires strengthening through the hidden, too.

–Rav Simcha Bonim of Pshischa, *A Torah of Joy*, p 57

Know that the previous generations and the early days, those of the fifth millennium, are not as these generations and these days. In those days, the gates of the wisdom were closed and locked. Hence, then Kabbalists were only a few. This is not so in this sixth millennium, when the gates of Lights, the gates of Mercy have been opened, since it is near the end of days. Now it is a joy of *Mitzva* (good deed) and great contentment in the eyes of the Creator to make the glory of His Eternal Kingdom known, and especially now, when the holy writings of the Ari Luria have been printed. This opened for us the gates of Light, which were sealed and locked. Now there is no obstacle or peril, just as with the revealed.

–*Sefer HaBrit* (*The Book of the Covenant*), Part 2, Article 12, Chapter 5

Only through the expansion of the wisdom of Kabbalah in the masses will we obtain complete redemption. ... Both the individual and the nation will not complete the aim for which they were created, except by attaining the inner part of the Torah and its secrets. Hence, it is the great expansion of the wisdom within the nation that we need first, to merit receiving the benefit from our Messiah. Thus, the expansion of the wisdom and the coming of our Messiah are interdependent. For this reason, we must establish seminaries and compose books, to hasten the dissemination of the wisdom throughout the nation.

–Rav Yehuda Ashlag, *The Book of Introductions*,
"Introduction to the Book, The Tree of Life," Item 5, pp 204-205

Now the time dictates acquiring much possessions in the inner Torah. *The Book of Zohar* breaks new paths, sets lanes, makes a highway in the desert, it, and all its crops are ready to open the doors of redemption.

–The Rav Raiah Kook, *Orot* (Lights), 57

Many thought that too much engagement in the secret is not good, since the practical Torah would be forgotten from Israel, the forbidden, the permitted, the non-kosher, and the kosher. And what shall become of this Torah had we all delved in the secrets of the Torah? ...Yet, those who despise it are not servants of the Creator whatsoever.

–Rav Moshe Cordovero (RAMAK), *Know the God of Thy Father*, 132

But if ...a person from Israel degrades the virtue of the internality of the Torah and its secrets, ...with regard to the virtue of the externality of the Torah, which discusses only the practical part... one causes degradation and decline of the internality of the world, which are the Children of Israel, and intensifies the domination of the externality of the world—the Nations of the World—over them. They will humiliate and disgrace the Children of Israel. ... Then they make all the ruin and the heinous slaughter... and the whole decline of the Children of Israel is because they had abandoned the internality of the Torah, degraded its merit, and made it seemingly redundant.

–Rav Yehuda Ashlag, *The Book of Introductions*, "Introduction to The Book of Zohar," Item 69, p 91

Woe unto them that make the spirit of the Messiah leave and depart from the world, and will not be able to return to the world. They are the ones who make the Torah dry, without the moist of understanding and knowledge, since they confine themselves to the practical part of the Torah, and do not wish to try to understand the wisdom of Kabbalah, to know and to learn the secrets of the Torah and the flavors of the *Mitzvot*. Woe unto them, for with these acts they make poverty, ruin, robbery, looting, killing, and destruction exist in the world.

–Rav Yehuda Ashlag, *The Book of Introductions*, "Introduction to The Book of Zohar," Item 70, p 91

The people of Israel are divided into three sects:

1. Populace servants of the Creator, who know Me not. These bring the world back to chaos, sustaining their bodies, and destroying their souls.

2. Wise disciples, who engage in the literal Torah, the sages of the literal. They despise engagement in the wisdom of truth and say that all there is in the Torah is the literal. These are sapient in doing harm, and do not know how to do good. And many a downfall come from them; they have no Light in their Torah.

3. Possessors of the wisdom of truth. These are called "sons."
>   –Rav Chaim Vital, *The Writings of the Ari, The Tree of Life*,
>   Part One, "Rav Chaim Vital's Introduction," 9-10

There is no doubt that those who engage only in Babylonian Talmud are like blind scraping the wall, in the dresses of the Torah. They have no eyes to see the secrets of the Torah that are hidden in it.
>   –Rav Chaim Vital, *The Writings of the Ari, The Tree of Life*,
>   Part One, "Rav Chaim Vital's Introduction," 9-10

Woe unto people from the affront of the Torah. For undoubtedly, when they engage only in the literal and in its stories, it wears its widow-garments, and covered with a bag. And all the nations shall say unto Israel: "What is thy Beloved more than another beloved? Why is your law more than our law? After all, your law, too, is stories of the mundane." There is no greater affront to the Torah than that.

Hence, woe unto the people from the affront of the Torah. They do not engage in the wisdom of Kabbalah, which honors the Torah, for they prolong the exile and all the afflictions that are about to come to the world... And what will the fools of our time do, as they are clever, and happy with their lot, rejoicing in their work? ... They do not know that it is for their fear of entering it that they avoid engaging in it.

Hence, these hills have been corrupted; their heart is a root that bears gall and wormwood, and the rust of mud has come upon them, to deny the wisdom of truth. They say that all there is in the Torah is but the literal and its clothes. ... Undoubtedly, they will have no share of the next world. ... And it is said about them, "My servants shall eat, but you shall be hungry."
>   –Rav Chaim Vital, *The Writings of the Ari, The Tree of Life*, Part One, "Rav Chaim Vital's Introduction," 11-12

We have learned how many virtues a whole man has over all that exists. And the opposite of that shall become clear, since when man sins, he has already violated the intention in his creation. Not only will he not be considered whole, he is the least of all creatures, even more than beasts and predators. As the RAMBAM wrote, "Any person who did not achieve the complete human form is not considered human, but a beast with a human form." This is because such a person has the ability to harm and create evil, which other animals do not, since the mind and the thought that were prepared for attaining perfection will be used for all sorts of trickery to inflict harm. Thus, he is lower than a beast.

–Rav Shimon Lavi, author of Ketem Paz (Fine Gold), "Man—Creation's Final Purpose"

This is the answer to the wiseacre fools, with vain wisdom, who speak against those who engage in the wisdom of Kabbalah and say about them that they hear the voice of words, yet see no image. Woe unto them and to their misfortune for their foolishness and wantonness, for they will not profit from it; they only move God's people from rising unto His Holy Mountain, since even the angels Above are weary and do not attain the actual glory.

And from all their craving, they strain to rise above their level, and they shout along the way saying, "with her love be thou ravished always," and it will not be considered a mistake for them. Even dwellers of clay houses, whose foundation is in the dust, their lust will not be considered a mistake, but only praise and glory and greatness. Because for one who strays seeking the King's house, and returns to know which way He is, it is considered righteousness, and he will be rewarded for his trouble by the King.

This is the truth, beyond any doubt. And them that proudly and scornfully prattle about those who engage in the books of Kabbalah are destined to pay the price: their lips shall be sealed in this and in the next. For the mouth of liars, who praise themselves on manmade gods with tangible proofs, as it appears to their blind eyes, without gazing at God's spiritual work, shall be blocked. This is so because He is a soul to the sensed, and their folly is punishment enough for their souls.

–Rav Shimon Lavi, author of Ketem Paz (Fine Gold), "Good and Evil Are Contained in Man"

The crown of the Torah is the wisdom of Kabbalah, from which the majority of the world retires, saying that you should observe what is permitted and that you have no dealings in the hidden. You, if you are fit for this teaching, reach out your hand, hold it, and do not move from it. This is because one who did not taste the flavor of this wisdom, has never seen Lights in his life, and he is walking in the dark. And woe unto the people from the affront of this Torah.

To explain the measure of the wrongdoing of those people who prevent those who want to from studying the wisdom of Kabbalah with their false arguments... this stumbling-block is not in the hands of the masses alone. Rather, the hand of the assistants and the wiseacres scheme with mutiny and embezzlement. And they not only loathe the knowledge of Godliness, they even began to scorn and condemn this wisdom. They walk in the dark and their name will be covered in darkness for gaping and saying, "Our hand is high in the revealed. Why do we need this wisdom? We settle for the literal Torah."

-*Sefer HaBrit* (*The Book of the Covenant*), Part 2, Article 12, Chapter 5

One who did not engage in the wisdom of truth, who did not want to learn it when his soul wanted to rise to the Garden of Eden, is rejected from there with disgrace. ... And do not follow the example of the greatest in the Torah in the revealed who do not want to engage in this wisdom, since the words of our sages in the Midrash and in *The Zohar* are truer than the greatest in this generation.

-*Sefer HaBrit* (*The Book of the Covenant*), Part 2, Article 12, Chapter 5

All who refrain from studying Kabbalah is rejected from among the righteous, and loses his world, and is not rewarded with seeing the Light of Life's King's countenance.

-Rav Yair Chayim Bacharach, *Havvot Yair* (*Villages of Yair*)

Many fools escape from studying the secrets of the Ari and *The Book of Zohar*, which are our lives. If my people heeded me in the time of the Messiah, when evil and heresy increase, they would delve in the study of *The Book of Zohar* and the *Tikkunim* and the writings of the Ari all their days. They would revoke all the harsh sentences and would extend abundance and Light. ... The life of the Israeli man depends on *The Book of Zohar* and the writings of the Ari, to study with sanctity, joy, and pleasantness, with fear and with love, each according to his attainment and holiness, and all of Israel are holy.

-Rav Yitzhak Yehudah Yehiel of Komarno,
Notzer Hesed (*Keeping Mercy*), Chapter 4, Teaching 20

He would say about those *Hassidim* that make much noise, but without depth and feeling, that they are chimneys without houses—emitting smoke without fire.

-*There Is None More Complete than a Broken Heart* (*Sayings of the Rav of Kotzk*), p 38

This is the panacea, and leaving it caused our fall. This is the thing that I, with my deficiency and bitterness of soul, am accustomed to repeating hundreds and thousands of times. We have left the internality of the Torah. ... Small and narrow people come and heal us with cold medicines of all kinds, but leave aside the principal potion of life.

-The Rav Raiah Kook, *Igrot (Letters)*, Vol. 2, 123

They are the ones who make the Torah dry, for they do not wish to delve in the wisdom of Kabbalah. Woe unto them, for thus they cause wretchedness, ruin, looting, killing, and destruction to the world.

-*The Book of Zohar, Tikkuney Zohar (The Zohar Corrections), Tikkun* no. 30

Anyone can attain what he is taught in his mother's womb. And one who could attain the secrets of the Torah and did not try to attain them is judged harshly, God forbid.

-The Vilna Gaon (GRA), *Even Shlemah (A Perfect and Just Weight)*, Chapter 24

Now you can understand the aridity and the darkness that have befallen us in this generation, such as we have never seen before. It is because even the workers of the Creator have abandoned the study of the secrets of the Torah.

-Rav Yehuda Ashlag, *The Book of Introductions*, "Introduction to The Book of Zohar," Item 57, p 88

The fool has no wish for wisdom, but for what appears in his heart, who follows the intoxication of the sordid world. He does little in studying the Torah and in delving into its hidden secrets, since this requires "wisdom," to deduce one thing from another. And the fool has no wish for laboring to understand, but for what appears in his heart, meaning for things that are seen by all, which require no effort to obtain. In his little mind, he thinks that he will understand them, although in truth, he does not even attain that.

-*Kabbalists' Interpretations of the Literal*, Part 2, p 459, RAMAK, *Dimmed Light*, Chapter 1

Indeed, when the wisdom is left bare, abstruse words without understanding, another evil is born from that: Great sages leave it aside, since it is the nature of the wise to seek sober understanding and to know the depth of the issues, and not consent to mere words. And when they saw that there was nothing in the words to fill their desire, they said, "Why should we waste our time with the unattainable?"

Others have harmed even more: They not only loathed it, but defamed it, considering it gullibility that people have assumed, to encounter obscene and unacceptable things. Moreover, they have come to deny its essence and negate the Holy *Zohar* being composed by Rashbi (Rabbi Shimon Bar-Yochai) and his friends. And all this was because the words of the sages were alien in their eyes, until they considered the Tanaaim, the foundations of the land, unworthy of attention.

–The Rav Moshe Chaim Luzzato (The Ramchal), *Shaarey Ramchal*
(*Gates of the Ramchal*), Introduction to the Article, "The Debate," p 37

But there is one darkness, which darkens the eyes of people, to immerse them in nature. Then, they no longer know that the Creator is the Higher Leader, who moves everything, but attribute it all to luck. This is the meaning of "that prepare a table for Fortune" (Isaiah 65:11). Despite that, they build all their thoughts and decisions according to nature.

Also, there are several external teachings following this nature, and they all immerse the people of the world in these notions. This removes them from knowing the Inner Guidance.

In the last generations, matters have come to the Torah being forgotten from Israel, and no one truly understands the Guidance, but all follow greed. I wish to say that even if they do not commit actual sins, they are like beasts carrying their load. And this rule is the darkness that does not permit seeing where is the root of Guidance.

–The Rav Moshe Chaim Luzzato (The Ramchal),
Adir BaMarom (*The Mighty One on High*), p 459

This is the reason why Rabbi Shimon Bar-Yochai so cried over it, and called upon those who engage in the literal Torah that they are asleep, for they do not open their eyes to see the love that the Creator loves them, as though they were, God forbid, ungrateful to Him. Moreover, they do not see and do not know the path of holiness and the *Dvekut* (adhesion) with Him at all.

But the Torah commands and says, "Cleave unto Him" (Deuteronomy 10:20). And even though they interpret it concerning one cleaving to a wise disciple, in the end, a text does not extend its literal meaning.

In truth, Israel must cleave unto Him with complete *Dvekut* (adhesion), to know His special ways according to His holiness, and to walk in them. Hence, they said, "The Song of Songs, the Holy of Holies" (*Midrash Rabba, Song of Songs*). This is because it is founded on this very matter, and he interprets this love and all the efforts the Creator is making to cling with His holiness with Israel, while Israel should correspond with a craving for Him, to genuinely cleave.

And this, unfortunately, is the product of the exile—Israel have forgotten this path, and they remain asleep, immersed in their slumber, oblivious to that. But the Torah is dressed in mourning for its plight, and we are in the dark, like the dead, virtually as blind scraping the wall. Praise is not comely for the just to walk in this way. Rather, it is to the contrary, to open blind eyes and to see the love of God, and to know Holiness and its ways, and be truly sanctified in it.

-The Rav Moshe Chaim Luzzato (The Ramchal),
Shaarey Ramchal (*Gates of the Ramchal*), "The Debate," p 97

A Prayer before a Prayer

May it please You, our Lord, God of our fathers, who hears the outcry of pleas and listens to the voice of the prayers of His people, Israel, with mercy, to prepare our hearts, establish our thoughts, and send our prayers in our mouths. Do lend Your ear to the voice of the prayer of Your servants, who pray to You with an outcry and a broken spirit.

You, merciful God, with Thy great mercy and graciousness, pardon, forgive, and atone for us and for the whole of Your people, House of Israel, all that we have sinned, perverted, condemned, and transgressed before You.

It is known to You that it is not at all with rebellion and deceit that we have defied You and the words of Your Law and Your Commandments. Rather, it is for the perpetual, unyielding, burning inclination within us, which brings us to the lusts of this lowly world and its vanities. It consistently baffles our minds, even when we wish to pray before You and beg for our souls. Time and time again, it confounds our thoughts with its ploys. And we cannot prevail over it, for our minds and reasons have grown so weak that the strength to endure has withered, from the troubles, the hardships, and the length of time.

Hence, You, Oh Merciful and Gracious God, do to us as You have promised us through Your trusted one: "And I will be gracious to whom I will be gracious, and will show mercy on whom I will show mercy." Our sages said, "Although he is not seemly and is not worthy," for this is Your way: to be good to the bad and to the good. Our sighs, our sorrow, and our conversations of our inability to bring ourselves closer to Your work, to truly cleave unto You are all known to You. Woe unto our souls; indeed, woe unto us.

Our Father in Heaven, now do awaken Your great and gracious mercy upon us, banish and root out our evil inclination from within us, and scold it so it will depart us and will not stray us from Your Work. Let no evil thought rise in our hearts, when we are awake and in the night's dream, too, and especially when we stand in prayer before You or when we study Your law. And while we engage in Your Commandments, let our thoughts be truly clear, lucid, sound, and as strong as Your good will for us.

Do awaken our hearts and the hearts of all of Israel, Your people, to unite with You in earnest truth and with love, to sincerely serve You, as it pleases Your Throne. And do fix Your Faith in our hearts forever and ever, and let Your Faith be tied to our hearts as a stake that will not fall, and remove all the screens that separate between us and You.

Our Father in Heaven, save us from all the failures and the errors; do not leave us, do not abandon us, and do not shame us. Be with our mouths when we speak, with our hands when we work, and with our hearts when we think. Grant us, our Father in Heaven, Merciful God, with devoting our hearts, our thoughts, our words, and our actions and all our movements and feelings, those that are known and those that are not known to us, the revealed and the concealed, to You alone, sincerely, without any ill thought.

Purify our hearts and sanctify us; throw upon us pure water and purify us with Your love and compassion, and plant Your love and fear in our hearts forever, with no end, at all times and at all places: when we walk, when we lay, and when we rise. And let the spirit of Your Holiness always burn within us.

We always rely on You, Your greatness, Your love, the fear of You, and Your law, written and oral, revealed and concealed, and Your Commandments, to unite with Your Mighty and Awful Name. And guard us from prejudice, pride, anger, and pedantry, sadness, gossip, and other vices, and from anything that lessens Your Holy and Pure Work, which we so care for.

Impart the spirit of Your Holiness upon us so we may cleave unto You and crave You always, more and more. And raise us from degree to degree so we may come to the merit of our holy fathers, Abraham, Isaac, and Jacob. May their virtue help us, and You will hear the voice of our prayers, so we will always be answered when we pray unto You, for us or for any one of Your people, Israel, one or many.

Rejoice and be proud of us, and we will bear fruit Above and root below. And remember not our sins, and especially the sins of our youth, as King David said, "Remember not the sins of my youth, nor my transgressions." Do turn our transgressions and sins to merits, and always impart upon us—from the world of repentance—thoughts of wholeheartedly returning unto You, to correct that which we have blemished in Your Holy and Pure Names.

Do save us from envy of one another, and let no envy for others come into our hearts, nor our envy of others. Rather, let our hearts see the virtues of our friends, and not their faults. And let us speak to each other in a way that is seemly and worthy before You, and let no hatred rise in one towards another, God forbid.

Brace our ties of love to You, as it is known to You, that all will be for bringing contentment unto You. This is our foremost aim. And should we not have the wit to aim our hearts to You, You will teach us, so we may truly know the aim of Your good will.

And for all that, Merciful and Gracious God, we pray before You to accept our prayers with mercy and good will. Amen, would that be so.

Spiritual Attainment

Divinity in Exile

It is written, "There is none else besides Him." This means that there is no other force in the world that has the ability to do anything against Him. And what one sees, that there are things in the world that deny the Higher Household, the reason is that this is His will.

And it is deemed a correction, called "the left rejects and the right adducts," meaning that which the left rejects is considered correction. This means that there are things in the world, which, to begin with, aim to divert a person from the right way, and through them he is rejected from Sanctity.

And the benefit from the rejections is that through them a person receives a need and a complete desire for the Creator to help him, since he sees that otherwise he is lost. Not only does he not progress in his work, but he sees that he regresses, that is, he lacks the strength to keep Torah and *Mitzvot* even in *Lo Lishma* (not for Her Name). That only by genuinely overcoming all the obstacles, above reason, can he keep the Torah and *Mitzvot*. But he does not always have the strength to overcome above reason; otherwise, he is forced to deviate, God forbid, from the way of the Creator, even from *Lo Lishma*.

And he, who always feels that the shattered is greater than the whole, meaning that there are many more descents than ascents, and he does not see an end to these states, and he will forever remain outside of holiness, for he sees that it is difficult for him to observe even as little as a jot, unless by overcoming above reason. But he is not always able to overcome, and what will become of him?

Then he comes to the decision that only the Creator Himself can help. This causes him to make a heartfelt demand for the Creator to open his eyes and heart, and truly bring him nearer to eternal adhesion with the Creator. It thus follows that all the rejections he had experienced came from the Creator.

This means that it was not because he was at fault, that he did not have the ability to overcome, that he had those rejections. Rather, for those people who truly want to draw near the Creator, and so they will not settle for little, so they will not remain as senseless children, he is therefore given help from Above, so he will not be able to say, "Thank God, I have Torah and *Mitzvot* and good deeds, and what else do I need?"

And only if that person has a true desire will he receive help from Above. And he is constantly shown that he is at fault in the present state. Namely, one is sent thoughts and views that are against the work. This is so he would see that he is not one with the Creator. And as much as he overcomes, he always sees how he is farther from holiness than others, who feel that they are one with the Creator.

But he, on the other hand, always has complaints and demands, and he cannot justify the Creator's behavior, and how He behaves with him. This pains him. Why is he not one with the Creator? Finally, he comes to feel that he has no part in holiness whatsoever.

Although he occasionally receives an awakening from Above, which momentarily revives him, soon after, he falls to a place of baseness. However, this is what causes him to come to realize that only the Creator can help and really bring him closer.

One should always try to go by a way of cleaving unto Him; namely, that all his thoughts will be about Him. That is to say, even if he is in the worst state, from which there cannot be a greater decline, he should not leave His domain, namely think that there is another authority, which prevents him from entering holiness, and which can bring benefit or harm.

That is, one must not think that there is the force of the *Sitra Achra* (Other Side), which does not let a person do good deeds and follow the ways of the Creator. Rather, one should think that all is done by the Creator.

It is as the Baal Shem Tov said, that one who says that there is another force in the world, namely *Klipot* (shells), that person is in a state of "serving other gods." It is not necessarily the thought of heresy that is the transgression, but if one thinks that there is another authority and force apart from the Creator, he is committing a sin.

Furthermore, he who says that man has his own authority, that is, he says that yesterday he himself did not want to follow the ways of the Creator, this, too, is considered committing the sin of heresy, meaning he does not believe that only the Creator is the leader of the world.

But when he has committed a sin, he must certainly regret it and be sorry for having committed it. But here, too, we should place the pain and sorrow in the right order: where does he place the cause of the sin? For that is the point that should be regretted.

Then, one should be remorseful and say: "I committed that sin because the Creator hurled me down from holiness to a place of filth, to the lavatory, the place of filth." That is to say, the Creator gave him a desire and craving to amuse himself and breathe air in a place of stench.

(And you might say of what is written in the books, that sometimes one comes incarnated as a pig, and receives a desire and craving to take liveliness from things he had already determined were litter. But now he wants to receive nourishment from them again.)

Also, when one feels that now he is in a state of ascent, and feels some good taste in the work, he must not say, "Now I am in a state that I understand that it is worthwhile to worship the Creator." Rather, one should know that now he was favored by the Creator, hence the Creator brought him closer, and for this reason he now feels good taste in the work. And one should be careful never to leave the domain of holiness and say that there is another who operates besides the Creator.

(But this means that the matter of being favored by the Creator, or the opposite, does not depend on the individual himself, but only on the Creator. And man, with his external mind, cannot comprehend why now the Creator has favored him and afterwards did not.)

Likewise, when he regrets that the Creator does not draw him near, he should also be careful that the sorrow would not concern him, that he is remote from the Creator. This is because by that, he becomes a receiver for his own benefit, and one who receives is separated from the Creator. Rather, one should regret the exile of the *Shechina* (Divinity), meaning that he is causing the sorrow of Divinity.

One should imagine that it is as though a small organ in the person is sore. Nonetheless, the pain is felt primarily in the mind and the heart. The heart and the mind are the whole of man. And certainly, the sensation of a single organ cannot resemble the sensation of a person's full stature, where the majority of the pain is felt.

Likewise is the pain that a person feels when he is remote from the Creator. This is because man is but a single organ of the Holy *Shechina*, for the Holy *Shechina* is the common soul of Israel. Hence, the individual sensation of pain does not resemble the collective sensation of the pain. This means that there is sorrow in the *Shechina* when the organs are detached from her, and she cannot nurture her organs.

(And perhaps this is the meaning of the verse: "When a person regrets, what does *Shechina* say? 'It is lighter than my head.'") By not relating the sorrow of remoteness to oneself, one is spared falling into the trap of the desire to receive for oneself, which is considered separation from holiness.

The same applies when one feels some closeness to holiness, when he feels joy at having been favored by the Creator. Then, too, one must say that his joy is primarily because now there is joy Above, in the Holy *Shechina*, because she could bring her private organ near her, and that she did not have to send her private organ away.

And one derives joy from being rewarded with pleasing the *Shechina*. This is in accord with the above calculation that when there is joy for the part, it is only a part of the joy of the whole. Through these calculations he loses his individuality and avoids being trapped by the net of the *Sitra Achra*, which is the will to receive for one's own sake.

Although the will to receive is necessary, since this is the whole of man, since anything that exists in a person apart from the will to receive does not belong to the creature, and we attribute it to the Creator, the will to receive pleasure should be corrected to being in order to bestow.

Namely, the pleasure and joy that the will to receive takes should be with the intention that there is contentment Above when the creatures feel pleasure, for this was the purpose of Creation—to benefit His creations. And this is called the joy of the *Shechina* Above.

For this reason, one must seek advice how he can bring contentment Above. And certainly, if he receives pleasure, contentment shall be felt Above. Therefore, he yearns to always be in the King's palace, and to have the ability to play with the King's treasures. And that will certainly bring contentment Above. It follows that one's longing should be only for the Creator.

The Reason for the Heaviness in the Work

We must know the reason for the heaviness felt when one wishes to work to annul one's "self" before the Creator, and to not care for one's own interest. One comes to a state as if the whole world stands still, and he alone is now seemingly absent from this world, and leaves his family and friends for the sake of annulling before the Creator.

There is but a simple reason for this, called "lack of faith." This means that one does not see before whom one nullifies, meaning he does not feel the existence of the Creator, and this causes him heaviness.

However, when one begins to feel the existence of the Creator, one's soul immediately yearns to be annulled and connected to the root, to be contained in it like a candle in a torch, without any mind or reason. However, this comes to one naturally, like a candle is annulled before a torch.

It therefore follows that the essence of one's work is only to come to the sensation of the existence of the Creator, to feel the existence of the Creator, that "the whole earth is full of His glory." This will be one's entire work, meaning all the vigor that he puts into the work will be only to achieve that, and not any other things.

One should not be misled into having to acquire anything else. Rather, there is only one thing a person needs, namely faith in the Creator. He should not think of anything, meaning that the only reward that he wants for his work should be to be rewarded with faith in the Creator.

We must know that there is no difference between a small illumination and a great one, which a person attains. This is because there are no changes in the Light. Rather, all the changes are in the vessels that receive the abundance, as it is written, "I the Lord change not." Hence, if one can magnify one's vessels, to that extent he magnifies the luminescence.

Yet, the question is, "With what can one magnify one's vessels?" The answer is, "To the extent that he praises and gives thanks to the Creator for having brought one closer to Him, so one would feel Him a little and think of the importance of the thing, meaning that he was rewarded with having some connection with the Creator."

As is the measure of importance that one pictures for oneself, so the measure of the luminescence grows in him. One must know that he will never come to know the true measure of the importance of the connection between man and the Creator, because one cannot assess its true value. Instead, to the extent that one appreciates it, he attains its merit and importance. There is a power in that, since thus one can be rewarded with having this illumination permanently.

Lishma Is an Awakening from Above

It is not in one's hands to understand how to be rewarded with *Lishma* (for Her Name). This is because the human mind cannot grasp how such a thing can be in the world. This is because one is only permitted to grasp that if one engages in Torah and *Mitzvot*, he will attain something. There must be self-gratification there, for otherwise, one is unable to do anything.

Instead, *Lishma* is an illumination that comes from Above, and only one who tastes it can know and understand. It is written about that, "Taste and see that the Lord is good."

Thus, we must understand why should one seek advice and counsel on how to achieve *Lishma*. After all, no counsel will help him, and if God does not give him the other nature, called "the Will to Bestow," no labor will help one to attain the matter of *Lishma*.

The answer is, as our sages said (*Avot*, 2:21), "It is not for you to complete the work, and you are not free to idle away from it." This means that one must give the awakening from below, since this is discerned as a prayer.

A prayer is considered a deficiency, and without a deficiency there is no fulfillment. Hence, when one has a need for *Lishma*, the fulfillment comes from Above, and the answer to the prayer comes from Above, meaning one receives fulfillment for one's need. It follows that one's work is needed to receive the *Lishma* from the Creator only in the form of a deficiency and a *Kli* (Vessel). Yet, one can never attain the fulfillment alone; it is rather a gift from the Creator.

However, the prayer must be a *whole* prayer, from the bottom of the heart. This means that one knows for certain that there is no one in the world who can help him but the Creator Himself.

Yet, how does one know that there is no one to help him but the Creator Himself? One can acquire that awareness precisely if he has exerted all the powers at his disposal to attain *Lishma*, and it did not help him. Thus, one must do every possible thing in the world to be rewarded with "for the Creator." Then one can pray from the bottom of one's heart, and then the Creator will hear his prayer.

However, one must know that when exerting to attain *Lishma*, one should take it upon himself to want to work entirely to bestow, completely, meaning only to bestow and to not receive anything. Only then does one begin to see that the organs do not agree to this idea.

From this, one can come to a clear awareness that he has no other counsel but to pour out his complaint before the Creator to help him so the body will agree to enslave itself to the Creator unconditionally, since one sees that he cannot persuade his body to annul its self entirely. It turns out that precisely when one sees that there is no reason to hope that his body will agree to work for the Creator by itself, one's prayer can be from the bottom of the heart, and then his prayer is accepted.

We must know that by attaining *Lishma*, one puts the evil inclination to death. The evil inclination is the will to receive, and acquiring the will to bestow cancels the will to receive from being able to do anything. This is considered putting it to death, since it removes it from its office; and it has nothing more to do since one no longer uses it. And when the evil inclination is revoked from its function, it is considered that one has put it to death.

And when one contemplates, "What profit hath man of all his labor... under the sun," he will see that it is not so difficult to enslave himself to His Name, for two reasons:

1. In any case, willingly or unwillingly, one must exert in this world, and what has one left of all the efforts he has made?
2. However, if one works *Lishma*, he receives pleasure during the work, as well.

This follows the proverb of the Sayer of Dubna about the verse, "Thou hast not called upon Me, O Jacob, neither hast thou wearied thyself about Me, O Israel." He said that it is like a rich man who departed the train with a small bag. He placed it where all the merchants place their baggage and the porters take the packages and bring them to the hotel where the merchants stay. The porter had thought that the merchant would certainly take a small bag by himself and there was no need for a porter for that, so the porter took a big package to the hotel.

The merchant wanted to pay him a small fee, as he usually pays for this small bag. But the porter did not want to take it, and said, "I put in the depository of the hotel a big bag; I could barely carry it, and it exhausted me, and you want to pay me so little for it?"

The lesson is that when one comes and says that he exerted extensively in keeping Torah and *Mitzvot*, the Creator tells him, "Thou hast not called upon Me, O Jacob." In other words, it is not my baggage that you took; this bag belongs to someone else. If you are saying you had great efforts in Torah and *Mitzvot*, you must have had a different landlord for whom you were working, so go to him to pay you.

This is the meaning of, "neither hast thou wearied thyself about Me, O Israel." In other words, one who works for the Creator has no labor whatsoever, but, on the contrary, pleasure and elated spirit.

But one who works for other goals cannot come to the Creator with complaints that the Creator does not give him vitality in the work, since he did not work for the Creator, for the Creator to pay him for his work. Instead, one can complain to those people that he had worked for, to administer him pleasure and vitality.

And since there are many goals in *Lo Lishma* (not for Her Name), one should demand of the goal for which he had worked that the goal would reward him, namely give him pleasure and vitality. It is said about them, "They that make them shall be like them, every one that trusts them."

However, according to that, it is perplexing. After all, we see that even when one takes upon oneself the burden of the Kingdom of Heaven without any other intention, he still feels no liveliness, to say that this liveliness compels him to assume the burden of the Kingdom of Heaven. And the reason one does assume the burden is only because of faith above reason.

In other words, one does it by way of coercive overcoming, unwillingly. Thus, we might ask, "Why does one feel exertion in this work, with the body constantly seeking a time when it can be rid of this work, as one does not feel any liveliness in the work?" And when one works in concealment, and has only the purpose of working in order to bestow, why does the Creator not impart him with flavor and vitality in the work?

The answer is that we must know that this is a great correction. Were it not for that, if Light and liveliness had illuminated as soon as one began to take upon himself the burden of the Kingdom of Heaven, one would have immediate liveliness in the work. In other words, the will to receive would consent to this work as well.

And why would it agree? Certainly, because it wishes to satisfy its craving, meaning it would work for its own benefit. Had that been so, it would never be possible to achieve *Lishma*, since one would be compelled to work for one's own benefit, as one would feel greater pleasure in the work of God than in corporeal desires. Thus, one would have to remain in *Lo Lishma*, since thus he would have had satisfaction in the work. And where there is satisfaction, one cannot do anything, as without profit, one cannot work. It follows that if one received satisfaction in this work of *Lo Lishma*, one would have to remain in that state.

This would be similar to what people say, that when people chase a thief to catch him, the thief, too, runs and yells, "Catch the thief." Then, it is impossible to tell who is the real thief, to catch him and retake the theft.

However, when the thief, the will to receive, does not feel any flavor or liveliness in the work of accepting the burden of the Kingdom of Heaven, if, in that state, one works with faith above reason, coercively, and the body becomes accustomed to this work against the desire of one's will to receive, then one has the means by which to come to a work that will be with the purpose of bringing contentment to one's Maker.

This is so because the primary requirement from a person is to achieve *Dvekut* (Adhesion) with the Creator through one's work, which is discerned as equivalence of form, where all of one's actions are in order to bestow.

It is as the verse says, "Then shalt thou delight thyself in the Lord." The meaning of "Then" is "before," that in the beginning of one's work, there was no pleasure. Instead, one's work was coercive.

However, afterwards, when one has already accustomed oneself to work in order to bestow, and to not examine oneself—if he is feeling a good taste in the work—but believes that he is working to bring contentment to his Maker through his work. And one should believe that the Creator accepts the labor of the lower ones regardless of how and how much is the form of their work. In everything, the Creator examines only the intention, and that this brings contentment to the Creator. Then one is granted with "delight thyself in the Lord."

Even during the work of God he will feel delight and pleasure, as now one really does work for the Creator, since the effort he had made during the coercive work qualifies one to be able to truly work for the Creator. You find that then, the pleasure that one receives relates to the Creator as well, meaning specifically for the Creator.

Support in the Torah

When a person is studying Torah and wants all his actions to be in order to bestow, one needs to try to always have support in the Torah. Support is considered nourishments, which are love, fear, elation, and freshness. And one should extract all that from the Torah. In other words, the Torah should give one these results.

However, when one studies Torah and does not have these results, it is not considered Torah. This is because Torah refers to the Light *clothed* in the Torah, as our sages said, "I have created the evil inclination, I have created the Torah as a spice." This refers to the Light in the Torah, since the Light in it reforms it.

We should also know that the Torah is divided into two discernments: 1-Torah, 2-*Mitzva*. In fact, it is impossible to understand these two discernments before one is rewarded with walking in the path of the Creator, by way of "The counsel of the Lord is with them that fear Him." This is so because when one is in a state of preparation to enter the Lord's Palace, it is impossible to understand the Path of Truth.

Yet, it is possible to give an example, which even a person in the preparation period may somewhat understand. It is written (*Sutah* 21), "Rabbi Yosef said, 'A *Mitzva* protects and saves while practiced, etc. The Torah protects and saves both when practiced and when not practiced.'"

"When practiced" means when one has some Light. One can use this Light he had obtained only while the Light is still in him, as now he is in gladness, since the Light shines for him. This is discerned as a *Mitzva*, meaning that he has not yet been rewarded with the Torah, but only elicits a life of *Kedusha* (holiness) from the Light.

This is not so with the Torah: When one attains some way in the work, one can use the way he has attained even when not practicing it, that is, while not engaging in it, meaning even while one does not have the Light. This is because only the luminescence has departed him, whereas one can use the way that one attained in the work even when the luminescence has departed him.

Still, one must also know that while practiced, a *Mitzva* is greater than the Torah when not practiced. "When practiced" means that now one receives the Light, which is called "practiced," when one receives the Light in it.

Hence, while one has the Light, a *Mitzva* is more important than the Torah when one has no Light, when there is no liveliness of the Torah. On the one hand, the Torah is important because one can use the way one has acquired in the Torah. Yet, it is without vitality, called "Light." And in a time of engaging in a *Mitzva*, one does receive vitality, called "Light." In this respect, a *Mitzva* is more important than the Torah.

Thus, when one is without sustenance, one is considered "evil." This is because now one cannot say that the Creator leads the world in a conduct of "Good that Doeth Good." It is considered that he is evil since he condemns his Maker, as now he feels that he has no vitality, and has nothing to be glad about so that he may say that now he is grateful for the Creator, for bestowing upon him delight and pleasure.

One cannot say that he believes that the Creator leads His Providence with others benevolently, since we understand the path of Torah as a sensation in the organs. If one does not feel the delight and pleasure, what does it give him that another person is experiencing sensations of delight and pleasure?

If one had really believed that Providence is revealed as benevolence to his friend, that belief should have brought him delight and pleasure from believing that the Creator leads the world in a guidance of delight and pleasure. And if this does not bring one liveliness and joy, what is the benefit in saying that the Creator does watch over one's friend with a guidance of benevolence?

The most important is what one feels in one's own body—either good or bad. One enjoys one's friend's pleasure only if he enjoys his friend's benefit. In other words, we learn only by the sensation of the body, regardless of the reasons. What is important is only if one feels good.

In that state, one says that the Creator is "good and does good." If one feels bad, one cannot say that the Creator behaves toward him in the form of the good who does good. Thus, precisely if one enjoys one's friend's happiness, and receives high spirits and gladness from that, then he can say that the Creator is a good leader. If one has no joy, he feels bad. Thus, how can he say that the Creator is benevolent?

Therefore, everything follows the state one is in. If one has no liveliness or gladness, he is in a state of having no love for the Creator, no ability to justify his Maker, and no gladness, as would be fitting for one who serves a great and important king.

And we must know that the Upper Light is in a state of complete rest. And any expansion of the Holy Names occurs by the lower ones. In other words, all the names that the Upper Light has, come from the attainment of the lower ones. This means that the Upper Light is named according to their attainments. Put differently, one names the Light according to the way one attains it, according to one's sensation.

If one does not feel that the Creator gives him anything, what name can he give to the Creator if he does not receive a thing from Him? Rather, when one believes in the Creator, every single state that one feels, he says that it comes to him from the Creator. And according to one's feeling, one names the Creator.

Thus, if one feels good in the state he is in, he says that the Creator is called "Benevolent," since that is what he feels—that he receives goodness from Him. In that state, one is called *Tzadik* (Righteous), since he *Matzdik* (justifies) his Maker.

And if one feels bad in the state he is in, he cannot say that the Creator sends him good. Therefore, in that state one is called *Rasha* (Evil), since he *Marshia* (Condemns) his Maker.

However, there is no such thing as in-between, when one says that he feels both good and bad in his state. Instead, one is either happy or unhappy.

Our sages wrote (*Berachot* 61), "The world was not created...but either for the complete wicked, or for the complete righteous." This is so because there is no such thing as feeling good and bad simultaneously.

When our sages say that there is in-between, it is that with the creatures, who have a discernment of time, you can say "in-between" about two times, one after the other, as we learn that there is a matter of ascents and descents. These are two times: once he is wicked, and once he is righteous. But in a single moment, for one to feel good and bad simultaneously, this does not exist.

It follows that when they said that the Torah is more important than a *Mitzva*, it is precisely at a time when he does not engage in it, when one has no vitality. Then the Torah is more important than a *Mitzva*, which has no vitality.

This is so because one cannot receive anything from a *Mitzva*, which has no vitality. But with the Torah, one still has a way in the work from what he had received while he was practicing the Torah. Although the vitality has departed, the way remains in him, and he can use it. And there is a time when a *Mitzva* is more important than the Torah: when there is vitality in the *Mitzva* and no vitality in the Torah.

Thus, when not practiced, when one has no vitality or gladness in the work, one has no other counsel but prayer. However, during the prayer, one must know that he is evil because he does not feel the delight and pleasure that exist in the world, although he calculates that he can believe that the Creator gives only goodness.

Yet, not all of one's thoughts are true in the way of the work. In the work, if the thought leads to action, meaning a sensation in the organs, so the organs feel that the Creator is benevolent, the organs should receive vitality and gladness from it. And if one has no vitality, what good are all the calculations if now the organs do not love the Creator because He imparts them with abundance?

Thus, one should know that if one has no vitality or gladness in the work, it is a sign that he is wicked, because he is unhappy. All the calculations are untrue if they do not yield an act, a sensation in the organs that one loves the Creator because He imparts delight and pleasure to the creatures.

Habit Becomes Second Nature

Through accustoming oneself to something, that thing becomes second nature for that person. Hence, there is nothing in the world that one cannot feel its existence. This means that although one has no sensation of the thing, by accustoming to that thing, one can still come to feel it.

We must know that there is a difference between the Creator and the creatures regarding sensations. For the creatures, there is the feeler and the felt, the attaining and the attained. This means that we have a feeler, which is connected to some reality.

However, a reality without a feeler is only the Creator Himself. In Him, "there is no thought and perception whatsoever." This is not so with a person: his whole existence is only through the sensation of reality, and even the validity of reality is evaluated only with respect to the one who senses the reality.

In other words, what the feeler tastes is what he considers true. If one tastes a bitter taste in reality, meaning he feels bad in the state he is in, and suffers because of that state, that person is considered wicked, in the work. This is because he condemns the Creator, since the Creator is called "the good who does good," because He bestows only goodness to the world. Yet, with respect to that person's feeling, the person feels that he has received the opposite from the Creator, meaning the state he is in is bad.

We should therefore understand what is written (*Berachot* p 61), "The world was created only for complete righteous or complete wicked." This means the following: either one tastes and feels a good taste in the world, and then one justifies the Creator and says that the Creator gives only goodness to the world, or, if one feels and tastes a bitter taste in the world, then one is wicked, since he condemns the Creator.

It turns out that everything is measured according to one's own sensation. However, all these sensations have no relation to the Creator, as it written in the *Poem of Unification*: "As she, so you will always be, shortage and surplus in you will not be." Hence, all the worlds and all the changes are only with respect to the receivers, according to the attaining individual.

The Difference between a Shade of Kedusha and a Shade of Sitra Achra

It is written (Song of Songs, 2), "Until the day breathes, and the shadows flee away." We must understand what are shadows in the work, and what is "two shadows." The thing is that when one does not feel His Providence, that the Creator leads the world in a manner of "Good that doeth good," it is regarded as a shadow hiding the sun.

In other words, as the corporeal shadow that hides the sun does not change the sun in any way, and the sun shines in its fullest power, so one who does not feel the existence of His Providence does not induce any change Above, as it is written, "I the Lord do not change."

Instead, all the changes are in the receivers. We must observe two discernments in this shade, in this concealment:

1. When one still has the ability to overcome the darkness and the concealments that one feels, justify the Creator, and pray to the Creator, that the Creator will open his eyes to see that all the concealments that one is feeling come from the Creator, that the Creator is doing all that to him so he would reveal his prayer and yearn to cleave unto Him.

   This is so because only through the suffering that one receives from Him, wishing to break free from one's trouble and escape the torments, then one does everything he can. Hence, when receiving the concealments and the afflictions, one is certain to make the known remedy: to do much praying for the Creator to help him and deliver him from the state he is in. In that state, one still believes in His Providence.

2. When one comes to a state where he can no longer prevail and say that all the suffering and pains one feels are because the Creator had sent them to him so as to have a reason to ascend in degree. Then one comes to a state of heresy, since one cannot believe in His Providence, and naturally, then one cannot pray.

It follows that there are two kinds of shades. And this is the meaning of, "and the shadows flee away," meaning that the shadows will flee from the world.

The shade of *Klipa* (Shell) is called "Another god is sterile and does not bear fruit." However, a shade of *Kedusha* (holiness) is called, "Under its shadow I delighted to sit, and its fruit was sweet to my palate." In other words, one says that all the concealments and the afflictions one feels are because the Creator has sent him these states, to have a place to work above reason.

And when one has the strength to say that, that is, that the Creator causes him all that, it is to one's benefit. This means that through it, one can come to work in order to bestow and not to benefit oneself. At that time, one comes to realize, meaning believe that the Creator enjoys specifically this work, which is built entirely above reason.

It follows that one does not pray to the Creator that the shadows will flee from the world. Rather, one says, "I see that the Creator wants me to serve Him in this manner, entirely above reason." Thus, in everything that one does, he says, "The Creator certainly enjoys this work, so why should I care if I work in a state of concealment of the face? After all, I want to work in order to bestow, that the Creator will enjoy. Hence, I have no abasement from this work, meaning a sensation of being in a state of concealment of the Face, that the Creator does not enjoy this work." Instead, one agrees to the leadership of the Creator, and one wholeheartedly agrees to however the Creator wants one to feel the existence of the Creator during the work. This is so because one does not consider what he can enjoy, but considers what the Creator can enjoy. Thus, this shade brings him life.

This is called, "Under its shadow I delighted," meaning one covets such a state where one can make some overcoming above reason. Thus, if one does not exert in a state of concealment, when there is still room to pray that the Creator will bring him closer, but he is negligent in that, hence one is sent a second concealment in which one cannot even pray. This is so because of the sin—that he did not exert with all his might to pray to the Creator. For this reason, one comes to such lowliness.

But after one has arrived at this state, one is pitied from Above, and he is given an awakening from Above once more. And the same order begins, until finally one strengthens in prayer, and the Creator hears his prayer and brings him closer and reforms it.

The Essence of One's Work

The essence of one's work should be how to come to feel taste in bestowing contentment upon one's Maker, since all that one does for oneself distances him from the Creator due to disparity of form. However, if one performs an act for the benefit of the Creator, even the smallest act, it is still considered a *Mitzva* (commandment/good deed).

Hence, one's primary exertion should be to acquire a force that feels taste in bestowing, which is through lessening the force that feels taste in self-reception. In that state, one slowly acquires the flavor in bestowing.

Lishma

In order for a person to obtain *Lishma* (for Her Name), one needs an awakening from Above because it is an illumination from Above, and it is not for the human mind to understand it. But he who tastes, knows. It is said about that, "Taste and see that the Lord is good."

Because of that, upon assuming the burden of the Kingdom of Heaven, one needs for it to be in utter completeness, meaning only to bestow and not at all to receive. And if a person sees that the organs do not agree with this view, he has no other counsel but prayer—to pour his heart out to the Creator, to help him make his body consent to enslaving itself to the Creator.

And one should not say that if *Lishma* is a gift from Above, then what good is one's strengthening in his work, and all the remedies and corrections that one performs in order to come to *Lishma*, if it depends on the Creator? Our sages said in that regard, "You are not free to rid yourself of it." Rather, one must offer the awakening from below, and this is considered "prayer." But there cannot be a true prayer if he does not know in advance that it is impossible to attain *Lishma* without prayer.

Therefore, the acts and remedies that he performs in order to obtain *Lishma* create the corrected vessels within him, to want to receive *Lishma*. And after all the actions and the remedies, then he can make an honest prayer, since he has seen that all his actions brought him no benefit. Only then can he make an honest prayer from the bottom of his heart, and then the Creator hears his prayer and gives him the gift of *Lishma*.

We should also know that by obtaining *Lishma*, one puts the evil inclination to death. This is because the evil inclination is called "receiving for one's own benefit." And by attaining the aim to bestow, one cancels the self-gratification.

And death means that one no longer uses one's vessels of reception for oneself. And since he has revoked the role of the evil inclination, it is considered dead.

If one considers what one receives for his work under the sun, one will find that it is not so difficult to subjugate oneself to the Creator, for two reasons:

1. One must strain oneself in this world in any case, whether one wants to or not.
2. Even during the work, if one works *Lishma*, one receives pleasure from the work itself.

It is as the Sayer from Dubna says about the verse, "Thou has not called upon Me oh Jacob, neither has thou worried thyself about me oh Israel." It means that he who works for the Creator has no effort. On the contrary, one has pleasure and elation.

But he who does not work for the Creator, but for other goals, cannot complain to the Creator for not giving him liveliness in the work, since he is working for another goal. One can complain only to the one he works for, and demand to be given vitality and pleasure during his work. It is said about him: "Anyone that trusts them shall be like them that maketh them."

Do not be surprised that when one assumes the burden of the Kingdom of Heaven, when he wants to work in order to bestow upon the Creator, that he still feels no vitality at all, and that this vitality would compel him to assume the burden of the Kingdom of Heaven. Rather, one should accept the burden of the Kingdom of Heaven coercively, feeling that it is not to his benefit. Meaning, the body does not agree to this work, why the Creator does not shower him with vitality and pleasure.

The reason for it is that this is a great correction. Were it not for that, the will to receive would agree to this work, and one would never have been able to achieve *Lishma*. Rather, he would always work for his own benefit, to satisfy his own desires. It is as people say, that the thief himself runs and yells, "Catch the thief!" And then you cannot tell which is the real thief, to catch him and reclaim the theft.

But when the thief, meaning the will to receive, does not find the work of accepting the burden of the Kingdom of Heaven tasteful, since the body accustoms itself to work against its own desire, one has the means by which to come to work only in order to bring contentment to one's Maker, since one's sole intention should be only for the Creator, as it is written, "Then shalt thou delight thyself in the Lord." Previously, when he was working for the Creator, he did not derive pleasure from his work. Rather his work was done by coercion.

But now that one has accustomed oneself to work in order to bestow, one is rewarded with delighting in the Creator, and the work itself renders one pleasure and vitality. And this is considered that the pleasure, too, is specifically for the Creator.

The Time of Ascent

When one feels oneself in a state of ascent, that he is high-spirited, when he feels that he has no desire but only for spirituality, it is then good to delve into the secrets of the Torah, to attain its internality. Even if one sees that although one exerts oneself to understand anything, and still does not know anything, it is still worthwhile to delve in the secrets of the Torah, even a hundred times in a single thing, and not despair, meaning say that it is useless, since he does not understand anything.

This is so for two reasons:

A) When one examines some issue and yearns to understand it, that yearning is called "a prayer." This is because a prayer is a lack, meaning that one is craving what he lacks, that the Creator will fill his lack.

The extent of the prayer is measured by the desire, since the greater desire is for the thing one needs most. According to the measure of the need, so is the measure of the yearning.

There is a rule that in the thing that one makes the most effort, the exertion increases the desire, and one wants to receive fulfillment for one's deficiency. Also, a lack is called "a prayer," or "the work in the heart," since "the Merciful One wants the hearts."

It turns out that then one can offer a true prayer. And when one studies the words of the Torah, the heart must be freed from other desires and give the mind the strength to be able to think and scrutinize. If there is no desire in the heart, the mind cannot scrutinize, as it is written, "One should always learn where one's heart desires."

For one's prayer to be accepted, it must be a complete prayer. Hence, when scrutinizing in a whole measure, one elicits a whole prayer from it, and then one's prayer can be accepted, because the Creator hears a prayer. But there is a condition: the prayer must be a whole prayer, and not have other things mixed in the middle of the prayer.

B) The second reason is that since one has separated from corporeality, and is somewhat closer to the quality of bestowal, it is a better time to connect with the internality of the Torah, which appears to those who have equivalence with the Creator. This is because the Torah, the Creator, and Israel are one. However, when one is in a state of self-reception, he belongs to the externality and not to the internality.

You Who Love the Lord Hate Evil

In the verse, "O ye that love the Lord, hate evil; He preserveth the souls of His followers; He delivered them out of the hand of the wicked," he interprets that it is not enough to love the Creator and to want to be granted adhesion with the Creator. One should also hate evil.

The matter of hatred towards evil is expressed by hating the evil, called "the will to receive." And one sees that one has no tactic to be rid of it, and at the same time one does not want to accept the situation. And one feels the losses that the evil causes him, and also sees the truth that one cannot annul the evil by himself, since it is a natural force by the Creator, who has imprinted the will to receive in man.

In that state, the verse tells us what one can do, meaning hate evil. And by that the Creator will keep him from that evil, as it is written, "He preserveth the souls of His followers." And what is the preservation? "He delivered them out of the hand of the wicked." In that state one is already a successful person, since he has some contact with the Creator, be it the tiniest connection.

In fact, the matter of evil remains and serves as *Achoraim* (Posterior) to the *Partzuf*. But this is done only by one's correction: through sincere hatred of evil, it is corrected into a form of *Achoraim*. The hatred comes because if one wants to obtain adhesion with the Creator, then there is a conduct among friends: if two people come to realize that each of them hates what and whom one's friend hates, and loves what and whom one's friend loves, then they come into perpetual bonding, like a stake that will never fall.

Hence, since the Creator loves to bestow, the lower ones should also adapt to want only to bestow. And as the Creator hates to be a receiver, since He is completely whole and does not need a thing, man, too, must hate the matter of reception for oneself.

It follows that one must bitterly hate the will to receive, for all the ruins in the world come only from the will to receive. And through the hatred, one corrects it and enters the *Kedusha* (holiness).

Raising the Slave through the Ministers

It is written, "for one higher than the high watcheth, and there are higher than they." As a fierce answer is required, I shall answer you that everyone believes in Private Providence, but does not adhere to it at all.

The reason is that an alien and foul thought cannot be attributed to the Creator, who is the epitome of the "Good that doeth Good." However, only to the true servants of the Creator does the knowledge of Private Providence open—that He caused all the reasons that preceded it, the good as well as the bad. Then they are cohesive with Private Providence, for all who are connected to the pure, are pure.

Since the Guardian is united with its guarded, there is no apparent division between bad and good. They are all loved and they are all clear, for they are all carriers of the Creator's vessels, ready to glorify the revelation of His uniqueness. It is known by sensing, and to that extent they have knowledge in the end that all the actions and the thoughts, both good and bad, are the carriers of the Creator's vessels. He has prepared them, from His mouth they have come, and this will be known to all at the end of correction.

However, in between it is a long and threatening exile. The biggest trouble is that when one sees some wrongful action, he falls from his degree, clings to the famous lie, and forgets that he is like an ax in the hand of the cutter. Instead, one considers oneself the owner of this act and forgets the reason for all consequences from whom everything comes, and that there is no other Operator in the world but Him.

This is the lesson. Although one knows it at first, still, in a time of need, one does not control this awareness, to unite everything with the cause, which sentences to a scale of merit. This is the whole reply to his letter.

I have already told you face to face a true allegory about these two concepts, where one elucidates the other. Yet, the force of concealment prevails and controls in between.

There is an allegory about a king who grew fond of his servant until he wanted to raise him above all the ministers, for he had recognized true and unwavering love in his heart.

However, it is not the royal manner to raise one to the highest level all at once, without an apparent reason. Rather, the royal manner is to reveal the reasons to all with great wisdom.

What did he do? He appointed the servant a guard at the city gate, and told a minister, who was a clever joker, to pretend to rebel against the kingship, and wage war to conquer the house while the guard was unprepared.

The minister did as the king had commanded, and with great wisdom and craftiness pretended to fight against the king's house. The servant at the gate risked his life and saved the king, fighting bravely and devotedly against the minister, until his great love for the king was evident to all.

Then the minister took off his clothes and there was great laughter, for he had fought so fiercely and bravely, and now realized that there was only fiction here, not reality. They laughed most when the minister told of the depth of the imaginings of his cruelty and the fear he had envisioned. And every item in this terrible war became a round of laughter and great joy.

However, he was still a servant; he was not scholarly. And how could he be raised above all the ministers and the king's servants?

Then the king thought, and said to that minister that he must disguise himself as a robber and a murderer, and wage fierce war against him. The king knew that in the second war he would discover a wondrous wisdom, and merit standing at the head of all the ministers.

Hence, he appointed the servant in charge of the kingdom's treasury, and that minister now dressed as a ruthless killer and came to loot the king's treasures.

The poor appointee fought fearlessly and devotedly, until the cup was full. Then the minister took off his clothes and there was great joy and laughter in the king's palace, even more than before.

The details of the minister's tricks aroused great laughter, since now the minister had to be smarter than before because now it was evidently known that no one was cruel in the king's domain, and all the cruel ones were only jokers. Therefore, the minister used great craftiness to acquire clothes of evil.

Yet, in the meantime, the servant inherited wisdom from after-knowledge, and love from fore-knowledge, and then he was erected for eternity.

In truth, all the wars in that exile are a wondrous sight, and everyone knows in their kind interior that it is all a kind of wit and joy that brings only good. Still, there is no tactic to ease the weight of the war and the threat.

I have spoken to you at length about it face to face, and now you have knowledge of one end of this allegory, and with the Creator's help you will understand it on its other end, as well.

And the thing you most want to hear me speak of is one to which I cannot answer anything. I have given you an allegory about it face to face, as well, for "the kingdom of the earth is as the kingdom of the firmament," and the true guidance is given to the ministers.

Yet, everything is done according to the king's counsel and his signature. The king himself does no more than sign the plan that the ministers devise. If he finds a flaw in the plan, he does not correct it, but places another minister in his place, and the first resigns from office.

So is man, a small world, behaving according to the letters imprinted in him, since kings rule the seventy nations in him. This is the meaning of what is written in the *Sefer Yetzira* (*Book of Creation*): "He crowned a certain letter." Each letter is a minister for its time, making evaluations, and the King of the world signs them. When the letter errs in some plan, it immediately resigns from office, and He crowns another letter in its place.

This is the meaning of, "Each generation and its judges." At the end of correction, that letter called Messiah will rule and will complete and tie all the generations to a crown of glory in the hand of God.

Now you can understand how I can interfere with your business of state, and each must uncover what he has been assigned to uncover, and all will become clear through the incarnations.

PARDESS

"Four entered a PARDESS,"[7] etc. Before the world was created, there was He is One and His Name One, because the souls were not considered souls, since the whole issue of name refers to when one turns one's face away from Him, He calls upon him to turn his face back.

And since prior to Creation, the souls were completely attached to Him, and He placed upon them crowns and wreaths, glory, majesty, and splendor, even what they did not evoke, since He knows their wishes by Himself, and grants them. Hence, it is certainly irrelevant to state a name, which relates to an awakening from below of some side. Hence, it is considered Simple Light, since everything is in utter simplicity, and this Light was understood by every simple person, even to those who have never seen any wisdom.

This is why sages and the wise called it *Peshat* (literal), since the *Peshat* is the root of everything. Authors and books do not discuss it, as it is one, simple, and famous concept. And although in the lower worlds, two divisions are detected in the *Reshimo* of this Simple Light, it is because of the division in their own hearts, by way of "and I am a smooth man."[8] Yet, in the above-mentioned place, there are no changes in any depiction you might make.

It is like a king who took his darling son and put him in his grand and wondrous grove. And when the son opened his eyes, he did not look at the place where he stood, since due to the great light in the grove, his eyes wandered far away, as the east is far from the west. And he cast his eyes only on the buildings and palaces far to his west, and he walked for days and months, wandering and wondering at the glory and the grandeur he was seeing to the west, before his eyes.

---

[7] Translator's note: In Hebrew, *Pardess* means grove, but in Kabbalah, this word is an acronym for *Pshat* (the literal Torah), *Remez* (intimation), *Drush* (interpretations), and *Sod* (secret).
[8] Translator's note: In Hebrew, *Halak* means both 'smooth' and 'part.'

After some months, his spirit rested and his desire was fulfilled, and he was satiated from looking to the west. He reconsidered and thought, "What can be found along the way I have traversed?" He turned his face eastward, the side through which he had entered, and he was startled. All the grandeur and all the beauty were right beside him. He could not understand himself, how he had failed to notice it thus far, and clung only to the Light that was shining to the west. From then on he was attached only to the Light that shines to the east, and he was wandering eastward until he returned right to the entrance gate.

Now do consider and tell me the difference between the days of entry and the days of exit, since all that he had seen in the latter months, he saw in the early months, as well. But in the beginning, he was not inspired, since his eyes and heart were taken by the Light that shines westward. And after he was satiated, he turned his face eastward and noticed the Light that shines towards the east. But how had it changed?

But being near the entrance, there is room for disclosing the second manner, which the sages call *Remez* (intimation), as in "What do thine eyes imply?" It is like a king who hints to his darling son and frightens him with a wink of his eye. And although the son does not understand at all, and does not see the inner fear that is hidden in this hint, still, due to his devout adherence to his father, he promptly jumps from there to another side.

This is the meaning of the second manner being called *Remez*, since the two manners, *Peshat* and *Remez*, are registered in the lower ones as one root, as the meticulous ones write, that there is not a word that does not have a two-letter root, called the "source of the word." This is so because no meaning can be deduced from a single letter; hence, the acronym for *Peshat* and *Remez* is *PR* (pronounced *Par*), which is the root of *Par Ben Bakar* (young bull) in this world. And *Pria* and *Revia* (multiplication) come from that root, as well.

Next appears the third manner, which the sages call *Drush* (interpretations). Hence, there was no *Drisha* (demand) for anything, as in "He is One and His Name One." But in this manner, there is subtraction, addition, interpretation (studying), and finding, as in "I labored and found," as you evidently know. This is why this place is ascribed to the lower ones, since there is an awakening from below there, unlike the illumination of the face of the east Upwards, which was by way of, "Before they call, I will answer." Rather, here there was a powerful call, and even exertion and craving, and this is the meaning of "the graves of lust."

Afterwards begins the fourth manner, which the sages call *Sod* (secret). In truth, it is similar to the *Remez*, but in the *Remez* there was no perception whatsoever; it was rather like a shadow following a person, and all the more so that the third manner, the *Drush*, has already clothed it.

Yet, here it is like a whisper, like a pregnant woman... you whisper in her ear that today is *Yom Kippur* (Day of Atonement), so the fetus would not be jolted and fall. And we might say, "Moreover, it is the concealment of the face, and not the face!" For this is the meaning of the words, "The counsel of the Lord is with them that fear Him; and His covenant, to make them know it." This is why he made several circles until a whispering tongue said this to him: "He hath given *Teref* (food) unto them that fear Him," and not *Trefa* (non-kosher food), as that soldier sneered.

You understood this answer by yourself, and you wrote me in your letter, though timidly, that you are a bachelor, and hence, naturally polite.

Since this verse came into your hands, I shall clarify it to you, as this is also the poet's question, "The counsel of the Lord is with them that fear Him." And why did he say so? It is as our sages' question, where we find that the text wastes (eight) twelve letters, to speak with a clean tongue, as it is written, "and of the beasts that are not clean," etc.

But your answer does not suffice the poet, for He could have given abundance to the souls, and with a clean tongue, as Laban said to Jacob, "Wherefore didst thou flee secretly, and outwit me; and didst not tell me, that I might have sent thee away with mirth and with songs, with tabret and with harp." The poet's answer to that is, "and His covenant, to make them know it."

This is the meaning of the cutting, the removal, and the drop of blood, meaning the individual thirteen covenants. Had the secret not been in this manner, but in another tongue, four corrections from the thirteen corrections of *Dikna* would be missing, and only the nine corrections of *Dikna* in ZA would remain. Thus, ZA would not be clothing AA, as it is known to those who know God's secret. This is the meaning of "and His covenant, to make them know it," and this is the meaning of "ancestral merit has ended, but ancestral covenant has not ended."

Let us get back to our issue, which is *PR* (pronounced *Par*), *PRD* (pronounced *Pered*), and *PRDS* (pronounced *Pardess*). This is their order and combination from Above downwards. Now you will understand these four sages who entered the *Pardess*, meaning the fourth manner, called *Sod* (secret), since the lower one contains the Upper Ones that preceded it. Hence, all four manners are included in the fourth manner, and they are to the right, left, front, and back.

The first two manners are the right and the left, meaning *PR* (this is the meaning of his words on the step at the Temple Mount: "All of Israel's sages are worthless in my eyes"). These are Ben Azai and Ben Zuma, as these souls nurtured off the two manners, *PR*. And the last two manners are the *Panim* (front) and *Achor* (back), which is Rabbi Akiva, who entered in peace and came out in peace. They correctly stated, "it indicates that for every thistle, mountains of laws can be learned."

Achor is Elisha Ben Avoia, who went astray (became heretical). Our sages said about that, "One shall not raise an evil dog within one's home," for it is going astray. Everything that was said about them—"peeped and died," "peeped and was hurt," "went astray"—is said of that generation when they have gathered closely together, but were all completely corrected, one by one, as it is known to those who know the secret of reincarnation.

Yet, after he saw the tongue of Hutzpit, the translator, he said, "Return, O backsliding children," except for the other, and Rabbi Meir, Rabbi Akiva's disciple, took his place. It is true that the Gemarah, too, finds it difficult: how did Rabbi Meir learn Torah from another? And they said, "He had found a pomegranate, ate its content, and threw its shell (another)." And some say that he corrected the *Klipa* (shell), too, as in, raising smoke over his grave.

Now you can understand Elisha Ben Avoia's words: "He who teaches a child, what is he like? Like ink, written on a new paper," meaning the soul of Rabbi Akiva. "And he who teaches an old man, what is he like? Like ink, written on used paper," he said of himself. This is the meaning of his warning to Rabbi Meir, "Thus far the Shabbat zone," for he understood and estimated his horse's steps, since he had never come off from his horse.

This is the meaning of "the transgressors of Israel, the fire of hell does not govern them, and they are as filled with *Mitzvot* (good deeds) as a pomegranate." He says that it is all the more so with the golden altar, which is merely as thick as a golden coin. It stood for some years, and the light did not govern it, etc., "the vain among you are as filled with *Mitzvot* as a pomegranate, all the more so," as he says, that the *Klipa*, too, is corrected.

Know that the great Rabbi Eliezer, and Rabbi Yehosha, too, are from the souls of *PR*, as are Ben Azai and Ben Zuma. But Ben Azai and Ben Zuma were in the generation of Rabbi Akiva, and were his students, among the 24,000. But Rabbi Eliezer and Rabbi Yehosha were his teachers.

This is why it is said that instead of Rabbi Eliezer, they were purifying the purifications (*Peshat*) that they had done over Achnai's oven, since they cut it into slices (eighteen slices) and placed sand between every two slices. In other words, the third manner, the sand, joins the first slice, which is the second manner, and the second slice, which is the fourth manner. And naturally, the sister and the awareness are conjoined as one. And Rabbi Tarfon and Rabbi Yehosha as one are disciples of the great Rabbi Eliezer. And Rabbi Akiva is seemingly included in them. This is because a second good day, with respect to the first good day, is like a weekday in the eyes of our sages, since the *Drush*, compared to the *Remez*, is like a candle at noon.

But the sages of his generation defiled all those purifications and burned them, and the great Rabbi Eliezer proved with the aqueduct whose water rose that Rabbi Yehosha was a great sage, and the walls of the Temple will prove. And they began to fall before the glory of Rabbi Eliezer, and they did not fall before the glory of Rabbi Yehosha. This is complete proof that there is no doubt that he is pure.

But the sages took Rabbi Yehosha for himself, and did not wish to rule as with Rabbi Eliezer, his teacher, until a voice came down that Rabbi Yehosha was really his disciple. But Rabbi Yehosha did not connect to his place, and said that you do not pay heed to a voice: "It is not in heaven," etc. Then, sages blessed him, for the Light of *Awzen* (ear) was cancelled from them, since they did not obey the rules of the great Rabbi Eliezer. And Rabbi Akiva, his favorite disciple, told him that his 24,000 disciples had died during the count, and the world was sickened, a third in olives, etc.

Elisha Ben Avoia and Rabbi Tarfon came from the same root. But Elisha Ben Avoia is the *Achoraim* (posterior) itself, and Rabbi Tarfon is the *Panim de Achoraim* (face of the posterior). To what is this likened? In one house lie bitter olives that are good for nothing; and in another house lays the beam of the oil-press, which is good for nothing. Then a man comes and connects the two. He places the beam over the olives and produces a wealth of oil.

It follows that the good oil that appears is the *Panim*, and the beam is the *Achoraim*. And the plain wooden tools are thrown away after they have completed their work.

Understand that this custom is in the expansion of the roots to the branches in worlds lower than itself. But at their root, they both appear at once, like a person who suddenly enters the oil-press and sees the beam, and under it, a large pile of olives with oil abundantly flowing from them. This is so because at the root, all is seen at once. This is why one is called "another" and the other is called "Tarfon." One is "a beam" and the other is "oil," which immediately flows through it.

This is also the meaning of going astray. After the desire has emerged, which is the soul of Rabbi Tarfon, the soul of "another" remained as "bad manners" in one's home. This is the meaning of the letter-combination *Sod* (secret): *Samech* is the head of the word *Sod* itself, the soul of "another," *Dalet* is the head of the word *Drush*, the soul of Rabbi Akiva, because they act, and the *Vav* in the middle is Rabbi Tarfon.

Sit and Do Nothing—Better

...I can no longer restrain myself with all that stands between us, so I will try the true, open admonition, for I need to know the true value of a word of truth in our land. This has always been my way—to meticulously delve into all of Creation's actions, to know their value, precisely whether it is good or bad.

My fathers have left me with only this boundary, and I have already found treasures in these passing, idle images, for there is a reason why this lot was placed before my eyes. These are lovely letters for phrasing every wisdom and every knowledge, which were created only for combinations of wisdom.

First, let us judge the attribute of indolence in this world. In general, it is not at all a bad and contemptible attribute. The proof of that is that our sages have already said, "Sit and do nothing—better." And although common sense and some texts deny this rule, to be properly accurate about it, I will show that "both are the words of the living God," and all will be settled.

It is certainly clear that there are no actions in the world except His actions. And all other kinds of actions, besides His, even in souls, if they concern one's own self, would be better off to not have been created. This is because it turns things upside-down, since one has not changed from receiving to bestowing. This is an unbreakable law, "and had he been there, he would not have been redeemed."

Thus, we need not discuss an operator or an operation whose doer is in the form of receiving, as this is complete vanity, and there is no doubt it would be better off sitting and doing nothing, since with such an act, one either harms oneself or others. It cannot yield any benefit, as we have said above.

I do not mind at all if some of your 248 organs feel uncomfortable about this ruling, and even openly protest against my words, as this is the nature of every word of truth: it does not require the consent of any woman born, great or small. And whoever is rewarded with the knowledge of the Torah becomes most insistent.

If I Am Not for Me, Who Is for Me?

I have already said in the name of the Baal Shem Tov that prior to making a *Mitzva*, one must not consider Private Providence at all. Instead, one should say, "If I am not for me, who is for me?" But after the fact, one must reconsider and believe that it is not "by my power and the might of my hand" that I did this *Mitzva*, but only by the power of the Creator, who planned it for me in advance, and thus I was compelled to do it.

This is also the order in worldly matters, for spirituality and corporeality are equal. Hence, before one leaves for work to make his daily earnings, he should remove his thoughts from Private Providence and say, "If I am not for me, who is for me," and do everything that is done in corporeality to earn one's living as they do.

But in the evening, when he returns home with his earnings, he should never think that his own resourcefulness has gotten him this profit. Rather, even if he were lying in the basement all day long, he would still earn his living, since this is what the Creator had planned for him in advance, and this is how it must be.

And even though it seems contradictory and unacceptable to the superficial mind, one must still believe so, as this is what the Creator has written of him in His law from books and from authors.

This is the meaning of the unification of *HaVaYaH-Elokim*. *HaVaYaH* is Private Providence, where the Creator does everything, and He does not need the help of dwellers of clay houses. *Elokim* (God), in *Gematria*, is "the nature." And one who behaves according to the nature He had imprinted in the systems of the corporeal heaven and earth, and keeps their laws like the rest of the corporeal ones, and at the same time believes in the name *HaVaYaH*, meaning

Private Providence, unites them, and they become one in his hand. Thus, he renders much contentment to his Maker and brings Light to all the worlds.

This is the meaning of the three discernments: *Mitzva* (good deed/commandment), transgression, and permission.

- **Mitzva** is the place of sanctity.
- **Transgression** is the place of the *Sitra Achra*.
- **Permission** is when it is neither *Mitzva* nor transgression. This is the battlefield over which the sanctity and the *Sitra Achra* struggle.

When one does what is permitted, and does not unite it with the authority of *Kedusha* (holiness), that whole place falls into the domain of the *Sitra Achra*. And when one prevails, and performs as many unifications as one can, where permitted, he brings permission back to the domain of *Kedusha*.

Thus I have explained what our sages said, "The healer has been given permission to heal." This means that although healing is undoubtedly in the hands of the Creator, and human trickery will not move Him from His place, still, the holy Torah states, "and shall cause him to be thoroughly healed," letting you know that this is permission, the battlefield between *Mitzva* and transgression.

Thus, we ourselves must conquer this "permission" and place it under the *Kedusha*. And how is it conquered? When one visits an expert physician, and the physician gives him a thoroughly tested medicine that has been tried a thousand times. And after one is healed he must believe that without the physician, the Creator would still heal him, for his lifespan has been predetermined. And instead of singing the praises of the human physician, one thanks and praises the Creator, and thus conquers the permission and places it in the domain of *Kedusha*.

It is similar in other matters of "permission." Thus, he expands the boundaries of *Kedusha* and increases the *Kedusha* to the fullest. And all of a sudden, he finds himself standing completely in the Holy Palace, since the boundaries of *Kedusha* have so expanded that it has reached his own place.

I have explained all that to you several times, since this matter is a stumbling block for quite a few people, who have no clear perception of Private Providence. "A slave is comfortable without responsibility," and instead of work, he wishes for the safest, and wishes even more to revoke the questions from his faith and acquire incontrovertible proof that is above nature. This is why they are punished and their blood is on their own heads, since after the sin of *Adam ha Rishon*, the Creator devised a correction for this sin in the form of the unification of *HaVaYaH-Elokim*, as I have explained.

And this is the meaning of "with the sweat of thy face shalt thou eat bread." It is human nature that when one achieves through great efforts, one finds it very difficult to say that it is the Creator's gift. Thus, one has room for work, to labor with complete faith in Private Providence, and to decide that he would obtain all that even without his work. Thus one corrects this transgression.

Walking the Path of Truth

Let me write to you with regard to the middle pillar in the work of God, so as to always be a target for you between right and left. This is because there is one who walks who is worse than he who sits idly. It is he who deflects from the road, for the path of truth is a very thin line that one walks until one comes to the King's palace.

And anyone who begins to walk at the beginning of the line needs great care to not stray to the right or to the left of the line, even as a hair's breadth. This is so because if at first the deviation is as a hair's breadth, even if one continues completely straight, it is certain that he will not come to the King's palace, as he is not stepping on the true line, and this is a true allegory.

Let me explain to you the meaning of the middle pillar, which is the meaning of "The Torah, the Creator, and Israel, are one." The purpose of the soul, when it comes into the body, is to be rewarded with returning to its root and to cleave unto Him, while still clothed in the body, as it is written, "to love the Lord your God, and to walk in all His ways, and to keep His commandments, and to cleave unto Him." You see that the matter ends in "to cleave unto Him," as it was prior to clothing in the body.

However, great preparation is required—which is to walk in all His ways. Yet, who knows the ways of the Creator? Indeed, this is the meaning of "Torah, that has 613 ways." He who walks by them will finally be purified until his body will no longer be an iron partition between him and his Maker, as it is written, "And I will take away the stony heart out of your flesh." Then he shall cleave unto his Maker just as he was before the clothing of the soul in the body.

It turns out that there are three discernments:

1. **Israel** is he who strains himself to return to his root.
2. The **Creator**, which is the root one longs for.

3. The **613 ways of the Torah,** by which one purifies one's soul and body. This is the spice, as it is written, "I have created the evil inclination, I have created for it the Torah as a spice."

However, these three are actually one and the same. In the end, any servant of the Creator attains them as single, united and unified discernment. They only appear to be divided into three because of one's incompleteness in the work of God.

Let me clarify it to you a little: you shall see its tip, but not its entirety, except when He delivers you. It is known that the soul is a part of God Above. Before it comes into a body, it is attached like a branch to the root. See in the beginning of *The Tree of Life*, that the Creator created the worlds because He wished to manifest His Holy Names, "Merciful" and "Gracious," and if there were no creatures, there would be no one to have mercy on.

However, as much as the pen permits, as they said, "The whole Torah is but the names of the Creator." The meaning of attainment is that "what we do not attain, we do not define by a name." It is written in the books that all these names are the reward of the souls, compelled to come into the body, for it is precisely through the body that it can attain the names of the Creator, and its stature is according to its attainment.

There is a rule: The sustenance of any spiritual thing is according to the merit of knowing it. A corporeal animal feels itself because it consists of mind and matter.

Thus, a spiritual sensation is a certain discernment, and the spiritual stature is measured by the amount of knowledge, as it is written, "One is praised according to one's mind." However, the animal knows; it does not feel at all.

Understand the reward of the souls: Before a soul comes into a body, it is but a tiny dot, though attached to the root as a branch to a tree. This dot is called "the root of the soul and its world." Had it not entered this world in a body, it would have had only its own world, meaning its own share of the root.

However, the more it is rewarded with walking in the paths of the Creator, which are the 613 ways of the Torah that return to being the actual Names of the Creator, the more its stature grows, according to the level of the names it has attained.

This is the meaning of the words, "the Creator imparts each and every righteous *Shay* (310 in *Gematria*) worlds." Interpretation: The soul consists of two righteous: Upper Righteous, and Lower Righteous, as the body is divided from the *Tabur* (navel) upward and from the *Tabur* downward. Thus it acquires the written Torah and the oral Torah, which are two times *Shay*, being *TaRaCh* (620 in *Gematria*). These are the 613 *Mitzvot* of the Torah and the seven *Mitzvot de Rabanan* (of our great Rabbis).

It is written in *The Tree of Life*, "The worlds were created only to disclose the names of the Creator." Thus, you see that since the soul came down to clothe this filthy substance, it could no longer cleave to its root, to its own world, as before it came to this world. Rather, it must increase its stature 620 times more than how it previously was in the root. This is the meaning of the whole perfection, the whole *NRNHY* up to *Yechida*. This is why *Yechida* is called *Keter*, implying the number 620.[9]

Thus, you see that the meaning of the 620 names, being the 613 *Mitzvot* of the Torah and the 7 *Mitzvot de Rabanan*, are in fact the five properties of the soul, meaning *NRNHY*. This is because the vessels of the *NRNHY* are from the above 620 *Mitzvot*, and the Lights of *NRNHY* are the actual Light of the Torah in each and every *Mitzvah*. It follows that the Torah and the soul are one.

However, the Creator is the Light of *Ein Sof*, clothed in the Light of the Torah, found in the above 620 *Mitzvot*, as the sages said, "the whole Torah is the names of the Creator." This means that the Creator is the whole, and the 620 names are parts and items. These items are according to the steps and degrees of the soul, which does not receive its Light at once, but gradually, one at a time.

From all the above, you find that the soul is destined to attain all 620 Holy Names, its entire stature, which is 620 more than it had before it came. Its stature appears in the 620 *Mitzvot* where the Light of the Torah is clothed, and the Creator is in the collective Light of the Torah. Thus you see that "the Torah, the Creator, and Israel" are indeed one.

Let us return to the issue that, before the completeness in the work of God, the Torah, the Creator and Israel appear as three discernments. At times, one wishes to complete one's soul and return it to its root, which is considered "Israel." And sometimes one wishes to understand the ways of the Creator and the secrets of the Torah, "for if one does not know the commandments of the Upper One, how will he serve Him?" This is considered "Torah."

And sometimes one wishes to attain the Creator, to cleave unto Him with complete cognizance, and essentially regrets only that, and does not agonize over attaining the secrets of the Torah, and also does not agonize over returning one's soul to its origin, as it was prior to its clothing in a body.

---

9 Translator's note: In Hebrew, *Keter* contains the same letters as *TaRaCh*.

Hence, one who walks upon the true line of preparing for the work of God must always test himself: Does he crave the three above discernments equally? Because the end of the act equalizes with its beginning. If one craves one discernment more than the second or the third, then one deflects from the path of truth.

Thus, you had better hold onto the goal of yearning for the commandment of the Upper One, for "one who does not know the ways of the Upper One and the commandments of the Upper One, which are the secrets of Torah, how will he serve Him?" Among all three, this is what guarantees the middle line most.

This is the meaning of, "Open for me one aperture of repentance, such as a needlepoint, and I will open for you gates where carts and coaches enter." Interpretation: the aperture of the needlepoint is not for entrance and exit, but to insert the thread for sewing and for work.

Similarly, you are to crave only the commandment of the Upper One, to work. And then I will open for you a door such as an entrance to a hall. This is the meaning of the Explicit Name in the verse, "but in very deed[10] as I live and all the earth shall be filled with the glory of the Lord."

---

10 Translator's note: the word 'indeed' is spelled like 'hall' in Hebrew.

One Is Where One Thinks

Keep your feet from suffering a man's jolt prematurely, since "one is where one thinks." Hence, when one is certain that he will not lack anything, he can focus his efforts in words of Torah, for "blessed cleave to blessed."

But with absence of confidence, he will have to toil, and any toil is from the *Sitra Achra*, "and the damned does not cleave to the blessed," since he will not be able to devote all his efforts to the words of Torah. But if one wishes to wander overseas, he must not consider these words at all, but return to one's routine as quickly as possible, as though by diabolic compulsion, so he will not scatter his sparks in times and places that are not yet properly unified.

And know that no flaw is ascribed to the lower ones except in a time and place that are permitted, as it is now. I wish to say that if one embezzles, regrets, or despairs in the current moment, he throws away all the times and all the places in the world. This is the meaning of "A moment's anger, what is its worth? A moment."

Hence, there can be no correction to a person unless one aligns all the present and future moments and dedicates them to His Great Name. And one who rejects the current moment because it is hard reveals his foolishness to all—that all the worlds and all the times are not for him, for the light of his face is not clothed in the changing times, though man's work is necessarily changed by them. For this reason, the belief and the confidence above reason have been prepared for us by merit of our holy patriarchs, which one uses effortlessly in dire times.

An Allegory about the Rich Man's Son in the Cellar

It would seem that one should be precise with the word *Teshuva* (repentance/return); it should have been named "wholeness"—that everything is predetermined and each soul is already in its utmost Light, benefit, and eternity.

It was only for the bread of shame that the soul emerged through the restrictions, until it clothed in the murky body, and only through it does it return to its root from before the restriction. Also, its reward for the terrible move it had undergone is that the real reward is the true *Dvekut* (adhesion). This means that it is rid of the bread of shame, since its vessel of reception has been turned into a vessel of bestowal and its form is equal to its Maker.

Now you understand that if the descent is for the purpose of ascension it is regarded as ascension and not as a descent. And indeed, the descent itself is the ascent, since the letters of the prayer themselves are filled with abundance, while with a short prayer the bounty falls short because the letters are missing. Also, our sages said, "Had Israel not sinned, they would have been given only the five books of Moses and the book of Joshua."

What is it like? It is like a wealthy man who had a young son. One day, the man had to travel far away for many years. The rich man feared lest his son would scatter his possessions unwisely; hence, he devised a plan and exchanged his possessions for gems and jewels and gold. He also built a cellar deep in the ground, and locked all his gold and gems in there, along with this son.

Then he called his loyal servants and commanded them to guard his son and not let him out of the cellar until he was twenty years of age. Every day, they were to bring him down his food and drink, but under no condition should they bring down fire and candles. And they should also inspect the walls for cracks, so no sunlight would penetrate. And for his health, they were to take him out of the cellar for one hour a day, and walk the streets with him, but carefully watching, so he would not escape. And when he turned twenty, they were to give him candles and open a window and let him out.

Naturally, the son's pain was immeasurable, especially when he walked outside and could see all the youths eating and drinking and rejoicing in the streets, without guards and without a time limit, while he was imprisoned with but a few moments of light. If he tried to run, he would be beaten mercilessly. And he was most hurt and depressed when he had heard that his father himself had brought all this pain upon him, for they were his father's servants, doing his father's command. Clearly, he thought his father was the cruelest man of all time, for who has ever heard of such a thing?

On the day of his twentieth birthday, the servants hung down one candle, as his father had commanded. The boy took the candle and began to examine his surroundings. And what did he see? Sacks filled with gold and every royal bounty.

Only then did he understand his father—that he was truly merciful—and that all he had done, he did for his own good. And he immediately realized that the guards would let him out of the cellar and go free. And so he did; he came out of the cellar, and there were no guards, no cruel servants, and he was the greatest of all the land's wealthy.

In fact, there is no innovation here at all, for it becomes apparent that he was of great wealth to begin with, all his days, and he only felt that he was poor and indigent, and utterly miserable. And now, in a single moment, he had been given immense wealth and rose from the lowest pit to the highest peak.

But who can understand this allegory? One who understands that the "sins" are the deep cellar and the careful guard that he will not escape. Thus, evidently, the cellar and the careful watch are the "merits" and the father's mercy over his son. Without them, it would have been impossible for him to become as rich as his father.

But the "sins" are "real sins," not "mistakes," and one must not be forced. Rather, before one returns to one's wealth, the aforementioned emotion rules in its fullest sense. But after one returns to one's wealth, he sees that all these were the father's mercies, and not cruelty at all.

We must understand that the whole connection of love between the father and his only son depends on the son's recognition of his father's mercy for him, concerning the issue of the cellar, the darkness, and the careful watch. This is because the son discovers great efforts and profound wisdom in these mercies of the father.

The Holy *Zohar*, too, speaks of it, saying that for one who is rewarded with repentance, the Holy Divinity appears like a kind-hearted mother who had not seen her child for many days. And they made great efforts to see each other, and as a result, suffered many a great danger.

In the end, the long-awaited freedom had come to them, and they were granted the meeting. And then the mother fell on him and kissed and comforted him, speaking softly to him all day and all night. She told him of the longing and the perils along her way, and how she was with him all along, and Divinity did not move, but suffered with him in all the places, only he could not see it.

These are the words of *The Zohar*: She tells him, "Here we slept; here we were assailed by bandits, and we were saved, and here we hid in a deep hole." And what fool would not understand the multitude of love, pleasantness, and delight that gushes out of these comforting stories?

In truth, before they met face to face, it felt like torments that are harder than death. But with a *Nega* (illness/pain), the *Ayin* (the last letter in the Hebrew word) is at the end of the word. Yet, when speaking comforting words, the *Ayin* is in the beginning of the word, which is certainly *Oneg* (pleasure).

But these are two points that shine only once they exist in the same world. And imagine a father and son who were waiting anxiously for each other for days and years. In the end they met, but the son was deaf and dumb, and they could not play with one another. Thus, the essence of love is in royal pleasures.

The Lord Is Thy Shade

The Baal Shem Tov gave a clear sign by which to know how much the Creator is playing with one—to examine one's own heart and see how much one is playing with the Creator. So are all the matters, by way of "the Lord is thy shade."

Hence, one who still feels a distinction between "knowing" and "cherishing" still needs to unite the heart. This is so because from the Creator's perspective, they are one and the same, and the Creator truly dwells in the heart of everyone from Israel. This is so from His perspective. Hence, does one need? Only to know it. The awareness changes and the awareness completes, and this is the meaning of "the Lord is thy shade."

The Labor Is the Most Important

My dear son, Baruch Shalom,

I have received your letter and I congratulate you for the *Semicha* (rabbinical ordination) that you have obtained. This was the first wall that blocked your path from marching forward. I hope that from this day forth you will begin to succeed and go from strength to strength, until you enter the King's Palace.

I would like you to obtain another *Semicha*, but from this day forth, hurry yourself to spend most of your time preparing your body to muster strength and courage "as an ox to the burden and as a donkey to the load" so as not to lose even a single moment.

And should you ask, "Where is this preparation?" I shall tell you that in the past, it was necessary to obtain all seven secular teachings and undergo terrible self-torments prior to attaining the Creator. Yet, not many were rewarded with the Creator's favor. But since we have been rewarded with the teachings of the Ari and the work of the Baal Shem Tov, it is truly within everyone's reach, and no further preparation is required.

Should your foot tread upon those two, and with God's mercy upon me, I have been favored by Him, and I have received them with both my hands, and my mind is as close to you as a father is close to his son. I will surely pass them on to you when you are fit for receiving mouth to mouth.

But the most important is the labor, to wish to toil in His work. This is because the ordinary work does not count at all, but only the bits that are beyond the ordinary, which are called "labor." It is like a person who needs a pound of bread for satiation—his whole meal is not considered a satiating meal, except the last bit of the pound. That bit, for all its smallness, makes the meal satiating. Similarly, from each work, the Creator draws only the surplus beyond the ordinary, and they will become the *Otiot* (letters) and the *Kelim* (vessels) for the reception of the Light of His face.

Association of Mercy with Judgment

The essence of the work is the choice, meaning "therefore choose life," which is *Dvekut* (adhesion), *Lishma* (for Her Name). Thus, one is rewarded with *Dvekut* with the Life of Lives.

But when there is open Providence, there is no room for choice. For this reason, the Upper One raised *Malchut*, which is *Midat ha Din* (quality of judgment) to the *Eynaim* (eyes). This created a concealment, meaning it became apparent to the lower one that there is a deficiency in the Upper One, that there is no *Gadlut* (greatness) in the Upper One. In that state, the qualities of the Upper One are placed with the lower one; that is, they are deficient.

It follows that these *Kelim* (vessels) are equal to the lower one: as there is no sustenance to the lower one, there is no sustenance to the Higher qualities. This means that there is no flavor in the Torah and *Mitzvot*; they are lifeless.

In that state, there is room for choice, meaning the lower one must say that all this concealment that one feels is because the Upper One restricted Himself in favor of the lower one. This is called, "when Israel is in exile, Divinity is with them." Thus, whatever flavor one tastes, one says that it is not his fault for not tasting liveliness, but that in his view there really is no life in the Upper One.

And if one becomes stronger and says that the bitter taste he finds in these nourishments is only because he does not have the proper vessels to receive the abundance, because his vessels are for reception and not for bestowal, and regrets the Upper One having to hide Himself, which allows the lower one to slander, this is considered *MAN* that the lower one raises. Through it, the Upper One raises its *AHP*, and ascent means that the Upper One can show the lower one the praise and delight in the vessels of *AHP* that the Upper One can disclose. Thus, with respect to the lower one, the Upper One raises the *GE* of the lower one, by the lower one's seeing of the Upper One's merit. It turns out that the lower one rises along with the *AHP* of the Upper One.

Thus, when the lower one sees the greatness of the Upper One, through it, the lower one itself grows. But in the beginning, the lower one is worthy of receiving only *Katnut* (smallness). And when the *Gadlut* (greatness) emerges in the Upper One, there is a division between the right and the left, between believing and knowing.

But the Upper One, too, is then diminished by the lower one, regarded as *Masach de Hirik*. In other words, for the lower one to receive the degrees of the Upper, to receive knowing only by the measure of faith, and not beyond, it is considered that the lower one restricts the Upper One's left line. That is, the lower one is the cause. And then, the lower one can exist because it is comprised of both knowing and believing. This is called "three lines," and it is specifically in this manner that the lower one receives perfection.

Society as a Condition for Attaining Spirituality

Matan Torah (The Giving of the Torah)

> "Love thy friend as thyself" (Leviticus 19:18)
> Rabbi Akiva says, "This is a great rule[11] in the Torah."

This statement of our sages demands explanation. The word *Klal* (collective/rule) indicates a sum of details that, when put together, form the above collective. Thus, when he says about the *Mitzva*, "love thy friend as thyself," that it is a great *Klal* in the Torah, we must understand that the rest of the 612 *Mitzvot* (precepts) in the Torah, with all their interpretations, are no more and no less than the sum of the details inserted and contained in that single *Mitzva* (singular for *Mitzvot*), "love thy friend as thyself."

This is quite perplexing, because you can say this regarding *Mitzvot* between man and man, but how can that single *Mitzva* contain all the *Mitzvot* between man and God, which are the essence and the vast majority of the laws?

2) And if we can still strain to find some way to reconcile these words, there comes before us a second saying, even more conspicuous, about a convert who came before Hillel (*Shabbat* 31) and told him: "Teach me the whole of the Torah while I am standing on one leg." And he replied: "Anything that you hate, do not do to your friend" (the translation of "love thy friend as thyself"), and the rest is its commentary; go study.

Here before us is a clear law, that in all 612 *Mitzvot* and in all the writings in the Torah there is none that is preferred to the *Mitzva*, "love thy friend as thyself." This is because they only aim to interpret and allow us to keep the *Mitzva* of loving others properly, since he specifically says—"the rest is its commentary; go study." This means that the rest of the Torah is interpretations of that one *Mitzva*, that the *Mitzva* to love your friend as yourself could not be completed were it not for them.

---

11 Translator's note: The word *Klal* in Hebrew means both 'rule' and 'collective.'

3) Before we delve into the heart of the matter, we must observe that *Mitzva*, since we were commanded: "love thy friend as thyself." The word 'thyself' tells us, "love your friend to the same extent you love yourself, not one bit less." In other words, you must constantly and vigilantly satisfy the needs of every person in the Israeli nation, no less than you are always vigilant to satisfy your own needs.

This is utterly impossible, for not many can satisfy their own needs during their daily work, so how can you tell them to work to satisfy the wishes of the entire nation? And we couldn't possibly think that the Torah exaggerates, for it warns us to not add or subtract, indicating that these words and laws were given with utter precision.

4) And if this is still not enough for you, I will tell you that the simple explanation of that *Mitzva* of loving your fellow person is even harsher, for we must put the needs of our friends before our own. It is as our sages wrote (*Kidushin* p 20) regarding the verse "because he is happy with thee" (Deuteronomy 15:16), regarding the Hebrew slave: "when sometimes he has but one pillow, if he lies on it himself and does not give it to his slave, he does not observe 'because he is happy with thee,' for he is lying on a pillow and the slave, on the ground. And if he does not lie on it, and does not give it to the slave, as well, it is Sodomite rule." It turns out that, against his will, he must give it to his slave, while the master himself lies on the ground.

We also find the same rule in our verse about the measure of loving our fellow person, for here, too, the text compares the satisfaction of the friend's needs to the satisfaction of one's own needs, as with the example of "because he is happy with thee" regarding the Hebrew slave. Thus, here too, if he has but one chair and his friend hasn't any, the law is that if he sits on it and does not give it to his friend, he breaks the *Mitzva*, "love thy friend as thyself," since he is not fulfilling the needs of his friend as he fulfills his own.

And if he does not sit on it and also does not give it to his friend, it is as evil as Sodomite rule. Therefore, he must let his friend sit on it while he himself sits on the ground or stands. Clearly, this is the law regarding all the needs that one has, and one's friend lacks. And now go and see if this *Mitzva* is in any way feasible.

5) We must first understand why the Torah was given specifically to the Israeli nation and not to all the peoples of the world equally. Is there, God forbid, nationalism involved here? Of course, only an insane person would think that. In fact, our sages have examined this question, and this is what they meant by their words (*Avoda Zarah* 2): "God gave it to every nation and tongue and they did not accept it."

But what they find bewildering is why, then, were we called "the chosen people," as it is written: "the Lord thy God has chosen thee" (Deuteronomy 7:6), since there was no other nation that wanted it? Moreover, there is a fundamental question in the matter: Can it be that the Creator came with His law in His hands to negotiate with those savage peoples? Such a thing has never been heard of and is completely unacceptable.

6) But when we fully understand the essence of the Torah and *Mitzvot* that were given to us, and their desired purpose, to the extent our sages have instructed us, which is the purpose of the great Creation that is set before our eyes, then we shall understand everything. For the first concept is that there is no act without a purpose. And there is no exception from this rule except for the lowest of the human species or infants. Therefore, it is certain that the Creator, whose exaltedness is beyond conception, would not act—be it a great or a small act—without a purpose.

Our sages tell us about that, that the world had not been created but for the purpose of keeping Torah and *Mitzvot*, meaning, as our sages have explained, that the aim of the Creator from the time He created His Creation is to reveal His Godliness to others. This is because the revelation of His Godliness reaches the creature as pleasant bounty that is ever growing until it reaches the desired measure.

And by that, the lowly rise with true recognition and become a chariot to Him, and to cleave unto Him, until they reach their final completion: "Neither has the eye seen a God beside thee" (Isaiah 64:3). And because of the greatness and glory of that perfection, the Torah and the prophecy, too, refrain from uttering even a single word of exaggeration here, as our sages said (*Berachot* 34), "All the prophets made their prophecies only for the days of the Messiah, but for the next world, neither has the eye seen a God beside thee."

This perfection is expressed in the words of the Torah and the prophecy and in the words of our sages in the simple word, *Dvekut* (adhesion). But for the widespread use of this word by the masses, it has lost almost all its content. But if you linger on that word for even an instant, you will be overwhelmed by its wondrous stature, for you will picture the exaltedness of the Creator and the lowliness of the creature. Then you will be able perceive the value of *Dvekut* of one with the other, and you will understand why we ascribe that word the purpose of the whole Creation.

It turns out that the purpose of the whole Creation is that the lowly creatures will be able, by keeping Torah and *Mitzvot*, to rise ever upward, ever developing, until they are rewarded with *Dvekut* with their Creator.

7) But here come the Kabbalists and ask, why were we not created in this high stature of adhesion to begin with? What reason did He have to burden us with this labor of Creation and the Torah and the *Mitzvot*? And they replied: "He who eats that which is not his, is afraid to look at his face." This means that one who eats and enjoys the labor of one's friend is afraid to look at his face because by doing so he becomes increasingly humiliated until he loses his human form. And because that which extends from His wholeness cannot be deficient, He gave us room to earn our exaltedness by ourselves, through our work in Torah and *Mitzvot*.

These words are most profound and I have already explained them in my book, *Panim Me'irot uMasbirot to the Tree of Life*, Branch One, and in the book, *The Study of the Ten Sefirot*, Inner Reflection, Part One. Here I will explain them briefly to make them understandable for all.

8) This matter is like a rich man who took a man from the market and fed him and gave him gold and silver and all desirables every day. And each day he showered him with more gifts than the day before. Finally, the rich man asked, "Do tell me, have all your wishes been fulfilled?" And he replied, "Not all of my wishes have been fulfilled, for how good and how pleasant it would be if all those possessions and precious things came to me through my own work, as they have come to you, and I would not be receiving the charity of your hand." Then the rich man told him: "In this case, there has never been born a person who could fulfill your wishes."

It is a natural thing, since on the one hand, he experiences greater and greater pleasure, the more he showers presents upon him, but on the other, it is hard for him to tolerate the shame for the excessive goodness that the rich bestows upon him. This is because there is a natural law that the receiver feels shame and impatience upon receiving gifts from the giver out of compassion and pity.

From here extends a second law, that never will anyone be able to satisfy the needs of his friend to the fullest, because ultimately he will not be able to give him the nature and the form of self-possession, as only with it is the desired perfection attained.

But this relates only to the creatures, whereas regarding the Creator, it is completely impossible and unacceptable. And this is the reason He has prepared for us the toil and the labor of Torah and *Mitzvot*, to produce our exaltedness by ourselves, because then the delight and pleasure that comes to us from Him, meaning everything that is included in the *Dvekut* with Him, will all be our own possession that has come to us through our own efforts. Then we will feel ourselves as the owners, without which there cannot be a sensation of wholeness.

9) Indeed, we need to examine the heart and the source of this natural law, and who it was that fathered the flaw of shame and impatience that we feel upon receiving charity from another. It is understood from a law that is known to scientists, that each branch bears the same nature as its root, and that the branch also desires, seeks, and craves, and benefits from all the conducts of the root. Conversely, all the conducts that are not in the root, its branch removes itself from them, cannot tolerate them, and is harmed by them. This law exists between each root and its branch and cannot be breached.

Now here opens before us a door to understand the source of all the pleasures and pains in our world. Since the Creator is the root of His creations, we feel all that exists in Him and extends to us directly from Him as pleasant and delightful, because our nature is close to our root. And everything that is not in Him, and does not extend to us directly from Him, but contradicts Creation itself, will be against our nature and difficult for us to tolerate. Thus, we love to rest and hate to move so much, that we do not make a single movement if not for the attainment of rest. That is because our root is immobile but at rest, and no motion exists in Him whatsoever. Therefore, it is against our nature and loathsome to us.

By the same token, we love wisdom, strength, and wealth, etc. because all those exist in Him who is our root. And hence, we hate their opposites, such as foolishness, weakness, and poverty, since they do not exist in our root at all. This makes us feel hateful and loathsome, and pains us immeasurably.

10) This is what gives us the foul taste of shame and impatience when we receive from others by way of charity, because in the Creator there is no such thing as reception of favors, because from whom would He receive? And because this element does not exist in our root, we feel it as repulsive and loathsome. On the other hand, we feel delight and pleasure every time we bestow upon others, since that conduct exists in our root, which it gives to all.

11) Now we have found a way to examine the purpose of Creation, which is to cleave unto Him, in its true appearance. This exaltedness and *Dvekut*, which is guaranteed to come to us through our work in Torah and *Mitzvot*, is no more and no less than the equivalence of the branches with their root. All the gentleness and pleasure and sublimity become a natural extension here, as

we have said above, that pleasure is only the equivalence of form with its Maker. And when we equalize in every conduct with our root, we sense delight.

Also, everything we encounter that is not in our root becomes intolerable, disgusting, or considerably painful to us, as is necessitated by that concept. And we naturally find that our very hope depends on the extent of our equivalence of form with our root.

12) These were the words of our sages (*Beresheet Rabba* 44) when they asked, "Why should the Creator mind whether one slaughters at the throat or at the back of the neck?" After all, the *Mitzvot* were given only to cleanse people, and that cleansing means the cleansing of the turbid body, which is the purpose that emerges from the observation of all the Torah and *Mitzvot*.

"A wild ass shall be turned into man" (Job 11:12), because when one emerges out of the bosom of Creation, one is in utter filth and lowliness, meaning a multitude of self-love that is imprinted in him, whose every movement revolves solely around himself, without a shred of bestowal upon others.

Thus, then one is at the farthest distance from the root, on the other end, since the root is all bestowal without a hint of reception, whereas the newborn is in a state of complete self-reception without a hint of bestowal. Therefore, his situation is regarded as being at the lowest point of lowliness and filth in our human world.

The more he grows, the more he receives from his environment portions of "bestowal upon others," depending on the values and development in that environment. And then one is initiated into keeping Torah and *Mitzvot* for the purpose of self-love, for reward in this world and in the next world, called *Lo Lishma* (not for Her name), since one cannot be accustomed any other way.

As one grows, he is told how to keep Torah and *Mitzvot Lishma* (for Her name), which is with an aim solely to bring contentment to his Maker. As the RAMBAM said, "Women and children should not be told of keeping Torah and *Mitzvot Lishma*, because they will not be able to bear it. But when they grow and acquire knowledge and wisdom, they are taught to work *Lishma*." It is as our sages said, "From lo *Lishma*, one comes to *Lishma*," which is defined by the aim to bring contentment to one's Maker and not for any self-love.

Through the natural remedy of the engagement in Torah and *Mitzvot Lishma*, which the Giver of the Torah knows, as our sages wrote (*Kidushin* 30b), "The Creator says, 'I have created the evil inclination, I have created for it the Torah as a spice.'" Thus, that creature develops and marches upward in degrees of the above spoken exaltedness, until he loses all remnants of self-love and all the *Mitzvot* in his body rise, and he performs all his actions only to bestow, so even the necessity that he receives flows in the direction of bestowal, so he can bestow. This is why our sages said, "The *Mitzvot* were given only to cleanse people with."

13) There are two parts in the Torah: 1) *Mitzvot* between man and God, and 2) *Mitzvot* between man and man. And they both aim for the same thing—to bring the creature to the final purpose of *Dvekut* with Him.

Furthermore, even the practical side in both of them is really one and the same, because when one performs an act *Lishma*, without any mixture of self-love, meaning without finding any benefit for himself, then one does not feel any difference whether one is working to love one's friend or to love the Creator.

This is so because it is a natural law for any being, that anything outside one's own body is regarded as unreal and empty. And any movement that a person makes to love another is performed with a Reflected Light, and some reward that will eventually return to him and serve him for his own good. Thus, such an act cannot be considered "love of another" because it is judged by its end. It is like rent that finally pays off. However, the act of renting is not considered love of another.

But making any kind of movement only as a result of love for others, without any spark of Reflected Light, and no hope for any kind of self-gratification in return, is completely impossible by nature. It is written in the *Tikkuney Zohar* about that with regard to the nations of the world: "Every grace that they do, they do for themselves."

This means that all the good deeds that they do, either toward their friends or toward their God, are not because of their love for others, but because of their love for themselves. And that is because it is completely unnatural.

Therefore, only those who keep Torah and *Mitzvot* are qualified for it, because by accustoming themselves to keeping Torah and the *Mitzvot* in order to bring contentment to their Maker, they gradually depart from the bosom of the natural creation and acquire a second nature, being the above-mentioned love of others.

This is what brought the sages of *The Zohar* to exclude the nations of the world from loving their fellow person, when they said, "Every act of grace that they do, they do for themselves," because they are not involved in keeping Torah and *Mitzvot Lishma*, and the only reason they serve their gods is for reward and salvation in this world and in the next. Thus, their worship of their gods is because of self-love, too, and they will never perform an action that is outside the boundaries of their own bodies, for which they will be able to lift themselves even a wisp above their basic nature.

14) Thus we can clearly see that toward those who keep Torah and *Mitzvot Lishma*, there is no difference between the two parts of the Torah, even on the practical side. This is because before one accomplishes it, one is compelled to feel any act of bestowal—either toward another person or toward the Creator—as emptiness beyond conception. But through great effort, one slowly rises and attains a second nature, and then one attains the final goal, which is *Dvekut* with Him.

Since this is the case, it is reasonable to think that the part of the Torah that deals with man's relationship with his friend is more capable of bringing one to the desired goal. This is because the work in *Mitzvot* between man and God is fixed and specific, and is not demanding, and one becomes easily accustomed to it, and everything that is done out of habit is no longer useful. But the *Mitzvot* between man and man are changing and irregular, and demands surround him wherever he may turn. Hence, their cure is much more certain and their aim is closer.

15) Now we can understand the words of Hillel Hanasi to the proselyte, that the essence of the Torah is, "Love thy friend as thyself," and the remaining six hundred and twelve *Mitzvot* are but an interpretation of it. And even the *Mitzvot* between man and God are regarded as a qualification of that *Mitzva*, which is the final aim emerging from the Torah and *Mitzvot*, as our sages said, "The Torah and *Mitzvot* were given only so as to cleanse Israel" (Item 12). This is the cleansing of the body until one attains a second nature defined as "love for others," meaning the one *Mitzva*: "Love thy friend as thyself," which is the final aim of the Torah, after which one immediately attains *Dvekut* with Him.

But one must not wonder why it was not defined in the words: "And thou shalt love the Lord thy God, with all thy heart and with all thy soul and with all thy might" (Deuteronomy 6:5). It is because indeed, with respect to a person who is still within the nature of Creation, there is no difference between the love of God and the love of his fellow person.

This is because anything that is not him is unreal to him. And because that proselyte asked of Hillel Hanasi to explain to him the desired outcome of the Torah, so his goal would be near, and he would not have to walk a long way, as he said, "Teach me the whole Torah while I am standing on one leg;" hence, he defined it for him as love of his friend because its aim is nearer and is revealed faster (Item 14), since it is mistake-proof and is demanding.

16) In the above words, we find a way to understand our concept from above (Items 3 and 4) about the contents of that *Mitzva*, "Love thy friend as thyself," how the Torah compels us to do something that cannot be done.

Indeed, know that for this reason, the Torah was not given to our holy fathers—Abraham, Isaac and Jacob—but was held until the exodus from Egypt, when they came out and became a whole nation of six hundred thousand men of twenty years of age or more. For then, each member of the nation was asked if he agreed to that exalted work. And once each and every one in the nation agreed to it in heart and soul, and said "We will do and we will hear," it then became possible to keep the whole of the Torah, and that which was previously impossible became possible.

This is because it is certain that if six hundred thousand men abandon their work for the satisfaction of their own needs and worry about nothing but standing guard so their friends will never lack a thing, and moreover, that they will keep it with a mighty love, with their very heart and soul, in the full meaning of the *Mitzva*, "Love thy friend as thyself," then it is beyond doubt that no man of the nation will need to worry about his own well being.

Because of that, he becomes completely free of securing his own survival and can easily keep the *Mitzva*, "Love thy friend as thyself," obeying all the conditions given in Items 3 and 4. After all, why would he worry about his own survival when six hundred thousand loyal lovers stand by, ready with great care to make sure he lacks nothing of his needs?

Therefore, once all the members of the nation agreed, they were immediately given the Torah, because now they were capable of keeping it. But before they have multiplied into a whole nation, and certainly during the time of the fathers, who were unique in the land, they were not qualified to truly keep the Torah in its desirable form. This is because with a small number of people, it is impossible to even begin with engagement in *Mitzvot* between man and man to the extent of "Love thy friend as thyself," as we have explained in Items 3 and 4. This is why they were not given the Torah.

17) From all the above, we can understand one of the most perplexing phrases of our sages: "All of Israel are responsible for one another." This seems to be completely unjust, for is it possible that if someone sins or commits a sin that upsets his Maker, and you have no acquaintance with him, the Creator will collect his debt from you? It is written, "Fathers shall not be put to death for children... every man shall be put to death for his own sin" (Deuteronomy 24:16),

so how can they say that you are responsible for the sins of even a complete stranger, of whom you know neither him nor his whereabouts?

And if that is not enough for you, see *Masechet Kidushin*, p 40b: "Rabbi Elazar, the son of Rabbi Shimon, says, 'Since the world is judged by its majority and the individual is judged by its majority, if he performed one *Mitzva*, happy is he, for he has sentenced the whole world to a scale of merit. And if he committed one sin, woe onto him, for he has sentenced himself and the whole world to a scale of sin, as it is said, 'one sinner destroys much good.'"

And Rabbi Elazar, son of Rabbi Shimon, has made me responsible for the whole world, since he thinks all the people in the world are responsible for one another, and each person brings merit or sin to the whole world with his deeds. This is twice as perplexing.

But according to the above said, we can understand their words very simply; we have shown that each of the 613 *Mitzvot* in the Torah revolves around that single *Mitzva*: "Love thy friend as thyself." And we find that such a state can only exist in a whole nation whose every member agrees to it.

THE ARVUT (MUTUAL GUARANTEE)

Continued from Matan Torah

> All of Israel are responsible for one another
> (*Sanhedrin*, 27b, *Shavuot* 39)

This is to speak of the *Arvut* (Mutual Guarantee), when all of Israel became responsible for one another. Because the Torah was not given to them before each and every one from Israel was asked if he agreed to take upon himself the *Mitzva* (precept) of loving others in the full measure, expressed in the words: "Love thy friend as thyself" (as explained in Items 2 and 3, examine it thoroughly there). This means that each and every one in Israel would take it upon himself to care and work for each member of the nation, and to satisfy their every need, no less than the measure imprinted in him to care for his own needs.

And once the whole nation unanimously agreed and said, "We shall do and we shall hear," each member of Israel became responsible that nothing shall be missing from any other member of the nation. Only then did they become worthy of receiving the Torah, and not before.

With this collective responsibility, each member of the nation was liberated from worrying about the needs of his own body and could keep the *Mitzva*, "Love thy friend as thyself" in the fullest measure, and give all that he had to any needy person, since he no longer cared for the existence of his own body, as he knew for certain that he was surrounded by six hundred thousand loyal lovers, who were standing ready to provide for him.

For this reason, they were not ready to receive the Torah at the time of Abraham, Isaac, and Jacob, but only when they came out of Egypt and became a complete nation. Only then was there a possibility to guarantee everyone's needs without any care and concern.

However, while they were still mingled with the Egyptians, a portion of their needs was necessarily given into the hands of these savages, permeated with self-love. Thus, the portion that is given into the hands of foreigners will not be secured for any person from Israel because his friends will not be able to provide for those needs, as they will not be in possession of them. Consequently, as long as the individual is troubled with concerns for himself, he is unfit to even begin to keep the *Mitzva*, "Love thy friend as thyself."

And you evidently find that the giving of the Torah had to be delayed until they came out of Egypt and became a nation of their own, so that all their needs were provided for by themselves, without dependence on others. This qualified them to receive the above *Arvut*, and then they were given the Torah. It turns out that even after the reception of the Torah, if a handful from Israel betray and return to the filth of self-love, without consideration of their friends, that same amount of need that is put in the hands of those few would burden Israel with the need to provide for it themselves.

This is because those few will not pity them at all; hence, the fulfillment of the *Mitzva* of loving one's friend will be prevented from the whole of Israel. Thus, these rebels cause those who keep the Torah to remain in their filth of self-love, for they will not be able to engage in the *Mitzva*, "Love thy friend as thyself," and complete their love for others without their help.

As a result, all of Israel are responsible for one another, both on the positive side and on the negative side. On the positive side, if they keep the *Arvut* until each cares and satisfies the needs of his friends, they can fully keep the Torah and *Mitzvot*, meaning bring contentment to their Maker (Item 13). And on the negative side, if a part of the nation does not want to keep the *Arvut*, but rather chooses to wallow in self-love, they cause the rest of the nation to remain immersed in their filth and lowliness without ever finding a way out of their filth.

18) Therefore, the Tana (Rabbi Shimon Bar Yochai) described the *Arvut* as two people on a boat, when one of them began to drill a hole in the boat. His friend asked, "Why are you drilling?" He replied, "What business is it of yours? I am drilling under me, not under you." So he replied, "Fool! We will both drown together!" (*VaYikra Rabba*, Chapter 4).

From this we learn that since those rebels wallow in self-love, by their actions they build an iron wall that prevents the observers of the Torah from even beginning to fully keep the Torah and *Mitzvot* in the measure of "Love thy friend as thyself," which is the ladder for reaching *Dvekut* (adhesion) with Him.

And how right were the words of the proverb that said, "Fool, we shall both drown together!"

19) Rabbi Elazar, son of Rashbi (Rabbi Shimon Bar-Yochai), clarifies this concept of *Arvut* even further. It is not enough for him that all of Israel be responsible for one another, but the whole world is included in that *Arvut*. Indeed, there is no dispute here, for everyone admits that to begin with, it is enough to start with one nation for the observance of the Torah for the beginning of the correction of the world. It was impossible to begin with all the nations at once, as they said that the Creator went with the Torah to every nation and tongue, and they did not want to receive it. In other words, they were immersed in the filth of self-love up to their necks, some with adultery, some with robbery and murder and so on, until it was impossible to conceive, in those days, to even ask if they agreed to retire from self-love.

Therefore, the Creator did not find a nation or a tongue qualified to receive the Torah, except for the children of Abraham, Isaac, and Jacob, whose ancestral merit reflected upon them, as our sages said, "The Patriarchs observed the whole Torah even before it was given." This means that because of the exaltedness of their souls, they had the ability to attain all the ways of the Creator with respect to the spirituality of the Torah, which stems from their *Dvekut*, without first needing the ladder of the practical part of the Torah, which they had no possibility of observing at all, as written in "Matan Torah," Item 16.

Undoubtedly, both the physical purity and the mental exaltedness of our Holy Fathers greatly influenced their sons and their sons' sons, and their righteousness reflected upon that generation, whose members all assumed that sublime work, and each and every one stated clearly, "We shall do and we shall hear." Because of that, we were chosen, out of necessity, to be a chosen people from among all the nations. Hence, only the members of the Israeli nation were admitted into the required *Arvut*, and not the nations of the world at all, because they did not participate in it. And this is the plain reality, and how could Rabbi Elazar disagree with it?

20) But the end of the correction of the world will only be by bringing all the people in the world under His work, as it is written, "And the Lord shall be King over all the earth; in that day shall the Lord be One, and His name one" (*Zechariah*, 14:9). And the text specifies, "on that day," and not before. And there are several more verses, "for the earth shall be full of the knowledge of the Lord..." (*Isaiah*, 11:9) "...and all the nations shall flow on to him" (*Isaiah*, 2:2).

But the role of Israel towards the rest of the world resembles the role of our Holy Fathers towards the Israeli nation: just as the righteousness of our fathers helped us develop and cleanse until we became worthy of receiving the Torah, were it not for our fathers, who observed the whole of Torah before it was given, we would certainly not be any better than the rest of the nations (Item 12).

Also, it is upon the Israeli nation to qualify itself and all the people of the world through Torah and *Mitzvot*, to develop until they take upon themselves that sublime work of the love of others, which is the ladder to the purpose of Creation, which is *Dvekut* with Him.

Thus, each and every *Mitzva* that each person from Israel performs in order to bring contentment to one's Maker, and not for any self gratification, helps, to some extent, with the development of all the people of the world. This is because it is not done at once, but by slow, gradual development, until it increases to such a degree that it can bring all the people in the world to the desired purity. And this is what our sages call "shifting the balance to virtue," meaning that the necessary weight of purity has been reached. And they compare it to weighing on a scale, where the shifting of the balance is the attainment of the desired weight.

21) These are the words of Rabbi Elazar, son of Rabbi Shimon, who said that the world is judged by its majority. He was referring to the role of the Israeli nation to qualify the world for a certain measure of purity, until they are worthy of taking upon themselves His work, no less than Israel were worthy at the time they received the Torah. In the words of our sages, it is considered that they had attained enough virtues to overcome the scale of sin, which is the filthy self-love.

Of course, if the scale of virtues, which is the sublime attainment of the benefit of loving others, transcends the filthy scale of sin, they become qualified for the decision and the agreement to say, "We shall do and we shall hear," as Israel said. But before that, before they obtained sufficient virtues, self-love would certainly prevail and sentence that they will refuse to assume His burden.

Our sages said, "Who performs one *Mitzva* is happy, for he has sentenced himself and the whole world to a scale of merit." This means that an individual from Israel finally adds his own part to the final decision, as one who weighs sesame seeds and adds them one by one to the scale, until the balance shifts. Certainly, everyone takes part in this shifting, and without him, the sentencing would never be completed. Similarly, it is said about the acts of an individual from Israel that he sentences the whole world to a scale of merit. This is because when the matter ends and the whole world has been sentenced to a scale of merit, each and every one will have a share in this shifting, for were it not for his actions, the shifting would have been deficient.

Thus you find that Rabbi Elazar, son of Rabbi Shimon, does not dispute the words of our sages that all of Israel is responsible for one another. Rather, Rabbi Elazar, the son of Rabbi Shimon, speaks of the correction of the whole world at the time of the end of correction, whereas our sages speak of the present, when only Israel has assumed the Torah.

22) And this is what Rabbi Elazar, son of Rabbi Shimon, quotes from the writings: "One sinner destroyeth much good." This is because it has already been explained (Item 20) that the impression that comes to a person when engaging in *Mitzvot* between man and God is completely the same as the impression he gets when engaging in *Mitzvot* between man and man. He is obliged to perform all the *Mitzvot Lishma* (for Her name), without any hope for self-love, meaning that no light or hope returns to him through his trouble in the form of reward or honor, etc. Here, in this exalted point, the love of the Creator and the love of his friend unite and actually become one (see Item 15).

Thus he affects a certain measure of advancement on the ladder of love for others in all the people of the world in general. This is because that degree, which that individual caused by his actions, whether large or small, ultimately joins the future in shifting the world to a scale of merit, since his share has been added and joins the shift (as written in Item 20 in the allegory about the sesame seeds).

And one who commits one sin, which means that he cannot overcome and conquer his filthy self-love, and hence steals or does something of the sort, sentences himself and the whole world to the scale of sin. This is because with the disclosure of the filth of self-love, the lowly nature of Creation is reinforced. Thus, he subtracts a certain amount from the sentencing to the final scale of merit. This is similar to a person removing from the scale that single sesame seed his friend had put there.

Thus, to that extent, he slightly elevates the scale of sin. It turns out that he regresses the world, as they said, "One sinner destroyeth much good." Because he could not overcome his petty lust, he pushed the spirituality of the whole world backwards.

23) With these words, we clearly understand what we said above (Item 5), about the Torah being given specifically to the Israeli nation, because it is certain and unequivocal, that the purpose of Creation lies on the shoulders of the whole of the human race, black, white or yellow, without any essential difference.

But because of the descent of human nature to the lowest degree, which is the self-love that unrestrictedly rules over all of humanity, there was no way to negotiate with them and persuade them to agree to take upon themselves, even as an empty promise, to exit their narrow world into the wide spaces of the love of others. The exception was the Israeli nation because they were enslaved in the savage kingdom of Egypt four hundred years in horrible torments.

Our sages said, "As salt sweetens meat, agony polishes man's sins." This means that they bring to the body great purification. And in addition, the purification of their Holy Fathers assisted them (see Item 16), which is the most important, as some of the verses of the Torah testify.

Because of these two forewords, they were qualified for it. And this is why the text refers to them in singular form, as it is written, "and there Israel camped before the mountain," which our sages interpret as "one man in one heart."

This is because each and every person from the nation completely detached himself from self-love, and wanted only to benefit his friend, as we have shown above (Item 16) regarding the meaning of the *Mitzva*, "Love thy friend and thyself." It turns out that all the individuals in the nation have come together and become one heart and one man, for only then were they qualified to receive the Torah.

24) Thus, because of the above necessity, the Torah was given specifically to the Israeli nation, solely to the descendents of Abraham, Isaac, and Jacob, for it was inconceivable that any stranger would take part in it. Because of that, the Israeli nation had been constructed as a sort of gateway by which the sparks of purity would shine upon the whole of the human race the world over.

And these sparks multiply daily, like one who gives to the treasurer, until they are filled sufficiently, that is, until they develop to such an extent that they can understand the pleasantness and tranquility that are found in the kernel of love of others. For then they will know how to shift the balance to the right, and will place themselves under His burden, and the scale of sin will be eradicated from the world.

25) Now there remains to complete what we have said above (Item 16) about the reason why the Torah was not given to our fathers, because the *Mitzva*, "Love thy friend as thyself," the axis of the whole Torah and around which all the *Mitzvot* revolve, so as to clarify and interpret it, cannot be observed by an individual, but only through the consent of an entire nation.

And this is why it took until they came out of Egypt, when they became worthy of observing it. And then they were first asked if each and every one of the nation agreed to take that *Mitzva* upon himself. And once they agreed to it, they were given the Torah. However, there still remains to clarify where we find in the Torah that the children of Israel were asked that question, and that they all agreed to it prior to receiving the Torah.

26) Bear in mind that these things are evident to every educated person in the invitation that the Creator had sent to Israel through Moses, prior to the reception of the Torah. It is as it is written (*Exodus*, 19:5), "'Now therefore, if ye will hearken unto My voice indeed, and keep My covenant, then ye shall be Mine own treasure from among all peoples; for all the earth is Mine; and ye shall be unto Me a kingdom of priests, and a holy nation. These are the words which thou shalt speak unto the children of Israel.' And Moses came and called for the elders of the people, and set before them all these words which the Lord commanded him. And all the people answered together, and said: 'All that the Lord hath spoken, we will do.' And Moses reported the words of the people unto the Lord."

These words do not seem to fit their role, because common sense dictates that if one offers one's friend to do some work, and he wants him to agree, he should give him an example of the nature of that work and its reward. Only then can the receiver examine it, whether to decline or to accept.

But here, in these two verses, we seem to find neither an example of the work nor its reward, because he says, "If ye will hearken unto My voice indeed, and keep My covenant," and he does not interpret the voice or the covenant and what they apply to. And then he says, "Then ye shall be Mine own treasure from among all peoples; for all the earth is Mine."

It is not clear whether He commands us to labor to be a treasure[12] from among all peoples, or whether this is a promise of good to us.

We must also understand the connection to the words, "for all the earth is Mine." All three interpreters—Unkalus, Yonatan Ben Uziel, and The Yerushalmi—and all the interpreters—Rashi, Ramban, etc.—try to correct the literal meaning of this writing. Even Ezra says, in the name of Rabbi Marinos, that the word "for" means "although," and he interprets, "then ye shall be Mine own treasure from among all peoples; although all the earth is Mine." Even Ezra himself tends to agree with it, but that interpretation does not coincide with our sages, who said that "for" serves for four meanings: "either," "lest," "but," and "that."

---

12 Translator's note: the Biblical text in Hebrew uses the word *Segula*, which actually means remedy, or power, but here the text translates as 'treasure.'

And he even adds a fifth interpretation: "although." And then the writing ends, "and ye shall be unto Me a kingdom of priests, and a holy nation." But here, too, it is not self-evident if this is a *Mitzva*, and one must delve into it, or a promise of benefit. Also, the words, "a kingdom of priests," are not repeated and are not explained anywhere in the Bible.

The important thing here is to determine the difference between "a kingdom of priests" and "a holy nation." For by the ordinary meaning of priesthood, it is one with sanctity, and it is thus obvious that a kingdom where all are priests must be a holy nation, so the words "holy nation" seem redundant.

27) However, by all that we have explained from the beginning of the essay until now, we learn the true meanings of the words as their roles should be—to resemble a negotiation of offer and consent. This means that with these words, He really does offer them the whole form and content of the work in Torah and *Mitzvot*, and its worthwhile reward.

The work in Torah and *Mitzvot* is expressed in the words, "and ye shall be unto Me a kingdom of priests." A kingdom of priests means that all of you, from youngest to oldest, will be like priests. Just as the priests have no land or any corporeal possessions because the Creator is their domain, so will the entire nation be organized so that the whole earth and everything in it will be dedicated to the Creator only. And no person should have any other engagement in it but to keep the *Mitzvot* of the Creator and to satisfy the needs of his fellow person. Thus he will lack none of his wishes, so that no person will need to have any worry about himself.

This way, even mundane works such as harvesting, sowing, etc. are considered to be precisely like the work with the sacrifices that the priests performed in the Temple. How is it different if I keep the *Mitzva* of making sacrifices to the Creator, which is a positive[13] *Mitzva*, or if I can keep the positive *Mitzva*, "Love thy friend as thyself"? It turns out that he who harvests his field in order to feed his fellow person is the same as he who sacrifices to the Creator. Moreover, it seems that the *Mitzva*, "Love thy friend as thyself," is more important than he who makes the sacrifice, as we have shown above (Items 14, 15).

Indeed, this is not the end of it yet, because the whole of the Torah and the *Mitzvot* were given for the sole purpose of cleansing Israel, which is the cleansing of the body (see Item 12), after which he will be granted the true reward, which is *Dvekut* with Him, the purpose of Creation (Item 15). And that reward is expressed in the words, "a holy nation." Through the *Dvekut* with Him, we have

---

13 Translator's note: a *Mitzva* to perform some action.

become sanctified, as it is written, "You shall be holy, for I the Lord your God am holy."

And you see that the words "a kingdom of priests" express the complete form of the work on the axis of "Love thy friend as thyself," meaning a kingdom that is all priests, that the Creator is their possession, and they have no self-possession of all the mundane possessions. And we must admit that this is the only definition through which we can understand the words, "a kingdom of priests." For you cannot interpret it with regard to the sacrifices on the altar, for that could not have been said of the whole nation, for who would be making the sacrifices?

Also, with regard to taking the gifts of the priesthood, who would be the givers? And also, to interpret the holiness of the priests, it has already been said, "a holy nation." Therefore, this must certainly mean that it is only that the Creator is their domain, that they lack any material possession for themselves, meaning the full measure of the words, "Love thy friend as thyself," which encompasses the whole of the Torah. And the words "a holy nation" express the full form of the reward, which is the *Dvekut*.

28) Now we fully understand the previous words, for he says, "Now therefore, if ye will hearken unto My voice indeed, and keep My covenant," meaning make a covenant on what I am telling you here, that ye shall be Mine own treasure from among all peoples. This means that you will be My treasure, and sparks of purification and cleansing of the body shall pass through you onto all the peoples and the nations of the world, for the nations of the world are not yet ready for it. And at any rate, I need one nation to start with now, so it will be as a remedy for all the nations. And therefore he ends, "for all the earth is Mine," meaning all the peoples of the earth belong to Me, as do you, and are destined to cleave to Me (Item 20).

But now, while they are still incapable of performing that task, I need a virtuous people. And if you agree to be the remedy for all the nations, I command you to "be unto Me a kingdom of priests," which is the love of others in its final form of "Love thy friend as thyself," which is the axis of all the Torah and *Mitzvot*. And "a holy nation" is the reward in its final form of *Dvekut* with Him, which includes all the rewards that can even be conceived.

These are the words of our sages in clarifying the ending, "These are the words which thou shalt speak unto the children of Israel." They made the precision, "These are the words," no more and no less. This is perplexing: How can you say that Moses would add or subtract from the words of the Creator to the point that the Creator had to warn him about it? And we find none like him in the whole of the Torah. On the contrary, the Torah says about him: "for he is the trusted one in all my house" (Numbers 12:7).

29) Now we can fully understand that concerning the form of work in its last manner, as explained in the words "a kingdom of priests," which is the final definition of "Love thy friend as thyself," it was indeed conceivable for Moses to restrain himself and refrain from disclosing the full outline of the work all at once, lest Israel would not want to detach themselves from all material possessions and give all their fortune and assets to the Creator, as instructed by the words, "a kingdom of priests."

It is much like the RAMBAM wrote, that women and small children must not be told the matter of the clean work, which must be in order to not be rewarded, and wait until they grow, become wise, and have the courage to execute it. Therefore, the Creator gave him the above warning, "no less," but offered them the true nature of the work, in all its sublimity, expressed in the words "a kingdom of priests."

And regarding the reward that is defined in the words "a holy nation," it was possible for Moses to contemplate interpreting and elaborating further about the pleasantness and the sublime subtleness that come with *Dvekut* with Him, to persuade them to accept this extreme, to completely detach themselves from any worldly possessions, as do priests. Hence, he was warned, "no more," but be vague and not explain the whole reward included in the words, "a holy nation."

The reason for it is, had he told them about the wondrous things in the essence of the reward, they would necessarily use and assume His work in order to obtain that wonderful reward for themselves. This would be considered working for themselves, for self-love. That, in turn, would falsify the whole purpose (Item 13).

Thus we see that regarding the form of the work expressed in the words "a kingdom of priests," he was told, "no less." And about the unclear measure of the reward, expressed in the words, "a holy nation," he was told, "no more."

The Peace

An empirical, scientific research about the necessity of the work of God

"The wolf also shall dwell with the lamb, and the leopard shall lay down with the kid; and the calf and the young lion and the fatling together; and a little child shall lead them. And it shall come to pass in that day, that the Lord shall set his hand again the second time to recover the remnant of his people, that shall be left, from Ashur, and from Egypt, from Patros, and from Kush, and from Elam, and from Shin'ar, and from Hamat, and from the islands of the sea" (*Isaiah* 11).

"Rabbi Shimon Ben Halafta said, 'God did not find a vessel to hold the blessing for Israel but peace, as it says: 'The Lord giveth strength to His people; the Lord blesseth His people with peace'" (end of *Masechet Okatzin*).

After having demonstrated in previous articles the general form of His work, whose essence is but the love of others, practically determined as "bestowal upon others," meaning that the actual manifestation of love of others is bestowal of goodness upon others, love of others should be determined as bestowal upon others, which is best suited for its content, aiming to ensure that we will not forget the aim.

Now that we know for certain the conduct of His work, there still remains to inquire whether this work is acceptable to us by faith alone, without any scientific, empirical basis, or whether we also have an empirical basis for it. This is what I want to demonstrate in the essay before us. But first I must thoroughly demonstrate the subject itself, meaning who it is who accepts our work.

But I am not an enthusiast of formative philosophy, since I dislike theoretically based studies, and it is well known that most of my contemporaries agree with me, for we are too familiar with such foundations, which are rickety foundations; and when the foundation fluctuates, the whole building tumbles.

Therefore, I have come here to speak only through critique of empirical reason, beginning from the simple recognition no one disagrees with, through proving analytically (separating the various elements in an issue), until we come to determining the uppermost topic. And it will be tested synthetically (the connection and unity between matters, such as inference and the "all the more so"), how His work is confirmed and reaffirmed by simple recognition from the practical aspect.

CONTRADICTIONS IN PROVIDENCE

Every reasonable person who examines the reality before us finds two complete opposites in it. When examining Creation, its reality and conducts, there is an apparent and affirmed leadership of great wisdom and skill, both regarding the formation of reality and the securing of its existence in general.

Let us take the making of a human being as an example: the love and pleasure of his progenitors is its first reason, guaranteed to perform its duty. And when the essential drop is extracted from the father's brain, Providence has very wisely secured a safe place for it, which qualifies it to receive life. Providence also gives it its daily bread in the exact amount, and it also prepares a wonderful foundation for it in the mother's womb so that no stranger may harm it.

It tends to its every need like a trained nanny who will not forget it even for a moment, until it has acquired the strength to emerge into our world. At that time, Providence briefly lends it just enough strength to break the walls that surround it, and like a trained, armed warrior it breaks an opening and emerges in the world.

Then, too, Providence does not abandon it. Like a loving mother, it brings it to such loving, loyal people it can trust, called "Mother" and "Father," to assist it through its days of weakness until it grows and is able to sustain itself. As man, so are all the animals, plants, and objects, all are wisely and mercifully cared for to ensure their own existence and the continuation of their species.

But those who examine that reality from the perspective of provision and persistence of existence can clearly see great disorder and confusion, as though there were no leader and no guidance. Everyone does that which is right in his own eyes, building himself on the ruin of others, the evil thrive and the righteous are trampled mercilessly.

Bear in mind that this oppositeness, set before the eyes of every sensible, educated person, has preoccupied humanity even in ancient days. And there are many methods to explain these two apparent opposites in Providence, which occupy the same world.

FIRST METHOD: NATURE

This method is an ancient one. Since they did not find a way and an outlet to bring these two conspicuous opposites closer, they came to assume that the Creator, who created all these, who watches mightily over His reality lest any of it be cancelled, is mindless and senseless.

Hence, although He watches over the existence of reality with wondrous wisdom, yet He Himself is mindless, and does all that senselessly. If there had been any reason and feeling in Him, He would certainly not leave such malfunctions in the provision of reality without pity and compassion for the tormented. For this reason, they named Him "Nature," meaning a mindless, heartless supervisor. And for that reason, they believe that there is no one to be angry at, to pray to, or to justify oneself to.

SECOND METHOD: TWO AUTHORITIES

Others were more clever. They found it difficult to accept the assumption of Nature's supervision, since they saw that the supervision over reality, to secure its existence, is a far deeper wisdom than any human culmination. They could not agree that the one who supervises all that will Himself be mindless, for how can one give that which he does not possess? And can one teach one's friend while he himself is a fool?

How can you say about He who performs before us such astute and wise deeds that he does not know what He is doing, and that He does it by chance? It is clearly evident that chance cannot arrange any orderly deed, devised in wisdom, much less secure its eternal existence.

In consequence, they came to a second assumption that there are two supervisors here: one creates and sustains the good, and the other creates and sustains the bad. And they have greatly elaborated that method with evidence and proof along their way.

THIRD METHOD: MULTIPLE GODS

This method was born out of the bosom of the method of two authorities. This is because they have divided and separated each of the general actions for itself, meaning strength, wealth, domination, beauty, famine, death, disorder, and so on. They appointed each its own supervisor, and expanded the system as they wished.

FIFTH METHOD: LEFT HIS OPERATION

Recently, when knowledge increased and they saw the tight linkage among all the parts of Creation, they recognized the concept of multiple gods to be completely impossible. Thus, the question of the oppositeness sensed in Creation reawakened.

This led them to a new assumption: that the Supervisor of reality is indeed wise and caring. Yet, because of His exaltedness, which is beyond conception, our world is deemed a grain of sand, nothing in His eyes. It is not worthwhile for Him to bother with our petty businesses, and this is why our livelihood is so disordered and every man does that which is right in his own eyes.

Alongside these methods, there existed religious methods of Godly unity. But this is not the place to examine them, as I wanted only to examine the origins from which the fouled methods and puzzling assumptions that vastly dominated and expanded in different times and places were taken.

We find that the basis on which all the above methods were born and emerged from the contradiction between the two types of Providence detectable in our world, and all these methods came about only to mend that great tear.

Yet, nothing is new under the sun. And not only was that great tear not mended; rather, it grows and expands before our eyes into a terrible chasm, without seeing or hoping for a way out of it. And when I look at all those attempts that humanity has been making for several thousand years to no avail, I wonder if we should not seek the mending of this great tear from the Supervisor's point of view at all, but rather accept that this great correction is in our own hands.

NECESSITY TO PRACTICE CAUTION WITH THE LAWS OF NATURE

We can all plainly see that the human species must lead a social life, meaning it cannot exist and sustain itself without the help of others. Therefore, imagine an event where one retires from society to a desolate location and lives there a life of misery and great pain due to his inability to provide for his needs. That person would have no right to complain about Providence or his fate. And if that person were to do that, meaning complain and curse his bitter fate, he would only be displaying his stupidity.

This is because while Providence has prepared for him a comfortable, desirable place in society, he has no justification to retire from it to a desolate place. Such a person must not be pitied, since he is going against the nature of Creation. And since he has the option to live as Providence has ordered him, he should not be pitied. That sentence is agreed upon by all of humanity without dispute.

And I can add and establish it on a religious basis, and give it such a form: since Providence extends from the Creator, who undoubtedly has a purpose in His actions, since there is no act without a purpose, we find that anyone who breaks a law from the laws of nature that He has imprinted in us, corrupts the purposeful aim.

Because the purpose is undoubtedly built over all the laws of nature, none excluded, just as the clever worker would not add or subtract even a hairsbreadth of the necessary actions to attain the goal, he who alters even a single law harms and damages the purposeful aim that the Creator has set, and will therefore be punished by nature. Hence, we, too, creatures of the Creator must not pity him because he is desecrating the laws of nature and defiles the purpose of the Creator. That, I believe, is the form of the sentence.

And I believe that it is not a good idea for anyone to contradict this form that I have given to the sentence, because the words of the sentence are one. For what is the difference if we say that the supervisor is called "nature," meaning mindless and purposeless, or saying that the supervisor is wise, wonderful, knowing, and feeling and has a purpose in his actions?

In the end, we all admit and agree that we are obliged to keep the commandments of Providence, meaning the laws of nature. And we all admit that one who breaks the commandments of Providence, meaning the laws of nature, should be punished by nature, and must not be pitied by anyone. Thus, the nature of the sentence is the same, and the only difference is in the motive: they maintain that the motive is necessary, and I maintain that it is purposeful.

To avoid having to use both tongues from now on—nature and a supervisor—between which, as I have shown, there is no difference regarding the following of the laws, it is best for us to meet halfway and accept the words of the Kabbalists that *HaTeva* (the nature) has the same numerical value (in Hebrew) as *Elokim* (God)—eighty-six. Then, I will be able to call the laws of God "nature's *Mitzvot* (commandments)," or vice-versa, for they are one and the same, and we need not discuss it further.

Now it is vitally important for us to examine nature's *Mitzvot*, to know what it demands of us, lest it would mercilessly punish us. We have said that nature obligates humankind to lead a social life, and this is simple. But we need to examine the *Mitzvot* that nature obliges us to keep in that respect, meaning with respect to the social life.

In general examination, we find that there are only two *Mitzvot* to follow in society. These can be called "reception" and "bestowal." This means that each member must, by nature, receive his needs from society and must benefit society through his work for its well-being. And if one breaks one of these two *Mitzvot*, he will be mercilessly punished.

We need not excessively examine the *Mitzva* (singular for *Mitzvot*) of reception, since the punishment is carried out immediately, which prevents any neglect. But in the other *Mitzva*, that of bestowal upon society, not only is the punishment not immediate, but it is given indirectly. Therefore, this *Mitzva* is not properly observed.

Thus, humanity is being fried in a heinous turmoil, and strife and famine and their consequences have not ceased thus far. And the wonder about it is that nature, like a skillful judge, punishes us according to our development. For we can see that to the extent that humankind develops, the pains and torments surrounding our sustenance and existence also multiply.

Thus you have a scientific, empirical basis that His Providence has commanded us to keep with all our might the *Mitzva* of bestowal upon others in utter precision, in such a way that no member from among us would work any less than the measure required to secure the happiness of society and its success. And as long as we are idle performing it to the fullest, nature will not stop punishing us and take its revenge.

And besides the blows we suffer today, we must also consider the drawn sword for the future. The right conclusion must be drawn—that nature will ultimately defeat us and we will all be compelled to join hands in following its *Mitzvot* with all the measure required of us.

PROOF OF HIS WORK BY EXPERIENCE

But he who wishes to criticize my words might still ask, "Although I have thus far proven that one must work to benefit people, where is the proof that it has to be done for the Creator?"

Indeed, history itself has troubled in our favor and has prepared for us an established fact, sufficient for a full appreciation and unequivocal conclusion: anyone can see how a large society such as the state of Russia, with hundreds of millions in population, more land than the whole of Europe, second to none wealth in raw materials, and which has already agreed to lead communal life and practically abolished private property altogether, where each worries only about the wellbeing of society, has seemingly acquired the full measure of the virtue of bestowal upon others in its full meaning, as far as the human mind can grasp.

And yet, go and see what has become of them: instead of rising and exceeding the achievements of the capitalist countries, they have sunk ever lower. Now, they not only fail to benefit the lives of the workers a little more than in the capitalist countries, they cannot even secure their daily bread and clothes on their flesh. Indeed, that fact puzzles us, because judging by the wealth of that country and its plentiful population, it seems unreasonable that it would come to that.

But this nation has sinned one sin which the Creator will not forgive: that all this precious and exalted work, namely bestowal upon others, which they have begun to perform, needs to be for the Creator and not for humanity. And because they do their work not for His name, from nature's point of view, they have no right to exist.

Try to imagine if every person in that society were anxious to keep the *Mitzvot* of the Creator to the extent of the verse: "And thou shalt love the Lord thy God with all thy heart, and with all thy soul, and with all thy might," and to that extent each would rush to satisfy the needs and wishes of one's friend in the full measure imprinted in man to satisfy his own wishes, as it is written, "Love thy neighbor as thyself."

If the Creator Himself were the goal of every worker while working for the well-being of society, meaning that the worker would expect this work for society would reward him with *Dvekut* (adhesion) with Him, the source of all goodness and truth and every pleasantness and softness, there is no doubt that within a few years they would rise in wealth over all the countries of the world put together. That is because then they would be able to utilize the raw materials in their rich soil, would truly be an example for all the countries, and would be considered blessed by the Creator.

But when all the work of bestowal upon others is based solely on the benefit of society, it is a rickety foundation, for who and what would obligate the individual to toil for society? In a dry, lifeless principle, one can never hope to find motivation even in developed individuals, much less for undeveloped people. Thus rises the question, "Where would the worker or the farmer find sufficient motivation to work?"

For his daily bread will not increase or decrease by his efforts, and there are no goals or rewards before him. It is well known to researchers of nature that one cannot perform even the slightest movement without motivation, without somehow benefiting oneself.

When, for example, one moves one's hand from the chair to the table, it is because one thinks that by putting his hand on the table he will enjoy it more. If he did not think so, he would leave his hand on the chair for the rest of his life without moving it at all. It is all the more so with greater efforts.

And if you say that there is a solution—to place them under supervision so that anyone who is idle at his work will be punished by denial of salary, I will ask, "Do tell me where the supervisors themselves should take the motivation for their work?" Because standing at one place and watching over people to motivate them to work is a great effort, too, perhaps more than the work itself. Therefore, it is as though one wishes to switch on a machine without fueling it.

Hence, they are doomed by nature, since nature's laws will punish them because they do not adapt to obeying its commands—performing these acts of bestowal upon others in the form of work for the Creator, to achieve through it to the purpose of Creation, which is *Dvekut* with Him. It was explained in the article, "Matan Torah" (Item 6), that this *Dvekut* comes to the worker in the measure of His pleasant and pleasurable bounty, which increases up to the desired measure for rising to know His genuineness, ever-developing until he is rewarded with the excessiveness implied in the words, "Neither hath the eye seen a God beside Thee."

And imagine that the farmer and the worker were to sense this goal before them while working for the well-being of society, they would certainly not need any supervisors, since they would already have sufficient motivation for a great effort, enough to raise society to the ultimate happiness.

Indeed, understanding that in such a way requires great care and proven conducts. But everyone can see that without it they have no right to exist from the perspective of the obstinate, uncompromising nature, and this is what I wanted to prove here.

Thus, I have evidently proven from the perspective of empirical reason—out of the practical history unfolding before our very eyes–that there is no other cure for humanity but the acceptance of the commandment of Providence: bestowal upon others in order to bring contentment to the Creator in the measure of the two verses.

The first is "love thy friend as thyself," which is the attribute of the work itself. This means that the measure of work to bestow upon others for the happiness of society should be no less than the measure imprinted in man to care for his own needs. Moreover, he should put his fellow person's needs before his own, as it written in the article, "Matan Torah" (Item 4).

And the other verse is, "And thou shalt love the Lord thy God with all thy heart, and with all thy soul, and with all thy might." This is the goal that must be before everyone's eyes when laboring for one's friend's needs. This means that he labors and toils only to be liked by the Creator, that He said and they do His will.

And if you wish to listen, you shall feed on the fruit of the land, for poverty and torment and exploitation shall be no more in the land, and the happiness of each and every one shall rise ever higher, beyond measure. But as long as you refuse to assume the covenant of the work for the Creator in the fullest measure, nature and its laws will stand ready to take revenge. And as we have shown, it will not let go until it defeats us and we accept its authority in whatever it commands.

Now I have given you practical, scientific research by the critique of empirical reason regarding the absolute necessity of all people to assume the work of God with all their hearts, and souls, and might.

CLARIFICATION OF THE PHRASE FROM THE MISHNAH: "EVERYTHING IS IN DEPOSIT, AND A FORTRESS SPREADS OVER ALL OF LIFE"

Now that we have learned all the above, we can understand an unclear phrase in *Masechet Avot* (Chapter 3, Item 20). It reads as follows: "He (Rabbi Akiva) would say, 'All is in deposit, and a fortress spreads over all of life. The store is open and the shopkeeper sells by deferred payment; the book is open and the hand writes. And all who wish to borrow may come and borrow, and the collectors return regularly, day-by-day, and collect from a person knowingly and unknowingly. And they have what to rely on, and the judgment is true, and all is ready for the feast.'"

That phrase did not remain an abstruse allegory without reason, without even a hint as to its meaning. It tells us that here there is great depth to delve into; indeed, the knowledge we have thus far acquired clarifies it very well indeed.

THE WHEEL OF TRANSFORMATION OF THE FORM

First, let me present the opinion of our sages concerning the unfolding of the generations of the world: although we see the bodies changing from generation to generation, this is only the case with the bodies. But the souls, which are the essence of the body's self, do not vanish, to be replaced, but move from body to body, from generation to generation. The same souls that were at the time of the flood came also during the time of Babylon, and in the exile in Egypt, and in the exodus from Egypt, etc., until this generation and until the end of correction.

Thus, in our world, there are no new souls the way bodies are renewed, but only a certain amount of souls that incarnate on the wheel of transformation of the form, because each time they clothe a new body and a new generation.

Therefore, with regard to the souls, all generations since the beginning of Creation to the end of correction are as one generation that has extended its life over several thousand years, until it developed and became corrected as it should be. And the fact that in the meantime each has changed its body several thousand times is completely irrelevant, because the essence of the body's self, called "the soul," did not suffer at all by these changes.

And there is much evidence pointing to that, and a great wisdom called "the secret of the incarnation of the souls." And while this is not the place to explain it, because of the great importance of the matter, it is worthwhile to point out to the uneducated that reincarnation occurs in all the objects of the tangible reality, and each object, in its own way, lives eternal life.

Although our senses tell us that everything is transient, it is only how we see it. In fact, there are only incarnations here—each item is not still and does not rest for a moment, but incarnates on the wheel of transformation of the form, losing nothing of its essence along its way, as physicists have shown.

And now we come to clarify the phrase: "All is in deposit." It has been compared with someone who lends money to his friend in order to make him a partner in the profit. To make sure that he does not lose his money, he gives it to him as collateral, and thus he is free from any uncertainty. The same applies to the creation of the world and its existence, which the Creator has prepared for humans to engage in and to eventually attain by it the exalted goal of *Dvekut* with Him, as it is explained in "Matan Torah" (Item 6). Thus, one must wonder, who would compel humanity to engage in His work, until they finally come to this exalted end?

Rabbi Akiva tells us about that, "All is in deposit." This means that everything that God had placed in Creation and given to people, He did not give to them licentiously, but secured Himself with collateral. And should you wonder what collateral He was given?

He responds to that by saying: "and a fortress spreads over all of life." This means that the Creator has cleverly devised a wonderful fortress and spread it over all of humanity, so no one will escape. All the living must be caught in that fortress and necessarily accept His work, until they attain their sublime goal. This is the collateral by which the Creator secured Himself, to guarantee that no harm would come to the deed of Creation.

Afterwards, he interprets it in detail and says, "The store is open." This means that this world seems to us like an open shop, without an owner, and anyone who passes through may receive abundantly, as much as one wishes, free of any charge. However, Rabbi Akiva warns us that the shopkeeper is selling by deferred payment. In other words, although you cannot see any shopkeeper here, know that there is a shopkeeper, and the reason that he is not demanding payment is because he sells it to you by deferred payment.

And should you say, "How does he know my debt?" To that he replies, "The book is open and the hand writes." Meaning there is a general book in which each act is written without losing even one. And the aim surrounds the law of development that the Creator has imprinted in humanity, which prompts us ever forward.

This means that the corrupt conducts in the states of humanity are the very ones that generate the good states. And each good state is nothing but the fruit of the work in the bad state that preceded it. Indeed, these values of good and bad do not refer to the value of the state itself, but to the general purpose: each state that brings humanity closer to the goal is considered good, and one that deflects them from the goal is considered bad.

By that standard alone is the "law of development" built—the corruption and the wickedness that appear in a state are considered the cause and the generator of the good state, so that each state lasts just long enough to grow the evil in it to such an extent that the public can no longer bear it. At that time, the public must unite against it, destroy it, and reorganize in a better state for the correction of that generation.

And the new state, too, lasts just as long as the sparks of evil in it ripen and reach such a level that they can no longer be tolerated, at which time it must be destroyed and a more comfortable state is built in its stead. And so the states clear up one by one and degree by degree until they come to such a corrected state that there will be no sparks of evil.

And you find that all the seeds from which the good states grow are only the corrupted deeds themselves, meaning that all the exposed evils that come from under the hands of the wicked in the generation join and accumulate to a great sum, until they weigh so heavily that the public can no longer bear them. Then, they rise up and ruin it and create a more desirable state. Thus you see that each wickedness becomes a condition for the driving force, by which the good state is developed.

These are the words of Rabbi Akiva: "The book is open and the hand writes." Any state that the generation is in is like a book, and all the evildoers are as writing hands because each evil is carved and written in the book until they accumulate to an amount that the public can no longer bear. At that time, they ruin that evil state and rearrange into a more desirable state. Thus, each and every act is calculated and written in the book, meaning in the state.

And he says, "All who wish to borrow may come and borrow." This means that he believes that this world is not like an open store without an owner, but that there is an owner present, a shopkeeper who stands in his store and demands of each customer the right price for the merchandise he is taking from the store, meaning toil in His work while he is nourished by that store, in a manner that is certain to bring him to the purpose of creation, as He pleases.

Such a person is regarded as one who wishes to borrow. Thus, even before he stretches his hand to take from this world, which is the store, he takes it as a loan, to pay its price. In other words, he takes it upon himself to work to achieve His goal during the time he lives off the store, in a way that he promises to pay his debt by achieving the desired goal. Therefore, he is deemed as one who wishes to borrow, meaning that he pledges to return the debt.

Rabbi Akiva depicts two kinds of people: the first are the "open store" type, which regard this world as an open store without a shopkeeper. He says about them, "The book is open and the hand writes." Meaning, although they do not see that there is an account, all their actions are nonetheless written in the book, as explained above. This is done by the law of development imprinted in Creation against humanity's will, where the deeds of the wicked themselves necessarily instigate the good deeds, as we have shown above.

The second type of people is called "those who want to borrow." They take the shopkeeper into consideration, and when they take something from the store, they only take it as a loan. They promise to pay the shopkeeper the desired price, meaning attain the goal by it. And he says about them, "All who wish to borrow may come and borrow."

And if you say, "What is the difference between the first type, whose goal comes to them from the law of development, and the other type, whose goal comes to them by self-enslavement to His work? Are they not equal in attaining the goal?"

In that regard, he continues, "and the collectors return regularly, day-by-day, and collect from a person knowingly and unknowingly." Thus, in truth, both pay their daily portion of the debt.

And just as the forces that emerge by engaging in His work are deemed the loyal collectors, who collect their debt in portions every day, until it is completely paid, the mighty forces imprinted in the law of development are also deemed as loyal collectors who collect their daily portions of the debt until it is paid in full. This is the meaning of, "and the collectors return regularly, day by day, and collect from a person."

However, there is a great difference and a great distance between them, meaning "knowingly and unknowingly." The first type, whose debt is collected by the collectors of the development, pay their debt unknowingly, but stormy waves come upon them, through the strong wind of development, and push them from behind, forcing them to step forward.

Thus, their debt is collected against their will and with great pains by manifestations of the evil forces, which push them from behind. But the second type pay their debt, which is the attainment of the goal knowingly, of their own accord, by repeating the actions that hasten the development of the sense of recognition of evil. And through this work they gain doubly.

The first gain that these forces, which appear out of His work, are set before them as a pulling, magnetic force. They chase it of their own free will, with the spirit of love. Needless to say, they are free from any kind of sorrow and suffering like the first type.

The second gain is that they hasten the desired goal, for they are the righteous and the prophets who attain the goal in each generation, as it is explained in the essay, "The Essence of the Wisdom of Kabbalah," in the section, What Does the Wisdom Revolve Around?

All is in deposit, and a fortress spreads over all of life. The store is open and the shopkeeper sells by deferred payment; the book is open and the hand writes. And all who wish to borrow may come and borrow, and the collectors return regularly, day by day, and collect from a person knowingly and unknowingly. And they have what to rely on, and the judgment is true, and all is ready for the feast.

Thus you see that there is a great distance between those who pay knowingly and those who pay unknowingly, as the supremacy of the light of delight and pleasure over the darkness of pain and agony. And he says further: "They have what to rely on, and the judgment is true." In other words, he promises all those who pay knowingly and willingly that "they have what to rely on," that there is great strength in His work to bring them to the sublime goal, and it is worthwhile for them to harness themselves under His burden.

And of those who pay unknowingly, he says, "and the judgment is true." Seemingly, one must wonder why Providence permits those corruptions and agonies to appear in the world, in which humanity is being fried mercilessly.

He says about it that this "judgment is true," since "all is ready for the feast," for the true goal. And the sublime delight that is destined to emerge with the revelation of His purpose in Creation, when all the trouble and toil and anguish that befall us through time will seem like a host who greatly troubles himself to prepare a great feast for the invited guests. And he compares the anticipated goal that must finally be revealed to a feast, whose guests attend with great delight. This is why he says, "and the judgment is true, and all is ready for the feast."

Such as that you will find in *Beresheet Rabba*, Chapter 6, regarding the creation of man: the angels asked of the Creator: "What is a man, that thou art mindful of him? And the son of man, that thou visitest him? Why do you need this trouble?"

And the Creator told them: "So why were Tzona and Alafim created?" There is an allegory about a king who had a tower filled with goods, but no guests. What pleasure does a king have in his full tower? They said unto Him: "Lord of the world, the Lord our master, how great is your name in all the land. Do that which pleases you."

Interpretation: The angels that saw all the pain and agony that was to befall humanity wondered "Why do you need this trouble?" And the Creator replied to them that indeed he had a tower full of goods, but only this humanity was invited to it. And of course, the angels weighed the pleasures in that tower, awaiting its guests, against the agony and trouble that awaited humanity.

And once they saw that it was worthwhile for humanity to suffer for the good that awaited them, they agreed to the creation of man, just as Rabbi Akiva said, "and the judgment is true, and all is ready for the feast." From the beginning of Creation, all people have reservations, and the Thought of the Creator necessitates them to come to the feast, knowingly or unknowingly.

And now all will see the truth in the words of the prophet (Isaiah 11) in the prophecy of peace: "The wolf shall dwell with the lamb, and the leopard shall lay down with the kid." And he reasoned that: "The earth shall be full of the knowledge of the Lord, as the waters cover the sea" (Isaiah 11:9).

Thus, the prophet conditions peace in the whole world with the filling of the whole world with the knowledge of God, just as we have said above, that the tough, egoistic resistance between people, along which international relationships deteriorate, all these will not cease from the world by any human counsel or tactic, whatever it may be.

Our eyes can see how the poor sick is turning over in dreadful, intolerable pains, and humanity has already thrown itself to the extreme right, as with Germany, or to the extreme left, as with Russia. But not only did they not ease the situation for themselves, they have worsened the malady and agony, and the voices rise up to the sky, as we all know.

Thus, they have no other choice but to come to accept His burden in knowledge of the Creator, meaning that they will aim their actions to the will of the Creator and to His purpose, as He had planned for them prior to Creation. And when they do that, it is plain to see that with His work, all envy and hatred will be abolished from humanity, as I have shown above. This is because then all members of humanity will unite into one body and one heart, full of the knowledge of the Lord. Thus, world peace and the knowledge of God are one and the same thing.

Immediately following, the prophet says, "And it shall come to pass in that day, that the Lord shall set His hand again the second time to recover the remnant of His people...and gather together the dispersed of Judah from the four corners of the earth" (Isaiah 11:12). Thus we learn that world peace comes before the gathering of the Diaspora.

Now you can understand the words of our sages at the end of *Masechet Okatzin*: "The Creator did not find a vessel to hold the blessing for Israel but peace," as it says: "The Lord shall give strength to His people, the Lord shall bless His people with peace" (Psalms 29:11). Seemingly, one should wonder at the allegory, "a vessel to hold the blessing for Israel." And also, how does one conclude that from these words?

But these words become clear to them like the prophecy of Isaiah that world peace precedes the gathering of the Diaspora. This is why the verse says, "The Lord shall give strength to His people," that in the future, when the Creator gives His people strength, meaning eternal resurrection, then "the Lord shall bless His people with peace." This means that He will first bless His people, Israel, with peace in the whole world, and then He will "set his hand again the second time to recover the remnant of his people."

Our sages said about the reason for the words: Therefore, the blessing of peace in the whole world precedes the strength, meaning the redemption, because "God did not find a vessel to hold the blessing for Israel but peace." Thus, as long as self-love and egoism exist among the nations, Israel, too, will not be able to serve the Creator in purity, as bestowal, as it is written in the explanation of the words, "And you shall be to me a kingdom of priests," in the essay, "The Arvut." And we see it from experience, for the coming to the land and the building of the Temple could not persist and receive the blessings that God has sworn to our fathers.

And this is why they said, "God did not find a vessel to hold the blessing," meaning thus far Israel did not have a vessel to hold the blessing of the fathers. Therefore, the oath that we can inherit the land for all eternity has not yet been fulfilled, because world peace is the sole vessel that enables us to receive the blessing of the fathers, as in the prophecy of Isaiah.

THE MESSAGE IN MATAN TORAH

In the three essays, "Matan Torah" (The Giving of the Torah), "The Arvut" (The Mutual Guarantee), and "The Peace," Baal HaSulam teaches us of the necessity for a large society to achieve the purpose of Creation. He demonstrates why a single person cannot achieve one's goals without the rest of the people in the world, and that only the right combination between social unity and the work of God will reward humanity with peace, prosperity, and the realization of our human potential.

In "Matan Torah," Item 14, he explicitly writes that the part of the Torah that concerns man and man is the most capable of bringing us to the desirable goal. At the end of the essay, he stresses and further expands upon the meaning of the reciprocal connection to a level of an entire nation when he says, "We have proven that each of the 613 *Mitzvot* in the Torah revolves around the single *Mitzva*, 'Love thy friend as thyself.'" He also says that this point is not feasible except when done by a whole nation whose every member is ready and willing for it.

In the essay, "The Arvut," Item 20, Baal HaSulam explains that the end of the world's correction will be when all the people in the world join in His work. But the first to enter God's work and lead the whole world after them are the children of Israel. "Israel's role with respect to the rest of the world is similar to the role of the Holy Patriarchs with respect to the Israeli nation... Also, the Israeli nation must... qualify itself and the rest of the peoples in the world to develop until they assume this sublime work of love of man, which is the ladder to the purpose of Creation. ...Thus, each *Mitzva* that an individual from Israel performs in order to bring contentment to one's Maker, and for no other reward and self-love, affects—to some extent—the evolution of the rest of the people of the world."

Further down the essay (Item 28) he defines the role of the children of Israel as the ones that should be the remedy through which the sparks of purity and cleansing of the body will pass on to all the nations of the world. This is because the rest of the nations of the world are not yet ready for it, and the Creator needs at least one nation to start with, so it will be chosen from among all nations.

All the nations of the world belong to Me [the Creator], as do you, and will eventually cleave to Me. But while they are still incapable of this task, I need a virtuous people. If you agree to be the chosen people, then I will command you to be unto Me a kingdom of priests, which is the ultimate form of love of others: "love thy friend as thyself."

In the essay, "The Peace," Baal HaSulam teaches us the real reason for the suffering of people in general, and the people of Israel in particular. He writes that the harsh, egoistic resistance to one another, which causes tension in relations among the members of the nation, will not cease by any human tactics. We can clearly see that we are already like a sick person turning from side to side in immeasurable pain, as humanity has already thrown itself to the extreme right, as with Germany, or to the extreme left, as with Russia. And not only did they not ease the situation, they only aggravated the pain, and the cries rise up to the heavens, as we all know.

From here he leads to the inevitable conclusion that people will have no other choice but to accept His burden, to know the Creator, and to aim their actions towards God's contentment and towards His goal, as He had planned for them prior to Creation. And when they do, it is evident that along with serving Him, any shred of envy or hatred will vanish from humanity, since then all members of humanity will unite into a single body and one heart, filled with the knowledge of God. Thus, world peace and the knowledge of God are one and the same thing.

To summarize his words in the three essays, we can point out a number of distinct messages:

1. The purpose of the whole Creation is for all creatures to cleave to their Maker. Thus, they will be rewarded with eternal delight and wholeness through their own doing.
2. It is possible to achieve this goal only through realizing the law: "Love thy friend as thyself."

This rule will be realized gradually, beginning with the unity of a few people, through a gradually growing group, up to a whole nation, which will eventually lead all the nations of the world to the work of God and the love of man.

3. The first nation that should carry out its role of realizing this idea is the Israeli nation.
4. The people of Israel are to set an example for all the nations and lead them to the same concepts.
5. Any individual, group, or nation that will refuse to tread this path will inflict terrible torment on themselves, which will direct them back to the right path—towards the end of correction.
6. Any individual, group, or nation that will dedicate itself to this goal will affect and accelerate the whole process and will be rewarded with the desired wholeness.
7. The following are the principles leading the group of Kabbalists, Bnei Baruch.

The members of this group lead a life of sharing and unity on a day to day basis, learning the writings of the great Kabbalists who have implemented these principles, and teaching what they learn throughout Israel and the world over. This is done through their many study groups, active all year long, dissemination of books of Kabbalists, and through live and archived Kabbalah lessons over the internet and TV. Their internet site, www.kabbalah.info, is the leading Kabbalah site on the web, and to date, features content in thirty-two languages. There are also Kabbalah papers and magazines published on a monthly basis in eight languages.

Bnei Baruch's primary goal is to present the complex Kabbalistic material in as simple terms as possible, so every person looking for life's purpose will be able to relate to them. Additionally, following Baal HaSulam's teachings, Bnei Baruch tries, with all the means at their disposal, to teach the whole of the people of Israel its historic role.

They teach the only message that can prevent suffering, pain, and war: the message called "There is none else besides Him."

It is clear to the members of Bnei Baruch that the political, economic, and global situation depends solely upon teaching this simple message. The only reason for the suffering in the world is to develop people and teach them to turn to the Creator and contact Him. The various attempts to avoid this mission of leading the world towards this conclusion inflict tremendous pain upon the Jews.

Human evolution is mandatory; it cannot be stopped. All we can do is understand the message and hurry its realization. Regrettably, the bloody history of the people of Israel teaches us where the obstinate refusal to carry out this mission leads.

The only thing we should keep in mind is that there is only one cause in the whole of reality. This cause appears to us in various ways, outside of us and within us. It contacts us through our feelings, thoughts, desires, and actions, and it appears in the same way to the rest of the people in the world. It is important to remember that only with its help will we be able to carry out the rule, "Love thy friend as thyself." All this can be achieved by simply changing our attitude towards reality; there is no need to make any external changes whatsoever.

If we succeed in teaching as many people as possible to relate to life in this manner, we will quickly find ourselves in a much more tranquil and peaceful world. The deep connection with the Creator will help each of us understand the purpose of our lives, the root of our souls, and how we can obtain endless enjoyment. By achieving that, we will be achieving the purpose of Creation and we will receive all the delight and pleasure that has been prepared for each of us.

Unity of Friends

Do what you can and the Lord's salvation is in the twinkling of an eye. The important thing that stands before you today is the unity of friends. Toil in that more and more, for it can compensate for all the faults.

It is written, "An exiled student; his Rav is exiled with him." Our sages were perplexed: How can complaints govern the student's Torah and work to the extent that repels him from being in God's domain, especially once he has become attached to a genuine Rav?

And they explained that when the student declines, it appears to him that the Rav has declined with him, as well. And because this is so, it is indeed so. That is, he will be able to benefit from his Rav only to the extent that he assumes in his heart. Hence, he only has a lowly and inferior Rav to the extent that he has measured him thus. And so, his Rav is exiled with him.

The beginning of the exile and enslavement in Egypt begins with the words, "Now there arose a new king over Egypt, who knew not Joseph." This means that a new dominion appeared in everyone's mind, a newly risen dominion, for they have fallen from their previous degree, as it is written, "An exiled student; his Rav is exiled with him." Thus, they did not know Joseph; that is, they attained him only to the extent that they assumed in their hearts.

For this reason, they pictured Joseph's image the same as they were, themselves. And for this reason, they did not know Joseph and the enslavement began. Otherwise, the righteous would certainly protect them and no exile and enslavement would be depicted for them.

Love of Friends

And what you wrote, that you inform me of the exile in Egypt, I wonder, you need further studying. "And they cried, and their cry came up unto God by reason of the bondage." Then, "and God knew." Without the knowledge of God in the exile, redemption is impossible. Moreover, the knowledge of the exile itself is the reason for the redemption. Thus, how can you wish to inform me at the time of redemption?

The truth shows its way and the grieving one declares his sorrow, and cannot restrain or hide it. Indeed, I feel you all, that within you, today has been replaced with tomorrow, and instead of "now" you say, "later." There is no cure for that but to strain to understand that error and perversion—that only those who need salvation today are salvaged by the Creator. And those who can wait for tomorrow will obtain their wit after their years, God forbid.

And this came upon you due to your negligence of my request to exert in love of friends, for I have explained to you in every possible manner that this remedy is sufficient to complement for your every deficiency. And if you cannot rise to heaven, I have given you ways on earth; and why have you not added in this work at all?

And besides the great power hidden in it, you should know that there are many sparks of sanctity in each person in the group. And when you collect all the sparks of sanctity into one place, as brothers, with love and friendship, you will certainly have a very high level of sanctity...

The Influence of the Environment on a Person

...We know that there is a custom, applied all over the world, that it is not good for a highly skilled professional to be among poorly skilled workers and learn from their actions. For example, when a cobbler is among unskillful cobblers, they let him understand that it is not worthwhile to make a good shoe, but do it however it comes out, and it is not worthwhile to make a good and handsome shoe.

Or a tailor, if he is skillful, when he is among unskillful tailors, they let him understand that it is not worthwhile to strain to make the clothing neat, tidy, and fitting its owner. Hence, he should be wary of being in contact with them.

But when a builder is among tailors, he cannot learn from their bad actions because there is no connection between them. But within the same profession, each one should watch himself and be in contact only with pure-hearted people.

According to the above, with any person that you consider a servant of the Creator, you should be watchful and see if he is a skilled professional, meaning wishes his work to be clean and pure and intended for His Name. At the very least, he should know that he is not a good worker and seek advice in his soul by which to be a skillful worker, and not an ordinary worker who aims only for the reward.

But a good, skillful worker is one who does not consider the reward, but enjoys his work. If, for example, a skillful tailor knows that the clothing fits its owner at every point, it gives him spiritual pleasure, more than the money he receives.

Thus, with people who are not from your profession, it is not important if you are among them, since you engage in building and they engage in tanning. But with people who engage in Torah, but are not meticulous about keeping the clothing fit for its owner, they only have a mind that is against the Torah, opposite from the view of Torah. And here you must always be watchful... and keep a good way off those people, as it were a bowshot. And this is not so with ordinary people.

- Hence, since you have no contact with the people of Mizrahi, you do not need such a careful watch.
- But from the people of Agudat Israel, you do need to keep away.
- And with Hassidim, you need even greater vigilance.
- And with people who were close to my father (Baal HaSulam) you need to keep a very watchful eye.

And this is the reason: In the world of *Nekudim*, *Melech ha Daat*, the level of *Keter*, which is the first *Melech* (king), fell lower than all the *Melachim* (kings) during the breaking. This is so because while the coarser is also higher when it has a *Masach*, it is the worst when losing the *Masach*. For this reason, it fell lower than all the *Melachim*.

And we can interpret these words. When they walk in the path of the Creator, they have a twofold will to receive: for corporeality, as well as for spirituality. Hence, those who were close to Baal HaSulam, while they were leaning, had a *Masach* and *Aviut* (coarseness). But now that they are not surrendering and have no interest in having a *Masach*, their whole work is on being "handsome Jews" or "Rebbes" (great rabbis).

Thus, this is *Aviut* without a *Masach*, and they naturally give off what they do. And as for me, I have no trust in them, and there is no one to hold them down. I am being brief because I do not wish to have them in my thoughts, for you know the rule: "One is where one thinks."

To understand the matter more clearly, I shall give you a brief example: It is known that between each two degrees there is a medium, made of both discernments together.

- Between the still and the vegetative, there is a medium called "corals."
- Between the vegetative and the animate, there is the stone of the field, which is an animal that is tied to the earth by its navel and nourishes off it.
- And between the animate and the speaking, there is the monkey.

Hence, there is a question: What is the medium between truth and falsehood? What is the point that is made of both discernments together?

Before I clarify, I shall add another rule: It is known that it is impossible to see a small object, and that it is easier to see a large object. Hence, when a person commits few lies, he cannot see the truth—that he is walking on a false path. Rather, he says that he is walking on the path of truth. But there is no greater lie than that. And the reason is that he does not have enough lies to see his true state.

But when a person has acquired many lies, the lies grow in him to an extent that he can see them if he wishes. Thus, now that he sees the lies—that he is walking on a false path—he sees his true state. In other words, he sees the truth in his soul and how to turn to the right path.

It follows that this point, which is a point of truth—that he is treading a false path—is the medium between truth and falsehood. This is the bridge that connects truth and falsehood. This point is also the end of the lie, and from here on begins the path of truth.

Thus, we can see that to be rewarded with *Lishma* (for Her Name), we first need to prepare the biggest *Lo Lishma* (not for Her Name), and then we can achieve *Lishma*. And similarly, *Lo Lishma* is called a "lie" and *Lishma* is called "truth." When the lie is small and the *Mitzvot* and good deeds are few, he has a small *Lo Lishma*, and then he cannot see the truth. Hence, in that state, he says that he is walking on the good and true path, meaning working *Lishma*.

But when he engages in Torah all day and all night in *Lo Lishma*, then he can see the truth, since by the accumulation of lies, his lie increases and he sees that he is indeed walking on a false path.

And then he begins to correct his actions. In other words, then he feels that everything he does is only *Lo Lishma*. From this point, one passes to the path of truth, to *Lishma*. Only here, at this point, does the issue of "from *Lo Lishma* one comes to *Lishma*" begins. But prior to that, he argues that he is working *Lishma*, and how can he change his state and his ways?

Hence, if a person is idle in the work, he cannot see the truth, that he is immersed in falsehood. But by increasing Torah in order to bestow contentment upon his Maker, one can then see the truth: that he is walking on a false path, called *Lo Lishma*. And this is the middle point between truth and falsehood. Hence, we must be strong and confident on our way, so every day will be to us as new, as we need to always renew our foundations, and then we shall march forward.

Purpose of Society

We have gathered here to establish a society for all who wish to follow the path and method of Baal HaSulam, the way by which to climb the degrees of man, and not remain as a beast, as our sages said (*Yevamot*, 61a) about the verse, "And ye My sheep, the sheep of My pasture, are men." And Rashbi said, "You are called 'men,' and idol worshipers are not called 'men.'"

To understand man's merit, we shall now bring a verse from our sages (*Berachot*, 6b) about the verse, "The end of the matter, all having been heard: fear God, and keep His commandments; for this is the whole man" (Ecclesiastes, 12:13). And the Gemarah asks, "What is 'for this is the whole man'? Rabbi Elazar said, 'The Creator said, 'The whole world was created only for that.' This means that the whole world was created for the fear of God.'"

Yet, we need to understand what the fear of God is, being the reason for which the world was created. From all the words of our sages, we learn that the reason for Creation was to do good to His creations. This means that the Creator wished to delight the creatures so they would feel happy in the world. And here our sages said about the verse, "for this is the whole man," that the reason for Creation was the fear of God.

But according to what is explained in the essay, "Matan Torah," it writes that the reason why the creatures are not receiving the delight and pleasure, even though it is the reason for Creation, is the disparity of form between the Creator and the creatures. The Creator is the giver and the creatures are the receivers. But there is a rule that the branches are similar to the root from which the branches were born.

And since there is no reception in our root, since the Creator is in no way deficient, needing to receive anything to satisfy His want, man feels unpleasantness when he needs to be a receiver. This is why every person is ashamed to eat the bread of shame.

And to correct that, the world had to be created. *Olam* (world) means *He'elem* (concealment), that the delight and pleasure must be concealed. Why is it so? The answer is, for fear. In other words, it is so man would fear using his vessels of reception, called "self love." This means that one should prevent oneself from receiving pleasures because one craves them, and should have the strength to prevail over the craving, the object of one's desire.

Instead, one should receive pleasures that bring contentment to the Creator. This means that the creature will want to bestow upon the Creator, and will have fear of the Creator, of receiving for oneself, since reception of pleasure—when one receives for one's own benefit—removes him from cleaving to the Creator.

Therefore, when a person performs one of the *Mitzvot* (commandments) of the Creator, one should aim that this *Mitzva* will bring him pure thoughts, that he will bestow upon the Creator by keeping God's *Mitzvot*. It is as our sages said, "Rabbi Hanania Ben Akashia says, 'The Creator wanted to cleanse Israel; hence, He gave them plentiful Torah and *Mitzvot*.'"

And this is why we gather here—to establish a society where each of us follows the spirit of bestowing upon the Creator. And to achieve bestowal upon the Creator, we must begin with bestowal upon man, which is called "love of others."

And love of others can only be with revoking one's self. Thus, on the one hand, each person should feel lowly, and on the other hand, be proud that the Creator has given us the chance to be in a society where each of us has but a single goal: for Divinity to be among us.

And although we have not yet achieved this goal, we have the desire to achieve it. And this, too, should be appreciated by us, for even though we are at the beginning of the way, we do hope to achieve the exalted goal.

Concerning Love of Friends

1) The need for love of friends.

2) What is the reason I chose specifically these friends, and why have the friends chosen me?

3) Should each of the friends disclose his love for the society, or is it enough to feel love in one's heart and practice love of friends in concealment, and thus not need to openly show what is in his heart?

It is known that being humble is a great thing. But we can also say the opposite—that one must disclose the love in his heart towards the friends, since by revealing it he evokes his friends' hearts toward the friends so they, too, would feel that each of them is practicing love of friends. The benefit from that is that in this manner, one gains strength to practice love of friends more forcefully, since every person's force of love is integrated in each other's.

It turns out that where a person has one measure of strength to practice love of friends, if the group consists of ten members, then he is integrated with ten forces of the need, who understand that it is necessary to engage in love of friends. However, if each of them does not show the society that he is practicing love of friends, then one lacks the force of the group.

This is so because it is very hard to judge one's friend to a scale of merit. Each one thinks that he is righteous and that only he engages in love of friends. In that state, one has very little strength to practice love of others. Thus, this work, specifically, should be public and not concealed.

But one must always remind oneself of the purpose of the society. Otherwise, the body tends to blur the goal, since the body always cares for its own benefit. We must remember that the society was established solely on the basis of achieving love of others, and that this would be the springboard for the love of God.

This is achieved specifically by saying that one needs a society so as to be able to give to one's friend without any reward. In other words, he does not need a society so the society would give him assistance and gifts, which would make the body's vessels of reception content. Such a society is built on self-love and prompts only the development of his vessels of reception, as now he sees an opportunity to gain more possessions through his friend's assistance to obtain corporeal possessions.

Instead, we must remember that the society was established on the basis of love of others, so each member would receive from the group the love of others and hatred of himself. And seeing that his friend is straining to annul his self and to love others would cause everyone to be integrated in their friends' intentions.

Thus, if the society is made of ten members, for example, each will have ten forces practicing self-annulment, hatred of self, and love of others. Otherwise, one remains with but a single force of love of others, since he does not see that the friends are practicing it, since the friends are practicing love of others in concealment. Moreover, the friends make him lose his strength in his desire to walk the path of loving others. In that state, he learns from their actions and falls into the dominion of self-love.

4) Should everyone know his friend's needs, specifically for each friend, so he would know how he can satisfy them, or is it enough to practice love of friends in general?

They Helped Every One His Friend

We must understand how one can help his friend. Is this where there are rich and poor, wise and fools, weak and strong? But when all are rich, smart, or strong, etc., how can one help another?

We see that there is one thing that is common to all—the mood. It is said, "A concern in one's heart, let him speak of it with others." This is because with regard to feeling high-spirited, neither wealth nor erudition can be of assistance.

Rather, it is one person who can help another by seeing that one's friend is low. It is written, "One does not deliver oneself from imprisonment." Rather, it is one's friend who can lift his spirit.

This means that one's friend raises him from his state into a state of liveliness. Then, one begins to reacquire strength and confidence of life and wealth, and he begins as though his goal is now near him.

It turns out that each and every one must be attentive and think how he can help his friend raise his spirit, because regarding the mood, anyone can find a needy place in one's friend, which he can fill.

Purpose of Society

Since man is created with a *Kli* called "self-love," where one does not see that an act will yield self-benefit, one has no motivation to make even a tiny movement. And without annulling self-love, it is impossible to achieve *Dvekut* (adhesion) with the Creator, meaning equivalence of form.

And since it is against our nature, we need a society that will form a great force so we can work together on annulling the will to receive, called "evil," as it hinders the achievement of the goal for which man was created.

For this reason, society must consist of individuals who unanimously agree that they must achieve it. Then, all the individuals become one great force that can fight against itself, since everyone is integrated in everyone else. Thus, each person is founded on a great desire to achieve the goal.

To be integrated in one another, each person should annul himself before the others. This is done by each seeing the friends' merits and not their faults. But one who thinks that he is a little higher than the friends can no longer unite with them.

Also, it is important to remain serious during the assembly so as not to lose the intention, as it is for this aim that they have gathered. And for walking humbly, which is a great thing, one should be accustomed to appear as though one is not serious. But in truth, a fire burns in their hearts.

Yet, to small people, during the assembly one should be wary of following words and deeds that do not yield the goal of the gathering—that thus they should achieve *Dvekut* with the Creator. And concerning *Dvekut*, see the essay, "Matan Torah."

But when one is not with the friends, it is best to show nothing of the intent in one's heart and appear to be like everyone else. This is the meaning of "walk humbly with the Lord your God." While there are higher interpretations of that, the simple explanation is also a great thing.

Hence, it is good that there will be equality among the friends who unite, so one can be annulled before the other. And there should be careful watch in the society, disallowing frivolity among them, since frivolity ruins everything. But as we have said above, this should be an internal matter.

But while there is someone who is not from this society, no seriousness should be shown, but to equalize with the person who had just come in. In other words, avoid speaking of serious matters, but only of things that suit the one who had just entered, who is called "an uninvited guest."

What Does "Love Thy Friend as Thyself" Give Us?

What does the law (*Klal*[14]), "love thy friend as thyself" give us? Through this law, we can come to love the Creator. If this is so, what does keeping the 612 *Mitzvot* give us?

First, we need to know what a law is. It is known that a collective (*Klal*) consists of many individuals. Without individuals, there cannot be a collective. For example, when we refer to an audience as "a sacred audience," we are referring to a number of individuals who have gathered and formed a unit. Afterwards, a head is appointed to the audience, etc., and this is called a *Minian* (ten/quorum) or a "congregation." At least ten people must be present, and then it is possible to say *Kedusha* (specific part of a Jewish prayer) at the service.

The Holy *Zohar* says about it: "Wherever there are ten, Divinity dwells." This means that in a place where there are ten men, there is a place for the dwelling of Divinity.

It therefore follows that the law, "Love thy friend as thyself," is built on 612 *Mitzvot*. In other words, if we keep the 612 *Mitzvot*, we will be able to achieve the law, "Love thy friend as thyself." It turns out that the particular elements allow us to achieve the collective, and when we have the collective, we will be able to achieve the love of the Creator, as it is written, "My soul yearns for the Lord."

However, one cannot keep all 612 *Mitzvot* alone. Take, for example, the redemption of the first-born. If one's first-born is a girl, he cannot keep the *Mitzva* of redemption of the first-born. Also, women are exempted from observing time-dependent *Mitzvot*, such as *Tzitzit* and *Tefillin*. But because "all of Israel are responsible for one another," through everyone, they are all kept. It is as though everyone keeps all the *Mitzvot* together. Hence, through the 612 *Mitzvot*, we can achieve the law, "Love thy friend as thyself."

---

14 Translator's note: In Hebrew, the word *Klal* means both "law" and "collective." The author alternates between the two meanings.

Love of Friends

"And a certain man found him, and behold, he was wandering in the field. And the man asked him, saying: 'What seekest thou?' And he said: 'I seek my brethren. Tell me, I pray thee, where they are feeding the flock'" (Genesis, 37).

A man "wandering in the field" refers to a place from which the crop of the field to sustain the world should spring. And the works of the field are plowing, sowing, and reaping. It is said about that: "They that sow in tears shall reap in joy," and this is called "a field which the Lord has blessed."

Baal HaTurim explained that a person wandering in the field refers to one who strays from the path of reason, who does not know the real way, which leads to the place he should reach, as in "an ass wandering in the field." And he comes to a state where he thinks that he will never achieve the goal he should achieve.

"And the man asked him, saying: 'What seekest thou?'" meaning, "How can I help you?" "And he said: 'I seek my brethren.'" By being together with my brothers, that is, by being in a group where there is love of friends, I will be able to mount the trail that leads to the house of God.

This trail is called "a path of bestowal," and this way is against our nature. To be able to achieve it, there is no other way but love of friends, by which everyone can help his friend.

"And the man said: 'They are departed hence.'" And Rashi interpreted that they had departed themselves from the brotherhood, meaning they do not want to bond with you. This, in the end, caused Israel's exile in Egypt. And to be redeemed from Egypt, we must take it upon ourselves to enter a group that wants to be in love of friends, and by that we will be rewarded with exodus from Egypt and the reception of the Torah.

According to What Is Explained Concerning "Love Thy Friend"

According to what is explained concerning "Love thy friend as thyself," all the details of the 612 *Mitzvot* are contained in this rule. It is as our sages say, "The rest is its commentary; go study." This means that by keeping the 612 *Mitzvot* we will be rewarded with the rule, "Love thy friend," and following, the love of God.

Thus, what does love of friends give us? It is written that by gathering a few friends together, since they each have but a small force of love of others, meaning they can carry out the love of others only in potential, when they implement it they remember that they have decided to relinquish self-love in favor of the love of others. But in fact, he sees that he cannot relinquish any pleasure of the will to receive in favor of another, not even a bit.

However, by assembling a few people who agree that they have to achieve love of others, when they annul themselves before one another, they are all intermingled. Thus, in each person there accumulates a great force, according to the size of the society. And then they can execute the love of others in actual fact.

Hence, what do the details of the 612 *Mitzvot* add to us, which we said are in order to keep the rule, since the rule is kept by love of friends? And we see that in reality there is love of friends among secular, too. They, too, gather in various circles in order to have love of friends. What then is the difference between religious and secular?

The verse says (Psalms 1), "nor sat in the seat of the scornful." We must understand the prohibition on "seat of the scornful." Is it due to slander or idle words? So the prohibition is not because of a "seat of scornful." What then does the "seat of scornful" add to us?

The meaning is that when a few people come together for the purpose of love of friends, with the intention that each and every one will help his friend improve his corporeal state, each anticipates that by having more meetings they will profit from society and improve their corporeal state.

However, after all the meetings, everyone calculates and sees how much he has received from society for the self-love, what the will to receive has gained by that, since he invested time and effort to benefit society, so what has he gained by it? He could probably succeed more if he had been occupied with self-benefit, at least the part of his own efforts. But "I entered the society because I thought that through the society, I would be able to gain more than I could gain alone. But now I see that I have gained nothing."

Then he regrets it and says, "I would be better off using my own little strength instead of giving my time to society. However, now that I have given my time to society, in order to gain more properties through help from the society, I finally realized that not only did I not gain anything from society, I even lost what I could have gained alone."

When there is someone who wishes to say that love of friends should be engaged in for the purpose of bestowal, that everyone will work to benefit others, everyone laughs and mocks it. It seems to them like a kind of joke, and this is a seat of seculars. It is said about it, "but sin is a reproach to any people, and every grace that they do, they do for themselves." Such a society detaches one from holiness. It casts one into the world of mockery, and this is the prohibition of the seat of the scornful.

Our sages said about such societies, "Disperse the wicked; better for them and better for the world." In other words, it is better that they do not exist. However, it is the opposite with the righteous: "Assemble the righteous; better for them and better for the world."

What is the meaning of "righteous"? It is those who want to keep the rule, "Love thy friend as thyself," whose sole intention is to exit self-love and assume a different nature of love of others. And although it is a *Mitzva* that should be kept, and one can force oneself to keep it, love is nonetheless something that is given to the heart, and the heart disagrees with it by nature. What then can one do to make love of others touch the heart?

This is why we were given the 612 *Mitzvot*: they have the power to induce a sensation in the heart. However, since it is against nature, that sensation is too small to have the ability to keep love of friends *de facto*, even though he has a need for it. Hence, now he must seek advice regarding how to actually implement it.

The advice for one to be able to increase his strength in the rule, "Love thy friend," is love of friends. If every one is nullified before his friend and mingles with him, they become one mass, where all the little parts that want the love of others unite in a collective force that consists of many parts. And when he has great strength, he can execute the love of others.

And then he can achieve the love of God. But the condition is that each will annul before the other. However, when he is separated from his friend, he cannot receive the share he should receive from his friend.

Thus, everyone should say that he is nothing compared to his friend. It is like writing numbers: If you first write "1" and then "0" it is ten times more. And when you write "00" it is a hundred times more. In other words, if his friend is number one, and the zero follows it, it is considered that he receives from his friend ten (10) times more. And if he says that he is double zero compared to his friend, he receives from his friend a hundred (100) times more.

However, if it is to the contrary, and he says that his friend is zero and he is one, then he is ten times less than his friend 0.1. And if he can say that he is one and he has two friends who are both zeros compared to him, then he is considered a hundred times less than them, meaning he is 0.01. Thus, his degree lessens according to the number of zeros he has from his friends.

Yet, even once he acquires that strength and can keep the love of others in actual fact, and feels his own gratification as bad for him, still, do not believe in yourself. There must be fear of falling into self-love in the middle of the work. In other words, should he be given a greater pleasure than he is used to receiving, although he can already work in order to bestow with small pleasures, and is willing to relinquish them, he lives in fear of great pleasures.

This is called "fear," and this is the gate to receive the Light of faith, called "The inspiration of Divinity," as it is written in *The Sulam*,[15] "by the measure of fear is the measure of faith."

Hence, we must remember that the matter of "Love thy friend as thyself" should be kept because it is a *Mitzva*, since the Creator commanded to engage in love of friends. And Rabbi Akiva only interprets this *Mitzva* that the Creator commanded. He intended to make this *Mitzva* into a rule by which all the *Mitzvot* would be kept because of the commandment of the Creator, and for self-gratification.

In other words, it is not that the *Mitzvot* should expand our will to receive, meaning that by keeping the *Mitzvot* we would be generously rewarded. Quite

---
15 Translator's note: *The Sulam* (Ladder) commentary on *The Book of Zohar*.

the contrary, by keeping the *Mitzvot* we will reach the reward of being able to annul our self-love and achieve the love of others, and subsequently the love of God.

Now we can understand what our sages said about the verse, "place them." It comes from the word, "potion[16]." "If granted, it is a potion of life; if not granted, it is a potion of death." Not granted means that one engages in Torah and *Mitzvot* to multiply self-love, so the body would acquire possessions in return for its work. If granted, one's self-love is nullified and he aims to receive a reward that is the strength for love of others, by which he will reach the love of the Creator—that his only wish will be to give contentment to the Creator.

---

16 Translator's note: In Hebrew the verb "to place" (*Ve Samtem*) is phonetically similar to the noun "potion" (*Sam*).

Which Keeping of Torah and Mitzvot Purifies the Heart

Question: Does keeping Torah and *Mitzvot* in order to receive reward purify the heart, too? Our sages said, "I have created the evil inclination, I have created the spice of Torah." This means that it does purify the heart. But is it so when one aims specifically at not receiving reward, or does it also purify the heart if one works in order to receive reward?

Answer: In the "Introduction to The Book of Zohar" (Item 44), it is written, "When one begins to engage in Torah and *Mitzvot*, even without any intention, meaning without love and fear, as is appropriate when serving the King, even in *Lo Lishma* (not for Her Name), the point in one's heart begins to grow and show its activity. This is so because *Mitzvot* do not require intention, and even actions without intention can purify one's will to receive, but in its first degree, called 'still.' And to the extent that one purifies the still part of the will to receive, one gradually builds the 613 organs of the point in the heart, which is the still of *Nefesh de Kedusha* (holiness)." Thus, we see that observing Torah and *Mitzvot*, even *Lo Lishma* purifies the heart.

Question: Is the path of observing Torah and *Mitzvot* in order to not be rewarded meant only for a chosen few, or can anyone walk this path of observing everything in order to not be rewarded, by which they will be rewarded with *Dvekut* (adhesion) with the Creator?

Answer: Although the will to receive for oneself alone emerged and came to be at the Thought of Creation, being given a correction that the souls will correct it to being in order to bestow, meaning observing Torah and *Mitzvot*, will turn our will to receive to be in order to bestow. This is given to everyone, without exception, for everyone was given this remedy, and not necessarily a chosen few.

But since this is a matter of choice, some advance more quickly and others more slowly. But as it is written in the "Introduction to The Book of Zohar" (Items 13, 14), in the end, everyone will achieve their complete perfection, as it is written, "He that is banished be not an outcast from him."

Still, when beginning to learn to observe Torah and *Mitzvot*, one begins in *Lo Lishma*. This is because man is created with a will to receive; hence, he does not understand anything that does not yield him self-benefit and he will never want to begin to observe Torah and *Mitzvot*.

It is as the Rambam wrote (*Hilchot Teshuva*, Chapter 10), "Sages said, 'one should always engage in Torah, even *Lo Lishma*, because from *Lo Lishma*, one comes to *Lishma*.' Hence, when teaching children and women and the populace, they are only taught to work out of fear and to receive reward. And when they gain knowledge and acquire wisdom, that secret is revealed to them bit by bit. They are accustomed to it calmly until they attain Him and serve Him with love." Thus, we see from the Rambam's words that everyone should achieve *Lishma*, but the difference is in the timing.

Question: If a person sees and feels that he is treading a path that leads to *Lishma*, should he try to influence others so others would tread the right path, too, or not?

Answer: This is a general question. It is like a religious person examining a secular person. If he knows that he can reform him, then he must reform him, due to the *Mitzva*, "Thou shalt surely rebuke thy neighbor." Similarly, in this case it can be said that you should tell your friend about the better way that one can go, provided your intention is only the *Mitzva*. But there are many times when a person rebukes another only for the purpose of dominating, and not in order to "rebuke thy neighbor."

And we learn from the above that everyone's desire that the other will tread the path of truth has created disputes between orthodox and secular, between *Litaim*[17] and Hassidim, and among the Hassidim themselves. This is because everyone thinks that he is in the right, and everyone is trying to persuade the other to tread the right path.

---

17 A faction of orthodox Judaism that started with the Vilna Gaon (GRA) in Vilna, Lithuania

Which Degree Should One Achieve?

Question: What is the degree one should achieve, so he will not have to reincarnate?

It is written in the book *Sha'ar Hagilgulim* (*Gate to Reincarnations*) that "All the children of Israel must reincarnate until they are complete with all the NRNHY. However, most people do not have all five parts called NRNHY, only *Nefesh*, which is from *Assiya*."

This means that each person must correct only one's own part and the root of one's own soul, and nothing more, and this completes what that person should correct.

The thing is that we must know that all the souls come from the soul of *Adam HaRishon*. After the sin of the Tree of Knowledge, Adam's soul broke into 600,000 souls. This means that the single Light that *Adam HaRishon* had in the Garden of Eden, which the Holy *Zohar* calls, "*Zihara Ilaa*" (Upper Light), has dispersed into many pieces.

In the book, *Panim Masbirot* (p 56), Baal HaSulam writes, "After the good mixed with the bad (after the sin), a great structure of *Klipot* was established, with the power to cling to *Kedusha* (Holiness)." In order to beware of them, the Light of the seven days of Creation was divided into very small pieces, which are too small for the *Klipot* to suck from.

This can be compared to a king who wished to deliver a great sum of money to his son who lived across the sea. Alas, all the people in the king's country were conniving thieves, and he could not find one loyal emissary. What did he do? He divided the money into pennies and sent them with a great number of emissaries. Thus, they found that the pleasure of theft was not worth dishonoring the kingship.

In this manner, over time and in many souls, through illumination of the days, it was possible to sort out all the holy sparks that were robbed by the *Klipot*, by the sin of the Tree of Knowledge.

"Many souls" refers to the division into Inner Lights, and many days is a division into many outer Lights. And the bits accumulate into the great amount of Light that *Adam ha Rishon* sinned in and then will bring the end of correction.

This leads to the conclusion that everyone is born with but a small piece of the soul of *Adam HaRishon*. When one corrects that piece, he no longer needs to reincarnate. This is why one can only correct that which belongs to one's own share.

It is written about it in the Ari's *The Tree of Life*, "There is not a day like another day, a moment like another moment, or a person like another person. And the *Helbona* (part of the sacred incense) will correct what the *Levona* (another part of the sacred incense) will not. Each must correct one's own part."

However, we must know that every person has a choice, for one is not born righteous. Our sages said (*Nida* 16b), "Rabbi Hanina Bar Pappa said, 'The angel appointed on conception is named *Laila* (Night). It takes a drop and places it before the Creator, and says, 'Dear Lord, this drop, what shall become of it—a hero or a weakling, a sage or a fool, rich or poor?' But it does not ask, 'righteous or wicked.'"

This means that one is not born righteous, for "it does not ask, 'righteous or wicked.'" This is left to our choice, each according to his labor in Torah and *Mitzvot*. Accordingly, one is rewarded with cleansing one's heart, with correcting what he must, according to the root of his soul, and then he is complete.

The First Degree When One Is Born

In *The Zohar, Mishpatim* (p 4, Item 11 in the *Sulam* commentary), it is written, "Come and see, when a person is born, he is given *Nefesh* from the side of the beast, the side of purity, from the side of those called 'Holy Angels,' meaning the world of *Assiya*. If he is rewarded further, he is given *Ruach* from the side of the 'Holy Animals,' meaning from the side of *Yetzira*. If further rewarded, he is given *Neshama* from the side of the *Kisse* (throne), meaning from the world of *Beria*. If rewarded further, he is given *Nefesh*, in the way of *Atzilut*. If rewarded further, he is given *Ruach de Atzilut* from the side of the middle pillar, and he is considered a son to the Creator, as it is written, 'Ye are the children of the Lord your God.' If further rewarded, he is given *Neshama* from the side of *Aba ve Ima*, which are *Bina*, about which it was said, 'Let the whole soul praise the Lord,' and with them, the name *HaVaYaH* is completed."

Thus, the perfection of the soul is having *NRN* from *BYA* and *NRN* from *Atzilut*. This is the perfection that *Adam ha Rishon* had prior to the sin. Only after the sin did he decline from his degree and his soul was divided into 600,000 souls.

This is the reason why man's spirituality is called *Neshama* (soul) even when one has only *Nefesh de Nefesh*, since there is a rule that when discussing anything, we always refer to its highest level. And since man's highest level is the degree of *Neshama*, man's spirituality is generally referred to as *Neshama*.

And although each person is born with the smallest degree, they said (*Shaar HaGilgulim* p 11b), "every person can be as Moses if he wishes to cleanse his actions. This is so because he can take another spirit, a higher one, with the height of *Yetzira*, as well as *Neshama* from the height of *Beria*."

Now you can also understand our sages' famous words: "The spirit of the righteous or their souls come and are impregnated in what is called *Ibur* (impregnation), to assist Him with work of God."

It is also presented in the *Sulam* (*Introduction of the Book of Zohar*, p 93): "The thing is that the donkey driver is the assistance to the souls of the righteous, sent to them from Above in order to elevate them from one degree to the next. Had it not been for this assistance, which the Creator sends to the righteous, they would have been unable to exit their degree and rise Higher. Hence, the Creator sends each righteous a High soul from Above, each according to his merit and degree, which helps him on his way. This is called 'the impregnation of the soul of a righteous,' and it is called 'disclosure of the soul of the righteous.'"

It follows that when it is said that there is no generation without the likes of Abraham, Isaac, and Jacob, it does not mean that they were born this way and do not have a choice in the matter. Rather, these are people who are trying to walk in the path of truth and make the necessary efforts. These people always receive help from Above through impregnation of the souls of the righteous, and they receive strength to climb the Higher degrees.

It turns out that everything that is given from Above is considered assistance, but not without any labor and choice. And the persistence of the world is through these righteous, who extend abundance from Above, and thus there is sustenance Above.

Concerning the Importance of Society

It is known that since man is always among people who have no connection to the work on the path of truth, but to the contrary, always resist those who walk on the path of truth, and since people's thoughts mingle, the views of those who oppose the path of truth permeate those with some desire to walk on the path of truth.

Hence, there is no other counsel but to establish a separate society for themselves, to be their framework, meaning a separate community that does not mingle with other people whose views differ from that society. And they should constantly evoke in themselves the issue of the purpose of society, so they will not follow the majority, because following the majority is our nature.

If the society isolates itself from the rest of the people, if they have no connection with other people in regard to spiritual matters, and their contact with them is only on corporeal matters, they do not mingle with their views, since they have no connection in matters of religion.

But when a person is among religious people, and begins to converse and argue with them, he immediately mingles with their views. Their views penetrate his mind below the threshold of his consciousness to such an extent that he will not be able to discern that these are not his own views, but what he received from the people he connected with.

Therefore, in matters of work on the path of truth, one should isolate oneself from other people. This is because the path of truth requires constant strengthening, since it is against the view of the world. The view of the world is knowing and receiving, whereas the view of Torah is faith and bestowal. If one strays from that, he immediately forgets all the work of the path of truth and falls into a world of self-love. Only from a society in the form of "They helped every man his friend" does each person in the society receives the strength to fight against the view of the world.

Also, we find the following in the words of *The Zohar* (*Pinechas*, p 31, Item 91, and in the *Sulam*): "When a person dwells in a city inhabited by evil people, and he cannot keep the *Mitzvot* of the Torah, and does not succeed in the Torah, he relocates and uproots himself from there and plants himself in a place inhabited by good people, with Torah and with *Mitzvot*. This is because the Torah is called 'Tree,' as it is written, 'She is a tree of life to them that lay hold upon her.' And man is a tree, as it is written, 'for is the tree of the field man.' And the *Mitzvot* in the Torah are likened unto fruits. And what does it say? 'Only the trees of which thou knows that they are not trees for food, them thou may destroy and cut down,' destroy from this world and cut down from the next world."

For this reason, he must uproot himself from the place where there are wicked, for he will not be able to succeed there in Torah and *Mitzvot*, and plant himself elsewhere, among righteous, and he will succeed in Torah and *Mitzvot*.

And man, whom *The Zohar* likens unto the tree of the field, like the tree of the field suffers from bad neighbors. In other words, we must always cut down the bad weeds around us that affect us, and we must also keep away from bad environments, from people who do not favor the path of truth. We need a careful watch so as to not be drawn to follow them.

This is called "isolation," when one has thoughts of the "single authority," called "bestowal," and not "public authority," which is self-love. This is called "two authorities"—the Creator's authority and one's own authority.

Now we can understand what our sages said (*Sanhedrin*, p 38), "Rav Yehuda said, 'Rav said, 'Adam ha Rishon* was heretic,' as it is written, 'And the Lord God called unto the man, and said unto him: 'Where art thou?'' Where has thine heart gone?'"

In Rashi's interpretation, "heretic" refers to a tendency for idol worshiping. And in the commentary, *Etz Yosef* (*Joseph's Tree*), it is written, "When it writes, 'Where, where has thine heart gone?' it is heresy, as it is written, 'that ye go not about after your own heart,' this is heresy, when his heart leans towards the other side."

But all this is very perplexing: How can it be said that *Adam ha Rishon* was inclined to idolatry? Or according to the *Etz Yosef* commentary, that he was in the form of "that ye go not about after your own heart," is it heresy? According to what we learn about the work of God, that it is solely about the aim to bestow, if a person works in order to receive, this work is foreign to us, for we need to work only to bestow, and he took everything in order to receive.

This is the meaning of what he said, that he failed in "go not about after your own heart." In other words, he could not take the eating from the Tree of Knowledge in order to bestow, but received the eating from the Tree of Knowledge in order to receive. This is called "heart," meaning the heart wishes only to receive for self-gratification. And this was the sin of the Tree of Knowledge.

To understand this matter, see the introduction to the book *Panim Masbirot*. And from this we can understand the benefits of the society—it can introduce a different atmosphere—working only in order to bestow.

Concerning the Importance of Friends

Concerning the importance of the friends in the society and how to appreciate them, meaning with which kind of importance everyone should regard his friend. Common sense dictates that if one regards one's friend as being at a lower degree than one's own, then he will want to teach him how to behave more virtuously than the qualities he has. Hence, he cannot be his friend; he can take the friend as a student, but not as a friend.

And if one sees one's friend as being at a higher degree than his own, and sees that he can acquire good qualities from him, then he can be his Rav, but not his friend.

This means that precisely when one sees one's friend as being at an equal degree to one's own, one can accept the other as a friend and bond with him. This is so because a friend means that they are both in the same state. This is what common sense dictates. In other words, they have the same views and thus decide to bond. Then, both of them act towards the goal that they both wish to achieve.

It is like two like-minded friends who are doing some business together, so this business will bring them profits. In that state, they feel that they have equal powers. But should one of them feel that he is more competent than the other, he will not want to accept him as an equal partner. Instead, they would create a proportional partnership according to the strength and qualities that one has over the other. In that state, the partnership is a thirty-three or twenty-five percent partnership, and it cannot be said that they are equal in the business.

But with love of friends, when friends bond to create unity among themselves, it explicitly means that they are equals. This is called "unity." For example, if they do business together and say that the profits will not be distributed equally, is this called "unity"? Clearly, a business of love of friends should be when all the profits and possessions that the love of friends yields will be equally controlled by them. They should not hide or conceal from one another, but everything will be with love, friendship, truthfulness, and peace.

But in the essay, "A Speech for the Completion of The Zohar," it is written, "The measure of the greatness comes under two conditions: 1) to always listen and receive the appreciation of society, to the extent of their greatness; 2) the environment should be great, as it is written, 'In the multitude of people is the king's glory.'"

To accept the first condition, each student must feel that he is the smallest among all the friends, and then he will be able to receive the appreciation of the greatness from everyone. This is so because the greater one cannot receive from the smaller one, much less be impressed by his words. Only the lower one is impressed by the appreciation of the greater one.

And for the second condition, each student must extol each friend's merit as though he were the greatest in the generation. Then the environment will affect him as a great environment should, since quality is more important than quantity.

It follows that in the matter of love of friends, they help each other, meaning it is enough for everyone to regard his friend as being of the same degree as his own. But because everyone should learn from his friends, there is the issue of Rav and disciple. For this reason, he should consider the friend as greater than himself.

But how can one consider one's friend as greater than himself, when he can see that his own merits are greater than his friend's, that he is more talented and has better natural qualities? There are two ways to understand this:

1. He is going with faith above reason: once he has chosen him as a friend, he appreciates him above reason.
2. This is more natural—within reason. If he has decided to accept the other as a friend, and works on himself to love him, than it is natural with love to see only good things. And even though there are bad things in one's friend, he cannot see them, as it is written, "love covers all transgressions."

We can see that a person may see faults in his neighbor's children, but not in his own children. And when someone mentions some faults in his children, he immediately resists his friend and begins to declare his children's merits.

And the question is, which is the truth? After all, there are merits to his children, and hence he is upset when others speak of his children. The thing is this, as I had heard it from my father: Indeed, each person has advantages and disadvantages. And both the neighbor and the father are saying the truth. But the neighbor does not treat the other's children like a father to his children, since he does not have the same love for the children as the father does.

Hence, when he considers the other's children, he sees only the children's faults, since this gives him more pleasure. This is because he can show that he is more virtuous than the other because his own children are better. For this reason, he sees only the other's faults. What he is seeing is true, but he sees only things he enjoys.

But the father, too, sees only the truth, except he regards only the good things that his children have. He does not see his children's faults, since it gives him no pleasure. Hence, he is saying the truth about what he sees in his children. And because he regards only the things that can please him, he sees only the virtues.

It turns out that if one has love of friends, the law in love is that you want to see the friends' merits and not their faults. Hence, if one sees some fault in one's friend, it is not a sign that his friend is at fault, but that the fault is in him, meaning that because he flawed the love of friends, he sees faults in his friend.

Therefore, now he should not see to his friend's correction. Rather, he himself needs correction. It follows from all the above that he should not care for the correction of his friend's faults, which he sees in his friend, but he himself needs to correct the flaw he has created in the love of friends. And when he corrects himself, he will see only his friend's merits and not his faults.

The Agenda of the Assembly

In the beginning of the assembly, there should be an agenda. Everyone should speak of the importance of the society as much as he can, describing the profits that society will give him and the important things he hopes society will bring him, which he cannot obtain by himself, and how he appreciates the society accordingly.

It is as our sages wrote (*Berachot* 32), "Rabbi Shamlai said, 'One should always praise the Creator, and then pray.' Where did we get that? From Moses, as it is written, 'And I besought the Lord at that time.' It is also written, 'O Lord God, Thou hast begun,' and it is written, 'Let me go over, I pray Thee, and see the good land.'"

And the reason we need to begin with praising the Creator is that it is natural that there are two conditions when one asks for something of another:

1. That he has what I ask of him, such as wealth, power, and repute as being wealthy and affluent.
2. That he will have a kind heart, meaning a desire to do good to others.

From such a person you can ask for a favor. This is why they said, "One should always praise the Creator, and then pray." This means that after one believes in the greatness of the Creator, that He has all sorts of pleasures to give to the creatures and He wishes to do good, then it is pertinent to say that he is praying to the Creator, who will certainly help him, since He wishes to bestow. And then the Creator can give him what he wishes. Then, also, the prayer can be with confidence that the Creator will grant it.

Similarly, with love of friends, at the very beginning of the assembly, when gathering, we should praise the friends, the importance of each of the friends. To the extent that we assume the greatness of the society, one can appreciate the society.

"And then pray," meaning that everyone should examine himself and see how much effort he is giving to the society. Then, when they see that you are powerless to do anything for the society, there is room for prayer to the Creator to help him, and give him strength and desire to engage in love of others.

And afterwards, everyone should behave the same as in the last three of the "Eighteen Prayer." In other words, after having pleaded before the Creator, the Holy *Zohar* says that in the last three of the "Eighteen Prayer," one should think as though the Creator has already granted his request, and he has departed.

In love of friends we should behave the same: After examining ourselves and following the known advice of praying, we should think as though our prayer has been answered and rejoice with our friends, as though all the friends are one body. And as the body wishes for all its organs to enjoy, we, too, want all our friends to enjoy themselves now.

Hence, after all the calculations comes the time of joy and love of friends. At that time, everyone should feel that he is happy, as though he had just sealed a very good deal that will earn him lots of money. And it is customary that at such a time he gives drinks to the friends.

Similarly, here everyone needs his friends to drink and eat cakes, etc. Because now he is happy, he wishes his friends to feel good, too. Hence, the dispersion of the assembly should be in a state of joy and elation.

This follows the way of "a time of Torah" and "a time of prayer." "A time of Torah" means wholeness, when there are no deficiencies. This is called "right," as it is written, "at His right hand was a fiery law."

But "a time of prayer" is called "left," since a place of deficiency is a place that needs correction. This is called "the correction of the *Kelim* (vessels)." But in the state of Torah, called "right," there is no room for correction, and this is why Torah is called a "gift."

It is customary to give presents to a person you love. And it is also customary to not love one who is deficient. Hence, at a "time of Torah," there is no room for thoughts of correction. Thus, when leaving the assembly, it should be as in the last three of the "Eighteen Prayer." And for this reason, everyone will feel wholeness.

STAGES *of* ATTAINMENT

Introduction to The Study of the Ten Sefirot

1) At the outset of my words, I find a great need to break an iron wall that has been separating us from the wisdom of Kabbalah, since the ruin of the Temple to this generation. It lies heavily on us and arouses fear of being forgotten from Israel.

However, when I begin to speak to anyone about this study, his first question is, "Why should I know how many angels are in the sky and what their names are? Can I not keep the whole Torah in all its details and intricacies without this knowledge?"

Second, he will ask, "The sages have already determined that one must first fill one's belly with Mishnah and Gemarah. Thus, how can one deceive himself that he has already completed the whole of the revealed Torah, and lacks only the wisdom of the hidden?"

Third, he is afraid that he will turn sour because of this engagement. This is because there have already been incidents of deviation from the path of Torah because of engagement in Kabbalah. Hence, "Why do I need this trouble? Who is so foolish as to place himself in danger for no reason?"

Fourth: Even those who favor this study permit it only to holy ones, servants of the Creator. And not all who wish to take the Lord may come and take.

Fifth, and most importantly, "There is a conduct in our midst that, when in doubt, keep this: Do as the people do," and my eyes see that all those who study Torah in my generation are of one mind, and refrain from studying the hidden. Moreover, they advise those who ask them that it is undoubtedly preferable to study a page of Gemarah instead of this engagement.

2) Indeed, if we set our hearts to answer but one very famous question, I am certain that all these questions and doubts will vanish from the horizon, and

you will look unto their place to find them gone. This indignant question is a question that the whole world asks, namely, "What is the meaning of my life?" In other words, these numbered years of our life that cost us so heavily, and the numerous pains and torments that we suffer for them, to complete them to the fullest, who is it who enjoys them? Or even more precisely, whom do I delight?

It is indeed true that historians have grown weary contemplating it, and particularly in our generation. No one even wishes to consider it. Yet the question stands as bitterly and as vehemently as ever. Sometimes it meets us uninvited, pecks at our minds and humiliates us to the ground before we find the famous ploy of flowing mindlessly in the currents of life as always.

3) Indeed, it is to resolve this great riddle that the verse writes, "Taste and see that the Lord is good." Those who keep the Torah and *Mitzvot* correctly are the ones who taste the taste of life. They are the ones who see and testify that the Lord is good, as our sages say, that He created the worlds to do good to His creations, since it is the conduct of The Good to do good.

Yet, those who have not yet tasted the taste of life in keeping Torah and *Mitzvot*, cannot feel and understand that the Lord is good, as our sages say, that when the Creator created us, His sole purpose was to benefit us. Hence, we have no other counsel but to keep the Torah and *Mitzvot* correctly.

It is written in the Torah (*Parashat Nitzavim*): "See, I have set before thee this day life and good, and death and evil." This means that prior to the giving of the Torah, we had only death and evil before us, as our sages say, "The wicked, in their lives, are called 'dead.'" This is because their death is better than their lives, as the pain and suffering they endure for their sustenance is many times greater than the little pleasure they feel in this life.

However, now we have been granted Torah and *Mitzvot*, and by keeping it we are rewarded with the real life, joyful and delightful to its owner, as it is written, "Taste and see that the Lord is good." Hence, the writing says, "See, I have set before thee this day life and good," which you did not have in reality at all prior to the giving of the Torah.

And the writing ends, "therefore choose life, that thou mayest live, thou and thy seed." There is a seemingly repeated statement here: "choose life, that thou mayest live." Yet, it is a reference to life in keeping Torah and *Mitzvot*, which is when there is real life. However, a life without Torah and *Mitzvot* is harder than death. This is the meaning of the words of our sages, "The wicked, in their lives, are called 'dead.'"

The writing says, "that thou mayest live, thou and thy seed." It means that not only is a life without Torah joyless to its owner, but one also cannot delight others. One finds no contentment even in one's progeny, since the life of his progeny is also harder than death. Hence, what gift does he leave for them?

However, not only does one who lives in Torah and *Mitzvot* enjoys his own life, but he is even happy to bear children and bequeath them this good life. This is the meaning of, "that thou mayest live, thou and thy seed," for he receives additional pleasure in the life of his progeny, of which he was the cause.

4) Now you can understand the words of our sages about the verse, "therefore choose life." It states, "I instruct you to choose the part of life, as one who says to his son: 'Choose for yourself a good part in my land.' He places him on the good part and tells him: 'Choose this for yourself.'" It is written about this, "O Lord, the portion of mine inheritance and of my cup, Thou maintainest my lot. You placed my hand on the good fate, to say, 'This take for you.'"

The words are seemingly perplexing. The verse says, "therefore choose life." This means that one makes the choice by himself. However, they say that He places him on the good part. Thus, is there no longer choice here? Moreover, they say that the Creator puts one's hand on the good fate. This is indeed perplexing, because if so, where then is one's choice?

Now you can see the true meaning of their words. It is indeed true that the Creator Himself puts one's hand on the good fate by giving him a life of pleasure and contentment within the corporeal life that is filled with torment and pain, and devoid of any content. One necessarily departs and escapes them when he sees a tranquil place, even if it seemingly appears amidst the cracks. He flees there from this life, which is harder than death. Indeed, there is no greater placement of one's hand by Him than this.

And one's choice refers only to the strengthening. This is because there is certainly a great effort and exertion here before one purifies one's body to be able to keep the Torah and *Mitzvot* correctly, not for his own pleasure, but to bring contentment to his Maker, which is called *Lishma* (for Her Name). Only in this manner is one endowed with a life of happiness and pleasantness that come with keeping the Torah.

However, before one comes to that purification there is certainly a choice to strengthen in the good way by all sorts of means and tactics. Also, one should do whatever his hand finds the strength to do until he completes the work of purification and will not fall under his burden midway.

5) According to the above, you will understand the words of our sages in the *Masechet Avot*: "Thus is the path of Torah: Eat bread with salt, drink little water, sleep on the ground, lead a sorrowful life, and labor in the Torah. If so you do, happy you will be; happy in this world and happy in the next world."

We must ask about their words: How is the wisdom of Torah different from the other teachings in the world, which do not require this asceticism and sorrowful life, but the labor itself is enough to acquire those teachings? Even though we labor extensively in the Torah, it is still not enough to acquire the wisdom of the Torah, except through the mortification of bread with salt and a sorrowful life.

The end of the words is even more surprising, as they said, "If so you do, happy you will be; happy in this world and happy in the next world." This is because it is possible that I will be happy in the next world. But in this world, while I torment myself by eating and drinking and sleeping, and lead a sorrowful life, would it be said about such a life, "happy in this world?" Is this the meaning of a happy life in this world?

6) However, it is explained above that engagement in Torah and *Mitzvot* correctly, in its strict condition, is to bestow contentment to one's Maker and not for self-gratification. And this is impossible to achieve except through great labor and exertion in purifying the body.

The first tactic is to accustom oneself to not receive anything for one's pleasure, even the permitted and necessary things for the existence of one's body, such as eating, drinking, sleeping, and other such necessities. Thus, one will detach oneself completely from any pleasure that comes to him, even in the necessities, in the fulfillment of one's sustenance, until he leads a sorrowful life in its literal meaning.

And after one becomes accustomed to that, and his body possesses no desire to receive any pleasure for itself, it is now possible for him to engage in the Torah and keep the *Mitzvot* in that manner, too, in order to bestow contentment upon his Maker and not at all for his own pleasure.

When one acquires that, one is rewarded with tasting the happy life, filled with goodness and delight without any blemish of sorrow, which appear in the practice of Torah and *Mitzvot Lishma*. It is as Rabbi Meir says (*Avot*, 6), "Anyone who engages in Torah *Lishma* is granted many things. Moreover, the whole world is rewarding to him, the secrets of Torah are revealed to him, and he becomes as a flowing spring."

It is about him that the verse says, "Taste and see that the Lord is good." One who tastes the flavor of the practice of Torah and *Mitzvot Lishma* is endowed with seeing the intention of Creation by himself, which it is to do only good to His creations, as it is the conduct of The Good to do good. Then he rejoices and delights in the number of years of life that the Creator has granted him, and the whole world is rewarding for him.

7) Now you will understand the two sides of the coin of engagement in Torah and *Mitzvot*: On the one hand, it is the path of Torah, meaning the extensive preparation one must make to prepare the purification of his body before he is actually rewarded with keeping Torah and *Mitzvot*.

In that state, he necessarily engages in Torah and *Mitzvot Lo Lishma* (not for Her name), but mixed with self-gratification. This is because he has not yet purified and cleansed his body from the will to receive pleasure from the vanities of this world. During this time, one must lead a sorrowful life and labor in the Torah, as it is written in the Mishnah.

However, after one completes the path of Torah, has already purified his body, and is now ready to keep the Torah and the *Mitzvot Lishma*, to bring contentment to his Maker, he comes to the other side of the coin. This is the life of pleasure and great tranquility, to which the intention of Creation—"to do good to His creations"—refers, meaning the happiest life in this world and in the next world.

8) This explains the great difference between the wisdom of Torah and the rest of the teachings in the world: Acquiring the other teachings in the world does not benefit life in this world whatsoever. This is because they do not even render mere gratification for the torments and suffering one experiences during life. Hence, one need not correct one's body, and the labor that he gives in return for them is quite sufficient, as with all other worldly possessions acquired in return for labor and toil.

However, the sole purpose of engagement in Torah and *Mitzvot* is to make a person worthy of receiving all the goodness in the intention of Creation, "to do good to His creations." Hence, one must necessarily purify one's body to merit that Godly goodness.

9) This also thoroughly clarifies the words of the Mishnah: "If so you do, happy you will be in this world." They made this precision deliberately, to indicate that a happy life in this world is only for those who have completed the path of Torah. Thus, the mortification in eating, drinking, sleeping, and

a sorrowful life that are mentioned here apply only while being on the path of Torah. This is why they meticulously stated, "Thus is the path of Torah."

And when one completes this path of *Lo Lishma* in sorrowful life and mortification, the Mishnah ends, "...happy are you in this world." This is because you will be granted that happiness and goodness in the intention of Creation, and the whole world will be rewarding for you, even this world, and all the more so the next world.

10) *The Zohar* (*Beresheet* p 31b) writes about the verse, "And God said: 'Let there be light,' and there was light," there was Light for this world and there was Light for the next world. This means that the acts of creation were created in their full stature and form, meaning in their fullest glory and perfection. Accordingly, the Light that was created on the first day came out in all its perfection, which contains the life of this world, too, in utter pleasantness and gentleness, as expressed in the words, "Let there be light."

However, to prepare a place of choice and labor, He stood and concealed it for the righteous at the end of days, as our sages say. Hence, they said in their pure tongue, "Let there be Light for this world." However, it did not remain so, but "let there be Light for the next world."

In other words, they who practice Torah and *Mitzvot Lishma* are rewarded with it only at the end of days, during the end of days, after the end of the purification of their body in the path of Torah. Then they are rewarded with that great Light in this world, too, as our sages said, "You shall see your world in your life."

11) However, we find and see in the words of the sages of the Talmud that they have made the path of Torah easier for us than the sages of the Mishnah. This is because they said, "One should always practice the Torah and *Mitzvot*, even *Lo Lishma*, and from *Lo Lishma* he will come to *Lishma*, because the Light in it reforms him."

Thus, they have provided us with a new means instead of the penance presented in the above- mentioned Mishnah, *Avot*: the "Light in the Torah." It bears sufficient power to reform one and bring him to practice Torah and *Mitzvot Lishma*.

They did not mention penance here, only that engagement in Torah and *Mitzvot* alone provides one with that Light that reforms, so one may engage in Torah and *Mitzvot* in order to bring contentment to his Maker and not at all for his own pleasure. And this is called *Lishma*.

12) Yet, it seems we must question their words. After all, we have found a few students whose practice in Torah did not help them to come to *Lishma* through the Light in it. Indeed, practicing Torah and *Mitzvot* in *Lo Lishma* means that one believes in the Creator, in the Torah, and in reward and punishment. And he engages in the Torah because the Creator commanded the engagement, but associates his own pleasure with bringing contentment to his Maker.

If, after all one's trouble in the practice of Torah and *Mitzvot*, he will learn that no pleasure or self-benefit came to him through this great exertion and strain, he will regret having made all these efforts. This is because from the very beginning, he has tortured himself thinking that he, too, would enjoy his exertion. This is called *Lo Lishma*.

Nonetheless, our sages permitted the beginning of the practice in Torah and *Mitzvot* in *Lo Lishma*, as well, because from *Lo Lishma* one comes to *Lishma*. However, there is no doubt that if this student has not been rewarded with faith in the Creator and in His law, but still dwells in doubt, it is not about him that our sages said, "from *Lo Lishma* he will come to *Lishma*." It is not about him that they said that by engaging in it, "the Light in it reforms" them.

This is so because the Light in the Torah shines only to those with faith. Moreover, the measure of that Light is as the measure of the force of one's faith. Yet, to those without faith it is the opposite, for they receive darkness from the Torah and their eyes darken.

13) Sages have already presented a nice allegory about the verse, "Woe unto you that desire the day of the Lord! Wherefore would ye have the day of the Lord? It is darkness, and not light" (Amos 5). There is an allegory about a rooster and a bat that were waiting for the Light. The rooster said to the bat: "I am waiting for the Light because the Light is mine. But you, why do you need the Light?" (*Sanhedrin* 98b).

Clearly, those students who were not endowed with coming from *Lo Lishma* to *Lishma*, due to their lack of faith, did not receive any Light from the Torah. Thus, in darkness they walk and shall die without wisdom.

Conversely, those who were imparted complete faith are guaranteed in the words of our sages that because they engage in the Torah, even in *Lo Lishma*, the Light in it reforms them. They will be imparted the Torah *Lishma*, which brings a happy and good life in this world and in the next world, even without the prior affliction and sorrowful life. It is about them that the verse writes, "Then shalt thou delight thyself in the Lord, and I will make thee to ride upon the high places of the earth."

14) Concerning such a matter as the above, I once interpreted the saying of our sages, "He whose Torah is his trade." The measure of his faith is apparent in his practice of Torah because the letters of the word, *Umanuto* (his trade), are the same (in Hebrew) as the letters of the word, *Emunato* (his faith).

It is like a person who trusts his friend and lends him money. He may trust him with a pound, and if he asks for two pounds he will refuse to lend him. He might also trust him with one hundred pounds, but not more. Also, he might trust him enough to lend him half his properties, but not all his properties. Finally, he may trust him with all his properties without a hint of fear. This last faith is considered "whole faith," and the previous forms are considered "incomplete faith." Rather it is partial faith, whether more or less.

Similarly, one allots oneself only one hour a day to practice Torah and work out of the measure of his faith in the Creator. Another allots two hours, according to the measure of one's faith in the Creator. The third does not neglect even a single moment of his free time without engaging in Torah and work. Thus, only the faith of the last one is whole, since he trusts the Creator with all his property. The previous ones, however, their faith is still incomplete.

15) Thus, it has been thoroughly clarified that one should not expect that engagement in Torah and *Mitzvot* in *Lo Lishma* will bring him to *Lishma*, except when one knows in one's heart that he has been granted faith in the Creator and in His Torah appropriately. This is because then the Light in it reforms him and he will attain "the day of the Lord," which is all Light. The sanctity of faith purifies one's eyes to enjoy His Light until the Light in the Torah reforms him.

Yet, those without faith are as bats. They cannot look at the Light of day because the daylight has been inverted for them to a more terrible darkness than the darkness of the night, as they are only fed in the darkness of night.

In this manner, the eyes of those without faith are blinded to the Light of God; hence, the Light becomes darkness to them. For them, the potion of life is turned into a potion of death. It is about them that the writing says, "Woe unto you that desire the day of the Lord! Wherefore would ye have the day of the Lord? It is darkness, and not light." Thus, first, one must make one's faith whole.

16) This answers yet another question in the *Tosfot* (*Taanit* p 7): "He who practices Torah *Lishma*, his Torah becomes to him a potion of life. And he who practices Torah *Lo Lishma*, his Torah becomes to him a potion of death." They asked, "Yet, they said, 'One will always practice the Torah, even in *Lo Lishma*, and from *Lo Lishma* he will come to *Lishma*.'"

According to the explained above, we should divide it simply: One who engages in Torah for the *Mitzva* of studying Torah, and believes in reward and punishment, but associating self-pleasure and benefit with the intention to bring contentment to his Maker, the Light in it will reform him and he will come to *Lishma*. And one who studies not for the *Mitzva* of studying Torah, because he does not believe in reward and punishment in that measure, to labor so for it, but exerts only for his own pleasure, it becomes a potion of death for him, since for him, the Light in it is turned to darkness.

17) Hence, the student pledges, prior to the study, to strengthen himself in faith in the Creator and in His guidance in reward and punishment, as our sages said, "Your employer is liable to reward you for your work." One should aim one's labor to be for the *Mitzvot* of the Torah, and in this way, he will be imparted the pleasure of the Light in it. His faith will strengthen and grow through the remedy in this Light, as it is written, "It shall be health to thy navel, and marrow to thy bones" (Proverbs 3:8).

Then one's heart shall rest assured that from *Lo Lishma* he will come to *Lishma*. Thus, even one who knows about himself that he has not been rewarded with faith, still has hope through the practice of Torah.

For if one sets one's heart and mind to attain faith in the Creator through it, there is no greater *Mitzva* than that, as our sages said, "Habakkuk came and stressed only that: 'the righteous shall live by his faith'" (*Makkot* 24).

Moreover, there is no other counsel than this, as it is written (*Masechet Baba Batra* p 16a), "Rabbi said: 'Job wished to rid the whole world of judgment. He said before Him: 'Oh Lord, Thou hath created the righteous; Thou hath created the wicked; who holds You down?'"

And Rashi interprets there: "Thou hath created righteous by means of the good inclination; Thou hath created wicked by means of the evil inclination. Hence, none are saved from Thine hand, for who holds You down? Coerced are the sinners." And what did the friends of Job reply (Job 15:4)? "Indeed, you do away with fear, and impair devotion before God, the Creator has created the evil inclination, He has created for it the spice of Torah."

Rashi interprets there: "Created the Torah, which is a spice that revokes 'thoughts of transgression,'" as it is written (*Kidushin* p 30), "If thou cometh across this villain, pull him to the *Beit Midrash* (seminary). If he is hard, he will soften. Hence, not coerced are they, for they could save themselves."

18) Clearly, they cannot rid themselves of the judgment if they say that they received that spice and still have thoughts of transgression, meaning that they

are still in doubt and the evil inclination has not yet melted. This is because the Creator, who created it and gave the evil inclination its strength, evidently knew to create the remedy and the spice liable to wear off the power of the evil inclination and eradicate it altogether.

And if one practices Torah and fails to remove the evil inclination from himself, it is either that he has been negligent in giving the necessary labor and exertion in the practice of Torah, as it is written, "I have not labored but found, do not believe," or perhaps one did put in the necessary amount of labor, but has been negligent in the quality.

This means that while practicing Torah, they did not set their minds and hearts to draw the Light in the Torah, which brings faith to one's heart. Rather, they have been absent-minded about the principal requirement demanded of the Torah, namely the Light that yields faith. And although they initially aimed for it, their minds went astray during the study.

Either way, one cannot rid oneself of the judgment by arguing coercion, for our sages strictly state, "I have created the evil inclination; I have created for it the spice of Torah." If there had been any exceptions in that, then Job's question would remain valid.

19) Through all that has been explained thus far, I have removed a great complaint about the words of Rabbi Chaim Vital in his introduction to *Shaar HaHakdamot* (*Gate to Introductions*) by the Ari, and the introduction to *The Tree of Life*. He writes, "Indeed, one should not say, 'I shall go and engage in the wisdom of Kabbalah before he engages in the Torah, Mishnah, and Talmud.' This is because our sages have already said, 'One should not enter the PARDESS[18] unless he has filled his stomach with meat and wine.'"

This is like a soul without a body: it has no reward or act or consideration before it is connected in a body, when it is whole, corrected in the *Mitzvot* of the Torah, in 613 *Mitzvot*.

Conversely, when one is occupied with the wisdom of the Mishnah and Babylonian Talmud, and does not give a share to the secrets of Torah and its concealments, as well, it is like a body that sits in the dark without a human soul, God's candle, which shines within it. Thus, the body is dry and does not draw from a source of life.

Thus, a wise disciple, who practices Torah *Lishma*, should first engage in the wisdom of the Bible, the Mishnah and the Talmud, as long as his

---
18 See explanation in the essay PARDESS.

mind can tolerate. Afterwards, he will delve into knowing his Maker in the wisdom of truth.

It is as King David commanded his son Solomon: "know thou the God of thy father and serve Him." And if that person finds the study of the Talmud heavy and difficult, he is better off leaving his hand off it once he has tested his luck in this wisdom, and engage in the wisdom of truth.

It is written, "A disciple who has not seen a good sign in his study within five years will also not see it" (*Hullin* p 24). Thus, every person whose study is easy must dedicate a portion of one or two hours a day to study the Halachah (Jewish code of laws), and explain and interpret the questions in the literal Halachah.

20) These words of his seem very perplexing: he is saying that before one succeeds in the study of the literal, one should already engage in the wisdom of truth. This contradicts his former words that the wisdom of Kabbalah without the literal Torah is as a soul without a body, having no deed, consideration, or reward.

The evidence he brings of a disciple who did not see a good sign is even more perplexing, for our sages said that he should therefore abandon the study of Torah. But certainly, it is to caution him to examine his ways and try with another Rav or in another portion. But he must certainly not leave the Torah, even the literal Torah.

21) It is even more difficult to understand, both in the words of Rabbi Chaim Vital and in the words of the Gemarah. It is implied in their words that one needs some specific preparation and merit to attain the wisdom of Torah. Yet, our sages said (*Midrash Raba*, Portion "And This Is the Blessing"), "The Creator said unto Israel: 'Regard, the whole wisdom and the whole Torah is easy: anyone who fears Me and observes the words of the Torah, the whole wisdom and the whole Torah are in his heart.'"

Thus, we need no prior merit here; and only by virtue of fear of God and the keeping of *Mitzvot* is one granted the whole wisdom of the Torah.

22) Indeed, if we examine his words they will clarify before us as pure heavenly stars. The text, "he is better off leaving his hand off it, once he has tested his luck in this [revealed] wisdom," does not refer to luck of wit and erudition. Rather, it is as we have explained above in the explanation, "I have created the evil inclination; I have created for it the spice of Torah." It means that one has delved and exerted in the revealed Torah, and still the evil inclination is in power and has not melted at all. This is because he is still not saved from thoughts of transgression, as Rashi writes above in the explanation, "I have created for it the spice of Torah."

Hence, he advises him to leave his hands off it and engage in the wisdom of truth, for it is easier to draw the light in the Torah while practicing and laboring in the wisdom of truth than in laboring in the literal Torah. The reason is very simple: the wisdom of the revealed is clothed in external, corporeal clothes, such as stealing, plundering, torts, etc. For this reason, it is difficult and heavy for any person to aim his mind and heart to the Creator while studying, so as to draw the Light in the Torah.

It is even more so for a person for whom the study in the Talmud itself is heavy and arduous. How can he remember the Creator during the study, since the scrutiny concerns corporeal matters, and cannot come in him simultaneously with the intention for the Creator?

Therefore, he advises him to practice the wisdom of Kabbalah, as this wisdom is entirely clothed in the names of the Creator. Then he will certainly be able to easily aim his mind and heart to the Creator during the study, even if he is the slowest learner. This is so because the study of the issues of the wisdom and the Creator are one and the same, and this is very simple.

23) Hence, he brings good evidence from the words of the Gemarah: "A disciple who has not seen a good sign in his study after five years will also not see it." Why did he not see a good sign in his study? Certainly, it is only due to the absence of the intention of the heart, and not because of any lack of aptitude, as the wisdom of Torah requires no aptitude.

Instead, as it is written in the above study: "The Creator said unto Israel, 'Regard, the whole wisdom and the whole Torah is easy: any one who fears Me and observes the words of the Torah, the whole wisdom and the whole Torah are in his heart.'"

Of course one must accustom oneself in the Light of Torah and *Mitzvot*, and I do not know how much. One might remain in waiting all his years. Hence the Braita warns us (*Hulin* 24) to not wait longer than five years.

Moreover, Rabbi Yosi says that only three years are quite sufficient to be granted the wisdom of the Torah. If one does not see a good sign within that length of time, one should not fool himself with false hopes and deceit, but know that he will never see a good sign.

Hence, one must immediately find himself a good tactic by which to succeed in achieving Lishma and to be granted the wisdom of the Torah. The Braita did not specify the tactic, but it warns to not remain seated in the same situation and wait longer.

This is the meaning of the Rav's words, that the surest and most successful tactic is the engagement in the wisdom of Kabbalah. One should leave one's hand entirely from engagement in the wisdom of the revealed Torah, since he has already tested his luck in it and did not succeed. And he should dedicate all his time to the wisdom of Kabbalah, where his success is certain.

24) This is very simple, for these words have no connection to the study of the literal Torah, in any thing that one must actually practice, for "it is not the ignorant who is pious, and a mistaken learning makes for evil, and one sinner destroyeth much good." Hence, one must necessarily repeat them as much as it is necessary to not fail in one's practice.

However, here it speaks only of the study of the wisdom of the revealed Torah, to explain and scrutinize questions that arise in the interpretation of the laws, as Rabbi Chaim Vital deduces there himself. It refers to the part of the study of the Torah that is not performed *de facto*, or to the actual laws.

Indeed, here it is possible to be lenient and study from the abbreviations and not from the origins. However, this, too, requires extensive learning, since one who knows from the origin is not like one who knows it from a brief scan of some abbreviation. In order to not err in that, Rabbi Chaim Vital says at the very outset of his words that the soul connects to the body only when it is corrected in the *Mitzvot* of the Torah, in 613 *Mitzvot*.

25) Now you see how all the questions that we presented in the beginning of the introduction are complete folly. They are the obstacles that the evil inclination spreads in order to hunt innocent souls, to dismiss them from the world, robbed and abused.

Examine the first question, where they imagine that they can keep the whole Torah without the knowledge of the wisdom of Kabbalah. I say to them: Indeed, if you can keep the study of Torah and the observance of the *Mitzvot* appropriately, *Lishma*, meaning only in order to bring contentment to the Maker, then indeed, you do not need to study Kabbalah. This is because then it is said about you, "One's soul shall teach him." This is because then all the secrets of the Torah will appear before you like a lush spring, as in the words of Rabbi Meir in the Mishnah (*Avot*), and you will need no assistance from the books.

However, if you are still engaged in learning *Lo Lishma*, but hope to merit *Lishma* by this means, then I ask you: "How many years have you been doing so?" If you are still within the five years, as the Tana Kama says, or within the three years, as Rabbi Yosi says, then you can still wait and hope.

But if you have been practicing the Torah in *Lo Lishma* for more than three years, as Rabbi Yosi says, and five years, as the Tana Kama says, then the Braita warns you that you will not see a good sign in this path you are treading! Why delude your souls with false hopes when you have such a near and sure tactic as the study of the wisdom of Kabbalah, as I have shown the reason above that the study in the issues of the wisdom and the Creator Himself are one?

26) Let us also examine the second question, which is that one must fill one's belly with Mishnah and Gemarah. Everyone agrees that it is indeed so. Yet, this is all true if you have already been endowed with learning *Lishma*, or even *Lo Lishma*, if you are still within the three years or the five years. However, after that time, the Braita warns you that you will never see a good sign, and so you must test your success in the study of Kabbalah.

27) We must also know that there are two parts to the wisdom of truth: The first, called the "secrets of Torah," should not be exposed except by implication, and from a wise Kabbalist to a disciple who understands in his own mind. *Maase Merkava* and *Maase Beresheet* belong to that part, as well. The sages of *The Zohar* refer to that part as "the first three *Sefirot*, *Keter*, *Hochma*, *Bina*," and it is also called "the *Rosh* (Head) of the *Partzuf*."

The second part is called the "flavors of Torah." It is permitted to disclose them and indeed, a great *Mitzva* to disclose them. *The Zohar* refers to it as the "seven lower *Sefirot* of the *Partzuf*," and it is also called the *Guf* (Body) of the *Partzuf*.

Every single *Partzuf de Kedusha* (of holiness) consists of ten *Sefirot*. These are called *Keter*, *Hochma*, *Bina*, *Hesed*, *Gevura*, *Tifferet*, *Netzah*, *Hod*, *Yesod*, *Malchut*. The first three *Sefirot* are considered the "*Rosh* of the *Partzuf*" and the seven lower *Sefirot* are named the "*Guf* of the *Partzuf*." Even the soul of the lower person contains the ten *Sefirot* in their above names, as well, and every single discernment, in the Upper and in the lower.

The reason why the seven lower *Sefirot*, which are the *Guf* of the *Partzuf*, are called "flavors of Torah" is as the meaning of the verse, "and the palate tasteth its food." The Lights that appear under the First three, namely the *Rosh*, are called *Taamim* (flavors), and *Malchut de* (of the) *Rosh* is called *Hech* (palate).

For this reason they are called *Taamim* of Torah. This means that they appear in the palate of the *Rosh*, which is the source of all the *Taamim*, which is *Malchut de Rosh*. From there down it is not forbidden to disclose them. Quite the contrary, the reward of one who discloses them is immeasurable and boundless.

Also, these First three *Sefirot* and these seven lower *Sefirot* expand both in the general and in the most particular segment that can be divided. Thus, even the First three *Sefirot* of the *Malchut* at the end of the world of *Assiya* belong to the section of the "secrets of Torah," which are not to be disclosed. And the seven lower *Sefirot* in the *Keter* of the *Rosh* of *Atzilut* belong to the section, "*Taamim* of Torah," which are permitted to be disclosed, and these words are written in the books of Kabbalah.

28) You will find the source of these words in the Mishnah *Pesachim* (p 119), as it is written (*Isaiah* 23), "And her gain and her hire shall be holiness to the Lord; it shall not be treasured nor laid up; for her gain shall be for them that dwell before the Lord, to eat their fill, and for stately clothing." "What is 'stately clothing'? This is what covers things that *Atik Yomin* covered. And what are those? The secrets of the Torah. Others say, this is what reveals things that *Atik Yomin* covered. What are those? The flavors of the Torah."

RASHBAM interprets, "*Atik Yomin* is the Creator," as it is written, "and *Atik Yomin* sits." The secrets of the Torah are *Maase Merkava* and *Maase Beresheet*. The meaning of "Name" is as it is written, "This is My Name for ever." The "clothing" means that He does not give them to any person, but only to those whose heart is anxious. "This is what reveals things that *Atik Yomin* covered" means covering the secrets of the Torah, which were initially covered, and *Atik Yomin* disclosed them, and gave permission to disclose them. And one who discloses them is granted what he said in this verse.

29) Now you evidently see the great difference between the secrets of Torah, where all who attain them receive this great reward for covering them and for not disclosing them. And it is to the contrary with the *Taamim* of the Torah, where all who attain them receive this great reward for disclosing them to others.

There is no dispute on the first opinion, but only examination of the different meanings between them. The Lishna Kama states the end, as it says, "stately clothing." Hence they interpret the attainment of the great reward for covering the secrets of Torah.

Others say it states the beginning, which reads, "eat their fill," meaning the *Taamim* of the Torah, as it is written, "and the palate tasteth its food." This is because the Lights of *Taamim* are called "eating"; hence, they interpret the attainment of the great reward mentioned in the text regarding one who discloses the *Taamim* of the Torah. (There is no dispute between them, but one speaks of the secrets of the Torah and the other speaks of the *Taamim* of the

Torah.) However, both think that the secrets of the Torah must be covered, and the *Taamim* of the Torah must be disclosed.

30) Thus you have a clear answer about the fourth and the fifth questions in the beginning of the introduction. And what you find in the words of our sages, as well as in the holy books, that it is only given to one whose heart is worried, meaning the part called "secrets of the Torah," considered the First three *Sefirot* and *Rosh*, that it is given to only concealed ones and under certain conditions, you will not find even a trace of them in all the books of Kabbalah, in writing and in print, since those are the things that *Atik Yomin* covered, as it is written in the Gemarah.

Moreover, do say if it is possible to even think and picture that all those holy and famous righteous, which are the greatest and best in the nation, such as *Sefer Yetzira* (*Book of Creation*), *The Book of Zohar*, and the Braita of Rabbi Ishmael, Rabbi Hai Gaon, and Rabbi Hamai Gaon, Rabbi Elazar of Garmiza, and the rest of the *Rishonim* (first ones) through the RAMBAN, and Baal HaTurim and the Baal Shulchan Aruch through the Vilna Gaon (GRA), and the Ladi Gaon, and the rest of the righteous may the memory of all be blessed.

From them we received the whole of the revealed Torah, and by their words we live, to know which act to perform so as to be favored by the Creator. All of them wrote and published books in the wisdom of Kabbalah. And there is no greater disclosure than writing a book, whose author does not know who reads the book. It is possible that utter wicked will scrutinize it. Hence, there is no greater uncovering of secrets of Torah than that.

And we must not doubt the words of these holy and pure, that they might infringe even an iota on what is written and explained in the Mishnah and the Gemarah, that are forbidden to disclose, as written in *Masechet Hagigah*.

Rather, all the written and printed books are necessarily considered the *Taamim* of the Torah, which *Atik Yomin* first covered and then uncovered, as it is written, "and the palate tasteth its food." Not only are these secrets not forbidden to disclose, on the contrary, it is a great *Mitzva* (very good deed) to disclose them (as written in *Pesachim* 119).

And one who knows how to disclose and discloses them, his reward is plentiful. This is because on disclosing these Lights to many, particularly to the many, depends the coming of Messiah soon in our days Amen.

31) There is a great need to explain once and for all why the coming of the Messiah depends on the study of Kabbalah in the masses, which is so prevalent in

The Zohar and in all the books of Kabbalah. The populace has already discussed it pointlessly and it has become unbearable.

The explanation of this matter is expressed in the *Tikkunim* (corrections) of *The Zohar* (*Tikkun* 30). Abbreviated translation: When the Holy Divinity went into exile, this spirit blows upon them who engage in the Torah because the Holy Divinity is among them. They are all as hay-eating beasts, every grace that they do, they do for themselves. Even all those who do study the Torah, every grace that they do, they do for themselves. In that time, the spirit leaves and does not return to the world. This is the spirit of the Messiah.

Woe unto them that make the spirit of the Messiah leave and not return to the world. They make the Torah dry and do not want to delve into the wisdom of Kabbalah. These people cause the sprouting of the wisdom, which is the *Yod* in the name *HaVaYaH*, to depart.

The spirit of the Messiah leaves, the spirit of holiness, the spirit of wisdom and understanding, the spirit of counsel and might, the spirit of knowledge, and of the fear of the Lord. "And God said: 'Let there be Light.'" This is the Light of love, the love of Mercy, as it is written, "I have loved thee with an everlasting love."

It is said about that, "if ye awaken, and if ye stir up love, until it please...," then it is love not in order to receive reward. This is because if fear and love are in order to receive reward, it is a handmaid... "a handmaid that is heir to her mistress."

32) We shall begin to explain the *Tikkunim* of *The Zohar* from toe to head. He says that the fear and the love one has in the practice of Torah and *Mitzvot* in order to receive reward, meaning while hoping for some benefit from the Torah and the work, this is considered the maid. It is written about her, "a handmaid that is heir to her mistress."

This is seemingly perplexing, for it is written: "One will always engage in Torah and *Mitzvot*, even *Lo Lishma*," and why "the earth doth quake?" In addition, we must understand the correlation of the engagement in *Lo Lishma* specifically to the handmaid, and also the parable that she inherits her mistress. What inheritance is there here?

33) You will understand the matter with everything that is explained above in this introduction, that they did not permit the study in *Lo Lishma* but only since from *Lo Lishma* one comes to *Lishma*, since the Light in it reforms. Hence, engagement in *Lo Lishma* is considered a helping handmaid, who assists and performs the ignoble works for her mistress, the Holy Divinity.

This is because at last, one will come to *Lishma* and will be imparted the inspiration of Divinity. Then the maid, which is the engagement in *Lo Lishma*, will also be considered a holy maid, for she supports and prepares the holiness, though she will be considered the world of *Assiya* of the *Kedusha* (holiness).

However, if one's faith is incomplete, and he does not engage in the Torah or in the work only because the Creator commanded him to study, then we have seen above that in such Torah and work the Light does not appear. This is because one's eyes are flawed, and like a bat turn the Light into darkness.

Such a study is no longer considered a maid of *Kedusha*, since he will not acquire *Lishma* through it. Hence, it comes to the domain of the maid of *Klipa* (shell), which inherits these Torah and work, and robs them for herself.

Hence, "the earth doth quake," meaning the Holy Divinity, called "earth." This is so because those Torah and work that should have come to her, as possessions of the Holy Divinity, that evil handmaid robs and lowers them to be a possession of the *Klipot* (shells). Thus, the handmaid is heir to her mistress.

34) The *Tikkunim* of *The Zohar* interpret the meaning of the oath, "if ye awaken, and if ye stir up love, until it please." The precision is that Israel will draw the Light of the Upper *Hesed* (Mercy), called "Love of Mercy," since this is what is desired. This is drawn particularly by the engagement in Torah and in *Mitzvot* not in order to receive reward. The reason is that the Light of the Upper Wisdom is extended to Israel through this Light of Mercy, appearing and clothing in this Light of Mercy, which Israel extends.

And this Light of Wisdom is the meaning of the verse, "And the spirit of the Lord shall rest upon him, the spirit of wisdom and understanding, the spirit of counsel and might, the spirit of knowledge and of the fear of the Lord" (Isaiah 11). It is said about the King the Messiah: "And He will set up an ensign for the nations, and will assemble the dispersed of Israel, and gather together the scattered of Judah from the four corners of the earth." This is because after Israel extends the Light of Wisdom through the Light of Mercy, the Messiah appears and assembles the dispersed of Israel.

Thus, everything depends on the practice of Torah and the work *Lishma*, which can extend the great Light of Mercy where the Light of Wisdom clothes and extends. This is the meaning of the oath, "if ye awaken, and if ye stir up." It is so because complete redemption and assembling the exiles are impossible without it, since so are the channels of holiness arranged.

35) They also interpreted "and the spirit of God hovered over the face of the waters." What is "the spirit of God"? During the exile, when Israel were still

occupied in Torah and *Mitzvot Lo Lishma*, if they are in this way because from *Lo Lishma* one comes to *Lishma*, then Divinity is among them, though in exile, since they still have not reached *Lishma*.

This is the meaning of the text when Divinity is in concealment. However, they are bound to attain the revelation of Divinity, and then the spirit of the Messiah King hovers on the engaging and awakens them to come to *Lishma*, as it is written, "the Light in it reforms them." She aids and prepares for the inspiration of Divinity, which is her mistress.

Yet, if this learning in *Lo Lishma* is not suitable to bring them to *Lishma*, Divinity regrets it and says that the spirit of man that rises upward is not found among those practicing the Torah. Rather, they suffice for the spirit of the beast, which descends, whose engagement in Torah and *Mitzvot* is only for their own benefit and pleasure.

The engagement in the Torah cannot bring them to *Lishma*, since the spirit of the Messiah does not hover on them, but leaves them and will not return, because the impure maid robs their Torah and inherits her mistress, since they are not on the way to come from *Lo Lishma* to *Lishma*.

Even though they do not succeed through the practice in the revealed Torah, since there is no Light in it, and it is dry due to the smallness of their minds, they could still succeed by engaging in the study of Kabbalah. This is because the Light in it is clothed in the clothing of the Creator—the Holy Names and the *Sefirot*. They could easily come to that form of *Lo Lishma*, which brings them to *Lishma*, and then the spirit of God would hover on them, as it is written, "the Light in it reforms them."

Yet, they have no wish at all for the study of Kabbalah. And thus they cause poverty, looting, ruin, killing, and destruction in the world, since the spirit of the Messiah leaves, the spirit of holiness, the spirit of wisdom and understanding.

36) We learn from the words of the *Tikkunim* of *The Zohar* that there is an oath that the Light of Mercy and love will not awaken in the world before Israel's deeds in Torah and *Mitzvot* will have the intention to not receive reward, but only to bestow contentment upon the Maker. This is the meaning of the oath, "I adjure you, O daughters of Jerusalem."

Thus, the length of the exile and affliction that we suffer depends on us and waits for us to merit the practice of Torah and *Mitzvot Lishma*. And if we only attain that, this Light of love and Mercy, which has the power to extend, will immediately awaken, as it is written, "And the spirit shall rest upon him, the spirit of wisdom and understanding." Then we will be granted complete redemption.

It has also been clarified that it is impossible for the whole of Israel to come to that great purity except through the study of Kabbalah, which is the easiest way, adequate even for commoners.

However, while engaging only in the revealed Torah, it is impossible to be rewarded through it, except for a chosen few and after great efforts, but not for the majority of the people (for the reason explained in Item 24). This thoroughly explains the irrelevance of the fourth and fifth questions at the beginning of the introduction.

37) The third question, which is the fear that one will turn sour, well, there is no fear at all here. This is because the deviation from the path of God that occurred before was for two reasons: Either they broke the words of our sages with things that they were forbidden to disclose, or because they perceived the words of the Kabbalah in their superficial meaning, as corporeal instructions, breaching "Thou shalt not make unto thee a graven image."

Hence, until this day there has indeed been a fortified wall around this wisdom. Many have tried to begin to study, but could not continue for lack of understanding and because of the corporeal appellations. This is why I have labored with the interpretation, *Panim Meirot* and *Panim Masbirot*, to interpret the great book, *The Tree of Life*, by the Ari, to make the corporeal forms abstract and to establish them as spiritual laws, above time and place. Thus, any novice can understand the matters, their reasons, and explanations with a clear mind and great simplicity, no less than one understands Gemarah through the interpretation of Rashi.

38) Let us continue to elaborate on the practice of Torah and *Mitzvot Lishma*. We must understand that name, "Torah *Lishma*." Why is desirable and whole work defined by the name, *Lishma*, and undesirable work named *Lo Lishma*?

The literal meaning implies that one who engages in Torah and *Mitzvot* to aim his heart to bring contentment to his Maker and not to himself should have been referred to as Torah *Lishmo* (for His Name) and Torah *Lo Lishmo* (not for His Name), meaning for the Creator. Why, then, is this defined by the name *Lishma* and *Lo Lishma*, meaning for the Torah?

There is certainly something more to understand here than the aforementioned, since the verse proves that Torah *Lishmo*, meaning to bring contentment to His Maker, is still insufficient. Instead, the study must be *Lishma*, meaning for the Torah. This requires explanation.

39) The thing is that it is known that the name of the Torah is "Torah of Life," as it is written, "For they are life unto those that find them" (Proverbs, 4:22); "For it is no vain thing for you; because it is your life" (Deuteronomy 32:47). Hence, the meaning of Torah *Lishma* is that the practice of Torah and *Mitzvot* brings one life and long days, and then the Torah is as its name.

And one who does not aim his heart and mind to the aforesaid, the practice of Torah and *Mitzvot* brings him the opposite of life and long days, meaning completely *Lo Lishma*, since its name is "Torah of Life." These words are explained in the words of our sages (*Taanit* 7a), "One who practices Torah *Lo Lishma*, his Torah becomes a potion of death for him; and one who practices Torah *Lishma*, his Torah becomes a potion of life for him."

However, their words require explanation, to understand how and through what does the Holy Torah becomes a potion of death for him? Not only is his work and exertion in vain, and he receives no benefit from his labor and strain, but the Torah and the work themselves become a potion of death for him. This is indeed perplexing.

40) First, we must understand the words of our sages (*Megillah* 6b), who said, "I labored and found—believe. I did not labor and found—do not believe."

We must ask about the words, "labored and found"; they seem to contradict each other, since labor refers to work and exertion that one gives in return for any desired possession. For an important possession, one makes great efforts; for a lesser possession, one makes lesser efforts.

Its opposite is the find. Its conduct is to come to a person absentmindedly and without any preparation in labor, toil, and price. Hence, how do you say, "labored and found"? And if there is effort here, it should have said, "labored and purchased" or "labored and acquired," etc., and not "labored and found."

41) *The Zohar* writes about the text "and those that seek Me shall find Me," and asks, "Where does one find the Creator?" They said that the Creator is found only in the Torah. Also, regarding the verse, "Verily Thou art a God that hidest Thyself," that the Creator hides Himself in the Holy Divinity.

We must thoroughly understand their words. It seems that the Creator is hidden only in corporeal things and conducts and in all the futilities of this world, which are outside the Torah. Thus, how can you say the opposite, that He hides Himself only in the Torah?

There is also the general meaning, that the Creator hides Himself in a way that He must be sought; why does He need this concealment? And also, "All that seek Him shall find Him," which we understand from the verse "and those that seek Me shall find Me." We must thoroughly understand this seeking and this finding, what are they and why are they?

42) Indeed, you should know that the reason for our great distance from the Creator, and that we are so prone to transgress His will, is for but one reason, which became the source of all the torment and the suffering that we suffer, and for all the sins and the mistakes that we fail in. Clearly, by removing that reason, we will instantly be rid of any sorrow and pain. We will immediately be granted adhesion with Him in heart, soul, and might. And I tell you that that preliminary reason is none other than the "lack of our understanding in His Providence over His creations," that we do not understand Him properly.

43) If, for example, the Creator were to establish open Providence with His creations in that, for instance, anyone who eats a forbidden thing would suffocate on the spot, and anyone who performs a *Mitzva* would discover such wonderful pleasures in it, like the finest delights in this corporeal world. Then, what fool would even contemplate tasting a forbidden thing, knowing that he would immediately lose his life because of it, just as one does not consider jumping into a fire?

Also, what fool would leave any *Mitzva* without performing it as quickly as possible, just as one who cannot retire from or linger with a great corporeal pleasure that comes into his hand, without receiving it as swiftly as he can? Thus, if Providence were open before us, all the people in the world would be complete righteous.

44) Thus you see that all we need in our world is open Providence. If we had open Providence, all the people in the world would be completely righteous. They would also cleave to Him with absolute love, for it would certainly be a great honor for any one of us to befriend and love Him with our heart and soul and cleave unto Him without losing even a minute.

However, since it is not so, and a *Mitzva* is not rewarded in this world, and those who defy His will are not punished before our eyes, but the Creator is patient with them, and moreover, sometimes think the opposite, as it is written (Psalms 73), "Behold, such are the wicked; and they that are always at ease increase riches." Hence, not all who want to take the Lord may come and take. Instead, we stumble every step of the way, until, as our sages wrote (*VaYikra Rabba*, 2) about the verse, "I have found one man out of a thousand, that a thousand enter a room, and one comes out to teach."

Thus, understanding His Providence is the reason for every good, and the lack of understanding is the reason for every bad. It turns out that this is the axis that all the people in the world circle, for better or for worse.

45) When we closely examine the attainment of Providence that people come to sense, we find four kinds there. Each and every kind receives specific Providence by the Creator, in a way that there are four discernments in the attainment of Providence here. In fact, they are only two: concealment of the face, and revelation of the face, but they are divided into four.

There are two discernments in Providence of concealment of the face, which are "single concealment" and "concealment within concealment," and two discernments in the Providence of revelation of the face: Providence of "reward and punishment," and "eternal Providence."

46) The verse says (Deuteronomy 31:17), "Then My anger shall be kindled against them in that day, and I will forsake them, and I will hide My face from them, and they shall be devoured, and many evils and troubles shall come upon them; so that they will say in that day: Are not these evils come upon us because our God is not among us? And I will surely hide My face in that day for all the evil which they shall have wrought, in that they are turned unto other gods."

When you regard these words, you will find that in the beginning it states, "Then My anger shall be kindled... ...and I will hide My face," meaning one concealment. Afterwards, it states, "and many evils and troubles shall come upon them... ...And I will surely hide My face," meaning double concealment. We must understand what is this "double concealment."

47) We must first understand what is the meaning of the "face of the Creator," about which the writing says, "I will hide My face." It can be thought of as a person who sees his friend's face and knows him right away. However, when he sees him from behind he is not certain of his identity. He might doubt, "Perhaps he is another and not his friend?"

So is the matter before us: Everyone knows and feels that the Creator is good and that it is the conduct of the good to do good. Hence, when the Creator generously bestows upon His creations, it is considered that His face is revealed to His creations. This is because then everyone knows and senses Him, since He behaves according to His name, as we have seen above regarding open Providence.

48) Yet, when He behaves with His creations the opposite from the above mentioned, meaning when they suffer affliction and torment in His world, it is considered the posterior of the Creator. This is because His face, meaning

His complete attribute of goodness, is entirely concealed from them, since this is not a conduct that suits His name. It is like a person who sees his friend from behind and might doubt and think, "Perhaps he is another?"

The writing says, "Then My anger shall be kindled... ...and I will hide My face." During the anger, when people suffer trouble and pains, it means that the Creator is hiding His face, which is His utter benevolence, and only His posterior is revealed. In that state, great strengthening in His faith is required, to beware of thoughts of transgression, since it is hard to know Him from behind. This is called "One Concealment."

49) However, when troubles and torments accumulate to a great extent, it causes a double concealment, which the books name "concealment within concealment." It means that even His posterior is unseen, meaning they do not believe that the Creator is angry with them and punishes them, but ascribe it to chance or to nature and come to deny His Providence in reward and punishment. This is the meaning of the verse, "And I will surely hide My face in that... they are turned unto other gods," that is, they become heretic and turn to idol worshiping.

50) However, before that, when the writing speaks only from the perspective of one concealment, the text ends, "they will say in that day: Are not these evils come upon us because our God is not among us?" This means that they still believe in Providence of reward and punishment, and say that the troubles and suffering come to them because they do not cleave to the Creator, as it is written, "these evils come upon us because our God is not among us." This is considered that they still see the Creator, but only from behind. For that reason it is called "One Concealment," only concealment of the face.

51) Now we have explained the two discernments of the perception of concealed Providence, which people sense: "one concealment" and "concealment within concealment." One concealment relates only to the concealment of the face, while the posterior is revealed to them. This means that they believe that the Creator gave them the affliction as a punishment. And although it is hard for them to always know the Creator through His posterior side, which brings them to transgress, even then they are considered "incomplete wicked." In other words, these transgressions are like mistakes, because they come to them as a result of the accumulation of the affliction, since, in general, they believe in reward and punishment.

52) Concealment within concealment means that even the posterior of the Creator is hidden from them, as they do not believe in reward and punishment.

These transgressions of theirs are considered sins. They are considered "complete evil" because they rebel and say that the Creator does not watch over His creations at all, and turn to idolatry, as it is written, "in that they are turned unto other gods."

53) We must know that the whole matter of the work in keeping Torah and *Mitzvot* by way of choice applies primarily to the two aforementioned discernments of concealed Providence. And Ben Ha Ha says about that time (*Avot*, Chapter 5): "The reward is according to the pain."

Since His Guidance is not revealed, it is impossible to see Him but only in concealment of the face, from behind, as one who sees one's friend from behind and might doubt and think he is another. In this manner, one is always left with the choice to either keep His will or break it. This is because troubles and the pains he suffers make him doubt the reality of His Guidance over His creations, whether in the first manner, which is the mistakes, or in the second manner, which are the sins.

In any case, one is still in great pain and labor. The writing says about this time: "Whatsoever thy hand attaineth to do by thy strength, that do" (Ecclesiastes 9). This is so because he will not be granted the revelation of the face, the complete measure of His goodness, before he exerts and does whatever is in his power to do, and the reward is according to the pain.

54) When the Creator sees that one has completed one's measure of exertion and finished everything he had to do in strengthening his choice in faith in the Creator, the Creator helps him. Then, one attains open Providence, meaning the revelation of the face. Then, he is rewarded with complete repentance, meaning he cleaves to the Creator once more with his heart, soul, and might, as though naturally drawn by the attainment of the open Providence.

55) These above attainment and repentance come to a person in two degrees: The first is the attainment of Providence of absolute reward and punishment. Besides attaining the reward for every *Mitzva* in the next world in utter clarity, he is also rewarded with the attainment of the wondrous pleasure in immediate observation of the *Mitzva* in this world.

In addition, besides attaining the bitter punishment that extends from every sin after one's death, one is also rewarded with the sensation of the bitter taste of every transgression while still being alive.

Naturally, one who is imparted this open Providence is certain that he will not sin again, as one is certain that he will not cut in his own flesh and cause himself terrible suffering. In addition, one is certain that he will not neglect a

Mitzva without performing it the instant it comes to his hand, as much as one is certain that he will not neglect any worldly pleasure or a great profit that comes into his hand.

56) Now you can understand the words of our sages, "What is repentance like? When He who knows all mysteries will testify that he will not turn back to folly." These are seemingly perplexing words, for who would rise to the heaven to hear the testimony of the Creator? Also, before whom should the Creator testify? Is it not enough that the Creator Himself knows that the person repented and will not sin again?

From the explanation, the matter becomes quite clear: In truth, one is not absolutely certain that he will not sin again before he is rewarded with the above attainment of reward and punishment, meaning the revelation of the face. And this revelation of the face, from the perspective of the Creator's salvation, is called "testimony," since His salvation in itself, to this attainment of reward and punishment, is what guarantees that he will not sin again.

It is therefore considered that the Creator testifies for him. It is written, "What is repentance like?" In other words, when will one be certain that he has been granted complete repentance? For this, one is given a clear sign: "when He who knows all mysteries testifies that he will not turn back to folly." This means that he will attain the revelation of the face, at which time one's own salvation will testify that he will not turn back to folly.

57) This above-mentioned repentance is called "repentance from fear." This is because although one returns to the Creator with his heart and soul, until He who knows all mysteries testifies that he will not turn back to folly, that certainty that he will not sin again is due to one's attainment and sensation of the terrible punishment and wicked torment extending from the transgressions. Because of that, one is certain that he will not sin, just as he is sure that he will not afflict himself with horrible suffering.

However, at last, these repentances and certainty are only because of the fear of punishment that extends from the transgressions. It turns out that one's repentance is only for the fear of punishment. Because of that, it is called "repentance from fear."

58) With this we understand the words of our sages: that one who repents from fear is rewarded with his sins becoming mistakes. We must understand how this happens. According to the above (Item 52), you can thoroughly understand that the sins one makes extend to him from the reception of Providence through

double concealment, namely concealment within concealment. This means that one does not believe in Providence of reward and punishment.

One concealment means that he believes in Providence of reward and punishment. Yet, because of the accumulation of the suffering, he sometimes comes to thoughts of transgression. This is because even though he believes that the suffering came to him as a punishment, he is still like one who sees his friend from behind, and might doubt and mistake him for another. And these sins are only mistakes, since, as a whole, he does believe in Providence of reward and punishment.

59) Hence, when one is granted repentance from fear, meaning a clear attainment of reward and punishment until he is certain that he will not sin again, the concealment within concealment is entirely corrected in him. This is because now he evidently sees that there is Providence of reward and punishment. It is clear to him that all the suffering he had ever felt was a punishment from His Providence for the sins he had committed. In retrospect, he made a grave mistake; hence, he uproots these sins.

However, this is not entirely so. They become sins. In other words, it is like the transgressions he made in one concealment, when he failed because of the confusion that came to him due to the multitude of torments that drive one out of one's mind. These are only regarded as mistakes.

60) Yet, in this repentance, he did not correct at all the first concealment of the face, which he had had before, but only from now on after he has attained the revelation of the face. In the past, however, before he had attained repentance, the concealment of the face and all the mistakes remained as they were, without any change or correction whatsoever. This is so because then, too, he believed that the troubles and the suffering came to him as punishment, as it is written, "they will say in that day: Are not these evils come upon us because our God is not among us?"

61) Therefore, he is still considered incomplete righteous because one who is awarded the revelation of the face, namely the complete measure of His goodness, as befits His Name, is called "righteous" (Item 55). This is so because he justifies His Providence as it truly is, that He is utterly good and utterly perfect with His creations, that He is good to the good and to the bad.

Hence, since he has been awarded the revelation of the face, from here on he merits the name "righteous." However, since he has not completed the correction, but only the concealment within concealment, and has not corrected the first concealment, but only from here on, that time, before he was awarded repentance, still does not merit the name "righteous." This is because then he is left with the concealment of the face, as before. For this reason, he is called "incomplete righteous," meaning one who still needs to correct his past.

62) He is also called "medium," since after he attains repentance from fear he becomes qualified, through his completion in Torah and good deeds, to attain repentance from love, as well. Then one attains being a "complete righteous." Hence, now one is the medium between fear and love, and is therefore named "medium." However, prior to that, he was not completely qualified to even prepare himself for repentance from love.

63) This thoroughly explains the first degree of attainment of the revelation of the face, the attainment and the sensation of Providence of reward and punishment in a way that He who knows all mysteries will testify that he will not turn back to folly. This is called "repentance from fear," when his sins become as mistakes. This is also called "incomplete righteous" and "medium."

64) Now we shall explain the second degree of the attainment of the revelation of the face, which is the attainment of the complete, true, and eternal Providence. It means that the Creator watches over His creations in the form of "Good that does good to the good and to the bad." Now one is considered "complete righteous" and "repentance from love," when one is granted turning his sins to virtues.

This explains all four discernments of perception of Providence that apply in the creations. The first three discernments, double concealment, single concealment, and attainment of Providence of reward and punishment are but preparations by which one attains the fourth discernment, which is the attainment of the true, eternal Providence.

65) But we have yet to understand why the third discernment is not enough for a person, namely attainment of the Providence of reward and punishment. We said that he has already been rewarded with He who knows all mysteries testifying that he will not sin again. Hence, why is he still called "medium" or "incomplete righteous," whose name proves that his work is still not desirable in the eyes of the Creator, and there is still a flaw and blemish in his Torah and work?

66) First, let us scrutinize what the interpreters asked about the *Mitzva* of loving the Creator. How did the Holy Torah oblige us to a *Mitzva* that we cannot keep at all? One can coerce and enslave oneself to anything, but no coercion or enslavement in the world will help with love.

They explained that when by keeping all 612 *Mitzvot* appropriately, the love of God extends to him by itself. Hence, it is considered possible to keep, since one can enslave and coerce oneself to keep the 612 *Mitzvot* appropriately, and then he will also attain the love of God.

67) Indeed, their words require elaborate explanation. In the end, the love of God should not come to us as a *Mitzva*, since there is no act or enslavement on our part in it. It rather comes by itself after completing the 612 *Mitzvot*. Hence, we are quite sufficient with the commandment of the 612 *Mitzvot*, and why was the *Mitzva* of love written?

68) To understand that, we must first acquire genuine understanding in the nature of the love of God itself. We must know that all the inclinations, tendencies, and properties instilled in a person, with which to serve one's friends, all these tendencies and natural properties are required for the work of God.

To begin with, they were created and imprinted in man only because of their final role, which is the ultimate purpose of man, as it is written, "he that is banished, be not an outcast from him." One needs them all so as to complement oneself in the ways of reception of abundance, and to complement the will of God.

This is the meaning of, "Every one that is called by My name, and whom I have created for My glory" (*Isaiah* 43:7), and also "The Lord hath made all things for His own purpose" (*Proverbs* 16:4). However, in the meantime, man has been given a whole world to develop and complete all these natural inclinations and qualities, by engaging in them with people, thus yielding them suitable for their purpose.

It is written, "One must say, 'The world was created for me,'" because all the people in the world are required for a person, as they develop and qualify the attributes and inclinations of every individual to become a fit tool for His work.

69) Thus, we must understand the essence of the love of God from the properties of love by which one person relates to another. The love of God is necessarily given through these qualities, since they were only imprinted in humans for His name to begin with. And when we observe the attributes of love between man and man, we find four measures of love, one atop the other, meaning two that are four.

70) The first is "conditional love." It means that because of the great goodness, pleasure, and benefit that one receives from one's friend, one's soul clings to one's friend with wondrous love.

There are two measures in that: the first is that before they met and began to love one another, they did harm to one another. However, now they do not want to remember it, for "love covereth all transgressions." The second measure is that they have always done good and helped one another and there is no trace of harm or detriment between them.

72) The second is "unconditional love." It means that one knows the virtue of one's friend to be sublime, beyond any imaginable measure. Because of that, his soul clings to him with endless love.

Here, too, there are two measures: the first measure is before one knows every conduct and deed of one's friend with others. At that time, this love is considered "less than absolute love."

This is because one's friend has dealings with others, and on the surface he seems to be harming others out of negligence. In this manner, if the lover saw them, the merit of his friend would be entirely blemished and the love between them would be corrupted. Yet, since he has not seen these dealings, his love is still whole, great, and truly wonderful.

73) The second attribute of unconditional love is the fourth attribute of love in general, which also comes from knowing the merit of his friend. Yet, in addition, now he knows all his dealings and conducts with every person, none missing. He has checked and found that not only is there not a trace of flaw in them, but his goodness is greater than anything imaginable. Now it is "eternal and complete love."

74) Note that these four attributes of love between man and man apply between man and God, as well. Moreover, here, in the love of God, they become degrees, by way of cause and consequence.

It is impossible to acquire any of them before one acquires the first attribute of conditional love. And after it is completely acquired, that first attribute causes one to acquire the second attribute. And after one has acquired the second attribute to the fullest, it causes him to acquire the third attribute. Finally, the third attribute to the fourth attribute, eternal love.

75) Hence the question arises, "How can one acquire the first degree of love of God, the first degree of conditional love, which is love that comes through the multitude of goodness that one receives from the loved one, when there is no reward for a *Mitzva* in this world?"

Moreover, according to the above, one must go through the first two forms of Providence by way of concealment of the face. In other words, His face, meaning His measure of goodness—the conduct of the good is to do good—is concealed at that time (Item 47). Therefore, at that time, one experiences pain and suffering.

Nevertheless, we learn that the whole practice of Torah and work out of choice is conducted primarily during that time, of concealment of the face. If so, how can it be that one will be awarded the second attribute of conditional love, being that the loved one has always done only wondrous and plentiful good, and never caused him any harm at all, and even more so when he attains the third degree or the fourth?

76) Indeed we dive into deep waters here. At the very least, we must fish out a precious gem from this. For that purpose, let us examine the words of our sages (*Berachot* 17), "You shall see your world in your life, and your end to the life of the next world."

We must understand why they did not say, "You will receive your world in your life," but only "see"? If they wanted to bless, they should have blessed wholly, meaning to acquire and receive his world in his life. We must also understand, why should one see his next world in his life? At least his end will be the life of the next world. Moreover, why did they place this blessing first?

77) First, we must understand how is this seeing of the next world in one's life? Certainly, we cannot see anything spiritual with corporeal eyes. It is also not the Creator's conduct to change the laws of nature. This is because the Creator originally arranged these conducts in this manner because they are the most successful for their purpose. Through them, one comes to cleave unto Him, as it is written, "The Lord hath made all things for His own purpose." Therefore, we must understand how one sees one's world in one's life?

78) I shall tell you that this seeing comes to a person through the opening of the eyes in the Holy Torah, as it is written, "Open Thou mine eyes, that I may behold wondrous things out of Thy law." It is about this that the soul is sworn before it comes to the body (*Nida* p 30), and "Even if the whole world says you are righteous, be wicked in your own eyes," specifically in your own eyes.

In other words, as long as you have not attained "opening of the eyes" in the Torah, regard yourself as wicked. Do not fool yourself with your reputation in the entire world as righteous.

Now you can also understand why they placed the blessing, "You shall see your world in your life," at the beginning of all the blessings. It is because prior to that, one is not even awarded the property of "Incomplete Righteous."

79) We have yet to understand, if a person knows within himself that he has already kept the whole Torah, and the whole world agrees with him in that, why is that not enough for him at all? Instead, he is sworn to continue regarding

himself as wicked. Is it because that wondrous degree of opening his eyes in the Torah is missing in him that you compare him to a wicked?

80) Indeed, the four measures of people's attainment of His Providence over them have already been explained. Two of them are in concealment of the face, and two are in disclosure of the face.

Also, the reason for the concealment of the face from the people has been explained: it is deliberately to give people room for labor and engage in His work in Torah and *Mitzvot* out of choice. This is because this increases the contentment of the Creator from their work in His Torah and *Mitzvot* more than His contentment from His angels above, who have no choice and whose work is coerced.

81) Despite the above praise for concealment of face, it is still not considered wholeness, but only as "transition." This is the place from which the longed-for wholeness is attained.

This means that any reward for a *Mitzva* that is prepared for a person is acquired only through one's labor in Torah and good deeds during the concealment of the face, when he engages out of "choice." This is so because then one feels sorrow out of his strengthening in His faith, in keeping His will. And one's whole reward is measured only according to the pain he suffers from keeping the Torah and the *Mitzva*, as it is written, "The reward is according to the pain."

82) Hence, every person must experience that transit period of concealment of the face. When he completes it, he is rewarded with open Providence, meaning the revelation of the face.

And before he is rewarded with revelation of the face, and although he sees the posterior side, he cannot refrain from ever committing a sin. Not only is he unable to keep all 613 *Mitzvot*, since love does not come by coercion and compulsion, but one is not complete even in the 612 *Mitzvot*, since even his fear is not fixed as it should be.

This is the meaning of the Torah being 611 in *Gematria* (any *Gematria* is the posterior side), that one cannot properly observe even 612 *Mitzvot*. This is the meaning of, "He will not always contend." In the end, one will be awarded the revelation of the face.

83) The first degree of the revelation of the face is the attainment of the Providence of reward and punishment in utter clarity. This comes to a person only through His salvation, when one is awarded the opening of eyes in the

Holy Torah in wonderful attainment, and becomes "a flowing spring" (*Avot*, 6). In any *Mitzva* in the Holy Torah that one has already kept of his own choice, one is granted seeing the reward of the *Mitzva* in it, intended for him in the next world, as well as the great loss in the transgression.

84) And although the reward is not yet in his hand, since the reward for a *Mitzva* is not in this world, the clear attainment is quite sufficient for him from now on, to feel the great pleasure while performing each *Mitzva*. This is so because, "All that is about to be collected is deemed collected."

For example, take a merchant who made a deal and gained a large sum, even though the profit will come to him after a long time. But if he is certain beyond any shadow of a doubt that the profit will come to him in time, he is as happy as if the money has come to him immediately.

85) Naturally, such Providence testifies that from now on he will cleave to Torah and *Mitzvot* with his heart, and soul, and might, and that he will retire from the sins as if escaping from a fire. And although he is not yet a complete righteous, since he has not acquired repentance from love, his great adhesion in the Torah and good deeds help him slowly be granted repentance from love, meaning the second degree of the revelation of the face. Then one can keep all 613 *Mitzvot* in full, and he becomes a complete righteous.

86) Now we thoroughly understand what we asked concerning the oath, that the soul is sworn before it comes to this world: "Even if the whole world says you are righteous, be wicked in your own eyes." We asked, "Since the whole world agrees that he is righteous, why must he still consider himself wicked? Does he not trust the entire world?"

We must also add, concerning the phrase, "Even if the whole world says." What is the connection between this and the testimony of the entire world, since one knows oneself better than the rest of the world? It should have sworn him, "Even if you know for yourself that you are righteous."

Yet, the most perplexing is that the Gemarah explicitly states (*Berachot* 61) that one must know in one's soul if he is righteous or not. Thus, there is an obligation and possibility to truly be completely righteous.

Moreover, one must delve and know this truth. If this is so, how is the soul sworn to always be wicked in its own eyes, and to never know the actual truth, when our sages have obligated the contrary?

87) The words are very precise indeed. As long as one has not been awarded the opening of eyes in the Torah in wondrous attainment, sufficient for him

for clear attainment of reward and punishment, he will certainly not be able to deceive himself and consider himself righteous. This is because he will necessarily feel that he lacks the two most comprehensive *Mitzvot* in the Torah, namely love and fear.

Even attaining complete fear, in a way that "He who knows all mysteries will testify that he will not turn back to folly," due to his great fear of punishment and the great loss from transgressing, is completely unimaginable before he is awarded complete, clear, and absolute attainment in Providence of reward and punishment.

This refers to the attainment of the first degree of revelation of the face, which comes to a person through the opening of eyes in the Torah. It is all the more so with love, which is completely beyond one's ability, since it depends on the understanding of the heart, and no labor or coercion will help here.

88) Hence, the oath states, "Even if the whole world says you are righteous." This is so because these two *Mitzvot*, love and fear, are given only to the individual, and no one else in the world can distinguish them and know them.

Thus, since they see that he is complete in 611 *Mitzvot*, they immediately say that he probably has the two *Mitzvot* of love and fear, too. And since human nature compels one to believe the world, one might fall into a grave mistake.

For that reason, the soul is sworn to that even before it comes into this world, and may it help us. Nonetheless, it is the individual himself who must certainly question and know in his heart if he is a complete righteous.

89) We can also understand what we asked, "How can even the first degree of love be attained when there is no reward for a *Mitzva* in this world (in this life)?" Now it is clear that one does not need to actually receive the reward for the *Mitzva* in his life, hence their precision, "You will see your world in your life, and your end to the life of the next world," indicating that the reward for a *Mitzva* is not in this world, but in the next world.

Yet, to know, to see, and to feel the future reward of the *Mitzva* in the next world, one must know it in complete certainty and clarity while in this life, through the wonderful attainment in the Torah. This is because then one still attains conditional love, which is the first degree of the exit from concealment of the face and the entrance to the revelation of the face, which one must have in order to keep Torah and *Mitzvot* correctly, in a way that, "He who knows all mysteries will testify that he will not turn back to folly."

90) And by laboring to observe Torah and Mitzvot in the form of conditional love, which comes to him from knowing the future reward in the next world, as in, "all that is about to be collected is deemed collected," one attains the second degree of revelation of the face—His Guidance over the world from His eternity and truthfulness, meaning that He is good and does good to the good and to the bad.

In that state, one attains unconditional love and the sins become as virtues for him. And from then on, he is called "complete righteous," since he can keep the Torah and Mitzvot with love and fear. And he is called "complete" because he has all 613 Mitzvot in completeness.

91) This answers what we asked: "One who attains the third measure of Providence, namely Providence of reward and punishment, when He who knows all mysteries already testifies that he will not turn back to folly, is still considered 'Incomplete Righteous.'" Now we thoroughly understand that one still lacks one Mitzva, the Mitzva of love. Of course, one is incomplete, since he must necessarily complete the 613 Mitzvot, which is necessarily the first step on the door of perfection.

92) With all that is said above, we understand what they asked, "How did the Torah obligate us to the Mitzva of love when this Mitzva is not even in our hands to engage in or even somewhat touch it?" Now you see and understand that it is about this that our sages warned us, "I have labored and did not find, do not believe," and also, "Let one always engage in Torah and Mitzvot in *Lo Lishma* because from *Lo Lishma* one comes to *Lishma*" (*Pesachim* 50). Also, the verse, "those that seek Me shall find Me" (Proverbs 8), testifies to that.

93) These are the words of our sages (*Megillah* p 6): "Rabbi Yitzhak said, 'If a person should tell you, 'I have labored and did not find,' do not believe; 'I did not labor and found,' do not believe; 'I labored and found,' believe.'" And we ask about, "I labored and found,' believe," that the words seem self-contradictory, since labor relates to possession, and a find is something that comes without labor at all, absentmindedly. He should have said, "I labored and bought."

However, you should know that this term, "find," mentioned here, relates to the verse, "those that seek Me shall find Me." It refers to finding the face of the Creator, as it is written in *The Zohar* that He is found only in the Torah, meaning that one is rewarded with finding the face of the Creator by laboring in the Torah. Hence, our sages were precise in their words, and said "I labored and found, believe," because the labor is in the Torah, and the finding is in the revelation of the face of His Providence.

They deliberately refrained from saying, "I labored and won, believe," or "I labored and bought." This is because then there would be room for error in the matters, since winning or possessing relate only to possession of the Torah. Hence, they made the precision of the word "found," indicating that it refers to another thing besides the acquisition of the Torah, namely the revelation of the face of His Providence.

94) That settles the verse, "I did not labor and found, do not believe." It seems puzzling, for who would think that it is possible to attain the Torah without having to labor for it? But since the words relate to the verse, "those that seek Me shall find Me" (*Proverbs* 8:17), it means that anyone, small or great, who seeks Him, finds Him immediately. This is what the word "seek" implies.

One might think that this does not require so much labor, and even a lesser person, unwilling to make any effort for it, will find Him, too. Our sages warn us in that regard to not believe such an explanation. Rather, the labor is necessary here, and not, "I labored and found, do not believe."

95) Now you see why the Torah is called "Life," as it is written, "See, I have set before thee this day life and good" (Deuteronomy 30:15), and also, "therefore choose life," and "For they are life unto those that find them" (Proverbs 4:22). This extends from the verse, "In the light of the king's countenance is life" (Proverbs 16), since the Creator is the source of all life and every good.

Hence, life extends to those branches that cleave to their source. This refers to those that have labored and found the Light of His face in the Torah, that have been imparted opening their eyes in the Torah in wonderful attainment, until they were imparted the revelation of the face, the attainment of the true Providence that befits His name, "Good," and the conduct of the Good is to do good.

96) And those that won can no longer retire from keeping the *Mitzva* correctly, as one cannot retire from a wonderful pleasure that comes to his hand. Hence, they run from transgression as one runs from a fire.

It is said about them: "But ye that did cleave unto the Lord your God are alive every one of you this day," as His love comes abundantly to them in natural love, through the natural channels prepared for one by the nature of Creation. This is so because now the branch is properly cleaved to its root, and life pours to him abundantly and incessantly from its origin. It is because of this that the Torah is called "Life."

97) For that reason, our sages warned us in many places concerning the necessary condition in the practice of Torah, that it will be specifically *Lishma*,

in a way that one will be awarded life through it, for it is a Torah of life, and this is why it was given to us, as it is written, "therefore choose life."

Hence, during the practice of Torah, every person must labor in it, and set his mind and heart to find "the light of the king's countenance" in it, that is, the attainment of open Providence, called "light of countenance." And any person is fit for it, as it is written, "those that seek Me shall find Me," and as it is written, "I labored and did not find, do not believe."

Thus, one needs nothing in this matter except the labor alone. It is written, "Anyone who practices Torah *Lishma*, his Torah becomes a potion of life for him" (*Taanit* 7a). It means that one should only set one's mind and heart to attain life, which is the meaning of *Lishma*.

98) Now you can see that the question the interpreters asked about the *Mitzva* of love, saying that this *Mitzva* is out of our hands, since love does not come by coercion and compulsion, is not at all a question. This is because it is entirely in our hands. Every person can labor in the Torah until he finds the attainment of His open Providence, as it is written, "I labored and found, believe."

When one attains open Providence, the love extends to him by itself through the natural channels. And one who does not believe that he can attain that through his efforts, for whatever reason, is necessarily in disbelief of the words of our sages. Instead, he imagines that the labor is not sufficient for each person, which is the opposite of the verse, "I labored and did not find, do not believe." It is also against the words, "those that seek Me shall find Me"; specifically, those that "seek," whomever they are, great or small. However, he certainly needs to labor.

99) From the above, you will understand the meaning of, "Anyone who practices Torah *Lo Lishma*, his Torah becomes a potion of death for him" (*Taanit* 7a), and the verse, "Verily Thou art a God that hidest Thyself," that the Creator hides Himself in the Torah.

We asked, "It seems reasonable that the Creator is hidden in this world, outside of the Torah, and not in the Torah itself, that only there is the place of the disclosure. And we asked further: This concealment that the Creator hides Himself, to be sought and found, why should I?"

100) From the above explained, you can thoroughly understand that this concealment that the Creator hides Himself so as to be sought is the concealment of the face, which He conducts with His creations in two manners: one concealment, and concealment within concealment.

The Zohar tells us that we should not even consider that the Creator wishes to remain in Providence of concealed face from His creations. Rather, it is like a person who deliberately hides himself, so his friend will seek and find him.

Similarly, when the Creator behaves in concealment of face with His creations, it is only because He wants the creatures to seek the disclosure of His face and find Him. In other words, there would be no way or inlet for people to attain the Light of the King's countenance had He not first behaved with them in concealment of face. Thus, the whole concealment is but a preparation for the disclosure of the face.

101) It is written that the Creator hides Himself in the Torah. Regarding the torments and pains one experiences during the concealment of the face, one who possesses few sins and has done little Torah and *Mitzvot* is not like one who has extensively engaged in Torah and good deeds. This is because the first is quite qualified to sentence his Maker to a scale of merit, to think that the suffering came to him because of his sins and scarceness of Torah.

For the other, however, it is much harder to sentence his Maker to a scale of merit. This is because in his mind, he does not deserve such harsh punishment. Moreover, he sees that his friends, who are worse than him, do not suffer so, as it is written, "the wicked, and they that are always at ease, increase riches," and also, "in vain have I cleansed my heart."

Thus, as long as one has not attained Providence of revelation of the face, the abundance of Torah and *Mitzvot* he has performed makes his concealment of the face much heavier. This is the meaning of, "the Creator hides Himself in the Torah."

Indeed, all that heaviness he feels through the Torah is but proclamations by which the Holy Torah itself calls him, awakening him to hurry and give the required measure of labor, to promptly endow him with the revelation of the face, as God wills it.

102) This is why it is written that all who learn Torah *Lo Lishma*, their Torah becomes a potion of death for them. Not only do they not emerge from concealment of the face to disclosure of the face, since they did not set their minds to labor and attain it, the Torah that they accumulate greatly increases their concealment of the face. Finally, they fall into concealment within concealment, which is considered death, being completely detached from one's root. Thus, their Torah becomes a potion of death for them.

103) This clarifies the two names the Torah is called by: "revealed" and "concealed." We must understand why we need the concealed Torah, and why is the whole Torah not revealed?

Indeed, there is a profound intention here. The concealed Torah implies that the Creator hides in the Torah, hence the name, "the Torah of the hidden." Conversely, it is called "revealed" because the Creator is revealed by the Torah.

Therefore, the Kabbalists said, and we also find it in the prayer book of the Vilna Gaon (GRA), that the order of attainment of the Torah begins with the concealed and ends with the revealed. This means that through the appropriate labor, where one first delves into the Torah of the hidden, he is thus granted the revealed Torah, the literal. Thus, one begins with the concealed, called *Sod* (secret), and when he is rewarded, he ends in the literal.

104) It has been thoroughly clarified how it is possible to attain the first degree of love, which is conditional love. We learned that even though there is no reward for a *Mitzva* in this world, the attainment of the reward for the *Mitzva* exists in worldly life nonetheless. It comes to a person by opening the eyes in the Torah. And this clear attainment is completely similar to receiving instantaneous reward for the *Mitzva*.

Hence, one feels the wonderful benefit contained in the Thought of Creation, which is to delight His creatures with His full, good, and generous hand. Because of the abundance of benefit that one attains, wondrous love appears between a person and the Creator. It pours to one incessantly, by the same ways and channels through which natural love appears.

105) However, all this comes to a person from the moment he attains onwards. Yet, one does not want to remember all the torment caused by the Providence in concealment of the face he had suffered before he attained the above disclosure of the face, since "love covereth all transgressions." Nevertheless, it is considered a great flaw, even with love among people, much less concerning the truthfulness of His Providence, since He is Good who does good to the good and to the bad.

Therefore, we must understand how one can attain His love in such a way that he will feel and know that the Creator has always done him wondrous good, since the day he was born onwards; that He has never, nor will ever cause him an ounce of harm, which is the second manner of love.

106) To understand that, we need the words of our sages. They said, "one who repents from love, his sins become as virtues." It means that not only does

the Creator forgive his sins, each sin and transgression one had made is turned into a *Mitzva* by the Creator.

107) Hence, after one attains the illumination of the face in such a measure that each sin he had committed, even the deliberate ones, is turned and becomes a *Mitzva* for him, one rejoices with all the torment and affliction he had ever suffered since the time he was placed in the two discernments of concealment of the face. This is because it is them that brought him all these sins, which have now become *Mitzvot*, by the illumination of His face, who performs wonders.

And any sorrow and trouble that drove him out of wits, and where he failed with mistakes, as in the first concealment, or failed with sins, as in the double concealment, has now become a cause and preparation for keeping a *Mitzva* and the reception of eternal and wondrous reward for it. Therefore, any sorrow has turned for him into great joy and any evil to wonderful good.

108) This is similar to a well-known tale about a Jew who was a house trustee for a certain landlord. The landlord loved him dearly. Once, the landlord went away, and left his business in the hands of his substitute, who was an anti-Semite.

What did he do? He took the Jew and struck him five times in front of everyone, to thoroughly humiliate him.

Upon the landlord's return, the Jew went to him and told him all that had happened to him. His anger was kindled, and he called the substitute and commanded him to promptly give the Jew a thousand coins for every time he had struck him.

The Jew took them and went home. His wife found him crying. She asked him anxiously, "What happened to you with the landlord?" He told her. She asked, "Then why are you crying?" He answered, "I am crying because he only beat me five times. I wish he had beaten me at least ten times, since now I would have had ten thousand coins."

109) Now you see that after one has been awarded repentance of the sins in a way that the sins became to him as virtues, one is then awarded achieving the second degree of love of the Creator, where the loved one never caused his loved one any harm or even a shadow of harm. Instead, He performs wondrous and plentiful good, always and forever, in a way that repentance from love and the turning of the sins into merits come as one.

110) Thus far, we examined only the two degrees of conditional love. Yet, we must still understand how one is awarded coming in the two manners of unconditional love with one's Maker.

For that, we must thoroughly understand what is written (*Kidushin* p 40), "One must always regard oneself half unworthy and half worthy. If he performs one *Mitzva*, happy is he, for he has sentenced himself to a scale of merit. If he commits one sin, woe unto him for he has sentenced himself to a scale of sin.

"Rabbi Elazar, son of Rabbi Shimon, says, 'Since the world is judged by its majority, and the individual is judged by the majority, if he performs one *Mitzva*, happy is he, for he has sentenced himself and the whole world to a scale of merit. If he commits one sin, woe unto him, for he has sentenced himself and the whole world to a scale of sin.' For this one sin that he had committed, the world and he have lost much good."

111) These words seem puzzling from beginning to end. He says that one who performs one *Mitzva*, immediately sentences to a scale of merit, for he is judged by the majority. Yet, this refers only to those who are half unworthy and half worthy. And Rabbi Elazar, son of Rabbi Shimon, does not speak of those at all. Thus, the essence is still absent.

Rashi interpreted his words as referring to the words, "One must always consider oneself half unworthy and half worthy." Rabbi Elazar, son of Rabbi Shimon, adds that one should also regard the whole world as though they are half unworthy and half worthy. Yet, the essence is still absent, and why did he change his words if the meaning is the same?

112) This is even more difficult on the object itself, meaning for one to see oneself as though he is half unworthy. This is a wonder: if one knows one's many iniquities, would he deceive oneself saying that he is only half this and half that?

The Torah states, "keep thee far from a false matter!" Moreover, it is written, "one sinner destroyeth much good." This is because one sin sentences the person and the entire world to a scale of sin. Thus, it is about the actual reality, not some false imagination by which a person should picture himself and the world.

113) And there is another bewilderment: can it be that there are not many people in each generation who perform one *Mitzva*? So how is the world sentenced to a scale of merit? Does that mean that the situation does not change at all, and there is nothing new under the sun? Indeed, great depth is required here, for the words cannot be understood superficially.

However, this does not concern a person who knows his sins are many, to teach him deception, that he is half this and half that, or to insinuate that he lacks only one *Mitzva*. This is not at all the way of the wise. Rather, this relates to one who feels and imagines himself as being completely and utterly righteous, and finds himself utterly whole. It is so because he has already been awarded the first degree of love by opening his eyes in the Torah, and He who knows all mysteries already testifies that he will not turn back to folly.

To him, the writing shows the way and proves that he is not yet righteous, but in between—half unworthy and half worthy. This is so because one still lacks one of the 613 *Mitzvot* in the Torah, namely the *Mitzva* of love.

The whole testimony of He who knows all mysteries that he will not sin again is only because of the clarity in one's attainment of the great loss in transgressing. This is considered fear of punishment, and is therefore called "repentance from fear."

114) We also learned above that this degree of repentance from fear still does not correct a person, but only from the time of repentance onwards. Yet, all the sorrow and the anguish one had suffered prior to being awarded the revelation of the face remain as they were, uncorrected. In addition, the transgressions one had made are not entirely corrected, but remain as mistakes.

115) This is why it is said that such a person, who is still short of one *Mitzva*, will regard himself as half unworthy and half worthy. Meaning, one should imagine that the time when he was granted repentance was in the middle of his years. Thus, he is still half unworthy, in that half of his years that had passed before he has repented. In that time, one is certainly unworthy, since repentance from fear does not correct them.

It follows, also, that he is also half worthy, in the half of his years since he has been awarded repentance onwards. At that time, one is certainly worthy, for he is certain that he will not sin again. Thus, in the first half of his years he is unworthy, and in the second half of his years, he is worthy.

116) He is told to think that if he performs one *Mitzva*, that *Mitzva* which he lacks from the number 613, he will be happy, for he has sentenced himself to a scale of merit. This is so because one who is granted the *Mitzva* of love by repentance from love, through it he is rewarded with turning his sins to merits.

Then, every sorrow and grief that he had ever suffered, prior to being awarded repentance, is turned into wondrous, endless pleasures for him. Moreover, he regrets not having suffered twice as much and more, as in the allegory about the landlord and the Jew who loved him.

This is called "sentencing to a scale of merit," since all of one's emotions, the mistakes and the sins, have been turned to merits. Thus, sentencing to a scale of merit means that the whole cup that was filled with sins has now been turned into a cup full of merits. In the words of the sages, this inversion is called "sentencing."

117) It further warns us and says that as long as one is in between, and has not been granted the one *Mitzva* that is missing from the number 613, one should not believe in oneself until one's dying day. He should also not rely himself on the testimony of the One who knows all mysteries, that he will not turn back to folly, but he might still transgress.

Hence, one should think for oneself that if he commits one sin, woe unto him, for he has sentenced himself to a scale of sin. This is because then he will immediately lose all his wonderful attainment in the Torah, and all the disclosure of the face that he has been granted, and he will return to concealment of the face. Thus, he will sentence himself to a scale of sin, for he will lose all the merits and the good, even from the latter half of his years. And as evidence, it brings the verse, "one sinner destroyeth much good."

118) Now you understand the addition that Rabbi Elazar, son of Rabbi Shimon, adds, and also why he does not bring the phrase, "half unworthy and half worthy." This is so because there it speaks of the second and third discernments of love, while Rabbi Elazar, son of Rabbi Shimon, speaks from the fourth discernment of love, the eternal love—the disclosure of face, as it truly is, Good and does good to the good and to the bad.

119) We learned there that it is impossible to attain the fourth discernment, except when one is proficient and knows all the dealings of the loved one, and how he behaves with all the others, none missing. This is also why the great privilege, when one is awarded sentencing himself to a scale of merit, is still not enough for one to attain whole love, meaning the fourth discernment. This is so because now he does not attain His merit as being good who does good to the good and to the bad, but only His Providence over him.

Yet, he still does not know of His Providence in this sublime and wonderful manner with the rest of the people in the world. Thus, we learned above that as long as one does not know the dealings of the loved one with others, until none of them is missing, the love is still not eternal. Hence, one must also sentence the entire world to a scale of merit, and only then does the eternal love appear to him.

120) This is what Rabbi Elazar, son of Rabbi Shimon, says, "Since the world is judged by its majority and the individual is judged by its majority," and since he relates to the whole world, he cannot say, as it is written, that he will regard

them as half unworthy, half worthy. This degree comes to a person only when he is granted the disclosure of the face and repentance from fear.

Yet, how is this said about the whole world, when they have not been granted this repentance? Thus, one must only say that the world is judged by its majority, and the individual is judged by its majority.

Explanation: One might think that one does not become a complete righteous, except when he has no transgressions and has never sinned. But those who failed with sins and transgressions no longer merit becoming complete righteous.

For that reason, Rabbi Elazar, son or Rabbi Shimon, teaches us that this is not so. Rather, the world is judged by its majority and so is the individual. This means that after one is no longer considered medium, after he has repented from fear, he instantaneously attains the 613 *Mitzvot* and is called "medium," meaning half his years he is unworthy, and in half his years he is worthy.

Afterwards, if one adds but a single *Mitzva*, the *Mitzva* of love, it is considered that he is mostly worthy and sentences everything to a scale of merit. Thus, the scale of sins becomes a scale of merits, too.

It turns out that even if one has a full scale of transgressions and sins, they all become merits. Then, one is as one who has never sinned, and is considered "complete righteous."

This is the meaning of the saying that the world and the individual are judged by the majority. Thus, the transgressions in one's hand from before the repentance are not taken into any account, for they have become merits. Accordingly, even "complete wicked" are considered "complete righteous" after they are granted repentance from love.

121) Therefore, he says that if an individual performs one *Mitzva*, meaning after the repentance from fear, then one is short of only one *Mitzva*, and "he is happy for he has sentenced himself and the whole world to a scale of merit." Thus, not only is he rewarded, through his repentance from love, with sentencing himself to a scale of merit, as the verse says, but he is even awarded sentencing the whole world to a scale of merit.

This means that he is awarded rising in wonderful attainments in the Holy Torah, until he discovers how all the people in the world will finally be awarded repentance from love. Then, they, too, will discover and see all that wonderful Providence, as he has attained for himself. And they, too, will be all sentenced to a scale of merit. At that time, "sins will cease out of the earth and the wicked be no more."

And even though the people in the world themselves have not yet been granted even repentance from fear, still, after an individual attains that sentencing to a scale of merit, destined to come to them in clear and absolute attainment, it is similar to, "You shall see your world in your life," said about one who repents from fear. We said that one is impressed and delighted by it as though he instantly had it, since "all that is about to be collected is deemed collected."

Also, here it is considered for that individual who attains the repentance of the whole world precisely as though they have been granted and came to repentance from love. Each of them sentenced their sins to merits sufficiently to know His dealings with every single person in the world.

This is why Rabbi Elazar, son of Rabbi Shimon, says, "Happy is he, for he has sentenced himself and the entire world to a scale of merit." From now on, one thoroughly knows all the conducts of His Providence, with every single creation, by way of disclosure of His real countenance, meaning the Good who does good to the good and to the bad. And since he knows it, he has therefore been granted the fourth discernment of love, namely "eternal love."

Like the verse, so Rabbi Elazar, son of Rabbi Shimon, warns that even after one has sentenced the whole world to a scale of merit, one should still not believe in himself until his dying day. Should he fail with a single transgression, he will immediately lose all his wonderful attainments, as it is written, "one sinner destroyeth much good."

This explains the difference in what Rabbi Elazar, son of Rabbi Shimon, writes. The writing speaks only from the second discernment and the third discernment of love; hence, it does not mention sentencing the whole world.

But Rabbi Elazar, son of Rabbi Shimon, speaks from the fourth discernment of love, which cannot be depicted except by attainment of sentencing the entire world to a scale of merit. However, we must still understand how we attain this wonderful attainment of sentencing the whole world to a scale of merit.

122) We must understand what is written (*Taanit* 11a), "When the public is in grief, one should not say, 'I shall go to my house and eat and drink, and have my soul at peace.' If one does that, the writing says about him, 'And behold joy and gladness, slaying oxen and killing sheep, eating flesh and drinking wine— Let us eat and drink, for tomorrow we shall die!' What does it say about that?

'And the Lord of hosts revealed Himself in mine ears: Surely this iniquity shall not be expiated by you till ye die.'

Thus far regarding the attribute of medium. But it is written about the attribute of wicked, 'Come ye, I will fetch wine, and we will fill ourselves with strong drink; and tomorrow shall be as this day.'

What does it say about that? 'The righteous perisheth, and no man layeth it to heart, ...that the righteous is taken away from the evil to come.' Instead, when one grieves with the public, one is granted the comfort of the public."

123) These words seem completely irrelevant. He wishes to bring evidence from the text, that one must pain oneself with the public. Hence, why should we divide and separate the attribute of medium from attribute of wicked? Furthermore, what is the precision that it makes regarding the attribute of medium and attribute of wicked? And why does it not say, "intermediate" and "wicked," and why do I need the attributes?

Also, where does it imply that the writing speaks of an iniquity when one does not pain oneself with the public? Still more, we do not see any punishment in the attribute of the wicked, but in what is written, "The righteous perisheth, and no man layeth it to heart." If the wicked sin, what does the righteous do that he should be punished, and why should the wicked cry if the righteous perisheth?

124) Yet, you should know that all these attributes, "medium," "wicked," and "righteous" are not in special people. Rather, all three are within every single person in the world. These three attributes are discernible in every person. During one's period of concealment of the face, even before one attains repentance from fear, he is discerned as being in the attribute of wicked.

Afterwards, if one is granted repentance from fear, he is considered medium. Then, if one is granted repentance from love, too, in its fourth discernment, meaning eternal love, he is considered "complete righteous." Hence, they did not say merely medium and righteous, but the attribute of medium and the attribute of wicked.

125) We should also remember that it is impossible to attain the above fourth discernment of love without first attaining the revelation of the face, which is destined to come to the entire world. That gives one strength to sentence the entire world to a scale of merit, as Rabbi Elazar, son of Rabbi Shimon says. And we have already learned that the matter of the disclosure of the face will inevitably turn every grief and sadness that came during the concealment of the face into wondrous pleasures, until one regrets having suffered so little.

Hence, we must ask, "When one sentences oneself to a scale of merit he certainly remembers all the grief and pains he had had during the concealment of the face." This is why it is possible that they will all be turned into wondrous pleasures for him, as we have said above. But when he sentences the entire world to a scale of merit, how does he know the measure of grief and pain that all the people in the world suffer, so as to understand how are they are sentenced to a scale of merit in the same manner we explained regarding one's own sentencing?

To avoid having the scale of merit of the entire world lacking, when one is qualified to sentence them to a scale of merit, one has no other tactic but to always pain himself with the troubles of the public, just as he suffers with his own troubles. Then the scale of sin of the entire world will be ready within him, like his own scale of sin. Thus, if he is granted sentencing himself to a scale of merit, he will be able to sentence the entire world to a scale of merit, too, and attain being "a complete righteous."

126) Thus, if one does not pain himself with the public, then even when he is granted repentance from fear, namely the attribute of medium, the writing says about him: "And behold joy and gladness." This means that one who has been granted the blessing, "You shall see your world in your life," and sees the entire reward for his *Mitzva*, which is prepared for the next world, is certainly "filled with joy and gladness." And he tells himself, "slaying oxen and killing sheep, eating flesh and drinking wine—Let us eat and drink, for tomorrow we shall die!"

In other words, he is filled with great joy because of his guaranteed reward in the next world. This is why he says so gladly, "for tomorrow we shall die," and I will collect my next world's life from The Whole after I die.

Yet, it is written about that: "And the Lord of hosts revealed Himself in mine ears: Surely this iniquity shall not be expiated by you till ye die." This means that the text rebukes him for the mistakes in his hand.

We learned that the sins of one who repents from fear become mere mistakes. Hence, since he did not pain himself with the public and cannot attain repentance from love, at which time the sins are turned to virtues, it is necessary that the mistakes in his hand will never be repented in his life. Thus, how can he rejoice in his life in the next world? This is why it is written, "Surely this iniquity shall not be expiated by you till ye die," meaning the mistakes, "until you die," meaning before he dies. Thus, he is devoid of repentance.

127) It is also written that this is the "attribute of medium," meaning that this text speaks of a time when one has repented from fear onwards. At that time, one is considered "medium."

Yet, what does it write about the "attribute of wicked"? In other words, what shall become of the time when he was in concealment of the face, which was then called "attribute of wicked"? We learned that repentance from fear does not correct one's past before he has repented.

Hence, the text brings another verse: "Come ye, I will fetch wine, and we will fill ourselves with strong drink; and tomorrow shall be as this day." This means that those days and years that have passed since the time of concealment of the face, which he has not corrected, called "attribute of wicked," they do not want him to die, since they have no part in the next world after the death, as they are the attribute of the wicked.

Therefore, at the time when the attribute of medium in him is glad and rejoicing, "for tomorrow we shall die," and will be rewarded with the life of the next world, at the same time the attribute of wicked in him does not say so. It rather says, "and tomorrow shall be as this day," meaning it wishes to live and be happy in this world forever, for it still has no part for the next world, since he has not corrected it, as it is only corrected by repentance from love.

128) It is written, "The righteous perisheth," meaning the attribute of complete righteous, which that person should merit, is lost from him. "And no man layeth it to heart …the righteous is taken away from the evil to come." This means that because that medium did not pain himself with the public, he cannot attain repentance from love, inverting sins to virtues and evils to wonderful pleasures. Instead, all the mistakes and the evil one had experienced before he acquired repentance from fear still stand in the attribute of wicked, who sense harm from His Providence. And because of these harms that they still feel, they cannot be awarded being complete righteous.

The writing says, "and no man layeth it to heart," meaning that that person does not take it to heart "from the evil to come." In other words, because of the harm that one still feels in His Providence from the past, "the righteous perisheth," meaning he lost the attribute of righteous. And he will die and pass away from the world as mere medium.

All that concerns he who does not pain himself with the public, and is not awarded seeing the comfort of the public, for he will not be able to sentence them to a scale of merit and see their consolation. Hence, he will never attain the attribute of righteous.

129) From all the aforementioned, we have come to know that there is no woman-born person who will not experience the three above attributes: attribute of wicked; attribute of medium; attribute of righteous.

They are called *Midot* (attributes) since they extend from the *Midah* (measure) of their attainment of His Providence. Our sages said, "one is measured to the extent that he measures" (*Sutah* 8). And they who attain His Providence in concealment of the face are considered wicked: either incomplete wicked from the perspective of the single concealment, or complete wicked from the perspective of the double concealment.

And because they feel and think that the world is conducted in bad guidance, it is as though they condemn themselves, since they receive torments and pains from His Providence and feel only bad all day long. And they condemn the most by thinking that all the people in the world are watched over like them, in bad guidance.

Hence, those who attain Providence from the perspective of concealment of the face are called "wicked," since that name appears in them out of the depth of their sensation. It depends on the understanding of the heart, and the words or the thought that justifies His Providence do not matter at all, when it opposes the sensation of every organ and sense, which cannot force themselves to lie, as it does.

Hence, they who are in this measure of attainment of Providence are considered to have sentenced themselves and the entire world to a scale of sin, as it is written in the words of Rabbi Elazar, son of Rabbi Shimon. This is because they imagine that all the people in the world are watched over in bad guidance, as would befit His Name, "The Good that does good to the good and to the bad."

130) They that are granted the sensation of His Providence in the form of the first degree of disclosure of the face, called "repentance from fear," are considered medium. This is because their emotions are divided into two parts, called "two cups of the scales."

Now that they have acquired the disclosure of the face, by way of "You shall see your world in your life," at the very least they have attained His Good Providence as befits His Name, "Good." Hence, they have a scale of merit.

Yet, all the sorrow and the bitter torments that were thoroughly imprinted in their feelings from all the days and years they received Providence of concealed face, from the time before they were awarded the above repentance, all remain standing and are called "a scale of sin."

And since they have these two scales standing one opposite the other, in a way that the scale of sin is set from the moment of their repentance and before, and the scale of merit is set and guaranteed to them from the moment of repentance onwards, the time of repentance stands "between" the merit and the sin, and hence they are called "medium."

131) And the ones who merit the disclosure of the face in the second degree, called "repentance from love," when sins become as merits to them, are considered to have sentenced the above scale of sin to a scale of merit. This means that all the sorrow and affliction engraved in their bones while being under the Providence of concealment of the face have now been inverted and sentenced to a "scale of merit."

This is because every sorrow and grief has now been turned into a wonderful, endless pleasure. Now they are called "righteous," for they justify His Providence.

132) We must know that the above attribute of medium applies even when one is under Providence of concealment of the face. By great exertion in faith in reward and punishment, a Light of great confidence in the Creator appears to them. For a time, they are granted a degree of disclosure of His face in the measure of the medium. But the drawback is that they cannot permanently remain in their degrees, since standing permanently in a degree is possible only through repentance from fear.

133) We should also know that what we said, that there is choice only when there is concealment of the face, does not mean that after one has attained Providence of revealed face, one has no further labor or exertion in the practice of Torah and *Mitzvot*. On the contrary, the proper work in Torah and *Mitzvot* begins primarily after one has been awarded repentance from love. Only then is it possible to engage in Torah and *Mitzvot* with love and fear, as we are commanded, and "The world was created only for the complete righteous" (*Berachot* 61).

It is rather like a king who wished to select for himself the most loyal of his subjects in the country and bring them in to work inside his palace. What did he do? He issued a decree that anyone who wished, young or old, would come to his palace to engage in the works inside his palace.

However, he appointed many of his servants to guard the palace gate and on all the roads leading to it, and ordered them to cunningly deflect all those nearing his palace and divert them from the way that leads to the palace.

Naturally, all the people in the country began to run to the king's palace. But the diligent guards cunningly rejected them. Many of them overpowered them and came near the palace gate, but the guards at the gate were the most diligent, and if someone approached the gate, they diverted him and turned him away with great craftiness, until one despaired and retuned as he had come.

And so they came and went, and regained strength, and came and went again, and so on and so forth for several days and years, until they grew weary of trying. And only the heroes among them, whose patience endured, defeated the guards and opened the gate. And they were instantly awarded seeing the King's face, who appointed each of them in his right place.

Of course, from that moment on, they had no further dealings with those guards, who diverted and mislead them and made their lives bitter for several days and years, running back and forth around the gate. This is because they have been rewarded with working and serving before the glory of the king's face inside His palace.

So it is with the work of the complete righteous. The choice applied during the concealment of the face certainly does not apply when they have opened the door to attain open Providence.

However, they begin their work primarily from the revealing of the face. At that time, they begin to march up the many rungs in the ladder set up on the earth, whose top reaches the heaven, as it is written, "The righteous shall go from strength to strength."

It is as our sages say, "Each and every righteous is covered by the cover of his friend." These works qualify them for the will of God, to realize His Thought of Creation in them, which is to "delight His creatures" according to His good and generous hand.

134) You should know this law, that there is disclosure only in a place where there was concealment. This is similar to matters of this world where the absence precedes the existence, since the growth of wheat appears only where it was sown and rotted.

It is the same with higher matters, where concealment and disclosure relate to each other as the wick to the light that catches it. This is because any concealment, once it is corrected, is a reason for disclosure of the Light related to that kind of concealment, and the Light that appears clings to it like light to a wick. Remember this on all your ways.

135) Now you can understand what our sages wrote, that the whole Torah is the names of the Creator. This seems puzzling, as there are many indecencies, such as names of wicked—Pharaoh, Balaam, etc., prohibition, impurity, ruthless curses in the two admonitions and so on. Thus, how can we understand that all these are names of the Creator?

136) To understand that, we must know that our ways are not His ways. Our way is to come from the imperfect to perfection. In His way, all the revelations come to us from perfection to the imperfect.

First, complete perfection emanates and emerges from Him. This perfection descends from His face and hangs down restriction by restriction, through several degrees, until it comes to the last, most restricted phase, suitable for our material world. And then the matter appears to us here in this world.

137) From the aforementioned, you will learn that the Holy Torah, whose Height is endless, did not emanate or emerge from before Him as it appears to us here in this world, since it is known that "The Torah and the Creator are one," and this is not at all apparent in the Torah of our world. Moreover, one who engages in it *Lo Lishma*, his Torah becomes a potion of death for him.

Rather, when it was first emanated from Him, it was emanated and emerged in utter perfection, meaning in the actual form of "The Torah and the Creator are one." This is called, "The Torah of *Atzilut*," in the Introduction to the Corrections of *The Zohar* (p 3), that "He, His Life, and His Self are one." Afterwards, it descended from His face and was gradually restricted through many restrictions, until it was given at Sinai, when it was written as it is before us here in this world, clothed in the crude dresses of the material world.

138) Yet, you should know that the distance between the dresses of the Torah in this world and the dresses of the Torah in the world of *Atzilut* is immeasurable. Yet, the Torah itself, meaning the Light within the dresses, is unchanged at all between the Torah of *Atzilut* and the Torah of this world, as it is written, "I the Lord change not" (*Malachi* 3:6).

Moreover, these crude dresses in our Torah of *Assiya* are not at all of inferior value with regard to the Light that is clothed in it. Rather, their importance is much greater, with respect to the end of their correction, than all its pure dresses in the Upper Worlds.

This is so because the concealment is the reason for the disclosure. After its correction, during the disclosure, the concealment is to the disclosure as a wick is to the light that grips it. The greater the concealment, the greater Light will cling to it when it is corrected. Thus, all these crude dresses that the Torah is clothed in, in this world, their value is not at all inferior to the Light that clothes it, but quite the contrary.

139) This is Moses' triumph over the angels with his argument, "Is there envy among you? Is the evil inclination among you?" (*Shabbat* 89). It means that the greater concealment discloses a greater Light. He showed them that in the pure clothes that the Torah clothes in, in the world of the angels, the greater Lights cannot appear through them as they can in dresses of this world.

140) We thus learn that there is no change whatsoever from the Torah *de Atzilut*, where "The Torah and the Creator are one" through the Torah in this world. The only difference is in the dresses, since the dresses of this world conceal the Creator and hide Him.

Know that because of His clothing in the Torah, it is called "Teaching." It tells you that even during the concealment of the face, and even during the double concealment, the Creator is instilled and clothed in the Torah. He is the "Teacher" and it is the Torah, but the crude clothes of the Torah before our eyes are as wings that cover and hide the Teacher who is clothed and hides in them.

However, when one is granted the revelation of the face in repentance from love in its fourth discernment, it is said about him, "yet shall not thy Teacher hide Himself any more, but thine eyes shall see thy Teacher" (Isaiah, 30:20). From then on, the clothes of the Torah no longer hide and conceal the "Teacher," and one discovers for all time that "The Torah and the Creator are one."

141) Now you can understand the meaning of the words, "Forsake Me and keep My law." They interpreted, "I wish that they had left Me and kept My Torah—the Light in it reforms them" (*Yerushalmi, Hagiga*, p 6b).

This is perplexing. They mean that they were fasting and tormenting to find the revelation of His face, as it is written, "they delight to draw near unto God" (*Isaiah* 58:2). Yet, the text tells them in the name of the Creator, "I wish you would leave Me, for all your labor is in vain and fruitless. I am found nowhere but in the Torah. Therefore, keep the Torah and look for Me there, and the Light in it will reform you and you will find Me," as it is written, "those that seek Me shall find Me."

142) Now we can somewhat clarify the essence of the wisdom of Kabbalah, enough for a reliable perception in the quality of that wisdom. Thus, one will not deceive oneself with false imaginations, as the masses envisage.

You should know that the Holy Torah divides into four discernments, which encompass the whole of reality. Three discernments are discerned in the general reality of this world. They are called "World," "Year," "Soul." The fourth discernment is the conduct of existence of the above three parts of reality, their nourishment, their conducts, and all their incidents.

143) The outer part of reality, like the sky and the firmaments, the earth and the seas, etc., that are written in the Torah, all these are called, "World." The inner part of reality—man and beast, animals and various birds, etc.—brought in the Torah, which exists in the above places, called "outer part," are called "Soul."

The evolution of reality throughout the generations is called "cause and consequence." For example, in the evolution of the heads of the generations from *Adam ha Rishon* through Joshua and Caleb, who came to the land, which are brought in the Torah, the father is considered the "cause" of the son, who is "caused" by him. This evolution of the details of reality by way of the above cause and consequence is called, "Year." Similarly, all the conducts of the existence of reality, both external and internal, in their every incident and conduct, brought in the Torah, are called "the existence of reality."

144) Know that the four worlds are named in the wisdom of Kabbalah, *Atzilut, Beria, Yetzira,* and *Assiya.* When they came out and evolved, they emerged from one another like a seal and imprint. This means that anything that is written in the seal necessarily appears in what is imprinted from it, no more and no less, and so it was in the evolution of the worlds, as well.

Thus, all four discernments, WYS (World, Year, Soul), with all their modes of sustenance, which were in the world of *Atzilut,* came out, were imprinted, and manifested in their image in the world of *Beria,* as well. It is the same from the world of *Beria* to the world of *Yetzira,* down to the world of *Assiya.*

Thus, all three discernments in the reality before us, called WYS, with all their modes of sustenance, which are set before our eyes here in this world, extended and appeared here from the world of *Yetzira,* and in *Yetzira* from its superior.

In this manner, the source of the numerous details before our eyes is in the world of *Atzilut.* Moreover, even with the innovations that appear in this world today, each novelty must first appear Above, in the world of *Atzilut,* and from there hang down and appear to us in this world.

This is the meaning of the words of our sages: "There is not a blade of grass below that does not have a fortune and a guard above, which strike it and tell it: 'Grow!'" (*Beresheet Rabba,* Chapter Ten). This is the meaning of the text, "One does not move one's finger below, before one is declared Above" (*Hulin* p 7).

145) Know that because of the clothing of the Torah in the three discernments of reality, "World," "Year," "Soul," and their existence in this material world, produce the prohibitions, impurities, and interdictions found in the revealed Torah. It has been explained above that the Creator is clothed in it by way of, "The Torah and the Creator are one," but in great concealment. This is because these material dresses are the wings that cover and hide Him.

However, the clothing of the Torah in the form of the pure WYS, and their existence in the three Upper Worlds, called *Atzilut*, *Beria*, *Yetzira*, are generally named, "The Wisdom of Kabbalah."

146) Thus, the wisdom of Kabbalah and the revealed Torah are one and the same. Yet, while a person receives from a Providence of concealed face, and the Creator hides in the Torah, it is considered that he is practicing the revealed Torah. In other words, he is incapable of receiving any illumination from the Torah of *Yetzira*, not to mention from Above *Yetzira*.

And when one is granted the revelation of the face, he begins to engage in the wisdom of Kabbalah. This is because the dresses of the revealed Torah themselves were purified for him, and his Torah became the Torah of *Yetzira*, called, "The Wisdom of Kabbalah."

Even for one who is granted the Torah of *Atzilut*, it does not mean that the letters of the Torah have changed for him. Rather, the very same dresses of the revealed Torah have purified for him and became very pure clothes. They have become like the verse, "yet shall not thy Teacher hide Himself any more, but thine eyes shall see thy Teacher." At that time, they become as, "He, His Life, and His Self are one."

147) Let me give you an example, so as to bring the matter a little closer to your mind. For instance: While one was in concealment of the face, the letters and the dresses of the Torah necessarily hid the Creator. Hence, he failed, due to the sins and the mistakes he had committed. At that time, he was placed under the punishment of the crude dresses in the Torah, which are impurity, prohibition, and interdictions.

However, when one is awarded open Providence and repentance from love, when his sins become as virtues, all the sins and the mistakes he had failed in while being under the concealment of the face have now shed their crude and very bitter clothes, and wore the clothes of Light, *Mitzva*, and merits.

This is so because the same crude clothes have turned to virtues. Now they are as clothes that extend from the world of *Atzilut* or *Beria*, and they do not cover or hide The Teacher. On the contrary, "thine eyes shall see thy Teacher."

Thus, there is no difference whatsoever between the Torah of *Atzilut* and the Torah in this world, between the wisdom of Kabbalah and the revealed Torah. Rather, the only difference is in the person who engages in the Torah. Two may study the Torah in the same portion and the same words, but to one, this Torah will be as the wisdom of Kabbalah and the Torah of *Atzilut*, while to the other, it will be the Torah of *Assiya*, the revealed.

148) Now you will understand the truth in the words of the Vilna Gaon in the prayer book, in the blessing for the Torah. He wrote that the Torah begins with *Sod* (secret), meaning the revealed Torah of *Assyia*, which is considered hidden, since the Creator is completely hidden there.

Then he moves on to the *Remez* (intimation), meaning that He is more revealed in the Torah of *Yetzira*. Finally, one attains the *Peshat* (literal), which is the Torah of *Atzilut*. It is called *Peshat*, for it is *Mufshat* (stripped) of all the clothes that conceal the Creator.

149) Once we have reached thus far, we can provide some idea and discernment in the four worlds, known in the wisdom of Kabbalah by the names, *Atzilut*, *Beria*, *Yetzira*, *Assiya* of *Kedusha* (holiness), and in the four worlds ABYA of the *Klipot*, arranged one opposite the other, opposite the ABYA of *Kedusha*.

You will understand that in the four discernments of attainment of His Providence, and in the four degrees of love. First, we shall explain the four worlds ABYA of *Kedusha*, and we shall start from below, from the world of *Assiya*.

150) We have already explained the first two discernments of Providence of concealment of the face. You should know that both are considered the world of *Assiya*. This is why it is written in the book, *The Tree of Life*, that the world of *Assiya* is mostly evil, and even the little good contained in it is mixed with evil and is unrecognizable.

From the perspective of the first concealment, it follows that it is mostly bad, meaning the torments and the pains that those who receive this Providence feel. And from the perspective of the double concealment, the good is mixed with the bad, as well, and the good is completely indiscernible.

The first discernment of revelation of the face is considered "the world of *Yetzira*." Hence, it is written in the book, *The Tree of Life* (Gate 48, Chapter Three), that the world of *Yetzira* is half good and half bad. This means that he who attains the first discernment of revelation of the face, which is the first form of conditional love, considered a mere "repentance from fear," is called "medium," and he is half unworthy, half worthy.

The second discernment of love is also conditional, but there is no trace of any harm or detriment between them. Also, the third discernment of love is the first discernment of unconditional love. Both are regarded as the world of *Beria*.

Hence it is written in the book, *The Tree of Life*, that the world of *Beria* is mostly good and only its minority is bad, and that minority of bad is indiscernible. This means that since the medium is awarded one *Mitzva*, he sentences himself to a scale of merit. And for this reason, he is considered "mostly good," meaning the discernment form of love.

The minute, indiscernible evil that exits in *Beria* extends from the third discernment of love, which is unconditional. Also, he has already sentenced himself to a scale of merit, but he has not yet sentenced the whole world; hence, a minority in him is bad, since this love is not yet considered eternal. However, this minority is indiscernible because he still did not feel any harm or detriment, even toward others.

The fourth discernment of love, the unconditional love, which is also eternal, is considered the world of *Atzilut*. This is the meaning of what is written in the book, *The Tree of Life*, that in the world of *Atzilut* there is no evil whatsoever, and there, "evil shall not sojourn with Thee."

This is because after one has sentenced the entire world to a scale of merit, too, love is eternal, complete, and no concealment and cover will ever be conceived. This is so because there is the place of the absolute revelation of the face, as it is written, "yet shall not thy Teacher hide Himself any more, but thine eyes shall see thy Teacher." This is because now he knows all of the Creator's dealings with all the people, as true Providence that appears from His name, "The Good who does good to the good and to the bad."

151) Now you can also understand the discernment of the four worlds *ABYA* of *Klipa*, set opposite the *ABYA* of *Kedusha*, as in, "God hath made even the one as well as the other." This is because the chariot of the *Klipot* of *Assiya* comes from the discernment of the concealed face in both its degrees. That chariot dominates to make man sentence everything to a scale of sin.

And the world of *Yetzira* of *Klipa* catches the scale of sin—which is not corrected in the world of *Yetzira* of *Kedusha*—in its hands. Thus, they dominate the medium, which receive from the world of *Yetzira*, by way of, "God hath made even the one as well as the other."

The world of *Beria* of *Klipa* has the same power to cancel the conditional love, to cancel only the thing that love hangs on, that is, the imperfection in the love of the second discernment.

And the world of *Atzilut* of *Klipa* is what captures in its hand that minority of evil whose existence in *Beria* is not apparent, due to the third discernment of love. And even though it is true love, by the force of the Good who does good to the good and to the bad, which is considered *Atzilut* of *Kedusha*, still, because he has not been awarded sentencing the whole world to a scale of merit, the *Klipa* has the strength to fail the love with regard to Providence over others.

152) This is the meaning of what is written in *The Tree of Life*, that the world of *Atzilut* of the *Klipot* stands opposite the world of *Beria*, not opposite the world of *Atzilut*. This is so because only the fourth discernment of love extends from the world of *Atzilut* of *Kedusha*. Hence, there is no dominion to the *Klipot* there at all, since he has already sentenced the whole world to a scale of merit, and knows all the conducts of the Creator in His Providence on people, too, from the Providence of His name, "The Good who does good to the good and to the bad."

However, in the world of *Beria*, from which extends the third discernment, there is still no sentencing of the whole world. Therefore, there is still a hold for the *Klipot*. Yet, these *Klipot* are considered the *Atzilut* of the *Klipa*, since they are opposite the third discernment, the unconditional love, and this love is considered *Atzilut*.

153) Now we have thoroughly explained the four worlds ABYA of *Kedusha* and the *Klipot*, which are the "vis-à-vis" of each and every world. They are considered the deficiency that exists in their corresponding world, in *Kedusha*, and they are the ones named "the four worlds ABYA of *Klipot*."

154) These words suffice for any observer to feel the essence of the wisdom of Kabbalah to some degree. You should know that most of the authors of Kabbalah books did not direct their books, but only to such readers that have already attained a disclosure of the face and all the sublime attainments.

We should not ask, "If they have already been awarded attainments, then they know everything through their own attainment. Why then would they still need to delve in books of Kabbalah by other authors?"

However, it is not wise to ask that question. It is like one who engages in the literal Torah who has no knowledge of the conducts of this world with respect to the World, Year, Soul of this world, and who does not know people's behavior and their conducts with themselves and with others. And also, he does not know the beasts and the birds in this world.

Would you even consider that such a person would be able to understand even a single issue in the Torah correctly? He would overturn the issues in the Torah from good to bad and from bad to good, and he would not find his hands or legs in anything.

So is the matter before us: Even if one has been awarded attainment, and even at the level of the Torah of *Atzilut*, he will still not perceive more than relates to his own soul. Yet, one must know all three discernments, World, Year, Soul, in their every incident and conduct in full consciousness, to be able to understand the issues in the Torah that relate to that world.

These issues are explained in *The Book of Zohar* and the genuine Kabbalah books with all their details and intricacies. Thus, every sage and one who understands with his own mind must contemplate them day and night.

155) Therefore we must ask, why then, did the Kabbalists obligate each person to study the wisdom of Kabbalah? Indeed, there is a great thing in it, worthy of being publicized: There is a wonderful, invaluable remedy to those who engage in the wisdom of Kabbalah. Although they do not understand what they are learning, through the yearning and the great desire to understand what they are learning, they awaken upon themselves the Lights that surround their souls.

This means that every person from Israel is guaranteed to finally attain all the wonderful attainments that the Creator had contemplated in the Thought of Creation to delight every creature. And one who has not been awarded in this life will be granted in the next life, etc., until one is awarded completing His Thought, which He had planned for him.

And while one has not attained perfection, the Lights that are destined to reach him are considered Surrounding Lights. That means that they stand ready for him, but are waiting for him to purify his vessels of reception, at which time these Lights will clothe the able vessels.

Hence, even when he does not have the vessels, when he engages in this wisdom, mentioning the names of the Lights and the vessels related to his soul, they immediately shine upon him to a certain extent. However, they shine for him without clothing the interior of his soul, for lack of able vessels to receive them. Yet, the illumination one receives time after time during the engagement draws upon him grace from Above, imparting him with abundance of sanctity and purity, which bring him much closer to achieving perfection.

156) Yet, there is a strict condition during the engagement in this wisdom—to not materialize the matters with imaginary and corporeal issues. This is because thus they breach, "Thou shalt not make unto thee a graven image, nor any manner of likeness."

In that event, one is rather harmed instead of receiving benefit. Therefore, our sages cautioned to study the wisdom only after forty years, or from a Rav, and other such cautions. All of that is for the above reason.

To rescue the readers from any materialization, I composed the book *Talmud Eser Sefirot* (*The Study of the Ten Sefirot*) by the Ari. There I collect from the books of the Ari all the principal essays concerning the explanation of the ten *Sefirot* in as simple and easy language as I could. I have also arranged the table of questions and table of answers for every word and issue. "...and that the will of God will succeed in his hand."

The Freedom

> "*Harut* (engraved) upon the tables"; do not pronounce it *Harut* (engraved), but rather *Herut* (freedom), to show that they are liberated from the angel of death.
>
> –*Midrash Shemot Raba*, 41

These words need to be clarified, because how is the matter of reception of the Torah related to one's liberation from death? Furthermore, once they have attained an eternal body that cannot die through the reception of the Torah, how did they lose it again? Can the eternal become absent?

FREEDOM OF WILL

To understand the sublime concept, "freedom from the angel of death," we must first understand the concept of freedom as it is normally understood by all of humanity.

It is a general view that freedom is deemed a natural law, which applies to all of life. Thus, we see that animals that fall into captivity die when we rob them of their freedom. This is a true testimony that Providence does not accept the enslavement of any creature. It is with good reason that humanity has been struggling for the past several hundred years to obtain a certain measure of freedom of the individual.

Yet, this concept, expressed in that word, "freedom," remains unclear, and if we delve into the meaning of that word, there will be almost nothing left. For before you seek the freedom of the individual, you must assume that any individual, in and of itself, has that quality called "freedom," meaning that one can act according to one's own free choice.

PLEASURE AND PAIN

However, when we examine the acts of an individual, we shall find them compulsory. He is compelled to do them and has no freedom of choice. In a sense, he is like a stew cooking on a stove; it has no choice but to cook. And it must cook because Providence has harnessed life with two chains: pleasure and pain.

The living creatures have no freedom of choice—to choose pain or reject pleasure. And man's advantage over animals is that he can aim at a remote goal, meaning to agree to a certain amount of current pain, out of choice of future benefit or pleasure, to be attained after some time.

But in fact, there is no more than a seemingly commercial calculation here, where the future benefit or pleasure seems preferable and advantageous to the agony they are suffering from the pain they have agreed to assume presently. There is only a matter of deduction here—that they deduct the pain and suffering from the anticipated pleasure, and there remains some surplus.

Thus, only the pleasure is extended. And so it sometimes happens, that we are tormented because we did not find the attained pleasure to be the surplus we had hoped for compared to the agony we suffered; hence, we are in deficit, just as merchants do.

And when all is said and done, there is no difference here between man and animal. And if that is the case, there is no free choice whatsoever, but a pulling force, drawing them toward any bypassing pleasure and rejecting them from painful circumstances. And Providence leads them to every place it chooses by means of these two forces, without asking their opinion in the matter.

Moreover, even determining the type of pleasure and benefit are entirely out of one's own free choice, but follow the will of others, as they want, and not he. For example: I sit, I dress, I speak, and I eat. I do all these not because I want to sit that way, or talk that way, or dress that way, or eat that way, but because others want me to sit, dress, talk, and eat that way. It all follows the desire and fancy of society, not my own free will.

Furthermore, in most cases, I do all these against my will. For I would be a lot more comfortable behaving simply, without any burden. But I am chained with iron shackles, in all my movements, to the fancies and manners of others, which make up the society.

So you tell me, where is my freedom of will? On the other hand, if we assume that the will has no freedom, then we are all like machines, operating and creating through external forces, which force them to act this way. This means that we are all incarcerated in the prison of Providence, which, using these two chains, pleasure and pain, pushes and pulls us to its will, to where it sees fit.

It turns out that there is no such thing as selfishness in the world, since no one here is free or stands on his own two feet. I am not the owner of the act, and I am not the performer because I want to perform, but I am performed upon, in a compulsory manner, and without my awareness. Thus, reward and punishment become extinct.

And it is quite odd not only for the orthodox, who believe in His Providence and can rely on Him and trust that He aims only for the best in this conduct. It is even stranger for those who believe in nature, since according to the above, we are all incarcerated by the chains of blind nature, with no awareness or accountability. And we, the chosen species, with reason and knowledge, have become a toy in the hands of the blind nature, which leads us astray, and who knows where?

THE LAW OF CAUSALITY

It is worthwhile taking some time to grasp such an important thing, meaning how we exist in the world as beings with a "self," where each of us regards himself a unique entity, acting on its own, independent of external, alien, and unknown forces. And does this being—the self—appear to us?

It is true that there is a general connection among all the elements of reality before us, which abide by the law of causality, by way of cause and effect, moving forward. And as the whole, so is each item for itself, meaning that each and every creature in the world from the four types—still, vegetative, animate, and speaking—abides by the law of causality by way of cause and effect.

Moreover, each particular form of a particular behavior, which a creature follows while in this world, is pushed by ancient causes, compelling it to accept that change in that behavior and not another whatsoever. And this is apparent to all who examine the ways of nature from a pure scientific point of view and without a shred of bias. Indeed, we must analyze this matter to allow ourselves to examine it from all sides.

FOUR FACTORS

Bear in mind that every emergence occurring in the beings of the world must be perceived not as extending existence from absence, but as existence from existence, through an actual entity that has shed its previous form and has robed its current one.

Therefore, we must understand that in every emergence in the world there are four factors where from the four of them together arises that emergence. They are called by the names:

A. The source.

B. The unchanging conduct of cause and effect, related to the source's own attribute.

C. Its internal conducts of cause and effect, which change by contact with alien forces.

D. The conducts of cause and effect of alien things, which affect it from the outside.

And I will clarify them one at a time:

THE FIRST REASON: THE SOURCE, THE FIRST MATTER

A) The "source" is the first matter, related to that being. For "there is nothing new under the sun," and anything that happens in our world is not existence from absence, but existence from existence. It is an entity that has stripped off its former shape and taken on another form, different from the first. And that entity, which shed its previous form, is defined as "the source." In it lies the potential destined to be revealed and determined at the end of the formation of that emergence. Therefore, it is clearly considered its primary cause.

THE SECOND REASON: CAUSE AND EFFECT THAT STEM FROM ITSELF

B) This is a conduct of cause and effect, related to the source's own attribute, and which is unchanging. Take, for example, a stalk of wheat that has rotted in the ground and arrived at a state of sowing many stalks of wheat. Thus, that rotten state is deemed the "source," meaning that the essence of the wheat has stripped off its former shape, the shape of wheat, and has taken on a new discernment, that of rotten wheat, which is the seed, called "the source," which has no shape at all. Now, after rotting in the ground, it has become fit for robing another form, the form of many stalks of wheat, intended to emerge from that source, which is the seed.

It is known to all that this source is destined to become neither cereal nor oats, but only equalize with its former shape, which has left it, being the single stalk of wheat. And although it changes to a certain degree in quality and quantity, for in the former shape it was a single stalk, and now there are ten stalks, and in taste and appearance, too, the essence of the shape of the wheat remains unchanged.

Thus, there is a conduct of cause and effect here, ascribed to the source's own attribute, which never changes. Thus, cereal will never emerge from wheat, as we have said, and this is called "the second reason."

THE THIRD REASON: INTERNAL CAUSE AND EFFECT

C) This is the conduct of the internal cause and effect of the source, which change upon encountering the alien forces in its environment. Thus, we find that from one stalk of wheat, which rots in the ground, many stalks emerge, sometimes larger and better wheat than prior to sowing.

Therefore, there must be additional factors involved here, collaborating and connecting with the force concealed in the environment, meaning the "source." And because of that, the additions in quality and quantity, which were absent in the previous form of wheat, have now appeared. Those are the minerals and the materials in the ground, the rain and the sun. All these operate on it by administering from their forces and joining the force within the source itself. And through the conduct of cause and effect, they have produced the multiplicity in quantity and quality in that emergence.

We must understand that this third factor joins with the internality of the source, since the force hidden in the source controls them. In the end, all these changes belong to the wheat and to no other plant. Hence, we define them as internal factors. However, they differ from the second factor, which is utterly unchanging, whereas the third factor changes in both quality and quantity.

THE FOURTH REASON: CAUSE AND EFFECT THROUGH ALIEN THINGS

This is a conduct of cause and effect of alien things that act upon it from the outside. In other words, they have no direct relation to the wheat, like minerals, rain, or sun, but are alien to it, such as nearby things or external events, such as hail, wind, etc.

And you find that four factors combine to the wheat throughout its growth. Each particular state that the wheat is subject to during that time becomes conditioned on the four of them, and the quality and quantity of each state is determined by them. And as we have portrayed in the wheat, so is the rule in every emergence in the world, even in thoughts and ideas.

If, for example, we picture to ourselves some conceptual state in a certain individual, such as a state of a person being religious or non religious, or an extreme orthodox or not so extreme, or midway, we will understand that that state is determined in that person by the above four factors.

HEREDITARY POSSESSIONS

The cause of the first reason is the source, which is its first substance. Man is created existence-from-existence, meaning from the minds of its progenitors. Thus, to a certain extent, it is like copying from book to book. This means that almost all the matters that were accepted and attained in the fathers and forefathers are copied here, as well.

But the difference is that they are in an abstract form, much like the sowed wheat, which is not fit for sowing until it has rotted and shed its former shape. So is the case with the drop of semen from which man is born: there is nothing in it of its forefathers' shapes, only abstract force.

For the same ideas that were concepts in his forefathers have turned into mere tendencies in him, called "instincts" or "habits," without even knowing why one does what he does. Indeed, they are hidden forces he had inherited from his ancestors in a way that not only do the material possessions come to us through inheritance from our ancestors, but the spiritual possessions and all the concepts that our fathers engaged in also come to us by inheritance from generation to generation.

And from here surface the manifold tendencies that we find in people, such as a tendency to believe or to criticize, a tendency to settle for material life or desiring only ideas, despising a life without aspirations, stingy, yielding, insolent, or shy.

All these pictures that appear in people are not their own property, which they have acquired, but mere inheritance that had been given to them by their ancestors. It is known that there is a special place in the brain where these hereditaments reside. It is called, "medulla oblongata" (the elongated brain), or "subconscious," and all the tendencies appear there.

But because the concepts of our ancestors, acquired through their experiences, have become mere tendencies in us, they are considered the same as the sowed wheat, which has taken off its former shape and remained bare, having only potential forces worthy of receiving new forms. In our matter, these tendencies will robe the forms of concepts. This is considered the first substance, and this is the primary factor, called "source." In it reside all the forces of the unique tendencies he had inherited from his progenitors, which are defined as "ancestral heritage."

Bear in mind that some of these tendencies come in a negative form, meaning the opposite of the ones that were in his ancestors. This is why they said, "All that is concealed in the father's heart emerges openly in the son."

The reason for it is that the source takes off its former shape in order to take on a new form. Hence, it is close to losing the shapes of the concepts of his ancestors, like the wheat that rots in the ground loses the shape that existed in the wheat. However, it still depends on the other three factors.

INFLUENCE OF THE ENVIRONMENT

The second reason is an unchanging, direct conduct of cause and effect, related to the source's own attribute. Meaning, as we have clarified with the wheat that rots in the ground, the environment in which the source rests, such as soil, minerals, and rain, air, and the sun affect the sowing by a long chain of cause and effect in a long and gradual process, state by state, until they ripen.

And the source retakes its former shape, the shape of wheat, but differing in quality and quantity. In their general aspect, they remain completely unchanged; hence, no cereal or oats will grow from it. But in their particular aspect, they change in quantity, as from one stalk emerge a dozen or two dozen stalks, and in quality, as they are better or worse than the former shape of the wheat.

It is the same here: man, as a "source," is placed in an environment, meaning in the society. And he is necessarily affected by it, as the wheat from its environment, for the source is but a raw form. Thus, through the constant contact with the environment and the society, he is gradually impressed by them through a chain of consecutive states, one by one, as cause and effect.

At that time, the tendencies included in his source are changed and take on the form of concepts. For example, if one inherits from his ancestors a tendency to stinginess, as he grows he builds for himself concepts and ideas that conclude decisively that it is good for a person to be stingy. Thus, although his father was generous, he can inherit from him the negative tendency—to be stingy, for the absence is just as inheritance as the presence.

Or, if one inherits from one's ancestors a tendency to be open-minded, he builds for himself ideas, and draws from them conclusions that it is good for a person to be open-minded. But where does one find those sentences and reasons? One takes all that from his environment unknowingly, for they impart to him their views and likings in the form of gradual cause and effect.

Hence, man regards them as his own possession, which he acquired through his free thought. But here, too, as with the wheat, there is one unchanging part of the source, which is that in the end, the tendencies he had inherited remain as they were in his forefathers. And this is called "the second factor."

HABIT TURNS TO SECOND NATURE

The third reason is a conduct of direct cause and effect, which affect the source and change it. Because the inherited tendencies in man have become concepts, due to the environment, they operate in the same directions that these concepts define. For example, a man of frugal nature, in whom the tendency for stinginess has been turned into a concept, through the environment, perceives frugality through some reasonable definition.

Let us assume that with this conduct, he protects himself from needing others. Thus, he has acquired a scale for frugality, and when that fear is absent, he can waive it. Thus, he has substantially changed for the better from the tendency he had inherited from his forefathers. And sometimes one manages to completely uproot a bad tendency. This is done by habit, which has the ability to become a second nature.

In that, the strength of man is greater than that of a plant. For wheat can change only in its private part, whereas man has the ability to change through the cause and effect of the environment, even in the general parts, that is, to completely invert a tendency and uproot it to its opposite.

EXTERNAL FACTORS

The fourth reason is a conduct of cause and effect that affects the source by things that are completely alien to it, and operates on it from the outside. This means that these things are not at all related to the source's growth conduct, to affect it directly, but rather operate indirectly. For example, monetary issues, burdens, or the winds, etc., have their own complete, slow, and gradual order of states by way of "cause and effect," and change man's concepts for better or for worse.

Thus, I have set up the four natural factors that each thought and idea that appears in us is but their fruits. And even if one were to sit and contemplate something all day long, he will not be able to add or to alter what those four factors give him. Any addition he can add is in the quantity: whether a great intellect or a small one. But in the quality, he cannot add one bit. This is because they are the ones that compellingly determine the nature and shape of the idea and the conclusion, without asking our opinion. Thus, we are at the hands of these four factors, as clay in the hands of a potter.

FREE CHOICE

However, when we examine these four factors, we find that although our strength is not enough to face the first factor, the "source," we still have the ability and the free choice to protect ourselves against the other three factors, by which the source changes in its individual parts, and sometimes in its general part, as well, through habit, which endows it with a second nature.

THE ENVIRONMENT AS A FACTOR

This protection means that we can always supplement in the matter of choosing our environment, which are the friends, books, teachers, and so on. It is like a person who inherited a few stalks of wheat from his father. From this small amount, he can grow dozens of stalks through his choice of the environment for his "source," which is fertile soil, with all the necessary minerals and raw materials that nourish the wheat abundantly.

There is also the matter of the work of improving the environmental conditions to fit the needs of the plant and the growth, for the wise will do well to choose the best conditions and will find blessing. And the fool will take from whatever comes before him, and will thus turn the sowing to a curse rather than to a blessing.

Thus, all its praise and spirit depends on the choice of the environment in which to sow the wheat. But once it has been sown in the selected location, the wheat's absolute shape is determined according to the measure that the environment is capable of providing.

So is the case with our topic, for it is true that the desire has no freedom. Rather, it is operated by the above four factors. And one is compelled to think and examine as they suggest, denied of any strength to criticize or change, as the wheat that has been sown in its environment.

However, there is freedom for the will to initially choose such an environment, such books, and such guides that impart to him good concepts. If one does not do that, but is willing to enter any environment that appears to him and read any book that falls into his hands, he is bound to fall into a bad environment or waste his time on worthless books, which are abundant and easier to come by. In consequence, he will be forced into foul concepts that make him sin and condemn. **He will certainly be punished, not because of**

his evil thoughts or deeds, in which he has no choice, but because he did not choose to be in a good environment, for in that there is definitely a choice.

Therefore, **he who strives to continually choose a better environment is worthy of praise and reward. But here, too, it is not because of his good thoughts and deeds, which come to him without his choice, but because of his effort to acquire a good environment, which brings him these good thoughts and deeds.** It is as Rabbi Yehoshua Ben Perachya said, "Make for yourself a Rav, and buy for yourself a friend."

THE NECESSITY TO CHOOSE A GOOD ENVIRONMENT

Now you can understand the words of Rabbi Yosi Ben Kisma (*Avot*, 6:9), who replied to a person who offered him to live in his town, and he would give him thousands of gold coins for it: "Even if you give me all the gold and silver and jewels in the world, I will live only in a place of Torah." These words seem too sublime for our simple mind to grasp, for how could he relinquish thousands of gold coins for such a small thing as living in a place where there are no disciples of Torah, while he himself was a great sage who needed to learn from no one? Indeed, a mystery.

But as we have seen, it is a simple thing, and should be observed by each and every one of us. For although everyone has "his own source," the forces are revealed openly only through the environment one is in. This is similar to the wheat sown in the ground, whose forces become apparent only through its environment, which is the soil, the rain, and the light of the sun.

Thus, Rabbi Yosi Ben Kisma correctly assumed that if he were to leave the good environment he had chosen and fall into a harmful environment, in a city where there is no Torah, not only would his former concepts be compromised, but all the other forces hidden in his source, which he had not yet revealed in action, would remain concealed. This is because they would not be subject to the right environment that would be able to activate them.

And as we have clarified above, **only in the matter of the choice of environment is man's reign over himself measured, and for this he should receive either reward or punishment.** Therefore, one must not wonder at a sage such as Rabbi Yosi Ben Kisma for choosing the good and declining the bad, and for not being tempted by material and corporeal things, as he deduces there: "When one dies, one does not take with him silver, or gold, or jewels, but only Torah and good deeds."

And so our sages warned, "Make for yourself a Rav, and buy for yourself a friend." And there is also the choice of books, as we have mentioned, for only in that is one rebuked or praised—in his choice of environment. But once he has chosen the environment, he is at its hands as clay in the hands of the potter.

THE MIND'S CONTROL OVER THE BODY

Some external contemporary sages, after contemplating the above matter and seeing how man's mind is but a fruit that grows out of the events of life, concluded that the mind has no control whatsoever over the body, but only life's events, imprinted in the physical tendons of the brain, control and activate man. And a man's mind is like a mirror, reflecting the shapes before it. And although the mirror is the carrier of these shapes, it cannot activate or move the shapes reflected in it.

So is the mind. Although life's events, in all their discernments of cause and effect, are seen and recognized by the mind, the mind is nonetheless utterly incapable of controlling the body, to bring it into motion, meaning to bring it closer to the good or remove it from the bad. This is because the spiritual and the physical are completely remote from one another, and there is no intermediary tool between them to enable the spiritual mind to activate and operate the corporeal body, as has been discussed at length.

But where they are smart, they disrupt. Man's imagination uses the mind just as the microscope serves the eye: without the microscope, he would not see anything harmful, due to its smallness. But once he has seen the harmful being through the microscope, man distances himself from the noxious factor.

Thus, it is the microscope that brings man to distance himself from the harm, and not the sense, for the sense did not detect the noxious factor. And to that extent, the mind fully controls man's body, to avert it from bad and bring it near the good. Thus, in all the places where the attribute of the body fails to recognize the beneficial or the detrimental, it needs only the mind's wit.

Furthermore, since man knows his mind, which is a true conclusion from life's experiences, **he can therefore receive knowledge and understanding from a trusted person and take it as law, although his life's events have not yet revealed these concepts to him.** It is like a person who asks the advice of a doctor and obeys him even though he understands nothing with his own mind. Thus, one uses the mind of others no less than one uses one's own.

As we have clarified above, there are two ways for Providence to make sure certain that man achieves the good, final goal:

A. The path of pain.

B. The path of Torah.

All the clarity in the path of the Torah stems from that. For these clear conceptions that were revealed and recognized after a long chain of events in the lives of the prophets and the men of God, there comes a man who fully utilizes them and benefits from them, as though these concepts were events of his own life. Thus, you see that one is exempted from all the ordeals one must experience before he can develop that clear mind by himself. Thus, one saves both time and pain.

It can be compared to a sick man who does not wish to obey the doctor's orders before he understands by himself how that advice would cure him, and therefore begins to study medicine. He could die of his illness before he learns medicine.

So is the path of pain vs. the path of Torah. One who does not believe the concepts that the Torah and prophecy advise him to accept without self-understanding, must come to these conceptions by himself by following the chain of cause and effect from life's events. These are experiences that greatly rush, and can develop the sense of recognition of evil in them, as we have seen, without one's choice, but because of one's efforts to acquire a good environment, which leads to these thoughts and actions.

THE FREEDOM OF THE INDIVIDUAL

Now we have come to a thorough and accurate understanding of the freedom of the individual. However, that relates only to the first factor, the "source," which is the first substance of every person, meaning all the characteristics we inherit from our forefathers and by which we differ from each other.

This is because even when thousands of people share the same environment in such a way that the other three factors affect all of them equally, you will still not find two people who share the same attribute. This is because each of them has his/her own unique source. This is like the source of the wheat: although it changes a great deal by the three remaining factors, it still retains the preliminary shape of wheat and will never take on the form of another species.

THE GENERAL SHAPE OF THE PROGENITOR IS NEVER LOST

So it is that each "source" that had taken off the preliminary shape of the progenitor and had taken on a new shape as a result of the three factors that were added to it, and which change it significantly, the general shape of the progenitor still remains, and will never assume the shape of another person who resembles him, just as oat will never resemble wheat.

This is so because each and every source is, in itself, a long sequence of generations comprised of several hundred generations, and the source includes the conceptions of them all. However, they are not revealed in it in the same ways they appeared in the ancestors, that is, in the form of ideas, but only as abstract forms. Therefore, they exist in him in the form of abstract forces called "tendencies" and "instincts," without him knowing their reason or why he does what he does. Thus, there can never be two people with the same attribute.

THE NECESSITY OF PRESERVING THE FREEDOM OF THE INDIVIDUAL

Know, that this is the one true possession of the individual that must not be harmed or altered. This is because the end of all these tendencies, which are included in the source, is to materialize and assume the form of concepts when that individual grows and obtains a mind of his own, as a result of the law of evolution, which controls that chain and prompts it ever forward, as explained in the article "The Peace." Also, we learn that each and every tendency is bound to turn into a sublime and immeasurably important concept.

Thus, anyone who eradicates a tendency from an individual and uproots it causes the loss of that sublime and wondrous concept from the world, intended to emerge at the end of the chain, for that tendency will never again emerge in any other body. Accordingly, we must understand that when a particular tendency takes the form of a concept, it can no longer be distinguished as good or bad. This is because such distinctions are recognized only when they are still tendencies or immature concepts, and in no way are any of them recognized when they assume the shape of true concepts.

From the above we learn what a terrible wrong inflict those nations that force their reign on minorities, depriving them of freedom without allowing them to live their lives by the tendencies they have inherited from their ancestors. They are regarded as no less than murderers.

And even those who do not believe in religion or in purposeful guidance can understand the necessity to preserve the freedom of the individual by watching nature's systems. For we can see how all the nations that ever fell, throughout the generations, came to it only due to their oppression of minorities and individuals, which had therefore rebelled against them and ruined them. Hence, it is clear to all that peace cannot exist in the world if we do not take into consideration the freedom of the individual. Without it, peace will not be sustainable and ruin shall prevail.

Thus, we have clearly defined the essence of the individual with utmost accuracy, after the deduction of all that he takes from the public. But now we face a question: "Where, in the end, is the individual himself?" All we have said thus far concerning the individual is perceived as only the property of the individual, inherited from his ancestors. But where is the individual himself, the heir and the carrier of that property, who demands that we guard his property?

From all that has been said thus far, we have yet to find the point of "self" in man, which stands before us as an independent unit. And why do I need the first factor, which is a long chain of thousands of people, one after the other, from generation to generation, with which we set the image of the individual as an heir? And what do I need the other three factors, which are the thousands of people, standing one besides the other in the same generation? In the end, each individual is but a public machine, forever ready to serve the public as it sees fit. Meaning, he has become subordinate to two types of public:

A. From the perspective of the first factor, he has become subordinate to a large public from past generations, standing one after the other.

B. From the perspective of the three other factors, he has become subordinate to his contemporary public.

This is indeed a universal question. For this reason, many oppose the above natural method, although they thoroughly know its validity. Instead, they choose metaphysical methods, or dualism, or transcendentalism, to depict for themselves some spiritual object and how it sits within the body, in man's soul. And it is that soul that learns and that operates the body, and it is man's essence, his "self."

And perhaps these interpretations could ease the mind, but the problem is that they have no scientific solution as to how a spiritual object can have any contact with physical atoms to bring them into any kind of motion. All their wisdom and delving did not help them find a bridge on which to cross that wide and deep crevice that spreads between the spiritual entity and the corporeal atom. Thus, science has gained nothing from all these metaphysical methods.

THE WILL TO RECEIVE—EXISTENCE FROM ABSENCE

To move a step forward in a scientific manner here, all we need is the wisdom of Kabbalah. This is because all the teachings in the world are included in the wisdom of Kabbalah. Concerning spiritual lights and vessels, we learn that the primary innovation, from the perspective of Creation, which He has created existence from absence, applies to one aspect only, defined as the "will to receive." All other matters in the whole of Creation are not innovations at all; they are not existence from absence, but existence from existence. This means that they extend directly from His essence, as the light extends from the sun. There, too, there is nothing new, since what is found in the core of the sun extends outwardly.

However, the will to receive is complete novelty. Meaning, prior to Creation such a thing did not exist in reality, since He has no aspect of desire to receive, as He precedes everything, so from whom would He receive?

For this reason, this will to receive, which He extracted as existence from absence, is complete novelty. But all the rest is not considered an innovation that could be called "Creation." Hence, all the vessels and the bodies, both from spiritual worlds and from physical worlds, are deemed spiritual or corporeal substance, whose nature is the will to receive.

TWO FORCES IN THE WILL TO RECEIVE: ATTRACTING FORCE AND REJECTING FORCE

You need to determine further that we distinguish two forces in that force called the "will to receive":

A. The attracting force.

B. The rejecting force.

The reason is that each body, or vessel, defined by the will to receive is indeed limited, meaning the quality it will receive and the quantity it will receive. Therefore, all the quantity and quality that are outside its boundaries appear to be against its nature; hence, it rejects them. Thus, that "will to receive," although it is deemed an attracting force, is compelled to become a rejecting force, as well.

ONE LAW FOR ALL THE WORLDS

Although the wisdom of Kabbalah mentions nothing of our corporeal world, there is still only one law for all the worlds (as written in the article, "The Essence of the Wisdom of Kabbalah," section, "The Law of Root and Branch"). Thus, all the corporeal entities in our world, that is, everything within that space, be it still, vegetative, animate, a spiritual object or a corporeal object, if we want to distinguish the unique, self aspect of each of them, how they differentiate from one another, even in the smallest of particles, it amounts to no more than a "desire to receive." This is its entire particular form, from the perspective of the generated Creation, limiting it in quantity and quality. As a result, there is an attracting force and the rejecting force in it.

Yet, anything other that exists in it besides these two forces is deemed the bounty from His essence. That bounty is equal for all creatures, and it presents no innovation, with respect to Creation, as it extends existence from existence.

Also, it cannot be ascribed to any particular unit, but only to things that are common to all parts of Creation, small or large. Each of them receives from that bounty according to its will to receive, and this limitation defines each individual and unit.

Thus, I have evidently—from a purely scientific perspective—proven the "self" (ego) of every individual in a scientific, completely criticism-proof method, even according to the system of the fanatic, automatic materialists. From now on, we have no need for those lame methods dipped in metaphysics.

And of course, it makes no difference whether this force, being the will to receive, is a result and a fruit of the material that had produced it through chemistry, or that the material is a result and a fruit of that force. This is because we know that the main thing is that only this force, imprinted in every being and atom of the "will to receive," within its boundaries, is the unit where it is separated and distinguished from its environment. And this holds true both for a single atom or for a group of atoms, called "a body."

All other discernments in which there is a surplus of that force are not related in any way to that particle or that group of particles, with respect to itself, but only with respect to the whole, which is the bounty extended to them from the Creator, which is common to all parts of Creation together, without distinction of specific created bodies.

Now we shall understand the matter of the freedom of the individual, according to the definition of the first factor, which we called the "source," where all previous generations, which are the ancestors of that individual, have imprinted their nature. As we have clarified, the meaning of the word, "individual," is but the boundaries of the will to receive, imprinted in its group of molecules.

Thus you see that all the tendencies he has inherited from his ancestors are indeed no more than boundaries of his will to receive, either related to the attracting force in him, or to the rejecting force in him, which appear before us as tendencies for stinginess or generosity, a tendency to mingle or to stay secluded, and so on.

Because of that, they really are his self (ego), fighting for its existence. Thus, if we eradicate even a single tendency from that individual, we are considered to be cutting off an actual organ from his essence. And it is also considered a genuine loss for all Creation, because there is no other like it, nor will there ever be like it in the whole world.

After we have thoroughly clarified the just right of the individual according to the natural laws, let us turn and see just how practical it is, without compromising the theory of ethics and statesmanship. And most important: how this right is applied by our holy Torah.

TAKING AFTER THE COLLECTIVE

Our scriptures say: "Take after the collective." That means that wherever there is a dispute between the collective and the individual, we are obliged to rule according to the will of the collective. Thus, you see that the collective has a right to expropriate the freedom of the individual.

But we are faced with a different question here, even more serious than the first. It seems as though this law regresses humanity instead of promoting it. This is because while most of humanity is undeveloped, and the developed ones are always a small minority, if you always determine according to the will of the collective, which are the undeveloped, and the reckless ones, the views and desires of the wise and the developed in society, which are always the minority, will never be heard and will not be taken into consideration. Thus, you seal off humanity's fate to regression, for it will not be able to make even a single step forward.

However, as is explained in the article, "The Peace," section, "Necessity to Practice Caution with the Laws of Nature," since we are ordered by Providence to lead a social life, we have become obligated to observe all the laws pertaining to the sustenance of society. And if we are somewhat negligent, nature will take its revenge in us, regardless of whether or not we understand the reasons for the laws.

And we can see that there is no other arrangement by which to live in society except following the law of "Taking after the collective," which sets every dispute and tribulation in society in order. Thus, this law is the only instrument that gives society sustainability. For this reason, it is considered one of the natural *Mitzvot* (commandments) of Providence, and we must accept it and guard it meticulously, regardless of our understanding.

This is similar to all the other *Mitzvot* in the Torah: all of them are nature's laws and His Providence, which come to us from Above downward. And I have already described ("The Essence of the Wisdom of Kabbalah," The Law or Root and Branch) how all the stubbornness we detect in the conduct of nature in this world is only because they are extended and taken from laws and conducts of Upper, Spiritual Worlds.

Now you can understand that the *Mitzvot* in the Torah are no more than laws and conducts set in Higher Worlds, which are the roots of all of nature's conducts in this world of ours. The laws of the Torah always match the laws of nature in this world as two drops in a pond. Thus, we have proven that the law, "Taking after the collective" is the law of Providence and nature.

A PATH OF TORAH AND A PATH OF PAIN

Yet, our question about the regression, which had emerged from this law, is as yet not settled by these words. Indeed, this is our concern—to find ways to mend that. But Providence, for itself, does not lose because of that, for it has enveloped humankind in two ways—the "Path of Torah," and the "Path of Pain"—in a way that guarantees humanity's continuous development and progress toward the goal without any reservations ("The Peace," Everything Is in Deposit). Indeed, obeying this law is a natural, necessary commitment.

THE COLLECTIVE'S RIGHT TO EXPROPRIATE THE FREEDOM OF THE INDIVIDUAL

We must ask further: things are justified when matters revolve around issues between people. Then we can accept the law of "Taking after the collective," through the obligation of Providence, which instructs us to always look after the well-being and happiness of the friends. But the Torah obliges us to follow the law of "Taking after the collective" in disputes between man and God, as well, although these matters seem completely unrelated to the existence of society.

Therefore, the question still stands: how can we justify that law, which obligates us to accept the views of the majority, which is, as we have said, undeveloped, and to reject and annul the opinion of the developed, which are always a small minority?

But as we have shown ("The Essence of Religion and Its Purpose," Conscious Development and Unconscious Development), the Torah and the *Mitzvot* were given only to purify Israel, to develop in us the sense of recognition of evil, imprinted in us at birth, which is generally defined as our self-love, and to come to the pure good defined as the "love of others," which is the one and only passage to the love of God.

Accordingly, the precepts between man and God are considered tools that detach man from self-love, which is harmful for society. It is thus obvious that the topics of dispute regarding *Mitzvot* between man and God relate to the problem of society's sustainability. Thus, they, too, fall into the framework of "Taking after the collective."

Now we can understand the conduct of discriminating between *Halachah* (Jewish law) and *Agadah* (legends). This is because only in *Halachot* (plural for *Halachah*), does the law, "individual and collective, *Halachah* (law) as the collective" apply. It is not so in the *Agadah*, since matters of *Agadah* stand above matters that concern the existence of society, for they speak precisely of the matter of people's conducts in matters concerning man and God, in that same part where the existence and physical happiness of society has no consequence.

Thus, there is no justification for the collective to annul the view of the individual and "every man did that which was right in his own eyes." But regarding *Halachot* that deal with observing the *Mitzvot* of the Torah, all of which fall under the supervision of society, since there cannot be any order, but through the law, "Take after the collective."

FOR SOCIAL LIFE, THE LAW, "TAKE AFTER THE COLLECTIVE"

Now we have come to a clear understanding of the sentence concerning the freedom of the individual. Indeed, there is a question: "Where did the collective take the right to expropriate the freedom of the individual and deny him of the most precious thing in life, freedom?" Seemingly, there is no more than brute force here.

But as we have clearly explained above, it is a natural law and the decree of Providence. And because Providence compels each of us to conduct a social life, it naturally follows that each person is obligated to secure the existence and well-being of society. And that cannot exist but through imposing the conduct of "Taking after the Collective," ignoring the opinion of the individual.

Thus, you evidently see that this is the origin of every right and justification that the collective has to expropriate the freedom of the individual against his will, and to place him under its authority. Therefore, it is understood that with regard to all those matters that do not concern the existence of the material life of the society, there is no justification for the collective to rob and abuse the freedom of the individual in any way. And if they do, they are deemed robbers and thieves who prefer brute force to any right and justice in the world, since here the obligation of the individual to obey the will of the collective does not apply.

IN SPIRITUAL LIFE, "TAKE AFTER THE INDIVIDUAL"

It turns out that as far as spiritual life is concerned, there is no natural obligation on the individual to abide by the society in any way. On the contrary, here applies a natural law over the collective, to subjugate itself to the individual. And it is clarified in the Article, "The Peace," that there are two ways by which Providence has enveloped and surrounded us, to bring us to the end:

A. A Path of Pain, which develops us in this manner unconsciously.

B. A Path of Torah and wisdom, which consciously develops us in this manner without any agony or coercion.

And since the more developed in the generation is certainly the individual, it follows that when the public wants to relieve themselves of the terrible agony and assume conscious and voluntary development, which is the path of Torah, they have no choice but to subjugate themselves and their physical freedom to the discipline of the individual, and obey the orders and remedies that he will offer them.

Thus you see that in spiritual matters, the authority of the collective is overturned and the law of "Taking after the Individual" is applied, that is, the developed individual. For it is plain to see that the developed and the educated in every society are always a small minority. It follows that the success and spiritual well-being of society is bottled and sealed in the hands of the minority.

Therefore, the collective is obliged to meticulously guard all the views of the few, so they will not perish from the world. This is because they must know for certain, in complete confidence, that the truer and more developed views are never in the hands of the collective in authority, but rather in the hands of the weakest, that is, in the hands of the indistinguishable minority. This is because every wisdom and everything precious comes into the world in small quantities. Therefore, we are cautioned to preserve the views of all the individuals, due to the collective's inability to tell wrong from right among them.

CRITICISM BRINGS SUCCESS; LACK OF CRITICISM CAUSES DECADENCE

We must further add that reality presents to our eyes extreme oppositeness between physical things and the concepts and ideas regarding the above topic. For the matter of social unity, which can be the source of every joy and success, applies particularly among bodies and bodily matters in people, and the separation between them is the source of every calamity and misfortune.

But with concepts and ideas, it is the complete opposite: unity and lack of criticism is deemed the source of every failure and hindrance to all the progress and didactic fertilization. This is because drawing the right conclusions depends particularly on the multiplicity of disagreements and separation between opinions. The more contradictions there are between opinions and the more criticism there is, the more the knowledge and wisdom increase and matters become more suitable for examination and clarification.

The degeneration and failure of intelligence stem only from the lack of criticism and disagreement. Thus, evidently, the whole basis of physical success is the measure of unity of the society, and the basis for the success of intelligence and knowledge is the separation and disagreement among them.

It turns out that when humankind achieves its goal, with respect to the success of the bodies, by bringing them to the degree of complete love of others, all the bodies in the world will unite into a single body and a single heart, as written in the article, "The Peace." Only then will all the happiness intended for humanity become revealed in all its glory.

But against that, we must be watchful to not bring the views of people so close that disagreement and criticism might be terminated from among the wise and scholarly, for the love of the body naturally brings with it proximity of views. And should criticism and disagreement vanish, all progress in concepts and ideas will cease, too, and the source of knowledge in the world will dry out.

This is the proof of the obligation to caution with the freedom of the individual regarding concepts and ideas. For the whole development of the wisdom and knowledge is based on that freedom of the individual. Thus, we are cautioned to preserve it very carefully, so each and every form within us, which we call "individual," that is, the particular force of a single person, generally named the "will to receive."

ANCESTRAL HERITAGE

All the details of the pictures that this will to receive includes, which we have defined as the "source," or the First Reason, whose meaning includes all the tendencies and customs inherited from his ancestors, which we picture as a long chain of thousands of people who once were alive, and who stand one atop of the other. Each of them is an essential drop of his ancestors, and that drop brings each person all the spiritual possessions of his ancestors into his "medulla oblongata" (the elongated brain), called "subconscious." Thus, the individual before us has, in his subconscious, all the thousands of spiritual legacies from all the individuals represented in that chain, which are his ancestors.

Thus, just as the face of each and every person differs, so their views differ. There are no two people on earth whose opinions are identical, because each person has a great and sublime possession inherited from his ancestors, and which others have no shred of them.

Therefore, all those possessions are considered the individual's property, and society is cautioned to preserve its flavor and spirit so as to not be blurred by its environment. Rather, each individual should maintain the integrity of his inheritance. Then, the contradiction and oppositeness between them will remain forever, to forever secure the criticism and progress of the wisdom, which is humanity's advantage and its true eternal desire.

And after we have come to a certain measure of recognition in man's selfishness, which we have determined as a force and a "will to receive," being the essential point of the bare being, we have also learned thoroughly clear, from all sides, the original possession of each body, which we have defined as "ancestral heritage." This pertains to all the potential tendencies and qualities that have come into his "source" by inheritance, which is the first substance of every person, that is, the initial seed of his forefathers. Now we shall clarify the two discernments in the will to receive.

TWO DISCERNMENTS: A) POTENTIAL, B) ACTUAL

First, we must understand that although this selfishness, which we have defined as the "will to receive," is the very essence of man, it cannot exist in reality even for a second. For what we call "potential," meaning before it emerges from potential to actual, exists only in our **thought**, meaning that only the **thought** can determine it.

But in fact, there cannot be any real force in the world that is dormant and inactive. This is because the force exists in reality only while it is revealed in action. By the same token, you cannot say about an infant that it is very strong when it cannot lift even the lightest weight, but you can say that you see in that infant that when it grows, it will manifest great strength.

However, we do say that that strength we find in man when he is grown was present in his organs and his body even when he was an infant, but that strength had been concealed and was not apparent. It is true that in our minds we could determine (the powers destined to manifest), since the mind asserts it. However, in the infant's actual body there is certainly no strength at all, since no strength manifests in the infant's actions.

So it is with appetite. This force will not appear in a man's body in the actual reality, when the organs cannot eat, meaning when he is satiated. But even when one is satiated, the force of appetite exists, but it is concealed in man's body. After some time, when the food had been digested, it reappears and manifests from potential to actual.

However, such a sentence, of determining a potential force that has not yet been revealed in actual fact, belongs to the conducts by which the thought perceives. But it does not exist in reality, since when satiated, we feel very clearly that the force of appetite is gone, and if you search for it, you will find it nowhere.

It turns out that we cannot display a potential as a subject that exists in and of itself, but only as a predicate. Thus, when an action occurs in reality, at that time the force manifests in the action.

Yet, we necessarily find two things here, in the perceiving process: a subject and a predicate, that is, potential and actual, such as the force of appetite, which is the subject, and the image of the dish, which is the predicate and the action. In reality, however, they come as one. It will never occur that the force of appetite will appear in a person without picturing the dish he wishes to eat. Thus, these are two halves of the same thing. The force of appetite must dress in that image. You therefore see that the subject and the predicate are presented at once, and become absent at once.

Now we understand that the will to receive, which we presented as selfishness, does not mean that it exists so in a person, as a craving force that wishes to receive in the form of a passive predicate. Rather, this pertains to the subject, which dresses in the image of the eatable object, and whose operation appears in the form of the thing being eaten, and in which it clothes. We call that action, "desire," meaning the force of appetite, revealed in the action of the imagination.

And so it is with our topic—the general will to receive, which is the very essence of man. It appears and exists only through dressing in the shapes of objects that are likely to be received. For then it exists as the subject, and in no other way. We call that action, "life," meaning man's livelihood, which means that the force of the will to receive dresses and acts within the desired objects. And the measurement of revelation of that action is the measurement of his life, as we have explained in the act we call, "desire."

TWO CREATIONS: A) MAN, B) A LIVING SOUL

From the above, we can clearly understand the verse: "And the Lord God formed man of the dust of the ground, and breathed into his nostrils the breath of life; and man became a living (*Chayah*) soul (*Nefesh*)" (Genesis 2:7). Here we find two creations:

A. Man himself;

B. The living soul itself.

And the verse says that in the beginning, man was created as dust of the ground, a collection of molecules in which resides the essence of man, meaning his will to receive. That force, the will to receive, is present in every element of reality, as we have explained above. Also, all four types: still, vegetative, animate and speaking emerged from them. In that respect, man has no advantage over any part of creation, and this is the meaning of the verse in the words: "dust of the ground."

However, we have already seen that this force, called "will to receive," cannot exist without dressing and acting in a desired object, and this action is called, "life." And accordingly, we find that before man has arrived at the human forms of reception of pleasure, which differ from those of other animals, he is still considered a lifeless, dead person. This is because his will to receive has no place in which to dress and manifest his actions, which are the manifestations of life.

This is the meaning of the verse, "and breathed into his nostrils the breath of life," which is the general form of reception suitable for humans. The word, *Nishmat*, (breath) comes from the word, *Samin*, (placing) the ground for him, which is like "value." And the origin of the word "breath" is understood from the verse (Job 33:4): "The spirit of God has made me, and the breath of the Almighty has given me life," and see the commentary of the MALBIM there. The word, "soul" (*Neshama*), has the same syntax structure as the words, "missing" (*Nifkad*), "accused" (*Ne'esham*), and "accused" (*Ne'eshama*—female term of *Ne'esham*).

And the meaning of the words, "and breathed into his nostrils" is that He instills a soul (*Neshama*) in his internality and an appreciation of life, which is the sum of the forms that are worthy of reception into his will to receive. Then, that force, the will to receive, enclosed in his molecules, has found a place in which to dress and act, meaning in those forms of reception that he had obtained from the Creator. And this action is called "life," as we have explained above.

And the verse ends, "and man became a living soul." This means that since the will to receive has begun to act by the measures of those forms of reception, life instantly manifested in it and it "became a living soul." However, prior to the attainment of those forms of reception, although the force of the will to receive had been imprinted in him, it is still considered a lifeless body, since it has no place in which to appear and to manifest in action.

As we have seen above, although man's essence is only the will to receive, it is still taken as half of a whole, as it must clothe in a reality that comes its way. For that reason, it and the image of possession it depicts are literally one, for otherwise it would not be able to exist for even a moment.

Therefore, when the machine of the body is at its peak, that is, until his middle-age, his "ego" stands upright in all the height imprinted in him at birth. Because of that, he feels within him a large and powerful measure of the will to receive. In other words, he craves great wealth and honor, and anything that comes his way. This is so because of the perfection of man's ego, which attracts shapes of structures and concepts that it dresses in and sustains itself through them.

But when half his life is through, begin the days of the decline, which, by their content, are his dying days. This is because a person does not die in an instant, just as he did not receive his life in an instant. Rather his candle, being his ego, withers and dies bit by bit, and along with it die the images of the possessions he wishes to receive.

He begins to relinquish many possessions he had dreamed of in his youth, and he gradually relinquishes great possessions, according to his decline over the years. Finally, in his truly old days, when the shadow of death hovers over all his being, a person finds himself in "times of no appeal," since his will to receive, his ego, has withered away. Only a tiny spark of it remains, hidden from the eye, from clothing in some possession. Therefore, there is no appeal or hope in those days for any image of reception.

Thus, we have proven that the will to receive, along with the image of the object expected to be received, are one and the same thing. And their manifestation is equal, their stature is equal, and so is the length of their lives.

However, there is a significant distinction here in the form of the yielding at the time of the decline of life. That yielding is not a result of satiation, like a person who relinquishes food when he is satiated, but a result of despair. In other words, when the ego begins to die during the days of decline, it senses its own weakness and approaching death. Therefore, a person lets go and gives up on the dreams and hopes of his youth.

Observe carefully the difference between that and the yielding due to satiation, which causes no grief and cannot be called "partial death," but is like a worker who completed his work. Indeed, relinquishment out of despair is full of pain and sorrow, and can therefore be called, "partial death."

FREEDOM FROM THE ANGEL OF DEATH

Now, after all that we have learned, we find a way to truly understand the words of our sages when they said, "'*Harut* (engraved) on the stones,' do not pronounce it *Harut* (engraved), but rather *Herut* (freedom), for they have been liberated from the angel of death."

It has been explained in the articles, "Matan Torah" and "The Arvut," that prior to the giving of the Torah, they had assumed the relinquishment of any private property to the extent expressed in the words, "a Kingdom of Priests," and the purpose of the whole of Creation—to cleave unto Him in equivalence of form with Him: as He bestows and does not receive, they, too, will bestow and not receive. This is the last degree of *Dvekut* (adhesion), expressed in the words, "Holy nation," as it is written at the end of the article, "The Arvut."

I have already brought you to realize that man's essence, meaning his selfishness, defined as the will to receive, is only half a thing, and can only exist when clothed in some image of a possession or hope for possession. For only then is our matter complete and can be called "man's essence."

Thus, when the children of Israel were rewarded with complete *Dvekut* on that holy occasion, their vessels of reception were completely emptied of any worldly possession and they were cleaved unto Him in equivalence of form. This means that they did not have any desire for any self-possession, but only to the extent that they could bestow contentment, so their maker would delight in them.

And since their will to receive had clothed in an image of that object, it had clothed in it and bonded with it into complete oneness. Therefore, they were certainly liberated from the angel of death, for death is necessarily an absence and negation of the existence of a certain object. But only while there is a spark that wishes to exist for its own pleasure is it possible to say about it that that spark does not exist because it has become absent and died.

However, if there is no such spark in man, but all the sparks of his essence clothe in bestowal of contentment upon their Maker, then it is neither absent nor dead. For even when the body is annulled, it is only annulled with respect to self-gratification, in which the will to receive is dressed and can only exist in it.

However, when he achieves the aim of Creation and the Creator receives pleasure from him, since His will is done, man's essence, which clothes in His contentment, is granted complete eternity, like Him. Thus, he has been rewarded with freedom from the angel of death. This is the meaning of the words of the Midrash (*Midrash Rabba, Shemot*, 41, Item 7): "Freedom from the angel of death." And in the Mishna (*Avot*, 6:2): "*Harut* (engraved) on the stones; do not pronounce it *Harut* (engraved), but rather *Herut* (freedom), for none are free, unless they engage in the study of Torah."

Concealment and Disclosure of the Face of the Creator

The second concealment, which the books refer to as "concealment within concealment," means that one cannot see even the back of the Creator. Instead, one says that the Creator has left him and no longer watches over him. He ascribes all the sufferings he feels to blind fate and to nature, since the ways of Providence become so complex in one's eyes that they lead one to denial.

This means (depiction) that one prays and gives charity for one's troubles but is not answered whatsoever. And precisely when one stops praying for one's troubles, one is answered. Whenever he overcomes, believes in Providence, and betters his deeds, luck turns away from him and he mercilessly falls back. And when he denies and begins to worsen his deeds, he becomes very successful and is greatly relieved.

One does not find one's sustenance in proper manners, but through deceit or through desecration of Shabbat. Or, all of one's acquaintances who keep Torah and *Mitzvot* (commandments) suffer poverty, illness, and are despised by people. These observers of *Mitzvot* seem impolite to him, innately brainless, and so hypocritical that he cannot bear to be among them for even a minute.

Conversely, all his wicked acquaintances, who mock his faith, are very successful, well to do, and healthy. They know no sickness; they are clever, virtuous, and good-tempered. They are carefree, confident, and tranquil all day, every day.

When Providence arranges things in this manner for a person, it is called "concealment within concealment." This is because then one collapses under one's weight and cannot continue to strengthen the belief that one's pains come from the Creator for some hidden reason. Finally, one fails, becomes heretic, and says that the Creator is not watching over His creations whatsoever, and all that transpires, transpires by fate and by blind nature. This is not seeing even the back.

DEPICTION OF CONCEALMENT OF THE FACE

1. Suffering torments such as deficient income, poor health, degradations, failing to accomplish one's plans, and emotional dissatisfaction such as keeping oneself from tormenting one's friend.
2. Praying without being answered. Declining when bettering one's actions, and succeeding when worsening them. Obtaining one's sustenance in improper manners: deception, stealing, or by desecrating the Shabbat.
3. All of one's honest acquaintances suffer poverty, ill health, and degradations of all kinds, and one's wicked acquaintances mock him every day and succeed in health, wealth, and lead carefree lives.
4. All of his righteous acquaintances who keep Torah and *Mitzvot* seem cruel, egotistical, odd or innately stupid and impolite, as well as hypocritical. He finds it repulsive to be with them, even in the Garden of Eden, and he cannot bear to be with them for even a moment.

First concealment (depiction): His Face is not revealed; that is, the Creator does not behave towards a person according to His Name—The Good who Does Good. Rather, it is to the contrary—one is afflicted by Him or suffers from poor income, and many people wish to collect their debts from him and make his life bitter. His whole day is filled with troubles and worries. Or, one suffers from poor health and disrespect from people. Every plan he begins he fails to complete, and he is constantly frustrated.

In this manner, of course one does not see the Creator's Good Face, that is, if he believes that the Creator is the one who does these things to him, either as punishment for transgressions or to reward him in the end. This follows the verse, "whom the Lord loves, He corrects," and also, "the righteous begin with suffering, since the Creator wishes to eventually impart them great peace."

Yet, one does not fail in saying that all this came to him by blind fate and by nature without any reason and consideration. Rather, one strengthens in believing that the Creator, with His Guidance, caused him all that. This is nonetheless considered seeing the Creator's back.

DEPICTION OF DISCLOSURE OF THE FACE

But once he has completely discovered the spice—the Light that one inhales into one's body—through strengthening in faith in the Creator, one becomes worthy of Guidance with His Face revealed. This means that the Creator behaves with him as is fitting to His Name, "The Good who Does Good."

Thus (depiction), he receives abundant good and great peace from the Creator and is always satisfied. This is because one obtains one's livelihood with ease and to the fullest, never experiencing trouble or pressure, knows no illness, is highly respected by people, effortlessly completes any plan that comes to his mind, and succeeds wherever he turns.

And when he wishes upon something, he prays and he is instantaneously answered, as He always answers anything that one demands of Him, and not a single prayer is denied. When one strengthens with good deeds, one succeeds even more, and when one is negligent, one's success proportionally decreases.

All of one's acquaintances are honest, of good income and health. They are highly respected in the eyes of people and have no worries at all. They are at peace all day and every day. They are smart, truthful, and so comely that one feels blessed to be among them.

Conversely, all of one's acquaintances who do not follow the path of Torah are of poor livelihood, troubled by heavy debts, and fail to find even a single moment's rest. They are sick, in pain, and despicable in the eyes of people. They seem to him mindless, ill-mannered, wicked and cruel towards people, deceitful and such sycophants that it is intolerable to be with them.

His Name shows us that He is benevolent to all His creations in all the forms of benefit, sufficient for every kind of receiver from among Israel. Certainly, the pleasure of one is not like the pleasure of another. For example, one who engages in wisdom will not enjoy honor and wealth, and one who does not engage in wisdom will not enjoy great achievements and inventions in the wisdom. Thus, He gives wealth and honor to one, and wondrous achievements in the wisdom to another.

One's request to become stronger in believing in His Guidance over the world during the concealment period brings one to contemplate the books, the Torah, and to draw from there the Light and the understanding how to strengthen one's faith in His Guidance. These illuminations and observations that one receives through the Torah are called "the spice of Torah." When they are collected to a certain amount, the Creator has mercy on him and pours upon him the spirit from Above, that is, the Higher Abundance.

DEPICTION OF DISCLOSURE OF THE FACE

1. Reception of abundant good and peace, and obtainment of one's livelihood with ease and to the fullest. One never feels paucity or ill health, he is respected wherever he turns, and successfully and easily accomplishes any plan that comes to his mind.

2. When one prays, he is immediately answered. When he betters his ways, he is very successful, and when he worsens his ways, he loses his success.

3. All one's acquaintances who walk on the right path are wealthy, healthy, know no sickness, are highly respected by people, and dwell in peace and tranquility. And acquaintances who do not follow the right path are of poor income, filled with troubles and pains, are ill, and are loathsome in the eyes of the people.

4. One considers all the righteous acquaintances as clever, reasonable, well-mannered, truthful, and so comely that it is most pleasurable to be among them.

Preface to The Book of Zohar

1) The depth of wisdom in the holy *Book of Zohar* is enclosed and caged behind a thousand locks, and our human tongue too poor to provide us with sufficient, reliable expressions to interpret one thing in this book to its end. Also, the interpretation I have made is but a ladder to help the examiner rise to the height of the matters and examine the words of the book itself. Hence, I have found it necessary to prepare the reader and give him a route and an inlet in reliable definitions concerning how one should contemplate and study the book.

2) First, you must know that all that is said in *The Book of Zohar*, and even in its legends, is denominations of the ten *Sefirot*, called KHB (*Keter, Hochma, Bina*), HGT (*Hesed, Gevura, Tifferet*), NHYM (*Netzah, Hod, Yesod, Malchut*), and their permutations. Just as the twenty-two letters of the spoken language, whose permutations suffice to uncover every object and every concept, the concepts, and permutations of concepts, in the ten *Sefirot* suffice to disclose all the wisdom in the book of Heaven. However, there are three boundaries that one must be very prudent with, and not exceed them while studying the words of the book.

3) First boundary: There are four categories in the conduct of learning, called "Matter," "Form in Matter," "Abstract Form," and "Essence." It is the same in the ten *Sefirot*. Know that *The Book of Zohar* does not engage at all in the Essence and the Abstract Form in the ten *Sefirot*, but only in the Matter in them, or in the Form in them, while clothed in Matter.

4) Second boundary: We distinguish three discernments in the comprehensive, Godly reality concerning the creation of the souls and the conduct of their existence:

- *Ein Sof* (Infinity);
- The world of *Atzilut*;
- The three worlds called *Beria, Yetzira*, and *Assiya*.

You should know that *The Zohar* engages only in the worlds, *BYA* (*Beria, Yetzira, Assiya*), and in *Ein Sof* and the world of *Atzilut*, to the extent that *BYA* receive from them. However, *The Book of Zohar* does not engage in *Ein Sof* and the world of *Atzilut* themselves at all.

5) Third boundary: There are three discernments in each of the worlds, *BYA*:

- The ten *Sefirot*, which are the Godliness that shines in that world;
- *Neshamot* (Souls), *Ruchot* (spirits), and *Nefashot* (life)[19] of people;
- The rest of reality in it, called "angels," "clothes," and "palaces," whose elements are innumerable.

Bear in mind that although *The Zohar* elucidates extensively on the details in each world, you should still know that the essence of the words of *The Zohar* always focuses on the souls of people in that world. It explains other discernments only to know the measure that the souls receive from them. *The Zohar* does not mention even a single word of what does not relate to the reception of the souls. Hence, you should learn everything presented in *The Book of Zohar* only in relation to the reception of the soul.

And since these three boundaries are very strict, if the reader is not prudent with them and will take matters out of context, he will immediately miscomprehend the matter. For this reason I have found it necessary to trouble and expand the understanding of these three boundaries as much as I could, in such a way that they will be understood by anyone.

6) You already know that there are ten *Sefirot*, called *Hochma, Bina, Tifferet,* and *Malchut*, and their root, called *Keter*. They are ten because the *Sefira* (singular for *Sefirot*) *Tifferet* contains six *Sefirot*, called *Hesed, Gevura, Tifferet, Netzah, Hod,* and *Yesod*. Remember that in all the places where we are used to saying ten *Sefirot*, which are *HB TM*.

In general, they comprise all four worlds *ABYA*, since the world of *Atzilut* is the *Sefira Hochma*; the world of *Beria* is the *Sefira Bina*; the world of *Yetzira* is the *Sefira Tifferet*; and the world of *Assiya* is the *Sefira Malchut*. In particular, not only does each and every world have ten *Sefirot HBTM*, but even the smallest element in each world has these ten *Sefirot HB TM*, as well.

7) *The Zohar* compared these ten *Sefirot*, *HB TM*, to four colors:

- White for the *Sefira Hochma*;
- Red for the *Sefira Bina*;

---

19 Translator's note: The usual translation for both *Neshama* and *Nefesh* is Souls, but here I had to choose a different word for *Nefesh* to distinguish it from *Neshama*.

- Green for the *Sefira Tifferet*;
- Black for the *Sefira Malchut*.

It is similar to a mirror that has four panes painted in the above four colors. And although the light in it is one, it is colored when traveling through the panes and turns into four kinds of light: white light; red light; green light; and black light.

Thus, the Light in all the *Sefirot* is simple Godliness and unity, from the top of *Atzilut* to the bottom of *Assiya*. The division into ten *Sefirot HB TM* is because of the *Kelim* (Vessels) called *HB TM*. Each *Kli* (singular for *Kelim*) is like a fine partition through which the Godly Light traverses towards the receivers.

For this reason, it is considered that each *Kli* paints the Light a different color. The *Kli* of *Hochma*, in the world *Atzilut*, transports white Light, meaning colorless. This is because the *Kli* of *Atzilut* is like the light itself, and the light of the Creator does not suffer any change while traversing it.

This is the meaning of what is written in *The Zohar* about the world of *Atzilut*, "He, His Life, and His Self are one." Hence, the Light of *Atzilut* is considered white light. But when it travels through the *Kelim* of the worlds *Beria*, *Yetzira*, and *Assiya*, the Light changes and dims as it travels through them to the receivers. For example, the red Light is for *Bina*, which is *Beria*; the green Light, like the light of the sun, is for *Tifferet*, which is the world of *Yetzira*; and the black Light is for the *Sefira Malchut*, which is the world of *Assiya*.

8) In addition to the above, there is a very important intimation in this allegory of the four colors. The Upper Lights are called *Sefer* (book), as it is written (*Book of Creation*, Chapter One, Section One), "He created His world in three books: A book, an author, and a story."

The disclosure of the wisdom in each book is not in the white in it, but only in the colors, in the ink, from which the letters in the book, in the permutations of wisdom, come to the reader. On the whole, there are three kinds of ink in the book: red, green, and black.

Correspondingly, the world of *Atzilut*, which is *Hochma*, is all Godliness, like the white in the book. This means that we have no perception in it whatsoever, but the whole disclosure in the book of Heaven is in the *Sefirot Bina*, *Tifferet*, and *Malchut*, which are the three worlds *BYA*, considered the ink in the book of Heaven.

The letters and their combinations appear in the three above-mentioned kinds of ink, and it is only through them that the Godly Light appears to the receivers. At the same time, we must note that the white in the book is the primary subject of the book, and the letters are all "predicates" on the white in the book. Thus, had it not been for the white, the existence of the letters and all the manifestations of *Hochma* in them would not be possible whatsoever.

Similarly, the world of *Atzilut*, which is the *Sefira Hochma*, is the primary subject of the manifestation of *Hochma*, which appears through the worlds *BYA*. This is the meaning of, "In wisdom hast Thou made them all."

9) We have said above, in the third boundary, that *The Zohar* does not speak of the world *Atzilut* in and of itself, since it is regarded as the white in the book, but according to its illumination in the three worlds *BYA*. This is so because it is like to the ink, the letters, and their permutations in the book, in two manners:

- Either the three worlds *BYA* receive the illumination of the world *Atzilut* in their own place, at which time the Light is greatly reduced, as it passes through the *Parsa* below the world *Atzilut*, until it is discerned as mere illumination of the *Kelim* of *Atzilut*.

- Or in the way the worlds *BYA* ascend above *Parsa*, to the place of *Sefirot Bina, Tifferet,* and *Malchut* of *Atzilut*. At that time, they clothe the world of *Atzilut* and receive the Light in the place where it shines.

10) Yet, the allegory and the lesson are not quite comparable, because in the book of wisdom in this world, both the white and the ink in its letters are lifeless. The disclosure of the wisdom induced by them is not in their essence itself, but outside of them, in the mind of the scrutinizer.

However, in the four worlds *ABYA*, which are the book of Heaven, all the Lights in the spiritual and corporeal realities are present in them and extend from them. Thus, you should know that the white in it, which is the subject in the book, is the learned subject matter itself, while the three colors of the ink elucidate that subject.

11) Here we should study these four manners of perception, presented above in the first boundary:

- Matter;
- Form Clothed in Matter;
- Abstract Form;
- Essence.

Yet, I shall first explain them using tangible examples from this world. For example, when you say that a person is strong, truthful, or deceitful, etc., you have the following before you:

- His matter, meaning his body;
- The form that clothes his matter—strong, truthful, or deceitful;
- The abstract form. You can shed the form of strong, truthful, or deceitful from the matter of that person, and study these three forms in and of themselves, unclothed in any matter or body, meaning examine the attributes of strength, truth, and deceitfulness and discern merit or demerit in them, while they are devoid of any substance.
- The person's essence.

12) Know that we have no perception whatsoever in the fourth manner, the essence of the person in itself, without the matter. This is because our five senses and our imaginations offer us only manifestations of the actions of the essence, but not of the essence itself.

For example, the sense of sight offers us only shadows of the visible essence as they are formed opposite the light.

Similarly, the sense of hearing is but a force of striking of some essence on the air. And the air that is rejected by it strikes the drum in our ear, and we hear that there is some essence in our proximity.

The sense of smell is but air that emerges from the essence and strikes our nerves of scent, and we smell. Also, the sense of taste is a result of the contact of some essence with our nerves of taste.

Thus, all that these four senses offer us are manifestations of the operations that stem from some essence, and nothing of the essence itself.

Even the sense of touch, the strongest of the senses, separating hot from cold, and solid from soft, all these are but manifestations of operations within the essence; they are but incidents of the essence. This is so because the hot can be chilled; the cold can be heated; the solid can be turned to liquid through chemical operations, and the liquid into air, meaning only gas, where any discernment in our five senses has been expired. Yet, the essence still exists in it, since you can turn the air into liquid once more, and the liquid into solid.

Evidently, the five senses do not reveal to us any essence at all, but only incidents and manifestations of operations from the essence. It is known that what we cannot sense, we cannot imagine; and what we cannot imagine, will never appear in our thoughts, and we have no way to perceive it.

Thus, the thought has no perception whatsoever in the essence. Moreover, we do not even know our own essence. I feel and I know that I take up space in the world, that I am solid, warm, and that I think, and other such manifestations of the operations of my essence. But if you ask me about my own essence, from which all these manifestations stem, I do not know what to reply to you.

You therefore see that Providence has prevented us from attaining any essence. We attain only manifestations and images of operations that stem from the essences.

13) We do have full perception in the first manner, which is **Matter**, meaning the manifestations of operations that manifest from each essence. This is because they quite sufficiently explain to us the essence that dwells in the substance in such a way that we do not suffer at all from the lack of attainment in the essence itself.

We do not miss it just as we do not miss a sixth finger in our hand. The attainment of the matter, meaning the manifestation of the operations of the essence, is quite sufficient for our every need and learning, both for attaining our own being and for attaining the all that exists outside of us.

14) The second manner, **Form clothed in Matter**, is a satisfactory and clear attainment, too, since we acquire it through practical and real experiments we find in the behavior of any matter. All our higher, reliable knowledge stems from this discernment.

15) The third manner is **Abstract Form**. Once the form has been revealed, while clothed in some matter, our imaginations can abstract it from any matter altogether and perceive it regardless of any substance. Such as that are the virtues and the good qualities that appear in moral books, where we speak of properties of truth and falsehood, anger, and strength, etc., when they are devoid of any matter. We ascribe them merit or demerit even when they are abstract.

You should know that this third manner is unacceptable to the prudent erudite, since it is impossible to rely on it one hundred percent, since being examined while not clothed in matter, they might err in them.

Take, for example, one with idealistic morals, meaning one who is not religious. Because of his intensive engagement in the merit of truth, while in its abstract form, that person might decide that even if he could save people from death by telling them a lie, he may decide that even if the whole world is doomed, he will not utter a deliberate lie. This is not the view of Torah, since nothing is more important than saving lives (*Yoma*, 82a).

Indeed, had one learned the forms of truth and falsehood when they are clothed in matter, he would comprehend only with respect to their benefit or harm to matter.

In other words, after the many ordeals the world has been through, having seen the multitude of ruin and harm that deceitful people have caused with their lies, and the great benefit that truthful people have brought by restricting themselves to saying only words of truth, they have agreed that no merit is more important than the quality of truth, and there is no such disgrace as the quality of falsehood.

And if the idealist had understood that, he would certainly agree to the view of Torah, and would find that falsehood that saves even one person from death is far more important than the entire merit and praise of the abstract quality of truth. Thus, **there is no certainty at all in those concepts** of the third manner, which are abstract forms, much less with abstract forms that have never clothed in any substance. Such concepts are nothing but a waste of time.

16) Now you have thoroughly learned these four manners—Matter, Form in Matter, Abstract Form, and Essence—in tangible things. It has been clarified that we have no perception whatsoever in the fourth manner, the essence, and the third manner is a concept that might mislead. Only the first manner, which is Matter, and the second manner, which is Form Clothed in Matter, are given to us by the Upper Governance for clear and sufficient attainment.

Through them, you will also be able to perceive the existence of spiritual objects, meaning the Upper Worlds *ABYA*, since there is not a tiny detail in them that is not divided by the four above manners. If, for example, you take a certain element in the world of *Beria*, there are *Kelim* there, which are of red color, through which the Light of *Beria* traverses to the dwellers of *Beria*. Thus, the *Kli* in *Beria*, which is the color red, is considered Matter, or object, meaning the first manner.

And even though it is only a color, which is an occurrence and manifestation of an operation in the object, we have already said that we have no attainment in the Essence itself, but only in the manifestation of an operation from the Essence. And we refer to that manifestation as Essence, or Matter, or body, or a *Kli*.

And the Godly Light, which travels and clothes through the red color, is the form clothed in the object, meaning the second manner. For this reason, the Light itself seems red, indicating its clothing and illumination through the object, considered the body and the substance, meaning the red color.

And if you want to remove the Godly Light from the object—the red color—and discuss it in and of itself, without clothing in an object, this already belongs to the third manner—Form removed from the Matter—which might be subject to errors. For this reason, it is strictly forbidden in studying the Upper Worlds, and no genuine Kabbalist would engage in that, much less the authors of *The Zohar*.

It is even more so with regards to the Essence of an element in *Beria*, since we have no perception whatsoever even in the essence of corporeal objects, all the more so in spiritual objects.

Thus you have before you four manners:

- The *Kli* of *Beria*, which is the red color, considered the object, or the substance of *Beria*;
- The clothing of the Godly Light in the *Kli* of *Beria*, which is the form in the object;
- The Godly Light itself, removed from the object in *Beria*;
- The essence of the item.

Thus, the first boundary has been thoroughly explained, which is that there is not even a single word of the third and fourth manners in the whole of *The Zohar*, but only from the first and second manners.

17) Along with it, the second manner has been clarified. Know that as we have clarified the four manners in a single item in the world of *Beria*, specifically, so are they in the general four worlds ABYA. The three colors—red, green, black—in the three worlds BYA, are considered the substance, or the object. The white color, considered the world of *Atzilut*, is the form clothed in the matter, in the three colors called BYA.

Ein Sof in itself is the essence. This is what we said concerning the first manner, that we have no perception in the essence, which is the fourth manner, concealed in all the objects, even in the objects of this world. When the white color is not clothed in the three colors in BYA, meaning when the Light of *Hochma* is not clothed in *Bina*, *Tifferet*, and *Malchut*, it is abstract form, which we do not engage in.

The Zohar does not speak in this manner whatsoever, but only in the first manner, being the three colors BYA, considered substance, namely the three *Sefirot Bina*, *Tifferet*, and *Malchut*, and in the second manner, which are the illumination of *Atzilut*, clothed in the three colors BYA, meaning Light of *Hochma*, clothed in *Bina*, *Tifferet*, and *Malchut*, which are in turn form clothed in matter. These are the two that *The Book of Zohar* is concerned with in all the places.

Hence, if the reader is not vigilant, restricting his thought and understanding to always learn the words of *The Zohar* strictly under the two above-mentioned manners, the matter will be immediately and entirely miscomprehended, for he will take the words out of context.

18) As the four manners in the general ABYA have been explained, so it is in each and every world, even in the smallest item of some world, both at the top of the world of *Atzilut* and at the bottom of the world of *Assiya*, because there is HB TM in it. You find that the *Sefira Hochma* is considered "a form," and *Bina* and TM are considered the "matter" in which the form clothes, meaning the first and second manners that *The Zohar* engages in. But *The Zohar* does not engage in the *Sefira Hochma* when stripped of *Bina* and TM, which is form without matter, and much less with the essence, considered the *Ein Sof* in that item.

Thus, we engage in *Bina*, *Tifferet*, and *Malchut* in every item, even in *Atzilut*, and we do not engage in *Keter* and *Hochma* of every item itself, even in *Malchut* of the end of *Assiya*, when they are not clothed, but only to the extent that they clothe *Bina* and TM. Now the first two boundaries have been thoroughly explained. All that the authors of *The Zohar* engage in is matter or form in matter, which is the first boundary, as well as in BYA, or the illumination of *Atzilut* in BYA, which is the second boundary.

19) Now we shall explain the third boundary. *The Zohar* engages in the *Sefirot* in each and every world, being the Godliness that shines in that world, as well as in every item of the SVAS (Still, Vegetative, Animate and Speaking), being the creatures in that world. However, *The Zohar* refers primarily to the Speaking in that world.

Let me give you an example from the conducts of this world. It is explained in the "Introduction to The Book of Zohar" (item 42) that the four kinds, Still, Vegetative, Animate and Speaking in each and every world, even in this world, are the four parts of the will to receive. Each of them contains these own four kinds of SVAS. Thus, you find that a person in this world should nurture and be nourished by the four categories SVAS in this world.

This is so because man's food, too, contains these four categories, which extend from the four categories SVAS in man's body. These are a) wanting to receive according to the necessary measure for one's sustenance; b) wanting more than is necessary for sustenance, craving luxuries, but restricting oneself solely to physical desires; c) craving human desires, such as honor and power; d) craving knowledge.

- These extend to the four parts of the will to receive in us:
- Wanting the necessary provision is considered the Still of the will to receive.
- Wanting physical lusts is considered the Vegetative of the will to receive, since they come only to increase and delight one's *Kli* (vessel), which is the flesh of the body.
- Wanting human desires is considered the Animate in the will to receive, since they magnify one's spirit.
- Wanting knowledge is the Speaking in the will to receive.

20) Thus, in the first category—the necessary measure for one's sustenance—and in the second category—the physical desires that exceed one's measure for sustenance—one is nourished by things that are lower than the person: the still, the vegetative, and the animate. However, in the third category, the human desires such as power and respect, one receives and is nurtured from his own species, his equals. And in the fourth category, knowledge, one receives and is nurtured by a higher category than one's own—from the actual wisdom and intellect, which are spiritual.

21) You will find it similar in the Upper, Spiritual Worlds, since the worlds are imprinted from one another from Above downward. Thus, all the categories of SVAS in the world of *Beria* leave their imprint in the world of *Yetzira*. And the SVAS of *Assiya* are imprinted from the SVAS of *Yetzira*. Lastly, the SVAS in this world is imprinted from the SVAS of the world of *Assiya*.

It has been explained in "Introduction to The Book of Zohar" (Item 42) that the still in the spiritual worlds are called *Heichalot* (Palaces), the vegetative is called *Levushim* (Clothes or Dresses), the animate is named *Mala'achim* (Angels), and the speaking is considered the *Neshamot* (Souls) of people in that world. And the Ten *Sefirot* in that world are the Godliness.

The souls of people are the center in each world, which are nourished by the spiritual reality in that world, as the corporeal speaking feeds on the entire corporeal reality in this world. Thus, the first category, which is the will to receive one's necessary sustenance, is received from the illumination of *Heichalot* and *Levushim* there. The second category, the animate surplus that increases one's body, is received from the category of *Mala'achim* there, which are spiritual illuminations beyond one's necessary measure for sustenance, to magnify the spiritual *Kelim* that his soul clothes in.

Thus, one receives the first category and the second category from lower categories than one's own, which are the *Heichalot*, *Levushim*, and the *Mala'achim* there, which are lower than human *Neshamot* (souls). The third category, which is human desires that increase one's spirit, is received in this world from one's own species. It follows that one receives from one's own species too, from all the *Neshamot* in that world. Through them, one increases the illumination of *Ruach* of his soul.

The fourth category of the desire, for knowledge, is received there from the *Sefirot* in that world. From them, one receives the *HBD* to one's soul.

It follows that man's soul, which is present in every single world, should grow and be completed with all the categories that exist in that world. This is the third boundary we have mentioned.

One must know that all the words of *The Zohar*, in every item of the Upper Worlds that are dealt with, the *Sefirot*, the *Neshamot*, and the *Mala'achim*, the *Levushim*, and the *Heichalot*, although it engages in them as they are for themselves, the examiner must know that they are spoken primarily with respect to the measure by which the human soul there receives from them and is nourished by them. Thus, all their words pertain to the needs of the soul. And if you learn everything according to that line, you will understand, and your path will be successful.

22) After all that, we have yet to explain all these corporeal appellations explained in *The Book of Zohar* concerning the ten *Sefirot*, such as that are up and down, ascent and descent, contraction and expansion, smallness and greatness, separation and mating, and numbers and the likes, which the lower ones induce through their good or bad deeds in the ten *Sefirot*.

These words seem perplexing. Can it be that Godliness would be affected, and would change in such ways because of the lower ones? You might say that the words do not refer to the Godliness itself, which clothes and shines in the *Sefirot*, but only to the *Kelim* of the *Sefirot*, which are not Godliness. Rather, they were generated with the creation of the souls, to conceal or reveal degrees of attainment in the proper ration and measure for the souls, to bring them to the desired end of correction. This resembles the mirror allegory with the four panes that are painted in four colors: white, red, green, and black. And there is also the white in the book, and the substance of the letters in the book.

All that is possible in the three worlds *BYA*, where the *Kelim* of the *Sefirot* are generated, and are not Godliness. However, it is not at all correct to comprehend that with respect to the world, *Atzilut*, where the *Kelim* of the ten *Sefirot* are also complete Godliness, one with the Godly Light in them.

It is written in the *Tikkunim* (corrections): "He, His Life, and His Self, are one." He pertains to the essence of the *Sefirot*, which is *Ein Sof*. His Life pertains to the Light that shines in the *Sefirot*, called "Light of *Haya*." This is so because the whole of the world, *Atzilut*, is considered *Hochma*, and the Light of *Hochma* is called the "Light of *Haya*." This is why it is called, "Life." His Self pertains to the *Kelim* of the *Sefirot*.

Thus, everything is complete Godliness and unity. How then is it possible to perceive these changes, which the lower ones induce there? At the same time, we must understand that if everything is Godliness in that world, and nothing of the generated creatures is to be found there, where then do we discern there the three above discernments in the *Tikkunim* of *The Zohar*, He, His Life, and His Self, since it is utter unity?

23) To understand that, you must remember the explained above, in Item 17. It explains that a necessary object is an essence that we have no perception of, even in the corporeal essences, and even in our own essence, all the more so in The Necessary One.

The world of *Atzilut* is a Form and the three worlds *BYA* are Matter. The illumination of *Atzilut* in *BYA* is Form clothed in Matter. Hence, you see that the name, *Ein Sof*, is not at all a name for the essence of The Necessary One, since what we do not attain, how can we define it by name or word?

Since the imagination and the five senses offer us nothing with respect to the essence, even in corporeality, how can there be a thought and a word in it, much less in The Necessary One Himself? Instead, we must understand the name, *Ein Sof*, as defined for us in the third boundary, that all that *The Book of Zohar* speaks of pertains precisely to the souls (Item 21).

Thus, the name, *Ein Sof*, is not at all The Necessary One Himself, but pertains to all the worlds and all the souls being included in Him, in the Thought of Creation, by way of "The end of an act is in the preliminary thought." Thus, *Ein Sof* is the name of the connection that the whole of Creation is connected in, until the end of correction.

This is what we name "the First State of the souls" ("Introduction to The Book of Zohar," Item 13), since all the souls exist in Him, filled with all the pleasure and the gentleness, at the final Height they will actually receive at the end of correction.

24) Let me give you an example from the conduct of this world: A person wants to build a handsome house. In the first thought, he sees before him an elegant house with all its rooms and details, as it will be when its building is finished.

Afterwards, he designs the plan of execution to its every detail. In due time, he will explain every detail to the workers: the wood, the bricks, the iron, and so on. Then he will begin the actual building of the house to its end, as it was arranged before him in the preliminary thought.

Know, that *Ein Sof* pertains to that first thought, in which the whole of Creation was already pictured before Him in utter completeness. However, the lesson is not quite like the example because in Him, the future and the present are equals. In Him, the thought completes, and He does not need tools of action, as do we. Hence, in Him, it is actual reality.

The world of *Atzilut* is like the details of the thought-out plan, which will later need to manifest when the building of the house actually begins. Know that in these two, the preliminary thought, which is *Ein Sof*, and the contemplated design of the details of the execution in its due time, there is still not even a trace of the creatures, since this is still in potential, not in actual fact.

It is likewise in humans: even though they calculate all the details—the wood, the bricks, and the metal—that will be required for carrying out the plan, it is essentially a mere conceptual matter. There is not even a trace of any actual wood or bricks in it. The only difference is that in a person, the contemplated design is not considered an actual reality. But in the Godly Thought, it is a far more actual reality than the actual, real creatures.

Thus, we have explained the meaning of *Ein Sof* and the world of *Atzilut*, that how all that is said about them is only with respect to the creation of the creatures. However, they are still in potential and their essence has not been revealed whatsoever, as with our allegory about the person who designed the blueprint, which does not contain any wood, and bricks, and metal.

25) The three worlds *BYA*, and this world, are considered the execution from potential to actual, such as one who builds one's house in actual fact and brings the wood, the bricks, and the workers until the house is complete. Hence, the Godliness that shines in *BYA* clothes the ten *Kelim KHB HGT NHYM* to the extent that the souls should receive in order to reach their perfection. These are

real *Kelim*, with respect to His Godliness, meaning they are not Godliness, but are generated for the souls.

26) In the above allegory, you find how the three discernments of one who contemplates building a house are interconnected by way of cause and consequence. The root of them all is the first thought, since no item appears in the planned blueprint except according to the end of the act, which emerged before him in the preliminary thought.

Also, one does not execute anything during the building, but only according to the details arranged before him in the blueprint. Thus you see, concerning the worlds, that there is not a tiny generation in the worlds that does not extend from *Ein Sof*, from the first state of the souls, which are there in their ultimate perfection of the end of correction, as in "The end of an act is in the preliminary thought." Thus, all that will manifest through the end of correction is included there.

In the beginning, it extends from *Ein Sof* to the world of *Atzilut*, as in the allegory, where the blueprint extends from the first thought. Each and every element extends from the world of *Atzilut* to the worlds *BYA*, as in the allegory, where all the details stem from the blueprint when they are actually executed during the building of the house.

Thus, there is not a single, tiny item, generated in this world, that does not extend from *Ein Sof*, from the first state of the souls. And from *Ein Sof*, it extends to the world of *Atzilut*, meaning specifically associated to the thing actually being generated in this world. And from the world of *Atzilut*, the generation extends to the three worlds *BYA*, where the generation appears in actual fact, where it stops being Godliness and becomes a creature, and to *Yetzira* and *Assiya*, until it extends to the lower one in this world.

It follows that there is no generation in the world, which does not extend from its general root in *Ein Sof*, and from its private root in *Atzilut*. Afterwards, it travels through *BYA* and adopts the form of a creature, and then it is made in this world.

27) Now you can understand that all these changes described in the world of *Atzilut* do not pertain to the Godliness itself, but only to the souls to the extent that they receive from *Atzilut* through the three worlds *BYA*. The meaning of the actuality of that world is in the relation of the blueprint to the preliminary thought, which is *Ein Sof*.

However, both in *Ein Sof* and in the world of *Atzilut*, there is still nothing in terms of souls, just like there is nothing of the actual wood, bricks, or metal in the blueprint of the person who designs it. The existence of the souls begins to manifest in the world *Beria*. For this reason, the *Kelim* of the ten *Sefirot*, which actually allot the ration to the souls, are necessarily not Godliness, but innovations. This is so because there cannot be any changes or numbering in the Godliness.

Hence, we ascribe the three colors—red, green, and black—to the *Kelim* of the ten *Sefirot* in BYA. It is inconceivable that they will be discerned as Godliness, since there is whatsoever no renewal in Him.

However, the Light clothed in the ten *Kelim* in BYA is simple Godliness and unity, unchanged at all. Even the Light clothed in the lowest *Kli* in *Assiya* is complete Godliness, without any change at all. This is because the Light itself is one, and all the changes made in its illumination are made by the *Kelim* of the *Sefirot*, which are not Godliness. In general, they comprise the three above shades; in particular, numerous changes were made of these three shades.

28) Yet, the *Kelim* of the ten *Sefirot* of BYA certainly receive from *Atzilut* every little item and detail of the changes, since there is the blueprint of all the details that will unfold in the actual building of the house in BYA. Hence, it is considered that the *Kelim* of the ten *Sefirot* HB TM in BYA receive from their corresponding feature in the HB TM in *Atzilut*, meaning from the blueprint there.

This is so because every detail in the execution stems from every detail in the blueprint. Hence, in this respect, we name the *Kelim* of *Atzilut* "white," although it is not at all a color.

Nevertheless, it is the source of all the colors. And like the white in the book of wisdom, where although there is no perception of the white in it, and the white in the book is meaningless to us, it is still the subject of the entire book of wisdom. This is because it shines around and inside each letter and gives each letter its unique shape, and every permutation its unique place.

And we might say the opposite: we have no perception of the substance of the red, green, or black letters, and all that we perceive and know of the substance of the letters of the book is only through the white in it. It is so because through its illumination around each letter and within each letter, it creates shapes in them, and these shapes reveal to us all the wisdom in the book.

We can compare it to the ten *Sefirot* of *Atzilut*: even though they resemble the white color, it is impossible to discern anything in them, neither a number nor any change such as the described. Yet, all the changes necessarily come from the ten *Kelim* of the *Sefirot* of *Atzilut* in the illumination of the white to the worlds BYA, which are the three colors of the substance of the letters, although for itself there are no *Kelim* there, as it is all white. It is like the allegory of the white in the book with respect to the letters and their permutations, since its illumination to *BYA* makes the *Kelim* in them.

29) From what has been explained, you will see that the *Tikkunim* of *The Zohar* divide the world of *Atzilut* into three discernments—He, His Life, and His Self—although it is simple unity there, and there is nothing of the creatures there. **He pertains to Godliness as it is in itself**, in which we have no perception, and cannot perceive any essence, even the corporeal ones (Item 12). **His Self pertains to the ten *Kelim* HB TM there**, which we have likened to the white in the book of wisdom.

Even a number cannot be noted in the white, since there is no one there to make a number, as it is all white. Yet, we not only ascribe to them a number, but the multitude of changes that appear in *BYA*, which are the substance of the letters, are first found in the *Kelim* HB TM in *Atzilut* itself.

It is the conduct of the white, which gives all the shapes of the letters in the book, while in itself it has no form. Thus, you find that the white is divided into myriad forms, although in itself it has no form. Similarly, the ten *Kelim* are detailed with numerous changes, according to their illumination in *BYA*, as in the blueprint, executed in the actual work of building the house.

Thus, all these changes, carried out in *BYA*, are only from the illumination of the *Kelim* of the ten *Sefirot* HB TM of *Atzilut*. And the multitude of changes we find in the white relate to the receivers in *BYA*. And with relation to *Atzilut* itself, it is like the white in and of itself, unclothed in the ink in the letters; no number and nothing at all is found in it. Thus, we have thoroughly explained the Self, which are the *Kelim*, which, in themselves, are simple unity, as is He.

30) **His Life pertains to the Light that is clothed in the white, which is the *Kelim*.** We understand this Light only with respect to the souls that receive from *Atzilut*, and not in the Godliness itself. "He" means that when the three worlds *BYA* rise to *Atzilut* with the souls of people, the Light that they receive there is considered the Light of *Hochma*, called "the Light of *Haya*."

It is in that respect that we name the Light there, "His Life." This is also the meaning of what is written in the *Tikkunim* of *The Zohar*, that He, His Life, and His Self are one. All these three discernments relate to the receivers, where His Self is the illumination of the *Kelim* in the place of *BYA* under the *Parsa* of *Atzilut*, since the Light of *Atzilut* will never go below the *Parsa* of *Atzilut*, but only the illumination of the *Kelim*. The category, "His Life," is the illumination of the Light of *Atzilut* itself, when *BYA* rise to *Atzilut*. And "He" pertains to the essence of Godliness, which is completely unattainable.

The *Tikkunim* of *The Zohar* say that although we, the receivers, should discern these three categories in *Atzilut*, it nonetheless pertains only to the receivers. Yet, with respect to the world of *Atzilut* itself, even "His Self" is considered "He," meaning the essence of Godliness. For this reason, there is no perception whatsoever in the world of *Atzilut* itself. This is the meaning of the white color, in which there is no perception for itself, and it is all utterly simple unity there.

31) *The Zohar* describes the *Kelim HB TM* in *Atzilut* as growing or diminishing by people's actions. Also, we find (*Zohar, Bo,* p 32b), "Israel... give anger and strength to the Creator," meaning it is not to be taken literally in Godliness itself, as there cannot be any changes in Godliness whatsoever, as it is written, "I the Lord change not."

Yet, since the Thought of Creation was to delight His creatures, it teaches us that He has a desire to bestow. We find in this world, that the givers' contentment grows when the receivers from Him multiply, and He wishes to proliferate the receivers. Hence, in this respect, we say that the Lights in *Atzilut* grow when the lower ones are given the bestowal of *Atzilut*, or that they nurture it. Conversely, when there are no lower ones worthy of receiving His abundance, the Lights diminish to that extent, meaning there is no one to receive from them.

32) You might compare it to a candle. If you light a thousand candles from it, or if you light none, you will not find that it caused any changes induced in the candle itself. It is also like *Adam ha Rishon*: if he had progeny of thousands of offspring like us today, or if he had no progeny at all, it would not induce any change at all on *Adam ha Rishon* himself.

Likewise, there is no change at all in the world *Atzilut* itself, whether the lower ones receive its great abundance lushly, or receive nothing at all. The above-mentioned greatness lies solely on the lower ones.

33) Thus, why did the authors of *The Zohar* have to describe all those changes in the world of *Atzilut* itself? They should have spoken explicitly only with respect to the receivers in *BYA*, and not speak so elaborately of *Atzilut*, forcing us to provide answers.

Indeed, there is a very trenchant secret here: this is the meaning of, "and by the ministry of the prophets have I used similitudes" (Hosea 12). The truth is that there is a Godly will here, that these similitudes, which operate only in the souls of the receivers, will appear to the souls as He Himself participates in them to greatly increase the attainment of the souls.

It is like a father who constrains himself to show his little darling child a face of sadness and a face of contentment, although there is neither sadness nor contentment in him. He only does this to impress his darling child and expand his understanding, so as to play with him.

Only when he grows will he learn and know that all that his father did was no more real than mere playing with him. So is the matter before us: all these images and changes begin and end only with the impression of the souls. Yet, by the will of God, they appear as though they are in Him Himself. He does that to enhance and expand the attainment of the souls to the utmost, in accordance with the Thought of Creation, to delight His creatures.

34) Let it not surprise you that you find such a conduct in our corporeal perception, too. Take our sense of sight, for example: we see a wide world before us, wondrously filled. But in fact, we see all that only in our own interior. In other words, there is a sort of a photographic machine in our hindbrain, which portrays everything that appears to us and nothing outside of us.

For that, He has made for us there, in our brain, a kind of polished mirror that inverts everything seen there, so we will see it outside our brain, in front of our face. Yet, what we see outside us is not a real thing. Nonetheless, we should be so grateful to His Providence for having created that polished mirror in our brains, enabling us to see and perceive everything outside of us. This is because by that, He has given us the power to perceive everything with clear knowledge and attainment, and measure everything from within and from without.

Without it, we would lose most of our perception. The same holds true with the Godly will, concerning Godly perceptions. Even though all these changes unfold in the interior of the receiving souls, they nevertheless see it all in the Giver Himself, since only in this manner are they awarded all the perceptions and all the pleasantness in the Thought of Creation.

You can also deduce that from the above parable. Even though we see everything as actually being in front of us, every reasonable person knows for certain that all that we see is only within our own brains.

So are the souls: Although they see all the images in the Giver, they still have no doubt that all these are only in their own interior, and not at all in the Giver.

35) Since these matters are at the core of the world, and I fear that the examiner will err in perceiving them, it is worth my while to trouble further and bring the golden words of *The Zohar* itself in these matters (*Parashat Bo*, item 215), and interpret them to the best of my ability: "Should one ask, 'It is written in the Torah, 'for ye saw no manner of form.' Thus, how do we depict names

and *Sefirot* in Him?' It will answer, 'I saw this form, as in the words, 'and the similitude of the Lord doth he behold.'"

This means that the *Sefira Malchut*, where all the souls and the words are rooted, since she is the root of all the *Kelim*, by way of, "The ones that receive from her, and must acquire the *Kelim* from her," she is considered a similitude to them. It is therefore said about her, "and the similitude of the Lord doth he behold."

Even this similitude, which we name in the *Sefira Malchut*, is not in her place with respect to herself, but only when the Light of *Malchut* descends and expands over the people. At that time, it appears to them, to each and every one, according to their own appearance, vision, and imagination, meaning only in the receivers and not at all in the *Sefira Malchut* herself.

This is the meaning of, "and by the ministry of the prophets have I used similitudes." Because of that, the Creator tells them: "Although I manifest to you in your forms, in vision and imagination, yet, 'To whom then will ye liken Me, that I should be equal?'" After all, before the Creator created a similitude in the world, and before He formed a form, the Creator was unique, formless and imageless.

And one who attains Him there, prior to the degree of *Beria*, which is *Bina*, where He is beyond any similitude, it is forbidden to ascribe Him a form and an image in the world, neither in the letter *Hey*, nor in the letter *Yod*, or even call Him by the holy name *HaVaYaH*, or by any letter and point.

This is the meaning of the verse, "for ye saw no manner of form." In other words, the verse, "for ye saw no manner of form," pertains to the ones rewarded with attaining Him above the degree of *Beria*, which is *Bina*. This is because there is no form and imagination whatsoever in the two *Sefirot Keter* and *Hochma*, meaning *Kelim* and boundaries (item 18). The *Kelim* begin from the *Sefira Bina* downward.

This is the reason why all the implications in letters, in points, or in the holy names are only from *Bina* downward. They are also not in the place of the *Sefirot* themselves, but only with respect to the receivers, as with the *Sefira Malchut*.

36) There seems to be a contradiction in their words: first they said that the forms extend to the receivers only from the *Sefira Malchut*, and here he says that the forms extend to the receivers from *Beria* down, meaning from *Bina* downwards. The thing is that indeed, the form and the similitude extend only from *Behina Dalet*, which is *Malchut*. From her the *Kelim* extend to the place of the receivers, and nothing from the first nine *Sefirot*, which are *Keter*, *Hochma*, *Bina*, and *Tifferet*.

Yet, the association of *Midat ha Rachamim* with *Din* was made in the World of *Tikkun*. This raised the *Sefira Malchut*, considered *Midat ha Din*, and brought her into the *Sefira Bina*, regarded as *Midat ha Rachamim*.

Hence, from that time on, the *Kelim* of *Malchut* have become rooted in the *Sefira Bina*, as he says here. For this reason, *The Zohar* begins to speak from the actual root of the pictures, which are the *Kelim*. It says that they are in *Malchut*, and then it says that they are in *Beria*, because of the association made for the correction of the world.

Our sages also said, "In the beginning the Creator created the world in *Midat ha Din*; He saw that the world cannot exist, He associated *Midat ha Rachamim* with her." Know that the ten *Sefirot KHBTM* have numerous appellations in *The Book of Zohar*, according to their manifold functions.

When they are called *Keter, Atzilut, Beria, Yetzira*, and *Assiya*, their function is to distinguish between the anterior *Kelim*, called *Keter* and *Atzilut*, meaning *Keter* and *Hochma*, and the posterior *Kelim*, called *Beria, Yetzira, Assiya*, meaning *Bina, Tifferet*, and *Malchut*. This discernment emerged in them by the association of *Midat ha Din* with *Midat ha Rachamim*.

The Zohar wishes to insinuate the matter of the association of *Malchut* in *Bina*. Hence, *The Zohar* calls the *Sefira Bina* by the name *Beria*. This is so because prior to that association, there was no image or form in *Bina*, even with respect to the receivers, but only in *Malchut*.

37) It continues there: After it made that form of the *Merkava* of the Upper Adam, it descended and clothed there. It is named in it in the form of the four letters *HaVaYaH*, meaning the ten *Sefirot KHBTM*. This is because the tip of the *Yod* is *Keter*, *Yod* is *Hochma*, *Hey* is *Bina*, *Vav* is *Tifferet*, and the last *Hey* is *Malchut*. This is so that they would attain Him through His attributes, meaning the *Sefirot*, in every single attribute in Him.

38) Explanation of the matters: From *Beria* on, meaning from *Bina*, after it had been associated with *Midat ha Din*, which is *Malchut*, the similitudes and the forms extend to the receivers, which are the souls. Yet, not in her own place, but only in the place of the receivers.

He says that at that time he made the form of the *Merkava* of the Upper Adam and descended and clothed in the form of this Adam. In other words, the whole form of Adam, in his 613 *Kelim*, extend from the *Kelim* of the soul, since the soul has 613 *Kelim*, called 248 organs and 365 spiritual tendons, divided into five divisions according to the four letters *HaVaYaH*:

- The tip of the *Yod*, her *Rosh*, is considered *Keter*;
- From the *Peh* to the *Chazeh* it is *Hochma*;
- From *Chazeh* to the *Tabur* it is *Bina*
- From *Tabur* to *Sium Raglin* it is the two *Sefirot Tifferet* and *Malchut*.

Additionally, the Torah, as a whole, is considered *Partzuf* Adam, pertaining to the 248 positive *Mitzvot*, corresponding to the 248 organs. And the 365 negative *Mitzvot* correspond to the 365 tendons. It contains five divisions, which are the five books of Moses, called "The image of the *Merkava* of the Upper Adam," meaning Adam of *Beria*, which is *Bina*, from which the *Kelim* begin to extend in the place of the souls.

He is called, "Upper Adam" because there are three categories of Adam in the *Sefirot*: Adam of *Beria*, Adam of *Yetzira*, and Adam of *Assiya*. In *Keter* and *Hochma*, however, there is no similitude at all, which could be named by some letter and point, or by the four letters *HaVaYaH*. Since here it speaks of the world of *Beria*, it makes the precision of saying Upper Adam.

At the same time, you must always remember the words of *The Zohar*, that these images are not in the place of the *Sefirot Bina*, *Tifferet*, and *Malchut*, but only in the place of the receivers. Yet, these *Sefirot* dispense these *Kelim* and *Levushim* (Dresses) so the souls would attain Him through the Light that extends to them by measure and boundary, according to their 613 organs. For this reason, we call the givers by the name "Adam," as well, although they are merely in the form of the white color (Item 8).

39) It should not be puzzling for you, since the four letters *HaVaYaH* and the tip of the *Yod*, are five *Kelim*, since the *Kelim* are always called "letters," and they are the five *Sefirot KHBTM*. Thus, it is clear that there are *Kelim* in *Keter* and *Hochma*, as well, implied by the tip of the *Yod* and the *Yod* of *HaVaYaH*.

The thing is that the similitudes and the attributes it speaks of, which are the *Kelim*, begin from *Beria* downward, meaning only the three *Sefirot Bina*, *Tifferet*, and *Malchut*, and not in *Keter* and *Hochma*, meaning from the perspective of the essence of the *Sefirot*.

Yet, it is known that the *Sefirot* are integrated in one another. There are ten *Sefirot KHBTM* in *Keter*, *KHBTM* in *Hochma*, *KHBTM* in *Bina*, as well as in *Tifferet*, and in *Malchut*.

Accordingly, you find that the three *Sefirot Bina*, *Tifferet*, and *Malchut*, that the *Kelim* come from, are found in each of the five *Sefirot KHBTM*. Now you see that the tip of the *Yod*, which is the *Kelim* of *Keter*, indicate *Bina* and *TM* that are incorporated in *Keter*.

The *Yod* of *HaVaYaH*, which is a *Kli* of *Hochma*, indicates *Bina* and *TM* incorporated in *Hochma*. Thus, the *Keter* and *Hochma* incorporated even in *Bina* and *ZON*, do not have *Kelim*, and in *Bina* and *TM* incorporated even in *Keter* and *Hochma*, there are *Kelim*.

In this respect, there really are five categories in Adam. The *Bina* and *TM* in all five *Sefirot* dispense in the form of the *Merkava* of Adam. For this reason, there is Adam in the category of *Keter*, called *Adam Kadmon*, and there is Adam in the category of *Hochma*, called "Adam of *Atzilut*." There is Adam in the category of *Bina*, called "Adam of *Beria*," *Adam* in the category of *Tifferet*, called "Adam of *Yetzira*," and *Adam* in the category of *Malchut*, called "Adam of *Assiya*."

40) He named Himself *El*, *Elokim*, *Shadai*, *Tzvaot*, and *Ekie*, so that every single attribute in Him would be known. The ten names in the Torah that are not to be erased pertain to the ten *Sefirot*, as it is written in *The Zohar* (*Vayikra*, item 168):

- The *Sefira Keter* is called *Ekie*;
- The *Sefira Hochma* is called *Koh*;
- And the *Sefira Bina* is called *HaVaYaH* (punctuated *Elokim*);
- The *Sefira Hesed* is called *Kel*;
- The *Sefira Gevura* is called *Elokim*;
- The *Sefira Tifferet* is called *HaVaYaH*;
- The two *Sefirot Netzah* and *Hod* are called *Tzvaot*;
- The *Sefira Yesod* is called *El Hay*;
- And the *Sefira Malchut* is called *Adni*.

41) Had His Light not expanded on all creations by seemingly clothing in these holy *Sefirot*, how would the creatures come to know Him? And how would they keep the verse, "the whole earth is full of His glory"? In other words, by that it explains the Godly desire to appear to the souls as if all these changes in the *Sefirot* are in Him. It is in order to give the souls room for sufficient knowledge and attainment in Him, for then the verse, "the whole earth is full of His glory" shall come true.

42) Yet, woe unto one who ascribes any measure to Him, who would say that there is a measure in Him for Himself, even in these spiritual measures by which

He appears to the souls. It is all the more so in the corporeal measures of the human nature, which are made of dust, and are transitory and worthless.

As we have said above, although it is a Godly wish for the souls to see that the changes in them are in the Giver, it should nonetheless be clear to the souls that there is no change and measurement in Him whatsoever. It is only a Godly wish that they will imagine so, as it is written, "and by the ministry of the prophets have I used similitudes."

And should they err in that, woe unto them, for they will instantly lose the Godly abundance. It is even more so with the fools who ascribe Him some incident of the transitory, worthless flesh and blood incidents.

Introduction to the Book, Panim Meirot uMasbirot[20]

1) It is written at the end of the Mishnah (*Okatzin*), "The Creator did not find a receptacle that holds a blessing for Israel, but peace, as it is written, 'The Lord will give strength unto His people; the Lord will bless his people with peace.'"

There is a lot to learn here: First, how did they prove that nothing is better for Israel than peace? Second, the text explicitly states that peace is the blessing itself, as it is written, "giving in strength and blessing in peace." According to them, it should have stated, "giving in peace." Third, why was this phrase written to end of the Mishnah? Also, we need to understand the meaning of the words "peace," "strength," and what they mean.

To interpret this article in its true meaning, we must go by a long way, for the heart of sayers is too deep to search. This means that all the issues of the Torah and the *Mitzva* bear revealed and concealed, as it is written, "A word fitly spoken is like apples of gold in settings of silver."

Indeed, the *Halachot* (collective name for Torah and *Mitzvot*) are like grails of wine. When one gives one's friend a gift, a grail of wine, then both the insides and the outside are important. This is because the grail has its own value, as does the wine inside it.

The legends, however, are as apples. Their interior is eaten and their exterior is thrown away, as the exterior is completely worthless. You find that all the worth and importance are only in the interior, the insides.

So is the matter with legends; the apparent superficiality seems meaningless and worthless. However, the inner content concealed in the words is built solely on the bedrock of the wisdom of truth, given to virtuous few.

---

20 *Shining and Welcoming Face*

Who would dare extract it from the heart of the masses and scrutinize their ways, when their attainment is incomplete in both parts of the Torah called *Peshat* (literal) and *Drush* (interpretation)? In their view, the order of the four parts of the Torah (PARDESS) begins with the *Peshat*, then the *Drush*, then *Remez* (insinuated), and in the end the *Sod* (Secret) is understood.

However, it is written in the Vilna Gaon prayer book that the attainment begins with the *Sod*. After the *Sod* part of the Torah is attained it is possible to attain the *Drush* part, and then the *Remez* part. When one is granted complete knowledge of these three parts of the Torah, one is awarded the attainment of the *Peshat* part of the Torah.

It is written in *Masechet Taanit*: "If one is rewarded, it becomes a potion of life to him; not rewarded, it becomes a potion of death to him." Great merit is required in order to understand the *Peshat* of the texts, since first we must attain the three internal parts of the Torah, which the *Peshat* robes, and the *Peshat* will not be parsed. If one has not been rewarded with it, one needs great mercy, so it will not become a potion of death for him.

It is the opposite of the argument of the negligent in attaining the interior, who say to themselves: "We settle for attaining the *Peshat*. If we attain that, we will be content." Their words can be compared to one who wishes to step on the fourth step without first stepping on the first three steps.

2) However, accordingly, we need to understand the great concealing applied in the interior of the Torah, as it is said in *Masechet Hagiga*, one does not study *Maase Beresheet* in pairs, and not the *Merkava* alone. Also, all the books at our disposal in this trade are sealed and blocked before the eyes of the masses. Only the few who are summoned by the Creator shall understand them, as they already understand the roots by themselves and in reception from mouth to mouth.

It is indeed surprising how the ways of wisdom and intelligence are denied of the people, for whom it is the life and the length of their days. It is seemingly a criminal offence, as about such our sages said in *Midrash Rabba, Beresheet*, about Ahaz, that he was called Ahaz (literally translated as "held" or "seized") for he had seized synagogues and seminaries, and this was his great iniquity.

Also, it is a natural law that one is possessive concerning dispensing one's capital and property to others. However, is there anyone who is possessive concerning dispensing one's wisdom and intelligence to others? Quite the contrary, more than the calf wants to eat, the cow wants to feed.

Indeed, we find such mysteries in the wisdom even in secular sages in previous generations. In Rav Butril's introduction to his commentary on *The*

Book of Creation, there is a text ascribed to Plato who warns his disciples as follows, "Do not convey the wisdom unto one who knows not its merit."

Aristotle, too, warned, "Do not convey the wisdom to the unworthy, lest it shall be robbed." He (Rav Butril) interprets that if a sage teaches wisdom to the unworthy, they rob the wisdom and destroy it.

The secular sages of our time do not do so. On the contrary, they exert in expanding the gates of their sagacity to the entire crowd without any boundaries and conditions. Seemingly, they strongly disagree with the first sages, who opened the doors of their wisdom to only a handful of virtuous few, which they had found worthy, leaving the rest of the people fumbling the walls.

3) Let me explain the matter. We distinguish four divisions in the Speaking species, arranged in gradations one atop the other. Those are the Masses, the Strong, the Wealthy, and the Sagacious. They are equal to the four degrees in the whole of reality, called "Still," "Vegetative," "Animate," and "Speaking."

The Still can educe the three properties, Vegetative, Animate and Speaking, and we discern three values in the quantity of the force, from the beneficial and detrimental in them.

The smallest force among them is the Vegetative. The flora operates by attracting what is beneficial to it and rejecting the harmful in much the same way as humans and animals do. However, there is no individual sensation in it, but a collective force, common to all types of plants in the world, which affects this operation in them.

Atop them is the Animate. Each creature feels itself, concerning attracting what is beneficial to it and rejecting the harmful. It follows that one animal equalizes in value to all the plants in reality. It is so because the force that distinguishes the beneficial from the detrimental in the entire Vegetative is found in one creature in the Animate, separated to its own authority.

This sensing force in the Animate is very limited in time and space, since the sensation does not operate at even the shortest distance outside its body. Also, it does not feel anything outside its own time, meaning in the past or in the future, but only at the present moment.

Atop them is the Speaking, consisting of an emotional force and an intellectual force together. For this reason, its power is unlimited by time and space in attracting what is good for it and rejecting what is harmful, like the Animate.

This is so because of its science, which is a spiritual matter, unlimited by time and place. One can teach others wherever they are in the whole of reality, and in the past and the future throughout the generations.

It follows that the value of one person from the Speaking equalizes with the value of all the forces in the Vegetative and the Animate in the whole of reality at that time, and in all the past generations. This is so because its power encompasses them and contains them within its own self, along with all their forces.

This ruling also applies to the four divisions in the human species, namely the Masses, the Strong, the Wealthy, and the Sagacious. Certainly, they all come from the Masses, which are the first degree, as it is written, "all are of the dust."

It is certain that the whole merit of the dust and its very right to exist is according to the merit of the three virtues it educes, Vegetative, Animate, and Speaking. Also, the merit of the Masses corresponds to the properties they educe from them. Thus, they, too, connect in the shape of a human face.

For that purpose, the Creator instilled three inclinations in the masses, called "envy," "lust," and "honor." Due to them, the Masses develop degree by degree to educe a face of a whole man.

The inclination for lust educes the Wealthy. The selected among them have a strong desire, and also lust. They excel in acquiring wealth, which is the first degree in the evolution of the Masses. Like the Vegetative degree in the general reality, they are governed by an alien force that deviates them to their inclination, as lust is an alien force in the human species borrowed from the Animate.

The inclination for honor educes the famous heroes from among them. They govern the synagogues, the town, etc. The most firm-willed among them, which also have an inclination for honor, excel in obtaining dominion. These are the second degree in the evolution of the Masses, similar to the Animate degree in the whole of reality, whose operating force is present in their own essence, as we have said above. This is because the inclination for honor is unique to the human species, and along with it the craving for governance.

The inclination for Envy elicits the sages from among them, as our sages said, "Author's envy increases wisdom." The strong-willed, with the inclination for envy, excel in acquiring wisdom and knowledge. It is like the Speaking degree in the whole of reality, in which the operating force is not limited by time and place, but is collective and encompasses every item in the world, throughout all times.

Also, it is the nature of the fire of envy to be general, encompassing all times and the whole reality. This is because it is the conduct of envy: if one had not seen the object in one's friend's possession, the desire for it would not have awakened in one at all.

You find that the sensation of absence is not for what one does not have, but for what one's friend has, who are the entire progeny of Adam and Eve throughout the generations. Thus, this force is unlimited and it is therefore fit for its sublime and elated role.

Yet, those who remain without any merit, it is because they do not have a strong desire. Hence, all three above-mentioned inclinations operate in them together, in mixture. Sometimes they are lustful, sometimes envious, and sometimes they crave honor. Their desire breaks to pieces, and they are like children, who crave everything they see, and cannot attain anything. Hence, their value is like the straw and bran that remain after the flour.

It is known that the beneficial force and the detrimental force go hand in hand. In other words, as much as something can benefit, so it can harm. Hence, since the force of one person is greater than all the beasts and the animals of all times, one's harmful force supersedes them all, as well.

Thus, as long as one does not merit one's degree in a way that one uses one's force only to do good, one needs a careful watch so he will not acquire great amounts of the human level, which is wisdom and science.

For this reason, the first sages hid the wisdom from the masses for fear of taking indecent disciples who would use the force of the wisdom to harm and damage. These would break and destroy the entire population with their lust and beastly savageness, using Man's great powers.

When the generations have lessened and their sages themselves had started to crave both tables, meaning a good life for their corporeality, too, their views drew near to the masses. They traded with them and sold the wisdom as prostitutes, for the price of a dog.

Since then, the fortified wall that the first had exerted on has been ruined and the masses have looted it. The savages have filled their hands with the force of men, seized the wisdom and tore it. Half was inherited by adulterers and half by murderers, and they have put it in eternal disgrace to this day.

4) From that you can deduce about the wisdom of truth, which contains all the secular teachings within it, which are its seven little maids. This is the entirety of the human species and the purpose for which all the worlds were created, as it is written, "If My covenant be not with day and night, if I have not appointed the ordinances of heaven and earth."

Hence, our sages have stated (*Avot* 4, *Mishnah* 7), "He who uses the Crown passes." This is because they have prohibited us from using it for any sort of worldly pleasure.

This is what has sustained us thus far, to maintain the armies and the wall around the wisdom of truth, so no stranger or foreigner would break in and put it in their vessels to go and trade it in the market, as with the secular sages. This was so because all who entered have already been tested by seven tests until it was certain beyond any concern and suspicion.

After these words and truth, we find what appears to be a great contradiction, from one extreme to the other, in the words of our sages. It is written in *The Zohar* that at the time of the Messiah, this wisdom will be revealed even to the young. However, according to the above, we learned that in the days of the Messiah, that whole generation will be at the highest level. We will need no guard at all, and the fountains of wisdom will open and water the whole nation.

Yet, in *Masechet Sutah*, 49, and *Sanhedrin* 97a, they said, "Impudence shall soar at the time of the Messiah, authors' wisdom shall go astray, and righteous shall be castaway." It interprets that there is none so evil as that generation. Thus, how do we reconcile the two statements, for both are certainly the words of the Living God?

The thing is that this careful watch and door-locking on the hall of wisdom is for fear of people in whom the spirit of writers' envy is mixed with the force of lust and honor. Their envy is not limited to wanting only wisdom and knowledge.

Hence, both texts are correct, and one comes and teaches of the other. The face of the generation is as the face of the dog, meaning they bark as dogs *Hav, Hav*, righteous are castaway and authors' wisdom went astray in them.

It follows that it is permitted to open the gates of the wisdom and remove the careful guard, since it is naturally safe from theft and exploitation. There is no longer fear lest indecent disciples might take it and sell it in the market to the materialistic plebs, since they will find no buyers for this merchandise, as it is loathsome in their eyes.

And since they have no hope of acquiring lust and honor through it, it has become safe and guarded by itself. No stranger will draw near, except lovers of wisdom and its dwellers. Hence, any examination shall be removed from those who enter, until even the very young will be able to attain it.

Now you can understand their words (*Sanhedrin* 98a): "The Son of David comes either in a generation that is all worthy, or all unworthy." This is very perplexing. Seemingly, as long as there are a few righteous in the generation, they detain the redemption. When the righteous perish from the land, the Messiah will be able to come. I wonder.

Indeed, we should thoroughly understand that this matter of redemption and the coming of the Messiah that we hope will be soon in our days, Amen, is the uppermost wholeness of attainment and knowledge, as it is written, "and they shall teach no more every man his neighbor, saying: 'Know the Lord'; for they shall all know Me, from the greatest of them unto the least of them." And with the completeness of the mind, the bodies are completed too, as it is written (Isaiah 65), "the youngest shall die a hundred years old."

When the Children of Israel are complemented with the complete knowledge, the fountains of intelligence and knowledge shall flow beyond the boundaries of Israel and water all the nations of the world, as it is written (Isaiah 11), "for the earth shall be full of the knowledge of the Lord," and as it is written, "and shall come unto the Lord and to His goodness."

The proliferation of this knowledge is the matter of the expansion of the Messiah King to all the nations. Yet, it is the opposite with the crude, materialistic plebs. Since their imagination is attached to the complete power of the fist, the matter of the expansion of the Kingdom of Israel is engraved in their imagination only as a sort of dominion of bodies over bodies, to take their fee from the whole with great pride, and to be haughty over all the people in the world.

And what can I do for them if our sages have already rejected them, and the likes of them, from among the congregation of the Lord, saying, "All who is proud, the Creator says, 'he and I cannot dwell in the same abode.'"

Conversely, some err and determine that as the body must exist prior to the existence of the soul and the complete perception, the perfection of the body and its needs precede in time the attainment of the soul and the complete perception. Hence, complete perception is denied of a weak body.

This is a grave mistake, harder than death, since a perfect body is inconceivable whatsoever before the complete perception has been attained. This is because, in itself, it is a punctured bag, a broken cistern. It cannot contain anything beneficial, neither for itself nor for others, except with the attainment of the complete knowledge.

At that time the body, too, rises to its completeness with it, literally hand in hand. This rule applies both in individuals and in the whole.

5) Now you will understand what is written in *The Zohar*: "With this composition, the Children of Israel will be redeemed from exile." Also, in many other places, only through the expansion of the wisdom of Kabbalah in the masses will we obtain complete redemption.

They also said, "The Light in it reforms him." They were intentionally meticulous about it, to show us that only the Light enclosed within it, "like apples of gold in settings of silver," in it lies the cure that reforms a person. Both the individual and the nation will not complete the aim for which they were created, except by attaining the internality of the Torah and its secrets.

And although we hope for the complete attainment at the coming of the Messiah, it is written, "Will give wisdom to the wise." It also says, "I have put wisdom in the heart of every wise-at-heart."

Hence, it is the great expansion of the wisdom of truth within the nation that we need first, so we may merit receiving the benefit from our Messiah. Consequently, the expansion of the wisdom and the coming of our Messiah are interdependent.

Therefore, we must establish seminaries and compose books to hasten the distribution of the wisdom throughout the nation. And this was not the case before, for fear lest unworthy disciples would mingle, as we have elaborated above. This became the primary reason for the prolonging of the exile for our many sins, to this day.

Our sages said, "Messiah, Son of David comes only in a generation that is all worthy..." meaning when everyone retires from pursuit of honor and lust. At that time, it will be possible to establish many seminaries to prepare them for the coming of the Messiah Son of David. "...or in a generation that is all unworthy," meaning in such a generation when "the face of the generation is as the face of the dog, and righteous shall be castaway, and authors' wisdom shall go astray in them." At such a time, it will be possible to remove the careful guard and all who remain in the house of Jacob with their hearts pounding to attain the wisdom and the purpose, "Holy" will be their names, and they shall come and study.

This is so because there will no longer be fear lest one might not sustain one's merit and trade the wisdom in the market, as no one in the mob will buy it. The wisdom will be so loathsome in their eyes that neither glory nor lust will be obtainable in return for it.

Hence, all who wish to enter may come and enter. Many will roam, and the knowledge will increase among the worthy of it. And by that we will soon be rewarded with the coming of the Messiah, and the redemption of our souls soon in our days, Amen.

With these words I unbind myself from a considerable complaint, that I have dared more than all my predecessors in disclosing the ordinarily covered rudiments of the wisdom in my book, which was thus far unexplored. This refers to the essence of the ten *Sefirot* and all that concerns them, *Yashar* and *Hozer*, *Pnimi* and *Makif*, the meaning of the *Hakaa* and the meaning of the *Hizdakchut*.

The authors that preceded me deliberately scattered the words here and there, and in subtle intimations, so one's hand would fail to gather them. I, through His Light, which appeared upon me, and with the help of my teachers, have gathered them and disclosed the matters clearly enough and in their spiritual form, above place and above time.

They could have come to me with a great argument: If there are no additions to my teachers here, then the Ari and Rav Chaim Vital themselves and the genuine authors, the commentators on their words, could have disclosed and explained the matters as openly as I. And if you wish to say that it was revealed to them, then who is this writer, for whom it is certainly a great privilege to be dust and ashes under their feet, who says that the lot given to him by the Creator is more than their lot?

However, as you will see in the references, I neither added to my teachers nor innovated in the composition. All my words are already written in the Eight Gates, in *The Tree of Life*, and in *Mavo Shearim* (*Entrance of the Gates*) by the Ari. I did not add a single word to them; but they aimed to conceal matters; hence, they scattered them one here and one there.

This was so because their generation was not yet completely unworthy and required great care. We, however, for our many sins, all the words of our sages are already true in us. They had been said for the time of the Messiah to begin with, for in such a generation there is no longer fear of disclosing the wisdom, as we have elaborated above; hence, my words are open and in order.

6) And now sons do hear me: The "Wisdom cries aloud in the streets, she utters her voice," "Whoso is on the Lord's side, let him come unto me," "For it is no vain thing for you; because it is your life, and the length of your days."

"You were not created to follow the act of the grain and the potato, you and your asses in one trough." And as the purpose of the ass is not to serve all its contemporary asses, man's purpose is not to serve all the bodies of the people of his time, the contemporaries of his physical body. Rather, the purpose of the ass is to serve and be of use to man, who is superior to it, and the purpose of man is to serve the Creator and complete His aim.

As Ben Zuma said, "All those were created only to serve me, and I, to serve my Maker." He says, "The Lord hath made all things for His own purpose," since the Creator yearns and craves our perfection.

It is said in *Beresheet Rabba*, *Parasha* 8, that the angels said to Him: "'What is man, that Thou art mindful of him, and the son of man, that Thou thinkest of him?' Why do You need this trouble? The Creator told them: 'Therefore, why sheep and oxen?'" What does it resemble? A king who had a tower filled abundantly, but no guests. What pleasure has the king from his fill? They promptly said unto Him: "O Lord, our Lord, how glorious is Thy name in all the earth! Do that which seems good to You."

Seemingly, we should doubt that allegory, since where does that tower filled abundantly stand? In our time, we really would fill it with guests to the rim.

Indeed, the words are earnest, since you see that the angels made no complaint about any of the creatures that were created during the six days of Creation, except about Man. This is because he was created in God's image and consists of the Upper and Lower together.

When the angels saw it, they were startled and bewildered. How would the pure, spiritual soul descend from its sublime degree, and come and dwell in the same abode with this filthy, beastly body? In other words, they wondered, "Why do You need this trouble?"

The answer that came to them is that there is already a tower filled abundantly, and empty of guests. To fill it with guests, we need the existence of this human, made of Upper and lower together. For this reason, this pure soul must clothe in the shape of this filthy body. They immediately understood it and said, "Do that which seems good to You."

Know that this tower, filled abundantly, implies all the pleasure and the goodness for which He has created the creatures, as they said, "The conduct of The Good is to do good." Hence, He has created the worlds to delight His creatures.

And since there is no past and future in Him, we must realize that as soon as He had Thought to create creatures and delight them, they came out and were instantly made before Him, they and all their fulfillments of delight and pleasure, as He had contemplated them.

It is written in the book, *Heftzi Bah* (*My Delight Is in Her*), by the Ari, that all the worlds, Upper and lower, are contained in the *Ein Sof* (Infinite), even before the *Tzimtzum* (restriction) by way of He is One and His Name One.

The incident of the *Tzimtzum*, which is the root of the worlds ABYA, confined to this world, occurred because the roots of the souls themselves yearn to equalize their form with the Emanator. This is the meaning of *Dvekut* (adhesion), as separation and *Dvekut* in anything spiritual is possible only in values of equivalence of form or disparity of form.

Since He wanted to delight them, the will to receive pleasure was necessarily imprinted in the receivers. Thus, their form has been changed from His, since this form is not at all present in the Emanator, as from whom would He receive?

The *Tzimtzum* and the *Gevul* (boundary/limitation) were made for this correction, until the emergence of this world to a reality of a clothing of a soul in a corporeal body. When one engages in Torah and work in order to bestow contentment upon one's Maker, the form of reception will be reunited in order to bestow once more.

This is the meaning of the text, "and to cleave unto Him," since then one equalizes one's form to one's Maker, and as we have said, equivalence of form is *Dvekut* in spirituality. When the matter of *Dvekut* is completed in all the parts of the soul, the worlds will return to the state of *Ein Sof*, as prior to the *Tzimtzum*.

"In their land they will inherit doubly." This is because then they will be able to receive once more all the pleasure and delight, prepared for them in advance in the world of *Ein Sof*. Moreover, now they are prepared for the real *Dvekut* without any disparity of form, since their reception is no longer for themselves, but to bestow contentment upon their Maker. You find that they have equalized in the form of bestowal with the Maker.

7) Now you will understand their words, that Divinity in the lower ones is a high need. This is a most perplexing statement, though it does go hand in hand with the above study.

They have compared the matter to a king who has a tower filled abundantly, and no guests. It is certain that he sits and waits for guests, or his whole preparation will be in vain.

It is like a great king who had a son when he was already old, and he was very fond of him. Hence, from the day of his birth he thought favorable thoughts about him, collected all the books and the finest scholars in the land, and built schools for him.

He gathered the finest builders in the land and built palaces of pleasure for him, collected all the musicians and the singers and built him concert halls. He assembled the best chefs and bakers in the land and served him every delicacy in the world, and so on and so forth.

Alas, the boy grew up to be a fool with no wish for knowledge. He was also blind and could not see or feel the beauty of the buildings; and he was deaf and could not hear the singers. Sadly, he was diabetic, and was permitted to eat only coarse-flour bread, arising contempt and wrath.

Now you can understand their words about the verse, "I, the Lord, will hasten it in its time." The *Sanhedrin* (98) interpreted, "Not rewarded—in its time; rewarded—I will hasten it."

Thus, there are two ways to attain the above-mentioned goal: through their own attention, which is called a "Path of Repentance." If they are awarded that, then "I will hasten it" will be applied to them. This means that there is no set time for it, but when they are awarded, the correction ends, of course.

If they are not awarded the attention, there is another way, called "Path of Suffering." As the *Sanhedrin* said (97), "I place upon them a king such as Haman, and they will repent against their will," meaning in its time, for in that there is a set time.

By that, they wanted to show us that His ways are not our ways. For this reason, the case of the flesh-and-blood king who had troubled so to prepare those great things for his beloved son and was finally tormented in every way, and all his trouble was in vain, bringing contempt and wrath, will not happen to Him.

Instead, all the deeds of the Creator are guaranteed and true, and there is no fraud in Him. This is what our sages said, "Not rewarded—in its time." What the will does not do, time will do, as it is written, "Canst thou send forth lightnings, that they may go, and say unto thee: 'Here we are'?"

There is a path of pain that can cleanse any defect and materialism until one realizes how to raise one's head out of the beastly crib, to soar and climb the rungs of the ladder of happiness and human success, for one will cleave to one's root and complete the aim.

8) Therefore, come and see how grateful we should be to our teachers, who impart us their sacred Lights and dedicate their souls to do good to our souls. They stand in the middle between the path of harsh torments and the path of repentance. They save us from the netherworld, which is harder than death,

and accustom us to reach the heavenly pleasures, the sublime gentleness and the pleasantness that is our share, ready and waiting for us from the very beginning, as we have said above. Each of them operates in his generation, according to the power of the Light of his Torah and sanctity.

Our sages have already said, "You have not a generation without such as Abraham, Isaac, and Jacob." Indeed, that Godly man, our Rav Isaac Luria, troubled and provided us the fullest measure. He did wondrously more than his predecessors, and if I had a tongue that praises, I would praise that day when his wisdom appeared almost as the day when the Torah was given to Israel.

There are not enough words to measure his holy work in our favor. The doors of attainment were locked and bolted, and he came and opened them for us. Thus, all who wish to enter the King's palace need only purity and sanctity, and to go and bathe and shave their hair and wear clean clothes, to properly stand before the sublime Kingship.

You find a thirty-eight-year-old who subdued with his wisdom all his predecessors through the Genius and through all times. All the elders of the land, the gallant shepherds, friends and disciples of the Godly sage, the RAMAK, stood before him as disciples before the Rav.

All the sages of the generations following them to this day, none missing, have abandoned all the books and compositions that precede him, the Kabbalah of the RAMAK, the Kabbalah of The First and the Kabbalah of The Genius, blessed be the memory of them all. They have attached their spiritual life entirely and solely to his Holy Wisdom. Naturally, it is not without merit that a total victory is awarded, as this young in years father of wisdom has.

Alas, the devil's work succeeded, and obstacles were placed along the path of expansion of his wisdom into a holy nation, and only very few have begun to conquer them.

This was so primarily because the words were written by hearsay, as he had interpreted the wisdom day-by-day before his disciples, who were already elderly and with great proficiency in *The Zohar* and the *Tikkunim* (Corrections). In most cases, his holy sayings were arranged according to the profound questions that they asked him, each according to his own interest.

For this reason, he did not convey the wisdom in a suitable order, as with compositions that preceded him. We find in the texts that the Ari himself had wished to bring the issues in order. In that regard, see the beginning of the sayings of Rashbi in the interpretation to the *Idra Zuta*, in a short introduction by Rav Chaim Vital.

There is also the short time of his teaching, since his entire time of his seminary was some seventeen months, as is said in the *Gate to Reincarnations*, Gate 8, p 49, since he arrived in Safed from Egypt soon before *Pesach* (Passover) in the year 1571, and at that time, Rav Chaim Vital was twenty-nine years of age. And in July 1572, on the eve of Shabbat, *Parashat Matot-Masaey*,[21] the beginning of the month of *Av*, he fell ill, and on Tuesday, fifth of *Av*, on the following week, he passed away.

It is also written in the *Gate to Reincarnations*, Gate 8, p 71a, that upon his demise, he ordered Rav Chaim Vital to not teach the wisdom to others, and permitted him to study only by himself and in a whisper. The rest of the friends were forbidden to engage in it altogether because he said that they did not understand the wisdom properly.

This is the reason why Rav Chaim Vital did not arrange the texts at all and left them unorganized. Naturally, he did not explain the connections between the matters, so it would not be as teaching others. This is the reason we find such great caution on his part, as is known to those proficient in the writings of the Ari.

The arrangements found in the writings of the Ari were arranged and organized by a third generation, in three times, and by three compilers. The first compiler was the sage MAHARI Tzemach. He lived at the same time of MAHARA Azulai, who passed away in the year 1644.

A large portion of the texts came by him, and he arranged many books from them. The most important among them is the book *Adam Yashar* (*Upright Man*), in which he collected the root and the essential teachings that were at his disposal. However, some of the books that this Rav had compiled were lost. In the introduction to his book, *Kol BeRama* (*A Loud Voice*), he presents all the books that he had compiled.

The second compiler is his disciple, MAHARAM Paprish. He did more than his Rav, since some of the books that were held by the sage MAHARASH Vital came by his hands, and he compiled many books. The most important among them are the books, *Etz haChaim* (*The Tree of Life*) and *Pri Etz haChaim* (*Fruit of the Tree of Life*). They contain the entire scope of the wisdom in its fullest sense.

The third compiler was the sage MAHARASH Vital, the son of MOHARAR Chaim Vital. He was a great and renowned sage. He compiled the famous *Eight Gates* from the patrimony his father had left him.

---

21 Translator's note: name of the weekly Torah portion.

Thus we see that each of the compilers did not have the complete writings. It heavily burdened the arrangement of the issues, which are unsuitable for those without true proficiency in *The Zohar* and the *Tikkunim*. Hence, few are those who ascend.

9) In return for that, we are privileged by Him to have been rewarded with the spirit of The Baal Shem Tov, whose greatness and sanctity are beyond any word and any utterance. He was not gazed upon and will not be gazed upon, except by those worthy that had served under his Light, and they, too, only intermittently, each according to what he received in his heart.

It is true that the Light of his Torah and Holy Wisdom are built primarily on the holy foundations of the Ari. However, they are not at all similar. I shall explain that with an allegory of a person who is drowning in the river, rising and sinking as drowning people do. Sometimes only the hair is visible, and then a counsel is sought to catch him by his head. Other times his body appears as well, and then a counsel is sought to catch him from opposite his heart.

So is the matter before us. After Israel has drowned in the evil waters of the exile in the nations, from then until now they rise and fall, and not all times are the same. At the time of the Ari, only the head was visible. Hence, the Ari had troubled in our favor to save us through the mind. At the time of The Baal Shem Tov, there was relief. Hence, it was a blessing for us to save us from opposite our heart, and that was a great and true salvation for us.

And for our many sins, the wheel has been turned over again in our generation and we have declined tremendously, as though from the zenith to the nadir.

In addition, there is the collision of the nations, which has confused the entire world. The needs have increased and the mind grew short and corrupted in the filth of materialism which apprehends the lead. Servants ride horses and ministers walk on the earth, and everything that is said in our study in the above-mentioned *Masechet Sutah* has come true in us, for our many sins. Again, the iron wall has been erected, even on this great Light of the Baal Shem Tov, which we have said illuminated as far as the establishment of our complete redemption.

And the wise-at-heart did not believe in the possibility that a generation would come when they could not see by his Light. Now, our eyes have darkened; we have been robbed of good, and when I saw this I said, "It is time to act!" Thus, I have come to open widely the gates of Light of the Ari, for he is indeed capable and fit for our generation, too, and "Two are better than one."

We should not be blamed for the brevity in my composition, since it corresponds and adapts to any wisdom lover, as too much wine wears off the flavor, and the attainment will become harder for the disciple.

Also, we are not responsible for those fat-at-heart, since the language to assist them has yet to be created. Wherever they rest their eyes, they find folly, and there is a rule that from the same source from which the wise draws his wisdom, the fool draws his folly.

Thus, I stand at the outset of my book and warn that I have not troubled at all for all those who love to look through the windows. Rather, it is for those who care for the words of the Creator and long for the Creator and His Goodness, to complete the purpose for which they were created, for with the will of God, the verse, "All those who seek Me shall find Me," shall come true in them.

10) Come and see the words of the sage, Rabbi Even Ezra in his book, *Yesod Mora*, p 8b: "And now note and know that all the *Mitzvot* that are written in the Torah or the conventions that the fathers have established, although they are mostly in action or in speech, they are all in order to correct the heart, 'for the Lord searches all hearts, and understands all the imaginations of the thoughts.'"

It is written, "to them that are upright in their hearts." Its opposite is, "A heart that deviseth wicked thoughts." I have found one verse that contains all the *Mitzvot*, which is, "Thou shalt fear the Lord thy God; and Him shalt thou serve."

The word "fear" contains all the negative *Mitzvot* in speech, in heart, and in action. It is the first degree from which one ascends to the work of God, which contains all the positive *Mitzvot*.

These will accustom one's heart and guide one until one cleaves to the Lord, as for that was man created. He was not created for acquiring fortunes or for building buildings. Hence, one should seek everything that will bring one to love Him, to learn wisdom and to seek faith.

And the Creator will open the eyes of his heart and will renew a different spirit within him. Then he will be loved by his Maker in his life.

Know that the Torah was given only to men of heart. Words are as corpses and the *Taamim* (flavors) as souls. If one does not understand the *Taamim*, one's whole effort is in vain, labor blown away.

It is as though one exerts oneself to count the letters and the words in a medicine book. No cure will come from this labor. It is also like a camel carrying silk; it does not benefit the silk, nor does the silk benefit it.

We draw only this from his words; hold on to the goal for which man was created. He says about it that this is the matter of the *Dvekut* with the Creator.

Hence, he says that one must search every means to bring one to love Him, to learn wisdom and to seek faith, until the Creator rewards one with opening one's eyes and renewing a different spirit within him. At that time, he shall be loved by his Maker.

He deliberately makes that precision, to be loved by his Maker in his life. It indicates that while he has not acquired that, his work is incomplete, and the work that was necessarily given to us to do today. It is as he ends it, that the Torah was only given to men of heart, meaning ones who have acquired the heart to love and covet Him. The sages call them "wise-at-heart," since there is no longer a descending, beastly spirit there, for the evil inclination is present only in a heart vacant from wisdom.

He interprets and says that the words are as corpses and the *Taamim*, as souls. If one does not understand the *Taamim*, it is similar to exerting oneself counting pages and words in a medicine book. This exertion will not yield a remedy.

He wishes to say that one is compelled to find the means to acquire the above-mentioned possession. It is because then one can taste the flavors of Torah, which is the interior wisdom and its mysteries, and the flavors of *Mitzva*, which are the interior love and the desire for Him.

Without it, one has only the words and the actions; dead bodies without souls. It is like one who labors counting pages and words in a medicine book, etc. Certainly, he will not perfect himself in medicine before he understands the meaning of the written medicine.

Even after one purchases it, for whatever price is asked, if the conduct of the study and the actions are not arranged to bring him to it, it is like a camel carrying silk; it does not benefit the silk and the silk does not benefit it, to bring it to complete the aim for which it was created.

11) According to these words, our eyes have been opened concerning the words of Rabbi Simon in *Midrash Rabba*, *Parasha* 6, about the verse, "Let us make man." When the Creator came to create man, He consulted the ministering angels, and they were divided into sects and groups. Some said, "Let him be created," and some said, "Let him not be created," as it is written, "Mercy and truth are met together; righteousness and peace have kissed each other."

- Mercy said, "Let him be created, for he does merciful actions."
- Truth said, "Let him not be created, for he is all lies."

- Righteousness said, "Let him be created, for he performs righteousness."
- Peace said, "Let him not be created, for he is all strife."

What did the Creator do? He took Truth and threw it to the ground, as it is written, "and it cast down truth to the ground." The angels said before the Creator: "Why do you disgrace your seal? Let Truth come up from the ground, as it is written, 'truth springeth out of the ground.'"

This text is difficult from all sides:

i. It does not explain the seriousness of the verse, "Let us make man." Is it a counsel that He needs, as it is written, "Deliverance in the heart of a counsel"?

ii. Regarding Truth, how can it be said about the entire human species that it is all lies, when there is not a generation without such as Abraham, Isaac, and Jacob?

iii. If the words of Truth are earnest, how did the angels of Mercy and Righteousness agree to a world that is all lies?

iv. Why is Truth called "Seal," which comes at the edge of a letter? Certainly, the reality exists primarily outside the seal. Is there no reality at all outside the borders of Truth?

v. Can true angels think of the True Operator that His operation is untrue?

vi. Why did Truth deserve such a harsh punishment to be thrown to the ground and into the ground?

vii. Why is the angels' reply not brought in the Torah, as their question is brought?

We must understand these two conducts set before our eyes, which are completely opposite. These are the conducts of the existence of the entire reality of this world and the conducts of the manners of existence for the sustenance of each and every one in the reality before us. From this end, we find a reliable conduct in utterly affirmed guidance, which controls the making of each and every creature in reality.

Let us take the making of a human being as an example. The love and pleasure are its first reason, certain and reliable for its task. As soon as it is uprooted from the father's brain, Providence provides it a safe and guarded place among the beddings in the mother's abdomen, so no stranger may touch it.

There Providence provides it with its daily bread in the right measure. It tends to its every need without forgetting it for even a moment, until it gains strength to come out to the air of our world, which is full of obstacles.

At that time, Providence lends it power and strength, and like an armed, experienced hero, it opens gates and breaks the walls until it comes to such people it can trust to help it through its days of weakness with love and great compassion to sustain its existence, as they are the most precious for it in the whole world.

Thus, Providence embraces it until it qualifies it to exist and to continue its existence onward. As is with man, so it is with the animate and the flora. All are wondrously watched, securing their existence, and every scientist of nature knows it.

On the other end, when we regard the order of existence and sustenance in the modes of existence of the whole of reality, large and small, we find confused orders, as if an army is fleeing the campaign sick, beaten, and afflicted by the Creator. Their whole life is as death, having no sustenance unless by tormenting first, risking their lives for their bread.

Even a tiny louse breaks its teeth when it sets off for a meal. How much frisking it frisks to attain enough food to sustain itself? As it is, so are all, great and small alike, and all the more so with humans, the elite of Creation, who is involved in everything.

12) We discern two opposites in the ten *Sefirot* of *Kedusha* (Holiness). The first nine *Sefirot* are in the form of bestowal, and *Malchut* means reception. Also, the first nine are filled with Light, and *Malchut* has nothing of her own.

This is the meaning of our discrimination of two discernments of Light in each *Partzuf*: *Ohr Pnimi* (Inner Light) and *Ohr Makif* (Surrounding Light), and two discernments in the *Kelim* (Vessels), which are the Inner *Kli* (Vessel) for *Ohr Pnimi* and an Outer *Kli* for *Ohr Makif*.

This is so because of the two above-mentioned opposites, as it is impossible for two opposites to be in the same subject. Thus, a specific subject is required for the *Ohr Pnimi* and a specific subject for the *Ohr Makif*.

However, they are not really opposite in *Kedusha*, since *Malchut* is in *Zivug* (Copulation) with the Upper nine, and its quality is of bestowal, too, in the form of *Ohr Hozer* (Reflected Light). But the *Sitra Achra* (Other Side) has nothing of the Upper nine. They are built primarily from the Vacant Space, which is the complete form of reception, on which the first *Tzimtzum* (Restriction) occurred.

That root remained without Light even after the illumination of the *Kav* (Line) reached inside the *Reshimo* (Reminiscence).

For this reason, they are two complete opposites, compared to life and *Kedusha*, as it is written, "God hath made even the one as well as the other"; hence they are called "dead."

It has been explained above, Item 6, that the whole issue of the *Tzimtzum* was only for the adornment of the souls, concerning the equalizing of their form to their Maker's, which is the inversion of the vessels of reception to the form of bestowal.

You find that this goal is still denied **from the perspective of the *Partzufim* of *Kedusha*** (Countenances of Holiness). This is because there is nothing there of the Vacant Space, which is the complete form of reception, over which was the *Tzimtzum*, hence, no correction will apply to it, as it does not exist in reality.

Also, there is certainly no correction here **from the perspective of the *Sitra Achra***, although it does have a Vacant Space, since it has a completely opposite interest, and everything it receives dies.

Hence, it is only a human in this world that we need. In infancy, he is sustained and supported by the *Sitra Achra*, inheriting the *Kelim* of the Vacant Space from it. When he grows, he connects to the structure of *Kedusha* through the power of Torah and *Mitzvot* to bestow contentment upon his Maker.

Thus, one turns the complete measure of reception he has already acquired to be solely arranged for bestowal. In that, he equalizes his form with his Maker and the aim comes true in him.

This is the meaning of the existence of time in this world. You find that first, these two above opposites were divided into two separate subjects, namely *Kedusha* and *Sitra Achra*, by way of, "even the one as well as the other." They are still devoid of the above correction, for they must be in the same subject, which is man.

Therefore, the existence of an order of time is necessary for us, since then the two opposites will come in a person one-by-one, meaning at a time of *Katnut* (infancy) and at a time of *Gadlut* (adulthood/maturity).

13) Now you can understand the need for the breaking of the vessels and their properties, as it is written in *The Zohar* and in the writings of the Ari, that two kinds of Light are present in each ten *Sefirot*, running back and forth.

- The first Light is *Ohr Ein Sof* (Light of Infinity), which travels from Above downward. It is called *Ohr Yashar* (Direct Light).

- The second Light is a result of the *Kli* of *Malchut*, returning from below Upward, called *Ohr Hozer* (Reflected Light).

Both unite into one. Know that from the *Tzimtzum* downward, the point of *Tzimtzum* is devoid of any Light and remains a Vacant Space. The Upper Light can no longer appear in the last *Behina* (discernment) before the end of correction, and this is said particularly about *Ohr Ein Sof*, called *Ohr Yashar*. However, the second Light, called *Ohr Hozer*, can appear in the last *Behina*, since the case of the *Tzimtzum* did not apply to it at all.

Now we have learned that the system of the *Sitra Achra* and the *Klipot* (Shells) is a necessity for the purpose of the *Tzimtzum*, in order to instill in a person the great vessels of reception while in *Katnut*, when one is dependent on her.

Thus, the *Sitra Achra* too needs abundance. Where would she take it if she is made solely of the last *Behina*, which is a space that is vacant of any Light, since from the *Tzimtzum* downward the Upper Light is completely separated from it?

Hence, the matter of the breaking of the vessels had been prepared. The breaking indicates that a part of the *Ohr Hozer* of the ten *Sefirot* of the world of *Nekudim* descended from *Atzilut* out to the Vacant Space. And you already know that *Ohr Hozer* can appear in the Vacant Space, as well.

That part, the *Ohr Hozer* that descended from *Atzilut* outwardly, contains thirty-two special *Behinot* (discernments) of each and every *Sefira* of the ten *Sefirot* of *Nekudim*. Ten times thirty-two is 320, and these 320 *Behinot* that descended, were prepared for the sustenance of the existence of the lower ones, which come to them in two systems, as it is written, "God hath made even the one as well as the other," meaning the worlds *ABYA* of *Kedusha* and opposite them the worlds *ABYA* of the *Sitra Achra*.

In the interpretation of the verse, "and the one people shall be stronger than the other people," our sages said that when one rises, the other falls, and *Tzor* is built only over the ruins of Jerusalem. This is so because all these 320 *Behinot* can appear for the *Sitra Achra*, at which time the structure of the system of *Kedusha*, with respect to the lower ones, is completely ruined.

Also, these 320 *Behinot* can connect solely to *Kedusha*. At that time, the system of the *Sitra Achra* is completely destroyed from the land, and they can divide more or less evenly between them, according to people's actions. And so they incarnate in the two systems until the correction is completed.

After the breaking of the vessels and the decline of the 320 *Behinot* of sparks of Light from *Atzilut* outwards, 288 of them were sorted and rose, meaning everything that descended from the first nine *Sefirot* in the ten *Sefirot* of *Nekudim*. Nine times thirty-two are 288 *Behinot*, and they are the ones that reconnected to building the system of *Kedusha*.

You find that only thirty-two *Behinot* remained for the *Sitra Achra* from what had descended from *Malchut* of the world of *Nekudim*. This was the beginning of the structure of the *Sitra Achra*, in its utter smallness, when she is as yet unfit for her task. The completion of her construction ended later, by the sin of *Adam ha Rishon* with the Tree of Knowledge.

Thus we find that there are two systems, one opposite the other, operating in the persistence and sustenance of reality. The ration of Light needed for that existence is 320 sparks. Those were prepared and measured by the breaking of the vessels. This ration is to be swaying between the two systems, and that is what the conducts of sustenance and existence of reality depend on.

You should know that the system of *Kedusha* must contain at least a ration of 288 sparks to complete her nine upper *Sefirot*, and then it can sustain and provide for the existence of the lower ones. This is what it had prior to the sin of *Adam ha Rishon*, and for that reason the whole of reality was then conducted by the system of *Kedusha*, since it had the full 288 sparks.

14) Now we have found the opening to the above study regarding the four sects, Mercy, Righteousness, Truth, and Peace, which negotiated with the Creator regarding man's creation. These angels are servants of man's soul; hence, He negotiated with them, since the whole act of Creation was created according to them, as each and every soul consists of ten *Sefirot* in *Ohr Pnimi* and *Ohr Makif*.

- Mercy is the *Ohr Pnimi* of the first nine of the soul.
- Righteousness is the *Ohr Pnimi* of the *Malchut* of the soul.
- Truth is the *Ohr Makif* of the soul.

We have already said that *Ohr Pnimi* and *Ohr Makif* are opposites, since the *Ohr Pnimi* is drawn by the law of the illumination of the *Kav*, which is prevented from appearing at the point of the *Tzimtzum*, which is the *Gadlut* form of reception.

The *Ohr Makif* extends from *Ohr Ein Sof*, which surrounds all the worlds, since there, in *Ein Sof*, great and small are equal. For this reason, the *Ohr Makif* shines and bestows upon the point of *Tzimtzum*, too, much less for *Malchut*.

Since they are opposites, two *Kelim* are needed. This is because the *Ohr Pnimi* illuminates in the Upper nine. Even to *Malchut*, it shines only according to the law of the Upper nine, and not at all to her own self. However, the

Ohr Makif shines in the *Kelim* that extend specifically from the point of the *Tzimtzum*, which is called "Outer *Kli*."

Now you can understand why Truth is called "Seal." It is a borrowed name from a seal at the edge of a letter, at the end of the matters. However, it asserts them and gives them validity. Without the seal they are worthless, and the whole text is wasted.

It is the same with the *Ohr Makif*, which bestows upon the point of the *Tzimtzum*, which is the *Gadlut* measure of reception, until it equalizes its form with its Maker in bestowal. Indeed, this is the purpose of all the limited worlds, Upper and lower.

The protest of Truth regarding man's creation is its claim that he is all lies. This is so because, from the perspective of the Creator, man does not have an Outer *Kli*, which he needs to draw from the point of *Tzimtzum*, as she has already been separated from His Light. Thus, the Angels of Truth could not help man obtain the *Ohr Makif*.

All the limited worlds, Upper and lower, were created solely for that completion, and this man must be its only subject. But since this man is unfit for his role, they are all abyss and falsehood, and the labor in them—useless.

It is the opposite with the angels of Mercy and Righteousness, which belong specifically to the *Ohr Pnimi* of the soul. Because he has nothing of the Vacant Space, they could bestow upon him all the Lights of *Neshama* abundantly, in the most sublime perfection.

Thus, they were happy to benefit him and wholeheartedly agreed to man's creation. Because they are *NHY* that enter by *Zivug de Hakaa* (Copulation in striking), they belong to the half of the *Ohr Makif* from the perspective of the *Ohr Hozer* in it.

The angels of Peace claimed that he is all strife. In other words, how will he receive the *Ohr Makif*? In the end, they cannot come in the same subject with the *Ohr Pnimi*, as they are opposite from each other, meaning all strife.

The *Ohr Makif* is discerned by two: the future *Ohr Hozer* and the future *Ohr Makif*. The Outer *Kli* for the *Ohr Hozer* is the *Masach* (Screen) and the Outer *Kli* for the *Ohr Makif* is the *Aviut* of *Behina Dalet* (Fourth Discernment) itself, namely the Stony Heart.

You find that *Adam ha Rishon* **lacked only the Outer *Kli*,** which belongs to the angels of Truth. He **did not lack the Outer *Kli*,** belonging to the angels of Peace.

Hence, they agreed to the Creation, but claimed that he is all strife, meaning that the *Ohr Yashar* cannot enter the Inner *Kli* since they are opposites.

15) Now we have been granted the understanding of the rest of the verses in the sin of the Tree of Knowledge of good and evil, which are most profound. Our sages, who disclosed a portion of them, concealed ten portions with their words.

As a foreword, it is written, "And they were both naked, the man and his wife, and were not ashamed." Know that clothing means an Outer *Kli*. Hence, the text precedes to demonstrate the reason for the sin of the Tree of Knowledge, as it is written in the verse, "Libel is terrible for the children of man, for in libel you come upon him."

This means that his sin had been prepared in advance, and this is the meaning of the words that *Adam* and his wife did not have an Outer *Kli* at the moment of creation, but only Inner *Kelim*, which extend from the system of *Kedusha*, hence they were not ashamed. This is why they did not feel their absence, as shame refers to a sensation of absence.

It is known that the sensation of absence is the first reason for the fulfillment of the deficiency. It is as one who feels one's illness and is willing to receive the medication. However, when one does not feel that he is ill, he will certainly avoid all medications.

Indeed, this task is for the Outer *Kli* to do. Since it is in the construction of the body and is empty of Light, as it comes from the Vacant Space, it begets the sensation of emptiness and dearth in it, by which one becomes ashamed.

Hence, one is compelled to return to fill the absence and draw the lacking *Ohr Makif*, which is about to fill that *Kli*. This is the meaning of the verse, "And they were both naked, the man and his wife," of the Outer *Kli*. For this reason, they were not ashamed, since they did not feel their absence. In that manner, they are devoid of the purpose for which they were created.

Yet, we must thoroughly understand the sublimity of that man, made by the hands of the Creator. Also, his wife, to whom the Creator has administered greater intelligence than him, as they have written (*Nidah* 45) in the interpretation to the verse, "And the Lord made the rib."

Thus, how did they fail and became as fools, not knowing to beware of the serpent's slyness? On the other hand, that serpent, of which the text testifies that it was more cunning than all the animals of the field, how did it utter such folly and emptiness that should they eat off the fruit of the Tree of Knowledge, they would be turned to God? Moreover, how did that folly settle in their hearts?

Also, it is said below that they did not eat because of their desire to become God, but simply because the tree is good to eat. This is seemingly a beastly desire!

16) We must know the nature of the two kinds of discernments customary for us:

- The first discernment is called "discernment of good and bad."
- The second discernment is called "discernment of true and false."

This means that the Creator has imprinted a discerning force in each creature that executes everything that is good for it and brings it to its desired perfection. The first discernment is the active, physical force. It operates using the sensation of bitter and sweet, which loathes and repels the bitter form, since it is bad for it, and loves and attracts the sweet because it is good for it. This operating force is sufficient in the Still, the Vegetative, and the Animate in reality, to bring them to their desired perfection.

Atop them is the human species, in which the Creator instilled a rational operating force. It operates in sorting the above second discernment, rejecting falsehood and emptiness with loathing to the point of nausea, and attracts true matters and every benefit with great love.

This discernment is called "discernment of true and false." It is implemented solely in the human species, each according to his own measure. Know that this second acting force was created and came to man because of the serpent. At creation, he had only the first active force, from the discernments of good and bad, which was sufficient for him at that time.

Let me explain it to you in an allegory: If the righteous were rewarded according to their good deeds, and the wicked punished according their bad deeds in this world, *Kedusha* would be determined for us in the reality of sweet and good, and the *Sitra Achra* would be defined in the reality of bad and bitter.

In that state, the commandment of choice would reach us, as it is written, "Behold, I have set before thee the sweet and the bitter; therefore choose sweet." Thus, all the people would be guaranteed to achieve perfection, for they would certainly run from the sin, as it is bad for them. They would be occupied in His *Mitzvot* day in and day out, ceaselessly, like today's fools regarding the bodily matters and its filth, since it is good and sweet to them. So was the matter of *Adam ha Rishon* when He created him.

"And put him into the Garden of Eden to dress it and to keep it." Our sages interpreted, "to dress it" are the positive *Mitzvot*, "and to keep it" are the negative *Mitzvot*. His positive *Mitzvot* were to eat and delight with all the trees of the Garden, and his negative *Mitzvot* were to not eat from the Tree of Knowledge of good and evil. The positive *Mitzvot* were sweet and nice, and the negative *Mitzvot* were retirement from the bitter fruit that is as hard as death.

Not surprisingly, these cannot be called *Mitzvot* and labor. We find the likes of that in our present chores, where through the pleasures of Shabbat and good days we are rewarded with sublime *Kedusha*. And we are also rewarded for retiring from reptiles and insects and everything that one finds loathsome.

You find that the choice in the work of *Adam ha Rishon* was by way of "therefore choose sweet." It follows that the physical palate alone was sufficient for all he needed, to know what the Creator commanded and what He did not command.

17) Now we can understand the serpent's craftiness, which our sages added, and notified us that SAM clothed in it, because its words were very high. It started with, "Yea, hath God said: 'Ye shall not eat of any tree of the garden?'" Meaning, it began to speak with her since the woman was not commanded by the Creator. Hence, it asked her about the modes of scrutiny, meaning how do you know that the Tree of Knowledge had been prohibited? Perhaps all the fruits of the Garden were forbidden for you, too? "And the woman said... 'Of the fruit of the trees of the garden we may eat'; ...Ye shall not eat of it, neither shall ye touch it, lest ye die."

There are two great precisions here:

A. The touching was never forbidden; hence, why did she add to the prohibition?

B. Did she doubt the words of the Creator? The Creator said, "thou shalt surely die," and the woman said, "lest ye die." Could it be that she did not believe the words of the Creator even prior to the sin?

Yet, the woman answered it according to the serpent's question. She knew what the Creator had prohibited, that all the trees of the Garden are sweet and nice and good to eat. However, she was already close to touching that tree inside the Garden, and tasted in it a taste that is as hard as death.

She herself had proven that by to her own observation, there is fear of death, even from mere touching. For this reason, she understood the prohibition further than she had heard from her husband, as there is none so wise as the experienced.

"Lest ye die" concerns the touching. The answer must have been quite sufficient, for who would interfere and deny another's taste? However, the serpent contradicted her and said, "Ye shall not surely die; for God doth know that in the day ye eat thereof, then your eyes shall be opened."

We must make the precision concerning the matter of the opening of the eyes to this place. Indeed, it informed her of a new thing, beyond her. It proved to them that it is folly to think that the Creator created something harmful and detrimental in His world. Thus, with respect to the Creator, it is certainly not a bad or harmful thing.

Instead, that bitterness that you will taste in it, when even close to touching, is only on your part, since this eating is to notify you of the height of your merit. Thus, it is additional *Kedusha* that you need during the act, so your sole aim will be to bring contentment to your Maker, to keep the aim for which you were created. For this reason, it seems evil to you, so you will understand the additional *Kedusha* required of you.

"For in the day that thou eatest thereof," meaning if the act is in *Kedusha* and purity as clear as day, then "ye shall be as God, knowing good and evil." This means that as it is certainly sweet to the Creator and completely equal, so the good and bad will be to you, in complete equivalence, sweet and gentle.

It is still possible to doubt the credibility of the serpent, since the Creator did not tell it that Himself. Therefore, the serpent first said, "for God doth know that in the day ye eat thereof, then your eyes shall be opened."

This means that it is not necessary for the Creator to notify you of that, since He knows that if you pay attention to that, to eat on the side of *Kedusha*, your eyes shall be opened by themselves, to understand the measure of His greatness. You will feel wondrous sweetness and gentleness in Him; hence, He does not need to let you know, as for that He instilled in you the scrutinizing force, that you may know what is to your benefit by yourselves.

It is written right after that: "And when the woman saw that the tree was good for food, and that it was a delight to the eyes." This means that she did not rely on His words, but went and examined with her own mind and understanding and sanctified herself with additional *Kedusha*, to bring contentment to the Creator in order to complete the aim desired of her, and not at all for herself. At that time, her eyes were opened, as the serpent had said, "And the woman saw that the tree was good for food."

In other words, by seeing that "it was a delight to the eyes," before she even touched it, she felt great sweetness and lust, when her eyes saw by themselves that she had not seen such a desirable thing in all the trees of the Garden.

She also learned that the tree is good for knowledge, meaning that there is far more to crave and covet in this tree than in all the trees of the Garden. This refers to knowing that they were created for this act of eating, and that this is the whole purpose, as the serpent had told her.

After all these certain observations "she took of the fruit thereof, and did eat; and she gave also unto her husband with her, and he did eat." The text accurately writes "with her," meaning with the pure intention to only bestow and not for her own need. This is the meaning of the words "and she gave also unto her husband with her," with her in *Kedusha*.

18) Now we come to the heart of the matter and the mistake that concerned his leg. This Tree of Knowledge of good and evil was mixed with the Vacant Space, meaning with the *Gadlut* form of reception upon, which the *Tzimtzum* was implemented, and from which the *Ohr Elyon* departed.

It has also been explained that *Adam ha Rishon* did not have any of the *Gadlut* form of reception in his structure, which extends from the Vacant Space. Instead, he extended solely from the system of *Kedusha*, concerned only with bestowal.

It is written in *The Zohar* (*Kedoshim*), that *Adam ha Rishon* had nothing of this world. For this reason, the Tree of Knowledge was forbidden to him, as his root and the whole system of *Kedusha* are separated from the *Sitra Achra*, due to their disparity of form, which is the separation.

Thus, he, too, was commanded and warned about connecting to it, as thus he would be separated from his holy root and die like the *Sitra Achra* and the *Klipot*, which die due to their oppositeness and separation from the *Kedusha* and the Life of Lives.

However, Satan, which is SAM, the angel of death that was clothed in the serpent, came down and enticed Eve with deceit in its mouth: "Ye shall not surely die." It is known that any lie does not stand if it is not preceded by words of truth. Hence, it started with a true word and revealed the purpose of Creation to her, which came only to correct that tree, meaning to invert the great vessels of reception to the side of bestowal.

It said to her that God had eaten from this tree and created the world, meaning looked at that matter in the form of "The end of an act is in the preliminary thought," and for this reason He has created the world. As we have seen above, the whole matter of the first *Tzimtzum* was only for man, destined to equalize the form of reception to bestowal.

This was the truth, which is why it succeeded and the woman believed it when she prepared herself to receive and enjoy solely in order to bestow. You find that at any rate, evil vanished from the Tree of Knowledge of good and evil, and the Tree of Knowledge of good remained.

This is because the evil there is only the disparity of form of reception for "self," which was imprinted in him. Yet, with reception in order to bestow, he is brought to his complete perfection, and thus you find that she has made the great unification, as it should be at the end of the act.

However, that sublime *Kedusha* was still untimely. She was only fit to endure it in the first eating but not in the second eating. I will explain to you that one who abstains oneself from pleasure before one has tasted and grown accustomed is not like one who abstains from pleasure after having tasted and become connected to it. The first can certainly abstain once and for all, but the other must exert to retire from one's craving bit-by-bit until the matter is completed.

So it is here, since the woman had not yet tasted from the Tree of Knowledge, and was completely in bestowal. For this reason, it was easy for her to perform the first eating in order to bestow contentment upon the Creator in absolute *Kedusha*. However, after she had tasted it, a great desire and coveting for the Tree of Knowledge was made in her, until she could not retire from her craving, since matters had gone out of her control.

This is why our sages said that she ate prematurely, meaning before it was ripe, before they acquired strength and power to rule over their desire. It is similar to what the sages said in *Masechet Yevamot*, "I have eaten and I shall eat more." This means that even when he had explicitly heard that the Creator was in wrath with him, he still could not retire from it, since the lust had already been connected to him. You find that the first eating was on the side of the *Kedusha*, and the second eating was in great filth.

Now we can understand the severity of the punishment of the Tree of Knowledge, for which all people are put to death. This death extends from eating it, as the Creator had warned him, "in the day that thou eatest thereof thou shalt surely die."

The thing is that the *Gadlut* form of reception extends into his limbs from the Vacant Space, and from the *Tzimtzum* onward it is no longer possible for it to be under the same roof with the *Ohr Elyon* (Upper Light). Hence, that eternal breath of life, expressed in the verse, "and breathed into his nostrils the breath of life," had to leave there and depend on a slice of bread for its transient sustenance.

This life is not an eternal life as before, when it was for himself. It is rather similar to a sweat of life, a life that has been divided into tiny drops, where each drop is a fragment of his previous life. And this is the meaning of the sparks of souls that were spread throughout his progeny. Thus, in all his progeny, all the people in the world in all the generations, through the last generation, which concludes the purpose of creation, are one long chain.

It follows that the acts of the Creator did not change at all by the sin of the Tree of Knowledge. Rather, this Light of life that came at once in *Adam ha Rishon* extended and stretched into a long chain, revolving on the wheel of transformation of form until the end of correction. There is no cessation for a moment, since the actions of the Creator must be alive and enduring; "Sanctity is raised, not lowered."

As is the case of man, so is the case with all the creatures in the world because they all descended from an eternal and general form, on the wheel of transformation of form, as did man.

Both man and the world have an inner value and an outer value. The external always ascends and descends according to the internal, and this is the meaning of "In the sweat of thy face shalt thou eat bread." Instead of the previous breath of life that the Creator had breathed in his nostrils, there is now a sweat of life in his nostrils.

19) Our sages said (*Babba Batra* 17), "He is the evil inclination, he is Satan, he is the angel of death. He descends and incites, ascends and complains, he cometh and he taketh his soul." This is because two general corruptions occurred because of the sin of the Tree of Knowledge.

The first corruption is the matter of "ascends and complains." He had been tempted to eat from the Tree of Knowledge and acquired a vessel of reception of the Vacant Space in the structure of his body. That, in turn, caused hatred and remoteness between the eternal Light of life that the Creator had breathed in Adam's nostrils, and Adam's body.

It is similar to what they said, "All who is proud, the Creator says, 'he and I cannot dwell in the same abode.'" This is so because pride stems from the vessels of reception of the Vacant Space, from which the *Ohr Elyon* had already departed from the time of the *Tzimtzum* onward.

It is written in *The Zohar* that the Creator hates the bodies that are built only for themselves. For this reason, the Light of life fled from him, and this is the first corruption.

The second corruption is the descent of the 288 sparks that were already connected in the system of *Kedusha*. They were given and descended to the system of *Sitra Achra* and the *Klipot* so the world would not be destroyed.

This is so because the system of *Kedusha* cannot sustain and nourish people and the world, due to the hatred that had been made between the *Kedusha* and the *Kelim* of the Vacant Space. This follows the law of opposites, "he and I can not dwell in the same abode." Hence, the 288 sparks were given to the system of the *Sitra Achra* so they would nurture and sustain man and the world all through the incarnations of the souls in the bodies, as it is written, "Ten thousand for a generation, and for a thousand generations," until the end of correction.

Now you can see why they are called *Klipot*. It is because they are like the peel on a fruit. The hard peel envelops and covers the fruit to keep it from any filth and harm until the fruit is eaten. Without it, the fruit would be corrupted and would not fulfill its purpose. Thus you find that the 288 sparks were given to the *Klipot*, to sustain and qualify reality until they connect and attain their desired goal.

The above-mentioned second corruption is the matter of "cometh and taketh his soul." I wish to say that even that tiny part of the soul that remains for a person, as "sweat of the previous life," is also robbed by the *Sitra Achra*, through that same bestowal that she gives him from the 288 sparks that have fallen into her.

To understand that, you need a clear picture of the *Sitra Achra* as she really is. Thus, you will be able to examine all her ways. All the parts of reality of the lower world are branches, extending from their roots like an imprint from a seal from the Upper World, and the Upper from the one Above it and that Upper from its own Upper.

Know that any discernment in branches about the roots is only on the basis of their substance. This means that the substances in this world are corporeal bases, and the substances in the world of *Yetzira* are spiritual bases, relating to the spirituality in *Yetzira*. So it is in each and every world.

However, the occurrences and the comportments in them have the same value from each branch to its root, like two drops in a pond, and like the imprint whose form is identical to the seal from which it was imprinted. And once you know that, we can seek that branch that the upper *Sitra Achra* has in this world, and through it, we will also know the root of the upper *Sitra Achra*.

We find in *The Zohar* (*Parashat Tazriya*) that the afflictions in people's bodies are branches of the upper *Sitra Achra*. Hence, let us take the Animate level and learn from that. We find that the spouting that occurs in its body through attainment of pleasure is what proliferates its life. For this reason, Providence has imprinted in the little ones, that every place they rest their eyes on gives them pleasure and contentment, even the most trifling things.

This is so because the level of the small must proliferate sufficiently to grow and sprout, and this is why their pleasure is copious. Thus you find that the Light of pleasure is the progenitor of life.

However, this law applies only in pleasures that come to the level as a whole. But in a pleasure of separation, when the pleasure is concentrated and received only by a separated part of the level of the Animal, we find the opposite rule. If there is a defective place in its flesh, which demands scratching and rubbing, the act of scratching carries its reward with it, as one feels great pleasure pursuing it. However, that pleasure is sodden with a drop of the potion of death: if one does not govern one's desire and pays the haunting demand, the payment will increase the debt.

In other words, according to the pleasure from scratching, so will the affliction increase and the pleasure will turn to pain. When it begins to heal again, a new demand for scratching appears, and at a greater extent than before. And if one still cannot govern one's desire and pays to saturate the demand, the affliction will grow as well.

Finally, it brings it a bitter drop, entirely poisoning the blood in that animal. You find that it died by receiving pleasure, since it is a pleasure of separation, received only by a separated part of the level. Hence, death operates in the level in the opposite manner from the pleasure administered to the entire level.

Here we see before us the form of the upper *Sitra Achra* from head to toe. Her head is the will to receive for herself alone, and to not bestow outside of herself, as is the property of the demand in the afflicted flesh with respect to the entire animal. The body of the *Sitra Achra* is a certain form of demand that is not going to be paid. The repayment one makes increases the debt and the affliction even more, as with the example of receiving pleasure by scratching.

The toe of the *Sitra Achra* is the drop of the potion of death, which robs it and separates it from the last spark of life it had left, like the drop of the potion of death that intoxicates all the blood in the animal.

This is the meaning of what our sages said, "in the end, it cometh and taketh his soul." In other words, they said that the angel of death comes with a drawn sword and a drop of poison at its tip; the person opens his mouth, he throws the drop inside, and he dies.

The sword of the angel of death is the influence of the *Sitra Achra*, called *Herev*[22] because of the separation that grows according to the measure of reception, and the separation destroys him. One is compelled to open one's mouth, since one must receive the abundance for sustenance and persistence from her hands. In the end, the bitter drop at the tip of the sword reaches him, and this completes the separation to the last spark of his breath of life.

20) As a result of these two corruptions, man's body was corrupted, too, as it is precisely adapted by Creation to receive the abundance of its sustenance from the system of *Kedusha*. This is so because in any viable act, its parts are guarded from any surplus or scarcity. An act that is not viable is because its parts are imbalanced and there is some shortage or surplus in them.

As he says in the Poem of Unification: "Of all Your work, not a thing You have forgotten; You did not add, and You did not subtract." It is a mandatory law that perfect operations stem from the perfect Operator.

However, when a person passes from the system of *Kedusha* to the system of the *Sitra Achra*, due to the barnacle attached to his construction by the Tree of Knowledge, many parts of him are already in surplus, needless. This is because they do not receive anything from the abundance of sustenance dispensed from the authority of the *Sitra Achra*, as we find with the *Luz* bone (*Zohar, Midrash HaNe'elam, Toladot*), and also in a certain portion of each and every organ.

Hence, one must receive sustenance into one's body more than is necessary, since the surplus joins every demand that rises from the body. Hence, the body receives for them. However, the surplus itself cannot receive its share; thus, its share remains in the body as surplus and litter that the body must later eject.

In consequence, the feeding and digesting tools exert in vain. They diminish and lessen to extinction because their sentence is predetermined, as that of any imbalanced act, destined to disintegrate. Thus you find that from the perspective of the construction of the body, too, its death depends on cause and effect from the Tree of Knowledge.

Now we have been awarded learning and knowing the two contradicting, opposite conducts (Item 11). The sustenance and keeping of the created beings has already passed from the system of *Kedusha* to the system of the *Sitra Achra*.

---

22 Translator's note: *Herev* means sword, but it comes from the Hebrew word *Harav* (destroyed)

This is so because of the barnacle of the great will to receive for oneself, connected to the created beings by the eating from the Tree of Knowledge. It induced separation, oppositeness, and hatred between the system of *Kedusha* and the structure of the bodies of the created beings in this world.

And when the *Kedusha* can no longer sustain and nurture them from the high table, to not destroy reality and to induce an act of correction for them, it gives the collective abundance of the sustenance of reality—her 288 sparks—to the system of the *Sitra Achra*, so they will provide for all creations in the world during the correction period.

For this reason, the conducts of existence are very confused, since evil sprouts from the wicked, and if the abundance is reduced to the created beings, it certainly brings ruin and destruction. And if abundance is increased, it brings excessive force of separation to the receivers, as our sages said, "He who has one hundred, wants two hundred; he who has two hundred wants four hundred."

It is like the separated pleasure that the separated and defected flesh senses, where increased pleasure increases separation and affliction. Thus, self-love greatly increases in the receivers, and one swallows one's friend alive. Also, the life of the body shortens, since the accumulation of reception brings the bitter drop at the end sooner, and wherever they turn they only condemn.

Now you can understand what is written in the *Tosfot* (*Ktubot* p104): "When one prays that Torah will enter one's body, one should pray that no delicacies will enter one's body." This is because the form of self-reception, which is the opposite of *Kedusha*, increases and multiplies by the measure of pleasure that one's body acquires.

Thus, how can one obtain the Light of Torah within one's body, when he is separated and in complete oppositeness of form from the *Kedusha*, and there is great hatred between them, as with all opposites: they hate each other and cannot be under the same roof.

Therefore, one must first pray that no delights or pleasures will enter one's body, and as the deeds in Torah and *Mitzvot* accumulate, one slowly purifies and inverts the form of reception to be in order to bestow. You find that one equalizes one's form with the system of *Kedusha*, and the equivalence and love between them returns, as prior to the sin of the Tree of Knowledge. Thus, one is awarded the Light of the Torah, since he entered the presence of the Creator.

21) Now it is thoroughly understood why the answer of the angels regarding man's creation, which we learned in the *Midrash* (Item 11), is not presented. It is because even the angels of Mercy and Righteousness did not agree to the present

man, since he has gone completely out of their influence and has become completely dependent on the *Sitra Achra*.

The *Midrash* ends: "He took Truth and threw it to the ground. They all said immediately, 'Let Truth spring out of the earth.'" This means that even the angels of Mercy and Righteousness regretted their consent, as they never agreed that Truth would be disgraced.

This incident occurred at the time of the eating from the Tree of Knowledge, when Truth was absent from the management of the sustenance of reality, since the scrutinizing force imprinted in man by Creation, which operates by the sensation of bitter and sweet, has weakened and failed (Item 17).

This is so because the provision for sustenance, which are 288 different *Behinot*, were already as clear as day, connected in the system of *Kedusha*. And "the palate tasteth its food," to attract in full all that is beloved and sweet, and to reject all that is bitter, so no man shall fail in them.

However, after the first tasting of the Tree of Knowledge, for which the *Gadlut* form of self-reception has stuck to them, their body and the *Kedusha* became two opposites. At that time, the abundance of sustenance, which is the 288 *Behinot*, went to the hands of the *Sitra Achra*.

You find that the 288 sparks that had already been sorted were remixed by the *Sitra Achra*. Thus, a new form was made in reality—the form whose beginning is sweet and whose end is bitter.

This was because the form of the 288 has been changed by the *Sitra Achra*, where the Light of pleasure brings separation and a bitter drop. This is the form of falsehood; the first and foremost progenitor of every destruction and confusion.

It is written, "He took Truth and threw it to the ground." Thus, because of the serpent, a new discernment was added to man—the active cognitive force. It operates by discernments of true and false, and one must use it throughout the correction period, for without it the benefit is impossible (Item 17).

Come and see all the confusion caused by the fall of the 288 sparks into the hands of the *Sitra Achra*. Before they tasted from the Tree of Knowledge, the woman could not even touch the forbidden thing (Item 17). By mere nearness to the Tree of Knowledge, she tasted bitterness that tasted like death. For this reason, she understood and added the prohibition on touching. And after the first eating, when the *Sitra Achra* and falsehood already controlled the sustenance of reality, the prohibition became so sweet in its beginning that they could no longer retire from it. This is why he said, "I have eaten and I shall eat more."

Now you understand why the reward in the Torah is intended only for the ripe bodies. It is because the whole purpose of the Torah is to correct the sin of the Tree of Knowledge, which induced the confusion of the conduct of the sustenance of reality.

It is for this correction that the Torah was given—to elevate the 288 sparks to *Kedusha* once more. At that time, the conduct of the sustenance will return to the *Kedusha* and confusions will cease from the modes of the sustenance of reality. Then, people will be brought to their desired perfection by themselves, solely by the discernment of bitter and sweet, which was the first operator, prior to the sin of the Tree of Knowledge.

The prophets, too, speak only of this correction, as it is said, "All the prophets prophesied only for the days of the Messiah." This is the meaning of the restoration of the modes of sustenance of the world under sorted Providence, as it was prior to the sin. "But for the next world" implies the end of the matter, which is the equivalence of form with the Maker, "neither hath the eye seen a God beside Thee." It is also written that in the days of the Messiah, if Egypt does not rise, it will not rain on them, meaning through discernments of good and bad.

22) Now we understand the words of our sages that the Creator did not find a vessel that holds a blessing for Israel but peace. We asked, "Why was this statement chosen to end the Mishnah?"

According to the above, we understand that the eternal soul of life that the Creator had blown in his nostrils, only for the needs of *Adam ha Rishon*, has departed because of the sin of the Tree of Knowledge. It acquired a new form, called "Sweat of Life," meaning the general has been divided into a great many particulars, tiny drops, divided between *Adam ha Rishon* and all his progeny through the end of time.

It follows, that there are no changes in the acts of the Creator, but there is rather an additional form here. This common Light of life, which was packed in the nose of *Adam ha Rishon* has expanded into a long chain, revolving on the wheel of transformation of form in many bodies, body after body, until the necessary end of correction.

It turns out that he died at the very day he ate from the Tree of Knowledge, and the eternal life departed him. Instead, he was tied to a long chain by the procreation organ (which is the meaning of the copulation, called "Peace").

You find that one does not live for oneself, but for the whole chain. Thus, each and every part of the chain does not receive the Light of life into itself, but only distributes the Light of life to the whole chain. This is also what you find in one's days of life: at twenty, he is fit to marry a woman; and ten years he may wait to bear sons; thus, he must certainly father by thirty.

Then he sits and waits for his son until he is forty years of age, the age of *Bina* (understanding), so he may pass onto him the fortune and knowledge he has acquired by himself, and everything he had learned and inherited from his forefathers, and he will trust him to not lose it for an ill matter. Then he promptly passes away, and his son grips the continuation of the chain in his father's place.

It has been explained (Item 15) that the incident of the sin of the Tree of Knowledge was mandatory for *Adam ha Rishon*, as it is written, "Libel is terrible for the children of men." This is so because one must add to one's structure an outer *Kli* to receive the Surrounding Light, so the two opposites will come in one subject, in two consecutive times. During the *Katnut* period, he will be dependent on the *Sitra Achra*. His vessels of reception of the Vacant Space will grow to their desired measure by the separated pleasures that one receives because of them.

Finally, when one reaches *Gadlut* and engages in Torah and *Mitzvot*, the ability to turn the great vessels of reception in order to bestow will be readily available. This is the primary goal, called "The Light of Truth," and "The Seal" (Item 14).

However, it is known that before one connects to the *Kedusha*, one must retire once more from any form of reception that he had received from the table of the *Sitra Achra*, as the commandment of love came to us, "with all thy heart and with all thy soul." Hence, what have the sages done by this correction if one loses everything he has acquired from the *Sitra Achra*?

For this reason, His Providence provided the proliferation of the bodies in each generation, as our sages said, "He saw that the righteous were few, He stood and planted them in each generation." This means that He saw that in the end, the righteous will repel the matter of self-reception altogether and thus their Surrounding Light would diminish, since the outer *Kli* that is fit for it will be repelled from them.

For this reason, He planted them in each and every generation, because in all generations, a large number of the people are created primarily for the righteous, to be the carriers of the *Kelim* of the Vacant Space for them. Thus, the Outer *Kli* would necessarily operate in the righteous involuntarily.

This is so because all the people in the world are attached to one another. They affect one another both in bodily inclinations and in opinions. Therefore, they necessarily bring the inclination for self-reception to the righteous, and in this manner they can receive the desired Surrounding Light.

However, accordingly, the righteous and the wicked should have been of equal weight in each generation. Yet, this is not so, and for each righteous, we find many thousands of vain ones. Yet, you must know that there are two kinds of governance in creation: a) a qualitative force; b) a quantitative force.

The force of those that hang about the feet of the *Sitra Achra* is meager, contemptible, and low, undesirable, and purposeless, and they are blown like chaff in the wind. Thus, how can such as those do anything to wise-hearted people whose way is clear with desire and aim, and a pillar of Upper Light shines before them day and night sufficiently to bring the tiny inclinations in their hearts?

Hence, He provided the quantitative force in Creation, as this force does not need any quality. I will explain it to you by the way we find the qualitative force in strength, such as in lions and tigers, where because of the great quality of their strength no man will fight them.

Opposite them, we find strength and power without any quality, as in the flies. But because of their numbers, no man will fight them. These wanderers roam man's house and set table freely and it is man who feels weak against them.

However, with wild flies, insects, and other such uninvited guests, although the quality of their strength is greater than the domestic flies, man will not rest until he entirely banishes them from his domain. This is so because nature did not allot them the reproduction ability of flies.

Accordingly, you can see that there must necessarily be a great multitude for every single righteous. They instill their crude inclinations in him through the power of their numbers, as they have no quality whatsoever.

This is the meaning of the verse, "The Lord will give strength unto His people." It means that the eternal Light of life, attained by the whole chain of creation, is called "Strength." The text guarantees that the Creator will surely give us that strength.

Yet, we should ask, How so? Since every person is not whole in and of himself, as our sages have written, 'It is better for one to not be born than to be born,' why then are we sure of His eternity?"

And the verse ends, "the Lord will bless his people with peace," meaning the blessing of the sons. It is as our sages said in *Masechet Shabbat*, "who makes peace in the house is idle." It is so because through the sons, this chain is tied and linked through the end of correction. At that time, all the parts will be in eternity.

For this reason, our sages said, "The Creator did not find a receptacle that holds a blessing for Israel, but peace." Because as His blessing is eternal, the receivers should be eternal.

Thus you find that through the sons, the fathers hold, and create among them the chain of eternity, fit to hold the blessing for eternity. It follows that it is peace that holds and conducts the wholeness of the blessing.

Hence, our sages ended the Mishnah with this verse, since peace is the vessel that holds the blessing of the Torah and all the *Mitzvot* for us until the complete and eternal redemption soon in our days Amen, and everything will come to its place in peace.

Matter and Form in the Wisdom of Kabbalah

As a whole, science is divided into two parts: one is called "material research" and the other, "formative research." This means that matter and form are perceived in every element of the entire reality before us.

For example, a table consists of matter, meaning the wood, and consists of form, the shape of a table. The matter, being the wood, is the carrier of the form: the table. Also, in the word "liar," there is matter, which is a person, and there is a form: the lie. The matter, which is the person, carries the form of a lie, meaning the custom of telling lies. And so it is in everything.

Hence, science, too, which researches the elements of reality, is divided into two parts: material research and formative research. The part of science that studies the quality of the substances in reality, both materials without their form, and materials along with their forms, is called "material research." This research is empirical, based on evidence and deductions derived from practical experimentation, and these practical experimentations are treated as a sound basis for valid deductions.

The other part of science studies only forms abstracted from materials, without any contact with the substances themselves. In other words, they shed the forms of true and false from the materials, which are the people who carry them, and engage only in research to know such values of superiority and inferiority in these forms of truth and falsehood as they are for themselves, bare, as though they were never clothed in any matter. This is called "formative research."

This research is not based on practical experiments, for such abstract forms do not appear in practical experiments, as they do not exist in the actual reality. This is because such an abstract form is imaginary, meaning only the imagination can picture it, even though it does not exist in the actual reality.

Hence, any scientific research of this kind is necessarily based solely on a theoretical basis. This means that it is not taken from practical experimentation, but only from a research of theoretical negotiations.

The whole of the higher philosophy belongs to this kind; hence, many contemporary intellectuals have left it, since they are displeased with any research built on a theoretical basis. They believe it is not a sound basis, for they consider only the experimental basis as sound.

And the wisdom of Kabbalah, too, is divided into these two parts: "material research" and "formative research." But here there is a great advantage over secular sciences: here, even the part of formative research is built entirely on the critique of practical reason, meaning on a practical, empirical basis.

This Is for Judah

That bread, which our fathers ate in the land of Egypt. The *Mitzva* of eating *Matza*[23] was given to the children of Israel even before they departed Egypt, relating to the future exodus, which was to be in haste. It follows that the *Mitzva* of eating a *Matza* was given to them while they were still enslaved, and the aim of the *Mitzva* was for the time of redemption, since then they departed in haste.

This is why we like to remember the eating of *Matzas* in Egypt even today, since we, too, are as when we were enslaved abroad. Also, with this *Mitzva*, we aim to extend the redemption that will happen soon in our days, Amen, just as our fathers ate in Egypt.

This year—here... next year—free. It is written above that with the aim of this *Mitzva* we can evoke the guaranteed redemption, destined for us, as in the *Mitzva* of eating the *Matza* of our fathers in Egypt.

We were slaves... It is written in *Masechet Pesachim* (p 116), "Begins with denunciation, and ends with praise." Concerning the denunciation, Rav and Shmuel were in dispute: Rav said to begin with "in the beginning, our fathers were idol worshipers," and Shmuel said to begin with "We were slaves." The practice follows Shmuel.

We need to understand this dispute. The reason for "beginning with denunciation and ending in praise" is, as it is written, "as far as light excelleth darkness." Hence, we must remember the issue of the denunciation, that through it we acquire thorough knowledge of the mercies of the Creator with us.

It is known that our whole beginning is only in denunciation, since "absence precedes presence." This is why "a wild ass's colt is born a man." And in the end, he acquires the shape of a man. This applies to every element in Creation, and this was so in the rooting of the Israeli nation, too.

---

23 Unleavened bread eaten by Jews during the holiday of Passover

The reason for it is that the Creator elicited Creation existence from absence. Hence, there is not a single creation that was not previously in absence. However, this absence has a distinct form in each element in creation, because when we divide reality into four types: still, vegetative, animate, and speaking, we find that the beginning of the still is necessarily complete absence.

However, the beginning of the vegetative is not complete absence, but merely its former degree, which, compared to itself, is considered absence. And in the matter of sowing and decay, which are necessary for any seed, it is received from the shape of the still. Also, it is the same with the absence of the animate and the speaking: the vegetative form is considered absence, with respect to the animate; and the animate form is considered absence, with respect to the speaking.

Hence, the text teaches us that the absence that precedes man's existence is the form of the beast. This is why it is written, "a wild ass's colt is born a man," as it is necessary for every person to begin in the state of a beast. And the writing says, "Man and beast Thou preserves, O Lord." And as a beast is given all that it needs for its sustenance and the fulfillment of its purpose, He also provides man with all that is necessary for his substance and the fulfillment of his purpose.

Therefore, we should understand where is the advantage of man's form over the beast, from the perspective of their own preparation. Indeed, it is discerned in their wishes, since man's wishes are certainly different from those of a beast. And to that extent, God's salvation of man differs from God's salvation of a beast.

Thus, after all the inquiries and scrutinies, we find that the only need in man's wishes, which does not exist in the whole of the animate species, is the awakening towards Godly *Dvekut* (adhesion). Only the human species is ready for it, and none other.

It follows that the whole issue of presence in the human species is in that preparation imprinted in him to crave His work, and in that, he is superior to the beast. And many have already said that even the intelligence in craftsmanship and in political conducts is present, with great wisdom, in many elements in the animal world.

Accordingly, we can also understand the matter of the absence that precedes the existence of man as the negation of the desire for God's proximity, since one is in the animate degree. Now we understand the words of the phrase that said, "Begins with denunciation, and ends with praise." This means that we must remember and research the absence that precedes our existence in a positive manner, as this is the denunciation that precedes the praise, and from it we will understand the praise more profoundly, as it is written, "Begins with denunciation, and ends with praise."

This is also the meaning of our four exiles, exile by exile, which precede the four redemptions, redemption by redemption, up to the fourth redemption, which is the complete perfection that we hope for soon in our days, Amen. Exile refers to "absence that precedes the presence," which is redemption. And since this absence is what prepares for the *HaVaYaH* ascribed to it, like the sowing that prepares the reaping, all the letters of redemption are present in exile, except for the *Aleph*, since this letter indicates the "*Aluph* (Champion) of the world."[24]

This teaches us that the form of the absence is but the negation of the presence. And we know the form of the presence—redemption—from the verse, "and they shall teach no more every man his neighbor ...for they shall all know Me, from the least of them unto the greatest of them." Hence, the form of the previous absence, meaning the form of exile, is only the absence of the knowledge of the Lord. This is the absence of the *Aleph*, which is missing in the *Gola* (exile), and present in the *Geula* (redemption)—the *Dvekut* with the "Champion of the world." This is precisely the redemption of our souls, no more and no less, as we have said that all the letters of *Geula* are present in *Gola*, but the *Aleph*, which is the Champion of the world.

To understand this weighty issue, that the absence in itself is what prepares the presence ascribed to it, we should learn from the conducts of this corporeal world. We see that in the concept of freedom, which is a sublime concept, only a chosen few perceive it, and even they require appropriate preparations. But the majority of the people are utterly incapable of perceiving it. Conversely, with regards to the concept of enslavement, the small and the great are equal: even the least among the people will not tolerate it.

(We saw that in Poland, they lost their kingdom only because the majority of them did not properly understand the merit of freedom and did not preserve it. Hence, they fell under the burden of subjugation under the Russian government for a hundred years. During that time, they all suffered under the burden of subjugation and desperately sought freedom from least to great. And although they did not yet assume the taste of freedom as it truly is, each of them imagined it as they wanted, but in the absence of freedom, which is subjugation, it was thoroughly engraved in their hearts to cherish freedom.

For this reason, when they were liberated from the burden of subjugation, many of them were bewildered, not knowing what they have gained by this

---

24 Translator's note: In Hebrew, the difference between the words *Galut* (exile) and *Ge'ula* (redemption) is in the addition of the letter *Aleph* to the latter.

freedom. Some of them even regretted it and said that their government was burdening them with even more taxes than the foreign government, and wished for their return. This was so because the force of absence did not sufficiently affect them.)

Now we can understand the dispute between Rav and Shmuel. Rav interprets the phrase as beginning with denunciation, so that through it the salvation will be thoroughly appreciated. Hence, he says to begin from the time of Terah. And he does not say what Shmuel does, since in Egypt, His love and work was already planted in a few within the nation. Also, the added difficulty of enslavement in Egypt is not a deficiency in itself in the life of the nation called "Adam."

And Shmuel interprets the phrase, saying that because the absence prepares the presence, it is considered a part of His salvation, and should be met with gratitude, as well. Hence, we should not begin with, "in the beginning, our fathers were idol worshipers," since that time is not even regarded as "absence that precedes the presence." This is because they are completely devoid of the human type of presence, since they were completely removed from His love, like the neuter, which is devoid of love.

Hence, we begin with the enslavement in Egypt, when the sparks of His love were burning in their hearts, to an extent, but due to impatience and hard work, it was being quenched every day. This is considered "absence that precedes the presence," and this is why he says to begin with "we were slaves."

And also, it is because the concept of the freedom of the nation in the knowledge of God is a very high concept, which only a chosen few understand, and even then it requires appropriate preparations, but the majority of the people have not attained that. Conversely, perceiving the hardships of enslavement is clear to all, as the Even Ezra wrote in the beginning of *Parashat Mishpatim*, "Nothing is harder for man than to be in the authority of another man like him."

The Acting Mind

Every person is obliged to attain the root of his soul. This means that the aspired-for purpose of the created being is *Dvekut* (adhesion) with His qualities, "As He is merciful, etc." His qualities are the Holy *Sefirot*, and this is the acting mind that guides His world and by which it allots them His benevolence and abundance.

But we must understand why this is called, "*Dvekut* with the Creator," as it seems to be mere study. I shall explain it with an allegory: In every act in the world, the mind of its operator remains in that act. In a table, one can attain the carpenter's dexterity and deftness in his craft, whether great or small. This is so because while working, he built it according to his mind, the qualities of his mind. And one who observes this act and considers the mind imprinted in it, during this act, he is attached to the mind that performed it, that is, they actually unite.

This is so because in fact, there is no distance and cessation between spirituals, even when they are in distinct bodies. But the mind in them cannot be distinguished, since what knife can cut the spiritual and leave it separated? Rather, the main difference between spirituals is in their qualities—praiseworthy or blameworthy—and the composition, since a mind that calculates astrology will not cling to one that contemplates natural sciences.

And there is great diversity even within the same teaching, for if one exceeds another in even one element, it separates the spirituals from one another. But when two sages contemplate the same teaching and bear the same measure of sagacity, they are in fact united, for what separates them?

Hence, when one contemplates another's action and attains the mind of the sage who performed it, they have the same mind and power. Thus, now they are completely united, like a man who met his beloved friend on the street, he embraces him and kisses him, and for their utter unity, they cannot be separated.

Hence, the rule is that in the Speaking, the mind is the best-adjusted force between the Creator and His creatures. It is considered the medium, meaning He conferred a spark of that force, and through that spark, everything returns to Him.

And it is written, "In wisdom hast Thou made them all," meaning that He created the whole world with His wisdom. Hence, one who is rewarded with attaining the manners by which He had created the world and its conducts is adhered to the Mind that performed them. Thus, he adheres to the Creator.

This is the meaning of the Torah being all the Names of the Creator, which belong to the creatures. And by their merit, the creature attains the Mind that affects everything, since the Creator was looking in the Torah when He created the world, and one achieves illumination through Creation and forever cleaves to that Mind; thus, he is adhered to the Creator.

Now we understand why the Creator has shown us His tools of craftsmanship. For do we need to create worlds? But from the above-mentioned, we gather that the Creator has shown us His conducts so we may know how to adhere to Him, which is "cleaving unto His qualities."

Introduction to the Book, From the Mouth of a Sage

It is known from books and from authors that the study of the wisdom of Kabbalah is an absolute must for any person from Israel. And if one studies the whole Torah and knows the Mishnah and the Gemarah by heart, and if one is also filled with virtues and good deeds more than all his contemporaries, but has not learned the wisdom of Kabbalah, he must reincarnate into this world to study the secrets of Torah and wisdom of truth. This is brought in several places in the writing of our sages.

This is what *The Zohar* writes in the interpretation to the *Song of Songs*, explaining the verse, "If thou know not, O thou fairest among women," which our sages interpreted as a soul that comes before the Thrown after one's demise.

The Creator tells it: "If thou know not, O thou fairest among women." Although you are the fairest among women and virtuous in good deeds more than all the souls, if you do not have knowledge in the secrets of Torah, "go thy way forth by the footsteps of the flock," leave here and never return to this world. "And feed thy kids, beside the shepherds' tents," go there to the seminaries and learn the secrets of Torah from the mouths of the disciples of our sages.

We must understand their words, conditioning one's perfection on the study of the wisdom of truth. Seemingly, how is it different from the other words of the revealed Torah? We found nowhere that one is obligated to understand all the subjects of the Torah, and that he will not be completed if one subject in the Torah is missing. Moreover, our sages said that it is not the study that is the most important, but the act. Our sages also said, "One does much, the other little, as long as they aim their hearts to Heaven," and there are many such sayings.

In order to attain the depth of their above words, we must first understand what has been written many times in *The Zohar* and the *Tikkunim* (Corrections of *The Zohar*), wisely and daintily: "The Torah, the Creator, and Israel, are one." This seems very perplexing.

Before I elucidate their words, I will notify you that our sages have defined a great rule for us, regarding all the holy names and appellations in the books. These are their golden words: "Anything that we do not attain, we do not define by a name."

Interpretation: It is known that there is no thought and perception in Him whatsoever, as it is written in the article "Elijah Started" in the beginning of the *Tikkunim* of *The Zohar*. For that reason, even the thought of the "Self" of the Creator is forbidden, much less the speech.

All the names we call Him do not refer to His Self, but only to His Lights, expanding from Him to the lower ones. Even the holy name, *Ein Sof* (Infinity), presented in the Kabbalah books, is also regarded as Light that expands from His Essence.

But since He determined that His Light, which expands from His Self, will be attained by the lower ones as *Ein Sof*, we shall therefore define it by that name. Yet, this does not refer to His Essence, since there is absolutely no perception or thought in Him. Thus, how shall we define Him by a name and a word, since all that we do not attain, we do not define by a name?

Any novice in the wisdom of truth must contemplate the above great rule before any scrutiny in a book of Kabbalah, that even the thought is forbidden in His Self, since there is no perception in Him whatsoever. Thus, how do we mention a name or a word in Him, which indicates attainment?

However, it is a great *Mitzva* to examine and research in His illuminations, which expand from Him, which are all the holy names and appellations brought in the books. It is an utter must for any person from Israel to study and understand the secrets of Torah and all the ways of His bestowal upon the lower ones, which are the gist of the wisdom of truth and the future reward of the souls at the end of correction.

It is written in the words of our sages, in *The Zohar*, and the *Tikkunim* that all the Upper Worlds and all the Holy *Sefirot* of the five worlds AK and ABYA have been prepared ahead of time in quantity and quality to complement the children of Israel. This is so because the soul of one from Israel is a part of God Above and "The end of an act is in the preliminary thought."

It arose in His Simple Will to delight with reward for their labor. And for that reason, the entire reality expanded before Him by way of a sequence of causes and their consequences in the descent of the degrees through the worlds AK and ABYA. Finally, they elicited two discernments clothed in one another: the soul from the concealments of heaven, which expands and robes the corporeal body.

The essence of reality expanded through the last degree, which is the corporeal body with a soul. Similarly, the concatenation was made by way of cause and consequence, relating to the essence of the existence of reality, which is the ways of His bestowal that hang down by gradations.

Thus, the Upper Light is Higher than High and will ultimately expand and come to the soul clothed in the corporeal body in this world, as it is written, "for the earth shall be full of the knowledge of the Lord, and they shall teach no more every man his neighbor, and every man his brother, saying: 'Know the Lord'; for they shall all know Me, from the least of them unto the greatest of them."

It is written by our sages and in *The Book of Zohar*, "The whole Torah is the names of the Creator." All the stories and the laws and the sentences, all are His Holy Names.

According to the explained above, that "Anything that we do not attain we do not define by a name," you will thoroughly understand the meaning of the Holy Names of the Creator. These are the attainments that expand from Him to His servants, the prophets and the righteous, each according to his merit, as it is written, "we are distinguished, I and Thy people, from all the people that are upon the face of the earth."

This distinguishing comes to us through the reception of the Torah and the keeping of *Mitzvot*, first only in the revealed way. It has the merit of purifying our bodies and enhancing our souls to such a measure that we become worthy of attaining the whole Torah and its *Mitzvot* as His Names. This is the whole reward intended for the souls at the end of correction. However, it is in this world, too, as it is written in the Gemarah, "You will see your world in your life."

That explains to us why he calls the 613 *Mitzvot* 613 counsels in several places in *The Zohar*, and in many other places in *The Zohar* he calls the 613 *Mitzvot* "613 deposits." This is so because at first, one must keep the Torah and the *Mitzvot* in order to purify his body and enhance his soul. At that time, the 613 *Mitzvot* are as 613 counsels for him, "tips" by which to gradually purify and be awarded coming before the King, and receiving the Light of his face. This is because keeping Torah and *Mitzvot* gradually purify him, until he is rewarded with the Light of the King's face.

Also, it is written similarly in the Gemarah: "The Creator cares not if one slaughters at the throat or slaughters at the back of the neck? Rather, we were given the Torah and *Mitzvot* only to purify Israel."

However, after one has been sufficiently purified and merits the Light of the King's face, one's eyes and soul open and he is awarded the attaining the 613 Sacred Lights found in the 613 *Mitzvot*. These are His Holy Names, the ones he can attain.

By keeping each of the *Mitzvot*, one takes the part of the Light deposited in that *Mitzva*, since the *Mitzva* is a *Kli* (vessel) where the Light is clothed, meaning a Holy Name that belongs specifically to that *Mitzva*. This is the meaning of "The *Mitzva* is a candle and the Torah—Light."

At that time, he calls the 613 *Mitzvot* "613 commandments (deposits)." It is like one who deposits good stones and gems in a vessel and says to his loved one: "Take this *Kli* for yourself but guard it from thieves and robbers." Thus, they only speak of the vessel, but their primary intention is the precious stones deposited there.

It is known in the books of Kabbalah that the meaning of the Holy Name, "The Holy One Blessed be He" or *Kudsha Brich Hu* (the same name in Aramaic) brought by our sages and in *The Zohar*, is named after the *HaVaYaH* (*Yod-Hey-Vav-Hey*). This Holy Name contains all the Holy Names until one Higher than High. Thus, we learn that "The Torah and the Creator are one," albeit the masses do not see Him in the Torah, but only stories, sentences, and laws.

Indeed, I have already explained that "apples of gold in settings of silver" is how the 613 deposits are called, as our sages said, "The whole Torah is the names of the Creator." Hence, the Torah and the Creator are one.

Yet, there are general and particular, where the Creator is the assembly of all the names, and the general Light, and the Torah is divided into 613 Lights. It follows that all of them together are one, and are the Creator Himself.

Now there still remains for us to explain the discernment of Israel. First, you must understand the matter of multiplicity of separate forms in spirituality, meaning how they are divided and in what. Corporeal things are separated by a knife and such, or time and place separate and distinguish them. Yet, this is unthinkable in spirituality, as it is known to be above time and place.

However, know that the whole difference in spirituality between the Upper Lights is only in the disparity of form. For example: the mental souls in people are certainly divided into separate souls. Each individual has a different soul.

Yet, the essential difference between them is nothing more then stemming out of their disparity in form, that the soul of one is good, the other's is bad; one has acquired wisdom, and the other folly, etc. Our sages say about that, "As their faces differ from one another, their views differ from one another."

Now we can understand that if all people were to come by equal concepts and inclinations, without any difference whatsoever, all the souls of all the people would be regarded as one soul. Its value would be like the light of the sun: the light clothes in all the inhabitants of the world, yet we do not discern that there are separate forms in the sunlight. Similarly, one conceptual soul would robe many bodies, since places do not separate at all in spiritual matters if there are no separate forms in their qualities.

Now we shall come to the actual scrutiny: It is known that the meaning of the souls of the children of Israel is that they are a part of God Above. The soul cascaded by way of cause and consequence and descended degree-by-degree until it became suitable to come into this world and clothe the filthy corporeal body.

By keeping the Torah and observing its *Mitzvot*, it ascends degree-by-degree until its stature is completed, and it is fit to receive its reward from The Whole. This has been prepared for it in advance, meaning attaining the holy Torah by way of the Names of the Creator, which are the 613 deposits.

Now you can see with your own eyes that "The Torah and Israel are one." And the only difference between the Torah and the soul is due to the disparity of form in the soul, which has been reduced to a very, very small Light, and the Torah is Simple Light that expands from His Essence, whose sublimity is endless, as it is written "The Torah and the Creator are one."

However, when the soul is complete in its full stature and receives the Torah by way of His Names, namely attains all the Light deposited in the Torah and *Mitzvot*, you find that, in any case, the Light of the soul is equal to the Light of Torah. This is because it has already attained all the Light in the Torah.

It is still considered incomplete as long as there is some deficit in attaining a small and subtle part of the general Light of the Torah. This is because all its Light has been prepared for the souls, as I have explained above, "All that we do not attain, we do not define by a name."

And since the Light has been prepared for the attainment of the soul, and the soul did not attain all of it, it is therefore deemed incomplete, as in, "I will keep the whole Torah except one thing. Certainly, he is a complete wicked."

However, such as that you can declare in the keeping of the Torah and *Mitzvot* in attaining the 613 deposits. It is incomplete when lacking even one thing, great or small.

Hence, it will finally come to complete perfection, namely attain the whole Light of the Torah. At that time, there will be no disparity of form between the Light of the soul and the Light of Torah anyhow. Thus, you find, daintily, that "The Torah and Israel are one," literally.

Because there is no difference or disparity of form between them, they are literally one. And since we have already proven that "The Creator and the Torah are one," and now we have proven that "The Torah and Israel are one," it is therefore evident that "The Torah and the Creator and Israel are one."

From all the above, you find that there are two parts in the Torah and *Mitzvot*:

A. The Torah and *Mitzvot* as they appear to all, being the keeping of *Mitzvot* and the study of Torah in the form of 613 counsels. These have the power to purify and cleanse the body, and enhance the merit of the soul, to be worthy and merit receiving the Light of the King's face, as the soul was in its root, before it diminished and came into this base body in the base world.

B. Keeping the *Mitzvot* and studying the Torah in the form of 613 deposits, namely the matter of attaining His Names and the full reward of the souls.

The merit of the latter part over the former is as the merit of Heaven over Earth. This is because the first part is mere preparation, and the second part is the actual completeness and the purpose of Creation.

This explains our above question about the words of our sages, that even if a person excels in Torah and good deeds more than all his contemporaries, if he has not learned the secrets of Torah and the wisdom of truth, he must reincarnate in the world.

We asked, "What is the difference between this subject in the wisdom of truth from other subjects in the Torah?" We found nowhere that one is compelled to engage in all the topics in the Torah. On the contrary, we have found opposition to that in many places, such as, "One does much, the other little, as long as they aim their hearts to Heaven," and also, "It is not the study that is important, but the act."

Now the matter is clarified—the whole part of the revealed Torah is but a preparation to become worthy and merit attaining the concealed part. It is the concealed part that is the very wholeness and the purpose for which man is created.

Hence, clearly, if a part of the concealed part is missing, although one may keep the Torah and observe its commandments in the revealed part, he will still have to reincarnate to this world and receive what he should receive, namely the concealed part, by way of 613 deposits. Only in that is the soul completed, the way the Creator had predetermined for it.

You can therefore see the utter necessity for anyone from Israel, whoever he may be, to engage in the internality of the Torah and in its secrets. Without it, the intention of Creation will not be completed in him.

This is the reason why we reincarnate, generation-by-generation through our current generation, which is the residue of the souls upon which the intention of Creation has not been completed, as they did not attain the secrets of the Torah in the past generations.

For this reason, they said in *The Zohar*: "The secrets of Torah and its mysteries are destined to be revealed at the time of the Messiah." It is clear to anyone who understands, that since they will be completing the intention of Creation, they will be awarded the coming of the Messiah. Hence, inevitably, the secrets of the Torah will be revealed among them openly, since if the correction is prevented they will be compelled to reincarnate.

This will explain to you what we should ask about this interpretation in general, for who am I and who are my fathers that I have been awarded making the interpretation to expand the knowledge of the hidden secrets in *The Zohar* and the writings of the Ari? Moreover, why have we thus far found no other to interpret this wisdom as openly as me?

Now you can see that because our generation is really the time of the Messiah, and we are all standing at the threshold of the complete correction, and the only prevention is the complete abandonment of the wisdom of truth in this generation, due to the difficulty of the language and the dispersion of the matters.

In addition to all that, there is the smallness of the mind and the abundant troubles in our generation. Hence, when the Lord wishes to hasten the redemption of our souls, He has passed a privilege onto my hand to disclose the measure in this interpretation, and the will of God succeeded in my hand.

And I had another reason for making this open interpretation, as it is written in *The Zohar*, "One must learn a little even from nonsense," as it is written, "as far as light excelleth darkness." After I completed my time in the city of Warsaw in the state of Poland, confined to my chamber, having nothing to do with the darkness of my surroundings, I have been blessed with settling in the Holy City of Jerusalem.

And when I walked among the people here, I saw the poverty of my people, the poverty of their mind. Their foolish laughter was in my ears as the noise of pots under the city, mocking and trampling the heart and soul of our yearnings, slandering the Lord, His Law, and His people in a loud voice, without any wisdom, understanding, and knowledge in the wisdom of Kabbalah at all. Rather, it is an assortment of words and names, no sense and no moral, only literal words.

It is a privilege to chatter idle words in the written text with complete faith that they are holy things, and that thus the purpose of Creation will be completed upon us. And when those who engage in the literal texts with complete faith increase in number, the Messiah King will come at once, for by that the whole correction will be completed, and nothing more is needed.

Finally, I met with the famous ones among them, people who have already worn out their years delving in the writings of the Ari and *The Zohar*. They have so succeeded that they have become proficient and conversant in all the writings of the Ari.

They have a reputation as being the holiest people in the land. I asked them if they had studied with a Rav who attained the internality of the matters. They answered: "Heavens, no! There is no internality here whatsoever, but accurate texts, given to us, and nothing more than that, God forbid."

I asked them if Rav Chaim Vital had attained the internality of the matters. They replied: "He certainly did not attain more than we do." I then asked them about the Ari himself. They answered: "He certainly did not know the internality more than us at all, and all that he knew, he had passed on to his disciple, Rav Chaim Vital, and thus they came into our hands."

I mocked them: "How then were the matters composed in the heart of the Ari without any understanding and knowledge?" They replied: "He received the composition of these matters from Elijah, and he knew the internality, since he is an angel." Here my wrath poured out on them, for my patience to be with them had ended.

And when I saw that their folly had found roots in nearly everyone engaging in this wisdom at this time, woe to the ears that so hear, "Will he even force the queen before me in the house?"

The Holy *Zohar* had already mourned bitterly the denial of the sinners in their souls, saying that there are no internal secrets in the Torah, as it is written in *Parashat Vayerah*: "Has the Torah come to show us fables and historic tales? Such stories and fables are found among other nations, too." Our sages said that they uproot the plantations, for they only take *Malchut*.

What would the authors of *The Zohar* say in view of the culture of such sinful people, denying that there is any knowledge or wisdom in the words of *The Zohar* and the wisdom of truth themselves? They say about the very secrets of the Torah that there is no knowledge or perception revealed in this world, but merely empty words. Thus, they have come to force the Holy Divinity inside the King's palace. Woe unto them, for they have caused their souls harm.

Our sages said that the Holy Torah mourns before the Creator: "Your sons have turned Me into a song in public-houses." But they do not even make of the Torah a semblance of a song, only frightening words to any listener that arise contempt and wrath.

Furthermore, they wish to be rewarded like Phinehas, saying that they do it in complete faith. The writing says about them: "Forasmuch as this people draw near, and with their mouth and with their lips do honor Me, but have removed their heart far from Me," and this is the reason for the ruin of the First Temple.

The devil still dances among us, precisely at the time of the Messiah, the time of the end of the secrets of the Torah. The zeal of the Lord of Hosts came as fire that will not quench in my bones. Because of that, I have been awakened to disclose the gown to such an extent that they will know that there is wisdom in Israel.

This has been among the primary reasons that made me come to this explanation. You must see in every purpose and every goal that it is utterly simple. All the wit, the cleverness, and the many issues form during the preparation, until the goal is reached. For example, when one wishes to sit in a house, he needs wit and knowledge in the design, in artisanship, and in the quality, and quantity of the rooms and the possessions.

The final goal is but a simple thing—to dwell there. This is the meaning of the words, "according to the beauty of a man, to dwell in the house." It is a simple thought, without any concepts and proliferation, and without wit, but a simple will.

Know that all the sophistications in the knowledge are mostly mistakes that should fall before the truth. Yet, the truth itself is simple, without any wit.

There is a secret in that, principally being the iron wall that separates us from our Father in Heaven: There are things that are hidden because of their great height and depth, and there are things that are hidden because of their extreme subtlety, like flies in the air, too thin to be seen.

Since His Light is such Simple Light that the human mind, which feels only a tiny portion of something, simply does not perceive. It is like the smaller things from that measure, requiring an actual tool to see.

This is so because although not all of the depth of the height and the depth of the width are perceived, you can nonetheless perceive the proximate. However, with subtle things, it seems as though they do not exist at all, since you do not attain even the slightest bit of them.

Introduction to the Preface to the Wisdom of Kabbalah

1) It is written in *The Zohar, Vayikra, Parashat Tazria*, p 40, "Come and see, all that exists in the world, exists for man, and everything exists for him, as it is written, 'Then the Lord God formed man,' with a full name, as we have established, that he is the whole of everything and contains everything, and all that is Above and below, etc., is included in that image."

Thus, it explains that all the worlds, Upper and lower, are included in man. And also, the whole of reality within those worlds is only for man. And we should understand these words: Is this world and everything in it, which serves him and benefits him, too little for man, that he needs the Upper Worlds and everything within them, too? After all, they were created solely for his needs.

2) To explain this matter to the fullest, I would have to introduce the whole of the wisdom of Kabbalah. But in general, matters will be sufficiently explained within the book, so as to understand them. The essence of it is that the Creator's intention in Creation was to delight His creatures. Certainly, as soon as He contemplated creating the souls and delighting them abundantly, they immediately emerged from before Him, complete in form and with all the delights He had planned to bestow upon them. This is because in Him, the thought alone completes, and He does not need actions as we do. Accordingly, we should ask, "Why did He create the worlds restriction by restriction down to this murky world, and clothe the souls in the murky bodies of this world?

3) The answer to that is written in *The Tree of Life*—"to bring to light the perfection of His deeds" (*The Tree of Life*, Branch One). Yet, we need to understand how could it be that incomplete operations would stem from a complete Operator, to the point that they would require completion through an act in this world?

The thing is that we should distinguish between Light and *Kli* (vessel) in the souls. The essence of the souls that were created is the *Kli* in them, and all the bounty that the He had planned to impart them with and delight them is the Light in them. This is because since He had planned to delight them, He necessarily made them as a desire to receive His pleasure, since the pleasure and delight increase according to the measure of desire to receive the abundance.

And know that that will to receive is the very essence of the soul with regard to the generation and elicitation existence from absence. This is considered the *Kli* of the soul, while the joy and the abundance are considered the Light of the soul, extending existence from existence from His essence.

4) Explanation: Creation refers to appearance of something that did not exist before. This is considered existence from absence. Yet, how do we picture something that is not included in Him, since He is almighty and includes all of them together? And also, one does not give what is not in Him.

As we have said, the whole Creation that He created is only the *Kelim* (plural for *Kli*) of the souls, which is the will to receive. This is quite clear, since He necessarily does not have a will to receive, as from whom would He receive? Hence, this is truly a new Creation, not a trace of which existed previously, and is hence considered existence from absence.

5) We should know that unification and separation applied in spirituality relate only to equivalence of form and disparity of form. This is because if two spiritual objects are of the same form, they are united, and they are one, and not two, since there is nothing to separate them from one another. They can only be discerned as two when there is some disparity of form between them.

Also, to the extent of their disparity of form, so is the measure of their distance from one another. Thus, if they are of opposite forms, they are considered as remote as the east from the west, meaning the greatest distance we can picture in reality.

6) But in the Creator, there is no thought or perception whatsoever, and we cannot utter or say anything with regard to Him. But since we know You by Your actions, we should discern that He is a desire to bestow, since He created everything in order to delight His creatures, and bestow His abundance upon us.

Thus, the souls are in oppositeness of form from Him, since He is all bestowal and has no will to receive anything, while the souls were imprinted with a will to receive for themselves. And we have already said that there is no greater oppositeness of form than that.

It follows that had the souls remained with the will to receive, they would forever remain separated from Him.

7) Now you will understand what is written (*The Tree of Life*, Branch One), that the reason for the creation of the worlds was that He must be complete in all His actions and powers, and if He did not execute His actions and powers in actual fact, He would seemingly not be considered whole. This seems perplexing, for how can incomplete actions emerge from a complete operator, to the extent that they would need correction?

From what has been explained, you can see that the essence of Creation is only the will to receive. On the one hand it is greatly deficient, since it is opposite in form from the Emanator, which is separation from Him, but on the other hand, this is the entire innovation and the existence from absence that He had created, by which to receive from Him what He had planned to bestow upon them.

Yet, had they remained separated from the Emanator, He would seemingly be incomplete, for in the end, complete operations must stem from the complete Operator.

For this reason, He restricted His Light and created the worlds restriction by restriction down to this world, and clothed the soul in a worldly body. And through the practice of Torah and *Mitzvot*, the soul obtains the perfection it lacked prior to Creation—the equivalence of form with Him. Thus, it will be fit to receive all the abundance and pleasure included in the Thought of Creation, and will also be in complete *Dvekut* (adhesion) with Him, in equivalence of form.

8) The matter of the *Segula* (power) of Torah and *Mitzvot* to bring the soul to *Dvekut* with Him applies only when the engagement in it is not in order to receive any reward, and only to bestow contentment upon his Maker. This is so because then the soul gradually acquires equivalence of form with its Maker, as will be written below concerning Rabbi Hanina's words in the beginning of the book ("Preface to the Wisdom of Kabbalah").

In all, there are five degrees—*Nefesh, Ruach, Neshama, Haya, Yechida* (NRNHY)—that come from the five worlds called *AK, Atzilut, Beria, Yetzira*, and *Assiya*. Also, there are five particular degrees NRNHY, which come from the five particular *Partzufim* (plural for *Partzuf*) in each of the five worlds. Then there are sub-particular NRNHY, which come from the ten *Sefirot* in each *Partzuf*, as will be written in the book.

And through Torah and *Mitzvot* to bestow contentment upon the Maker, one is gradually rewarded with the *Kelim* in the form of desire to bestow, which come in these degrees, degree by degree, until they achieve complete equivalence of form with Him. In that state, the Thought of Creation, to receive all the pleasure, tenderness, and abundance that He had planned for them is carried out. Additionally, they receive the greatest reward, since they are awarded the true *Dvekut*, since they have obtained the desire to bestow, like their Maker.

9) Now it will not be difficult for you to understand the above words of *The Zohar*, that all the worlds, Upper and lower and everything within them, was created only for man. This is so because all these degrees and worlds came only to complement the souls in the measure of *Dvekut* that they lacked with respect to the Thought of Creation.

In the beginning, they were restricted and hung down degree-by-degree and world after world, down to our material world, to bring the soul into a body of this world, which is entirely to receive and not to bestow, like animals and beasts. It is written, "A wild ass's colt is born a man." This is considered the complete will to receive, which has nothing in the form of bestowal. In that state, a man is regarded as the complete opposite of Him, and there is no greater remoteness than that.

Afterwards, through the soul that clothes within one, he engages in Torah and *Mitzvot*. Gradually and slowly, from below Upwards, he obtains the same form of bestowal as his Maker, through all those discernments that hung down from Above downwards, which are but degrees and measures in the form of the desire to bestow.

Each Higher degree means that it is farther from the will to receive, and closer to being only to bestow. In the end, one is awarded being entirely to bestow and to not receive anything for himself. At that time, one is completed with true *Dvekut* with Him, for this is the only reason why man was created. Thus, all the worlds and everything in them were created only for man.

10) Now that you have come to know all that, you are permitted to study this wisdom without any fear of materialization. This is because the students are very confused: on the one hand, it is said that the ten *Sefirot* and the *Partzufim*, from the beginning of the ten *Sefirot* of *Atzilut* to the end of the ten *Sefirot* of *Assiya*, are complete Godliness and unity.

But on the other hand, it is said that all these worlds are generated and appear after the *Tzimtzum* (restriction); but how can this even be conceived in Godliness? And there are also the numbers and Above and below and other such changes and ascents and descents and *Zivugim* (couplings). But it is written, "I the Lord do not change."

11) From what is clarified before us, it is clear that all these ascents, descents, restrictions, and the numbers are only regarded as *Kelim* (vessels) of the receivers—the souls. And we should distinguish between the potential and the actual in them, like a person who builds a house—the end of the act is in his preliminary thought.

But the quality of the house in his mind does not resemble the house that should actually be built, since the conceived house is spirituality, a conceptual substance, and is considered the substance of the thinking person. At that time, the house is only a potential. But when the building of the house begins in actual fact, it acquires an entirely different substance—that of wood and bricks.

Similarly, we should discern potential and actual in the souls. The beginning of their emergence from the Emanator into "actual" souls begins only in the world of *Beria*. And their integration in *Ein Sof*, prior to the *Tzimtzum*, with respect to the Thought of Creation, as written in Item 2, concerns only the "potential," without any actual manifestation.

In that sense, it is said that all the souls were integrated in *Malchut de Ein Sof*, called "the middle point," since this point is included in "potential" in all the *Kelim* of the souls that are destined to "actually" emerge from the world of *Beria* downwards. And the first restriction occurred only in this middle point, meaning precisely in that discernment and measure considered the "potential" of the future souls, and not at all in itself.

You should know that all the *Kelim* of the *Sefirot* and the worlds, through the world of *Beria*, which hang down and emerge from this point, or due to its *Zivug de Hakaa*, called *Ohr Hozer*, are also considered mere potential, without any essence of the souls. But these changes are destined to subsequently affect the souls whose essence begins to emerge from the world of *Beria* down, since there they have not yet departed the essence of the Emanator.

12) And I shall give you an allegory from the conducts of this world. For example, if a person who covers and hides himself behind clothes and garments so his friend would not see him and notice him, can it even be conceived that he himself would be affected by the concealment made by all the garments he is covered with?

Similarly, take the ten *Sefirot* we call **Keter, Hochma, Bina, Hesed, Gevura, Tifferet, Netzah, Hod, Yesod, Malchut** as an example. These are only ten coverings by which *Ein Sof* is covered and concealed. The souls that are destined to receive from it will be compelled to receive by those measures that the ten *Sefirot* allot them. Thus, the receivers are affected by this number of ten *Sefirot*, and not by His Light, which is one, unique, and unchanging.

The receivers divide into ten degrees, precisely according to the qualities of these names. Moreover, even these coverings we spoke of pertain only to the world of *Beria* and below, since this is where the souls that receive from these ten *Sefirot* are found. But in the worlds AK and *Atzilut*, there is no existence even to the souls, since there they are only in potential.

Hence, the ten above coverings in the ten *Sefirot* govern only in the three lower worlds, called *Beria*, *Yetzira*, and *Assiya*. But in the worlds BYA, the ten *Sefirot* are considered Godliness through the end of *Assiya*, just as in AK and ABYA, and as prior to the *Tzimtzum*.

The only difference is in the *Kelim* of the ten *Sefirot*: in AK and *Atzilut*, they do not even disclose their dominance, since they are only in "potential" there, and only in BYA do the *Kelim* of the ten *Sefirot* begin to manifest their concealing and covering force. But in the Light in the ten *Sefirot*, there is no change whatsoever due to these coverings, as was written in the allegory. This is the meaning of "I the Lord do not change."

13) We might ask, "Since there is no disclosure of the essence of the souls of the receivers in AK and *Atzilut*, what do those *Kelim*, called ten *Sefirot*, serve for, and whom do they conceal and cover in those measures?"

There are two answers to that: The first is the hanging down, as you will find inside the book. The second is that the souls, too, are destined to receive from those ten *Sefirot* in AK and *Atzilut*, through the ascension of the three worlds BYA to them (as will be written in Item 163 in the "Preface to the Wisdom of Kabbalah"). Hence, we should discern these changes in the ten *Sefirot* in AK and *Atzilut*, as well, according to the Light that they are destined to shine upon the souls once they rise there with the worlds BYA, for then they will receive according to the degree in those ten *Sefirot*.

14) Thus, we have thoroughly clarified that the worlds, the generation, the changes, and the number of degrees, etc., were said only with respect to the *Kelim* that give to the souls, and conceal and measure for them, so they can gradually receive from the Light of *Ein Sof* in them. But they do not affect the Light of *Ein Sof* itself in any way, since no coverings affect the one who is covered, but only the other, who wishes to feel it and receive from it, as said in the allegory.

15) In general, we should discern these three discernments in the *Sefirot* and *Partzufim* wherever they are: *Atzmuto* (His Self/Essence), *Kelim*, and Lights.

In *Atzmuto*—there is no thought or perception whatsoever. In the *Kelim*—there are always two opposite discernments: concealment and disclosure. This is so because in the beginning, the *Kli* covers *Atzmuto* in a way that these ten *Kelim* in the ten *Sefirot* are ten degrees of concealments.

But once the souls receive these *Kelim* under all the conditions in them, these concealments become disclosures for the attainments of the souls. Thus, the *Kelim* contain two opposite discernments, which are one. This is because the measure of disclosure in the *Kli* is precisely like the measure of concealment in the *Kli*, and the coarser the *Kli*, the more it conceals *Atzmuto*, and reveals a Higher degree. Thus, these two opposites are one.

And the Lights in the *Sefirot* refer to that measure of degree suitable for appearing for the attainment of the souls. Since everything extends from *Atzmuto*, and yet, there is no attainment in Him, but only in the qualities of the *Kelim*, there are necessarily ten Lights in these ten *Kelim*, meaning degrees of revelation to those receiving in the qualities of those *Kelim*.

Thus, His Light and His Essence are indistinguishable, except that in His Essence, there is no attainment or perception whatsoever, except for what comes to us from Him through clothing in the *Kelim* of the ten *Sefirot*. And in that respect, we refer to anything that we attain by the name, "Lights."

The Evolution of the Worlds

Foreword to the Preface to the Wisdom of Kabbalah

INTRODUCTION TO THE PREFACE TO THE WISDOM OF KABBALAH

1) All the worlds, Above and below, are within man, and the whole of reality was created for man alone. This is written in *The Book of Zohar*. So why do we feel different? We feel that we are within reality, not that reality is within us. Moreover, why is this world not enough for us? Why do we need the Upper Worlds?

2) The reason for the creation of reality is **the Creator's desire to benefit His creations**. Hence, the Creator created the creature with a nature of wanting to enjoy what the Creator wishes to bestow upon it. The Creator is above time and place; His Thought operates like the act itself.

Hence, when He wished and contemplated creating the creations, so as to fill them with delights, the creatures were immediately created, filled with all the pleasures they had received from the Creator. Yet, we do not feel that state, since it is merely our root, which we must achieve, according to the design of creation.

In creating the sequence of the worlds from the world of *Ein Sof* through this world, the Creator removed the creature from Himself down to the lowliest state. It is important to understand why He did that. Does this act indicate imperfection in His actions?

The Ari answers this question in the book, *The Tree of Life*: "to reveal the perfection of His deeds," so the creatures would perfect themselves and achieve the Creator's degree, which is the only true perfection. To help them, the Creator created the ladder of worlds. The souls climb down this ladder down to the lowest degree, where they clothe in corporeal bodies of this world. Then, through the study of Kabbalah, the souls themselves begin to rise and climb up that ladder, by which they had descended, until they return to the Creator.

3) The soul consists of Light and *Kli*. The Light of the soul comes from the Creator, from *Atzmuto* (His Essence). Through this Light, the *Kli* (vessel) of the soul was created, being the desire to receive Light, to enjoy the Light. Hence, the *Kli* perfectly fits the Light that comes to fill it.

The Light is a part of the Creator. The soul is the actual *Kli*. Hence, only the *Kli* is considered a creation. It was created from absence, meaning there was no desire before the Creator decided to create it. And because the Creator wished to give the perfect pleasure to this *Kli*, as is becoming of Him, He created this *Kli*—the will to receive—enormous, according to the measure of Light (pleasure) that He wished to give it.

4) Creation means initiation, something new that did not previously exist, and this initiation is called "existence from absence." But if the Creator is complete, how could something not be included in Him? From what has already been said, it is clear that prior to creation, there was no will to receive in the Creator, since the Creator is whole and wishes only to bestow. Hence, what is not in Him, and should be created, is only the desire to receive the pleasure from Him.

The will to receive is the whole of reality. Hence, the only difference between the elements of reality is in the measure of desire to receive in each element, and no two elements contain the same desire.

5) There are no physical bodies in spirituality. The spiritual world is a world of desires, "raw" forces, devoid of material clothing of any kind. Hence, all the words used in the wisdom of Kabbalah are actually appellations of the desire to enjoy, or its impressions of the fulfillment of the Light within it.

The Creator is the desire to bestow, and the creature is the desire to enjoy the Creator's bestowal. If the creature enjoys only because the Creator enjoys its reception, such an act is considered bestowal, according to its intention, and not as an act of receiving. This is regarded as the Creator's desire and creature's desire being equal, with nothing to separate them.

Thus, following the spiritual law of equivalence of form, as a result of equalizing their qualities (desires), they become one. In that state, they are not two identical desires, but are literally one. That spiritual state is called "equivalence of form" or *Dvekut* (adhesion).

However, if they do not have the same desire, the same intention, they do not have the same goal and they are separated. Because they have different qualities (desires), they are two, and not one. In spirituality, that state is called, "disparity of form."

The measure of equivalence of form between Creator and creature determines how their closeness and measure of disparity of form determine their distance from each other. In the beginning, the Creator's desire to bestow and the creature's desire to receive are equal, since the creature's will to receive was born from the Creator's desire to bestow. Hence:

- If all their desires (intentions) are the same, they are one;
- If all their desires (intentions) are opposite, they are as far as two extremes;
- If, of all the desires (intentions), they have only one common desire, then they are touching one another through that common desire;
- If some of the desires (intentions) are similar, they are as far or near as their measure of equivalence of form or disparity of form.

6) We have no attainment in the Creator Himself, in *Atzmuto*, since we attain only the sensation of the Light in the *Kli*, the filling in our desire. And what we do not attain, we cannot call by any name, since we assign names according to our impressions of the filling. Hence, we cannot say a single word or assign any name to *Atzmuto*. All our names and appellations, with respect to the Creator, are only reflections of what we feel towards Him.

We can feel Him and His actions only by the measure of equivalence of form (desire, intention) with Him. Hence, to the extent that we are similar to the Creator, we feel His desires and actions, and we name the Creator accordingly. When we feel them, we can name Him according to what we feel of Him. This is called "By Your actions, we know You."

7) Kabbalists are people who are living in this world and connect to the Creator according to their measure of equivalence of form while living in this world. Worlds are the different measures of sensation of the Creator. A "world" is the measure of disclosure or concealment of the Creator towards the creatures; and complete concealment is called "this world."

The beginning of the sensation of the Creator is the transition between this world and the spiritual world. The transition itself is called "barrier." There are 125 degrees of revelations of parts of the Creator to the creatures between concealment and complete disclosure. These parts are called "worlds."

Kabbalists climb the spiritual worlds by correcting their desires (intentions). They tell us—verbally or in text—that the Creator has only the desire to benefit. He created everything to give us all His abundance. This is why He created us with a desire to receive, so that we can receive what He wishes to give us.

The desire to receive for ourselves is our very nature. But in that nature, we are opposite in form from the Creator, since the Creator is only a desire to bestow, and does not possess a desire to receive. Hence, if we remain in the will to receive for ourselves, we will remain forever far from the Creator.

Kabbalists tell us that the Creator's purpose is to bring the whole of Creation to Himself, and that He is the absolute goodness. For this reason, He wishes to bestow upon everyone.

They also say that the reason for the creation of the worlds is that the Creator must be complete in all His actions and forces. And if He does not execute His forces in complete actions, He is seemingly considered incomplete.

But how could imperfect operations stem from the perfect Creator to the point that His actions would require correction by the creatures? We are His actions! If we must correct ourselves, does it not mean that His actions are imperfect?

The Creator created only the desire to receive, called "the creature." But when the creature receives what the Creator wishes to bestow upon it, it is separated from the Creator, since the Creator is the Giver and the creature is the receiver, and in that, they are opposites. In spirituality, equivalence of form is determined by equivalence of desires (qualities, intentions). And if the creature remains separated from the Creator, the Creator, too, will not be complete, since perfect operations stem from a perfect operator.

To grant the creature the possibility of achieving perfection of its own free choice, the Creator restricted Himself—His Light—and created worlds, restriction by restriction, down to this world. Here man is completely subordinate to the desire to enjoy, but not to enjoy the Light of God, but rather the beastly clothes on top of it. The whole of humanity is developing from the desire for pleasure that animals have, as well, through desires for wealth, honor, domination, and knowledge, until the Creator implants a desire to enjoy something unknown within these desires, something beyond the clothes of this world.

The new desire prompts man to seek fulfillment until he comes to the study of Kabbalah. During the study, he begins to understand the Creator's intention towards him. In that state, he studies not in order to receive knowledge, but to draw on himself the Light that reforms ("Introduction to The Study of the Ten Sefirot," Item 155).

Through that Light, a person begins to correct his desires. In all, man has 613 desires, which are generally called *Guf* (body). The correction of the desires is done by using each desire with the intention to bestow upon the Creator, just as the Creator bestows upon man. The correction of each desire and the reception of the Light in it is called "keeping a *Mitzva* (good deed/commandment)." The Light that a person receives within the common, corrected desire is called, "Torah." And the Light that corrects (reforms) man's desires is the means by which the creature obtains its perfection (see "Walking the Path of Truth").

The perfection is in that the creature obtains equivalence of form (qualities) with the Creator by itself. This is because then it is worthy of receiving all the delight and pleasure included in the Thought of Creation. In other words, it enjoys the Light and the status of the Creator Himself, since it achieved equivalence of form in desires and thoughts.

It turns out that only through the study of Kabbalah can one correct oneself and achieve the goal for which man was created. This is what all the Kabbalists write. The only difference between the holy books (Torah, Prophets, Hagiographa, Mishnah, Talmud, etc.) is in the intensity of the Light within them, which can correct a person. The Light in Kabbalah books is the greatest; this is why Kabbalists recommend studying them specifically.

"There is no other way for the populace to achieve spiritual elevation and redemption except through the study of Kabbalah, which is an easy and accessible way. However, only a few can achieve the goal using other parts of the Torah."

–Rav Yehuda Ashlag, "Introduction to The Study of the Ten Sefirot," Item 36

"Attainment begins with the wisdom of the hidden, and only then are the other parts in the Torah attained. In the end, the revealed Torah is attained."

–The Vilna Gaon (GRA), Prayer Book

"The prohibition on studying Kabbalah was only for a limited time, until 1490. But since 1540, everyone should be encouraged to engage in *The Book of Zohar*, since only by studying *The Zohar* will humanity achieve its spiritual salvation and the coming of the Messiah. Hence, we must not avoid the study of Kabbalah."

–Avraham Ben Mordechai Azulai, *Ohr HaChama* (*Light of the Sun*)

"Woe unto those who do not wish to study *The Zohar*, for thus they cause wretchedness, ruin, looting, killing, and destruction to the world."

–*The Book of Zohar, Tikkuney Zohar* (*Corrections of The Zohar*), *Tikkun* no. 30

"The study of *The Book of Zohar* is above and is preferable to any other study."

-The Chidah

"Redemption and the coming of the Messiah depend only on the study of Kabbalah."

- The Vilna Gaon (GRA), *Even Shlemah* (*A Perfect Weight*)

"There are no limitations on the study of *The Zohar*."

-The Chafetz Chaim

"If my contemporaries heeded me, they would study *The Book of Zohar* at the age of nine, and would thus acquire fear of heaven instead of superficial knowledge."

-Rav Yitzhak Yehudah Yehiel of Komarno, *Notzer Hesed* (*Keeping Mercy*)

"I call upon every person to dedicate time to the study of Kabbalah every day, as this is what the cleansing of your souls depends on."

-Rav Yitzhak Kaduri

"In the future, only by merit of *The Book of Zohar* will the children of Israel be redeemed from exile."

-*The Book of Zohar*, *Parashat Nasso*

(There are many more such excerpts in the chapter, "Kabbalists Write about the Wisdom of Kabbalah.")

8) There is a "power" in the study of Torah and *Mitzvot*. This power is the spiritual force that brings a person to equalize one's desire with the Creator's desire. But this power appears and acts in a person only when one engages in Torah and *Mitzvot* in order to not receive any reward for oneself. Instead, he works only to bestow contentment upon the Creator. Only on that condition does one gradually acquire equivalence of form with the Creator.

Man's correction of equivalence of form with the Creator is gradual, generally consisting of five degrees: *Nefesh*, *Ruach*, *Neshama*, *Haya*, *Yechida*. Each degree is considered a world, since if one draws some degree in the process of his correction, he feels the Creator's existence according to the measure of his correction. These corrections are called "worlds" because they reveal the Creator according to one's measure of correction, and conceal the Creator according to the—as yet—uncorrected *Kelim* (desires), from the total of 613 desires.

It follows that one receives these five degrees on one's way to perfection from the five worlds: *Assiya*, *Yetzira*, *Beria*, *Atzilut*, and *Adam Kadmon*. Within each world are five *Partzufim*, and in each of them are five *Sefirot*, hence the total of 125 degrees in "Jacob's Ladder" from this world to the top of the ladder.

By keeping Torah and *Mitzvot* in order to give contentment to one's Maker, a person is gradually rewarded with the *Kelim* of the desire to bestowal, degree by degree. Thus, one climbs the rungs, one at a time, finally achieving complete equivalence of form with the Creator. At that time, the Thought of Creation is realized in a person—to receive the complete delight and wholeness that the Creator had planned for him. Additionally, one is rewarded with the greatest benefit of all—true *Dvekut*—by having obtained the desire to bestow, like the Creator.

9) Now we will try to understand the above-written, "All the worlds, Above and below, and everything within them, were created for man alone." All these degrees and worlds come only to complement each desire in a person with the aim to bestow, so man would acquire equivalence of form with the Creator. This equivalence of form is absent in man by the nature of his creation.

In the beginning, the worlds were restricted and the degrees cascaded degree-by-degree and world-by-world, down to our material world, to come to a "body of this world." This is the name Kabbalah ascribes to the will to receive for oneself. At the degree of "this world," a person is like a beast, since he is incapable of any bestowal. In that state, man is opposite from the Creator, and there is no greater distance than that.

A person who studies Kabbalah awakens a "Surrounding Light" on oneself in proportion to one's desire for spirituality. This is the Light that exists outside, or around one's *Kli* (desire/soul). The Surrounding Light corrects the *Kli* in such a way that its intention will be to bestow. The intention to bestow upon the Creator and not to oneself turns an act of reception into an act of bestowal.

Following its nature, the *Kli* remains a desire to enjoy, but the aim changes the essence of the act from reception to bestowal. Then the Surrounding Light can enter the corrected *Kli* with the aim to bestow upon the Creator. It is precisely during the study of Kabbalah that the Surrounding Light can correct one's desires until they are worthy of receiving it as "Inner Light."

One obtains the desire to bestow gradually, from Above downwards, from a small desire, which is easier to correct, to the greatest one, following the same order by which the degrees hung down from Above downwards.

All the degrees are measures of the desire to bestow. The ladder of degrees is arranged in such a way that the Higher the degree, the farther it is from the will to receive for oneself, and the closer it is to the desire to bestow. A person gradually acquires all the degrees of bestowal until one is rewarded with having only the aim to bestow, without any self-reception.

At that time, a person is complete, in true *Dvekut* with the Creator. This is the purpose of Creation, and man was created for that alone. This is why all the worlds and everything within them were not created for themselves, but only to assist man in climbing the ladder of degrees. When one corrects oneself and is filled with Light, the entire system of the worlds and everything within them is included in him.

10) A person who knows and remembers what has been said here is permitted to study Kabbalah without any fear of materializing it. This is because studying the wisdom of Kabbalah without proper guidance confuses the learner. On the one hand, all the *Sefirot* and *Partzufim* from the world of *Atzilut* to the world of *Assiya* are complete Godliness, in unity with the Creator, and on the other hand, how can there be changes, ascents, descents, and *Zivugim* (couplings) in Godliness and unity?

11) From what has been explained, it is clear that all these changes—ascents, descents, restrictions, and *Zivugim*—are discerned only with respect to the *Kelim* of the souls that receive the Light. Reality can be divided into two parts: potential and actual.

This is similar to a person who wants to build a house and already has the blueprint of the house in mind. But the blueprint of the house is not like the completed house—a blueprint that has been executed. This is because the thought about the house is made of conceptual substance and exists in potential. But when the house begins to emerge from thought to action, it turns into a different substance—bricks and wood.

In the same manner, we should distinguish between potential and actual in the souls. The "actual" elicitation of souls from the Creator begins only from the world of *Beria*. This is why all the changes and everything that occurs prior to the world of *Beria* are considered "potential," without any actual distinction from the Creator.

This is the reason why it is said that all the souls are included in *Malchut de Ein Sof*, in the middle point of reality, since this point "potentially" contains all the *Kelim* (plural for *Kli*) of the souls that are destined to emerge in actuality from the world of *Beria* downwards. And *Tzimtzum Aleph* (first restriction), too, occurred in the middle point, only on the "potential," with respect to the future souls.

With respect to the souls, all the *Kelim* of the *Sefirot* and worlds that emerge and hang down from the middle point, after *Tzimtzum Aleph* and down the world of *Beria*, are only in potential. When the souls begin to emerge in fact, from the world of *Beria* downwards, only then do the changes in the degrees of the worlds affect them.

12) This is similar to a person who hides and conceals himself with clothes and coverings, so he will not be seen or noticed. But to himself, he remains as he was. Thus, the ten *Sefirot*, *Keter*, *Hochma*, *Bina*, *Hesed*, *Gevura*, *Tifferet*, *Netzah*, *Hod*, *Yesod*, and *Malchut* are only ten coverings that cover *Ein Sof* and conceal it from the souls.

The Light of *Ein Sof* is in complete rest; hence, it shines within the coverings. But because the souls receive the Light of *Ein Sof* through the coverings, they feel as though there are changes in the Light. For this reason, the souls that receive Light are divided into ten degrees, too, according to the division in the coverings.

All the coverings are only from the world of *Beria* downwards, since only from there down are there souls that receive from the ten *Sefirot* through the coverings. In the worlds *Adam Kadmon* (AK) and *Atzilut* there is still no presence of souls, since there they are only in potential.

Although the ten coverings in the ten *Sefirot* govern only the worlds BYA—*Beria*, *Yetzira*, *Assiya*—the ten *Sefirot* there are considered Godliness, too, as prior to *Tzimtzum Aleph*. The difference is only in the *Kelim* of the ten *Sefirot*: in AK and in *Atzilut* they are in potential; and from BYA the *Kelim* of the ten *Sefirot* begin to disclose their force of concealment and covering. This is so although the coverings inflict no changes in the Light itself.

13) This brings up a question: If, within the worlds AK and *Atzilut*, there is still no actual disclosure of the souls that receive Light from the worlds, what is the purpose of the *Kelim* of AK and *Atzilut*, and towards whom do they conceal and cover the Light of *Ein Sof*, according to their measures? In the future, the souls will rise to AK and *Atzilut*, along with the worlds BYA, and receive Light from them. Hence, changes occur in AK and *Atzilut*, as well, according to the

qualities of the souls, as they are destined to shine to the souls that will rise to them in the future.

14) It follows that the worlds, initiations, changes, and degrees all relate only to the *Kelim*, which affect the souls and gauge them so they can receive from the Light of *Ein Sof*. But when the souls rise in degrees, they do not induce any changes in the Light of *Ein Sof* itself, since the coverings do not affect the thing being covered, only the one who wishes to sense what is covered and receive from it.

15) We should make three discernments in the *Sefirot* and *Partzufim*, wherever they are—*Atzmuto*, *Kelim*, and Lights.

1. In *Atzmuto*, the receivers have no thought or perception.

2. In the *Kelim*, there are always two opposite discernments: concealment and disclosure. First, the *Kli* conceals itself so the ten *Kelim* in the ten *Sefirot* are ten degrees of concealment. But after the souls receive the same conditions as in the *Kelim*, these concealments become disclosures, attainments of the souls. In that state, the two opposite discernments in the *Kelim* become as one, since the measure of disclosure in the *Kli* is just as the measure of concealment in the *Kli*. And the coarser the *Kli*, when it hides more of its *Atzmuto*, it discloses a Higher Level.

3. The Lights in the *Sefirot* are the specific measure that should appear for the attainment of the souls. Although everything extends from *Atzmuto*, the attainment in the Light is only in the qualities of the *Kli*. Hence, there are necessarily ten Lights in these ten *Kelim*, meaning ten degrees of disclosure. Thus, the Light cannot be distinguished from *Atzmuto*, but only in that there is no perception or attainment in *Atzmuto*. What is revealed to us is only what reaches us from the Creator through His clothing in the *Kelim* of the ten *Sefirot*. Hence, we refer to anything we attain by the name, "Lights."

FOUR STAGES IN THE DEVELOPMENT OF THE KLI

The Kabbalists attained spirituality and wrote it down in Kabbalah books. They perceived that the root of the whole of reality is a Higher Force, which they called *Atzmuto* (His Self), since they could not attain it in itself. They did, however, attain that a thought and intention originates from *Atzmuto*—to create creations and delight them. They called that thought and intention the "Thought of Creation" or "Upper Light." Thus, with respect to the creature, the Light is the

Creator, since *Atzmuto* is unattainable. Hence, the Creator-creature connection exists through the Upper Light.

To summarize: Light emits from *Atzmuto* and wishes to create a creature and delight it by filling it with pleasure. In other words, the Light's goal is to create a creature that will feel the Light as pleasure. This is why the Kabbalists named the creature, *Kli*, and the Light, "filling." The Light that stems from *Atzmuto*, to create the creature, is called *Behinat Shoresh* (Root discernment), since it is the root of the whole of reality. This Light creates a desire to enjoy it, and the desire to enjoy the Light is called "the will to receive" Light.

The measure of pleasure depends on the measure of desire to receive it. As in our world, one may have an empty stomach, but no desire to eat. Hence, the desire is the *Kli* for the filling, and without desire, there is no pleasure. There is no coercion in spirituality, and the filling always follows the desire.

The Light emerges from *Atzmuto*, creates a *Kli*, and fills it. The pleasure experienced in the creature by the reception of Light is called *Ohr Hochma* (Light of Wisdom). The desire born by the Light that fills it is called *Behina Aleph* (first discernment). It is given that name since this is the first discernment of the future *Kli*.

Yet, this desire is still not autonomous, since it is directly created by the Light. A real created being is one that wants to enjoy all the Light emitted from the Creator **by itself**. In other words, its desire and decision to enjoy the Light should come from within it, instead of being instilled in it by the Creator.

To want to receive Light, the creature must first know the amount of pleasure that exists in the Light. Hence, it must be filled with Light and then feel what it is like being without Light. In that state, a true desire for the Light is created in it.

It is similar to situations we know from life. When a person is given some unfamiliar fruit to taste, initially, one has no desire for it. But after one tastes the fruit, and experiences the pleasure that stems from it, and the fruit is taken away, one begins to crave it and wishes to re-experience the pleasure. This craving is the new desire that was born in a person, which one feels as one's autonomous desire.

Hence, it is impossible to build the *Kli* all at once. Instead, for the desire to know what to enjoy, for it to feel that it wants to enjoy, it must undergo the entire order of evolution. In Kabbalah, this condition is presented as a law: **"The expansion of the Light** inside the desire to receive **and its departure** from there **make the *Kli* fit for its task** of receiving all the Light and enjoying it." The states of the development of the desire are called *Behinot* (discernments), since they are new observations in the will to receive.

Therefore, a Light that fills the *Kli* gives it, along with the pleasure, its quality of giving. And while the *Kli* enjoys the Light, it suddenly discovers that it wishes to bestow, like the nature of the Light that fills it. The reason for it is that the Creator intentionally prepared for the Light the ability to convey to the *Kli* the desire to bestow, along with the pleasure.

It follows that once the Light created *Behina Aleph* and filled it, it felt that it wished to be similar to the Creator. And because this was a new desire, it was a new discernment, called *Behina Bet* (second discernment).

Behina Bet is a desire to give. The pleasure it feels from being similar to the Creator is called *Ohr Hassadim* (Light of Mercy). We therefore see that *Behina Aleph* is opposite from *Behina Bet* in the sense that the desire in *Behina Aleph* is to receive, and the desire in *Behina Bet* is to give. The Light in *Behina Aleph* is *Ohr Hochma*, and in *Behina Bet* it is *Ohr Hassadim*.

When the will to receive in *Behina Aleph* begins to enjoy the Light that fills it, it immediately senses that the Light is the giver of the pleasure and that it (*Behina Aleph*) is the receiver of the pleasure. In consequence, it begins to want to be like the Light itself, not wanting to receive the pleasure, but to give it, like the Light. For this reason, the desire to receive in it disappears and remains empty of *Ohr Hochma*, since pleasure is sensed only in a desire for it.

The will to receive cannot remain without *Ohr Hochma*, since *Ohr Hochma* is its Light of life. Hence, it is forced to receive some *Ohr Hochma*. Thus, this new desire, called *Behina Gimel* (third discernment) consists of two desires: 1) a desire to be similar to the Light; and 2) a desire to receive a little bit of *Ohr Hochma*.

In that state, the *Kli* feels two Lights: Light of *Hassadim*—in the desire to bestow—and Light of *Hochma*—in the desire to receive.

When *Behina Gimel* receives Light, it feels that of its two Lights, the *Ohr Hochma*, the Light of life, suits its nature. Then it decides to receive it in full, and thus a new, independent desire to receive that pleasure, *Ohr Hochma*, is born. This is the same pleasure that the Creator wishes to fill the creature with.

We therefore see that the Light that emerges from *Atzmuto* creates for itself a *Kli* in four steps. Hence, this final desire, called *Behina Dalet* (fourth discernment), is the only creature. All its preceding stages are but the stages of its development. In fact, the whole of Creation is *Behina Dalet*. Everything that exists in reality besides the Creator is *Behina Dalet*. *Behina Dalet* is called *Malchut* (Kingship), since the will to receive reigns in it.

FOUR BEHINOT

Behina Dalet is the only creature. *Behina Dalet* is divided into externality, whose parts are *Sefirot*, *Partzufim* (plural for *Partzuf*), worlds, and our world—still, vegetative, and animate—and to internality: the souls of people. The difference between all these parts is only in the measure of desire to receive within them.

Behina Dalet, which was completely filled with *Ohr Hochma*, is called "the world of *Ein Sof*" (no end), since there is no end to its desire to receive the Light. *Behina Dalet* receives Light through its four preceding *Behinot*—*Shoresh*, *Aleph*, *Bet*, *Gimel*. Thus, it is internally divided into five *Behinot* of desire to receive: desires for Lights in the *Behinot* preceding itself, and the desire for the Light that comes to her.

THE FOUR BEHINOT PRIOR TO BEHINA DALET, WITH FIVE BEHINOT WITHIN IT

Summary: Light emits from the Creator, *Behinat Shoresh*. The Light creates a creature, *Behina Dalet*, in four stages. The essence of the creature is the desire to receive pleasure. The pleasure is the sensation of Light within the desire. *Behina Dalet* itself divides into four parts, which receive Light from the previous *Behinot*. *Behina Dalet*, which is filled with *Ohr Hochma*, is called "the world of *Ein Sof*." The parts of *Behina Dalet* are called "souls" and "worlds." The worlds contain *Partzufim*, *Sefirot*, and everything other than the souls.

TZIMTZUM ALEPH, MASACH, PARTZUF

When *Ohr Hochma* fills the will to receive in *Behina Aleph*, it gives the will to receive its nature—the desire to bestow. This is the reason why, at its end, *Behina Aleph*—after she felt the nature of the Light that fills her—changed her desire from wanting to receive to wanting to bestow.

Once *Behina Dalet* departed *Behina Gimel* and was filled with her Light, which is *Ohr Hochma*, too, the Light affected her in such a way that she began to want to bestow, similar to the nature of the Light within her. Hence, the will to receive disappeared from *Behina Dalet*.

But why does the *Ohr Hochma* give the *Kli* a desire to bestow when it fills it? This is so because the *Kli* feels not only the pleasure from the Light, but the desire of the Giver, too. The Creator could have created a *Kli* that would not feel

Him as the Giver, but only the pleasure of reception. In our world, this is what people feel when their will to receive is still undeveloped, like that of children, crude people, or the mentally unwell.

As a child grows, it becomes ashamed of receiving. In man, this sensation is so developed that one would prefer any pain in the world to the suffering of shame. The Creator created this quality in us deliberately, so that **through it, we would be able to rise above our nature**, the will to receive.

To be ashamed and suffer from receiving, one must feel that one is receiving. This is possible only if you feel the giver, that there is a giver. If I cannot feel the host, I will not be ashamed. But if the host is in front of me, I will be ashamed.

I cannot receive directly because I will have to relate to him. I will feel that I must give something in return for receiving from him. In that case, I will no longer be receiving, but I would change places with him and become a giver, since then he, too, would be receiving from me.

The sensation of the Creator evokes such great suffering from reception in *Malchut*, it decides to never use her will to receive for reception of pleasures for herself. This decision in *Malchut*, to not receive Light for herself, is called *Tzimtzum* (restriction). The name, *Tzimtzum Aleph* (first restriction), indicates that this operation occurred for the first time.

Thus, *Malchut* stopped receiving Light. By that, she stopped being a receiver, but she was still not giving anything to the Creator; she still did not fulfill her wish to become like the Light, the giver of pleasure. By not receiving pleasure from the Creator, *Malchut* did not obtain equivalence of form. Hence, we see that the act of *Tzimtzum Aleph* was not a goal, but a means to acquire the ability to give.

The Creator's purpose in Creation was for *Malchut*, the created being, to receive pleasures. The Thought of Creation is constant and absolute. Hence, the Creator, the Light, continued to pressure *Malchut* to receive it. *Malchut* sensed that the act of restriction was insufficient to achieve the act of bestowal. Yet, how could the creature, whose only quality is to receive, give to the Creator, as He does?

By sensing the qualities of the Upper nine within her—the qualities of the Creator that she feels within, which, to her, form the Creator's attitude towards her—*Malchut* begins to understand how she can come to bestow upon the Creator. She decides that if she receives the Light and enjoys it only because the Creator enjoys her delight in it, her reception would be tantamount to bestowal. Reception of pleasure by the receiver in order to benefit the giver turns an act of reception into one of bestowal. Thus, if *Malchut* receives all the Light (pleasure) that the Creator has prepared for her, she would be giving to Him, just as He is giving to her.

Take, for example, a visiting guest. The host treats the guest with food, precisely in the amount and flavor that the guest wishes it (the desire is in perfect match with the Light, in flavor and quantity, since the Light-pleasure created the *Kli*-desire in accordance with itself).

Yet, even though the guest is hungry, the presence of the host creates shame in him, which stops him from receiving. The shame stems from the sensation of himself as a receiver, and the host as a giver. And the shame is so powerful that he can no longer receive.

Yet, the host's imploring of him to eat, since He has prepared everything for him, persuades the guest that the host would enjoy his eating. Then, it seems to the guest that if he were to receive the pleasure, after having rejected it several times, this reception would be regarded as him giving and benefiting the host. Thus, the guest would become a giver, and the host would become the receiver.

In Kabbalah, the hunger, the desire to receive delight and pleasure, is called *Kli* (vessel). The pleasure that comes from the Creator is called *Ohr Yashar* (Direct Light). The force that repels the pleasure that comes from the Creator is called *Masach* (screen). The Light repelled from the *Masach* is called *Ohr Hozer* (Reflected Light).

Using the force of the *Masach*—the power to resist self-gratification and delight the Creator—the *Kli* can resist its own will to receive. We can understand that the *Kli* rejects the Light, but it is truer to say that the *Kli* rejects using the desire to enjoy for itself.

The *Kli* cannot return Light to the Creator; it can only change its intention. The aim created in the *Kli* to delight the Creator is called *Ohr Hozer* (Reflected Light). *Ohr* (Light) is another name for pleasure. *Ohr Yashar* is the pleasure that the Creator wishes to give to the creature, and *Ohr Hozer* is the pleasure that the creature wishes to bestow upon the Creator.

Once the *Kli* (guest) is certain that it will not receive (enjoy) for itself, it examines the intensity of its *Ohr Hozer* (the measure of its desire to bestow pleasure upon the Creator—Host), and decides to receive the abundance that comes by it from the *Ohr Yashar* (the delicatessen and delights the Host is imparting), but only as much as it can receive in order to delight the Creator (Host).

Kabbalists are people who feel the Light emitted from the Creator and all its actions. But when they write about spirituality, they convey their sensations in a language of "technical" terms and definitions. Hence, only if the reader has a *Masach* and the forces that the books speak of, can one "translate" the words into feelings, by performing the same actions he reads about within himself.

The Light comes directly from the Creator (hence its name, *Ohr Yashar*) and wishes to clothe within the *Kli*. Yet, it encounters the *Masach*. The *Masach* repels the Light (refuses to receive it in order to receive), thus keeping the condition of *Tzimtzum Aleph*: to not receive for oneself. Once the *Kli* is certain that it will not receive for itself, it calculates (using the *Masach*) how much it can receive in order to bestow (delight the Creator). The sensation in the Light and the decision how much to receive is done prior to receiving it. For this reason, this part in the *Kli* is called *Rosh* (head). The place of calculation, where the *Masach* stands, is called *Peh* (mouth).

Following the decision in the *Rosh*, the *Kli* receives the Light in the *Toch* (interior). The *Toch* is the part of the *Kli* in which the reception of Light (sensation of pleasure inside the desire to enjoy) occurs de facto. *Ohr Hochma* (the pleasure) is received with the aim to delight the Creator in this manner. This aim is called *Ohr Hassadim* (Light of Mercy). In the language of Kabbalah, *Ohr Yashar* dresses in *Ohr Hozer*, and *Ohr Hochma* dresses in *Ohr Hassadim*.

The *Kli* can receive only a small portion of the Light that comes from the Creator, since the *Masach* hasn't the power to receive all the Light. Thus, a part (of the desires) in it is filled and a part remains empty. The part that remains empty is called *Sof* (end, conclusion). We therefore see that the creature consists of three parts: *Rosh*, *Toch*, and *Sof*. Together, they are called *Partzuf* (face, countenance). The *Guf* of the *Partzuf* (all its desires) divides into *Toch*, the receiving part, and *Sof*, which remains empty.

- **The boundary in the *Guf* of the *Partzuf*, where the reception of Light ends, is called *Tabur* (navel).**
- **The part of the Light received within the *Partzuf* is called *Ohr Pnimi* (Inner Light).**
- **The part of the Light that remains outside the *Kli* is called *Ohr Makif* (Surrounding Light).**
- **Through the *Masach*, the *Ohr Yashar* divides into *Ohr Pnimi* and *Ohr Makif*.**

Malchut comprises five *Behinot* (discernments). The *Masach* decides how much to receive in each *Behina*. Each *Behina* divides into a part that receives and a part that does not receive. Hence, there are five *Behinot* in the *Toch*, and five *Behinot* in the *Sof*.

Summary: When the Light corrects the *Kli*, it gives the desire of the Creator to the *Kli*. This, in fact, is what we are lacking: for the Light (the Surrounding Light, which we evoke during the study, if we wish to achieve the purpose of Creation) to come and correct us, so that we may want our actions to be like the Creator's (bestowing). This is the uniqueness of the study of Kabbalah, and this is also its importance. The study evokes the Surrounding Light, which corrects a person.

EXPANSION AND DEPARTURE OF LIGHTS

After *Malchut* decided to receive a part of the *Ohr Yashar*, and received it in the *Toch*, she stopped receiving. *Malchut* always calculates, in the *Rosh* of the *Partzuf*, what is the maximum Light she can receive in order to bestow. Depending on the force of the *Masach*, *Malchut* receives only a very small part of the whole of the *Ohr Yashar*, since receiving in order to benefit the Creator is against her nature.

The part of the *Ohr Yashar* that remains outside the *Kli* is called *Ohr Makif*. It continues to pressure the *Masach*, which limits its expansion in the *Partzuf* and wishes to break through the *Masach* and fill the entire *Kli*, including the *Sof* of the *Partzuf*, as prior to the *Tzimtzum*.

The *Partzuf* understands that if it received only a part, meaning filled itself only to the *Tabur*, and remained in that state, the Thought of Creation would not be realized. To realize the Thought of Creation, all the Light that filled *Malchut* prior to the *Tzimtzum* must be received with the aim to bestow. But if the *Partzuf* were to receive more, below *Tabur*, it would be reception in order to receive, since it does not have a *Masach* to receive in order to bestow over those *Kelim*.

For this reason, the *Partzuf* decides to leave the reception of Light altogether and return to its state from before the reception. This decision is made at the *Rosh* of the *Partzuf*, as with all decisions. Following the decision, the *Masach* that descended from *Peh* to *Tabur* and stood there, begins to rise from *Tabur* to *Peh*. The ascension of the *Masach* causes the Lights to depart the *Partzuf* through the *Peh* to the *Rosh*.

The decision to stop receiving the Light was made because the *Masach* that stood at the *Tabur* was pressured by the *Ohr Makif* that wanted to be received in the *Partzuf*, as well as by the *Ohr Pnimi*. These two Lights wish to cancel the *Masach*, which is like a limit on the expansion of the Light. Their pressure on the *Masach* is called "*Bitush* (beating) of *Ohr Pnimi* an *Ohr Makif*."

These two Lights pressure the *Masach* at the *Tabur*, which limits the reception of Light in the *Partzuf*. They want the *Masach* to descend from *Tabur* to the *Sium* (end) of the *Partzuf*, and that thus, the whole of the *Ohr Makif* would be able to enter.

This state is similar to a person who received a part of what his host had served him. He feels great pleasure in what he has received, and that weakens him because he feels what great pleasures exist in what he did not receive.

As a result, the *Masach* returns from *Tabur* to *Peh*, and the *Partzuf* is emptied from Light. Just as the Light entered the *Partzuf* through the *Peh*, it leaves the *Partzuf* through the *Peh*. The expansion of Light from Above downwards, from *Peh* to *Tabur*, is called *Taamim* (flavors). The departure of Light in the *Partzuf* from *Toch* to *Rosh* is called *Nekudot* (points). When the Light departs the *Partzuf*, it leaves an impression of itself, called *Reshimo* (memory/recollection). A *Reshimo* from the Lights of *Taamim* is called *Tagin* (tags), and a *Reshimo* from the Lights of *Nekudot* is called *Otiot* (letters).

The expansion of Light and its departure make the *Kli* fit for its task, since only after the *Kli* feels the pleasure and the pleasure departs, does a true desire for this pleasure appear in the *Kli*. After the departure of the Light, a *Reshimo* remains in the *Kli*. This is a *Reshimo* of the pleasure that was there, of the *Nekudot*. Once the *Kli* is emptied of Light, the *Reshimo* determines the desire and craving of the *Kli*. Hence, the *Reshimo* from the departure of the Light is called *Otiot*, or *Kli*.

Prior to the *Tzimtzum*, *Behina Dalet* receives Lights from all of its four preceding *Behinot*. Light comes to her from *Atzmuto* through *Behinot Shoresh*, *Aleph*, *Bet*, *Gimel*, and *Dalet*. Hence, *Behina Dalet* contains five internal *Behinot*. Each internal *Behina* of *Behina Dalet* receives Light from its corresponding *Behina*:

- *Behinat Shoresh* in *Behina Dalet* receives *Ohr Yechida* (Light of *Yechida*) from *Behinat Shoresh*.
- *Behina Aleph* in *Behina Dalet* receives *Ohr Haya* from *Behina Aleph*.
- *Behina Bet* in *Behina Dalet* receives *Ohr Neshama* from *Behina Bet*.
- *Behina Gimel* in *Behina Dalet* receives *Ohr Ruach* from *Behina Gimel*.
- *Behina Dalet* in *Behina Dalet* receives *Ohr Nefesh* from *Behina Dalet*.

Only *Behina Dalet* in *Behina Dalet* feels that the will to receive pleasure is hers. Hence, only this *Behina* is regarded as a "creature." The rest of the *Behinot* in *Behina Dalet*, preceding *Behina Dalet* in *Behina Dalet*, are desires that *Behina Dalet* received from *Behinot Shoresh*, *Aleph*, *Bet*, and *Gimel* that preceded it. Although the desires in its preceding *Behinot* are desires to receive, they come from the Creator and not from *Behina Dalet* herself.

Behina Dalet consists of five *Behinot*; this is her structure and it is unchanging. These *Behinot* may divide, fill, join for actions of reception of Lights within them, but their structure remains the same. It is called **the tip of the Yod, Yod, Hey, Vav, Hey**.

The worlds, and everything in them besides people, emerge from the *Behinot* that precede *Behina Dalet* in *Dalet*. They have no independent desire to receive. They are operated by the desires that the Creator imprinted in them, and are therefore not defined in Kabbalah as "creatures." Only the souls of people were made of *Behina Dalet* in *Dalet*, where the will to receive exists in her independently. Hence, only souls of people are considered "creatures."

A true desire to receive for oneself appears only in *Behina Dalet* in *Behina Dalet*. She is the only one that perceives herself as receiving. Hence, she is the only one that decides to restrict the reception of the Light. But the Light departs from the rest of the *Behinot* in *Behina Dalet*, too, since only *Dalet* in *Dalet* receives, while the preceding *Behinot* only develop her will to receive. When she stops receiving, the Light disappears from all of them, since all five *Behinot* are one *Kli*, **the tip of the Yod, Yod, Hey, Vav, Hey**.

After the *Tzimtzum*, when *Malchut* receives those five Lights through the *Masach*—within her five *Behinot*—they enter those five parts of *Malchut*. The order in which Lights enter the *Partzuf* is from the smallest Light to the greatest Light: *Nefesh, Ruach, Neshama, Haya,* and *Yechida*. Hence, these Lights are called NRNHY.

ENTRANCE AND DEPARTURE OF LIGHTS IN A PARTZUF

The five parts of *Malchut* are called *Behinot Shoresh, Aleph, Bet, Gimel,* and *Dalet*. Following the *Tzimtzum*, when these parts receive Lights through the *Masach*, they are called *Sefirot* (sapphires, illuminations) because the Light shines in them. Hence, instead of *Behinot*, we call them *Sefirot*.

Keter = *Shoresh*

Hochma = *Aleph*

Bina = *Bet*

Zeir Anpin (ZA) = *Gimel*

Malchut = *Dalet*

The *Reshimot* (plural for *Reshimo*) from the departing Lights are called *Otiot* (letters). After the departure of the five Lights, **Nefesh, Ruach, Neshama, Haya, and Yechida,** from the five *Sefirot*, **Keter, Hochma, Bina,**

Zeir Anpin*, and *Malchut, five *Reshimot*, or *Otiot* remain: **the tip of the *Yod*, *Yod*, *Hey*, *Vav*, *Hey***.

Later in this article, we will learn how Kabbalists use symbols to depict spiritual forces in writing. They build letters, words, and names out of dots and lines. This is how all the holy books were written. It turns out that the writing is information about spiritual forces and operations. When Kabbalists read books, they can act according to the instructions in them.

Yet, when we examine holy books, they seem to discuss historic events. But it is written in the Torah that the whole of the Torah is names of the Creator. This means that all the words in the Torah tell us either about the *Kelim* or about their actions. In other words, the whole of the Torah is the same wisdom of Kabbalah that we must learn today, written in a different language.

There are four languages to the Torah: the language of the Torah, the language of legends, the language of the Talmud, and the language of Kabbalah. All of them were invented by Kabbalists who attained spirituality, to tell us how we can achieve the purpose of Creation.

OVERVIEW

The Creator wishes to benefit His creatures. The creatures are meant to receive the Creator's benefit by themselves. For this purpose, the Creator created an independent creature, completely detached from Him. The creature does not feel the Creator because the Light is Higher than the *Kli*, and when it fills the *Kli*, it controls it and determines what the *Kli* will want.

Hence, the creature must be born in concealment from the Light so as to be independent, without the sensation of spirituality and the existence of the Creator. It is born at the farthest degree from the Creator, in a degree called "this world." Yet, when the creature is independent from the influence of the Upper Light (the Creator), it also lacks the power to understand its state, its reality, the purpose of its life. It follows that the Creator must prepare the right environment for the creature to develop and grow:

1. He must restrict His Light to the minimum, restriction by restriction. This is how the degrees were built from Above downwards, from the degree of *Ein Sof*, the closest to the Creator, to the degree of "this world," the lowest and farthest from the Creator. This act is called "the expansion of the worlds and the *Partzufim*."

2. Once the starting point has been prepared for the creature, it must be given a possibility to rise from that state and reach the Creator's degree.

But how can this be done, if after *Tzimtzum Aleph* no Light reaches the *Kli*—the creature—who is at the degree of "this world"? For this reason, the Creator provided us in this world with a *Segula* (power, remedy): *Ohr Makif* (Surrounding Light), which shines even to the restricted *Kli*.

Rav Yehuda Ashlag wrote about this *Segula* in Item 155 of his "Introduction to The Study of the Ten Sefirot": "Therefore we must ask, why then, did the Kabbalists obligate each person to study the wisdom of Kabbalah? Indeed, there is a great thing in it, worthy of being publicized: There is a wonderful, invaluable remedy to those who engage in the wisdom of Kabbalah. Although they do not understand what they are learning, through the yearning and the great desire to understand what they are learning, they awaken upon themselves the Lights that surround their souls.

"This means that every person from Israel is guaranteed to finally attain all the wonderful attainments that the Creator had calculated in the Thought of Creation to delight every creature. One who has not been awarded in this life will be granted in the next life, etc., until one is awarded completing the Creator's Thought, which He had planned for him.

"And while one has not attained perfection, the Lights that are destined to reach him are considered Surrounding Lights. This means that they stand ready for him, but are waiting for him to purify his vessels of reception, at which time these Lights will clothe the able vessels.

"Hence, even when one does not have the vessels, when one engages in this wisdom, mentioning the names of the Lights and the vessels related to one's soul, they immediately shine upon him to a certain measure. However, they shine for him without clothing the interior of his soul for lack of able vessels to receive them.

"Yet, the illumination one receives time after time during the engagement in the wisdom of Kabbalah draws upon one grace from Above, imparting one with abundance of sanctity and purity, which bring one closer, until he achieves perfection.

"Yet, there is a strict condition during the engagement in this wisdom, to not materialize the matters with imaginary and corporeal things, as thus they breach, 'Thou shalt not make unto thee a graven image, nor any manner of likeness.' In that event, one is rather harmed instead of benefited."

Thus, only proper study of the wisdom of Kabbalah can bring man to the purpose of his life. This is what Kabbalists are saying, and who knows about reality more than they?

Ohr Makif is the power with which any person can begin to rise from this world to the spiritual world. Without the help of the illumination of this *Ohr Makif*, we would have no possibility of transcending our state, since the *Kli* can be corrected only by the Light, and the Upper Light cannot reach this world. Hence, we need the *Ohr Makif*.

To help beginners avert failures on their way, we added a table of questions and answers, a glossary, abbreviations, and various media files. We do not intend to delve deep or expand the explanation and the amount of information, but to direct the student towards obtaining the drive to progress correctly. It should be clear that the purpose of the study is to achieve *Dvekut* (adhesion) with the Creator. This must be before our eyes, since only then do we evoke upon ourselves the Surrounding Lights, and through their impact, we will enter the Upper World.

The glossary is intended for the correct understanding of basic terms. But only if one knows how to interpret the words one is reading correctly, in their true, spiritual meaning, unlike the way we usually interpret them in our world, only to that extent is one permitted to learn and read anything in the Torah. Otherwise, one might perceive the books of Torah as historic narratives.

When a Kabbalist attains spirituality, it is indescribable in words, since spirituality contains only sensations. This is why Kabbalah books are written in the language of branches, using worldly words to describe spiritual concepts.

The spiritual world is an abstract place, "virtual," where only forces and emotions exist, without bodily clothing. We must constantly renew and repeat the spiritual concepts because until we achieve emotional connection with spirituality, we will be reading in the Kabbalah books without any understanding of what stands behind the words.

The primary mistake is that there are "Kabbalists" who teach that there is some connection between the human body and the spiritual *Kli*, as though the spiritual *Kli* clothes in a human body, as if within each corporeal organ clothes a spiritual organ. In their view, if one performs a physical act or any physical motion whatsoever, it seemingly contains spiritual content. They think that in so doing, one actually performs a spiritual action.

Their mistake stems from the Kabbalists' use of the language of the branches, using worldly words to name and define spiritual terms. This is the reason for the strict prohibition in the Torah, "Thou shalt not make unto thee a graven image, nor any manner of likeness." In other words, it is forbidden to imagine spirituality in corporeal shapes, not because this could inflict harm Above, but because the false image would prevent one from understanding the Creator's ways and approaching the goal.

Hence, the student must constantly repeat the key concepts of Kabbalah, such as "place," "time," movement," "no absence," *Guf* (body), "body parts" or "organs," *Zivug* (coupling), "kiss," "embrace" until each concept is perceived correctly. This is what Baal HaSulam writes in his "Introduction to The Study of the Ten Sefirot." Those who want to study Kabbalah the right way are advised to leave all the books on this subject, except for *The Book of Zohar*, the writings of the Ari, the writings of Baal HaSulam, and the writings of Rabash.

Interpreting the Torah as a historic narrative contradicts the verse that says that the whole Torah is the names of the Creator, that it is the Torah of the world of *Atzilut*, and that all the words in it are Holy Names. It is important to remember that it does not speak of this world, and the people in it (see "Introduction to The Book of Zohar," Item 58).

All the names in the Torah are holy, even such names as Pharaoh, Balaam, Balak. For example, one who is called up to stand next to the Ark of the synagogue during service, kisses the book of Torah without first checking to see if he mistakenly kissed the name Pharaoh or Laban. *The Zohar* explains that each name symbolizes a spiritual degree: Pharaoh corresponds to *Malchut*, Laban to the Higher *Loven* (whiteness), *Partzuf* of Upper *Hochma*, etc.

RESHIMOT

To perform the correct operation, the *Kli* must know what it wants, how to get what it wants, and have the strength to get what it wants.

Besides the Creator, there is only one Creation: the will to receive pleasure. Hence, the whole of reality contains only Light and *Kli*, pleasure and desire, *Hitlabshut* (clothing) and *Aviut* (coarseness/desire to receive).

In each spiritual act, following the departure of Light from the *Kli*, meaning after the transition from a state where the *Kli* is filled with Light to a state where the *Kli* is empty, it leaves behind it two "recollections" of the previous state. They are called *Reshimo de Hitlabshut* (recollection of the clothing)—a *Reshimo* of the Light that was in the *Kli* and departed, and *Reshimo de Aviut* (recollection of the desire to receive)—a *Reshimo* of the *Kli* on the *Masach* that remains to be used.

These two *Reshimot* (plural for *Reshimo*) are considered one *Reshimo*. If no *Reshimo* is left, the *Kli* will not know what to want or how to get what it wants.

The whole process of reality's cascading from its initiation in *Malchut de* (of) *Ein Sof*, through its end in this world, are different states of *Malchut de Ein Sof*. It undergoes this sequence of states with the help of the Light that surrounds it, which evokes the *Reshimot* that remain in it after each state.

The state in which *Behina Dalet* is filled with Light is called *Malchut de Ein Sof*. After *Behina Dalet* experienced herself as a "receiver," she decided to restrict the reception of Light. The Light departed and a *Reshimo* of the Light that was in it remained in *Malchut*. Even after the *Tzimtzum*, Light came to fill *Malchut*, but she calculated and decided to receive only as much as she could receive with the aim to bestow upon the Creator.

The required data for this calculation are (a) the *Reshimo* from the *Hitlabshut* of the Light in the previous state, and (b) the desire to receive in order to bestow. Once *Malchut* calculates these *Reshimot* in the *Rosh*, she receives what she has decided to receive in the *Guf*. And when the *Kli* completes the reception of the part of the Light that it decided to receive, the *Ohr Makif* batters the *Masach* and forces it to return to the *Peh*. Thus, the *Partzuf* is emptied of its filling.

When the *Masach* rises from *Tabur de Galgalta* to its *Peh*, the *Ohr Pnimi* exits *Galgalta* and leaves the *Masach* of the *Guf* with a *Reshimo* of the Light that it had, called *Reshimo de Hitlabshut*. But the *Reshimo* of the strength of the *Masach* that received the Light does not stay, since the *Masach* had decided to stop receiving the Light, and disqualified itself from working with its strength. Hence, the *Reshimo* of the *Masach* disappears.

The *Masach* rose from *Tabur* back to the *Peh*. Hence, it feels the Upper Light in the *Rosh*, which pressures it with a demand to receive it. As a result, the desire to receive Light in order to bestow is reawakened in *Malchut*. This is the beginning of the birth of a new *Partzuf* on the remaining *Reshimot* from the previous state.

Summary: A *Reshimo* of the Light is a part of the Light, which the Light leaves after its departure. It is the nucleus, the root of the birth of the next *Partzuf*. The *Reshimo* from the *Masach* is lost, and the *Zivug* is done on a new *Reshimo*.

The Reshimot on which the Partzufim Emerge

World/Partzuf	Name	Reshimo de Hitlabshut	Reshimo de Aviut
World of Adam Kadmon:			
Partzuf Keter	Galgalta	Dalet	Dalet
Partzuf Hochma	AB	Dalet	Gimel
Partzuf Bina	SAG	Gimel	Bet
Partzuf ZA	MA	Bet	Aleph
Partzuf Malchut	BON	Aleph	Shoresh
Partzuf Nekudot de SAG:			
Partzuf Nekudot de SAG		Bet	Bet
World of Nekudim:			
Partzuf Katnut (smallness/infancy)		Bet	Aleph
Partzuf Gadlut (greatness/adulthood)		Dalet	Gimel
World of Atzilut:			
Partzuf Keter	Atik	Dalet	Dalet
Partzuf Hochma	AA	Dalet	Gimel
Partzuf Bina	AVI	Gimel	Bet
Partzuf ZA	ZA	Bet	Aleph
Partzuf Malchut	Nukva	Aleph	Shoresh
World of Beria:			
Partzuf Keter	Atik	Dalet	Dalet
Partzuf Hochma	AA	Dalet	Gimel
Partzuf Bina	AVI	Gimel	Bet
Partzuf ZA	ZA	Bet	Aleph
Partzuf Malchut	Nukva	Aleph	Shoresh
World of Yetzira:			
Partzuf Keter	Atik	Dalet	Dalet
Partzuf Hochma	AA	Dalet	Gimel
Partzuf Bina	AVI	Gimel	Bet
Partzuf ZA	ZA	Bet	Aleph
Partzuf Malchut	Nukva	Aleph	Shoresh
World of Assiya:			
Partzuf Keter	Atik	Dalet	Dalet
Partzuf Hochma	AA	Dalet	Gimel
Partzuf Bina	AVI	Gimel	Bet
Partzuf ZA	ZA	Bet	Aleph
Partzuf Malchut	Nukva	Aleph	Shoresh

Reshimot of the Aviut de Masach of the Worlds

World of *Keter*	World of *Adam Kadmon*	*Aviut Dalet*
World of *Hochma*	World of *Atzilut*	*Aviut Gimel*
World of *Bina*	World of *Beria*	*Aviut Bet*
World of *ZA*	World of *Yetzira*	*Aviut Aleph*
World of *Malchut*	World of *Assiya*	*Aviut Shoresh*

When the whole of reality expands until no *Reshimo* is left in the *Masach*, this is the end of the world of *Assiya*. *Malchut* of the world of *Atzilut* begets yet another *Partzuf*, called *Adam ha Rishon*, which shatters into pieces that fall below the world of *Assiya*, to a place called "this world."

The smallest *Reshimo* in the smallest broken *Kli* is called "the point in the heart." This is what a person feels as a desire for spirituality when being awakened from Above. These *Reshimot* clothe in certain people in our world and give them no rest, until they correct them with a *Masach* and fill them with Light.

If a person feels that *Reshimo*, he or she is worthy of achieving spirituality, of experiencing the Upper World and knowing the whole of reality. The guidance for achieving it is found in books of Kabbalah. Each generation has its own books of Kabbalah, written for that generation, for the particular kind of souls that descend in it.

The books that are to guide our generation into spirituality are the books of Rav Yehuda Ashlag (Baal HaSulam), and Rav Baruch Ashlag (the Rabash). Besides studying in these books, there are two more necessary conditions for proper learning: studying in a group, whose goal is to achieve the purpose of Creation, which is headed by a Kabbalist teacher (Rav).

In the cascading of reality from Above downwards, a ladder of degrees was formed, on which a person climbs back. One who achieves a certain degree discovers in it *Reshimot* from a Higher degree, and can thus continue to climb. *Reshimot* from Higher degrees appear in people in our world, too. These are *Reshimot* from the closest spiritual degree to that person. By working with these *Reshimot*, a person exits our world and enters the spiritual world.

THE BIRTH OF THE PARTZUFIM

Behina Dalet is called *Malchut*, since it hosts the biggest will to receive. When filled with Light, she is called *Ein Sof* (no end), since she receives the Light without putting an end to it. *Malchut* is the only created being. Her parts are called *Olamot* (worlds), since they *Maalimim* (conceal) the Creator's Light from the creatures. The concealment in each world corresponds to the measure by which the creatures can receive the Light using the *Masach*.

When *Behina Dalet* received the Light of *Ein Sof*, she felt that the Light was coming from the Giver. The sensation of the Giver evoked such shame and agony in her that she decided never to be a receiver.

A decision in a Higher One becomes a binding law for all its subsequent states. Thus, even if a part of *Malchut* does want to receive for itself, it will not be able to receive, since *Malchut* controls all its parts. Each new decision comes from the weakness of the degree; hence, each decision affects only the lower degrees.

Following *Tzimtzum Aleph*, *Reshimo* of the Light and the *Kli* remained in *Malchut*. The Light returned to *Malchut* and wanted to fill it, since the Creator's intention to delight the creature is constant. It is only this Thought of the Creator that operates in every act in Creation, even when it seems to us that reality is not in our favor.

Malchut, which stands at the *Peh* of the *Rosh* of the *Partzuf*, senses the Creator's goal to benefit her, as in the example of the guest and the host. *Malchut* feels that if she does not receive from the Creator, she will not be giving Him anything. Hence, she decides to receive, so the Creator will enjoy her reception.

With the help of the *Reshimot de Hitlabshut* and *de Aviut* from the previous filling, *Malchut* can accurately calculate how much she can receive, not according to her desire to enjoy, but in order to delight the Creator.

The *Reshimo de Hitlabshut* is a *Reshimo* from the Light that was in *Malchut*. The *Masach*, on which *Malchut* received that Light, has been purified. There was no power in the *Masach* to once again receive the same Light from which the *Reshimo de Hitlabshut* remained. Thus, the *Rosh de Hitlabshut* of the next *Partzuf* was born on the *Reshimo de Hitlabshut*. Afterwards, the *Masach* made a *Zivug* on the *Reshimo de Aviut*, begetting the second *Rosh*, called *Rosh de Aviut*, from which the *Guf* expanded. This is the clothing of the Light in *Malchut*.

The part in which *Malchut* decides how much of the Upper Light she can receive in order to bestow is called *Rosh*. Following the decision in the *Rosh*, *Malchut* receives the amount of Light she has decided, within the *Partzuf*. This Light is called *Taamim* (flavors).

When the Light of *Taamim* completes its entrance to the *Guf*, the *Masach* that extended it stops the expansion of the Light into the *Partzuf*. The *Masach* does not allow the Light to continue entering, since *Malchut's* decision is a decision on the maximum amount she can receive not in order to delight herself. If she receives more, it will be in order to receive pleasure for herself.

Hence, in a place where the *Masach* stops and does not receive anymore, *Malchut* senses once more the prompting of the Upper Light to receive it. This place is called *Tabur* (navel). If *Malchut* receives more Light, it will be for her own pleasure. Hence, she has no choice but to stop receiving Light altogether.

All decisions are made only at the *Rosh* of the *Partzuf*, and are then executed in the *Guf*. Here, too, following the decision in the *Rosh* to stop receiving, the *Masach* rises from *Tabur* to *Peh* and deports the Lights from the *Guf* of the *Partzuf*.

The *Masach* comes to the *Peh* with a *Reshimo* of the Light that filled the *Partzuf*, and a *Reshimo* of the *Aviut* that remained in the *Masach*. By the meeting of the *Masach* with the Upper Light at the *Rosh* of the *Partzuf*, the desire to receive Light in order to bestow is reawakened in the *Masach*, which awaken *Reshimot* in it. The *Masach* makes a *Zivug de Hakaa* with the Upper Light and begets the next *Partzuf*.

There are two *Masachim* (plural for *Masach*) in each *Partzuf*: a *Masach* that rejects the Light, and a *Masach* that receives the Light. The *Masach* that rejects the Light always stands at the *Peh* of the *Partzuf*, repelling all the Light that wishes to penetrate the *Partzuf*, and thus meets the condition of *Tzimtzum Aleph*.

Once the first *Masach* repels all the Light and is certain that it will not receive for itself, but only with the aim to bestow upon the Creator, it activates the second *Masach*, which weighs how much of the Upper Light that comes to it can be received with the aim to bestow.

Following the decision, the *Masach* begins to receive Light. It descends from the *Peh* down, and following it, the Light enters the *Partzuf*. When the measure of Light within the *Partzuf* reaches the measure that the *Masach* of the *Rosh* had decided on, the *Masach* that descended to the *Guf* stops. This is so because the *Masach* of the *Guf* always follows orders and decisions made by the *Masach* of the *Rosh*. Thus, the next *Partzuf* is born out of the former.

The calculation is done at the *Masach* in the *Rosh*. But because its *Aviut* is less than in the previous *Partzuf*, the *Masach* descends to the *Chazeh* of the *Partzuf*, and does not stand at the *Peh*. This is because the *Chazeh* is the level of *Aviut Gimel* of the *Guf*, as opposed to the *Peh*, which is *Dalet*.

Hence, once the *Masach* rises from *Tabur* to *Peh*, where it receives a desire to make a new *Zivug*, it descends to the *Chazeh* and calculates how much to receive. That calculation begets the second *Rosh* of the *Partzuf*. Following the decision, the *Masach* descends from the *Peh* down to the place it chose as the place through which it would receive Light. That place will become the *Tabur* of the next *Partzuf*.

Below *Tabur* and through the *Sium Raglin* of the next *Partzuf*, there remain empty *Kelim* that the *Masach* does not fill due to absence of resistance power. The second *Partzuf*, and the rest of the *Partzufim* of the world of *Adam Kadmon*, cannot descend below *Tabur* of the first *Partzuf*, due to the absence of power in their *Masach*.

After the second *Partzuf*, AB de AK, emerged and received what it decided in the *Rosh*, on the *Masach* that descended into its *Tabur*, too, there was a *Bitush* of *Ohr Pnimi* and *Ohr Makif*. Here, too, the *Masach* understands that it cannot remain at the *Tabur* because it does not have the strength to receive more, and were it to remain in its state, it would not achieve the purpose of Creation.

Hence, the *Masach* of the second *Partzuf*, too, decides to purify, and rises to the *Peh*. Here, too, a *Reshimo* remains in the *Masach*. When it reaches the *Peh* and is integrated in the *Masach* of the *Peh*, it reawakens to receive Light. The last *Reshimo de Aviut*, from *Behina Gimel*, disappears from the *Masach*, and *Reshimo de Behina Bet* appears. Hence, the *Masach* descends to the *Chazeh*, where it makes a *Zivug de Hakaa* for begetting the new *Partzuf*, called *Partzuf* SAG of AK.

Here, too, once *Partzuf* SAG emerged, its *Masach de Guf* is purified by the *Bitush* of *Ohr Pnimi* and *Ohr Makif* on it. The *Masach* rises to the *Peh*, descends to the *Chazeh*, and begets the next *Partzuf* at the level of *Aviut Aleph*, called "Upper MA."

When *Partzuf* Upper MA stops the expansion of the Light within it, it senses the *Bitush* of the Inner and Surrounding Lights within it, and decides to purify. It returns to the *Peh* with *Aviut Shoresh*, since the *Masach* no longer has the strength of *Kashiut* (hardness) to receive Light. It cannot beget a *Partzuf*, but only a *Rosh*, and thus stops the process of the birth of the *Partzufim*.

THE OVERALL REALITY

Following the *Tzimtzum*, *Malchut* decides to receive in order to bestow upon the Creator. This intention is called *Masach* (screen). Following, a sequence of *Partzufim* emerges on the *Masach* in *Malchut*:

- A *Partzuf* called *Galgalta* emerges on a *Masach* with the strength to receive Light on *Aviut Dalet*.
- A *Partzuf* called AB emerges on a *Masach* with the strength to receive Light on *Aviut Gimel*.

- A *Partzuf* called SAG emerges on a *Masach* with the strength to receive Light on *Aviut Bet*.
- A *Partzuf* called MA emerges on a *Masach* with the strength to receive Light on *Aviut Aleph*.
- A *Partzuf* called BON emerges on a *Masach* with the strength to receive Light on *Aviut Shoresh*.

The names of the *Partzufim* are determined by the quantity and quality of the Lights that fill them. *Malchut* emerged as *Behina Dalet*, meaning the fifth in the evolution of the Light of *Atzmuto*. Hence, she receives from the previous *Behinot* and contains them. For this reason, within *Malchut de Ein Sof* are five *Behinot* of the desire, from the smallest desire in *Behinat Shoresh* to the greatest desire in *Behina Dalet*, and she receives Light inside of her unboundedly.

After the *Tzimtzum*, *Malchut* decides to receive Light only in order to bestow upon the Creator. Reception in this manner is contrary to her natural desire; hence, she cannot receive unboundedly. She cannot receive all the Light at once, as before. Thus, she decides to receive all this Light in smaller portions. In the end, she will be completely filled and will achieve the purpose of Creation.

Each tiny part of *Malchut* is like the whole of *Malchut*, containing five parts of will to receive. This is so because there cannot be a desire if there are no four degrees of expansion of Lights preceding it.

For this reason, each *Kli* has a fixed structure, according to the five parts of *Aviut*: **Shoresh, Aleph, Bet, Gimel,** and **Dalet**, called *Sefirot* **Keter, Hochma, Bina, ZA,** and **Malchut**, called *Otiot* **Tip of the Yod, Yod, Hey, Vav,** and **Hey**.

The whole of *Malchut* is divided into five main parts, called five worlds: **AK (Adam Kadmon), Atzilut, Beria, Yetzira,** and **Assiya**. Each world is divided into five *Partzufim*: **Atik, AA (Arich Anpin), AVI (Aba ve Ima), ZA (Zeir Anpin),** and **Nukva (Malchut)**. Each *Partzuf* contains five *Sefirot*: **Keter, Hochma, Bina, ZA,** and **Malchut**.

The five worlds contain 5x5=25 *Partzufim*. Each *Partzuf* contains five *Sefirot*. Hence, in all the worlds there are 25x5=125 *Sefirot* or degrees each soul must experience, from this world to the world of *Ein Sof*, in order to achieve *Dvekut* with the Creator.

Each degree, *Sefira* (singular for *Sefirot*), *Partzuf*, world—a part of *Malchut de Ein Sof*, the smallest fraction of reality—comprises five parts of the will to receive, a *Masach* above it, and Light, which it receives through the *Masach*. Hence, the difference between all the parts of Creation is only in the measure of the will to receive and the *Masach* atop it. The measure of the *Masach* determines the kind and level of the implementation of the desire.

Our body contains the same parts. The difference between the parts is in their filling (stronger, smarter, or more skillful). Thus, the same parts exist in all the spiritual *Partzufim*: **the tip of the *Yod*, *Yod*, *Hey*, *Vav*, *Hey*.**

These letters are called "the name of the Creator," since He created the creature in this pattern. The creature senses its Creator by the way it is filled with Light—the Creator—and ascribes names to the Creator accordingly.

The name of each *Kli* follows the extent to which the *Kli* senses the Creator. Hence, each degree bears its own name, from this world to the world of *Ein Sof*. The souls rise to attain the purpose of Creation, beginning with this world, which is the lowest degree. When a soul ascends to a certain degree, it means that it receives the Light in that degree. In other words, it fills its *HaVaYaH* with a certain filling of Light of *HaVaYaH*, which, along with the filling, creates the name of the degree.

It is written that everyone must come to be like Moses. This means that everyone must achieve the degree called "Moses." All the names in the Torah are Holy Names, since they are depictions of the revelation of the Light, the Creator. Hence, the whole Torah is called "the names of the Creator," including such names as Pharaoh, Balaam, Balak, etc.

The name of the degree is determined by the Light that fills the *Partzuf*, the *HaVaYaH*. For example, if the *Kli* is filled with *Ohr Hochma*, and the symbol of that Light is the letter *Yod*, the filling of the letters *Yod*, *Hey*, *Vav*, *Hey* is *Yod*, *Hey* (a *Yod* in the *Hey*), *Viv* (a *Yod* in the *Vav*), *Hey* (a *Yod* in the *Hey*).

This is because each letter in the Hebrew alphabet has its own number:

Aleph = 1	*Zayin* = 7	*Mem* = 40	*Kof* = 100
Bet = 2	*Het* = 8	*Nun* = 50	*Reish* = 200
Gimel = 3	*Tet* = 9	*Samech* = 60	*Shin* = 300
Dalet = 4	*Yod* = 10	*Ayin* = 70	*Tav* = 400
Hey = 5	*Chaf* = 20	*Peh* = 80	
Vav = 6	*Lamed* = 30	*Tzadi* = 90	

Thus, if we sum up the letters in the name *HaVaYaH*: **Yod, Hey, Vav, Hey = Yod** (10+6+4) + **Hey** (5+10) + **Viv** (6+10+6) + **Hey** (5+10) = 72, which is the letters AB (Ayin+Bet). This is why *Partzuf Hochma* is called AB.

A *Partzuf* that receives Light of *Hassadim* is called SAG:

Yod, Hey, Vav, Hey = 63 = SAG (Samech+Gimel).

This is how all the degrees in the whole of reality are named. Hence, to know the name of each degree, we need only know the names of each type of Light. Then, when we read the Torah, we will understand which spiritual actions and which places and degrees in the Upper Worlds are being discussed.

Then we will no longer mistakenly think that the Torah discusses anything below the spiritual world. We will not think that the Torah speaks of our corporeal lives, of history, or of how to manage ourselves in our material lives. Instead, we will know that all books of Torah are actually instructions telling us how to achieve the purpose of our lives while still living in this world, so we will not have to return to this world cycle-by-cycle and repeatedly suffer this vain, purposeless, and useless life.

A *Partzuf* is ten *Sefirot*: *Keter, Hochma, Bina, ZA,* and *Malchut*

A *Partzuf* in letters is *Yod* (*Hochma*), *Hey* (*Bina*), *Vav* (*ZA*), and *Hey* (*Malchut*).

But the level of a *Partzuf—Nefesh, Ruach, Neshama, Haya, Yechida—*is not explained by the name *HaVaYaH*, since the letters *HaVaYaH* are ten *Sefirot* of the skeleton of the *Kli*. They clarify the state of the empty *Kli*, without fulfillment with the Upper Light. The level of the *Kli*, the spiritual degree of the *Kli*, is determined by the measure of the *Masach*. The *Masach* fills the ten *Sefirot* of *HaVaYaH* with Lights. The *Masach* can fill the *Kli* with Light of *Nefesh, Ruach, Neshama, Haya,* or *Yechida*. The Light in the *Kli* determines the *Kli*'s degree on the ladder of degrees.

There are only two Lights in reality: *Ohr Hochma* (Light of Wisdom) and *Ohr Hassadim* (Light of Mercy). The symbol for *Ohr Hochma* is the letter *Yod*, and the symbol for *Ohr Hassadim* is the letter *Hey*.

1. The registration of the level of *Yechida* (*Kli Keter*) is simple *HaVaYaH*, without filling: **Yod, Hey, Vav, Hey** = 10+5+6+5 = 26.

2. The registration of the level of *Haya* (*Kli Hochma*) is *HaVaYaH* filled with *Yod*: **Yod, Hey, Viv, Hey** = (10+6+4) + (5+10) + (6+10+6) + (5+10) = 72.

3. The registration of the level of *Neshama* (*Kli Bina*) is *HaVaYaH* filled with *Hey*, except that the letter *Vav* is filled with *Aleph*, and the letter *Hey* is filled with *Yod*: **Yod, Hey, Vav, Hey** = (10+6+4) + (5+10) + (6+1+6) + (5+10) = 63.

4. The registration of the level of *Ruach* (*Kli ZA*) is *HaVaYaH* filled with *Hey*, except that the letter *Vav* of *HaVaYaH* is filled with *Aleph*: **Yod, He, Vav, He** = (10+6+4) + (5+1) + (6+1+6) + (5+1) = 45.

5. The registration of the level of *Nefesh* (*Kli Malchut*) is *HaVaYaH* filled with *Hey*, except the letter *Vav* of *HaVaYaH*, which remains without filling: **Yod, Hh, Vv, Hh** = (10+6+4) + (5+5) + (6+6) + (5+5) = 52.

This is the source of the names, AB, SAG, MA, BON.

NEKUDOT DE SAG

After *Tzimtzum Aleph*, *Malchut* decides to fill herself in order to bestow using the *Reshimot* that remained from the world of *Ein Sof*. Reception in order to bestow is against the creature's nature. Hence, *Malchut* cannot instantaneously receive all the Upper Light that filled her in the world of *Ein Sof*, but only in small portions, called *Partzufim*. Thus, *Malchut* receives five portions of Light: *Galgalta*, AB, SAG, Upper MA, and Upper BON. This completes the exit of all the *Reshimot* in her, and the chain of expansion is stopped.

The third *Partzuf* to emerge is *Partzuf SAG*. Its nature is that of *Bina*, so it does not want to receive anything for itself; it "delights in mercy." For this reason, this *Partzuf* can descend below *Tabur de Galgalta* and fill the end of *Galgalta* with its Lights.

Partzuf SAG emerged on *Reshimot* of *Hitlabshut Gimel* and *Aviut Bet*. Hence, there is illumination of *Hochma* in its *Taamim*. For this reason, the *Taamim* of SAG cannot descend below *Tabur de Galgalta*. But when *Partzuf SAG* begins to purify, the *Ohr Hochma* immediately vanishes, and as the *Masach* purifies from *Tabur* to *Peh*, *Partzuf Nekudot de SAG* emerges, and this *Partzuf* contains only *Ohr Hassadim*. Thus, this *Partzuf* can descend below *Tabur de Galgalta* and fill the *Sof* (end) of *Galgalta* with *Ohr Hassadim*.

The whole of reality emerges from *Behinat Shoresh*, the Creator's desire to benefit His creatures. In accordance with this desire, the Light expands as a cause and effect sequence to execute the Thought of Creation within the *Kli*, so it will receive it.

In *Behina Aleph*, which is the whole of the Light and the *Kli*, there is the whole of the Creator's intention to make a *Kli* and fill it with Light. Everything that emerges after *Behina Aleph* emerges from it. Thus the thought of the Creator appears in actual fact. The Creator imprinted the possibility to bring Creation to its goal of rising to the degree of the Creator within the nature of the *Kelim* and the Lights, from the outset.

After *Tzimtzum Aleph*, *Malchut de Ein Sof* decided to receive through the *Masach* and generated five *Partzufim*: *Galgalta*, AB, SAG, Upper MA, and Upper

BON. This completes the elicitation of all the *Reshimot*, and exhausted the force of the *Masach*, although only part of *Malchut* was filled.

Had *Nekudot de SAG* not descended to fill the *Sof* of *Galgalta*, *Malchut de Ein Sof* would never have been filled. This is so because *Malchut* is only a desire to receive, without any mixture of desires to bestow. And here, when *Nekudot de SAG*—which are *Bina*—descend to the *Sof* of *Galgalta*—which is *Malchut*—it creates a mixture of *Malchut* with *Bina*. Thus, *Malchut* is given an opportunity to acquire the desire (*Kli*) for bestowal, to correct herself and be filled with Light.

Following *Tzimtzum Aleph*, *Malchut de Ein Sof* decided to receive only by means of a *Masach*, that is, according to her ability to receive in order to bestow. She makes a *Zivug* on *Reshimot* of *Hitlabshut Dalet* and *Aviut Dalet*, which remained in her after the *Tzimtzum*, and received a part of the Light of *Ein Sof*. The part of *Malchut de Ein Sof* that was filled by this *Zivug* is called *Galgalta* or *Keter*.

Subsequently, *Malchut* receives yet another share of the Light of *Ein Sof*, in order to bestow. The part of *Malchut* that was filled by this *Zivug* on the *Masach* with *Reshimot* of *Hitlabshut Dalet* and *Aviut Gimel* that remained after *Galgalta* is called AB, or *Partzuf Hochma*.

The part of *Malchut de Ein Sof* that was filled by the *Zivug* on the *Reshimot* in the next stage—*Hitlabshut Gimel* and *Aviut Bet* that remained after *Partzuf AB*—is called SAG, or *Partzuf Bina*. *Partzuf SAG* is the same *Malchut*, will to receive, except it cannot receive in order to bestow, through the *Masach*, like *Partzufim Galgalta* and AB; it can only make itself similar to *Behina Bet*, *Bina*.

By its nature, *Bina* does not want to receive Light; she wishes only to bestow. There are no limitations on the act of giving; hence, *Partzuf SAG* can fill with its *Ohr Hassadim*, the whole part of *Malchut* that remained empty.

Bina comprises three parts:

1. Expansion of *Ohr Hochma*.

2. *Bina's* decision that it does not want *Ohr Hochma*, but wishes only to bestow. This is why *Ohr Hassadim* spreads in this part.

3. *Bina* receives some *Ohr Hochma*, but not for herself, to pass it on to *Partzuf ZA*.

The first part in *Bina* is still *Hochma*. Only from the second part in *Bina* does the desire to bestow begin to manifest. Hence, she can fill the part of *Malchut de Ein Sof*, the part where there is a desire to bestow with *Ohr Hassadim*, below the general *Tabur*, which has not yet been filled.

Partzuf SAG begins to receive Light in its *Toch* through a *Zivug* on *Hitlabshut Gimel* and *Aviut Bet*. The presence of *Reshimo* of *Gimel de Hitlabshut* induces the expansion of *Ohr Hochma* in its *Taamim*. For this reason, this part of *Malchut* cannot descend below *Tabur de Galgalta*.

But once *Masach de SAG* begins to purify and rises from *Tabur* to *Peh*, a part of the *Partzuf*, which is only *Bina*, can descend below *Tabur de Galgalta*. The Light that departs from *Partzuf* SAG can also descend below *Tabur de Galgalta*, since it is *Ohr Hassadim*, without *Ohr Hochma*.

For this reason, the part of *Partzuf* SAG, called *Nekudot de SAG*, which includes the second and third parts of *Partzuf Bina*, descends below *Tabur de Galgalta* and clothes over its *Sof*.

TZIMTZUM BET

Nekudot de SAG descended below *Tabur de Galgalta* and there filled the empty *Kelim* of *Sof de Galgalta* with *Ohr Hassadim*. They sensed that there are *Reshimot* from the Light that filled the *Sof* of *Galgalta* prior to its *Hizdakchut* (purification) in *Galgalta*'s empty *Kelim*.

The Light that filled the *Sof de Galgalta* was *Ohr Hassadim* with a little bit of *Hochma*, and *Reshimot* remained there after the *Hizdakchut* of the *Masach*: *Reshimo* from the Light of *Dalet de Hitlabshut*, and *Reshimo* from the *Masach* on *Gimel de Aviut*. The *Sof* of *Galgalta* repelled the Light from spreading in it, like *Bina*, and in that, it became similar to *Nekudot de SAG*. Hence, *Nekudot de SAG* mingled with the *Sof de Galgalta* and filled her empty *Kelim*.

By mixing *Nekudot de SAG* with the *Sof* of *Galgalta*, they received *Reshimot* that remained in the *Sof* of *Galgalta*. The *Reshimot* from *Galgalta* were larger than the *Masach* of *Nekudot de SAG*, and in consequence, *Nekudot de SAG* began to want to receive the pleasure that was in *Galgalta* for themselves.

The rule is that if the pleasure being sensed in the will to receive is greater than the force of the *Masach*, the *Kli* wants it for itself, since the stronger one—*Masach* or desire—determines.

All the worlds and *Partzufim* are parts of *Malchut de Ein Sof*. This *Malchut* made a *Tzimtzum* and decided never to receive for herself. Hence, now that a desire to receive for itself appeared in *Partzuf Nekudot de SAG*, *Malchut* that made the *Tzimtzum Aleph* rose and stood at the *Sium* of *Galgalta*, up to the place where *Partzuf Nekudot de SAG* stands. This is the place from which *Nekudot de SAG* began to want to receive the Light for themselves.

Each *Partzuf* contains ten *Sefirot*: *Keter, Hochma, Bina, Hesed, Gevura, Tifferet, Netzah, Hod, Yesod, Malchut*. *Nekudot de SAG* is *Partzuf Bina*, and *Bina* divides into two parts:

1. *Bina's* Upper parts are the *Sefirot* **Keter, Hochma, Bina, Hesed, Gevura, Tifferet**. These *Sefirot* want only to give, and to not receive a thing.

2. The bottom parts of *Bina* are the *Sefirot* **Netzah, Hod, Yesod, Malchut**.

These *Sefirot* do not belong to *Bina*. Their role in *Bina* is to receive *Ohr Hochma* from *Hochma*, and pass it onto the lower one. This means that *Sefirot* **Netzah, Hod, Yesod, and Malchut** in *Bina* have a desire to receive Light. They have a *Masach* to receive the Light not for themselves, but only to pass it on to the lower one. But if the *Masach* is lost, the *Sefirot*—these desires—immediately want to receive it for themselves, without giving it to others.

Example: A certain person was used to receiving a regular sum of money and pass it to people who were destitute. All of a sudden, he received a much larger sum than usual, and felt that he could not deliver the money; he wanted it for himself. He could not resist such a great pleasure.

As long as the pleasure in the money was smaller than his *Masach*, he resisted the pleasures because the pleasure of giving the money was greater than the pleasure of delighting himself (stealing). But when the pleasure from reception became greater than the pleasure from giving, he immediately wanted to receive for himself.

This is how the will to receive operates in every person and in every creature because our very substance is the will to receive. If we perform acts of bestowal, it is only because they bring us more benefit than acts of reception.

This is also what happened in *Partzuf Nekudot de SAG*: When the part of the *Partzuf* that received in order to deliver to the lower ones was exposed to greater pleasure than the power of the *Masach*, the *Masach* was immediately cancelled and the *Partzuf* wanted to receive for itself.

The will to receive for self evoked in *Partzuf Nekudot de SAG* from the *Sefira Tifferet* downwards. This is so because *Sefirot Keter, Hochma, Bina* are *Sefirot* of *Rosh*, which do not want to receive, and *Hesed, Gevura, Tifferet* are like *Sefirot Keter, Hochma, Bina*, except they are in *Guf* of the *Partzuf*. *Hesed* is like *Keter*, *Gevura* is like *Hochma*, and *Tifferet* is like *Bina*. Thus, the *Sefira Tifferet* is *Bina* of the *Guf* of the *Partzuf*.

Each *Sefira* comprises ten internal *Sefirot*. Hence, the *Sefira Tifferet* is divided in its ten internal *Sefirot* into two parts, like *Bina*: 1) *Kelim* that "do not receive"— *Sefirot Keter, Hochma, Bina, Hesed, Gevura, Tifferet*; 2) *Kelim* that "receive in order to bestow," which are the lower part of *Bina*, *Sefirot Netzah, Hod, Yesod, Malchut*.

Partzuf Nekudot de SAG divides into vessels of bestowal and vessels of reception. The separating line between them is in the internal *Sefira* of *Tifferet*, of the *Sefira Tifferet*. This place is called "the *Chazeh* of *Partzuf Nekudot de SAG*."

Now, a part of the *Kelim* of *Nekudot de SAG* received a desire that was greater than their *Masach*; hence, *Malchut de Tzimtzum Aleph*, which maintains *Tzimtzum Aleph*, rose specifically to this place. It stood there and did not allow Light to permeate below it. The boundary on the expansion of Light that was made here is called *Parsa*.

Malchut's ascent to the place of *Chazeh* of *Nekudot de SAG*, to limit the expansion of Light downwards, is called *Tzimtzum Bet* (second restriction). *Tzimtzum Aleph* (first restriction) is the ban on receiving *Ohr Hochma* in order to receive, and *Tzimtzum Bet* is a ban on any reception of *Ohr Hochma*, since there is no strength to receive *Ohr Hochma* in order to bestow from *Partzuf Nekudot de SAG* down. This is why any dealing with it is forbidden.

"A desire in the Upper One becomes a binding law in the lower one." Hence, in all the *Partzufim* that emerge after *Tzimtzum Bet*, the *Parsa* in them does not allow the Upper Light—*Ohr Hochma*—to go through it and down to the vessels of reception. For this reason, the place below *Tabur de Galgalta* was divided into four parts:

1. The place of the world of *Atzilut*, where *Ohr Hochma* can shine.
2. The place of the world of *Beria*, under the *Parsa*, where *Ohr Hochma* cannot appear, but only *Ohr Hassadim*.
3. The place of the world of *Yetzira*, below the place of the world of *Beria*.
4. The place of the world of *Assiya*, below the place of the world of *Yetzira*.

The *Sium* (end) of the world of *Assiya* is also the end of *Kedusha* (holiness). Below the *Kedusha* there are (1) the barrier—the boundary between spirituality and corporeality, separating the world of *Assiya* from the point of the world; (2) the place of this world; and (3) our world.

THE WORLD OF NEKUDIM

The whole process of the descent of *Nekudot de SAG* below *Tabur de Galgalta*, their mingling with the *Sof* of *Galgalta*, and *Tzimtzum Bet* took place during the ascension of the *Masach de SAG* from *Tabur* to *Peh*. Hence, when the *Masach* reached *Peh de SAG*, the *Reshimot* from all that had happened from *Nekudot de SAG* upwards and from *Tabur de Galgalta* downwards were already in it.

Following the *Hizdakchut* (purification) of *Partzuf Galgalta*, there remain a *Reshimo de Hitlabshut Dalet* of the Light that was in *Galgalta* and a *Reshimo de Aviut Gimel* of the remaining *Masach*. Following the *Hizdakchut* of *Partzuf AB*, *Reshimot* of *Hitlabshut Gimel* and *Aviut Bet* remained in the *Masach*. Thus, we see that after the *Hizdakchut* of the *Partzuf*, a pair of *Reshimot* remain in it: *Reshimo de Hitlabshut* and *Reshimo de Aviut*.

But following the *Hizdakchut* of *Partzuf SAG*, three pairs of *Reshimot* remained in the *Masach* that reached from *Tabur* to *Peh*, on which the *Masach* made three *Zivugim*, by order of importance:

1. A *Zivug* on *Reshimot Bet de Hitlabshut* and *Aleph de Aviut* from *Taamim de SAG*. They create a *Partzuf* at the level of ZA, above *Tabur*, called "Upper MA."

2. A *Zivug* on *Reshimot Bet de Hitlabshut* and *Aleph de Aviut* from *Nekudot de SAG* that have spread below *Tabur de Galgalta*. These *Reshimot* are subsequent to *Tzimtzum Bet* that was made in *Nekudot de SAG*, below *Tabur*.

    Everything that was in the *Partzuf* moves to the *Reshimot*. Hence, the prohibition on using the vessels of reception from *Tzimtzum Bet* is registered in the *Reshimot* from *Nekudot de SAG*. To keep this condition according to the demand of the *Reshimot*, the *Masach de Rosh de SAG* rises from *Peh* to *Nikvey Eynaim*, where it makes a *Zivug de Hakaa* with the Upper Light on *Reshimot Bet de Hitlabshut* and *Aleph de Aviut*.

    The place at the *Rosh* where the *Masach* makes a *Zivug de Hakaa* with the Upper Light determines the uniqueness of the expansion of Lights in the *Guf* of the *Partzuf*.

3. A *Zivug* on *Reshimot Dalet de Aviut* and *Gimel de Hitlabshut*. This will be discussed later in the essay.

The *Masach* rose to *Nikvey Eynaim* (NE) due to the ban on reception of Light in the vessels of reception. The Light can only expand through the *Chazeh* in each *Partzuf*, since the vessels of bestowal are present only through the *Chazeh*, and from the *Chazeh* down begin the vessels of reception in the *Partzuf*.

The *Masach* that makes a *Zivug* on the restricted *Reshimot* begets a *Partzuf*. The Light spreads in this *Partzuf* and fills only the vessels of bestowal. It does not fill the *Kelim* for the reception of the Light, and they remain empty. The *Partzuf* can use only a part of its *Kelim*, which is why it is considered "small."

Question: Why does the *Masach* rise from *Peh* to *Nikvey Eynaim* and makes the *Zivug* there, according to the demand of the *Reshimot*?

Answer: This is so because the *Reshimot* require a *Zivug* only on the vessels of bestowal. For this reason, the *Masach* should rise to half of *Bina de Rosh de SAG*, where the vessels of bestowal of the *Rosh* end, and make a *Zivug* on *Reshimot Bet de Hitlabshut* and *Aleph de Aviut*.

The *Reshimot* from below *Tabur* demand to extend Light only in vessels of bestowal, but how can a *Partzuf* be born only with vessels of bestowal? There cannot be a *Partzuf* that does not comprise ten *Sefirot*. However, there can be a *Partzuf* that is not using some of its desires—*Sefirot*. Hence, *Rosh de SAG* must beget a *Partzuf* whose vessels of reception will be inactive. These *Kelim* in the *Partzuf* are the bottom half of *Bina*, *ZA*, and *Malchut*.

The *Masach* of SAG must beget the *Partzuf* in such a way that, from the outset, it will not use the vessels of reception in its *Toch*, so these vessels in the *Partzuf* will not be filled. For this to happen, the *Masach* must make a *Zivug* for delivering the *Partzuf*, only with the vessels of bestowal in the *Rosh*.

The *Kelim* of the *Rosh* are as follows:

Keter = Galgalta

Hochma = Eynaim

Bina = Awznaim

ZA = Hotem

Malchut = Peh

THE DIVISION OF ROSH DE SAG INTO FIVE BEHINOT

The *Kelim*, *Keter*, *Hochma*, and Upper half of *Bina* together are called *Galgalta ve Eynaim* (GE), or "vessels of bestowal." The Upper half of *Bina* belongs to the vessels of bestowal since she is filled with *Ohr Hochma*, and hence does not want to receive anything, but craves *Ohr Hassadim*. But *Bina*'s lower half does want to receive Light for ZA. *Partzuf Nekudot de SAG* is *Partzuf Bina*. From the bottom half of *Partzuf Bina*, that is, from the *Sefira Tifferet de Nekudot de SAG* down, there are vessels of reception:

- The bottom half of *Bina* wishes to receive Light for ZA.
- ZA wishes to receive *Ohr Hassadim* in illumination of *Ohr Hochma*.
- *Malchut* wishes to receive the full *Ohr Hochma*.

For this reason, this part of *Partzuf Nekudot de SAG* received a desire to receive in order to receive.

THE DIVISION OF PARTZUF NEKUDOT DE SAG INTO GE AND AHP

The place where the *Masach de Rosh* stands determines the shape of the *Partzuf* that will be born:

- If the *Masach* wishes to beget a *Partzuf* that will receive Light in all of its ten *Sefirot*, it must make a *Zivug* in the *Peh*. Once the *Masach* stands at the *Peh*, the *Kashiut* (hardness) of the *Masach* determines the level of the *Partzuf* (size and height), that is, the extent to which the *Masach* will use its five *Kelim*.

- If the *Masach* wishes to beget a *Partzuf* that will receive Light only in vessels of bestowal, that is, in only half of the *Partzuf*, it should stand at *Nikvey Eynaim*, and not at the *Peh de Rosh*, since there is the Upper half of the *Rosh*. Then the vessels of bestowal will be above the *Masach*, meaning they will be taken into the calculation of the *Masach*.

Once the *Masach* stands at *Nikvey Eynaim*, its *Kashiut* determines the size (height) of the *Partzuf*, that is, the percentage of its vessels of bestowal that the *Partzuf* will use. The *Partzuf* that is born under these conditions is called "*Katnut* of the world of *Nekudim*."

Once a *Zivug* on the restricted *Reshimot* of *Bet de Hitlabshut* and *Aleph de Aviut* is made in *Rosh de SAG*, the newly born *Partzuf* descends to the place from which the *Reshimot* rose. It descends below *Tabur de Galgalta* and spreads there in *Rosh* and *Guf*. The *Rosh de Hitlabshut* is called *Keter*, *Rosh de Aviut* is called *Aba ve Ima* (AVI), and the *Guf* is called ZON.

Its structure contains *Rosh* and *Guf*, and each part in it is divided into two parts: GE and AHP:

- GE are always vessels of bestowal. They can always be used because the *Tzimtzum* was only on *Ohr Hochma*.

- AHP are always vessels of reception. Once *Tzimtzum Bet* was made in *Partzuf Nekudot de SAG*, no *Partzuf* that emerges has the strength to receive *Ohr Hochma* in the *Kelim* of AHP in order to bestow.

The third pair of *Reshimot*, which rose with the *Masach* to *Rosh de SAG*, are *Reshimot* that moved to *Nekudot de SAG* from the *Sof* of *Galgalta*: *Dalet de Hitlabshut* and *Gimel de Aviut*. *Partzuf Nekudot de SAG* was integrated with these *Reshimot* when it filled the *Sof de Galgalta*, and these *Reshimot* demand to receive *Ohr Hochma*.

After *Partzuf Katnut* of the world of *Nekudim* descended to its place, from *Tabur de Galgalta* through *Parsa*, *Rosh de SAG* gave it the remaining *Reshimo*, *Dalet* de *Hitlabshut* and *Gimel de Aviut*. By the demand of these *Reshimot*, the *Masach* that stood at *Nikvey Eynaim de Rosh AVI* descended to *Peh de AVI*, where it made a *Zivug* on *Reshimot Dalet-Gimel*. As a result of this *Zivug*, *Ohr Hochma* descended to the *Guf*, reached the *Parsa*, and went through it.

Rosh de AVI thought that according to the current awakening of *Reshimot Dalet-Gimel*, the vessels of reception below the *Parsa* could now receive in order to bestow. Hence, *AVI* made a *Zivug* on *Gadlut*, that is, on *Reshimot Dalet-Gimel*. For this purpose, they joined the *Kelim* of *GE* with the *AHP* in their *Rosh*, as well as in their *Guf*, which are *ZON*, and *Ohr Hochma* expanded from them down to *ZON*.

THE BIRTH OF A PARTZUF FROM THE UPPER ONE, PARTZUF KATNUT DE NEKUDIM, AND PARTZUF GADLUT DE NEKUDIM

The *Roshim* (plural for *Rosh*) of *Keter* and *AVI* have no knowledge that the Light of *AB-SAG* that came from above and gave strength to the *Kli* to shift from *Katnut* to *Gadlut*, could not descend below the *Parsa*. This is why the *Parsa* was not cancelled. When *Ohr Hochma* began to fill the *Kelim* below the *Parsa*, the *Kelim* began to break, since they remained in the will to receive in order to receive.

When *Rosh* of *AVI* made a *Zivug* on *Reshimot* of *Dalet de Hitlabshut* and *Gimel de Aviut*, *Ohr Hochma* came out of them and entered the *Guf* of *Nekudim*. The Light extended through *GE*, wishing to go through the *Parsa* and enter the *AHP* of the *Guf*. At that time, the *Kelim* of *AHP* began to receive the *Ohr Hochma* in order to receive. The *Kelim* of *GE*, which stand above the *Parsa*, joined the *Kelim* of *AHP* below the *Parsa* into a single *Guf*. For this reason, the *GE*–vessels of bestowal–broke along with the *AHP*–vessels of reception.

The first *Partzuf* of *Gadlut de Nekudim* was made when *Ohr Hochma* came out of *Peh de AVI* and expanded through the *Guf* of *Nekudim*, which include *GE* and *AHP*. And it broke—(a) the *Kelim de Guf* lost the *Masach*, and (b) they fell from their previous state, since they wanted to receive in order to receive.

As a result of the shattering, the *Masach* of the first *Partzuf de Gadlut*, *Partzuf AVI*, purified and rose with *Reshimot Gimel-Bet* that remained in it, to *Peh de Rosh AVI*. There, it made a *Zivug de Hakaa* on these *Reshimot* and generated the next *Partzuf*, whose *Rosh* is called YESHSUT. Once the *Rosh* emerged, it calculated and produced a *Guf*.

Partzuf YESHSUT broke and died, too. Hence, the *Masach* purified and rose to the *Peh* of YESHSUT with the *Reshimot Bet-Aleph*. A *Guf* cannot emerge on these *Reshimot*, since there is not enough *Aviut* to receive Light.

Thus, we see that the two *Partzufim* that emerged, AVI and YESHSUT, broke. As each *Partzuf* purified, four *Partzufim* of *Nekudot* emerged. Thus, in all, eight *Partzufim* emerged, called "the eight *Melachim*" (kings), since *Malchut*, the will to receive in order to receive, governs them.

Each *Partzuf* comprises *HaVaYaH*, four parts. This is the structure of every creation. Each *Partzuf* contains its own ten *Sefirot*; hence, the total number of parts is 8x4x10=320. In *Gematria*, this number is called *Shach* (*Shin* + *Chaf*), since the letter *Shin* equals 300 and the letter *Chaf* equals 20.

The breaking occurred at all the *Sefirot*. All the *Sefirot* were mingled and integrated in one another, so each broken part comprised 320 parts. Hence, the whole work in the *Tikkun* (correction) is to sort out each of the parts of the broken *Kelim*.

The least broken of the 320 parts should be taken first, and then sort out the parts of *Malchut* that caused the breaking from among its broken pieces. In total, the 320 broken pieces are the nine *Sefirot* of ZON de Nekudim. *Malchut* is the tenth part in these ten *Sefirot*, meaning that within the 320 parts are 32 parts of *Malchut*.

Sorting the parts of *Malchut* is done by the *Ohr Hochma*. When *Ohr Hochma* shines to all 320 broken pieces, it can only shine to the nine *Sefirot*, meaning to 288 (320-32) of the pieces, and not for the tenth *Sefira*, the 32 parts of *Malchut*. This is how the sorting is done.

Malchut is the only evil part, preventing us from entering spirituality. Our nature is to distance ourselves from the bad. This is why one comes to hate evil. Because in spirituality the separator is hatred, one is separated from this evil, the will to receive for oneself.

- The 288 pieces that are fit for correction are called *Rapach* (*Reish* = 200 + *Peh* = 80 + *Het* = 8).
- The 32 pieces unfit for correction are called *Lev ha Even* (stony heart). *Lev* is written with *Lamed* (30) and *Bet* (2). Thus *Lamed* (30) + *Bet* (2) = 32.

Therefore, after the sorting of the *Lamed-Bet* (32) *Malchuts* that are not to be used, the *Rapach* (288) broken pieces remain to be corrected. These are the broken pieces of the first nine *Sefirot*. Of those, the first ones to be sorted are the vessels of bestowal, GE. They comprise the ZON of the world of *Atzilut*.

As there are ten *Sefirot* in the *Hitpashtut* (expansion) of the Light in the *Kli* from Above downwards, there are also ten *Sefirot* in the thickness of the *Kli*.

These come from the *Hitkalelut* (mingling) of the *Sefirot* through the *Ohr Hozer*. The ten *Sefirot* at the thickness of the *Partzuf* are called:

Keter — Mocha

Hochma — Atzamot

Bina — Gidin

ZA — Bassar

Malchut — Or

Here, too, the law of *Tzimtzum Bet* applies just as in the *Sefirot* of the length.

THE WORLD OF TIKKUN (CORRECTION)

Following the shattering of the world of *Nekudim*, the **Lights** that filled *Partzuf Gadlut de Nekudim* departed to the *Rosh* of *Partzuf Nekudim*. The **Reshimot** that remained in the *Masach* rose to the *Rosh* of *Partzuf Nekudim*, and then to *Rosh de SAG*. The **Nitzotzin**, parts of *Ohr Hozer* (pieces of the broken *Masach*), fell into the broken *Kelim*, which lost the *Masach* and returned to the will to receive in order to receive. It is considered that they fell to the place of *BYA*, below the *Parsa*.

The difference between the *Hizdakchut* of the *Partzuf* through the *Bitush* of *Ohr Pnimi* and *Ohr Makif*, and the *Hizdakchut* of the *Partzuf* through the shattering is that after the shattering, the *Kelim* must be mended first, and only then can *Zivugim* be made on them, to bear new *Partzufim*, meaning to fill them with Light.

The intention of the *Rosh* of the world of *Nekudim* was to receive all the Light of the purpose of Creation in order to bestow, by filling the whole *Sof* of *Galgalta*. Thus, it would achieve the complete filling of *Malchut de Ein Sof*. Hence, when the shattering of the vessels is corrected, it corrects all the vessels of reception, so they work in order to bestow, and *Gmar Tikkun* (the end of correction) is achieved.

Yet, this will not make the whole of *Malchut de Ein Sof* corrected, but only a part of it, its *Behinot Shoresh*, *Aleph*, *Bet*, and *Gimel*, excluding *Behina Dalet*. *Behina Dalet* is the only creature. *Behinot Shoresh*, *Aleph*, *Bet*, and *Gimel* in it come from the *Hitkalelut* of the Upper nine in her, from the Creator's influence on her, while a "creature" is a desire that is completely detached from the Creator and stands in its own right.

Only *Behina Dalet* in *Behina Dalet* is a will to receive in order to receive that feels independent. Hence, it is only she who restricts her will to receive. After the *Tzimtzum*, all the *Partzufim* and all the worlds emerge to fill desires *Shoresh*, *Aleph*, *Bet*, and *Gimel* in *Behina Dalet*, and not *Behina Dalet* in *Dalet*.

But if what requires correction is *Behina Dalet* in *Dalet*, and not *Behinot Shoresh*, *Aleph*, *Bet*, and *Gimel* in *Dalet*, why are Lights received in these desires? These desires are not the creature's desires; they are the qualities of the Creator, the forces of the Creator. Using them, He guides the creature—*Behina Dalet* in *Behina Dalet*. These forces fill the spiritual worlds, except for Adam's soul.

Behina Dalet herself, Adam's soul, cannot really correct herself into receiving in order to bestow. Rather, the very correction of the creature is in examining all its qualities opposite all of the Creator's qualities, and in all cases, preferring to be like the Creator. The creature does not use its own quality—the stony heart— but only the Upper nine, the 248 *Behinot* that it sorts out and elevates after the breaking, towards unity with the Creator.

All the *Zivugim* performed after *Tzimtzum Aleph* are made on these desires. The *Partzufim*, worlds, and everything within the worlds are born out of these *Zivugim*, and spread from Above downwards. All five worlds, with the five *Partzufim* in each world, become a ladder of degrees from the Creator—the Giver—to the creature—the receiver. The rungs of the ladder are measures of equivalence of desires between the creature and the Creator.

The cascading of the *Partzufim* and the worlds from Above downwards builds the degrees, which are like coverings over the Light of *Ein Sof*. Each *Partzuf* covers the Light and conceals it from the *Partzufim* below it, to the extent that it receives in order to bestow.

We can compare the *Partzufim* and the worlds to onion skins: round, encircling one another, and the more internal the skin, the more the Light is covered. Thus, the point of darkness is at the end of the ladder, in the middle of all these circles.

To allow the creature's desire freedom of action, and for the creature to achieve equivalence with the Creator and cleave to Him out of free choice, and also, to enable the creature to develop and rise from its state to the degree of the Creator, the creature must be born in the middle point of all the worlds, the point of darkness. Also, the possibility of correcting its desire must be prepared for it, although due to the creature's weakness, the correction is not instantaneous, but gradual.

For this purpose, a ladder of degrees has been prepared, with five worlds, five *Partzufim* in each world, and five *Sefirot* in each *Partzuf*. In total, there are

125 degrees from the creature's initial state to its completion. Hence, the worlds have two roles:

1. To gradually hide the Light of *Ein Sof*. This is done by the cascading of the worlds from Above downwards. This is why the degrees of concealment are called *Olamot* (worlds), from the word *Haalama* (concealment).

2. Providing the creature (souls) with corrections with which they can climb the degrees of the worlds from below Upwards. Each degree it acquires is a *Partzuf*, created during the cascading from Above downwards. To climb the spiritual degrees, the creature must be assisted by the degree for which it aspires. When the creature is assisted by that degree, it uses this auxiliary force to acquire a *Masach* and rise to that stage. When the creature rises to that degree, it is given the name of that degree.

From this, we learn that all the worlds and what fills them are but a ladder prepared by the Creator for man's ascension. When one climbs those degrees, all the souls rise along with him, since all the worlds and everything that fills these worlds is within us. Hence, other than the attaining individual, the creature, there is only the Creator!

Around us is only Simple, Upper Light, in complete rest. This means that the Creator's intention is unchanging, and it is the same in all His Actions—to benefit man. A person feels the Creator only to the extent of one's equivalence of qualities with the Creator's quality of bestowal:

- If qualities—desires, intentions—totally contradict those of the Creator, one does not feel the Creator. According to one's sensation, a person calls that state "this world."

- If one succeeds in changing a certain quality and makes it somewhat similar to the Creator's quality of bestowal, it is considered that that person has gone from the state of "this world" to the state of "the spiritual world." Thus, one enters the first degree of the ladder of degrees towards nearing the Creator.

All the changes are only within man, in one's vessels of reception. They depend on the measure of correction of one's *Masach* within him. But other than man, there is only the Upper Light, where there are no changes. By obtaining a part of the Upper Light, one attains and feels a part of the Creator. And according to this feeling, one names the sensation of the Creator: "Merciful," "Gracious," "Terrible," etc.

The whole of the Torah is only registrations of sensations of a person who attains spirituality, who approaches the Creator. It follows that the whole Torah is names of the Creator. This is why it is written that the whole Torah is His Holy Names. A person who attains the Torah attains a part of the Common Light. The degrees of attainment of Light are called by the names of the *Sefirot* (*Partzufim*, worlds) or by the Lights that one receives (*NRNHY*).

Besides man, there is only the Creator. Hence, anything each of us feels, thinks, and wants comes to us from the Creator. What each person in the world feels is only the Creator.

When the creature climbs from the lowest point, from which one begins to approach the Creator (the point of this world), to the time one achieves complete equivalence of form with the Creator (*Gmar Tikkun*), one traverses 620 degrees, called "the 613 *Mitzvot* of the Torah" and the "Seven *Mitzvot* of our great sages."

A *Zivug* with the Upper Light in the *Masach* is called a *Mitzva*. The Light that the attaining individual receives in one's *Kli* is called *Ohr Pnimi* (Inner Light), or *Ohr Taamim* (Light of Flavors), or "Torah." This is why Kabbalists tell everyone, "taste and see that the Lord is good."

The creature, *Behina Dalet* in *Behina Dalet*, corrects its will to receive so it would receive in order to bestow. The *Tikkun* (correction) is not on the desire to receive itself, but on how it is used—with the aim to bestow. That *Tikkun*, placing the aim to bestow, is made on small portions of the creature's desire, from the smallest part to the largest, and not on all of it. By that, the creature rises from degree to degree on the ladder of degrees. The worlds are degrees on which one ascends from below Upwards.

The *Tikkun* of the will to receive, to receive only in order to bestow, is a very difficult *Tikkun*, since it is opposite to the intention. It is opposite to the creature's nature. Hence, the Creator divided the whole way into 613 small degrees, and split the creature itself into 600,000 small pieces, called "souls." When all the souls unite, they are called "the common soul" or *Adam ha Rishon* (the first man).

But the correction work begins even before that, in a lower state, called "our world," where all the parts of Creation exist in a reality where there is no Creator and no spirituality. They do not even feel that they lack the sensation of absence of knowledge of the Creator. Everyone is born in this degree, which is only a will to receive the pleasures available to our five senses.

The whole world is led by the Creator's commandments. This leadership is called "nature," since the desire to receive pleasure in each of the states—still, vegetative, animate, and speaking—necessarily determines every reaction. This is so because the law is that every creature always chooses the greatest pleasure and escapes suffering.

In each generation, there are people in whom the Creator "plants" a point in the heart—a desire to feel the Creator. Such a person begins to seek fulfillment for this new desire in him, not knowing that it is a desire for the Creator and that it can be filled only with the Upper Light.

The *Partzufim* that emerged after the breaking are called "the world of *Tikkun*." Everything that happens must appear in Creation and is necessary for the development of the creature, so it can obtain the perfection of the Creator's actions and enjoy what the Creator has prepared for it.

Hence, both the breaking in the world of *Nekudim*, called "the breaking in the worlds," and the breaking in *Adam ha Rishon*, called "the breaking in the souls," were preordained. In the breaking of the world of *Nekudim*, vessels of reception mingled with vessels of bestowal. The broken parts are in such a mixture that each of them is included in all the others. Thus, each of the 320 pieces (desires) contains all the others within it. As a result, 1) the vessels of reception will be corrected due to the mingling with the vessels of bestowal, and 2) NRNHY Lights will appear in each desire (instead of the Light of *Nefesh*, which was there previously).

Without the mixture, obtained by the breaking, the vessels of reception would have no way of receiving Light, since the *Parsa* would separate them from the place in which the Upper Light could begin to spread. But now, after the breaking, they can be elevated to *Atzilut* (raised AHP) and be filled there.

The breaking in the world of *Nekudim* is called "the breaking of the worlds," since *Malchut de Ein Sof* comprises five parts. Four of them beget the worlds and everything within them, as they spread from Above downwards. They contain the whole of Creation besides man, who was created from *Behina Dalet* in *Dalet*, from *Malchut's* last part—the actual, independent will to receive, completely detached from the Creator's desire to bestow.

Hence, only man is the purpose and the goal of Creation. Besides him, the rest of the parts of Creation are not independent. They belong to the Creator's desire, since the Creator determines their conduct, as the still, vegetative, and animate exist in our world.

In our world, man's desire is not essentially different from that of animals. Only a person in whom the desire for the Creator emerged (a part of the desire of *Adam ha Rishon*) is called "Adam" (Man). A person with such a desire can correct it by acquiring a *Masach* and achieving the desire to bestow. And if no such desire appears in a person, one has nothing to correct and such a person feels no inclination to draw near to the Creator.

The whole of reality in this world is divided into the four parts of Creation: still, vegetative, animate, and speaking, according to the measure of the will to receive, and hence according to the measure of the beneficial and detrimental powers.

A person in this world must undergo four stages of development: still, vegetative, animate, and speaking, to develop and intensify the desire to receive in him, until the Creator "plants" the point in him, meaning the desire for the Creator, to reach the goal. For this reason, for millennia, humanity has been pulverized under nature's press—the evolution of the will to receive from the "still" degree through the "speaking" degree. This is the evolution of the generations we know.

The whole of humanity, and each soul—from generation to generation—undergo four stages of development of the will to receive:

1. Plebs: The "still" in the human species. Through a propensity for wealth, they develop into the degree of "wealthy."

2. Wealthy: The "vegetative" in the human species. Through a propensity for honor (power), they develop into the degree of "strong."

3. Strong: The "animate" in the human species. Through a propensity for knowledge, they develop into the degree of "knowledgeable."

4. Knowledgeable: The "speaking" in the human species. In the speaking in man, the desire is unlimited by time or place. A person is envious of people who lived in previous generations, in things one has no need for, but that others have and he does not. Hence, he can increase his will to receive, since he wants what he sees in others. Thus, one can enhance one's will to receive unboundedly, and this makes one a suitable candidate for achieving the purpose of Creation.

5. If the Creator plants a point in the heart in this "speaking," such a person begins to awaken toward the goal and seeks the root of one's soul.

The order of corrections from Above downwards is as follows:

- Receiving in order to receive—exists in our world.
- Bestowing in order to receive—exists in our world.
- Bestowing in order to bestow—exists in the worlds *BYA*.
- Receiving in order to bestow—exists in the world of *Atzilut*.

The whole system of Creation achieves *Gmar Tikkun* only through the world of *Atzilut*. This is why the world of *Atzilut* is called "the world of *Tikkun*" (the world of correction).

THE WORLD OF ATZILUT

Following the breaking, the *Masach* purified and rose with the *Reshimot* to the *Rosh* of AVI de *Nekudim*. The *Reshimot* in the *Masach* demand correction so a *Zivug* can be made on them for reception of the Light. But the *Rosh* of AVI de *Nekudim* returned to the state of *Katnut* and could not do it. Hence, the *Masach* rose to the *Rosh* of the Higher *Partzuf*, *Rosh de SAG*.

There is no difference between a *Masach* that is purified by the *Bitush* of its internal and surrounding Lights and a *Masach* that is purified by the breaking. Even after the breaking, *Reshimot* remain in the *Masach* and demand to be filled:

- Restricted *Reshimot de Hitlabshut Aleph* and *Shoresh de Aviut* that remained from *Partzuf Nekudim*;
- *Reshimot Dalet de Hitlabshut* and *Gimel de Aviut* from the *Sof* of *Partzuf Galgalta*.

The restricted *Reshimot Aleph de Hitlabshut* and *Shoresh de Aviut* come from *Partzuf Nekudim* itself. Hence, the *Masach* makes the first *Zivug* on them. After a *Partzuf* is born on them, the *Masach* will provide for the demands of *Reshimot Dalet-Gimel* that caused the elicitation of the *Gadlut* of the *Partzuf*. Hence, once the *Masach* rose to *Rosh de SAG*, it rose according to the restricted *Reshimo de Aviut Shoresh*, to *Bina* of *Keter de Rosh SAG*.

The five *Behinot* of the *Rosh* are called:

Keter–Galgalta–Aviut de Shoresh

Hochma–Eynaim–Aviut Aleph

Bina–Awznaim–Aviut Bet

ZA–Hotem–Aviut Gimel

Malchut–Peh–Aviut Dalet

In each of the *Sefirot* in the *Rosh* are five particular *Sefirot*: *Keter*, *Hochma*, *Bina*, *ZA*, *Malchut*. The *Reshimo* of restricted *Aviut de Shoresh* demands a *Zivug* only on the vessels of bestowal in *Aviut Shoresh*. The *Reshimo* demands that a *Partzuf* will be born, which works only with vessels of bestowal, GE, de *Aviut*

Shoresh. Hence, the *Masach* that begets this *Partzuf* must make a *Zivug* only on the vessels of bestowal of *Aviut de Shoresh* at the *Rosh*.

Accordingly, the *Masach* rises from the *Peh* to the *Sefira Keter de Rosh de SAG*, and from there Higher still, to *Bina de Keter*, standing after the *Sefirot KHB HGT de Keter*. It follows that Above the *Masach* there are only vessels of bestowal of *Keter*, meaning *Aviut Shoresh*. The place where the *Masach* stands is called *Metzach* (forehead).

The *Partzuf*, born out of the *Zivug* on the *Reshimo* of the restricted *Aviut de Shoresh*, is called *Ubar* (fetus). In spirituality, there cannot be less than this degree. Put differently, this is the minimal spiritual degree. After its birth, the newly born *Partzuf* descends to the place from which the *Reshimot* rose, below *Tabur de Galgalta*, and spreads there from *Tabur* down.

After the *Partzuf Ubar* spreads into its place, *Reshimot Dalet de Hitlabshut* and *Gimel de Aviut* (from the *Sof* of *Galgalta*) awaken in it. The *Gadlut* of the *Partzuf* emerges on these *Reshimot*: the *Masach* makes a *Zivug* with the Upper Light on *Reshimot Dalet-Gimel*, and the level of *Gadlut* spreads from *Tabur de Galgalta* through *Parsa*. This *Partzuf* is called *Atik*, since it is *Ne'etak* (detached) from the attainment of the lower ones (souls).

Partzuf Atik is the first *Partzuf* in a new series of five *Partzufim*, called "the world of *Atzilut*." Hence, *Partzuf Atik* is the *Keter* of the world of *Atzilut*.

After *Partzuf Atik* emerged in *Gadlut*, *Rosh de SAG* gave it all the *Reshimot* that rose to it after the breaking. Of all the *Reshimot*, *Atik* chose the purest *Reshimo*, made a *Zivug* on it, and generated the next *Partzuf*, first creating it at the *Ubar* level and then making a *Zivug* on *Gadlut* (*Dalet-Gimel*). This *Partzuf* expanded from *Peh de Atik* through *Parsa*, and it is called *Partzuf Hochma*, or *Arich Anpin* (AA).

Once *Gadlut de Partzuf AA* emerges, *Atik* gives it all the remaining *Reshimot*, from the ones that rose to *Rosh de SAG* after the breaking. Of those, AA chooses the purest, makes a *Zivug* on them, and this generates *Partzuf Bina* of the world of *Atzilut*, first at the *Ubar* level and finally in *Gadlut*. This *Partzuf* spreads from *Peh de AA* to *Tabur de AA*. It is called *Aba ve Ima* (AVI).

After *Partzuf AVI* emerges in *Gadlut*, AA gives it all the remaining *Reshimot*. Of the *Reshimot* that AA gave it, AVI chooses the purest *Reshimot* and makes a *Zivug* on them, thus generating *Partzuf ZA* of the world of *Atzilut*. Here, for the first time, there are three states: *Ubar*, *Katnut* (infancy, smallness), and *Gadlut* (maturity, greatness). *Partzuf ZA* takes its place from *Tabur* of AA through the *Parsa*.

Once *Partzuf* ZA emerges, AVI gives it all the remaining *Reshimot*. ZA makes a *Zivug* on them and generates *Malchut* of the world of *Atzilut*. This completes the *Zivugim* that can emerge on the *Reshimot* that rose to *Rosh de* SAG following the breaking of the vessels.

The constant state of *Atzilut* is *Katnut*—GE—vessels of bestowal. There cannot be less than that in it. In this state, it precisely matches the *Katnut* of the world of *Nekudim*, prior to the breaking. However, the world of *Atzilut* emerged in order to bring the whole of Creation to *Gmar Tikkun*, so *Malchut de Ein Sof* would be filled with the Light of *Ein Sof* with the aim to bestow. And this has not yet been achieved.

In the breaking, the vessels of reception were mixed with the vessels of bestowal. Hence, four discernments were made in each *Kli*:

1. Vessels of bestowal.
2. Vessels of bestowal within vessels of reception.
3. Vessels of reception within vessels of bestowal.
4. Vessels of reception.

First sorting: Vessels of bestowal are sorted out from the mixture and constitute the *Katnut* of the world of *Atzilut*.

Second sorting: Vessels of bestowal within vessels of reception are sorted out from the mixture and comprise the worlds BYA. These worlds are vessels of bestowal, GE, like the world of *Atzilut*, but they remain contained in the AHP, the vessels of reception. For themselves, these are vessels of bestowal; hence, Light can spread within them.

Thus, once the world of *Atzilut* emerged, *Malchut* of the world of *Atzilut* rose to AVI and made a *Zivug* on the vessels of bestowal within the vessels of reception. She generated the world of *Beria*, then the world of *Yetzira*, and finally, the world of *Assiya*.

- The world of *Beria* emerged in the *Zivug* on GE that are in vessels of reception of *Aviut Bet*.
- The world of *Yetzira* emerged in the *Zivug* on GE that are in vessels of reception of *Aviut Gimel*.
- The world of *Assiya* emerged in the *Zivug* on GE that are in vessels of reception of *Aviut Dalet*.

Third sorting: Vessels of reception within vessels of bestowal are sorted out from the mixture. This sorting and correction is done by souls of people. They sort out these *Kelim* and elevate them above the *Parsa* to the world of *Atzilut*.

This work is called "awakening from below," since it is done by the souls. The broken *Kelim* that rise to *Atzilut* are called "raised *AHP*."

Fourth sorting: Vessels of reception that were not mingled with vessels of bestowal are examined, verifying that they remained in their qualities, and are hence banned from being used. These *Kelim* are called *Klipot* (shells), or *Lev ha Even* (stony heart), since they cannot be corrected until *Gmar Tikkun*.

THE WORLDS BYA

The *Zivug* for begetting the world of *Beria* was made in *Bina de Atzilut*. Hence, the world of *Beria* expands in the place of ZA *de Atzilut*.

The world of *Yetzira*, born after the world of *Beria*, expands from it down in the place of *Malchut de Atzilut*. *Partzuf Malchut de Atzilut* clothes only the four *Sefirot* NHYM of *Partzuf* ZA. Thus, only the first four *Sefirot* of *Partzuf Malchut—KHB* and *Hesed—*are in *Atzilut*, opposite the four *Sefirot* NHYM *de* ZA. The *Sefirot Gevura, Tifferet*, and NHYM *de Partzuf Malchut* are below the *Parsa*.

Therefore, when the world of *Yetzira* was born, its first four *Sefirot* clothed the first four *Sefirot* of *Malchut*, while its last six *Sefirot* clothed in the place of the first six *Sefirot* of the place of BYA.

The place of BYA comprises thirty *Sefirot*. In the future, after the sin of *Adam ha Rishon*, the worlds BYA will fall into this place. The place where the last six *Sefirot* of the world of *Yetzira* end is called "*Chazeh* of the place of the world of *Beria*." This is where *Chazeh de Beria* will be after the sin of *Adam ha Rishon*.

After the world of *Yetzira* was born and expanded to its place, *Malchut de Atzilut* generated the world of *Assiya*, which spreads below the world of *Yetzira* from the *Chazeh* of the place of the world of *Beria* to the *Chazeh* of the place of the world of *Yetzira*.

The *Chazeh* of the place of the world of *Yetzira* is called "*Chazeh* of the place of the worlds BYA." This is the place where the expansion of the worlds BYA ends. Below the *Chazeh* of the place of the world of *Yetzira*, it is empty of Light. This place, from the *Chazeh* of the place of BYA downwards through the *Sium*, is the place of the *Klipot*, called *Mador ha Klipot* (the shell section). Below it is a place called "the point of this world."

In spirituality, a "place" means a "desire." The point of this world is a desire to receive (enjoy) in order to receive (for oneself), a desire to enjoy pleasures in dresses of this world: sex, honor, power, envy. The *Klipot* are considered Higher, since they wish to receive pleasure from the Creator, which corresponds to *Kedusha* (holiness).

The wisdom of Kabbalah always speaks from the perspective of the perceiving individual. Hence, one who perceives that his desires are only to receive in order to receive, and not to bestow, can be said to have attained, that he is in a state called "this world." But one who did not attain that all his desires are to receive in order to receive is not in this place (desire). Such a person is lower down (before this revelation), in a place (desire) called "our world," where people are unaware (of their desires), and do not feel their unawareness.

The whole of humanity is at the degree of "our world," unaware. From this degree, the desire to receive begins to develop in a person. Evolution occurs by nature's prompting everyone towards correction by the force of harsh judgment.

The entire history of humanity is a generation-by-generation evolution of the will to receive by three elements: pride, honor, and envy. Suffering brings man, and humanity as a whole, to the decision to exit the will to receive, since it is the reason for all suffering.

Those whose will to receive has developed sufficiently receive a drive from Above to want what is beyond this world. Following this drive, a person begins to search for a source of pleasure that will fill the new desire, until one finds the right teacher. This search may take years, or even more than one lifetime, but if the Creator brings a person to a place where Kabbalah is being taught, as it happened with me (Michael Laitman), it is a sign that you are given an opportunity from Above to correct your soul and reach the goal.

THE STATES OF THE PARTZUFIM IN THE WORLDS ABYA

Adam ha Rishon

Adam ha Rishon is a separate entity from everything that preceded it. He is the only one that was created from *Malchut de Ein Sof*; hence, he is the only one who merits the title, "creature." He, too, was generated by *Malchut de Atzilut*, which rose to AVI. She procreated *Partzuf Adam ha Rishon*, just as she procreated the worlds BYA, and for this reason, *Adam ha Rishon* is always within the worlds BYA.

When the worlds BYA were born, they stood from AVI through the *Chazeh* of the place of the world of *Yetzira*. When *Adam ha Rishon* was born, he was within them at the level of all three worlds BYA, receiving the Lights NRN from BYA. *Adam ha Rishon* received additional Lights, *NRN de Atzilut*, since BYA were in *Atzilut*.

The state of the worlds when *Adam ha Rishon* was born is called "eve of Shabbat." Afterwards, through an awakening from Above, the worlds rose the first ascension, one degree Higher—ten *Sefirot*—along with *Adam ha Rishon*, so the *Sium* of the worlds BYA, with *Adam ha Rishon* within them, rose to the *Chazeh* of the place of the world of *Beria*.

In that state, *Adam ha Rishon* wanted to receive all the Lights in order to bestow, as in the state that preceded the breaking of the vessels in the world of *Nekudim*. There, in *Nekudim*, *Rosh de AVI* did not understand that the part of ZON did not have *Tikkun Kavim* (correction of lines); hence, they gave the Light of *Gadlut* and ZON broke.

The same occurred here with *Adam ha Rishon*: there was no understanding that a shattering would occur. But after the first time he mistakenly received in order to receive, he wanted to receive again, this time deliberately. He could no longer stop himself from enjoying.

As a result, *Klipot* were born of this breakage, desires to receive in order to receive. Also, the worlds BYA descended below the *Parsa*, to their constant state, from *Parsa* to the general *Sium*. It is called "the constant state" because the worlds BYA cannot be in a lower state than that. But they are not "permanently" fixed to that place; they can rise and descend to their constant place.

Besides the decline of the worlds BYA to their constant place, a result of the shattering of *Partzuf Adam ha Rishon*, the impure BYA were born. These are three worlds that contain the deficiencies in BYA and stand opposite BYA. Hence, BYA, which are clean of desires to receive in order to receive, are called "the pure BYA" and their corresponding deficiencies are called "impure BYA."

The three impure worlds are called:

- *Esh Mitlakachat* (blazing fire)—corresponding to the world of *Beria*.
- *Anan Gadol* (great cloud)—corresponding to the world of *Yetzira*.
- *Ruach Se'ara* (stormy wind)—corresponding to the world of *Assiya*.

After the sin, *Partzuf Adam ha Rishon* was broken into 600,000 pieces. The shattering continued deeper into the broken pieces (additional breakages are referred to in the Torah as "the killing of Abel," "the generation of the flood," the generation of Babylon," etc.).

Finally, all the pieces in his *Partzuf* remained only in their will to receive in order to receive, with the spark of Light that was in it. These pieces, the desires with the sparks in them, clothe people in our world and prompt them to awaken towards spirituality, to the Light, the Creator. Thus, we are made to come into a group of people who are studying Kabbalah, learning the method by which to achieve the goal.

There is yet another *Klipa* (singular for *Klipot*): *Klipat* (*Klipa* of) *Noga*. These are desires mixed of good and evil. "Mixed" means they receive Light in their good part and transfer it to their bad part, too. The *Tikkun* of the whole of reality focuses on the *Tikkun* of *Klipat Noga*—detaching it from the three impure

Klipot (*Ruach Se'ara*, *Anan Gadol*, and *Esh Mitlakachat*), to which it is tied in its evil part, and joining its good part to *Kedusha*, to *Atzilut*.

THE ASCENSION OF THE WORLDS

The worlds' real place is that of the second state, prior to the sin:

- ZA in the place of AA;
- *Malchut* in the place of AVI;
- *Beria* in the place of YESHSUT;
- *Yetzira* in the place of ZA.
- The first four *Sefirot* of the world of *Assiya* in the place of the first four *Sefirot* of *Nukva de Atzilut*, clothing TNHYM of the world of *Yetzira*;
- The last six *Sefirot* of the world of *Assiya* in the place of the six *Sefirot* of the world of *Beria*, below the *Parsa*;
- The first six *Sefirot* of the place of the world of *Beria*, meaning the place from *Parsa* to *Chazeh* of the place of the world of *Beria*, is called "outskirts of the city," since they belong to the world of *Atzilut*, which is called "a city." Also, *Parsa* is called "the wall of the city."
- There are twenty-four *Sefirot* from the *Chazeh* of the place of the world of *Beria* through the general *Sium*. This is a void that is empty of Light.
- The sixteen *Sefirot* from *Parsa* to *Chazeh de Yetzira* are called "Shabbat zone." It contains the "outskirts of the city," plus ten *Sefirot* from *Chazeh de Beria* to *Chazeh de Yetzira*. Each ten *Sefirot* are called 2,000 *Amma* (about ¾ of a yard). Hence, the whole place of the worlds BYA is called 6,000 *Amma* or 6,000 years of the life of the world.
- The fourteen *Sefirot* from *Chazeh de Yetzira* through the general *Sium* are called "the shell section." This is where the *Klipot* were prior to the sin of *Adam ha Rishon*. But after the sin, they became the four impure worlds ABYA.

THE SEQUENCE OF CAUSE AND CONSEQUENCE

Four *Behinot* (stages) of *Ohr Yashar*:

- **Behinat Shoresh:** Light emits from *Atzmuto*—His desire to do good to His creations. As a result of His desire to benefit, He creates *Behina Aleph*, the will to receive, the desire to enjoy the Light.
- **Behina Aleph:** Once she feels she is receiving, she decides that she does not want to receive. This new desire is *Behina Bet*.

- **Behina Bet**: Once she is completely emptied of *Ohr Hochma*, *Behina Bet* feels its absence and decides that she wants to receive some *Ohr Hochma* within the *Ohr Hassadim*. This is *Behina Gimel*.
- **Behina Gimel**: At its end, when she receives *Ohr Hochma* as well as *Ohr Hassadim*, *Behina Gimel* decides that she wants to receive all the Light. This is *Behina Dalet*, called *Malchut*, since she is governed by the will to receive. She feels the desire to receive Light, the same as in *Behina Aleph*, but with an addition. This additional desire is a new *Kli*, called "craving." *Malchut* senses that her desire is an independent one, which comes from her.
- **Behina Dalet**: She receives all the Light without limitations, hence her title, "the world of *Ein Sof*."

Tzimtzum Aleph: *Behina Dalet* makes the *Tzimtzum Aleph*. The restricted *Behina Dalet* is called "the world of *Tzimtzum*."

The work of the Masach: *Behina Dalet*, *Malchut*, decides to receive Light in the desires to bestow, her *Behinot Shoresh*, *Aleph*, *Bet*, and *Gimel*, and not in her *Behina Dalet*, which is a pure desire to receive.

Partzuf Galgalta: Through the *Masach* with *Reshimot Dalet de Hitlabshut* and *Dalet de Aviut*, *Malchut* makes a *Zivug* with the Upper Light, which parted due to the *Tzimtzum*. In the *Zivug* with the Light, the *Masach* decides how much Light it will receive into *Malchut*.

Following the decision, the *Masach* descends to the *Guf* with the amount of Light it had decided to receive. The Lights that enter the *Partzuf* are called *Taamim*. The place in which the *Masach* stops descending and limits the reception of Light is called *Tabur*.

The Light that enters the *Partzuf* is called *Ohr Pnimi* (Inner Light). The general Light that remained outside the *Kli* is called *Ohr Makif* (Surrounding Light). Subsequently, a *Bitush* (beating) between the *Ohr Pnimi* and *Ohr Makif* occurs on the *Masach* that stands at the *Tabur*, since they both wish to cancel the limitation on the reception.

The *Masach* decides to not use the *Reshimot de Aviut Dalet* and purify. It rises from *Tabur* to *Peh* and the *Ohr Pnimi* departs the *Partzuf*. The departing Lights are called *Nekudot* (points). The whole *Partzuf*, from the *Zivug* at the *Rosh* to the end of its *Hizdakchut*, is called *Partzuf Galgalta*.

Partzuf AB: The *Masach de Guf de Galgalta* that rose to *Peh de Rosh de Galgalta* is integrated in the perpetual *Zivug* at the *Masach* in the *Peh*. The encounter between the *Masach* and the Upper Light at the *Rosh* causes the *Masach* to want to receive a part of the Light in the *Rosh*, but according to the *Reshimot* in it, *Dalet de Hitlabshut* and *Gimel de Aviut*. The last *Reshimo de Aviut* (for extension of Light) vanishes, a result of the decision to depart from reception.

The *Masach* descends to *Chazeh de Galgalta*, according to *Reshimo Gimel de Aviut*, and makes a *Zivug* on *Reshimot Dalet de Hitlabshut* and *Gimel de Aviut*. This is the place of the *Peh* of the next *Partzuf*. After the *Zivug*, the *Masach* descends from the *Peh* down to the *Tabur* of the new *Partzuf*, and the Lights of *Taamim* enter the *Toch*.

Subsequently, there is a *Bitush* of *Ohr Pnimi* and *Ohr Makif* on the *Masach* at the *Tabur*, to cancel the limitation of the *Masach*. The *Masach* decides to purify, the *Reshimo* of *Aviut Gimel* disappears, and the *Masach* rises from *Tabur* to *Peh*. The departing Lights are called *Nekudot de AB*.

Partzuf SAG: When the *Masach* comes to the *Peh*, it is integrated in the perpetual *Zivug* with the Upper Light that exists there, and wishes to receive a part of the Light that is in the *Rosh*. Hence, the *Masach* descends to *Chazeh de Partzuf AB*, according to the *Reshimo*, and there makes a *Zivug* with the Light on *Reshimot Gimel de Hitlabshut* and *Bet de Aviut*. It receives Light and stops at the place it determined in the *Rosh–Tabur*. An immediate *Bitush* of *Ohr Pnimi* and *Ohr Makif* is applied to the *Masach*, as they want to cancel the limitation on the reception that the *Masach de Toch* creates. The *Masach* decides to purify and rises to the *Peh*.

Nekudot de SAG: The Lights, which emerge during the *Hizdakchut* of the *Masach*, are called *Nekudot*. *Nekudot de SAG* are *Bet de Hitlabshut* and *Bet de Aviut*. This is *Bina's* quality. These Lights can appear anywhere (any desire). For this reason, the Lights of *Nekudot* descend below *Tabur de Galgalta* and fill the *Sof de Galgalta*.

Sof de Galgalta and *Nekudot de SAG* mingle and *Partzuf Nekudot de SAG*, which is *Partzuf Bina*, divides into *GAR de Bina* and *ZAT de Bina*. *ZAT de Bina*, being vessels of reception, are affected by the *Reshimot* at the *Sof de Galgalta* and want to receive those Lights in order to receive. This is so because the force of the *Masach de Nekudot de SAG* is *Bet de Aviut*, and the *Reshimot* at the *Sof de Galgalta* are *Dalet-Gimel*, more than the resistance power in the *Masach*.

Hence, a desire to receive in order to receive is formed from the *Chazeh de Nekudot de SAG* downwards. This forces *Malchut*, which performed *Tzimtzum Aleph*, to rise from *Sium de Galgalta* to the place of *Chazeh de Nekudot de SAG* and limit the expansion of the Light so it reaches only the *Chazeh*.

All the processes at *Nekudot de SAG* unfold during the ascension of the *Masach de Guf de SAG* from *Tabur de SAG* to its *Rosh*, except that *Reshimot* from *Tzimtzum Bet* and from *Sof de Galgalta* were added to it.

Tzimtzum Bet (second restriction): The ascension of *Malchut de Tzimtzum Aleph* to *Chazeh de Nekudot de SAG* is called *Tzimtzum Bet*.

MA and BON above *Tabur de Galgalta*: When the *Masach de Guf de SAG* reaches the *Peh*, it makes a *Zivug* on *Reshimot Bet de Hitlabshut* and *Aleph de Aviut* that remained of the Lights of *Taamim de SAG* Above *Tabur*, generating *Partzuf* Upper MA, from *Peh de SAG* through *Tabur de Galgalta*. After the *Hizdakchut* of *Partzuf* Upper MA, *Partzuf* Upper BON is born from it, from *Peh de MA* through *Tabur de Galgalta*.

The World of *Nekudim* (*Katnut*): When *Masach de Guf de SAG* purifies and rises to *Peh de SAG*, it wishes to make a *Zivug* on the *Reshimot* in it (*Bet de Hitlabshut* and *Aleph de Aviut* from below *Tabur de Galgalta*). It ascends, following the demand of the *Reshimot*, from *Peh* to *Nikvey Eynaim* (NE) *de Rosh de SAG*, since *Reshimot Bet-Aleph* are restricted, demanding to receive Light only in vessels of bestowal.

Hence, the *Masach* stands below the vessels of bestowal in the *Rosh*, below *Keter* and *Hochma* at the *Rosh de SAG*. The *Masach* always makes a *Zivug* only on the *Behinot Rosh* that are above it. For this reason, it stands at the *Rosh*, the place from which it wishes to receive Light into the *Guf*.

After the *Zivug*, the *Masach* actively passes to the *Guf* what it had received in the *Rosh* in potential. The Light spreads to the place from which the restricted *Reshimot Bet-Aleph* rose, meaning from below *Tabur de Galgalta*. This *Partzuf* is called *Partzuf Nekudim*, since it emerged on *Reshimot* from *Nekudot de SAG*.

This *Partzuf* includes:

- *Rosh de Hitlabshut*, called *Keter*;
- *Rosh de Aviut*, called *Aba ve Ima* (AVI);
- *Guf*, called ZON (*Zeir Anpin* and *Nukva*).

In each of them, only the vessels of bestowal are active; their vessels of reception are concealed (within them).

Gadlut of the world of Nekudim: After the elicitation of the *Katnut* of the world of *Nekudim*, the *Masach* in *Rosh de SAG* descended, following the demand of *Reshimot Dalet de Hitlabshut* and *Gimel de Aviut*, into the *Peh de SAG*, and made a *Zivug*. As a result of this *Zivug*, *Ohr Hochma* came to the *Rosh* of *Keter de Nekudim* and to *Aba* of *Rosh AVI*.

Ima is *Bina*, which does not want to receive *Ohr Hochma* except by *ZON*'s request. *Ohr Hochma* shines from *Rosh de Nekudim* to *Sof de Galgalta*, and from there comes a request—through *ZON de Nekudim*—to ask *AVI* for *Gadlut*, *Ohr Hochma*. When *ZON* ask of *AVI*, they mate and bring *ZON Ohr Hochma*.

The breaking of the vessels: *Ohr Hochma* spreads from *Rosh de AVI* into *ZON*, through the *GE* of *ZON* and to the *Parsa*. When the Light wishes to cross the *Parsa* and fill the *Kelim* of *AHP de ZON*, it encounters the will to receive and departs Upwards. The *Kelim GE* and *AHP* break and 320 broken pieces fall below the *Parsa*.

In the breaking, the vessels of bestowal (*GE*) mix with the vessels of reception (*AHP*); hence, in each broken piece there are four types of *Kelim*:

1. *GE*—which formed *GE de ZON de Atzilut*;
2. *Hitkalelut* of *GE* in *AHP*—which formed the worlds *BYA*;
3. *Hitkalelut* of *AHP* in *GE*—which formed the raised *AHP*;
4. *AHP*—which formed the *Klipot*, which are desires to receive in order to receive, unfit for reception of Light. These are the (32, *Lamed Bet*) *Malchuts* of the (320 *Shach*) pieces that cannot be corrected until *Gmar Tikkun*, and receive in order to bestow in them. The thirty-two *Malchuts* are called *Lev ha Even* (the stony heart). Their correction is in being sorted from all 320 pieces and not being used.

288 pieces (320-32) of the 320 that exist in each broken piece can be corrected, since they are not parts of *Malchut*, but are parts of the Upper nine *Sefirot*. Some, those that belong to *GE de ZON*, should be sorted out of the mixture, since they are vessels of bestowal. These are the ones that build the *Katnut* (*GE*) *de ZON de Atzilut*.

EMERGING OF THE WORLD OF ATZILUT

Atik: The *Masach*, with the *Reshimot*, rose to *Rosh de Nekudim* and from there to *Rosh de SAG*. The *Masach* sorted the purest *Reshimot*, *Aleph de Hitlabshut* and *Shoresh de Aviut*, rose from *Peh* to the *Sefira Keter de Rosh de SAG*, and from there it went further up to *Bina* in *Keter*, where it stood behind the *Sefirot KHB HGT de Keter*.

Thus, above the *Masach* are only *Keter*'s vessels of bestowal of *Aviut Shoresh*. This place is called *Metzach* (forehead), and it is where the *Masach* makes a *Zivug*, from which *Partzuf Keter de Atzilut* is born, called *Partzuf Atik*.

The *Partzuf* born of this *Zivug* is called *Ubar*, since it has only vessels of bestowal in *Aviut Shoresh*, the least that can be in spirituality. After its birth, this *Partzuf* descends to the place from which the *Reshimot* rose, below *Tabur de Galgalta*.

When *Partzuf Atik* is born and descends to its place, *Reshimot Dalet-Gimel* awaken in it and demand that this *Partzuf* obtain *Gadlut*. The *Masach* makes a *Zivug* with the Upper Light on these *Reshimot* and builds the level of *Atik* in *Gadlut*. This *Partzuf* spreads from *Tabur de Galgalta* to *Sium de Galgalta*, crossing the *Parsa*, since it is *Partzuf Keter*, which still belongs to *Tzimtzum Aleph*. This is why it is named *Atik*, because it is *Ne'etak* (detached) from the attainment of the lower ones.

AA: Once *Partzuf Atik* in *Gadlut* emerges, *Rosh de SAG* passes it all the *Reshimot* it received after the breaking. Of all the *Reshimot*, *Atik* chooses the purest *Reshimo*, makes a *Zivug* on it and begets the next *Partzuf*—*Hochma*—at the level of *Ubar*, and subsequently in *Gadlut*. This *Partzuf* spreads from *Peh de Atik* to the *Parsa* and is called *Partzuf Arich Anpin* (AA).

AVI: Once *Gadlut* of *Partzuf AA* emerges, *Atik* gives it all the *Reshimot* that remained of those that rose to *Rosh de SAG* after the breaking. Of those, AA chooses the purest *Reshimot* and makes a *Zivug* on them. This *Zivug* produces *Partzuf Bina de Atzilut*, first at the level of *Ubar* and subsequently in *Gadlut*. This *Partzuf* spreads from *Peh de AA* through its *Tabur*.

ZA: Once *Partzuf AVI* emerges in *Gadlut*, AA gives it all the remaining *Reshimot*. AVI chooses the purest *Reshimot* of all the *Reshimot* it had received, makes a *Zivug* on them, and begets *Partzuf ZA de Atzilut*, at the levels of *Ubar* (*Katnut*) and then *Gadlut*. *Partzuf ZA* takes its place from *Tabur de AA* through the *Parsa*.

Malchut: After *Partzuf ZA* in *Katnut* emerges, AVI give it all the remaining *Reshimot*, which have not been corrected by the previous *Partzufim*. Of those, ZA chooses those that suit it, makes a *Zivug*, and begets *Partzuf Malchut de Atzilut* as a *Nekuda* (point), as it was in the world of *Nekudim*. This completes the correction of all the *Reshimot de Katnut de Nekudim* that rose to *Rosh de SAG* after the breaking.

EMERGING OF THE WORLD BYA

The *Partzufim* of GAR of the world of *Atzilut* emerged on *Reshimot de Rosh de Nekudim*, which was only purified, but not broken. From *ZON de Nekudim* downwards, the birth of the *Partzufim* is done by sorting and correcting the broken pieces. This is so because through the breaking in the world of *Nekudim*, vessels of bestowal from Above the *Parsa* mingled with the vessels of reception

from below the *Parsa* and were integrated in one another. Thus, in each of the 320 broken pieces are four types of *Kelim*:
1. Vessels of bestowal;
2. Vessels of bestowal integrated with vessels of reception;
3. Vessels of reception integrated with vessels of bestowal;
4. Vessels of reception.

First, only the vessels of bestowal are sorted and corrected (*Zivugim* are made on them) from all 320 pieces by order of *Aviut*, from pure to coarse. The *Masach* that descends from *Rosh de SAG* begets all the *Partzufim* of the world of *Atzilut*, first in *Katnut* and then in *Gadlut*. *Katnut* of the world of *Atzilut* emerges opposite the *Katnut* of the world of *Nekudim*.

Subsequently, ZON *de Atzilut* rise to AVI *de Atzilut*, ZA becomes like *Aba*, and *Malchut* becomes like *Ima*. The lower one that rises to the Upper One becomes like it; hence, *Malchut* received the degree of *Bina* so it could make a *Zivug* on *Ohr Hochma* and beget new *Partzufim*. When *Malchut de Atzilut* rose to *Ima*, she sorted the vessels of bestowal that were integrated with vessels of reception from each of the 320 broken pieces, by order of *Aviut*—from pure to coarse. In this order, she generated new *Partzufim*:

- Five *Partzufim* were made of the sorting and *Zivug* made on the vessels of bestowal (GE) that fell in the part of *Bina* that was below the *Parsa* (GE integrated in *Aviut Bet de AHP*): Keter–*Atik*, Hochma–AA, Bina–AVI, ZA–ZA, and Malchut–*Nukva* of the world of *Beria*.

- Five *Partzufim* were made of the sorting and *Zivug* made on the vessels of bestowal (GE) that fell in the *Kelim de* ZA below the *Parsa* (GE integrated in *Aviut Gimel de AHP*): Keter–*Atik*, Hochma–AA, Bina–AVI, ZA–ZA, and Malchut–*Nukva* of the world of *Yetzira*.

- Five *Partzufim* were made of the sorting and *Zivug* made on the vessels of bestowal (GE) that fell to *Malchut* below the *Parsa* (GE integrated in *Aviut Dalet de AHP*): Keter–*Atik*, Hochma–AA, Bina–AVI, ZA–ZA, and Malchut–*Nukva* of the world of *Assiya*.

Malchut de Atzilut made these *Zivugim* while standing at the place of *Ima de Atzilut*. For this reason, the world of *Beria*, which she created, stands below her, occupying the place of ZA *de Atzilut*.

The world of *Yetzira*, born of *Malchut de Atzilut* after the world of *Beria*, emerged from her and occupied the place below the world of *Beria* in the place of the four *Sefirot* of *Malchut de Atzilut* and six *Sefirot* of the place of the world of *Beria*.

The world of *Assiya*, born of *Malchut de Atzilut* after the world of *Yetzira*, emerged from her and occupied the place below the world of *Yetzira*, from *Chazeh* of the place of the world of *Beria* to *Chazeh* of the place of the world of *Yetzira*.

All the worlds end at the *Chazeh* of the world of *Yetzira*, since of all the broken pieces, the ones that were sorted are the vessels of bestowal and the vessels of bestowal, integrated with vessels of reception. This corresponds to the *Chazeh* of the place of the worlds BYA, since there is where their GE end.

Below *Chazeh de Yetzira* begins the AHP of the place of BYA, the place of the vessels of reception that were integrated with the vessels of bestowal, and the vessels of reception (*Lev ha Even*).

Raised AHP: The sorting and correcting of the vessels of reception that were integrated in the vessels of bestowal adds *Kelim* of AHP in the world of *Atzilut*. The Light that spreads in these *Kelim* is *Ohr Hochma*, and the world of *Atzilut* receives *Gadlut*.

Ohr Hochma spreads only in real vessels of reception, while here there are vessels of reception integrated with vessels of bestowal during the breaking. Hence, the Light that appears on the *Zivugim* of these *Kelim* is not *Ohr Hochma* (Light of *Hochma*), but only *He'arat* (illumination, smaller Light) of *Hochma*.

There is a special *Tikkun* at the *Rosh* of the world of *Atzilut* ensuring that there will never be another breaking in the world of *Atzilut*, as it happened in the world of *Nekudim*. There is a limitation at *Rosh* of *Partzuf AA*, so there is no *Zivug* on *Malchut* herself below *Partzuf AA*, but only on the *Hitkalelut* (integration) of *Malchut* in the *Sefirot* Above her, in desires to bestow.

As a result, the world of *Atzilut* was born only in *Katnut*, and each *Partzuf* has only vessels of bestowal, *Kelim de GE*. The vessels of reception, AHP, are below the *Parsa*. It is impossible to add AHP to GE and make a *Zivug* on all ten *Sefirot* in their place, as it was in the world of *Nekudim*, as this was the cause of the breaking.

Hence, each addition of vessels of reception in *Atzilut* is done by raising a few vessels of reception, which are integrated in vessels of bestowal. The ascent is from below the *Parsa* to Above the *Parsa*, so that pieces of AHP are added to *Atzilut*. This, in turn, prompts illumination of *Hochma* in the world of *Atzilut*.

Thus, pieces of the vessels of reception rise from below the *Parsa* and join *Atzilut*. All the vessels of reception that can join the vessels of *Atzilut*, which are the vessels of reception that are integrated in the vessels of bestowal, rise in order from pure to coarse.

Correction of *Lev ha Even* is done only by the Light of the Messiah: After all the above-mentioned corrections are completed, all that remains in *BYA* are vessels of reception, called *Lev ha Even*. These are not included in vessels of reception and hence cannot be corrected. Their correction is in being excluded each time a sorting is done on one of the 320 broken pieces. Thus, the thirty-two pieces of *Lev ha Even* are removed. When using the remaining 288 pieces for building the *Partzufim*, we must sort out and decide that we do not want to use the *Lev ha Even* that belongs in that part.

After the *Tikkun* of all 288 pieces, a special *Ohr Hochma* will come from Above called "Messiah," and will correct these *Kelim* in the *Masach*. At that time, the whole of *Malchut de Ein Sof* will be corrected with a *Masach*. This state in *Malchut* is considered its *Gmar Tikkun* (end of correction).

All the pieces in the worlds *BYA*, except for *Lev ha Even*, are corrected by order of from pure to coarse. In each of the worlds *BYA* there are 2,000 stages of correction, called "years" or "degrees." In all, there are 6,000 degrees in the three worlds *BYA*, called "the six weekdays," since the worlds *BYA* are considered weekdays, while the world of *Atzilut* is considered "the Holy Shabbat."

- When all the worlds *BYA* are corrected, as well as *Lev ha Even*, the world of *Atzilut* will spread below the *Parsa* through this world. This state will be called "the seventh millennium."
- Afterwards, the worlds *ABYA* will rise to *SAG*, and this will be called "the eighth millennium."
- Afterwards, the worlds *ABYA* will rise to *AB*, and this will be called "the ninth millennium."
- Afterwards, the worlds *ABYA* will rise to *Galgalta*, and this will be called "the tenth millennium."

In other words, after the correction of the whole of *Malchut de Ein Sof*, it will be filled just as it was prior to *Tzimtzum Aleph*. In addition, it will receive additions from the infinite ascensions in the degrees of bestowal upon the Creator.

Yet, since the wisdom of Kabbalah teaches a person only what concerns one's own correction, what one must do, these states are not taught. They do not appear in books of Kabbalah, since they belong to the part that is forbidden to reveal, called "secrets of Torah." Only a chosen few engage in them, and under strict conditions.

Adam ha Rishon: In all of *Malchut's* corrections mentioned thus far, *Malchut* of *Malchut*, the central point of all the worlds, has not been filled. All that has thus far unfolded—*Tzimtzum Aleph*, *Tzimtzum Bet*, the breaking of the vessels, the *Tikkun* of the *Kelim*—happened in the Upper nine *Sefirot* of *Malchut*, not on *Malchut* herself, *Behina Dalet* in *Behina Dalet*. This is so because there was a *Tzimtzum* on her, so she would not receive within her, in the will to receive. What is received after *Tzimtzum Aleph* is received only in vessels of bestowal, in the *Kelim* of *Malchut de Ein Sof*, which were impressed by the Upper nine, the Upper Light's desire to bestow.

Malchut in *Malchut* will be corrected and filled with *Ohr Hochma*, as prior to *Tzimtzum Aleph*, only if desires to bestow enter that *Malchut* and mingle with *Malchut's* desires to receive. In the breaking of the vessels in the world of *Nekudim*, *Malchut* mingled with the nine *Sefirot* preceding it. As a result, the worlds, the externality of reality, emerged. But this did not correct anything in *Malchut* herself, since she did not mingle with the desire to bestow.

After the birth of the worlds BYA, *Malchut de Atzilut*, which stands at the place of *Ima*, made a *Zivug* on *Katnut* on joining the vessels of bestowal with *Behina Dalet de Dalet*. The result of this *Zivug* is *Partzuf Katnut*, GE, whose AHP is *Behina Dalet de Dalet*. Hence, this *Partzuf* is forbidden to use its vessels of reception, its AHP. This *Partzuf* is called *Adam ha Rishon* (First Man), who was forbidden to eat from the Tree of Knowledge, that is, to make a *Zivug* on the vessels of reception—AHP.

At the birth of *Adam ha Rishon*, the worlds BYA expanded through the place of *Chazeh de Yetzira*. Afterwards, Light from *Ein Sof*, called "awakening from Above," came and elevated all the worlds by one degree. Thus, the *Sium* of the world of *Assiya* rose from the place of *Chazeh de Yetzira* to the place of *Chazeh de Beria*. Afterwards arrived more Light of awakening from *Ein Sof*, by which all the worlds rose one more degree, so the *Sium* of the world of *Assiya* rose above the *Parsa*.

Adam ha Rishon is inside the worlds BYA; hence, he rose to *Atzilut* along with them. *Adam ha Rishon* thought that now he could receive in order to bestow all the Light in his vessels of reception, in the AHP, in *Behina Dalet* in *Behina Dalet*.

But just as it happened with the breaking of the vessels in the world of *Nekudim*, when he extended Light into the vessels of reception, he broke. He lost his *Masach*, his aim to bestow. His whole *Guf* was divided into 600,000 pieces, called "organs" or "souls," which fell to the *Klipot* and received the desire to receive.

All the pieces together, and each piece in particular, fell lower still (as described in the sins that the Torah narrates in the first generations following

Adam). These parts clothe in people in our world. Those in whom broken pieces of *Partzuf Adam ha Rishon* are clothed, feel—specifically in this part—a desire to rise and unite with their Source, which was in *Adam ha Rishon*. That Source is called "the root of one's soul."

For the creature to merit the title "creature," it must stand in its own right, that is, be unaffected by the Creator. This is why the Creator hides Himself. By doing so, He helps the creatures equalize with Him through their own efforts. It turns out that a person in our world, in whom a piece of *Adam ha Rishon* is clothed, is defined as a "creature."

A creature is a part of *Adam ha Rishon* that exists in a person in our world. All the creatures, all the souls, are parts of the *Guf* of *Adam ha Rishon*. They should all partake in correcting its shattering. By doing so, they return to the state that preceded the sin and add *Dvekut* (adhesion) with the Creator. They sort out all the pieces from the *Klipot*. Thus, each person must reach the root of his or her soul while still living in our world. One who does not, reincarnates into our world until one achieves the purpose for which one was created.

Preface to the Wisdom of Kabbalah

While studying, it is recommend to examine the drawings at the end of the essay, Hallan

THE THOUGHT OF CREATION AND THE FOUR PHASES OF DIRECT LIGHT

1) Rabbi Hanania Son of Akashia says, "The Creator wished to cleanse Israel; hence, He has given them plentiful Torah and *Mitzvot* (commandments), as it is written, 'The Lord was pleased, for His righteousness' sake, to make the teaching great and glorious'" (*Makot*, 23b). It is known that "cleansing" is derived from the (Hebrew) word, "purifying." It is as our sages said, "The *Mitzvot* were only given for the purification of Israel" (*Beresheet Rabba*, *Parasha* 44). We must understand this cleansing, which we achieve through Torah and *Mitzvot*, and what is the *Aviut* (thickness/coarseness/will to receive) within us, which we should cleanse using Torah and *Mitzvot*.

Since we have already discussed it in my book, *Panim Masbirot*, and in *The Study of the Ten Sefirot*, I shall briefly reiterate that the Thought of Creation was to delight the creatures, in accordance with His abundant generosity. For this reason, a great desire and craving to receive His abundance was imprinted in the souls.

This is so because the will to receive is the *Kli* (vessel) for the measure of pleasure in the abundance, since the measure and strength of the will to receive the abundance precisely corresponds to the measure of pleasure and delight in the abundance. And they are so connected that they are indivisible, except in what they relate to: the pleasure is related to the abundance, and the great desire to receive the abundance is related to the receiving creature.

These two necessarily extend from the Creator, and necessarily came in the Thought of Creation. However, they should be divided in the above-mentioned manner: the abundance comes from His Essence, extending existence from existence, and the will to receive included there is the root of the creatures. This means that it is the root of initiation, that is, emergence existence from absence, since there is certainly no form of will to receive in His Essence.

Hence, it is considered that the above-mentioned will to receive is the whole substance of Creation from beginning to end. Thus, all the creatures, all their innumerable instances and conducts that have appeared and that will appear, are but measures and various denominations of the will to receive. All that exists in those creatures, that is, all that is received in the will to receive imprinted in them, extends from His Essence existence from existence. It is not at all a new creation, since it is not new at all. Rather, it extends from His Endlessness existence from existence.

2) As we have said, the will to receive is innately included in the Thought of Creation with all its denominations, along with the great abundance He had planned to delight them and impart to them. And know that these are the *Ohr* (Light) and *Kli* that we discern in the Upper Worlds. They necessarily come tied together and cascade together degree by degree. And the extent to which the degrees descend from the Light of His Face and depart from Him is the extent of the materialization of the will to receive contained in the abundance.

We could also state the opposite: to the extent that the will to receive in the abundance materializes, it descends degree by degree to the lowest of all places, where the will to receive is fully materialized. This place is called "the world of *Assiya*," the will to receive is considered "man's body," and the abundance one receives is considered the measure of "vitality in that body."

It is similar in other creatures in this world. Thus, the only difference between the Upper Worlds and this world is that as long as the will to receive included in His Abundance has not fully materialized, it is regarded as being in the spiritual worlds, Above this world. And once the will to receive has fully materialized, it is regarded as being in this world.

3) The above-mentioned order of cascading, which brings the will to receive to its final form in this world, follows a sequence of four discernments that exist in the four-letter-name, *HaVaYaH*. This is because the four letters, *HaVaYaH* (*Yod, Hey, Vav, Hey*), in His Name contain the whole of reality, without any exception.

In general, they are described in the ten *Sefirot*, *Hochma, Bina, Tifferet, Malchut*, and their *Shoresh* (Root). They are ten *Sefirot* because the *Sefira Tifferet* contains six internal *Sefirot*, called *HGT NHY* (*Hesed-Gevura-Tifferet Netzah-Hod-Yesod*), and the Root, called *Keter*. Yet, in essence, they are called *HB TM* (*Hochma-Bina Tifferet-Malchut*).

And they are four worlds, called *Atzilut, Beria, Yetzira,* and *Assiya*. The world of *Assiya* contains this world within it. Thus, there is not a creature in this world, which is not initiated in the world of *Ein Sof*, in the Thought of Creation to delight His creatures. Hence, it is innately comprised of Light and *Kli*, meaning a certain measure of abundance with the will to receive that abundance.

The measure of abundance extends existence from existence from His Essence, and the will to receive the abundance is initiated existence from absence.

But for that will to receive to acquire its final quality, it must cascade along with the abundance within it through the four worlds—*Atzilut, Beria, Yetzira,* and *Assiya*. This completes the Creation with Light and *Kli*, called *Guf* (body), and the "Light of life" within it.

4) The reason why the will to receive must cascade by the four abovementioned discernments in *ABYA* (*Atzilut, Beria, Yetzira, Assiya*) is that there is a great rule concerning the *Kelim* (plural for *Kli*): **the expansion of the Light and its departure make the Kli fit for its task.** This means that as long as the *Kli* has not been separated from its Light, it is included in the Light and is annulled within it like a candle in a torch.

This annulment is because they are completely opposite from one another, on opposite ends. This is so because the Light extends from His Essence existence from existence. From the perspective of the Thought of Creation in *Ein Sof*, it is all towards bestowal and there is no trace of will to receive in it. Its opposite is the *Kli*, the great will to receive that abundance, which is the root of the initiated creature, in which there is no bestowal whatsoever.

Hence, when they are bound together, the will to receive is annulled in the Light within it, and can determine its form only once the Light has departed thence once. This is so because following the departure of the Light from it, it begins to crave it, and this craving properly determines and sets the shape of the will to receive. Subsequently, when the Light dresses in it once more, it is regarded as two separate matters: *Kli* and Light, or *Guf* and Life. Observe closely, for this is most profound.

5) Hence, the four discernments in the name *HaVaYaH*, called *Hochma, Bina, Tifferet,* and *Malchut*, are required. **Behina Aleph (Phase One)**, called *Hochma*, is indeed the whole of the emanated being, Light and *Kli*. In it is the

great will to receive with all the Light included in it, called *Ohr Hochma* (Light of Wisdom) or *Ohr Haya* (Light of *Haya*), as it is all the *Hayim* (life) in the emanated being, dressed in its *Kli*. However, this *Behina Aleph* is considered all Light and the *Kli* in it is barely noticeable, as it is mingled with the Light and annulled in it as a candle in a torch.

Following it comes Behina Bet (Phase Two), since at its end, the *Kli* of *Hochma* prevails in equivalence of form with the Upper Light in it. This means that a desire to bestow upon the Emanator appears in it, according to the nature of the Light within it—entirely to bestow.

Then, using this desire, which has awakened in it, a new Light extends to it from the Emanator, called *Ohr Hassadim* (Light of Mercy). As a result, it becomes almost entirely separated from the *Ohr Hochma* that the Emanator imprinted in it, since *Ohr Hochma* can only be received in its own *Kli*—a desire to receive that has grown to its fullest measure.

Thus, the Light and *Kli* in *Behina Bet* are utterly different from those in *Behina Aleph*, since the *Kli* in it is the desire to bestow. The Light within it is considered *Ohr Hassadim*, a Light that stems from the *Dvekut* (adhesion) of the emanated in the Emanator, as the desire to bestow induces its equivalence of form with the Emanator, and in spirituality equivalence of form is *Dvekut*.

Next follows Behina Gimel (Phase Three). Once the Light had diminished in the emanated being into *Ohr Hassadim* without any *Hochma*, while it is known that *Ohr Hochma* is the essence of the emanated being, hence, at the end of *Behina Bet*, it awakened and drew within it a measure of *Ohr Hochma*, to shine within its *Ohr Hassadim*. This awakening re-extended a certain measure of the will to receive, which forms a new *Kli* called *Behina Gimel* or *Tifferet*. And the Light in it is called "Light of *Hassadim* in illumination of *Hochma*," since the majority of that Light is *Ohr Hassadim*, and its lesser part is *Ohr Hochma*.

Following it came Behina Dalet (Phase Four), since the *Kli* of *Behina Gimel*, too, awakened at its end to draw the complete *Ohr Hochma*, as it occurred in *Behina Aleph*. Thus, this awakening is considered "craving" in the measure of the will to receive in *Behina Aleph*, and exceeding it, since now it has already been separated from that Light, as the Light of *Hochma* is no longer clothed in it, but craves it. Thus, the form of the will to receive has been fully determined, since the *Kli* is determined following the expansion of the Light and its departure from there. Later, when it returns, it will receive the Light once more. It turns out that the *Kli* precedes the Light, and this is why this *Behina Dalet* is considered the completion of the *Kli*, and it is called *Malchut* (Kingship).

6) These four above discernments are the ten *Sefirot*, discerned in each emanation and each creature, in the whole, which are the four worlds, and even in the smallest part in reality. *Behina Aleph* is called *Hochma* or "the world of *Atzilut*"; *Behina Bet* is called *Bina* or "the world of *Beria*"; *Behina Gimel* is called *Tifferet* or "the world of *Yetzira*"; and *Behina Dalet* is called *Malchut* or "the world of *Assiya*."

Let us explain the four discernments applied in each soul. When the soul exits from *Ein Sof* and comes into the world of *Atzilut*, it is *Behina Aleph* of the soul. Yet, there, it is still not discerned by that name, since the name *Neshama* (soul) implies that there is some difference between her[25] and the Emanator, and that through that difference, she departed *Ein Sof* and has been revealed as its own authority.

But as long as it does not have a form of a *Kli*, there is nothing to distinguish it from His Essence, to merit her own name. You already know that *Behina Aleph* of the *Kli* is not considered a *Kli* at all, and is entirely annulled in the Light. And this is the meaning of what is said about the world of *Atzilut*, that it is complete Godliness, as in "He, His Life, and His Self are One." Even the souls of all living creatures, while traversing the world of *Atzilut*, are still considered attached to His Essence.

7) This above-mentioned *Behina Bet* rules in the world of *Beria*—the *Kli* of the desire to bestow. Hence, when the soul cascades into the world of *Beria* and achieves the *Kli* that exists there, it is considered a *Neshama* (soul). This means that it has already separated from His Essence and merits its own name—*Neshama*. Yet, this is a very pure and fine *Kli*, as it is in equivalence of form with the Emanator. For this reason, it is considered complete spirituality.

8) The above-mentioned *Behina Gimel* rules in the world of *Yetzira*, containing a little bit of the form of the will to receive. Hence, when the soul cascades into the world of *Yetzira* and achieves that *Kli*, it exits the spirituality of the *Neshama* and is then called *Ruach*. This is because here its *Kli* is already mingled with some *Aviut*, meaning the little bit of will to receive within it. Yet, it is still considered spiritual because this measure of *Aviut* is insufficient to completely separate it from His Essence and merit the name, "body," which stands in its own right.

9) *Behina Dalet* rules in the world of *Assiya*, which is the complete *Kli* of the great will to receive. Hence, it obtains a completely separated and distinguished body from His Essence, which stands in its own right. The Light in it is called

---

25 Translator's note: in Hebrew, a *Neshama* is considered female. In general, every object and being receives a specific gender, though in Kabbalah, each term (*Partzuf*, world, etc.) may change its gender according to its functionality at that time: active/giving is male, and passive/receiving is female.

Nefesh (from the Hebrew word 'rest'), indicating that the Light is motionless in and of itself. You should know that there is not a single element in reality that is not comprised of the whole ABYA.

10) Thus, you find that this *Nefesh*, the Light of Life that is dressed in the body, extends from His Very Essence, existence from existence. As it traverses the four worlds ABYA, it becomes increasingly distant from the Light of His Face, until it comes into its designated *Kli*, called *Guf* (body). This is considered that the *Kli* has completed its desirable form.

And even if the Light in it has so diminished that its origin becomes undetectable, through engagement in Torah and *Mitzvot* in order to bestow contentment upon the Maker, one purifies one's *Kli*, called *Guf*, until it becomes worthy of receiving the great abundance in the full measure included in the Thought of Creation, when He created it. This is what Rabbi Hanania meant by "The Creator wished to cleanse Israel; hence, He has given them plentiful Torah and *Mitzvot*."

11) Now you can understand the real difference between spirituality and corporeality: anything that contains a complete desire to receive, in all its aspects, which is *Behina Dalet*, is considered "corporeal." This is what exists in all the elements of reality before us in this world. Conversely, anything above this great measure of desire to receive is considered "spirituality." These are the worlds ABYA–Above this world–and the whole reality within them.

Now you can see that the whole issue of ascents and descents described in the Upper Worlds does not relate to an imaginary place, but only to the four discernments in the will to receive. The farther it is from *Behina Dalet*, the Higher it is considered to be. And conversely, the closer it is to *Behina Dalet*, the lower it is considered to be.

12) We should understand that the essence of the creature, and of Creation as a whole, is only the will to receive. Anything beyond it is not part of Creation, but extends from His Essence by way of existence from existence. Thus, why do we discern this will to receive as *Aviut* (thickness) and turbidity, and we are commanded to cleanse it through Torah and *Mitzvot*, to the point that without it we will not achieve the sublime goal of the Thought of Creation?

13) The thing is that as corporeal objects are separated from one another by remoteness of location, spirituals are separated from each other by the disparity of form between them. This can be found in our world, too. For example, when two people share similar views, they like each other and the remoteness of location does not cause them to draw far from one another.

Conversely, when their views are far, they are hateful of each other, and proximity of location will not bring them any closer. Thus, the disparity of form in their views removes them from each other, and the proximity of form in their views brings them closer to each other. If, for example, one's nature is the complete opposite of another's, they are as far from one another as the east from the west.

Similarly, all matters of nearness and remoteness, coupling and unity that unfold in spirituality are but measures of disparity of form. They depart from one another according to their measure of disparity of form, and become attached to one another according to their measure of equivalence of form.

Yet, you should understand that although the will to receive is a mandatory law in the creature, as it is the essence of the creature and the proper *Kli* for reception of the goal of the Thought of Creation, it nonetheless completely separates it from the Emanator. This is so because there is disparity of form to the point of oppositeness between itself and the Emanator. This is because the Emanator is complete bestowal without a shred of reception, and the creature is complete reception without a shred of bestowal. Thus, there is no greater oppositeness of form than that. It therefore follows that this oppositeness of form necessarily separates it from the Emanator.

14) To save the creatures from this titanic separation, the *Tzimtzum Aleph* (First Restriction) took place. It essentially separated *Behina Dalet* from the rest of the *Partzufim* (faces/countenances) of *Kedusha* (holiness) in such a way that that great measure of reception remained an empty void, a space devoid of Light.

This is so because all the *Partzufim* of *Kedusha* emerged with a *Masach* (screen) erected in their *Kli Malchut* so they would not receive in this *Behina Dalet*. Then, when the Upper Light was extended and spread to the emanated being, this *Masach* rejected it. This is regarded as striking between the Upper Light and the *Masach*, which raises *Ohr Hozer* (Reflected Light) from below Upwards, clothing the ten *Sefirot* of the Upper Light.

That part of the Light that is rejected and pushed back is called *Ohr Hozer* (Reflected Light). As it dresses the Upper Light, it becomes a *Kli* for reception of the Upper Light instead of *Behina Dalet*, since afterwards the *Kli* of *Malchut* had expanded by the measure of *Ohr Hozer*—the rejected Light—which rose and dressed the Upper Light from below Upwards, and expanded from Above downwards, too. Thus, the Lights were clothed in the *Kelim* (plural for *Kli*), within that *Ohr Hozer*.

This is the meaning of the *Rosh* (head) and *Guf* (body) in each degree. The *Zivug de Hakaa* (coupling of striking) from the Upper Light in the *Masach* raises

Ohr Hozer from below Upwards and dresses the ten *Sefirot* of the Upper Light in the form of ten *Sefirot de* (of) *Rosh*, meaning the roots of *Kelim* (vessels). This is because there cannot be actual clothing there.

Subsequently, when *Malchut* expands with that *Ohr Hozer*, from Above downwards, the *Ohr Hozer* ends and becomes *Kelim* for the Upper Light. At that time, there is clothing of the Lights in the *Kelim*, and this is called the *Guf* of that degree, that is, complete *Kelim*.

15) Thus, new *Kelim* were made in the *Partzufim* of *Kedusha* instead of *Behina Dalet* after *Tzimtzum Aleph* (first restriction). They were made of the *Ohr Hozer* of the *Zivug de Hakaa* in the *Masach*.

Indeed, we should understand this *Ohr Hozer* and how it became a vessel of reception, since initially it was but a rejected Light. Thus, it is now serving in an opposite role from its own essence.

I shall explain that with an allegory from life. Man's nature is to cherish and favor the quality of bestowal, and to despise and loathe reception from one's friend. Hence, when one comes to one's friend and he (the host) invites him for a meal, he (the guest) will decline, even if he is very hungry, since in his eyes it is humiliating to receive a gift from his friend.

Yet, when his friend sufficiently implores him until it is clear that by eating he would do a big favor to his friend, he consents to eat, as he no longer feels that he is receiving a gift and that his friend is the giver. On the contrary, he (the guest) is the giver, who is doing his friend a favor by receiving this good from him.

Thus, you find that although hunger and appetite are vessels of reception designated to eating, and that that person had sufficient hunger and appetite to receive his friend's meal, he still could not taste a thing, due to the shame. Yet, as his friend implored him and he rejected him, new vessels for eating began to form within him, since the power of his friend's pleading and the power of his own rejections, as they accumulate, finally accumulate into a sufficient amount that turns the measure of reception into a measure of bestowal.

In the end, he can see that by eating, he will be doing a big favor and bring great contentment to his friend by eating. In that state, new vessels of reception to receive his friend's meal were made within him. Now it is considered that the power of his rejection has become the essential vessel in which to receive the meal, and not the hunger and appetite, although they are actually the usual vessels of reception.

16) From the above allegory between two friends, we can understand the matter of *Zivug de Hakaa* and the *Ohr Hozer* that rises through it, which then becomes new vessels of reception for the Upper Light instead of *Behina Dalet*.

We can compare the Upper Light, which strikes the *Masach* and wants to expand into *Behina Dalet*, to the pleading to eat, because as he yearns for his friend to receive his meal, the Upper Light desires to spread to the receiver. And the *Masach*, which strikes the Light and repels it, can be resembled to the friend's rejection and refusal to receive the meal, since he rejects his favor.

And just as you find here that it is precisely the rejection and refusal that became the proper vessels to receive his friend's meal, you can imagine that the *Ohr Hozer*, which rises by the striking of the *Masach* and the rejection of the Upper Light, becomes the new vessel of reception for the Upper Light, instead of *Behina Dalet*, which served as the vessel of reception prior to the first restriction.

However, this was placed only in the *Partzufim* (plural for *Partzuf*) of *Kedusha* (holiness) of ABYA, not in the *Partzufim* of the *Klipot* (shells), and in this world, where *Behina Dalet* herself is considered the vessel of reception. Hence, they are separated from the Upper Light, since the disparity of form in *Behina Dalet* separates them. For this reason, the *Klipot* are considered wicked and dead, as they are separated from the Life of Lives by the will to receive within them.

FIVE DISCERNMENTS IN THE MASACH

17) Thus far we have clarified the three basic elements in the wisdom. The first is the Light and the *Kli*, where the Light is a direct extension of His Essence, and the *Kli* is the will to receive, which is necessarily included in that Light. One departs the Emanator and becomes an emanated being to the extent of that desire. Also, this will to receive is considered the *Malchut* discerned in the Upper Light. This is why it is called *Malchut*, by way of "He is One and His Name, One," as His name in *Gematria* is *Ratzon* (desire).

The second matter is the clarification of the ten *Sefirot* and four worlds ABYA, which are four degrees one below the other. The will to receive must hang down through them until it is completed—*Kli* and content.

The third matter is the *Tzimtzum* and the *Masach* placed on this vessel of reception, which is *Behina Dalet*, in return for which new vessels of reception were made in the ten *Sefirot*, called *Ohr Hozer*. Understand and memorize these three foundations and their reasons, as they had appeared before you, since without them there is no understanding of even a single word in this wisdom.

18) Now we shall explain the five discernments in the *Masach*, by which the levels change during the *Zivug de Hakaa* performed with the Upper Light. First, we must thoroughly understand that even though *Behina Dalet* was banned from being a vessel of reception for the ten *Sefirot* after the *Tzimtzum*, and the *Ohr Hozer* that rises from the *Masach* through the *Zivug de Hakaa* became the vessel of reception in

its stead, it must still accompany the *Ohr Hozer* with its power of reception. Had it not been for that, the *Ohr Hozer* would have been unfit to be a vessel of reception.

You should also understand that from the allegory in Item 15. We demonstrated there that the power to reject and decline the meal became the vessel of reception instead of the hunger and appetite. This is because hunger and appetite, the usual vessels of reception, were banned from being vessels of reception in this case, due to the shame and disgrace of receiving a gift from one's friend. Only the powers of rejection and refusal have become vessels of reception in their stead, as through the rejection and refusal, reception has become bestowal, and through them he achieved vessels of reception suitable to receive one's friend's meal.

Yet, it cannot be said that he no longer needs the usual vessels of reception, namely the hunger and the appetite, as it is clear that without appetite for eating he will not be able to satisfy his friend's will and bring him contentment by eating at his place. But the thing is that the hunger and appetite, which were banned in their usual form, have now been transformed by the forces of rejection and decline into a new form—reception in order to bestow. Thus, the humiliation has been turned into dignity.

It turns out that the usual vessels of reception are still as active as ever, but have acquired a new form. You will also conclude, concerning our matter, that it is true that *Behina Dalet* has been banned from being a *Kli* for reception of the ten *Sefirot* because of its *Aviut*, meaning the difference of form from the Giver, which separates from the Giver. Yet, through correcting the *Masach* in *Behina Dalet*, which strikes the Upper Light and repels it, her previous, faulty form has been transformed and acquired a new form, called *Ohr Hozer*, like the transformation of the form of reception into a form of bestowal.

The content of its initial form has not changed; it still does not eat without appetite. Similarly, all the *Aviut*, which is the force of reception in *Behina Dalet*, has come inside the *Ohr Hozer*, hence the *Ohr Hozer* becomes suitable for being a vessel of reception.

Therefore, two discernments must always be made in the *Masach*:

1. *Kashiut* (hardness), which is the force within it that rejects the Upper Light;
2. *Aviut*, which is the measure of will to receive from *Behina Dalet* included in the *Masach*. By the *Zivug de Hakaa* through the force of the *Kashiut* in it, its *Aviut* is turned to purity, meaning reception is transformed into bestowal.

These two forces in the *Masach* act in five discernments: the four *Behinot HB TM* and their root, called *Keter*.

19) We have already explained that the first three discernments are still not considered a *Kli*, but only *Behina Dalet* is considered a *Kli*. Still, because the first three discernments are its causes and induce the completion of *Behina Dalet*, once *Behina Dalet* is completed, four measures are registered in its quality of reception.

- *Behina Aleph* in it is the slightest measure of the quality of reception.
- *Behina Bet* is somewhat thicker (having more *Aviut*) than *Behina Aleph* in terms of its quality of reception.
- *Behina Gimel* is thicker than *Behina Bet* in its quality of reception.
- And finally, *Behina Dalet* is the thickest of all, and its quality of reception is perfect in every way.
- We should also discern that the root of the four *Behinot* (plural for *Behina*), which is the purest of them all, is included in it, too.

These are the five discernments of reception contained in *Behina Dalet*, which are called by the names of the ten *Sefirot KHB* (*Keter-Hochma-Bina*) *TM*, included in *Behina Dalet*, since the four phases are *HB TM*, and the root is called *Keter*.

20) The five discernments of reception in *Behina Dalet* are called by the names of the *Sefirot KHB TM*. This is so because prior to the *Tzimtzum*, while *Behina Dalet* was still the vessel of reception for the ten *Sefirot* included in the Upper Light by way of "He is One and His Name One," since all the worlds are included there, its clothing of the ten *Sefirot* in that place followed these five *Behinot*. Each *Behina* of the five *Behinot* in her clothed its corresponding *Behina* in the ten *Sefirot* in the Upper Light.

- *Behinat Shoresh* (Root Phase) in *Behina Dalet* clothed the light of *Keter* in the ten *Sefirot*;
- *Behina Aleph* in *Behina Dalet* clothed the Light of *Hochma* in the ten *Sefirot*;
- *Behina Bet* in her clothed the Light of *Bina*;
- *Behina Gimel* in her clothed the Light of *Tifferet*;
- And her own *Behina* clothed the Light of *Malchut*.

Hence, even now, after the first restriction, when *Behina Dalet* has been banned from being a vessel of reception, the five discernments of *Aviut* in her are named after the five *Sefirot KHB TM*.

21) And you already know that in general, the substance of the *Masach* is called *Kashiut*, which means something very hard, which does not allow anything to push into its boundary. Similarly, the *Masach* does not let any of the Upper Light through

it and into *Malchut*, *Behina Dalet*. Thus, it is considered that the *Masach* halts and repels the entire measure of Light that should clothe the *Kli* of *Malchut*.

It has also been made clear that those five *Behinot* of *Aviut* in *Behina Dalet* are included and come in the *Masach*, and join its measure of *Kashiut*. Hence, five kinds of *Zivug de Hakaa* are discerned in the *Masach*, corresponding to the five measures of *Aviut* in it:

- A *Zivug de Hakaa* on a complete *Masach* with all the levels of *Aviut* raises sufficient *Ohr Hozer* to clothe all ten *Sefirot*, up to the level of *Keter*.
- A *Zivug de Hakaa* on a *Masach* that lacks the *Aviut* of *Behina Dalet*, and contains only *Aviut* of *Behina Gimel*, raises sufficient *Ohr Hozer* to clothe the ten *Sefirot* only up to the level of *Hochma*, lacking *Keter*.
- And if it has only *Aviut* of *Behina Bet*, its *Ohr Hozer* diminishes and suffices only to clothe the ten *Sefirot* up to the level of *Bina*, lacking *Keter* and *Hochma*.
- If it contains only *Aviut* of *Behina Aleph*, its *Ohr Hozer* diminishes even further and suffices only to clothe up to the level of *Tifferet*, lacking *KHB*.
- And if it lacks *Aviut* of *Behina Aleph*, too, and is left with only *Aviut* of *Behinat Shoresh*, its striking is very faint and suffices to clothe only up to the level of *Malchut*, lacking the first nine *Sefirot*, which are *KHB* and *Tifferet*.

22) Thus you see how the five levels of ten *Sefirot* emerge though five kinds of *Zivug de Hakaa* of the *Masach*, applied on its five measures of *Aviut* in it. And now I shall tell you the reason, for it is known that Light is not attained without a *Kli*.

Also, you know that these five measures of *Aviut* come from the five measures of *Aviut* in *Behina Dalet*. Prior to the *Tzimtzum*, there were five *Kelim* in *Behina Dalet*, clothing the ten *Sefirot KHB TM* (Item 18). After *Tzimtzum Aleph*, they were incorporated in the five measures of the *Masach*, which, along with the *Ohr Hozer* it elevates, return to being five *Kelim*, with respect to the *Ohr Hozer* on the ten *Sefirot KHB TM*, instead of the five *Kelim* in *Behina Dalet* itself prior to the *Tzimtzum*.

Accordingly, it is clear that if a *Masach* contains all these five levels of *Aviut*, it contains the five *Kelim* to clothe the ten *Sefirot*. But when it does not contain all five measures, since the *Aviut* of *Behina Dalet* is absent in it, it contains only four *Kelim*. Hence, it can only clothe four Lights: *HB TM*, and lacks one Light—the Light of *Keter*—just as it lacks one *Kli*–*Aviut* of *Behina Dalet*.

Similarly, when it lacks *Behina Gimel*, too, and the *Masach* contains only three measures of *Aviut*, meaning only up to *Behina Bet*, it contains only three

Kelim. Thus, it can only clothe three Lights: *Bina*, *Tifferet*, and *Malchut*. In that state, the level lacks the two Lights, *Keter* and *Hochma*, just as it lacks the two *Kelim*, *Behina Gimel* and *Behina Dalet*.

And when the *Masach* contains only two measures of *Aviut*, that is, *Behinat Shoresh* and *Behina Aleph*, it contains only *Kelim*. Hence, it clothes only two Lights: the Light of *Tifferet* and the Light of *Malchut*. Thus, the level lacks the three Lights *KHB*, just as it lacks the tree *Kelim*, *Behina Bet*, *Behina Gimel*, and *Behina Dalet*.

And when the *Masach* has but one level of *Aviut*, which is only *Behinat Shoresh* of the *Aviut*, it has only one *Kli*. Hence, it can clothe only one Light: the Light of *Malchut*. This level lacks the four Lights *KHB* and *Tifferet*, just as it lacks the four *Kelim*, *Aviut* of *Behina Dalet*, *Behina Gimel*, *Behina Bet*, and *Behina Aleph*.

Thus, the level of each *Partzuf* precisely depends on the measure of *Aviut* in the *Masach*. The *Masach* of *Behina Dalet* elicits the level of *Keter*, *Behina Gimel* elicits the level of *Hochma*, *Behina Bet* elicits the level of *Bina*, *Behina Aleph* elicits the level of *Tifferet*, and *Behinat Shoresh* elicits the level of *Malchut*.

23) Yet, we must still find out why is it that when the *Kli* of *Malchut*—*Behina Dalet*—is missing from the *Masach*, it lacks the Light of *Keter*, and when the *Kli* of *Tifferet* is missing, it lacks the Light of *Hochma*, etc. It would seem that it should have been to the contrary, that when the *Kli* of *Malchut*, *Behina Dalet*, is absent in the *Masach*, only the Light of *Malchut* would be missing in the level and it would have the four Lights *KHB* and *Tifferet*. Also, in the absence of two *Kelim*, *Behina Gimel* and *Behina Dalet*, it would lack the Lights of *Tifferet* and *Malchut*, and the level would have the three Lights *KHB*, etc.

24) The answer is that there is always an inverse relation between Lights and vessels. In the *Kelim*, the Higher Ones grow first in the *Partzuf*: first *Keter*, then the *Kli* of *Hochma*, etc., and the *Kli* of *Malchut* grows last. This is why we name the *Kelim* by the order *KHB TM*, from Above downwards, as this is the order of their growth.

It is to the contrary with the Lights. In the Lights, the lower Lights are the first to enter the *Partzuf*. First enters *Nefesh*, which is the Light of *Malchut*, then *Ruach*, which is the Light of ZA, etc., and the Light of *Yechida* is the last to enter. This is why we name the Lights by the order *NRNHY*,[26] from below Upwards, as this is the order by which they enter—from below Upwards.

Thus, when only one *Kli* has grown in the *Partzuf*, which is necessarily the Highest *Kli*—*Keter*—the Light of *Yechida*, ascribed to that *Kli*, does not enter the

---

26 Translator's note: *Nefesh*, *Ruach*, *Neshama*, *Haya*, *Yechida*, pronounced *NaRaNHaY*.

Partzuf, but only the lowest Light—the Light of *Nefesh*. Thus, the Light of *Nefesh* clothes in the *Kli* of *Keter*.

And when two *Kelim* grow in the *Partzuf*, which are the Highest two—*Keter* and *Hochma*—the Light of *Ruach* enter it, as well. At that time, the Light of *Nefesh* descends from the *Kli* of *Keter* to the *Kli* of *Hochma*, and the Light of *Ruach* clothes in the *Kli* of *Keter*.

Similarly, when a third *Kli* grows in the *Partzuf*—the *Kli* of *Bina*—the Light of *Neshama* enters it. At that time, the Light of *Nefesh* descends from the *Kli* of *Hochma* into the *Kli* of *Bina*, the Light of *Ruach* to the *Kli* of *Hochma*, and the Light of *Neshama* clothes in the *Kli* of *Keter*.

And when a fourth *Kli* grows in the *Partzuf*—the *Kli* of *Tifferet*—the Light of *Haya* enters the *Partzuf*. At that time, the Light of *Nefesh* descends from the *Kli* of *Bina* to the *Kli* of *Tifferet*, the Light of *Ruach* to the *Kli* of *Bina*, the Light of *Neshama* to the *Kli* of *Hochma*, and the Light of *Haya* to the *Kli* of *Keter*.

And when a fifth *Kli* grows in the *Partzuf*, the *Kli* of *Malchut*, the Light of *Yechida* enters it. At that time, all the Lights enter their respective *Kelim*. The Light of *Nefesh* descends from the *Kli* of *Tifferet* to the *Kli* of *Malchut*, the Light of *Ruach* to the *Kli* of *Tifferet*, the Light of *Neshama* to the *Kli* of *Bina*, the Light of *Haya* to the *Kli* of *Hochma*, and the Light of *Yechida* to the *Kli* of *Keter*.

25) Thus, as long as not all five *Kelim KHB TM* have grown in a *Partzuf*, the Lights are not in their designated places. Moreover, they are in inverse relation: in the absence of the *Kli* of *Malchut*, the Light of *Yechida* is absent, and when the two *Kelim*, *TM*, are missing, *Yechida* and *Haya* are absent there, etc. This is so because in the *Kelim*, the Higher ones emerge first, and in the Lights, the last ones are the first to enter.

You will also find that each new Light that reenters dresses only in the *Kli* of *Keter*. This is so because the receiver must receive in its purest *Kli*, the *Kli* of *Keter*.

For this reason, upon reception of each new Light, the Lights that are already dressed in the *Partzuf* must descend one degree from their place. For example, when the Light of *Ruach* enters, the Light of *Nefesh* must descend from the *Kli* of *Keter* to the *Kli* of *Hochma*, to make room in the *Kli* of *Keter* to receive the new Light, *Ruach*. Similarly, if the new Light is *Neshama*, *Ruach*, too, must descend from the *Kli* of *Keter* to the *Kli* of *Hochma*, to clear its place in *Keter* for the new Light, *Neshama*. As a result, *Nefesh*, which was in the *Kli* of *Hochma*, must descend to the *Kli* of *Bina*, etc. All this is done to make room in the *Kli* of *Keter* for the new Light.

Keep this rule in mind and you will always be able to discern in each issue if it is referring to the *Kelim* or to the Lights. Then you will not be confused, because there is always an inverse relation between them. Thus we have thoroughly clarified the matter of the five discernments in the *Masach*, and how, through them, the levels change one below the other.

THE FIVE PARTZUFIM OF AK

26) Thus we have thoroughly clarified the issue of the *Masach* that has been placed in the *Kli* of *Malchut*—the *Behina Dalet* after having been restricted—and the issue of the five kinds of *Zivug de Hakaa* within it, which produce five levels of ten *Sefirot* one below the other. Now we shall explain the five *Partzufim* of AK, which precede the worlds ABYA.

You already know that this *Ohr Hozer*, which rises through the *Zivug de Hakaa* from below Upwards and dresses the ten *Sefirot* of the Upper Light, suffices only for the roots of the *Kelim*, called "ten *Sefirot de Rosh* (head) of the *Partzuf*." To complete the *Kelim*, *Malchut* of the *Rosh* expands from those ten *Sefirot* of *Ohr Hozer* that clothed the ten *Sefirot de Rosh* and spread from it and within it from Above downwards to the same extent as in the ten *Sefirot de Rosh*. This spreading completes the *Kelim*, called "the *Guf* of the *Partzuf*." Hence, we should always distinguish two discernments of ten *Sefirot* in each *Partzuf*: *Rosh* and *Guf*.

27) In the beginning, the first *Partzuf* of AK emerged. This is because immediately following *Tzimtzum Aleph*, when *Behina Dalet* was banned from being a receptacle for the Upper Light, and was erected with a *Masach*, the Upper Light was drawn to clothe in the *Kli* of *Malchut*, as before. Yet, the *Masach* in the *Kli* of *Malchut* halted it and repelled the Light. Through this striking in the *Masach* of *Behina Dalet*, it raised *Ohr Hozer* up to the level of *Keter* in the Upper Light, and this *Ohr Hozer* became a clothing and the roots of the *Kelim* for the ten *Sefirot* in the Upper Light, called "ten *Sefirot de Rosh*" of "the first *Partzuf* of AK."

Subsequently, *Malchut* with the *Ohr Hozer* expanded from her and within her by the force of the ten *Sefirot de Rosh* into ten new *Sefirot* from Above downwards. This completed the *Kelim* of the *Guf*. Then, the full measure that emerged in the ten *Sefirot de Rosh* clothed in the ten *Sefirot de Guf*, as well. This completed the first *Partzuf* of AK, *Rosh* and *Guf*.

28) Subsequently, that same *Zivug de Hakaa* repeated itself on the *Masach* erected in the *Kli* of *Malchut*, which has only *Aviut* of *Behina Gimel*. And then, only the level of *Hochma*, *Rosh* and *Guf*, emerged on it, since the absence of the *Masach* in *Aviut* of *Behina Dalet* caused it to have only four *Kelim*, KHB Tifferet. Hence, the *Ohr Hozer* has room to clothe only four Lights, HNRN (*Haya, Neshama, Ruach, Nefesh*), lacking the Light of *Yechida*. This is called AB de AK.

Following, that same *Zivug de Hakaa* repeated itself on the *Masach* in the *Kli* of *Malchut* that contains only *Aviut* of *Behina Bet*. Thus, ten *Sefirot*, *Rosh* and *Guf*, at the level of *Bina* emerged on it. This is called *Partzuf SAG* of *AK*. It lacks the two *Kelim*, *ZA* and *Malchut*, and the two Lights, *Haya* and *Yechida*.

Afterward the *Zivug de Hakaa* emerged on a *Masach* that has only *Aviut* of *Behina Aleph*. Thus, ten *Sefirot*, *Rosh* and *Guf*, emerged at the level of *Tifferet*, lacking the three *Kelim*, *Bina*, *ZA*, and *Malchut*, and the three Lights, *Neshama*, *Haya*, and *Yechida*. It has only the Lights *Ruach* and *Nefesh*, dressed in the *Kelim Keter* and *Hochma*. This is called *Partzuf MA* and *BON* of *AK*. Remember the inverse relation between the *Kelim* and the Lights (as mentioned in Item 24).

29) Thus we have explained the emergence of the five *Partzufim* of *AK*, called *Galgalta*, *AB*, *SAG*, *MA*, and *BON*, one below the other. Each inferior lacks the Higher *Behina* of its superior. Thus, *Partzuf AB* lacks the Light of *Yechida*, *Partzuf SAG* lacks the Light of *Haya*, as well, which its superior, *AB*, has. *Partzuf MA* and *BON* lacks the Light of *Neshama*, which its superior, *SAG*, has.

This is so because it depends on the measure of *Aviut* in the *Masach* on which the *Zivug de Hakaa* occurs (Item 18). Yet, we must understand who and what caused the *Masach* to gradually diminish its *Aviut*, *Behina* by *Behina*, until it divided into the five levels that exist in these five kinds of *Zivugim* (plural for *Zivug*—coupling).

THE HIZDAKCHUT OF THE MASACH TO THE ATZILUT OF THE PARTZUF

30) To understand the issue of the concatenation of the degrees by five levels one below the other, explained above concerning the five *Partzufim* of *AK*, as well as in all the degrees appearing in the five *Partzufim* of each world of the four worlds *ABYA*, through *Malchut* of *Assiya*, we must thoroughly understand the issue of the *Hizdakchut* (purification) of the *Masach de Guf*, implemented in each of the *Partzufim* of *AK*, the world of *Nekudim*, and the world of *Tikkun* (correction).

31) The thing is that there is no *Partzuf*, or any degree at all, that does not contain two Lights, called *Ohr Makif* (Surrounding Light) and *Ohr Pnimi* (Inner Light), and we shall explain them in *AK*. The *Ohr Makif* of the first *Partzuf* of *AK* is the Light of *Ein Sof*, which fills the whole of reality. Following *Tzimtzum Aleph* and the *Masach* that has been erected in *Malchut*, there was a *Zivug de Hakaa* from the Light of *Ein Sof* on that *Masach*. And using the *Ohr Hozer* that the *Masach* raised, it redrew the Upper Light to the restricted world in the form of ten *Sefirot* of *Rosh* and ten *Sefirot* of *Guf* (Item 25).

Yet, this extension from *Ein Sof* in *Partzuf AK* does not fill the whole of reality, as prior to the *Tzimtzum*. Rather, it is discerned with a *Rosh* and a *Sof*:

- From Above downwards—its Light stops at the point of this world, which is the concluding *Malchut*, as in the verse, "And His feet shall stand... upon the Mount of Olives."

- And from within outwards, for as there are ten *Sefirot KHB TM* from Above downwards, and *Malchut* concludes the *AK* from below, there are ten *Sefirot KHB TM* from within outwards, called *Mocha, Atzamot, Gidin, Bassar,* and *Or*. The *Or* is *Malchut*, which ends the *Partzuf* from the outside. In that respect, *Partzuf AK* is considered a mere thin line compared to *Ein Sof*, which fills the whole of reality. This is so because *Partzuf Or* ends it and limits it from all sides, from the outside, and it cannot expand and fill the entire restricted space. Thus, only a thin line remains standing in the middle of the space.

And the measure of the Light received in *AK*, the thin line, is called *Ohr Pnimi*. The difference between the *Ohr Pnimi* in *AK* and the Light of *Ein Sof* from before the *Tzimtzum* is called *Ohr Makif*, since it remains as *Ohr Makif* around *Partzuf* of *AK*, as it could not clothe within the *Partzuf*.

32) This thoroughly clarifies the meaning of the *Ohr Makif* of *AK*, whose immensity is immeasurable. Yet, this does not mean that *Ein Sof*, which fills the whole of reality, is in itself considered the *Ohr Makif* of *AK*. Rather, it means that a *Zivug de Hakaa* was made on the *Malchut* of the *Rosh* of *AK*, that *Ein Sof* struck the *Masach* positioned there. In other words, it wished to dress in *Behina Dalet de AK*, as prior to the *Tzimtzum*, but the *Masach* in *Malchut de Rosh AK* struck it. This means that it detained it from spreading in *Behina Dalet* and repelled it (Item 14). This *Ohr Hozer* that emerged from the pushing of the Light back became *Kelim* for clothing the Upper Light, as well.

However, there is a big difference between the reception in *Behina Dalet* prior to the *Tzimtzum* and the reception of the *Ohr Hozer* after the *Tzimtzum*, as now it clothed only a thin line in *Rosh* and *Sof*. This is what the *Masach* did through its striking on the Upper Light. And the measure that was rejected from *AK* by the *Masach*, the full measure of Upper Light from *Ein Sof* that wanted to clothe in *Behina Dalet*—had it not been for the *Masach* that halted it—became the *Ohr Makif* surrounding *AK*.

The reason is that there is no change or absence in the spiritual. And since the Light of *Ein Sof* is drawn to *AK*, to clothe in *Behina Dalet*, it must therefore be so.

Hence, even though the *Masach* has now detained it and repelled it, it does not negate the extension of *Ein Sof*. On the contrary, it sustains it but in a different manner: through multiplication of *Zivugim* (plural for *Zivug*) in the five worlds AK and ABYA, until the end of correction, when *Behina Dalet* is completely corrected through them. At that time, *Ein Sof* will clothe in her as in the beginning.

Thus, no change or absence has been effected there by the striking of the *Masach* in the Upper Light. This is the meaning of what is written in *The Zohar*, "The *Zivug* of *Ein Sof* does not descend until it is given its pair." Meanwhile, that is, until that time, it is considered that this Light of *Ein Sof* has become *Ohr Makif*, meaning it will clothe in it in the future. For now, it circles it and shines upon it from the outside with a certain illumination. This illumination accustoms it to expand by the right laws that will bring it to receive this *Ohr Makif* in the measure that *Ein Sof* was initially drawn to it.

33) Now we shall clarify the issue of the *Bitush* (beating) of *Ohr Pnimi* and *Ohr Makif* on one another, which yields the *Hizdakchut* (purification) of the *Masach* and the loss of the last *Behina* of *Aviut*. As these two Lights are opposites, yet connected through the *Masach* in *Malchut* of the *Rosh* of AK, they beat and strike one another.

Interpretation: The *Zivug de Hakaa* in the *Peh* (mouth) *de Rosh de AK*, in the *Masach* in *Malchut de Rosh*, called *Peh*, which was the reason for clothing the *Ohr Pnimi* of AK by the *Ohr Hozer* it raised, is also the reason for the exit of the *Ohr Makif* of AK. Because it detained the Light of *Ein Sof* from clothing in *Behina Dalet*, the Light came out in the form of *Ohr Makif*.

In other words, that whole part of the Light that the *Ohr Hozer* cannot clothe, like the *Behina Dalet* herself, came out and became *Ohr Makif*. Thus, the *Masach* in the *Peh* is the reason for the *Ohr Makif*, as it is the reason for the *Ohr Pnimi*.

34) We have learned that both the *Ohr Pnimi* and the *Ohr Makif* are connected to the *Masach*, but in opposite actions. And just as the *Masach* extends part of the Upper Light into the *Partzuf* through the *Ohr Hozer* that clothes it, it drives the *Ohr Makif* away from clothing in the *Masach*.

And since the part of the Light that remains outside as *Ohr Makif* is very large, due to the *Masach* that stops it from clothing in AK, it is considered that it strikes the *Masach* that removes it, since it wants to clothe within the *Partzuf*. In contrast, it is considered that the force of *Aviut* and *Kashiut* in the *Masach* strikes the *Ohr Makif*, which wants to clothe within it, and detains it, as it strikes the Upper Light during the *Zivug*. These beatings that the *Ohr Makif* and the

Aviut in the *Masach* beat on each other are called the *Bitush* of the *Ohr Makif* and *Ohr Pnimi*.

Yet, this *Bitush* between them occurred only in the *Guf* of the *Partzuf*, since the clothing of the Light in the *Kelim*, which leaves the *Ohr Makif* outside the *Kli*, is apparent there. However, this *Bitush* does not apply to the ten *Sefirot de Rosh*, since the *Ohr Hozer* is not considered *Kelim* there whatsoever, but as mere thin roots. For this reason, the Light in them is not regarded as limited *Ohr Pnimi*, to the point of distinction between that and the Light that remains outside as *Ohr Makif*. And since this distinction between them does not exist, there is no beating of *Ohr Pnimi* and *Ohr Makif* in the ten *Sefirot de Rosh*.

Only once the Lights extend from the *Peh* down to the ten *Sefirot de Guf*, where the Lights clothe in *Kelim*, which are the ten *Sefirot* of *Ohr Hozer* from the *Peh* down, is there beating there between the *Ohr Pnimi* inside the *Kelim* and the *Ohr Makif* that remained outside.

35) This *Bitush* continued until the *Ohr Makif* purified the *Masach* from all its *Aviut* and elevated it to its Upper Root in *Peh de Rosh*. This means that it purified all the *Aviut* from Above downwards, called *Masach* and *Aviut de Guf*, leaving it with only the *Shoresh* (root) *de Guf*, the *Masach* of *Malchut de Rosh*, called *Peh*. In other words, it had been purified of its entire *Aviut* from Above downwards, which is the divider between the *Ohr Pnimi* and the *Ohr Makif*, leaving only the *Aviut* from below Upwards, where the distinction between the *Ohr Pnimi* and *Ohr Makif* has not yet taken place.

It is known that equivalence of form merges spirituals into one. Hence, once the *Masach de Guf* has been purified of all the *Aviut de Guf*, leaving in it only *Aviut* that is equal to the *Masach* of *Peh de Rosh*, its form was equalized with the *Masach de Rosh*. Thus, it was integrated and became literally one with it, since there was nothing to divide them into two. This is considered that the *Masach de Guf* rose to *Peh de Rosh*.

And since the *Masach de Guf* was integrated in the *Masach de Rosh*, it is re-included in the *Zivug de Hakaa* in the *Masach* of *Peh de Rosh*, and a new *Zivug de Hakaa* was made on it. Consequently, ten new *Sefirot*, at a new level, emerged in it, called *AB de AK* or *Partzuf Hochma de AK*. This is considered "a son," an offspring of the first *Partzuf* of AK.

36) And after *Partzuf AB de AK* emerged, complete with *Rosh* and *Guf*, the *Bitush* of *Ohr Makif* and *Ohr Pnimi* repeated itself there, too, as it was explained above concerning the first *Partzuf* of AK. Its *Masach de Guf* was purified from all

its *Aviut de Guf*, as well, until it equalized its form with its *Masach de Rosh* and was then included in the *Zivug* in its *Peh de Rosh*.

Subsequently, a new *Zivug de Hakaa* was made on it, producing a new level of ten *Sefirot* at the level of *Bina*, called *SAG de AK*. This is considered a son and an offspring of *Partzuf AB de AK*, since it emerged from its *Zivug* in *Peh de Rosh*. And the *Partzufim* from *SAG de AK* downwards emerged in a similar manner.

37) Thus we have explained the emergence of the *Partzufim* one below the other by the force of the *Bitush* of *Ohr Makif* and *Ohr Pnimi*, which purifies the *Masach de Guf* until it brings it back to the state of *Masach de Peh de Rosh*. At that time, it is included there in a *Zivug de Hakaa*, which unfolds in the *Peh de Rosh*, and through this *Zivug* emits a new level of ten *Sefirot*. This new level is considered the son of the previous *Partzuf*.

In this manner, AB emerged from *Partzuf Keter*, SAG from *Partzuf AB*, MA from *Partzuf SAG*, and so on with the rest of the degrees in *Nekudim* and *ABYA*. Yet, we should still understand why the ten *Sefirot de AB* emerged only on *Behina Gimel*, and not on *Behina Dalet*, and why was SAG only on *Behina Bet*, etc., meaning that each lower one is inferior to its superior by one degree. Why did they not all emerge from one another at the same level?

38) First, we must understand why the ten *Sefirot* of AB are considered an offshoot of the first *Partzuf* of AK, since it emerged from the *Zivug* in *Peh de Rosh* of the first *Partzuf*, like the ten *Sefirot* of the *Guf* of the *Partzuf* itself. Thus, in what way did it come out of the first *Partzuf*, to be considered a second *Partzuf* and its offshoot?

Here you must understand the big difference between the *Masach de Rosh* and the *Masach de Guf*. There are two kinds of *Malchut* in the *Partzuf*:

1. The Mating *Malchut*—with the Upper Light—by the force of the *Masach* erected in her.

2. The Ending *Malchut*—the Upper Light in the ten *Sefirot* of the *Guf*—by the force of the *Masach* erected in her.

The difference between them is as great as the difference between the Emanator and the emanated. *Malchut de Rosh*, which mates in a *Zivug de Hakaa* with the Upper Light, is considered "the Emanator of the *Guf*," since the *Masach* erected in her did not reject the Upper Light as it struck it. On the contrary, through the *Ohr Hozer* that it raised, it clothed and extended the Upper Light in the form of ten *Sefirot de Rosh*. Thus, it expands from Above downwards, until the ten *Sefirot* of the Upper Light clothed in the *Kli* of *Ohr Hozer*, called *Guf*.

For this reason, the *Masach* and the *Malchut* of the *Rosh* are considered Emanator of the ten *Sefirot* of the *Guf*, and no limitation and rejection are apparent in that *Masach* and *Malchut*. Yet, the *Masach* and the *Malchut de Guf*, that is, after the ten *Sefirot* expanded from *Peh de Rosh* from Above downwards, spread only down to the *Malchut* in those ten *Sefirot*. This is because the Upper Light cannot spread into *Malchut de Guf* because of the *Masach* positioned there, which stops it from spreading into *Malchut*. For this reason, the *Partzuf* stops there, and the end and conclusion of the *Partzuf* are made.

Thus, the whole power of the *Tzimtzum* and limitation appears only in this *Masach* and *Malchut* of the *Guf*. For this reason, the whole *Bitush* of *Ohr Makif* and *Ohr Pnimi* is only done in the *Masach* of the *Guf*, as this is what limits and pushes the *Ohr Makif* away from shining in the *Partzuf*. This is not so in the *Masach de Rosh*, since the *Masach de Rosh* only extends and clothes the Lights, but the power of the limitation is still completely concealed in it.

39) It follows that by the force of the *Bitush* of *Ohr Makif* and *Ohr Pnimi*, the *Masach* of the ending *Malchut* became the *Masach* and *Malchut* of the mating *Malchut* once more (Item 35). This is because the *Bitush* of *Ohr Makif* purified the ending *Masach* from all its *Aviut de Guf*, leaving in it only fine *Reshimot* (records) of that *Aviut*, equal to the *Aviut de Masach de Rosh*.

It is also known that equivalence of form attaches and unites the spirituals to one another. Hence, once the *Masach de Guf* equalized the form of its *Aviut* to the *Masach de Rosh*, it was immediately included in it and they became seemingly one *Masach*. In that state, it received the strength for *Zivug de Hakaa*, like the *Masach* of the *Rosh*, and ten *Sefirot* of the new level emerged on it.

Yet, along with this *Zivug*, the *Reshimot* of the *Aviut de Guf*, which were in it from the beginning, were renewed in its *Masach de Guf*. In that state, the disparity of form between itself and the *Masach de Rosh* included in it appeared in it once more, to an extent. The acknowledgement of this difference separates and removes it from the *Peh de Rosh* of the Upper One, since after it returned and its origin—from *Peh* of the Upper One downwards—has become known, it could not continue to stand above the *Peh* of the Upper One, as the disparity of form separates the spirituals from one another. It follows that it was compelled to decline from there to the place from the *Peh* of the Upper One downwards.

Hence, it is necessarily considered a second entity with respect to the Upper One, as even the *Rosh* of the new level is considered merely the body of the new level, since it extends from its *Masach de Guf*. Thus, this disparity of form distinguishes them into two separate entities. And since the new level is entirely a result of the *Masach de Guf* of the previous *Partzuf*, it is considered its offspring, like a branch extending from it.

40) And there is another difference between the lower and the Upper: Each lower one emerges with a different level than in the five *Behinot* in the *Masach* (Item 22). Also, each lower one lacks the Highest *Behina* of the Lights of the Upper One, and the lowest *Behina* of the *Kelim* of the Upper One. The reason is that it is the nature of the *Bitush* of the *Ohr Makif* in the *Masach* to exclude the last *Behina* of its *Aviut*.

For example, in the first *Partzuf de AK*, whose *Masach* contains all five levels of *Aviut*, down to *Behina Dalet*, the *Bitush* of *Ohr Makif* in the *Masach de Guf* completely purifies the *Aviut* of *Behina Dalet*, not leaving even a *Reshimo* (singular for *Reshimot*) of that *Aviut*. And only the *Reshimot* from the *Aviut* of *Behina Gimel* and Above remain in the *Masach*.

Hence, when that *Masach* is included in the *Rosh* and receives a *Zivug de Hakaa* on the *Aviut* that remained in its *Reshimot* from the *Guf*, the *Zivug* emerges only on *Behina Gimel de Aviut* in the *Masach*. This is because the *Reshimo de Aviut* of *Behina Dalet* is gone from there. Therefore, the level that emerges on that *Masach* is only at the level of *Hochma*, called *HaVaYaH de AB de AK*, or *Partzuf AB de AK*.

We have already learned, in Item 22, that the level *Hochma* that emerges on the *Masach* of *Behina Gimel* lacks the *Malchut de Kelim* and the discernment of the Light of *Yechida* from the Lights, which is the Light of *Keter*. Thus, *Partzuf AB* lacks the last discernment of the *Kelim* of the Upper One and the Highest discernment of the Lights of the Upper One. And because of this great disparity of form, the lower one is considered a separate *Partzuf* from the Upper One.

41) Similarly, once *Partzuf AB* expanded in *Rosh* and *Guf* and there was the *Bitush* of *Ohr Makif* on the *Masach* of the *Guf de AB*, which is *Masach de Behina Gimel*, this *Bitush* cancels and annuls the *Reshimo de Aviut* of the last *Behina* in the *Masach*, which is *Behina Gimel*. It turns out that during the ascension of the *Masach* to the *Peh de Rosh* and its inclusion in the *Zivug de Hakaa*, the beating occurred only on *Aviut* of *Behina Bet* that remained in that *Masach*, since *Behina Gimel* has disappeared from it. Hence, it elicits only ten *Sefirot* at the level of *Bina*, called *HaVaYaH de SAG de AK*, or *Partzuf SAG*, lacking *ZA* and *Malchut* in *Kelim*, and *Haya* and *Yechida* in Lights.

Similarly, when this *Partzuf SAG* expanded in *Rosh* and *Guf*, there was the *Bitush* of *Ohr Makif* in its *Masach de Guf*, which is *Masach* of *Behina Bet*. This

Bitush cancels and annuls the last *Behina* of *Aviut* in the *Masach*—*Behina Bet*—leaving only the *Reshimot de Aviut* from *Behina Aleph* and Above in the *Masach*.

Hence, during the ascension of the *Masach* to the *Peh de Rosh*, and the inclusion in the *Zivug de Hakaa* there, the beating occurred only on the *Masach* of *Behina Aleph* that remained in the *Masach*, since *Behina Bet* had already disappeared from it. For this reason, it elicits only ten *Sefirot* at the level of *Tifferet*, called "the level of ZA," lacking *Bina*, ZA, and *Malchut* in the *Kelim*, and *Neshama*, *Haya*, and *Yechida* in the Lights, etc., similarly.

42) This thoroughly clarifies the reason for the decline of the levels one below the other during the concatenation of the *Partzufim* from one another. It is because the *Bitush* of *Ohr Makif* and *Ohr Pnimi*, applied in each *Partzuf*, always cancels the last *Behina* of *Reshimo* of *Aviut* in there. Yet, we should know that there are two discernments in the *Reshimot* that remain in the *Masach* after its *Hizdakchut* (purification):

3. *Reshimo de Aviut*
4. *Reshimo de Hitlabshut* (clothing)

For instance, once the *Masach de Guf* of the first *Partzuf* in AK has been purified, we said that the last *Behina* of the *Reshimot de Aviut*, the *Reshimo* of *Behina Dalet*, was lost, and that all that remained in the *Masach* was the *Reshimo* of *Aviut de Behina Gimel*. Yet, although the *Reshimo* of *Behina Dalet* contains two discernments, as we have said—*Hitlabshut* and *Aviut*—only the *Reshimo de Aviut* of *Behina Dalet* had disappeared from the *Masach* by that *Hizdakchut*. But the *Reshimo de Hitlabshut* of *Behina Dalet* remained in that *Masach* and did not disappear from it.

Reshimo de Hitlabshut refers to a very subtle *Behina* (discernment) from the *Reshimo* of *Behina Dalet*, which does not contain sufficient *Aviut* for *Zivug de Hakaa* with the Upper Light. This *Reshimo* remains from the last *Behina* in each *Partzuf* during its *Hizdakchut*. And our saying that the last *Behina* disappears from each *Partzuf* during its *Hizdakchut* refers only to the *Reshimo de Aviut* in it.

43) The remainder of the *Reshimot de Hitlabshut* from the last *Behina* that remained in each *Masach*, prompted the elicitation of two levels—male and female—in the heads of all the *Partzufim*: beginning in AB de AK, SAG de AK, MA and BON de AK, and in all the *Partzufim* of *Atzilut*. This is so because in *Partzuf AB de AK*, where there is only *Reshimo* of *Aviut de Behina Gimel* in the *Masach*, which elicits ten *Sefirot* at the level of *Hochma*, the *Reshimo de Hitlabshut* from *Behina Dalet*, which remained there in the *Masach*, is unfit for *Zivug* with the Upper Light, due to its purity. Yet, it is included with the *Aviut* of *Behina*

Gimel and becomes a single *Reshimo*, at which time the *Reshimo de Hitlabshut* acquires the strength for mating with the Upper Light. For this reason, the *Zivug de Hakaa* with the Upper Light emerged on her, eliciting ten *Sefirot* at nearly the level of *Keter*.

This is so because she had *Hitlabshut* of *Behina Dalet*. This *Hitkalelut* (mingling/integration) is called *Hitkalelut* of the female in the male, since the *Reshimo de Aviut* from *Behina Gimel* is called "female," as it carries the *Aviut*. And the *Reshimo de Hitlabshut* of *Behina Dalet* is called "male," as it comes from a Higher place, and because it is purified from *Aviut*. Thus, although the *Reshimo* of the male is insufficient for a *Zivug de Hakaa* in itself, it becomes fit for a *Zivug de Hakaa* through the *Hitkalelut* of the female in it.

44) Subsequently, there is *Hitkalelut* of the male in the female, too. This means that the *Reshimo de Hitlabshut* is integrated with the *Reshimo de Aviut*. This produces a *Zivug de Hakaa* only at the level of the female, the level of *Behina Gimel*, which is the level of *Hochma*, called *HaVaYaH de AB*. The Upper *Zivug*, when the female is included in the male, is considered the level of the male, which is nearly the level of *Keter*. And the lower *Zivug*, when the male is included in the female, is considered the female level, which is only the level of *Hochma*.

Yet, the *Aviut* in the male level does not come from himself, but by means of *Hitkalelut* with the female. And although it suffices to elicit the level of ten *Sefirot* from below Upwards, called *Rosh*, this level still cannot spread from Above downwards in the form of a *Guf*, which would mean clothing of Lights in the *Kelim*. This is so because a *Zivug de Hakaa* on *Aviut* that comes from *Hitkalelut* is insufficient for the expansion of *Kelim*.

Hence, the male level contains only a discernment of *Rosh*, without a *Guf*. The *Guf* of the *Partzuf* extends only from the female level, which has her own *Aviut*. For this reason, we name the *Partzuf* only after the female level, meaning *Partzuf AB*. This is so because the core of the *Partzuf* is its *Guf*—the clothing of the Lights in the *Kelim*. And this emerges only from the female level, as we have explained. This is why the *Partzuf* is named after her.

45) And as we have explained concerning the two levels—male and female—at the *Rosh* of *Partzuf AB*, these two emerge in precisely the same manner in the *Rosh* of SAG. But there, the male level is nearly the level of *Hochma*, as it is from the *Reshimo de Hitlabshut* of *Behina Gimel* in the *Hitkalelut* of the *Aviut* of *Behina Bet*. And the female level is at the level of *Bina*, from *Aviut* of *Behina Bet*. And here, too, the *Partzuf* is named solely after the female level, since the male is a *Rosh* without a *Guf*.

Similarly, in *Partzuf* MA *de* AK, the male level is nearly the level of *Bina*, called "the level of YESHSUT," as it is from the *Reshimo* of *Behina Bet de Hitlabshut*, with *Hitkalelut* of *Aviut* from *Behina Aleph*, while the female level is only the level of ZA, as it is only *Behina Aleph de Aviut*. And here, too, the *Partzuf* is named solely after the female, that is, *Partzuf* MA or *Partzuf* VAK, since the male is a *Rosh* without a *Guf*. You will find it likewise in all the *Partzufim*.

TAAMIM, NEKUDOT, TAGIN, AND OTIOT

46) Now we have clarified the *Bitush* of *Ohr Makif* and *Ohr Pnimi*, occurring after the expansion of the *Partzuf* into a *Guf*. This causes the *Masach de Guf* to purify, all the Lights of the *Guf* to depart, and the *Masach* with the *Reshimot* that remain in it rise to *Peh de Rosh*, where they are renewed with a new *Zivug de Hakaa*, and produce a new level in the measure of *Aviut* in the *Reshimot*. Now we shall explain the four types of Lights, TANTA (*Taamim, Nekudot, Tagin, Otiot*), occurring with the *Bitush* of *Ohr Makif* and the ascents of the *Masach* to *Peh de Rosh*.

47) It has been explained that through the *Bitush* of *Ohr Makif* in the *Masach de Guf*, it purifies the *Masach* of all the *Aviut de Guf* until it is purified and equalizes with the *Masach de Peh de Rosh*. The equivalence of form with the *Peh de Rosh* unites them as one, and it is included in the *Zivug de Hakaa* in it.

However, the *Masach* is not purified at once, but gradually: first from *Behina Dalet* to *Behina Gimel*, then from *Behina Gimel* to *Behina Bet*, then from *Behina Bet* to *Behina Aleph*, and then from *Behina Aleph* to *Behinat Shoresh*. Finally, it is purified from all its *Aviut* and becomes as pure as the *Masach de Peh de Rosh*.

Now the Upper Light does not stop shining for even a moment, and mates with the *Masach* at every stage of its *Hizdakchut*. This is because once it has been purified of *Behina Dalet* and the level of *Keter* has been entirely removed, and the *Masach* came to *Aviut* of *Behina Gimel*, the Upper Light mates with the *Masach* on the remaining *Aviut* of *Behina Gimel* and produces ten *Sefirot* at the level of *Hochma*.

Afterwards, when the *Masach* departs from *Behina Gimel*, too, and the level of *Hochma* departs, as well, leaving only *Behina Bet* in the *Masach*, the Upper Light mates with it on *Behina Bet* and produces ten *Sefirot* at the level of *Bina*. Then, when it has been purified of *Behina Bet*, too, and this level has departed, leaving only *Aviut* of *Behina Aleph* in it, the Upper Light mates with the *Masach* on the remaining *Aviut* of *Behina Aleph*, and produces ten *Sefirot* at the level of ZA. And when it has been purified of *Aviut de Behina Aleph*, too, and the level of ZA has departed, it remains with only the *Shoresh* (root) of the *Aviut*.

In that state, the Upper Light makes a Zivug on Aviut Shoresh that remains in the Masach, and produces ten Sefirot at the level of Malchut. And when the Masach is purified of Aviut Shoresh, too, the level of Malchut departs thence, too, since no Aviut de Guf remains there. In that state, it is considered that the Masach and its Reshimot rose and united with the Masach de Rosh, became included there in a Zivug de Hakaa there, and produced new ten Sefirot over it, called a "child" and a "consequence" of the first Partzuf.

Thus we have explained that the Bitush of Ohr Makif and Ohr Pnimi that purifies the Masach de Guf of the first Partzuf of AK and elevates it to its Peh de Rosh, by which the second Partzuf, AB de AK, emerges, is not done at once. Rather, it occurs gradually, as the Upper Light mates with it at each state in the four degrees it traverses during its Hizdakchut, until it equalizes with the Peh de Rosh.

And as it has been explained regarding the elicitation of the four levels during the Hizdakchut of the Guf of the first Partzuf for AB's purpose, three levels emerge during the Hizdakchut period of the Masach de Guf of Partzuf AB, as it emanates Partzuf SAG, and similarly in all the degrees. The rule is this: A Masach does not purify at once, but gradually. And the Upper Light, which does not stop spreading to the lower one, mates with it at each degree along its purification.

48) Yet, these levels, which emerge on the Masach during its gradual Hizdakchut, are not considered Hitpashtut of real degrees, like the first level that emerged before the beginning of the Hizdakchut. Rather, they are considered Nekudot, and they are called Ohr Hozer and Din (judgment), since the Din force of the Lights' departure is already mingled in them. This is so because in the first Partzuf, as soon as the Bitush began to occur, and purified the Masach de Guf from Behina Dalet, it is considered as having been completely purified, since there is no "some" in the spiritual.

And since it began to purify, it had to purify completely. Yet, since the Masach purifies gradually, there is time for the Upper Light to mate with it at each degree of Aviut that the Masach assumes during its Hizdakchut, until it is completely purified. Hence, the departure force is mingled with the levels that emerge during its departure, and they are considered as only Nekudot and Ohr Hozer and Din.

This is why we discern two types of levels in each Partzuf: Taamim and Nekudot. This is so because the first ten Sefirot de Guf that emerge in each Partzuf are called Taamim, and the levels that emerge in the Partzuf as it purifies, after the Masach had already begun to purify until it reaches Peh de Rosh, are called Nekudot.

49) The Reshimot that remain below, in the Guf, after the departure of the Lights of Taamim, are called Tagin, and the Reshimot that remain from the

levels of *Nekudot* are called *Otiot*, which are *Kelim*. Also, the *Tagin*, which are the *Reshimot* from the Lights of *Taamim*, hover over the *Otiot* and the *Kelim* and sustain them.

Thus we have learned the four types of Light, called *Taamim, Nekudot, Tagin, Otiot*. The first level to emerge in each *Partzuf* of the five *Partzufim* called *Galgalta, AB, SAG, MA*, and *BON*, is called *Taamim*. The levels that emerge in each *Partzuf* once it has started to purify, until it is completely purified, are called *Nekudot*. The *Reshimot* that remain of the Lights of *Taamim* in each level, after their departure, are called *Tagin*, and the *Reshimot* that remain from the Lights of the levels of *Nekudot* after their departure are called *Otiot* or *Kelim*. Remember that in all five *Partzufim* called *Galgalta, AB, SAG, MA*, and *BON*, for in all of them there is *Hizdakchut* and they all have these four types of Lights.

THE ROSH, TOCH, SOF IN EACH PARTZUF AND THE ORDER OF HITLABSHUT OF THE PARTZUFIM IN ONE ANOTHER

You already know the difference between the two *Malchuts* in each *Partzuf*—the mating *Malchut* and the ending *Malchut*. Ten *Sefirot* of *Ohr Hozer* emerge from the *Masach* in the mating *Malchut*, clothing the ten *Sefirot* of Upper Light, called "ten *Sefirot de Rosh*," that is, only roots. From there down, the ten *Sefirot de Guf* of the *Partzuf* expand in the form of *Hitlabshut* (clothing) of Lights in complete *Kelim*.

These ten *Sefirot de Guf* are divided into two discernments of ten *Sefirot*: ten *Sefirot de Toch* (insides), and ten *Sefirot de Sof* (end/conclusion). The position of the ten *Sefirot de Toch* is from the *Peh* to the *Tabur* (navel), the place of the clothing of the Lights in the *Kelim*. The ten *Sefirot* of the end of the *Partzuf* are positioned from the *Tabur* down to the *Sium Raglin* (end of the legs/feet).

This means that *Malchut* ends each *Sefira* until it reaches itself, which is unfit to receive any Light, hence the *Partzuf* ends there. This cessation is called "the end of the *Etzbaot Raglin* (toes) of the *Partzuf*," and from there down it is an empty space, a void without Light.

Know that these two kinds of ten *Sefirot* extend from the root ten *Sefirot*, called *Rosh*, since both are included in the mating *Malchut*. This is so because there is the clothing power there—the *Ohr Hozer* that rises and clothes the Upper Light. There is also the *Masach's* detaining force over *Malchut* so it would not receive the Light, by which the *Zivug de Hakaa* that raises *Ohr Hozer* was done. At the *Rosh*, these two forces are only roots.

Yet, when they expand from Above downwards, the first force, which is a clothing force, is executed in the ten *Sefirot de Toch*, from the *Peh* down to the *Tabur*.

And the second force, which detains *Malchut* from receiving Light, is executed in the ten *Sefirot de Sof* and *Sium*, from *Tabur* down to the end of the *Etzbaot Raglin*.

These two kinds of ten *Sefirot* are always called HGT NHYM. All ten *Sefirot de Toch*, from *Peh* to *Tabur*, are called HGT, and all ten *Sefirot de Sof* from *Tabur* down are called NHYM.

51) We should also know that the issue of the *Tzimtzum* was only on the *Ohr Hochma*, whose *Kli* is the will to receive that ends at *Behina Dalet*, where the *Tzimtzum* and the *Masach* occurred. Yet, there was no *Tzimtzum* at all on the *Ohr de Hassadim* there, since its *Kli* is the will to bestow, in which there are no *Aviut* and disparity of form from the Emanator, and which does not need any corrections.

Hence, in the ten *Sefirot* of the Upper Light these two Lights, *Hochma* and *Hassadim*, are linked together without any difference between them, since they are one Light that expands according to its quality. For this reason, when they come to clothe in the *Kelim* after the *Tzimtzum*, the *Ohr Hassadim* (Light of Mercy) stops at *Malchut*, too, even though it was not restricted. This is so because had the *Ohr Hassadim* expanded in a place where the *Ohr Hochma* (Light of Wisdom) could not expand even a bit—the ending *Malchut*—there would be shattering in the Upper Light, as the *Ohr Hassadim* would have to be completely separated from the *Ohr Hochma*. Hence, the ending *Malchut* became an empty space, devoid of even the *Ohr Hassadim*.

52) Now we can understand the content of the ten *Sefirot de Sof* of the *Partzuf* from *Tabur* down. It cannot be said that they are only considered *Ohr Hassadim*, without any *Hochma* at all, since the *Ohr Hassadim* is never completely separated from the *Ohr Hochma*. Rather, there is necessarily a small illumination of the *Ohr Hochma* in them, as well. You should know that we always call this small illumination "VAK without a *Rosh*." Thus, the three discernments of ten *Sefirot* in the *Partzuf*, called *Rosh*, *Toch*, and *Sof* have been explained.

53) And now we shall explain the order of the clothing of the *Partzufim Galgalta, AB*, and *SAG de AK* on each other. Know that each lower one emerges from the *Masach* of the *Guf* of the Upper One, once it has been purified and has equalized its form with the *Malchut* and the *Masach* at the *Rosh*. This is so because then it is included in the *Masach* at the *Rosh*, in the *Zivug de Hakaa* in it.

And once it undergoes the *Zivug de Hakaa* in the two *Reshimot—Aviut* and *Hitlabshut*—that remain in the *Masach de Guf*, its *Aviut* is recognized as *Aviut de Guf*. Through this recognition, it is discerned that the level emerges from the *Rosh* of the first *Partzuf de AK*, descends, and clothes its *Guf*, meaning at her root, since she is from the *Masach de Guf*.

Indeed, the *Masach* with the mating *Malchut* of the new *Partzuf* had to descend to the place of *Tabur* of the first *Partzuf*, since the *Masach de Guf* with the ending *Malchut* of the first *Partzuf* begins there. Also, the root of the new *Partzuf* and its grip are there. Yet, the last *Behina* of *Aviut* has vanished from the *Masach* by the *Bitush* of *Ohr Pnimi* and *Ohr Makif* (Item 40), and only *Aviut* of *Behina Gimel* remained in the *Masach*. This *Behina Gimel de Aviut* is called *Chazeh* (chest). For this reason, the *Masach* and the mating *Malchut* of the new *Partzuf* have no hold and root in the *Tabur* of the Upper One, but only in its *Chazeh*, where it is attached like a branch to its root.

54) Hence, the *Masach* of the new *Partzuf* descends to the place of the *Chazeh* of the first *Partzuf*, where it elicits ten *Sefirot de Rosh* from it and above it through a *Zivug de Hakaa* with the Upper Light, up to the *Peh* of the Upper One—*Malchut de Rosh* of the first *Partzuf*. But the lower one cannot clothe the ten *Sefirot de Rosh* of the Upper *Partzuf* at all, since it is considered merely the *Masach de Guf* of the Upper One. Subsequently, it produces ten *Sefirot* from Above downwards, called "ten *Sefirot de Guf*" at the *Toch* and the *Sof* of the lower one.

Their place is only from the *Chazeh* of the Upper *Partzuf* down to its *Tabur*, since from *Tabur* down is the place of the ten *Sefirot* of the *Sium* of the Upper One, being *Behina Dalet*. The lower one has no hold of the last *Behina* of the Upper One, since it loses it during its *Hizdakchut* (Item 40). For this reason, that lower *Partzuf*, called *Partzuf Hochma* of AK, or *Partzuf AB de AK*, must end above the *Tabur* of the first *Partzuf* of AK.

Thus, it has been thoroughly clarified that any *Rosh*, *Toch*, *Sof* of *Partzuf AB de AK*, which is the lower one of the first *Partzuf* of AK, stand from the place below the *Peh* of the first *Partzuf* down to its *Tabur*. Thus, the *Chazeh* of the first *Partzuf* is the place of *Peh de Rosh* of *Partzuf AB*, the mating *Malchut*, and the *Tabur* of the first *Partzuf* is the place of *Sium Raglin* of *Partzuf AB*, that is, the ending *Malchut*.

55) As has already been explained regarding the order of the emergence of *Partzuf AB* from the first *Partzuf* of AK, it is the same in all the *Partzufim*, through the end of the world of *Assiya*. Each lower one emerges from the *Masach de Guf* of its Superior, after it has been purified and included in the *Masach de Malchut de Rosh* of the Upper One in the *Zivug de Hakaa* there.

Afterwards, it comes out of there to its gripping point in the *Guf* of the Upper One, and elicits the ten *Sefirot de Rosh* from below Upwards in its place, through a *Zivug de Hakaa* with the Upper Light. Also, it expands from Above downwards into ten *Sefirot de Guf* in *Toch* and *Sof*, as has been explained in

Partzuf AB de AK. Yet, there are differences concerning the end of the *Partzuf*, as it is written elsewhere.

TZIMTZUM BET, CALLED TZIMTZUM NHY DE AK

56) Thus we have thoroughly explained the issue of *Tzimtzum Aleph* (the first restriction), carried out on the *Kli* of *Malchut—Behina Dalet—*so it would not receive the Upper Light within it. We have also explained the issue of the *Masach* and its *Zivug de Hakaa* with the Upper Light, which raises *Ohr Hozer*. This *Ohr Hozer* became new vessels of reception instead of *Behina Dalet*.

Also explained was the *Hizdakchut* of the *Masach de Guf*, made in the *Gufim* (plural for *Guf*) of each *Partzuf* by the *Bitush* of *Ohr Makif* and *Ohr Pnimi*, which produces the four discernments TANTA of the *Guf* of each *Partzuf* and raises the *Masach de Guf* to be considered *Masach de Rosh*. It qualifies it for a *Zivug de Hakaa* with the Upper Light, on which another *Partzuf* is born, one degree lower than the previous *Partzuf*. Finally, we have explained the elicitation of the first three *Partzufim* of AK, called *Galgalta*, AB, SAG, and their clothing order on one another.

57) Know that in these three *Partzufim*, *Galgalta*, AB, and SAG *de AK*, there is not even a root for the four worlds ABYA, since there is not even room for the three worlds BYA here. This is because the inner *Partzuf* of AK extended down to the point of this world, and the root of the desirable correction, which was the cause for the *Tzimtzum*, has not been revealed. This is so because the purpose of the *Tzimtzum* that unfolded in *Behina Dalet* was to correct it, so there would be no disparity of form within it, as it receives the Upper Light (Item 14).

In other words, to create Adam's *Guf* of that *Behina Dalet*, he will turn the reception force in *Behina Dalet* to being in order to bestow, through his engagement in Torah and *Mitzvot* in order to bestow contentment upon his Maker. By that he will equalize the form of reception with complete bestowal, and that would be the end of correction, since this would bring *Behina Dalet* back to being a vessel of reception for the Upper Light, while being in complete *Dvekut* (adhesion) with the Light, without any disparity of form.

Yet, thus far, the root of this correction has not been revealed, as this requires that man (Adam) will be included with the higher *Behinot*, above *Behina Dalet*, so as to be able to perform good deeds of bestowal. And had Adam departed the state of the *Partzufim* of AK, he would have been completely in the state of empty space. This is because then the whole of *Behina Dalet*, which should be the root of Adam's *Guf*, would have been below AK's *Raglaim* (feet), in the form of empty and dark space, as it would be of opposite form from the Upper Light. Thus, it would be considered separated and dead.

And had Adam been created from that, he would not have been able to correct his actions whatsoever, since there would be no sparks of bestowal in him at all. He would be deemed a beast that has nothing of the form of bestowal, and whose life is only for himself. This would be like the wicked who are immersed in the lust of self-reception, "and even the grace that they do, they do for themselves." It is said about them, "the wicked—during their lives are called 'dead,'" since they are in oppositeness of form from the Life of Lives.

58) This is the meaning of our sages' words: "In the beginning, He contemplated creating the world with the quality of *Din* (judgment). He saw that the world does not exist and preceded the quality of *Rachamim* (mercy), and associated it with the quality of *Din*" (*Beresheet Rabba*, 12). This means that every "first" and "next" in spirituality refers to cause and consequence.

This is why it is written that the first reason for the worlds, meaning the *Partzufim* of *AK*, emanated before all the worlds, were emanated in the quality of *Din*, that is, in *Malchut* alone, called *Midat ha Din* (quality of judgment). This refers to *Behina Dalet* that has been restricted and departed as an empty space and the conclusion of the *Raglaim* of *AK*, that is, the point of this world, below the *Sium* of *AK's Raglaim*, in the form of empty space, devoid of any Light.

"He saw that the world does not exist" means that in this way, it was impossible for Adam, who was to be created from this *Behina Dalet*, to acquire acts of bestowal so the world would be corrected in the desired amount through him. This is why he "associated the quality of *Rachamim* with the quality of *Din*."

Explanation: The *Sefira* (singular for *Sefirot*) *Bina* is called *Midat ha Rachamim* (quality of mercy), and the *Sefira Malchut* is called *Midat ha Din*, since the *Tzimtzum* was made on her. The Emanator raised *Midat ha Din*, which is the concluding force made in the *Sefira Malchut*, and elevated it to *Bina—Midat ha Rachamim*. He associated them with one another, and through this association, *Behina Dalet—Midat ha Din—*was incorporated with the sparks of bestowal in the *Kli* of *Bina*.

This allowed Adam's *Guf*, which emerged from *Behina Dalet*, to be integrated with the quality of bestowal, too. Thus, he will be able to perform good deeds in order to bestow contentment upon his Maker, until he turns the quality of reception in him to being entirely in order to bestow. Thus, the world will achieve the desired correction by the creation of the world.

59) This association of *Malchut* in *Bina* occurred in *Partzuf SAG de AK* and prompted a second *Tzimtzum* in the worlds from itself downwards. This is because a new *Sium* on the Upper Light was made on it, that is, in *Bina*'s place. It follows that the ending *Malchut*, which stood at the *Sium Raglaim* of *SAG de AK*, above the point of this world, rose and ended the Upper Light at half of *Bina de Guf de SAG de AK*, called *Tifferet*, since *KHB de Guf* is called *HGT*. Thus, *Tifferet* is *Bina de Guf*.

Also, the mating *Malchut*, which stood at the *Peh de Rosh de SAG de AK*, rose to the place of *Nikvey Eynaim* (pupils) *de AK*, which is half of *Bina de Rosh*. Then, a *Zivug* for the MA *de AK* was made there, at the *Nikvey Eynaim*, called "the world of *Nekudim*."

60) This is also called *Tzimtzum NHY de AK*. This is because *SAG de AK*, which ended equally with *Partzuf Galgalta de AK*, above the point of this world, ends above the *Tabur* of the inner AK through the association and the ascent of *Malchut* to the place of *Bina*, at half the *Tifferet*, which is half the *Bina de Guf* of the inner AK. This is so because the ending *Malchut* rose to that place and detained the Upper Light from spreading from it downwards.

For this reason, an empty space was made there, devoid of Light. Thus, the TNHY (*Tifferet, Netzah, Hod, Yesod*) *de SAG* became restricted and devoid of the Upper Light. This is why *Tzimtzum Bet* (second restriction) is called *Tzimtzum NHY de AK*, since through the new *Sium* at the place of *Tabur*, NHY *de SAG de AK* were emptied of their Lights.

It is also considered that AHP of *Rosh de SAG* departed the degree of *Rosh de SAG* and became its *Guf*, since the mating *Malchut* rose to *Nikvey Eynaim* and the ten *Sefirot de Rosh* emerged from the *Masach* at *Nikvey Eynaim* and Above. Also, from *Nikvey Eynaim* downwards it is considered the *Guf* of the *Partzuf*, since it can only receive illumination from *Nikvey Eynaim* and below, which is considered *Guf*.

The level of these ten *Sefirot* that emerged at the *Nikvey Eynaim de SAG de AK* are the ten *Sefirot* called "the world of *Nekudim*." They came down from the *Nikvey Eynaim de SAG* to their place below the *Tabur* of the inner AK, where they expanded with *Rosh* and *Guf*. Know that this new *Sium*, made at the place of *Bina de Guf*, is called *Parsa*. Also, there is internality and externality here, and only the ten external *Sefirot* are called "the world of *Nekudim*," while the ten inner *Sefirot* are called MA and BON *de AK* itself.

61) Yet, we should understand that since the ten *Sefirot* of *Nekudim* and the MA *de AK* were emanated and emerged from the *Nikvey Eynaim de Rosh de SAG*,

they should have clothed the *SAG* from its *Peh de Rosh* and below, as with the other *Partzufim*, where each inferior clothes its superior from the *Peh de Rosh* downwards. Why was it not so? Why did they descend and clothe the place below *Tabur de AK*? To understand that, we must thoroughly understand how this association came about, when *Bina* and *Malchut* were connected into one.

62) The thing is that during the emergence of *Partzuf SAG*, it ended entirely above *Tabur* of the inner *AK*, as has been explained concerning *Partzuf AB de AK*. They could not spread from *Tabur* down, since the government of *Behina Dalet* of the inner *AK* begins there, in its ten *Sefirot de Sium*, and there is nothing of *Behina Dalet* whatsoever in *Partzufim AB* and *SAG* (Item 54).

Yet, when *Nekudot de SAG de AK* began to emerge, after the *Masach de SAG*, which is *Behina Dalet de Aviut*, has been purified through the *Bitush* of *Ohr Makif* in it, and came to *Behina Bet de Hitlabshut* and *Behina Aleph de Aviut*, the *Taamim de SAG* departed. Then, the level of *Nekudot* emerged on the *Aviut* that remained in the *Masach*, in *VAK* without a *Rosh*.

This is so because the ten *Sefirot* that emerge on *Behina Aleph de Aviut* are the level of ZA, lacking GAR. Also, there is no *Bina* at the male level, which is *Behina Bet de Hitlabshut*, but only nearly that. This is considered *VAK de Bina*.

Hence, this form of the level of *Nekudot de SAG* has been equalized with the ten *Sefirot de Sium* below *Tabur de AK*, considered *VAK* without a *Rosh*, too (Item 52). It is known that equivalence of form unites the spirituals into one. Hence, this level subsequently descended below *Tabur de AK* and mingled there with ZON *de AK*, where they were as one, since they are of equal levels.

63) We might wonder at the fact that there is still a great distance between them with respect to their *Aviut*, since *Nekudot de SAG* come from *Aviut* of *Behina Bet* and have nothing of *Behina Dalet*. And although they are the level of ZA, it is not like the level of ZA below *Tabur de AK*, which is ZA of *Behina Dalet*. Thus, there is a big difference between them.

The answer is that the *Aviut* is not apparent in the *Partzuf* during the clothing of the Light, but only after the departure of the Light. Hence, when *Partzuf Nekudot de SAG* appeared at the level of ZA, descended, and clothed at the level of ZON from *Tabur de AK* downwards, *Behina Bet* was mingled with *Behina Dalet* and caused *Tzimtzum Bet*. This created a new *Sium* at the place of *Bina de Guf* of that *Partzuf*, as well as prompted a change in the place of the *Zivug*, making it the *Peh de Rosh* instead of the *Nikvey Eynaim*.

64) Thus, you find that the source of the association of *Malchut* in *Bina*, called *Tzimtzum Bet*, occurred only below *Tabur de AK*, by the expansion of

Partzuf Nekudot de SAG in that place. Hence, this level of ten *Sefirot de Nekudim*, which comes from *Tzimtzum Bet*, could not spread above *Tabur de AK*, since there is no force and ruling that can appear above its source. And since the place where *Tzimtzum Bet* was created was from *Tabur* down, the level of *Nekudim* had to expand there, as well.

THE PLACE FOR THE FOUR WORLDS ABYA, AND THE PARSA BETWEEN ATZILUT AND BYA

65) Thus we have learned that *Tzimtzum Bet* occurred only in *Partzuf Nekudot de SAG*, positioned from *Tabur de AK* downwards, through its *Sium Raglin*, that is, above the point of this world. Know that all the changes that followed the second restriction came only in that *Partzuf Nekudot de SAG*, and not Above it.

When we said that Above, that through *Malchut's* ascent to half of *Tifferet de AK*, where she ended the *Partzuf*, the lower half of *Tifferet* and NHYM de AK came out in the form of empty space, this did not occur in TNHY de AK itself, but only in TNHY of *Partzuf Nekudot de SAG de AK*. Yet, these changes are considered a mere raising of MAN in AK itself. In other words, it clothed in these changes to emanate the ten *Sefirot de Nekudim* themselves, though no change was prompted in AK itself.

66) And as soon as the *Tzimtzum* occurred, during the ascent of *Malchut* to *Bina*, even before the raising of MAN and the *Zivug* that was made at the *Nikvey Eynaim de AK*, it caused *Partzuf Nekudot de SAG de AK* to divide into four divisions:

1. KHB HGT up to its *Chazeh* are considered the place of *Atzilut*;
2. The two lower thirds of *Tifferet*, from the *Chazeh* down to the *Sium* of *Tifferet* became the place of the world of *Beria*;
3. Its three *Sefirot*, NHY, became the place of the world of *Yetzira*;
4. The *Malchut* in it became the place of the world of *Assiya*.

67) The reason for it is that the place of the world of *Atzilut* means the place worthy of the expansion of the Upper Light. And because of the ascension of the ending *Malchut* to the place of *Bina de Guf*, called *Tifferet*, the *Partzuf* ends there and the Light cannot traverse from there downwards. Thus, the place of *Atzilut* ends there, at half the *Tifferet*, on the *Chazeh*.

And you already know that this new *Sium*, made here, is called "the *Parsa* below the world of *Atzilut*." And there are three divisions in the *Sefirot* below the *Parsa*. This is because indeed, only two *Sefirot*, ZON de Guf, called NHYM, needed to emerge below the *Atzilut*. This is so because since the *Sium* was made at the *Bina de Guf*, which is *Tifferet*, only the ZON below *Tifferet* are below the *Sium*, and not *Tifferet*, although half of the lower *Tifferet* went out to below the *Sium*, as well.

The reason is that *Bina de Guf* consists of the ten *Sefirot* KHB ZON, too. And since these ZON de *Bina* are the roots of the inclusive ZON de *Guf*, which were included in *Bina*, they are considered like them. Hence, ZON de *Bina* came out below the *Parsa de Atzilut*, as well, along with the inclusive ZON. For this reason, the *Sefira Tifferet* was cracked across it at the place of the *Chazeh*, since the *Malchut* that rose to *Bina* is standing there and brings out the ZON de *Bina*, that is, the two thirds of *Tifferet* from the *Chazeh* down to its *Sium*.

Yet, there is still a difference between the two thirds of *Tifferet* and the NHYM, since the two thirds of *Tifferet* truly belong to the *Bina de Guf* and never emerged below the *Sium de Atzilut* because of themselves, but only because they are the roots of ZON. Hence, their flaw is not so great, since they did not come out because of themselves. Thus, they have become separated from the NHYM and became a world in and of themselves, called "the world of *Beria*."

68) ZON de *Guf*, too, called NHYM, are divided into two discernments: since *Malchut* is considered *Nukva* (female), her flaw is greater, and she becomes the place of the world of *Assiya*. ZA, who is NHY, became the world of *Yetzira*, above the world of *Assiya*.

Thus we have explained how *Partzuf Nekudot de SAG* was divided by *Tzimtzum Bet* and became the place of four worlds: *Atzilut*, *Beria*, *Yetzira*, and *Assiya*. KHB HGT, down to its *Chazeh*, became the place of the world of *Atzilut*. The lower half of *Tifferet*, from the *Chazeh* to the *Sium* of *Tifferet*, became the place of the world of *Beria*, the NHY in it—the world of *Yetzira* and its *Malchut*—the world of *Assiya*. Their place begins from the point of *Tabur de AK* and ends above the point of this world, that is, through the *Sium Raglin de AK*, which is the end of the clothing of *Partzuf Nekudot de SAG* over *Partzuf Galgalta de AK*.

THE KATNUT AND GADLUT INITIATED IN THE WORLD OF NEKUDIM

69) Now that you know about the *Tzimtzum Bet* that occurred in *Partzuf Nekudot de SAG* for the purpose of emanating the ten *Sefirot* of the world of *Nekudim*, the fourth *Partzuf* of AK, we shall go back to explaining the elicitation of the ten particular *Sefirot* of *Nekudim*. The elicitation of one *Partzuf* from the next has already been explained. Each inferior *Partzuf* is born and originates from the

Masach de Guf of the Upper One, after its *Hizdakchut* and ascension for renewing the *Zivug* in the *Peh* of the Upper One. And the cause of this *Hizdakchut* is the *Bitush* of *Ohr Makif* in the *Masach* of the Upper *Partzuf*, which purifies the *Masach* from its *Aviut de Guf*, and equalizes it with the *Aviut de Rosh* (Item 35).

In this manner, *Partzuf AB de AK* emerged from *Partzuf Keter de AK*, *Partzuf SAG de AK* from *Partzuf AB de AK*, and the fourth *Partzuf de AK*, called "ten *Sefirot* of the world of *Nekudim*," was born and emerged from its superior, being *SAG de AK*, in the same way.

70) Yet, there is another issue here. In the previous *Partzufim*, the *Masach* was made only of the *Reshimot de Aviut* of the *Guf* of the Upper One, during the *Hizdakchut* of the *Masach* to the *Peh de Rosh* of the Upper One. But here, in the *Hizdakchut* of the *Masach de SAG de AK* for *Nekudim*, this *Masach* was made of two kinds of *Reshimot*. Besides being made of its own *Reshimot de Aviut*, with respect to the *Sefirot de Guf de SAG de AK*, it is included with the *Reshimot de Aviut de ZON de AK* below *Tabur*, too. This is because of their mixture below *Tabur de AK*, as it is written (Item 61) that *Nekudot de SAG* descended below *Tabur de AK* and mixed with the *ZON de AK* there.

71) Thus, the matter of *Katnut* (smallness) and *Gadlut* (adulthood) has been initiated here in *Partzuf Nekudim*. With respect to the *Reshimot de Aviut* in the *Masach*, ten *Sefirot* of *Katnut Nekudim* emerged over them. And with respect to the *Reshimot de ZON de AK* below *Tabur*, which mingled and connected with the *Reshimot* of the *Masach*, the ten *Sefirot de Gadlut* of *Nekudim* emerged over them.

72) You should also know that the ten *Sefirot* of *Katnut Nekudim* that emerged on the *Masach* are considered the core of *Partzuf Nekudim*, since they emerged gradually, that is, from the core of the *Masach de Guf* of the Upper One, the same as the three previous *Partzufim de AK* emerged. But the ten *Sefirot de Gadlut* of *Nekudim* are regarded as mere addition to *Partzuf Nekudim*. This is because they only emerged from the *Zivug* on the *Reshimot de ZON de AK* below the *Tabur*, which did not appear gradually, but were added and connected to the *Masach* because of the decline of *Partzuf Nekudot de SAG* below *Tabur de AK* (Item 70).

73) We shall first clarify the ten *Sefirot de Katnut Nekudim*. You already know that following the *Hitpashtut* (spreading/expansion) of *SAG de AK*, it underwent the *Bitush* of *Ohr Makif* and *Ohr Pnimi* on its *Masach*, which gradually purified it. The levels that emerged as it purified are called *Nekudot de SAG*, and they descended below *Tabur de AK* and mingled with the *Behina Dalet* there (Item 62). After it completed its purification of all the *Aviut de Guf* in the *Masach* and remained with only *Aviut de Rosh*, it is considered to have risen to *Rosh de SAG*,

where it received a new *Zivug* on the measure of *Aviut* that remained in the *Reshimot* in the *Masach* (Item 35).

74) And here, too, it is considered that the last *Behina* of *Aviut*, *Aviut de Behina Bet* that was in the *Masach*, completely vanished, leaving only the *Reshimo de Hitlabshut*. Thus, nothing was left of the *Aviut* but *Behina Aleph*. Hence (Item 43), the *Masach* received two kinds of *Zivugim* (plural for *Zivug*) in *Rosh de SAG*:

1. *Hitkalelut* of *Behina Aleph de Aviut* within *Behina Bet de Hitlabshut* (clothing), called "*Hitkalelut* of the female *Reshimo* in the male *Reshimo*," produced a level at nearly the degree of *Bina*, which is the degree of VAK de *Bina*. This level is called "the *Sefira Keter de Nekudim*."

2. *Hitkalelut* of the male with the *Reshimo* of the female, the *Reshimo* of *Behina Bet de Hitlabshut* in *Behina Aleph de Aviut*, produced the level of ZA, considered VAK without a *Rosh*, called *Aba ve Ima de Nekudim* back to back."

These two levels are called GAR *de Nekudim*, that is, they are considered ten *Sefirot de Rosh Nekudim*, since each *Rosh* is called GAR or KHB. But there is a difference between them: *Keter de Nekudim*, which is at the male level, does not spread into the *Guf* and shines only at the *Rosh*. Only AVI *de Nekudim*, which are the female level, called "seven lower *Sefirot de Nekudim*" or HGT NHY *de Nekudim*" expand to the *Guf*.

75) Thus, there are three degrees one below the other:

1. *Keter de Nekudim*, with the level of VAK *de Bina*.
2. The level of AVI (*Aba* and *Ima*) *de Nekudim*, which has the level of ZA. These are both considered *Rosh*.
3. ZAT *de Nekudim*, HGT NHYM, considered *Guf de Nekudim*.

76) Know, that by *Malchut*'s ascent to *Bina*, these two degrees of *Nekudim* split into two halves upon their exit, called *Panim* (face) and *Achoraim* (back). This is so because since the *Zivug* was made at the *Nikvey Eynaim*, there are only two and a half *Sefirot* at the *Rosh*—*Galgalta*, *Eynaim* (eyes) and *Nikvey Eynaim*, that is, *Keter*, *Hochma*, and the Upper half of *Bina*. These are called *Kelim de Panim* (frontal *Kelim*).

The *Kelim de AHP*, which are the lower half of *Bina*, ZA, and *Nukva*, emerged from the ten *Sefirot de Rosh* and were considered the degree below the *Rosh*. Hence, *Kelim de Rosh*, which departed the *Rosh*, are considered *Kelim de Achoraim* (posterior *Kelim*). Each degree was split in this manner.

77) It follows that there is not a single degree that does not have *Panim* and *Achoraim*. This is because the *AHP* of the male level, the *Keter de Nekudim*, emerged from the degree of *Keter* and descended to the degree of *AVI de Nekudim*, the female level. And *AHP* of the female level—*AVI de Nekudim*—descended and fell to their degree of *Guf*, the degree of the seven lower *Sefirot HGT NHY de Nekudim*.

It turns out that *AVI* comprise two *Behinot Panim* and *Achoraim*: within them are the *Achoraim* of the *Keter* degree, that is, the *AHP de Keter*, and atop them clothe the *Kelim de Panim de AVI* themselves, that is, their own *Galgalta*, *Eynaim*, and *Nikvey Eynaim*. Also, ZAT *de Nekudim* comprise *Panim* and *Achoraim*: the *Kelim de Achoraim de AVI*, which are their *AHP*, are within the ZAT, and the *Kelim de Panim de ZAT* clothe them from without.

78) This issue of the division into two halves made the degrees of *Nekudim* unable to contain more than *Behinat Nefesh Ruach*, meaning VAK without GAR. This is because each degree is deficient of the three *Kelim*, *Bina* and ZON, hence the absence of Lights of GAR there, being *Neshama*, *Haya*, *Yechida* (Item 24). Thus we have thoroughly explained the ten *Sefirot de Katnut de Nekudim*, which are the three degrees called *Keter*, *AVI*, and *ZAT*. Each degree contains only *Keter Hochma* in *Kelim* and *Nefesh Ruach* in Lights, since the *Bina* and ZON of each degree fell to the degree below it.

RAISING MAN AND THE ELICITATION OF THE GADLUT DE NEKUDIM

79) Now we shall explain the ten *Sefirot de Gadlut* (adulthood/greatness) of *Nekudim*, which emerged on the MAN *de Reshimot* of ZON *de AK* below its *Tabur* (Item 71). First, we must understand the raising MAN. Thus far, we have only discussed the ascent of the *Masach de Guf* to the *Peh de Rosh* of the Upper One, once it has purified. Also, there was a *Zivug de Hakaa* on the *Reshimot* included in it, which produces the level of ten *Sefirot* for the needs of the lower one. Now, however, the issue of raising *Mayin Nukvin* (MAN/female water) has been renewed, for these Lights, which rose from below *Tabur de AK* to the *Rosh de SAG*, which are the *Reshimot de ZON de Guf de AK*, are called "raising MAN."

80) Know, that the origin of raising MAN is from the ZA and *Bina* of the ten *Sefirot* of *Ohr Yashar* (Direct Light) (Item 5). It is explained there that *Bina*, considered *Ohr Hassadim*, reunited with *Hochma* when she emanated the *Sefira Tifferet*, called *Behina Gimel*, and extended illumination of *Hochma* from it for *Tifferet*, which is ZA. The majority of ZA emerged from the *Ohr Hassadim* of *Bina*, and its minority with illumination of *Hochma*.

This is where the connection between ZA and *Bina* was made, as every time the *Reshimot de* ZA rise to *Bina*, *Bina* connects with *Hochma* and extends illumination of *Hochma* from it, for ZA. This ascension of ZA to *Bina*, which connects it with *Hochma*, is always called "raising MAN." Without the ascent of ZA to *Bina*, *Bina* is not considered *Nukva* to *Hochma*, since she herself is only *Ohr Hassadim* and does not need to receive *Ohr Hochma*.

She is always considered back-to-back with *Hochma*, which means that she does not want to receive from *Hochma*. Only when ZA rises to her does she become *Nukva* for *Hochma* once more, to receive illumination of *Hochma* from it, for ZA. Thus, the ascent of ZA make her a *Nukva*, and this is why its ascent is called *Mayin Nukvin*, as the ascent of ZA brings her face-to-face once more. This means that she receives from him the way *Nukva* does from the male. Thus we have thoroughly clarified the raising of MAN.

81) You already know that *Partzuf AB de AK* is *Partzuf Hochma*, and *Partzuf SAG de AK* is *Partzuf Bina*. This means that they are discerned according to the Highest *Behina* of their level. AB, whose Highest *Behina* is *Hochma*, is considered all *Hochma*. SAG, whose Highest *Behina* is *Bina*, is considered all *Bina*.

Thus, when the *Reshimot de ZON de Guf* below *Tabur de AK* rose to *Rosh de SAG*, they became MAN to the SAG there, for which SAG, which is *Bina*, mated with *Partzuf AB*, which is *Hochma*. Subsequently, AB gave to SAG a new Light for ZON's needs, below the *Tabur* that rose there.

And once ZON *de AK* received this new Light, they descended back to their place below *Tabur de AK*, where there are the ten *Sefirot de Nekudim*, where they illuminated the new Light within the ten *Sefirot de Nekudim*. This is the *Mochin* (Light) *de Gadlut* of the ten *Sefirot de Nekudim*. Thus we have explained the ten *Sefirot de Gadlut* that emerged on the second type of *Reshimot*, which are the *Reshimot de ZON* below *Tabur de AK* (Item 71). Indeed, it is these *Mochin de Gadlut* that caused the breaking of the vessels, as will be written below.

82) It has been explained above (Item 74) that there are two degrees at the *Rosh de Nekudim*, called *Keter* and *AVI*. Hence, when ZON *de AK* shone the new Light of AB SAG to the ten *Sefirot de Nekudim*, it first shone to *Keter de Nekudim* through its *Tabur de AK*, where *Keter* clothes, and completed it with GAR in Lights and *Bina* and ZON in *Kelim*. Subsequently, it shone to *AVI de Nekudim* through *Yesod de AK*, where *AVI* clothe, and completed them with GAR in Lights and *Bina* and ZON in *Kelim*.

83) First, let us explain the *Gadlut*, which this new Light caused in the ten *Sefirot* of *Nekudim*. The thing is that we should ask about what is written

in Item 74, that the level of *Keter* and *AVI de Nekudim* were considered *VAK* because they emerged on *Aviut* of *Behina Aleph*. But we have said that through the descent of *Nekudot de SAG* below *Tabur de AK*, *Behina Dalet* joined with the *Masach de Nekudot de SAG*, which is *Bina*. Thus, this *Masach* contains a *Reshimo* of *Behina Dalet de Aviut*, as well. In that case, during the *Hitkalelut* of the *Masach* in *Rosh de SAG*, ten *Sefirot* should have emerged at the level of *Keter* and the Light of *Yechida*, and not at the level of *VAK de Bina* in the *Sefira Keter*, and the level of *VAK* without a *Rosh* in *AVI*.

The answer is that the place is the cause. Since *Behina Dalet* is included in *Bina*, which is *Nikvey Eynaim*, *Aviut Dalet* disappeared there in the internality of *Bina*, as though it is not there at all. Hence, the *Zivug* was made only on the *Reshimot* of *Behina Bet de Hitlabshut* and *Behina Aleph de Aviut*, which are essentially only from *Masach de Bina* (Item 74), and only two levels emerged there: *VAK de Bina* and complete *VAK*.

84) Therefore, now *ZON de AK* below *Tabur* extended the new Light through their *MAN* from *AB SAG de AK*, and illuminated it to the *Rosh de Nekudim* (Item 81). And since *Partzuf AB de AK* has no connection with this *Tzimtzum Bet*, which elevated the *Behina Dalet* to the place of *Nikvey Eynaim*, when its Light was drawn to *Rosh de Nekudim*, it re-cancelled the *Tzimtzum Bet* within it, which elevated the place of the *Zivug* to *Nikvey Eynaim*. Also, it lowered the *Behina Dalet* back to its place at the *Peh*, as prior to *Tzimtzum Aleph*, that is, the place of *Peh de Rosh*.

Thus, the three *Kelim*—*Awzen* (ear), *Hotem* (nose), and *Peh* (mouth)—that fell from the degree because of *Tzimtzum Bet* (Item 76), now returned to their place—their degree—as before. At that time, the place of the *Zivug* descended once more from *Nikvey Eynaim* to *Behina Dalet* at the place of *Peh de Rosh*. And since *Behina Dalet* is already at her place, ten *Sefirot* emerged there at the degree of *Keter*.

Thus it has been explained that through the new Light, which *ZON de AK* extended to *Rosh de Nekudim*, it gained the three Lights *Neshama*, *Haya*, *Yechida*, and the three *Kelim AHP*, which are *Bina* and *ZON* that were missing when it first emerged.

85) Now we have thoroughly clarified the *Katnut* and *Gadlut de Nekudim*. *Tzimtzum Bet*, which raised the lower *Hey*—*Behina Dalet*—to the place of *Nikvey Eynaim*, where it was concealed, caused the level of *Katnut de Nekudim*—the level of *VAK* or *ZA* in Lights of *Nefesh Ruach*. There they were lacking *Bina* and *ZON* in *Kelim* and *Neshama*, *Haya*, *Yechida* in Lights. And through the approaching of a new Light of *AB SAG de AK* to the *Nekudim*, *Tzimtzum Aleph* returned to its place.

Bina and *ZON* of the *Kelim* returned to the *Rosh*, since the lower *Hey* descended from the *Nikvey Eynaim* and returned to her place—*Malchut*, called *Peh*. Then a *Zivug* was made on *Behina Dalet*, which returned to her place, and ten *Sefirot* at the level of *Keter* and *Yechida* emerged. This completed the *NRNHY* of Lights and the *KHB ZON* of *Kelim*.

For short, we will henceforth refer to *Tzimtzum Bet* and the *Katnut* by the name "ascension of the lower *Hey* to *Nikvey Eynaim* and the descent of *AHP* below." Also, we refer to the *Gadlut* by the name "the approaching of the Light of *AB SAG*, which lowers the lower *Hey* from the *Nikvey Eynaim* and brings the *AHP* back to their place." Remember this above explanation.

You should also remember that *GE* (*Galgalta Eynaim*) and *AHP* are names of the ten *Sefirot KHB ZON de Rosh*, and the ten *Sefirot de Guf* are called *HGT NHYM*. They, too, are divided into *GE* and *AHP*, since *Hesed* and *Gevura* and the Upper third of *Tifferet*—through the *Chazeh*—are *Galgalta ve* (and) *Eynaim* and *Nikvey Eynaim*, and the two thirds of *Tifferet* and *NHYM* are *AHP*, as has been written above.

Also, remember that *Galgalta*, *Eynaim*, and *Nikvey Eynaim*, or *HGT* up to the *Chazeh*, are called *Kelim de Panim* (anterior *Kelim*). And *AHP*, or the two lower thirds of *Tifferet* and *NHYM* from the *Chazeh* down are called *Kelim de Achoraim* (posterior *Kelim*), as written in Item 76. And you should also remember the fissuring of the degree that occurred with *Tzimtzum Bet*, which left only *Kelim de Panim* in the whole degree. And finally, each inferior contains within it the *Kelim de Achoraim* of the Upper One (Item 77).

EXPLAINING THE THREE NEKUDOT HOLAM, SHURUK, HIRIK

86) Know, that the *Nekudot* (dots) are divided into three *Behinot*—*Rosh*, *Toch*, and *Sof*, which are

- Upper *Nekudot*, above the *Otiot* (letters), included in the name, *Holam*;
- Middle *Nekudot*, inside the *Otiot*, included in the name, *Shuruk* or *Melafom*, meaning *Vav* and a point within it;
- Lower *Nekudot*, below the *Otiot*, included in the name, *Hirik*.

87) This is their explanation: *Otiot* are *Kelim*, that is, *Sefirot* of the *Guf*. This is because the ten *Sefirot de Rosh* are but roots to the *Kelim*, not actual *Kelim*. *Nekudot* mean Lights, which sustain the *Kelim* and move them, meaning *Ohr Hochma*, called *Ohr Haya*.[27] This is considered a new Light, which *ZON de AK* received from *AB SAG* and illuminated the *Kelim de Nekudim*, bringing down the

---
27 Translator's note: *Haya* comes from the word *Hayim* (life).

lower *Hey* back to the *Peh* of each degree, and returning the *AHP de Kelim* and *GAR* of Lights to each degree.

Thus, this Light moves the *Kelim de AHP* and elevates them from the lower degree, connecting them to the Upper One, as in the beginning. This is the meaning of the *Nekudot* that move the *Otiot*. And since this Light extends from *AB de AK*, which is *Ohr Haya*, it revives those *Kelim de AHP* through clothing in them.

88) You already know that *ZON de AK* shone this new Light to the ten *Sefirot de Nekudim* through two places: It illuminated the *Keter de Nekudim* through the *Tabur*, and illuminated the *AVI de Nekudim* through the *Yesod*.

Know that this illumination through the *Tabur* is called *Holam*, which shines for the *Otiot* above them. It is so because the illumination of *Tabur* reaches only *Keter de Nekudim*, the male level of *Rosh de Nekudim* (Item 74). And the male level does not expand into the lower seven of the *Nekudim*, which are the *Kelim de Guf*, called *Otiot*, hence it is considered to be shining on them only from its place above, without expanding in the *Otiot* themselves.

This illumination through the *Yesod* is called *Shuruk*, that is, *Vav* with a point that stands inside the line of the *Otiot*. The reason is that this illumination comes to *AVI de Nekudim*, which are the female level of *Rosh de Nekudim*, whose Lights expand into the *Guf*, as well, which are the *ZAT de Nekudim*, called *Otiot*. This is why you will find the point of *Shuruk* inside the line of *Otiot*.

89) Thus, the *Holam* and *Shuruk* have been thoroughly explained. The illumination of a new Light through the *Tabur*, which lowers the lower *Hey* from *Nikvey Eynaim de Keter* to the *Peh*, and elevates the *AHP de Keter* once more, is the point of *Holam* above the *Otiot*. The illumination of a new Light through the *Yesod*, which lowers the lower *Hey* from *Nikvey Eynaim de AVI* to their *Peh* and returns their *AHP*, is the point of *Shuruk* inside the *Otiot*. This is because these *Mochin* also come in *ZAT de Nekudim*, called *Otiot*.

90) *Hirik* is considered the new Light that the *ZAT* themselves receive from *AVI*, to bring down the ending lower *Hey*, which stands at their *Chazeh*, to the place of *Sium Raglin de AK*. Thus, their *AHP*, namely the *Kelim* from the *Chazeh* downwards, which became the place of *BYA*, return to them. At that time, *BYA* will once again be as *Atzilut*.

But *ZAT de Nekudim* could not bring the lower *Hey* down from the *Chazeh* and completely revoke *Tzimtzum Bet*, the *Parsa*, and the place of *BYA*. Rather, when they extended the Light into *BYA*, all the *Kelim de ZAT* immediately broke, since the force of the ending lower *Hey*, which stands at the *Parsa*, was mingled with these *Kelim*.

Thus, the Light had to instantaneously depart there and the *Kelim* broke, died, and fell into *BYA*. Also, their *Kelim de Panim*, above the *Parsa*, the *Kelim* above the *Chazeh*, broke as well, since all the Light departed thence, too. Thus, they broke and fell into *BYA*, due to their joining into one *Guf* with the *Kelim de Achoraim*.

91) Thus you see that the point of *Hirik* could not emerge and control in the world of *Nekudim*, since, moreover, it caused the breaking of the vessels. This was because she wanted to clothe inside the *Otiot*, in the *TNHYM* below *Parsa de Atzilut*, which became *BYA*.

However, later, in the world of *Tikkun*, the point of *Hirik* received its correction, since she was corrected into shining below the *Otiot*. This means that when *ZAT de Atzilut* receive the Light of *Gadlut* from *AVI*, which should lower the ending lower *Hey* from the place of the *Chazeh* to *Sium Raglin de AK*, and connect the *Kelim de TNHYM* to *Atzilut*, the Lights will spread down to *Sium Raglin de AK*. Yet, they do not do so, but raise these *TNHY* from the place of *BYA* to the place of *Atzilut*, above the *Parsa*, and receive the Lights while they are above *Parsa de Atzilut*, so that no breaking of vessels would occur in them again, as in the world of *Nekudim*.

This is considered that the point of *Hirik*, which raises the *Kelim de TNHY de ZAT de Atzilut*, stands below the *Kelim de TNHYM* that she raised, that is, she stands in the place of *Parsa de Atzilut*. Thus, the point of *Hirik* serves under the *Otiot*. This explains the three points, *Holam*, *Shuruk*, *Hirik*, in general.

THE ASCENT OF MAN DE ZAT DE NEKUDIM TO AVI AND THE EXPLANATION OF THE SEFIRA DAAT

92) It has already been explained that due to the lower *Hey's* ascent to *Nikvey Eynaim*, which occurred in *Tzimtzum Bet*, when the *Katnut* of the ten *Sefirot de Nekudim* emerged, each degree was divided into two halves.

- *Galgalta ve Eynaim* remained in the degree; hence, they are called *Kelim de Panim* (anterior *Kelim*).
- *Awzen*, *Hotem*, and *Peh*, which fell from the degree to the one below it, are therefore called *Kelim de Achoraim* (posterior *Kelim*).

Thus, each degree is now made of internality and externality, since the *Kelim de Achoraim* of the Upper degree fell to the internality of its own *Kelim de Panim*. And the fallen *AHP de Keter Nekudim* are clothed inside *Galgalta ve Eynaim de AVI*, and the fallen *AHP de AVI* are clothed inside *Galgalta ve Eynaim de ZAT de Nekudim* (Item 76).

93) In consequence, when the new Light of *AB SAG de AK* comes to the degree, and lowers the lower *Hey* back to her place at the *Peh*, during the *Gadlut de Nekudim*, the degree brings her *AHP* back to her, and her ten *Sefirot de Kelim* and ten *Sefirot* of Lights are completed. It is then considered that the lower degree, too, which was attached to the *AHP* of the Upper One, rises along with them to the Upper One.

This is so because the rule is that "there is no absence in the spiritual." And as the lower one was attached to the *AHP* of the Upper One during the *Katnut*, they are not separated from each other during the *Gadlut* as well, when the *AHP* of the Upper One return to their degree. It turns out that the lower degree has now actually become a Higher degree, since the lower one that rises to the Upper One becomes like Him.

94) It turns out that when *AVI* received the new Light of *AB SAG* and lowered the lower *Hey* from the *Nikvey Eynaim* back to their *Peh*, and raised their *AHP* to them, the ZAT, too, which clothe these *AHP* during the *Katnut*, now rose along with them to *AVI*. Thus, the ZAT became a single degree with *AVI*. This ascent of the ZAT to *AVI* is called "raising MAN." And when they are at the same degree as *AVI*, they receive the Lights of *AVI*, as well.

95) And it is called MAN since the ascent of ZA to *Bina* brings her back to being face-to-face with the *Hochma* (Item 80). It is known that every ZAT are ZON. Hence, when the ZAT rose with the *AHP de AVI* to the degree of *AVI*, they became MAN to the *Bina* of the *Sefirot de AVI*. Then she returns to being face-to-face with the *Hochma de AVI* and provides ZON, which are the ZAT *de Nekudim* that rose to them, with illumination of *Hochma*.

96) Despite the above-mentioned ascent of ZAT to *AVI*, it does not mean that they were altogether absent from their place and rose to *AVI*, since there is no absence in the spiritual. Also, any "change of place" in spirituality does not mean that it has departed its former place and moved to a new location, as one relocates in corporeality. Rather, there is merely an addition here: they came to the new location, while remaining in the former one. Thus, although the ZAT rose to *AVI* to MAN, they still remained in their place, at their lower degree, as before.

97) Similarly, you can understand that even though we say that once ZON rose to MAN to *AVI* and received their Lights there, and left there and returned to their place below, here, too, it does not mean that they departed their place above and moved to the place below. Had ZON been absent from their place above in *AVI*, the face-to-face *Zivug de AVI* would stop instantaneously, and they

would return to being back-to-back as before. This would stop their abundance, and ZON, below, would lose their *Mochin*, too.

It has already been explained above that *Bina* naturally craves only *Ohr Hassadim*, as in, "for he delights in mercy." She has no interest whatsoever in receiving *Ohr Hochma*; hence, she is back-to-back with *Hochma*. Only when ZON ascend to them for MAN does *Bina* return in a face-to-face *Zivug* with *Hochma*, to bestow illumination of *Hochma* to ZA (Item 80).

Hence, it is necessary that the ZON will always remain there, to give sustenance and subsistence to the face-to-face *Zivug de AVI*. For this reason, it cannot be said that ZON are absent from the place of AVI when they come to their place below. Rather, as we have said, any "change of place" is but an addition. Thus, although ZON descended from their place, they still remained above, as well.

98-99) Now you can understand the *Sefira Daat* that was initiated in the world of *Nekudim*. In all the *Partzufim* of AK, through *Nekudim*, there are only ten *Sefirot* KHB ZON. But from the world of *Nekudim* onwards, there is the *Sefira Daat*, which we regard as KHBD ZON.

The thing is that there was no ascension of MAN in the *Partzufim* of AK, but only the ascent of the *Masach* to *Peh de Rosh* (Item 79). But you should know that the *Sefira Daat* extends from the ascension of MAN *de* ZON to AVI, as it has been clarified that ZON, which rose there to MAN to *Hochma* and *Bina*, remain there even after their exit from there to their place below, to provide sustenance and subsistence to the face-to-face *Zivug de AVI*. These ZON, which remain in AVI, are called "the *Sefira Daat*." Hence, now HB have the *Sefira Daat*, which sustains and positions them in a face-to-face *Zivug*. These are the ZON that rose to MAN there and remained there even after the exit of ZON to their place.

Hence, from now on we call the ten *Sefirot* by the names KHBD ZON. But in the *Partzufim* of AK, prior to the world of *Nekudim*, before the raising of MAN, there was no *Sefira Daat* there. You should also know that the *Sefira Daat* is always called "five *Hassadim* and five *Gevurot*," since the ZA that remains there is considered five *Hassadim*, and the *Nukva* that remained there is considered five *Gevurot*.

100) We might ask about what is written in the *Book of Creation*, that the ten *Sefirot* are "ten and not nine, ten and not eleven." It was said that the *Sefira Daat* was initiated in the world of *Nekudim*; thus, there are eleven *Sefirot* KHBD ZON.

The answer is that this is not at all an addition to the ten *Sefirot*, since we have learned that the *Sefira Daat* is ZON that rose to MAN and remained there. Hence, there is no addition here, but rather two discernments in ZON:

1. The ZON in their place below, which are considered *Guf*;
2. The ZON that remained in *Rosh de AVI*, since they were already there during the raising of the MAN, and there is no absence in the spiritual. Thus, there is no addition to the ten *Sefirot* here, whatsoever, for in the end, there are only ten *Sefirot* KHB ZON here. And if the discernment of ZON remains in *Rosh* in AVI, it does not add a thing to the ten *Sefirot*.

THE BREAKING OF THE VESSELS AND THEIR FALL TO BYA

101) Now we have thoroughly explained the raising of MAN and the *Sefira Daat*, which are considered the *Kelim de Panim de ZAT de Nekudim* that extended and rose to AVI. This is because AVI received the new Light of AB SAG de AK from ZON de AK in the form of the point of *Shuruk*. They lowered the lower *Hey* from their *Nikvey Eynaim* to the *Peh*, and raised their *Kelim de Achoraim*, which were fallen in the ZAT *de Nekudim*. As a result, the *Kelim de Panim de ZAT*, which were attached to the *Kelim de Achoraim de AVI* (Items 89-94), rose, too, and the ZAT *de Nekudim* became MAN there, and returned AVI to being face-to-face.

And since the lower *Hey*, which is *Behina Dalet*, had already returned to her place at the *Peh*, the *Zivug de Hakaa* that was made on that *Masach of Behina Dalet* produced ten complete *Sefirot* at the level of *Keter* in the Light of *Yechida* (Item 84). Thus, ZAT, which are included there as MAN, received those great Lights of AVI, too. Yet, all this is only regarded as being from Above downwards, since AVI are considered the *Rosh de Nekudim*, where the *Zivug* that produces ten *Sefirot* from Above downwards occurs.

Subsequently, they expand into a *Guf*, too, from Above downwards (Item 50). At that time, the ZAT extend with all the Lights they had received in AVI to their place below, and the *Rosh* and *Guf* of *Partzuf Gadlut de Nekudim* ends. This *Hitpashtut* is considered the *Taamim of Partzuf Gadlut de Nekudim* (Item 26).

102) The four *Behinot—Taamim, Nekudot, Tagin, Otiot*—are discerned in *Partzuf Nekudim*, too (Item 47). This is so because all the forces that exist in the Upper Ones must exist in the lower ones, as well. But in the lower one, there are additional matters to the Upper One. It has been explained that the heart of the *Hitpashtut* of each *Partzuf* is called *Taamim*. After it expands, the *Bitush* of *Ohr Makif* and *Ohr Pnimi* occurs in it, and through this *Bitush*, the *Masach* is gradually purified until it equalizes with the *Peh de Rosh*.

And since the Upper Light does not stop, the Upper Light mates with the *Masach* in each state of *Aviut* along its purification. This means that when it purifies from *Behina Dalet* to *Behina Gimel*, the level of *Hochma* emerges on it. And when it comes to *Behina Bet*, the level of *Bina* emerges on it. When it comes to *Behina Aleph*, the level of *ZA* emerges on it, and when it comes to *Behinat Shoresh*, the level of *Malchut* emerges on it. All those levels that emerge on the *Masach* through its purification are called *Nekudot*.

The *Reshimot* that remain of the Lights, once they have departed, are called *Tagin*. The *Kelim* that remain after the departure of the Lights from them are called *Otiot*, and once the *Masach* has been completely purified of its *Aviut de Guf*, it is included in the *Masach de Peh de Rosh* in the *Zivug* there, and a second *Partzuf* emerges on it.

103) And here in *Partzuf Nekudim* it was done in precisely the same manner. Here, too, two *Partzufim* emerge—AB and SAG—one below the other. And in each of them are *Taamim, Nekudot, Tagin*, and *Otiot*.

The only difference is that the issue of the *Hizdakchut* of the *Masach* was not done here because of the *Bitush* of *Ohr Makif* and *Ohr Pnimi*, but because of the force of *Din* in the ending *Malchut*, included in those *Kelim* (Item 90). For this reason, the empty *Kelim* did not remain in the *Partzuf* after the departure of the Lights, as in the three *Partzufim Galgalta, AB, SAG de AK*, but broke and died and fell to *BYA*.

104) *Partzuf Taamim*, which emerged in the world of *Nekudim*, which is the first *Partzuf* in *Nekudim*, which emerged at the level of *Keter*, emerged with *Rosh* and *Guf*. The *Rosh* came out in AVI, and the *Guf* is the *Hitpashtut* of ZAT from *Peh de AVI* downwards (Item 101). This *Hitpashtut* from *Peh de AVI* down is called *Melech ha Daat* (King *Daat*).

And this is indeed the whole of the ZAT *de Nekudim* that re-expanded to their place after the raising of MAN. But since their root remained in AVI for sustenance and subsistence to the face-to-face of AVI (Item 98), called *Moach ha Daat*, which couples AVI, their expansion from Above downwards into a *Guf* is also called by that name—*Melech ha Daat*. This is the first *Melech* (king) of *Nekudim*.

105) It is known that all the quantity and quality in the ten *Sefirot de Rosh* appears in the *Hitpashtut* from Above downwards to the *Guf*, as well. Hence, as in the Lights of the *Rosh*, the mating *Malchut* returned and descended from the *Nikvey Eynaim* to the *Peh*. Then, GE (*Galgalta Eynaim*) and *Nikvey Eynaim*, which are the *Kelim de Panim*, reunited their *Kelim de Achoraim*, their AHP, and the Lights expanded in them. Similarly, as they expanded from Above downwards

to the *Guf*, the Lights were drawn to their *Kelim de Achoraim*, too, which are the *TNHYM* in *BYA*, below *Parsa de Atzilut*.

However, since the force of the ending *Malchut* in *Parsa de Atzilut* is mixed in those *Kelim*, as soon as the Lights of *Melech ha Daat* met this force, they all departed the *Kelim* and rose to their root. Then, all the *Kelim* of *Melech ha Daat* broke face and back, died, and fell to *BYA*, since the departure of the Lights from the *Kelim* is like the departure of vitality from the corporeal body, called "death." At that time, the *Masach* was purified from the *Aviut de Behina Dalet*, since these *Kelim* have already broken and died, and only *Aviut de Behina Gimel* remained in it.

106) And as the *Aviut* of *Behina Dalet* was revoked from the *Masach de Guf* by the breaking, that *Aviut* was revoked in the mating *Malchut* of the *Rosh* in *AVI*, too. This is so because *Aviut de Rosh* and *Aviut de Guf* are the same thing, except one is potential and the other is actual (Item 50). Hence, the *Zivug* at the level of *Keter* stopped at the *Rosh* in *AVI*, too, and the *Kelim de Achoraim*, the *AHP* that completed the level of *Keter*, fell once more to the degree below it—the *ZAT*. This is called "revoking the *Achoraim* of the level of *Keter* from *AVI*." It turns out that the whole level of *Taamim de Nekudim*, *Rosh* and *Guf*, has departed.

107) And since the Upper Light does not stop shining, it mated once more on the *Aviut de Behina Gimel* that remained in the *Masach de Rosh* in *AVI*, producing ten *Sefirot* at the level of *Hochma*. The *Guf* from Above downwards expanded to the *Sefira Hesed*, and this is the second *Melech* of *Nekudim*. It, too, extended to *BYA*, broke, and died, at which time the *Aviut* of *Behina Gimel* was revoked from the *Masach de Guf* and *de Rosh*, as well. Also, the *Kelim de Achoraim*, the *AHP* that completed this level of *Hochma* of *AVI*, were revoked once more, and fell to the degree below it, to *ZAT*, as it happened at the level of *Keter*.

Following, the *Zivug* was made on *Aviut* of *Behina Bet* that remained in the *Masach*, producing ten *Sefirot* at the level of *Bina*. The *Guf*, from Above downwards, expanded in the *Sefira Gevura*, and this is the third *Melech* of *Nekudim*.

It, too, extended into *BYA*, broke, and died, revoking the *Aviut* of *Behina Bet* in *Rosh* and *Guf*, too, ending the *Zivug* at the level of *Bina* in the *Rosh*, too. The *Achoraim* of the level of *Bina de Rosh* fell to the degree below her in the *ZAT*, and then the *Zivug* was made on the *Aviut* of *Behina Aleph* that remained in the *Masach*, producing ten *Sefirot* at the level of *ZA* on her. Also, its *Guf*, from Above downwards, spread in the Upper third of *Tifferet*. Yet, it, too, did not last and its Light departed it. Thus, the *Aviut* of *Behina Aleph* has been purified with *Guf* and *Rosh*, and the *Achoraim* of the level of *ZA* fell to the degree below her, to *ZAT*.

108) This completes the descent of all the *Achoraim de AVI*, which are the *AHP*. This is so because with the breaking of *Melech ha Daat*, only the *AHP* that belong to the level of *Keter* were cancelled in *AVI*. And with the breaking of *Melech ha Hesed*, only the *AHP* that belong to the level of *Hochma* were cancelled in *AVI*. And with the breaking of *Melech ha Gevura*, the *AHP* that belong to the level of *Bina* were cancelled; and with the departure of the Upper third of *Tifferet*, the *AHP* of the level of *ZA* were cancelled.

It follows that the whole *Gadlut* of *AVI* was cancelled, and only *GE de Katnut* remained in them, and only *Aviut Shoresh* remained in the *Masach*. Afterwards, the *Masach de Guf* was purified from all its *Aviut*, and equalized with the *Masach de Rosh*. At that time, it was included in a *Zivug de Hakaa* of the *Rosh*, and the *Reshimot* in it were renewed, apart from the last *Behina* (Item 41). And by this renewal, a new level emerged on it, called YESHSUT.

109) And since the last *Behina* was lost, all that was left was *Behina Gimel*, on which ten *Sefirot* at the level of *Hochma* emerged. And when its *Aviut de Guf* was recognized, it left the *Rosh* of *AVI*, descended, and clothed the place of the *Chazeh de Guf de Nekudim* (Item 55). It produced the ten *Sefirot de Rosh* from the *Chazeh* upwards, and this *Rosh* is called YESHSUT. It produced its *Guf* from the *Chazeh* down from the two thirds of *Tifferet* through the *Sium* of *Tifferet*. This is the fourth *Melech* of *Nekudim*, and it, too, extended to *BYA*, broke and died. Thus, *Aviut* of *Behina Gimel* has been purified *Rosh* and *Guf*. Its *Kelim de Achoraim* of the *Rosh* fell to the degree below it, in the place of their *Guf*.

Subsequently, the *Zivug* was made on *Aviut* of *Behina Bet*, which remained in it, producing the level of *Bina* on it. Its *Guf*, from Above downwards, expanded in the two *Kelim Netzah* and *Hod*, which are both one *Melech*—the fifth *Melech* of *Nekudim*. And they, too, extended to *BYA*, broke, and died. Thus, the *Aviut* of *Behina Bet* has been purified *Rosh* and *Guf*, and the *Kelim de Achoraim* of the level fell to the degree below it: the *Guf*.

Afterwards, the *Zivug* was made on the *Aviut* of *Behina Aleph* that remained in it, and produced the level of *ZA*. Its *Guf*, from Above downwards, expanded in the *Kli de Yesod*, and this is the sixth *Melech* of *Nekudim*. It, too, expanded into *BYA*, broke, and died. Thus, the *Aviut* of *Behina Aleph* has been purified in *Rosh* and *Guf*, as well, and the *Kelim de Achoraim* at the *Rosh* fell to the degree below them, to the *Guf*.

Then there was the *Zivug* on the *Aviut* of *Behinat Shoresh* that remained in the *Masach*, producing the level of *Malchut*. Its from Above downwards extended into the *Kli* of *Malchut*, and this is the seventh *Melech* of *Nekudim*. It, too, expanded into *BYA*, broke, and died. Thus, *Aviut Shoresh* was purified in *Rosh* and *Guf*, as well, and the *Achoraim de Rosh* fell to the degree below it, in the *Guf*. Now all the *Kelim de Achoraim* of *YESHSUT* have been cancelled, as well as the breaking of the vessels of the whole *ZAT de Nekudim*, called "the seven *Melachim* (kings)."

110) Thus we have explained the *Taamim* and *Nekudot* that emerged in the two *Partzufim AVI* and *YESHSUT de Nekudim*, called *AB SAG*. In *AVI*, four levels emerged one below the other:

- The level of *Keter* is called "gazing of the *Eynaim de AVI*."
- The level of *Hochma* is called *Guf de Aba*.
- The level of *Bina* is called *Guf de Ima*.
- The level of *ZA* is called *Yesodot* (foundations) *de AVI*.

Four bodies expanded from them:

- *Melech ha* (king of) *Daat*;
- *Melech ha Hesed*;
- *Melech ha Gevura*;
- The *Melech* of the Upper third of *Tifferet*, through the *Chazeh*.

These four *Gufim* (plural for *Guf*) broke in both *Panim* and *Achoraim*. But with respect to their *Roshim* (plural for *Rosh*), that is, the four levels in *AVI*, all their *Kelim de Panim* remained in the levels, that is, the *GE* and *Nikvey Eynaim* of each level, which were in them since the *Katnut de Nekudim*. Only the *Kelim de Achoraim* in each degree, which joined them during the *Gadlut*, were re-cancelled by the breaking, fell to the degree below them, and remained as they were prior to the emergence of *Gadlut de Nekudim* (Items 76-77).

111) The emergence of the four levels, one below the other, in *Partzuf YESHSUT* was in precisely the same manner:

- The first level is the level of *Hochma*, called "gazing of the *Eynaim de YESHSUT* at one another."
- The level of *Bina*;
- The level of *ZA*;
- The level of *Malchut*.

Four *Gufim* expanded from them:

- The *Melech* of the two lower thirds of *Tifferet*;
- *Melech* of *Netzah* and *Hod*;

- *Melech* of *Yesod*;
- *Malchut*.

Their four *Gufim* broke in both *Panim* and *Achor* (back). But in the *Roshim*, that is, in the four levels of YESHSUT, the *Kelim de Panim* in them remained, and only their *Achoraim* were cancelled by the breaking, and fell to the degree below them. After the cancellation of the two *Partzufim* AVI and YESHSUT, the level of MA *de Nekudim* emerged. And since all that expanded from her to the *Guf* were only corrections of *Kelim*, I will not elaborate here.

The World of *Tikkun* and the New MA that Emerged from the *Metzach de* AK

112) From the beginning of the preface to this point we have thoroughly explained the first four *Partzufim* AK:

- The first *Partzuf* of AK is called *Partzuf Galgalta*, whose *Zivug de Hakaa* is performed on *Behina Dalet* and its ten *Sefirot* are at the level of *Keter*.
- The second *Partzuf* of AK is called AB *de* AK. The *Zivug de Hakaa* in it is made on *Aviut* of *Behina Gimel*, and its ten *Sefirot* are at the level of *Hochma*. It clothes from *Peh de Partzuf Galgalta* downward.
- The third *Partzuf* of AK is called SAG *de* AK. The *Zivug de Hakaa* in it occurs on *Aviut* of *Behina Bet*, and its ten *Sefirot* are at the level of *Bina*. It clothes *Partzuf* AB *de* AK from the *Peh* down.
- The fourth *Partzuf de* AK is called MA *de* AK. The *Zivug de Hakaa* in it occurs on *Aviut* of *Behina Aleph*, and its ten *Sefirot* are at the level of ZA. This *Partzuf* clothes SAG *de* AK from the *Tabur* down, and is divided into internality and externality. The internality is called MA and BON *de* AK, and the externality is called "the world of *Nekudim*." This is where the association of *Malchut* in *Bina*, called *Tzimtzum Bet*, takes place, as well as the *Katnut*, *Gadlut*, the raising of MAN, and the *Daat*, which determines and mates the HB face-to-face, and the issue of the breaking of the vessels. This is so because all these were initiated in the fourth *Partzuf* of AK, called MA or "the world of *Nekudim*."

113) These five discernments of *Aviut* in the *Masach* are named after the *Sefirot* in the *Rosh*, that is, *Galgalta Eynaim* and AHP:

- *Aviut* of *Behina Dalet* is called *Peh*, on which the first *Partzuf* of AK emerges.
- *Aviut* of *Behina Gimel* is called *Hotem*, on which *Partzuf* AB *de* AK emerges.
- *Aviut* of *Behina Bet* is called *Awzen*, on which *Partzuf* SAG *de* AK emerges.

- *Aviut* of *Behina Aleph* is called *Nikvey Eynaim*, on which *Partzuf MA de AK* and the world of *Nekudim* emerge.
- *Aviut* of *Behinat Shoresh* is called *Galgalta* or *Metzach*, on which the world of *Tikkun* (correction) emerges, called "the new MA," since the fourth *Partzuf* of *AK* is the core of *Partzuf MA de AK*, as it stemmed from the *Nikvey Eynaim* at the level of ZA, called *HaVaYaH de MA*.

But the fifth part of *AK*, which emerged from the *Metzach*, that is, *Behinat Galgalta*, considered *Aviut Shoresh*, actually has only the level of *Malchut*, called BON. Yet, because *Behina Aleph de Hitlabshut*, considered ZA, remained there, it, too, is called MA. Yet, it is called MA that emerged from the *Metzach de AK*, which means it is from the *Hitkalelut* of *Aviut Shoresh*, called *Metzach*. It is also called "the new MA," to distinguish it from the MA that emerged from *Nikvey Eynaim de AK*. And this new *Partzuf* MA is called "the world of *Tikkun*" or "the world of *Atzilut*."

114) Yet we should understand why the first three levels of *AK*, called *Galgalta*, *AB*, and *SAG* are not considered three worlds but three *Partzufim*, and how the fourth *Partzuf* of *AK* differs to merit the name "world." This also concerns the fifth *Partzuf* of *AK*, since the fourth *Partzuf* is called "the world of *Nekudim*" and the fifth *Partzuf* is called "the world of *Atzilut*" or "the world of *Tikkun*."

115) We should know the difference between a *Partzuf* and a world. Any level of ten *Sefirot* that emerges on a *Masach de Guf* of an Upper One, after it has been purified and included in the *Peh de Rosh* of the Upper One (Item 50), is called *Partzuf*. After its departure from the *Rosh* of the Upper One, it expands into its own *Rosh*, *Toch*, and *Sof*, and it also contains five levels one below the other, called *Taamim* and *Nekudot* (Item 47). Yet, it is named only after the level of *Taamim* in it. And the first three *Partzufim* of *AK*—*Galgalta*, *AB*, *SAG* (Item 47)—emerged in that manner. But a world means that it contains everything that exists in the world Above it, like seal and imprint, where everything that exists in the seal is transferred to its imprint in its entirety.

116) Thus you see that the first three *Partzufim*, *Galgalta*, *AB*, and *SAG de AK* are considered one world, the world of *AK*, which emerged in the first restriction. But the fourth *Partzuf* of *AK*, where *Tzimtzum Bet* occurred, became a world in and of itself, due to the duality that occurred in the *Masach de Nekudot de SAG* in its descent from *Tabur de AK*. This is because it was doubled by the *Aviut de Behina Dalet*, in the form of the lower *Hey* in the *Eynaim* (Item 63).

During the *Gadlut*, *Behina Dalet* returned to its place at the *Peh* and produced the level of *Keter* (Item 84), and this level equalized with the first *Partzuf* of *AK*.

And after it spread into *Rosh*, *Toch*, *Sof*, in *Taamim* and *Nekudot*, a second *Partzuf* emerged on it, at the level of *Hochma*, called YESHSUT, which is similar to the second *Partzuf* of AK, called AB de AK. And following its *Hitpashtut* into *Taamim* and *Nekudot*, a third *Partzuf* emerged, called MA de Nekudim (Item 111), which is similar to the third *Partzuf* de AK.

Thus, everything that existed in the world of AK appeared here in the world of *Nekudim*, that is, three *Partzufim* one below the other. Each of them contains *Taamim* and *Nekudot* and all their instances, like the three *Partzufim* Galgalta, AB, SAG de AK in the world of AK. This is why the world of *Nekudim* is regarded as an imprint of the world of AK.

Also, for this reason it is considered a complete world in and of itself. (And the reason why the three *Partzufim* of *Nekudim* are not called Galgalta, AB, SAG, but rather AB, SAG, MA is that the *Aviut* of *Behina Dalet* that was joined with a *Masach de* SAG is incomplete, due to the *Hizdakchut* that occurred in the first *Partzuf* of AK. This is why they descended into being AB, SAG, and MA.)

117) Thus we have learned how the world of *Nekudim* was imprinted from the world of AK. Similarly, the fifth *Partzuf* of AK, that is, the new MA, was entirely imprinted from the world of *Nekudim*. Thus, although all the discernments that served in *Nekudim* were broken and cancelled there, they were renewed in the new MA. This is why it is considered a separate world.

Also, it is called "the world of *Atzilut*" because it ends completely above the *Parsa* that was created in the second restriction. It is also called "the world of *Tikkun*" (correction) because the world of *Nekudim* could not persist because of the breaking and cancelling that occurred in it. Only afterwards, in the new MA, when all those *Behinot* that were in the world of *Nekudim* returned and came in the new MA, they were established and persisted there.

This is why it is called "the world of *Tikkun*," for indeed, it is actually the world of *Nekudim*, but here, in the new MA, it receives its correction from the Whole. This is because through the new MA, all the *Achoraim* that fell from AVI and YESHSUT to the *Guf*, as well as the *Panim* and *Achoraim* of all the ZAT that fell into BYA and died, reunite and rise through it to *Atzilut*.

118) The reason for it is that each lower *Partzuf* returns and fills the *Kelim* of the Upper One, after the departure of their Lights during the *Hizdakchut* of the *Masach*. This is because after the departure of the Lights of the *Guf* of the first *Partzuf* of AK, because of the *Hizdakchut* of the *Masach*, the *Masach* received a new *Zivug* at the level of AB, which refilled the empty *Kelim* of the *Guf* of the Upper One, that is, the first *Partzuf*.

Also, following the departure of the Lights of *Guf de AB* because of the *Hizdakchut* of the *Masach*, the *Masach* received a new *Zivug* at the level of SAG, which refilled the empty *Kelim* of the Upper One, which is AB. Additionally, after the departure of the Lights of SAG, due to the *Hizdakchut* of the *Masach*, the *Masach* received a new *Zivug* at the level of MA, which emerged from *Nikvey Eynaim*, being the *Nekudim*, which refilled the empty *Kelim* of the Upper One, being *Nekudot de SAG*.

And just so, following the departure of the Lights of *Nekudim* because of the cancellation of the *Achoraim* and the breaking of the vessels, the *Masach* received a new *Zivug* at the level of MA, which emerged from the *Metzach* of *Partzuf SAG de AK*. This fills the empty *Kelim* of the *Guf* of the Upper One, which are the *Kelim de Nekudim* that were cancelled and broken.

119) Yet, there is an essential difference here in the new MA: It became a male, and an Upper One to the *Kelim de Nekudim*, which it corrects. Conversely, in previous *Partzufim*, the lower one does not become a male and an Upper One to the *Kelim de Guf* of the Upper One, even though it fills them through its level. And that change is because in previous *Partzufim* there was no flaw in the departure of the Lights, for only the departure of the *Masach* caused their departure.

But here, in the world of *Nekudim*, there was a flaw in the *Kelim*, since the force of the ending *Malchut* was mixed with the *Kelim de Achoraim de ZAT*, making them unfit to receive the Lights. This is the reason why they broke and fell into BYA. Hence, they are completely dependent on the new MA to revive them, sort them, and raise them to *Atzilut*. As a result, the new MA is regarded as male and giver.

And these *Kelim de Nekudim*, sorted by it, become *Nukva* (female) to the MA. For this reason, their name has been changed to BON, meaning they had become *Tachton* (lower one) to the MA, even though they are superior to the new MA, since they are *Kelim* from the world of *Nekudim* and are considered MA and *Nikvey Eynaim*, whose Highest *Behina* is VAK de SAG de AK (Item 74). Even so, they now became *Tachton* (lower one) to the new MA, for which reason they are called BON.

THE FIVE PARTZUFIM OF ATZILUT AND THE MA AND BON IN EACH PARTZUF

120) It has been explained that the level of the new MA expanded into a whole world in itself, as well, like the world of *Nekudim*. The reason is, as it has been explained regarding the level of *Nekudim*, the doubling of the *Masach* from

Behina Dalet, too (Item 116). This is because the illumination of *ZON de AK* that shone through the *Tabur* and the *Yesod* to *GAR de Nekudim* brought *Tzimtzum Aleph* back to its place, and the lower *Hey* descended from her *Nikvey Eynaim* to the *Peh*, which caused all these levels of *Gadlut de Nekudim* to emerge (Item 101). Yet, all these levels were cancelled and broken once more, and all the Lights departed them. For this reason, *Tzimtzum Bet* returned to its place, and *Behina Dalet* was reunited with the *Masach*.

121) Hence, in the new *MA*, too, which emerged from the *Metzach*, there are the two *Behinot* of *Katnut* and *Gadlut*, too, as in the world of *Nekudim*. The *Katnut* emerges first, according to the *Aviut* disclosed in the *Masach*, which is the level of *ZA de Hitlabshut*, called *HGT*, and the level of *Malchut de Aviut*, called *NHY*, due to the three lines made in *Malchut*. The right line is called *Netzah*, the left line is called *Hod*, and the middle line is called *Yesod*.

Yet, since there is only *Hitlabshut* in *Behina Aleph*, without *Aviut*, it has no *Kelim*. Thus, the level of *HGT* is devoid of *Kelim*, clothing in *Kelim de NHY*, and this level is called **Ubar** (embryo). This means that there is only *Aviut de Shoresh* there, which remained in the *Masach* after its *Hizdakchut*, during its ascension for *Zivug* at the *Metzach* of the Upper One. And the level that emerges from there is only the level of *Malchut*.

Yet, within her is the concealed lower *Hey*, regarded as "the lower *Hey* at the *Metzach*." Once the *Ubar* receives the *Zivug* of the Upper One, it descends from there to its place (Item 54), and receives the **Mochin de Yenika** from the Upper One, which are *Aviut* of *Behina Aleph*, considered "the lower *Hey* in *Nikvey Eynaim*." Thus, it acquires *Kelim* for *HGT*, too, and *HGT* spread from *NHY* and it has the level of *ZA*.

122) Afterwards, it rises for *MAN* to the Upper One once again. This is called *Ibur Bet* (second conception/impregnation), where it receives *Mochin* from *AB SAG de AK*. At that time *Behina Dalet* descends from *Nikvey Eynaim* to her place at the *Peh* (Item 101), and a *Zivug* is made on *Behina Dalet* at her place, producing ten *Sefirot* at the level of *Keter*. Thus, the *Kelim de AHP* rise back to their place at the *Rosh*, and the *Partzuf* is completed with ten *Sefirot* of Lights and vessels. And these *Mochin* are called *Mochin de Gadlut* of the *Partzuf*. This is the level of the first *Partzuf de Atzilut*, called *Partzuf Keter* or *Partzuf Atik de Atzilut*.

123) And you already know that after the breaking of the vessels, all the *AHP* fell from their degrees, each to the degree below it (Items 77, 106). Thus, the *AHP* of the level of *Keter de Nekudim* are in *GE* of the level of *Hochma*, and the *AHP* of the level of *Hochma* is in the *GE* of the level of *Bina*, etc. Therefore, during *Ibur*

Bet de Gadlut of the first *Partzuf* of *Atzilut*, called *Atik*, which elevated its *AHP* once more, *GE* of the level of *Hochma* rose along with them. They were corrected along with the *AHP* of the level of *Atik*, and received the first *Ibur* there.

124) And once *GE de Hochma* received their level of *Ibur* and *Yenika* (nursing) (Item 121), they rose to *Rosh de Atik* again, where they received a second *Ibur* for *Mochin de Gadlut*. *Behina Gimel* descended to her place at the *Peh*, produced ten *Sefirot* on her, at the level of *Hochma*, and their *Kelim de AHP* rose back to their place at the *Rosh*. Thus, *Partzuf Hochma* was completed with ten *Sefirot* of Lights and *Kelim*. This *Partzuf* is called *Arich Anpin de Atzilut*.

125) The *GE* of the level of *Bina* rose along with these *AHP de AA*, where they received their first *Ibur* and *Yenika*. Afterwards, they rose to the *Rosh* of *AA* for a second *Ibur*, raised their *AHP*, received the *Mochin de Gadlut*, and *Partzuf Bina* was completed with ten *Sefirot*, Lights and vessels. This *Partzuf* is called AVI and YESHSUT, since the GAR are called AVI, and the ZAT are called YESHSUT.

126) And *GE de ZON* rose along with these *AHP de AVI*, where they received their first *Ibur* and *Yenika*. This completes the ZON in the state of VAK to ZA and *Nekuda* (point) to the *Nukva*. Thus we have explained the five *Partzufim* of the new MA that emerged in the world of *Atzilut*, in the constant state, called Atik, AA, AVI, and ZON.

- *Atik* emerged at the level of *Keter*;
- AA—at the level of *Hochma*;
- AVI—at the level of *Bina*;
- And ZON in VAK and *Nekuda*, which is the level of ZA.

Also, there can never be any diminution in these five levels, since the acts of the lower ones never reach the GAR in a way that they can blemish them. The actions of the lower ones do reach ZA and *Nukva*, that is, their *Kelim de Achoraim*, which they obtain during the *Gadlut*. But the actions of the lower ones cannot reach the *Kelim de Panim*, which are GE in Lights of VAK and *Nekuda*. Hence, these five levels are considered constant *Mochin* in *Atzilut*.

127) The order of their clothing of each other and on *Partzuf AK* is that *Partzuf Atik de Atzilut*, although it emerged from *Rosh de SAG de AK* (Item 118), it still cannot clothe from the *Peh of SAG de AK* downwards, but only below *Tabur*. This is because above *Tabur de AK* it is considered *Tzimtzum Aleph*, *Akudim*.

Since *Partzuf Atik* is the first *Rosh* of *Atzilut*, *Tzimtzum Bet* does not control it, so it should have been worthy of clothing above *Tabur de AK*. But since *Tzimtzum*

Bet had already been established in its *Peh de Rosh*, for the rest of the *Partzufim de Atzilut*, from it downwards, it can only clothe from *Tabur de AK* downwards.

It turns out that the level of *Atik* begins at *Tabur de AK* and ends equally with the *Raglaim de AK*, that is, above the point of this world. This is so because of its own *Partzuf*. Yet, because of its connection to the rest of the *Partzufim* of *Atzilut*, from whose perspective it is regarded as being included in *Tzimtzum Bet*, as well, in that respect, it is considered that its *Raglaim* end above *Parsa de Atzilut*, since *Parsa* is the new *Sium* (end) of *Tzimtzum Bet* (Item 68).

128) The second *Partzuf* in the new MA, called AA, which was emanated and came out of the *Peh de Rosh Atik*, begins from the place of its emergence, from *Peh de Rosh de Atik*, and clothes the ZAT *de Atik*, which end above *Parsa* of *Atzilut*. The third *Partzuf*, called AVI, which emerged from *Peh de Rosh de AA*, begins from *Peh de Rosh de AA* and ends above the *Tabur de AA*. And the ZON begin in *Tabur de AA* and end equally with the *Sium* of AA, that is, above the *Parsa de Atzilut*.

129) You should know that each level of these five *Partzufim* of the new MA sorted and connected to itself a part of the *Kelim de Nekudim*, which became its *Nukva*. Thus, when *Partzuf Atik* emerged, it took and connected to itself all the GAR *de Nekudim* that remained complete during the breaking of the vessels. This refers to the GE in them, which emerged during their *Katnut*, called *Kelim de Panim* (Item 76). In the *Katnut* of *Nekudim*, only the Upper half of each degree came with them, that is, GE and *Nikvey Eynaim*. The bottom half of each, called AHP, descended to the lower degree.

Hence, it is considered that *Partzuf Atik* of the new MA took the Upper half of *Keter* from the *Kelim* of *Nekudim*, as well as the Upper half of HB, and the seven roots of ZAT, included in GAR *de Nekudim*. And these became a *Partzuf Nukva* to the *Atik* of the new MA, and joined with one another. They are called MA and BON *de Atik de Atzilut*, since *Atik*'s male is called MA, and the *Kelim de Nekudim* that joined it are called BON (Item 119). They are arranged face and back: *Atik de MA* at the *Panim*, and *Atik de BON* in its *Achor*.

130) *Partzuf* AA of the new MA, which emerged at the level of *Hochma*, sorted and connected to itself the lower half of *Keter de Nekudim*—the AHP *de Keter*—which, during the *Katnut*, were at the degree below *Keter*, that is, in *Hochma* and *Bina de Nekudim* (Item 77). It became a *Nukva* to the AA of the new MA, and they were joined. Their stance is right and left: AA *de* MA, which is the male, stands at the right, and AA *de* BON, which is the *Nukva*, stands at the left.

And the reason why *Partzuf Atik de* MA did not take the lower half of *Keter de Nekudim*, as well, is that since *Atik* is the first *Rosh de Atzilut*, whose level is very high, it connected to itself only the *Kelim de Panim de GAR de Nekudim*, where no flaw occurred during the breaking. This is not so at the bottom half of *Keter*, the *AHP* that were fallen in *HB* during the *Katnut*. Afterwards, during the *Gadlut*, they rose from *HB* and were joined in *Keter de Nekudim* (Item 84). Then, after the breaking of the vessels, they fell from *Keter de Nekudim* once more and were cancelled. Thus, they were flawed by their fall and cancellation, and are therefore unworthy of *Atik*. This is why *AA de MA* took them.

131) And the new *Partzuf AVI*, at the level of *Bina*, sorted and connected to themselves the lower half of *HB de Nekudim*, which are the *AHP de HB* that fell in the *ZAT de Nekudim* during the *Katnut*. But afterwards, during the *Gadlut de Nekudim*, they rose and joined with *HB de Nekudim* (Item 94). During the breaking of the vessels they fell into *ZAT de Nekudim* once more and were cancelled (Item 107), and *AVI de MA* sorted them into being their *Nukva*.

They are called *ZAT de Hochma* and *VAT de Bina de BON*, since *Hesed de Bina* remained with the *GAR de HB de BON* in *Partzuf Atik*, and only the lower *Vav*, from *Gevura* downwards, remained at the bottom half of *Bina*. It turns out that the male of *AVI* is the level of *Bina de MA*, and the *Nukva de AVI* is *ZAT* of *HB de BON*. They stand at the right and the left: *AVI de MA* on the right, and *AVI de BON* on the left. And *YESHSUT de MA*, which are the *ZAT de AVI*, took the *Malchuts* of *HB de BON*.

132) And *Partzuf ZON* of the new *MA*, at the level of *VAK* and *Nekuda*, sorted and connected to themselves the *Kelim de Panim* of *ZAT de Nekudim*, out of their shattering in *BYA*, that is, the *Behinat GE* of the *ZAT de Nekudim* (Item 78). They became *Nukva* to *ZON de MA* and stand on the right and on the left: *ZON de MA* on the right, and *ZON de BON* on the left.

133) Thus we have explained the *MA* and *BON* in the five *Partzufim* of *Atzilut*. The five levels of the new *MA* that emerged in the world of *Atzilut* sorted the old *Kelim* that worked in the *Nekudim*, and made them into *Nukvas* (females), called *BON*.

- *BON de Atik* were sorted and made of the Upper half of *GAR de Nekudim*.
- *BON de AA* and *AVI* were sorted and made of the bottom half of *GAR de Nekudim*, which served them during the *Gadlut de Nekudim* and were cancelled once again.
- *BON de ZON* were sorted and made of the *Kelim de Panim* that emerged during the *Katnut de Nekudim*, which broke and fell along with their *Kelim de Achoraim* during their *Gadlut*.

A GREAT RULE CONCERNING THE CONSTANT MOCHIN AND THE ASCENTS OF THE PARTZUFIM AND THE WORLDS DURING THE SIX THOUSAND YEARS

134) It has already been explained that the emergence of the *Gadlut* of the *GAR* and *ZAT de Nekudim* came in three sequences, by way of the three points *Holam*, *Shuruk*, *Hirik* (Item 86). From this you can understand that there are two kinds of completion of ten *Sefirot* for reception of *Mochin de Gadlut*.

The first is through ascension and integration in the Upper One, that is, when *ZON de AK* illuminated the new Light through the *Tabur* into the *Keter de Nekudim* and lowered the lower *Hey* from *Nikvey Eynaim de Keter* to its *Peh*. Thus, the fallen *AHP de Keter* that were in *AVI* rose and returned to their degree in *Keter*, completing its ten *Sefirot*.

It is considered that at that state, *GE de AVI* attached to *AHP de Keter* rose along with them. Hence, *AVI*, too, are included in the ten complete *Sefirot* of *Keter*, since the lower one that rises to the Upper One becomes like it (Item 93). It is therefore considered that *AVI*, too, obtained the *AHP* that they lacked to complete their ten *Sefirot*, by their integration in *Keter*. This is the first kind of *Mochin de Gadlut*.

135) The second kind is a degree that was completed into ten *Sefirot* by itself when *ZON de AK* illuminated the new Light through the *Yesod de AK*, called "the point of *Shuruk*," to *AVI*, and lowered the lower *Hey* from *Nikvey Eynaim de AVI* themselves to their *Peh*. By that, they elevated the *Kelim de AHP de AVI* from the place to which they fell in *ZAT* to the *Rosh de AVI*, and completed their ten *Sefirot*. Thus, now *AVI* are completed by themselves, since now they have obtained the actual *Kelim de AHP* that they lacked.

Yet, in the first kind, when they received their completion from the *Keter* through *Dvekut* with its *AHP*, they were actually still deficient of the *AHP*. But owing to their *Hitkalelut* in *Keter*, they received an illumination from their *AHP*, which sufficed only to complete them in ten *Sefirot* while they were still in the place of *Keter*, and not at all when they departed thence to their own place.

136) Similarly, there are two kinds of completions in the *ZAT*, too:

1. During the illumination of *Shuruk* and the ascension of *AHP de AVI*, at which time the *GE de ZAT* that are attached to them rose along with them to *AVI*, too, where they received an *AHP* to complete their ten *Sefirot*. These *AHP* are no longer their real *AHP*, but only illumination of *AHP*, sufficient to complete the ten *Sefirot* while they are in *AVI*, and not at all upon their descent to their own place.

2. The completion of the ten *Sefirot*, which the ZAT obtained during the *Hitpashtut* of *Mochin* from AVI to the ZAT, by which they, too, lowered their ending lower *Hey* from their *Chazeh* to the *Sium Raglin* of AK and elevated their *TNHY* from BYA and connected them to their degree, to *Atzilut*. Then, had they not been broken and died, they would have been completed with ten complete *Sefirot* by themselves, since now they have obtained the actual AHP that they lacked.

137) In the four *Partzufim* that emerged from AVI into *Kelim de* HGT, as well as in the four *Partzufim* that emerged from YESHSUT to the *Kelim de* TNHYM (Items 107-109), there are these two kinds of completions of ten *Sefirot*, too. This is because first, each of them was completed by their adhesion with the AHP de AVI and YESHSUT while they were still at the *Rosh*. This is the first kind of completion of the ten *Sefirot*. Afterwards, when they expanded to BYA, they wanted to be completed by completing the second kind of ten *Sefirot*. This applies to the *Sefirot* within *Sefirot*, too.

138) You should know that these five *Partzufim* of *Atzilut*, *Atik*, AA, AVI, and ZON were established in permanence,[28] and no diminution applies to them (Item 126). *Atik* emerged at the level of *Keter*; AA at the level of *Hochma*; AVI at the level of *Bina*; and ZON at the level of ZA, VAK without a *Rosh*.

Thus, the *Kelim de* AHP that were sorted for them, from the period of *Gadlut*, were considered the completion of the first kind of ten *Sefirot*, by way of the point of *Holam* that shown in *Keter de Nekudim*. At that time AVI, too, were completed by the *Keter* and obtained illumination of *Kelim de* AHP (Item 134). Hence, even though *Atik*, AA, and AVI all had ten complete *Sefirot* at the *Rosh*, no GAR expanded from it to their *Gufim*. Even *Partzuf Atik* had only VAK, without a *Rosh*, at the *Guf*, and so did AA and AVI.

The reason for this is that the pure is sorted first. Hence, only the completion of the first kind of ten *Sefirot* was sorted in them, from the perspective of its ascension to the Upper One, that is, the illumination of the *Kelim de* AHP, which suffices to complete the ten *Sefirot* in the *Rosh*. But there is still no *Hitpashtut* from the *Rosh* to the *Guf*, since when AVI were included in *Keter de Nekudim*, they settled for the illumination of AHP by the power of *Keter*, and not at all for their *Hitpashtut* to their own place, from *Peh de Keter de Nekudim* downwards (Item 135). And since the bodies of *Atik* and AA and AVI were in VAK without a *Rosh*, it is all the more so with ZON themselves, considered the common *Guf de Atzilut* that emerged in VAK without a *Rosh*.

---

28 Translator's note: "in permanence" is also referred to as "the constant state."

139) Yet, this was not so in AK. Rather, the whole quantity that emerged in the *Roshim* of the *Partzufim* of AK expanded to their *Gufim*, too. Hence, all five *Partzufim* of *Atzilut* are regarded as merely VAK of the *Partzufim* of AK. This is why they are called "the new MA" or "MA of the five *Partzufim* of AK," that is, the level of ZA, which is MA without GAR. GAR are *Galgalta*, AB, SAG, since the heart of the degree is measured according to its expansion to the *Guf*, from the *Peh* down. And since the first three *Partzufim* do not spread into the *Guf*, but only VAK without a *Rosh*, they are considered MA, which is the level of VAK without a *Rosh*, with respect to the five *Partzufim de* AK.

140) Thus, **Atik de Atzilut**, with the level of *Keter* at the *Rosh*, is considered VAK to *Partzuf Keter de* AK, and lacks *Neshama, Haya, Yechida de Keter de* AK. **AA de Atzilut**, having the level of *Hochma* at the *Rosh*, is considered VAK to *Partzuf* AB *de* AK, which is *Hochma*, lacking *Neshama, Haya, Yechida de* AB *de* AK.

AVI de Atzilut, with the level of *Bina* at the *Rosh*, are considered VAK of *Partzuf* SAG *de* AK, and lack *Neshama, Haya, Yechida de* SAG *de* AK. **ZON de Atzilut** are considered VAK *de Partzuf* MA and BON *de* AK, and lack *Neshama, Haya, Yechida de* MA and BON *de* AK. And **YESHSUT** and **ZON** are always on the same degree—one being the *Rosh* and the other being the *Guf*.

141) The completion of the AHP of the ten *Sefirot* of the second kind are sorted through raising MAN from good deeds of the lower ones. This means that they complete AVI, with respect to themselves, as in the point of *Shuruk*. At that time, AVI themselves lower the lower *Hey* from their *Nikvey Eynaim* and raise their AHP to them. Then they have the strength to bestow upon the ZAT, as well, which are ZON, that is, to the *Gufim* from Above downwards. This is because the GE *de* ZON, attached to the AHP *de* AVI, are drawn along with them to AVI, and receive the completion of their ten *Sefirot* from them (Item 94).

At that time, the full amount of *Mochin* in AVI are given to the ZON that rose along with them to their AHP, as well. Hence, when the five *Partzufim de Atzilut* receive this completion of the second kind, there is GAR to the *Gufim* of the first three *Partzufim*—*Atik*, AA, and AVI *de Atzilut*—as well as to ZON *de Atzilut*, the common *Guf de Atzilut*.

At that time, the five *Partzufim* of *Atzilut* rise and clothe the five *Partzufim* of AK. This is because during the *Hitpashtut* of GAR to the *Gufim* of the five *Partzufim* of *Atzilut*, they equalize with the five *Partzufim* of AK:

- *Atik de Atzilut* rises and clothes *Partzuf Keter de* AK
- AA clothes AB *de* AK

- AVI–SAG de AK
- And ZON clothes MA and BON de AK.

And then each of them receives *Neshama*, *Haya*, and *Yechida* from its corresponding *Behina* in AK.

142) Yet, with respect to ZON de Atzilut, these *Mochin* are regarded as merely the first kind of completion of ten *Sefirot*. This is because these AHP are not complete AHP, but mere illumination of AHP, which they receive through AVI while they are at the place of AVI. But in their expansion to their own place, they still lack their own AHP (Item 136).

For this reason, all the *Mochin* that ZON obtains in the 6,000 years are considered "*Mochin* of ascension," since they can obtain *Mochin de GAR* only when they rise to the place of GAR, as then they are completed by them. But if they do not rise to the place of GAR, they cannot have *Mochin*, since the ZON still have to sort the second kind of *Mochin*, and this will happen only at the end of correction.

143) Thus we have explained that the *Mochin* of the five permanent *Partzufim* in *Atzilut* are from the first kind of sorting of *Kelim de AVI*. In the world of *Nekudim*, this illumination is called "illumination of *Tabur*" or "the point of *Holam*." Even AVI have only the first kind of completion; hence, no illumination of GAR spreads from the *Roshim* of *Atik*, AA, and AVI to their own *Gufim* and to ZON, since ZAT *de Nekudim*, too, received none of that illumination of the *Holam* (Item 88).

And the *Mochin* of the 6,000 years, through the end of correction, which come through the lower ones' raising of MAN, are considered sorting of *Kelim* to complete the second kind of ten *Sefirot de AVI*. In the world of *Nekudim*, this illumination is called "illumination of the *Yesod*" or "the point of *Shuruk*," since then AVI raise their own AHP, to which the GE *de ZAT* are attached, as well. Hence, ZAT, too, receive *Mochin de GAR* in the place of AVI. Thus, these *Mochin* reach the *Gufim* of the five *Partzufim* of *Atzilut* and the common ZON, except they must be above, in the place of GAR, and clothe them.

In the future, at the end of correction, ZON will receive the completion of the second kind of ten *Sefirot*, and will lower the concluding lower *Hey* from their *Chazeh*, which is *Parsa de Atzilut*, to the place of *Sium Raglin de AK* (Item 136). At that time TNHY *de ZON* in BYA will connect to the degree of ZON *de Atzilut*, and *Sium Raglin de Atzilut* will equalize with *Sium Raglin de AK*. Then the Messiah King will appear, as it is written, "And His feet shall stand... upon the mount of Olives." Thus, it has been thoroughly clarified that there is no correction to the worlds during the 6,000 years, except through ascension.

EXPLAINING THE THREE WORLDS BERIA, YETZIRA, AND ASSIYA

144) There are seven basic points to discern in the three worlds BYA:

1. From where was the place for these three worlds made?
2. The levels of the *Partzufim* BYA and the initial stance of the worlds when they were created and emanated from the *Nukva de Atzilut*.
3. All the levels from the added *Mochin* and the stance they had obtained prior to the sin of *Adam ha Rishon*.
4. The *Mochin* that remained in the *Partzufim* BYA and the place to which the worlds fell after they were flawed by the sin of *Adam ha Rishon*.
5. The *Mochin de Ima* that the *Partzufim* BYA received after their fall below *Parsa de Atzilut*.
6. The *Partzufim* of *Achor* of the five *Partzufim* of *Atzilut*, which descended and clothed the *Partzufim* BYA and became what is discerned as *Neshama* to *Neshama* for them.
7. The *Malchut de Atzilut* that descended and became *Atik* to the *Partzufim* BYA.

145) The first discernment has already been explained (Item 66): Because of the ascension of the ending *Malchut*, which was below the *Sium Raglin* of AK, to the place of *Chazeh de ZAT de Nekudot de SAG*, which occurred during *Tzimtzum Bet*, the two lower thirds of *Tifferet* and NHYM fell below the new point of *Sium* at *Chazeh de Nekudot*. Thus, they are no longer worthy of receiving the Upper Light, and the place of the three worlds BYA was made of them:

- The place of the world of *Beria* was made of the two lower thirds of *Tifferet*;
- The place of the world of *Yetzira* was made of the three *Sefirot* NHY;
- The place of the world of *Assiya* was made of *Malchut*.

146) The second discernment is the levels of the *Partzufim* BYA and their stance upon their exit and birth from the *Nukva de Atzilut*. Know that at that time, ZA had already obtained the *Behinat Haya* from *Aba*, and the *Nukva* had already obtained the *Behinat Neshama* from *Ima*.

And you already know that the ZON receive the *Mochin* from AVI only by ascension and clothing (Item 142). Hence, ZA clothes *Aba de Atzilut*, called Upper AVI, the *Nukva* clothes *Ima de Atzilut*, called YESHSUT, and then *Nukva de Atzilut* sorted and emanated the world of *Beria* with its five *Partzufim*.

147) And since the *Nukva* stands at *Ima's* place, she is considered having *Ima's* degree, since the lower one that rises to the Upper One becomes like it. Hence, the world of *Beria*, which was sorted by her, is considered the degree of ZA, since it is an inferior degree to the *Nukva*, considered *Ima*, and the one lower to *Ima* is ZA. Then the world of *Beria*, which stands at the place of ZA *de Atzilut*, is below *Nukva de Atzilut*, which was then considered *Ima de Atzilut*.

148) Thus, it is considered that the world of *Yetzira*, which was sorted and emanated by the world of *Beria*, is then at the degree of *Nukva de Atzilut*. This is because it is the degree below the world of *Beria*, which was then considered ZA of *Atzilut*. And the one below ZA is considered *Nukva*. However, not all ten *Sefirot* of the world of *Yetzira* are considered *Nukva de Atzilut*, but only the first four of *Yetzira*. The reason is that there are two states to the *Nukva*: face-to-face and back-to-back:

- When she is face-to-face with ZA, her level is equal to that of ZA;
- And when she is back-to-back, she occupies only the four *Sefirot* TNHY *de* ZA.

And since at that time the state of all the worlds was only back-to-back, there were only four *Sefirot* in the *Nukva*. Hence, the world of *Yetzira*, too, has only its first four *Sefirot* at the place of *Nukva de Atzilut*. And the bottom six of *Yetzira* were at the first six *Sefirot* of the current world of *Beria*, according to the qualities in the place of BYA in the first discernment (Item 145), where the worlds BYA fell after the sin of *Adam ha Rishon*, and this is now their permanent place.

149) The world of *Assiya*, which was sorted by the world of *Yetzira*, is considered the current degree of *Beria*. Since the world of *Yetzira* was previously at the degree of *Nukva de Atzilut*, the degree below it—the world of *Assiya*—is considered the current world of *Beria*. But since only the first four of *Yetzira* were considered *Nukva de Atzilut* and its lower six were in the world of *Beria*, as well, only the first four of the world of *Assiya* below it are regarded as the bottom four *Sefirot* of the world of *Beria*. And the bottom six of the world of *Assiya* were in the place of the first six of the current world of *Yetzira*.

At that time, the fourteen *Sefirot*—NHYM of the current *Yetzira* and all ten *Sefirot* of the current world of *Assiya*—were devoid of any *Kedusha* (holiness), and became *Mador ha Klipot* (the shell section). This is so because there were only *Klipot* (shells) in the place of these fourteen *Sefirot*, since the worlds of *Kedusha* ended at the place of *Chazeh* of the current world of *Yetzira*. Thus we have learned the levels of the *Partzufim* BYA and the place of their stance upon their first emergence.

150) Now we shall explain the third discernment—the levels of the *Partzufim* BYA and the stance they had had from the added *Mochin* prior to the sin of *Adam ha Rishon*. This is because through the illumination of the addition of Shabbat, they had two ascensions.

1. On the fifth hour on the eve of Shabbat, when *Adam ha Rishon* was born. At that time, the illumination of Shabbat begins to shine in the form of the fifth of the sixth day. At that time:

- ZA obtained *Behinat Yechida* and rose and clothed AA de *Atzilut*;
- And *Nukva—Behinat Haya*, and rose and clothed AVI de *Atzilut*;
- *Beria* rose to YESHSUT;
- The whole of *Yetzira* rose to ZA;
- The first four *Sefirot* of *Assiya* rose to the place of *Nukva de Atzilut*;
- And the bottom six of *Assiya* rose to the place of the first six of *Beria*.

2. On the eve of Shabbat, at dusk. Through the addition of Shabbat, the bottom six of *Assiya* rose to the place of *Nukva de Atzilut*, as well, and the worlds of *Yetzira* and *Assiya* stood in the world of *Atzilut*, in the place of ZON de *Atzilut*, in the form of face-to-face.

151) And now we shall explain the fourth discernment—the level of *Mochin* that remained in BYA, and the place to which they fell after the sin. Because of the flaw of the sin of the Tree of Knowledge, all the added *Mochin* that they had obtained through the two ascensions departed the worlds, and ZON returned to being VAK and *Nekuda*. And the three worlds BYA were left with merely the *Mochin* with which they initially emerged. The world of *Beria* was at the degree of ZA, which means VAK, and *Yetzira* and *Assiya* in the above-mentioned measure, too (Item 148).

Additionally, the discernment of *Atzilut* had completely left them and they fell below *Parsa de Atzilut*, to the quality of the place of BYA, prepared by *Tzimtzum Bet* (Item 145). Thus, the bottom four of *Yetzira* and the ten *Sefirot* of the world of *Assiya* fell and stood at the place of the fourteen *Sefirot* of the *Klipot* (Item 149), called *Mador ha Klipot*.

152) The fifth discernment is the *Mochin de Ima* that BYA received at the place to which they fell. After BYA departed *Atzilut* and fell below *Parsa de Atzilut*, they had only VAK (Item 151). Then YESHSUT clothed in ZON de *Atzilut*, and YESHSUT mated for the purpose of clothing in ZON, and imparted *Mochin de Neshama* to the *Partzufim* BYA in their place:

- The world of *Beria* received from them ten complete *Sefirot* at the level of *Bina*;

- The world of *Yetzira* received VAK from them;
- And the world of *Assiya*, only the discernment of back-to-back.

153) The sixth discernment is the *Neshama* to *Neshama*, which the *Partzufim* BYA obtained from the *Partzufim* of *Achor* of the five *Partzufim* of *Atzilut*. This is because during the lunar diminution, the *Partzuf* of *Achor de Nukva de Atzilut* fell and clothed in the *Partzufim* BYA. It contains three *Partzufim*, called *Ibur*, *Yenika*, *Mochin*.

- *Behinat* (discernment of) *Mochin* fell into *Beria*;
- *Behinat Yenika* fell into *Yetzira*;
- And *Behinat Ibur* fell into *Assiya*.

They became *Behinat Neshama* to *Neshama* to all the *Partzufim* BYA, which is considered *Haya*, with respect to them.

154) The seventh discernment is the *Nukva de Atzilut*, which became the RADLA and the illumination of *Yechida* in BYA. This is because it has been explained that during the lunar diminution, the three discernments—*Ibur*, *Yenika*, *Mochin*—of *Partzuf Achor de Nukva de Atzilut* fell and clothed in BYA. They are regarded as the *Achoraim* of the bottom nine of *Nukva*, which are *Ibur*, *Yenika*, and *Mochin*:

- NHY is called *Ibur*;
- HGT is called *Yenika*;
- HBD is called *Mochin*.

However, the *Achor* of *Behinat Keter de Nukva* became *Atik* to the *Partzufim* BYA, in a way that the Lights of the current *Partzufim* BYA are primarily from the remnants, left in them after the sin of *Adam ha Rishon*, which is the VAK of each of them (Item 151).

- They received *Behinat Neshama* from *Mochin de Ima* (Item 152);
- And they received *Behinat Neshama* to *Neshama*, which is *Behinat Haya*, from the bottom nine of *Partzuf Achor de Nukva*;
- And they received *Behinat Yechida* from *Behinat Achor de Keter de Nukva de Atzilut*.

EXPLAINING THE ASCENSIONS OF THE WORLDS

155) The main difference between the *Partzufim* of AK and the *Partzufim* of the world of *Atzilut* is that the *Partzufim* of AK are from *Tzimtzum Aleph*, where each degree contains ten complete *Sefirot*. Also, there is only one *Kli* in the ten *Sefirot*—the *Kli* of *Malchut*, but the first nine *Sefirot* are only considered Lights.

The *Partzufim* of *Atzilut*, however, are from *Tzimtzum Bet*, as it is written, "in the day that the Lord God made earth and heaven," when He associated *Rachamim* (mercy) with *Din* (judgment) (Item 59). *Midat ha Din* (quality of judgment), which is *Malchut*, rose and connected to *Bina*, which is *Midat ha Rachamim* (quality of mercy), and they were conjoined. Thus, a new *Sium* was placed over the Upper Light in *Bina's* place. The *Malchut* that ends the *Guf* rose to *Bina de Guf*, which is *Tifferet*, at the place of the *Chazeh*, and the coupling *Malchut* at the *Peh de Rosh* rose to the *Bina de Rosh*, called *Nikvey Eynaim*.

Thus, the level of the *Partzufim* diminished into GE, which are *Keter Hochma* in *Kelim*, at the level of VAK without a *Rosh*, which is *Nefesh Ruach* in Lights (Item 74). Hence, they are deficient of the AHP *de Kelim*, which are *Bina* and ZON, and the Lights *Neshama*, *Haya*, and *Yechida*.

156) It has been explained (Item 124) that by raising MAN for the second *Ibur*, the *Partzufim* of *Atzilut* obtained the illumination of *Mochin* from AB SAG de AK, which lowers the lower *Hey* from *Nikvey Eynaim* back to her place at the *Peh*, as in *Tzimtzum Aleph*. Thus, they regain the AHP *de Kelim* and the *Neshama*, *Haya*, *Yechida* of Lights. Yet, this helped only to the ten *Sefirot* of the *Rosh* of the *Partzufim*, but not to their *Gufim*, since these *Mochin* did not spread from the *Peh* down to their *Gufim* (Item 138).

Therefore, even after the *Mochin de Gadlut*, the *Gufim* remained in *Tzimtzum Bet*, as during the *Katnut*. For this reason, all five *Partzufim de Atzilut* are considered to have only the level of the ten *Sefirot* that emerge on *Aviut* of *Behina Aleph*, the level of ZA, VAK without a *Rosh*, called "the level of MA." They clothe the level of MA of the five *Partzufim* of AK, that is, from *Tabur* of the five *Partzufim* of AK downwards.

157) Thus, **Partzuf Atik de Atzilut** clothes *Partzuf Keter de AK* from its *Tabur* down, and receives its bounty from the level of MA of *Partzuf Keter de AK*, which is there. **Partzuf AA de Atzilut** clothes *Partzuf AB de AK* from *Tabur* down and receives its bounty from the level of MA de AB de AK, which is there. **AVI de Atzilut** clothe *Partzuf SAG de AK* from *Tabur* down, and receive their bounty from the level of MA de SAG, which is there. **ZON de Atzilut** clothe *Partzuf* MA and BON *de AK* from *Tabur* down, and receive their bounty from the level of MA of *Partzuf* MA and BON *de AK*.

Thus, each of the five *Partzufim* of *Atzilut* receives from its corresponding *Partzuf* in AK, only VAK without a *Rosh*, called "the level of MA." And even though there is GAR in the *Roshim* of the five *Partzufim* of *Atzilut*, only the

Mochin that expand from the *Peh* down into their *Gufim*, which are merely *VAK* without a *Rosh*, are taken into consideration (Item 139).

158) This does not mean that each of the five *Partzufim* of *Atzilut* clothes its corresponding *Behina* (discernment) in *AK*. This is impossible, since the five *Partzufim* of *Atzilut* clothe one atop the other, and so do the five *Partzufim* of *Atzilut*. Rather, this means that the level of each *Partzuf* of the *Partzufim* of *Atzilut* is aiming towards its corresponding *Behina* in the five *Partzufim* of *AK*, from which it receives its bounty (*HaIlan*, Image no. 3).

159) For the *Mochin* to flow from the *Peh* down to the *Gufim* of the five *Partzufim* of *Atzilut*, it has been explained (Item 141) that raising MAN from the lower ones is required. This is because then the completion of the ten *Sefirot* of the second kind are given to them, which suffices for the *Gufim*, as well.

And there are three discernments in these MAN that the lower ones raise:

- When they raise MAN from *Aviut de Behina Bet*, ten *Sefirot* at the level of *Bina* emerge, called "the level of SAG." These are *Mochin* of Light of *Neshama*.

- When they raise MAN from *Aviut de Behina Gimel*, ten *Sefirot* at the level of *Hochma* emerge, called "the level of AB." These are *Mochin* of the Light of *Haya*.

- When they raise MAN from *Aviut de Behina Dalet*, ten *Sefirot* at the level of *Keter* emerge, called "the level of *Galgalta*." These are *Mochin* of the Light of *Yechida* (Item 29).

160) Know that the lower ones that are suitable for raising MAN are only considered NRN (*Nefesh, Ruach, Neshama*) *de Tzadikim* (righteous), which are already included in BYA and can raise MAN to ZON *de Atzilut*, considered their Upper One. At that time the ZON raise MAN to their Upper One, which are AVI, and AVI Higher still, until they reach the *Partzufim* of AK. Then the Upper Light descends from *Ein Sof* to the *Partzufim* of AK on the MAN that rose there, and the level of ten *Sefirot* emerges, according to the measure of *Aviut* of the MAN that they raised.

- If it is from *Behina Bet*, it is at the level of *Neshama*;
- If it is from *Behina Gimel*, it is the level of *Haya*.

And from there, the *Mochin* descend degree by degree through the *Partzufim* of AK, until they arrive at the *Partzufim* of *Atzilut*. And they also travel degree by degree, through all the *Partzufim* of *Atzilut*, until they arrive at the *Partzufim* ZON *de Atzilut*, which impart these *Mochin* upon the NRN *de Tzadikim* that raised these MAN from BYA.

And this is the rule: any initiation of *Mochin* comes only from *Ein Sof*, and no degree can raise MAN or receive bounty except from its adjacent Upper One.

161) This tells you that it is impossible for the lower ones to receive anything from ZON *de Atzilut* before all the Higher *Partzufim* in the world of *Atzilut* and the world of AK are brought into *Gadlut* by them. This is because it has been explained that there is no initiation of *Mochin* except from *Ein Sof*.

Yet, the NRN *de Tzadikim* can only receive them from their adjacent Upper One, which are ZON *de Atzilut*. Hence, the *Mochin* must cascade through the Upper Worlds and *Partzufim*, until they reach the ZON, which then give to the NRN *de Tzadikim*.

You already know that there is no absence in the spiritual, and that transference from place to place does not mean becoming absent from the first place and arriving at the next place, as in corporeality. Rather, they remain in the first place even after they have moved and arrived at the next place, as though lighting one candle from another, without the first being deficient.

Moreover, the rule is that the essence and the root of the Light remains in the first place, and only a branch of it extends to the next place. Now you can see that the bounty that traverses the Upper Ones until it reaches the NRN *de Tzadikim* remains in each degree it had traversed. Thus, all the degrees grow because of the bounty that they pass onto the NRN *de Tzadikim*.

162) Now you can understand how the actions of the lower ones cause ascents and descents in the Upper *Partzufim* and worlds. This is because when they better their deeds and raise MAN and extend bounty, all the worlds and degrees through which the bounty passed grow and rise Higher, because of the bounty that they pass. And when they corrupt their deeds once more, the MAN is corrupted, and the *Mochin* depart the Higher degrees, too, since the transference of bounty from them to the lower ones stops, and they descend once more to their permanent state as in the beginning.

163) And now we shall explain the order of the ascensions of the five *Partzufim* of *Atzilut* to the five *Partzufim* of AK, and the three worlds BYA to YESHSUT and ZON *de Atzilut*, beginning with their constant state and up to the level that can be reached during the 6,000 years before the end of correction. Overall, there are three ascensions, but they are divided into many details.

The constant state of the worlds AK and ABYA has already been explained above: the first *Partzuf* that was emanated after *Tzimtzum Aleph* is *Partzuf Galgalta de AK*, clothed by the four *Partzufim* of AK: *AB*, *SAG*, *MA*, and *BON*, and the *Sium Raglin* of AK is above the point of this world (Items 27, 31). It is circled by the surroundings of AK from *Ein Sof*, whose magnitude is infinite and immeasurable (Item 32). And just as *Ein Sof* surrounds it, it clothes within it, and it is called "the line of *Ein Sof*."

164) And within *MA* and *BON de AK* lies *Partzuf TNHYM de AK*, called *Nekudot de SAG de AK* (Item 63, 66). During *Tzimtzum Bet*, the ending *Malchut*, which stood above the point of this world, rose and determined its place at the *Chazeh* of this *Partzuf*, below its Upper third of *Tifferet*, where it created a new *Sium* on the Upper Light, so it would not spread from there down. This new *Sium* is called "*Parsa* below *Atzilut*" (Item 68).

Also, these *Sefirot* from the *Chazeh* down of *Partzuf Nekudot de SAG de AK* that remained below the *Parsa* became a place for the three worlds BYA:

- The two thirds of *Tifferet* through the *Chazeh* became the place of the world of *Beria*;
- *NHY* became the place of the world of *Yetzira*;
- And *Malchut*, the place of the world of *Assiya* (Item 67).

It turns out that the place of the three worlds BYA begins below the *Parsa* and ends above the point of this world.

165) Thus, the four worlds, *Atzilut*, *Beria*, *Yetzira*, and *Assiya* begin from the place below *Tabur de AK* and end above the point of this world. This is because the five *Partzufim* of the world of *Atzilut* begin from the place below *Tabur de AK*, and end above the *Parsa*. And from the *Parsa* down to this world stand the three worlds BYA. This is the permanent state of the worlds AK and ABYA, and there will never be any diminution in them.

And it has already been explained (Item 138) that in that state, there is only *Behinat VAK* without a *Rosh* in all the *Partzufim* and the worlds. This is so because even in the first three *Partzufim* of *Atzilut*, in whose *Roshim* there is GAR, they are still not imparted from their *Peh* downwards, and all the *Gufim* are VAK without a *Rosh*, all the more so in the *Partzufim* BYA. Even the *Partzufim* of AK, with respect to their surroundings, are regarded as lacking GAR (Item 32).

166) Hence, over all there are three ascensions to complete the worlds in the three levels, *Neshama*, *Haya*, and *Yechida*, which they lack. And these ascensions depend on the lower ones' raising of MAN.

The first ascension is when the lower ones raise MAN from the *Behinat Aviut* of *Behina Bet*. At that time, the *AHP* of the level of *Bina* and *Neshama*, with respect to the ten *Sefirot* of the second kind, are sorted, from the illumination of the point of *Shuruk* (Item 135). These *Mochin* shine to the ZAT and the *Gufim*, as well, like in the *Partzufim* of AK, when the full quantity that exists in the ten *Sefirot* in the *Roshim* of the *Partzufim* of AK traverses and spreads to the *Gufim*, as well.

167) It turns out that when these *Mochin* travel through the *Partzufim* of *Atzilut*, each of the five *Partzufim* of *Atzilut* receives *Mochin de Bina* and *Neshama*, called *Mochin de SAG*, which illuminate GAR to their *Partzufim*, as well, as in AK. Hence, it is then considered that they grow and rise and clothe the five *Partzufim* of AK, to the extent of the *Mochin* that they achieved.

168) Thus, when *Partzuf Atik de Atzilut* obtained these *Mochin de Bina*, it rises and clothes *Partzuf Bina de AK*, opposite the level of *SAG de Partzuf Galgalta de AK*, from which it receives its *Behinat Neshama de Yechida de AK*, which shines for his ZAT, too.

And when the **Mochin** come to **Partzuf AA de Atzilut**, it ascends and clothes the *Rosh de Atik* of the constant state, opposite the level of *SAG* of *Partzuf AB de AK*, from which it receives *Behinat Neshama de Haya de AK*, which shines for its ZAT. And when the **Mochin** come to **Partzuf AVI de Atzilut**, it ascends and clothes the constant GAR *de AA*, opposite the level of *Bina* of *SAG de AK*, from which it receives *Behinat Neshama de Neshama de AK*, which shines to their ZAT, too. And when these **Mochin** come to the **YESHSUT** and **ZON de Atzilut**, they ascend and clothe the constant AVI, opposite the level of *Bina de Partzuf MA* and *BON de AK*, from which they receive *Behinat Neshama de Nefesh Ruach de AK*. Then the *NRN de Tzadikim* receive the *Mochin de Neshama de Atzilut*.

And when the **Mochin** come to the **Partzufim** of the world of **Beria**, the world of *Beria* ascends and clothes *Nukva de Atzilut*, from which it receives *Behinat Nefesh de Atzilut*. And when the **Mochin** come to the world of **Yetzira**, it ascends and clothes the constant world of *Beria*, from which it receives *Behinat Neshama* and *GAR de Beria*. And when the **Mochin** come to the world of **Assiya**, it ascends and clothes the world of *Yetzira*, from which it receives *Behinat Mochin de VAK* that are in *Yetzira*. Thus we have explained the first ascension that each *Partzuf* in *ABYA* obtained by the *MAN de Behina Bet*, which the lower ones raised (*Hallan*, Image no 7).

169) The second ascension occurs when the lower ones raise MAN from *Aviut de Behina Gimel*. At that time the *AHP* of the level of *Hochma* and *Haya* are sorted with respect to the completion of the second kind of ten *Sefirot*. These *Mochin* shine for the ZAT and the *Gufim*, too, as in the *Partzufim* of AK. And when the *Mochin* pass through the *Partzufim* ABYA, each *Partzuf* rises and grows through them, according to the *Mochin* it had attained.

170) Thus, when the **Mochin** came to **Partzuf Atik de Atzilut**, it rose and clothed the GAR of *Partzuf Hochma de AK*, called *AB de AK*, opposite the level of *AB de Galgalta de AK*, from which it receives the Light of *Haya de Yechida*. And when the **Mochin** reach **Partzuf AA de Atzilut**, it rises and clothes GAR *de SAG de AK*, opposite the level of *AB de Partzuf AB de AK*, from which it receives the Light of *Haya de Haya de AK*. And when the **Mochin** reach the **Partzufim AVI de Atzilut**, they rise and clothe the constant GAR *de Atik*, opposite the level of *AB* of *Partzuf SAG de AK*, from which they receive the Light of *Haya de Neshama de AK*, which shines for the ZAT and the *Gufim*, as well. And when the **Mochin** reach **YESHSUT de Atzilut**, they rise and clothe the constant GAR *de AA*, opposite the level of *AB de MA de AK*, from which they receive the Light of *Haya de MA de AK*. And when the **Mochin** reach **ZON de Atzilut**, they rise to GAR *de AVI*, opposite the level of *AB de BON de AK*, from which they receive the Light of *Haya de BON de AK*. Also, they receive the souls of the righteous from ZON.

And when the **Mochin** reach the world of **Beria**, it rises and clothes ZA *de Atzilut*, from which it receives *Behinat Ruach de Atzilut*. And when the **Mochin** reach the world of **Yetzira**, *Yetzira* ascends and clothes *Nukva de Atzilut*, and receives from her the Light of *Nefesh de Atzilut*. And when the **Mochin** reach the world of **Assiya**, it rises and clothes the world of *Beria*, and receives from it *Behinat GAR* and *Neshama de Beria*. At that time, the world of *Assiya* is completed with the full *NRN de BYA*. Thus we have explained the second ascension of each *Partzuf* of the *Partzufim* ABYA that rose and grew by the MAN of *Behina Gimel*, which the *NRN de Tzadikim* raised. (HaIlan, Image no. 8)

171) The third ascension is when the lower ones raise MAN from *Aviut* of *Behina Dalet*. At that time the *AHP* of the level of *Keter de Yechida* are sorted, with respect to the completion of the second kind of ten *Sefirot*. These *Mochin* shine to the ZAT and their *Gufim*, too, as in the *Partzufim* of AK. And when these *Mochin* traverse the *Partzufim* ABYA, each *Partzuf* rises, grows, and clothes its Superior, according to the measure of that *Mochin*.

172) Thus, when the **Mochin** reach **Partzuf Atik de Atzilut**, it rises and clothes the GAR of *Partzuf Galgalta de AK*, and receives its Light of *Yechida de Yechida* from there. And when the **Mochin** reach **Partzuf AA de Atzilut**, it rises and clothes the GAR de *Partzuf AB de AK*, and receives the Light of *Yechida de Haya de AK* from there. And when the **Mochin** reach **Partzuf AVI de Atzilut**, they rise and clothe GAR de *SAG de AK*, and receive the Light of *Yechida de Neshama de AK* from there. And when the **Mochin** reach **Partzuf YESHSUT**, they rise and clothe the GAR de *MA de AK*, and receive the Light of *Yechida de MA de AK* from there. And when the **Mochin** reach **ZON de Atzilut**, they rise and clothe GAR de *BON de AK*, and receive the Light of *Yechida de BON de AK* from there. And then the *NRN de Tzadikim* receive the Light of *Yechida* from the *ZON de Atzilut*.

And when the **Mochin** reach the world of **Beria**, it rises and clothes *Partzuf YESHSUT de Atzilut*, and receives *Neshama de Atzilut* from there. And when the **Mochin** reach the world of **Yetzira**, it rises and clothes *Partzuf ZA de Atzilut*, and receives *Behinat Ruach de Atzilut* from it. And when the **Mochin** reach the world of **Assiya**, it rises and clothes *Nukva de Atzilut*, and receives *Behinat* Light of *Nefesh de Atzilut* from her (*HaIlan*, Image no. 9).

173) It turns out that now, during the third ascension, the five *Partzufim* of *Atzilut* have each been completed with three levels, *Neshama*, *Haya*, and *Yechida* from AK, which they lacked in the constant state. It is therefore considered that these five *Partzufim* rose and clothed the five *Partzufim* of AK, each in its corresponding *Behina* in the *Partzufim* of AK.

Also, the *NRN de Tzadikim* received the GAR that they lacked. The three worlds BYA that were under the *Parsa de Atzilut* had only NRN of Light of *Hassadim* in the constant state, departed from *Hochma* by the force of the *Parsa* atop them. Now, however, they have risen above the *Parsa* and clothed YESHSUT and ZON *de Atzilut*, and have NRN *de Atzilut*, when the Light of *Hochma* shines in their *Hassadim*.

174) We should know that the *NRN de Tzadikim* permanently clothe only the *Partzufim* BYA below the *Parsa*:

- *Nefesh* clothes the ten *Sefirot* of *Assiya*;
- *Ruach*—the ten *Sefirot* of *Yetzira*;
- And *Neshama*—the ten *Sefirot* of *Beria*.

It turns out that although they receive from ZON *de Atzilut*, it still reaches them only through the *Partzufim* BYA, which clothe over them. Thus, the

NRN *de Tzadikim*, too, rise along with the ascensions of the three worlds BYA. It turns out that the worlds BYA, too, grow only according to the measure of reception of abundance by the NRN *de Tzadikim*, that is, according to the MAN, sorted by them.

175) Thus, it has been made clear that in the constant state, there is only VAK without a *Rosh* in all the worlds and *Partzufim*, each according to its *Behina*. Even the NRN *de Tzadikim* are only considered VAK, since although they have GAR *de Neshama* from the world of *Beria*, these GAR are regarded as VAK, compared to the world of *Atzilut*, since they are considered Light of *Hassadim*, separated from *Hochma*.

Also, the *Partzufim* of *Atzilut*, although there is GAR in their *Roshim*, they are merely regarded as VAK, since they do not shine to the *Gufim*. And all the *Mochin* that reach the worlds, which are more than the VAK, come only through the MAN that the *Tzadikim* (righteous) raise.

Yet, these *Mochin* can only be accepted in the *Partzufim* through the ascension of the lower one to the place of the Upper One. This is so because although they are considered completion of the second kind of ten *Sefirot*, with respect to the *Gufim* and the ZAT themselves, they are still regarded as sorting of AHP of the first kind, which are not completed in their own place, but only when they are at the place of the Upper One (Item 142). Hence, the five *Partzufim* of *Atzilut* cannot receive *Neshama*, *Haya*, and *Yechida de AK*, except when they rise and clothe them.

Also, the NRN and the three worlds BYA cannot receive NRN *de Atzilut*, except when they ascend and clothe YESHSUT and ZON *de Atzilut*. This is because these AHP of the second kind, which belong to ZAT, and expand from Above downwards to the place of ZAT, will only be sorted at the end of correction. Hence, when the three worlds BYA rise and clothe YESHSUT and ZON *de Atzilut*, their constant place, from *Parsa* downwards, remains utterly vacant of any Light of *Kedusha*.

And there is a difference between from the *Chazeh* upwards of the world of *Yetzira*, and from its *Chazeh* downwards. This is because it has been explained above that from the *Chazeh* of the world of *Yetzira* downwards, it is the permanent place of the *Klipot* (Item 149). But because of the flaw of the sin of *Adam ha Rishon*, the bottom four of *Yetzira* of *Kedusha* and the ten *Sefirot* of *Assiya* of *Kedusha* descended and clothed there (Item 156). Hence, during the ascensions of BYA to *Atzilut*, there is neither *Kedusha* nor *Klipot* from the *Chazeh de Yetzira* upwards. But from the *Chazeh de Yetzira* downwards, there are *Klipot*, as this is their section.

176) And since the additional *Mochin* from the levels of VAK come only through MAN of the lower ones, they are not constantly present in the *Partzufim*, as they are dependent on the actions of the lower ones. When they corrupt their actions, the *Mochin* leave (Item 162). However, the constant *Mochin* in the *Partzufim*, which were established by the force of the Emanator Himself, will never suffer any change, since they are not augmented by the lower ones, and are hence not flawed by them.

177) Do not wonder about AA de BON being considered *Keter de Atzilut*, and AVI as AB (Item 130). This is because AA is the bottom half of *Keter de BON*, and AVI are the bottom half of *HB de Nekudim*. Hence, its corresponding *Behina de AA* in AK should have been *Partzuf Keter de AK*, and the *Behina* corresponding AVI in AK should have been AB de AK.

The answer is that the *Partzufim* of BON are females, having no reception of their own, except what the males—the *Partzufim* of MA—impart them. Hence, all these discernments in the ascensions, which mean obtaining *Mochin* from the Upper One, are discerned only in the males, which are the *Partzufim* of MA. And since AA de MA does not have anything from *Behinat Keter*, but only the level of *Hochma*, and AVI de MA have nothing of *Behinat Hochma*, but only the level of *Bina* (Item 126), it is considered that their corresponding *Behina* in AK is AB de AK to AA, and SAG de AK to AVI. And *Partzuf Keter de AK* relates only to *Atik*, which took the whole of the level of *Keter de MA*.

178) You should also note what is said, that the ladder of degrees, as they are in the permanent *Mochin*, never changes by all these ascensions. After all, it has been explained that the reason for all these ascents was that the NRN de *Tzadikim*, which stand at BYA, cannot receive anything before all the Higher *Partzufim* transfer it to them from *Ein Sof*. To that extent, the Upper Ones themselves, through *Ein Sof*, grow and ascend, as well, each to their own Upper One (Item 161).

It turns out that to the extent that one degree rises, all the degrees through *Ein Sof* must rise, as well. For example, when ZON rise from their constant state, below *Tabur de AA*, clothing the *Chazeh de AA* downwards, then AA, too, rose one degree above his constant state, from *Peh de Atik* downwards, clothing GAR de Atik. Following him, all his internal degrees rose, too: his HGT rose to the place of the constant GAR, and his from the *Chazeh* to *Tabur* rose to the place of the constant *HGT*, and his from the *Tabur* down rose to the place from the *Chazeh* through *Tabur*.

Accordingly, ZON, which rose to the place from the *Chazeh* through *Tabur* of the constant AA, is still below *Tabur de AA*. This is because at that time, the below *Tabur de AA* had already ascended to the place from the *Chazeh* to *Tabur*. (*HaIlan*, Image no. 4: the ascensions of ZON in the constant state of the five *Partzufim* of *Atzilut*, which rise and clothe during the obtainment of *Neshama* to GAR *de* YESHSUT, over the from *Peh de AVI* downwards, over the from *Chazeh de AA* downwards.)

However, all the *Partzufim* of *Atzilut* rise at that time (*HaIlan*, Image no. 7). For this reason, you will find that there, the ZON still clothes YESHSUT from the *Peh* down, atop from *Chazeh de AVI* downwards, atop from *Tabur de AA* downwards. Thus, the ladder of degrees has not changed at all by the ascension. And it is likewise in all the ascensions (*HaIlan*, Images no. 3-last).

179) We should also know that even after the ascension of the *Partzufim*, they leave their entire degree in the permanent place, or in the place they were in the beginning, since there is no absence in the spiritual (Item 96). Thus, when GAR *de* AVI rise to GAR *de* AA, GAR *de* AVI still remain in the permanent place from *Peh de AA* downwards. And YESHSUT rise atop the HGT of the raised AVI, and receive from the actual GAR *de* AVI, which were there prior to the ascension.

Moreover, it is considered that there are three degrees together there. The raised GAR *de* AVI stand at the place of the constant GAR *de* AA, and bestow upon their permanent place from *Peh de AA* downwards, where YESHSUT are now present. Thus, GAR *de* AA and AVI and YESHSUT illuminate at the same time in the same place.

This is also the manner with all the *Partzufim de* AK and ABYA during the ascensions. For this reason, when a *Partzuf* ascends, we should always note the meaning of the ascension with respect to the Upper Ones in their constant state, and its value towards the Upper Ones, who also rose by one degree. (Examine all that in the book *HaIlan*. In Image no. 3, you will find the state of the *Partzufim* in their constant state. And in Images 4-6 you will find the three ascensions of ZA by the value of the five constant *Partzufim* of *Atzilut*. In images 7-9 you will find the three ascensions of all five *Partzufim* of *Atzilut*, by the value of the five permanent *Partzufim* of AK. And in images 10-12 you will find the three ascensions of all five *Partzufim* of AK in relation to the line of the permanent *Ein Sof*.)

THE DIVISION OF EACH PARTZUF INTO KETER AND ABYA

180) We should know that the general and the particular are equal. Also, what is discerned in the general, is also present in its details, and even in the smallest detail that can be. Also, the general reality is discerned in five worlds, AK and ABYA, where the world of AK is considered the *Keter* of the worlds, and the four worlds ABYA are regarded as *HB ZON* (Item 3). Similarly, there is not a single item in all four worlds ABYA that does not comprise these five: The *Rosh* of each *Partzuf* is considered its *Keter*, corresponding to the world of AK; and the *Guf*, from *Peh* to *Chazeh* is considered the *Atzilut* in it. From the place of *Chazeh* through *Tabur*, it is considered its *Beria*, and from *Tabur* down to its *Sium Raglin*, it is considered its *Yetzira* and *Assiya*.

181) And you should know that there are many appellations to the ten *Sefirot KHB, HGT, NHYM*. Sometimes they are called *GE* and *AHP*, or *KHB* and *ZON*, or *NRNHY*, or the tip of the *Yod* and the four letters, *Yod, Hey, Vav, Hey*, or simple *HaVaYaH* and *AB, SAG, MA*, and *BON*, being the four kinds of fillings in *HaVaYaH*:

- The filling of *AB* is *Yod, Hey, Viv, Hey* (the *Aleph* in *Vav* is replaced by a *Yod*);
- The filling of *SAG* is *Yod, Hey, Vav, Hey*;
- The filling of *MA* is *Yod, He* (*Aleph* replaces the *Yod*), *Vav, He*;
- The filling of *BON* is *Yod, Heh* (*Hey* replaces the *Yod*), *Vav, Heh*;

They are also called *AA, AVI*, and *ZON*. *AA* is *Keter*, *Aba* is *Hochma*, *Ima* is *Bina*, *ZA* is *HGT NHY*, and *Nukva de ZA* is *Malchut*.

And they are also called *AK* and *ABYA*, or *Keter* and *ABYA*. *Malchut de Keter* is called *Peh*, *Malchut de Atzilut* is called *Chazeh*, *Malchut de Beria* is called *Tabur*, *Malchut de Yetzira* is called *Ateret Yesod*, and the general *Malchut* is called *Sium Raglin*.

182) Know that you should always distinguish two instructions in these different names of the ten *Sefirot*:

1. Its equality to the *Sefira* to which it relates;
2. How it differs from that *Sefira* to which it relates, for which its name changed in the specific appellation.

For example, *Keter* of the ten *Sefirot* of Direct Light is *Ein Sof*, and each *Rosh* of a *Partzuf* is also called *Keter*. Similarly, all five *Partzufim* of AK are called *Keter*, too. *Partzuf Atik* is also called *Keter*, and *AA* is also called *Keter*. Hence, we should consider this: if they are all *Keter*, why do their names change to be called by these appellations? And also, if they all relate to *Keter*, should they not be equal to *Keter*?

Indeed, in a sense, they are all equal to *Keter*, as they are considered *Ein Sof*, for the rule is that as long as the Upper Light has not clothed in a *Kli*, it is considered *Ein Sof*. Hence, all five *Partzufim* of AK are regarded as Light without a *Kli* with respect to the world of *Tikkun*, since we have no perception in the *Kelim de Tzimtzum Aleph*. For this reason, for us, its Lights are considered *Ein Sof*.

Also, *Atik* and AA *de Atzilut* are both considered *Keter de Nekudim*. Yet, from a different angle, they are remote from one another, since *Keter de Ohr Yashar* is one *Sefira*, but in AK it contains five complete *Partzufim*, each of which contains *Rosh, Toch, Sof* (Item 142). Also, *Partzuf Atik* is only half of the Upper half of *Keter de Nekudim*, and *Partzuf AA* is half of the bottom half of *Keter de Nekudim* (Item 129). Similarly, these two instructions should be discerned in all the appellations of the *Sefirot*.

183) Know that the special instruction in these appellations of the ten *Sefirot* named *Keter* and ABYA is to show that it refers to the division of the ten *Sefirot* into *Kelim de Panim* and *Kelim de Achoraim*, made because of *Tzimtzum Bet* (Item 60). At that time, the ending *Malchut* rose to the place of *Bina de Guf*, called "*Tifferet* at the place of the *Chazeh*," where she ended the degree and created a new *Sium*, called "*Parsa* below the *Atzilut*" (Item 68).

And the *Kelim* from the *Chazeh* down went outside of *Atzilut*, and they are called BYA. The two thirds of *Tifferet* from *Chazeh* to *Sium* are called *Beria*; NHY are called *Yetzira*; and *Malchut* is called *Assiya*. It has also been explained that for this reason, each degree was divided into *Kelim de Panim* and *Kelim de Achoraim*: from the *Chazeh* upwards it is called *Kelim de Panim*, and from the *Chazeh* downwards it is called *Kelim de Achoraim*.

184) Hence, this discernment of the *Parsa* at the place of the *Chazeh* splits the degree into four special *Behinot*, called ABYA: *Atzilut*–through the *Chazeh*, and BYA–from the *Chazeh* down. And the beginning of the distinction is in AK itself. But there, the *Parsa* descended through its *Tabur* (Item 68); hence, the *Atzilut* in it is the AB SAG that end above its *Tabur*.

From its *Tabur* down it is its BYA, the place of the two *Partzufim* MA and BON in it. This is how the five *Partzufim* of AK are divided into ABYA by the force of the *Sium* of *Tzimtzum Bet*, called *Parsa*: *Galgalta* is the *Rosh*, AB SAG through its *Tabur* are *Atzilut*, and the MA and BON from its *Tabur* down is BYA.

185) Similarly, all five *Partzufim* of the world of *Atzilut* are divided into their own *Keter* and ABYA:

- AA is the *Rosh* of the whole of *Atzilut*.

- The Upper *AVI*, which are *AB*, clothing from *Peh de AA* down to the *Chazeh*, are *Atzilut*. And there, at the point of *Chazeh*, stands *Parsa*, which ends the *Behinat Atzilut* of the world of *Atzilut*.
- *YESHSUT*, which are *SAG*, clothing from *Chazeh de AA* through its *Tabur*, are *Beria de Atzilut*.
- *ZON*, which are *MA* and *BON*, clothing from *Tabur de AA* through the *Sium* of *Atzilut*, are *Yetzira* and *Assiya de Atzilut*.

Thus, the world of *Atzilut*, too, with its five *Partzufim*, is divided into *Rosh* and *ABYA*, as do the five *Partzufim* of *AK*. But here stands the *Parsa* at its place in *Chazeh de AA*, which is its true place (Item 127).

186) However, in the worlds in general, all three *Partzufim Galgalta, AB, SAG de AK* are regarded as the general *Rosh*. And the five *Partzufim* of the world of *Atzilut*, which clothe from *Tabur de AK* down to the general *Parsa*, being the *Parsa* that was made at the *Chazeh de Nekudot de SAG* (Item 66), are the general *Atzilut*. And the general three worlds *BYA* stand from *Parsa* down (Items 67-68).

187) In this very way, each particular degree in each of the worlds *ABYA* is divided into *Rosh* and *ABYA*, even *Malchut de Malchut de Assiya*, because it contains a *Rosh* and a *Guf*.

- The *Guf* is divided into *Chazeh, Tabur*, and *Sium Raglin*.
- The *Parsa*, below the *Atzilut* of that degree, stands at its *Chazeh* and ends the *Atzilut*.
- From *Chazeh* to *Tabur*, it is considered the *Beria* of the degree, which the point of *Tabur* concludes.
- From *Tabur* down to its *Sium Raglin*, it is considered *Yetzira* and *Assiya* of the degree.

And with respect to the *Sefirot*, *HGT* through *Chazeh* are considered *Atzilut*; the two bottom thirds of *Tifferet* from *Chazeh* to *Tabur* are considered *Beria*; *NHY* is *Yetzira*, and *Malchut* is *Assiya*.

188) For this reason, the *Rosh* of each degree is ascribed to *Behinat Keter*, or *Yechida*, or *Partzuf Galgalta*. The *Atzilut* in it, from *Peh* to *Chazeh*, is ascribed to *Hochma*, to *Ohr Haya*, or to *Partzuf AB*. The *Beria* in it, from *Chazeh* to *Tabur*, is ascribed to *Bina*, to *Ohr Neshama*, or to *Partzuf SAG*. And the *Yetzira* and *Assiya* in it, from *Tabur* downwards, are ascribed to *ZON*, to Lights *Ruach Nefesh*, or to *Partzuf MA* and *BON*. (Examine the book, *HaIlan*, from Image no. 3 onwards, how each *Partzuf* is divided by these *Behinot*.)

HaIlan (The Tree)

Illustrations and References

DIAGRAM 1

- Item 1 depicts the *Rosh, Toch, Sof* of *Partzuf Keter de AK*.

- Item 2 depicts *Partzuf AB de AK* in *Rosh, Toch, Sof* and how it clothes *Partzuf Keter de AK* from its *Peh* down.

- Item 3 depicts *Partzuf SAG de AK* in *Rosh, Toch, Sof* and how it clothes *Partzuf AB de AK* from its *Peh* down.

DIAGRAM 1, ITEM 1

This is *Partzuf Keter de AK*, the first ten *Sefirot* that expanded from *Ein Sof* into the space after the *Tzimtzum*. Its *Rosh* touches *Ein Sof*, Above, and its *Sium Raglin* is in the middle, central point, which is this world. It contains three *Behinot* of ten *Sefirot*: ten *Sefirot de* (of) *Rosh*, ten *Sefirot de Toch*, and ten *Sefirot de Sof*.

The ten *Sefirot de Rosh* are called "the roots of the ten *Sefirot*," since there is the beginning of their creation, through the meeting of the ten *Sefirot de Ohr Yashar* by the *Zivug de Hakaa* in the *Masach* in *Malchut de Rosh*, which raises ten *Sefirot de Ohr Hozer* that clothe the ten *Sefirot de Ohr Yashar*, which extend from *Ein Sof* (as it is written in *The Tree of Life*, Gate 47, Chapter 1). The ten *Sefirot de Ohr Yashar* are arranged from Above downwards, and their opposite is the *Ohr Hozer*, where they are arranged from below Upwards. *Malchut* of the ten *Sefirot de Rosh* is called *Peh*.

The ten *Sefirot de Toch* in the *Partzufim* of AK is called *Akudim*, in *Partzuf Keter*, in AB, as well as in SAG. Yet, in *Partzuf Keter*, the Upper Light was not yet distinguished in ten *Sefirot*, and the difference between them was only in impressions (as the Ari wrote in *The Tree of Life*, Section *Present and Not Present*, Chapter 1). Also, *Malchut* of the ten *Sefirot de Toch* is called *Tabur*.

The ten *Sefirot de Sof* are considered the *Sium* of each *Sefira* of the ten *Sefirot* through *Malchut*. The *Partzuf* ends in the *Sefira* of *Malchut*, which is why she is called *Sium Raglin*.

DIAGRAM 1, ITEM 2

This is *Partzuf AB de AK*, the second *Hitpashtut* of ten *Sefirot* from *Ein Sof* into the space, after the *Tzimtzum*. It begins from *Hochma*, and lacks the Light of *Keter*. It is emanated and comes out of *Malchut de Rosh* of *Partzuf Keter*, which is called *Peh*. Hence, it clothes *Partzuf Keter* from its *Peh* down to *Tabur* of *Partzuf Keter*.

Its ten *Sefirot de Rosh* are like the ten *Sefirot de Rosh* of *Partzuf Keter de AK*, except that it lacks *Keter*. The elicitation of these ten *Sefirot* is elaborated on in *The Tree of Life*, Section *Present and Not Present*, Chapters 1 and 2, as well as in *Talmud Eser Sefirot*, Part 5, where these words of the Ari are thoroughly explained.

Here, the ten *Sefirot de Toch* become more conspicuous than the ten *Sefirot de Toch* in *Partzuf Keter*, since here there were ten entrances and ten exits in the order of *Present and Not Present* (as it is written in *The Tree of Life*, Section *Present and Not Present*, and in *Talmud Eser Sefirot*, Part 5). In the *Sefira Keter* of the ten *Sefirot de Toch*, there are two *Kelim*, called *Yod-Hey*. This is so in their *Sefira Hochma*, too, but in the *Sefira Bina*, the *Yod-Hey* are only in one *Kli*, and the *Vav* is in the *Kli* of *Yesod*, and the bottom *Hey* is in *Malchut*.

The ten *Sefirot de Sof* are the same as in *Partzuf Keter de AK*, except its *Sium Raglin* is above the *Tabur* of *Partzuf Keter*.

DIAGRAM 1, ITEM 3

This is *Partzuf SAG de AK*, the third expansion of ten *Sefirot* from *Ein Sof* into the space after the *Tzimtzum*, in *Rosh, Toch, Sof*. It is emanated and comes out of the *Peh* of *Partzuf AB de AK*. It begins from *Bina* and lacks the Lights *Keter* and *Hochma*, and clothes from the *Peh* of *Partzuf AB de AK* downwards, although below it is longer than it, since it expanded downwards, to the same level as the *Sium Raglin* of *Partzuf Keter de AK*.

DIAGRAM 2, ITEM 1

This is the state of *Partzuf SAG de AK* during *Tzimtzum Aleph*. It is presented above, in Diagram 1, Item 3, but here there is the additional distinction of its own two *Partzufim*: *Partzuf Taamim*, from *Peh* to *Tabur*, and *Partzuf Nekudim*, from *Tabur* down. You will find their explanation in *Talmud Eser Sefirot*, Part 6, p 390.

Thus far, the three lower worlds *Beria*, *Yetzira*, and *Assiya* did not come to any existence, since *SAG de AK*, too, extended through the point of this world. It follows that it was considered *Atzilut* down to the point of this world.

DIAGRAM 2, ITEM 2

This is the state of *SAG de AK* during *Tzimtzum Bet*, prior to the *Zivug* in *Nikvey Eynaim*, which was done in order to emanate the ten *Sefirot de Nekudim*. Because of the descent of *SAG* into the inner *MA* and *BON de AK*, *Bina* received the *Behinat Malchut*. Thus, the ending *Malchut*, which stood at the point of this world, rose to the place of *Tabur*, and the mating *Malchut*, which stood at *Peh de Rosh de SAG*, rose to the place of *Nikvey Eynaim de Rosh de SAG*, and the *Awzen, Hotem, Peh de Rosh* descended to *Behinat Guf de SAG*. Also, the Light was emptied from *Tabur* down, and this, in general, is *Partzuf SAG*.

And there is *Rosh, Toch, Sof*, called *HBD, HGT, NHYM* in its own *Partzuf Nekudot de SAG*, standing entirely below the *Tabur* (see above, diagram 2, Item 1). In it, too, as in general, it is considered that the ending *Malchut* rose to *Bina de Guf*, called *Tifferet*, in the place of its *Chazeh*, where the line of *Ein Sof* ended, and below it the *Parsa* was established, since this is where *Behinat Atzilut* ended.

From there down, it became the place of the three worlds *Beria, Yetzira*, and *Assiya*. The world of *Beria* was made of the two bottom thirds of *Tifferet*, down to its *Sium*. The world of *Yetzira* was made of *Netzah, Hod*, and *Yesod*, and the world of *Assiya* was made of *Malchut*. This is thoroughly explained in the words of the Ari, p 8, and in *Ohr Pashut* there.

DIAGRAM 2, ITEM 3

This is the state in *SAG de AK* during the *Zivug* that was made in *Nikvey Eynaim*: the *Awzen, Hotem, Peh* came out of *Behinat Rosh* and into *Guf*, below the place of the *Zivug de Rosh*. Yet, since there is no absence in the spiritual, two kinds of *Awzen, Hotem*, and *Peh* are discerned here: the first are the *Awzen, Hotem, Peh* at their exit spot, their place at the *Rosh*, as in the beginning. The second are the *Awzen, Hotem, Peh* that descended into actual *Behinat Guf* below *Peh de Rosh de SAG*. They are called *Awzen, Hotem, Peh* not in the place of their exit. And all those are called "inner *Awzen, Hotem, Peh*."

Here, the ten *Sefirot de Toch* through *Tabur* are called *Akudim*, as prior to *Tzimtzum Bet*, since the ten *Sefirot* that came out of the *Zivug de Nikvey Eynaim* could only manifest below *Tabur*. These are called "ten *Sefirot de Nekudim*," and they came out primarily outside of *Partzuf SAG*, although their internality emerged in *AK* itself.

Also, they are called MA and BON de AK, since the internality of the Upper three of *Nekudim* is called MA *de* AK and the internality of the lower seven of *Nekudim* is called BON *de* AK. They end at the point of *Sium* of *Tzimtzum Bet*, called "the *Parsa* between *Atzilut* and *Beria*." Below it are the three worlds, lower *Beria*, *Yetzira*, and *Assiya*.

DIAGRAM 2, ITEM 4

This is an external *Partzuf Awzen, Hotem, Peh de SAG de AK*, through *Tabur*. From *Tabur* down, it is *Partzuf* of ten *Sefirot de Nekudim*, which end at the *Parsa*. Below *Parsa* stand the three worlds, lower *Beria*, *Yetzira*, and *Assiya*.

In the external ones, the *Awzen, Hotem, Peh* are divided into two *Behinot Awzen, Hotem, Peh*: external *Awzen, Hotem, Peh*, at the place of their elicitation, standing above the *Peh*, and external *Awzen, Hotem, Peh*, not in their elicitation place, standing from below the *Peh* through *Tabur*. Their Upper three are attached to the bottom lip. It is called *Shibolet ha Zakan* (the bit of hair under the bottom lip), and the Upper three are primarily the Light of *Awzen*, but their *Behinot Hotem, Peh* are included in them, too. These are the roots of the Upper three of *Nekudim*.

Their lower seven, which are the actual *Hotem* and *Peh*, stand below *Shibolet ha Zakan* and spread through the *Tabur*. These external *Awzen, Hotem, Peh* are also called *Dikna* (beard) *de SAG de AK*, and you will find a detailed explanation of them in *Talmud Eser Sefirot*, Part 6, p 409, Item 20.

The ten *Sefirot de Nekudim* stand from *Tabur* downwards. Their First three are in *Tikkun Kavim* and clothe MA *de* AK, and their bottom seven are one below the other, as in *Tzimtzum Aleph*, clothing BON *de* AK. Below them are the *Parsa* and the three worlds *Beria*, *Yetzira*, and *Assiya*, under the *Parsa*.

DIAGRAM 3, ITEM 1

This is the constant state of the five *Partzufim* of AK, from which the five *Partzufim* of the new MA emerged, called "the five constant *Partzufim* of *Atzilut*." Once they were established, no diminution will ever occur in them.

It also explains the division of each *Partzuf* into *Keter, Atzilut, Beria, Yetzira*, and *Assiya*, which are also called *Keter*, AB, SAG, MA, and BON, or *Yechida, Haya, Neshama, Ruach*, and *Nefesh*. Each *Rosh*, through the *Peh*, is called *Keter* or *Yechida*. From *Peh* through *Chazeh* in each of them, it is called *Atzilut* or AB or *Haya*. And from *Chazeh* to *Tabur* in each of them, it is called *Beria* or *Neshama* or SAG. And from *Tabur* down to each of them, it is called *Yetzira* and *Assiya*, or MA and BON, or *Ruach-Nefesh*.

Additionally, it explains their clothing within one another. Each clothes its Superior from the *Peh* of its Superior downwards in such a way that the *Rosh* of each lower one clothes the *AB* and *Atzilut* of the Upper One, and *AB* and *Atzilut* of the lower one clothe the *SAG* and *Beria* of its Superior.

Also, *SAG* and *Beria* of each lower one clothe *MA* and *BON*, which is *Yetzira* and *Assiya* of the Upper One. Thus, the *Peh* of the Upper One is considered the *Galgalta* of the lower one, and the *Chazeh* of the Upper One is considered *Peh* of the lower one, and *Tabur* of the Upper One is considered the *Chazeh* of the lower one.

Also, it explains the elicitation of the new MA in each of the five *Partzufim* of *Atzilut*, the MA in its corresponding *Partzuf* in AK.

DIAGRAM 4
The state of ZA during its ascension to obtain *Neshama*, with respect to the constant five *Partzufim* of AK and *Atzilut*, and how it takes and nourishes off *Beria de BON de AK*—its corresponding *Partzuf* in AK.

DIAGRAM 5
The state of ZA during its ascension to obtain *Haya*, with respect to the constant five *Partzufim* of AK and *Atzilut*, and how it takes and nourishes off *Atzilut de BON de AK*—its corresponding *Partzuf* in AK.

DIAGRAM 6
The state of ZA during its ascension to obtain *Yechida*, with respect to the constant five *Partzufim* of AK and *Atzilut*, and how it takes and nourishes off *Rosh de BON de AK*—its corresponding *Partzuf* in AK.

DIAGRAM 7
The states of the five *Partzufim* of *Atzilut* upon their ascent to obtain *Neshama*, with respect to the five constant *Partzufim* of AK, and how each takes and nourishes off its corresponding *Partzuf* in AK.

DIAGRAM 8
The states of the five *Partzufim* of *Atzilut* upon their ascent to obtain *Haya*, with respect to the five constant *Partzufim* of AK, and how each takes and nourishes off its corresponding *Partzuf* in AK.

DIAGRAM 9
The states of the five *Partzufim* of *Atzilut* upon their ascent to obtain *Yechida*, with respect to the five constant *Partzufim* of AK, and how each takes and nourishes off its corresponding *Partzuf* in AK.

DIAGRAMS 10, 11, 12

These depict how the ladder of degrees never changes, and the degrees, as a whole, always remain as they were in their beginning, at the time of the elicitation of the new MA, as in the constant state. This is so because when ZA ascends and obtains *Neshama*, all the degrees rise along with it—the five *Partzufim* of AK and *Atzilut*—and each obtains the *Behinat Neshama* related to it. It is similar in obtaining *Haya de* ZA and obtaining *Yechida de* ZA.

Diagram 10 is the state of the five *Partzufim* of AK as they ascend to obtain *Neshama*. Diagram 11 depicts their state when they obtain *Haya*, and Diagram 12 is their state when they obtain *Yechida*.

Diagram no. 1

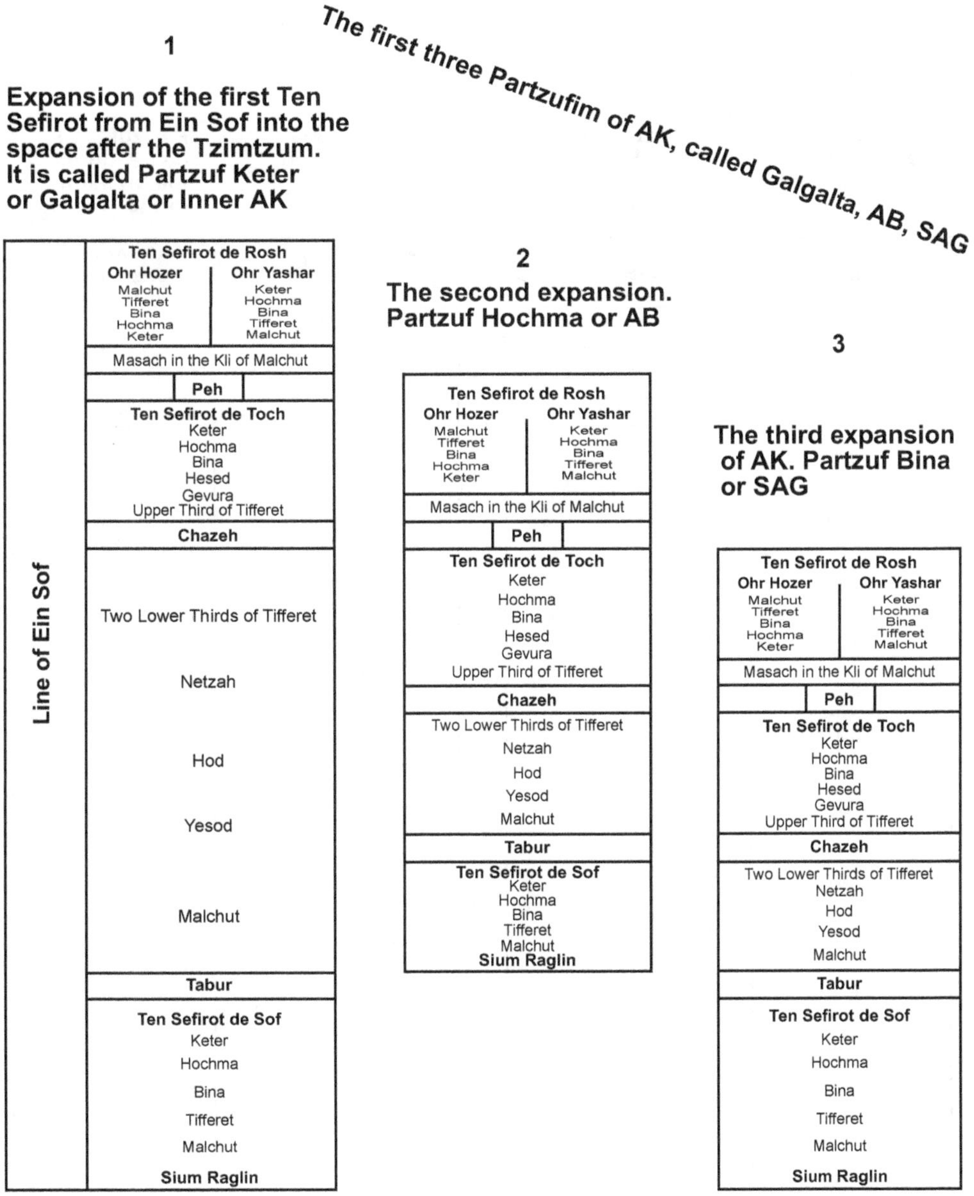

The first three Partzufim of AK, called Galgalta, AB, SAG

1

Expansion of the first Ten Sefirot from Ein Sof into the space after the Tzimtzum. It is called Partzuf Keter or Galgalta or Inner AK

Line of Ein Sof	Ten Sefirot de Rosh	
	Ohr Hozer	Ohr Yashar
	Malchut Tifferet Bina Hochma Keter	Keter Hochma Bina Tifferet Malchut
	Masach in the Kli of Malchut	
	Peh	
	Ten Sefirot de Toch Keter Hochma Bina Hesed Gevura Upper Third of Tifferet	
	Chazeh	
	Two Lower Thirds of Tifferet	
	Netzah	
	Hod	
	Yesod	
	Malchut	
	Tabur	
	Ten Sefirot de Sof Keter Hochma Bina Tifferet Malchut Sium Raglin	

2

The second expansion. Partzuf Hochma or AB

Ten Sefirot de Rosh	
Ohr Hozer	Ohr Yashar
Malchut Tifferet Bina Hochma Keter	Keter Hochma Bina Tifferet Malchut
Masach in the Kli of Malchut	
Peh	
Ten Sefirot de Toch Keter Hochma Bina Hesed Gevura Upper Third of Tifferet	
Chazeh	
Two Lower Thirds of Tifferet	
Netzah	
Hod	
Yesod	
Malchut	
Tabur	
Ten Sefirot de Sof Keter Hochma Bina Tifferet Malchut Sium Raglin	

3

The third expansion of AK. Partzuf Bina or SAG

Ten Sefirot de Rosh	
Ohr Hozer	Ohr Yashar
Malchut Tifferet Bina Hochma Keter	Keter Hochma Bina Tifferet Malchut
Masach in the Kli of Malchut	
Peh	
Ten Sefirot de Toch Keter Hochma Bina Hesed Gevura Upper Third of Tifferet	
Chazeh	
Two Lower Thirds of Tifferet Netzah Hod Yesod Malchut	
Tabur	
Ten Sefirot de Sof Keter Hochma Bina Tifferet Malchut Sium Raglin	

Diagram no. 2

1	2	3	4
Partzuf SAG de AK during Tzimtzum Aleph	**Partzuf SAG de AK during the ascent to Tzimtzum Bet**	**Partzuf SAG de AK during the Katnut**	**Partzuf SAG de AK during the breaking of the vessels**

Column 1: Partzuf SAG de AK during Tzimtzum Aleph

Ten Sefirot de Rosh
- Galgalta - Keter
- Eynaim - Hochma
- Awzen - Bina
- Hotem - Tifferet
- Peh - Malchut

Peh

Taamim de SAG
- Keter
- Hochma
- Bina
- Hesed
- Gevura
- Tifferet
- Netzah
- Hod
- Yesod
- Malchut

Tabur

Nekudot de SAG
- Keter
- Hochma
- Bina

- - - - - - - - - -
- Hesed
- Gevura
- Upper Third of Tifferet
- - - - - - - - - -

Chazeh

- Two Lower Thirds of Tifferet
- - - - - - - - - -
- Netzah
- Hod
- Yesod
- - - - - - - - - -
- Malchut

Column 2: Partzuf SAG de AK during the ascent to Tzimtzum Bet

Ten Sefirot de Rosh
- Galgalta - Keter
- Eynaim - Hochma

Nikvey Eynaim
- Awzen - Bina
- Hotem - Tifferet
- Peh - Malchut

Peh

Tabur

Place of the World of Atzilut

Parsa

Place of the World of Beria

Place of the World of Yetzira

Place of the World of Assiya

Column 3: Partzuf SAG de AK during the Katnut

Ten Sefirot de Rosh
- Galgalta - Keter
- Eynaim - Hochma

Nikvey Eynaim
- Awzen - Bina
- Hotem - Tifferet
- Peh - Malchut

Chazeh

YESHSUT
First Rosh of the World of Nekudim

Tabur

Katnut of the World of Nekudim
Keter

Bina	Hochma

- Hesed
- Gevura
- Tifferet
- Netzah
- Hod
- Yesod
- Malchut

Parsa

Column 4: Partzuf SAG de AK during the breaking of the vessels

Ten Sefirot de Rosh
- Galgalta - Keter
- Eynaim - Hochma
- Awzen - Bina
- Hotem - Tifferet
- Peh - Malchut

Peh

Chazeh

YESHSUT
First Rosh of the World of Nekudim

Tabur

Gadlut of the World of Nekudim
Keter

Bina	Hochma

- Daat
- Hesed
- Gevura
- Upper Third of Tifferet

Parsa

- Two Lower Thirds of Tifferet

Hod	Netzah

- Yesod

- Malchut

Breaking of the Vessels

Point of this world

Diagram no. 3

The constant state of the five Partzufim of AK and the five Partzufim of Atzilut, which are never reduced from this level

Dotted lines extending from each Rosh of the five Partzufim of Atzilut to its corresponding Partzuf in AK indicate the level from which they take and nourish

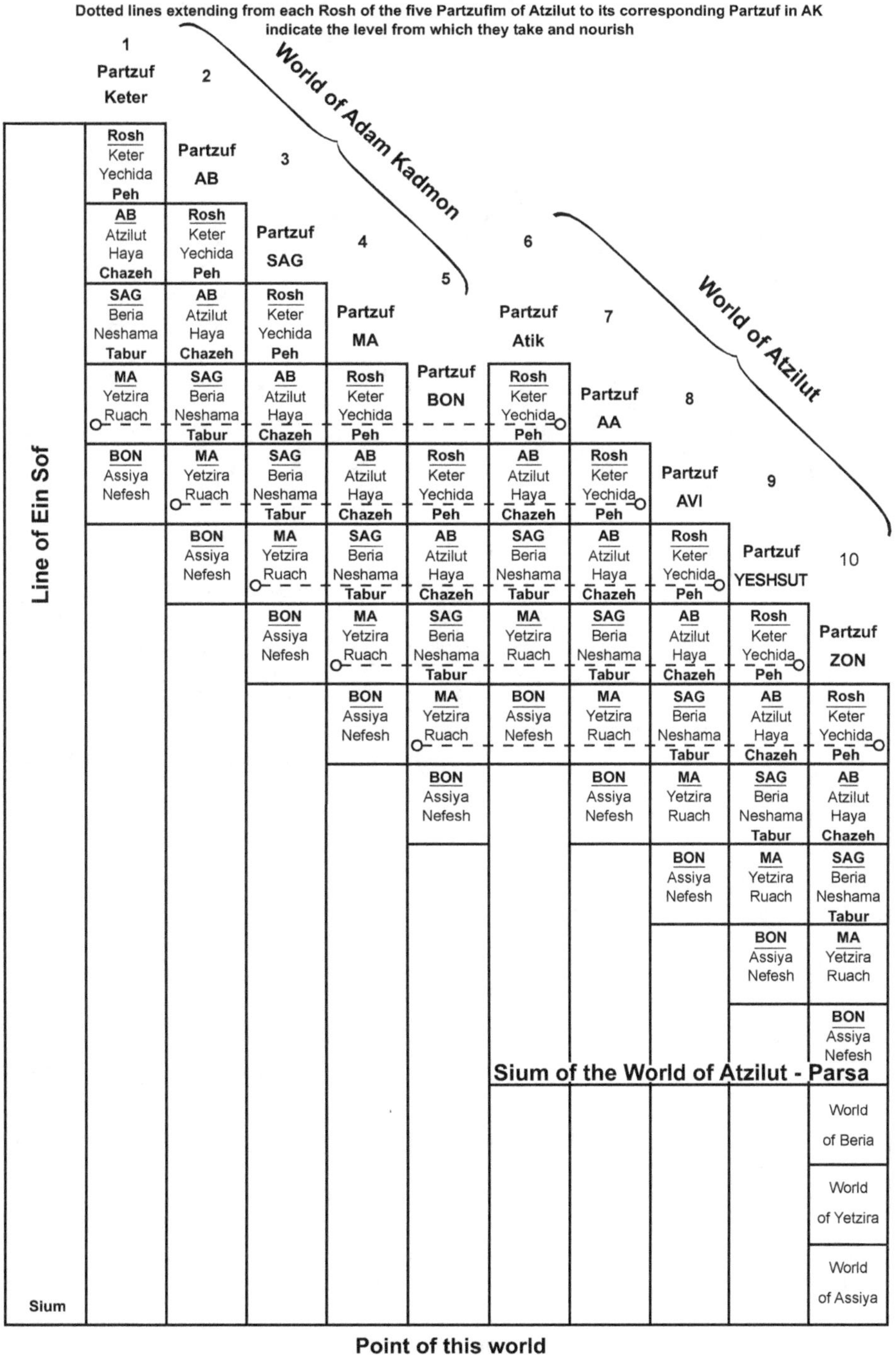

#	Partzuf (AK)	#	Partzuf (Atzilut)
1	Partzuf Keter	6	Partzuf Atik
2	Partzuf AB	7	Partzuf AA
3	Partzuf SAG	8	Partzuf AVI
4	Partzuf MA	9	Partzuf YESHSUT
5	Partzuf BON	10	Partzuf ZON

World of Adam Kadmon
World of Atzilut

Line of Ein Sof

Partzuf structure levels (repeated across columns):
- Rosh / Keter / Yechida / Peh
- AB / Atzilut / Haya / Chazeh
- SAG / Beria / Neshama / Tabur
- MA / Yetzira / Ruach
- BON / Assiya / Nefesh

Sium of the World of Atzilut – Parsa

- World of Beria
- World of Yetzira
- World of Assiya

Sium

Point of this world

Diagram no. 4

Position of ZA after obtaining **Neshama** in the constant state of the five Partzufim of AK and Atzilut

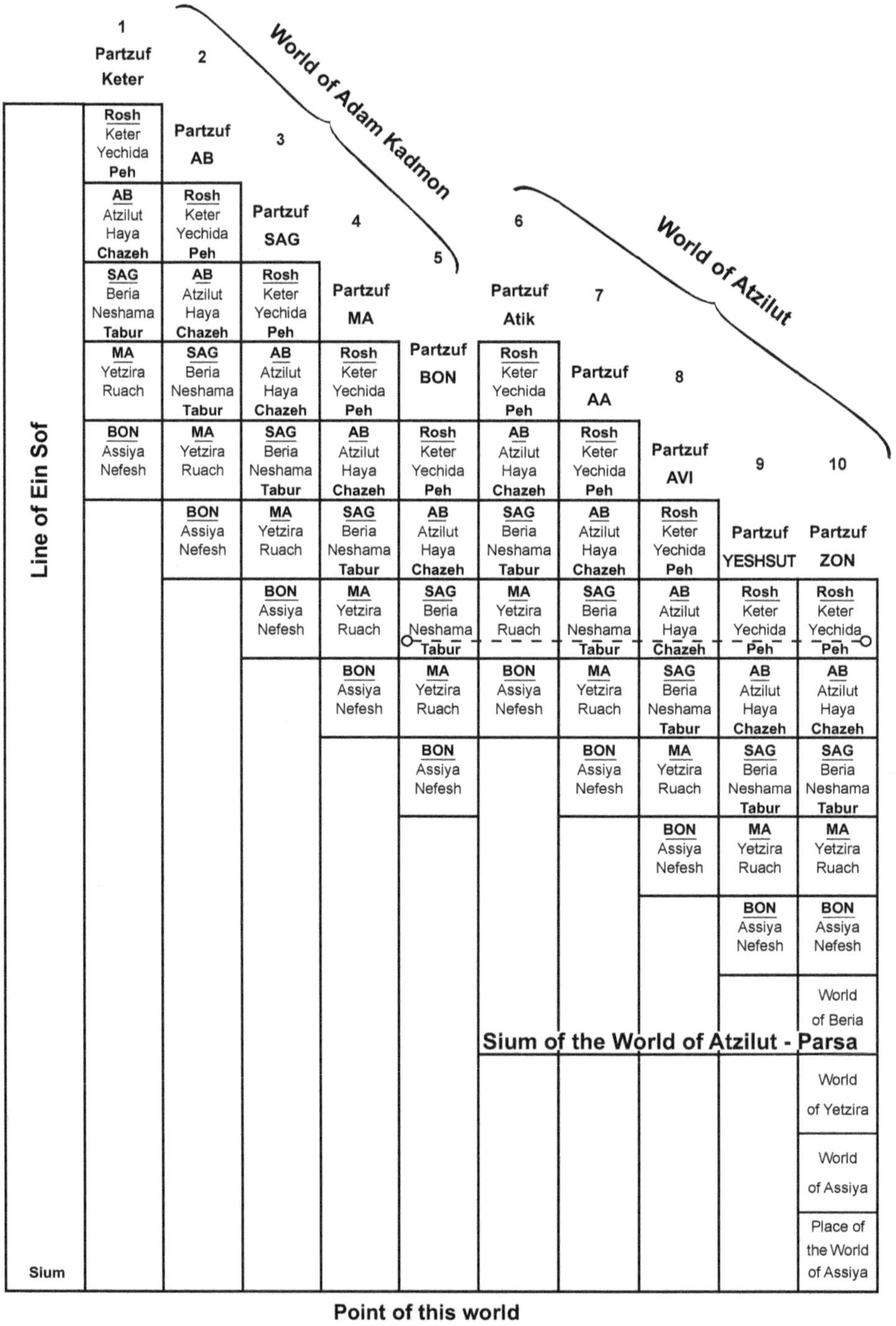

Diagram no. 5

Position of ZA after obtaining **Haya** in the constant state of the five Partzufim of AK and Atzilut

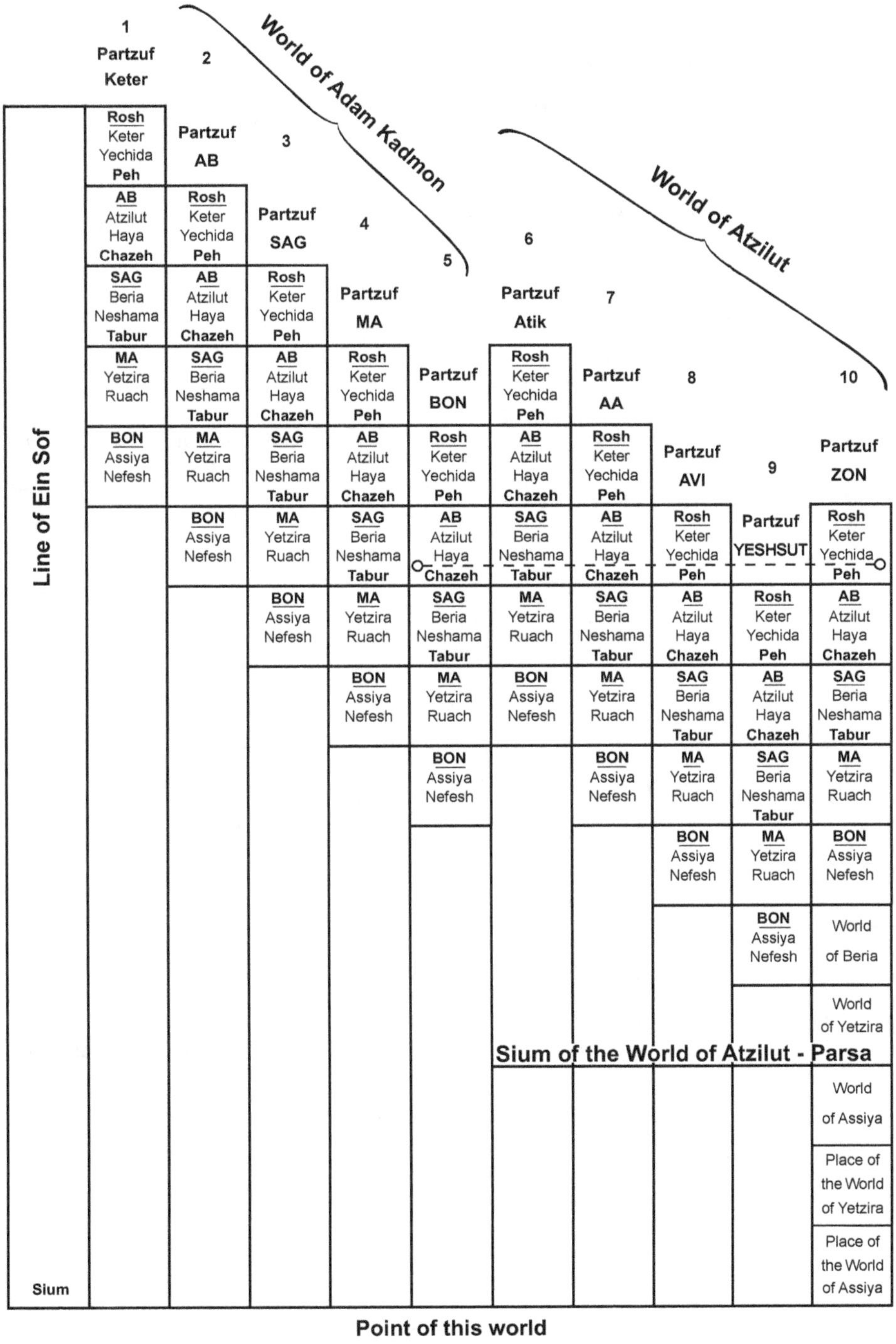

World of Adam Kadmon — *World of Atzilut*

Line of Ein Sof	1 Partzuf Keter	2 Partzuf AB	3 Partzuf SAG	4 Partzuf MA	5 Partzuf BON	6 Partzuf Atik	7 Partzuf AA	8 Partzuf AVI	9 Partzuf YESHSUT	10 Partzuf ZON
	Rosh / Keter / Yechida / Peh									
	AB / Atzilut / Haya / Chazeh	Rosh / Keter / Yechida / Peh								
	SAG / Beria / Neshama / Tabur	AB / Atzilut / Haya / Chazeh	Rosh / Keter / Yechida / Peh							
	MA / Yetzira / Ruach	SAG / Beria / Neshama / Tabur	AB / Atzilut / Haya / Chazeh	Rosh / Keter / Yechida / Peh		Rosh / Keter / Yechida / Peh				
	BON / Assiya / Nefesh	MA / Yetzira / Ruach	SAG / Beria / Neshama / Tabur	AB / Atzilut / Haya / Chazeh	Rosh / Keter / Yechida / Peh	AB / Atzilut / Haya / Chazeh	Rosh / Keter / Yechida / Peh			
		BON / Assiya / Nefesh	MA / Yetzira / Ruach	SAG / Beria / Neshama / Tabur	AB / Atzilut / Haya / Chazeh ─o─	SAG / Beria / Neshama / Tabur	AB / Atzilut / Haya / Chazeh	Rosh / Keter / Yechida / Peh		Rosh / Keter / Yechida / Peh ─o─
			BON / Assiya / Nefesh	MA / Yetzira / Ruach	SAG / Beria / Neshama / Tabur	MA / Yetzira / Ruach	SAG / Beria / Neshama / Tabur	AB / Atzilut / Haya / Chazeh	Rosh / Keter / Yechida / Peh	AB / Atzilut / Haya / Chazeh
				BON / Assiya / Nefesh	MA / Yetzira / Ruach	BON / Assiya / Nefesh	MA / Yetzira / Ruach	SAG / Beria / Neshama / Tabur	AB / Atzilut / Haya / Chazeh	SAG / Beria / Neshama / Tabur
					BON / Assiya / Nefesh		BON / Assiya / Nefesh	MA / Yetzira / Ruach	SAG / Beria / Neshama / Tabur	MA / Yetzira / Ruach
								BON / Assiya / Nefesh	MA / Yetzira / Ruach	BON / Assiya / Nefesh
									BON / Assiya / Nefesh	World of Beria
										World of Yetzira

Sium of the World of Atzilut - Parsa

	World of Assiya
	Place of the World of Yetzira
	Place of the World of Assiya

Sium

Point of this world

Diagram no. 6

Position of ZA after obtaining **Yechida** in the constant state of the five Partzufim of AK and Atzilut

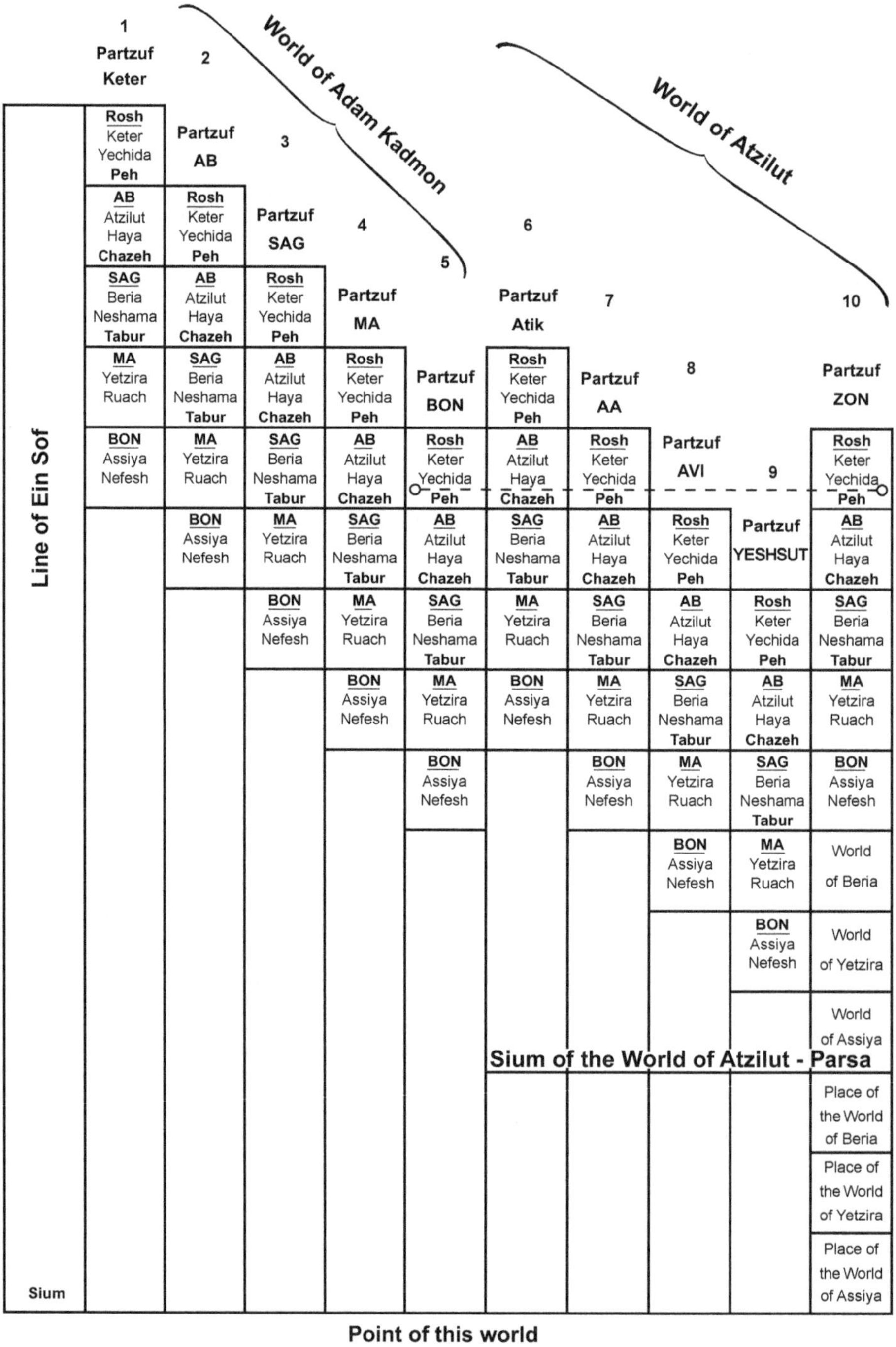

World of Adam Kadmon | *World of Atzilut*

1 Partzuf Keter	2 Partzuf AB	3 Partzuf SAG	4 Partzuf MA	5 Partzuf BON	6 Partzuf Atik	7 Partzuf AA	8 Partzuf AVI	9 Partzuf YESHSUT	10 Partzuf ZON
Rosh / Keter / Yechida / Peh									
AB / Atzilut / Haya / Chazeh	Rosh / Keter / Yechida / Peh								
SAG / Beria / Neshama / Tabur	AB / Atzilut / Haya / Chazeh	Rosh / Keter / Yechida / Peh							
MA / Yetzira / Ruach	SAG / Beria / Neshama / Tabur	AB / Atzilut / Haya / Chazeh	Rosh / Keter / Yechida / Peh		Rosh / Keter / Yechida / Peh				Partzuf ZON
BON / Assiya / Nefesh	MA / Yetzira / Ruach	SAG / Beria / Neshama / Tabur	AB / Atzilut / Haya / Chazeh	Rosh / Keter / Yechida / Peh	AB / Atzilut / Haya / Chazeh	Rosh / Keter / Yechida / Peh			Rosh / Keter / Yechida / Peh
	BON / Assiya / Nefesh	MA / Yetzira / Ruach	SAG / Beria / Neshama / Tabur	AB / Atzilut / Haya / Chazeh	SAG / Beria / Neshama / Tabur	AB / Atzilut / Haya / Chazeh	Rosh / Keter / Yechida / Peh		AB / Atzilut / Haya / Chazeh
		BON / Assiya / Nefesh	MA / Yetzira / Ruach	SAG / Beria / Neshama / Tabur	MA / Yetzira / Ruach	SAG / Beria / Neshama / Tabur	AB / Atzilut / Haya / Chazeh	Rosh / Keter / Yechida / Peh	SAG / Beria / Neshama / Tabur
			BON / Assiya / Nefesh	MA / Yetzira / Ruach	BON / Assiya / Nefesh	MA / Yetzira / Ruach	SAG / Beria / Neshama / Tabur	AB / Atzilut / Haya / Chazeh	MA / Yetzira / Ruach
				BON / Assiya / Nefesh		BON / Assiya / Nefesh	MA / Yetzira / Ruach	SAG / Beria / Neshama / Tabur	BON / Assiya / Nefesh
							BON / Assiya / Nefesh	MA / Yetzira / Ruach	World of Beria
								BON / Assiya / Nefesh	World of Yetzira
									World of Assiya

Line of Ein Sof

Sium of the World of Atzilut - **Parsa**

Place of the World of Beria

Place of the World of Yetzira

Place of the World of Assiya

Sium

Point of this world

Diagram no. 7

Position of all five Partzufim of Atzilut and the three worlds BYA after obtaining their **Neshama** in the constant state of the five Partzufim of AK

Dotted lines extending from each Rosh of the five Partzufim of Atzilut to its corresponding Partzuf in AK indicate the level from which they take and nourish

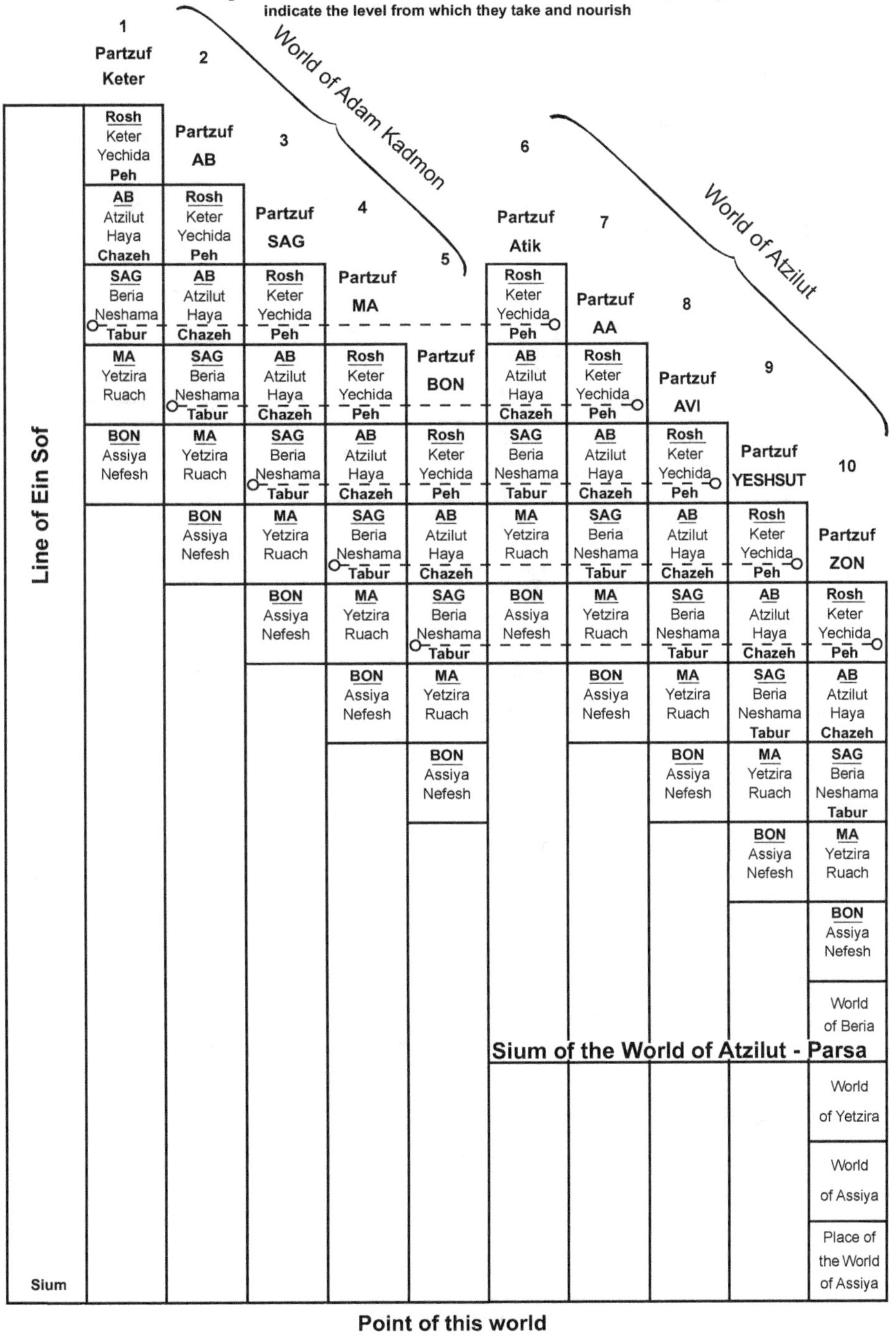

World of Adam Kadmon (columns 1–5: Partzuf Keter, Partzuf AB, Partzuf SAG, Partzuf MA, Partzuf BON)

World of Atzilut (columns 6–10: Partzuf Atik, Partzuf AA, Partzuf AVI, Partzuf YESHSUT, Partzuf ZON)

1	2 Partzuf Keter	3 Partzuf AB	4 Partzuf SAG	5 Partzuf MA	6 Partzuf BON	7 Partzuf Atik	8 Partzuf AA	9 Partzuf AVI	10 Partzuf YESHSUT / ZON
Line of Ein Sof	Rosh — Keter / Yechida / Peh								
	AB — Atzilut / Haya / Chazeh	Rosh — Keter / Yechida / Peh							
	SAG — Beria / Neshama / Tabur	AB — Atzilut / Haya / Chazeh	Rosh — Keter / Yechida / Peh						
	MA — Yetzira / Ruach	SAG — Beria / Neshama / Tabur	AB — Atzilut / Haya / Chazeh	Rosh — Keter / Yechida / Peh		Rosh — Keter / Yechida / Peh			
	BON — Assiya / Nefesh	MA — Yetzira / Ruach	SAG — Beria / Neshama / Tabur	AB — Atzilut / Haya / Chazeh	Rosh — Keter / Yechida / Peh	AB — Atzilut / Haya / Chazeh	Rosh — Keter / Yechida / Peh		
		BON — Assiya / Nefesh	MA — Yetzira / Ruach	SAG — Beria / Neshama / Tabur	AB — Atzilut / Haya / Chazeh	SAG — Beria / Neshama / Tabur	AB — Atzilut / Haya / Chazeh	Rosh — Keter / Yechida / Peh	
			BON — Assiya / Nefesh	MA — Yetzira / Ruach	SAG — Beria / Neshama / Tabur	BON — Assiya / Nefesh	SAG — Beria / Neshama / Tabur	AB — Atzilut / Haya / Chazeh	Rosh — Keter / Yechida / Peh
				BON — Assiya / Nefesh	MA — Yetzira / Ruach		BON — Assiya / Nefesh	MA — Yetzira / Ruach	AB — Atzilut / Haya / Chazeh
					BON — Assiya / Nefesh			BON — Assiya / Nefesh	SAG — Beria / Neshama / Tabur
									MA — Yetzira / Ruach
									BON — Assiya / Nefesh

Sium of the World of Atzilut — Parsa

- World of Beria
- World of Yetzira
- World of Assiya
- Place of the World of Assiya

Sium

Point of this world

Diagram no. 8

Position of all five Partzufim of Atzilut and the three worlds BYA after obtaining their *Haya* in the constant state of the five Partzufim of AK

Dotted lines extending from each Rosh of the five Partzufim of Atzilut to its corresponding Partzuf in AK indicate the level from which they take and nourish

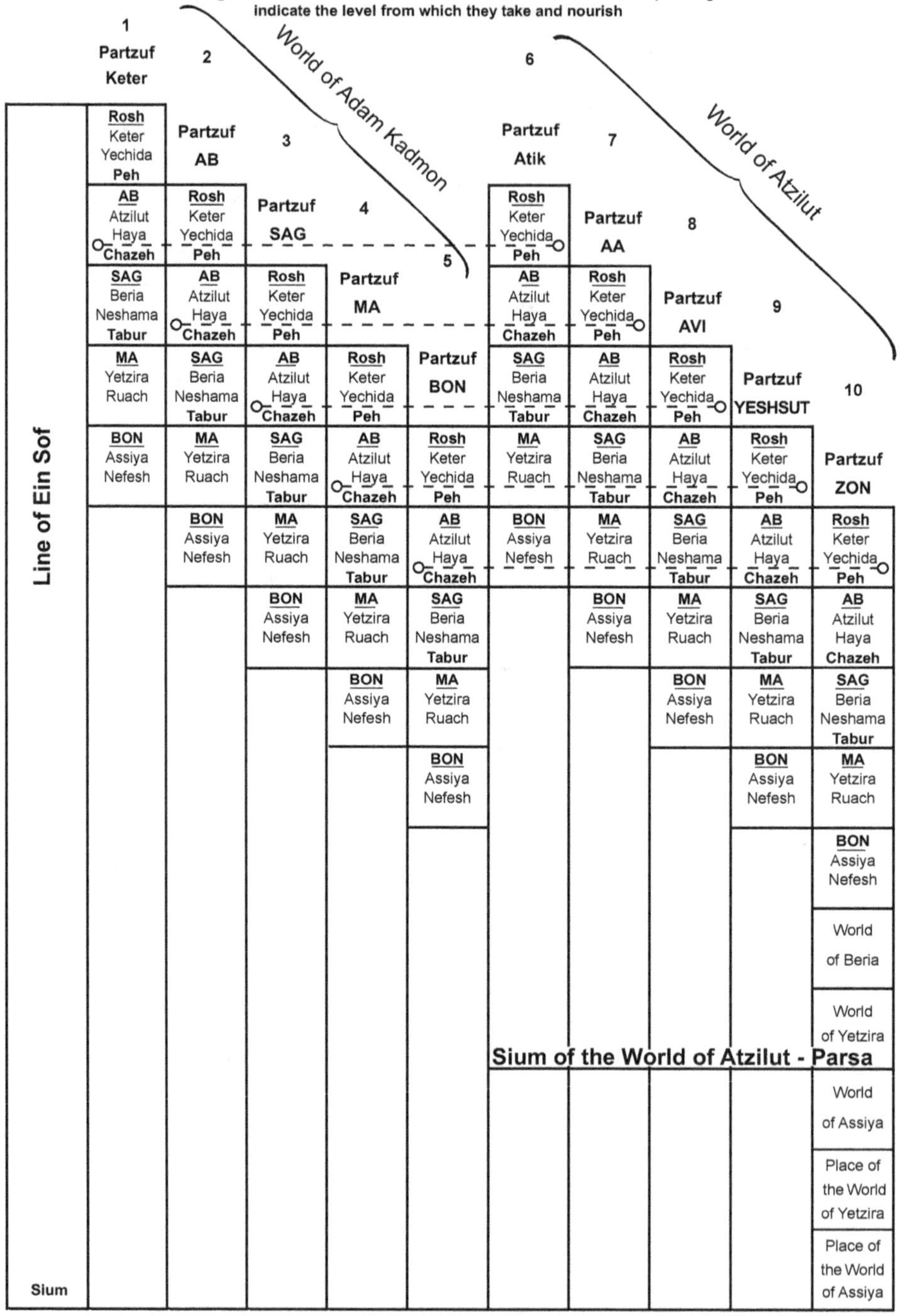

	1 Partzuf Keter	2	World of Adam Kadmon		6		World of Atzilut		
	Rosh Keter Yechida Peh	Partzuf AB	3		Partzuf Atik	7			
	AB Atzilut Haya Chazeh	Rosh Keter Yechida Peh	Partzuf SAG	4	Rosh Keter Yechida Peh	Partzuf AA	8		
	SAG Beria Neshama Tabur	AB Atzilut Haya Chazeh	Rosh Keter Yechida Peh	Partzuf MA	5	AB Atzilut Haya Chazeh	Rosh Keter Yechida Peh	Partzuf AVI	9
	MA Yetzira Ruach	SAG Beria Neshama Tabur	AB Atzilut Haya Chazeh	Rosh Keter Yechida Peh	Partzuf BON	SAG Beria Neshama Tabur	AB Atzilut Haya Chazeh	Rosh Keter Yechida Peh	Partzuf YESHSUT	10
Line of Ein Sof	BON Assiya Nefesh	MA Yetzira Ruach	SAG Beria Neshama Tabur	AB Atzilut Haya Chazeh	Rosh Keter Yechida Peh	MA Yetzira Ruach	SAG Beria Neshama Tabur	AB Atzilut Haya Chazeh	Rosh Keter Yechida Peh	Partzuf ZON
		BON Assiya Nefesh	MA Yetzira Ruach	SAG Beria Neshama Tabur	AB Atzilut Haya Chazeh	BON Assiya Nefesh	MA Yetzira Ruach	SAG Beria Neshama Tabur	AB Atzilut Haya Chazeh	Rosh Keter Yechida Peh
			BON Assiya Nefesh	MA Yetzira Ruach	SAG Beria Neshama Tabur		BON Assiya Nefesh	MA Yetzira Ruach	SAG Beria Neshama Tabur	AB Atzilut Haya Chazeh
				BON Assiya Nefesh	MA Yetzira Ruach			BON Assiya Nefesh	MA Yetzira Ruach	SAG Beria Neshama Tabur
					BON Assiya Nefesh				BON Assiya Nefesh	MA Yetzira Ruach
										BON Assiya Nefesh
										World of Beria
										World of Yetzira
					Sium of the World of Atzilut - **Parsa**					
										World of Assiya
										Place of the World of Yetzira
Sium										Place of the World of Assiya

Point of this world

Diagram no. 9

Position of all five Partzufim of Atzilut and the three worlds BYA after obtaining their Yechida in the constant state of the five Partzufim of AK

Dotted lines extending from each Rosh of the five Partzufim of Atzilut to its corresponding Partzuf in AK indicate the level from which they take and nourish

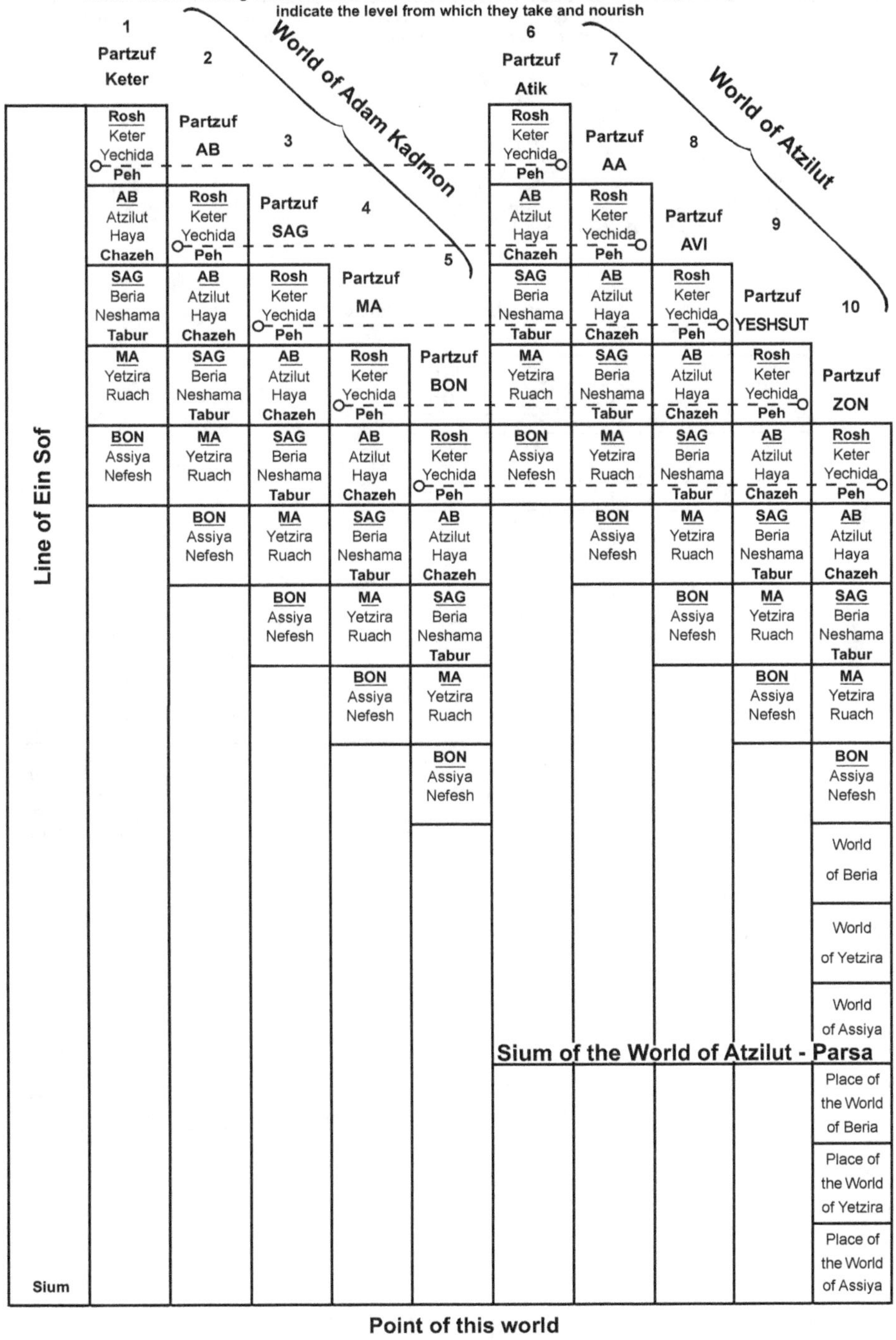

World of Adam Kadmon (columns 1–5): Partzuf Keter (1), Partzuf AB (2), Partzuf SAG (3), Partzuf MA (4), Partzuf BON (5)

World of Atzilut (columns 6–10): Partzuf Atik (6), Partzuf AA (7), Partzuf AVI (8), Partzuf YESHSUT (9), Partzuf ZON (10)

Line of Ein Sof	Partzuf Keter	Partzuf AB	Partzuf SAG	Partzuf MA	Partzuf BON	Partzuf Atik	Partzuf AA	Partzuf AVI	Partzuf YESHSUT	Partzuf ZON
	Rosh Keter Yechida Peh					Rosh Keter Yechida Peh				
	AB Atzilut Haya Chazeh	Rosh Keter Yechida Peh				AB Atzilut Haya Chazeh	Rosh Keter Yechida Peh			
	SAG Beria Neshama Tabur	AB Atzilut Haya Chazeh	Rosh Keter Yechida Peh			SAG Beria Neshama Tabur	AB Atzilut Haya Chazeh	Rosh Keter Yechida Peh		
	MA Yetzira Ruach	SAG Beria Neshama Tabur	AB Atzilut Haya Chazeh	Rosh Keter Yechida Peh		MA Yetzira Ruach	SAG Beria Neshama Tabur	AB Atzilut Haya Chazeh	Rosh Keter Yechida Peh	
	BON Assiya Nefesh	MA Yetzira Ruach	SAG Beria Neshama Tabur	AB Atzilut Haya Chazeh	Rosh Keter Yechida Peh	BON Assiya Nefesh	MA Yetzira Ruach	SAG Beria Neshama Tabur	AB Atzilut Haya Chazeh	Rosh Keter Yechida Peh
		BON Assiya Nefesh	MA Yetzira Ruach	SAG Beria Neshama Tabur	AB Atzilut Haya Chazeh		BON Assiya Nefesh	MA Yetzira Ruach	SAG Beria Neshama Tabur	AB Atzilut Haya Chazeh
			BON Assiya Nefesh	MA Yetzira Ruach	SAG Beria Neshama Tabur			BON Assiya Nefesh	MA Yetzira Ruach	SAG Beria Neshama Tabur
				BON Assiya Nefesh	MA Yetzira Ruach				BON Assiya Nefesh	MA Yetzira Ruach
					BON Assiya Nefesh					BON Assiya Nefesh
										World of Beria
										World of Yetzira
										World of Assiya

Sium of the World of Atzilut - Parsa

										Place of the World of Beria
										Place of the World of Yetzira
										Place of the World of Assiya

Sium

Point of this world

Diagram no. 10

Position of all the worlds and Partzufim the five Partzufim of AK, the five Partzufim of Atzilut, and the three worlds BYA after obtaining their Neshama in the constant state of Kav Ein Sof

Dotted lines extending from each Rosh of the five Partzufim of Atzilut to its corresponding Partzuf in AK indicate the level from which they take and nourish

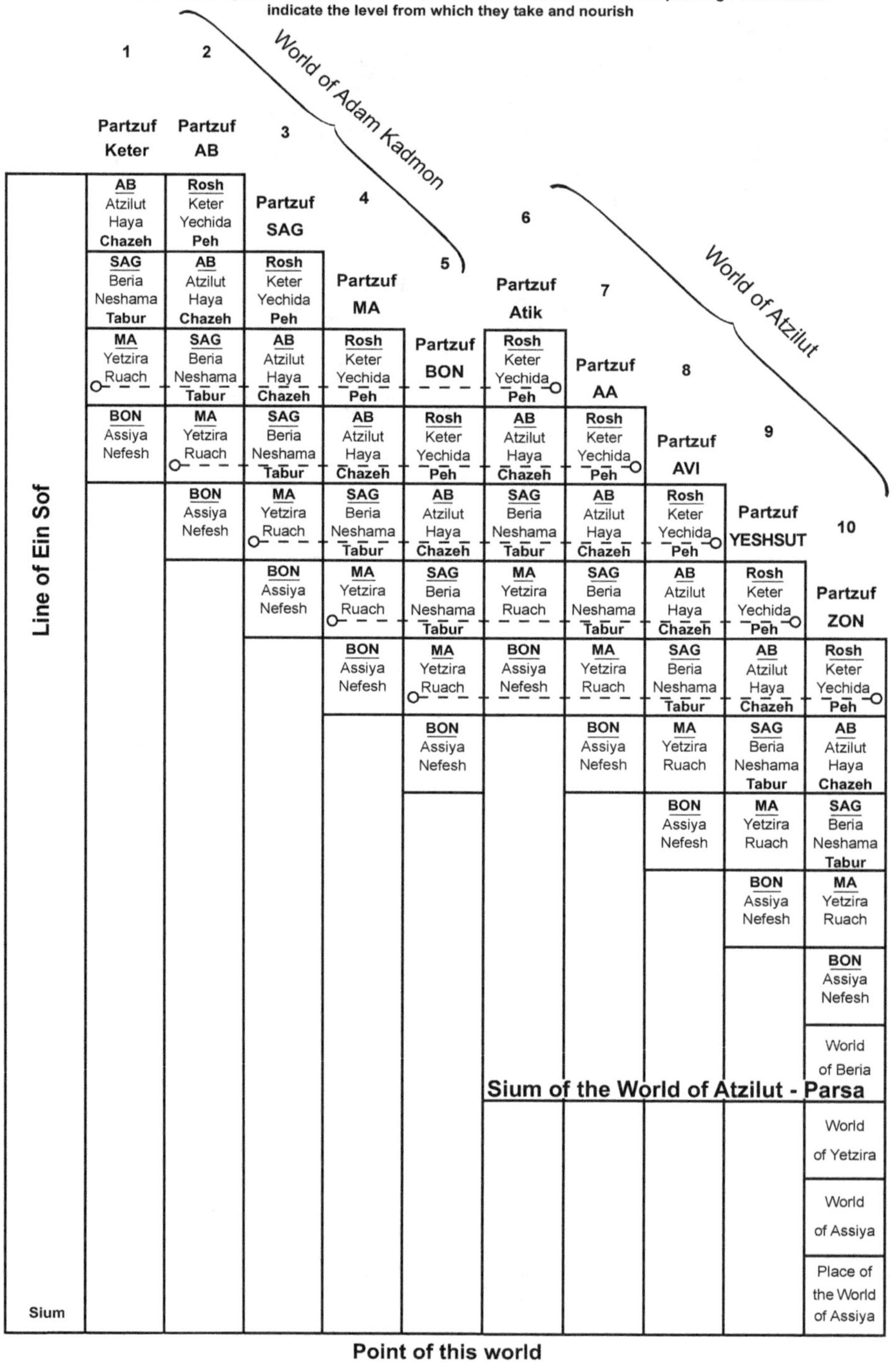

World of Adam Kadmon
World of Atzilut

Columns (left to right):

1. Partzuf Keter
- AB / Atzilut / Haya / Chazeh
- SAG / Beria / Neshama / Tabur
- MA / Yetzira / Ruach
- BON / Assiya / Nefesh

2. Partzuf AB
- Rosh / Keter / Yechida / Peh
- AB / Atzilut / Haya / Chazeh
- SAG / Beria / Neshama / Tabur
- MA / Yetzira / Ruach
- BON / Assiya / Nefesh

3. Partzuf SAG
- Rosh / Keter / Yechida / Peh
- AB / Atzilut / Haya / Chazeh
- SAG / Beria / Neshama / Tabur
- MA / Yetzira / Ruach
- BON / Assiya / Nefesh

4. Partzuf MA
- Rosh / Keter / Yechida / Peh
- AB / Atzilut / Haya / Chazeh
- SAG / Beria / Neshama / Tabur
- MA / Yetzira / Ruach
- BON / Assiya / Nefesh

5. Partzuf BON
- Rosh / Keter / Yechida / Peh
- AB / Atzilut / Haya / Chazeh
- SAG / Beria / Neshama / Tabur
- MA / Yetzira / Ruach
- BON / Assiya / Nefesh

6. Partzuf Atik
- Rosh / Keter / Yechida / Peh
- AB / Atzilut / Haya / Chazeh
- SAG / Beria / Neshama / Tabur
- MA / Yetzira / Ruach
- BON / Assiya / Nefesh

7. Partzuf AA
- Rosh / Keter / Yechida / Peh
- AB / Atzilut / Haya / Chazeh
- SAG / Beria / Neshama / Tabur
- MA / Yetzira / Ruach
- BON / Assiya / Nefesh

8. Partzuf AVI
- Rosh / Keter / Yechida / Peh
- AB / Atzilut / Haya / Chazeh
- SAG / Beria / Neshama / Tabur
- MA / Yetzira / Ruach
- BON / Assiya / Nefesh

9. Partzuf YESHSUT
- Rosh / Keter / Yechida / Peh
- AB / Atzilut / Haya / Chazeh
- SAG / Beria / Neshama / Tabur
- MA / Yetzira / Ruach
- BON / Assiya / Nefesh

10. Partzuf ZON
- Rosh / Keter / Yechida / Peh
- AB / Atzilut / Haya / Chazeh
- SAG / Beria / Neshama / Tabur
- MA / Yetzira / Ruach
- BON / Assiya / Nefesh

Sium of the World of Atzilut – Parsa

- World of Beria
- World of Yetzira
- World of Assiya
- Place of the World of Assiya

Line of Ein Sof (left side)

Sium

Point of this world

Diagram no. 11

Position of all the worlds and Partzufim the five Partzufim of AK, the five Partzufim of Atzilut, and the three worlds BYA after obtaining their *Haya* in the constant state of Kav Ein Sof

Dotted lines extending from each Rosh of the five Partzufim of Atzilut to its corresponding Partzuf in AK indicate the level from which they take and nourish

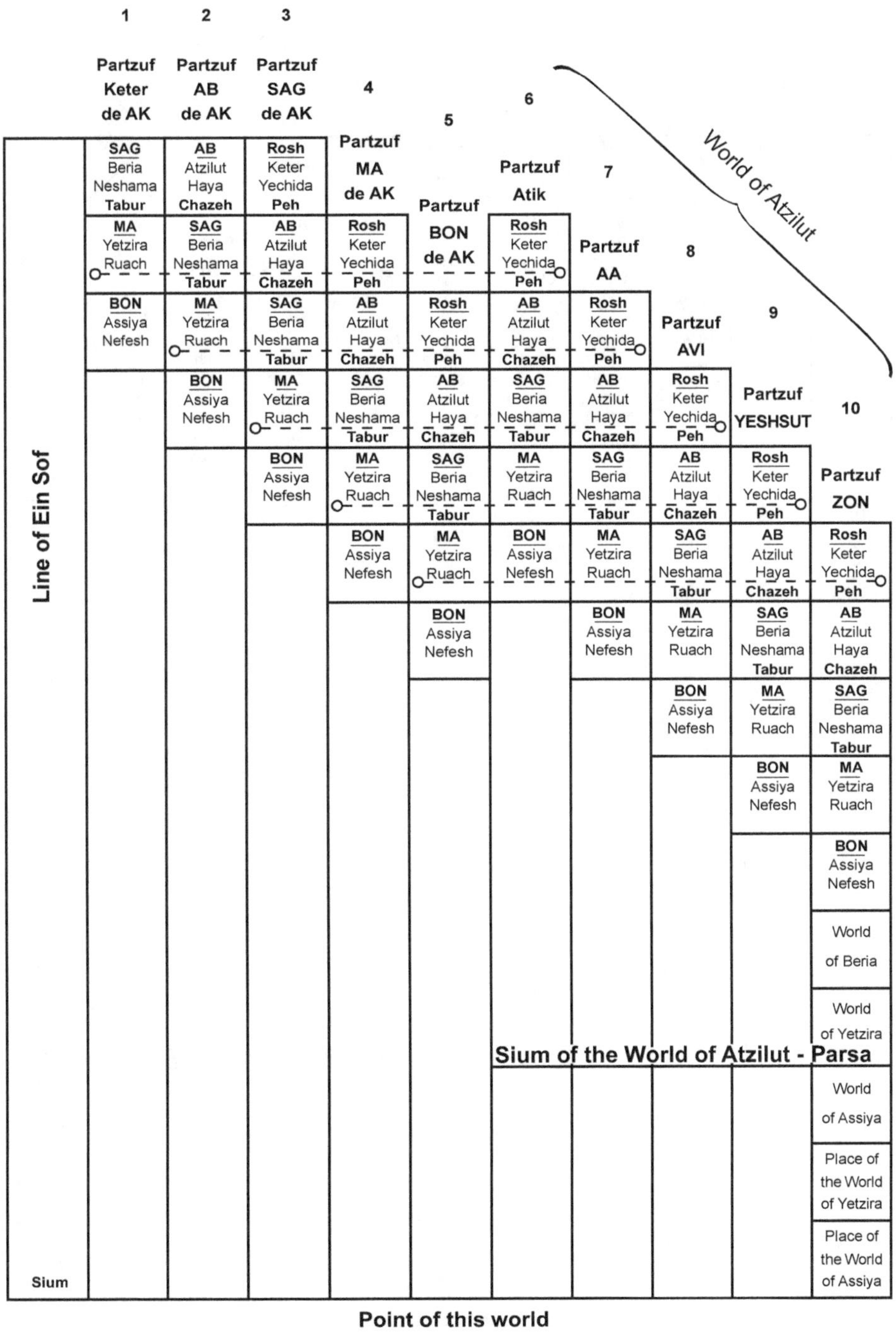

	1	2	3	4	5	6	7	8	9	10
	Partzuf Keter de AK	Partzuf AB de AK	Partzuf SAG de AK	Partzuf MA de AK	Partzuf BON de AK	Partzuf Atik	Partzuf AA	Partzuf AVI	Partzuf YESHSUT	Partzuf ZON

World of Atzilut

Line of Ein Sof

Sium of the World of Atzilut - Parsa

World of Beria
World of Yetzira
World of Assiya
Place of the World of Yetzira
Place of the World of Assiya

Sium

Point of this world

Diagram no. 12

Position of all the worlds and Partzufim
the five Partzufim of AK, the five Partzufim of Atzilut, and the three worlds BYA after obtaining their Yechida in the constant state of Kav Ein Sof

Dotted lines extending from each Rosh of the five Partzufim of Atzilut to its corresponding Partzuf in AK indicate the level from which they take and nourish

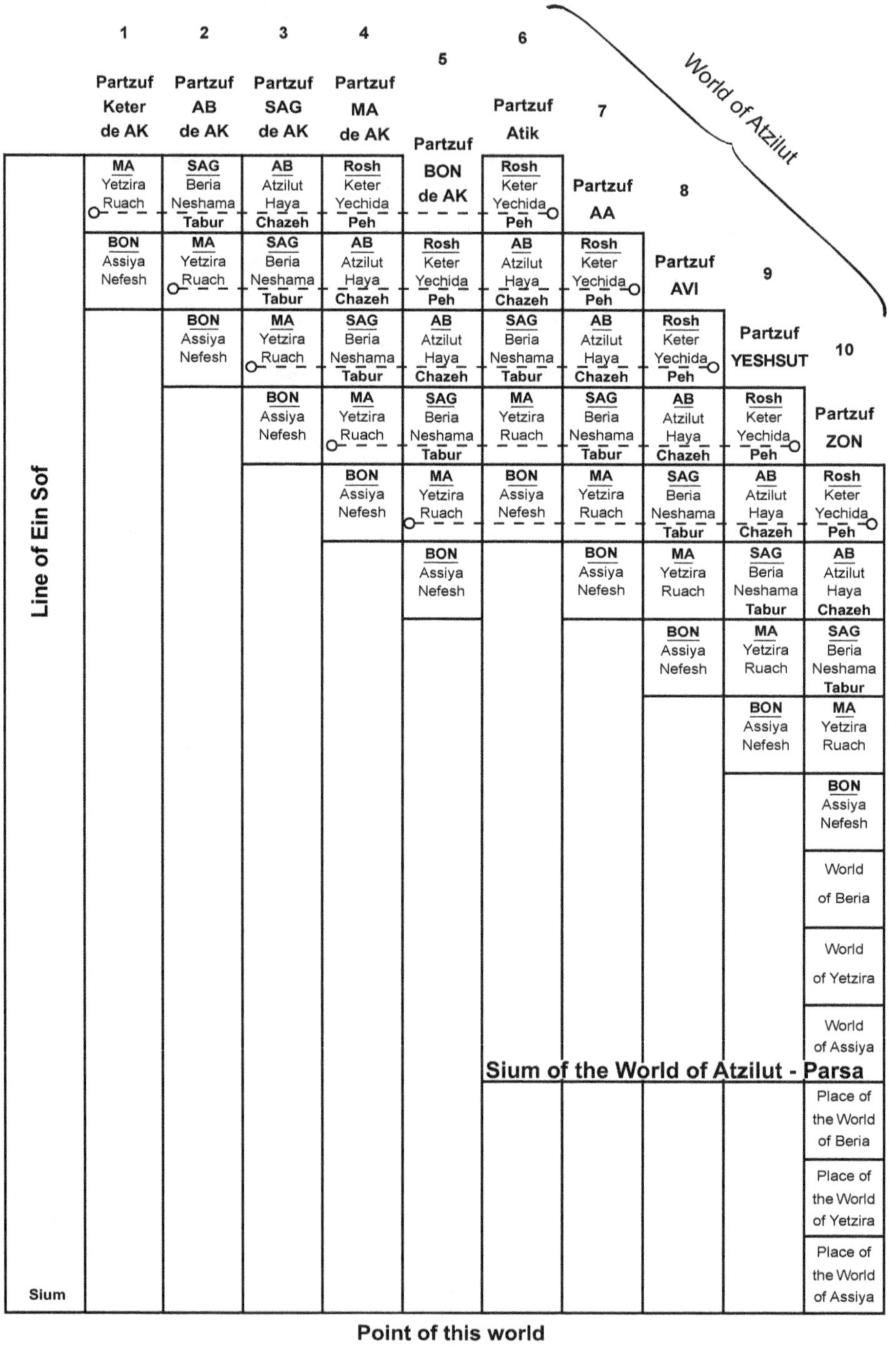

World of Atzilut

	1	2	3	4	5	6	7	8	9	10
	Partzuf Keter de AK	Partzuf AB de AK	Partzuf SAG de AK	Partzuf MA de AK	Partzuf BON de AK	Partzuf Atik	Partzuf AA	Partzuf AVI	Partzuf YESHSUT	Partzuf ZON
Line of Ein Sof	MA / Yetzira / Ruach	SAG / Beria / Neshama / Tabur	AB / Atzilut / Haya / Chazeh	Rosh / Keter / Yechida / Peh		Rosh / Keter / Yechida / Peh				
	BON / Assiya / Nefesh	MA / Yetzira / Ruach	SAG / Beria / Neshama / Tabur	AB / Atzilut / Haya / Chazeh	Rosh / Keter / Yechida / Peh	AB / Atzilut / Haya / Chazeh	Rosh / Keter / Yechida / Peh			
		BON / Assiya / Nefesh	MA / Yetzira / Ruach	SAG / Beria / Neshama / Tabur	AB / Atzilut / Haya / Chazeh	SAG / Beria / Neshama / Tabur	AB / Atzilut / Haya / Chazeh	Rosh / Keter / Yechida / Peh		
			BON / Assiya / Nefesh	MA / Yetzira / Ruach	SAG / Beria / Neshama / Tabur	MA / Yetzira / Ruach	SAG / Beria / Neshama / Tabur	AB / Atzilut / Haya / Chazeh	Rosh / Keter / Yechida / Peh	
				BON / Assiya / Nefesh	MA / Yetzira / Ruach	BON / Assiya / Nefesh	MA / Yetzira / Ruach	SAG / Beria / Neshama / Tabur	AB / Atzilut / Haya / Chazeh	Rosh / Keter / Yechida / Peh
					BON / Assiya / Nefesh		BON / Assiya / Nefesh	MA / Yetzira / Ruach	SAG / Beria / Neshama / Tabur	AB / Atzilut / Haya / Chazeh
								BON / Assiya / Nefesh	MA / Yetzira / Ruach	SAG / Beria / Neshama / Tabur
									BON / Assiya / Nefesh	MA / Yetzira / Ruach
										BON / Assiya / Nefesh
										World of Beria
										World of Yetzira
										World of Assiya

Sium of the World of Atzilut - Parsa

										Place of the World of Beria
										Place of the World of Yetzira
Sium										Place of the World of Assiya

Point of this world

Explanation of the Article, Preface to the Wisdom of Kabbalah

FOUR PHASES OF DIRECT LIGHT

The learning begins with a discernment called "The connection between the Creator and the creatures," since we do not speak of the Creator Himself and we cannot attain Him. Instead, "By Your actions we know You," meaning the attainment is only in the operations extending from Him.

This connection is also called "the purpose of Creation." Our sages perceived that His wish and goal were to benefit His creations. Hence, the order of evolution begins from this discernment until it reaches the souls, whose root is the soul of *Adam ha Rishon*, which extends from the internality of the worlds *BYA*.

Allegorically speaking, when the Creator wished to benefit His creatures, He wanted to give them 100 kilograms of pleasure. Hence, He had to create such creations that would want to receive it. We learned that the desire to receive delight and pleasure is the very essence of the creature and the reason why Creation is called "existence from absence." And He created it so His Thought of delighting His creations would be realized.

And for the will to receive to be born, there had to be an order of four discernments, since one can enjoy something only according to one's desire for it. This is why we call the *Kli* (vessel) by the name, "will to receive" or "craving." Thus, according to the measure of the need is the measure of the craving to satisfy the need.

There are two conditions for the making of a craving:
1. One should know what to crave. One cannot crave something one has never seen or heard of.
2. One will not have the desired thing, since if he has already obtained his wish, he loses the craving.

To realize these two conditions, four phases/discernments emerged in the will to receive, which are actually five, along with their root. The fifth discernment is called a *Kli*, suitable for reception of delight and pleasure.

They follow this order:

1) *Keter*: His desire to benefit His creations.

2) *Hochma*: His desire to benefit His creations created a deficiency—existence from absence—and along with it, created the Light. Thus, the abundance and the desire to receive the abundance came together. This is so because the desire still did not know what to want; hence, it was born along with its filling. But if it has its filling, it loses the desire for filling, as the second condition requires. This discernment is called *Behina Aleph* (first discernment) *de Aviut* (of the desire).

3) *Bina*: Since the Light comes from the Giver, the force of bestowal is included in it. Hence, at its end, *Hochma* wishes to equalize its form, meaning to not be a receiver, but a giver. There is a rule in spirituality: "Any generation of a form is considered a new discernment." Hence, this discernment is given its own name—*Bina*, and this is *Behina Bet* (second discernment) *de Aviut*. We also learned that the Light that spreads while the lower one wishes to equalize its form is *Ohr Hassadim* (Light of Mercy), and this is the Light that shines in *Bina*.

Question: If *Bina* craves to bestow, why is it considered *Aviut Bet* (second degree of *Aviut*)? On the contrary, it seems like it should have been purer than *Behina Aleph de Aviut* (first degree of *Aviut*).

Answer: I explain it with an allegory: A person gives his friend a present and the friend receives it. Afterwards, he reconsiders and decides that it is not in his interest to receive, and returns the gift. In the beginning, he was under the influence and domination of the giver; hence, he received. But once he received, he felt that he was the receiver, and that sensation caused him to return the gift.

Lesson: in *Behina Aleph*, he received due to the domination of the giver, but he still did not feel like a receiver. And when he saw and felt that he was the receiver, he stopped receiving, and this is *Behina Bet*. In other words, in that state, he felt that he was the receiver, and hence wanted to bestow upon the giver. This is why *Behina Bet* is called *Bina*, for it *Hitbonena* (examined/observed) herself being a receiver and hence wanted to bestow. This is also why we learn that the beginning of the learning is from *Bina* down.

4) ZA: At its end, *Bina* received a kind of drive that stems from the purpose of Creation, which she must receive because the purpose of Creation was not for the creatures to engage in bestowal. On the other hand, she also wanted

equivalence of form, bestowal. Therefore, she compromised: she would receive *Hassadim* (mercy) and illumination of the *Ohr Hochma* (Light of Wisdom).

This is called *Behina Gimel de Aviut*, since she already extends *Hochma*, but there are still *Hassadim* in her. This is the reason for the name *Zeir Anpin* (small face). **Hochma is called Panim** (face), as in, "A man's wisdom makes his face shine," but it receives this *Ohr Hochma* in a **Zeir, meaning very small extent**. But this discernment is still not considered a *Kli* (vessel), since if it can bestow and receive only an illumination of the *Ohr Hochma*, it is a sign that its craving to receive is incomplete, since it still has the strength to engage in bestowal, too.

5) *Malchut*: At its end, *Behina Gimel* is prompted from Above to receive abundantly because of His desire to benefit His creations. After all, the purpose of Creation was not for the lower ones to receive in *Zeir Anpin*. Hence, this awakening causes *Malchut* to have a desire and craving to receive the *Ohr Hochma* as it shone in *Behina Aleph*, when she had all the *Ohr Hochma*.

But the difference between *Behina Aleph* and *Behina Dalet* is that in *Behina Aleph*, it could not be said that she was enjoying the *Ohr Hochma*, since she still did not possess the craving and deficiency, since the *Kli* and the abundance came together. But *Behina Dalet* craves the *Ohr Hochma* when she does not have it; hence, when she receives, she feels the delight and pleasure that come with fulfilling her wish.

Only this *Behina* is called a *Kli*, since it wishes only to receive. All the *Behinot* (plural for *Behina*) prior to it are considered "Light without a *Kli*." And when this *Behina Dalet* receives the Light, it is a state called **"the world of Ein Sof,"** and also **"filling the whole of reality."**

Question: If we are dealing with spirituality, where there is no time and no place, what does "filling the whole of reality" mean?

Answer: Let us return to our allegory from the beginning of this explanation, the allegory that He wanted to give His creatures 100 kg of pleasure and therefore had to create 100 kg of deficiency and desire to receive in the creatures, corresponding to the pleasure. When the 100 kg of desire receive the 100 kg of filling, this is called **"filling the whole of reality,"** meaning no deficiency is left unfulfilled.

And now we will explain the meaning of the name **Malchut de Ein Sof**: This *Malchut*, which craves to receive abundance to fill her deficiency, is called "receiving in order to receive." This means that she receives in order to satisfy her lack. At a later stage, she put an end and *Tzimtzum* (restriction) on using this *Kli*. But in the initial stage, which we are dealing with, she still did not make that **Sof (end) and Sium (conclusion)**; hence, this state is still called **Ein Sof (no end)**.

We learned that, at its end, after receiving the abundance, a desire to bestow awakened in **Hochma**, fitting the Emanator's wish to bestow. Also, once **Malchut** received the Light, it evoked within her a desire to bestow, since this Light possesses the power of bestowal. **Bina** wished to bestow, but failed because in *Bina*'s way, the purpose of Creation is missing. Even her subsequent reception of illumination in ZA was not enough, since the Creator's desire to benefit His creations was for abundance, not for ZA. Hence, how could **Malchut achieve equivalence of form and obtain the purpose of Creation, too?**

It is said about that that she invented something new: *Malchut* was to receive everything, but unlike *Ein Sof*, where it was all in order to receive, she would do it in order to bestow. Thus, on the one hand she would be realizing the purpose of Creation of benefiting His creations, since she would be receiving, and on the other hand her aim would be to bestow, which is equivalence of form.

TZIMTZUM ALEPH

Malchut's decision that she did not want to receive in order to receive is considered that she repelled the Light. This state is called *Tzimtzum* (restriction). There is a rule in spirituality that any appearance of a new form is considered a new discernment. Therefore, we should discern two states:

1. When *Behina Dalet* received all the Light with a *Kli* called "craving." This is called "filling the whole of reality." It is also called "the world of *Ein Sof*."
2. After she wanted equivalence of form, this state is considered a different world, called "the world of *Tzimtzum*," from which the Light departed.

Hence, as we discerned that *Hochma* received and *Bina* reflected the Light, *Malchut* remained as she was, in the state of the world of *Ein Sof*, receiving all the Light. And now we discern a new *Malchut*, which reflects the Light.

We should know that in the first state, called *Ein Sof*, it was "He is One and His Name One," meaning the Light and the *Kli* were one discernment. Only after the *Tzimtzum* was there a distinction of the four phases, or the ten *Sefirot*, since the Light departed from them.

Question: With this *Tzimtzum*, the Light departed from all ten *Sefirot*. This is perplexing, since the *Tzimtzum* was on reception in order to receive, which is *Behina Dalet*, and not on the other *Behinot*!

Answer: The first three *Behinot* are not considered *Kelim*, they only prompt an order of development, at the end of which the *Kli*, called receiving in order to receive, is born and becomes separated from the Giver. But the first three *Behinot* are still not separated from the Giver.

After *Malchut* was born, she obtained her causes. Hence, it cannot be said that after the *Tzimtzum*, the Light remained in the Upper Nine, since they are not *Kelim*. The only *Kli* is *Malchut*, and if she does not want to receive, all the Light departs and she does not receive a thing.

The Ari also says, "The *Tzimtzum* was equal," without distinction of degrees.

Question: If this is so, why did we say that the four *Behinot* became distinct after the *Tzimtzum*?

Answer: The distinction was made with respect to cause and consequence, but there was no distinction of Above and below.

Question: What do Above and below mean in spirituality?

Answer: Importance—whereas cause and consequence do not imply importance. For example, the Vilna Gaon was a consequence of his father, but who was more important, the cause or the consequence?

We need to understand why there was no distinction of Above and below. *Malchut* received the Light that "fills the whole of reality," and this is not considered a deficiency or inferiority in importance. Hence, she could have remained in that state, had she not chosen to make the *Tzimtzum*.

This is what the Ari wishes to imply when he says that the *Tzimtzum* was equal, that *Malchut* was not of inferior importance, but that the *Tzimtzum* was made through her own choice. But afterwards, when *Malchut* does not receive due to the prohibition, she becomes inferior in importance. Then, what is farther from *Malchut* becomes **of Higher importance**, and what is nearer to *Malchut* becomes of **lower importance**.

THE TEN SEFIROT DE IGULIM (CIRCLES) AND THE LINE OF EIN SOF THAT FILLS THEM

After the *Tzimtzum*, the *Kelim* were left empty, and within them *Reshimot* (recollections/memories) of the Light that they'd had. They are called "the ten *Sefirot de Igulim* in the world of *Tzimtzum*." They are called *Igulim* to imply that the issue of Above and below does not apply to them, as it is in a corporeal circle.

And since *Malchut* is the operator, since she is the actual *Kli*, *Malchut de Igulim* returned and extended the Light to receive it in order to bestow. And here we learn a new rule: "A desire in the Upper One becomes a binding law in the lower one." Hence, now she is forbidden to receive.

I once offered an allegory about that: The eve of a new month is a time for saying the small *Yom Kippur* (Day of Atonement) prayer and for awakening to repent. Sometimes, a person debates whether or not to fast on that day. It is not mandatory to fast and there is no prohibition on the food, as well. Hence, the choice is in one's own hands.

If, in the end, a person decides to fast, and later regrets and wishes to eat, the rule is that the food is now forbidden, so "he shall not break his word" concerning the oath. Thus, we see that initially, there was no prohibition on the food, but after he had chosen to avoid eating, the food became forbidden.

Lesson: In the beginning, *Malchut* did not want to receive through her own choice. But now that she extends the Light again, it is prohibited to receive the Light. And if there is prohibition, there is Above and below in importance. Hence, this extension is called "a line that extends from *Ein Sof* from Above downwards."

We also learned that even though the *Igulim* extended the Light, they received it only from the line. We must understand why this is so: Any new form in spirituality is a new discernment. Hence, there are two kinds of *Kelim* (plural for *Kli*):

1. *Kelim* in which there is no prohibition on reception.
2. *Kelim* that extend now, with the extension of the Light, and whose *Malchut* is called *Malchut de Yosher* (directness), on which there is a prohibition to receive, due to the rule: A desire in the Upper One becomes a binding law in the lower one.

We also learn that the *Igulim* should receive Light from what they had drawn anew. This Light is called "a line." It contains Above and below in importance, and there is no other Light. This is the meaning of the *Igulim* having no Light but from the line.

Yet, there is a great difference between *Malchut de Igulim* and *Malchut* of the line. *Malchut de Igulim* had the Light in the form of "filling the whole of reality," while *Malchut de Yosher* never had any Light, nor will it ever have Light in its *Kli*, called "receiving in order to receive."

THE LINE AND THE ZIVUG DE HAKAA

Thus far, we have discussed three states:

1. The will to receive that was created in the world of *Ein Sof*, and which received all the Light.
2. In the world of *Tzimtzum*, it became apparent that the will to receive must be corrected for the purpose of decoration.
3. In the line, it is apparent that the *Kli* must be corrected due to the deficiency. Otherwise, the Light does not expand to it.

Explanation of the Preface to the Wisdom of Kabbalah

And now we shall speak of the line. We have already learned that the line has Above and below in importance, since *Malchut* of the line was forbidden to receive because she is regarded as receiving in order to receive. The rule is that in all the degrees, *Malchut's* name was not changed, which is "receiving in order to receive." And her Light is *Ohr Hozer*, meaning she wishes to bestow upon the Upper One.

And when the Light extends to *Malchut*, she made a *Zivug de Hakaa*, a *Masach*, which implies ending the Light and making calculations. For example, she assumed that she could receive only twenty percent of the Light in order to bestow. Hence, she decided to clothe only that much Light.

However, she felt that there was too much pleasure in the remaining eighty percent, and if she were to receive it, it would be in order to receive. Hence, she decided to not receive that part of the Light. So what is the difference between a *Tzimtzum* and a *Masach* (screen)?

- A *Tzimtzum* occurs through choice, as we learned that *Malchut* had all the Light and she chose to not receive it.
- A *Masach* is the domination of the Upper One on it. Thus, even if the lower one wished to receive, the Upper One would not let it.

The meaning of the term *Zivug de Hakaa* (coupling of striking) is as follows: In corporeality, it sometimes happens that when people disagree, they strike each other. In spirituality, when two things contradict each other, it is considered that they strike each other.

And what is the dispute? The Upper One, who wishes to benefit His creations, evokes in the lower ones a desire to receive all the Light. But the lower one wishes the contrary, to equalize its form, and hence does not wish to receive at all. This is the striking that unfolds between the Upper One and the lower one.

In the end, they equalize with one another and create a union and *Zivug* between them. In other words, the lower one receives the Light as the Upper One wishes, but only as much of it as it can receive in order to bestow, as the lower one wishes. Thus, there are two things here: 1) equivalence of form, and 2) reception of the Light.

However, the *Zivug* is possible only if a striking preceded it, since without the striking, and with the lower one's desire to receive the Light, this would be oppositeness and separation from the Creator. This process of *Zivug de Hakaa* is called **Rosh** (head). A *Rosh* means root, a potential, which needs a process of realization. The **Rosh** exists because of the existence of the **Sof**, the prohibition on reception. Hence, *Malchut* is compelled to calculate, and this is called a *Rosh*, preceding the actual reception.

Accordingly, we can understand the Ari's words in the beginning of *Talmud Eser Sefirot* (*The Study of the Ten Sefirot*): "Behold that before the emanations were emanated and the creatures were created, etc., and there was no such part as head, or end," etc. This is so because in *Ein Sof*, there was still no prohibition on receiving; hence, it immediately received it. But now that there was an end, we should distinguish between the *Rosh*, which is the potential, and the *Guf* (body), which is the realization.

And afterwards it actually receives, meaning the twenty percent that it receives in order to bestow are called the **Toch (interior) of the degree**, and the place of the expansion of the Light is called **from Peh (mouth) to Tabur (navel)**. And *Malchut de* (of) *Toch* stands at the *Tabur*, saying, "What I receive from here on, meaning the eighty percent, will be in order to receive. Hence, I do not want to receive, so I will not be separated." Thus, the Light departs, and this discernment is called **the Sof of the degree**.

THE BITUSH BETWEEN INTERNAL AND SURROUNDING IN THE PARTZUF

Everything discussed here concerning the *RTS* (*Rosh, Toch, Sof*) concerns the first *Partzuf*, called *Galgalta*, which uses the *Aviut* of *Behina Dalet*. And we learned that *Galgalta* received the maximum it could receive in order to bestow. It could not receive more. Yet, we learned that in the Thought of Creation, the *Kli* received everything. This is so because the *Kli* of reception in order to receive was created by the Creator, while in the *Kli* that the lower one makes, called "in order to bestow," there is a limit to the amount it can receive. It follows that there is no *Kli* that can receive the eighty percent of Light that remained outside the *Partzuf*.

So what shall become of them? To correct that, a **Bitush of Internal and External** was created. These are the Ari's words concerning this issue (*Talmud Eser Sefirot*, Part 4, Chapter 1, Item 4): "When the Inner Lights connect to the Surrounding Lights, they connect inside the *Peh*. Hence, when they emerge together outside the *Peh*, tied together, they strike and beat on each other, and their beatings beget the *Kelim*." Thus, **it is through the beatings that the Kelim are made**.

And we need to understand why 1) the *Ohr Pnimi* (Inner Light) and *Ohr Makif* (Surrounding Light) beat on each other, and 2) why this beating creates the *Kelim*.

Answer: We have already said that in spirituality, a beating occurs when two things are in opposition to one another. But we also need to understand why the beating occurs "when they emerge together outside the *Peh*."

At the *Rosh* of the degree, 100 percent of the Light expands without a distinction of Internal and Surrounding. This is because His desire to benefit His creations is complete. But the lower one, who is limited, calculates and decides, for example, that it can only receive twenty percent in order to bestow. This occurs in the *Rosh*, in potential. **"When they emerge together outside the *Peh*"**: Emergence, in spirituality, is called "revelation," when what was in potential is revealed in actuality. At that time, it receives a part and repels a part, to become *Ohr Makif*.

This *Ohr Makif* seemingly comes to the *Masach* and argues, "Your conduct, meaning the fact that you have erected the *Masach*, is not good, since how will the purpose of Creation of benefiting His creations be implemented? Who will receive the Light?"

On the other hand, the *Ohr Pnimi* agrees with the *Masach*, since the very expansion of the Light within is through the *Masach* and the *Ohr Hozer* (Reflected Light). **This dispute is called *Bitush* of *Ohr Makif* and *Ohr Pnimi*, or *Bitush* of *Ohr Makif* in the *Masach*.**

In truth, the *Ohr Makif* is on the right; hence, the *Masach* agrees with it. And since it agrees, it can no longer repel and raise *Ohr Hozer*, and hence can no longer receive in order to bestow. Thus, the Light departs and the *Masach* is purified, meaning stops receiving. This state is called *Din* (judgment) and *Achoraim* (posterior).

And since each *Behina* (discernment) consists of four *Behinot*, the *Masach* departs **gradually**, beginning with *Behina Dalet* in *Behina Dalet*, then from *Behina Gimel* in *Behina Dalet*, etc., until it rises to *Peh de Rosh*, the source from which the *Masach de Guf* arrived. In other words, it stops receiving altogether.

As it rises, it uses a smaller *Aviut* each time, and thus receives smaller Lights in order to bestow. For example, when it ascends to *Behina Aleph*, it can only receive the Light of *Ruach*. When it rises to *Behinat Shoresh* (root), it can only receive the Light of *Nefesh* in order to bestow. Finally, it cannot receive anything in order to bestow and thus stops receiving altogether.

Question: What is the benefit of the *Ohr Makif*, which wants to shine because of the purpose of Creation, and therefore wishes for the *Masach* to receive more? After all, things are unfolding in contrast to its will, meaning **the *Masach* loses even what it had**!

Answer: All the degrees that appeared during the departure are not residue of what it had in the beginning, since there is a rule: "There is no generation of Light that does not extend from *Ein Sof*." This means that each discernment that appears is a new discernment. Thus, in the beginning, it could not receive anything more. But now that *Behina Dalet* has departed, it can receive more from *Behina Gimel*.

This is the meaning of **the *Kelim* were made through the *Bitush***, that is, prior to the *Bitush*, it did not have any more *Kelim* for reception, since it received all it could with the aim to bestow. But after the *Bitush*, when the *Masach* of *Behina Dalet* was purified, there was room to receive on *Behina Gimel*, since it departed from *Behina Dalet* and had nothing. And when it departed *Behina Gimel*, it could receive on *Behina Bet*.

But this still leaves the question: What is the benefit, if it receives less each time?

Answer: There is no absence in spirituality. This means that anything that appears remains, except he does not see it, and cannot currently enjoy it, but only from the present. But when the work is done, all the Lights will appear at once. Thus, in the end, it is benefitting.

Baal HaSulam once said an allegory about it: Two people who were childhood friends separated as adults. One of them became a king, and the other, indigent. After many years, the poor one heard that his friend became a king and decided to go to his friend's country and ask for help. He packed his few belongings and went.

When they met, he told the king that he was destitute, and this touched the king's heart. The king said to his friend: "I will give you a letter to my treasurer to allow you into the treasury for two hours. In those two hours, whatever you manage to collect is yours." The poor man went to the treasurer, armed with his letter, and received the longed for permit. He walked into the treasury with the box he was used to using for his beggary, and within five minutes, he filled his box to the rim and merrily stepped out of the treasury.

But the treasurer took his box from him and spilled its entire contents. Then the treasurer told the sobbing indigent, "Take your box and fill it up again." The poor man walked into the treasury once more and filled his box. But when he stepped outside, the treasurer spilled its contents as before.

This cycle repeated itself, until the two hours were through. The last time the beggar came out, he told the treasurer: "I beg you, leave me what I have collected. My time is through and I can no longer enter the treasury." Then the treasurer told him: "The contents of this box is yours, and so is everything that I have spilled out of your box for the past two hours. I have been spilling your money every time because I wanted to benefit you, since **each time, you were coming with your tiny box full and you had no room for anything more.**"

Lesson: Each reception of Light in order to bestow remains. But if the Light remained, we would not want to receive anymore, since we would not be able to receive in order to bestow on more than we had received. Hence, each degree must depart, and each time we correct a *Kli* of will to receive with the aim to bestow, until all is corrected. Then, all the Lights will shine at once.

And now let us return the purification of the *Masach*. The first expansion that emerged from the *Peh* down is called **Taamim (flavors)**, from the verse, "as the palate tastes its food." After the *Bitush* of *Ohr Makif*, the *Masach* began to purify, and on its way, produced a new degree each time. These degrees are called **Nekudot (points)**.

I have already explained the Ari's words, that the *Kelim* were made through the *Bitush*, since now it has the ability to receive more Light. But Baal HaSulam interprets the making of the *Kelim* (plural for *Kli*) differently: While the Light was in the *Kli*, the Light and the *Kli* were mingled in each other. Through the *Bitush*, the Light departed, and then the *Kli* became apparent.

Interpretation: While the Light shines in the *Kli* the deficiency of the *Kli* is indistinguishable; hence, it does not merit the name *Kli*. This is because without the *Kli*, the Light cannot shine. Hence, they are of equal importance. But once the Light departs, the *Kli* is distinguished as a *Kli*, and the Light, as Light.

The *Nekuda* (point) of *Tzimtzum* is the reason why the degrees emerging during the purification are called *Nekudot*.

And what is the *Nekuda* of the *Tzimtzum*? The Holy *Zohar* says that *Malchut* is called "a black point without any white in it." This means that during the darkness, *Malchut* is called "a point." And when there is *Tzimtzum*, and it is forbidden to receive in order to receive, it becomes dark. In other words, **the point of Tzimtzum is present wherever it is impossible to receive in order to bestow and there is a desire to receive in order to receive.**

To return to our subject, when the *Masach* was purified from *Behina Dalet*, *Behina Dalet* was forbidden to receive. This is the meaning of the point of *Tzimtzum* being over her. But *Behina Gimel* could still receive, and when the *Masach* was purified from *Behina Gimel*, too, this became the point of *Tzimtzum*.

We should also explain the difference between *Rosh*, *Toch*, and *Sof*: **Rosh is considered "potential,"** meaning there is no reception there. Two parts spread from the *Rosh*:

- One part can receive the Light, and it is called **ten *Sefirot de Toch***. The Light is the abundance that enters the *Kelim*, and it is called *Ohr Pnimi*, which is *Ohr Hochma*—the Light of His desire to benefit His creations.

- The second part that spreads from the *Rosh* is the part of the desire to receive in order to receive, which it does not want to use. It says that it does not want to receive there, meaning it ends it. Hence, this part is called **ten *Sefirot de Sof***.

Question: We learned that the word *Sefirot* comes from the word 'sapphire,' meaning it shines. But if *Malchut de Guf*, called *Malchut de Tabur*, does not want to receive and puts a *Sof* over the Light, why is this part called *Sefirot*?

Answer: They are called ten *Sefirot* because, in truth, the Light did shine for them. An explanation of that can be found in Part 4, Chapter 5, Item 1, where he explains the difference between *Toch* and *Sof*: "From *Peh de AK* emerged ten internal *Sefirot* and ten surrounding *Sefirot*. They extend from opposite the *Panim* through opposite the *Tabur de AK*. This is the essential Light, but it also shines through the sides and all around that Adam," meaning not necessarily opposite the *Panim*, but also from the sides.

In Item 2, he interprets the Ari's words as follows: "In short, we will explain that **from *Tabur* up it is called *Panim***. This is because the Light of *Hochma*, considered the essential Light, spreads there, **and from *Tabur* down it is called *Achor* (posterior)**, since it is considered receiving in order to receive. Hence, the Light of *Hochma* does not spread there, but **comes through the sides**."

Further down that page, it continues, "...because through the *Ohr Hozer* that *Behina Dalet* brings to the *Partzuf*, which is *Ohr Hassadim*." This means that **Malchut de Tabur does not want to receive there, since there it is a will to receive in order to receive. Instead, it wants equivalence of form, called Hassadim**. "Thus, she receives illumination of *Hochma*, as well, though in the form of 'female Light,' meaning only receiving and not bestowing." **"Receiving and not bestowing"** means that she does not want to bestow the Light upon herself, but, to the contrary, she says that she does not want to receive.

And through this *Dvekut* (adhesion), an illumination of the Light of *Hochma* shines upon her, and this is called "illumination of *Hochma*." Accordingly, **the difference between *Toch* and *Sof* is that the *Ohr Hochma* shines in the *Toch* and in the *Sof* as long as she does not want to receive, for the purpose of equivalence of form, the Light that shines is *Ohr Hassadim* in illumination of *Hochma*.**

And we still need to explain why the names in *Ohr Hassadim* are "right" and "left," and in the *Ohr Hochma* they are called "long" and "short." When the Light shines, in *Hassadim*, it is called "right," and in *Hochma*, "long." And when it does not shine, in *Hassadim*, it is called "left," and in *Hochma*, "short." What do these names mean?

Answer: We learned that *Ohr Hochma* shines in the vessels of reception in order to bestow, of course. Hence, the measure of illumination depends on its measure of *Aviut*. This is called "Above" and "below," and this is why the names in *Ohr Hochma* are "long" and "short." But *Ohr Hassadim* is not extended through *Aviut* and is not dependent on it. Hence, the names in *Ohr Hassadim* relate to width: "right" and "left," implying that **they shine in the same level**, and it does not matter to them if there is more *Aviut* or less *Aviut*.

AN INNER PARTZUF

Thus far we have discussed the first *Partzuf* of AK, called *Galgalta* or the Inner *Partzuf de AK*. Now we will explain the inner *Partzuf*. There is a rule that in all the worlds, there are inner *Partzufim* (plural for *Partzuf*), with four clothes. We will explain it in AK: *Partzuf Galgalta* has complete *HaVaYaH* within its degree, and a complete degree emerges from each letter in this *HaVaYaH*.

- Its *Rosh*, called *Keter* or "the tip of the *Yod*," is unattainable.
- From *Peh* to *Chazeh*, it is called *Yod de HaVaYaH*, and from there emerges *Partzuf AB de AK*, which clothes it.
- From its first *Hey*, called *Bina*, emerges *Partzuf SAG*, from the *Chazeh* down.

  Thus, the **Yod-Hey**, which are AB and SAG, clothe it from *Tabur* up. And below *Tabur*, it is **Vav-Hey** *de HaVaYaH*.

- The **Vav** is called the Upper third of NHY, called *Partzuf MA*, and from it, emerges the world of *Nekudim*, which clothes there.
- From its last **Hey**, called *Malchut*, which are the two lower thirds of NHY *de AK*, emerged *Partzuf BON*, called "the world of *Atzilut*," which uses *Aviut Shoresh*.

THE RESHIMOT

When the Light departs *Partzuf Galgalta*, empty *Kelim* remain, and in them are *Reshimot* from the Lights that shone within the *Kelim*. The meaning of *Reshimot* is as we see in corporeality: when a person eats a delightful dish or hears of something pleasant, a taste remains of what he had experienced, evoking him to re-extend what he had had. Similarly, a *Reshimo* (singular for *Reshimot*) is a **desire for what he had had**.

There are two discernments in the *Reshimot*: 1) the pure Light in the *Reshimo*, and 2) the coarse Light in the *Reshimo*.

This means that as the general *Ohr Yashar* shone in *Kelim* called "general *Ohr Hozer*," when the *Ohr Yashar* departs, it leaves a *Reshimo* that is a part of the *Ohr Yashar*. This *Reshimo* clothes in part of the *Ohr Hozer* that was there, meaning it leaves a recollection of the fact that it worked with the aim to bestow. This is called **Reshimo from the Ohr Hozer**.

- What remains of the *Ohr Yashar* is called **"the pure Light in the Reshimo"**;
- And what remains of the *Ohr Hozer* is called **"the coarse Light in the Reshimo."**

Both are clothed in the general *Ohr Hozer*, called *Kli*, and both are one discernment.

Explanation: When the Light shines in the *Kelim*, we say that the Light and the *Kli* are mixed in one another until the Light and the *Kli* become indistinguishable. **This means that they are performing the same action, and one cannot be without the other.** It is like meal and appetite: they both perform the same action, since it is impossible to eat if there is appetite but no meal, and it is also impossible to eat if there is a meal but no appetite. But afterwards, when the Light departs, we discern the *Kli*, meaning the *Ohr Hozer* receives a *Kli* there.

So it is concerning the *Reshimot*: when the pure Light and the coarse Light are together, **they are both called Light and they are mingled in one another**. And when the pure Light is separated from the coarse Light, the coarse Light receives a new name: **Nitzotzin (sparks)**.

We should understand why it is that when the general *Ohr Yashar* departs, the general *Ohr Hozer* is called **Kli**, but when the *Ohr Yashar* in the *Reshimo* departs, the coarse Light in the *Reshimo* is called **Nitzotz (spark)**, meaning a spark of Light.

Answer: We should say that when the general *Ohr Yashar* departs, **it does not shine at all**. But when the *Ohr Yashar* in the *Reshimo* departs, **it shines from afar**.

Now we can understand the matter of the root of the *Kelim* and the root of the Lights: there is a rule that all the worlds emerge in the form of seal and imprint. This means that as the discernment emerged the first time, the worlds expand from Above downwards by that same order. The first time that *Kelim* emerged was in *Partzuf Galgalta*. This is why it is considered "the root of the *Kelim*."

This means that when the Light shines in the *Kelim*, they are mixed. For this reason, it is impossible to distinguish the Light from the *Kli*. But after the departure of the Light, the *Kelim* appear. Also, *Reshimot* from the Light remain in the *Kelim*: a *Reshimo* of the Light of *Keter* in the *Kli* of *Keter*, a *Reshimo* of the Light of *Hochma* in the *Kli* of *Hochma*, etc. Hence, when we speak of the *Kelim*, we begin with KHB.

And when the second *Partzuf* emerged, called AB, where the Light of *Hochma* shines, following the rule that each Light that comes shines in the purest *Kli*, called *Keter*, now the Light of *Hochma* shines in the *Kli* of *Keter*. This is called "the root of the Lights," which are arranged in this order, the order of HBD. Thus we can understand why he sometimes starts the ten *Sefirot* with KHB and sometimes with HBD.

TAGIN AND OTIOT

Now we shall explain the matter of *Tagin* and *Otiot*. We learned that the *Reshimot* that remained from the *Taamim* are called *Tagin*. Sometimes it calls the *Reshimot* that remain of the *Nekudot* by the name *Otiot*. The reason for it is that when the whole of *Partzuf Galgalta* purifies, which is *Behina Dalet de Aviut*, the *Masach* was included with the *Reshimot* of all the levels that departed. This level rose to the *Rosh* of the degree and asked for the powers it had lost. And since the last *Behina* is lost, due to the *Bitush de Ohr Makif* that weakened the force of the *Masach*, it could not overcome *Behina Dalet*, but only *Behina Gimel*, which is similar to *Nekudot*.

And we learned that two kinds of *Reshimot* remained—a *Reshimo* from the Light of *Keter* that was clothed in the *Kelim*, called **Dalet de Hitlabshut** (clothing). However, it lost the *Reshimo* from the powers and intensifications. It is said about that, "the last *Behina* is lost," and what remains is only the **Gimel de Aviut**.

It follows that when the *Masach de Guf de Galgalta* rose to the *Rosh de Galgalta*, it asked for the power of the *Masach* for both kinds of *Reshimot*:

1. On *Dalet*, the *Reshimo* from the level of *Taamim*.

2. On the *Aviut* of the level of *Nekudot*.

Hence, two *Zivugim* were made at the *Rosh* of the degree:

1. On the *Dalet de Hitlabshut* at the level of *Keter*.

2. On the *Gimel de Aviut* at the level of *Hochma*.

We also learned that *Dalet de Hitlabshut* shines only at the *Rosh* of the degree of the lower one, the *Rosh de AB*. But *Gimel de Aviut* has *Hitpashtut* in the *Guf*, as well. And since the *Guf* is called *Kelim* and *Otiot*, **the Reshimo de**

Aviut, meaning the Reshimo de Nekudot, is called Otiot. This is so because afterwards, *Kelim* spread from this *Reshimo*, while the **Reshimo de Hitlabshut remains as Tagin, shining only at the Rosh of the degree.**

Orally, he explained it in this manner: *Gimel de Aviut de AB*, and *Gimel de Galgalta* are not identical, since *Gimel de AB* is the *Gimel* of the general *Aviut*, while *Gimel de Galgalta* is the *Gimel* of *Dalet de Aviut*. But even so, *Gimel de AB* still extends from *Gimel de Galgalta*. Hence, here he ascribes the *Reshimo de Aviut* on which *Partzuf AB* emerged to *Reshimo de Nekudot*, whose Highest *Behina* is *Gimel*.

THE CONTINUANCE OF THE SEQUENCE

Let us return to clarifying the rest of the sequence. Once the *Ohr Makif* cancelled the *Masach de Guf de Galgalta*, the *Masach de Guf* rose to the *Rosh*. And since the last *Behina* was lost, there was a *Zivug* at the *Rosh de Galgalta* on *Reshimot Dalet Gimel* only, spreading from *Peh* to *Chazeh*.

And since the *Masach de Tabur* is included in the *Aviut de Rosh*, while it is at the *Rosh*, there are two discernments to make in it:

1. Its own *Behina*—*Masach de Tabur*;
2. *Aviut de Rosh*.

Once this *Masach* descended from *Peh* to *Chazeh*, which is *Behina Gimel*, it is considered that the Light of *AB* shines in the internality of *Kelim de Galgalta*. This means that the inner *AB* made a *Zivug* on what was included in the *Aviut de Rosh*. From *Chazeh* to *Peh de Galgalta*, a new degree emerged, called "*Rosh* of the outer *AB*," and from *Chazeh* to *Tabur* emerged the *Guf de AB*.

Question: This is perplexing. After all, there is a rule that the next degree should fill the empty *Kelim* of the previous degree. So why does *AB* not expand below *Tabur de Galgalta*?

Answer: It is because it does not have a *Masach* on *Behina Dalet*. Hence, were it to expand below and see the will to receive that is present there, it would not be able to overcome it. This is why it remained above the *Tabur*.

In *Partzuf AB*, too, there was a *Bitush* of *Ohr Makif*, and *Partzuf SAG* emerged from the *Reshimot* of *Partzuf AB*. These are still the *Reshimot* from above *Tabur de AK*, but the *Reshimot* from below *Tabur de AK* have not yet been fulfilled.

And this *Partzuf SAG* emerged on *Reshimot Gimel de Hitlabshut* and *Bet de Aviut*, and filled the empty *Kelim* of *Partzuf AB*, as well. However, it could not descend below *Tabur de Galgalta* and fill the empty *Kelim* there, since it has

Gimel de Hitlabshut, which are *Kelim* for extension of *Hochma*. It follows that this discernment, called *Taamim de SAG*, expanded through *Tabur de AK*.

But *Nekudot de SAG*, considered merely *Hassadim*, since they do not have the above-mentioned *Behina Gimel*, could expand below *Tabur de Galgalta*, although there is *Behina Dalet de Aviut* there, which is a vessel of reception on which it is impossible to put a *Masach*. Still, because *Nekudot de SAG* are vessels of bestowal, they have no interest in vessels of reception. Hence, they expanded below *Tabur de Galgalta* and filled the empty *Kelim* that were there.

Yet, since they saw the will to receive that was there, they wanted to receive in order to receive, as they did not have a *Masach* on *Behina Dalet*. And since we learned that there was a *Tzimtzum* on receiving in order to receive, the Light immediately departed them.

Question: We learned that *Nekudot de SAG* are vessels of bestowal. Thus, how were they restricted?

Answer: There is a difference between GAR *de Bina* and ZAT *de Bina*, since we learned that ZAT *de Bina* should receive *Hochma* in order to bestow upon ZA, but GAR *de Bina* engage solely in bestowal.

Now we can understand why GAR *de Bina*, which are GE, were not mixed, which left GE in the degree, unrestricted, while ZAT *de Bina*, called AHP, departed the degree because they wanted to receive in order to receive. This is called *Tzimtzum Bet* (second restriction).

It follows that in HBD, HGT *de Nekudot de SAG*, which are GE, there is no mixture of *Behina Dalet*. Hence, their place is still considered the place of *Atzilut*. And below *Tabur de Nekudot de SAG*, clothing the two bottom thirds of NHY *de AK*, the reception in order to receive governs.

And when *Partzuf* SAG rose to *Peh de Rosh*, two *Zivugim* were made there at *Rosh de SAG*:

1. A *Zivug* on *Reshimot de Taamim de SAG* that did not descend below *Tabur de AK*, and from which the *Partzuf* of the Upper MA emerged.

2. A *Zivug* on *Reshimot de Nekudot de SAG* that were restricted and mingled with *Behina Dalet* below *Tabur de AK*, from which MA emerged—the world of *Nekudim*. This *Zivug* unfolded on half a degree of *Aleph de Aviut* and on *Bet de Hitlabshut*.

Therefore, we must understand that *Malchut* does not extend Light on her own vessels of reception, but only on vessels of bestowal, due to the *Tzimtzum*. Because of it, were she to use the vessels of reception, it would be in order to receive.

And here, too, we learn that the Light expands in both the inner *Kelim de SAG*, and in the outer *Kelim de SAG*. And we should know that as a rule, he does not speak of the Upper *MA*, since we are speaking primarily about the association of *Midat ha Rachamim* (quality of mercy) in the *Din* (judgment), which begins in *Partzuf MA*, which is the world of *Nekudim*.

We learned that there are two *Roshim* (plural for *Rosh*) in the world of *Nekudim*: 1) from the *Aviut*, and 2) from the *Hitlabshut* (clothing). *Keter* is called *Bet de Hitlabshut*, and *AVI* are *Aleph de Aviut*. And since *Bet de Hitlabshut* cannot extend Light, since there is no deficiency there, it needs the association with the *Aviut*, which has the power to extend Light. We also learned that the level of Light that shines there is *VAK de Bina*, in the form of "for He delights in Mercy," which liberates the degree from the need for *Hochma*.

This Light is also called *Tikkun Kavim* (correction of lines). Hence, we learned that the *Tikkun Kavim* shines only at the *Rosh*, since the *Hitlabshut* does not have *Hitpashtut* (expansion) in the *Guf*. But the *Guf* had only a small illumination, and it was not satisfied with the state of *Katnut*. Hence, when the Light achieved *Gadlut*, the vessels of bestowal of the *Guf* broke, as well.

Preface to the Sulam Commentary

TEN SEFIROT

1) First, we must know the names of the ten *Sefirot*: *KHB, HGT, NHYM*. These are acronyms of *Keter, Hochma, Bina, Hesed, Gevura, Tifferet, Netzah, Hod, Yesod, Malchut*. These are also the ten coverings of His Light, established so the lower ones can receive His Light.

This is like the light of the sun, which is impossible to look at unless through darkened glass that diminishes its light and makes it suitable for the eyes' ability to see. Similarly, had His Light not been covered by these ten coverings, called "ten *Sefirot*," in which each lower one further covers His Light, the lower ones would have been unable to obtain it.

2) These ten *Sefirot* are the ten Holy Names in the Torah: the name *Ehyeh* (pronounced *Ekyeh*), is the *Sefira Keter*; the name *Yah* (pronounced *Koh*) is the *Sefira Hochma*; and the name *HaVaYaH* with punctuation of *Elokim* is *Bina*. The name *El* (pronounced *Kel*) is *Hesed*; the name *Elohim* (pronounced *Elokim*) is *Gevura*; and the name *HaVaYaH* with punctuation of *Shvah, Holam, Kamatz* is *Tifferet*. The name *Tzvaot* is *Netzah* and *Hod*; the name *Shadai* (pronounced *Shadi*) is *Yesod*; and the name *Adonay* (pronounced *Adni*) is *Malchut* (*The Zohar, VaYikra*, Items 157-163, 166-177).

3) And although we count ten *Sefirot*, there are no more than five *Behinot* (discernments) in them, called *Keter, Hochma, Bina, Tifferet,* and *Malchut*. The reason why we count ten *Sefirot* is because the *Sefira Tifferet* contains six *Sefirot*, called *Hesed, Gevura, Tifferet, Netzah, Hod,* and *Yesod*, which makes them ten (*Introduction of the Book of Zohar*, "Mirrors of the Sulam," p 5).

And these five *Behinot*, *KHB TM* are discerned in each emanated and in each creature, in all the worlds—the five worlds, called *Adam Kadmon, Atzilut,*

Beria, *Yetzira*, and *Assiya*, which correspond to the five *Behinot KHB TM*—as well as in the smallest item in reality. We discern that the *Rosh* (head) in it is *Keter*; from its *Rosh* to *Chazeh* (chest) it is *Hochma*; from *Chazeh* to *Tabur* (navel) it is *Bina*; and from *Tabur* down it is *Tifferet* and *Malchut*.

WHY TIFFERET INCLUDES HGT NHY

4) When the five *Behinot KHB TM* emerged, they were incorporated in one another in such a way that each of them contained *KHB TM*. However, in the *Sefira Tifferet*, the level of the *Sefirot* descended from being GAR, hence the names of the *KHB TM* included in it changed to *HGT NH*, and *Yesod*, which contains them. Therefore, when we say that *Tifferet* contains six *Sefirot*, it is not because of its merit over the first three *Sefirot*, but to the contrary, it is the lack of Light of GAR in it that caused the five *Behinot KHB TM* to receive different names: *HGT NH*.

Thus, *Hesed*, is *Keter*, *Gevura*, is *Hochma*, and *Tifferet* is *Bina*, *Netzah* is *Tifferet*, and *Hod* is *Malchut*. The *Sefira Yesod* is added to them, but it is not an additional *Behina* (singular to *Behinot*) to the five *Behinot*. Rather, it is a container, which contains all five *Sefirot HGT NH* within it. Also, they are always called *VAK*, which is an acronym for *Vav* (six) *Ktzavot* (ends/edges), which are the six *Sefirot HGT NHY*. And since this descent of the five *Behinot* to *HGT NHY* occurred only in ZA, we ascribe the five changed *Behinot* only to ZA.

LIGHT AND KLI

5) It is impossible to have Light without a *Kli* in any of the worlds. Initially, there was only one *Kli* in the ten *Sefirot*—*Malchut*. The reason why we say that there are five *Behinot KHB TM* is that they are all parts of *Malchut*, called *Behina Dalet*. This means that they are arranged by their proximity to the complete *Kli*, which is *Malchut*, called *Behina Dalet*.

But after *Tzimtzum Aleph* (the first restriction), a *Masach* (screen) was erected in the *Kli* of *Malchut*, which stops the Upper Light from dressing in it. Hence, when the Upper Light reaches the *Masach*, the *Masach* strikes it and repels it. This striking is called "*Zivug de Hakaa* (coupling by striking) of the Upper Light with the *Masach* in the *Kli* of *Malchut*," and the repelled Light is called "ten *Sefirot* of *Ohr Hozer* (Reflected Light)."

This is so because the repelled Light rises from below Upwards and clothes the ten *Sefirot* in the Upper Light, called "ten *Sefirot* of *Ohr Yashar* (Direct Light)." And new *Kelim* were made of this *Ohr Hozer*, to clothe the Upper Light instead of *Malchut*, which had been restricted so as not to receive Light. The content of those new *Kelim* (plural for *Kli*) is called "ten *Sefirot* of *Ohr Hozer*."

ROSH-TOCH-SOF, PEH-TABUR-SIUM RAGLIN

6) And because of the new *Kelim* (vessels) of *Ohr Hozer*, each *Partzuf* is discerned with three parts, called *Rosh, Toch, Sof* (Head, Interior, End). It has been explained that by the force of the *Masach* that stops the Light from reaching *Malchut*, there was a *Zivug de Hakaa* with the Light, which produced the ten *Sefirot de* (of) *Ohr Hozer* and clothed the ten *Sefirot de Ohr Yashar* in the Upper Light.

These ten *Sefirot de Ohr Yashar* and *Ohr Hozer* are called "ten *Sefirot de Rosh*." However, these ten *Sefirot de Ohr Hozer*, which emerged from the *Masach* upwards and clothe the ten *Sefirot de Ohr Yashar*, are still not actual *Kelim*. This is because the name, *Kli*, indicates the *Aviut* in it, that is, the force of *Din* (judgment, restriction) in the *Masach*, which prevents the clothing of the Light in *Malchut*.

There is a rule that the *Din* force operates only from the place of the emergence of the *Din* downwards, not from the place of the emergence of the *Din* Upwards. And since the ten *Sefirot de Ohr Hozer* emerged from the *Masach* Upwards, the *Din* force is not apparent in the *Ohr Hozer* and is unfit to be a *Kli*. For this reason, these ten *Sefirot de Ohr Hozer* are called *Rosh*, that is, a root for the *Kelim*, and not actual *Kelim*.

And *Malchut*, in which the *Masach* for the *Zivug de Hakaa* had been established, is therefore called *Peh* (mouth). This implies that as in a corporeal mouth, where *Otiot* (letters) are made through a *Zivug de Hakaa* of the five outlets of the mouth, the spiritual *Peh* contains a *Zivug de Hakaa* to produce ten *Sefirot de Ohr Hozer*, being the five *Behinot KHB TM*, which are the *Kelim* for the ten *Sefirot de Ohr Yashar*, and *Kelim* are called *Otiot*. Thus, the ten *Sefirot de Rosh* have been explained.

7) Thus, the ten *Sefirot de Ohr Yashar* and ten *Sefirot de Ohr Hozer* had to expand from the *Masach* downwards, at which time the ten *Sefirot de Ohr Hozer* became *Kelim* that receive and clothe the ten *Sefirot de Ohr Yashar*. This is because now there is a *Masach* over the ten *Sefirot de Ohr Hozer*. For this reason, its thickness controls the ten *Sefirot de Ohr Hozer*, and by that the *Kelim* were made.

Also, these ten *Sefirot*, which are actual *Kelim*, are called *Toch* and *Guf* (body), that is, they are the very insides of the *Guf* of the *Partzuf*. And *Malchut* of the *Toch* is called *Tabur*, as in the phrase, "the *Tabur* (navel, center) of the land," referring to the center and the middle. This indicates that *Malchut de Toch* is the central *Malchut*, and it is from her *Ohr Hozer* that the actual *Kelim* of the *Guf* were made.

It can also be said that *Tabur* comes from the words, *Tov Ohr* (Good Light), indicating that thus far the Light is good, as it is dressed in *Kelim* that are suitable to receive it. Thus we have explained the ten *Sefirot de Toch* through the *Tabur*.

8) Thus, we find two discernments in *Malchut de Rosh*:

- The Ending *Malchut*: the *Masach's* detaining of the Upper Light from clothing in the *Kli* of *Malchut*.

- The Mating *Malchut*: Had it not been for the *Zivug* of the Upper Light with the *Masach* through a *Zivug de Hakaa*, which raises *Ohr Hozer* to clothe the Upper Light, there would be no vessels of reception in the Upper Light, and there would be no Light in reality, since there is no Light without a *Kli*.

But in *Malchut* of the *Rosh*, these two discernments are only two roots. The ending *Malchut* is the root of the *Malchut* that ends the degree, and the mating *Malchut* is the root of the clothing of Light in the *Kelim*.

Both these actions appeared and occurred in the *Guf* of the *Partzuf*:

- From *Peh* to *Tabur*, the mating *Malchut* shows its strength there, and the Upper Light is clothed in *Kelim*.

- And from *Tabur* down, the ending *Malchut* shows its strength and produces ten *Sefirot de Sium* (ending). Each *Sefira* emerges with illumination of only *Ohr Hozer*, without the Upper Light. And when it reaches the *Malchut* of these ten *Sefirot de Sium*, the entire *Partzuf* ends. This is because this *Malchut* is the ending *Malchut*, which does not receive anything, and hence ends the expansion of the *Partzuf*.

And we call this *Malchut*, *Malchut de Sium Raglin*, which cuts the Light and ends the *Partzuf*. And these ten *Sefirot de Sium* that expand from the *Tabur* down to its *Sium Raglin* are called "ten *Sefirot de Sof*" (end), and they are all parts of the *Malchut* of *Sof* and *Sium*. Also, when we say that there is only *Ohr Hozer* in them, it does not mean that they have no *Ohr Yashar* at all. Rather, it means that they do have some illumination of *Ohr Yashar*, but it is considered VAK without a *Rosh*.

CHAZEH

9) Thus far we have discussed the *Partzufim* (plural for *Partzuf*) of *Adam Kadmon*. But in the *Partzufim* of the world of *Atzilut*, another *Sium* was added in the ten *Sefirot de Toch*: *Malchut de Toch*, called *Tabur*, rose to *Bina* of the ten *Sefirot de Toch*, and ended the ten *Sefirot* of the *Toch* degree there. This *Sium* is called *Chazeh*, and the *Parsa* has been set there.

This means that the new *Sium* that was made by the ascension of *Malchut* to *Bina* at the place of the *Chazeh* is called *Parsa* (diaphragm, midriff), as in the firmament that separates the Higher Waters—*Keter* and *Hochma* that remained in the *Toch* degree—from *Bina* and *TM*, which departed from the degree of ten *Sefirot de Toch* and became the degree of ten *Sefirot de Sof*.

For this reason, the ten *Sefirot de Toch* were divided into two degrees:

- From *Peh* to *Chazeh* it is considered ten *Sefirot de Toch*, *Atzilut*, GAR of the *Guf*.
- From the *Chazeh* down to *Tabur*, it is considered ten *Sefirot de Sof*, *Beria*, VAK without a *Rosh*, like the ten *Sefirot de Sof*.

INVERSE RELATION BETWEEN KELIM AND LIGHTS

10) There is always an inverse relation between Lights and *Kelim*. In the *Kelim*, the order is that Upper Ones are the first to grow in a *Partzuf*. First, *Keter* comes to the *Partzuf*, then *Hochma*, then *Bina*, then *Tifferet*, and then *Malchut*. For this reason, we name the *Kelim* KHB TM, that is, from Above downwards, because so is their order of appearance in the *Partzuf*.

But the Lights are opposite. The order of the Lights is that the lower ones enter the *Partzuf* first. The first to enter is the Light of *Nefesh*, then the Light of *Ruach*, then the Light of *Neshama*, then the Light of *Haya*, and then the Light of *Yechida*.

Thus, in the beginning comes the Light of *Nefesh*, which is the Light of *Malchut*, the smallest of all the Lights. And the last to come is the Light of *Yechida*, the biggest of all the Lights. This is why we always name the Lights NRNHY, that is, from below Upwards, as this is their order of entering the *Partzuf*.

11) It therefore follows that while there is only one *Kli* in the *Partzuf*, which is necessarily the Highest *Kli*—*Keter*—which is the first to emerge, the great Light related to *Keter*, the Light of *Yechida*, does not enter the *Partzuf*. Rather, the Light that enters and clothes in *Kli de Keter* is the smallest Light, the Light of *Nefesh*.

And when two *Kelim* grow in the *Partzuf*, which are the greater *Kelim*—*Keter* and *Hochma*—the Light of *Ruach* enters, too. In that state, the Light of *Nefesh* descends from *Kli de Keter* to *Kli de Hochma*, and the Light of *Ruach* clothes in *Kli de Keter*. Similarly, when the third *Kli* grows in the *Partzuf*—the *Kli* of *Bina*—the Light of *Neshama* enters the *Partzuf*. In that state, the Light of *Nefesh* descends from the *Kli* of *Hochma* to the *Kli* of *Bina*, the Light of *Ruach* leaves the *Kli* of *Keter* and enters the *Kli* of *Hochma*, and the Light of *Neshama* dresses in the *Kli* of *Keter*.

And when a fourth *Kli* grows in the *Partzuf*, being the *Kli* of *Tifferet*, the Light of *Haya* enters the *Partzuf*. In that state, the Light of *Nefesh* descends from the *Kli* of *Bina* to the *Kli* of *Tifferet*, the Light of *Ruach* to the *Kli* of *Bina*, the Light of *Neshama* to the *Kli* of *Hochma*, and the Light of *Haya* to the *Kli* of *Keter*.

And when a fifth *Kli* grows in the *Partzuf*, the *Kli* of *Malchut*, all the Lights enter their respective *Kelim*. This is because then the Light of *Yechida* is drawn into the *Partzuf*: the Light of *Nefesh* descends from *Kli de Tifferet* to the *Kli* of *Malchut*, the Light of *Ruach* descends from *Kli de Bina* and enters the *Kli* of *Tifferet*, the Light of *Neshama* descends from *Kli de Hochma* and enters the *Kli* of *Bina*, and the Light of *Haya* descends from *Kli de Keter* and comes into the *Kli* of *Hochma*, and the Light of *Yechida* comes and clothes in the *Kli* of *Keter*.

12) You find that as long as not all five *Kelim* KHB TM have grown in the *Partzuf*, the Lights are not in their designated places. Moreover, they are in inverted ratio, since if the *Kli* of *Malchut*—the smallest *Kli*—is lacking in the *Partzuf*, the Light of *Yechida*—the greatest Light—will be missing. And if the two bottom *Kelim*—*Tifferet* and *Malchut*—are missing, the two greatest Lights—*Haya* and *Yechida*—will be missing. And if the three bottom *Kelim*—*Bina*, *Tifferet*, and *Malchut*—are missing, the three greatest Lights—*Neshama*, *Haya*, and *Yechida*—will be missing, etc.

Thus, as long as not all five *Kelim* KHB TM have grown in a *Partzuf*, there is an inverse relation between the *Kelim* and the Lights. If one Light and one *Kli* are missing, then the greatest Light, the Light of *Yechida*, will be missing. And it is the opposite in the *Kelim*: the smallest *Kli* will be missing—the *Kli* of *Malchut*.

13) Now you can see why we say that through *Malchut's* ascension to *Bina*, the degree has ended under the *Hochma*. And for this reason, only two *Sefirot* remained in the degree—*Keter* and *Hochma*, while *Bina* and TM of the degree were cancelled and descended from the degree. Yet, this relates only to the *Kelim*. But it is the opposite in the Lights: the Lights *Nefesh-Ruach* remained in the degree, and the Lights *Neshama*, *Haya*, and *Yechida* were cancelled from the degree.

14) Now you can understand why *The Zohar* sometimes says that with the ascension of *Malchut* to *Bina*, the five *Otiot* (letters) of the name *Elokim* were divided in a way that the two *Otiot* MI (Mem, Yod) remained in the degree and the three *Otiot* ELEH (Aleph, Lamed, Hey) departed and were cancelled in the degree.

But sometimes *The Zohar* says the opposite, that when *Malchut* rose to *Bina*, the two *Otiot* EL (Aleph, Lamed) remained in the degree, and the three *Otiot* HYM (Hey, Yod, Mem) were cancelled and descended from the degree. The thing is that the five *Otiot Elokim* are the five *Sefirot* KHB TM or five Lights NRNHY. And when *Malchut* rises to *Bina*, only the *Kelim Keter* and *Hochma*, which are the two *Otiot* EL, remain in the degree, and the three *Otiot* HYM descend from the degree.

In the Lights it is to the contrary: the two bottom *Otiot MI*, which imply the two lowest Lights, *Nefesh-Ruach*, remained in the degree, and the three Higher *Otiot*, *ELEH*, which imply *Yechida*, *Haya*, *Neshama*, departed and were cancelled from the degree.

Hence, in the *Introduction of the Book of Zohar*, *The Zohar* speaks of five Lights *NRNHY*, implied in the five *Otiot Elokim*. This is why it says that *MI* remained and *ELEH* departed the degree. Also, in *The Zohar* (*Beresheet*, 1), it speaks of five *Kelim KHB TM*, implied in the five *Otiot Elokim*.

For this reason, it states the opposite: *EL* remained in the degree and the three *Otiot HYM* departed the degree. We should remember these words and examine every place to see if it speaks of Lights or of *Kelim*, and this will resolve many apparent contradictions.

MALCHUT'S ASCENSION TO BINA

15) We should thoroughly understand the issue of the sweetening of *Malchut* with *Bina*, as it is the root of the whole wisdom. *Malchut* is *Midat ha Din* (quality of judgment), in which the world cannot exist. For this reason, the Emanator elevated it to the *Sefira* of *Bina*, which is *Midat ha Rachamim* (quality of mercy). Our sages hinted about that: "In the beginning, He contemplated creating the world in *Midat ha Din*," that is, only in *Malchut*, which is *Midat ha Din*. "He saw that the world does not exist, preceded *Midat ha Rachamim* and associated it with *Midat ha Din*" (*Beresheet Rabba*, 12).

Through *Malchut's* ascent to *Bina*, *Malchut* acquires *Bina's* form, which is *Midat ha Rachamim*, and then *Malchut* leads the world in *Midat ha Rachamim*. This issue of *Malchut's* ascent to *Bina* occurs in each and every degree, from the top of the world of *Atzilut* to the bottom of the world of *Assiya*, since there is no degree without ten *Sefirot KHB*, *HGT*, *NHYM*. And the *Malchut* in each degree rose to *Bina* in that degree and was sweetened there.

THE DIVISION OF EACH DEGREE INTO TWO HALVES

16) It is known that *Malchut* ends each *Sefira* and each degree. This means that by the *Tzimtzum* (restriction) that was made on her, of not receiving the Upper Light, *Malchut* stops the Light in the degree from spreading into it. Hence, the Light of the degree extends only through *Malchut* and stops when it reaches the *Masach* in *Malchut*, and a *Zivug de Hakaa* with the Light is performed on the *Masach* in *Malchut*.

Therefore, since *Malchut* of the degree has risen to *Bina* in that degree, *Malchut* ends the Light in the place to which it climbed, that is, in the middle of *Bina*. Thus, half of *Bina*, *Tifferet*, and *Malchut*, which are under the ending *Malchut*, exit their degree and become another degree, below *Malchut*.

Thus, by *Malchut's* ascension to *Bina*, each degree is cut in two: *Keter*, *Hochma*, and half of *Bina* above the *Malchut* remain in the degree, and half of *Bina*, *Tifferet* (including *HGT NHY*), and *Malchut* exit the degree and become a degree below it. This ending that *Malchut* created in the middle of *Bina* is called *Parsa*.

17) Each degree must have five Lights, called *Yechida*, *Haya*, *Neshama*, *Ruach*, and *Nefesh* clothed in five *Kelim*, called *Keter*, *Hochma*, *Bina*, *Tifferet* (including *HGT NHY*), and *Malchut*. And since due to *Malchut's* ascension to *Bina*, only two complete *Kelim* remained in the degree—*Keter* and *Hochma*—and three *Kelim*, *Bina*, *Tifferet*, and *Malchut* are missing in it, only two Lights remain in it—*Nefesh*, *Ruach*—clothing the two *Kelim*, *Keter* and *Hochma*. And the three Lights *Neshama*, *Haya*, and *Yechida* are missing in it, since they have no *Kelim* in which to clothe.

It turns out that the degree is deficient of the first three *Sefirot*, since due to *Malchut's* ascent to *Bina*, the degree was cut into two halves: half of it remained in the degree—*Keter-Hochma* in the *Kelim* and *Nefesh-Ruach* in the Lights—and half of it departed the degree—*Bina* and *TM* in *Kelim*, and *Neshama*, *Haya*, *Yechida* in Lights. This is why this ascension of *Malchut* to *Bina* is implied by the *Yod* that entered the Light of the degree, and the *Ohr* (Light) became *Avir* (air). As a result of *Malchut's* ascent to *Bina*, the degree lost the Light of its first three *Sefirot* and remained at the level of *Ruach Nefesh*, called *Avir*. This matter is also implied in the five letters of the name, *Elokim*, divided into two halves: *MI-ELEH*. The two letters *MI* imply the two Lights *Ruach Nefesh*, clothed in the two *Kelim Keter Hochma* that remained in the degree, and the three letters *ELEH* imply the three *Kelim Bina*, *Tifferet*, and *Malchut* that departed the degree.

MALCHUT'S DESCENT FROM BINA TO ITS PLACE

18) However, through raising *Mayin Nukvin* from Torah and prayer of the lower ones, Higher Illumination is drawn from *Hochma* and *Bina de AK*, which brings *Malchut* out of *Bina* in all the degrees, and lowers it to its place (*The Zohar*, *VaYikahel*, p 41). The three *Kelim*, *Bina*, *Tifferet*, and *Malchut* previously departed the degree because of the entrance of the *Yod*, which is *Malchut*, into the Light of the degree, thus ending the degree under *Hochma* and turning the *Ohr* (Light) into *Avir* (air).

But now, after *Malchut* has descended from there and departed the *Avir*, the *Kelim* return to their degree. Thus, once again there are five *Kelim KHB TM* in the degree. And since there are five *Kelim*, all five Lights *Yechida*, *Haya*, *Neshama*, *Ruach*, *Nefesh* return and clothe in them, and the *Avir* becomes *Ohr* once more, since the level of the first three, called *Ohr*, has returned to the degree.

A TIME OF KATNUT AND A TIME OF GADLUT

19) Thus, it has been explained that because of *Malchut's* ascent to *Bina*, two times were made in each degree: a time of *Katnut* (smallness, infancy) and a time of *Gadlut* (greatness, adulthood). With *Malchut's* ascent to *Bina*, it ends the degree under the *Hochma*, and *Bina*, *Tifferet*, and *Malchut* of the degree depart the degree and come to the degree below it. Hence, only *Keter Hochma* in *Kelim* and *Ruach Nefesh* in Lights remain in the degree, lacking the GAR (first three). This is the time of *Katnut*.

But after the lower ones raise *Mayin Nukvin* and extend illumination from *Hochma Bina de* (of) *AK*, which brings *Malchut* out of *Bina*, the three *Kelim Bina* and *TM* that fell to the degree below it return and rise from there to their initial degree. And since there are now five *Kelim KHB TM* in the degree, five Lights return and clothe in them: *Nefesh*, *Ruach*, *Neshama*, *Haya*, and *Yechida*. This is the *Gadlut* time of the degree. Thus we have explained that due to the fall of *Bina* and *TM* of the degree to the degree below it, the degree is in *Katnut*, lacking GAR. And through *Bina* and *TM's* return to the degree, the degree is in *Gadlut*, that is, with filling of GAR.

HOW THE LOWER ONE RISES TO ITS HIGHER ONE

20) By this ascension of *Malchut* to *Bina*, the connection and the possibility of raising each lower one to its Upper One have been prepared. This is because the rule is that when the Upper One descends to the lower one, it becomes like it. And also, when the lower one rises to the Upper One, it becomes like it.

Hence, in the degree's state of *Katnut*, when the ending *Malchut* rises to *Bina*, it drives *Bina* and *TM* outside the degree and into the degree below it. Then, these *Bina* and *TM* become one degree with the degree below it, since the Upper One that descends to the lower one becomes like it. For this reason, in the degree's state of *Gadlut*, when *Malchut* returns and exits *Bina* and comes to its place, *Bina* and *TM* that fell from *Bina* return to their degree and take the lower degree in which they were while they were fallen, along with them.

Because they have now become one degree with the lower one, when they were fallen, and became as one with it, they take it with them upon their return to the degree and elevate the lower degree to the Upper Degree. According to the rule that the lower one that rises to the Upper One's place becomes like it, now the lower degree receives all the Lights and *Mochin* that exist in the Upper Degree.

Thus it has been clarified how the ascension of *Malchut* to *Bina* induced the connection between the degrees, so each degree can rise to the degree above it. Thus, even the lowest degree can rise to the Highest Level through this connection made by the fall of *Bina* and *TM* from each degree to the degree below it (*The Zohar, VaYikahel*, p 41).

KATNUT AND GADLUT OF YESHSUT AND ZON

21) Once the issue of *Malchut's* ascension to *Bina*, applied in each and every degree in the four worlds *ABYA*, has been explained in general, I will now explain them in detail. Let us take two degrees, called *YESHSUT* and *ZON* in the world of *Atzilut*, as an example. Through the ascent of *Malchut de YESHSUT* to *Bina de YESHSUT* in the state of *Katnut*, the three *Sefirot*, *Bina* and *TM de YESHSUT* departed and fell into the degree below *YESHSUT*, being *ZON*. And these *Bina* and *TM* clung to the degree of *ZON* during their fall.

Hence, upon the arrival of the time of *Gadlut*, *Malchut* departed *Bina de YESHSUT* back to her own place. Thus, *Bina* and *TM de YESHSUT* rose from their fall and came to the degree of *YESHSUT*. And along with them, they brought *ZON*, since they were attached to them during the *Katnut*, when they were fallen. It turns out that *ZON*, too, rose and became the degree of *YESHSUT*, receiving the same Lights and *Mochin* fit for the degree of *YESHSUT*.

HAD IT NOT BEEN FOR MALCHUT'S ASCENT TO BINA, ZON WOULD NOT HAVE BEEN WORTHY OF MOCHIN

22) And here we should know that for themselves, *ZON* are unworthy of receiving *Mochin* at all, since the origin of *ZON* is below *Tabur de AK*, where *Malchut* of *Midat ha Din* rules, which is governed by the force of *Tzimtzum* and is unfit to receive the Upper Light. Yet, now that *Bina* and *TM de YESHSUT* elevated *ZON* to the degree of *YESHSUT*, *ZON* became as the degree of *YESHSUT* and can receive the Upper Light as they do.

23) Now you can thoroughly understand why our sages said (*Beresheet Rabba, Parasha* 12): "In the beginning, He contemplated creating the world in *Midat ha Din*," that is, with *Malchut* of the first restriction, which is *Midat ha Din*. And "world" should be understood as *ZON de Atzilut*, called "world." And it should also be understood as "this world," which receives from *ZON de Atzilut*. This is because all that is received in *ZON de Atzilut* can be received by people in this world, and all that is not received in *ZON* is not received by people in this world, as we cannot receive above the degree of *ZON*.

Hence, since the root of *ZON* is below *Tabur de AK*, where *Malchut* of *Midat ha Din* rules, they cannot receive the Upper Light and exist, since they are under the *Tzimtzum* in *Malchut*. All the more so, this world cannot exist.

This is the meaning of, "He saw that the world does not exist, preceded *Midat ha Rachamim* and associated it with *Midat ha Din*." This means that He elevated *Malchut* of each degree, which is *Midat ha Din*, to the *Bina* of the degree, which is *Midat ha Rachamim*. It follows that *Malchut de YESHSUT* rose to *Bina de YESHSUT*, by which *Bina* and *TM de YESHSUT* fell to the degree below it, which is ZON, and clung to them.

For this reason, during the *Gadlut* of YESHSUT, when *Malchut* descended from *Bina de YESHSUT* and returned to her place, and the three *Kelim Bina* and *TM de YESHSUT* returned to their place, YESHSUT, as in the beginning, they took the ZON that were attached to them along with them, and raised them to the degree of YESHSUT. Thus, ZON became like the degree of YESHSUT, that is, they became worthy of receiving the Upper Light like YESHSUT. For this reason, they receive the Upper Light of YESHSUT and give to this world, and now the world can exist.

But had it not been for the association of *Midat ha Din* with *Midat ha Rachamim*, meaning if *Malchut de YESHSUT* had not risen to *Bina de YESHSUT*, *Bina* and *TM de YESHSUT* would not have fallen to ZON, and there would be no possibility for ZON to rise to YESHSUT. In that state, they would not be able to receive the Upper Light for the world, and the world would not be able to exist. Thus we have explained the issue of *Malchut*'s ascension to *Bina*.

TIKKUN KAVIM

24) In the first three *Partzufim de AK*, called *Galgalta*, AB, SAG *de AK*, the *Sefirot* were in a single line, one below the other. But in the world of *Nekudim*, clothing from *Tabur de AK* downwards, there was a *Tikkun Kavim* (correction of lines) in their GAR, but not in the seven lower *Sefirot*. And in the world of *Atzilut*, there was a *Tikkun Kavim* in the seven lower *Sefirot*, as well.

TWO DISCERNMENTS IN TIKKUN KAVIM

25) The reason for it is that the *Tikkun Kavim* performed in the ten *Sefirot* extends from *Malchut*'s ascent to *Bina*, which became *Nukva* (female) to *Hochma*. As a result, two sides were made in the ten *Sefirot*:

- The *Malchut* that was mingled into each *Sefira* became the left side of the *Sefira*;
- The actual *Sefira* is considered the right line in the *Sefira*.

Also, the left line blemished the right line. In that state, the Upper Light mated on the *Masach* of the *Dinim* (plural for *Din*) in this *Malchut*, and the level of *Hassadim* that emerged in the *Zivug de Hakaa* of the Upper Light on the *Masach* of that *Malchut* became the middle line, uniting and equalizing the two lines with one another. Were it not for the *Dinim* in *Malchut*, there would be no *Zivug de Hakaa*, nor would there be the many *Hassadim*. Hence, *Malchut*, which is left, became as important as the actual *Sefira*, which is the right.

It is known that the beginning of the *Tikkun* of *Malchut*'s ascent to *Bina* was in the world of *Nekudim*, which emerged after *Partzuf SAG de AK*. Hence, the *Tikkun* of the three *Kavim* begins in the world of *Nekudim*, too, for one is dependent on the other. But in the first three *Partzufim*, *Galgalta*, *AB*, *SAG* that preceded the world of *Nekudim*, where there was no such issue as *Malchut*'s ascent to *Bina*, hence, there weren't three lines in them, but only one line.

26) And all of this is possible only in GAR of the world of *Nekudim*, considered GAR *de Bina*, whose *Hassadim* are GAR, since they are *Ohr Hassadim* by their very essence, since they never receive *Ohr Hochma*. For this reason, the level of *Hassadim* that emerged on the *Masach* of *Malchut* is sufficient to unite the two lines, right and left, with one another, and return the GAR to the *Sefirot*.

Yet, this is not so in the seven lower *Sefirot* in the world of *Nekudim*, which are considered ZA, whose essence is illumination of *Hochma* in *Hassadim*, since they need *Hochma*. And since the *Malchut* is involved in all the *Sefirot*, they cannot receive *Hochma*. For this reason, they are deficient and flawed as long as *Hochma* does not shine in them.

Thus, the level of *Hassadim* that emerged on *Masach de Malchut* does not help them at all to equalize the two lines, right and left, with one another. This is because the *Dinim* in the left, which are the *Dinim* of *Malchut* that rose to *Bina*, blemish the right line and remove the Light of GAR from it. Thus, the *Tikkun Kavim de* GAR does not help at all in correcting the two lines, right and left in VAK, since the VAK in all the *Sefirot* is from the *Hitkalelut* (mixture, integration) of ZA there. And as long as it does not have illumination of *Hochma*, it is deficient and flawed.

TIKKUN KAVIM IN ZAT AND IN YESHSUT

27) Hence, the first *Tikkun* the lower seven *Sefirot* need is to remove the *Dinim* in *Malchut* that has been mingled in the *Sefirot*, that is, to simply extend illumination from *Hochma Bina de AK*, which lowers the *Malchut* from *Bina* and returns it to its place. At that time, the three *Kelim Bina* and *TM* return to the *Sefira* and become the left line, and *Keter* and *Hochma* that remained, become the right line. And since the degree is completed with five *Kelim*, *KHB TM*, all

five Lights *NRNHY* return to it, and the Light of *Hochma* returns to the degree. Then the middle line can unite the two lines in one another and complete the degree with all its corrections.

28) The second *Tikkun* is to strengthen the *Parsa*, which is the ending force of *Malchut* that rose to *Bina*, so it will never be cancelled. And even when *Malchut* descends from *Bina*, her ending force remains in *Bina's* place. Then *Bina* and *TM*, which unite with the degree, should rise above the *Parsa* and unite there with the degree. Yet, when they are below the *Parsa*, they cannot connect to the degree, even though *Malchut* has already descended from there, since her ending force remains after her descent from there, as well.

29) And when *Bina* and *TM* rise above the *Parsa* and connect to the degree, they do not actually become one degree with the two *Kelim Keter* and *Hochma*. This is because there remains a difference between the two *Kelim Keter* and *Hochma*, which were never blemished because they have never left their degree, and the three *Kelim Bina* and *TM* that departed their degree, were blemished during the *Katnut*, and have now returned. And that difference turns them into two lines, right and left, where *Keter* and *Hochma* of the degree become the right line, and *Bina* and *TM* of the degree become the left line.

30) This difference and these right and left do not refer to a location because the spiritual is above place and above time. Instead, a difference means that they do not want to bond with one another. Also, right refers to *Ohr Hassadim* and left refers to *Ohr Hochma*.

The thing is that *Keter* and *Hochma* of the degree, which remain in it during the *Katnut*—with *Ohr Hassadim*—settle for this *Ohr Hassadim* during the *Gadlut*, as well, after *Malchut* has descended from *Bina*. This is because this Light was not flawed. They do not want to receive the *Ohr Hochma* and *GAR* that have now returned to the degree, with the return of *Bina* and *TM* to the degree. For this reason, *Keter* and *Hochma* are considered the right line, meaning *Ohr Hassadim*.

Also, these *Bina* and *TM*, which, upon their return to the degree, introduce *Ohr Hochma* and *GAR* to the degree, do not want to bond with *Keter* and *Hochma*, since they keep to the *Ohr Hassadim* that they had had during the *Katnut*. *Bina* and *TM* have higher regard for the *Ohr Hochma* that has now come to the degree; hence, they are considered the left line, since they keep to the *Ohr Hochma*.

31) And this difference between the right line and the left line is also considered the division of the right from the left. The right line keeps to the *Hassadim*, and wishes to cancel the *Ohr Hochma* in the left line, and ordain

the *Ohr Hassadim* alone. Conversely, the left line, which keeps to *Ohr Hochma*, wishes to cancel the *Ohr Hassadim* in the right line and ordain only the *Ohr Hochma*. Because of this dispute, neither of them shines, since the *Ohr Hassadim* in the right line is deficient of *Ohr Hochma*, like a *Guf* without a *Rosh*, and the *Ohr Hochma* in the left line is complete darkness because *Ohr Hochma* cannot shine without *Hassadim*.

32) And there is no correction to this dispute except through the middle line, created by the lower one that ascends there for MAN, in the form of the middle line. A *Zivug* from the Upper Light is made on the *Masach* of the lower one, called *Masach de Hirik*, and the level of *Hassadim* emerges on it, and this is the middle line. On the one hand, this *Masach* diminishes the GAR of the left line, and on the other hand, it increases the *Ohr Hassadim*. By these two, it compels the left line to unite with the right line.

Thus, the Light of VAK *de Hochma* of the left line clothes the *Hassadim* in the right line, and now it can shine. Also, this completes the left line, and the *Ohr Hassadim* in the right line unites with the *Hochma* in the left line, thus obtaining the Light of GAR, which completes the right line. Thus, you see how the middle line completes the two lines, right and left. This explains in general terms the *Tikkun* of the three lines that was established in the seven lower *Sefirot*.

THE EMERGENCE OF THE THREE LINES IN YESHSUT

33) Now we shall explain the order of emergence of the three lines in one particular degree. And from it, you will be able to deduce about all the degrees.

Take the degree of YESHSUT, for example, that is, the seven bottom *Sefirot* of *Bina*. GAR *de Bina de AA* were established in the Upper AVI, and ZAT *de Bina de AA* were established in YESHSUT. The first to emerge was the right line of YESHSUT–*Keter* and *Hochma de* YESHSUT. It was established during the ascent of *Malchut de* YESHSUT to *Bina de* YESHSUT, which ended the degree of YESHSUT under the *Hochma*, and *Bina* and TM *de* YESHSUT fell below, to the degree of ZA.

Then, these two *Kelim*, *Keter* and *Hochma*, remained in the degree of YESHSUT and became the right line. And since there are only two *Kelim* there, *Keter* and *Hochma*, they have only two Lights, *Nefesh Ruach*, lacking GAR.

34) Then the left line emerged–the three *Kelim* of *Bina* and TM of YESHSUT–after they returned and rose from their fall. It was established by the illumination of *Hochma* and *Bina de AK*, which brought the ending *Malchut*

from *Bina de YESHSUT*, and returned it to her place. At that time, *Bina* and *TM de YESHSUT* rise back to their degree.

And since the five *Kelim* in the *Partzuf* are now completed, the full NRNHY clothe in them. At that time they become the left line *de YESHSUT*. Also, with the emergence of the left line, there is a division between the right and the left: the right wishes to cancel the left and rule by itself, and the left, too, wishes to cancel the right and rule by itself. For this reason, neither can shine as long as the middle line, which unites them, has not been erected.

35) Afterwards emerged the middle line. It emerged by the *Masach* of the lowest degree in YESHSUT, ZA, which rose as MAN to YESHSUT. It rose to YESHSUT along with the three *Kelim Bina* and *TM* when they rose back to their degree.

The level of Light that emerges on this *Masach* unites the right and left in YESHSUT into one. However, the right shines from Above downwards and the left shines from below Upwards. In that state, the *Hochma* is dressed with *Hassadim* and can shine, while the *Hassadim* are included in the illumination of *Hochma* and are completed with GAR.

Thus, you find that before the establishment of the middle line, the right line and the left line were in dispute. They wanted to revoke one another: the right line, being unflawed and the root of the degree, wished to revoke the dominion of the left and subdue it, as is the root's relation to its branch. And since the left line holds the *Ohr Hochma*, which is greater than the *Ohr Hassadim* in the right line, its power is therefore great to revoke the *Ohr Hassadim* in the right line. This is why neither could shine, since *Hochma* cannot shine without clothing of *Hassadim*, and *Hassadim* without illumination of *Hochma* are VAK without a *Rosh*.

36) The reason *Hochma* cannot shine without *Ohr Hassadim* is that it is YESHSUT—the seven lower *Sefirot* of *Bina*—HGT NHYM *de Bina*. And these HGT NHYM *de Bina* are not the actual *Bina*, but from the *Hitkalelut* of ZA in *Bina*. This is because all ten *Sefirot* are included in one another and each *Sefira* contains ten *Sefirot*.

For example, the *Sefira Bina* is comprised of all ten *Sefirot* KHB TM, and its *Bina* is discerned as its self. *Keter* and *Hochma* in it are from *Keter* and *Hochma* that were included in it, and *Tifferet* and *Malchut*, which are its HGT NHYM, are from the *Hitkalelut* of ZON in it. And it is known that the *Sefira ZA* from its source in the ten *Sefirot de Ohr Yashar* is primarily *Ohr Hassadim*, but the *Ohr Hochma* shines in its *Hassadim*. Hence, it is impossible that *Hochma* will shine without *Hassadim* in all seven lower *Sefirot*, since they lack the core and the carrier of the illumination of *Hochma*—the *Hassadim*—the essence of ZA of the ten *Sefirot de Ohr Yashar*, which is the root of every seven lower *Sefirot* included in all the degrees.

Hence, the rule is that *Hochma* can shine without *Hassadim* only in the Light of the first three *Sefirot*. But in the seven lower *Sefirot*, wherever they are, they are considered ZA, and *Hochma* cannot shine without *Hassadim*, since the *Hassadim* are its main essence. For this reason, if *Hochma* is deficient of *Hassadim*, it is darkness and not Light.

37) But because of the Height of the *Hochma* that the left is holding, the left line does not surrender whatsoever to unite with the *Hassadim* in the right line. Moreover, it fights it and wishes to revoke it. It does not surrender to the right, unless by the two forces that rise from the middle line, which act on it and subdue it:

1. The *Masach* of *Behina Aleph* in the middle line, which is ZA. This *Masach* diminishes the level of *Hochma* in the left line from the level of GAR *de Hochma* to the level of VAK *de Hochma*. This is so that *Hochma* would not expand and shine from Above downwards, but would shine from below Upwards. This illumination is regarded as only VAK *de Hochma*.

2. The *Zivug* of the Upper Light on this *Masach de Behina Aleph*, which extends the level of *Ohr Hassadim*. Then, on the one hand, the level of *Hochma* in the left descended into VAK *de Hochma*, by the force of the *Masach*; and on the other hand, the *Hassadim* on the left line increased from two sides: from the side of the right line and from the side of the *Zivug* of the Upper Light on the *Masach* in the middle line. At that time, the left line surrenders and unites with the *Hassadim* in the right line and in the middle line. However, as long as the *Masach* in the middle line does not diminish the level of GAR *de Hochma*, there is no power in the world that can unite it with the right line.

38) We should know that two forces operate in this *Masach* of the middle line, to diminish the level of GAR *de Hochma* in the left line. This is because in themselves ZON are unfit to receive *Mochin*, as they are controlled by *Malchut* of *Midat ha Din*, who is ridden by the force of *Tzimtzum*, so as to not receive illumination of *Hochma*. We call this *Malchut* of *Midat ha Din*, *Man'ula* (lock). But afterwards, *Malchut* was associated with *Midat ha Rachamim*, *Bina*, and in *Behinat Malchut* that is associated with *Bina*, they are worthy of receiving

Mochin—Light of *Hochma*. And we call this *Malchut*, which is associated with *Bina*, *Miftacha* (key).

Hence, in *Masach de ZA*, too, which is their middle line, there are these two forces of *Miftacha* and *Man'ula*. In the beginning, when it needs to diminish the GAR of the left line, it works in this *Masach* of *Man'ula*, that is, in *Malchut* of *Midat ha Din*. Wherever it appears, the Upper Light flees. But since it wishes VAK *de Hochma* to remain, it subsequently removes this *Masach de Man'ula*, and operates with the *Masach de Miftacha*, being *Malchut* that is associated with *Bina*. And through its force, an illumination of VAK *de Hochma* remains, nevertheless.

Thus, we have thoroughly explained how ZA rises along with *Bina* and TM *de YESHSUT* to the degree of YESHSUT, and through its *Masach*, unites and completes the two lines, right and left in YESHSUT, where it becomes a middle line. And these three lines in YESHSUT are called *Hochma*, *Bina*, *Daat de YESHSUT*. The two lines, right and left, are called HB, and ZA, the middle line that decides between them, is called *Daat*.

HOLAM, SHURUK, HIRIK

39) These three lines are also called "the three points, *Holam*, *Shuruk*, *Hirik*." The right line is the point of *Holam*, the left line is the point of *Shuruk*, the *Melafom*, which is a *Vav* with a point within it, and the middle line is the point of *Hirik*. The reason for it is that points imply illumination of *Hochma*, which revive and move the *Otiot* (letters), which are the *Kelim*.

Hence, the right line, erected during *Malchut's* ascent to *Bina*, which lacks *Hochma*, is implied by the point of *Holam*, which stands above the *Otiot*. This indicates that the point, which is *Hochma*, is not clothed in the *Kelim*, which are the *Otiot*, but is above the *Kelim*.

And the left line is made of *Bina* and TM, which have *Ohr Hochma*, after they have returned to their degree. For this reason, it is implied by the point of *Shuruk*, which is a *Vav* with a dot within it. This indicates that the point, which is *Hochma*, is clothed inside the *Kelim*, called *Otiot*. And the middle line is made of the degree below it, which rose to the Higher Degree, deciding and completing its two lines.

Had it not been for the middle line, *Hochma* would never have been able to shine. And since this *Tikkun* comes from the degree below it, it is implied by the point of *Hirik*, which stands below the *Otiot*—the *Kelim*—as it is its inferior degree. And because of it, we always refer to the *Masach* of the middle line as *Masach de Hirik*.

THE MIDDLE LINE ABOVE THE TWO LINES

40) Indeed, there is a middle line above the two lines, in the first *Roshim* (heads) of *Atik*, where the *Reisha de lo Etyada* decides and unites the two lines, right and left, which are the two *Roshim*, *Keter* and *Hochma Stimaa de AA*, which are below it. But although they were erected as the root for the three lines, in all three lines, the middle line comes from below, except in these.

And you find that there are three *Behinot* (discernments) of *Tikkun Kavim*:

1. *Tikkun Kavim* in the three *Roshim de Atik*, where the middle line is above the two lines.
2. *Tikkun Kavim* in GAR, where there is no appearance of *Hochma* even in the left line (Item 26).
3. *Tikkun Kavim* in the seven lower *Sefirot*, where there is appearance of *Hochma* in the left line (Items 27-39).

THREE KINDS OF HOCHMA IN ATZILUT

41) There are three *Hochmas* in *Atzilut*:

1. *Hochma* in the ten *Sefirot de Ohr Yashar*, which, in the *Partzufim*, is *Hochma Stimaa de AA*;
2. GAR *de Bina*, which, in the *Partzufim*, is AVI, and is called "*Hochma* of the right";
3. ZAT *de Bina*, which, in the *Partzufim*, is YESHSUT, and is called "*Hochma* of the left."

The first two *Hochmas* are blocked and do not shine to the lower ones. Only the third *Hochma*, the *Hochma* of the left, is apparent at the place of *Malchut*, and shines to ZON and to the lower ones.

42) You already know that AA is *Hochma de Atzilut*, and AVI are GAR *de Bina de Atzilut*, and YESHSUT are the seven lower *Sefirot de Bina de Atzilut*. And it is known that there are only two *Sefirot*, *Keter* and *Hochma*, in *Rosh de AA*, called *Kitra* and *Hochma Stimaa*.[29] Its *Bina* departed its *Rosh* and became a *Guf* without a *Rosh* because of the ending *Malchut* that rose and ended the *Rosh* under its *Hochma*.

For this reason, *Bina* and TM are below the ending *Malchut* in the *Rosh* (Item 33), and hence was discerned as a *Guf*. Also, these *Bina* and TM are all named after the Highest *Behina* in them, which is *Bina*. And since it departed

---

29 Translator's note: these names are in Aramaic. *Kitra* is the *Sefira Keter*, and *Hochma Stimaa* means blocked *Hochma*.

the *Rosh* to form a *Guf* without a *Rosh*, it is no longer worthy of receiving *Hochma* until it returns to *Rosh de AA*.

43) This *Bina* is divided into two *Behinot*, GAR and ZAT, since the flaw of the absence of *Hochma* that was made in it by its exit from *Rosh* of AA does not affect the GAR *de Bina* whatsoever, since they are always in the state of "for he delights in mercy." Thus, *Bina* craves only *Ohr Hassadim*, and not *Ohr Hochma*. Even when it was at *Rosh de AA*, its GAR did not receive *Hochma*, but only *Hassadim*.

This extended to it from *Bina de Ohr Yashar*, whose essence is *Hassadim* without *Hochma*. For this reason, GAR *de Bina* are not flawed in any way by their exit from the *Rosh*, and they are considered completely perfect while still at the *Rosh de AA*. Hence, GAR *de Bina* were separated into a degree in and of themselves. Also, Upper AVI, clothing from *Peh de AA* downwards, which are always considered GAR, are made of them, although they are below the *Rosh* of AA.

But the seven lower *Sefirot de Bina* are not *Bina*'s essence, but are from the *Hitkalelut* of ZON in *Bina*. And the essence of ZA is the illumination of *Hochma* in *Hassadim*. Hence, they need illumination of *Hochma* in order to give to ZON. And since they are not worthy of receiving *Hochma* for ZON upon their exit from *Rosh de AA*, they are considered flawed.

For this reason, they were separated from the complete GAR *de Bina* and became a separate degree in itself, from which *Partzuf* YESHSUT *de Atzilut* that clothes from *Chazeh de AA* downwards was made. Also, they are considered VAK without a *Rosh*, until *Bina* returns to *Rosh de AA*, at which time they obtain GAR.

44) Thus, you see that *Hochma* is primarily at the *Rosh de AA*, called *Hochma Stimaa*, since this initial *Hochma* was blocked at the *Rosh* of AA and does not shine to the lower ones, below *Rosh de AA*. And AVI and YESHSUT are the original *Bina de Atzilut*, called "the level of SAG de MA," whose essence is *Hassadim* and not *Hochma*.

And upon the exit of *Bina* from *Rosh de AA*, only ZAT *de Bina*—YESHSUT—were flawed, and hence remained without GAR. They are completed only upon the return of *Bina* to *Rosh de AA*, at which time *Hochma* receives for ZON.

At that time, they are regarded as *Hochma* of the left line. This means that this *Hochma* appears only through the three lines that emerge in YESHSUT, where the *Hochma* appears in the left line of these three lines (Item 34).

Even though GAR and ZAT *de Bina*, which are AVI and YESHSUT, returned to *Rosh de AA*, YESHSUT do not receive the *Hochma* directly from *Hochma Stimaa* in *Rosh de AA*, since each degree receives only from its adjacent

Superior. Thus, *AVI* receive the *Hochma* from *Hochma Stimaa* at the *Rosh de AA*, and give to *YESHSUT*.

45) *AVI* are regarded as *Hochma* of the right. This is because even when they are below the *Rosh*, they are as complete as they were at the *Rosh*. They are always united with the *Hochma Stimaa* at the *Rosh de AA*, but do not receive from it, since they are always in the state of, "for he delights in mercy."

This thoroughly explains that the essence of *Hochma* is at the *Rosh de AA*, but it is blocked and does not shine at all below its *Rosh*. Also, the illumination of *Hochma Stimaa*, included in *AVI*, is considered *Hochma* of the right, although they do not actually receive it. And upon their return to the *Rosh*, they are called *Hochma Ilaa* (Upper *Hochma*).

And the reason they are considered *Hochma*, although they do not receive it, is that their unification with the *Hochma* turns the *Hassadim* in *AVI* into complete *GAR*. Also, the *Hochma* that shines in *YESHSUT* is the *Hochma* of the left, since it shines only in the left line. This *Hochma* of the left is called "Thirty-two paths of *Hochma* (wisdom)," and this is the *Hochma* that appears to *ZON* and to the lower ones.

But the *Hochma* of the right does not shine any *Hochma* at all, but only *Hassadim*, since *AVI* do not receive the *Hochma*, much less the *Hochma de Ohr Yashar* in the *Rosh de AA*, which does not shine below its *Rosh*. This is why it is called *Hochma Stimaa*. Thus, illumination of *Hochma* does not appear, but only *Hochma* of the left, even though this is not the actual *Hochma*, but *Bina* that receives *Hochma* for *ZON*.

THREE OTIOT, MEM, LAMED, TZADIK IN TZELEM

46) The *Mochin de Gadlut*—after *Malchut* came back down from *Bina's* place to her own, and *Bina* and *TM* returned to their degree, and the degree was completed with five *Kelim KHB TM* and five Lights *NRNHY*. This is considered that *Malchut*, which is the *Yod* that entered the *Ohr* (Light) and turned it into *Avir* (air), returned and departed the *Avir*, and the *Avir* went back to being *Ohr*. There are three degrees to discern in these *Mochin*, implied by the three *Otiot* (letters)—*Mem, Lamed, Tzadik*—which is *Tzelem*.

First Degree: This is the *GAR de Bina* that were established in Upper *AVI*. They are in a state of "for he delights in mercy," and never receive *Hochma*. For this reason, it is discerned in them that the *Yod* does not leave their *Avir*. This is because *Avir* implies the level of *Ruach, Hassadim*, and in *AVI* these *Hassadim* are regarded as actual *GAR*, and they have no interest in removing the *Yod* from their *Avir*.

Also, they are called *Mem de Tzelem*, since this letter implies that they contain four *Mochin*: *Hochma*, *Bina*, the right of *Daat*, and the left of *Daat*. Each *Moach* (singular for *Mochin*) comprises ten *Sefirot*, hence they are forty *Sefirot*. It also implies that the *Mochin* are closed as though by a ring, which is the form of the *Mem*, so as to not receive *Hochma*.

47) **Second Degree:** This is the seven lower *Sefirot* of *Bina* that were erected in YESHSUT, which require *Hochma* in order to give to ZON. Hence, during the *Gadlut*, the *Yod* leaves their *Avir* and the *Ohr Hochma* returns to them in order to give to ZON. Yet, they, too, do not receive *Hochma* for themselves, since they are from *Bina*, and every *Bina*, whether GAR or ZAT, is from *Ohr Hassadim*. The only difference is in the ZAT, which receive *Hochma* in order to give to ZON.

This degree is called *Lamed de Tzelem*. This letter implies that there are three *Mochin* in them: *Hochma*, *Bina*, and *Daat*. Each *Moach* contains ten *Sefirot*, hence they are thirty *Sefirot*. This is because the right in *Daat* and the left in *Daat* are regarded as one here, since they are considered the middle line, uniting *Hochma* and *Bina*.

48) The third degree is ZON, in which the *Hochma* appears from the *Chazeh* down, since the place where *Hochma* appears is in them. It is called *Tzadik de Tzelem*, after the nine *Sefirot* in ZON. Each comprises ten, hence they are ninety.[30] Thus we have explained the three *Otiot Mem, Lamed, Tzadik* (MLTz) in the three *Partzufim* AVI, YESHSUT, and ZON in the world of *Atzilut* in general. Yet, this is so in every detail, too, since there is no degree in which these three *Behinot* MLTz are not discerned, since each of them contains MLTz.

49) Yet, the place where *Hochma* appears is not in ZA, but in *Malchut*. When we say that *Hochma* appears from the *Chazeh de ZA* downwards, it is because from *Chazeh de ZA* downwards it is considered *Malchut*. Thus, *Hochma* does not appear in the first nine *Sefirot*, but only in *Malchut*. This is why *Malchut* is called *Hochma Tataa* (lower *Hochma*).

TWO DISCERNMENTS IN RAISING MAN

50) There are two *Behinot* (discernments) in raising MAN de ZA: 1) Since GAR de *Bina*, which are the Upper AVI, are always in *Achoraim* to *Hochma*. This means that they do not want to receive *Hochma*, but *Hassadim*, as it is written, "for he delights in mercy." Also, YESHSUT cannot receive *Hochma* from AA, but only through AVI (Item 44). Hence, YESHSUT cannot receive *Hochma* through AVI,

---
30 Translator's note: in *Gematria*, the numeric value of *Tzadik* is 90.

unless ZA rises to YESHSUT for MAN. At that time, AVI remove their *Achoraim* from the *Hochma*, and *Hochma* passes through AVI to YESHSUT.

This awakening extends from *Bina de Ohr Yashar*, which extends illumination of *Hochma* in *Hassadim* for ZA *de Ohr Yashar*. And therefore, whenever ZA rises for MAN, AVI awaken to extend *Hochma* for it.

51) The second discernment in the raising of MAN by ZA is to unite the two lines, right and left, in YESHSUT (Item 35). This is because when the left line of YESHSUT emerges, a division is made between the right and the left. For this reason, neither shines until ZA unites them with one another through the middle line, and then they both shine.

THREE COME OUT OF ONE, ONE EXISTS IN THREE

52) Thus, it has been explained that the second discernment in raising MAN *de* ZA to YESHSUT is to unite the two lines of YESHSUT, right and left. They can only shine through the *Masach de Hirik* in ZA (Item 39), which completes the middle line in them and determines the two lines of *Bina*. This is considered that three lines emerge in *Bina* through the *Masach de* ZA, called *Hochma*, *Bina*, and *Daat*.

The rule is that the lower one is rewarded with the full illumination that it causes in the Upper One. Hence, since ZA, with its *Masach*, caused the emergence of the three lines *Hochma*, *Bina*, and *Daat* in YESHSUT, ZA, too, is rewarded with the three lines, *Hochma*, *Bina*, and *Daat*. This is the meaning of what is written in *The Zohar*: "Three come out of one, one exists in three" (*Beresheet*, 1, Item 363).

THE ROOT OF NUKVA DE ZA, MEANING THE MALCHUT

53) During the *Katnut* of the world of *Nekudim*, ZA, which is HGT NHY *de Nekudim*, had six *Kelim*, HBD HGT. This is because from the perspective of the Lights, where the small ones grow first, they are called HGT NHY and they lack GAR. And from the perspective of the *Kelim*, where the Higher Ones grow first, they are called HBD HGT and they lack NHY *de Kelim*.

Thus, it lacked NHY *de Kelim* because of *Malchut's* ascent to the place of *Bina de* ZA, namely the *Sefira Tifferet*, since HGT *de* ZA are KHB (Item 9), that is, on the Upper third of *Tifferet*, in the place of the *Chazeh*. And the two thirds, *Bina* and TM, which, in ZA, are called the two thirds *Tifferet* and NHY, fell from its degree to the degree below it, to the worlds *Beria*, *Yetzira*, and *Assiya*, below ZA *de Atzilut*.

For this reason, only *HBD HGT de Kelim* through the point of *Chazeh* remained in it. And the point of *Chazeh* is the *Malchut* that ends the degree in the place of *Bina*, and lowers *Bina* and *TM*, called *TNHY*, to the degree below it (Item 16). This is why *ZON* in *Katnut* are always called *VAK* and *Nekuda*, since the six *Kelim HBD HGT* in it are called *VAK*, meaning *Vav Ktzavot* (six ends), and the point of *Chazeh*, which is the *Malchut* that ends its degree is called *Nekuda* (point). From the perspective of the Lights, where the smaller ones grow first, they are called *HGT NHY*, and the ending *Malchut* is called "*Nekuda* under the *Yesod*."

54) For this reason, *Malchut* took all the *Kelim* in *BYA* into her own domain, which is the point of the *Chazeh*. This is because this point took the *Kelim de TNHY de ZA* out to *BYA*. Also, she returned these *Kelim* to the degree of *Atzilut* when the *Gadlut de Nekudim* emerged, before they broke. This is because during the *Gadlut*, the ending *Malchut* declined from the place of the *Chazeh* back to her own place, under *NHY de Kelim de ZA*. Then the *Kelim de Bina* and *TM* that fell to *BYA*, which are *TNHY*, rose back to *Atzilut*. And since *ZA* acquired the complete *TNHY de Kelim*, it had Lights of *GAR*.

And since there is no absence in the spiritual, it is considered that even now *Malchut* remains in the place of *Chazeh de ZA* as before, and that only the force of *Din* and *Sium* (ending) in her descended to the point of this world. Hence, those *Kelim TNHY de ZA* that were under its authority during the *Katnut*, and now returned and united with *ZA*, unite with her during the *Gadlut*, as well, after they have been united and completed the *TNHY de ZA*.

Also, they become her lower nine *Sefirot*, since the point of *Chazeh*, which is the root of *Malchut* that she has had since the time of *Katnut*, has become *Keter*. And in the three *Kelim NHY de ZA*, each *Kli* was divided into three thirds. The three thirds of *Netzah de ZA* became *Malchut, Hochma, Hesed, Netzah*. And the three thirds of *Hod de ZA* became *Malchut, Bina, Gevura, Hod*, and the three thirds of *Yesod de ZA* became *Malchut, Daat, Tifferet, Yesod*. Thus, these *TNHY de ZA* that rose from *BYA* during the *Gadlut*, and united with its degree, causing its *GAR* of Lights, unite with *Malchut*, too, and become her nine lower *Sefirot* in *Kelim* and the first nine in Lights.

55) And you find that the root of *Nukva de ZA* is the point of the *Chazeh*, which is not absent in it even during the *Katnut*. And it is called by the name *Keter* of *Malchut*. These *Kelim TNHY de ZA* that fell into *BYA* during the *Katnut* and return to *Atzilut* during the *Gadlut*, divide into two *Partzufim*: *ZA* and

Malchut. This is because they serve as *TNHY de Kelim* for *ZA* and *HBD HGT NHY de Kelim* for *Malchut*.

FROM CHAZEH DE ZA DOWN, IT BELONGS TO NUKVA

56) This yields the rule that from *Chazeh de ZA* downwards, that is, the *Kelim TNHY de ZA*, are considered *Malchut*, called "the separated *Nukva de ZA*." This is because all bottom nine *Sefirot* of *Malchut* are made of these *TNHY de ZA* after they unite with it, during the *Gadlut*. Also, we thoroughly understand what we say, that in *Katnut*, *ZA* and *Malchut* are in the form of *Vav* and *Nekuda*, meaning *HBD HGT de Kelim* and *Nekuda* of *Chazeh*. *ZA* lacks *GAR* of Lights because of the absence of *NHY de Kelim*, and *Malchut* lacks the first nine *Sefirot* of Lights due to the absence of the lower nine in the *Kelim*.

Thus, it has been thoroughly clarified that the root of the *Nukva de ZA* in *Katnut* and *Gadlut* is from the *Katnut* and *Gadlut* of the world of *Nekudim*. And although the *Kelim de Nekudim* broke, they still returned and were corrected in the world of *Atzilut*, in both these times of *Katnut* and *Gadlut*. Thus, both *ZA* and *Malchut de Atzilut* are *VAK* and *Nekuda* in *Katnut*, as in the *Katnut* of the seven *Sefirot de Nekudim*.

At that time, *TNHY de ZA de Atzilut* are fallen in *BYA*, and this point is the root of the *Nukva*. During the *Gadlut*, they return to their degree in *ZA de Atzilut* and complete *NHY de Kelim* to *ZA* and the lower nine of *Kelim* to its *Nukva*, which is *Malchut*, as in *Katnut* and *Gadlut* of the world of *Nekudim*. Thus, these *TNHY de ZA* from its *Chazeh* down are the roots of *Gadlut de Nukva*.

TWELVE PARTZUFIM IN ATZILUT

57) Each degree that contains three times ten *Sefirot*—ten *Sefirot de Rosh*, ten *Sefirot de Toch*, and ten *Sefirot de Sof*—is called a *Partzuf*. It is discerned by its Highest *Behina*. If the Highest *Behina* is *Keter*, all thirty *Sefirot* in it are named *Keter*; and if the Highest *Behina* is *Hochma*, they are all called *Hochma*, etc.

Also, there are five *Partzufim* whose level is measured by the *Zivug de Hakaa* on the five *Behinot* in the *Masach*. A *Zivug de Hakaa* on *Masach de Behina Dalet* extends the level of *Keter*; *Masach de Behina Gimel* extends the level of *Hochma*; *Masach de Behina Bet* extends the level of *Bina*; *Masach de Behina Aleph* extends the level of *ZA*; and *Masach de Behinat* (*Behina of*) *Shoresh* extends the level of *Malchut*.

58) Yet, there are twelve *Partzufim* in *Atzilut*: the four *Partzufim* of *Keter*, called *Atik* and *Nukva*, and *Arich* and *Nukva*; the four *Partzufim* of *Bina*, called Upper *AVI* and *YESHSUT*; and the four *Partzufim* of *ZON*, called "the big *ZON*"

and "the little ZON." The reason they are divided in this manner is that each *Partzuf* in *Atzilut* comprises two kinds of *Kelim*:

- *Kelim* that emerged in the world of *Atzilut* in the *Zivugim de Hakaa* (plural for *Zivug de Hakaa*). Those are called *Kelim de MA*.
- *Kelim* that broke in the world of *Nekudim*, called *Kelim de BON*. They are corrected and rise from BYA, and connect to the levels that emerged through a *Zivug de Hakaa* in the world of *Atzilut*, called MA. Also, the *Kelim de MA* are considered "male" and the *Kelim de BON* are considered "female." Hence, each *Partzuf* contains male and female.

59) In addition, each *Partzuf* is divided into GAR and ZAT. It turns out that there is male and female in the GAR of the *Partzuf* and there is male and female in the ZAT of the *Partzuf*. For this reason, four *Partzufim* emerged in each *Partzuf*.

The two *Partzufim* of GAR of *Keter* are called *Atik* and *Nukva*, where *Atik* is MA and *Nukva* is BON. The two *Partzufim* of ZAT de *Keter* are called *Arich Anpin* and *Nukva*, where *Arich Anpin* is MA and *Nukva* is BON. The two *Partzufim* of GAR de *Bina* are called Upper AVI, the two *Partzufim* of ZAT de *Bina* are called YESHSUT, the two *Partzufim* of GAR de ZON are called "the big ZON," and the two *Partzufim* of ZAT in ZON are called "the little ZON."

60) The reason we do not count four *Partzufim* in *Hochma* is that AA is the level of *Hochma de MA*, but the *Hochma* in it has been blocked inside its *Keter*, by way of "one inside the other." Also, *Hochma* never shines in *Atzilut* at all. Instead, all the *Hochma* that shines in *Atzilut* is from *Bina* that returned to *Rosh de AA* and became *Hochma*. This *Bina* clothed in AVI and YESHSUT. And AVI are regarded as *Hochma* of the right, and YESHSUT are regarded as *Hochma* of the left (Item 41). Hence, we do not count four *Partzufim* in *Hochma*, but in *Bina*, which is also considered *Hochma*, which shines in ZA and *Malchut* in all the worlds.

A GREAT RULE IN TIME AND PLACE

61) Know that all the expressions in the wisdom of Kabbalah that are with time and place do not refer to the imaginary time and place in corporeality, since here everything is above time and above space. Rather, "before" and "after" refer to cause and consequence. We refer to the cause as "before," and to the consequence as "after," since every cause precedes its consequence.

Also, "above," "below," "ascent," and "descent" are measures of *Aviut* and *Zakkut* (purity).[31] This is because "ascension" means *Hizdakchut*, and "descent"

---

31 Translator's note: In Kabbalah, *Zakkut* refers to the power of the *Masach*, rather than to the traditional meaning of the word: purity.

means *Hit'abbut* (increasing the *Aviut*). And when we say that a lower degree rose, it means that the lower one has been purified and became as pure as the Higher Degree. Hence, it is considered to have clung to it because equivalence of form attaches the spirituals to one another.

Also, when we say that the lower one clothes the Upper One, it means that an equivalence of form with the externality of the Upper One has been made in it. This is because we call the *Dvekut* to the externality of the Upper One "clothing the Upper One." And it is the same in all other things perceived in time or in space. Study them in this manner, that is, in spiritual meanings, according to the issue.

TWO DIFFERENCES BETWEEN THE PARTZUFIM OF GAR AND THE PARTZUFIM OF VAK

62) Each *Partzuf* is emanated and born from the *Masach de Guf* of the Higher *Partzuf* by way of cause and consequence. This applies to all the *Partzufim*, from *Partzuf Keter de AK*, which emerged after the first restriction, to the end of the *Partzufim* of *Assiya*. Also, they clothe each other; that is, each lower one clothes the *Guf* of its Upper One.

63) The *Partzufim* are divided into *Partzufim* of GAR—*Partzuf Keter*, *Partzuf Hochma*, and *Partzuf Bina*—and *Partzufim* of VAK—*Partzuf ZAT de Bina*, called YESHSUT, *Partzuf ZA*, and *Partzuf Malchut*. These three *Partzufim* are always considered *Partzufim* of VAK. And even when they receive GAR, they do not stop being VAK, since they lack KHB from their very root. And there is a difference between the *Partzufim* of GAR and the *Partzufim* of VAK, both in their emergence and birth and in how they clothe the *Guf* of the Upper One.

The *Partzufim* of GAR exit from *Peh de Rosh* of their adjacent Upper One. This begins in *Partzuf Keter de AK*, since once *Partzuf Keter de AK* has emerged in *Rosh* and *Guf*, there was the *Bitush* of *Ohr Makif* (Surrounding Light) and *Ohr Pnimi* (Inner Light) in the ten *Sefirot* of the *Guf*.

This means that that Light, which the *Aviut* of the *Masach* detained from entering the *Guf* of the *Partzuf*, is called *Ohr Makif*. It struck the *Aviut* of the *Masach*, whose *Ohr Pnimi* is dressed in its *Ohr Hozer* (Reflected Light), and through this striking of the *Ohr Makif* in the *Aviut* on the *Masach*, the *Masach* in the *Guf* was purified and its form was equalized with the mating *Masach* at the *Rosh* of the *Partzuf*. This is considered that the *Masach de Guf* rose and was included in the *Masach* at the *Peh de Rosh*, inside the *Zivug* there, since equivalence of form is considered *Dvekut* (adhesion/attachment).

Hence, through its *Hitkalelut* (inclusion/mixture) in the *Zivug* of the *Rosh*, all the *Behinot* (discernments) of *Aviut* in the *Masach* were renewed, apart for the last *Behina*. Then, a *Zivug de Hakaa* on the measure of *Aviut* that remained in the *Masach*—*Aviut de Behina Gimel*—emerged on it from the Upper Light in the *Rosh*, and the level of *Partzuf Hochma* emerged on it.

At that time, it was recognized that the *Masach* was from another *Behina*, since the Upper One is *Partzuf Keter*, and this level that was renewed on the *Masach* is the level of *Hochma*, since the last *Behina* had been lost. And this recognition is considered "birth," meaning it departed the level of *Keter* and became a distinct *Partzuf* that has only the level of *Hochma*. Thus, the source of the newly born *Partzuf Hochma* is the *Masach de Guf* of the level of *Keter*, which purified and rose to the *Peh de Rosh*, and the exit, birthplace, is *Peh de Rosh* of *Partzuf Keter*.

And after *Partzuf Hochma* was born and emerged from *Peh de Rosh* of *Partzuf Keter*, it is considered clothing only the *Guf* of *Partzuf Keter*, that is, the GAR *de Guf*, which is HGT. This is because the *Masach de Guf* is the root from which it was born. Also, it clothes only the externality of the *Guf* of *Partzuf Keter*, since the level of *Behina Gimel* is external to *Partzuf Keter*, whose level is from the *Ohr Hozer* of *Behina Dalet*. Hence, this is regarded as clothing, indicating *Dvekut* in the externality.

64) As has been explained concerning the birth of *Partzuf Hochma de AK* from *Peh de Rosh* of *Partzuf Keter de AK*, *Partzuf Bina* emerged from *Peh* and *Rosh* of *Partzuf Hochma* in precisely this manner. After *Partzuf Hochma* had been completed with *Rosh* and *Guf*, there was another *Bitush* of *Ohr Makif* and *Ohr Pnimi*, which purifies the *Aviut* of the *Masach* and equalizes its form with the *Masach de Malchut* of the *Rosh*. And since it is included in the *Zivug* of the *Rosh*, the *Behinat Aviut* in it has been renewed, except for the last *Behina*, which was lost.

Then, ten *Sefirot* emerged on the remaining *Aviut* in it, *Aviut de Behina Bet*, at the level of *Bina*. And since it has been recognized that it is a lower level than *Partzuf Hochma*, it was discerned as separated from it and was born into its own domain. Yet, it clothes the *Guf* of the Upper One, which is its root. And it also clothes the GAR *de Guf*, at the place of HGT.

65) The three *Partzufim* of VAK—YESHSUT, ZA, and *Malchut*—emerged in this very way, except there are two differences in them:

1. Their lower one does not emerge from the *Peh de Rosh* of its adjacent Upper One, but from the *Peh de Rosh* of the one Above its Upper One. For example, ZA does not emerge from *Peh de Rosh de* YESHSUT, but only after YESHSUT has become one *Partzuf* with AVI, which are one Above its Upper One. Similarly, *Nukva* does not emerge from *Peh de Rosh* of ZA, but only after ZA has risen to AVI. Likewise, *Partzuf Atik de Atzilut*

did not emerge from the first *Rosh* of *Nekudim*, but from the *Rosh* of *SAG de AK*. The reason is that these *Roshim* (plural for *Rosh*), considered VAK from their very root, are unfit for *Zivug* with the Upper Light in a way that they can emanate a lower *Partzuf*.

2. This concerns the clothing: The *Partzufim* of VAK do not clothe the GAR *de Guf* of their Upper One, HGT, but the VAK of the *Guf* of the Upper One, which is NHY from the *Chazeh* downwards. Since they are VAK at their root, they cannot cling to the GAR *de Guf* of the Upper One. Thus, the two differences between the *Partzufim* of GAR and the *Partzufim* of VAK have been thoroughly clarified:

- One concerns the emergence, where only *Partzufim* of GAR emerge from the *Peh* of their adjacent Upper One. This is not so in the *Partzufim* of VAK, which emerge from the one Above their Upper One.

- And the other concerns the clothing, that only *Partzufim* of GAR can cling to the HGT of the Upper One, which are GAR *de Guf*, but not the *Partzufim* of VAK, which cling only from the *Chazeh* downwards, in the VAK *de Guf*.

THREE CONDITIONS FOR THE EMERGENCE OF A LOWER PARTZUF

66) There are three conditions for a *Zivug* to beget a lower *Partzuf*:

The first condition is the *Masach* that mates with the Upper Light in *Zivug de Hakaa* and raises *Ohr Hozer*, which clothes the Upper Light. The level of the lower one is according to the measure of clothing of *Ohr Hozer*. Similarly, after the *Masach* elicited all the *Partzufim* and degrees in the world of *Nekudim*, they did not persist but broke and cancelled, and the *Masach* was purified of all five *Behinot Aviut* in it, returned to *Rosh de SAG*, and all the degrees that emerged in *Nekudim* left their *Reshimot* in the *Masach*.

Hence, when the *Masach* was included in the *Zivug* in *Rosh de SAG*, its previous *Reshimot* were renewed in it. Initially, the *Masach* elicited the Highest *Behina* in it, the *Reshimo* of *Partzuf Keter*, called *Atik de Atzilut*, at *Aviut* of *Behina Dalet*. The rest of the *Reshimot*, which remained in the *Masach*, emerged along with the birth of *Atik* to the place of *Atik*.

And once *Atik* had been completed, there was a *Zivug de Hakaa* in it, on the Highest *Behina* in the remainder of the *Masach* within it, which is *Behina Gimel*, and elicited the level of AA on it. And the rest of the *Reshimot* in the *Masach*, on which the *Zivug de Hakaa* has not yet been made, descended along with the birth of AA to the place of AA.

And when AA was completed, a *Zivug* was made in it on the Highest *Behina* in the remainder of the *Masach*, which is *Behina Bet*, and elicited the level of AVI, etc., similarly. Thus, all the *Partzufim* emerge through a *Zivug de Hakaa* of the Upper Light with the *Masach*.

67) **The second condition** is that *Keter* and *Hochma* of each lower one are attached to the *Bina* and *TM* of their Upper One. Hence, when the Upper One is completed and raises its *Bina* and *TM*, *Keter* and *Hochma* of the lower one rise along with them to the place of the Upper One and are included in the *Zivug* of the Upper One. Thus, each lower one receives its level from the *Zivug* of the *Rosh* of the Upper One.

68) **The third condition** is that ZA rises to YESHSUT and completes and unites the Lights of the right and left of YESHSUT. Had it not been for the ascent of ZA for MAN, the right and left of YESHSUT would have been unable to shine. It follows that the ascent of ZA to YESHSUT caused the elicitation of the three lines, right, left, and middle, which are HBD de YESHSUT.

There is a rule: the lower one is rewarded with the full measure of Light that it causes its illumination in the Upper One. Hence, ZA receives the same *Mochin de HBD* from YESHSUT. This is the meaning of "Three emerge from one; one exists in three." Thus, we have explained the three conditions for the *Zivug* to elicit the lower one.

69) In essence, the *Zivug* to elicit the lower one emerges from the *Zivug de Hakaa* of Upper Light on the *Masach*, since this measures the level of the lower one. Yet, it requires an awakening of MAN of the lower one, and this awakening is done by *Keter* and *Hochma* of the lower one, which are attached to *Bina* and *TM* of the Upper One. Therefore, both are required for eliciting a lower *Partzuf*.

Yet, in ZA there is an additional matter: its *Masach* does not extend *Kelim de GAR*, since it is a *Masach* of *Behina Aleph*. Thus, the Upper One cannot give it *Mochin* from a *Zivug* of the *Masach* in the Upper Light. Hence, the third condition is required—to receive the *Mochin* by inducing *Mochin* in its Upper One, as in "three emerge from one; one exists in three."

THREE STAGES IN THE ELICITATION OF THE TEN SEFIROT

70) **The first stage** is in the first *Partzufim* of AK, where all ten *Sefirot* emerged at once. In the *Zivug de Hakaa* on the *Masach de Behina Dalet*, the ten *Sefirot* of the level of *Keter* emerged. And in the *Zivug de Hakaa* on the *Masach de Behina Gimel*, ten *Sefirot* at the level of *Hochma* emerged. And in the *Zivug de Hakaa* on the *Masach de Behina Bet*, ten *Sefirot* at the level of *Bina* emerged.

71) **The second stage** is the world of *Nekudim*, which emerged on a *Masach de Behina Aleph*, connected with the *Malchut*, and in which ten *Sefirot* emerged in two times. First, *Malchut* rose to *Bina de SAG de AK*. Then, when the *Masach* of SAG purified into *Behina Aleph*, called *Nikvey Eynaim*, *Malchut* rose and conjoined with *Behina Aleph*, ending the degree under the *Hochma*, called *Eynaim*. It follows that only two *Kelim* remained in the degree, *Keter* and *Hochma*, with two Lights, *Ruach* and *Nefesh*. And the three *Kelim Bina* and *TM* fell from the degree. This is called *Katnut* (smallness) *de Nekudim*.

At the time of *Gadlut* (greatness, adulthood), the three *Kelim Bina* and *TM* returned to the degree and the five *Kelim KHB TM* in the degree were completed with the five Lights *NRNHY*. Thus, it has been clarified that in the world of *Nekudim*, the ten *Sefirot* did not emerge at once, as in the first three *Partzufim de AK*, but rather emerged at two times—a time of *Katnut* and a time of *Gadlut*. During the *Katnut*, only two *Sefirot* emerged, and during the *Gadlut*, the remaining three *Sefirot* emerged.

72) The third stage is the world of *Atzilut*, in which the ten *Sefirot* emerged in three times, called *Ibur* (conception), *Yenika* (nursing), and *Mochin*. It is so because here the *Hizdakchut* of the *Masach* at the last degree was added to the world of *Atzilut*. This is because the *Masach* was purified from *Behina Aleph*, called *Nikvey Eynaim*, into a *Masach* with *Aviut* of *Behinat Shoresh*, whose *Ohr Hozer* clothes only the level of the Light of *Malchut* in the *Kli* of *Keter*, called *Metzach*. Hence, this Light is called "MA that emerges from the *Metzach* (forehead)." This is because *KHB TM de Rosh* are called *Galgalta, Eynaim, AHP*, and *Metzach* is *Galgalta*.

Hence, two descents of *Malchut* are required here:

1. A decline from the *Metzach* to *Nikvey Eynaim*, called *Yenika*.
2. A decline from the *Nikvey Eynaim* to her place at the *Peh*. This is called *Mochin*.

Thus, the first level that emerges on the *Masach* of *Aviut Shoresh* is called *Ibur*. The second level, emerging on the *Masach* after *Malchut's* descent to *Behina Aleph*, is called *Yenika*. And the third level, emerging on the *Masach* after *Malchut's* decline to her place, is called *Mochin*. Thus, it has been clarified that in the world of *Atzilut*, the ten *Sefirot* emerge at three times, called *Ibur, Yenika*, and *Mochin*.

IBUR, YENIKA, MOCHIN DE ACHOR, AND IBUR, YENIKA, MOCHIN DE PANIM

73) It has already been explained that the level that emerges on a *Masach* with mere *Aviut Shoresh* is called "the level of *Ibur*." This is the level of the Light of *Nefesh* in the *Kli* of *Keter*. With respect to its three lines, it is called "the level of NHY." Yet, there is the level of *Ruach* in it, too, called "the level of HGT," except it is without *Kelim*. For this reason, HGT must clothe in *Kelim de* NHY, which is why the level of *Ibur* is called "three inside three," meaning HGT inside NHY.

74) The meaning of it is that although the *Hizdakchut* of the *Masach* causes the loss of the last *Behina*, for which the five levels are one below the other, the last *Behina* is not entirely lost, but a *Reshimo de Hitlabshut* of it remains in the *Masach*. For example, when the *Masach* of *Partzuf Keter de AK* was purified and rose to *Peh de Rosh*, it was included in the *Zivug* there, and its *Reshimot* were renewed. With respect to the *Aviut* in the *Masach*, on which the *Zivug de Hakaa* was made, only the *Reshimo* of *Aviut de Behina Gimel* remained in the *Masach*, since the last *Behina*, *Behina Dalet*, had been lost. But the part of the *Hitlabshut* of *Behina Dalet* still remained in the *Masach*.

It follows that there are two Upper *Behinot* in the *Masach* that are fit for *Zivug*:

1. The *Aviut* of *Behina Gimel*, which detains the Upper Light and receives the *Zivug de Hakaa*, on which the level of *Hochma* emerges.
2. The *Hitlabshut* of *Behina Dalet*. Even though it is unfit for *Zivug de Hakaa*, since it has no *Aviut* that detains the expansion of the Light, when it is included and associated with *Aviut de Behina Gimel*, a *Zivug de Hakaa* is done on it, too, producing nearly the level of *Keter*.

These two levels are called "male" and "female." The level that emerged on *Behina Dalet de Hitlabshut*, associated with *Behina Gimel de Aviut* is called "male," and the level that emerged on only *Behina Gimel de Aviut* is called "female."

Similarly, when the *Masach de Guf* of *Partzuf Hochma de AK* purified and rose to its *Peh de Rosh*, two *Reshimot* remained in it—male and female. This is because the *Reshimo de Behina Gimel de Hitlabshut*, associated with *Behina Bet de Aviut*, produces nearly the level of *Hochma*. This is considered the male. And the *Reshimo de Behina Bet de Aviut*, which is the primary one that receives the *Zivug de Hakaa*, produces the level of *Bina*. This is considered a female.

In the same way, there are male and female in the *Hizdakchut* of the *Masach de Guf de Partzuf Nekudim*. The male, that is, the *Reshimo de Behina Aleph de Hitlabshut* that remained in the *Masach*, is associated with *Behinat Aviut de Shoresh* at nearly the level of *Behina Aleph*, meaning the level of *ZA*, which is the level of *Ruach*, *HGT*. And the female, which is the *Aviut* of *Behinat Shoresh*, which receives the *Zivug de Hakaa*, is at the level of the Light of *Nefesh*, *Malchut*, which, from the perspective of the three lines, is called *NHY*.

75) Therefore, we discern two levels at the level of *Ibur*: the level of *HGT* and the level of *NHY*. The level of *HGT*, which is male, emerges on the *Reshimot de Behina Aleph de Hitlabshut*, which is joined with *Aviut de Shoresh*. And the level of *NHY*, which is female, emerges only on the *Reshimo de Aviut Shoresh*.

And since the *Reshimo de Hitlabshut* is unfit to receive a *Zivug de Hakaa*, except through association with *Aviut Shoresh*, the level of *HGT* does not stand on its own, but must clothe inside the *NHY*. For this reason, the level of *Ibur*, which is *HGT* and *NHY* together, is regarded as "three within three," that is, *HGT* within *NHY*.

76) And after the two levels *HGT* within *NHY* emerged in the *Hitkalelut* of the *Zivug de Rosh* of the Upper One, and it was recognized that they are new levels, different from the Upper One, this recognition is considered "birth." This means it has been recognized that a new *Partzuf* has been born here, different from the Upper One, and they decline and clothe the *Guf* of the Upper One. If they are *Partzufim* of GAR, they clothe the GAR *de Guf*, which are *HGT*, and if they are *Partzufim* of VAK, they clothe the VAK *de Guf*, which are *TNHYM* from the *Chazeh* downwards.

Also, they suck the Light from the Upper *Partzuf*, a suction that makes for *Malchut's* descent from the *Metzach* to the *Nikvey Eynaim*. At that time, it receives *Aviut de Behina Aleph* once more, which is connected to *Malchut*, as it was in the *Partzufim of Nekudim*. Then the level of *HGT* acquires *Behinot Kelim*, as well, and they no longer need the *Kelim de NHY*. It is therefore considered that through the suction, *HGT* expand and exit the *NHY*. And then it has the complete level of *Ruach*.

For example, in *Partzuf Atik de Atzilut*, the *Masach de Nekudim* rose first—through its *Hizdakchut*—to *Rosh de SAG de AK*. And after the last *Behinat* (*Behina* of) *Aviut* in it had been lost, the *Masach* remained with *Aviut de Behinat Shoresh*, called *Metzach*, and *Reshimo de Hitlabshut de Behina Aleph*. And then two levels, *HGT NHY*, emerged on it, three within three, since *HGT* has no *Kelim*.

When they were recognized as a new level, it is considered that they had departed and were born and came to their place, to clothe from *Tabur de AK* downwards. Since it is *Partzuf VAK*, it clothes only *VAK de Guf*, and this is called *Partzuf Atik*.

Afterwards, through *Yenika*, which it sucks from *SAG de AK*, it lowers the *Masach* from the *Metzach* to *Nikvey Eynaim*. Following, the *Kelim* come out to its *HGT*, as well, expanding from within the *NHY*. Thus, the two *Behinot*, called *Ibur* and *Yenika*, have been clarified.

77) Now we shall explain *Partzuf Mochin*. After the *Partzuf* received the two *Behinot Ibur* and *Yenika*, it rises for MAN to the Upper One and brings *HB* of the Upper One back to being face-to-face. Then they give the lower one the illumination that lowers *Malchut* from *Nikvey Eynaim* to her own place—the *Peh*.

At that time, these three *Kelim*, *Bina* and *TM*, which fell because of *Malchut's* ascent to *Bina* rise back to their degree, and the *Partzuf* is completed with five *Kelim KHB TM* and five Lights *NRNHY*. This is called *Partzuf Mochin*, since the first three Lights *Neshama*, *Haya*, *Yechida* are called *Mochin*.

For example, after *Atik* received the complete two *Behinot Ibur* and *Yenika*, which are the levels of *Nefesh* and *Ruach*, it rises back to *Rosh de SAG* for MAN, and returns the *Hochma* and *Bina* there to being face-to-face. And since the *Bina* in *Partzuf Hochma de AK* is not mixed with *Malchut*, when *Atik* receives its illumination it lowers its *Malchut* from its *Bina*, too. At that time, it raises the three *Kelim Bina* and *TM*, which fell by the mixture of *Malchut* in *Bina*, to its own degree, and now it has *KHB TM de Kelim*, in which the Lights *NRNHY* can clothe.

78) And when these *Mochin* emerge for the first time, it causes a rift between the right and the left. This is because the left line, which carries the illumination of *Hochma*, wishes to cancel the right line, which carries the Light of *Hassadim*. Because of this rift and *Bitush* (beating) of right and left that occur in these *Mochin*, they are called *Mochin de Achor*. Thus, the three *Behinot Ibur*, *Yenika*, and *Mochin de Achor* have been clarified.

79) This *Bitush* of left and right causes the *Partzuf* to return to raising MAN to the Upper One. This is because the illumination of the left, which is illumination of *Hochma*, strikes and purifies all the *Aviut* in the *Partzuf* until the *Masach* becomes as pure as it was when it first rose to the *Rosh* of the Upper One. This means that only *Aviut Shoresh* and *Reshimo de Hitlabshut de Behina Aleph* remained in it. And through this equivalence, it adheres to the *Rosh* of the Upper One.

Once it is incorporated in the *Zivug de Rosh* of the Upper One, it receives a *Zivug de Hakaa* from the Upper Light once more, on the *Aviut of Behinat Shoresh* and *Behina Aleph de Hitlabshut* that were renewed in the *Masach*. This elicits the level of three within three on it once more, meaning the level of *HGT*, clothed in the level of *NHY*, called "the level of *Ibur*." Thus we have explained that the *Bitush* of the left and the right that occurred in *Mochin de Achor* caused the *Partzuf* to return to the Upper One and receive a new *Behina* of *Ibur* from the Upper One.

80) And once it received the new *Behinat Ibur*, it departed the *Rosh* of the Upper One once more and clothed the *Guf* of the Upper One. And through this clothing, it sucked the Lights from the Upper One once more.

These Lights of *Yenika* lowered the *Aviut de Shoresh* into *Aviut* of *Behina Aleph*. They lowered the *Malchut* from the *Metzach* to the place of *Nikvey Eynaim*, at which time a complete level of *Behina Aleph* emerged n the *Masach*. This is regarded as the *Hitpashtut* (expansion) of *HGT* from within the *NHY*. It follows that it has obtained a new *Behina* of *Yenika*, which is the level of *Ruach*.

81) And after it obtained new *Ibur* and *Yenika*, it rises for *MAN* to the Upper One once more, and this ascension is by itself, since by leaving its root attached to *Bina* and *TM* of the Upper One (Item 67), it can now return there whenever it needs. It unites the *HB* that are there face-to-face, and they bestow upon it the illumination that lowers the *Malchut* from *Nikvey Eynaim* to its place. At that time, *Bina* and *TM* rise and unite in it as before, and it obtains *KHB TM de Kelim* and *NRNHY* of Lights.

To prevent the rift of right and left from reawakening, the middle line rises from below and unites the right and the left so they shine together: the *Hochma* on the left will clothe in the *Hassadim* on the right, and the *Hassadim* on the right will be integrated in the *Hochma* on the left (Item 37). Then the *Mochin* shine in their fullest perfection, and they are called *Mochin de Panim*. Thus we have explained how due to the *Bitush* of left and right in the *Mochin de Achor*, the three *Behinot Ibur, Yenika*, and *Mochin de Panim* reemerged.

82) Hence, a *Partzuf* is complete only after it receives *Ibur, Yenika*, and *Mochin de Achor* and *Ibur, Yenika*, and *Mochin de Panim*. Because of the *Hizdakchut* of the *Masach* that was added in *Atzilut* to the degree of *Aviut* of *Behinat Shoresh*, the *Partzufim* of *Atzilut* will not be able to receive their ten *Sefirot*, except after three consecutive times, called *Ibur, Yenika, Mochin*. And since at the first elicitation of *Mochin* there was the *Bitush* of right and left, until the left purified all the *Aviut* in the *Masach*, all the Lights, *Ibur, Yenika*, and *Mochin* it had received departed.

This is so because when the *Aviut* in the *Masach* is cancelled, the *Zivug* is cancelled and the Lights depart. The *Partzuf* returns to the *Rosh* of the Upper One for an *Ibur*, receiving new three within three. Then it is born and receives a new *Yenika*, which lowers the *Malchut* from *Metzach* to *Eynaim*, the *HGT* exit the *NHY*, and it receives the level of *Ruach* once more. Subsequently, it rises for MAN and receives *Neshama, Haya, Yechida* once more, in which there is already the middle line, which unites the right and the left with each other. This is called *Mochin de Panim*, and then they shine and persist. Thus, before the *Mochin* is obtained for the second time, they cannot persist.

PANIM AND ACHOR (FACE-TO-BACK), AND PANIM BE PANIM (FACE-TO-FACE)

83) Even while the *Partzuf* has already received the *Mochin de Panim*, the *Hochma* and *Bina* there are still in a state of *Panim* and *Achor*. This means that only *Hochma* receives the *Mochin de Panim*. But *Bina* is always in a state of delighting in mercy and wants *Hassadim* and not *Hochma*; hence, it is considered that its *Achoraim* are towards the *Hochma*, and it does not want to receive the *Mochin de Panim* from it.

Hochma and *Bina* are at that state of *Panim* and *Achor* until ZA rises to them for MAN. Also, there is a connection between *Bina de Ohr Yashar*, imparting illumination of *Hochma* to ZA *de Ohr Yashar*. Hence, when ZA rises for MAN to *Bina*, *Bina* immediately turns her *Panim* back to *Hochma* to receive the *Mochin de Panim* from it—which are *Mochin* of illumination of *Hochma*—for ZA, as it does in the five *Behinot* of *Ohr Yashar*. Then it is discerned that *Hochma* is already *Panim be Panim* with *Bina*.

WHO MEASURES THE LEVEL IN ATZILUT?

84) And we should ask this: "The *Masach de Atzilut* has only *Behinat Shoresh de Aviut*, called *Metzach*, having only the level of *Ohr Nefesh*. Thus, who caused the emergence of the five *Partzufim* in *Atzilut, Atik, AA, AVI*, and *ZON*, where *Atik* is the level of *Yechida*, AA—the level of *Haya*, AVI—the level of *Neshama*, and ZON—the level of *Ruach*?" This question applies also to the world of *Nekudim*, since only *Aviut de Behina Aleph* remained in the *Masach*, called *Nikvey Eynaim*. Thus, how could five *Partzufim* emerge in *Nekudim*?

85) The thing is that *Behina Dalet*, too, was connected in the *Masach de Nekudim* and in the *Masach de Atzilut* by the force of *Malchut* that rose to *Nekudot de SAG de AK*. And had *Behina Dalet* not been associated in the *Masach* in them, no *Partzuf* would have been able to emerge on that *Masach*. This is because even the *Aviut de Behina Aleph* in *Nekudim* is regarded as "thin *Histaklut*" (looking), from which the *Zivug de Hakaa* does not produce any *Partzuf*. It is all the more

so in the *Aviut de Metzach* in *Atzilut*: it is unfit for a *Zivug de Hakaa* for the elicitation of a *Partzuf*.

But since *Behina Dalet* conjoined with their screens, they became fit for *Zivug de Hakaa*. Now we may ask, "In that case, the level of *Keter* should have emerged on the *Masach*, since *Behina Dalet* is attached to the *Masach*!"

86) The answer is that *Behina Dalet* does not produce the level of *Keter*, except when it is at the place of *Malchut*. At that time, the *Ohr Hozer* that rises from the *Zivug de Hakaa* on it clothes the five *Kelim KHB TM* over the five Lights *NRNHY*. But if *Behina Dalet* stands at the place of *ZA*, where there are only four *Kelim KHB Tifferet*, the *Ohr Hozer* draws only four Lights *NRNH* in four *Kelim KHB* and *Tifferet*.

And if *Behina Dalet* stands at the place of *Bina*, where there are only three *Kelim KHB*, the *Ohr Hozer* draws only three Lights *NRN*. And if *Behina Dalet* stands at the place of the *Kli de Hochma*, where there are only two *Kelim*—*Keter* and *Hochma*—its *Ohr Hozer* draws only two Lights, *Nefesh Ruach*.

This is what happened in *Nekudim*, where the *Zivug* was made at the *Nikvey Eynaim*, which is the *Kli de Hochma*. Hence, only the level of *Nefesh Ruach* emerged in *Katnut*.

And if *Behina Dalet* stands at the place of *Keter*, where there is but one *Kli*, its *Ohr Hozer* draws only one Light: *Nefesh*. This is what happened in *Atzilut*—only the level of *Nefesh* emerged in the *Ibur*, since the *Zivug* was at the place of the *Metzach*, which is the *Kli de Keter*.

Yet, after the illumination of *Yenika*, which *Behina Dalet* rejected to the place of *Behina Aleph*, called *Nikvey Eynaim*, the level of *Ruach* emerged. But then, through illumination of *HB Panim be Panim* of the Upper One, which lowered *Behina Dalet* to her place in *Malchut*, which raises the fallen *Bina* and *TM* to their degree, there are five *Kelim KHB TM* there once again. At that time, *Behina Dalet* elicits the level of *Keter* in the Light of *Yechida*, and this is the level of *Atik de Atzilut*.

87) Now we need to explain how the rest of the *Partzufim* below *Atik* came out. In the beginning, after the breaking of the vessels, *Masach de Nekudim* rose to *Rosh de SAG*. It was purified of all five *Behinot Aviut* that emerged in it in five *Partzufim*, until it equalized with the *Masach of Rosh de SAG*. Yet, the *Reshimot* from the *Aviut* of the five *Partzufim* that emerged in it remained in it, except for the last *Behina*, which was lost, as it is written about all the *Partzufim*. Thus, when it was included in the *Zivug* of the *Masach of Rosh de SAG*, the *Aviut* of all five *Partzufim* was renewed in the *Masach de Nekudim*, and a *Zivug de Hakaa* emerged on the *Aviut* in the *Masach*.

However, not all the *Behinot* in the *Aviut* participated in the *Zivug de Hakaa*, but only its Highest *Behina*, which is *Aviut de Metzach*, connected to *Behina Dalet*. And through the three *Behinot Ibur*, *Yenika*, and *Mochin*, its ten *Sefirot* were completed at the level of *Keter*.

The other *Reshimot*, from the rest of the *Partzufim de Nekudim* that were in the *Masach*, did not receive anything from this *Zivug* at the *Rosh de SAG*, since they are below the level of *Keter*; hence, they are waste compared to its value. For this reason, upon the emergence of *Atik* from *Rosh de SAG*, all the *Reshimot* from the rest of the *Partzufim* that were not included in its *Zivug* came down with it.

And after *Atik* was completed in *Ibur*, *Yenika*, *Mochin de Panim*, the Upper Light shone on the Highest *Behina* from the *Reshimot* that remained in it, which is *Aviut de Behina Gimel*. And through the three *Behinot*, *Ibur*, *Yenika*, and *Mochin*, ten *Sefirot* at the level of *Hochma* emerged. This is *Partzuf AA*.

It is the same here; all the *Reshimot de Aviut* that are less than *Aviut de Behina Gimel* are waste compared to the value of the *Zivug* at the level of *Behina Gimel* that emerged in *Rosh de Atik*. Hence, when AA was born and departed *Rosh de Atik* to its place, all those *Reshimot* were drawn to its place along with it.

And after AA obtained all three *Behinot Ibur*, *Yenika*, *Mochin* in completeness, the Upper Light shone on the Highest *Behina* that remained in those *Reshimot*, which is *Aviut de Behina Bet*. Then, through the three *Behinot Ibur*, *Yenika*, *Mochin*, ten *Sefirot* at the level of *Bina* emerged on it. This is *Partzuf AVI*, and the rest of the *Partzufim* emerged similarly. Thus we have explained how the *Partzufim* of *Atzilut* emerged from one another.

TWO STATES IN MALCHUT

88) *Malchut* is the *Nukva de ZA*. Her root begins in *Malchut de Tzimtzum Bet*, which ended the seven *Sefirot de Katnut de ZA de Nekudim*. And it is a separate degree from ZA, since ZA includes HGT NHY *de Nekudim*, and the degree below it is *Malchut*, which ends the *Nekudim*. Hence, this *Malchut* is considered a separate *Nukva* from ZA and a lower degree than ZA.

And there is also *Behinat Nukva* in the *Guf* of ZA, since the left side of ZA is considered its *Nukva*. Yet, this *Nukva* is considered ZA's own *Guf* (body), since ZA is the middle line, which receives from the two lines, right and left, of *Bina*. The right in it receives from *Bina*'s right line, which is *Ohr Hassadim*, considered the male side in it, and the left side in it receives from the left line of *Bina*, which is *Ohr Hochma*, considered the *Nukva* side in it. Yet, both are one degree, included in one another.

It is known that in the beginning, the sun and the moon, which are the separate *Nukva* and ZA, were considered the two great lights. The level *Nukva* was equal to that of ZA, and she was as big as him. But then the moon—the *Nukva* that is separated from ZA—complained and said, "Two kings cannot use the same *Keter* (crown)." Then she was told, "Go, diminish yourself." Thus she became the small light.

Thus, you find two states here in *Nukva*:

- In the first state, she was with ZA, in the state of the two great lights, equal to ZA;
- The second state is after the *Nukva* was diminished and became the small light.

Explanation: In the beginning of the correction of the separate *Nukva de* ZA, the Emanator connected her with the *Nukva* in the *Guf* of ZA, which is the left side in it, and the two became one *Nukva* for ZA. When *Mochin* of right and left were drawn for them from *Bina*, ZA, which is the right in it, took the Lights of the right of *Bina*, and the separate *Nukva* took the Lights of the left line of *Bina*, like the *Nukva* in the *Guf* of ZA, since she was joined into a single *Nukva* with her.

And you already know that the Lights of the right line *de Bina* are *Hassadim*, and the Lights of the left line *de Bina* are *Hochma*. It follows that now ZA received the *Hassadim* of the right of *Bina* without *Hochma*, and the separate *Nukva* received the *Hochma* of the left of *Bina* without *Hassadim*, and it is known that *Hochma* cannot shine without *Hassadim*. For this reason, the *Hochma* froze in it and she became darkness and not Light.

This is the meaning of the moon's complaint, saying that two kings cannot use the same *Keter*. This is because when they both use the same *Keter*, which is *Bina*, considered their *Keter*, ZA becomes *Hassadim* without *Hochma*, and the *Nukva* becomes *Hochma* without *Hassadim*, which is darkness, and she could not tolerate that state.

We could ask, "But before the separate *Nukva* joined with the *Nukva* in his *Guf*, the right in it, which is the male, did receive *Hassadim*, and the left in it, which is the *Nukva* in his *Guf* received *Hochma*; yet, the *Nukva* in his *Guf* could tolerate it and was not darkness!" The thing is that the *Nukva* in his *Guf* is ZA's own self. Hence, the *Hochma* in her is not separated from the *Hassadim* in ZA. But this is not so with the separate *Nukva*, which is truly a different degree from ZA. But because it joined with the *Nukva* in his *Guf*, she received the *Hochma* of the left of *Bina* like her. Hence, after she received the *Hochma* within her, the *Hochma* was separated from the *Hassadim*, since she had no connection with the *Hassadim de* ZA.

Thus, we thoroughly explained the first state of the separate *Nukva*. To be able to shine for the lower ones, she was told, "Go, diminish yourself," meaning diminish yourself from that great degree of being equal with the degree of ZA and receiving from *Bina*. Rather, she is to descend below *Yesod de* ZA, as she was at her root: below the whole degree of ZA, and receive all of her Lights from ZA.

And since she receives her Lights from ZA, which is the middle line, the *Hochma* that he gives her is integrated with *Hassadim* and she can shine. This is the second state of the separate *Nukva*. What she received in the first state is regarded as *Nefesh, Ruach, Neshama de Achor*, meaning they do not shine. And what she receives in the second state is regarded as *Nefesh, Ruach, Neshama de Panim*, meaning they shine in completeness (*The Zohar, Beresheet* 1, Items 111-116; *Idra Raba*, Item 323-325).

There are merits to her first state, since then her Highest level was *Bina* and she could receive *Hochma* from her, and she did not need to receive from ZA. Yet, she could not shine to the lower ones, due to the absence of *Hassadim*. For this reason, it is considered *Achoraim*.

But in the second state, after she was diminished under the *Masach of Yesod de* ZA, she was no longer worthy of receiving *Hochma*, since the *Masach de Yesod* ZA detained her. Hence, she had to receive *Hochma* in *Kelim de Achoraim*, which remained in her from the first state. But there are more merits to the second state than to the first state, since then she could shine both *Hochma* and *Hassadim* to the lower ones, whereas in the first state, she could not shine to the lower ones.

Talmud Eser Sefirot, Part One, Histaklut Pnimit[32]

First, you must know that when dealing with spiritual matters that have no concern with time, space and motion, and moreover when dealing with Godliness, we do not have the words by which to express and contemplate. Our entire vocabulary is taken from sensations of imaginary senses. Thus, how can they assist us where sense and imagination do not reign?

For example, if you take the subtlest of words, namely "lights," it nonetheless resembles and borrows from the light of the sun, or an emotional light of satisfaction. Thus, how can they be used to express Godly matters? They would certainly fail to provide the reader with anything true.

It is even truer in a place where these words should disclose the negotiations in the wisdom in print, as is done in any research of wisdom. If we fail with even a single inadequate word, the reader will be instantly disoriented and will not find his hands and legs in this whole matter.

For that reason, the sages of the Kabbalah have chosen a special language, which we can call "the language of the branches." There is not an essence or a conduct of an essence in this world that does not begin in its root in the Upper World. Moreover, the beginning of every being in this world starts from the Upper World and then hangs down to this world.

Thus, the sages have found an adequate language without trouble by which they could convey their attainments to each other by word of mouth and in writing from generation to generation. They have taken the names of the branches in this world, where each name is self-explanatory, as though pointing to its Upper Root in the system of the Upper Worlds.

That should appease your mind regarding the perplexing expressions we often find in books of Kabbalah, and some that are even foreign to the human spirit. It

---

32 *The Study of the Ten Sefirot*, Part One, Inner Reflection

is because once they have chosen this language to express themselves, namely the language of the branches, they could no longer leave a branch unused because of its inferior degree. They could not avoid using it to express the desired concept when our world suggests no other branch to be taken in its place.

Just as two hairs do not feed off the same foramen, we do not have two branches that relate to the same root. It is also impossible to exterminate the object in the wisdom that is related to that inferior expression. Such a loss would inflict impairment and confusion in the entire realm of the wisdom, since there is no other wisdom in the world where matters are so intermingled by cause and effect, reason and consequence as in the wisdom of Kabbalah. Matters are interconnected and tied to each other from top to bottom like one long chain.

Thus, there is no freedom of will here to switch and replace the bad names with better ones. We must always provide the exact branch that points to its Upper Root, and elaborate on it until the accurate definition is provided for the scrutinizing reader.

Indeed, those whose eyes have not been opened to the sights of Heaven, and have not acquired the proficiency in the connections of the branches of this world with their roots in the Upper Worlds are like the blind scraping the walls. They will not understand the true meaning of even a single word, for each word is a name of a branch that relates to its root.

Only if they receive an interpretation from a genuine sage who makes himself available to explain it in the spoken language, which is necessarily like translating from one language to another, from the language of branches to the spoken language. Only then will he be able to explain the spiritual term as it is.

This is what I have troubled to do in this interpretation, to explain the ten *Sefirot* as the Godly sage the Ari had instructed us, in their spiritual purity, devoid of any tangible terms. Thus, any beginner may approach the wisdom without failing in any materialization and mistake. With the understanding of these ten *Sefirot*, one will also come to examine and know how to comprehend the other issues in this wisdom.

CHAPTER ONE

"Know that before the emanations were emanated and the creatures created, an Upper Simple Light had filled the whole of reality" (*The Tree of Life*). These words require explanation: How was there a reality that the Simple Light had filled before the worlds were emanated? Also, the issue of the appearance of the desire to be restricted in order to bring the perfection of His deeds to light. It is implied in the book that there was already some want there.

Also, the issue of the middle point in Him, where the restriction occurred, is quite perplexing, for he had already said that there is neither start nor end there, so how is there a middle? Indeed these words are deeper than the ocean, and I must therefore elaborate on their interpretation.

There is not one thing in the whole of reality that is not contained in Ein Sof. The contradicting terms in our world are contained in Him in the form of One, Unique, and Unified.

1) Know that there is not an essence of a single being in the world, both the ones perceived by our senses and the ones perceived by our mind's eye, that is not included in the Creator, for they all come to us from Him, and can one give that which is not in Him?

We must understand the concepts that are separated or opposite for us. For example, the term, "wisdom," is regarded as different from the term, "sweetness," as wisdom and sweetness are two separate terms. Similarly, the term, "operator," certainly differs from the term, "operation." The operator and its operation are necessarily two separate concepts. It is even more so with opposite terms such as "sweet" and "bitter"; these are certainly examined separately.

However, in Him, wisdom, pleasure, sweetness and pungency, operation and operator, and other such different and opposite forms are all contained as one in His Simple Light. There are no differentiations among them whatsoever, as is the term "One, Unique, and Unified."

"One" indicates a single evenness. "Unique" implies that everything that extends from Him, all these multiplicities are in Him as single as His Essence. "Unified" shows that although He performs many operations, there is one Force that performs all these, and they all return and unite in the form of One. Indeed, this one form swallows all the forms that appear in His Operations.

This is a very subtle matter and not every mind can tolerate it. The Ramban had already explained to us the matter of His uniqueness, as expressed in the words, "One, Unique, and Unified."

There is a difference between "One," "Unique," and "Unified":

- When He unites to act with One Force, He is called "Unified."
- When He divides to act His act, each part of Him is called "Unique."
- When He is in a single evenness, He is called "One."

Interpretation: "Uniting to act with One Force," when He works to bestow, as is fitting of His Oneness, and His operations are unchanging, when He "divides to act His act," meaning when His operations differ, and He seems to be doing good and bad, then He is called "Unique," since all His different operations have a single outcome: benefitting.

We find that He is unique in every single act and does not change by His various operations. When He is in a single evenness, He is called "One." One points to His Essence, where all the opposites are in a single evenness. It is as the Rambam wrote, "In Him, knower, known and knowledge are one, for His Thoughts are far Higher than our thoughts, and His ways Higher than our ways."

Two discernments in bestowal: before it is received and after it is received.

2) We should learn from those who ate the manna. Manna is called "Bread from the sky" because it did not materialize when clothing in this world. Our sages said that each and every one tasted everything he or she wanted to taste in it.

That means that it had to have opposite forms in it: one person tasted sweet and the other tasted it as acrid and bitter. Thus, the manna itself had to have been contained of both opposites together, for can one give what is not in one? Thus, how can there be two opposites in the same carrier?

It is therefore a must that it is simple and devoid of both flavors, but is only included in them in such a way that the corporeal receiver might discern the taste he or she wants. In the same way, you can perceive anything spiritual: it is unique and simple in itself, but consists of the entire multiplicity of forms in the world. When falling in the hand of a corporeal, limited receiver, the receiver discerns a separate form in it, unlike all other forms united in that spiritual essence.

We should therefore always distinguish two discernments in His bestowal:

1. The form of the Essence of that Higher Abundance before it is received, when it is still inclusive Simple Light.

2. After the Abundance has been received, and thus acquired one separate form according to the properties of the receiver.

How can we perceive the soul as a part of Godliness?

3) Now we can come to understand what the Kabbalists write about the essence of the soul: "The soul is a part of God Above and is not at all changed from the Whole, except in that the soul is a part and not the Whole." It is like

a stone that is carved off a mountain: the essence of the stone and the essence of the mountain are the same and there is no distinction between the stone and the mountain, except that the stone is but a part of the mountain, and the mountain is the whole.

These words seem utterly perplexing. It is most difficult to understand how parts and differences can be discerned in Godliness to the point of resembling it to a stone that is carved off a mountain. The stone is carved off the mountain by an ax and a sledgehammer. But in Godliness, how and what would separate them from one another?

The spiritual is divided by disparity of form, as the corporeal is divided by an ax.

4) Before we come to clarify the matter, we shall explain the essence of the separation in spirituality: Know that spiritual entities become separated from one another only by disparity of form. In other words, if one spiritual entity acquires two forms, it is no longer one, but two.

Let me explain it in souls of people, which are also spiritual: It is known that the form of the spiritual law is simple. Certainly, there are as many souls as there are bodies, where the souls shine. However, they are separated from one another by the disparity of form in each of them, as our sages said, "As their faces are not the same, their opinions are not similar." The body can discern the form of the souls and tell if each specific soul is a good soul or a bad soul and likewise with the various forms.

And you see that as a corporeal matter is divided, cut, and becomes separated by an ax and motion that increase the distance between each part, a spiritual matter is divided, cut, and separated by the disparity of form between each part. According to the measure of disparity, so is the distance between each two parts.

How can there be disparity of form in Creation with respect to Ein Sof?

5) It is now clear in this world, in souls of people. However, in the soul, which is a part of God Above, it is still unclear how it is separated from Godliness to the point that we can call it "a Godly Part." We should not say, "by disparity of form," since we have already said that Godliness is Simple Light, which contains the whole multiplicity of forms and opposite forms in the world in His Simple Uniqueness, as in "One, Unique, and Unified." Hence, how can we depict disparity of form in the soul, making it different from Godliness, rendering it distinct, to acquire a part of Him there?

Indeed, this question applies primarily to the Light of *Ein Sof* prior to the *Tzimtzum* (restriction), for in the reality before us, all the worlds, Upper and lower, are discerned by two discernments:

1. The first is the form of this whole reality, as it is prior to the *Tzimtzum*. At that time, everything was without bounds and without end. This discernment is called, "the Light of *Ein Sof*."
2. The second discernment is the form of this entire reality from the *Tzimtzum* downwards. Then everything became limited and measured. This discernment is called the four worlds, *Atzilut, Beria, Yetzira, Assiya*.

It is known that there is no thought and perception whatsoever in His Essence, and no name and appellation is in Him. And what we do not attain, how can we define by a name? A name implies attainment, indicating that we have attained it as that name.

Thus, it is certain that there no name and appellation whatsoever in His Essence. Instead, all the names and appellations are but in His Light, which expands from Him. The expansion of His Light prior to the *Tzimtzum*, which filled the whole of reality unboundedly and without end is called *Ein Sof*. Thus we should understand how the Light of *Ein Sof* is defined in and of itself and has departed His Essence, so we may define it by a name, as we have said about the soul.

> *Explanation of the words: "Hence, work and labor have been prepared for the reward of the souls, since 'One who eats that which is not one's own, is afraid to look at one's face.'"*

6) To somewhat understand this sublime place, we must go into further detail. We shall research the axis of the entire reality before us and its general purpose. Is there an Operator without a purpose? And what is that purpose, for which He has invented this whole reality before us in the Upper Worlds and in the lower worlds?

Indeed, our sages have already instructed us in many places that all the worlds were created only for Israel, who keep Torah and *Mitzvot*. However, we should understand this question of our sages, who asked about it: "If the purpose of the creation of the worlds is to delight His creatures, why did He create this corporeal, turbid, and tormented world? Without it, He could certainly delight the souls as much as He wanted; so why did He bring the soul into such a foul and filthy body?"

They explained it with the verse, "One who eats that which is not one's own is afraid to look at one's face." It means there is a flaw of shame in any free gift. To spare the souls this blemish, He created this world, where there is work. And we will enjoy their labor, for they take their pay from the Whole in return for their work, and are thus spared the blemish of shame.

What is the ratio between working seventy years and eternal delight, as there is no greater free gift than this?

7) These words of theirs are perplexing through and through. First bewilderment: our primary aim and prayer is, "Spare us a free gift." Our sages said that the treasure of a free gift is prepared only for the greatest souls in the world.

Their answer is even more perplexing: They said that there is a great flaw in free gifts, namely the shame that encounters every receiver of a free gift. To mend this, the Creator has prepared this world where there is work and labor, to be rewarded for their labor and work in the next world.

But that answer is odd indeed. What is this like? It is like a person who says to his friend, "Work with me for just a minute, and in return I will give you every pleasure and treasure in the world for the rest of your life." There is indeed no greater free gift than that, since the reward is utterly incomparable with the work, since the work is in this world, a transient, worthless world compared to the reward and the pleasure in the eternal world.

What value is there to the passing world compared to the eternal world? It is even more so with regard to the quality of the labor, which is worthless compared to the quality of the reward.

Our sages have said, "The Creator is destined to bequeath each righteous 310 worlds." We cannot say that the Creator gives some of the reward in return for their work and the rest as a free gift, for then what good would that do? The blemish of shame would remain in the rest of the gift! Indeed, their words are not to be taken literally, for there is a profound meaning here.

The whole of reality was emanated and created with a single Thought. It is the Operator, it is the very Operation, it is the sought-after reward, and it is the Essence of the labor.

8) We must understand His Thought in creating the worlds and the reality before us. His Operations did not emerge by many thoughts, as is our way. This is because He is One, Unique, and Unified. And as He is Simple, His Lights, which extend from Him, are Simple and Unified, without any multiplicity of forms, as it is written, "My thoughts are not your thoughts, neither are your ways My ways."

You must therefore understand and perceive that all the names and appellations and all the worlds, Upper and lower, are all One Simple Light,

Unique, and Unified. In the Creator, the Light that extends, the Thought, the Operation and the Operator and anything the heart can think and contemplate, are in Him one and the same thing.

Thus, you can judge and perceive that this entire reality, Upper and lower as one, in the final state of the end of correction, was emanated and created by a Single Thought. That Single Thought performs all the operations, is the Essence of all the operations, the ultimate Objective, and the Essence of the labor. It is by itself the very perfection and the sought-after reward, as the Ramban wrote, "One, Unique, and Unified."

The issue of the Tzimtzum explains how an incomplete operation emerged from the Perfect Operator.

9) The Ari elaborated on the matter of *Tzimtzum Aleph* (first restriction), for it is a most serious matter. That is because it is necessary that all the corruptions and all the various shortcomings extend and come from Him, as it is written, "I form the light, and create darkness." But the corruptions and the darkness are the complete opposite of Him, so how can they stem from one another? Also, how could they come together with the Light and the pleasure in the Thought of Creation?

We cannot say that they are two separate thoughts. Thus, how does all that extend from Him down to this world, which is so filled with scum, torment, and filth, and how do they exist together in the single thought?

CHAPTER TWO

Explaining the Thought of Creation.

10) Now we shall come to clarify the Thought of Creation. It is certain that "The end of the act is in the preliminary thought." Even in corporeal humans with their many thoughts, the act ends in the preliminary thought. For example, when one builds one's house, we understand that the first thought in this engagement is the shape of the house to dwell in.

Therefore, it is preceded by many thoughts and many operations until this shape that one had pre-designed is completed. This shape is what appears at the end of all his operations; thus, the act ended in the preliminary thought.

The final act, which is the axis and the purpose for which all these were created, is to delight His creations. It is known that His Thought ends and acts immediately, for He is not a human, obliged to act, but the Thought itself completes the entire act at once.

Hence, we can see that as soon as He contemplated the creation in order to delight His creatures, this Light immediately extended and expanded from

Him in the full measure and form of the pleasures He had contemplated. It is all included in that Thought, which we call "The Thought of Creation." Know that we call this Thought of Creation, "The Light of *Ein Sof*," since we do not have a single word or utterance in His Essence to define Him by any name.

The will to bestow in the Emanator necessarily begets the will to receive in the emanated, and it is the Kli in which the emanated receives His Abundance.

11) The Ari said that in the beginning, an Upper Simple Light had filled the whole reality. This means that since the Creator contemplated delighting the creations, and the Light seemingly expanded from Him and departed Him, the desire to receive His Pleasures was immediately imprinted in this Light.

You can also determine that this desire is the full measure of the expanding Light. In other words, the measure of His Light and Abundance is as the measure of His Desire to delight, no more and no less.

For this reason, we call the essence of that will to receive, imprinted in this Light through the power of His Thought, by the name, "place." For instance, when we say that a person has a stomach big enough to eat two pounds of bread, while another person cannot eat more than one pound of bread, which place are we talking about? It is not the size of the intestines, but the measure of appetite. You see that the measure for the place of the reception of the bread depends on the measure and the desire to eat.

It is all the more so in spirituality, where the desire to receive the abundance is the place of the abundance, and the abundance is measured by the intensity of the desire.

The will to receive contained in the Thought of Creation brought it out of His Essence, to acquire the name Ein Sof.

12) Now you see how the Light of *Ein Sof* departed His Essence, in which we cannot utter any word, and became defined by the name *Ohr* (Light of) *Ein Sof*. It is because of this above discernment that in that Light there is the will to receive, incorporated in it from His Essence.

This is a new form that is not included whatsoever in His Essence, for whom would He receive from? This form is also the full measure of this Light.

*Prior to the **Tzimtzum**, the disparity of form in the will to receive was indiscernible.*

13) In His Almightiness, this new form would not have been defined as a change from His Light, as it is written, "Before the world was created, there were He is One and His Name One."

"He" indicates the Light in *Ein Sof*, and "His Name" implies the "Place," which is *Malchut de* (of) *Ein Sof*, being the will to receive from His Essence, contained in the Light of *Ein Sof*. He tells us that He is One and His Name One. His Name, which is *Malchut de Ein Sof*, being the desire, namely the will to receive that has been immersed in the entire reality contained in the Thought of Creation, prior to the *Tzimtzum*, no disparity of form and difference from the Light was discerned in it. And the Light and the place are literally one. Had there been any difference and deficiency in the place, compared to the Light of *Ein Sof*, there would certainly be two discernments there.

Tzimtzum means that Malchut de Ein Sof diminished the will to receive in her. Then the Light disappeared because there is no Light without a Kli.

14) Regarding the *Tzimtzum*: The will to receive that is contained in the Light of *Ein Sof*, called *Malchut de Ein Sof*, which is the Thought of Creation in *Ein Sof*, which contains the whole of reality, embellished herself to ascend and equalize her form with His Essence. Hence, she diminished her will to receive His Abundance in *Behina Dalet* in the desire. Her intention was that by so doing, the worlds would emanate and be created down to this world.

Thus, the form of the will to receive would be corrected and return to the form of bestowal, and that would bring her to equivalence of form with the Emanator. Then, after she had diminished the will to receive, the Light departed, for it is already known that the Light depends on the desire, and the desire is the place of the Light, for there is no coercion in spirituality.

CHAPTER THREE

Explanation of the origin of the soul.

15) Now we shall explain the matter of the origin of the soul. It has been said that it is a part of God Above. We asked, "How and in what does the form of the soul differ from His Simple Light, which separates it from The Whole?" Now we can understand that there really is a great disparity of form in it. Although He contains all the conceivable and imaginable forms, still, after the above words, you find one form that is not contained in Him, namely the form of the will to receive, for whom would He receive from?

However, the souls, whose creation came about because He wanted to delight them, which is the Thought of Creation, were necessarily imprinted with this law of wanting and yearning to receive His Abundance. That is where they differ from Him, since their form has changed from His. It has already been explained that a corporeal essence is separated and divided by the force of motion and remoteness of location, and a spiritual essence is separated and divided by disparity of form.

The measure of disparity of form determines the distance between one another. If the disparity of form becomes complete oppositeness, from one extreme to the other, they become completely severed and separated until they can no longer nourish from one another, for they are considered alien to one another.

CHAPTER FOUR

After the Tzimtzum and the Masach (screen) that was placed on the will to receive, it was disqualified from being a Kli (vessel) for reception and departed the system of Kedusha (Holiness). In its stead, the Ohr Hozer (Reflected Light) serves as a vessel for reception, and the Kli of the will to receive was given to the impure system.

16) After the *Tzimtzum* and the *Masach* were placed on that *Kli*, called "will to receive," it was canceled and departed from the pure system, and the *Ohr Hozer* became the vessel of reception in its place.

Know that this is the whole difference between the pure *ABYA* and the impure *ABYA*. The vessels of reception of the pure *ABYA* are from *Ohr Hozer* that is corrected in equivalence of form with *Ein Sof*, while the impure *ABYA* use the will to receive that was restricted, which is the opposite form from *Ein Sof*. That makes them separated and cut off from the "Life of Lives," namely *Ein Sof*.

Humanity feeds on the leavings of the Klipot (shells), and thus uses the will to receive as they do.

17) Now you can understand the root of the corruption, which was promptly incorporated in the Thought of Creation, which is to delight His creatures. After the cascading of the five general worlds, *Adam Kadmon* and *ABYA*, the *Klipot* appeared in the four impure worlds *ABYA*, too, as in "One before the other hath God made them."

In that state, the turbid corporeal body is set before us, about which it is written, "Man's heart is evil from his youth." This is so because its entire sustenance from its youth comes from the leavings of the *Klipot*. The essence of *Klipot* and impurity is their form of wanting only to receive. They have nothing of the will to bestow.

In that, they are opposite from Him, for He has no will to receive whatsoever, and all He wants is to bestow and delight. For that reason, the *Klipot* are called "dead," since their oppositeness of form from the Life of Lives cuts them off from Him and they have nothing of His Abundance.

Hence, the body, too, which feeds on the leavings of the *Klipot*, is also severed from life and is filled with filth. And all of that is because of the will to only receive and to not bestow imprinted in it. Its desire is always open to receive the whole world into its stomach. Thus, "The wicked are called 'dead' during their lives," since their fundamental disparity of form from their root, where they have nothing of the form of bestowal, severs them from Him and they become literally dead.

Although it seems that the evil, too, have the form of bestowal when they give charity, etc., it has been said about them in *The Zohar*, "Any grace that they do aims primarily for themselves and for their own glory." But the righteous, who keep Torah and *Mitzvot* in order to not be rewarded, but to bestow contentment upon their Maker, thus purify their bodies and invert their vessels of reception to the form of bestowal.

That makes them completely adherent with Him, for their form is identical to their Maker without any disparity of form. Our sages said about the verse, "Say unto Zion: 'Thou art My people,'" that you are with Me in partnership. This means that the righteous are partners with the Creator, since He started Creation, and the righteous finish it by turning the vessels of reception into bestowal.

The whole of reality is contained in Ein Sof and extends existence from existence. Only the will to receive is new and extends existence from absence.

18) Know that the very initiation that the Creator had initiated in this Creation, which He brought out existence from absence, applies only to the form of desire to enjoy, imprinted in every creature. Nothing more was generated in Creation, and this is the meaning of "I form the light, and create darkness." The Ramban interprets the word, "Creator," as an indication of renewal, meaning something that did not exist before.

You see that it does not say, "create Light," since there is no innovation in it, as in existence from absence. This is because the Light and everything contained in the Light, all the pleasant sensations and conceptions in the world, extend existence from existence. This means that they are already contained in Him and are therefore not an innovation. This is why it is written, "form the light," indicating that there are no innovations or creations in Him.

However, it is said of the darkness, which contains every unpleasant sensation and conception, "and create darkness." That is because He invented them literally existence from absence. In other words, it does not exist in His reality whatsoever, but was generated now. The root of all of them is the form of the "desire to enjoy," included in His Lights, which expand from Him.

In the beginning, it is only darker than the Upper Light and is therefore called "darkness," compared to the Light. But finally, the *Klipot*, *Sitra Achra*, and the wicked hang down and emerge because of it, which are completely cut off from the Root of Life by it, as it is written, "and her legs descend unto death." "Her legs" indicate the end of something. And he says that in the end, death hangs down from the legs of *Malchut*—the desire to enjoy, found in the expansion of His Light—to the *Sitra Achra* and to those that feed off her and follow her.

Because we are branches that extend from Ein Sof, the things that are in our Root are pleasurable to us, and those that are not in our Root are burdensome and painful to us.

19) We can ask, "Since this disparity of form of the will to receive must be in the creatures, for how else would they extend from Him and shift from being Creator to being creatures?" This is only possible by the above-mentioned disparity of form.

Furthermore, this form of the will to enjoy is the primary essence of Creation, the axis of the Thought of Creation. It is also the measure of the delight and pleasure, for which it is called "a place."

Thus, how can we say about it that it is called "darkness" and extends to the *Behina* (discernment) of death, since it creates separation and interruption from the Life of Lives in the receiving lower ones? We should also understand what is the great worry that comes to the receivers because of the disparity of form from His Essence, and why the great wrath.

To explain, we must first know the origin of all the pleasures and sufferings felt in our world. It is known that the nature of every branch is equal to its root. Therefore, every conduct in the root is desired and loved and coveted by the branch, as well, and any matter that is not in the root, the branch, too, removes itself from them, does not tolerate them, and hates them.

This is an unbreakable law that abides between every branch and its root. Because He is the root of all His creations, everything in Him and that extends from Him directly is pleasurable and pleasant to us, for our nature is close to our Root. Also, everything that is not in Him and does not extend to us directly from Him, but is rather opposite to Creation itself will be against our nature and will be hard for us to tolerate.

For example, we love rest and vehemently hate motion, to the point that we do not make even a single movement if not to find rest. This is because our Root is motionless and restful; there is no movement in Him whatsoever. For this reason, it is against our nature and hated by us.

Similarly, we love wisdom, strength, wealth, and all the virtues because they are included in Him, Who is our Root. We hate their opposites, such as folly, weakness, poverty, ignominy and so on, since they are not at all in our Root, which makes them despicable, loathsome, and intolerable to us.

We should still examine how can there be any extension that does not come directly from Him, but is opposite to Creation itself? It is like a wealthy man who called upon a poor fellow, fed him and gave him drinks, silver, and gold every single day, and each day more than the day before.

Note that this man tastes two distinct flavors in the great gifts of the rich: On the one hand, he tasted immeasurable pleasure due to the multitude of his gifts. On the other hand, it is hard for him to tolerate the plentitude of benefits and is ashamed upon receiving it. This causes him impatience due to the plentitude of presents showered on him every time.

It is certain that his pleasure from the gifts extends directly from the wealthy benefactor, but the impatience that he felt in the presents did not come from the wealthy benefactor, but from the very essence of the receiver—the shame awakened in him by reason of the reception and the free gift. The truth is that this, too, comes to him from the rich man, of course, but indirectly.

Because the will to receive is not in our Root, we feel shame and intolerance in it. Our sages wrote that to correct that, He has "prepared" for us labor in Torah and Mitzvot in this world, to invert the will to receive into a will to bestow.

20) We learn that all the forms that indirectly extend to us from Him present a difficulty for our patience and are against our nature. By that, you will see that the new form that was made in the receiver, namely the desire to enjoy, is not in any way inferior or deficient compared to Him. Moreover, this is the primary axis of His Creation. Without that, there would be no Creation here at all. However, the receiver, who is the carrier of that form, feels the intolerance due to his "self," since this form does not exist in his Root.

Now we can understand the answer of our sages that this world was created because "one who eats that which is not one's own, is afraid to look at one's face." They referred to the disparity of form of the desire to enjoy, which necessarily exists in the souls, since "one who eats that which is not one's own is afraid to look at one's face."

Thus, any receiver of a present is ashamed when receiving it, due to the disparity of form from the Root, since the Root does not contain that form of reception. To correct that, He created this world, where the soul comes and clothes a body. And through the practice in Torah and *Mitzvot* in order to bring contentment to His Maker, the soul's vessels of reception turn to vessels of bestowal.

Thus, for herself, she did not want the distinguished abundance, yet she receives the abundance in order to bring contentment to her Maker, who wishes for the souls to enjoy His Abundance. Because she is cleansed from the will to receive for herself, she is no longer afraid to look at His face, and thus reveals the complete perfection of the creature. And the need and the necessity to hang down all the way to this world, with the great labor of turning the form of reception into the form of bestowal, can only be conceived in this world.

The wicked are doubly destroyed, and the righteous doubly inherit.

21) Come and see that the wicked are doubly destroyed, for they hold both ends of the rope. This world is created with a want and emptiness of all the good abundance, and to acquire possessions we need movement.

However, it is known that profusion of movement pains man, for it is an indirect extension from His Essence. However, it is also impossible to remain devoid of possessions and good, for that, too, is in contrast with the Root, since the Root is filled abundantly. Hence, we choose the torment of movement in order to acquire the fulfillment of possessions.

However, because all their possessions are for themselves alone, and "he who has a hundred wants two hundred," one finally dies with less than "half one's desire in one's hand." In the end, they suffer from both sides: from the pain of increased motion, and from the pain of deficiency of possessions, half of which they lack.

But the righteous inherit doubly in their land. In other words, once they turn their will to receive into a will to bestow, and what they receive is in order to bestow, then they inherit doubly. Not only do they attain the perfection of the pleasures and diverse possessions, they also acquire the equivalence of form with their Maker. Thus, they come to true *Dvekut* (Adhesion) and are at rest, too, since the abundance comes to them by itself, without any movement or effort.

CHAPTER FIVE

The Thought of Creation compels every item in reality to stem from one another until the end of correction.

22) Now we understand the power of His Uniqueness, that His Thoughts are not our thoughts and all the multiplicity of matters and forms we perceive in this reality before us is united in Him within a Single Thought, being the Thought of Creation to delight His creatures. This Singular Thought encompasses the

whole of reality in perfect unity through the end of correction, for this is really the very purpose of Creation, and this is the Operator, like the Force that operates in the operated. This is because what is merely a Thought in Him is a binding law in the creatures. And since He contemplated delighting us, it necessarily occurred in us that we receive His Good Abundance.

And it is the operation. This means that after this law of the will to receive pleasure has been imprinted in us, we define ourselves by the name, "operation." This is so because through this disparity of form, we stop being a Creator and become a creature, stop being the Operator and become the operation.

And it is the labor and the work. Due to the force that operates in the operated, the desire to receive increases in us as the worlds hang down, until we become a separated body in this world, opposite in form from the Life of Lives, which does not bestow outside itself at all, and brings death to the bodies and every kind of torment and labor to the soul.

This is the meaning of serving the Creator in Torah and *Mitzvot*. Through the illumination of the line in the restricted place, the Holy Names—Torah and *Mitzvot*—extend. By laboring in Torah and *Mitzvot* to bestow contentment to the Maker, our vessels of reception gradually become vessels of bestowal, and this is the whole sought-after reward.

The more corrupted our vessels of reception are, the more we cannot open our mouths to receive His Abundance. This is so due to the fear of disparity of form, as in "One who eats that which is not one's own, is afraid to look at one's face." This was the reason for *Tzimtzum Aleph*, but when we correct our vessels of reception to being in order to bestow, we thus equalize our *Kelim* with their Maker and become fit to receive His Abundance unboundedly.

Thus you see that all these opposite forms in the whole of Creation before us, namely the form of operator and operated, and the form of the corruptions and corrections, and the form of the labor and its reward, all are included in His Single Thought. In simple words, it is "to delight His creatures," precisely that, no more and no less.

The entire multiplicity of concepts is also included in that Thought, both the concepts in our Holy Torah, and those of secular teachings. All the many creations and worlds and various conducts in each and every one, stem from this Single Thought.

Malchut de Ein Sof means that Malchut does not put up any end there.

23) Yet, can we recognize a *Malchut* in *Ein Sof*? That would mean that there are the Upper Nine *Sefirot* there, too! From our words, it becomes very clear

that the will to receive that is necessarily included in the Light of *Ein Sof* is called *Malchut de Ein Sof*. There, however, *Malchut* did not place a boundary and an end on that Light of *Ein Sof*, since the disparity of form due to the will to receive had not become apparent in her. That is why it is called *Ein Sof*, meaning *Malchut* does not put a stop there. Conversely, from the *Tzimtzum* downwards, an end was made in each *Sefira* and *Partzuf* by the force of *Malchut*.

CHAPTER SIX

It is impossible for the will to receive to appear in any essence, except in four Behinot (discernments), which are the four letters of HaVaYaH.

24) Let us fully understand the end that occurred in *Malchut*. First, we will explain what the Kabbalists have determined, that there is no Light, great or small, in the Upper Worlds or in the lower worlds, that is not arranged by the order of the four-letter name, *HaVaYaH*.

This goes hand in hand with the law that there is no Light in the worlds that is not clothed in a *Kli*. I have already explained the difference between His Essence and the Light that expands from Him. That happens only due to the will to enjoy that is contained in His expanding Light, being a disparity of form from His Essence, Who does not have that desire.

The expanding Light is defined by the name "emanated" because this disparity of form stops the Light from being Emanator to being emanated. It is also explained that the will to enjoy, included in His Light, is also the measure of the greatness of the Light. It is called the "place of the Light," meaning it receives its abundance according to its measure of will to receive and craving, no more and no less.

It also explains that this will to receive is the very novelty that was generated in the creation of the worlds by way of making existence from absence. This is so because this form alone is not at all included in His Abundance, and the Creator has only now created it for the purpose of Creation. This is the meaning of "and create darkness," since this form is the root for darkness, due to the disparity of form in it. For this reason, it is darker than the Light that expands within her and because of her.

Now you see that any Light that expands from Him instantly consists of two discernments:

1. The first is the essence of the expanding Light before the form of "desire to enjoy" appears in it.

2. The second one is after the form of "desire to enjoy" appears in it, at which time it becomes coarser and somewhat darker, due to the acquisition of disparity of form.

Thus, the first discernment is the Light and the second discernment is the *Kli*. For this reason, any expanding Light consists of four *Behinot* in the impression on the *Kli*. This is so because the form of the will to receive, called "a *Kli* to the expanding Light," is not completed all at once, but by way of operator and operated.

There are two *Behinot* in the operator and two *Behinot* in the operated. They are called "potential" and "actual" in the operator, and "potential" and "actual" in the operated, which make up four *Behinot*.

The will to receive does not permeate the emanated except through his own awakening to receive of his own choice.

25) Because the *Kli* is the root of darkness, as it is opposite from the Light, it must therefore begin to operate slowly, gradually, by way of cause and consequence, as it is written, "The waters were conceived and begotten darkness" (*Midrash Rabba, Shemot* 80, 22).

The darkness is a result of the Light itself and is operated by it, as in conception and birth, which are potential and actual. This means that in any expanding Light, the will to receive is necessarily incorporated, though it is not regarded as disparity of form before this desire is clearly set in the Light.

The will to receive that is incorporated in the Light by the Emanator is not enough for that. Rather, the emanated himself must independently discover the will to receive in him, in action, meaning of his own choice. This means that he must extend abundance through his own will, more than the measure of Light of the expansion in him by the Emanator.

After the emanated is operated by his own choice in increasing the measure of his desire, the craving and the will to receive become fixed in him, and the Light can permanently clothe this *Kli*.

It is true that the Light of *Ein Sof* seemingly expands over all four *Behinot*, reaching the full measure of the desire by the emanated himself, which is *Behina Dalet*. This is because he would not extend his own essence anyway and acquire a name for himself, meaning *Ein Sof*.

However, the form did not change at all because of the will to receive in His Almightiness, and there is no change distinguished there between the Light and the place of the Light, which is the will to enjoy; they are one and the same thing.

It is written, "Before the world was created, there were He is One and His Name One." It is indeed difficult to understand this double reference "He" and "His Name." What has His Name got to do there before the world was created? It should have said, "Before the world was created, He was One."

However, this refers to the Light of *Ein Sof*, which is prior to the *Tzimtzum*. Even though there is a place there and a will to receive the Abundance from His Essence, it is still without change and distinction between the Light and the "Place."

"He is One" means that Light of *Ein Sof* and His Name are one. This refers to the will to enjoy included there without any change whatsoever. You must understand what our sages implied, that the "His Name" is desire in *Gematria*, meaning the "will to enjoy."

All the worlds in the Thought of Creation are called "the Light of Ein Sof," and the sum of the receivers there is called Malchut de Ein Sof.

26) It has already been explained regarding "The end of an act is in the preliminary thought," that it is the Thought of Creation, which expanded from His Essence in order to delight His creatures. We have learned that in Him, the Thought and the Light are one and the same thing. It therefore follows that the Light of *Ein Sof* that expanded from His Essence contains the whole of reality before us through the end of the future correction, which is the end of the act.

In Him, all the creations are already complete with all their perfection and joy that He wished to bestow upon them. This complete reality is called "the Light of *Ein Sof*," and that which contains them is called *Malchut de Ein Sof*.

CHAPTER SEVEN

Although only Behina Dalet was restricted, the Light left the first three Behinot, as well.

27) It has already been explained that the middle point, which is the inclusive point of the Thought of Creation, namely the will to enjoy in it, embellished herself to enhance her equivalence of form with the Emanator. Although there is no disparity of form in His Almightiness from the perspective of the Emanator, the point of the desire felt it as a kind of indirect extension from His Essence, as with the allegory about the rich man. For this reason, she diminished her desire from the last *Behina*, which is the complete enormity of the will to receive, to increase the *Dvekut* by way of direct extension from His Essence.

Then the Light was emptied from the entire place, meaning from all four degrees that exist in the place. Even though she diminished her Light only from *Behina Dalet*, it is the nature of the spiritual that it is indivisible.

*Afterwards, he re-extended a line of Light from the first three Behinot,
and Behina Dalet remained a vacant space.*

28) Afterwards, the Light of *Ein Sof* extended once more to the place that was emptied, but did not fill the whole place in all four *Behinot*, but only three *Behinot*, as was the desire of the point of *Tzimtzum*. Hence, the middle point that has been restricted remained empty and hollow, since the Light illuminated only through *Behina Dalet*, but not all the way, and the Light of *Ein Sof* stopped there.

We will henceforth explain the matter of the *Hitkalelut* (mingling) of the *Behinot* in one another, applied in the Upper Worlds. Now you see that the four *Behinot* are integrated in one another in such a way that within *Behina Dalet* itself there are all four *Behinot*, as well. Thus, the Light of *Ein Sof* reached the first three *Behinot* in *Behina Dalet*, too, and only the last *Behina* in *Behina Dalet* remained empty and without Light.

CHAPTER EIGHT

*Hochma is called Light, and Hassadim, "Water." Bina is called
"Upper Water," and Malchut, "lower water."*

29) Now we shall explain the meaning of the four *Behinot* of cause and consequence, necessary to complete the form of the will to receive. There are two *Behinot* of Light in *Atzilut*. The first *Behina* is called "Light," namely *Ohr Hochma*, and the second *Behina* is called "Water," which is *Hassadim*.

The first *Behina* extends from Above downwards without any assistance from the lower one. The second *Behina* extends with the help of the lower one, hence the name, "water," for it is the nature of the Light to be Above, and the nature of the water to be below.

There are also two *Behinot* in the water itself: Upper Water, by *Behina Bet* in the four *Behinot*, and lower water, by *Behina Dalet* in the four *Behinot*.

*Explanation of the expansion of Ohr Ein Sof into the four Behinot
in order to uncover the Kli, which is the will to receive.*

30) For this reason, any expansion of *Ohr Ein Sof* consists of *Eser Sefirot*. This is because the *Ein Sof*, which is the Root and the Emanator, is called *Keter*. The Light of the expansion itself is called *Hochma*, and this is the entire measure of expansion of the Light from Above, from *Ein Sof*.

It has already been said that the will to receive is incorporated in every expansion of Light from Above. However the form of the desire does not actually become apparent before the desire awakens in the emanated, to extend more Light than the measure of its expansion.

Thus, because the will to receive is included as potential immediately in the Light of the expansion, the Light is compelled to bring the potential to the actual. Consequently, the Light awakens to extend additional Abundance, more than the measure of its expansion from *Ein Sof*. Thus, the will to receive actually appears in that Light and acquires the new form in disparity of form, for by that it becomes darker than the Light, as it grew coarser by the new form, since it has become thicker by the new form.

Also, this part, which has become thicker, is called *Bina*. In truth, *Bina* is a part of *Hochma*, meaning the very Light of expansion of *Ein Sof*. But because she increased her desire and drew more Abundance than the measure of the expansion in her from *Ein Sof*, she thus acquired disparity of form and grew a little thicker than the Light. Thus, she acquired her own name, which is "the *Sefira Bina*."

The essence of the additional Abundance that she extended from *Ein Sof* by the power of the strengthening of her desire is called *Ohr Hassadim*, or "Upper Water." This is because this desire does not extend directly from *Ein Sof* like *Ohr Hochma*, but through assistance of the emanated, who intensified the desire. Hence, it merits its own name, to be called *Ohr Hassadim* or "water."

Now you find that the *Sefira Bina* consists of three discernments of Light:

1. Light of *Bina's* essence, which is a part of the *Ohr Hochma*.
2. The thickening and the disparity of form in her, acquired by the intensification of the desire.
3. The *Ohr Hassadim* that came to her through her own extension from *Ein Sof*.

However, that still does not complete the entire vessel of reception, since *Bina* is essentially *Hochma*, who is indeed transcendent, being a direct expansion from *Ohr Ein Sof*. Consequently, only the root for the vessels of reception and the operator for the operation of the *Kli* appeared in *Bina*.

Afterwards, that same *Ohr Hassadim* that she extended through the power of her intensification extended from her once more, and some illumination of *Hochma* was added. This expansion of *Ohr Hassadim* is called *Zeir Anpin*, or *HGT*.

This Light of *Hitpashtut* also increased its desire to extend new abundance, more than the measure of illumination of *Hochma* in its expansion from *Bina*. This expansion is also regarded as two *Behinot*, since the Light of expansion itself is called *ZA* or *VAK*, while its intensification in it is called *Malchut*.

This is how we come by the ten *Sefirot*: *Keter* is *Ein Sof*; *Hochma* is the Light of expansion from *Ein Sof*; *Bina* is the *Ohr Hochma* that intensified in order to increase abundance, by which it gained *Aviut*. ZA, which consists of *HGT NHY*, is *Ohr Hassadim* with illumination of *Hochma*, which expands from *Bina*; and *Malchut* is the second intensification to add *Hochma* more than there is in ZA.

The four Behinot in the desire are the four letters HaVaYaH,
which are KHB TM.

31) This is the meaning of the four letters in the four-letter Name: The tip of the *Yod* is *Ein Sof*, meaning the operating force included the Thought of Creation, which is to delight His creatures, namely the *Kli* of *Keter*.

Yod is *Hochma*, meaning *Behina Aleph*, which is the actual in the potential that is contained in the Light of the expansion of *Ein Sof*. The first *Hey* is *Bina*, *Behina Bet*, which is the actualization of the potential, meaning the Light that has grown thicker by the *Hochma*.

Vav is *Zeir Anpin* or *HGT NHY*, meaning the expansion of *Ohr Hassadim* that emerged through *Bina*. This is *Behina Gimel*, the force for the performance of the operation. The lower *Hey* in *HaVaYaH* is *Malchut*, meaning *Behina Dalet*. It is the manifestation of the complete act in the vessel of reception that has intensified to extend more abundance than the measure of its expansion from *Bina*. That completes the form of the will to receive, and the Light that clothes its *Kli*, being the will to receive that is completed only in this fourth *Behina* and not before.

Now you can easily see that there is no Light in the Upper Worlds or lower worlds that is not arranged under the four-letter Name, being the four *Behinot*. Without it, the will to receive that should be in every Light is incomplete, for this will is the place and the measure of the Light.

The letters Yod and Vav of HaVaYaH are thin because they are
discerned as mere potential.

32) This might surprise us, since *Yod* implies *Hochma* and *Hey* implies *Bina*, and the whole essence of the Light that exists in the ten *Sefirot* exists in the *Sefira Hochma*, while *Bina*, *Zeir Anpin*, and *Malchut* are merely clothes, with respect to *Hochma*. Thus, *Hochma* should have taken the greater letter in the four-letter Name.

The thing is that the letters of the four-letter Name do not imply or indicate the amount of Light in the ten *Sefirot*. Instead, they indicate measures of impact on the *Kli*. The white in the parchment of the scroll of Torah implies the Light, and the black, being the letters in the scroll of Torah, indicates the quality of the *Kelim*.

Thus, because *Keter* is only discerned as the root of the root of the *Kli*, it is implied only in the tip of the *Yod*. *Hochma*, which is the force that has not actually appeared in actuality, is implied by the smallest of the letters, namely the *Yod*.

Bina, where the force is carried out in action, is indicated by the widest letter, the *Aleph*. ZA is only the force for the performance of the act; hence, it is implied by a long and narrow letter, which is *Vav*. Its thinness indicates that the essence of the *Kli* is as yet in concealed potential in it, and its length indicates that at the end of its expansion, the complete *Kli* appears through it.

Hochma did not manage to manifest the entire *Kli* in her expansion, for *Bina* is an incomplete *Kli*, but the operator of the *Kli*. Hence, the leg of the *Yod* is short, implying that it is still short, and did not manifest the entire *Kli* through its expansion and through the force concealed in it.

Malchut is also implied by the letter *Hey*, like *Bina*, which is a wide letter, appearing in its complete form. It should not surprise you that *Bina* and *Malchut* have the same letters, since in the World of *Tikkun* they are indeed similar and lend their *Kelim* to one another, as in the verse, "So they two went."

CHAPTER NINE

Spiritual movement means renewal of disparity of form.

33) We should still understand the meaning of time and movement that we come across in almost every word in this wisdom. Indeed, you should know that spiritual movement is not like tangible movement from place to place. Rather, it refers to a renewal of form.

We denominate every renewal of form by the name "movement." It is that renewal, that disparity of form that was renewed in the spiritual, unlike its general preceding form in that spiritual, is regarded as having been divided and distanced from that spiritual, and departed with its own name and authority. In that, it is exactly like a corporeal essence that some part departed it and moves about from place to place. Hence, the renewal of form is called "movement."

Spiritual time means a certain number of renewals of disparity of form that stem from one another. Former and latter mean cause and consequence.

34) Concerning the spiritual definition of time: Understand that for us, the spiritual definition of time is only a sensation of movements. Our imagination pictures and devises a certain number of movements, which it discriminates one by one and translates them like a certain amount of "time."

Thus, if one had been in a state of complete rest with one's environment, he would not even be aware of the concept of time. So it is in spirituality: A certain amount of renewals of forms is considered as "spiritual movements." Those are intermingled in one another by way of cause and consequence, and they are called "time" in spirituality. Also, "before" and "after" are always referred to as "cause and consequence."

CHAPTER TEN

The entire substance that is ascribed to the emanated is the will to receive.
Any addition in it is ascribed to the Emanator.

35) Know that the will to receive in the emanated, which is his *Kli*, is also all the general substance ascribed to the emanated, in a way that all that exists besides it is ascribed to the Emanator.

The will to receive is the first form of every essence. We define the first form as "substance" because we have no attainment in the essence.

36) Although we perceive the will to receive as an incident and a form in the essence, how is it we perceive it as the substance of the essence? Indeed, it is the same with essences that are near us. We name the first form in the essence by the name "the first substance in the essence," since we have no attainment or perception whatsoever in any substance, as all of our five senses are completely unfit for it. The sight, sound, smell, taste, and touch offer the scrutinizing mind mere abstract forms of "incidents" of the essence, formulating through collaboration with our senses.

For example, if we take even the smallest, microscopic atoms in the smallest elements of any essence, separated through a chemical process, they, too, are merely abstract forms that appear that way to the eye. More accurately, we distinguish and examine them by the ways of the will to receive and to be received that we find in them.

Following these proceedings, we can distinguish and separate these various atoms to the very first matter of that essence. However, even then they would be no more than forces in the essence, not a substance.

Thus you find that even in corporeality we have no other way to understand the first matter, except by assuming that the first form is the first matter, which carries all other incidents and forms that follow it. It is all the more so in the Upper Worlds, where tangible and imaginary do not abide.

GENERAL PREFACE

To the proficient in The Tree of Life, and to everyone, as in, "First, learn; then, comprehend."

1) Our sages said, "There is not a blade of grass below that does not have an angel above that strikes it and tells it, 'Grow!'" This seems very perplexing, for why would the Creator trouble an angel from Above with striking and nursing a tiny, insignificant blade of grass?

Yet, this saying is of one of Creation's secrets that are too long to interpret. This is so because the heart of the infinitely wise wishes to reveal a portion and conceal two portions with their golden allegories, as they are wary of revealing the Torah to an unworthy disciple. It is for this reason that our sages said that one does not learn from legends, as legends are sealed and blocked before the masses, and are revealed only to a chosen few in a generation.

And we also find in *The Book of Zohar*, that Rashbi (Rabbi Shimon Bar-Yochai) instructed Rabbi Aba to write the secrets, because he knew how to reveal with intimation. See in the *Idra*, where it is written that for each secret that Rashbi disclosed in the wisdom, he would cry and say, "Woe if I tell; woe if I do not tell. If I do not tell, my friends will lose that word; and if I tell, the wicked will know how to serve their Master."

This means that he was in distress from both angles: if he did not reveal the secrets of the Torah, the secrets would be lost from the true sages, who fear God. And if he did reveal the secrets, people of no merit would fail in them, for they would not understand the root of the matters and would eat unripe fruit.

Hence, Rashbi chose Rabbi Aba to write, because of his wisdom in allegories, to arrange things in such a way that it would be sufficiently revealed to those who are worthy of understanding them, and hidden and blocked from those unworthy of understanding them. This is why he said that Rabbi Aba knew how to reveal with intimation. In other words, although he revealed, it still remains a secret to the unworthy.

However, in *The Zohar*, they promised us that this wisdom is destined to be completely revealed at the end of days, even for little ones. And they also said that with this composition, the children of Israel would be redeemed from exile, meaning that with the appearance of the wisdom of truth, Israel will be rewarded with complete redemption. And we also see that the words of *The Zohar* and the hidden secrets in the wisdom of truth are being gradually revealed, generation by generation, until we are rewarded with revealing all this wisdom, and at that time we will be rewarded with complete redemption.

To clarify the text with which we began, we shall first explain the verse in the famous *Book of Creation*, where it is written of the ten *Sefirot* being ten and not nine, ten and not eleven. Most of the interpreters have already examined it, but we will explain it our own way, so matters will be revealed to all who seek the word of God.

It is known that the ten *Sefirot* are called *Keter, Hochma, Bina, Hesed, Gevura, Tifferet, Netzah, Hod, Yesod, Malchut*. It is written in the Ari's *Gate to Introductions*, in the section "HaDaat," that they are actually five *Behinot* (discernments): *Keter, Hochma, Bina, Zeir Anpin,* and *Malchut*; but *Zeir Anpin* comprises six *Sefirot HGT NHY*. I have written at length about the ten *Sefirot* within this composition, so here I would briefly say that in this general preface, I wish to give the student a true and general knowledge of the majority of this expansive wisdom, and true orientation in the style of study.

In the book, *The Tree of Life*, most students fail to understand the matters, since the spiritual concepts are above time and above place, but they are expressed in corporeal terms, pictured and set in times and places. Additionally, in the writings of the Ari, no order for beginners is arranged in this wisdom. The books were composed by the holy words that he would say before his students day-by-day, and the students themselves were proficient in the wisdom of truth.

Hence, there is no text—long or short—in all the books that were written, which does not require true proficiency in the wisdom in general. For this reason, the students grow weary and cannot connect matters altogether.

Thus, I have come out with this preface, to connect the matters and the foundations of the wisdom in a concise manner, so it will be readily available to the student with every text he may wish to study in the writings of the Ari. And for this reason, I do not elaborate or interpret each matter to the fullest, for this will be clarified within my composition. Instead, I summarize sufficiently for my purpose. And our sages said, "First, learn; then, comprehend."

The Ari wrote that the ten *Sefirot* KHB, HGT, NHYM are actually five *Behinot*, KHB, ZA, and *Malchut*. This is the meaning of the four-letter-name, *Yod, Hey, Vav, Hey*. The tip of the *Yod* is *Keter*; the *Yod* is *Hochma*; *Hey* is *Bina*, *Vav* is *Zeir Anpin*—containing six *Sefirot* HGT NHY—and the last *Hey* is *Malchut*.

You should know that the *Otiot* (letters) and the *Sefirot* are one thing. But following the rule that no Light expands without a *Kli* (vessel), when we speak of both together, that is, when the Light is clothed in the *Kli*, they are called *Sefirot*. And when we speak of the *Kelim* (plural for *Kli*) alone, they are called *Otiot*.

It is written about the Light that the white in the book of Torah implies the Light, and the black in the book of Torah, meaning the letters, implies the *Kelim*. This means, as the Ramban interprets concerning "I form the light, and create darkness," that the matter of eliciting existence from absence is called "Creator," since it is an innovation, something that did not exist prior to its creation. And in the Light, and all the delight and pleasure included in the Light, it is not an innovation and elicitation existence from absence, but rather existence from existence, for the Light and all the abundance are already included in His Essence.

For this reason, it is said, "form the light," for it is not a matter of creation, but of formation, that is, forming the Light in a way that the dwellers below can receive it. But the darkness is an innovation that was generated with Creation, in eliciting existence from absence, meaning it is not included in His Essence. This is why it is said, "and create darkness." But the darkness is the real opposite from the Light; hence, we should understand how darkness can extend from the Light.

In *Panim Masbirot* (A Welcoming Face), "Branch One," I have elaborated on this point, and here I shall only brush through it. It is known that it is written in *The Zohar* that the purpose of Creation is to delight His creatures, since it is the conduct of The Good to do good. Clearly, every wish in Him is a mandatory law for the creatures. It follows that since the Creator contemplated delighting His creations, a mandatory nature of wanting to receive His pleasure was immediately imprinted in the creatures, that is, the great desire to receive His Abundance. Know that this craving is called a *Kli*, with respect to its root.

For this reason, Kabbalists have said that there is no Light without a *Kli*, since the will to receive included in each emanated being and creature is the *Kli*, and it is also the full measure of the Light. In other words, it receives precisely the measure that it wishes, no more and no less, since there is no coercion in spirituality, and even in the corporeals it is not from the side of *Kedusha* (holiness).

Clearly, the *Kli's* form is different from the Light's. This is why it is called *Kli* and not Light. But we need to understand the meaning of this disparity of form. Indeed, the will to receive for oneself is a great disparity of form, since this form does not apply to the Emanator whatsoever, as from whom would He receive? Rather, it has been initiated in the first emanated by its existence-from-absence making. In it, the will to receive is the Cause of Causes (*Panim Masbirot*, "Branch One").

This clarifies what is written in the Holy *Zohar* that the Upper *Keter* is darkness compared to the Cause of Causes. They are referring to the will to receive included in the first emanation; and they call this disparity of form, "darkness," since it does not exist in the Emanator. For this reason, it is the root of the darkness, which is the color black, compared to the Light, and opposite from it.

Also, it has been explained in *Panim Masbirot* that as corporeal things are separated from one another by an axe and a hammer, the spirituals are separated from one another by the disparity of form between them. And when the disparity of form increases to the point of oppositeness, from one extreme to the other, complete separation is created between them.

For this reason, it has been explained there that the form of the will to receive is immediately included in all the Light that expands from Him, but as a hidden, potential force. This force is not revealed to the emanated except when the emanated intensifies the desire to want additional abundance, more than the measure that has expanded in it by the Emanator.

For example, when the food is tasty, one's desire for more food increases more than one's eating. Hence, after the emanated increases the desire to extend additional abundance, more than the measure of its expansion, the actual vessels of reception appear. And the thing is that because this disparity of form does not apply in Him, but in the creature, it is completed only by the awakening of the emanated, and understand thoroughly.

2) Hence, the expansion of His Light does not extend the boundary of being an Emanator and becomes an emanated until it goes through the four *Behinot*, called *Hochma*, *Bina*, *Zeir Anpin*, and *Malchut*. This is so because the expansion of His Light is called *Hochma*, which is the full measure of the essence of the Light of that emanated. And when it intensifies and extends more abundance

than the measure of its expansion, it is considered *Behina* (singular for *Behinot*) *Bet* (a second *Behina*), called *Bina*.

Also, three discernments should be made in the second *Behina*: **First discernment:** The essence of the *Sefira Bina* is *Hochma*. **Second discernment:** The intensification of the desire that it manifested, for which the root of the vessel of reception was revealed in her. In that sense, there is disparity of form in her, meaning *Aviut* (will to receive), compared to the *Ohr* (Light of) *Hochma*. This is called Upper *Gevura*.

Third discernment: This is the essence of the abundance that she has acquired through an awakening of her own desire. This Light is given its own name—*Ohr Hassadim*, which is much lower than the *Ohr Hochma*, which expands solely from the Emanator. *Ohr Hassadim* is associated with the intensification of the emanated, as it was mentioned, that the *Gevura*, which is a Light that has been made coarser, became the root of the *Ohr Hassadim*. These three discernments together are called *Bina*, and the second *Behina* from *Hochma*. Thus, the two *Sefirot*, *Hochma* and *Bina*, have been clarified, and the *Keter* is the *Ein Sof* (Infinity), the root of the emanated.

And although *Behina Bet* manifested an intensified desire towards the Operator, she is still unfit to be a complete vessel of reception. The thing is that in spirituality, the *Kli* with the Light in it are very close, virtually interdependent. When the Light disappears, the *Kli* is cancelled, and when the *Kli* disappears, the Light is cancelled. Thus, the importance of the *Kli* is as the importance of the Light.

Hence, the form of the vessel of reception was not completed in *Bina*, since her essence is the *Ohr Hochma*. For this reason, the *Ohr Hassadim*, which she extended through her own intensification, was annulled before her essence as a candle before a torch. Thus, this *Ohr Hassadim* expanded further from *Bina* outwards from herself and gained strength to extend additional abundance, more than the measure of its expansion through *Bina*. At that time, the vessel of reception was completed.

Hence, we discern two more *Behinot*, *Behina Gimel* (third discernment) and *Behina Dalet* (fourth discernment), which are expansions that extend from *Bina*, where the vessel of reception is still hidden, in potential, as long as it did not intensify for addition, and this is called *Zeir Anpin*. And its intensification for more abundance is called "the *Kli* of *Malchut*," which is a vessel of reception that was completed in that emanated, which is now made of Light and *Kli*. By that, it stops being considered an Emanator and is discerned as emanated.

These are the four *Behinot* known as *HB*, *ZA*, and *Malchut*, which are the four-letter-name. *HB* are *Yod-Hey*, and *ZON* are *Vav-Hey*. They are considered ten *Sefirot* because *Zeir Anpin* contains six *Sefirot*, which are *Hesed*, *Gevura*, *Tifferet*, *Netzah*, *Hod*, *Yesod*.

The thing is that the essence of *ZA* is the Light of *Hesed* and *Gevura*, meaning the two *Behinot Ohr Hassadim* and Upper *Gevura*, which expanded from *Bina* outwardly. And we should note here that in *Bina*, *Gevura* is the first and the root of the *Ohr Hassadim*. But in *Tifferet* it is to the contrary: *Hesed* precedes the Light of *Gevura*, since the main Light that expands is *Hesed*, and the *Gevura* is ancillary within it, in *Bina*.

Now you can understand what was written in *The Tree of Life* and by Rashbi, that in the world of *Nekudim*, *Gevura de* (of) *ZA* preceded its *Hesed*, since the *ZON de Nekudim* are considered *ZON de Bina*, and not the actual *ZON*, as in the two bottom *Behinot* of the four above-mentioned *Behinot*. This is why *Gevura de ZA* precedes its *Hesed*.

Also, the *Sefira Tifferet de ZA* is the unification of the above *Hochma* and *Gevura* to the act of the *Kli* of *Malchut*. It is called *Tifferet* since the Light *Mitpaer* (boasts) itself on the *Behina Aleph* (first *Behina*), which is *Hochma*, whose desire did not suffice to make a *Kli*. But *Behina Gimel*, which is *Hassadim* and *Gevurot* (plural for *Gevura*) that expand from *Bina* outwardly, sufficed to make the *Kli* of *Malchut*. This is the meaning of "according to the beauty (*Tifferet*) of a man, to dwell in the house." This explains the three *Sefirot HGT de ZA*, and they are called "the three patriarchs," since they are the essence of *ZA*. Also, *Netzah*, *Hod*, and *Yesod* are called "sons," since they expand from *HGT*.

The thing is that because of *Tzimtzum Aleph* (the first restriction), which is thoroughly explained inside the book, a hard *Masach* (screen) was made in the *Kli* of *Malchut*. This means that *Behina Dalet* (the fourth *Behina*) in the *Kli Malchut* detains the Upper Light from spreading into *Behina Dalet*, due to the disparity of form there, as it is written there.

Yet, the Light expands and wishes to come to *Behina Dalet*, too, as the nature of the Upper Light is to expand to the lower ones until it is almost separated from its place, as it is written in *Panim Masbirot*. Hence, a *Zivug de Hakaa* (coupling by striking) was made between the Upper Light that spreads into the *Kli* of *Malchut* and the detaining *Masach* in the *Kli* of *Malchut*.

This is like sunlight hitting a mirror, with sparks being reflected. Hence, ten new *Sefirot* emerged from this *Zivug de Hakaa*, called ten *Sefirot de* (of) *Ohr Hozer* (Reflected Light). It turns out that there are two sets of ten *Sefirot* in each emanated being: ten *Sefirot de Ohr Yashar* (Direct Light) over the four *Behinot*, and ten *Sefirot de Ohr Hozer*.

Know that this is the Upper Light that re-expanded from *HGT de ZA* for *Zivug de Hakaa* in the *Masach* in *Kli Malchut*. They are called *Netzah, Hod, Yesod*.

Now you can understand what is written in *Tikkunney Zohar* (*Corrections of The Zohar*), that *Malchut* is fourth to the fathers and seventh to the sons. This means that when she is first emanated, *Malchut* is discerned from the act of *Tifferet de ZA* and follows the *HGT*, which are called "Fathers." And from the perspective of the illumination of the *Ohr Hozer* in her *Masach*, she follows the *NHY* that expanded to her for *Zivug de Hakaa*. And the *NHY* are called "the sons of *HGT*"; hence it is seventh to the sons.

Thus we have properly explained the essence of the ten *Sefirot KHB, HGT, NHY*, and *Malchut* at their root. This is the first concept in the wisdom of truth, and it must always be before the eyes of the student while delving in this wisdom.

Now we understand the sound warning in *The Book of Creation*, "ten and not nine." It means that since a detaining *Masach* was made in *Behina Dalet* from the *Tzimtzum* (restriction) downwards, it is impossible to mistakenly say that *Behina Dalet* is excluded from the ten *Sefirot*, and only nine *Sefirot* remain in *Kedusha* (holiness). For this reason, it warns, "ten and not nine."

And it warns further, "ten and not eleven." This means that you should not mistakenly say that *Behina Dalet* became a vessel of reception after the *Tzimtzum*. Thus, there are two *Sefirot* in one *Malchut*: one is the *Masach* that always raises *Ohr Hozer*, and a vessel of reception to receive the *Ohr Yashar*, as well. This is why it states, "ten and not eleven."

3) There are five prominent discernments in the ten above-mentioned *Sefirot*, which should not move from your eyes and will straighten your ways in studying the wisdom. **The first discernment** is the Light of *Atzmut* (self, essence), which is the comprehensive Light from *Ein Sof* that exists in that emanated. This is the essence, since the lower one does not participate here whatsoever; and it is called *Hochma de Ohr Yashar*.

The second discernment is the *Ohr Hassadim* that extends from Above downwards. This Light is conjoined with the awakening of the *Gevura* of the emanated of *Behina Bet*, which is the Light of *Bina* that she drew. **The third discernment** is the *Ohr Hassadim* that rises from below Upwards through a *Zivug de Hakaa*. It is called *Ohr Hozer* that rises and extends only from the emanated, due to the above-mentioned detainment.

The fourth discernment is the Light of Upper *Gevura*, meaning *Behina Bet*, which is *Aviut de Bina* that she acquired by her intensification. **The fifth discernment** is the lower *Gevura*, meaning *Behina Dalet*, where the intensification of the desire is activated in the *Ohr Hassadim* that was added by the emanated. This is called "the *Kli* of *Malchut de Ohr Yashar*," and this *Gevura* is the *Kli* of ten *Sefirot*, and remember that.

Know that the *Masach* in *Kli Malchut* is the root of darkness, because of the detaining force that exists in the *Masach*, to stop the Upper Light from spreading in *Behina Dalet*. This is also the root of the labor in order to receive reward, since labor is an involuntary act, for the worker feels comfortable only when resting. But because the landlord is paying his salary, he cancels his will before the will of the landlord.

Know that here in this world, there is no being or conduct that is not rooted in the Upper Worlds, from which branches expand to the lower worlds, until they are revealed to us in this world. And you see that in general, work and labor are rooted in the *Masach* in the *Kli* of *Malchut*, which detains the Upper Light that she covets, due to the Emanator, Who wishes to bestow delight, and everything that is a Thought in the Emanator is a mandatory law in the emanated. Naturally, He needs no actions, but His Thought completes. Hence, she chooses to not receive the Upper Light, lest it will come to disparity of form (*Panim Masbirot*, "Branch One").

It follows that the detaining force in the *Masach* is equal to the labor. And the reward that the landlord gives to the worker is rooted in the *Ohr Hozer* emitted by the *Zivug de Hakaa*, where by the *Masach*, a root was made for the *Ohr Hozer*. It turns out that she returns to being *Keter* to these ten *Sefirot de Ohr Hozer*, as well as to *Ohr Yashar*. As will be explained below, all this profit came to her because of this act of detaining.

From the above-mentioned, it follows that the ten *Sefirot* are really one *Kli*, called *Malchut*. But to complete its form, it is discerned with three roots: the three *Behinot Hochma*, *Bina*, and *ZA* that extend from one another. You should know that this *Malchut* is still contained in the *Ohr Ein Sof* from before the *Tzimtzum*, called *Malchut de Ein Sof*, in which was the first restriction.

As it is written in *Panim Masbirot*, "Branch One," because of the equivalence of form with the Emanator, her desire rose from wanting to receive in *Behina Dalet*, and the Light of the *Kav* (line) extended to her from *Ein Sof*. The Light of the *Kav* contains all the Light that extends into the five worlds, called *Adam Kadmon*, *Atzilut*, *Beria*, *Yetzira*, and *Assiya*. This Light is generally referred to as

Kav, from the word *Kav Midah* (measurement), as it extends into the worlds by measure and a rationed number in each world, according to the form of the *Kli* of *Malchut* in that world, as it is elaborated within.

And the matter of the five above-mentioned worlds are truly the matter of the *Keter* and the four known *Behinot* in the ten *Sefirot*. Thus, the world of *AK* is the world of *Keter*; the world of *Atzilut* is the world of *Hochma*; the world of *Beria* is the world of *Bina*; the world of *Yetzira* is the world of *Zeir Anpin*; and the world of *Assiya* is the world of *Malchut*. However, in each world, there are ten *Sefirot*, and each *Sefira* of the ten *Sefirot* of that world comprises ten *Sefirot*, as well, as it is written inside.

They are divided into the five above-mentioned worlds because the *Kli* of *Malchut* should first be integrated in each *Sefira*, through *Keter*. This occurs in *Hitpashtut Aleph* (first expansion) of *AHP de AK*, where she was integrated in ZON. In *Hitpashtut Bet* (second expansion) *de AHP*, she was integrated in *Bina*. And in the world of *Nekudim*, she was integrated in *Hochma*, and in the world of *Atzilut* she was integrated in *Keter*.

And since *Malchut* has been integrated in each *Sefira*, the world of *Tikkun* (correction) begins: Its *Rosh* (head) is the above-mentioned world of *Atzilut*, where the Light of *Ein Sof* dresses in *Behina Aleph*. Then the Light of *Ein Sof* dresses in *Behina Bet*, creating the world of *Beria*. Following, it dresses in *Behina Gimel*, creating the world of *Yetzira*, and then it dresses in *Behina Dalet*, creating the world of *Assiya*. It will be elaborated inside how they all stem from one another by a mandatory manner of cause and consequence, and how they are tied to one another.

4) First, we need to understand the quality of each of the worlds *AK* and *ABYA*, which I will explain one at a time. Let us begin with the world of *Keter*, which is the world of *Adam Kadmon*. Its first *Kli* is the world of *Akudim* (tied). In *The Gate of Akudim*, Chapter Three, the Ari wrote that all ten *Sefirot* emerged, but not all of them emerged together. In the beginning, only *Malchut* came out in the world of *Akudim*. And this *Malchut* came out in the form of *Nefesh*. Following it, the rest of the parts emerged, through *Keter*.

And when *Keter* came, *Malchut* was completed with all five Inner Lights—*Nefesh*, *Ruach*, *Neshama*, *Haya*, and *Yechida*. Yet, they were still missing all the above *Sefirot*, which emerged incomplete. Hence, they had to climb back to the Emanator to be completed. But now, on the return, *Keter* returned first.

And when *Keter* rose, the Light of *Hochma* rose to the place of *Keter*, *Bina* to the place of *Hochma*, ZA to the place of *Bina*, and *Malchut* to the place of

ZA. Subsequently, *Hochma* rose to the Emanator, too. Then *Bina* rose to *Keter*, following *Hochma*, ZA to *Hochma*, and *Malchut* to *Bina*. Then *Bina* rose, too, and ZA rose to *Keter*, *Malchut* to *Hochma*. Finally, ZA rose and *Malchut* rose to *Keter*, until *Malchut*, too, rose to the Emanator.

After that, the Light returned from the Emanator and expanded in them, though not in their initial order. Instead, the Light of *Keter* did not return but departed and remained missing. Hence, the Light of *Hochma* came out in the *Kli* of *Keter*, the Light of *Bina* in the *Kli* of *Hochma*, the Light of ZA in the *Kli* of *Bina*, and the Light of *Malchut* in the *Kli* of ZA. The *Kli* of *Malchut* remained without Light at all, thus far his words in brief. Additionally, the ten *Sefirot de Akudim* emerged from below Upwards. *Malchut* emerged first, then ZA, then *Bina*, then *Hochma*, and finally *Keter*, thus far his words.

We should thoroughly understand the matter of the elicitation of the ten *Sefirot* from Above downwards and from below Upwards, mentioned in the Ari's words. Certainly, this is not about measures of Above, below, before, and after in time and place. Rather, it is in terms of reason and result, cause and consequence. Hence, how can *Malchut* emerge first, followed by ZA, followed by *Bina*, until *Keter*—the root of them all—emerges last? This seems perplexing. And who and what gave and inverted the Upper to be lower and the lower to be Above?

The thing is that the order of the ten *Sefirot de Ohr Yashar* has already been explained above, being five degrees one below the other, by the measure of *Hizdakchut* (purification) of each of them from the coarse Light whose form has changed, that is, the *Behina Dalet*. *Behina Aleph*, since it is considered a hidden potential, is the most important in the degree. And *Behina Bet* has already moved from potential to actual by intensifying with a worse desire than in *Behina Aleph*. *Behina Gimel* is worse than *Behina Bet*, and *Behina Dalet*, *Malchut* is the worst, since the *Aviut* in her is greater than in the rest.

Also, it is known that once the *Kli* of *Malchut* emerged, it experienced the *Tzimtzum Aleph* of not receiving in *Behina Dalet*. This detaining force is called *Masach* (screen), and when the *Ohr Yashar* that descends from *Ein Sof* strikes the *Masach* in *Malchut*, there is a *Zivug de Hakaa*, and thus ten *Sefirot de Ohr Hozer* emerge, as it is written inside (Branch Three).

Within these ten *Sefirot de Ohr Hozer*, the degrees are inverted compared to the value of the ten *Sefirot de Ohr Yashar*. In the ten *Sefirot de Ohr Yashar*, the purer is Higher in merit and better. But in the ten *Sefirot de Ohr Hozer*, the coarser is Higher and better. This is so because *Malchut* is the *Keter* and the root of these ten *Sefirot de Ohr Hozer*, since her coarse *Masach* detains the Light from descending into her *Behina Dalet*. Thus, *Malchut* returns to being *Keter* by way of its end is in its beginning, as it is written in *Panim Masbirot*, Branch Three.

It turns out that ZA receives the Light from *Keter de Ohr Hozer*; hence, ZA is considered a degree of *Hochma*, and *Bina* is considered a degree of *Bina* because she receives from ZA, who returns to being *Hochma*. Also, *Hochma de Ohr Yashar* is considered ZA, in the *Ohr Hozer*, since it receives the *Ohr Hozer* from *Bina*. And *Keter de Ohr Yashar* is considered *Malchut* in the *Ohr Hozer*, since it receives from ZA. Thus, you find that the purer in the degree will be lower in praise and merit, and understand that thoroughly.

Yet, the ten *Sefirot de Ohr Hozer* join and integrate in the ten *Kelim*. When they join as one, all the degrees are of equal merit, since *Malchut's* level is equal to that of *Keter* from the perspective of the *Ohr Hozer*, where *Malchut* returns to being *Keter*. Also, ZA is equal to *Hochma*, since ZA is considered *Hochma de Ohr Hozer*. And the level of *Hochma* is equal to that of *Keter*, since *Keter* receives the *Ohr Hozer* from her, as *Hochma* receives the *Ohr Yashar* from *Keter*.

And since the level of ZA is equal to *Hochma*, and *Hochma* to *Keter*, it follows that the level of ZA is equal to that of *Keter*, too. It follows that by the elicitation of the ten *Sefirot de Ohr Hozer* from *Behina Dalet*, all the degrees in the ten *Sefirot* have been equalized, having the same level through *Keter*.

5) But the ten *Sefirot* of the world of *Akudim* disappeared once more. And we need to understand the reason for their departure. The Ari says that the reason is that when they emerged, they emerged incomplete and hence departed once more to receive their completion.

However, we need to understand the deficiency and the *Tikkun* (correction) that came to them through this departure. Here the Ari wrote that the deficiency was because *Keter* emerged only in *Behinat Nefesh*. And in another place, he wrote that the deficiency was because the *Ohr Pnimi* (Inner Light) and the *Ohr Makif* (Surrounding Light) came from the same foramen, and were beating on each other, as he writes in *Heichal AK, Shaar Vav, Shaar Akudim*, Chapter One.

Following, the lower *Taamim* came, below the *Otiot* (letters), which are Lights that emerge through the *Peh* of AK, and from there outwards. And here the Lights have been completely joined, since they come out through a single channel. And since the Surrounding Lights and Inner Lights have conjoined, here begins the making of the *Kelim*.

For this reason, the five Inner Lights and the Surrounding Lights emerged tied together. This is why they are called *Akudim*, from the verse, "and bound Isaac." Thus, when they emerge together outside of the *Peh* (mouth), tied together, they beat and strike each other, and their beatings beget the existence of the *Kelim*.

This means that the Lights of *Awzen* and *Hotem* where the *Ohr Pnimi* expands through the left foramens of the *Awzen* and the *Hotem*, and *Ohr Makif* expanded through the right foramens of *Awzen* and *Hotem*. Hence, they persisted and did not leave, since there is a special *Kli* for the *Ohr Pnimi* and a special *Kli* for the *Ohr Makif*.

But in the Light of the *Peh*, where there is only one foramen, the *Ohr Pnimi* and the *Ohr Makif* were in the same *Kli*. Hence, they were beating on each other, as a result of which the Light departed and the *Kelim* fell down. In other words, they fell from their degree, and further *Aviut* was added to the previous *Aviut*, and this created the *Kelim*, since the departure of the Light completes the *Kelim*.

To thoroughly understand the issue of the two foramens of *Awzen* and *Hotem de AK*, the issue of the single foramen in the *Peh de AK*, and the meaning of the five internal and five surrounding, the *Bitush* and the *Kelim* and the *Ibuy* (adding *Aviut*), I need to elaborate, since the Ari's words on these matters are quite succinct.

It is even more so concerning the surrounding, where he seemingly contradicts himself in each and every section. Once he says that they had Inner Lights *KHB ZON* and the five Surrounding Lights *KHB ZON* from the *Hotem* upwards, but from the *Peh* down, the Surroundings of *Bina* and *ZON* ceased and only two surrounding, *Keter* and *Hochma* remained, and the five *Partzufim KHB ZON*. And another time, he said that from the world of *Nekudim* downwards, the lower surrounding have stopped, but there are still five Surrounding Lights and five Inner Lights in the Lights of the *Peh*. And another time, he says that there are five Inner and five Surrounding in the whole of *ABYA*, and other such contradictions.

6) I will elaborate inside the book, and here I will be brief so as to not stray from the issue. It is explained in Branch One and in Branch Four in the order of the ten *Sefirot*, concerning the four *Behinot* of ten *Sefirot de Ohr Yashar* and *Ohr Hozer*, that in every ten *Sefirot*, there are two discernments of *Hitpashtut* (expansion) and two discernments of *Hitaabut* (increasing the *Aviut*), which expand from the root, which is the *Keter* of these ten *Sefirot*.

Hochma, considered broad *Hitpashtut*, emerges first. This means that this *Hitpashtut* contains all the Light that extends from *Ein Sof* to that emanated. And the *Kli*, called *Ohr ha Av* (the thick Light), meaning the will to receive contained in the *Hitpashtut* of the Light, for which it acquires disparity of form from the Emanator, in whom there is no form of reception, and for which it becomes darker than the Light, is still not revealed in this broad *Hitpashtut*. This is so as long as its desire does not intensify, craving additional abundance more than the measure of its *Hitpashtut*. Instead, it is included in the above-mentioned coarse Light from the perspective of the Emanator, who wishes to bestow upon it.

For this reason, it must reveal its vessels of reception and realize it from potential to actual. Hence it grows thicker as it spreads, meaning its desire to extend more abundance than its measure of *Hitpashtut* increases. And the *Hitaabut* that was made in this *Hitpashtut* is given its own name, due to its intensification. It is called *Bina* because it is darker than the *Ohr Hochma*, in which the will to receive was revealed in actual fact.

This *Bina* is still unfit to be an actual *Kli*, since its essence is from *Hochma*; but it is the root of the *Kli*, for the *Kli* can only be completed from the *Hitaabut* (thickening) made in the second *Hitpashtut*. It is called "*Hitpashtut* through a window," meaning that the additional abundance that *Bina* drew through her intensification spreads from her outwards. This is called *Ohr Hassadim*, the opposite of the broad *Hitpashtut Aleph* (first *Hitpashtut*), called *Ohr Atzmut* (Light of Self/Essence).

The *Hitpashtut* through a window that spreads from *Bina* is called ZA, and it thickens as it spreads, like the first *Hitpashtut*. This means that it, too, intensifies to extend additional abundance, more than the measure of its *Hitpashtut* from *Bina*. By that, it actualizes the vessels of reception contained in it. This second *Hitaabut* is given its own name, since through this intensification, it grew darker than the Light of *Hitpashtut*, and it is called *Malchut*.

Behina Dalet, which is the *Hitaabut* created at the *Hitpashtut* through the window, called *Malchut*, is the complete vessel of reception, and not the three *Behinot* preceding it, which cascaded only to reveal this fourth *Behina*. It is her that undergoes the first restriction, preventing herself from receiving abundance in this *Behina Dalet*, due to the disparity of form revealed in her. This detaining force is called *Masach* (screen) or *Pargod* (curtain), which means that it detains the abundance from shining and spreading within it.

Also, this is the whole difference between the first *Hitaabut* made in the broad *Hitpashtut*, and the *Hitaabut* that was done in a *Hitpashtut* through a window. This is because so in the first *Hitaabut*, the *Tzimtzum* does not govern; hence it is fit for reception of Light. This is why she is called "a window," meaning receiving, as the house receives the daylight through the window in it. But in the second *Hitaabut*, the force of *Tzimtzum* governs her and she prevents herself from receiving the abundance in her *Aviut*. Hence, he is called a *Masach*, detaining the Light.

And after *Behina Dalet* appeared with her *Masach*, the Light spreads to her again, and the *Masach* detains it, as mentioned above. Consequently, a *Zivug de Hakaa* is made on it, and ten *Sefirot de Ohr Hozer* emerge, as it is written in Branch Three. The arrangement of these ten *Sefirot* is opposite from the ten *Sefirot de Ohr Yashar*, which emerge from below Upwards, since the *Masach* that elicited that great Light, and which is its root, has become *Keter*.

This is the meaning of "their end is imbedded in their beginning. Just as *Keter* is the beginning and the *Rosh* (head) of the ten *Sefirot de Ohr Yashar*, the end, which is *Malchut*, has become the beginning and the *Rosh* of the ten *Sefirot de Ohr Hozer*.

Thus, *Malchut* has returned to being a *Keter* to these ten *Sefirot*, and ZA of the ten *Sefirot de Ohr Yashar* has now become *Hochma*, since the first receiver from the root is called *Hochma*. It is similarly with the rest, through *Keter de Ohr Yashar*, which becomes *Malchut* in the ten *Sefirot de Ohr Hozer*, since it receives from ZA *de Ohr Hozer*, which is *Hochma de Ohr Yashar*.

It turns out that in the ten *Sefirot* KHB ZON *de Ohr Yashar*, the degrees are measured according to the purity from the coarse Light, where the purer is Higher and more important. But in the ten *Sefirot* KHB ZON *de Ohr Hozer*, the degrees are measured by the *Aviut*, where the greater the *Aviut* in the degree, the Higher it is and more important. This makes the Higher ones in the ten *Sefirot de Ohr Yashar* lower in the ten *Sefirot de Ohr Hozer*, and the lower ones in the ten *Sefirot de Ohr Yashar* Higher in the ten *Sefirot de Ohr Hozer*.

The first ten *Sefirot* that spread from *Ein Sof* are called *Adam Kadmon*. These are the roots of the *Kelim de Rosh*, hence the ten *Sefirot* are named after the *Kli de Rosh*: *Galgalta* (skull), *Eynaim* (eyes), *Awznaim* (ears) are the KHB of the ten *Sefirot de AK*, and *Hotem* (nose) and *Peh* (mouth) are ZA and *Malchut* of the ten *Sefirot de AK*. Also, it is known that the ten *Sefirot* are integrated in one another, as it is written inside. Hence, each of the above-mentioned *Galgalta*, *Eynaim*, and *AHP*, expanded into ten *Sefirot*.

It is forbidden to speak of the ten *Sefirot* that expanded in *Galgalta ve* (and) *Eynaim*, which are *Keter* and *Hochma* of the ten *Sefirot de AK*, and we have no dealings with them. We begin to speak from the *AHP* down, from *Bina* and ZON *de AK*.

Also, it is known that the ten *Sefirot* are *Keter* and the four *Behinot* HB ZON, and there are *Ohr Pnimi* and *Ohr Makif* in them. This means that what has already been clothed in the *Kli* is called *Ohr Pnimi*, and what has not yet been clothed in the *Kli* is called *Ohr Makif*. Thus, in each of the ten *Sefirot de AHP de AK* are five internals, *KHB ZON*, and five surrounding *KHB ZON*.

7) Now we shall explain the inherent quality of the *Ohr Pnimi* and *Ohr Makif* of the ten *Sefirot de AK*. The matter of the ten *Sefirot de Ohr Yashar* and ten *Sefirot de Ohr Hozer* that exist in each ten *Sefirot* has already been explained. In these ten *Sefirot de AK*, too, there are ten *Sefirot de Ohr Yashar* from *Keter* to *Malchut*, and likewise, ten *Sefirot de Ohr Hozer* from *Malchut* to *Keter*, and the *Ohr Yashar* extends and arrives in completeness to that emanated. Yet, the ten *Sefirot de Ohr Hozer* are not fully and immediately extended to that emanated. Instead, it is extended through all the *Partzufim* emanated after *Adam Kadmon*. The thing is that everything that extends from the Emanator extends complete and full. These are the ten *Sefirot de Ohr Yashar*.

But the ten *Sefirot de Ohr Hozer* that extend from the emanated, from the detaining force in *Behina Dalet*, called *Masach*, does not immediately emerge in full. Instead, each emanated being has a part of it, and is multiplied according to the multiplication of the emanated, as it is written inside. Now you can see that the ten *Sefirot de Ohr Yashar* and a part of the ten *Sefirot de Ohr Hozer* are the *Ohr Pnimi*, while the whole of the *Ohr Hozer* is the *Ohr Makif*.

Also, it has already been explained above that there are two *Nukvaot* (plural for *Nukva*) in the ten *Sefirot*: *Hitaabut* in the broad *Hitpashtut*, and *Hitaabut* in the *Hitpashtut* through a window, called *Bina* and *Malchut*. You should know that *Bina* is discerned as an inner *Kli*, in which all the *Ohr Pnimi* is clothed, and *Malchut* is the outer *Kli*, in which all the *Ohr Makif* is clothed. This means that the *Ohr Makif* is tied to her, since she has a *Masach* that is unfit for reception, due to the detaining force in it. Instead, it is the root of the ten *Sefirot de Ohr Hozer*.

Thus, the content of the *Ohr Pnimi* and *Ohr Makif* has been thoroughly explained, as well as the content of the inner *Kli* and the outer *Kli*. Now we can understand the Ari's words, brought above in Item 5 concerning the five internals and five externals that emerged tied to one another through the *Peh de AK*. This concerns what he had explained in *Shaar TANTA*, Chapter One, that the *Ohr Pnimi* and *Ohr Makif* of the ten *Sefirot de Awznaim*, and the *Ohr Pnimi* and *Ohr Makif* of the ten *Sefirot de Hotem* emerged in two *Kelim*: an inner *Kli* for *Ohr Pnimi* and an outer *Kli* for *Ohr Makif*.

Also, they are remote from one another, since the five surrounding *KHB ZON* emerge from the foramen of the right *Awzen*, and the five internal *KHB ZON* emerge from the foramen of the left *Awzen*, and similarly in the *Hotem*.

Hence, he tells us here, in the ten *Sefirot de Peh de AK*, that there are no two distinct *Kelim* here, but both, the five internal and the five surrounding, emerged tied to a single *Kli*—the *Peh*, called *Malchut de AK*, meaning *Behina Dalet*. Yet, the inner *Kli*, which is *Behina Bet* and *Behinat Bina*, does not exist here.

We could ask about it: How is it possible for the *Ohr Pnimi*, which is the ten *Sefirot de Ohr Yashar*, to clothe in the *Kli de Peh*, which is *Behina Dalet* that was erected with a *Masach*, and is unfit for reception? The thing is that *Malchut* herself is discerned with four distinct *Behinot*, called *Atzamot* (bones), *Gidin* (tendons), *Bassar* (flesh), and *Or* (skin). The *Atzamot* of *Malchut* indicate the *Etzem* (bone, but also core) of her structure. This is the actual *Behinat ZA*, meaning the *Hitpashtut* through a window, except it has gained *Aviut* along its *Hitpashtut* due to the intensification of the desire to extend more abundance than in its *Hitpashtut* from *Bina*.

For this reason, it is defined by a name according to itself. Thus, two *Behinot* are discerned in her: *Behina Aleph* is the *Atzamot* in her, the part of *ZA*, and *Behina Bet* is the *Aviut* added to her by her intensification. This is called *Gidin*. And what she takes from the force of *Tzimtzum*—the detaining force so as to not receive abundance in this coarse Light—called a *Masach*, the one with the *Zivug* of the ten *Sefirot de Ohr Hozer*, is *Behina Dalet* in *Malchut*, called *Or*. And the *Ohr Hozer* that rises from the *Masach* by the force of the *Zivug* is called *Bassar*, and this is the *Behina Gimel* of *Malchut*.

Thus, you find that *Malchut* is contained of the *Hitpashtut* of *Bina*, too. Moreover, it is in fact the essence of its structure. Now you will understand that the *Atzamot* in *Malchut* become the inner *Kli* to the internal five in the Lights of the *Peh*, and the *Behinat Or* in her becomes an outer *Kli* for the surrounding five in the Lights of the *Peh*. Now it has been thoroughly clarified how the five internal *KHB ZON* and five surrounding *KHB ZON* emerged in a single *Kli*—*Malchut*—in which there are two *Kelim*, as well, internal and external, though connected to each other, since all four *Behinot* are but one *Kli*: *Malchut*.

8) And now we shall explain the issue of the striking and the *Bitush* that occurred between the *Ohr Makif* and the *Ohr Pnimi* due to their being tied in one *Kli*. See in *The Tree of Life*, *Heichal AK*, *Shaar 2*, p 3, as well as in *Shaar Akudim*, Chapter Two, that the nature of the *Ohr Pnimi* is to purify the *Kli* that is clothed in her. Hence, since in the ten *Sefirot de Peh de AK* the *Ohr Pnimi* and *Ohr Makif* were tied in a single *Kli* in *Malchut*, the *Ohr Pnimi* was purifying the *Kli Malchut* degree-by-degree. This is the reason for the departure of the ten *Sefirot de Peh*, called "the world of *Akudim*."

The thing is that it has already been explained in Item 6 and Item 4, that the ten *Sefirot de Ohr Hozer* are of opposite value to the ten *Sefirot de Ohr Yashar*. This is so because in the ten *Sefirot de Ohr Yashar*, the degrees rise one above the other according to their purity, up to their root, which is the purest among them. But in the ten *Sefirot de Ohr Hozer*, the degrees rise one above the other according to their *Aviut*, up to the root, which is the coarsest among them. This is the *Behina Dalet*, and *Malchut* that became *Keter* again. Also, *Behina Gimel* is *Hochma*, *Behina Bet* is *Bina*, *Behina Aleph* is ZA, and *Keter* is considered *Malchut*.

In the beginning, the *Masach* was purified by one degree. This means that the coarse form of Light of *Behina Dalet* was purified, and reacquired the form of *Aviut de Behina Gimel*. This is considered that the Light of *Malchut* departed its place and rose to *Kli de* ZA, since then, too, the *Ohr Yashar* expanded from *Ein Sof* on the *Masach*, and the detaining force controlled the *Masach* until a *Zivug de Hakaa* was made and the ten *Sefirot de Ohr Hozer* emerged from the *Masach de Behina Gimel*.

However, they are no longer at the level of *Keter*, as they were initially, but are at the level of *Hochma*. This is because the *Aviut* of *Behinat* ZA and *Behina Gimel de Ohr Yashar* has the value of *Hochma* in the *Ohr Hozer*. It turns out that the *Masach* did not return to being *Keter* due to the *Ohr Hozer*, but returned to being *Hochma*.

Afterwards it purified further, and received the purification of *Behina Bet*, which is *Bina*. There, too, the *Ohr Yashar* expanded to it up to the *Zivug de Hakaa* and the raising of *Ohr Hozer*, though at the level of *Bina*. And as the *Aviut de Behina Gimel* and *Behina Dalet* were lost, she lost the first two *Sefirot de Ohr Hozer*.

Subsequently, it purified further, and received the purification of *Behina Aleph*, the *Ohr Yashar* from *Ein Sof* mated in it, and the *Ohr Hozer* rose, though at the level of ZA, lacking *Behinat Bina*, too. After that it purified even more, up to the form of *Shoresh* (root), which rose to the level of *Keter*.

At that time, there was no *Aviut* left in the *Masach* at all; hence there was no more *Zivug de Hakaa* on the *Ohr Yashar* in it. For this reason, the *Ohr Hozer* completely disappeared from the ten *Sefirot de Akudim*, and see inside in Branch Three and Branch Four, where it is all explained elaborately.

Thus, it has been clarified that since the *Ohr Pnimi* is clothed in the *Kli* of *Malchut*, it purifies it degree-by-degree, and along with its purification, the ten *Sefirot KHB ZON de Ohr Hozer* vanish, too. This is so because during her ascension to *Behinat Keter*, the *Masach* loses all its power to raise *Ohr Hozer*. Thus, the ten *Sefirot de Ohr Yashar* depart it, too, since the *Ohr Yashar* and *Ohr Hozer* are interdependent and tied to one another.

9) To explain that, I shall first explain the state of the *Sefirot* with a picture of the *Taam* (singular for *Taamim*—punctuation marks) *Segolta*, like this: ∴, that is, the *Keter* is on top, below it on the right is *Hochma*, and at its left—*Bina*. We need to understand that, for God forbid that we should understand it as a depiction of places that the tangible eye perceives. Also, the matter of *Panim be Panim* (face-to-face) and *Achor be Achor* (back-to-back) that apply in the ten *Sefirot*, God forbid that there should back and front here.

The thing is that it has already been explained in the four *Behinot* of *Ohr Yashar* that expand from *Ein Sof*, which is *Keter*, that the expansion of the *Keter* is called *Hochma*. Also, it thickens as it expands, meaning the intensification of the desire to extend abundance more than the measure of its expansion. Hence, it is regarded as two discernments: *Behina Aleph* is the whole of the Light that expands from *Ein Sof* to that emanated, called *Hochma*, and *Behina Bet* is the *Hitaabut*, given to it by the intensification of the desire to extend new abundance, called *Bina*.

For this reason, there are three discernments in the *Sefira Bina*: the first discernment is her own structure, which is a part of *Hochma* itself. The second discernment is the Light that had thickened in her through her intensification to extend new abundance from *Keter*. The third discernment is the essence of the abundance that she draws from *Keter*, called *Ohr de Hassadim*, which is much lower than the *Ohr Hochma* that extends directly from the Emanator. But the Light of *Bina* that she draws from *Keter* is associated by her initial intensification, which was thickened for it.

And when *Bina* draws the Light of *Hassadim* from *Keter*, she does not draw the Light of *Hochma* from the *Sefira* of *Hochma*. Hence, she is considered to be *Achor be Achor* (back to back) with *Hochma*. It turns out that the *Ohr Hochma*, which is the Light of *Atzmut* of the general ten *Sefirot* in that emanated, ceases from it, for *Bina* has turned her *Panim* to draw *Ohr Hassadim* from *Keter*.

Yet, when *Behina Dalet* appears, and the ten *Sefirot de Ohr Hozer* that extend from her, considered even more *Ohr Hassadim* than the *Ohr Hassadim* in *Bina*, *Bina* no longer needs to draw the *Ohr Hassadim* from *Keter*, since she receives abundantly from the *Ohr Hozer de Malchut*. For this reason, she turns her *Panim* back to *Hochma* and draws *Ohr Hochma* once more. At that time, the *Ohr Hochma*, too, is drawn abundantly in the general ten *Sefirot* in that emanated. This is called *Panim be Panim* of HB, which they gained through the *Ohr Hozer* that rises from the *Malchut*.

However, prior to the exile of the *Kli* of *Malchut*, *Bina* turned her *Panim* to *Keter*, which is the state of the *Taam Segolta*, where *Bina* is below *Keter*, like *Hochma*, but *Hochma* draws the Light of *Atzmut* from *Keter*, and *Bina* draws Light of *Hassadim* from *Keter*. And since the Light of *Atzmut* is the collective Light in the emanated, *Hochma* is considered "right," and the Light of *Hassadim* is considered "left," as it is associated with *Gevura*.

Thus we have explained that the Light of *Atzmut* cannot spread in the whole of the ten *Sefirot de Ohr Yashar*, since *Bina* is *Achor be Achor* with it, except during a *Zivug de Hakaa* in the *Masach* in *Kli Malchut*. At that time, *Bina* no longer needs the *Ohr Hassadim* and returns to being *PBP* (*Panim be Panim*) with *Hochma*.

It turns out that when the ten *Sefirot de Ohr Hozer* depart from the world of *Akudim*, the Light of *Atzmut* of the ten *Sefirot de Ohr Yashar* depart along with it. This is because the *Ohr Hochma* and the *Ohr Hozer* are interdependent, and only *Achoraim de Bina* remains there in the world of *Akudim*, meaning Light of *Hassadim* and her *Gevura*.

Now you will understand the Ari's words we brought above, that the nature of the *Ohr Pnimi* is to purify the *Kli* it is clothed in, since it revolves around the *Ohr Hochma* that clothes in the internality of the emanated through the *Bina* that returns to being *PBP* with it. Thus, the *Achoraim de Bina* are purified, and since the *Achoraim de Bina*, which is *Behina Bet*, is the root of *Behina Dalet*, since the root is purified, the branch, *Behina Dalet*, is purified along with it.

10) Now we shall explain the issue of the *Bitush* of the Inner Lights with the Surrounding Lights, since they are tied to one another, which I introduced above in Item 5. I shall also bring the Ari's words in *Shaar Akudim*, Chapter Five, where he himself explains the issue of the *Bitush* at length. This is what he wrote, in brief: It follows that there are three kinds of Light [in the *Hitpashtut* of Light in the world of *Akudim* and its departure back to the Emanator]. The first Light is the Lights of *Akudim*, called *Taamim*. The second is the *Reshimo* of that Light, which remains after its departure, and it is called *Tagin*. The third is the Light that comes to it through the ascension of the *Sefirot*, at which time it is through the *Achoraim*, which is *Din*. This is called *Nekudot*.

And when the third Light, called *Nekudot*, comes and strikes the second Light, called *Reshimo*, which is *Rachamim*, they strike and beat on each other. This is because they are opposites: one is *Ohr Yashar*, which is *Rachamim*, and the other is *Ohr Hozer*, which is *Din*. And then *Nitzotzin* (sparks) fall from the descending *Ohr Hozer*, which is *Din*, and these *Nitzotzin* are another, fourth Light, called *Otiot*. These are the four discernments—*Taamim, Nekudot, Tagin,*

Otiot—all of which are included here in the *Akudim*. Also, these *Nitzotzin* that fell from the descending *Ohr Hozer* are like the 248 *Nitzotzin* of the breaking of the vessels in the world of *Nekudim*.

Interpreting his words: According to what has been explained above concerning the order of the expansion of the Light in the world of *Akudim*, first the Light expands from *Ein Sof* to the *Zivug de Hakaa* in the *Masach* in the *Kli* of *Malchut*. Following, ten *Sefirot de Ohr Hozer* emerge from it, from below Upwards, as written in Item 6. They have an inverse ratio, where the Upper Ones in *Ohr Yashar* are below in the *Ohr Hozer*, since in the ten *Sefirot de Ohr Hozer* the degrees diminish according to the purity.

Thus, ZA, which is purer than *Malchut*, is of a lower degree than *Malchut*. But this is so only with respect to the *Hochma* in the ten *Sefirot de Ohr Hozer*. And *Bina*, which is purer than ZA, was diminished in the degree, and she possesses only the value of *Bina*. *Hochma*, which is purer than *Bina*, is diminished in her degree and has only the value of ZA. And *Keter* has the value of *Malchut*, as it is written there and inside, in Branch Three.

But once the *Ohr Yashar* and *Ohr Hozer* unite and join together, it creates an equal value, where the level of each of the ten *Sefirot* reaches the level of *Keter*, as written in Item 4. And the whole of the world of *Akudim*, the expansion and return of the Light of *Ein Sof* from *Keter* to *Malchut* and from *Malchut* to *Keter*, and the *Ohr Hozer* that conjoins with the *Ohr Yashar* at an equal level through *Keter*, is called *Taamim* or *Hitpashtut Aleph de Akudim*.

It has been explained above (Item 8) that because the *Ohr Pnimi* dresses in the *Kli* of *Malchut*, whose nature is to purify the *Kli*, it causes the purification of the *Masach* degree by degree. In the beginning, it receives the purification as in *Behina Gimel*. This is considered that the *Masach* rose to ZA. At that time, the *Ohr Ein Sof* expands once more from *Keter* to the *Masach* in *Kli* ZA, and from ZA to *Keter*. This diminishes the value of the *Ohr Hozer* that rises from the *Masach* to the degree of *Hochma*, similar to the value of ZA *de Ohr Hozer*. Similarly, the degrees descend in the *Hizdakchut* of the *Masach* through the *Hizdakchut* of *Behinat Keter de Ohr Yashar*, at which time the *Masach* is cancelled and the *Zivug de Hakaa* ceases.

Thus, all this *Ohr Hozer*, which descends degree by degree until it completely disappears, is called "the Light of *Nekudot*." This is so because the *Masach* extends from the point of *Tzimtzum*, and hence detains the *Ohr Yashar*, too, from approaching and expanding in it. It is like the middle point of *Tzimtzum Aleph* that decorated itself and departed the Light in it, and assertively chose the

Hizdakchut from its *Aviut*, in order to equalize her form with the Emanator, as has been explained in detail in *Panim Masbirot*, Branch One. Hence, this force, the desire to be purified, is imprinted in the *Masach*.

Now we shall explain the meaning of the *Reshimo*—the Light of *Tagin*. It is known that even though the Light departs, it still leaves a *Reshimo* behind it. Hence, the first *Hitpashtut* in the world of *Akudim*, which expanded and returned from *Keter* to *Malchut* and from *Malchut* to *Keter*, eliciting ten *Sefirot* whose level equals *Keter* in *Ohr Pnimi*, and similarly, ten *Sefirot de Ohr Makif*, as written in Item 7 [note that here there was no distinct *Kli* for *Ohr Pnimi* and a distinct *Kli* for *Ohr Makif*]. That *Kli*, as a whole, is called *Kli de Keter*. This is so because all ten *Sefirot* were at the level of *Keter*. Hence, even though this *Hitpashtut* departed once more, a *Reshimo* of it remained nevertheless, which keeps and sustains the previous form there, so it would not be altogether revoked due to the departure of the Light.

Accordingly, you can see how the Light of *Reshimo*, which remained from *Hitpashtut Aleph*, and the descending *Ohr Hozer*, which is the Light of *Nekudot*, are two opposites, striking and beating each other. This is so because the Light of *Reshimo* is strengthened by *Hitpashtut Aleph*, where the *Ohr Yashar* expanded through the *Masach de Behina Dalet*, and wished very much for the *Masach* to remain specifically in *Aviut* of *Behina Dalet*, since only through the power in the excessive *Aviut* in *Behina Dalet* does it have the value of the level of *Keter*. However, the Light of *Nekudot*, the *Masach* itself, intensifies with all its might only to be purified from its coarse Light, discerned as *Din*, and wishes to be utterly purified and equalize its form with the Emanator, since the first beginning of the point of *Tzimtzum* has been imprinted in it, and this is its root.

11) Now we can understand the fourth Light, which fell through the *Bitush* of the Light of *Reshimo* with the Light of *Nekudot*, called *Otiot*. They are like the 248 *Nitzotzin* in the breaking of the vessels in the world of *Nekudim*.

You should know that in every place in *The Zohar*, the *Tikkunim* (corrections of *The Zohar*), and in the writings of the Ari, the word *Nitzotzin* or *Natzatzin* or *Hitnotzetzut* indicates *Ohr Hozer*. This is because the illumination of *Ohr Yashar* is defined by the names *Orot* or *Nehorin*, and the illumination of *Ohr Hozer* is defined by the name *Nitzotzin* or *Zikin* or *Hitnotzetzut*. Thus, you see that the issue of the *Nitzotzin* that fell through the *Bitush* of the *Reshimo* in the descending *Ohr Hozer* is also considered *Reshimo*, though it is a *Reshimo de Ohr Hozer*, and hence defined by the name *Nitzotzin*.

The order of the descent of the *Ohr Hozer* has been explained above (Item 8). In the beginning, it received for the purification of ZA and was detached from *Behina Dalet*, which is the actual *Kli* of *Malchut*. And when the *Ohr Ein Sof* expands to the *Masach* in *Kli* ZA once again, this Light of *Malchut* will be at the level of *Hochma*, lacking the *Behinat Keter* from the general Light of *Akudim*, since the *Malchut* in ZA does not return to being *Keter*, but *Hochma*. [It has been explained that the essential giver of the level in the ten *Sefirot* of the emanated is the Light of *Malchut*, as above-mentioned (*Panim Masbirot*, Branch Four).]

It follows that the real *Kli* of *Malchut* is without Light, and two *Reshimot* should have stayed in it. The first *Reshimo* is from the Light of *Taamim*, which keeps and sustains the *Aviut* of *Behina Dalet* as much as it can. The second *Reshimo* is from the Light of *Nekudot*, meaning the Light ascribed to the *Masach* and which craves the *Hizdakchut*.

However, both cannot remain together, since they are opposites. This is because the place of the *Reshimo de Taamim* is called *Kli de Keter*, since its ten *Sefirot* are at the level of *Keter*. And the place of the *Reshimo* of the descending *Ohr Hozer* is called *Kli de Hochma* or "below *Keter*." Hence, her own *Reshimo* has departed *Malchut*, too, and rose to the *Kli* of ZA. And the *Reshimo* of the descending *Ohr Hozer* remained in its place. Thus, here the *Reshimo* for the *Nitzotzin de Ohr Hozer* were rejected. However, from here onwards the *Nitzotzin de Ohr Hozer* are rejected, for the Light of *Reshimo*.

Afterwards, in the ascension of the *Masach* to the place of *Bina*, when it received the purification of *Behina Bet*, and the *Ohr Ein Sof* expands once more from *Keter* to *Bina* and from *Bina* to *Keter*, *Behinat Hochma* is withdrawn, too. Then the *Kli* of ZA remains without Light, and two *Reshimot* are left there, too, from the Light of *Taamim* and from the *Ohr Hozer*, which are opposites. And here the *Reshimo* overpowers the *Nitzotzin de Ohr Hozer*, since the *Reshimo de Taamim* remained in *Kli* ZA; hence, it remained in the form of *Kli de Keter*.

Yet, the *Reshimo de Ohr Hozer*, which are the *Nitzotzin de Kli Hochma*, are rejected below *Tabur*, below the *Kli de Keter*, since the *Hitpashtut* of the world of *Akudim* is through *Tabur*, as *Malchut de Akudim* is called *Tabur*. Also, it is already known that *Nitzotzin de Keter* of the descending *Ohr Hozer*, whose value is considered *Keter de Hochma*, remain there since the *Reshimo de Malchut de Taamim*, which are verily *Behinat Keter*, rose to ZA. And the *Nitzotzin* that fell from *Kli* ZA, which are the *Nitzotzin de Hochma* in *Hochma*, fell below *Tabur*, where there is *Keter de Hochma*.

Similarly, in the ascent of the *Masach* to *Hochma*, when it purified into *Behina Aleph*, the *Ohr Ein Sof* was still expanding from *Keter* to *Hochma* and from *Hochma* to *Keter*, and this Light is at the level of ZA. Hence, the level of *Bina* has been withdrawn, as well, and the *Kli* of *Bina* remained empty, without Light. This left two *Reshimot*, as written above: *Reshimo de Taamim* that remained in their place, and *Reshimo* of the descending *Ohr Hozer* that were rejected and fell below the *Nitzotzin de Hochma* below *Tabur*.

Subsequently, it was purified up to *Behinat Keter*, the *Shoresh* (root), and hence lost all the *Behinot Aviut* in it. Thus, the *Zivug de Hakaa* was naturally cancelled, having no more *Ohr Hozer*. It turns out that no *Nitzotzin* fell from *Behinat Keter* at all, and only the *Reshimo de Taamim* remained there.

Thus we have thoroughly explained the oppositeness between the *Reshimo* and the descending *Ohr Hozer*, for which the package was broken, and the *Reshimo* of the ten *Sefirot de Taamim* that remain in their places. These are considered *Kelim KHB ZON de Keter*, through *Tabur de AK*. And the *Nitzotzin*, which are *Reshimo* of the descending *Ohr Hozer*, fell outside the degree they were in. They are regarded as being below *Tabur*, meaning below *Malchut de Akudim*, which are considered *Kelim KHB ZON de Hochma*, as we have said above, that they are called *Otiot*.

12) The reason for the *Hizdakchut* has already been explained above, at the end of Item 9: The *Ohr Pnimi* is connected to the *Kli* of *Malchut*, which is actually only an external *Kli* for the *Ohr Makif*, as it is written in Item 7. Hence, when the *Ohr Hozer* rises and brings HB back to PBP, as written in Item 9, *Aviut de Bina* leaves it, for it returns to being one with the *Hochma*, as they initially were. And when the *Aviut* in the root is cancelled, the *Aviut* in the branch is cancelled, too. Thus, when *Bina* becomes one object with *Hochma*, she purifies the *Masach* along with her, and it, too, rises degree by degree, through her and because of her, until it disappears.

At the beginning of the entrance of the *Ohr Hozer* to *Bina*, she begins to turn her *Panim* back to *Hochma*. Thus, the *Masach* rises from *Behina Dalet* and *Behina Gimel*. And when she draws the *Ohr Hochma* from *Panim de Hochma*, the *Masach* rises to *Behina Bet*. And when she becomes one object with the *Hochma*, the *Masach* rises to *Behina Aleph*, until it rises to *Behinat Shoresh*. This is the meaning of what is mentioned in the *Idra Raba*, "the spark was sucked."

It follows that the *Ohr Hochma*, which is the primary Light of *Atzmut* in the first emanated, meaning the world of *Akudim*, and the *Ohr Hozer* that rises from the *Kli* of *Malchut*, are tied to one another and chase one another. This is because without the *Ohr Hozer*, the *Ohr Hochma* would not able to expand in the emanated, since the *Bina* turns her face to suck *Ohr Hassadim* from *Keter*, and her back to *Hochma*. This means she will not suck the *Ohr Atzmut* from it.

However, when the *Ohr Hozer* comes out, *Bina* turns her face back to *Hochma*, and only then can the Light of *Atzmut* expand in the emanated. Thus, the Light of *Atzmut* depends on the *Ohr Hozer*. But when *HB* return to being *PBP*, and her nursing off *Keter* ceases, her *Aviut* is cancelled, which naturally cancels the *Aviut* in the branch, which is the *Masach*. Thus, the *Ohr Hozer* disappears, as well. Thus, the *Ohr Hozer* is repelled and chased because of the Light of *Atzmut*.

This will thoroughly explain the Ari's words, which I presented above, Item 5, that the *Ohr Pnimi* and *Ohr Makif* beat on each other, and their beating begets the *Kelim*. This is because the *Ohr Pnimi* is the *Ohr Hochma* that expands in the emanated due to the *Ohr Hozer*. And the *Ohr Makif* is the *Masach*, which is the outer *Kli*, which is tied to all the *Ohr Makif* that is destined to come out in the worlds by way of *Ohr Hozer*, as written in Item 7.

And although they are interdependent, the *Ohr Pnimi* that spreads through returning *HB PBP* beats on the *Ohr Makif*. This purifies the *Masach* and causes the departure of the Light from the world of *Akudim*. Thus, the *Reshimot de Taamim* and *de Ohr Hozer* are separated from each other, the *Reshimo de Ohr Hozer* is rejected outside her presence, meaning below *Tabur*, called *Otiot*, and these are the *Kelim*.

13) Thus, we have thoroughly clarified the reason for the departure, due to the gradual *Hizdakchut* of the *Masach* until all the *Ohr Hozer* disappeared, and along with it, the Light of *Atzmut* of *Keter* and *Hochma de Ohr Yashar*. Yet, it did not remain so: following the disappearance of the Light of *Atzmut*, *Bina* turned its *Panim* back to *Keter*, for abundance of *Ohr Hassadim*, and hence, the previous *Achoraim* and *Aviut* returned to her; hence, her *Aviut* returned to the *Masach*, as well, which are her branch.

Also, it is known that the *Ohr Yashar* from the Emanator does not stop flowing to the emanated for even a moment. Hence, after the *Masach* regained its *Aviut*, the *Ohr Yashar de Ein Sof* was renewed on the four above-mentioned *Behinot*, up to the *Zivug de Ohr Hozer*. And once again, the ten *Sefirot de Ohr Yashar* and *Ohr Hozer* expanded in the world of *Akudim*. This is called *Hitpashtut Bet* of the world of *Akudim*.

Yet, since *HB* returned to being *PBP* through the above-mentioned *Ohr Hozer*, the *Aviut* and *Achoraim de Bina* purified once more, and with it, the *Aviut de Masach*, which is her branch. And once again, the *Zivug de Hakaa* and the

Ohr Hozer were cancelled, and *Bina* returns to drawing *Ohr Hassadim* from *Keter*. Thus, the Light of *Atzmut* left as before.

Similarly, once the *Achoraim* and *Aviut* returned to *Bina*, the *Aviut* was drawn on the *Masach*, as well, and naturally, the *Ohr Yashar* was renewed on the *Masach*. Through it, the Light of *Atzmut* expanded, too.

This is repeated similarly: when the *Ohr Hozer* comes, the Light of *Atzmut* spreads once more. And when the Light of *Atzmut* comes, the *Ohr Hozer* leaves. And when the *Ohr Hozer* leaves, the *Masach* regains its *Aviut*, and the *Ohr Hozer* is renewed, and the Light of *Atzmut* spreads once more, and so on. It turns out that this second *Hitpashtut* is like a constant flame moving to and fro. This is why the Ari says that *Ohr Pnimi* and *Ohr Makif* that are tied in one *Kli* strike and beat on each other.

This clarifies the big difference between *Hitpashtut Aleph de Akudim* that was at the level of *Keter*, since the *Ohr Yashar* mated with the *Masach de Behina Dalet*, and the current *Hitpashtut*, which is only at the level of *Hochma*. It is because the whole *Aviut* of the *Masach* is only a *Hitpashtut* from the *Aviut* of *Bina*, as in the *Aviut de ZA*, which extends only the level of *Ohr Hochma*, as written in Item 8. But this Light, too, is not constant. Rather, it is like a flame that moves to and fro. This thoroughly explains that the matter of *Hitpashtut Bet de Akudim* is continued from the departure of *Hitpashtut Aleph* itself.

14) Now we understand the Ari's words in *Shaar Akudim*, Chapters One and Two, that *AK* restricted itself and raised all the Lights from below *Tabur* to *Tabur* and Above, and they rose as MAN to AB de Galgalta. There, it placed a boundary (curtain) in its internals and the Light that rose from NHY departed through the *Eynaim*, extended below *Tabur*, and spread into the ten *Sefirot* of the world of *Nekudim*.

And from the Light that was renewed by raising MAN, it spread and fissured the *Parsa*, and descended below *Tabur*, extending through the *Nekavim* (holes) of *Tabur* and *Yesod*, into the ten *Sefirot* of the world of *Nekudim*. These two Lights comprise the ten *Sefirot* of *Nekudim*. These two Lights and this new *Tzimtzum* require great detail, which will be done in its time. Here I shall explain as needed in this place.

It has already been explained that the Lights below *Tabur de AK* are the *Otiot* and *Nitzotzin* that fell through the *Bitush* of the *Reshimo de Keter* and the *Taamim* in the *Reshimo de Hochma* and *Nekudot*. They departed below the whole *Reshimo de Keter*, and this exit place is called NHY and "below *Tabur*."

Now, after *Hitpashtut Bet*—which is only *Ohr Hochma* in *Kli de Keter*—returned to the world of *Akudim*, the equivalence between the *Reshimot de Taamim* and the *Reshimot de Nekudot* was made once more. This is because they are both considered *Hochma*, and hence all the *KHB ZON de Reshimot de Nekudot* below *Tabur* were drawn, rose, and reconnected with the *Reshimot* Above *Tabur*. This is why the Ari says that *AK* raised the Light from below its *Tabur* to Above its *Tabur*.

However, we need to understand why it is called *Tzimtzum*. The thing is that there are two discernments in these *Nitzotzin* that rose. The first is a *Nitzotzin* of *Keter* of the descending *Ohr Hozer* that remained in *Tabur* itself, which is *Malchut de Akudim* and *Behina Dalet*. The Light of *Hitpashtut Bet* does not reach it, since it is from *Behina Gimel*, and has *Aviut* from the *Hitpashtut* of *Achoraim de Bina*. The second discernment is *Nitzotzin de HB* and *ZON* from *Behina Gimel*, as it is written in Items 11 and 12.

Hence, once *HB ZON de Nitzotzin* rose, the Lights increased there more than before, due to the *Aviut* that was added to them by their fall below *Tabur*. Hence, the *Nitzotzin de Keter* in the *Tabur*, which are *Behina Dalet*, extended in there, too. And naturally, the Light of the *Ohr Yashar de Ein Sof*, which never stops, was renewed upon them. Thus, the *Zivug de Ohr Hozer* was made in *Behina Dalet*, and as a result, ten new *Sefirot* emerged at the level of *Keter*, as in *Hitpashtut Aleph*.

Thus, you see how two *Behinot* of ten *Sefirot* were made of the *Nitzotzin* that rose: ten *Sefirot* at the level of *Hochma* were made from the *HB ZON de Nitzotzin* that were corrected only in their ascent, since they are from *Behina Gimel*, like *Hitpashtut Bet*, and ten new *Sefirot* at the level of *Keter* were made of the *Nitzotzin de Keter*.

These two *Partzufim* are the roots of the *Partzufim AVI* and *YESHSUT de Atzilut*. The new *Partzuf* at the level of *Keter* is *AVI*, and is called *Hochma* and *Aba de Atzilut*. And the *Partzuf* of the old Light, at the level of *Hochma*, is *YESHSUT*, and is called *Bina* and *Ima de Atzilut*.

With these roots you will understand what is written in the *Idra Zuta*, that *Aba* brought *Ima* out because of her son, and *Aba* himself was built as a kind of male and female. This is so because the Upper *Partzuf*, which is at the level of *Keter*, called *Aba*, was built as a kind of male and female, since he raised *Behina Dalet*—*Nukva* and *Malchut*—to him. And *Bina*, the lower *Partzuf*, whose level is below *Keter*, departed *Aba* because of the *Nukva*, which is *Behina Dalet*, which ends and detains the Upper Light from expanding below her. This is why this *Behina Dalet* is called *Parsa*, without the *Nekev* (hole) that exists in *Behina Bet*. And because of this *Parsa*, *YESHSUT* does not clothe the Light of *Keter*.

It turns out that *Behina Bet*, which is *Bina*, on which the *Tzimtzum Aleph* did not apply at all, has now become deficient, since she was restricted, too, as she is below *Behina Dalet*. This is why the Ari said that AK restricted himself by raising Light from below *Tabur*, concerning *Behina Bet* that has now been restricted due to the ascension of MAN.

15) You should know the big difference between *Rosh* and *Guf*. The *Rosh* is called GAR, and the *Guf* is called VAK, ZAT, or ZON. The *Guf* itself is divided into GAR and ZON, too.

The root of this division is that up to the *Peh—Malchut*—the structure is made essentially of *Ohr Yashar*. And the *Ohr Hozer* that rises and joins it is but clothing over it. The opposite of that is the *Guf*, which is a *Hitpashtut* of the *Masach* itself, to the extent that it clothes the *Sefirot de Rosh*. Hence, it is made primarily of *Ohr Hozer*, and the ten *Sefirot de Ohr Yashar* are like its branches.

Although it is called ZON, it is essentially only *Malchut*. This is so because there is no Light of *Malchut* in reality at all, except with NHY de ZA that unite with it in a *Zivug de Hakaa*. Hence, they are regarded as one that expands through the *Ohr Hozer*. And it has already been explained above that the detaining *Masach* and the *Ohr Hozer* that emerges as a result of it are not ascribed to the Emanator, but only to the emanated. For this reason, the *Rosh* is regarded as the *Atzmut* of the Light of the Emanator, and the *Guf* is regarded only as the act of the emanated itself.

Now you understand the five inclusive *Partzufim* of AK, called *Galgalta*, AB, SAG, MA, and BON, and the order of their creation and clothing of one another, how they are interconnected and emerge from one another by way of cause and consequence. This is so because of His one, unique, and unified Thought—thoroughly explained in *Panim Masbirot*, Branch One—which is to delight His creations. This Thought is the root of the *Kli*, and of *Tzimtzum Aleph* that occurred in *Behina Dalet*, though indirectly, as it is written there in Item 7, as in the allegory about the rich man. See in Item 8, that this single Thought encompasses the whole of reality, all the worlds, and all the many forms and conducts through the end of correction, when they all reunite with the Light of *Ein Sof* from before the *Tzimtzum*, in simple unity, in the one form that stands Above us—"to delight His creatures."

And immediately following the *Tzimtzum* in *Behina Dalet*, which is the *Gadlut* (maturity, ripeness) of the desire in *Malchut de Ein Sof*, four forms of gradations appeared in the *Reshimo* that has been emptied of the Light—in the

Kli. They are called *HB*, *ZA*, and *Malchut*, and they contain *Ohr Pnimi* and *Ohr Makif*, thus twelve forms.

Afterwards, the Light extended on the above-mentioned *Reshimo*, down to the point of *Tzimtzum*, since His Light does not stop at all, and remember that. Then the thin line extended into the *Reshimo*, and it is called "thin" because the Light of *Atzmut* extends to the emanated only in the *Ohr Hozer* that rises in a *Zivug* from the *Masach*. And by the power of the *Ohr Hozer*, the *Tzelem* of *AK* was revealed in the form of *Partzuf Galgalta*, which is called, in the example, "the beginning of the line."

It expands over the twenty-five *Behinot*, since there are *KHB ZON* at the length and there are *KHB ZON* in thickness. As we have said, because *Malchut* returned to being *Keter*, each of the *KHB ZON* expands into ten *Sefirot* through *Keter*, and it is called in the example, *Galgalta*, *Eynaim*, *AHP*, or *Galgalta*, *AB*, *SAG*, *MA*, and *BON*. The level of each of them reaches *Galgalta*, and its Lights emerge from the internality of this emanated, as it has been explained in *Panim Masbirot*, Branch Three, Item 2, p 32, concerning the order of elicitation of Lights due to the *Hizdakchut* of the *Masach*.

16) And thus begins *AB*'s elicitation. Elicitation concerns deficiency. Due to the *Hizdakchut* of *Behina Dalet* of the Inner *AK*, called *Peh*, she received *Aviut de Behina Gimel*. And after the Light of *Ein Sof* was drawn over this *Masach*, new ten *Sefirot* emerge at the level of *Hochma*, called *AB*. It turns out that the *AB* that comes out is subtracted from the *AB* that remains within *AK*, at the level of *Keter*.

Thus, *Keter* of the external *AB* clothes *Hochma de Galgalta*, and spreads through *Tabur* of the Inner *AK*. And it, too, contains twenty-five *Behinot* of its ten *Sefirot de Ohr Yashar*, which are its *Galgalta*, *Eynaim*, *Awzen*, *Hotem*, *Peh*, each of which spreads by the power of the *Ohr Hozer* over the five *Behinot*, through *Keter de AB*.

Yet, the general *Keter* of the Inner *AK* remains revealed, and it is discerned with *Rosh* and *Guf*. From the *Peh* down, it is called *Guf*, since it is only *Hitpashtut* of the *Masach*. Hence, the *Ohr Pnimi* and *Ohr Makif* are tied there only in the *Behina Dalet*. This is why they had to depart once more, and this is called "the world of *Nekudim*," being *ZON* and *Guf* of the Outer *AB*.

Also, it has already been explained that the *Aviut* returned to the *Masach* after the *Histaklut* of its *Guf*, and a second *Hitpashtut* occurred there, as it is written in Items 13 and 14. It extends the Lights from below *Tabur* to Above *Tabur*, and by this ascension, the Upper *AVI* are corrected. A *Parsa* is spread beneath them, and YESHSUT is from the *Parsa* to the *Tabur*. All this ascension is called "the Outer *Partzuf* SAG," meaning it had departed its previous degree, which, in the outer AB was *Bina* at the level of *Keter Hochma*, which is the Light of *Awzen* through *Shibolet ha Zakan*.

However, at this *Partzuf*, which was made of the *Nitzotzin* that fell from the Lights of *Peh* of the Outer AB, *Bina* of this *Partzuf* is below the whole ten *Sefirot* of the Upper AVI, hence it is deficient of the *Keter*. Thus, its place is from *Peh* down, meaning from *Shibolet ha Zakan*, which is its *Galgalta*.

And as the Outer AB clothes only *Malchut* of the general *Keter* and the Upper Nine remain revealed, the Outer SAG, too, clothes only *Malchut de Keter de AB*, from *Peh* down, while its Upper Nine—the whole of the *Rosh*—remain revealed. And as the AB elicited its branches through the *Se'arot* (hair) *Rosh*, this SAG elicited its branches through the *Se'arot* AHP, which will be explained in their place. This is the meaning of the Light that is withdrawn from them due to their exit, compared to the Upper One that remains there in the *Se'arot* as surrounding, as in returning surrounding.

And this SAG clothes the AK from *Shibolet ha Zakan* through its end. This means that its *Behinat Rosh*, which are GAR, extend through *Tabur*, which are at the value of *Galgalta*, *Eynaim*, *Awzen*, and *Hotem*. Its *Peh* expands into ten *Sefirot de Guf* in itself, as in the *Peh* of the Outer AB. And the case of the Lights of the *Peh* of the outer SAG, as in the case of the Lights *de Peh* of the Outer AB, due to their being tied in a single *Kli*, there was gradual *Hizdakchut* in them, as well, until it purified into *Behinat Keter*, and the whole *Hitpashtut* disappeared.

This is the meaning of the breaking of the vessels and the fall of the 248 *Nitzotzin*. Yet, this happened only in their ZON, and not in their GAR, due to the correction of the *Parsa*, as will be explained in its place. Afterwards, the *Nitzotzin* that fell from *Peh* of the Outer SAG extended and rose in the form of MAN, the new MA came out, and the ten *Sefirot de Atzilut* were established in the form of twelve *Partzufim*.

Thus, all the previous *Behinot* are included in the world of *Atzilut*, as it is written in *The Tree of Life*, And the world of *Beria* was imprinted from the world of *Atzilut*, in a way that all that exists in *Atzilut* is imprinted in *Beria*. *Yetzira* is imprinted from *Beria*, *Assiya* is imprinted from *Yetzira*, and hence there is no conduct or being in the lower ones that is not directly related to the Upper Ones from which it stems and extends through its inferior essence.

This is why our sages said, "There is not a blade of grass below that does not have an angel Above that strikes it and tells it, 'Grow!'" This is so because all that extends from a Higher world to a lower one, extends through *Zivugim* (plural for *Zivug*). But the worlds are divided into internality and externality. The internality of the worlds, from *Atzilut* down, does not extend through a *Zivug de Hakaa* in the *Masach*, but through *Zivug de Yesodot* (plural for *Yesod*). But the externality, which extends from world to world, extends through a *Zivug de Hakaa*.

This is the meaning of the striking, and this is why our sages meticulously stated that the angel in the world of *Yetzira*, which is the root of the blade of grass in the world of *Assiya*, bestows upon it and nurtures it in the form of *Zivug de Hakaa*. In other words, it strikes it and tells it, "Grow!" since saying means bestowing.

Thus, the matter of cause and consequence in *Galgalta*, *AB*, *SAG de AK* has been thoroughly explained, and the quality of their clothing over one another. Each lower one has the value of *ZON* of the Upper One, which extends only from the *Nitzotzin* of the Lights of the *Peh* of the Upper One.

And it has been clarified that in the emergence of *AB*, the *Masach* was included in *Behina Gimel*. And in the emergence of *SAG*, the *Masach* was included in *Behina Bet*, to *Nukva de Aba*. And in the emergence of MA from inside out, the *Masach* was included in *Behina Aleph*. This will be explained in its place.

Also, *Malchut de Behina Gimel* is called *Tabur*, of *Behina Bet* is called *Parsa*, and of *Behina Aleph* is called *Kruma* (crust). There is nothing more to add here; I only tied the matters at their roots in an easy and brief manner. This is my intention in this place; but inside the book, the matters are explained elaborately.

Appendix A:
Kabbalah Glossary

2,000 *Amma*, Shabbat Zone	The actual place of the worlds is like the second *Behina*, prior to the sin: ZA is at the place of AA; *Malchut*—at the place of AVI; *Beria*—at the place of YESHSUT; and *Yetzira*—at the place of ZA. The first four *Sefirot* of *Assiya* are at the place of *Nukva*, clothing the world of *Yetzira*.
	The last six *Sefirot* of *Assiya* are at the place of the six *Sefirot* of the world of *Beria*. The first six *Sefirot* of the place of the world of *Beria*, from *Parsa* to the *Chazeh* of the world of *Beria*, are called "Outskirts of the city." They belong to the city—*Atzilut*—since this is where the bottom six of *Assiya* remained during the ascension. From *Chazeh* of *Beria* through the *Sium*, twenty-four *Sefirot* remained in a space devoid of Light.
	The Shabbat Zone is the ten *Sefirot* from *Chazeh de Beria* through *Chazeh de Yetzira*, which is 2,000 *Amma*. Fourteen *Sefirot* from *Chazeh de Yetzira* through the *Sium* are called *Mador ha Klipot* (the shell section). The city is the world of *Atzilut*; *Parsa*—the edge of the city.
6,000 Years	The world of *Assiya* is called "2,000 years of *Tohu*," since *Tohu* is *Klipot*, and the whole of the world of *Assiya* is in *Klipot*. The world of *Yetzira* is called "2,000 years of Torah," since *Yetzira* is considered ZA, which is the written Torah (law). The world of *Beria* is called "2,000 years of the days of the Messiah," since *Beria* is considered *Bina* (*Ima*), which is Leah, the mother of the Messiah, son of David, from whom the whole redemption comes.

AA	*Partzuf* whose essence is *Ohr Hochma*. A diminutive illumination of *Hochma* is called ZA.
Abdomen	The bottom third of *Tifferet* in each *Partzuf*. In *Nukva*, it is the place of conception and delivery.
Above	The lower one's equivalence of form with its Upper One.
Abroad	*Assiya* of this world. *Beria* is the place of the Temple, and *Yetzira* is *Eretz Ysrael*.
Absence	Concealment of *Ohr Hochma* is called "absence"; presence of *Ohr Hochma* is called "presence."
ABYA de *Klipot*	Stand opposite ABYA de *Kedusha* (holiness, purity), but standing opposite ZON de *Atzilut* and below. The *Klipot* stand under the *Kedusha*, in the vacant space under the *Sium* of the *Kav*, under the *Malchut* that ends the whole of *Kedusha*. After *Tzimtzum Aleph*, their place is under the *Raglaim* of AK. In *Tzimtzum Bet*, the ending *Malchut* rose to *Bina* in *Guf de Nekudot de SAG*, where the *Parsa* that ends the *Kedusha* was spread. Under the *Parsa*, a vacant place was made for the worlds BYA. Since that place has no *Kedusha*, the *Klipa* took the whole of that place. The shattering occurred because *Ohr Hochma* came from *Rosh de SAG* and wanted to expand below the *Parsa*, through the *Sium* of *Galgalta* in all ten *Sefirot*, as prior to *Tzimtzum Bet*. This occurred because GE joined with AHP in both the *Rosh* and *Guf* of *Partzuf Nekudim*. But before the Light traversed to the place of the vacant space, the *Kelim* broke and died because the *Parsa* was not cancelled. The Light departed and rose, and the *Kelim* fell below the *Parsa*, mingling with the *Klipot* in the place of BYA. *Kelim* that fell under the *Parsa* are AHP of the *Guf* of *Nekudim* and not AHP of the *Rosh*. This is why the *Klipot* begin only from ZON de *Atzilut* downwards.
Achor/Achoraim (Posterior)	1. A *Kli* where no *Ohr Hochma* clothes. 2. A *Kli* or a part of a *Kli* that does not work to bestow or to receive. 3. The part of the *Kli* below the *Chazeh*.

Achoraim de Nukva	Sefirot NHY of Nukva end the Atzilut; hence they are adjacent to the Klipot. The Klipot begin from them downwards. The Klipot grip primarily in the Achoraim, as long as Ohr Hochma is deficient there.
Adam Kadmon	The first world to emerge after Tzimtzum Aleph, which receives from Ein Sof and stretches from it through this world. It is called Adam because its Sefirot de Yosher (directness), with the Light of bestowal, are the root of Adam in this world, and it is called Kadmon (primordial) because Tzimtzum Aleph acts in it.
Afterwards	'Before' is the cause; 'afterwards' is its consequence.
Air (Avir)	Light of Ruach, Ohr Hassadim.
Aleph	Numeric value: 1
Armies of Malchut	Partzufim that stem from Malchut in the worlds BYA.
Ascent	Hizdakchut, because it rises in equivalence of form with Ein Sof. The rule is that all that is purer is Higher, and all that is coarser is lower.
Assembly of Israel (Knesset Ysrael)	Partzuf GAR of Malchut, which receives (assembles/gathers) Lights from GAR de ZA, called Ysrael.
Assiya	The ten Sefirot of the level of Malchut that she receives from ZA.
Atzmut	Ohr Hochma is called by that name because it is the livelihood and the essence (Atzmut) of the emanated.
Augmentation	Transition from a state of Katnut into a state of Gadlut.
Aviut	The measure of the will to receive with intense craving, which is the Kli for extension of Light. For this reason, it is called "internality of the Kli."
Awzen	The level of ten Sefirot de Rosh in Behina Bet, which is Bina.
Ayin	Numeric value: 70
Back to Back (ABA, Achor be Achor)	Correction through the Light of Bina, Hafetz Hesed (delighting in mercy). When a Kli is deficient of Ohr Hochma, it receives a Tikkun through the Light of Bina, which provides it with wholeness.

Back to Face (ABP, Achor be Panim)	A *Tikkun* for *Nukva*: the *Panim* of *Malchut* are only *Hochma*. Hence, she could not receive *Ohr Hochma*, since *Ohr Hochma* can only be received in *Ohr Hassadim*. For this reason, ZA corrects her through a *Zivug Achor be Panim*, which gives her *Panim Ohr Hassadim* from his *Achoraim*.
Bassar (Flesh)	*Behina Gimel*, called ZA, in the ten *Sefirot*, whose level is equal from within outwards: *Mocha*, *Atzamot*, *Gidin*, *Bassar*, and *Or*.
Before	'Before' is the cause and 'after' is its consequence.
Before and After	When speaking of relations of cause and consequence between two emanated beings, we refer to the cause as 'before' and to the consequence as 'after.'
Beginning (*Resheet*)	*Hochma de ZA*.
Below	Of inferior degree compared to another.
Bet	Numeric value: 2
Bina	Observing of conducts of cause and consequence.
Birth	Recognition of the *Aviut* of ZA itself, which is different from the *Aviut* of *Ima*. It is regarded as born and departed due to the disparity of form, which is like relocation in corporeality.
Birth-Blood	When MAN of ZA rise to AVI, the MAN of all the *Partzufim* that will later emerge from ZA rise along with the MAN of ZA, through the last *Partzuf* in the world of *Assiya*. During the months of pregnancy, the MAN of ZA is sorted out from the rest of the MAN, its *Ibur Partzufim* emerge on the MAN of ZA, and then it is born. During delivery, all the MAN that does not belong to ZA exits in the form of birth-blood. The birth-blood is also called "impure blood."
Blood (*Dam*)	*Aviut* in *Malchut* that is under *Tzimtzum Aleph* so as to not receive Light within it. In that state, *Malchut* is halted and stilled from receiving Light; hence, she is called *Dam*.[33] When this *Aviut* is in NHY, it is called "blood at the source," and it is under the prohibition on reception. But when this *Aviut* rises to HGT, not in her place, she is sweetened and turns into milk.

---

[33] There is similarity in sound between the Hebrew words *Dam* (blood) and *Domem* (still), hence the connection.

Blood at the Source	*Dam* (blood)—*Aviut* in *Malchut* that is under *Tzimtzum Aleph* so as to not receive Light within it. In that state, *Malchut* is halted and stilled from receiving Light; hence she is called *Dam*.[34] When this *Aviut* is in *NHY*, it is called "blood at the source" and it is under the prohibition on reception. But when this *Aviut* rises to *HGT*, not in her place, she is sweetened and turns into milk.
Blood Turned to Milk	Blood is the *Aviut* in *Malchut*. This *Aviut* is under *Tzimtzum Aleph*, so as to not receive Light within it. This "stills" *Malchut* from receiving Light; hence its name, *Dam* (from the word *Domem*—still). When this *Aviut* is in *NHY*, it is called "blood at the source" and it is under the prohibition on reception. But when this *Aviut* rises to *HGT*, not in her place, she is sweetened and turns into milk.
Bohu	Called AA, in which there is attainment. *Tohu* is called *Atik*, and there is no attainment in it.
Borrowing	The *Kelim* of *NHY de Ima*, which she gives to ZA. ZA receives its Light in these *Kelim*.
Boundary (*Gevul*)	The *Masach* in a degree.
Brain (*Moach*)	The *Sefira Keter* in ten *Sefirot* of equal level. A *Kli* for Light of *Neshama* that stands in GAR.
Breaking	Cancelling of the boundary in the *Masach*. Also, the fall of the *Kelim* to the *Klipot*. The fall of the souls to the *Klipot* is called "the falling of organs."
Breaking of a *Kli*	When the *Kli* is banned from receiving Light.
Breasts	In the *Dadim* (young breasts) there is *Ohr Hassadim*. When *Ohr Hochma* appears in them, they are called *Shadaim* (mature breasts).
BYA in this world	The place of the Temple—*Beria*; *Eretz Israel*—*Yetzira*; Abroad (outside of Israel)—*Assiya*; Ruin—*Klipot*.
Came Up in the Desire	*Zivug* on a *Masach* with *Aviut Shoresh*
Cancelled	When two spirituals are of completely equal form, without any disparity of form between them, they return to being one, and the small is "cancelled" in the big.
Cause	Causing a *Zivug*
Chaf	Numeric value: 20

[34] There is similarity in sound between the Hebrew words *Dam* (blood) and *Domem* (still), hence the connection.

Chaf-Bet (22)	The twenty-two letters of the alphabet. Letters are *Kelim* in which the Light clothes. There are twenty-two primary discernments by which all the *Partzufim* are discerned.
Chaf-Zayin (27)	The twenty-seven letters of the alphabet—twenty-two letters of the alphabet plus the five final letters MANTZEPACH (*Mem, Nun, Tzadi, Peh, Chaf*). Using the five *Behinot Sium* of the *Masach* at the *Rosh*, Lights spread to the *Guf* and beget *Kelim*, meaning the rest of the twenty-two letters. They are called "the five outlets of the mouth" of the *Partzuf*, and they are only written, not pronounced.
Chair/Throne (*Kisse*)	The world of *Beria*. It comes from the word *Kisui* (covering) and *Haalama* (concealing), since the *Ohr Hochma* is concealed there. It is called *Kisse* also because *Ohr Hassadim* that passes through the *Parsa* is considered *Ohr VAK*, sitting, as opposed to the *Ohr Hochma*, which is *Ohr GAR* and standing.
Chazeh (Chest)	The *Sium* of *Tzimtzum Bet*. Hence, *Tzimtzum Bet* does not apply Above the *Chazeh*, in the *Kelim de Panim*.
Circling Light	*Ohr Yashar* (Direct Light) was created during the Upper Light's descent to the *Kelim*, precisely matching the craving in the *Kelim*, according to their *Behina Dalet*. This resembles a heavy object falling directly to the ground. In *Kelim* that have no *Aviut*—craving—the Light is circled, since they have no gravitational power that attracts.
City	The state of the world of *Atzilut* when the worlds rise to it.
Cleaning Waste	The *Aviut* in the MAN of the lower one rises and is included in the *Zivug* of the Upper *Partzuf*, where it is sorted and corrected by obtaining the *Masach* from the Upper One. At that time, the lower one itself is worthy of a *Zivug*. It all depends on the *Zivug* in the Upper One: if the *Zivug* is carried out on *Aviut Aleph* in the *Masach*, only *Behina Aleph* of the whole *Aviut* is sorted. The rest of the *Behinot* are not sorted, and depart as waste, since the *Masach* did not correct them. This is why this *Zivug* is called "cleaning waste." Only the amount of waste that the *Masach* absorbs is corrected and worthy of *Zivug*.
Clinging of the *Klipot*	The *Klipot* cling to the *Achoraim* of *Malchut*, since she stops the Upper Light, so it is dark from her downwards. Hence, at the point of *Sium* in *Malchut*, there is equivalence with the *Klipot*. This is considered that the *Klipot* cling there.

Clothing	ZA that was separated from the *Ohr Pnimi* and became *Ohr Makif*. Also, each inferior *Partzuf* is considered "clothing" with respect to its Superior.
Connecting	*Malchut* of the Upper One becomes *Keter* of the lower one. By doing so, she connects two degrees, since equivalence of form between them has now been made. Thus, the connection between all the degrees is made.
Connection (*Hitkashrut*)	The ten *Sefirot* of *Ohr Hozer* that rise from the *Masach de Rosh* upwards, clothe the ten *Sefirot de Ohr Yashar*, and connect to them, since there the Lights precede the *Kelim*.
Connection (*Kesher*)	A title for *Tikkun Kavim* is called by that name since all the *Sefirot* connect, until there is no oppositeness between them.
Connection (*Kesher*) of the *Sefirot*	Ascent of the lower *Hey* to the *Eynaim* connects the *Sefirot* to one another.
Corporeality	Everything that the five senses imagine and perceive, or that takes up time and space.
Covenant	The place of *Masach* and *Aviut*, where the *Zivug* with the Upper Light occurs.
Creation	Generation of existence from absence, appearing below the *Parsa*, like *Aviut* and desire to receive.
Creator (*Borreh*)	This name relates only to the generation of the desire to receive, existence from absence.
Cutting/ Clipping	Separation of the lower *Hey* from the *Kelim* that fell to BYA. The whole *Tikkun* depends on that.
Dadei Behama (Udders)	Illumination of *Malchut* without the sweetening of *Rachamim*. The bottom thirds of NH of *Atik*, which stand in the world of *Beria*.
Dadim (Breasts)	The medium between Upper and lower. The Upper One's attitude towards the lower one, even when it is unworthy of rising to the Upper One.
Dalet	Numeric value: 4
Darkness	*Behina Dalet* in the will to receive, which does not receive Light because of the force of the *Tzimtzum*.
Days of Old	*Sefirot* of *Atik*, in which there is *Malchut* of *Tzimtzum Aleph*, which was concealed from the rest of the *Partzufim* of *Atzilut*.

Death	Where there is departure of Light of *Atzilut* from the *Kli*, it is considered death. *Ohr Hochma* is called "Light of life," Light of *Haya*, since there is no life to the *Kli* except in *Ohr Hochma*.
Death (the place of death)	The place below the *Sium* of the Upper Light, below the point of *Tzimtzum*, below the *Parsa*. The *Kelim* that fell below the *Parsa* are called "dead," since they are separated from the Light of Life.
Death of the *Melachim* (Kings)	Since they cannot receive *Ohr Hochma*, they are separated from the line of the Upper Light and are considered that they have fallen into BYA and died, since the Light ends in *Atzilut*.
Decline	Decline from the degree: in the second *Hitpashtut*, when *Ohr Hochma* comes and clothes in the *Kli* of *Keter*. It follows that the degree of *Keter* descended to the degree of *Hochma*, *Hochma* to *Bina*, etc.
Departure from the Upper Light	The closer it is to the place of empty space, the farther it is considered to be from the Upper Light.
Descent to the *Klipot*	ZON rise to AVI to receive new Light, through the MAN that the souls raise to ZON. If the souls corrupt their actions, ZON lose the Light (*Mochin*). The Light comes to ZON only through the MAN of the souls, which causes the ascent of *Kelim* from BYA, which are sorted and clothe over the ZON. But when the MAN departs, the Light departs, and ZON return to their place. At that time, the *Kelim* of NHY de ZA and the bottom nine of *Nukva* that rose from BYA and clothed ZON, the *Klipot*.
Desert	(Also: Ruin.) The place of *Klipot* in this world.
Diminution of the Moon	*Malchut*'s state in the world of *Atzilut*, where she cannot receive Lights due to absence of *Tikkunim*.
Dormita (Sleep)	When a *Partzuf* rises to its Superior, as in MAN, all its Lights leave it and it is then considered that the *Partzuf* remained below with little livelihood. This livelihood is considered sleep.
Drop (as of water)	Intermittent extension of Light, and for brief periods.
Drop of Procreation	*Ohr Hesed* of *Aba*, which lowers the lower *Hey* from the *Eynaim*.

Dvekut (Adhesion)	Equivalence of form between two spirituals.
Earth (Soil)	*Malchut* of each degree or of a world.
Emanator (*Maatzil*)	Any cause, with respect to its consequence. *Malchut de Rosh* is considered *Maatzil* with respect to the *Guf*, and so is any Superior Degree with respect to its inferior degree.
Embrace of the Left	Dispensing of force from ZA to *Malchut*, so she can bring down the lower *Hey* and raise the *AHP*.
Empty Air (*Avir*)	*Ohr Hassadim* before it clothes the *Ohr Hochma*.
Ending *Malchut*	*Malchut de Guf*.
Equivalence	When there is no distinction between the four degrees of the will to receive.
ET	*Malchut* is called *ET* because she comprises all the letters from *Aleph* to *Tav*.[35]
Exedras	External rooms, *NHY* of ZA. When there is illumination of *Hochma*, there is a desire to disclose it. Disclosure of illumination of *Hochma* is called "external rooms."
Existence	Presence of *Ohr Hochma* is called "existence." Concealment of *Ohr Hochma* is called "absence."
Exit	Change of form. When disparity of form occurs in a part of the *Partzuf*, it is considered that that part has come out of the *Partzuf* into a new authority of its own. Yet, this does not inflict any change in the first one.
Exit of Light through the *Eynaim*	When *Malchut* rises to *NE* and a *Zivug* is made on her, Light is emitted from the *Zivug* through the *NE* and not through the *Peh*.
Extended	Descent of Light by the force of the *Aviut*—the force of craving in the emanated—is called "extended" or "extension."
External *Kelim* (*Kelim de Achoraim*)	*Kelim* below the *Chazeh* in the *Partzuf*.
Externality	The purest in the *Kli*, the *Kli* for the *Ohr Makif*.
Face to Face (*PBP Panim be Panim*)	When *Nukva* receives Upper Light from the male's *Panim* into her *Kelim de Panim*.

---

[35] In Hebrew, the letter combination *Aleph-Tav* is pronounced *ET*. *Aleph* is the first letter of the Hebrew alphabet, and *Tav* is the last.

Facing Downwards	When the Light is dispensed according to the measure of *Aviut*, to come and clothe in the *Aviut*.
Facing Upwards	During the *Hizdakchut* of the *Masach*. They are called by that name because they turn to a finer *Aviut*.
Fall	Descent of a degree to a lower one, because it has become like it.
Fall of Organs	The fall of souls into the *Klipot*. In the *Kelim*, the fall into the *Klipot* is called "breaking."
Fall of Organs of *Adam ha Rishon*	Prior to the sin, *Adam ha Rishon* had NRN of *Atzilut*. After the sin, all the organs of his soul fell, and only Light of *Nefesh* remained in the *Kelim* of the 100 *Ketarim* (plural for *Keter*).
Falling	When ZA is worthy, *Tevuna* rises to *Ima*, makes a *Zivug* on *Aviut Bet*, and gives to ZA. This is called "supporting the fallen," ZON, since they give them GAR.
Far/Distant	A large measure of disparity of form. Also, diminutive illumination of *Ohr Hochma*. Near means extensive illumination of *Ohr Hochma*.
Female (*Nukva*)	*Malchut* of the world of *Atzilut* is called by that name because she receives Light from ZA through a *Nekev* (hole) in his *Chazeh*, where the Light is diminished.
Female Face	*Kelim de Panim* related to reception of *Hochma*.
Female Light	Light that the *Partzuf* receives from its adjacent Superior, and not as bestowal from *Ein Sof*. It is also called *Ohr Nefesh* or *Ohr Malchut*.
Filling	The measure of *Aviut* in the *Masach* is called by that name since this is the reason for the filling of the *Kli*.
Filling of *HaVaYaH*	The name *HaVaYaH* is ten *Sefirot*: Yod–*Hochma*, First Hey–*Bina*, Vav–ZA, lower Hey–*Malchut*. But this name does not indicate the level of the ten *Sefirot*. The level could be *Nefesh*, *Ruach*, *Neshama*, *Haya*, or *Yechida*.
	The level is determined by its filling. The filling indicates the Light in the ten *Sefirot* of the *HaVaYaH*: the level of *Nefesh* of *HaVaYaH* is filled with Hey–Gematria BON; the level of *Ruach* with the filling of Aleph–Gematria MA; the level of *Neshama* with the filling of Yod, where only Vav is filled with Aleph–Gematria SAG; and the level of *Haya* is completely filled with Yod, including the Vav of *HaVaYaH*–Gematria AB.

Filling of Names	Indicates the level of the degree. The punctuation of the letters indicates the source of each particular degree in them, whether it is *Hitkalelut* with the Upper One, lower one, or itself.
Fillings	A *Partzuf* is ten empty *Sefirot*: *Keter*, *Hochma*, *Bina*, *ZA*, and *Malchut*. They are marked in the name *HaVaYaH*: *Yod* is *Hochma*, *Hey* is *Bina*, *Vav* is *ZA*, and *Hey* is *Malchut*. In *Gematria*, *Yod-Hey-Vav-Hey* = 10+5+6+5=26 (*Chaf-Vav*). However, all that does not indicate their level: *Nefesh*, *Ruach*, *Neshama*, *Haya*, or *Yechida*. The level is determined by the filling of Light in the ten *Sefirot*. At the level of *Haya*, it is filled entirely with *Yod*, including in the *Vav* of *HaVaYaH*. Its *Gematria* is *Ayin-Bet* (AB): *Yod-Hey-Viv-Hey* = (10+6+4) + (5+10) + (6+10+6) + (5+10) = AB = 72. At the level of *Neshama*, it is filled with *Yod*, and only the *Vav* is filled with *Aleph*. Its *Gematria* is *Samech-Gimel* (SAG): *Yod-Hey-Vav-Hey* = (10+6+4) + (5+10) + (6+1+6) + (5+10) = SAG = 63. At the level of *Ruach*, it is filled with *Hey*, and only the *Vav* is filled with *Aleph*. Its *Gematria* is *Mem-Hey* (MA): *Yod-He-Vav-He* = (10+6+4) + (5+1) + (6+1+6) + (5+1) = MA = 45. At the level of *Nefesh*, it is filled with *Hey*, and only the *Vav* is without filling. Its *Gematria* is *Bet-Nun* (BON): *Yod-Heh-Vv-Heh* = (10+6+4) + (5+5) + (6+6) + (5+5) = BON = 52.
Firmament (*Rakia*)	*Yesod de ZA* is called by that name because it is the *Sium* of *ZA*—Upper Water—and the beginning of *Nukva*—lower water.
First *Ibur*	*Zivug* for the mere existence of the *Partzuf*.
Force of the *Klipa*	Clothes of Lights depart their *Kelim* due to a mixture of evil in them, and fall to the *Klipot* with the residue of Light. This adds strength to the *Klipa*.
Form	The four *Behinot Aviut* in *Malchut*, called *Hochma*, *Bina*, *ZA*, and *Malchut* are called "four forms."
Four Forms	The *Aviut* or desire in the creature is considered its substance. The four *Behinot* in the *Aviut* are called "four forms."

Four Rudiments	*Dalet Behinot* in the *Aviut* of *Kli Malchut*
From Above Downwards	Light that extends from pure to coarse, called *Ohr Yashar*. Also, from *Behina Aleph* through *Behina Dalet*. *Behina Dalet* remained without Light, hence she is considered the lowest. *Behina Aleph* is Above them all since her desire is the smallest.
From Below Upwards	Light that extends from coarse to pure, called *Ohr Hozer*.
Full	When there is no deficiency and nothing to add to its completeness.
Gadlut (Greatness/ Adulthood/ Maturity)	*Ohr Hochma* in the degree.
Galgalta	*Partzuf Keter*, the *Kli* that clothes the Light of *Yechida*.
GAR	Lights of *Rosh* that preceded the *Kelim*, which are the *Sefirot* KHB, called *Rosh* of the *Partzuf*.
GAR of the *Guf*	HGT
Garden of Eden	*Malchut de Atzilut*. Eden is *Hochma*, and Garden is *Malchut*. The whole of the world of *Atzilut* is *Hochma*. This is why *Malchut de Atzilut* is called "Garden of Eden."
Gidin (Tendons)	*Kli* of *Bina* in ten *Sefirot* whose level is equal.
Gimel	Numeric value: 3
Giving Lights	From *Sefira* to *Sefira*, through *Hizdakchut* of the *Masach*, all the Lights come to *Keter*. When *Behina Gimel de Keter* purifies into *Behina Bet*, she gives Lights to *Hochma*. When *Aviut Hochma* purifies from *Behina Bet* to *Behina Aleph*, she gives Lights to the *Kli* of *Bina*, etc.
Great/Adult/ Mature	Disclosure of *Ohr Hochma*. Absence of *Ohr Hochma* makes a *Partzuf* small.
Grip/Hold	As a branch wishes to suck through its grip, the *Klipa* grips to a place devoid of *Kedusha*. The lack is the hose through which it sucks strength and livelihood according to the measure of deficiency of *Kedusha*.
Guf (Body)	The real vessels of reception in each degree, which expand by the force of the *Ohr Hozer* in the *Masach* from it downwards. This is where the reception of Lights occurs in actual fact.

Hair (Se'arot)	Lights that the *Moach* cannot tolerate due to absence of *Tikkunim*. For this reason, they exit on *Galgalta*. They are also called *Motrey* (Surplus) *Mocha* (surplus of *Mocha*).
Hakaa (Striking/ Beating)	The encounter between the Upper Light and the *Masach* is comparable to the encounter of two hard objects, where one wishes to breach the bounds of the other, and the other resists and does not let the first enter.
HaVaYaH-ADNY	*Zivug Panim be Panim* of ZA and *Nukva* implied in the anagram YADONEHY. *Yod* of *HaVaYaH*, which is ZA, at the start of the anagram, implying the *Hochma* in ZA. *Yod* of ADNY, at the end of the anagram, implies the *Hochma* in *Nukva*.
Haya	*Ohr Hochma*
Head to Foxes	The *Rosh* of the lower degree. It is also a tail to lions—the *Sium* (end) of the Superior degree.
Hearing	The Light of *Bina de Rosh*.
Heart	*Kli* for the Light of *Ruach*; stands at HGT.
Het	Numeric value: 8
Hevel	*Ohr Hozer* that rises from the *Masach* upwards.
Hey	Numeric value: 5
Histaklut (Looking)	*Hitpashtut* of Light from *Ein Sof* to the *Masach*. A Light that comes from *Ein Sof* is always *Ohr Hochma*, or *Ohr Eynaim*, or vision, or *Histaklut*.
Histaklut Aleph (First Looking)	*Hitpashtut* of Light from *Ein Sof* to the *Masach*. A Light that comes from *Ein Sof* is always *Ohr Hochma*, or *Ohr Eynaim*, or vision, or *Histaklut*.
Histaklut Bet (second looking)	*Hitpashtut* of Light of *Ein Sof* to the *Masach* that rises from *Tabur* to *Peh* and makes *Zivugim* along its way, generating *Partzufim* of *Nekudot*.
Hitpashtut (Expansion)	Light that is emitted from the Emanator and comes to the emanated through the extension of the emanated being's will to receive, which extends the *Hitpashtut* to itself according to the measure of its craving for the Light.
Hitpashtut Aleph (First Expansion)	Lights of *Taamim*

Hitpashtut Bet (Second Extension)	The second entrance of Lights after the *Hizdakchut* of the *Masach*. Then there are already *Kelim*, according to the rule, "the expansion of the Light and its departure makes the *Kli* fit for its task."
Hochma	The Light of *Atzmuto* of the emanated. Also, knowing the purposeful result of all the details in reality.
Hochma of the Thirty-Two Paths	*Ohr Hochma* that *Bina* receives for ZON, including *Bina's* twenty-two *Otiot*, and the ten *Sefirot* for ZON in *Bina*.
Holam	The Lights above the *Otiot*.
Hose/Conduit (*Tzinor*)	*Kelim de Yosher* are called by that name because they extend and limit the Light within their boundaries.
Hotem (Nose)	*Sefira* ZA *de Rosh*.
House (*Bayit*)	Or *Heichal* (hall)—*Behinat Malchut* that was separated from the inner *Kelim* and became a *Kli* for the *Ohr Makif*.
Hurva (Ruin)	The place of the *Klipot* in this world (deserts, too).
Ibur	*Zivug* of *Katnut*
Idrin	Internal rooms, HGT of ZA, filled with *Ohr Hassadim*, not disclosing illumination of *Hochma*. This is why they are called "inner."
Image (*Demut*)	*Tzelem* (also image) means clothes of *Mochin* of ZA, and *Demut* means clothes of *Mochin* of *Nukva*. The *Otiot Yod*, *Hey*, *Vav* of the Name *HaVaYaH* are *Tzelem*, and the last *Hey* of *HaVaYaH* is the *Demut*.
Impure Blood	Also known as "birth-blood."
In the Future	Lights of Upper *Bina* are called by that name since they are set in ZA for the future. The Lights of *Tvuna* enter ZON permanently, and are therefore called "the next world."
Internal (*Pnimi*)	*Partzufim Ibur*, *Yenika*, and *Mochin* clothed in a way that the bigger one is also more internal.
Internal *Zivug* of *Atzilut*	The inner *Kelim* of *Atzilut* are KHB, called *Mocha*, *Atzamot*, *Gidin*, with Lights of NRN. The Lights *Haya* and *Yechida* clothe into the Light of *Neshama*. The *Kelim* ZA and *Malchut* were separated from the *Partzuf*, hence they are called *Bassar* and *Or*. These are not real, complete *Kelim*, but only surround the *Kelim* of the *Guf* from without. They receive

	their Lights—*Ruach* and *Nefesh*—from the inner *Kelim*.
	For this reason, there are Lights *Ruach-Nefesh* in the inner *Kelim*, and Lights *Ruach-Nefesh* in the outer *Kelim*. Souls of people are born from the *Zivug* of the inner *Kelim*, and the souls of angels are born from the *Zivug* of the outer *Kelim*. Hence, souls of people are considered the internality of the worlds, as they emerge on the inner *Kelim* of the *Partzuf*, and angels are considered the externality of the worlds, since they emerge from the outer *Kelim* of the *Partzuf*.
Internality	The *Aviut* in the *Masach* is called by that name because this is the place for giving of abundance.
Jerusalem	The external *Yesod* of *Malchut*.
Kamatz (punctuation mark)	*Kmitza* (condensing) of Lights. This indicates the ten *Sefirot de Rosh*, which are condensed in the *Kelim de Guf* prior to their clothing. The *Hitpashtut* of Lights in the *Guf* is called *Patach* (opened), since it opens an entrance to the Light.
Katnut (Smallness)	The two *Partzufim Ibur* and *Yenika* in each *Partzuf* are called by that name since they lack *Rosh* or *Mochin*.
Kelim de Achoraim (External *Kelim*)	*Kelim* below the *Chazeh* in the *Partzuf*.
Kelim de Panim	*Kelim* Above the *Chazeh* in the *Partzuf*.
Keter	Placement of the root on the degree. It comes from the word *Machtir*, meaning "encircles," as it is purer than any degree and hence surrounds the *Partzuf* from Above.
Kisse Din (Throne of judgment)	*Malchut* of *Mochin de Ima*, which clothes in *Malchut* of the world of *Beria*. It is called *Techelet* (azure) and *Sandalfon*.
Kisse Rachamim (Throne of Mercy)	The Upper nine of *Mochin de Ima*.
Kissing (*Neshikin*)	*Zivug* of two internal *Partzufim ZA* and *Nukva*, also called "*Zivug* of voice and speech."
Kista de Hayuta (Cista (Chest) of Life-Force)	A *Reshimo* of past Light. This is what remains in the *Partzuf* in its place, as it rises to the Upper One for MAN, and has "departure of *Mochin*."

Kli	The will to receive in the emanated being.
Kli for Ohr Makif	The outer, purer half of the wall in the Kli. The inner, coarser half of the wall in the Kli, serves as a Kli for the Ohr Pnimi.
Kli for Ohr Pnimi	The inner, coarser half of the wall in the Kli. The Kli for the Ohr Makif is the outer, purer half of the Kli.
Kli Malchut	Behina Dalet of the Ohr Yashar, on which there was the Tzimtzum Aleph so as to not receive Light.
Kli that Raises MAN	AHP of the Upper One during Gadlut.
Klipat Noga (The Noga Shell)	Nitzotzin that contain a mixture of good and bad. When Noga receives Light in her good part, she gives of the Light to her bad part, too.
Klipot (Shells)	A contradicting desire to the Upper Light, which is only about bestowal, meaning a desire to only receive. Hence, they are separated from the Life of Lives and are considered "dead."
Kof	Numeric value: 100
Lamed	Numeric value: 30
Lamed-Bet (32) Gods of the Act of Creation	Thirty-two paths of Hochma, which come from Bina, called Elokim (God). It sorts Reish-Peh-Het (288) out of the Shin-Chaf (320) Nitzotzin, which are the Upper nine, leaving Malchut below, as waste.
Land of Edom (Eretz Edom)	Malchut included in Bina is called Bina, "the land of Edom."
Land of Israel (Eretz Ysrael)	Yetzira of this world
Length	The distance between two edges of a degree, from the purest Behina (Highest) to the coarsest (lowest).
Light of Atzilut	Ohr Hochma
Light of Beria	Ohr Hassadim, without Ohr Hochma
Light of Malchut	Light that the Partzuf receives from its adjacent Superior, and not as bestowal from Ein Sof. It is also called Ohr Nefesh or "Female Light."
Light of Reshimo	What remains after the departure of the Light from the Kli.
Light that is limited in the Kli.	When the Light is gripped and dependent upon the measure of Aviut in the Kli, so it cannot expand there more, or less, than the measure of Aviut in the Kli.

Line (*Kav*)	Indicating a distinction of "from Above downwards," which did not exist previously, as well as that its illumination is much smaller than the previous value. Also, ten *Sefirot de Yosher* are called *Tzinor* (hose), from the perspective of the *Kelim*, and *Kav*, from the perspective of the Lights.
Live/Animate	*Yesod*, because it elevates nine *Sefirot* of *Ohr Hozer* and receives nine *Sefirot* of *Ohr Yashar* in them.
Liver	In internal *Kli* with the Light of *Nefesh*.
Long	Abundance of *Hochma*. Short–scarcity of *Hochma*. Wide–abundance of *Hassadim*; Narrow–scarcity of *Hassadim*.
Looking in the Face	Bestowing *Ohr Hochma*.
Lower Eden	*Yesod* of the world of *Assiya*
Lower Garden of Eden	*Yesod de Malchut* in the world of *Assiya*.
Lower *Hochma*	*Hochma* in *Nukva*.
Lower *Ima*	*Malchut de Atzilut*
Lower Land	*Malchut*
Luck (*Mazal*)	*Yesod*. It is called *Mazal* because it gives off *Ohr Hochma* intermittently, like drops.
MA	*HaVaYaH* filled with *Alephs*: *Yod-He-Vav-He*. All the levels that emerge in *Atzilut* emerge at the level of MA. *Atzilut* is considered the new MA with respect to the Lights—the *Nitzotzin* and the *Kelim* of *Nekudim* that connect to it. They are considered older than it, since they had already been used in the previous *Partzuf* of *Nekudim*.
Malchut	The last *Behina*. It is called by that name because assertive and firm guidance extends from her, in complete governance.
Malchut Has No Light	The *Masach* is purified and only *Aviut Shoresh* remains, insufficient for a *Zivug*. Hence, she can receive only from the *Zivug* made in ZA.
Male (*Zachar*)	A *Partzuf* that receives Lights from its Superior in completeness, as they were in the Upper One.
Male Face	Bestowal of *Hochma*.

MAN	What causes the *Zivug*. Also, the *GE* of the lower one were attached in the same degree with the *AHP* of the Upper One, which were fallen in them in the state of *Katnut*. Hence, as a result of the *Dvekut* during the time of *Katnut*, when the Upper One came by *Gadlut*, because its *AHP* rose and became a new *NHY*, within its *AHP* are the *GE* of the lower one. Like the *Masach* and *Reshimot de AB*, included in *Rosh de Galgalta* and generating *AB*, this is what happened in *Tzimtzum Bet*, through the *Ibur*, except the *Zivug* is on *Yesod*.
MANTZEPACH	*Behinot Masach* and *Aviut* of the *Partzuf* that remained in it from the time of its *Katnut*. MAN of the lower one are attached to the *AHP* of *Partzuf Nukva*, in the MAN of *Nukva* herself, which remained for her from her *Ibur*. From the *Masach* of her *Ibur*, the lower one receives the level of *Ibur*. Hence, MAN of the *Ibur* was included in the MANTZEPACH of *Nukva*, as she raises them to ZA. At that time, an *Ibur* was made on his MAN, and he receives his level.
Masach	The force of *Tzimtzum* awakened in the emanated toward the Upper Light, stopping it from descending into *Behina Dalet*. Thus, the minute it reaches and touches *Behina Dalet*, that force immediately awakens, strikes it, and repels it. And this force is called *Masach*.
Mating Malchut	*Malchut de Rosh*.
Mayin Nukvin	As *Nekudot de SAG* expanded below the *Tabur*, two *Reshimot* were joined—of the first five of *SAG*, and of the lower *Hey* of *Galgalta*. The *Masach* is an inclusion of two females: *Bina* and *Malchut*. This is why the *Masach* is called *Mayin Nukvin*, as from here onwards there are always two females included in each of its *Zivugim*.
Mazla (Aramaic: luck)	*Se'arot Dikna* are called by that name because their Lights drip like drops until they join the great Lights in the worlds.
Me (Ani)	When *Malchut* is revealed, she is called "I" or "Me." When she is concealed, she is called "He" or "Him."
Mem	Numeric value: 40
Metzach	*Bina de Keter*.

Metzach of the Desire	During the *Zivug* of *Gadlut*, when *Ohr Hochma* shines through the Light of *AB-SAG*, the *Se'arot* depart and the time of good will appears.
MI	Bina
Middle Point	*Behina Dalet* in *Ein Sof* is called by that name because it is in unity with the Light of *Ein Sof*.
Middle/Medium	Connecting and deciding between two remote edges
Milk	Lights of *Hassadim*, which *Bina* gives to ZA after its birth. These Lights return to being *Hochma*, and this is called "milk that becomes blood."
Mochin	Lights of GAR or Lights of *Rosh*.
Mochin de Gadlut	The *Mochin* that ZA receives through its ascent to MAN after nine years. It is called *Ibur Gimel*, as well as "*Mochin* of procreation," since ZON make a *Zivug Panim be Panim* and can procreate souls.
Mochin de Holoada (procreation)	The *Mochin* that ZA receives through its ascent to MAN after nine years. At that time, ZON make a *Zivug Panim be Panim* and can procreate souls. It is also called *Mochin de Gadlut* and *Ibur Gimel*. Also, it is Light of *Haya* that ZA receives from *AVI* at the level of *AB*. Through these *Mochin*, ZA begets the GAR of the souls.
Months of Conception (*Ibur*)	(Also: the time of conception). Time and space are initiations of form. A *Partzuf* is completed through many *Zivugim* and Lights, which are seven, nine, or twelve months, according to the number of Lights that join the completion.
Moshe and Israel	GAR *de* ZA.
Motion	Any regeneration of form from a previous form.
Motrey (Surplus) *Mocha*	Lights that the *Moach* cannot tolerate due to absence of *Tikkunim*. Hence, they exit on *Galgalta*. They are also called *Se'arot* (hair).
Muteness-Speech	Ten *Sefirot* of Light that traverse from *Malchut de Rosh*, called *Peh*, into the *Toch*. The inner *Partzuf* of *Nukva* is called "Speech." If it departs and she remains with only the outer *Partzuf*, it is then considered "muteness," since the inner *Partzuf* is GAR and the outer is VAK.

Name	A description of how the Light, which is implied in a name, is attained. The name of each degree describes the manners of attainment in that degree.
Narrow	Scarcity of *Hassadim*. Wide—abundance of *Hassadim*. Scarcity of *Hochma* is called "short" and abundance of *Hochma* is called "long."
Near	Proximity of form to one's friend.
Nefesh	Light that the *Partzuf* receives from its adjacent Superior and not as bestowal from *Ein Sof*. It is also called "female Light."
Nehiro	*Ohr Yashar*
Nehiro Dakik	Fine and small illumination, which revives the *Klipot*.
Nekuda	*Malchut* in which there is no *Zivug*, and which does not raise *Ohr Hozer*, remains dark, without Light, because of the *Tzimtzum* made in the middle point.
Nekudot	Four levels that emerge on the *Zivug* in the *Masach* during its *Hizdakchut*. Lights of *Tabur—Nekudot* Above the *Otiot—Holam*. Lights of *Yesod—Nekudot* inside the *Otiot—Melafom*. Light of *Sium Raglaim—Nekudot* below the *Otiot*.
Neshama	Light that clothes in the *Kli* of *Bina* is called *Neshima* (breathing), from the word *Linshom* (to breath), because ZA receives the Light of the spirit of life from *Bina* by rising and falling, as in breathing.
Nesira (Sawing Off)	Separation of *Nukva* from ZA.
New Light	Any Light emerging from the correction of the *Kelim* in the world of *Atzilut*.
New Souls	1) Completely new, extending from *Hochma de Ohr Yashar*. These do not come into the world of *Tikkun*. 2) Regeneration of souls, which come from *Hochma* of the thirty-two paths, from *Bina* included in *Hochma*. However, they are new with respect to ZON, since they come from the new MA (and only souls of BON are old).

In them, too, there are two *Behinot*: 1) New souls of *Panim be Panim*, applied during the Temple, when ZA was permanently at the level of AB, and *Beria*, considered the souls, was in *Atzilut*. For this reason, the souls, too, were in the world of *Atzilut*, and were regarded as *Panim be Panim*. 2) After the |

	ruin, when *Beria* descended to its place under the *Parsa*, and does not have Light of *Atzilut*, but *Achor be Achor*. Hence, with respect to *Achor be Achor*, these souls are considered new.
Next World	Lights of *Tevuna*, which come in ZON permanently. In the future—Lights of Upper *Bina*. They are called by that name since they are set in ZA for the future.
Nikvey (Holes of) *Awzen*, *Hotem*, *Eynaim*	In *Tzimtzum Bet*, *Malchut* rose to the *Sefira Hochma* in each *Sefira*, and made holes in the *Hotem*, *Awzen*, and *Eynaim*. Prior to *Malchut's* ascent, there was only one hole in each *Sefira*, in the *Peh*.
Nikvey Eynaim	*Behina Aleph* in the *Rosh*, since *Hochma* is called *Eynaim*, and by the force of the ascent of the lower *Hey* to the *Eynaim*, a *Nukva* was made in *Hochma*, too.
Nitzotzin	The *Reshimot* that remained of the Lights of *Nekudim* after their departure from the broken *Kelim*. There are two kinds of Lights in them: 1) *Ohr Yashar*, pure, called "Lights," which remained in *Atzilut*, and 2) *Ohr Hozer*, coarse, called *Nitzotzin*, which descended to BYA with the *Kelim*.
Nourishments	These must be from a Higher Degree, since they provide strength to permanently rise and clothe the Upper One.
NRNHY	The *Kelim* of the ten *Sefirot* are called *KHB ZON*. The Lights of the ten *Sefirot* are called *Nefesh*, *Ruach*, *Neshama*, *Haya*, *Yechida*. The *Kelim* are regarded as being from Above downwards, and the Lights—from below Upwards, in order of growth.
Nukva	The height of its growth: in the future, she will be *Panim be Panim* with ZA, in one *Keter*. Its greatest diminution—a point under *Yesod de ZA*.
Nun	Numeric value: 50
Ohr (Light)	Everything received in *Behina Dalet*; includes everything but the will to receive.
Ohr Eynaim	Light that emerges on the *Masach* in NE in *Behinat Aviut Aleph*. Also, *Hitpashtut* Light from *Ein Sof* to the *Masach*. A Light that comes from *Ein Sof* is always *Ohr Hochma*, *Ohr Eynaim*, vision, or *Histaklut*.

Ohr Hochma	Light that extends from the Creator to the creature, the entirety and the sustenance of the emanated being.
Ohr Hozer (Reflected Light)	Light that was not received in *Behina Dalet* and was repelled by the *Masach*. After *Tzimtzum Aleph*, it serves as a vessel of reception in all the *Partzufim*, instead of *Behina Dalet*. Also, Light that extends from coarse to pure, called "from below Upwards."
Ohr Makif	Any Light that is repelled from reception in the *Sof* of the *Partzuf*, due to the weakness of the *Masach*. Surrounds the *Partzuf* and pressures the *Masach* in order to be clothed within it in the future.
Ohr Nefesh	Light that the *Partzuf* receives from its adjacent Superior, and not as bestowal from *Ein Sof*. It is also called "Female Light" or *Ohr Malchut*.
Ohr Panim	*Ohr Hochma*
Ohr Pnimi (Inner Light)	Light clothed in a *Kli*.
Ohr Yashar	Light that extends from *Ein Sof* to the *Partzufim*. It does not affect the *Igulim* (circles), but only the *Sefirot* of *Yosher* (directness), according to the desire to receive in them: the Giver gives to a coarser desire, to *Behina Dalet*. Also, Light that extends from pure to coarse, called "from Above downwards."
Old Light	Light that remained in the world of *Nekudim* after the breaking of the vessels.
One	Upper Light that spreads from *Atzmuto*, from Above downwards, without any change in form.
Opening of the Eyes	Illumination of *Hochma*.
Organs	*Sefirot de Guf*.
Origin of the Lights	*Malchut de Rosh* is called by that name since it creates *Ohr Hozer*, which clothes the Light and brings it into the *Guf*.
Origin of the Soul	The will to receive that was imprinted in the souls, which separates them from the Upper Light. The transition between the world of *Atzilut* and the world of *Beria*.

Oscillating	VAK is called by that name because until the *Partzuf* achieves GAR, it oscillates between *Din* and *Rachamim*.
Other Gods	The grip of the *Klipot* on the *Achoraim de Nukva*, since she is not entirely sorted prior to *Gmar Tikkun*.
Otiot (Letters)	Kelim
Outskirts of the City	The first six *Sefirot* of the world of *Beria*, protruding from the world of *Atzilut* downwards.
Panim	The place in the *Kli* that is intended to receive or to bestow.
Parsa	A boundary that divides the *Partzuf* into vessels of bestowal and vessels of reception.
Partitions	The *Guf* of the *Partzuf*.
Partzuf	Ten *Sefirot*, one below the other, which come through *Malchut*'s ascension to the Emanator.
Patach (punctuation mark)	*Hitpashtut* of Lights in the *Guf* is called by that name because it opens an entrance for the Light. *Kamatz* is *Kemitza* (condensing) of Lights, indicating the ten *Sefirot de Rosh*, which are condensed prior to their clothing in the *Kelim de Guf*.
Patriarchs (*Avot*)	The *Sefirot* HGT with respect to the *Sefirot* NHY, which are their offspring.
Peh	*Malchut de Rosh*.
Peh	Numeric value: 80
Permanent *Zivug*	*Zivug* of AVI in their place.
Place	The will to receive in the emanated. Also, time, space, and motion are all one issue.
Place of BYA	Prepared during *Tzimtzum Bet*.
Place of Conception	The bottom third of the *Sefira Tifferet de AVI*, while they are one *Partzuf* with YESHSUT.
Place of Darkness	The *Sefira Malchut*, which ends the *Partzuf* due to the force of *Tzimtzum* in her, makes darkness from her outwards.
Place of Settlement	As the place of the worlds BYA is divided into GE *de* BYA, the place of *Kedusha*, and the fourteen *Sefirot* of *Mador ha Klipot*, this world is divided into a place of settlement, which includes BYA—the place of the Temple, *Eretz Ysrael*, and abroad—and the place of ruin, which are the deserts, in which people do not settle.

Place where the *Klipot* Grip	A place of deficiency in *Kedusha* (Holiness).
Preparation to Receive	When there is a *Masach* in the *Partzuf* in the right measure for *Zivug* and extension of Light.
Primordial *Hochma*	*Hochma* in AA, which does not shine in *Atzilut*. Rather, only *Hochma* of the thirty-two paths shines.
Proliferation of Light	Many *Reshimot* that were not regenerated in a *Zivug*, and hence, demand their correction and rise to MAN for a new *Zivug*.
Protruding	Illumination of *Hochma*.
Punctuation of *Otiot* (Letters)	Indicates the source of each degree within them, whether it is from *Hitkalelut* with the Upper One, with the lower one, or with herself. The filling of the names indicates the level of the degree.
Quality of the place	The quantity of the place is the number of degrees that exist in that place. The quality of the place is the importance of the degree present in the place.
Quantity of the Place	Quantity of the place is the number of degrees in that place. The quality of the place is the importance of the degree in that place.
Rachel	*Nukva de ZA*, from his *Chazeh* down.
RADLA	Ten *Sefirot* of *Rosh de Atik* are called *Reisha de Lo Etyada* (RADLA) because they use *Malchut de Tzimtzum Aleph*.
Regeneration of Souls	Bestowal of *Ohr Hochma* to the souls, as they had had during the *Gadlut* of the world of *Nekudim*, and which was removed by the shattering. It is also as they had had the second time, prior to the sin of *Adam ha Rishon* and the second departure through the falling of the organs of the soul.
Reish	Numeric value: 200
Removal/Distancing	A *Tikkun* in which the *Kli* distances itself from receiving *Ohr Hochma* and instead chooses *Ohr Hassadim*.
Reshimo	What the Light leaves after its departure. This is the nucleus and the root of the birth of another *Partzuf* off it.
Residue/Remainder (*She'er*)	A *Zivug* to revive the worlds.

Return to the Emanator	Departure of Light in the *Hizdakchut* of the *Masach* to *Malchut de Rosh*, the Emanator of the ten *Sefirot de Guf*.
Revival of the Dead	Return from *BYA* to the world of *Atzilut* is given that name because exit from the world of *Atzilut* is called "death."
Rib	*Nukva's* name when she is attached *Achor be Achor* to the *Achoraim* of *Chazeh de ZA*, since she is attached to its *Guf*, and they serve one *Keter*.
Roof	*Keter* in each degree.
Rosh (Head)	The part in the emanated that is the most equal to the form of the *Shoresh*. It is also the ten *Sefirot* of the Upper Light that expand to the *Masach* in *Malchut*, to raise *Ohr Hozer*. It is called by that name because they precede the *Masach* and the *Ohr Hozer*. Also, it is ten *Sefirot de Ohr Yashar* that clothe in the ten *Sefirot de Ohr Hozer*.
Round	When there is no distinction of Above and below between the four *Behinot* in the desire. For this reason, the four *Behinot* are called "four round *Igulim* (circles)" one inside the other, as there is no Above and below among them.
Ruach	*Ohr Hassadim*. It is a Light that clothes in *Kli de ZA*, since its conduct is to rise to *Bina* to suck Light from her and to descend in order to give it to *Malchut*.
Said to His world, "Enough! Spread no further."	*Malchut*, which ends the *Hitpashtut* of Upper Light in the *Chazeh* of the world of *Yetzira*, places this boundary there.
Samech	Numeric value: 60
Seal (*Hotam*)	*Ohr Hozer* that rises from the *Masach* upwards, clothing the ten *Sefirot de Rosh*. *Nechtam* (imprint)—the same ten *Sefirot* as they go from the *Rosh* to the *Guf*.
Sealed	The same ten *Sefirot* that go from the *Rosh* to the *Guf*, since a seal is *Ohr Hozer* that rises from the *Masach* upwards, clothing the ten *Sefirot de Rosh*.
Second *Ibur*	*Zivug* for adding *Ohr Hochma* in the *Partzuf*.
Sefira	Ten *Sefirot de Ohr Yashar* clothed in ten *Sefirot de Ohr Hozer*, which emerge on one *Zivug*, are called "one *Sefira*," after the Highest *Sefira* in the level, although it contains ten *Sefirot* in length and thickness.

Segol	An indication that there are three *Nekudot HBD* when *HB* are *Panim be Panim*.
Separating the *Sigim* (Dross)	*Sigim* are lower *Hey* that was mingled in the seven *Melachim* and caused the breaking of the world of *Nekudim*. Hence, the *Tikkun* is the need to remove the lower *Hey* from all the broken *Kelim*. This is done by *Ohr Hochma*, Light of *Aba*. This *Tikkun* is called "separation of the *Sigim*."
	Also: a *Tikkun* that is done by *Ohr Hochma*, Light of *Aba*, which should remove the lower *Hey* from all the broken *Kelim*. This is so because *Sigim* is the lower *Hey* that was mingled with the seven *Melachim* and caused the breaking of the world of *Nekudim*.
Separation	Two degrees without equivalence of form between them, from any side.
Shabbat Zone	An end on the Upper Light by the force of *Malchut*.
Shin	Numeric value: 300
Shoresh (Root)	All the *Behinot* in *Keter*; ten *Sefirot de Rosh*.
Short	Scarcity of *Hochma*. Wide—abundance of *Hassadim*. Narrow—scarcity of *Hassadim*. Long—abundance of *Hochma*.
Side-lock	*Malchut* is called by that name because she is the last of the *Sefirot*.
Sigim (Dross)	Lower *Hey* that mingled with the seven *Melachim* (kings) and caused the breaking of the world of *Nekudim*.
Simple (*Pashut*)	Without distinction of degrees and sides.
Sium Kelim de Panim	*Chazeh*
Sium of Tzimtzum Aleph	Above the point of this world
Sium of Tzimtzum Bet	The *Parsa* that ends *Atzilut*.
Sium Raglaim de Adam Kadmon	The point of *Sium* of this world. This is the end of the line of *Ein Sof* and the middle point of all the worlds.
Sium Raglaim de Atzilut	*Bina* of *NHY de Adam Kadmon*.
Sleep	When a *Partzuf* ascends for MAN, its place is considered to be in a state of slumber, without *Mochin*. It remains with *Kista de Hayuta* (cista (chest) of life-force).

Slow	Gradual extension of Lights by way of cause and consequence.
Smell	The Light in *ZA de Rosh*, called *Hotem* (nose).
Sof/Sium (Ending)	Done by the repelling force in *Behina Dalet*. The Upper Light stops shining there because she does not receive it. *Behina Dalet* is called *Sium* (end) because it stops receiving the Upper Light, and by so doing ends the degree.
Son	A lower one, with respect to the Upper One.
Sorting and Correcting	Sorting means the lowering of the thirty-two *Nitzotzin*—thirty-two *Malchuts*—as waste, so only 288 remain for the construction of *Kedusha*. It is corrected by the illumination of *Aba*, and this is called "sorting the Lights." But without *Malchut*, there is no degree. Hence, *Hitkalelut* of both the first *Hey* and the lower *Hey* are received from the *Masach* of *Ima*, and this is called "the association of the quality of *Din* with the quality of *Rachamim*." From this *Hitkalelut*, thirty-two new *Malchuts* are completed, to complete the 320 *Nitzotzin*. This sorting is made possible only through the Light of *Aba*, since it does not shine to *Behina Dalet*, and thus the waste is sorted out. But the *Tikkun* is through the Light of *Ima*. Sorting means to sort out the parts of *Behina Dalet*, which obstruct the reception of the Upper Light.
Souls of *Adam ha Rishon*	Prior to the sin—*NRN* from *BYA* in *Atzilut*. After the sin—Light of *Nefesh* remained in *Kli de Keter* of each of the *Sefirot de BYA*, except for *AVI* of *Beria*.
Souls of Angels	The inner *Kelim* of *Atzilut* are *KHB*, called *Mocha*, *Atzamot*, and *Gidin*, with Lights of *NRN*. Lights of *Haya* and *Yechida* clothe within the Light of *Neshama*. The *Kelim* ZA and *Malchut* were separated from the *Partzuf*; hence, they are called *Bassar* and *Or*. These are not real, complete *Kelim*, but only surround the *Kelim* of the *Guf* from without. The Lights within them are *Ruach* and *Nefesh*, and they receive from the inner *Kelim*. There are Lights of *Ruach-Nefesh* in the inner *Kelim* and Lights of *Ruach-Nefesh* in the outer *Kelim*. Souls of people

	are born from the *Zivug* of the inner *Kelim*, and souls of angels are born from the *Zivug* of the outer *Kelim*.
	The souls are considered the internality of the worlds, since they emerge on the inner *Kelim* of the *Partzuf*. Angels are considered the externality of the worlds, since they emerge from the outer *Kelim* of the *Partzuf*.
Souls of People	The inner *Kelim* of *Atzilut* are KHB, called *Mocha*, *Atzamot*, and *Gidin*, with Lights of NRN. Lights of *Haya* and *Yechida* clothe within the Light of *Neshama*.
	The *Kelim* ZA and *Malchut* were separated from the *Partzuf*; hence, they are called *Bassar* and *Or*. These are not real, complete *Kelim*, but only surround the *Kelim* of the *Guf* from without. The Lights within them are *Ruach* and *Nefesh*, and they receive from the inner *Kelim*.
	There are Lights of *Ruach-Nefesh* in the inner *Kelim*, and Lights of *Ruach-Nefesh* in the outer *Kelim*. Souls of people are born from the *Zivug* of the inner *Kelim*, and souls of angels are born from the *Zivug* of the outer *Kelim*.
	The souls are considered the internality of the worlds, since they emerge on the inner *Kelim* of the *Partzuf*. Angels are considered the externality of the worlds, since they emerge from the outer *Kelim* of the *Partzuf*.
Space/Void	*Behina Dalet*, which is emptied of Light due to *Tzimtzum Aleph* is not absent from the emanated, but there is an empty space in it, without Light.
Spark (*Netzitzo*)	*Ohr Hozer*
Speech	Ten *Sefirot* of Light that pass through *Malchut* from her and down into the *Guf*.
	Also, ten *Sefirot* of Light that pass from *Malchut de Rosh*, called *Peh*, into the *Toch*. The inner *Partzuf* of *Nukva* is called "speech." If it departs and she remains with only the outer *Partzuf*, then it is called "muteness" because the inner *Partzuf* is GAR and the outer is VAK.
Spiritual *Zivug*	A *Zivug* that stems from *Rosh SAG* to *Rosh de Nekudim*, which corrects the GAR of *Partzuf Nekudim*, but does not expand to the *Guf* of *Nekudim*. It is also called *Zivug de Neshikin* (*Zivug* of kisses).

Spirituality	Devoid of any corporeal state, such as time, space, and motion.
Square	*Zivugim* made on *Malchut* during her *Hizdakchut* from *Behina Dalet* to *Behina Gimel*, from *Behina Gimel* to *Behina Bet*, and until she arrives at the *Peh*. They are given that name after the four kinds of purification of the *Masach*.
Strength	A discernment that is like the seed from which a tree will grow.
Substance/ Matter (*Homer*)	The *Aviut* in a *Partzuf* of *Behina Dalet* in the desire. It, too, has length, width, depth, and six edges—above, below, east, west, north, and south.
Suction of the *Klipot*	The substance of the *Klipot* is complete evil; they cannot receive any Light. But during the breaking of the vessels, vessels of bestowal fell into the *Klipot* and have become their soul and livelihood.
Suffering	Where the *Kli* is worthy of clothing Light, but does not clothe it due to its own choice.
Sun in Its Sheath	NHY of ZA that clothe within *Nukva*.
Supplement of Shabbat	The ascent of the worlds from the fifth hour on the eve of Shabbat.
Sweetening/ Mitigation	If the *Kelim* are flawed by the breaking, they need the Light to "sweeten" their bitterness, their *Din* (judgment) forces, so there will not be a grip for the externals in them.
Taamim	*Hitpashtut* of Light from Above downwards, from *Peh* to *Tabur*.
Tabur	*Malchut de Guf*, from which the actual limitation and rejection of Light begins.
Tabur of the Heart	The place of the *Chazeh* (chest).
Tail to Lions	The *Sium* (end) of the Superior Degree, which becomes the degree of "head to foxes," the *Rosh* (head) of the lower degree.
Tav	Numeric value: 400
Tefillin	*Tzitzit* (Zizith) is *Se'arot de ZA*, which shine in *Rosh de Nukva*, which educes *Behinat Tefillin* in her *Metzach*.

Temple (*Beit ha Mikdash*)	*Beria* of this world
Tet	Numeric value: 9
The End of All	*Behina Dalet* in *Behina Dalet*—the coarsest of all—is called *Sof* (end) because all the degrees come only to correct her.
Thirty Degrees in *Guf de Nukva*	*Ibur, Yenika, Mochin* in *Achor de Nukva*, in each of which are ten *Sefirot*.
Throne	Ten *Sefirot* of Light of *Ima*, which spread in the world of *Beria*: GAR is called *Kisse* and VAK is called "six rungs of the throne." *Malchut* that clothes in *Malchut* of *Beria* is called *Din, Techelet* (azure), and *Sandalfon*.
Through the Sides	Limited bestowal.
Time	A certain amount of *Behinot* (discernments) that stem from one another by way of cause and consequence.
Time of Good Will	During the *Zivug* on *Gadlut*, *Ohr Hochma* shines through the Light of AB-SAG, the *Se'arot* depart, and the *Metzach* of the desire appears.
Toenails	The *Sium* of every *Partzuf*.
Tohu	*Bohu* is called AA, where there is attainment. *Tohu* is called *Atik*, where there is no attainment.
Torah	Light of ZA.
Touching (Tangential)	Insufficient disparity of form of a degree to separate two degrees at the root.
Trail	*Yesod de Aba* is given that name because it is long and narrow.
Tree	*Yesod de ZA*, the middle line, the place of *Zivug*.
Tree of Knowledge (*Etz ha Daat*)	The place from the *Chazeh* downwards, called *Assiya*. Its primary part is *Yesod*, which is a middle line, called *Etz* (tree).
Tree of Knowledge of Good and Evil	From *Chazeh de ZA* downwards, since there is illumination of *Hochma* there. Hence, in that place there is a hold for the *Klipot*, called "evil."
Tree of Life (*Etz Chaim*)	The place from the *Chazeh* Upwards. There are covered *Hassadim* there, the Light of *Achoraim de Bina*, and hence, no hold for the *Klipot*.
Triangle	A degree with only the first three *Behinot* in the desire.

Tzadi	Numeric value: 90
Tzelem	*Ohr Hozer* that rises on the *Hitkalelut* MAN of the lower one in the *Masach* and *Aviut* of the Upper One, clothing the ten *Sefirot* of *Ohr Yashar*. This *Ohr Hozer* belongs to the Upper One, but since the Upper One makes a *Zivug* for the needs of the lower one, on the *Aviut* of the lower one, this *Ohr Hozer* descends to the lower one along with the *Ohr Yashar*. To receive it, the lower one must diminish it by three degrees, called *Mem-Lamed-Tzadi*, or as it reads from below Upwards *Tzadi-Lamed-Mem* (*Tzelem*).
Tzere (punctuation mark)	Implying HB when *Bina* is in *Achoraim* to *Hochma*, and they have no point of *Daat* under them, to bring them into *Zivug*. *Bina*, too, is called *Tzere*, since all the organs of ZA receive their form through her *Masach de Aviut*.
Tzimtzum	Who conquers his desire, detains himself and does not receive, despite the great desire to receive.
Tzimtzum Aleph	*Tzimtzum* of *Malchut*; *Tzimtzum* on *Behina Dalet*. Hence, the line of *Ein Sof* stops at *Malchut de NHY*.
Tzimtzum Bet	*Tzimtzum NHY de Adam Kadmon*; *Tzimtzum* on *Behina Bet*. For this reason, the line of *Ein Sof* stops at *Bina* of *NHY de AK*, from which the place of the worlds BYA was made. *Tzimtzum Bet* is the association of *Midat ha Rachamim*, *Bina*, with *Midat ha Din*, *Malchut*.
Tzitzit	*Se'arot de ZA*, which shine in *Rosh de Nukva*, which educes *Behinat Tefillin* in her *Metzach*.
Unification (*Yhud*)	Two different *Behinot* that have equalized their forms to one another.
Unique	The Upper Light that produces a multiplicity of degrees for equalizing them. United—when in the end everything becomes unique.
United	When, in the end, everything becomes one. One—the Upper Light that brings equivalence to the multitude of degrees.
Upper	More important.
Upper Eden	*Yesod* of the world of *Beria*.
Upper Garden of Eden	In the world of *Beria*, which is *Bina*.

Upper *Hochma*	*Hochma* in ZA
Upper Land	*Bina*. *Malchut* is the lower land. When *Malchut* is included in *Bina*, *Bina* is called *Eretz Edom*.
Upper Whiteness	Before it is clothed in a *Kli*, the Light is white, since all the colors come only from the *Kelim*.
Vacant	A place that is ready to undergo corrections.
Vacant Place and a Space	When ZA rises to AA, which is its real place from the perspective of *Nekudim*, a vacant space remains in BYA, since there is no Light of the wholeness of *Atzilut* there, until at *Gmar Tikkun*, *Atzilut* will descend below the *Parsa*.
Vacant Space	By the force of *Tzimtzum Aleph*, *Malchut* ends the Upper Light. This *Sium* stands above the point of this world. Through *Tzimtzum Bet*, the place of *Tzimtzum* rose from *Sium Galgalta* to the *Chazeh* of *Partzuf Nekudim*. And from there down, an empty place was made, and the place of the *Klipot*. Yet, by the fall of vessels of bestowal below the *Chazeh* of the place of BYA, only fourteen *Sefirot* remained for *Mador ha Klipot*. Through the sin of *Adam ha Rishon*, the point of *Sium* of *Kedusha* descended to *Bina* of *Malchut* of the world of *Assiya*, called "the ground of the lower Garden of Eden," from which the place of the empty space was made. It follows that the space was diminished by the breaking of the vessels and the sin of *Adam ha Rishon*, since it descended from the place of *Parsa* to *Bina* of *Malchut* of *Assiya*. But the *Klipot* obtained the strength to build four worlds.
VAK and *Nekuda* of the *Klipot* of *Atzilut*	Prior to the sin of *Adam ha Rishon*, once all the worlds rose to *Atzilut*, there were *Klipot* in the fourteen *Sefirot* of *Mador ha Klipot* (shell section). They did not have a *Partzuf*, only VAK for ZA of the *Klipa*, and *Nekuda* for the *Nukva* of the *Klipa*.
Vav	Numeric value: 6
Vision (*Re'iah*)	*Hitpashtut* of Light from *Ein Sof* to the *Masach*. A Light that comes from *Ein Sof* is always *Ohr Hochma* or *Ohr Eynaim*, or *Re'iah* (vision), or *Histaklut*, *Ohr Hochma de Rosh*.
Voice and Speech	*Zivug* of the two internal *Partzufim* ZA and *Nukva*. It is also called *Zivug de Neshikin* (kissing).

Wall (*Dofen*)	The *Aviut* of the *Masach* is the *Kli* that receives Light. It is called "the wall of the *Kli*" because the whole *Kli* is only its walls. The four *Behinot* of *Aviut* are four layers in the thickness of the wall, positioned one atop the other and considered internality and externality. The thickest *Behina* in the wall of the *Kli* extends more abundance and is considered the internality of the *Kli*. The rest of the *Behinot*, the purer ones, are considered the externality of the *Kli*, where *Behina Dalet* is the internal, compared to *Behina Gimel*, *Behina Gimel* is internal compared to *Behina Bet*, etc.
Wall (*Kotel*)	A *Masach* of *Achoraim* of *Ima*, which detains the *Ohr Hochma* from reaching ZON, when they are in *Katnut*, by the force of being *Hafetz Hesed* (delighting in mercy).
Waste	The *Sigim* left after the scrutinies.
Well (of water)	*Yesod de Nukva*, from which *Ohr Hozer* rises, as though from a well.
Wheels	*Sefirot de Igulim* (circles) are called by that name because the Lights in them become round, since there is no purity and *Aviut* (coarseness) there.
Wide	Abundance of *Hassadim*. Narrow—scarcity of *Hassadim*. Scarcity of *Hochma* is called "short" and abundance of *Hochma* is called "long."
Window	The force of the *Ohr Hozer* that opens the reception of Light in the *Kli*.
Wings	*Malchut de Ima* is always in *Katnut*, interrupting ZON from the external ones. By doing so, she guards ZON, since only illumination of *Hochma* passes through her. *Parsa*, below *Atzilut*, is also made of *Malchut de Ima*, and she is called "shoe," protecting ZON's feet. No illumination of *Hochma* passes through her.
World (*Olam*)	The name *Olam* begins with *Partzuf* BON of the world of *Adam Kadmon*, since ZA and *Malchut* of the inner *Kelim* of *Behina Dalet* disappeared and became *Kelim* for *Ohr Makif*, called *Levush* and *Heichal*. Also, *Olam* means *He'elem* (concealment).

Worlds and Souls	AVI make two *Zivugim*: 1) *Achor be Achor*, to revive the worlds with *Ohr Hassadim*; 2) *Panim be Panim*, to procreate souls. A *Levush* extends from the first, external *Zivug*, and from the second, internal *Zivug*, extends *Ohr Hochma* to the souls. This is why there are three *Partzufim*: external and medium—from the first *Zivug*, and internal—from the second *Zivug*.
Yaakov (Jacob)	VAK of ZA, external *Partzuf*.
Yashar (Straight)	Descent of Upper Light in the *Kelim* precisely according to the craving in the *Kelim*, according to their *Behina Dalet*, like a heavy object that falls straight to the ground. In *Kelim* without *Aviut*—craving—the Light is circled, since they have no attracting, pulling force.
Yechida	The Light clothed in the *Sefira* of *Keter*.
YESHSUT	ZAT or AHP of AVI. When AVI make a *Zivug Panim be Panim*, AVI and YESHSUT are regarded as one *Partzuf*. When AVI make a *Zivug Achor be Achor*, YESHSUT depart AVI into a separate *Partzuf*.
Yod	Numeric value: 10
Yod-Aleph (11) Signs of the Incense.	Sparks of Light that remained to revive the stony heart.
Yosef (Joseph)	*Yesod de* ZA.
Yotzer (creating)	Bestowal of Light upon the worlds; includes everything besides the will to receive.
Ysrael (Israel)	(Also: *Moshe* (Moses) and Israel.) GAR of ZA or inner *Partzuf*.
Zayin	Numeric value: 7
Zeir Anpin	It means "small face," since the majority of ZA is *Ohr Hassadim*, and its minority—*Ohr Hochma*. *Ohr Hochma* is called *Panim* (face). Hence, *Keter* is called *Arich Anpin*, which means "long face," having *Ohr Hochma*.
Zion (*Tzion*)	The inner *Yesod* of *Nukva* is called by that name from the word *Yetzia* (exit).
Zivug de Guf	A complete *Zivug*—*Zivug* AVI to give the souls Light and procreation for ZON.
Zivug de Hakaa (Coupling of Striking)	The *Masach*'s action of repelling the Light from *Behina Dalet* to its root. There are two opposite matters in this act: *Hakaa* (striking) of the Light, and a subsequent *Zivug* with it, which induces its acceptance in the *Kli*, since the Light rejected

	from *Behina Dalet* becomes *Ohr Hozer*, which becomes the clothing *Kli*, which discloses the Light in the *Partzuf*.
Zivug de Neshikin	A *Zivug* that stems from *Rosh SAG* to *Rosh de Nekudim*, which corrects the GAR of *Partzuf Nekudim* but does not expand to the *Guf* of *Nekudim*. It is also called "a spiritual *Zivug*."
Zivug de Yesodot (plural for *Yesod*)	Corrects the ZAT of the *Partzuf*. Also called "lower *Zivug*" and *Zivug* of the *Guf*.

Appendix B:
Acronyms and Abbreviations

(Because the acronyms are of Hebrew words, the letters in English may not match the words they represent)

AA	*Arich Anpin*
AB	*HaVaYaH filled with Yod*
ABA	*Achor be Achor*
ABYA	*Atzilut, Beria, Yetzira, Assiya*
AHP	*Awzen, Hotem, Peh*
AN	*Atik and Nukva*
Ari	*The Godly, Rabbi, Isaac*
AVI	*Aba ve Ima*
BON	*HaVaYaH filled with Hey*
BYA	*Beria, Yetzira, Assiya*
GE	*Galgalta Eynaim*
HB	*Hochma, Bina*
HBD	*Hochma, Bina, Daat*
HHN	*Hochma, Hesed, Netzah*
KH	*Keter, Hochma*
KHB	*Keter, Hochma, Bina*
KHB TM	*Keter, Hochma, Bina, Tifferet, Malchut*
KHBD	*Keter, Hochma, Bina, Daat*
Lamed Bet	number (32)
MA	*HaVaYaH filled with Aleph*
MAD	*Mayin Duchrin*
MAN	*Mayin Nukvin*

Matatron	Name of an angel
MI	Two letters from the Name *E-L-O-H-I-M*
NE	*Nikvey Eynaim*
NHY	*Netzah, Hod, Yesod*
NHYM	*Netzah, Hod, Yesod, Malchut*
NR	*Nefesh, Ruach*
NRN	*Nefesh, Ruach, Neshama*
NRNHY	*Nefesh, Ruach, Neshama, Haya, Yechida*
OBDAM	*Or, Bassar, Gidin, Atzamot, Mocha*
OH	*Ohr Hozer*
OM	*Ohr Makif*
OP	*Ohr Pnimi*
OY	*Ohr Yashar*
PARDESS	*Peshat, Remez, Drush, Sod*
PBA	*Panim be Achor*
PBP	*Panim be Panim*
RADLA	*Reisha de Lo Etyada*
Ramak	Rabbi Moshe Kordovero
Ramchal	Rabbi Moshe Chaim Luzzato
RAPACH	number (288)
Rashbi	Rabbi Shimon Bar Yochai
RIU	number (216)
RTS	*Rosh, Toch, Sof*
SAG	*HaVaYaH* filled with *Yod*, and *Aleph* in the *Vav*
SNGLH	*Shoresh, Neshama, Guf, Levush, Heichal*
SVAT	Still, Vegetative, Animate, Speaking
TANTA	*Taamim, Nekudot, Tagin, Otiot*
TD	*Tikkuney Dikna*
VAK	Six Edges (Ends)
VAT	Bottom Six
YESHSUT	*Ysrael Saba ve Tevuna*
YHNRN	*Yechida, Haya, Neshama, Ruach, Nefesh*
ZA	*Zeir Anpin*
ZAT	Bottom Seven
ZON	*Zeir Anpin* and *Nukva*

Appendix C:
Diagrams of the Spiritual Worlds

In order of the "Preface to the Wisdom of Kabbalah."

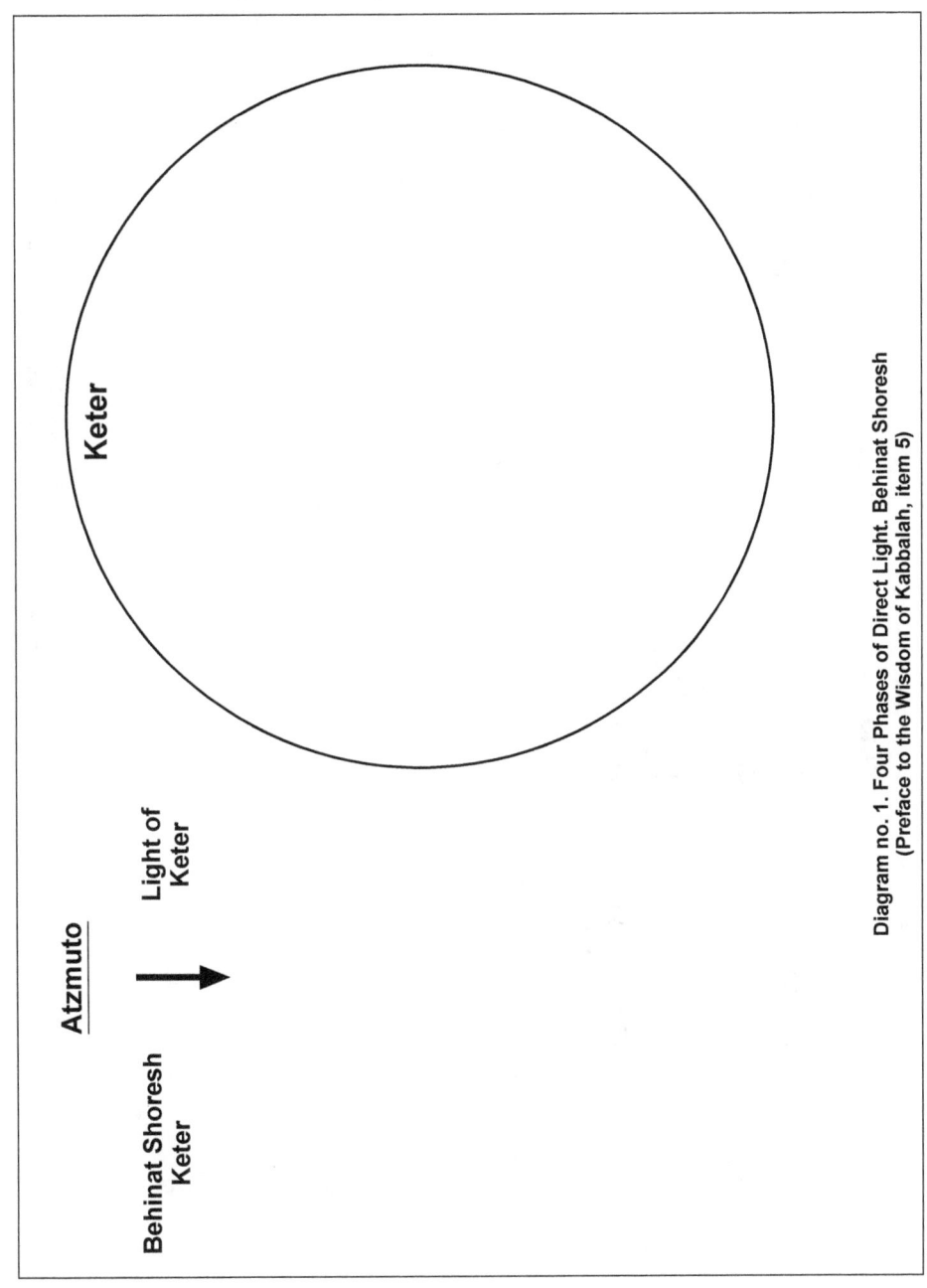

Diagram no. 1. Four Phases of Direct Light. Behinat Shoresh (Preface to the Wisdom of Kabbalah, item 5)

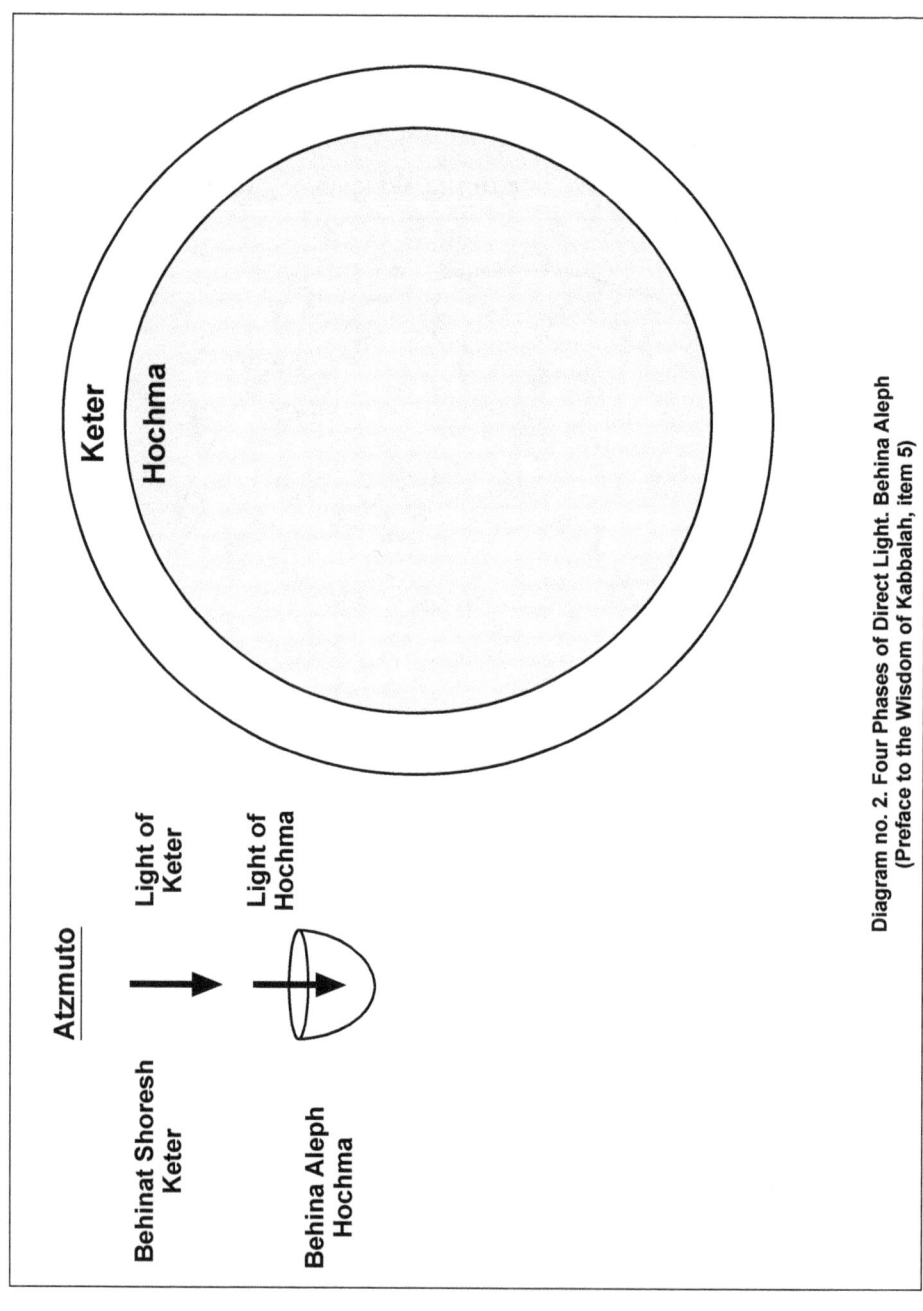

Diagram no. 2. Four Phases of Direct Light. Behina Aleph (Preface to the Wisdom of Kabbalah, item 5)

Appendix C: Diagrams of the Spiritual Worlds

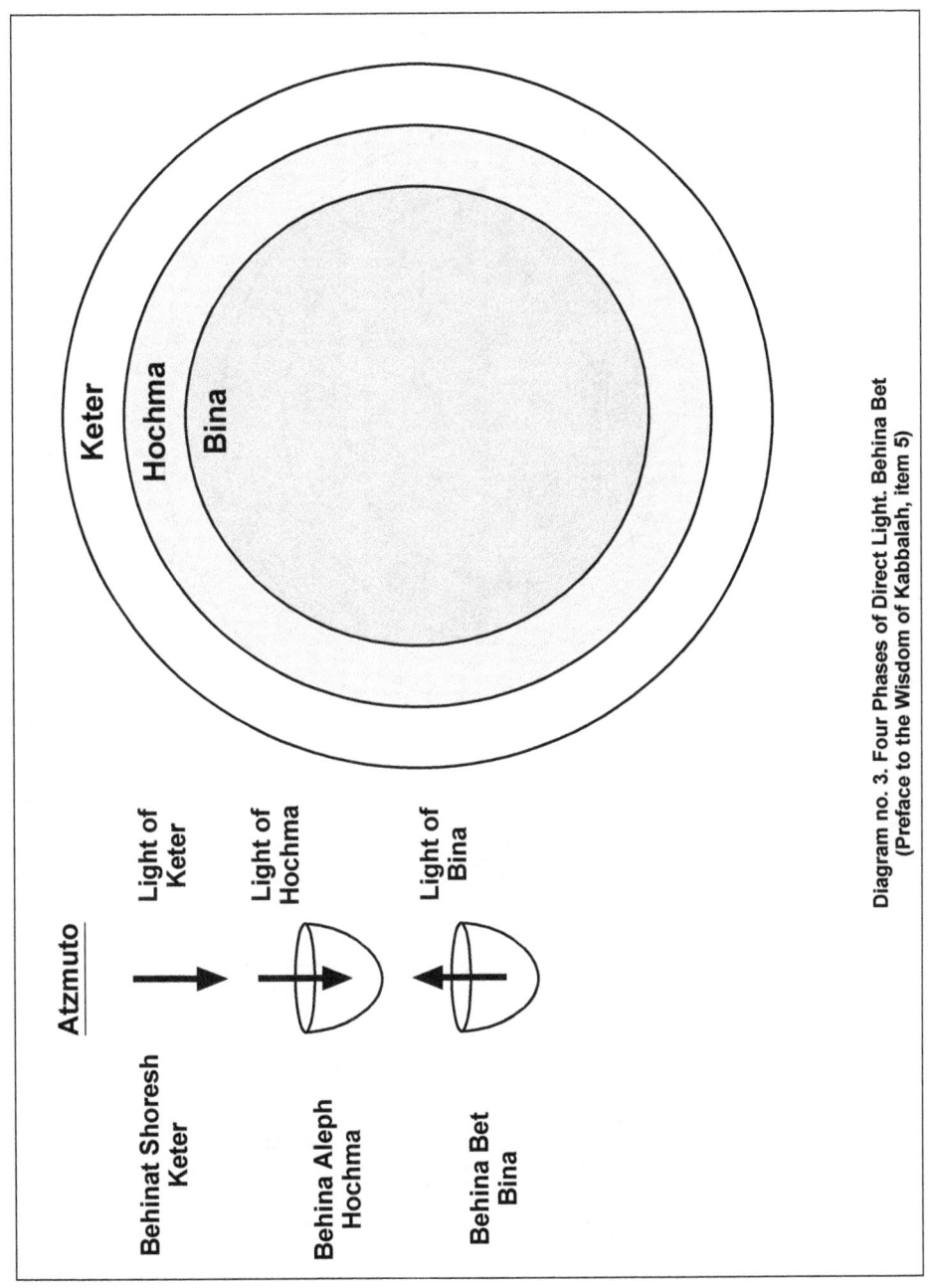

Diagram no. 3. Four Phases of Direct Light. Behina Bet (Preface to the Wisdom of Kabbalah, item 5)

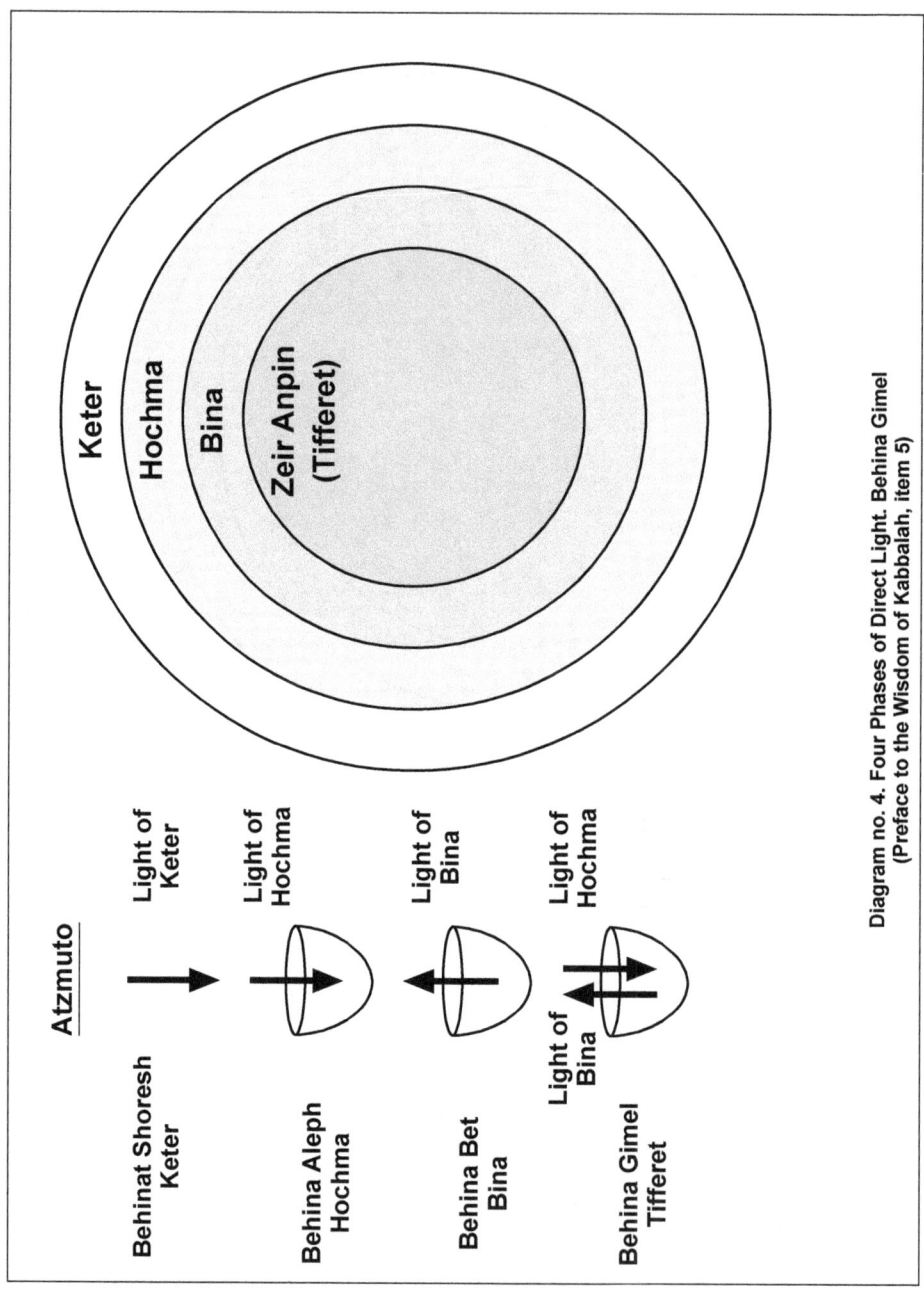

Diagram no. 4. Four Phases of Direct Light, Behina Gimel
(Preface to the Wisdom of Kabbalah, item 5)

Appendix C: Diagrams of the Spiritual Worlds 817

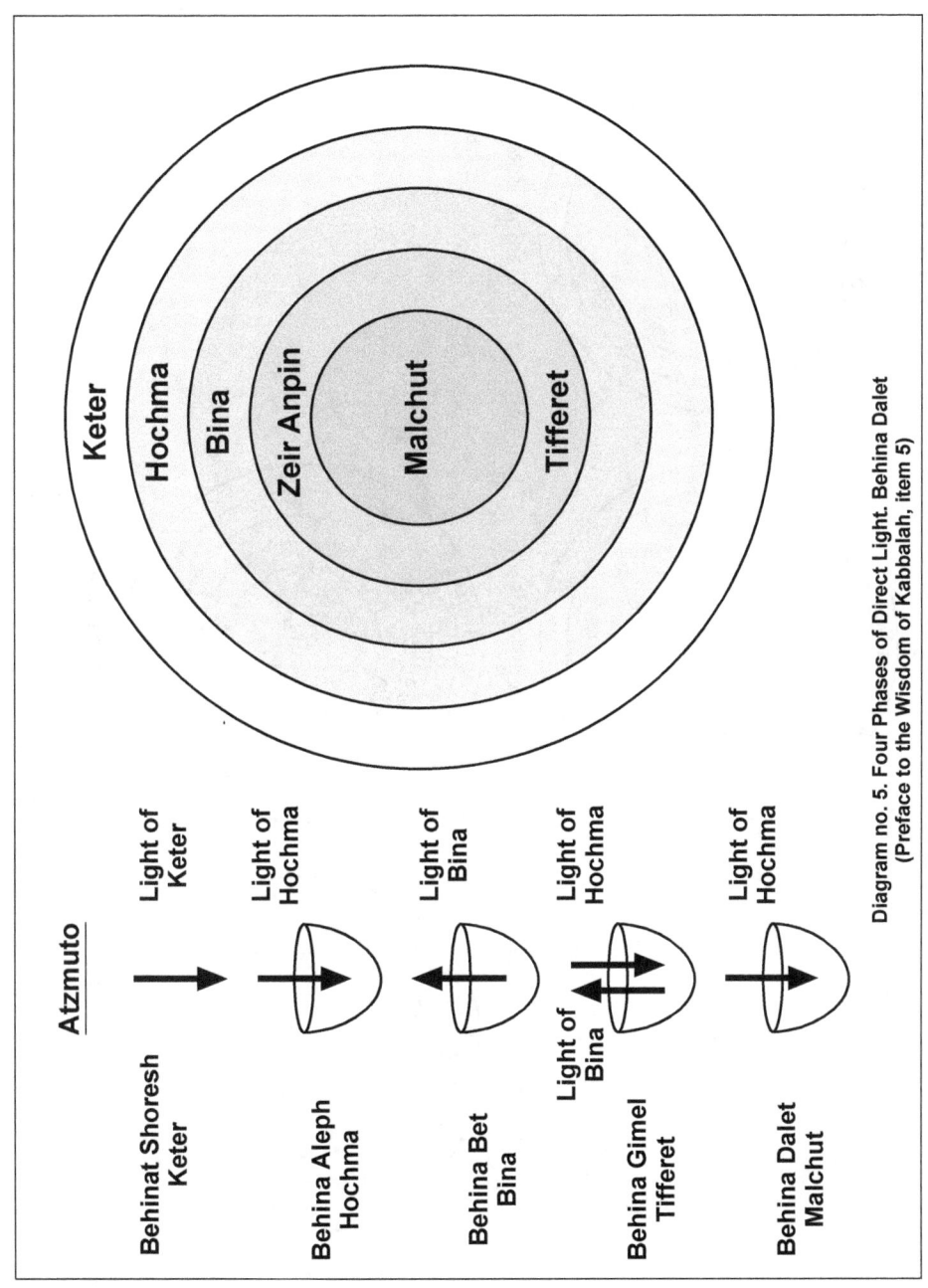

Diagram no. 5. Four Phases of Direct Light. Behina Dalet (Preface to the Wisdom of Kabbalah, item 5)

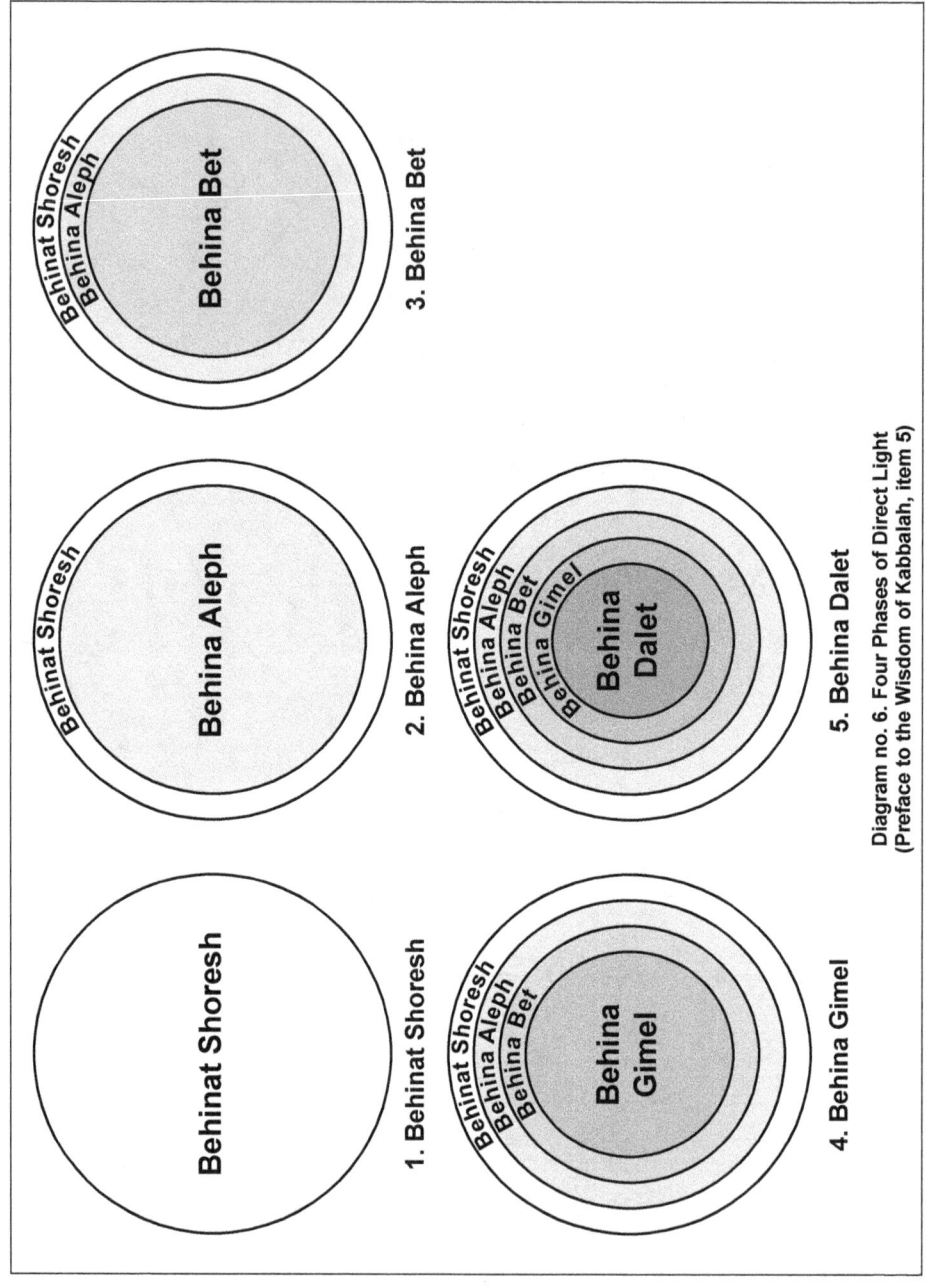

Diagram no. 6. Four Phases of Direct Light
(Preface to the Wisdom of Kabbalah, item 5)

APPENDIX C: DIAGRAMS OF THE SPIRITUAL WORLDS

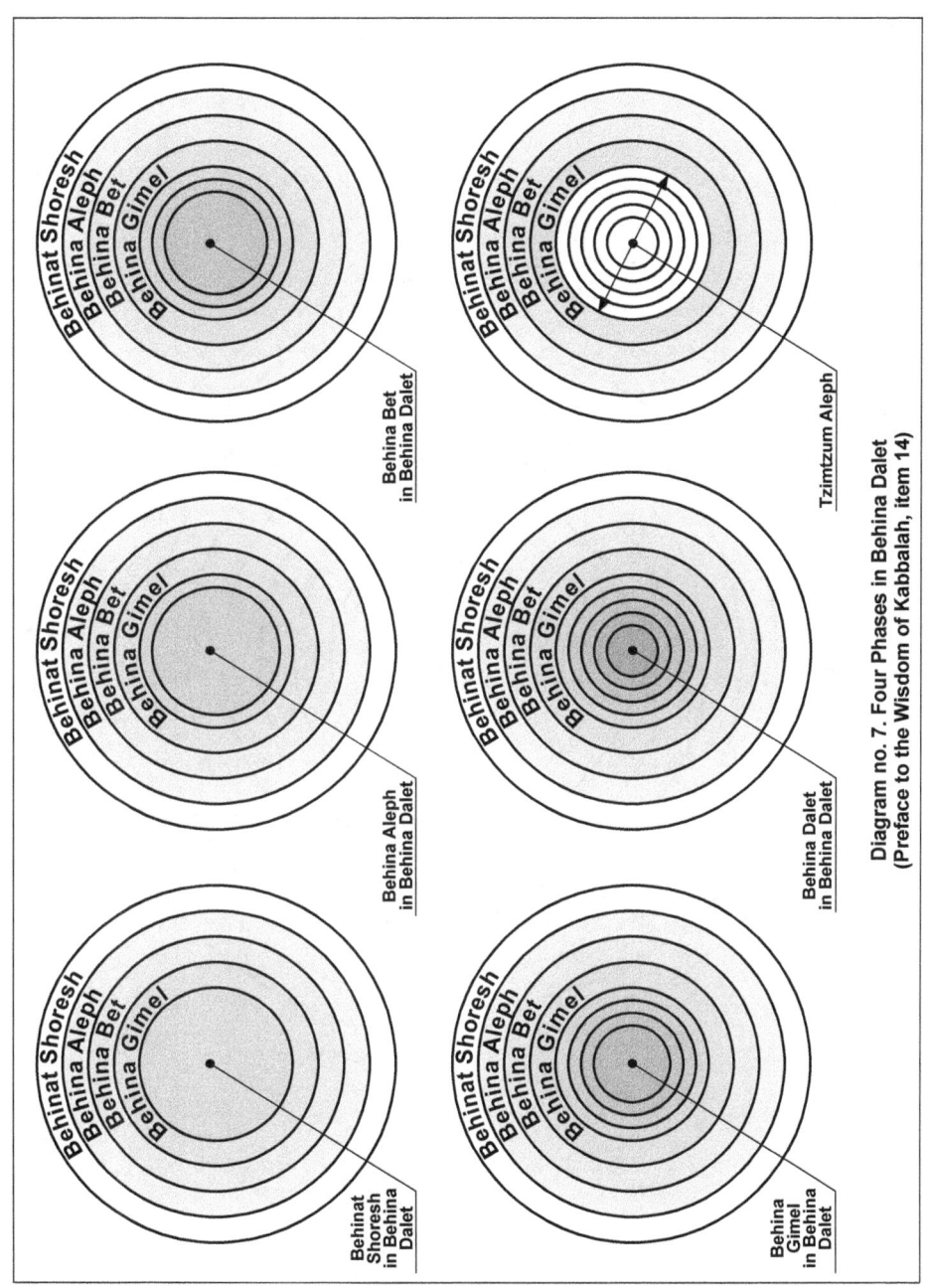

Diagram no. 7. Four Phases in Behina Dalet
(Preface to the Wisdom of Kabbalah, item 14)

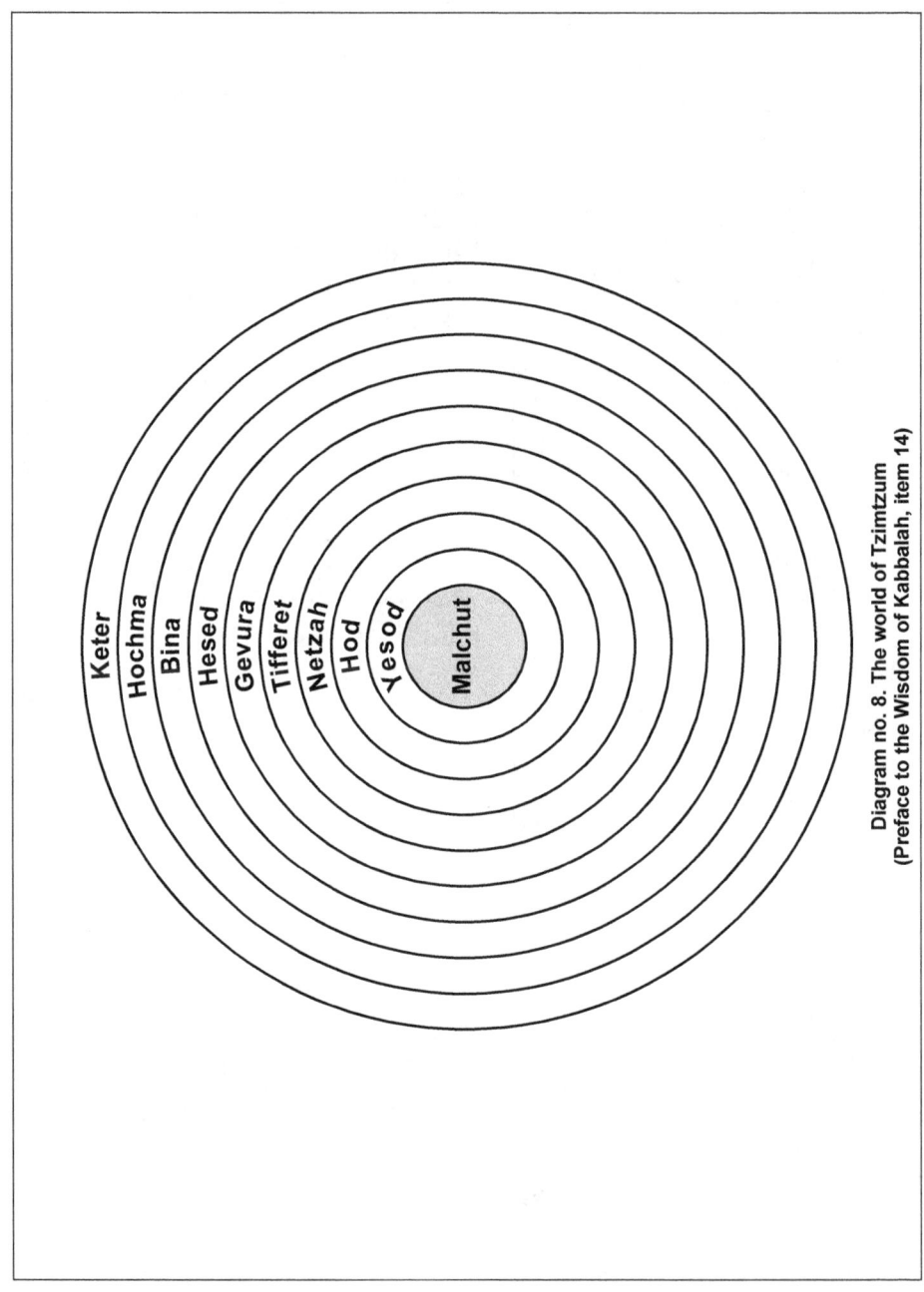

Diagram no. 8. The world of Tzimtzum (Preface to the Wisdom of Kabbalah, item 14)

Appendix C: Diagrams of the Spiritual Worlds 821

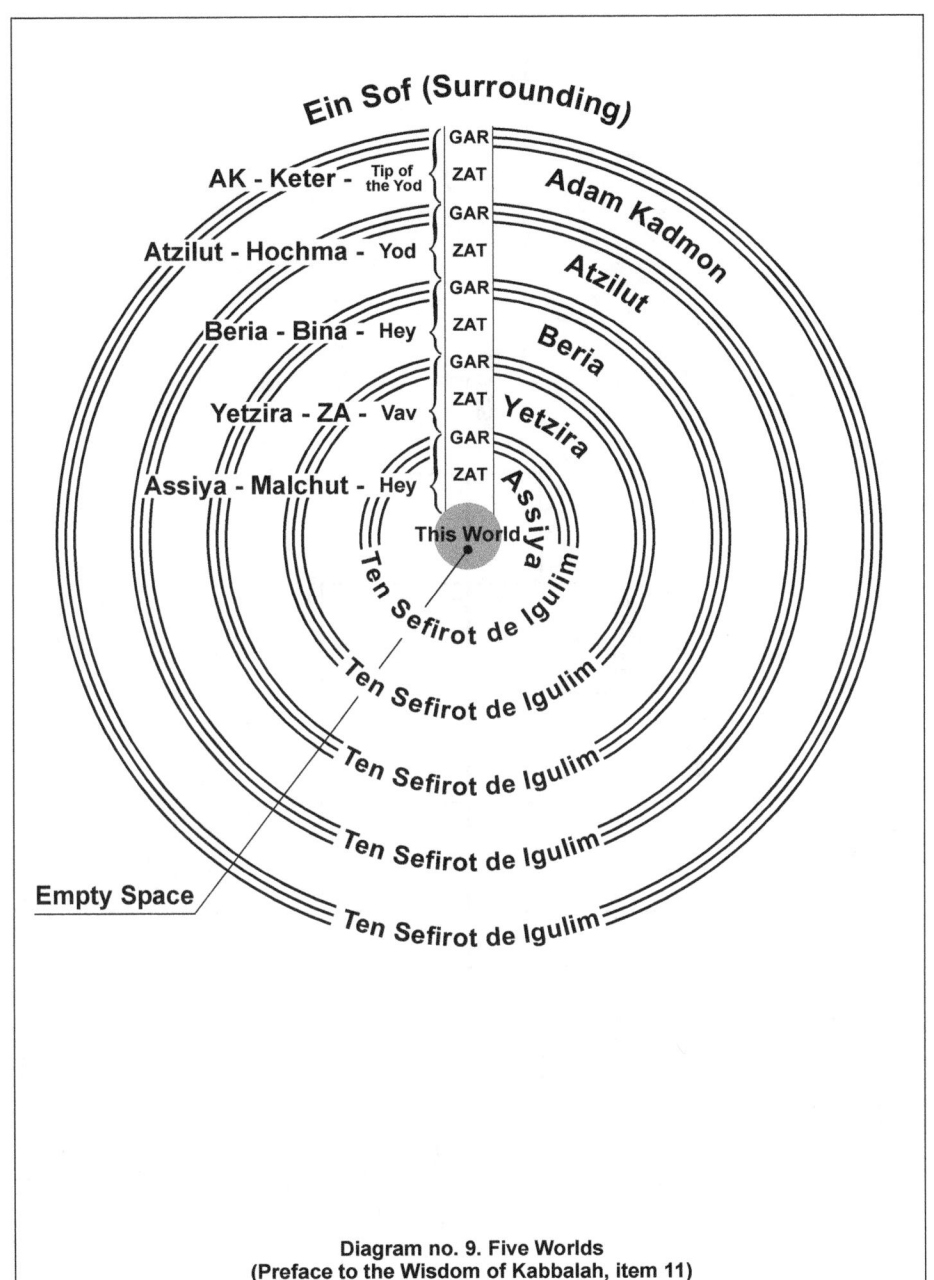

Diagram no. 9. Five Worlds
(Preface to the Wisdom of Kabbalah, item 11)

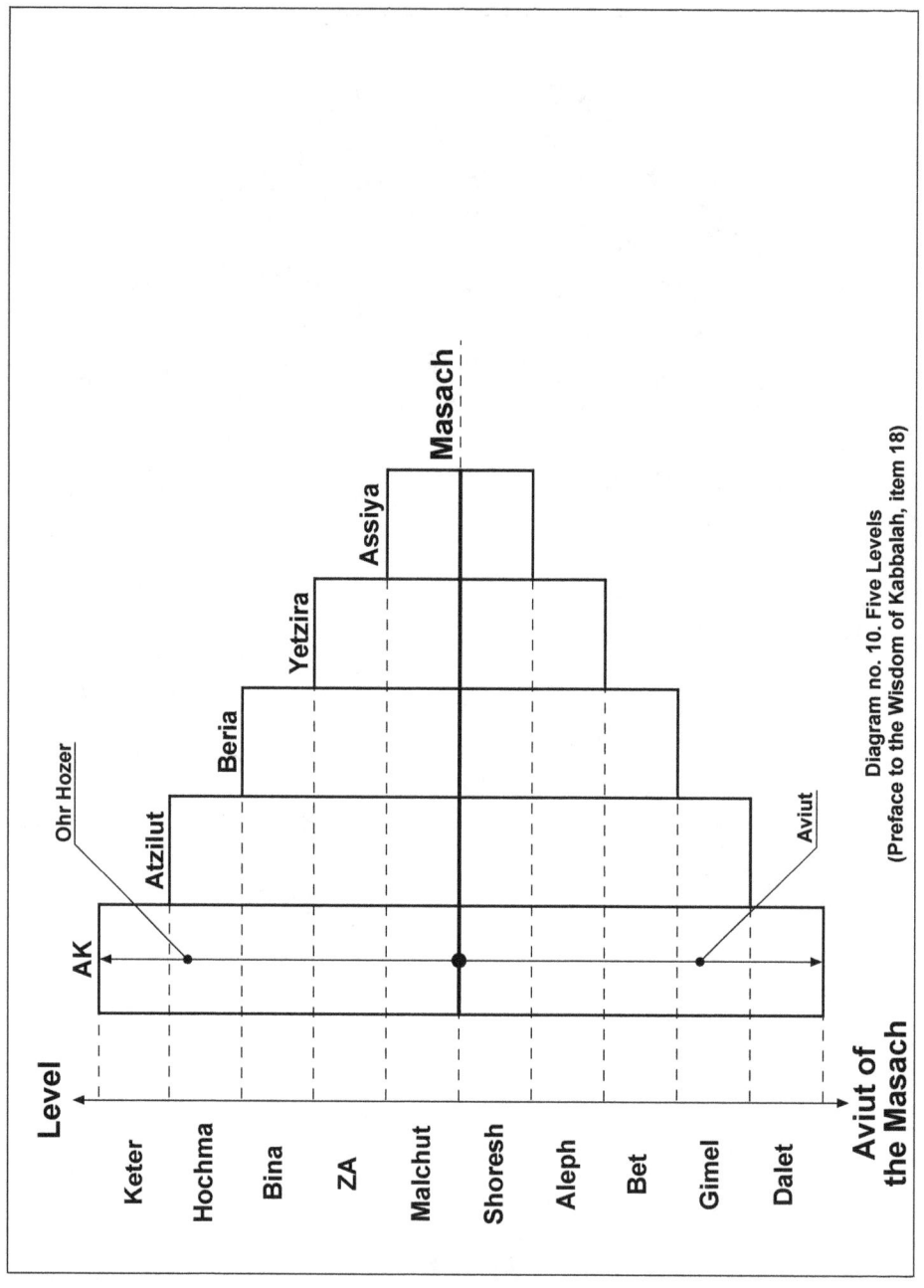

Diagram no. 10. Five Levels
(Preface to the Wisdom of Kabbalah, item 18)

APPENDIX C: DIAGRAMS OF THE SPIRITUAL WORLDS 823

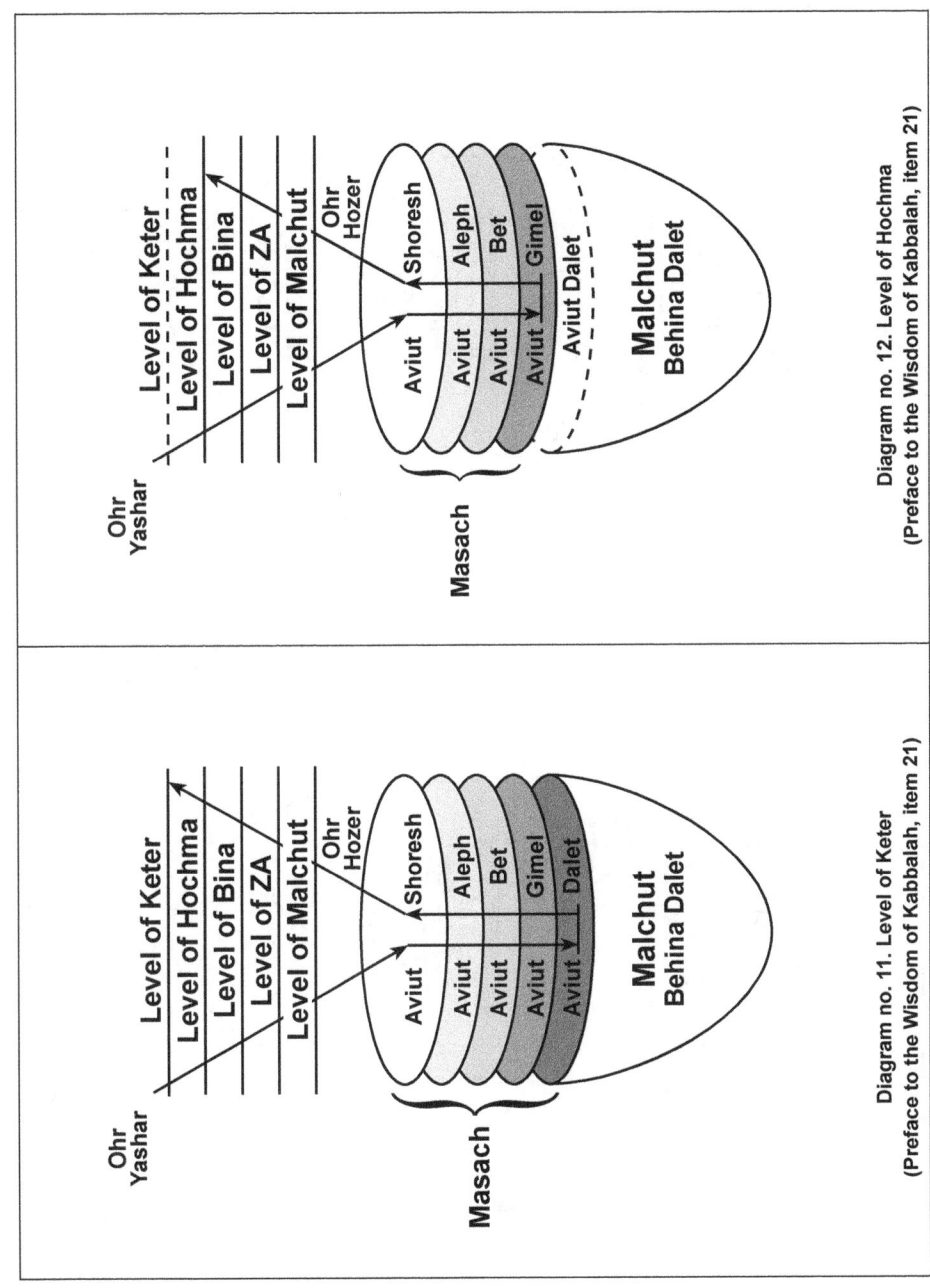

Diagram no. 11. Level of Keter
(Preface to the Wisdom of Kabbalah, item 21)

Diagram no. 12. Level of Hochma
(Preface to the Wisdom of Kabbalah, item 21)

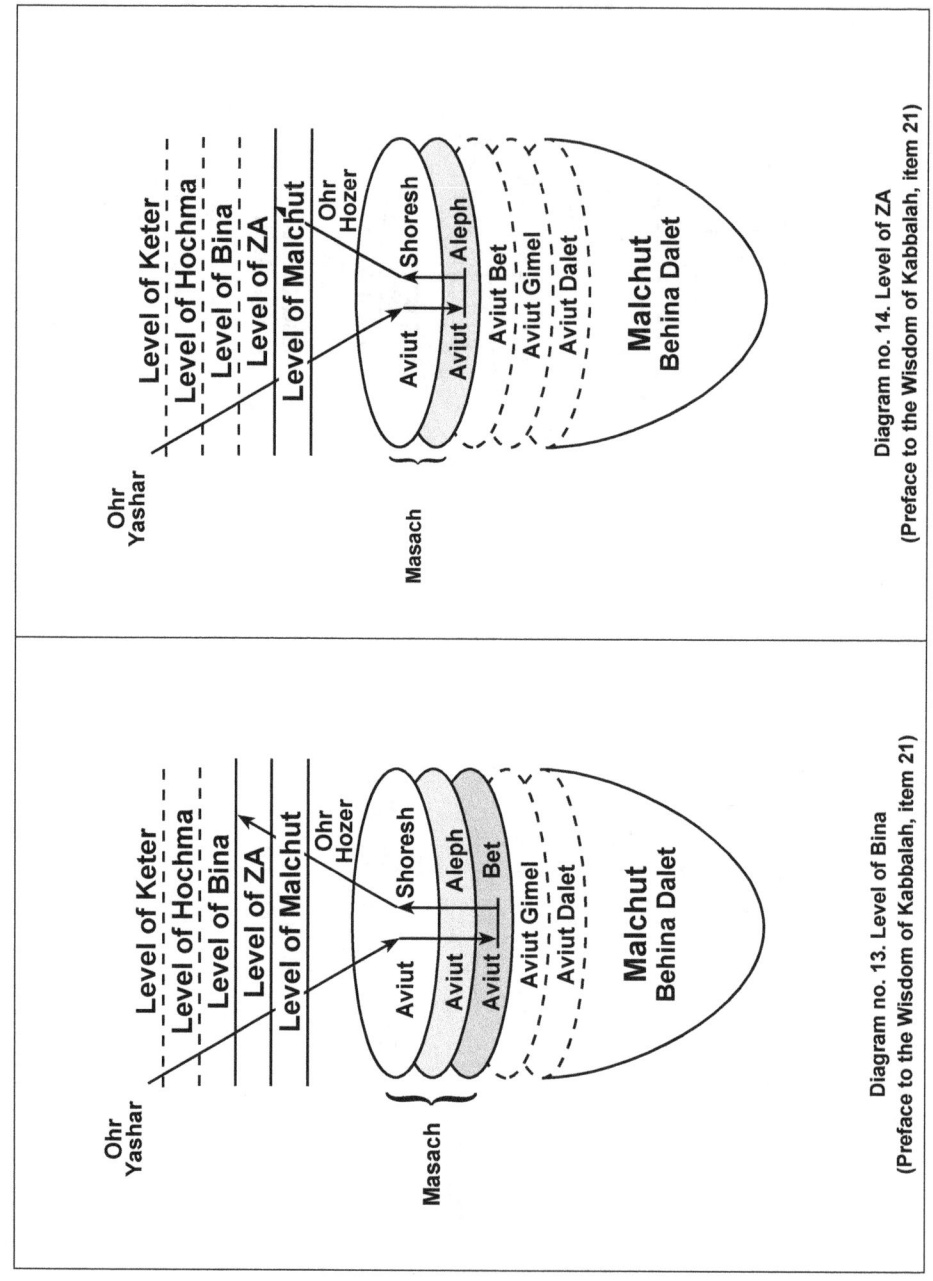

Diagram no. 14. Level of ZA
(Preface to the Wisdom of Kabbalah, item 21)

Diagram no. 13. Level of Bina
(Preface to the Wisdom of Kabbalah, item 21)

APPENDIX C: DIAGRAMS OF THE SPIRITUAL WORLDS   825

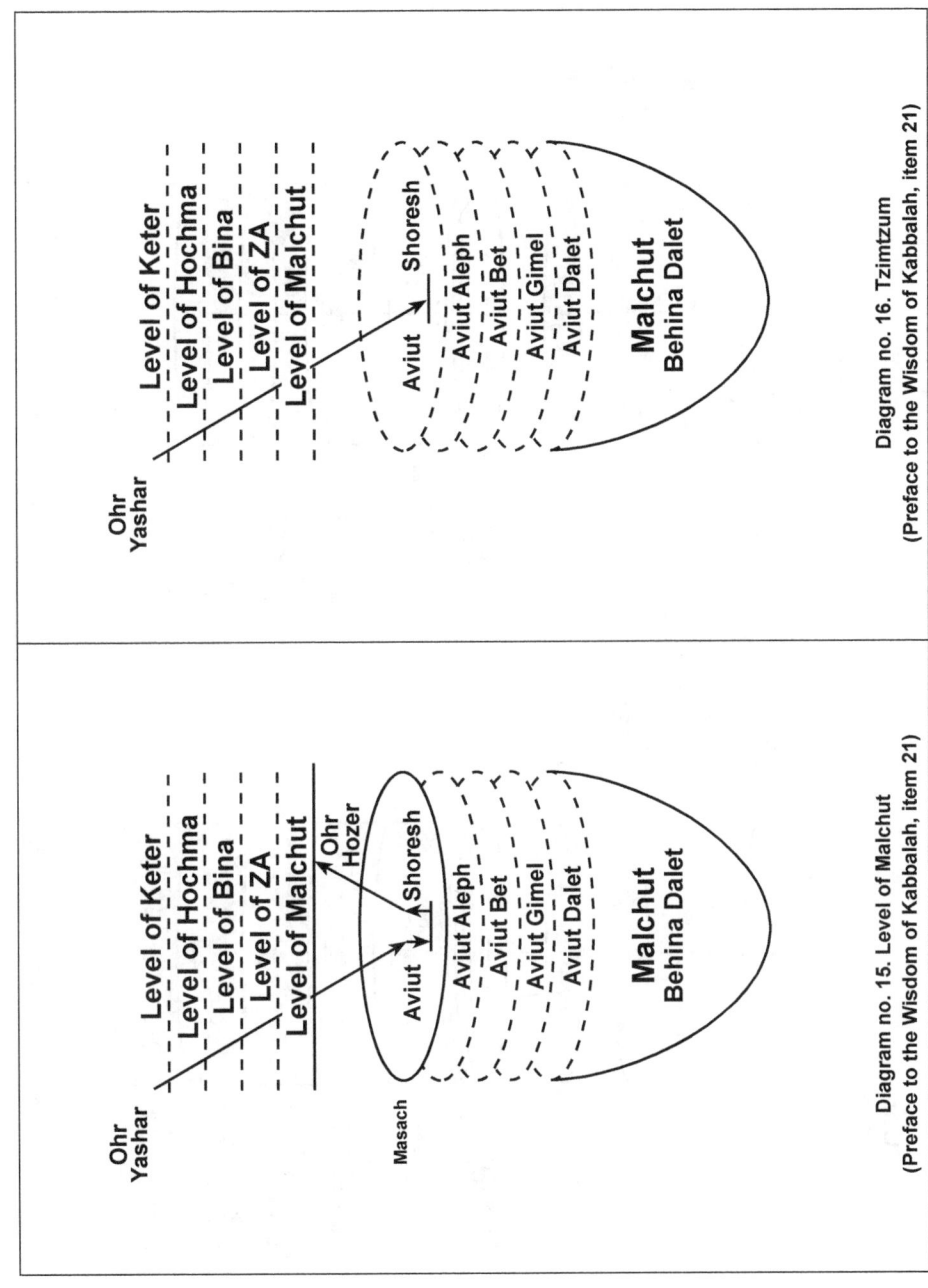

Diagram no. 15. Level of Malchut
(Preface to the Wisdom of Kabbalah, item 21)

Diagram no. 16. Tzimtzum
(Preface to the Wisdom of Kabbalah, item 21)

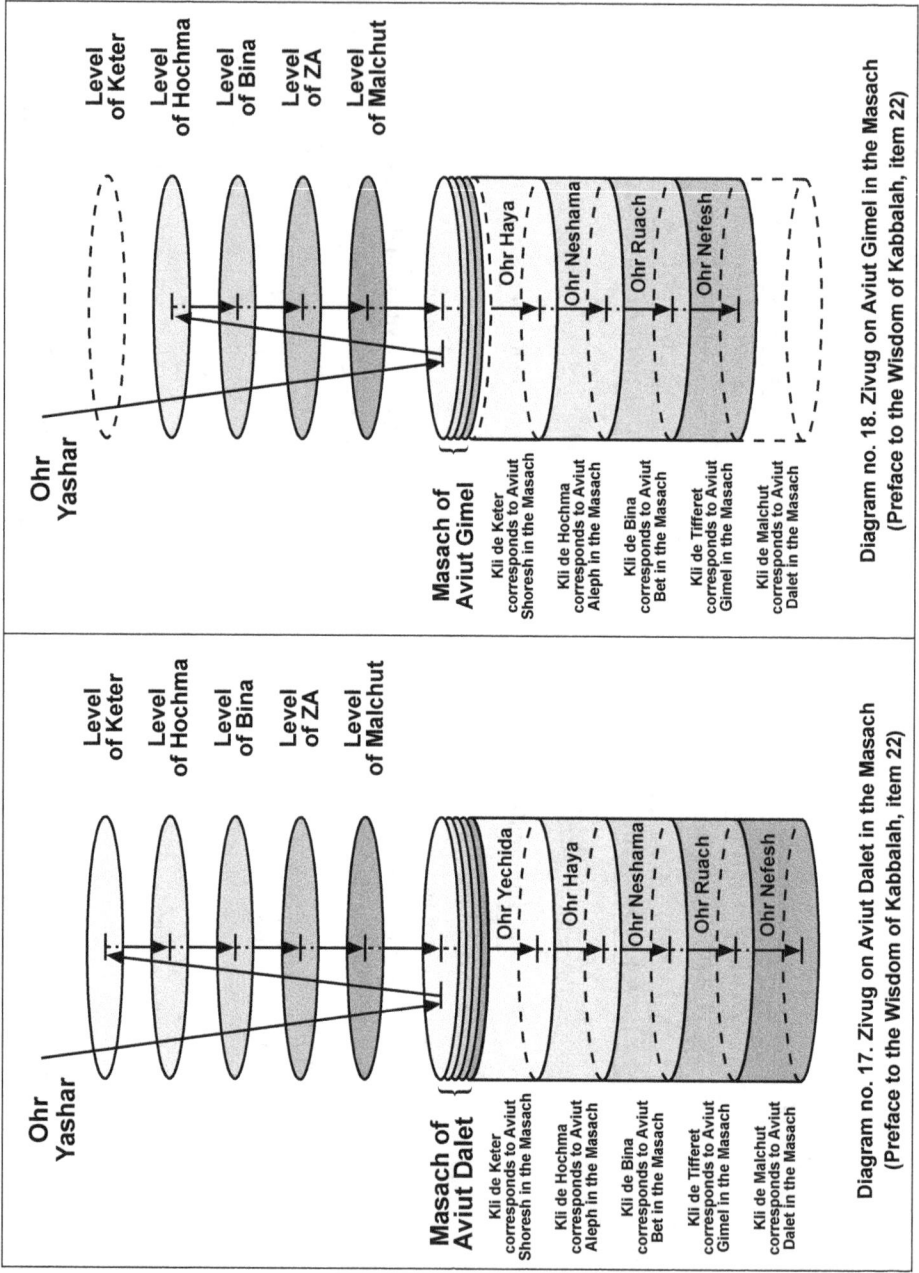

Diagram no. 17. Zivug on Aviut Dalet in the Masach
(Preface to the Wisdom of Kabbalah, item 22)

Diagram no. 18. Zivug on Aviut Gimel in the Masach
(Preface to the Wisdom of Kabbalah, item 22)

APPENDIX C: DIAGRAMS OF THE SPIRITUAL WORLDS

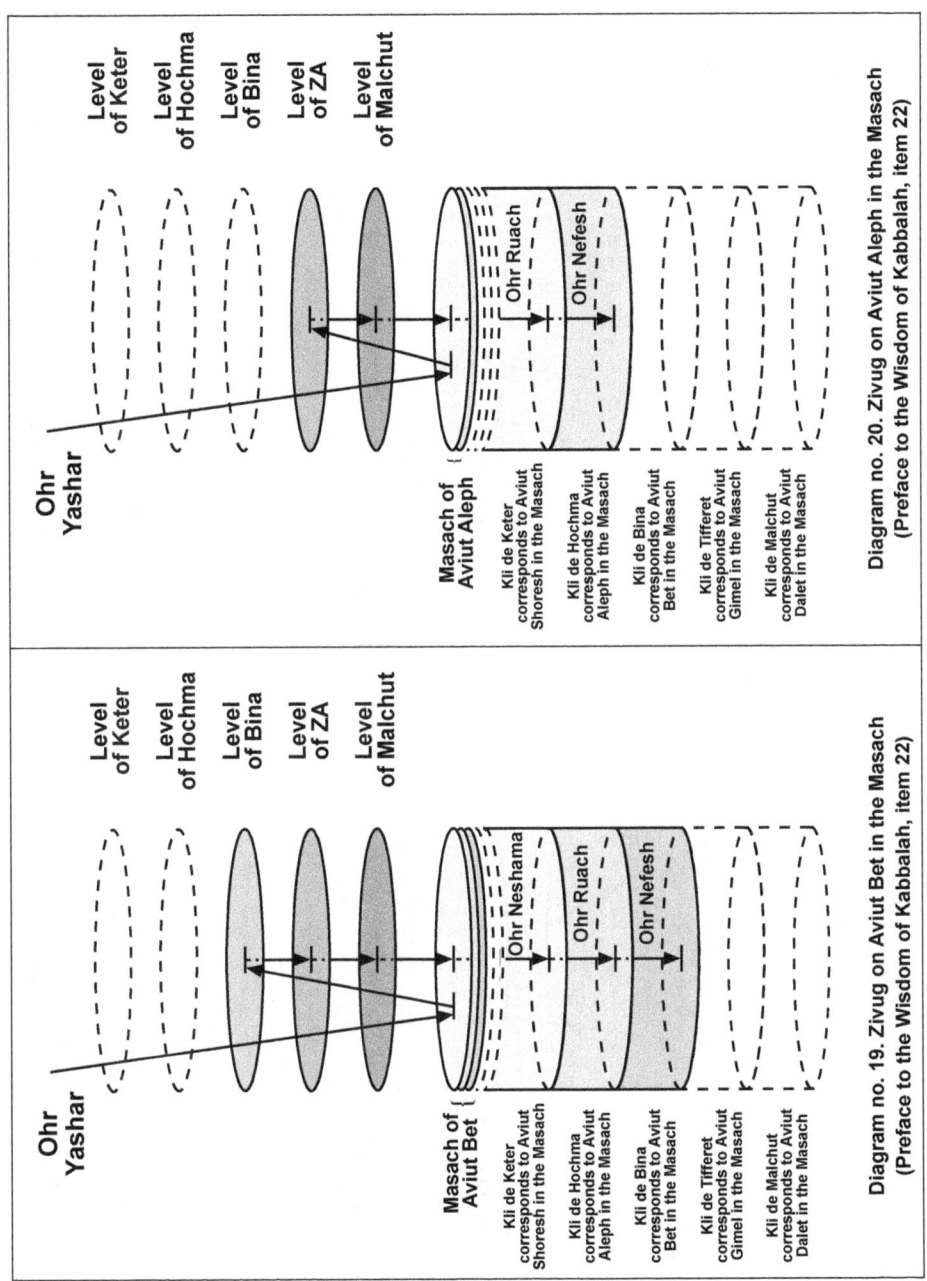

Diagram no. 20. Zivug on Aviut Aleph in the Masach
(Preface to the Wisdom of Kabbalah, item 22)

Diagram no. 19. Zivug on Aviut Bet in the Masach
(Preface to the Wisdom of Kabbalah, item 22)

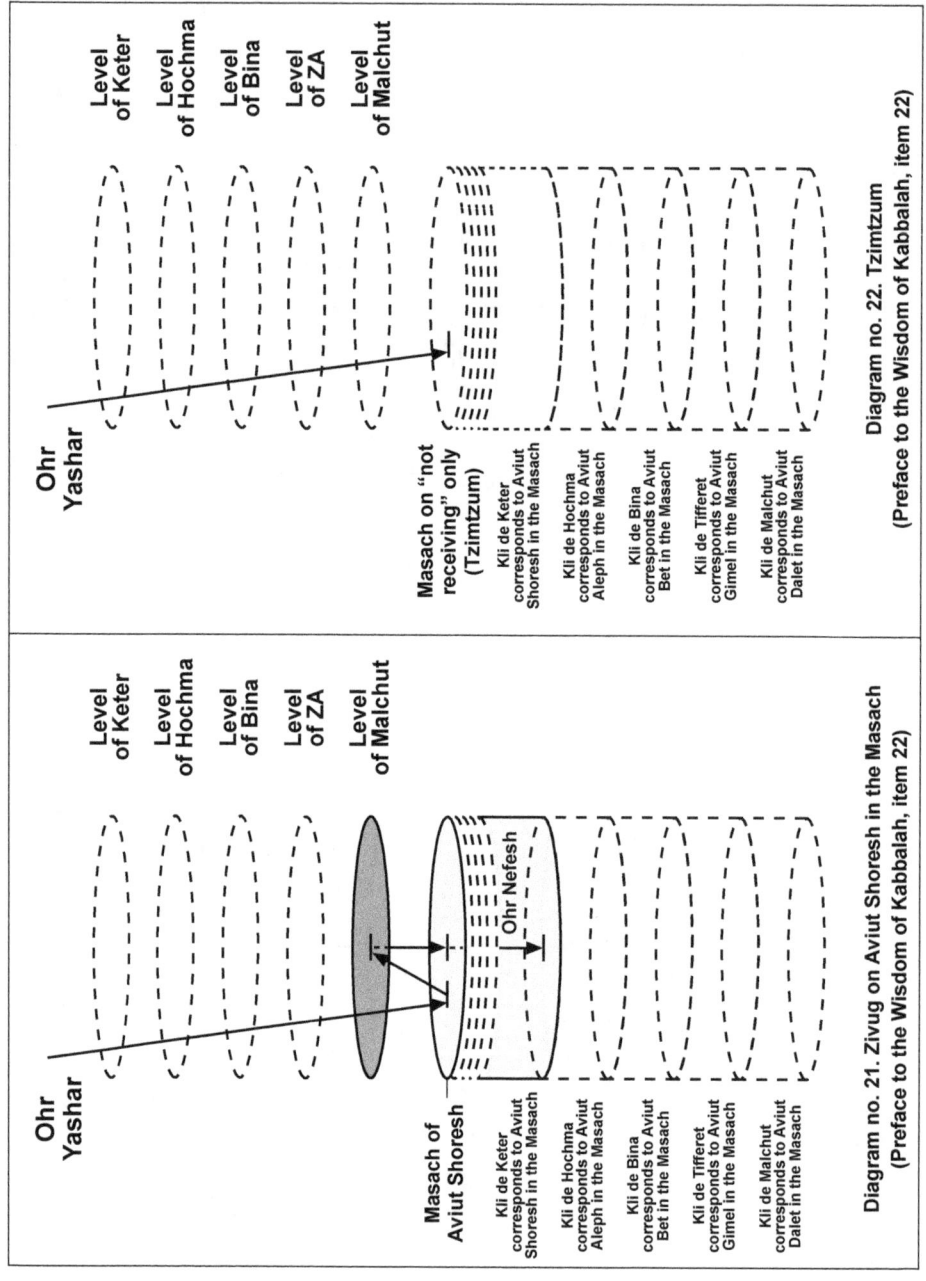

Diagram no. 21. Zivug on Aviut Shoresh in the Masach
(Preface to the Wisdom of Kabbalah, item 22)

Diagram no. 22. Tzimtzum
(Preface to the Wisdom of Kabbalah, item 22)

Appendix C: Diagrams of the Spiritual Worlds

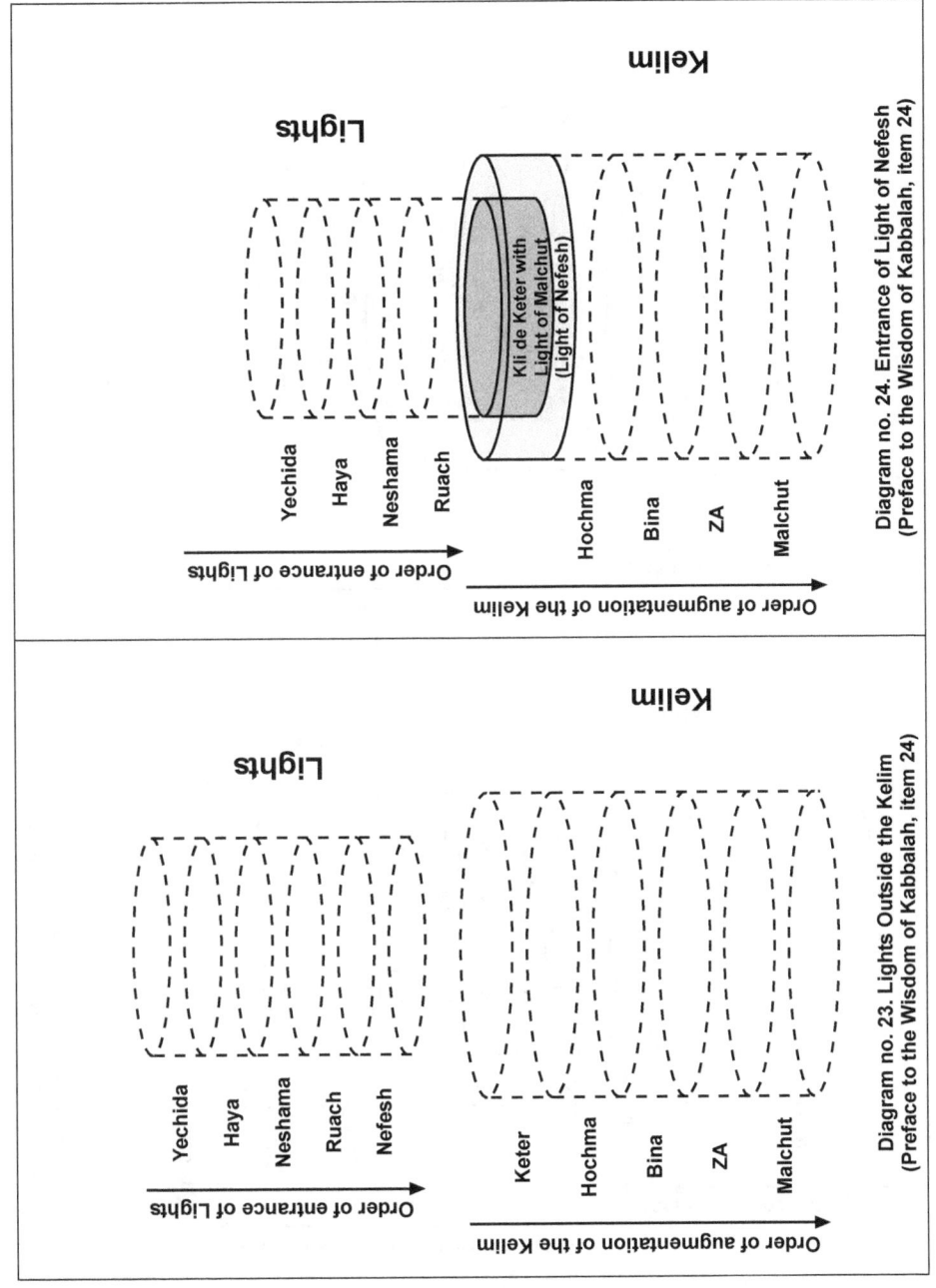

Diagram no. 24. Entrance of Light of Nefesh
(Preface to the Wisdom of Kabbalah, item 24)

Diagram no. 23. Lights Outside the Kelim
(Preface to the Wisdom of Kabbalah, item 24)

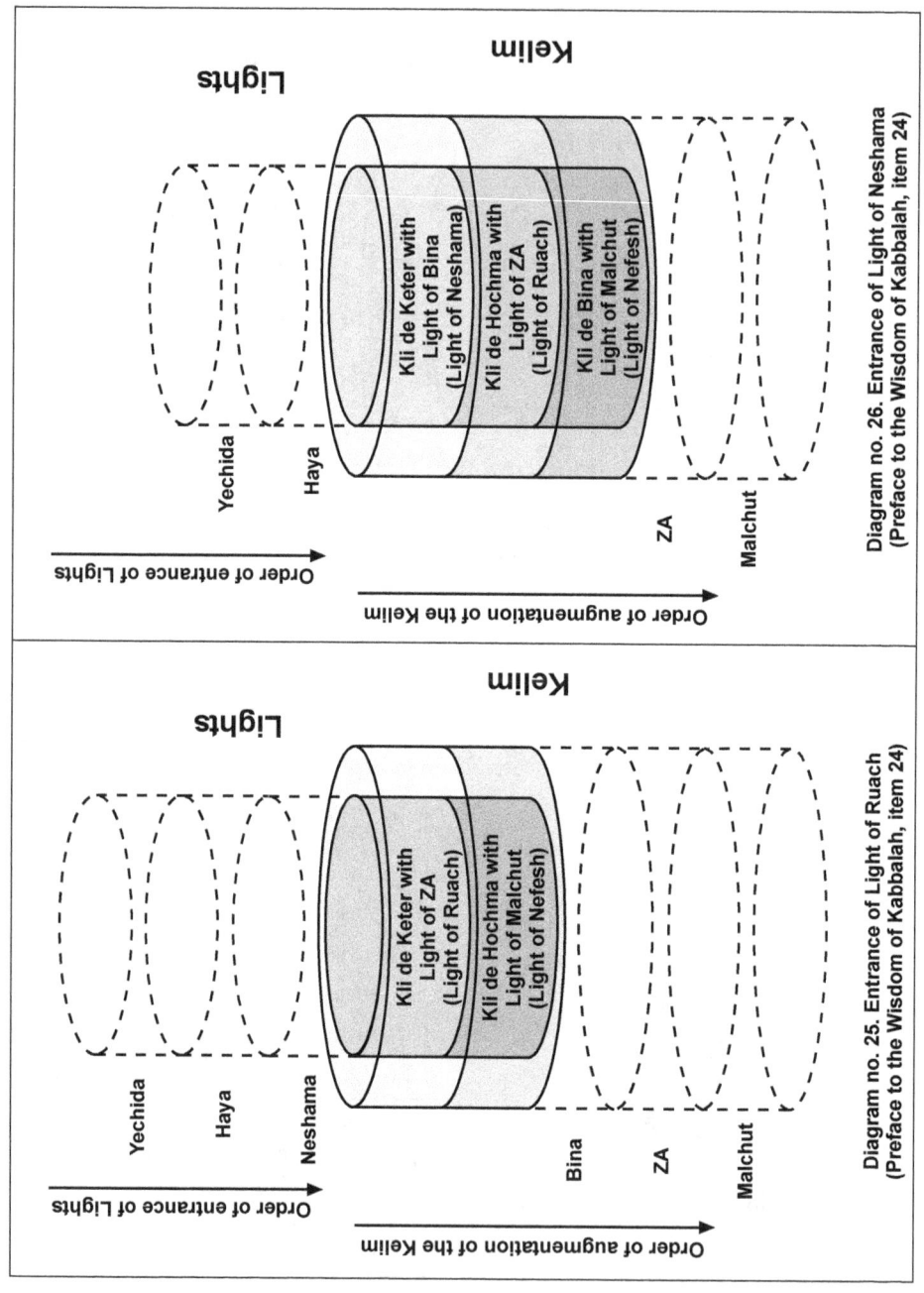

Diagram no. 26. Entrance of Light of Neshama
(Preface to the Wisdom of Kabbalah, item 24)

Diagram no. 25. Entrance of Light of Ruach
(Preface to the Wisdom of Kabbalah, item 24)

Appendix C: Diagrams of the Spiritual Worlds 831

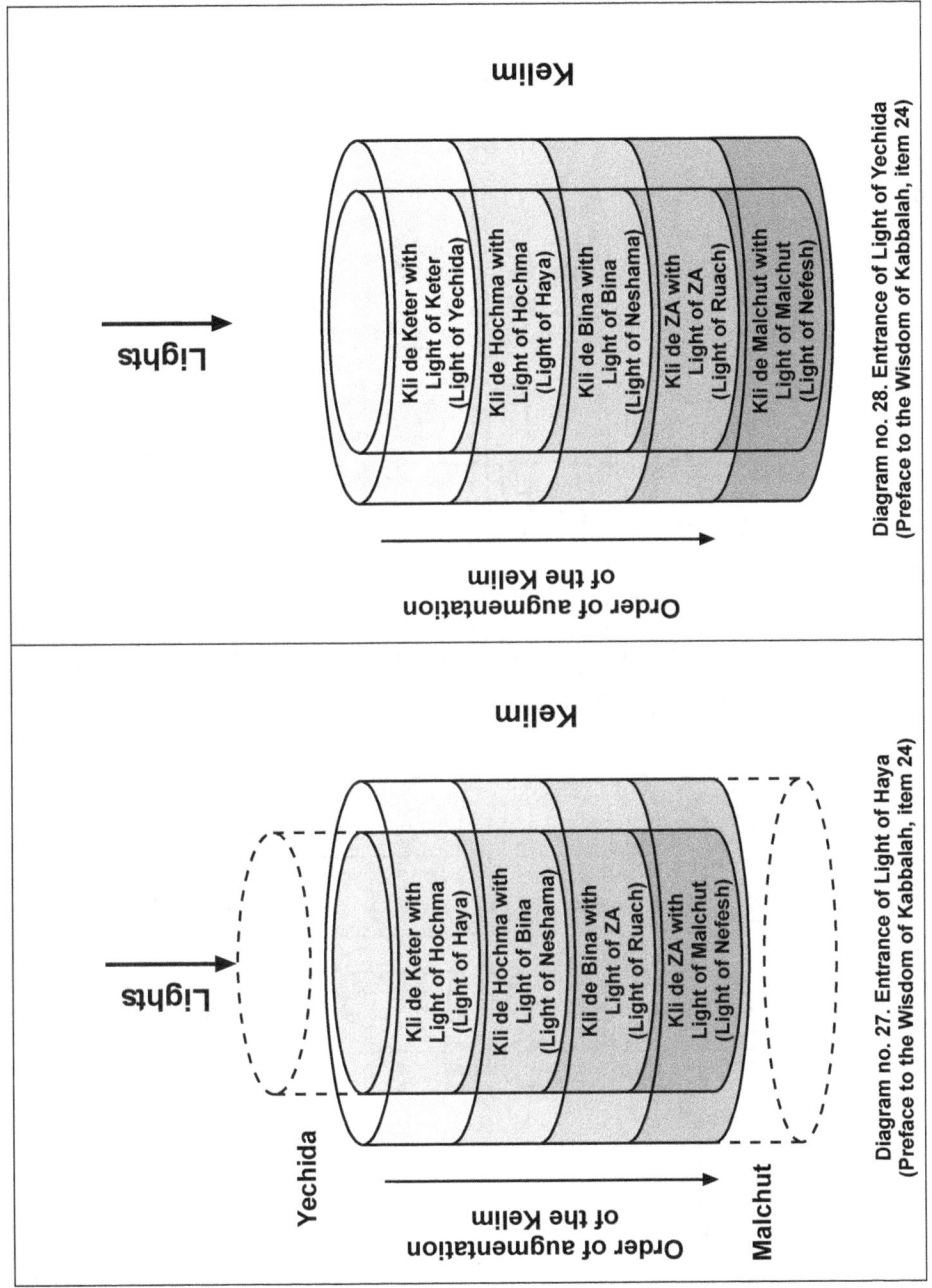

Diagram no. 28. Entrance of Light of Yechida
(Preface to the Wisdom of Kabbalah, item 24)

Diagram no. 27. Entrance of Light of Haya
(Preface to the Wisdom of Kabbalah, item 24)

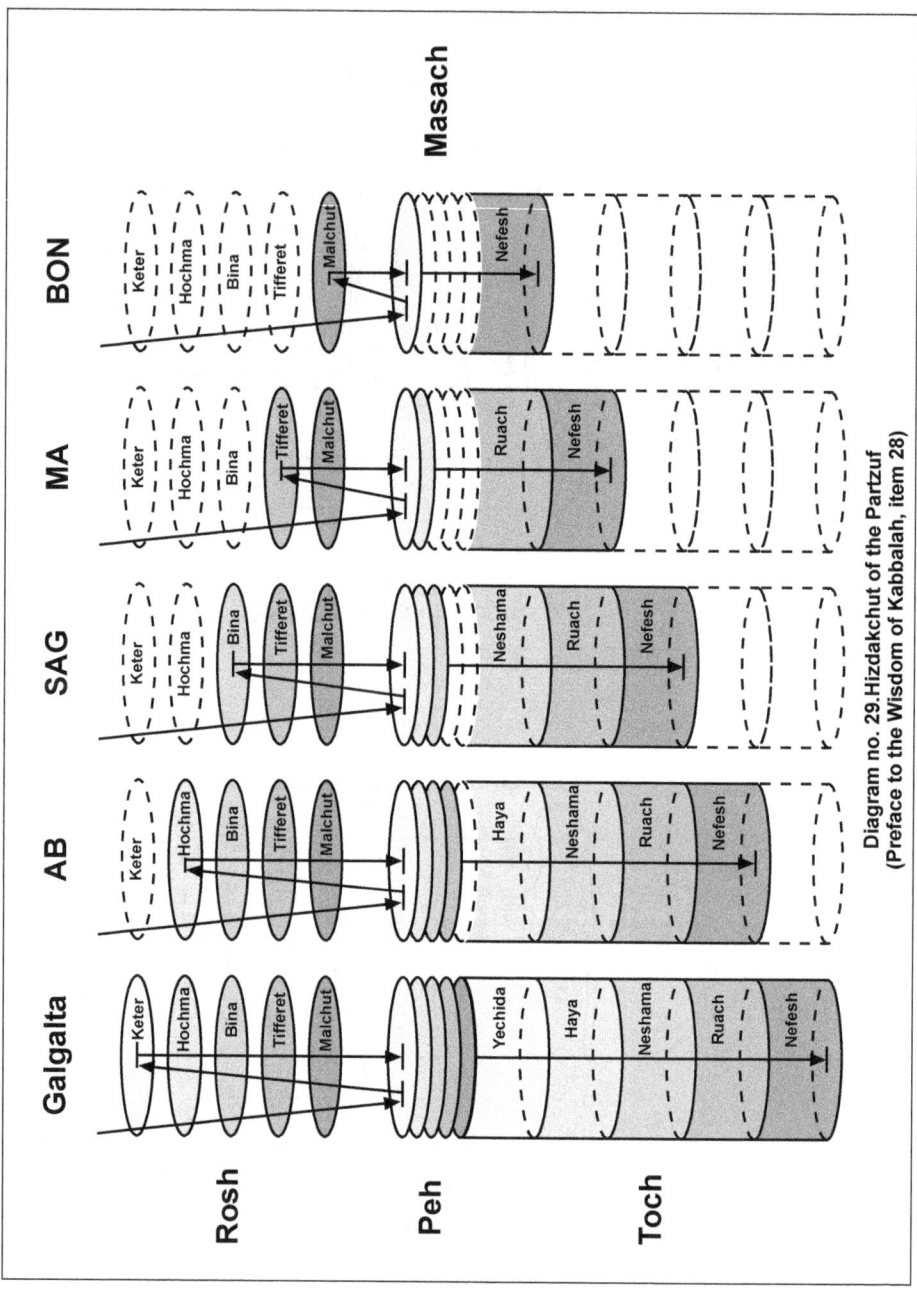

Diagram no. 29. Hizdakchut of the Partzuf
(Preface to the Wisdom of Kabbalah, item 28)

Appendix C: Diagrams of the Spiritual Worlds

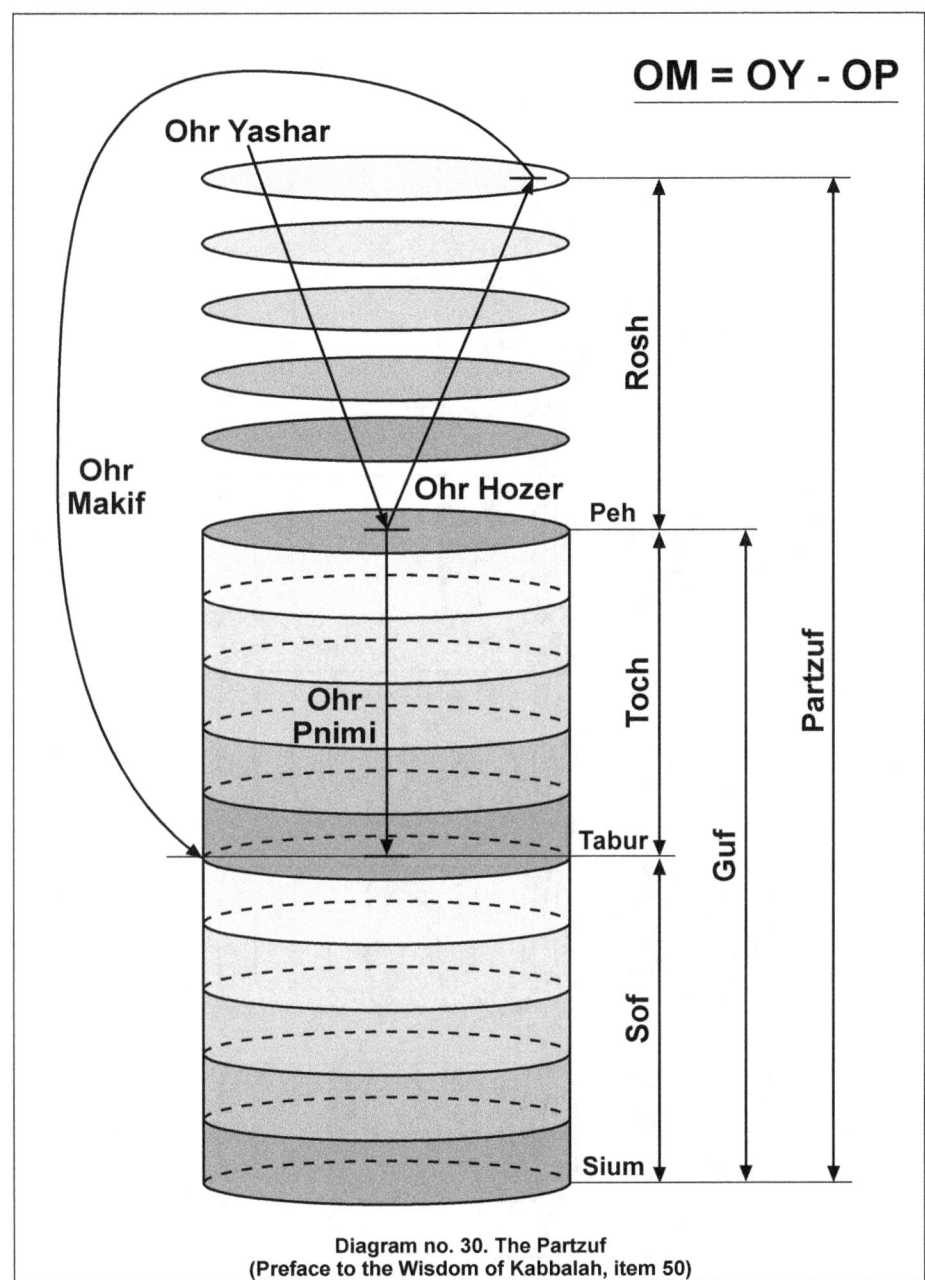

Diagram no. 30. The Partzuf
(Preface to the Wisdom of Kabbalah, item 50)

834   Kabbalah for the Student

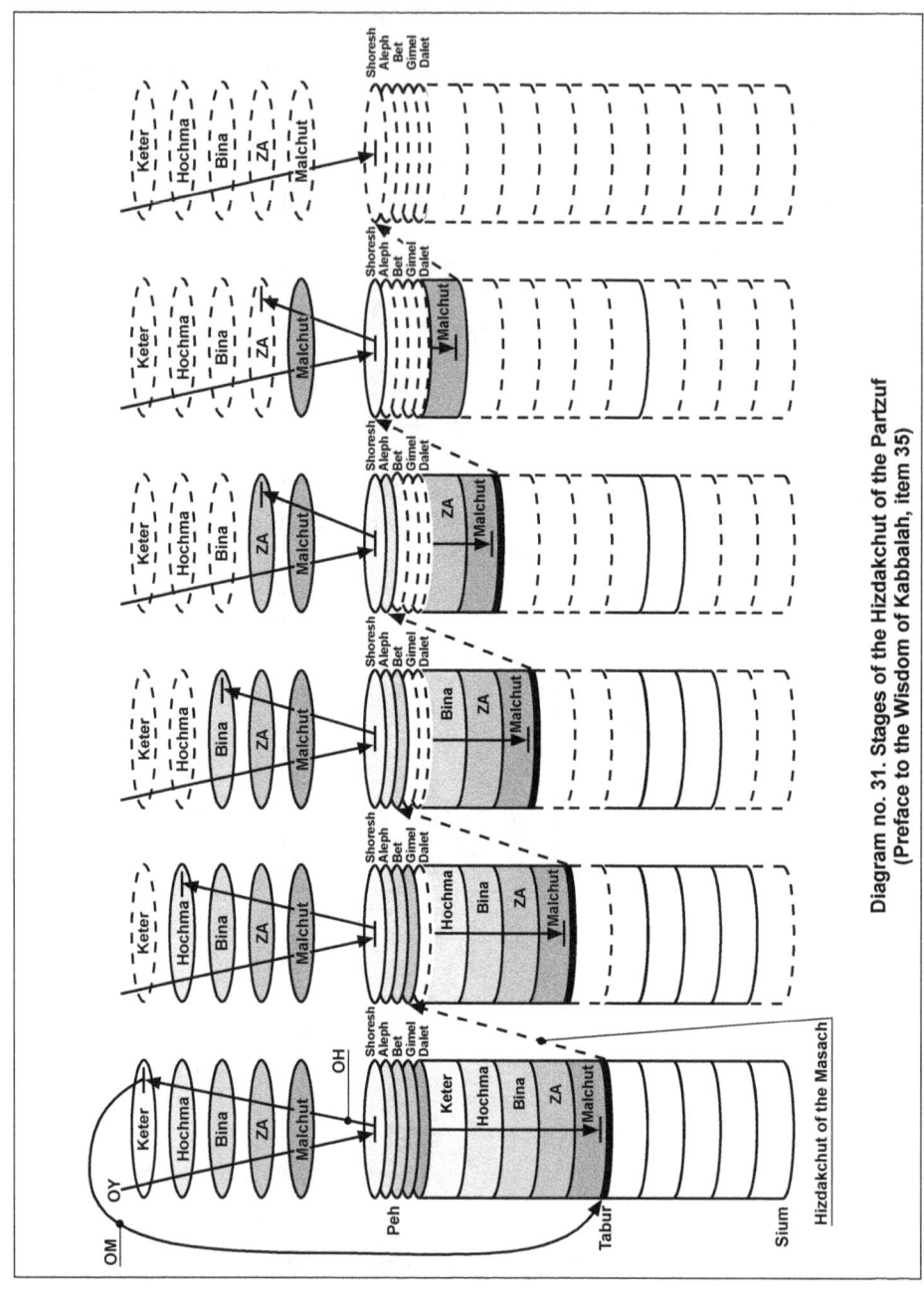

Diagram no. 31. Stages of the Hizdakchut of the Partzuf
(Preface to the Wisdom of Kabbalah, item 35)

APPENDIX C: DIAGRAMS OF THE SPIRITUAL WORLDS

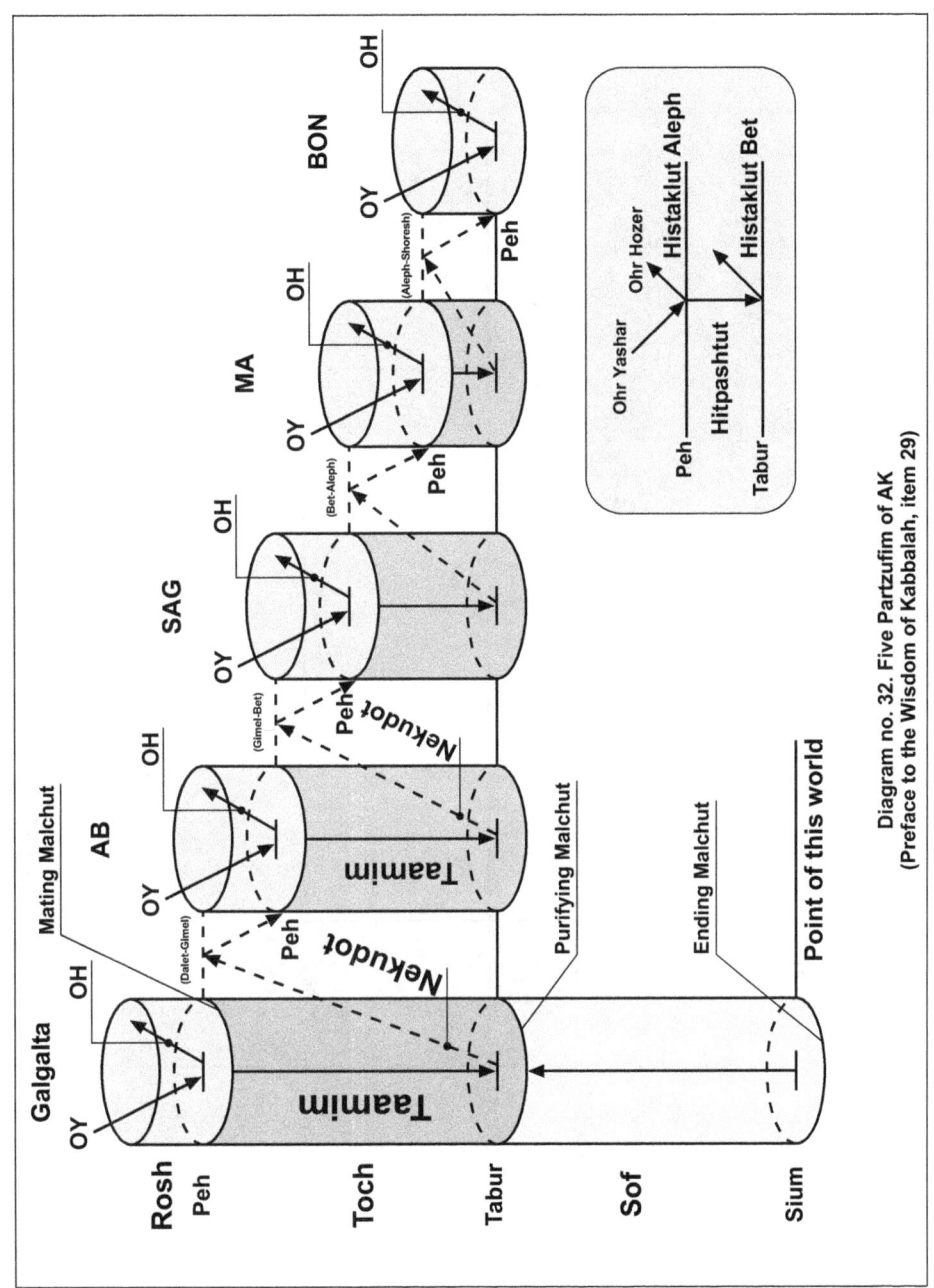

Diagram no. 32. Five Partzufim of AK
(Preface to the Wisdom of Kabbalah, item 29)

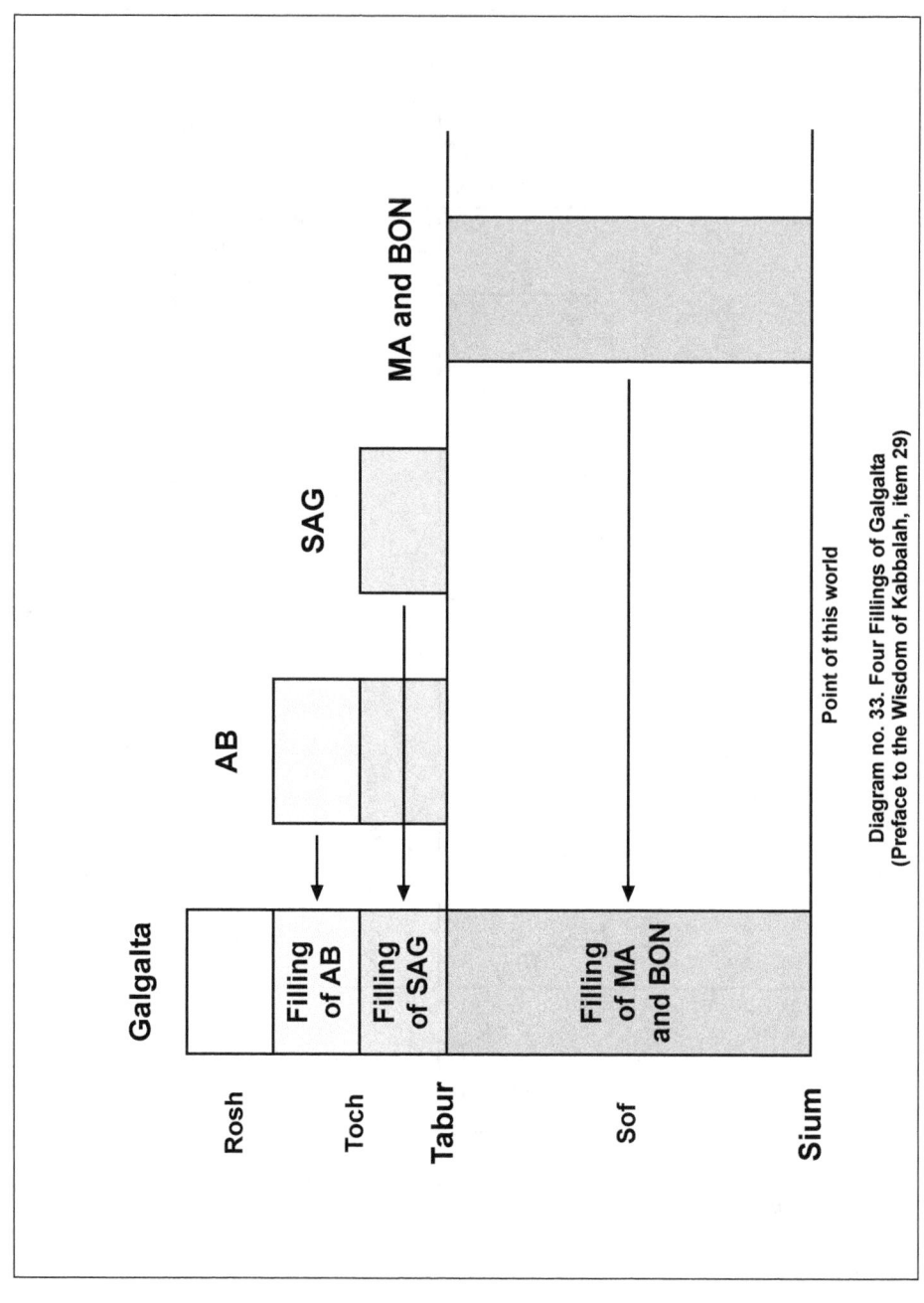

Diagram no. 33. Four Fillings of Galgalta
(Preface to the Wisdom of Kabbalah, item 29)

Appendix C: Diagrams of the Spiritual Worlds 837

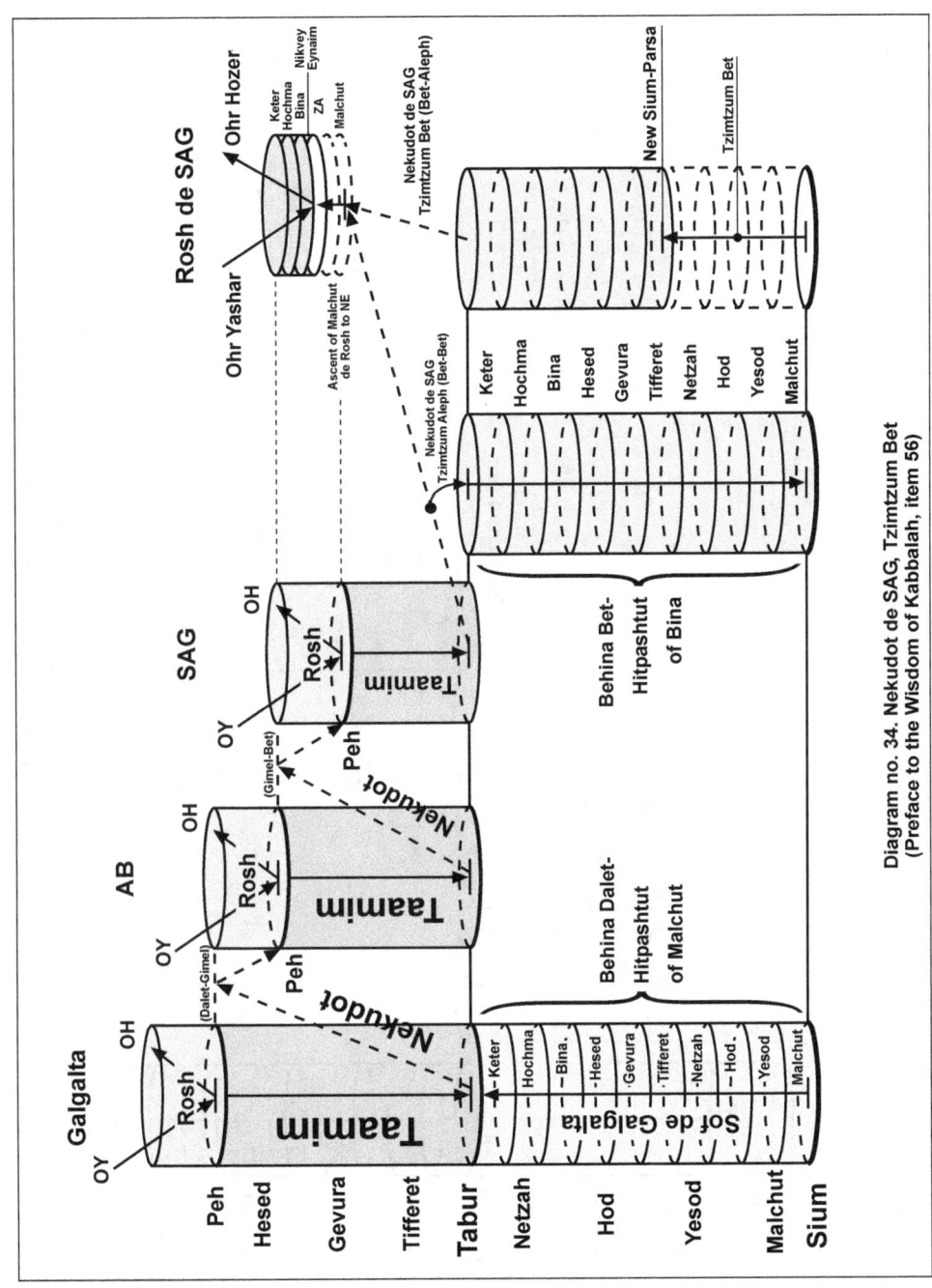

Diagram no. 34. Nekudot de SAG, Tzimtzum Bet
(Preface to the Wisdom of Kabbalah, item 56)

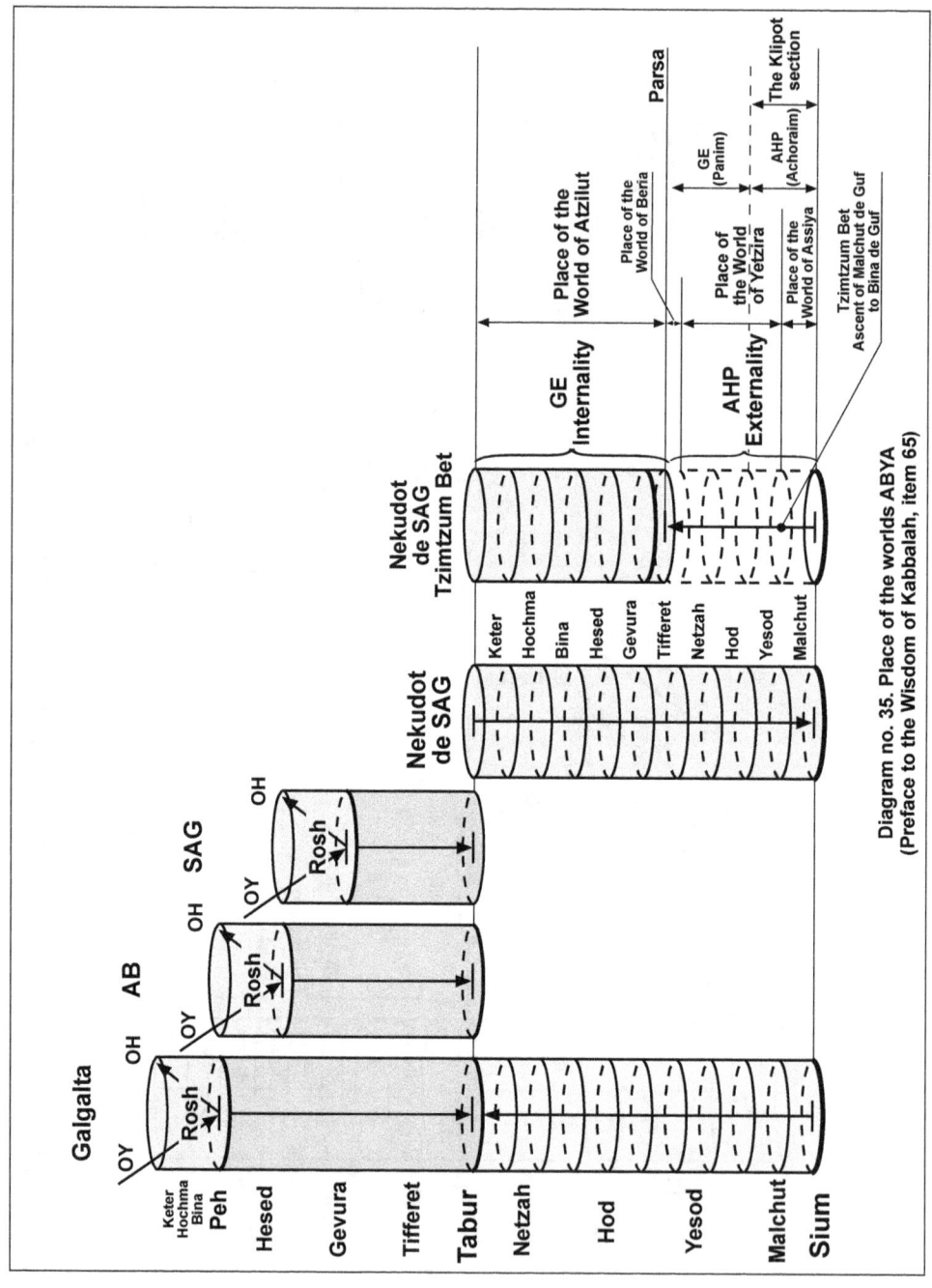

Diagram no. 35. Place of the worlds ABYA
(Preface to the Wisdom of Kabbalah, item 65)

APPENDIX C: DIAGRAMS OF THE SPIRITUAL WORLDS

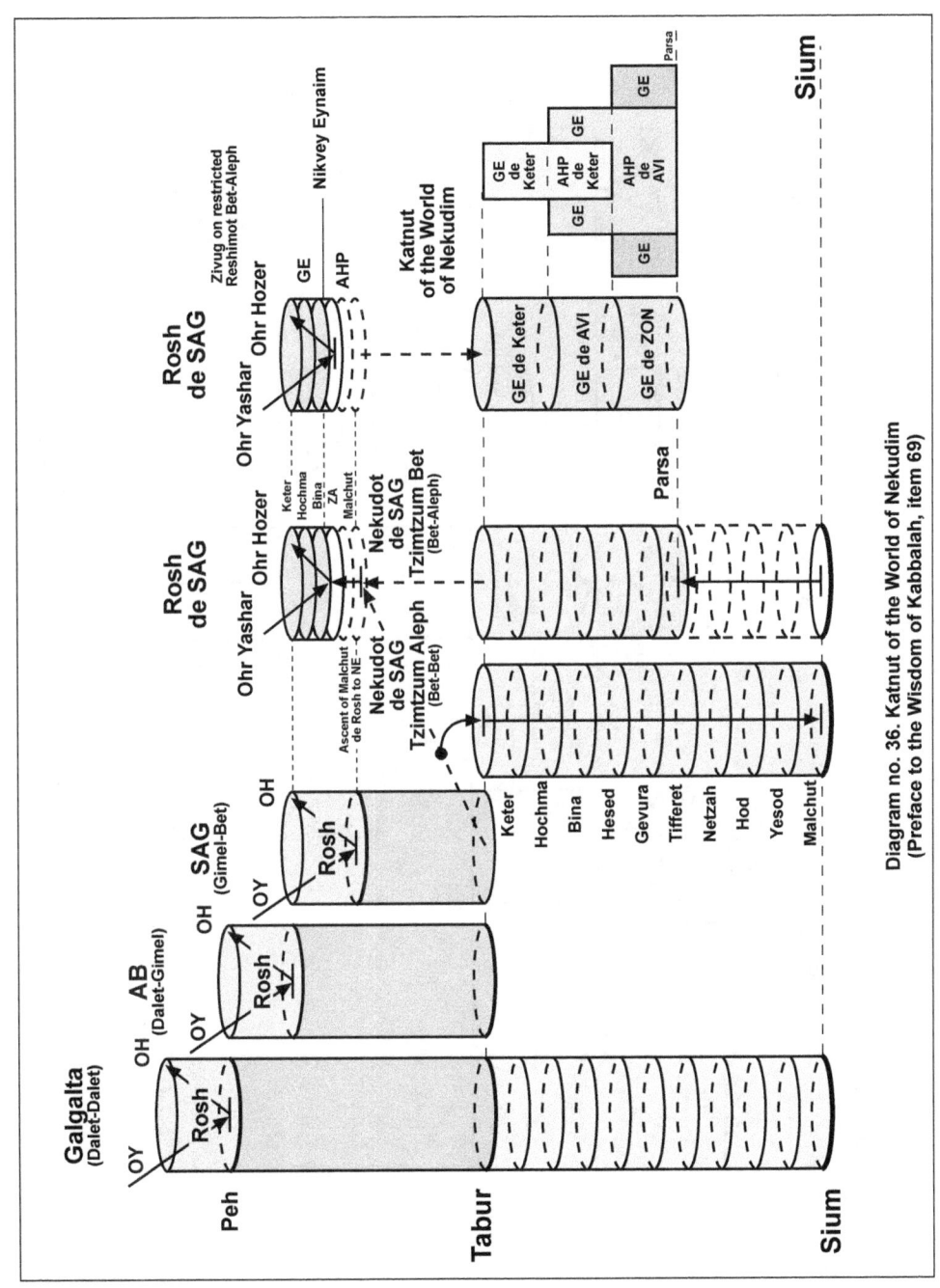

Diagram no. 36. Katnut of the World of Nekudim (Preface to the Wisdom of Kabbalah, item 69)

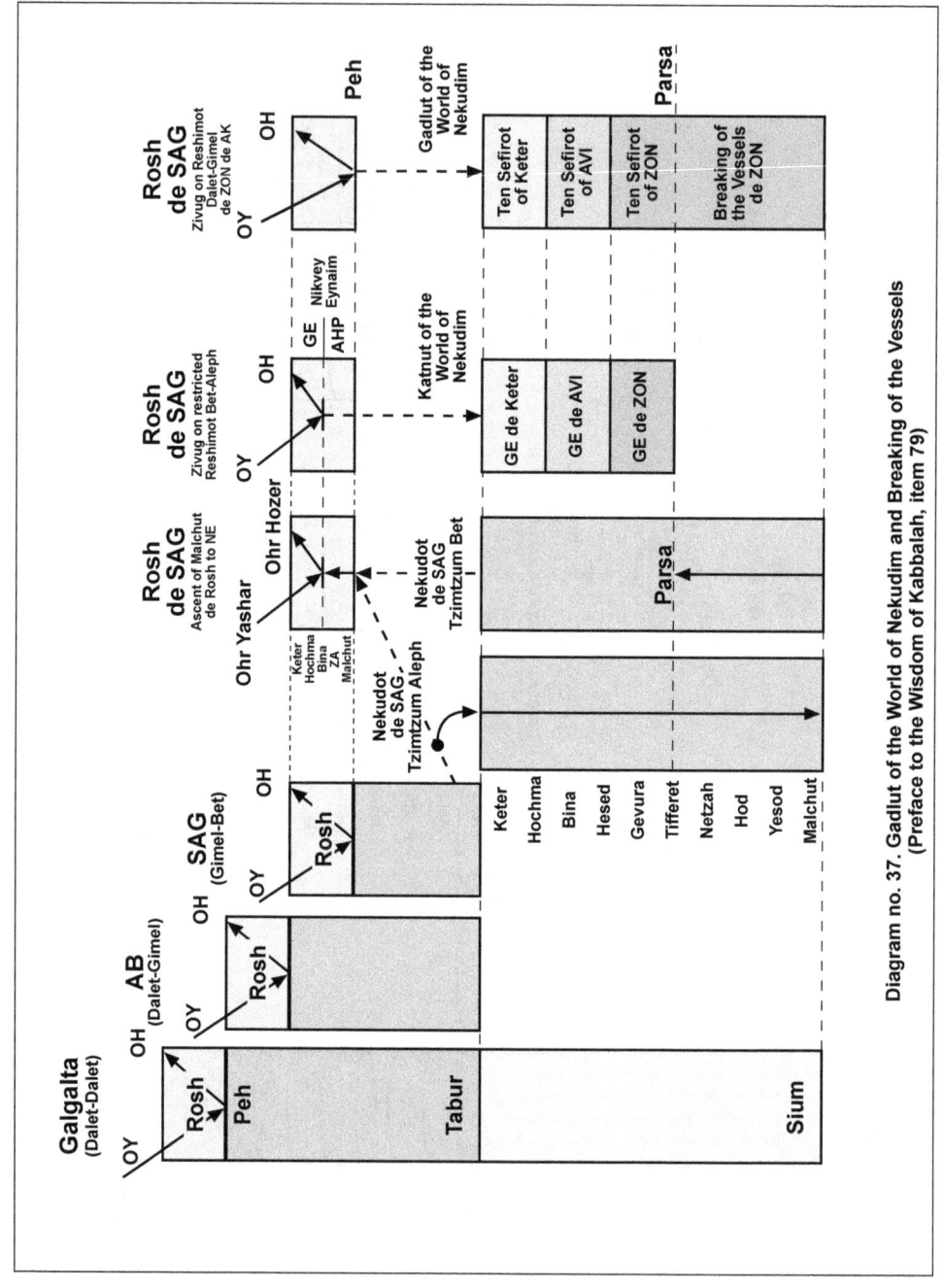

Diagram no. 37. Gadlut of the World of Nekudim and Breaking of the Vessels (Preface to the Wisdom of Kabbalah, item 79)

APPENDIX C: DIAGRAMS OF THE SPIRITUAL WORLDS 841

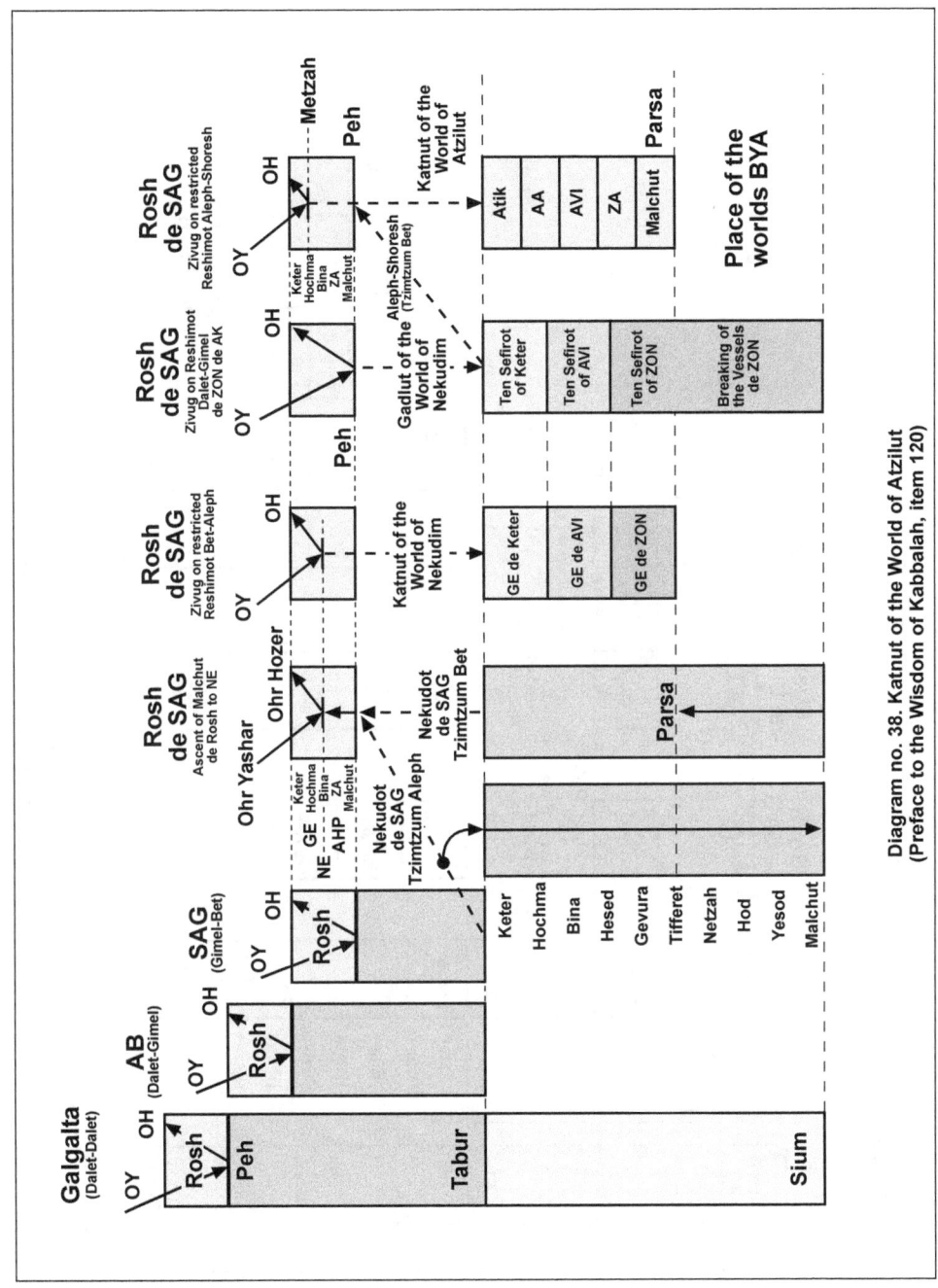

Diagram no. 38. Katnut of the World of Atzilut
(Preface to the Wisdom of Kabbalah, item 120)

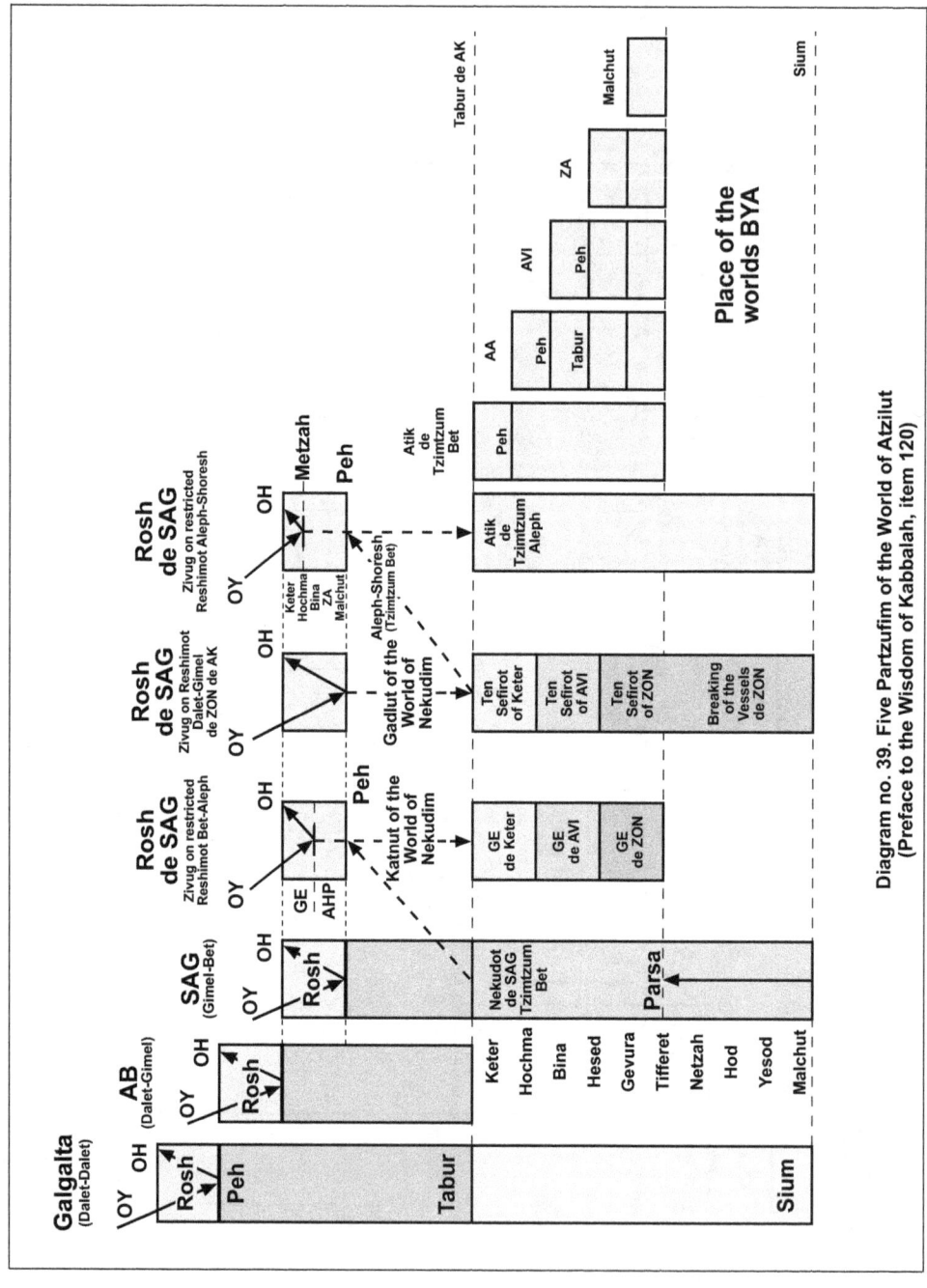

Diagram no. 39. Five Partzufim of the World of Atzilut
(Preface to the Wisdom of Kabbalah, item 120)

Appendix C: Diagrams of the Spiritual Worlds

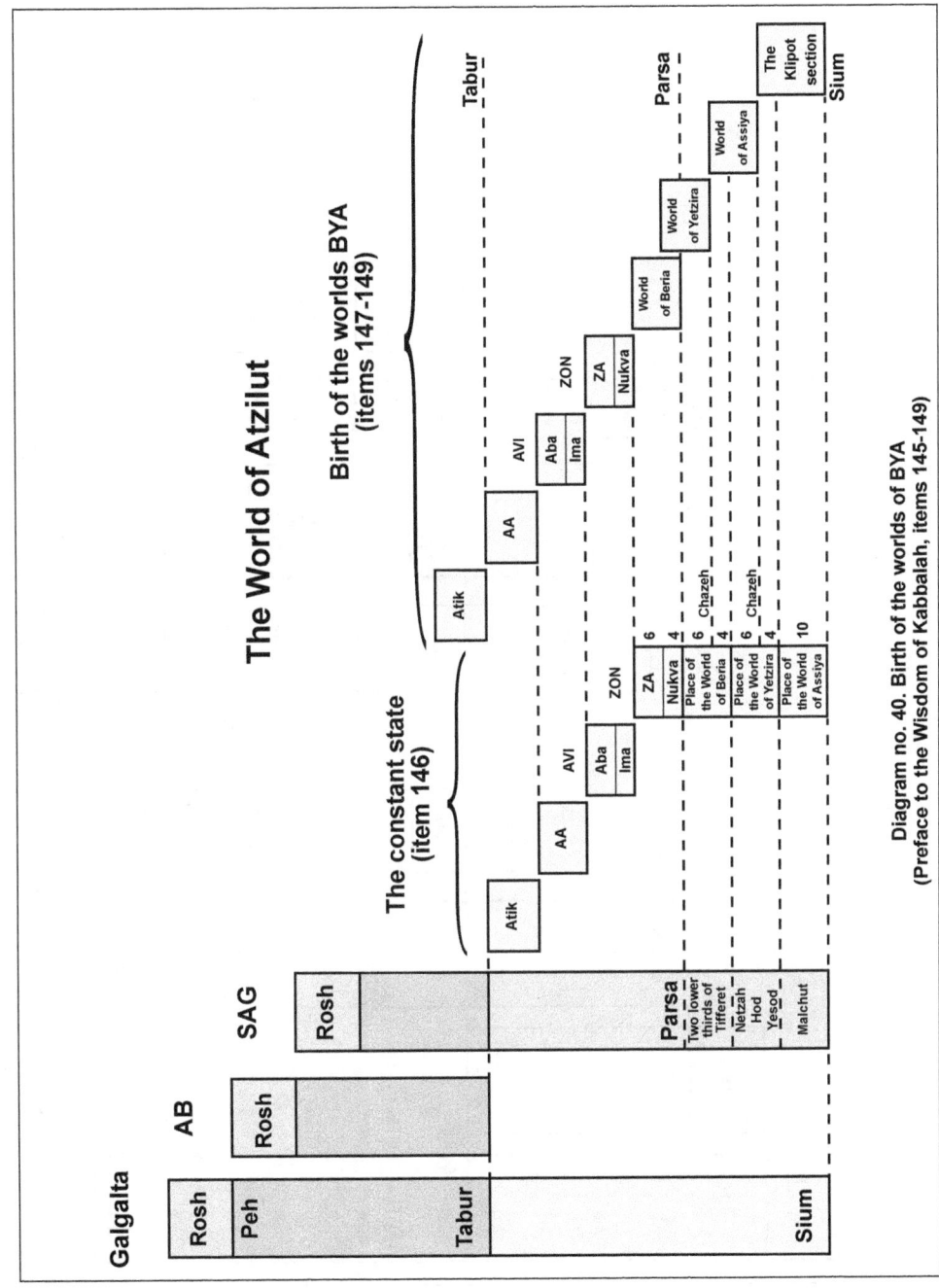

Diagram no. 40. Birth of the worlds of BYA
(Preface to the Wisdom of Kabbalah, items 145-149)

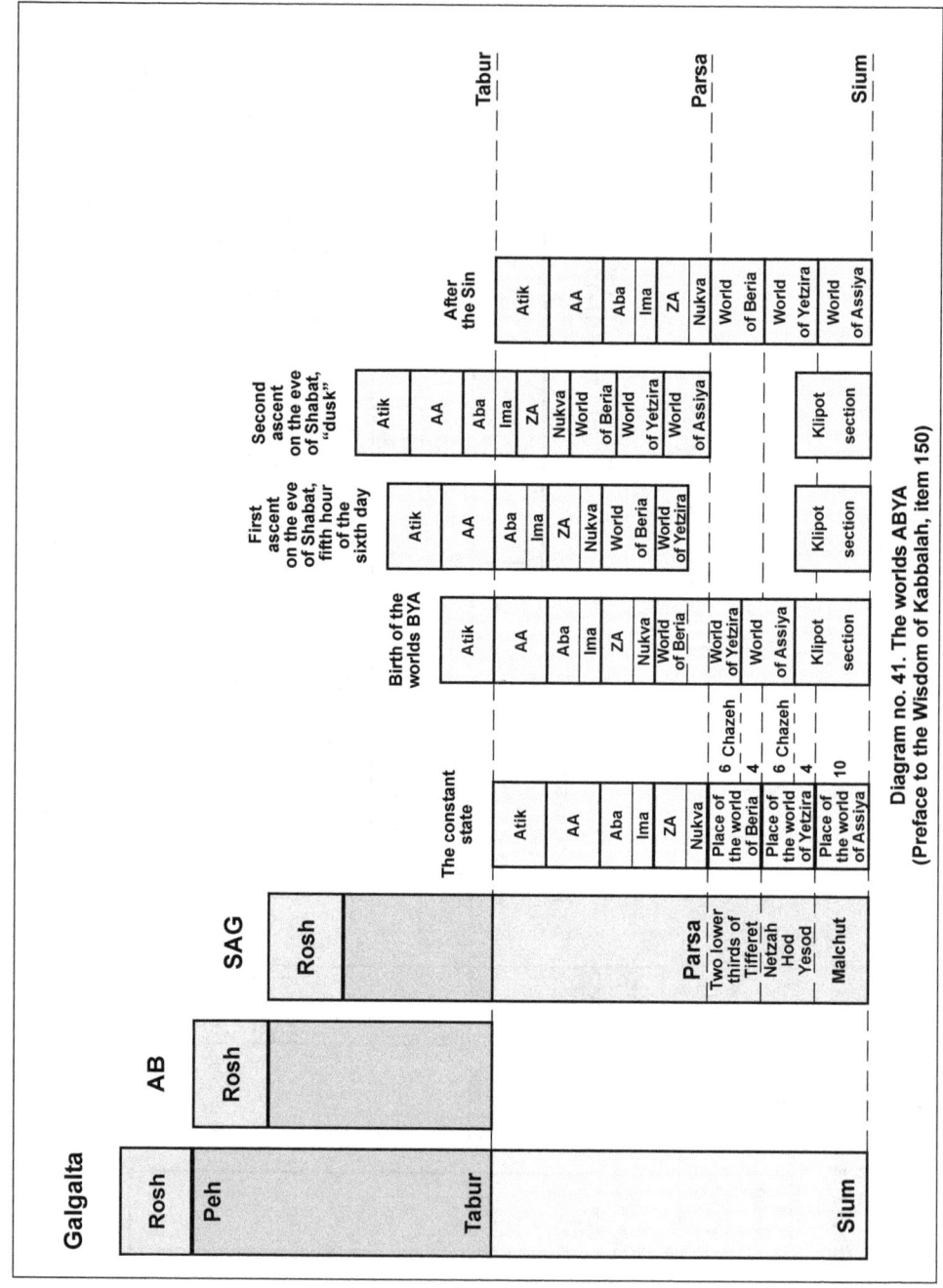

Diagram no. 41. The worlds ABYA
(Preface to the Wisdom of Kabbalah, item 150)

Appendix C: Diagrams of the Spiritual Worlds

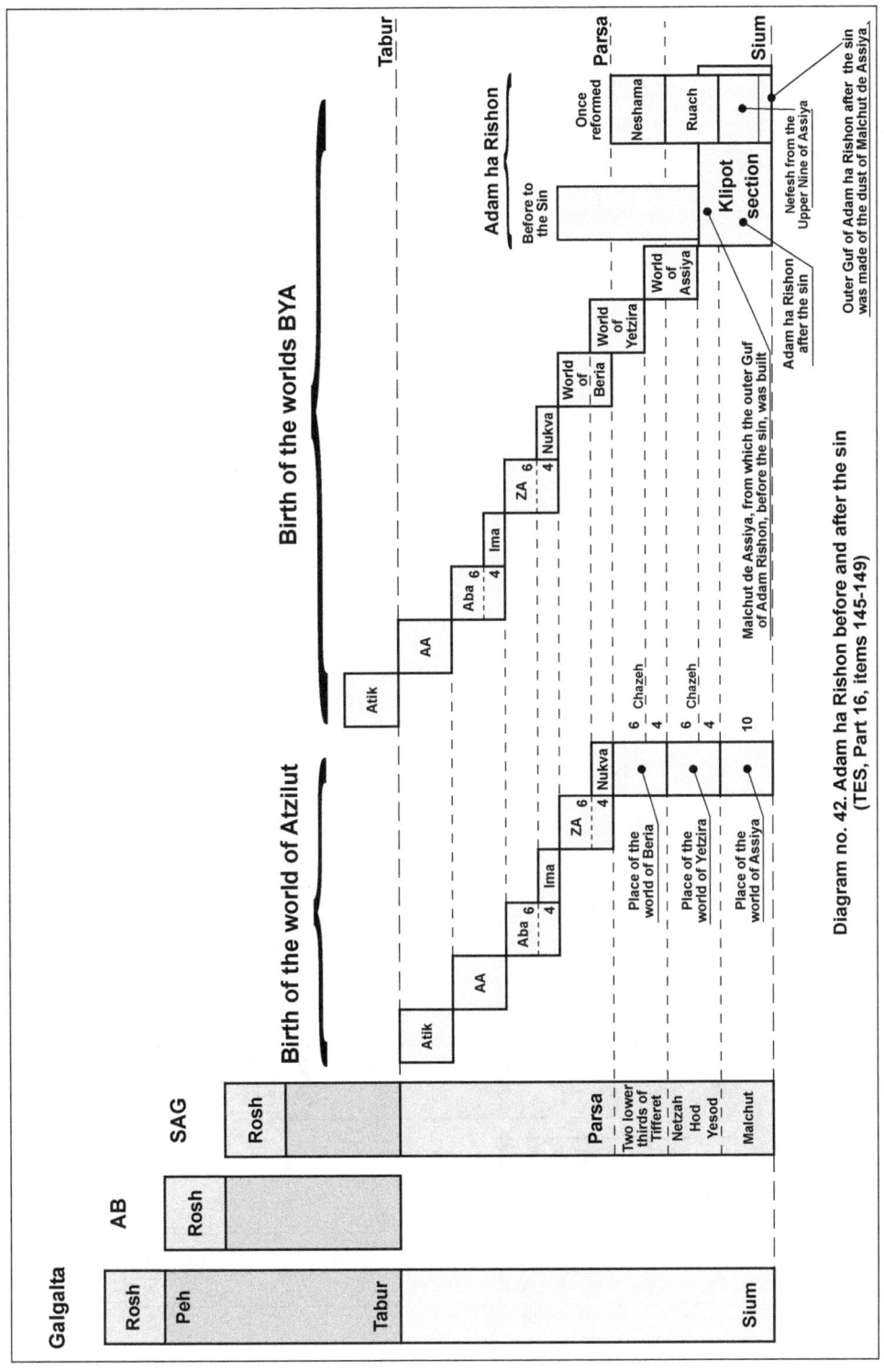

Diagram no. 42. Adam ha Rishon before and after the sin
(TES, Part 16, items 145-149)

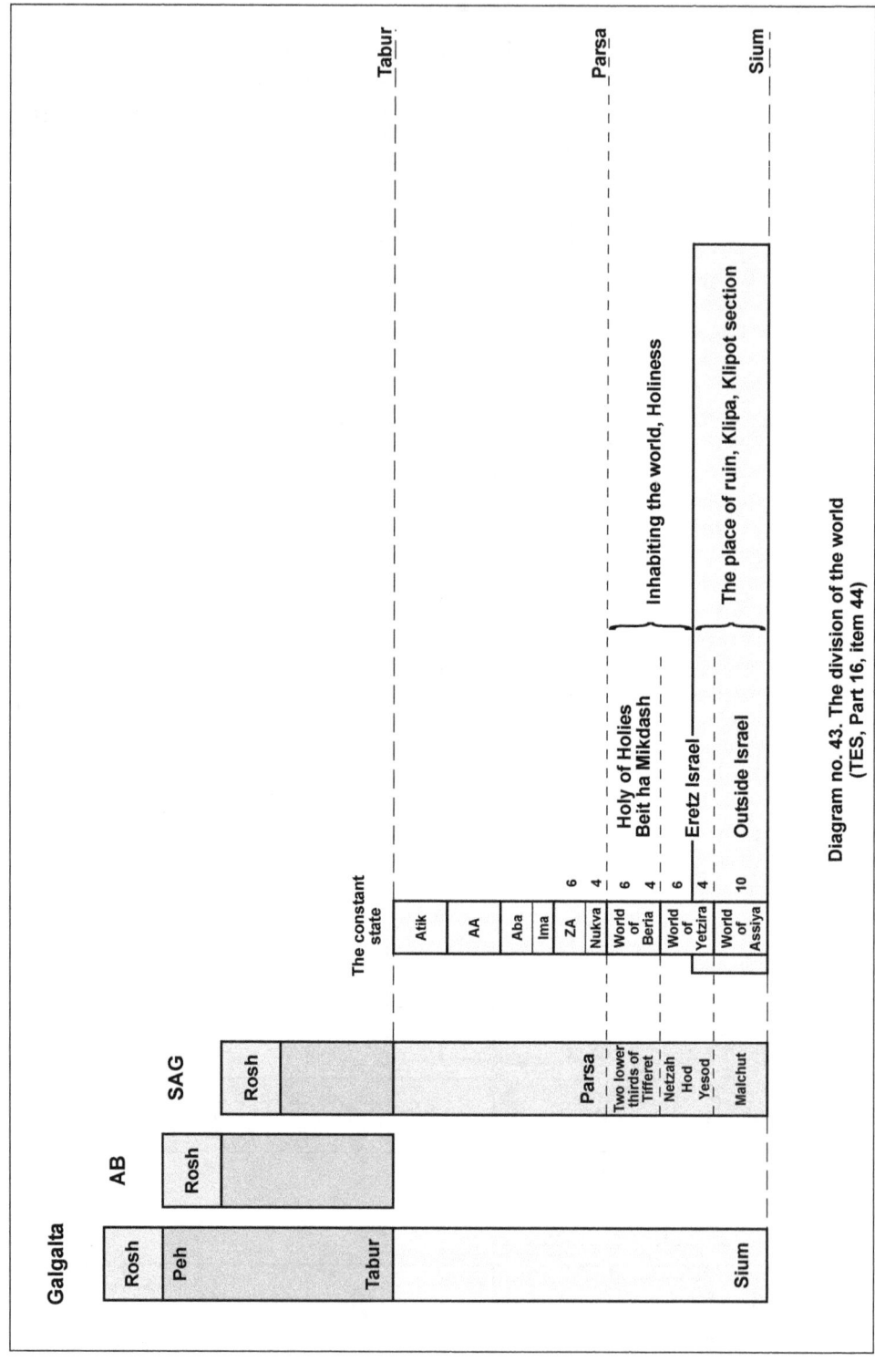

Diagram no. 43. The division of the world
(TES, Part 16, item 44)

APPENDIX C: DIAGRAMS OF THE SPIRITUAL WORLDS 847

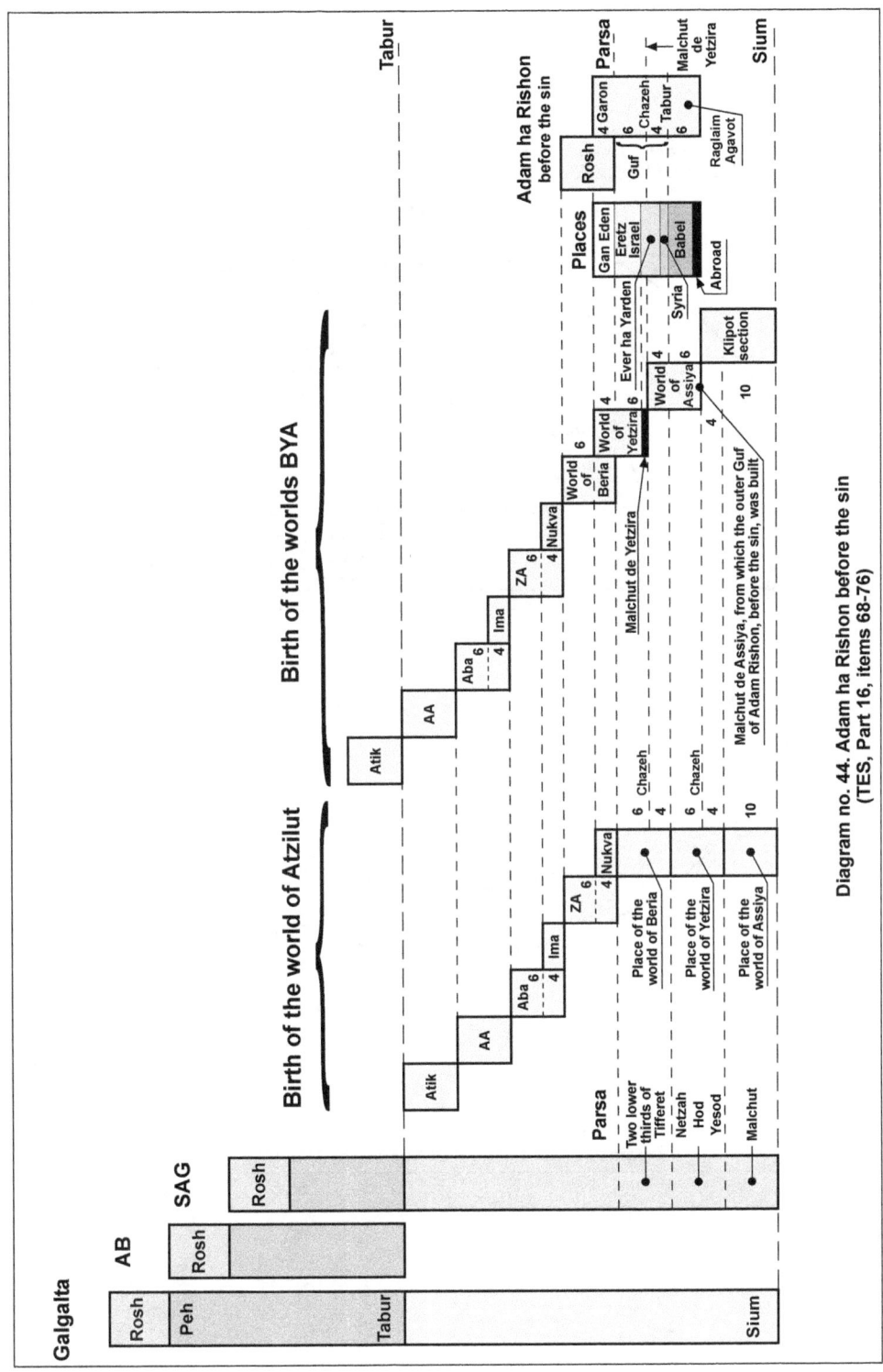

Diagram no. 44. Adam ha Rishon before the sin
(TES, Part 16, items 68-76)

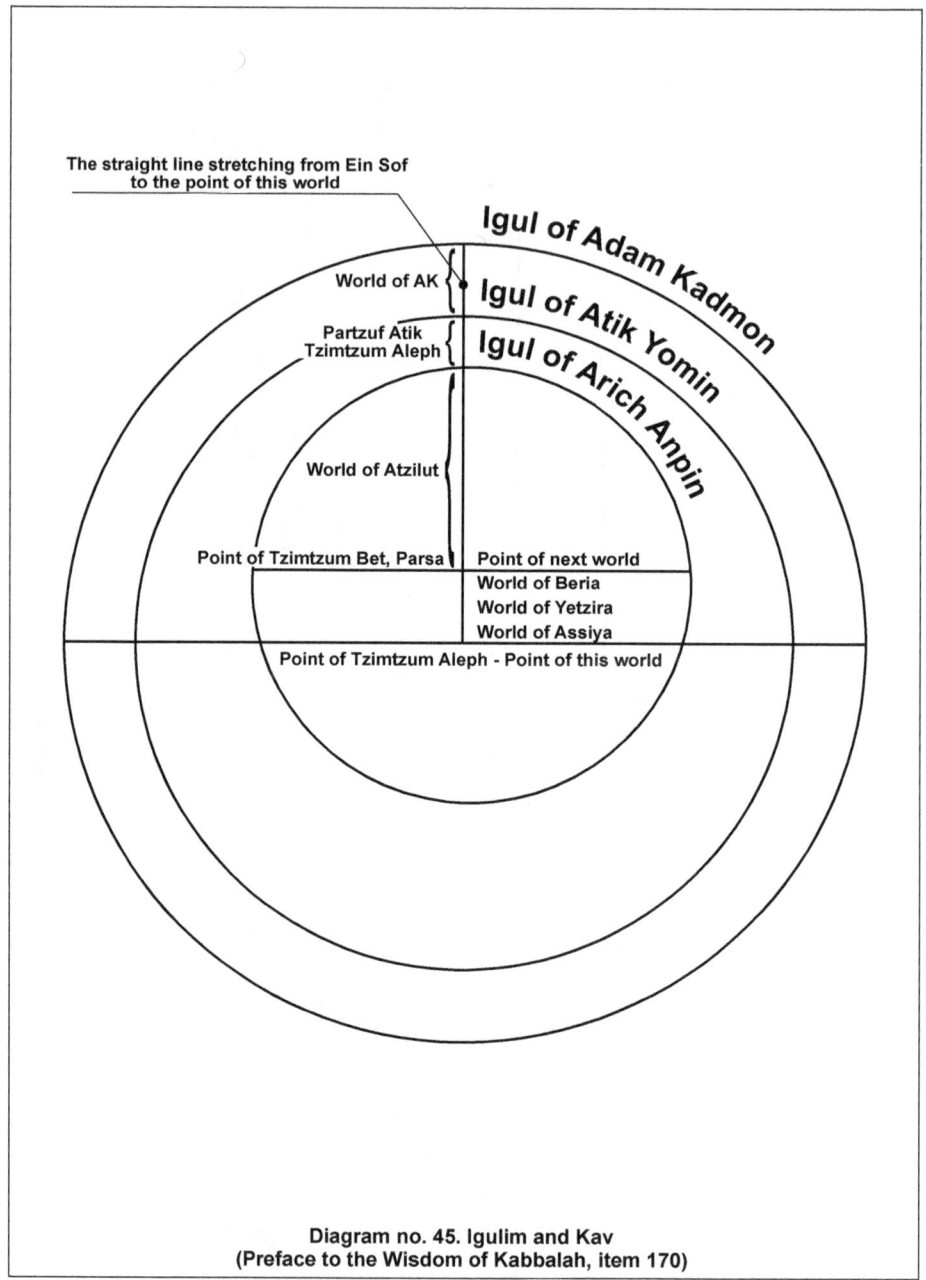

Diagram no. 45. Igulim and Kav
(Preface to the Wisdom of Kabbalah, item 170)

Appendix C: Diagrams of the Spiritual Worlds

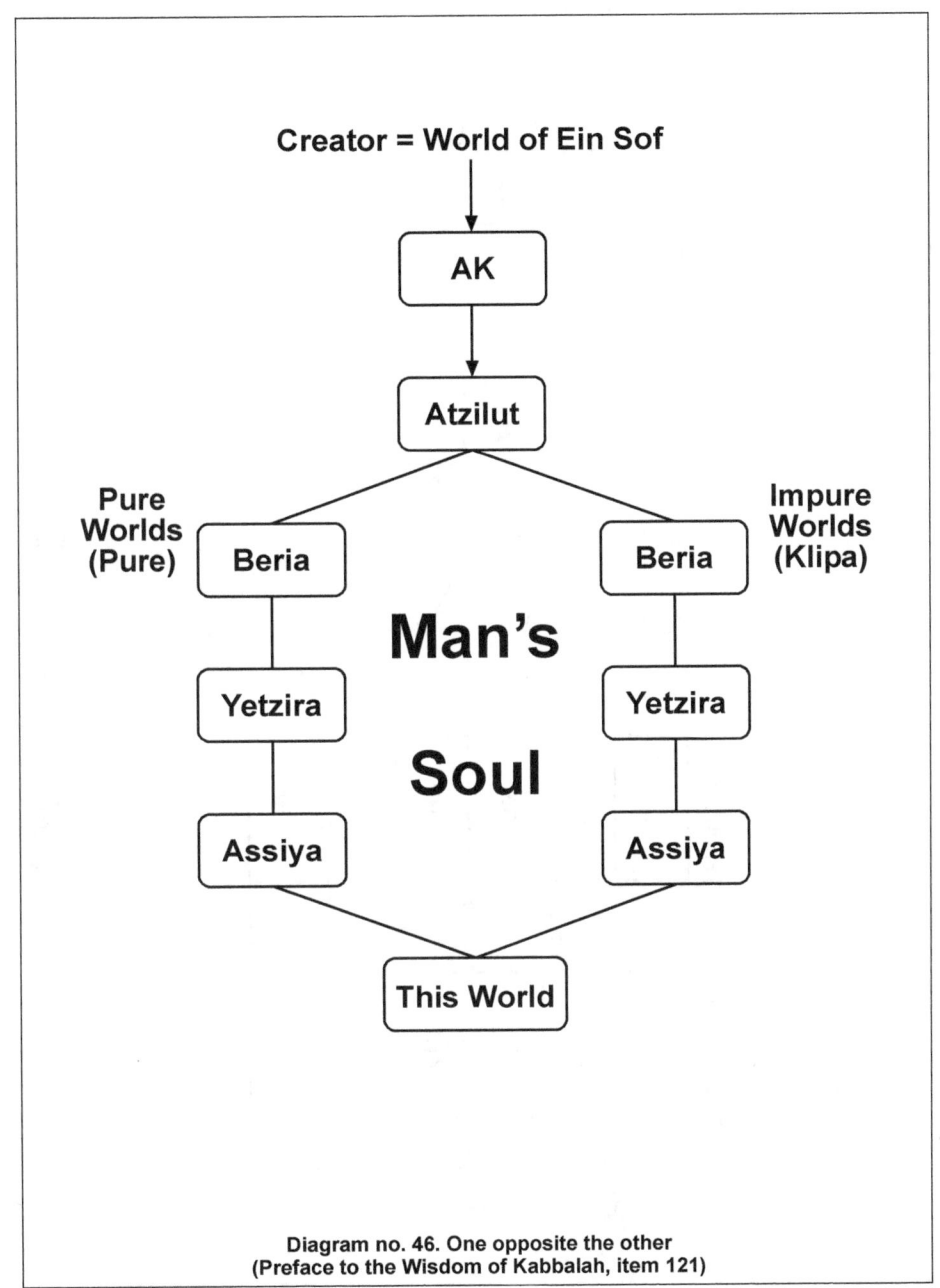

Diagram no. 46. One opposite the other
(Preface to the Wisdom of Kabbalah, item 121)

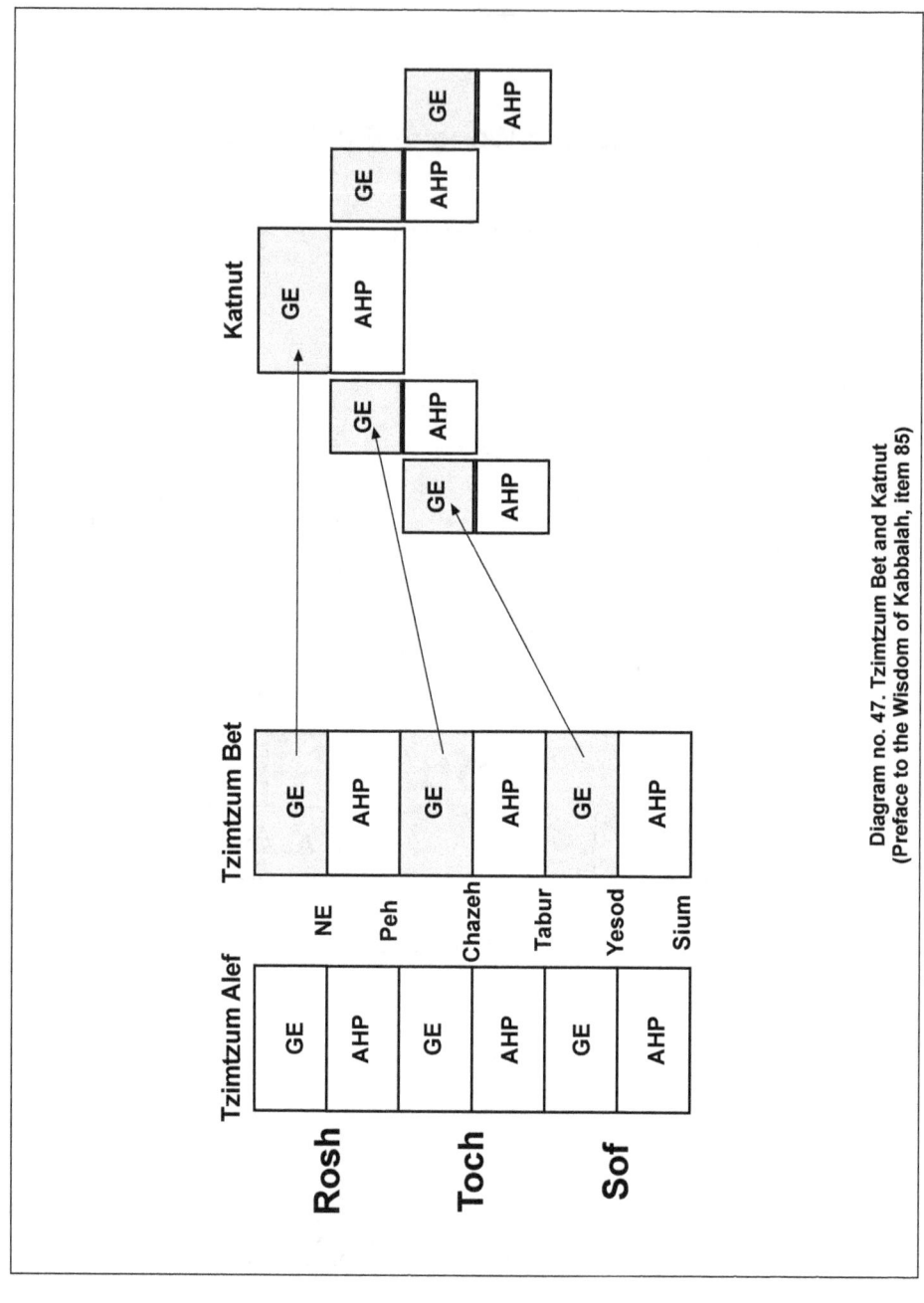

Diagram no. 47. Tzimtzum Bet and Katnut
(Preface to the Wisdom of Kabbalah, item 85)

APPENDIX C: DIAGRAMS OF THE SPIRITUAL WORLDS

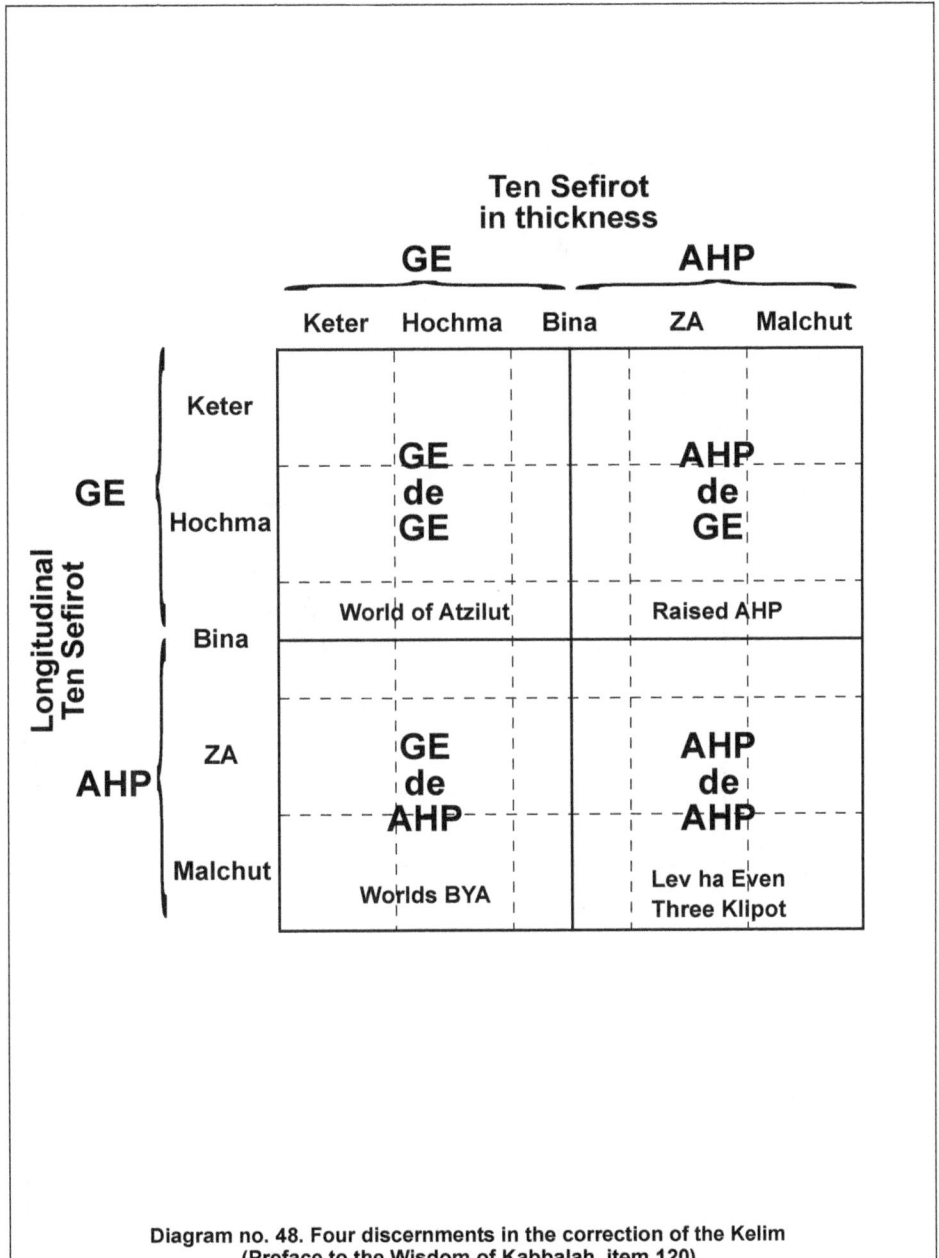

Diagram no. 48. Four discernments in the correction of the Kelim
(Preface to the Wisdom of Kabbalah, item 120)

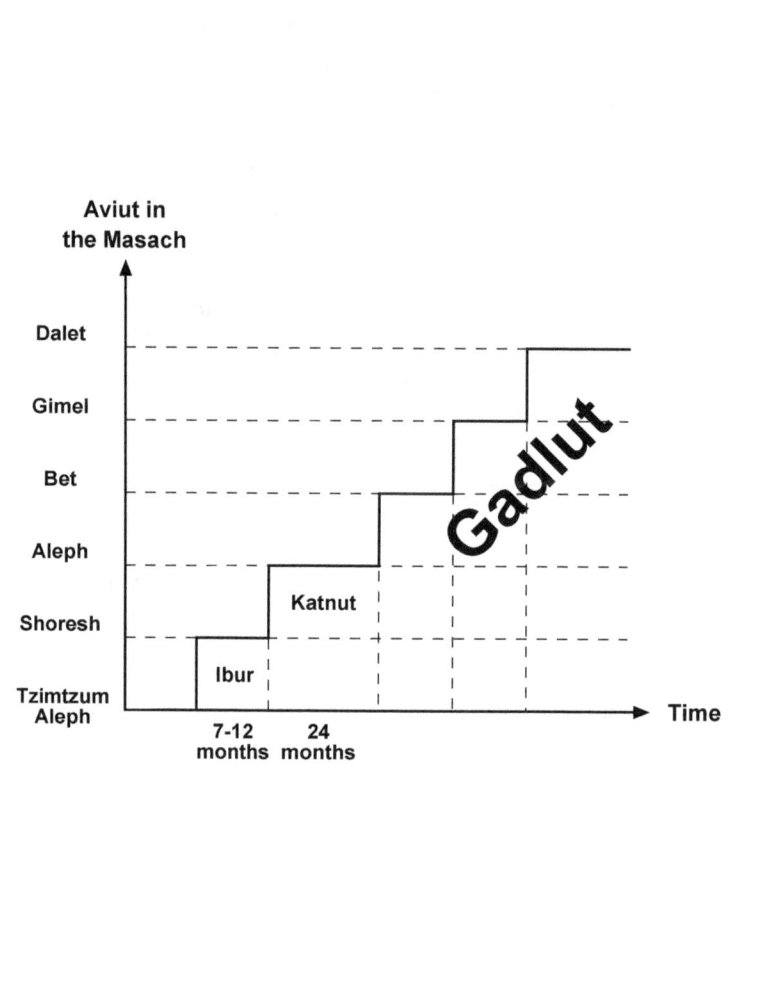

Diagram no. 49. Stages in the development of the Partzuf
(Preface to the Wisdom of Kabbalah, item 121)

Appendix C: Diagrams of the Spiritual Worlds

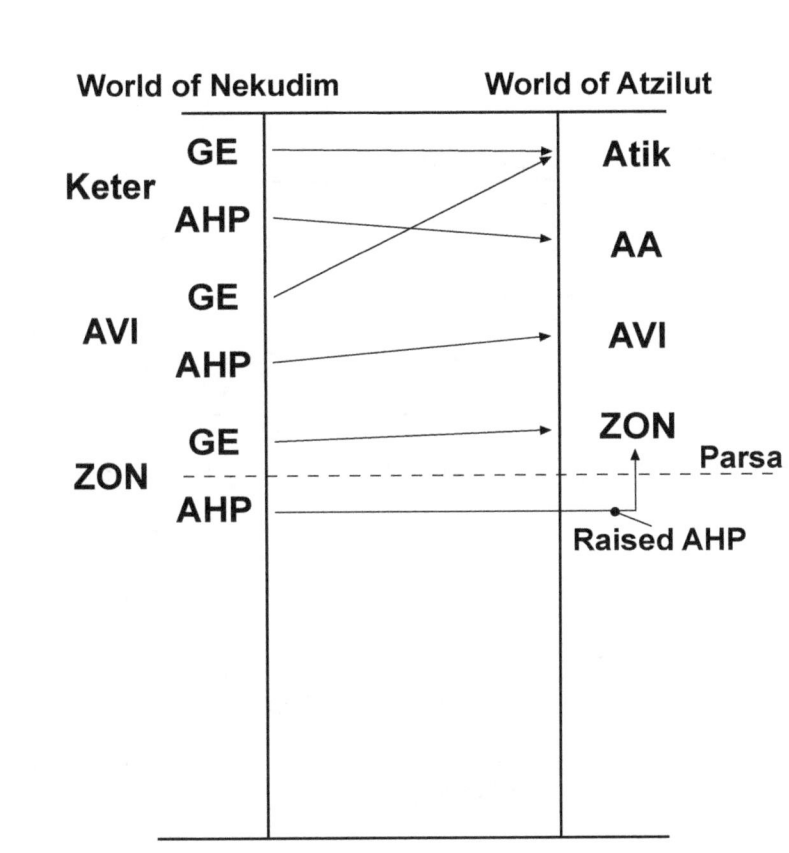

Diagram no. 50. Sorting of the Kelim after the breaking
(Preface to the Wisdom of Kabbalah, item 101)

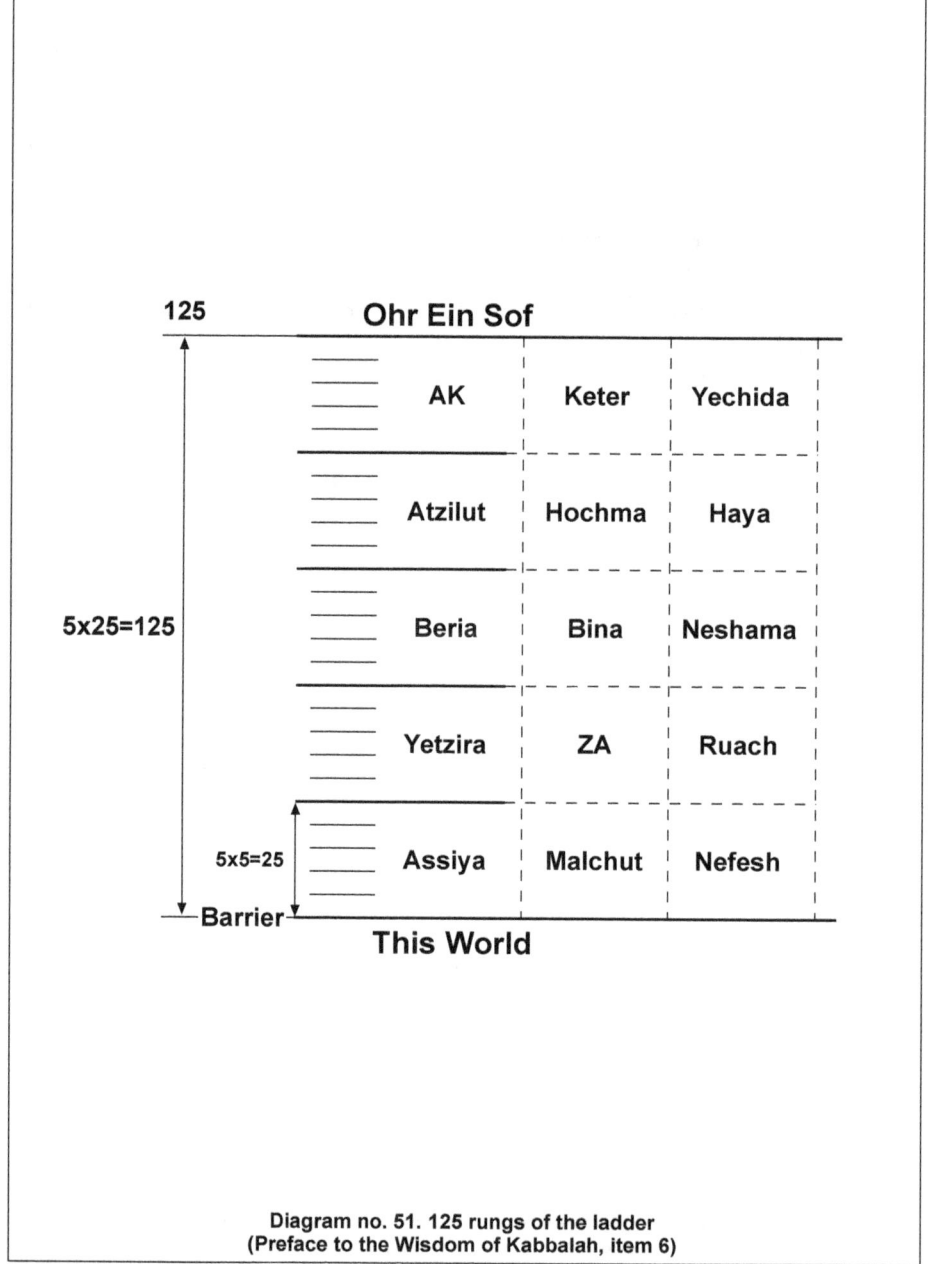

Diagram no. 51. 125 rungs of the ladder
(Preface to the Wisdom of Kabbalah, item 6)

Appendix C: Diagrams of the Spiritual Worlds

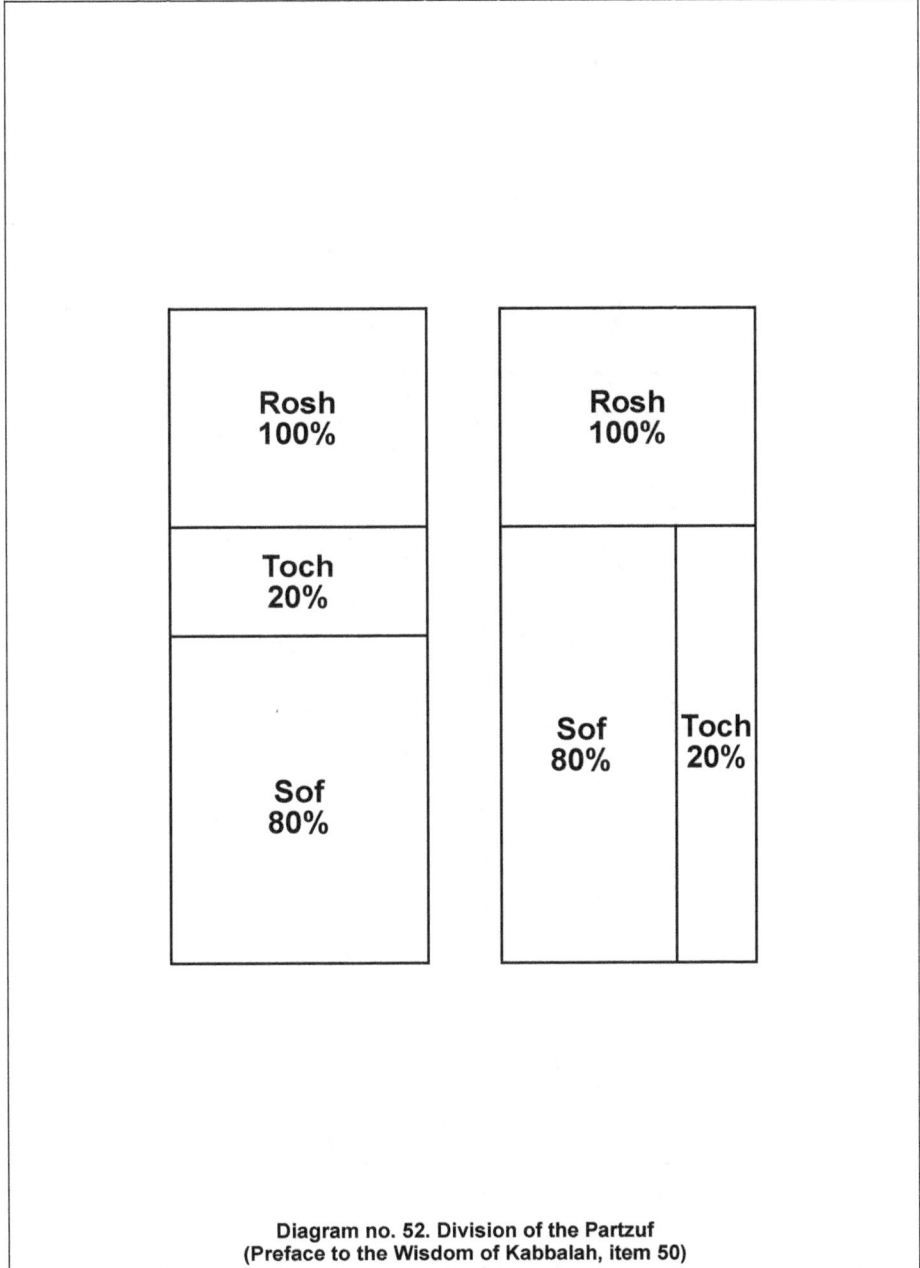

Diagram no. 52. Division of the Partzuf
(Preface to the Wisdom of Kabbalah, item 50)

Behinot	HaVaYaH	Sefirot	Parts of the Rosh	Senses	Partzufim	Worlds	Lights	TANTO	Four Behinot in Nature	Man: Four Behinot in Man	Man: Medium Behina in Man	Man: Spirituality in Man	Man: Man's Guf	Man: Man's Levush	Man: Man's Home	SVAS	Medium Behina in Nature	Direct
Shoresh	Tip of the Yod	Keter	Gulgolet		Galgalta	AK	Yechida			(Shoresh)		Yechida	Moach					
Aleph	Yod	Hochma	Eynaim	Sight	AB	Atzilut	Haya	Taamim	Fire	Inner Man (Neshama)	Dam	Haya	Atzamot	Kutonet	Bayit	Speaking	Monkey	Sou (hot dr
Bet	Hey	Bina	Awzen	Hearing	SAG	Beria	Neshama	Nekudot	Wind	Guf	Se'arot Tzipornayim	Neshama	Gidin	Michnasayim	Hatzer	Animate	Dog of the Field	Nor (cold dam
Gimel	Vav	ZA	Hotem	Smell	MA	Yetzira	Ruach	Tagin	Water	Levush	Ohalim	Ruach	Bassar	Mitznefet	Sadeh	Vegetative	Corals	We (hot dam
Dalet	Hey	Malchut	Peh	Speech	BON	Assiya	Nefesh	Otiot	Dust	Bayit		Nefesh	Or	Avnet	Midbar	Still		Ea (cold dr

Diagram no. 53. General names
(TES, Part 3, Chapters 4-5)

About Bnei Baruch

Bnei Baruch is an international group of Kabbalists who share the wisdom of Kabbalah with the entire world. The study materials (in over 30 languages) are authentic Kabbalah texts that were passed down from generation to generation.

HISTORY AND ORIGIN

In 1991, following the passing of his teacher, Rav Baruch Shalom HaLevi Ashlag (The Rabash), Michael Laitman, Professor of Ontology and the Theory of Knowledge, PhD in Philosophy and Kabbalah, and MSc in Medical Bio-Cybernetics, established a Kabbalah study group called "Bnei Baruch." He called it Bnei Baruch (Sons of Baruch) to commemorate his mentor, whose side he never left in the final twelve years of his life, from 1979 to 1991. Dr. Laitman had been Ashlag's prime student and personal assistant, and is recognized as the successor to Rabash's teaching method.

The Rabash was the firstborn son and successor of Rav Yehuda Leib HaLevi Ashlag, the greatest Kabbalist of the 20th century. Rav Ashlag authored the most authoritative and comprehensive commentary on *The Book of Zohar*, titled *The Sulam* (Ladder) *Commentary*. He was the first to reveal the complete method for spiritual ascent, and thus was known as Baal HaSulam (Owner of the Ladder).

Bnei Baruch bases its entire study method on the path paved by these two great spiritual leaders.

THE STUDY METHOD

The unique study method developed by Baal HaSulam and his son, the Rabash, is taught and applied on a daily basis by Bnei Baruch. This method relies on authentic Kabbalah sources such as *The Book of Zohar*, by Rabbi Shimon

Bar-Yochai, *The Tree of Life*, by the Ari, and *The Study of the Ten Sefirot*, by Baal HaSulam.

While the study relies on authentic Kabbalah sources, it is carried out in simple language and uses a scientific, contemporary approach. The unique combination of an academic study method and personal experiences broadens the students' perspective and awards them a new perception of the reality they live in. Those on the spiritual path are thus given the necessary tools to study themselves and their surrounding reality.

Bnei Baruch is a diverse movement of tens of thousands of students worldwide. Students can choose their own paths and intensity of their studies according to their unique conditions and abilities.

THE MESSAGE

The essence of the message disseminated by Bnei Baruch is universal: unity of the people, unity of nations and love of man.

For millennia, Kabbalists have been teaching that love of man should be the foundation of all human relations. This love prevailed in the days of Abraham, Moses, and the group of Kabbalists that they established. If we make room for these seasoned, yet contemporary values, we will discover that we possess the power to put differences aside and unite.

The wisdom of Kabbalah, hidden for millennia, has been waiting for the time when we would be sufficiently developed and ready to implement its message. Now, it is emerging as a solution that can unite diverse factions everywhere, enabling us, as individuals and as a society, to meet today's challenges.

ACTIVITIES

Bnei Baruch was established on the premise that "only by expansion of the wisdom of Kabbalah to the public can we be awarded complete redemption" (Baal HaSulam). Therefore, Bnei Baruch offers a variety of ways for people to explore and discover the purpose of their lives, providing careful guidance for beginners and advanced students alike.

Internet

Bnei Baruch's international website, www.kab.info, presents the authentic wisdom of Kabbalah using essays, books, and original texts. It is by far the most expansive source of authentic Kabbalah material on the Internet, containing a unique, extensive library for readers to thoroughly explore the wisdom of

Kabbalah. Additionally, the media archive, www.kabbalahmedia.info, contains thousands of media items, downloadable books, and a vast reservoir of texts, video and audio files in many languages.

Bnei Baruch's online Learning Center offers free Kabbalah courses for beginners, initiating students into this profound body of knowledge in the comfort of their own homes.

Dr. Laitman's daily lessons are also aired live on www.kab.tv, along with complementary texts and diagrams.

All these services are provided free of charge.

Television

In Israel, Bnei Baruch established its own channel, no. 66 on both cable and satellite, which broadcasts 24/7 Kabbalah TV. The channel is also aired on the Internet at www.kab.tv. All broadcasts on the channel are free of charge. Programs are adapted for all levels, from complete beginners to the most advanced.

Conferences

Twice a year, students gather for a weekend of study and socializing at conferences in various locations in the U.S., as well as an annual convention in Israel. These gatherings provide a great setting for meeting like-minded people, for bonding, and for expanding one's understanding of the wisdom.

KABBALAH BOOKS

Bnei Baruch publishes authentic books, written by Baal HaSulam, his son, the Rabash, as well as books by Dr. Michael Laitman. The books of Rav Ashlag and Rabash are essential for complete understanding of the teachings of authentic Kabbalah, explained in Laitman's lessons.

Dr. Laitman writes his books in a clear, contemporary style based on the key concepts of Baal HaSulam. These books are a vital link between today's readers and the original texts. All the books are available for sale, as well as for free download.

PAPER

Kabbalah Today is a free paper produced and disseminated by Bnei Baruch in many languages, including English, Hebrew, Spanish, and Russian. It is apolitical, non-commercial, and written in a clear, contemporary style. The purpose of *Kabbalah Today* is to expose the vast knowledge hidden in the wisdom of Kabbalah at no cost and in a clear, engaging style for readers everywhere.

KABBALAH LESSONS

As Kabbalists have been doing for centuries, Laitman gives a daily lesson. The lessons are given in Hebrew and are simultaneously interpreted into seven languages—English, Russian, Spanish, French, German, Italian, and Turkish—by skilled and experienced interpreters. As with everything else, the live broadcast is free of charge.

FUNDING

Bnei Baruch is a non-profit organization for teaching and sharing the wisdom of Kabbalah. To maintain its independence and purity of intentions, Bnei Baruch is not supported, funded, or otherwise tied to any government or political organization.

Since the bulk of its activity is provided free of charge, the prime sources of funding for the group's activities are donations and tithing—contributed by students on a voluntary basis—and Dr. Laitman's books, which are sold at cost.

HOW TO CONTACT BNEI BARUCH

1057 Steeles Avenue West, Suite 532
Toronto, ON, M2R 3X1
Canada

Bnei Baruch USA,
2009 85th street, #51,
Brooklyn, New York, 11214
USA

E-mail: info@kabbalah.info
Web site: www.kabbalah.info

Toll free in USA and Canada:
1-866-LAITMAN
Fax: 1-905 886 9697